W9-APH-608

YOUR SUCCESS

ESSENTIAL ON YOUR ROAD TO ACHIEVEMENT.

- ❯ **Student-Centered**

- ❯ **Imaginative Writing**

- ❯ **Emphasis on Practicality**

- ❯ **Resources that Work**

management

A PRACTICAL INTRODUCTION

fourth edition

management
A PRACTICAL INTRODUCTION

fourth edition

Angelo Kinicki

Arizona State University

Brian K. Williams

McGraw-Hill Irwin

Boston   Burr Ridge, IL   Dubuque, IA   New York   San Francisco   St. Louis
Bangkok   Bogotá   Caracas   Kuala Lumpur   Lisbon   London   Madrid   Mexico City
Milan   Montreal   New Delhi   Santiago   Seoul   Singapore   Sydney   Taipei   Toronto

The McGraw·Hill Companies

McGraw-Hill
Irwin

MANAGEMENT: A PRACTICAL INTRODUCTION
Published by McGraw-Hill/Irwin, a business unit of The McGraw-Hill Companies, Inc., 1221 Avenue of
the Americas, New York, NY, 10020. Copyright © 2009, 2008, 2006, 2003 by The McGraw-Hill
Companies, Inc. All rights reserved. No part of this publication may be reproduced or distributed in any
form or by any means, or stored in a database or retrieval system, without the prior written consent of
The McGraw-Hill Companies, Inc., including, but not limited to, in any network or other electronic
storage or transmission, or broadcast for distance learning.

Some ancillaries, including electronic and print components, may not be available to customers outside the
United States.

This book is printed on acid-free paper.
Printed in China
2 3 4 5 6 7 8 9 0 CTP/CTP 0 9

ISBN   978-0-07-338148-0
MHID   0-07-338148-9

Vice president and editor-in-chief: *Brent Gordon*
Senior sponsoring editor: *Michael Ablassmeir*
Developmental editor II: *Laura Griffin*
Editorial coordinator: *Kelly Pekelder*
Senior marketing manager: *Anke Braun Weekes*
Marketing coordinator: *Michael Gedatus*
Senior project manager: *Harvey Yep*
Full service project manager: *Jodi Dowling, Aptara,® Inc.*
Lead production supervisor: *Michael R. McCormick*
Designer: *Matthew Diamond*
Senior photo research coordinator: *Lori Kramer*
Photo researcher: *Ira C. Roberts*
Senior media project manager: *Susan Lombardi*
Cover design: *Matt Diamond*
Cover image: *©Getty Images*
Interior design: *Pam Verros*
Typeface: *10.5/12 Times New Roman*
Compositor: *Aptara®, Inc.*
Printer: *CTPS*

Library of Congress Cataloging-in-Publication Data

Kinicki, Angelo.
    Management : a practical introduction / Angelo Kinicki, Brian K. Williams.—4th ed.
      p. cm.
    Includes index.
    ISBN-13: 978-0-07-338148-0 (alk. paper)
    ISBN-10: 0-07-338148-9 (alk. paper)
    1. Management. I. Williams, Brian K., 1938- II. Title.
  HD31.K474 2009
  658—dc22
                                                        2008031090

www.mhhe.com

brief contents

ABOUT THE
authors

Angelo Kinicki Angelo is a professor of management at the W. P. Carey School of Business at Arizona State University. He also was awarded the Weatherup/Overby Chair in Leadership in 2005. He has held his current position since 1982, when he received his doctorate in organizational behavior from Kent State University.

Angelo is recognized for both his teaching and research. As a teacher, Angelo has been the recipient of several awards, including the Outstanding Teaching Award— MBA and Master's Programs (2007–2008) the John W. Teets Outstanding Graduate Teacher Award (2004–2005), Graduate Teaching Excellence Award (1998–1999), Continuing Education Teaching Excellence Award (1991–1992), and Undergraduate Teaching Excellence Award (1987–1988). He also was selected into Who's Who of American Colleges and Universities and Beta Gamma Sigma. Angelo is an active researcher. He has published over 80 articles in a variety of leading academic and professional journals and has coauthored six college textbooks (18, counting revisions). His textbooks have been used by hundreds of universities around the world. Angelo's experience as a researcher also resulted in his selection to serve on the editorial review boards for the *Academy of Management Journal, the Journal of Vocational Behavior,* and the *Journal of Management.* He received the "All-Time Best Reviewer Award" from the *Academy of Management Journal* for the period of 1996–1999.

Angelo also is an active international consultant who works with top management teams to create organizational change aimed at increasing organizational effectiveness and profitability. He has worked with many Fortune 500 firms as well as numerous entrepreneurial organizations in diverse industries. His expertise includes facilitating strategic/operational planning sessions, diagnosing the causes of organizational and work-unit problems, implementing performance management systems, designing and implementing performance appraisal systems, developing and administering surveys to assess employee attitudes, and leading management/executive education programs. He developed a 360° leadership feedback instrument called the Performance Management Leadership Survey (PMLS) that is used by companies throughout the United States and Europe.

One of Angelo's strengths is his ability to teach students at all levels within a university. He uses an interactive environment to enhance undergraduates' understanding about management and organizational behavior. He focuses MBAs on applying management concepts to solve complex problems; PhD students learn the art and science of conducting scholarly research.

Angelo and his wife, Joyce, have enjoyed living in the beautiful Arizona desert for 25 years but are natives of Cleveland, Ohio. They enjoy traveling, golfing, and hiking.

Brian Williams has been managing editor for college textbook publisher Harper & Row/Canfield Press in San Francisco; editor-in-chief for non-fiction trade-book publisher J. P. Tarcher in Los Angeles; publications & communications manager for the University of California, Systemwide Administration, in Berkeley; and an independent writer and book producer based in the San Francisco and Lake Tahoe areas. He has a B.A. in English and an M.A. in communication from Stanford University. He has coauthored 20 books (50, counting revisions), which include such best-selling college texts as *Using Information Technology* with his wife, Stacey C. Sawyer, being revised in its eight edition with McGraw-Hill. He has also written a number of other information technology books, college success books, and health and social science texts. In his spare time, he and Stacey enjoy travel, music, cooking, hiking, and exploring the wilds of the American West.

dedication

To Leslie and Master Chaz Turner, for their entrepreneurial spirit, caring for others, and love and devotion to their children.

—A.K.

To my wife, Stacey, for her 23 years of steadfast, patient support and for her collaboration and shared adventures; and to my beloved children and their families—Sylvia, Scott, and Atticus; and Kirk, Julia, Nicolas, and Lily.

—B.K.W.

A promise: To make learning management easy, efficient, and effective

The fourth edition of *Management: A Practical Introduction*—a concepts book for the introductory course in management—uses a wealth of instructor feedback to identify which features from prior editions worked best and which should be improved and expanded. By blending Angelo's scholarship, teaching, and management-consulting experience with Brian's writing and publishing background, we have again tried to create a research-based yet highly readable, innovative, and practical text.

Our primary goal is simple to state but hard to execute: to make learning principles of management as easy, effective, and efficient as possible. Accordingly, the book integrates writing, illustration, design, and magazine-like layout in **a program of learning that appeals to the visual sensibilities and respects the time constraints and different learning styles of today's students**. In an approach initially tested in our first edition and fine-tuned in the subsequent editions, **we break topics down into easily grasped portions** and incorporate **frequent use of various kinds of reinforcement techniques**. Our hope, of course, is to make a difference in the lives of our readers: to produce a text that students will enjoy reading and that will provide them with practical benefits.

The text covers the principles that most management instructors have come to expect in an introductory text—planning, organizing, leading, and controlling—plus the issues that today's students need to be aware of to succeed: customer focus, globalism, diversity, ethics, information technology, entrepreneurship, work teams, the service economy, and small business.

Beyond these, our book has **four features that make it unique:**

1. A student-centered approach to learning
2. Imaginative writing for readability and reinforcement
3. Emphasis on practicality
4. Resources that work

> "K & W offers an incredibly student-centered, highly accessible, and practically focused textbook on management and organizational behavior. The text offers numerous practical examples of exemplary managers and organizations that illustrate the four functions of management. Much more so than my current book, K & W offers an impressive range of supplementary materials that aid instructors and students."
>
> —**Kevin S. Groves,**
> *California State University,*
> *Los Angeles*

A Student-Centered Approach to Learning

CHAPTER OPENERS: Designed to help students read with purpose

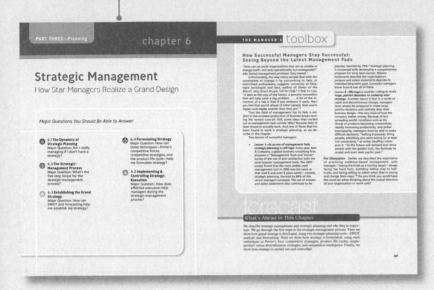

Each chapter begins with four to eight provocative, motivational **Major Questions,** written to appeal to students' concern about "what's in it for me?" and help them read with purpose and focus.

Instead of opening with the conventional case, as most texts do, we open with **The Manager's Toolbox,** a motivational device offering practical nuts-and-bolts advice pertaining to the chapter content students are about to read—and allowing for class discussion. Fourteen of the 16 toolboxes are new to or repurposed in this edition.

CHAPTER SECTIONS:

Structured into constituent parts for easier learning

Chapters are organized to cover each major question in turn, giving students bite-sized chunks of information. Each section begins with a recap of the **Major Question** and includes **"The Big Picture,"** which presents students with an overview of how the section they are about to read answers the Major Question.

"The Kinicki/Williams text is extremely student centered. . . . This text provides students with an understanding of the critical management concepts in a way that is easy to understand and apply. . . . The authors have taken into consideration how students think about reading textbooks in preparing this management text."

—Erika E. Small, *Coastal Carolina University*

Chapter tools help students learn how to learn

In focus groups, symposiums, and reviews, instructors told us that many students do not have the skills needed to succeed in college. To support students in acquiring these skills, we offer the following:

A One-Minute Guide to Success in This Class

Got one minute to read this section? It could mean the difference between getting an A instead of a B. Or a B instead of a C.

Four Rules for Success

There are four rules that will help you be successful in this (or any other) course.

- **Rule 1:** Attend every class. No cutting allowed.
- **Rule 2:** Don't postpone studying, then cram the night before a test.
- **Rule 3:** Read or review lectures and readings more than once.

"A One-Minute Guide to Success in This Class," found on page I, lays down four rules for student success in class and suggestions for how to use this book most effectively.

"Getting Control of Your Time: Dealing with the Information Deluge in College & in Your Career," at the end of Chapter I, gives students a crash course in time management skills, solid study habits, memory aids, learning from lectures, and becoming effective test takers.

Taking Something Practical Away from this Chapter

Getting Control of Your Time: Dealing with the Information Deluge in College & in Your Career

One great problem most college students face—and that all managers face—is how to manage their time. This first box describes skills that will benefit you in college and later in your career.

"I've managed to ratchet my schedule down so I can have an outside life," says Doug Shoemaker, a San Francisco architect who tries to be home by 6:00 every night. "I'm a highly organized guy, I really focus on tasks, and I get them done."[69]

Professionals and managers all have to deal with this central problem: how not to surrender their lives to their jobs. The place to start, however, is in college.

If you can learn to manage time while you're still a student, you'll find it will pay off not only in higher grades and more free time but also in more efficient information-handling skills that will serve you well as a manager later on.

Developing Study Habits: Finding Your "Prime Study Time"

Each of us has a different energy cycle. The trick is to use it effectively. That way your hours of best performance will coincide with your heaviest academic demands. For example, if your energy level is high during the evenings, you should plan to do your studying then.

Why Learn about International Management?

International management is management that oversees the conduct of operations in or with organizations in foreign countries, whether it's through a multinational corporation or a multinational organization.

- A *multinational corporation*, or multinational enterprise, is a business firm with operations in several countries. Our publisher, McGraw-Hill, is one such "multinational" (see the 17 foreign cities listed on our book's title page). In terms of revenue, the real behemoths in multinational corporations include the American firms Wal-Mart, ExxonMobil, General Motors, Ford Motor Co., General Electric, and Citigroup. The largest foreign companies are BP (Britain), Royal Dutch/Shell (Netherlands/Britain), DaimlerChrysler (Germany/USA), and Toyota (Japan).
- A *multinational organization* is a nonprofit organization with operations in several countries. Examples are the World Health Organization, the International Red Cross, the Church of Latter Day Saints.

Key terms are highlighted and terms and definitions are in boldface, to help students build their management vocabulary.

Other devices to help students develop understanding:

- Important **scholar names in boldface** so students remember key contributors to the field of management.
- Frequent use of **advance organizers, bulleted lists, and headings** to help students grasp the main ideas.
- **Illustrations positioned close to relevant text discussion** so students can refer to them more easily and avoid flipping pages.

- **Characteristic of both—high need for achievement.** Both entrepreneurs and managers have a high need for achievement. However, entrepreneurs certainly seem to be motivated to pursue moderately difficult goals through their own efforts in order to realize their ideas and, they hope, financial rewards. Managers, by contrast, are more motivated by promotions and organizational rewards of power and perks.
- **Also characteristic of both—belief in personal control of destiny.** If you believe "I am the captain of my fate, the master of my soul," you have what is known as *internal locus of control,* the belief that you control your own destiny, that external forces will have little influence. (External locus of control means the reverse—you believe you don't control your destiny, that external forces do.) Both entrepreneurs and managers like to think they have personal control over their lives.
- **Characteristic of both, but especially of entrepreneurs—high energy level and action orientation.** Rising to the top in an organization probably requires that a manager put in long hours. For entrepreneurs, however, creating a new enterprise may require an extraordinary investment of time and energy. In addition, while some managers may feel a sense of urgency, entrepreneurs are especially apt to be impatient and to want to get things done as quickly as possible, making them particularly action oriented.
- **Characteristic of both, but especially of entrepreneurs—high tolerance for ambiguity.** Every manager needs to be able to make decisions based on ambiguous—that is, unclear or incomplete—information. However, entre-

Test Your Knowledge:
Characteristics of Successful Entrepreneurs

"*Kinicki and Williams is currently the best book on the market. My students like it and so do I. The writing best meets the reading style of today's students. Keep up the good work.*"

—**Stephen F. Hallam,** *The University of Akron*

Imaginative Writing for Readability

Research shows that textbooks written in **an imaginative, people-oriented style significantly improve students' ability to retain information.** We employ a number of journalistic devices to make the material as engaging as possible for students.

We **use colorful facts, attention-grabbing quotes, biographical sketches, and lively tag lines** to get students' attention as they read.

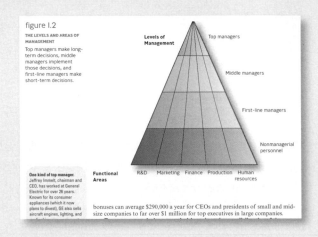

figure I.2

THE LEVELS AND AREAS OF MANAGEMENT
Top managers make long-term decisions, middle managers implement those decisions, and first-line managers make short-term decisions.

Levels of Management
- Top managers
- Middle managers
- First-line managers
- Nonmanagerial personnel

Functional Areas
R&D Marketing Finance Production Human resources

One kind of top manager. Jeffrey Immelt, chairman and CEO, has worked at General Electric for over 26 years. Known for its consumer appliances (which it now plans to divest), GE also sells aircraft engines, lighting, and

bonuses can average $290,000 a year for CEOs and presidents of small and mid-size companies to far over $1 million for top executives in large companies.

Example

Informal Groups & Informal Learning: Getting Workers to Share Their Know-How with One Another

As a manager, what would you think if you saw employees making brief conversation near the lunchroom coffeepot? "The assumption was made that this was chitchat, talking about their golf game," said a training director at the Siemens Power Transmission and Distribution plant in Wendell, North Carolina, where managers worried about workers gathering so often in the cafeteria. "But there was a whole lot of work activity."[14]

And indeed a 2-year study by the Center for Workplace Development found that 70% of workplace learning is informal.[15] As a result of the study conclusions, Siemens managers alerted supervisors about the informal meetings and even placed overhead projectors and empty pads of paper in the lunchroom to facilitate the exchange of information.

What about when employees are in far-flung places and can't gather in a cafeteria? "Sales reps are out in the field and they're kind of on islands," pointed out an executive at ExactTarget, an Indianapolis-based software firm. "It's a challenge to keep everyone connected."[16] So what was the company to do when the 75 reps started overwhelming the sales-support staff with questions about product details and client information? To ease the strain, ExactTarget leveraged the knowledge of its sales force by creating a Web site on which the reps could post and answer questions in an informal peer-to-peer learning setting.

Talking it out. Ever worked in a job in which you got a lot of informal training through conversations over coffee?

Our emphasis on practicality and applications extends to the **Example Boxes,** "mini-cases" that use snapshots of real-world instructions to explain text concepts. **"Your Call" invites student critical thinking and class discussion at the end of each example.** Suggestions for how to use the example boxes are found in the Instructor's Manual. See page 409 for the remainder of this box on worker chit-chat as informal training.

> "KW ... offers a succinct, current, and readable treatment of topics related to effective management in a global marketplace. It offers adequate treatment of key elements of the management foundation without overwhelming the reader. It is well supported by other resources available through the text website."
>
> —**Pamela A. Dobies,** University of Missouri, Kansas City

An Emphasis on Practicality

We want this book to be a "keeper" for students, a resource for future courses and for their careers—so we give students **a great deal of practical advice** in addition to covering the fundamental concepts of management. Application points are found not only throughout the text discussion but also in the following specialized features.

Practical Action

Going Green: How Businesses & Individuals Can Fight Global Warming

"When Wal-Mart became the largest retailer in the world," says Adam Werbach, "they didn't understand the responsibility that came with it, or the attention they'd get by being that symbol. But now they've reinvented what is possible. Whether you love or hate Wal-Mart, it has done more for sustainability than any environmental organization I've ever worked for."[69]

What makes this remark especially interesting is that not only is Werbach a former head of the Sierra Club, the environmental organization, whose members tend to revile Wal-Mart, but that Werbach's San Francisco environmental consulting firm, Act Now Productions, took on Wal-Mart as a client. Why? Because, Werbach says, the challenge gave him the opportunity

Practical Action boxes, appearing one or more times in each chapter, offer students practical and interesting advice on issues students will face in the workplace. Detailed discussions of how to use these sections appear in the Instructor's Manual. See page 89 for the rest of this box.

End-of-Chapter Resources that reinforce applications

Each chapter continues our strategy of repetition for learning reinforcement. We include various unique pedagogical features to help students take away the most significant portions of the chapter's content:

Management in Action cases depict how companies students are familiar with respond to situations or issues featured in the text. Discussion questions are included for ease of use in class, as reflection assignments, or over online discussion boards.

Self-Assessment Exercises enable students to personally apply chapter content. These exercises include objectives for ease in assigning, instructions for use, guidelines for interpreting results, and questions for further reflection. They can also be found on the text Web site.

Ethical Dilemmas present cases—often based on real events—that require students to think through how they would handle the situation, helping prepare them for decision making in their careers.

Resources that Work

No matter the course you teach, on campus, hybrid, or online courses, we set out to provide you with the most comprehensive set of resources to enhance your Principles of Management course.

First of all, you asked for ways to tie resources to specific chapters, so we did it! Target icons in the text margins denote **specific places where chapter content is augmented by a review activity, exercise, Test Your Knowledge activity, self-assessment, or Hot Seat video** as part of our online resources supporting this text, allowing you to help guide your students in remediation and making connections between concepts.

Audio visuals for your visual students: We present the richest and most diverse video program on the market to engage your students in the important management concepts covered in this text:

Principles of Management Video DVD Vol. I & NEW! Vol. 2—Now offering more than 70 video clips from sources such as BusinessWeek TV, PBS, NBC, BBC, CBS, & McGraw-Hill are provided on two DVD sets. These company videos are organized by the four functions of management and feature companies such as PlayStation, Panera Bread, Patagonia, Mini Cooper, the Greater Chicago Food Depository, Employer-Subsidized Commuting, Grounded: Are U.S. Airlines Safe? Using Facebook at Work, Adult Bullies, and Encore Careers in 2½- to 15-minute clips. Corresponding video cases and a guide that ties the videos closely to the chapter can be found in the Instructor's Manual and online.

Management in the Movies DVD. This faculty DVD makes it easy to bring that captivating power of big-screen movies to your classroom! Each video clip illustrates a specific management topic in less than 2½ minutes via a scene from major movies or TV show. For example, Groups—*13 Going On 30*, Ethics—*John Q*, Global Management—*Gungo Ho*. This DVD is exclusively reserved for McGraw-Hill users and is supported by an IM with summaries and discussion questions.

Manager's Hot Seat Online! Enhanced and expanded! Now you can put your students in the hot seat with access to our interactive program. After reviewing the

situation and related management materials, students watch 21 real managers apply their years of experience when confronting unscripted issues. Students are prompted to make decisions along with the manager. At the end students watch a post-interview with the manager and then submit a report critiquing the manager's choices while defending their own. Access to the online program is an optional package with this text.

Assurance of Learning Ready

Educational institutions are often focused on the notion of assurance of learning, an important element of many accreditation standards. This edition is designed specifically to support your assurance of learning initiatives with a simple, yet powerful, solution.

Each test bank question for this edition maps to a specific chapter learning outcome/objective listed in the text. You can use our test bank software, EZ Test, to easily query for learning objectives that directly relate to the learning objectives for your course. You can use the reporting features of EZ Test to aggregate student results in a similar fashion, making the collection and presentation of assurance of learning data quick and easy.

The **Online Learning Center** is located at **www.mhhe.com/kw4e.** At this site, students can take chapter quizzes to review concepts, access a career corner, and review chapter PowerPoint slides. Students can easily upgrade to a richer set of Premium Online Resources right on this site.

Premium Online Resources: Organized chapter by chapter, the online content is designed to reinforce and build on the text content. As students read the book, they can go online to take self-grading quizzes, review material, watch video clips relating to the chapter, complete video cases, based on clips, or work through interactive exercises such as the Management History Timeline, Self-Assessments, or Test Your Knowledge Exercises. Unique to this text, a complete study guide supports students in their learning. Chapter quizzes, narrated slides, and most videos are available for iPod download. The Premium Online Resources can be delivered in multiple ways—professors and students can access them directly through the textbook Web site at **www.mhhe.com/kw4e,** through PageOut, or within a course management system (e.g., WebCT, Blackboard, D2L, eCollege).

The Instructor's Resource CD includes multiple resources to make your teaching life easier.

- The **Instructors Manual,** authored by two-time "Excellence in Teaching" award-winner Kimberly Jaussi of SUNY Binghamton, was revised and updated to include thorough coverage of each chapter as well as time-saving features such as an outline on incorporating PowerPoint® slides, lecture enhancers that supplement the textbook, video cases and video notes, and answers to all end-of-chapter exercises.

- Also included is a set of **PowerPoint slides** prepared by Brad Cox of Midlands Technical College, improved and streamlined for this edition. In addition to providing comprehensive lectures notes, these slides also include questions for the class as well as company examples not found in the textbook.

- Finally, the **Test Bank** by Carol Johnson of the University of Denver includes more than 100 questions per chapter in a variety of formats; it has been revised for accuracy and expanded to include a greater variety of comprehension and application (scenario-based) questions as well as tagged Bloom's Taxonomy levels and AACSB requirements.

AACSB Statement

The statements contained in this edition are provided only as a guide for the users of this text. The AACSB leaves content coverage and assessment clearly within the realm and control of individual schools, the mission of the school, and the faculty. The AACSB does also charge schools with the obligation of doing assessment against their own content and learning goals. While this text and the teaching package make no claim of any specific AACSB qualification or evaluation, we have labeled selected questions within the text according to the six general knowledge and skills areas. The labels or tags are as indicated. There are, of course, many more within the test bank, the text, and the teaching package which may be used as a standard for your course.

Always at the forefront of learning innovation, McGraw-Hill has taken another leap forward....

2008 SIIA //CODiE// WINNER

- Use our online course tools to help launch your program.

- Enhance your current online curriculum with our assets.

- Use our courses in conjunction with the textbook of your choice.

- Customize our online content to meet your specific course needs.

McGraw-Hill Online Learning's range of online course solutions is designed to empower you to teach your online course the way you want to. These online course tools provide instructional design, animation, streaming video, interactive activities, and audio narration that enliven the content and motivate the learner. And our online course content integrates with major learning management systems, allowing professors and IT staff to make their courses unique. Recognizing our approach to educational technology, members of the Software & Information Industry Association elected McGraw-Hill's online learning content as 2008 SIIA CODiE Award winners for Best Postsecondary Instructional Solution *and* Best Postsecondary Course/Content Management Solution.

PageOut ®

Create a custom course website with **PageOut**, free to instructors using a **McGraw-Hill textbook**.

To learn more, contact your McGraw-Hill publisher's representative or visit www.mhhe.com/solutions.

McGraw-Hill/Irwin's PageOut enables you to **create a Web site for your management course** that incorporates your course materials and syllabus to build a Web site to your specifications—no HTML coding or graphic design knowledge needed! Simply fill in a series of boxes, click on one of our available designs, and in no time your course is online. For more information, visit **www.pageout.net.**

e-book Options

e-books are an innovative way for students to save money and to "go green." McGraw-Hill's e-books are typically 55% of bookstore price. Students may choose between McGraw-Hill's **2 types of e-books:** *CourseSmart* (online e-book) and *VitalSource* (downloadable e-book).

- **Online e-book via *CourseSmart*:**

  CourseSmart is the online option for e-books. Through *CourseSmart*, students have the flexibility to access an exact replica of their textbook from any computer that has Internet service without plug-ins or special software. Access to the CourseSmart e-book is *1 year*.

  Features: *CourseSmart* e-books allow students to highlight, take notes, organize notes, and share the notes with other *CourseSmart* users. Students can also search terms across all e-books in their purchased *CourseSmart* library. *CourseSmart* e-books can be printed (5 pages at a time).

  More info and purchase: Please visit **www.coursesmart.com** for more information and to purchase access to our online e-book. *CourseSmart* allows students to try one chapter of the e-book, free of charge, before purchase. Instructors should contact their McGraw-Hill rep for their 1-year free access.

- **Downloadable e-book via *VitalSource*:**

  VitalSource is the downloadable option for e-books. When students purchase a *VitalSource* e-book, it is theirs to keep *permanently* or unitl they delete it from their computer. *VitalSource* e-books can be downloaded on up to two computers. Download and installation of the free "Bookshelf" application to the computer is required to access the e-book.

  Features: *VitalSource* e-books allow students to copy and paste e-book text into other documents (includes the citation information), students can highlight (with multiple colors), take notes, organize notes, and share notes with other *VitalSource* users. Pages are "reflowable," meaning students can customize views, fonts, etc. *VitalSource* includes a search feature that allows students to search across all *VitalSource* e-books within their purchased library. *VitalSource* e-books can be printed (2 pages at a time).

  More info and purchase: Students can purchase a *VitalSource* e-book and "Bookshelf" application at **www.textbooks.VitalSource.com.** *VitalSource* allows students and instructors to download the entire book free for a 7-day trial. Instructors should contact their McGraw-Hill rep for permanent access to their *VitalSource* textbook.

acknowledgments

We could not have completed this product without the help of a great many people. The first edition was designed by Karen Mellon, to whom we are very grateful. Sincere thanks and gratitude also go to our former executive editor John Weimeister and to our present senior sponsoring editor Michael Ablassmeir. Among our first-rate team at McGraw-Hill, we want to acknowledge key contributors Laura Griffin, developmental editor II, and editorial coordinator Kelly Pekelder; Anke Braun Weekes, senior marketing manager, and Michael Gedatus, marketing coordinator; Harvey Yep, senior project manager; lead production supervisor Michael R. McCormick; designer Matt Diamond; senior photo research coordinator Lori Kramer; senior media project manager Susan Lombardi. In addition, we would like to acknowledge project manager Jodi Dowling of Aptara; photo researcher Ira C. Roberts; interior designer Pam Verros; and our former developmental editor Kirsten Guidero, for her work on the marginal icon material. We would also like to thank Kimberly Jaussi for her work on the Instructor's Manual; Brad Cox for the PowerPoint slides; and Carol Johnson for the test bank.

Warmest thanks and appreciation go to the individuals who provided valuable input during the developmental stages of this edition, as follows:

Randy Blass, *Florida State University*

Susan M. Bosco, *Roger Williams University*

Pamela A. Dobies, *University of Missouri—Kansas City*

Ron Dougherty, *Ivy Tech Community College/Columbus Campus*

Kevin S. Groves, *California State University, Los Angeles*

Stephen F. Hallam, *The University of Akron*

Nancy M. Johnson, *Madison Area Technical College*

Robert Scott Taylor, *Moberly Area Community College*

Erika E. Small, *Coastal Carolina University*

Joseph Tomkiewicz, *East Carolina University*

We would also like to thank the following colleagues who served as manuscript reviewers during the development of previous editions:

G. Stoney Alder, *Western Illinois University*

Phyllis C. Alderdice, *Jefferson Community College*

Scott Anchors, *Maine Business School*

John Anstey, *University of Nebraska at Omaha*

Maria Aria, *Camden County College*

James Bell, *Texas State University-San Marcos*

Victor Berardi, *Kent State University*

David Bess, *University of Hawaii*

Stephen Betts, *William Paterson University*

Danielle Beu, *Louisiana Tech University*

Larry Bohleber, *University of Southern Indiana*

Melanie Bookout, *Greenville Technical College*

Robert S. Boothe, *University of Southern Mississippi*

Roger Brown, *Western Illinois University*

Marit Brunsell, *Madison Area Technical College*

Neil Burton, *Clemson University*

Jon Bryan, *Bridgewater State College*

Pamela Carstens, *Coe College*

Glen Chapuis, *St. Charles Community College*

Rod Christian, *Mesa Community College*

Mike Cicero, *Highline Community College*

Jack Cichy, *Davenport University*

Anthony Cioffi, *Lorain County Community College*

Deborah Clark, *Santa Fe Community College*

Sharon Clinebell, *University of Northern Colorado*

Ron Cooley, *South Suburban College*

Gary Corona, *Florida Community College*

Ajay Das, *Baruch College*

Kathleen DeNisco, *Erie Community College*

David Dore, *San Francisco City College*

Lon Doty, *San Jose State University*

Scott Droege, *Western Kentucky University*

Steven Dunphy, *University of Akron*

Linda Durkin, *Delaware County Community College*

Subhash Durlabhji, *Northwestern State University*

Jack Dustman, *Northern Arizona University*

Ray Eldridge, *Freed-Hardeman University*

Judy Fitch, *Augusta State University*

David Foote, *Middle Tennessee State University*

Tony Frontera, *Broome Community College*

Michael Garcia, *Liberty University*

Evgeniy Gentchev, *Northwood University*

James Glasgow, *Villanova University*

Kris Gossett, *Ivy Tech State College*

Joyce Guillory, *Austin Community College*

Charles T. Harrington, *Pasadena City College*

Santhi Harvey, *Central State University*

Samuel Hazen, *Tarleton State University*

Jack Heinsius, *Modesto Junior College*

Kim Hester, *Arkansas State University*

Mary Hogue, *Kent State University*

Edward Johnson, *University of North Florida*

Rusty Juban, *Southeastern Louisiana University*

Dmitriy Kalyagin, *Chabot College*

Heesam Kang, *Bacone College*

Marcella Kelly, *Santa Monica College*

Bobbie Knoblauch, *Wichita State University*

Rebecca Legleiter, *Tulsa Community College*

David Leonard, *Chabot College*

David Levy, *United States Air Force Academy*

Beverly Little, *Western Carolina University*

Mary Lou Lockerby, *College of DuPage*

Paul Londrigan, *Charles Stewart Mott Community College*

Tom Loughman, *Columbus State University*

Brenda McAleer, *University of Maine at Augusta*

David McArthur, *University of Nevada Las Vegas*

Tom McFarland, *Mount San Antonio College*

Joe McKenna, *Howard Community College*

Jeanne McNett, *Assumption College*

Spencer Mehl, *Coastal Carolina Community College*

Mary Meredith, *University of Louisiana*

Douglas Micklich, *Illinois State University*

Christine Miller, *Tennessee Tech University*

Val Miskin, *Washington State University*

Gregory Moore, *Middle Tennessee State University*

Rob Moorman, *Creighton University*

Robert Myers, *University of Louisville*

Francine Newth, *Providence College*

Jack Partlow, *Northern Virginia Community College*

Don A. Paxton, *Pasadena City College*

John Paxton, *Wayne State College*

Sheila Petcavage, *Cuyahoga Community College*

Barbara Petzall, *Maryville University*

Leah Ritchie, *Salem State College*

Barbara Rosenthall, *Miami Dade Community College/Wolfson Campus I*

Gary Ross, *Barat College of DePaul University*

Cindy Ruszkowski, *Illinois State University*

William Salyer, *Morris College*

Diane R. Scott, *Wichita State University*

Marianne Sebok, *Community College of Southern Nevada*

Randi Sims, *Nova Southeastern University*

Gerald F. Smith, *University of Northern Iowa*

Mark Smith, *University of Southwest Louisiana*

Jeff Stauffer, *Ventura College*

Raymond Stoudt, *DeSales University*

Virginia Anne Taylor, *William Patterson University*

Jerry Thomas, *Arapahoe Community College*

Robert Trumble, *Virginia Commonwealth University*

Isaiah Ugboro, *North Carolina Agricultural & Technical State University*

Anthony Uremovic, *Joliet Junior College*

Barry Van Hook, *Arizona State University*

Susan Verhulst, *Des Moines Area Community College*

Annie Viets, *University of Vermont*

Tom Voigt, *Jr., Aurora University*

Bruce C. Walker, *University of Louisiana at Monroe*

Charles Warren, *Salem State College*

Allen Weimer, *University of Tampa*

James Whelan, *Manhattan College*

John Whitelock, *Community College of Baltimore/Catonsville Campus*

Wendy Wysocki, *Monroe County Community College*

The following professors also participated in an early focus group that helped drive the development of this text. We appreciate their suggestions and participation immensely:

Rusty Brooks, *Houston Baptist University*

Kerry Carson, *University of Southwestern Louisiana*

Sam Dumbar, *Delgado Community College*

Subhash Durlabhji, *Northwestern State University*

Robert Mullins, *Delgado Community College*

Carl Phillips, *Southeastern Louisiana University*

Allayne Pizzolatto, *Nicholls State University*

Ellen White, *University of New Orleans*

We would also like to thank the following students for participating in a very important focus group to gather feedback from the student reader's point of view:

Marcy Baasch, *Triton College*

Diana Broeckel, *Triton College*

Lurene Cornejo, *Moraine Valley Community College*

Dave Fell, *Elgin Community College*

Lydia Hendrix, *Moraine Valley Community College*

Kristine Kurpiewski, *Oakton Community College*

Michelle Monaco, *Moraine Valley Community College*

Shannon Ramey, *Elgin Community College*

Arpita Sikand, *Oakton Community College*

Finally, we would like to thank our wives, Joyce and Stacey, for being understanding, patient, and encouraging throughout the process of writing this edition. Your love and support helped us endure the trials of completing this text.

We hope you enjoy reading and applying the book. Best wishes for success in your career.

Angelo Kinicki   **Brian K. Williams**

contents

part 2
The Environment of Management

Chapter Three

The Manager's Changing Work Environment & Ethical Responsibilities: Doing the Right Thing 70

Chapter Four

Global Management: Managing across Borders 104

part 3
Planning

Chapter Five

Planning: The Foundation of Successful Management 138

Chapter Six

Strategic Management: How Star Managers Realize a Grand Design 166

Chapter Seven

Individual & Group Decision Making: How Managers Make Things Happen 200

Chapter Nine

Human Resource Management: Getting the Right People for Managerial Success 274

Chapter Ten

Organizational Change & Innovation: Lifelong Challenges for the Exceptional Manager 310

A One-Minute Guide to Success in This Class

Got one minute to read this section? It could mean the difference between getting an A instead of a B. Or a B instead of a C.

Four Rules for Success

There are four rules that will help you be successful in this (or any other) course.

LIST HEAD FOUR RULES FOR SUCCESS

- **Rule 1:** Attend every class. No cutting allowed.
- **Rule 2:** Don't postpone studying, then cram the night before a test.
- **Rule 3:** Read or review lectures and readings more than once.
- **Rule 4:** Learn how to use this book.

How to Use This Book Most Effectively

When reading this book, follow the steps below:

- Get an overview of the chapter by reading over the first page, which contains the section headings and Major Questions.
- Read "Forecast: What's Ahead in This Chapter."
- Look at the Major Question at the beginning of each section before you read it.

If you follow these steps consistently, you'll probably absorb the material well enough that you won't have to cram before an exam; you'll need only to lightly review it before the test.

Read the "The Big Picture," which summarizes the section.

Read the section itself (which is usually only 2–6 pages), *trying silently to answer the Major Question.* This is important!

After reading all sections, use the Key Terms and Summary at the end of the chapter to see how well you understand the major concepts. Reread any material you're unsure about.

Got one minute to read this section? It could mean the difference between getting an A instead of a B. Or a B instead of a C.

The Exceptional Manager

What You Do, How You Do It

Major Questions You Should Be Able to Answer

1.1 Management: What It Is, What Its Benefits Are
Major Question: What are the rewards of being an exceptional manager—of being a star in my workplace?

1.2 Six Challenges to Being a Star Manager
Major Question: Challenges can make one feel alive. What are six challenges I could look forward to as a manager?

1.3 What Managers Do: The Four Principal Functions
Major Question: What would I actually *do*—that is, what would be my four principal functions—as a manager?

1.4 Pyramid Power: Levels & Areas of Management
Major Question: What are the levels and areas of management I need to know to move up, down, and sideways?

1.5 Roles Managers Must Play Successfully
Major Question: To be an exceptional manager, what roles must I play successfully?

1.6 The Entrepreneurial Spirit
Major Question: Do I have what it takes to be an entrepreneur?

1.7 The Skills Star Managers Need
Major Question: To be a terrific manager, what skills should I cultivate?

How to Become a Star in the Workplace

It is our desire *to make this book as practical as possible for you.* One place we do this is in the **Manager's Toolbox,** like this one, which appears at the beginning of every chapter and which offers practical advice appropriate to the subject matter you are about to explore.

The purpose of this book is to help you become a successful, competent manager—indeed, a *star manager*—an *exceptional manager,* as this chapter's title has it, whose performance is far superior to that of other managers. People who are stars at their jobs "are made, not born," says Robert E. Kelley. "They have a fundamentally different conception of what work is." Here are the nine "star strategies" Kelley has identified, which average performers can adopt to become star performers—to become exceptional managers:[1]

- **Initiative:** Initiative, says Kelley, is doing something outside your regular job that makes a difference to the company's core mission—doing something beyond your job description that helps other people. Initiative means you need to see the activity through to the end and you may need to take some risks.

- **Networking:** Exceptional performers use networking to multiply their productivity, to do their current job better. "Average performers wait until they need some information, then cold-call someone to get it," Kelley says. "Stars know that you can't get work done today without a knowledge network and that you've got to put it in place beforehand."

- **Self-management:** Exceptional managers know how to get ahead of the game instead of waiting for the game to come to them. They look at the big picture and think about managing their whole life at work. They understand who they are and how they work best.

- **Perspective:** Average performers tend to see things just from their own points of view, says Kelley. Exceptional performers try to think how things look through the eyes of their boss, co-workers, clients, and competitors.

That depth of perspective can lead to better solutions.

- **Followership:** Stars know not only how to stand out but also how to help out—to be a follower as well as a leader. The idea is that if you help others, they will later look out for you.

- **Leadership:** Exceptional performers lead by understanding other people's interests and by using persuasion to bring out the best in people. People want leaders who are knowledgeable, who bring energy to a project and create energy in other people.

- **Teamwork:** Stars join only workplace teams in which they think they will make a difference, and they become very good participants. They "make sure, once the team is put together, that it actually gets the job done," says Kelley.

- **Organizational savvy:** Average performers think of office politics as being dirty. Stars avoid getting needlessly involved in office melodramas, but they learn how to manage these interests to achieve their work goals. They learn not that one perspective is right but that there are different perspectives.

- **Show and tell:** In both formal and informal meetings, exceptional performers learn how to craft their messages and to time them so that people pay attention. To excel at "show and tell," they learn to match the language of their communication to the language that people speak, and then deliver the message in a way that works for them.

The good news is that these nine strategies can be learned. Just as you develop skills in a sport, you identify the areas in which you need to improve and then practice every day.

For Discussion   Which two of these qualities do you think you need to work on most to develop into an exceptional performer?

forecast

What's Ahead in This Chapter

We describe the rewards, benefits, and privileges managers might expect. We also describe the six challenges to managers in today's world. You'll be introduced to the four principal functions of management—planning, organizing, leading, and controlling—and levels and areas of management. Then we consider the contributions of entrepreneurship. Finally, we describe the three types of roles and three skills required of a manager.

1.1 MANAGEMENT: WHAT IT IS, WHAT ITS BENEFITS ARE

major question? What are the rewards of being an exceptional manager—of being a star in my workplace?

THE BIG PICTURE

Management is defined as the pursuit of organizational goals efficiently and effectively. Organizations, or people who work together to achieve a specific purpose, value managers because of the multiplier effect: Good managers have an influence on the organization far beyond the results that can be achieved by one person acting alone. Managers are well paid, with the CEOs and presidents of even small and midsize businesses earning good salaries and many benefits.

Judy McGrath, from a blue-collar Irish neighborhood in Scranton, Pennsylvania, was 26 when she arrived in New York in 1978 with an English degree. After a period of writing articles for women's magazines, she was hired to create promotional materials for MTV. Today at age 54 she is chairwoman and chief executive officer (CEO) of MTV Networks, which was launched in 1981 as a music video channel but now comprises TV channels, Web sites, and wireless services reaching 514 million households in 162 countries.[2] What brought about her rise to the top of this $7 billion company?

One quality she brought to her job is a strong sense of community. If she has been "smart or lucky at one thing," she says, "it has been [picking] good people." Another quality is perseverance. "It's a really undervalued asset," she points out, "but if you really want something, you've got to hang in there." A third quality: encouraging an anything-is-possible spirit by creating an atmosphere in which people feel safe and are not afraid to fail. "Falling flat is a great motivator, " she says. "So is accident."[3]

In an era of broadband, iPods, and an "Always On" online generation, MTV faces a slew of threats. The company will now have to deliver services across new broadband channels, over cell phones, and via video games. Two important rules in the McGrath playbook, therefore, are "Make change part of your DNA" and "Companies don't innovate, people do."

Being prepared for surprises and change is important to any manager's survival, and continuing change—in the world and in the workplace—is a major theme of this book.

MTV's Judy McGrath. As chairwoman and CEO, McGrath must understand the unique needs of customers from Stockholm to Toronto to Chicago, as well as how to reach them with MTV's offerings. If you were in her shoes, what would you consider to be the key component of managerial success? A strong sense of community? Perseverance? Making people not afraid to fail?

The Art of Management Defined

Is being an exceptional manager—a star manager—a gift, like a musician having perfect pitch? Not exactly. But in good part it may be an art. Fortunately, it is one that is teachable.

Management, said one pioneer of management ideas, is "the art of getting things done through people."[4]

Getting things done. Through people. Thus, managers are task oriented, achievement oriented, and people oriented. And they operate within an *organization*—a group of people who work together to achieve some specific purpose.

More formally, *management* is defined as (1) the pursuit of organizational goals efficiently and effectively by (2) integrating the work of people through (3) planning, organizing, leading, and controlling the organization's resources.

Note the words *efficiently* and *effectively,* which basically mean "doing things right."

- *Efficiency—the means.* Efficiency is the means of attaining the organization's goals. **To be *efficient* means to use resources—people, money, raw materials, and the like—wisely and cost-effectively.**

- *Effectiveness—the ends.* Effectiveness is the organization's ends, the goals. **To be *effective* means to achieve results, to make the right decisions and to successfully carry them out so that they achieve the organization's goals.**

Good managers are concerned with trying to achieve both qualities. Often, however, organizations will erroneously strive for efficiency without being effective.

Example

Efficiency versus Effectiveness: Won't Someone Answer the Phone—*Please?*

We're all now accustomed to having our calls to companies answered not by people but by a recorded "telephone menu" of options. Certainly this arrangement is *efficient* for the companies, since they no longer need as many telephone receptionists. But it's not *effective* if it leaves us, the customers, fuming and not inclined to continue doing business.

The cost for self-service via an automated phone system averages $1.85, whereas the cost of using a live customer-service representative is $4.50, according to the Gartner Group.[5] Nevertheless, automated technologies often don't allow completion of transactions, because of customer confusion and technological glitches, so this leads to "ping-ponging"—customers calling back trying to find a live representative.

Thus, Scott Broetzmann, president of CustomerCare Measurement Consulting, a firm that does surveys on customer service, says that 90% of consumers say they want nothing to do with an automated telephone system. "They just don't like it," he says. The most telling finding is that 50% of those surveyed had become so aggravated that they were willing to pay

Effective? Is this irate customer dealing with a company phone system that is more efficient than effective?

an additional charge for customer service that avoids going through an automated phone system.[6]

Richard Shapiro, head of a firm that evaluates the experiences of customers calling in to toll-free call centers, says that companies "create more value through a dialogue with a live agent. A call is an opportunity to build a relationship, to encourage a customer to stay with the brand. There can be a real return on this investment.[7] Recognizing this, Netflix, the DVD-by-mail rental company, recently added 24/7 live operators to deal with customers' problems.[8]

Your Call
Paul English, chief technology officer for a travel search engine business, was so fed up with automated voice services and other awful customer service that he started Get Human to "change the face of customer service." The Web site, **www.gethuman.com,** publishes the unpublicized codes for reaching a company's human operators, a list of the best and worst companies, and cut-through-automation tips.[9] What recent unpleasant customer experience would you want to post on this Web site?

Why Organizations Value Managers: The Multiplier Effect

Some great achievements of history, such as scientific discoveries or works of art, were accomplished by individuals working quietly by themselves. But so much more has been achieved by people who were able to leverage their talents and abilities by being managers. For instance, of the top 10 great architectural wonders of the world named by the American Institute of Architects, none was built by just one person. All were triumphs of management, although some reflected the vision of an individual. (The wonders are the Great Wall of China, the Great Pyramid, Machu Picchu, the Acropolis, the Coliseum, the Taj Mahal, the Eiffel Tower, the Brooklyn Bridge, the Empire State Building, and Frank Lloyd Wright's Falling Water house in Pennsylvania.)

Good managers create value. The reason is that in being a manager you have a *multiplier effect:* your influence on the organization is multiplied far beyond the results that can be achieved by just one person acting alone. Thus, while a solo operator such as a salesperson might accomplish many things and incidentally make a very good living, his or her boss could accomplish a great deal more—and could well earn two to seven times the income. And the manager will undoubtedly have a lot more influence.

Star managers are in high demand. "The scarcest, most valuable resource in business is no longer financial capital," says a recent *Fortune* article. "It's talent. If you doubt that, just watch how hard companies are battling for the best people. . . . Talent of every type is in short supply, but the greatest shortage of all is skilled, effective managers.[10]

Financial Rewards of Being a Star Manager

How well compensated are managers? According to the U.S. Bureau of Labor Statistics, the median weekly wage in 2007 for American workers of all sorts was $700, or $36,400 a year.[11] Education pays: The average 2006 income for full-time workers with a bachelor's degree was $43,143 and with a master's degree was $52,390. (For high-school graduates, it was $26,505.)

The business press frequently reports on the astronomical earnings of top chief executive officers such as Lee R. Raymond, chairman and chief executive of the oil giant ExxonMobil, who was compensated more than $686 million from 1993 to 2005, which works out to $144,573 a day.[12] However, this kind of compensation isn't common. More usual is the take-home pay for the head of a small business: In 2007, the median salary for a small business chief executive was $233,500. (A small business was classified as a company with up to 500 full-time employees.) The national median salary for a CEO with 500 to 5,000 employees was $500,000, and $849,375 for those at companies with more than 5,000 employees.[13]

Managers farther down in the organization usually don't make this much, of course; nevertheless, they do fairly well compared to most workers. At the lower rungs, managers may make between $25,000 and $50,000 a year; in the middle levels, between $35,000 and $110,000.

There are also all kinds of fringe benefits and status rewards that go with being a manager, ranging from health insurance to stock options to large offices. And the higher you ascend in the management hierarchy, the more privileges may come your way: personal parking space, better furniture, lunch in the executive dining room, on up to—for those on the top rung of big companies—company car and driver, corporate jet, and even executive sabbaticals (months of paid time off to pursue alternative projects).

What Are the Rewards of Studying & Practicing Management?

Are you studying management but have no plans to be a manager? Or are you trying to learn techniques and concepts that will help you be an exceptional management practitioner? Either way there are considerable rewards.

The Rewards of Studying Management Students sign up for the introductory management course for all kinds of reasons. Many, of course, are planning business careers, but others are taking it to fulfill a requirement or an elective or just to fill a hole in their course schedule. Some students are in technical fields,

Lee Raymond. The former ExxonMobil CEO earned about $144,573 a day in the years before retirement—equivalent to the yearly salary of a well-paid middle manager. The company's shares rose an average of 13% a year on Raymond's watch. What do you think your chances are of making $400 million, as Raymond did in his final year?

such as accounting, finance, computer science, and engineering, and never expect to have to supervise other people.

Here are just a few of the payoffs of studying management as a discipline:

- **You will understand how to deal with organizations from the outside.** Since we all are in constant interaction with all kinds of organizations, it helps to understand how they work and how the people in them make decisions. Such knowledge may give you some defensive skills that you can use in dealing with organizations from the outside, as a customer or investor, for example.

- **You will understand how to relate to your supervisors.** Since most of us work in organizations and most of us have bosses, studying management will enable you to understand the pressures managers deal with and how they will best respond to you.

- **You will understand how to interact with co-workers.** The kinds of management policies in place can affect how your co-workers behave. Studying management can give you the understanding of teams and teamwork, cultural differences, conflict and stress, and negotiation and communication skills that will help you get along with fellow employees.

- **You will understand how to manage yourself in the workplace.** Management courses in general, and this book in particular, give you the opportunity to realize insights about yourself—your personality, emotions, values, perceptions, needs, and goals. We help you build your skills in areas such as self-management, listening, handling change, managing stress, avoiding groupthink, and coping with organizational politics.

Manager's Hot Seat:
Office Romance:
Groping for Answers

The Rewards of Practicing Management It's possible you are planning to be a manager. Or it's possible you will start your career practicing a narrow specialty but find yourself tapped for some sort of supervisory or leadership position. However you become a management practitioner, there are many rewards—apart from those of money and status—to being a manager:

Mentoring. Being a manager is an opportunity "to counsel, motivate, advise, guide, empower, and influence" other people. Does this sense of accomplishment appeal to you?

- **You and your employees can experience a sense of accomplishment.** Every successful goal accomplished provides you not only with personal satisfaction but also with the satisfaction of all those employees you directed who helped you accomplish it.

- **You can stretch your abilities and magnify your range.** Every promotion up the hierarchy of an organization stretches your abilities, challenges your talents and skills, and magnifies the range of your accomplishments.

- **You can build a catalog of successful products or services.** Every product or service you provide—the personal Eiffel Tower or Empire State Building you build, as it were—becomes a monument to your accomplishments. Indeed, studying management may well help you in running your own business.

Finally, points out Odette Pollar, who owns Time Management Systems, a productivity-improvement firm in Oakland, California, "Managers are able to view the business in a broader context, to plan and grow personally. Managers can play more of a leadership role than ever before. This is an opportunity to counsel, motivate, advise, guide, empower, and influence large groups of people. These important skills can be used in business as well as in personal and volunteer activities. If you truly like people and enjoy mentoring and helping others to grow and thrive, management is a great job."[14] ●

Challenges can make one feel alive. What are six challenges I could look forward to as a manager?

THE BIG PICTURE

Six challenges face any manager: You need to manage for competitive advantage—to stay ahead of rivals. You need to manage for diversity in race, ethnicity, gender, and so on, because the future won't resemble the past. You need to manage for the effects of globalization and of information technology. You always need to manage to maintain ethical standards. Finally, you need to manage for the achievement for your own happiness and life goals.

The ideal state that many people seek is an emotional zone somewhere between boredom and anxiety, in the view of psychologist Mihaly Csikzentmihalyi.[15] Boredom, he says, may arise because skills and challenges are mismatched: You are exercising your high level of skill in a job with a low level of challenge, such as licking envelopes. Anxiety arises when one has low levels of skill but a high level of challenge.

As a manager, could you achieve a balance between these two states? Certainly managers have enough challenges to keep their lives more than mildly interesting. Let's see what they are.

Challenge #I: Managing for Competitive Advantage— Staying Ahead of Rivals

Competitive advantage is the **ability of an organization to produce goods or services more effectively than competitors do, thereby outperforming them.** This means an organization must stay ahead in four areas: (1) being responsive to customers, (2) innovation, (3) quality, and (4) efficiency.

I. Being Responsive to Customers The first law of business is: *take care of the customer*. Without customers—buyers, clients, consumers, shoppers, users, patrons, guests, investors, or whatever they're called—sooner or later there will be no organization. Nonprofit organizations are well advised to be responsive to their "customers," too, whether they're called citizens, members, students, patients, voters, rate-payers, or whatever, since they are the justification for the organizations' existence.

2. Innovation Finding ways to **deliver new or better goods or services** is called *innovation.* No organization, for-profit or nonprofit, can allow itself to become complacent—especially when rivals are coming up with creative ideas. "Innovate or die" is an important adage for any manager.

We discuss innovation in Chapter 3.

3. Quality If your organization is the only one of its kind, customers may put up with products or services that are less than stellar (as they have with some airlines whose hub systems give them a near-monopoly on flights out of certain cities), but only because they have no choice. But if another organization comes along and offers a better-quality travel experience, TV program, cut of meat, computer software, or whatever, you may find your company falling behind. Making improvements in quality has become an important management idea in recent times, as we shall discuss.

Example

Losing Competitive Advantage: Network Television Battles "On-Demand" Technologies

The four major television networks—ABC, CBS, NBC, and Fox—have felt extreme pressure on revenues as the mass audience they used to take for granted has fragmented, causing the networks to lose their competitive advantage. During the past dozen years, their share of the viewing audience has fallen from 72% to about 41%; indeed, it lost an entire 5% just between 2006 and 2007.[16] This has been caused by three developments, says television critic David Friend.[17]

First has been the rise of cable television, supported by its two revenue streams, advertisers and subscribers, and its offerings, which, says Friend, "made even the best network shows look strangely antique." Examples have been the HBO hits "The Sopranos" and "Deadwood," Comedy Central's "South Park," and FX's "The Shield." The major networks responded by premiering shows not just in the fall but throughout the year, by putting on serial dramas and reality shows, and by running shows in short series of only 10 or 12 episodes. However, these tactics adversely affected the ability of the networks to sell hit shows into syndication (reruns), causing them to lose further revenues.

Second has been further audience fragmentation occasioned by the change from a "linear" viewing model to an "on-demand" model. In the linear model, according to Friend, people watch a show at the time the network airs it, such as "Desperate Housewives" at 9 P.M.

on ABC. In the on-demand model, viewers tune in whenever they want to, using ad-skipping digital video-recorders (TiVo systems), iPods, personal computers, and cell phones. This has two results: on-demand viewers frequently become distracted by other offerings (including "grassroots" content, such as skateboard wipeouts created by sk8hed), and they frequently skip or delete commercials. As many as 20–40% of viewers may now be in a position to zap ads.[18] This phenomenon has forced the networks to resort to more "product (or brand) integration," in which products are placed in scenes visible to viewers and advertisers are given roles in plots of shows, such as "a desperate housewife showing off a Buick at a shopping mall," in one description.[19]

Third has been the networks' obsession with beating other hit shows, moving successful shows around to different time slots in order to try to outdraw rivals. "By obsessing about whether 'Chicago Hope' will beat 'ER,'" says Friend, "the execs are making a classic *Time* vs. *Newsweek* . . . mistake: grappling with their longtime rival, oblivious of their surroundings, they all fall over the cliff together."

Your Call

As the networks go, will cable follow? What do you think the effect will be of iPods, DVRs, HDTV, video-on-demand, and the like on the cable industry?[20]

4. Efficiency   Whereas a generation ago organizations rewarded employees for their length of service, today the emphasis is on efficiency: Companies strive to produce goods or services as quickly as possible using as few employees (and raw materials) as possible. While a strategy that downgrades the value of employees will probably backfire—resulting in the loss of essential experience and skills and even customers—an organization that is overstaffed may not be able to compete with leaner, meaner rivals. This is the reason why, for instance, today many managers—aided by their desktop computers—do much of their own correspondence and filing. Secretarial staffs have been reduced, but of course the secretarial work remains.

Challenge #2: Managing for Diversity—The Future Won't Resemble the Past

During the next half-century, the mix of American racial or ethnic groups will change considerably, with the United States becoming half minority. Nonhispanic whites are projected to decrease from 69% of the population at the turn of the 21st century to 50% in 2050. African Americans will increase from 13% to 15%, Asians and Pacific Islanders from 4% to 8%, and Hispanics (who may be of any race) from 13% to 24%.[21] In addition, in the coming years there will be a different mix of women, immigrants, and older people in the general population, as well as in the workforce. For instance, in 2006, Hispanics accounted for nearly one-quarter of all U.S. births.[22]

Some scholars think that diversity and variety in staffing produce organizational strength, as we consider elsewhere.[23] Clearly, however, the challenge to the manager of the near future is to maximize the contributions of employees diverse in gender, age, race, and ethnicity. We discuss this matter in more detail in Chapter 3.

Challenge #3: Managing for Globalization—The Expanding Management Universe

"In Japan it is considered rude to look directly in the eye for more than a few seconds," says a report about teaching Americans how to behave abroad, "and in Greece the hand-waving gesture commonly used in America for goodbye is considered an insult."[24]

The point: Gestures and symbols don't have the same meaning to everyone throughout the world. Not understanding such differences can affect how well organizations manage globally.

American firms have been going out into the world in a major way, even as the world has been coming to us—leading to what *New York Times* columnist Thomas Friedman has called, in his 2005 book *The World Is Flat,* a phenomenon in which globalization has leveled (made "flat") the competitive playing fields between industrial and emerging-market countries.[25] Indeed, despite political outcries about white-collar jobs disappearing overseas to places such as India, foreigners actually send far more office work to the United States than American companies send abroad.[26] Managing for globalization will be a complex, ongoing challenge, as we discuss at length in Chapter 4.

Challenge #4: Managing for Information Technology

The challenge of managing for information technology, not to mention other technologies affecting your business, will require your unflagging attention. Perhaps

The famous golden arches. This McDonald's store in Beijing is an example of globalization.

most important is the *Internet,* **the global network of independently operating but interconnected computers, linking hundreds of thousands of smaller networks around the world.**

By 2010, according to International Data Corp., Internet trade between businesses will surpass $10 trillion worldwide.[27] This kind of *e-commerce,* or electronic commerce—**the buying and selling of goods or services over computer networks**—is reshaping entire industries and revamping the very notion of what a company is. More important than e-commerce, the information technology has facilitated *e-business,* **using the Internet to facilitate *every* aspect of running a business.** As one article puts it, "at bottom, the Internet is a tool that dramatically lowers the cost of communication. That means it can radically alter any industry or activity that depends heavily on the flow of information."[28]

Some of the implications of e-business that we will discuss throughout the book are as follows:

- **Far-ranging e-management and e-communication.** Using wired and wireless telephones, fax machines, electronic mail, or *e-mail*—**text messages and documents transmitted over a computer network**—as well as *project management software*—**programs for planning and scheduling the people, costs, and resources to complete a project on time**—21st-century managers will find themselves responsible for creating, motivating, and leading teams of specialists all over the world. This will require them to be masters of organizational communication, able to create concise, powerful e-mail and voice-mail messages.

- **Accelerated decision making, conflict, and stress.** The Internet not only speeds everything up, it also, with its huge, interconnected *databases*—**computerized collections of interrelated files**—can overwhelm us with information, much of it useful, much of it not. For example, recent studies show that employees lose valuable time and productivity when dealing with excessive and unimportant e-mail volume and increasing amounts of cell phone spam.[29] Among the unavoidable by-products are increased conflict and stress, although, as we will show, these can be managed.

- **Changes in organizational structure, jobs, goal setting, and knowledge management.** With computers and telecommunications technology, organizations and teams become "virtual"; they are no longer as bound by time zones and locations. Employees, for instance, may *telecommute,* **or work from home or remote locations using a variety of information technologies.** Meetings may be conducted via *videoconferencing,* **using video and audio links along with computers to let people in different locations see, hear, and talk with one another.** In addition, *collaborative computing,* **using state-of-the-art computer software and hardware, will help people work better together.** Goal setting and feedback will be conducted via Web-based software programs such as eWorkbench, which enables managers to create and track employee goals. All such forms of interaction will require managers and employees to be more flexible, and there will be an increased emphasis on *knowledge management*—**the implementing of systems and practices to increase the sharing of knowledge and information throughout an organization.**

Challenge #5: Managing for Ethical Standards

With the pressure to meet sales, production, and other targets, managers can find themselves confronting ethical dilemmas. What do you do when you learn

Perp walk. Handcuffed former Enron CEO Jeffrey Skilling, escorted by an FBI agent, arrives at the federal courthouse in Houston in 2004. He was charged with nearly three dozen counts of fraud, insider trading, and other crimes that led to his company's colossal collapse. If you're tempted to stretch your ethics in order to pass a college course, do you think you'd do the same in business, where the pressures can be even worse?

Manager's Hot Seat:
Ethics: Let's Make a
Fourth-Quarter Deal

an employee dropped a gyroscope but put it in the helicopter anyway in order to hold the product's delivery date? How much should you allow your sales reps to knock the competition? How much leeway do you have in giving gifts to prospective clients in a foreign country to try to land a contract? In an era of global warming and rising sea levels, what is your responsibility to "act green"—avoid company policies that are damaging to the environment?

Ethical behavior is not just a nicety, it is a very important part of doing business. This was made clear during the period 2003–2004 as executives from Enron, Tyco, WorldCom, Adelphia, and other companies were paraded in handcuffs before television cameras. Not since sociologist Edwin Sutherland invented the term "white-collar crime" in the 1930s were so many top-level executives being hauled into court. We consider ethics in Chapter 3 and elsewhere in the book.

Challenge #6: Managing for Your Own Happiness & Life Goals

Ann Garcia had the view that good managers push decision making down, spread the compliments, and take the blame, but after being given a team to manage at her technology company, she gave it up. "I'm just not a big enough person all the time to want to do that," she said. "Many of us realize that we don't want the career path that corporate America has to offer."[30]

Regardless of how well paid you are, you have to consider whether in meeting the organization's challenges you are also meeting the challenge of realizing your own happiness. Many people simply don't find being a manager fulfilling. They may complain that they have to go to too many meetings, that they can't do enough for their employees, that they are caught in the middle between bosses and subordinates. They may feel, at a time when Dilbert cartoons have created such an unflattering portrayal of managers, that they lack respect.[31] They may decide that, despite the greater income, money cannot buy happiness, as the adage goes.

In the end, however, recall what Odette Pollar said: "If you truly like people and enjoy mentoring and helping others to grow and thrive, management is a great job." And it helps to know, as she points out, that "one's experience in management is greatly affected by the company's culture."[32] Culture, or style, is indeed an important matter, because it affects your happiness within an organization, and we discuss it in detail in Chapter 8. ●

1.3 WHAT MANAGERS DO: THE FOUR PRINCIPAL FUNCTIONS

What would I actually *do*—that is, what would be my four principal functions—as a manager?

major question?

THE BIG PICTURE

Management has four functions: *planning, organizing, leading,* and *controlling.*

What do you as a manager do to "get things done"—that is, achieve the stated goals of the organization you work for? You perform what is known as the ***management process,** also called the **four management functions:** **planning, organizing, leading, and controlling.** (The abbreviation "POLC" may help you to remember them.)

As the diagram below illustrates, all these functions affect one another, are ongoing, and are performed simultaneously. *(See Figure 1.1.)*

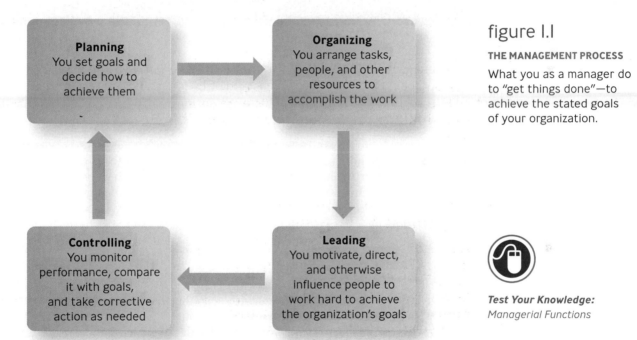

figure 1.1

THE MANAGEMENT PROCESS

What you as a manager do to "get things done"—to achieve the stated goals of your organization.

Test Your Knowledge:
Managerial Functions

Although the process of management can be quite complex, these four functions represent its essential principles. Indeed, as a glance at our text's table of contents shows, they form four of the part divisions of the book. Let's consider what the four functions are, using the management (or "administration," as it is called in nonprofit organizations) of your college to illustrate them.

Planning: Discussed in Part 3 of This Book

***Planning** is defined as **setting goals and deciding how to achieve them.** Your college was established for the purpose of educating students, and its present managers, or administrators, now must decide the best way to accomplish this. Which of several possible degree programs should be offered? Should the college be a residential or a

Leading. Steve Jobs, cofounder and CEO of Apple Computer and Pixar Animation, is famous for being an innovative leader. Do you think you have the ability to take the kind of risks he has?

commuter campus? What sort of students should be recruited and admitted? What kind of faculty should be hired? What kind of buildings and equipment are needed?

Organizing: Discussed in Part 4 of This Book

Organizing **is defined as arranging tasks, people and other resources to accomplish the work.** College administrators must determine the tasks to be done, by whom, and what the reporting hierarchy is to be. Should the institution be organized into schools with departments, with department chairpersons reporting to deans who in return report to vice presidents? Should the college hire more full-time instructors than part-time instructors? Should English professors teach just English literature or also composition, developmental English, and "first-year experience" courses?

Leading: Discussed in Part 5 of This Book

Leading **is defined as motivating, directing, and otherwise influencing people to work hard to achieve the organization's goals.** At your college, leadership begins, of course, with the president (who would be the chief executive officer, or CEO, in a for-profit organization). He or she is the one who must inspire faculty, staff, students, alumni, wealthy donors, and residents of the surrounding community to help realize the college's goals. As you might imagine, these groups often have different needs and wants, so an essential part of leadership is resolving conflicts.

Controlling: Discussed in Part 6 of This Book

Controlling **is defined as monitoring performance, comparing it with goals, and taking corrective action as needed.** Is the college discovering that fewer students are majoring in nursing than they did 5 years previously? Is the fault with a change in the job market? with the quality of instruction? with the kinds of courses offered? Are the Nursing Department's student recruitment efforts not going well? Should the department's budget be reduced? Under the management function of controlling, college administrators must deal with these kinds of matters. ●

1.4 PYRAMID POWER: LEVELS & AREAS OF MANAGEMENT

What are the levels and areas of management I need to know to move up, down, and sideways?

major question?

THE BIG PICTURE

Within an organization, there are managers at three levels: *top, middle,* and *first-line*. Managers may also be *general managers,* or they may be *functional managers,* responsible for just one organizational activity, such as Research & Development, Marketing, Finance, Production, or Human Resources. Managers may work for for-profit, non-profit, or mutual-benefit organizations.

The workplace of the future may resemble a symphony orchestra, famed management theorist Peter Drucker said.[33] Employees, especially so-called knowledge workers—those who have a great deal of technical skills—can be compared to concert musicians. Their managers can be seen as conductors.

In Drucker's analogy, musicians are used for some pieces of music—that is, work projects—and not others, and they are divided into different sections (teams) based on their instruments. The conductor's role is not to play each instrument better than the musicians but to lead them all through the most effective performance of a particular work.

This model is in sharp contrast to the traditional pyramid-like organizational model, where one leader sits at the top, with layers of managers beneath. We therefore need to take a look at the traditional arrangement first.

The Traditional Management Pyramid: Levels & Areas

A new Silicon Valley technology startup company staffed by young people in sandals and shorts may be so small and so loosely organized that only one or two members may be said to be a manager. General Motors or the U.S. Army, in contrast, has thousands of managers doing thousands of different things. Is there a picture we can draw that applies to all the different kinds of organizations that describes them in ways that make sense? Yes: by levels and by areas, as the pyramid on the next page shows. *(See Figure 1.2.)*

Three Levels of Management

Not everyone who works in an organization is a manager, of course, but those who are may be classified into three levels—top, middle, and first-line.

Top Managers   Their offices may be equipped with expensive leather chairs and have lofty views. Or, as with one Internet service provider (ISP), they may have plastic lawn chairs in the CEO's office and beat-up furniture in the lobby. Whatever their decor, an organization's top managers tend to have titles such as "chief executive officer (CEO)," "chief operating officer (COO)," "president," and "senior vice president."

Some may be the stars in their fields, the men and women whose pictures appear on the covers of business magazines, people such as MySpace co-founders Tom Anderson and Chris DeWolfe or PepsiCo CEO Indra Nooyi, who appeared on the front of *Fortune* in 2006, or former eBay CEO Meg Whitman or AT&T CEO Ed Whitacre, who were on the cover of *Forbes* in 2007. The salaries and

figure I.2

THE LEVELS AND AREAS OF MANAGEMENT

Top managers make long-term decisions, middle managers implement those decisions, and first-line managers make short-term decisions.

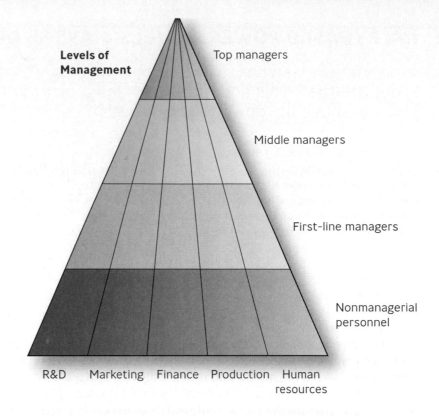

Levels of Management

Top managers

Middle managers

First-line managers

Nonmanagerial personnel

Functional Areas

R&D   Marketing   Finance   Production   Human resources

One kind of top manager. Jeffrey Immelt, chairman and CEO, has worked at General Electric for over 26 years. Known for its consumer appliances (which it now plans to divest), GE also sells aircraft engines, lighting, and medical imaging equipment. Do you see yourself joining a company and staying with it for life, as Immelt did, or is that even possible anymore?

bonuses can average $290,000 a year for CEOs and presidents of small and mid-size companies to far over $1 million for top executives in large companies.

Top managers **make long-term decisions about the overall direction of the organization and establish the objectives, policies, and strategies for it.** They need to pay a lot of attention to the environment outside the organization, being alert for long-run opportunities and problems and devising strategies for dealing with them. Thus, executives at this level must be future oriented, dealing with uncertain, highly competitive conditions.

These people stand at the summit of the management pyramid. But the nature of a pyramid is that the farther you climb, the less space remains at the top. Thus, most pyramid climbers never get to the apex. However, that doesn't mean that you shouldn't try. Indeed, you might end up atop a much smaller pyramid of some other organization than the one you started out in—and happier with the result.

Middle Managers   *Middle managers* **implement the policies and plans of the top managers** above them and **supervise and coordinate the activities of the first-line managers below them.** In the nonprofit world, middle managers may have titles such as "clinic director," "dean of student services," and the like. In the for-profit world, the titles may be "division head," "plant manager," and "branch sales manager." Their salaries may range from under $50,000 up to $110,000 a year.

Sometimes the titles have become more creative, in accordance with the changing face of management. For instance, now there are titles such as chief security officer, chief sales officer, chief revenue officer, and chief investment officer. A company may also have a "chief learning officer" in charge of training, a "chief green (or sustainability) officer" in charge of environmental concerns, and even a "chief beer officer," a position created by the Sheraton Hotels Four Points chain for a person who selects beers for hotel menus and leads brewery tours.[34]

First-Line Managers   The job titles at the bottom of the managerial pyramid tend to be on the order of "department head," "foreman" or "forewoman," "team leader," or "supervisor"—clerical supervisor, production supervisor, research supervisor, and so on. Indeed, *supervisor* is the name often given to first-line managers as a whole. Their salaries may run from $25,000 to $50,000 a year.

Following the plans of middle and top managers, *first-line managers* **make short-term operating decisions, directing the daily tasks of nonmanagerial personnel,** who are, of course, all those people who work directly at their jobs but don't oversee the work of others.

No doubt the job of first-line manager will be the place where you would start your managerial career. This can be a valuable experience because it will be the training and testing ground for your management ideas.

Top managers of another sort. Entrepreneurs Larry Page (left) and Sergey Brin, former graduate students who founded the highly popular search engine Google in a Menlo Park, California, garage, became instant billionaires before age 30 when they took their company public in 2004. Do you think a top manager is always adventurous?

Areas of Management: Functional Managers versus General Managers

We can represent the levels of management by slicing the organizational pyramid horizontally. We can also slice the pyramid vertically to represent the organization's departments or functional areas, as we did in Figure 1.2.

In a for-profit technology company, these might be *Research & Development, Marketing, Finance, Production,* and *Human Resources.* In a nonprofit college, these might be *Faculty, Student Support Staff, Finance, Maintenance,* and *Administration.* Whatever the names of the departments, the organization is run by two types of managers—functional and general. (These are line managers, with authority to direct employees. Staff managers mainly assist line managers, as we discuss later.)

Functional Managers   If your title is Vice President of Production, Director of Finance, or Administrator for Human Resources, you are a functional manager. **A** *functional manager* **is responsible for just one organizational activity.** Danamichele Brennan, now chief technology officer for McGettigan Partners, was previously with Rosenbluth Travel, where her title—indicative of the trend in some companies toward use of more flexible job titles—was Chief Travel Scientist. Her job was heading a research team that developed services to turn reservation agents into travel consultants. The goal: not just cheaper travel but better travel.[35] Leading this specialized sort of research-and-development activity makes her a functional manager.

General Managers   If you are working in a small organization of, say, 100 people and your title is Executive Vice President, you are probably a general manager over several departments, such as Production and Finance and Human Resources. **A** *general manager* **is responsible for several organizational activities.** At the top of the pyramid, general managers are those who seem to be the subject of news stories in magazines such as *BusinessWeek, Fortune, Forbes, Inc.,* and *Fast Company.* Examples are big-company CEOs Jeffrey R. Immelt of General Electric and Anne Mulcahy of Xerox Corp. It also includes small-company CEOs such as Gayle

Martz, who heads Sherpa's Pet Trading Co., a $4 million New York company with 10 employees that sells travel carriers for dogs and cats. But not all general managers are in for-profit organizations.

Dr. Rick Aubrey is president of Rubicon Programs, a San Francisco–area nonprofit formed after California state psychiatric hospitals were closed in 1973. The organization funds training, housing, and employment programs that have helped thousands of former patients and disabled, impoverished, and homeless people reenter society. Rubicon funds 59% of its $13.9 million annual budget from its rental properties, enterprises, and services, such as the Rubicon Bakery and Rubicon Landscape Services, which also provide job training. Aubrey makes a point of running Rubicon like a business, reflecting the strategic vision of a top-level general manager.[36] Rubicon was a recipient of *Fast Company* magazine's 2008 Social Capitalist awards.[37]

Managers for Three Types of Organizations: For-Profit, Nonprofit, Mutual-Benefit

There are three types of organizations classified according to the three purposes for which they are formed—*for-profit, nonprofit, and mutual-benefit.*[38]

Nonprofit manager. A general manager is responsible for several organizational activities. Rick Aubrey oversees a nonprofit organization with a $13.9 million budget. Do you think managerial skills are different for nonprofit and for-profit organizations?

I. For-Profit Organizations: For Making Money   For-profit, or business, organizations are formed to make money, or profits, by offering products or services. When most people think of "management," they think of business organizations, ranging from Allstate to Zenith, from Amway to Zagat.

2. Nonprofit Organizations: For Offering Services   Managers in nonprofit organizations are often known as "administrators." Nonprofit organizations may be either in the public sector, such as the University of California, or in the private sector, such as Stanford University. Either way, their purpose is to offer services to some clients, not to make a profit. Examples of such organizations are hospitals, colleges, and social-welfare agencies (the Salvation Army, the Red Cross).

One particular type of nonprofit organization is called the *commonweal organization.* Unlike nonprofit service organizations, which offer services to *some* clients, commonweal organizations offer services to *all* clients within their jurisdictions. Examples are the military services, the U.S. Postal Service, and your local fire and police departments.

3. Mutual-Benefit Organizations: For Aiding Members   Mutual-benefit organizations are voluntary collections of members—political parties, farm cooperatives, labor unions, trade associations, and clubs—whose purpose is to advance members' interests.

Do Managers Manage Differently for Different Types of Organizations?
If you become a manager, would you be doing the same types of things regardless of the type of organization? Generally you would be; that is, you would be performing the four management functions—planning, organizing, leading, and controlling—that we described in Section 1.3.

The single biggest difference, however, is that in a for-profit organization, the measure of its success is how much profit (or loss) it generates. In the other two types of organization, although income and expenditures are very important concerns, the measure of success is usually the effectiveness of the services delivered—how many students were graduated, if you're a college administrator, or how many crimes were prevented or solved, if you're a police chief. ●

1.5 ROLES MANAGERS MUST PLAY SUCCESSFULLY

To be an exceptional manager, what roles must I play successfully?

major question ?

THE BIG PICTURE

Managers tend to work long hours at an intense pace; their work is characterized by fragmentation, brevity, and variety; and they rely more on verbal than on written communication. According to management scholar Henry Mintzberg, managers play three roles—*interpersonal, informational,* and *decisional.* Interpersonal roles include figurehead, leader, and liaison activities. Informational roles are monitor, disseminator, and spokesperson. Decisional roles are entrepreneur, disturbance handler, resource allocator, and negotiator.

Clearly, as MTV Networks CEO Judy McGrath's experience suggests, being a successful manager requires playing several different roles and exercising several different skills. What are they?

The Manager's Roles: Mintzberg's Useful Findings

Maybe, you think, it might be interesting to shadow some managers to see what it is, in fact, they actually do. That's exactly what management scholar **Henry Mintzberg** did when, in the late 1960s, he followed five chief executives around for a week and recorded their working lives.[39] And what he found is valuable to know, since it applies not only to top managers but also to managers on all levels.

Consider this portrait of a manager's workweek: "There was no break in the pace of activity during office hours," reported Mintzberg about his subjects. "The mail (average of 36 pieces per day), telephone calls (average of five per day), and meetings (average of eight) accounted for almost every minute from the moment these executives entered their offices in the morning until they departed in the evening."[40]

Only five phone calls per day? And, of course, this was back in an era before e-mail, which nowadays can shower some executives with 100, even 300, messages a day. Indeed, says Ed Reilly, who heads the America Management Association, all the e-mail, cell phone calls, text messaging, and so on can lead people to end up "concentrating on the urgent rather than the important."[41]

Obviously, the top manager's life is extraordinarily busy. Here are three of Mintzberg's findings, important for any prospective manager:

Multitasking. Multiple activities are characteristic of a manager—which is why so many managers carry a personal digital assistant or smart phone to keep track of their schedules. Many students already use these. Do you?

I. A Manager Relies More on Verbal Than on Written Communication Writing letters, memos, and reports takes time. Most managers in Mintzberg's research tended to get and transmit information through telephone conversations and meetings. No doubt this is still true, although the technology of e-mail now makes it possible to communicate almost as rapidly in writing as with the spoken word.

2. A Manager Works Long Hours at an Intense Pace "A true break seldom occurred," wrote Mintzberg about his subjects.

A Mintzberg manager.
Charles Schwab, founder of the financial services firm, relies more on verbal than on written communication, works long hours, and experiences an "interrupt-driven day." Interestingly, Schwab is successful despite having had lifelong dyslexia, the common language-related learning disability. What kind of personal obstacles do you need to overcome?

"Coffee was taken during meetings, and lunchtime was almost always devoted to formal or informal meetings."

Long hours at work are standard, he found, with 50 hours being typical and up to 90 hours not unheard of. A 1999 survey by John P. Kotter of the Harvard Business School found that the general managers he studied worked just under 60 hours per week.[42]

Are such hours really necessary? Three decades following the Mintzberg research, Linda Stroh, Director of Workplace Studies at Loyola University Chicago, did a study that found that people who work more also earn more. "Those managers who worked 61 hours or more per week had earned, on average, about two promotions over the past five years," she reported.[43] However, researchers at Purdue and McGill universities have found that more companies are allowing managers to reduce their working hours and spend more time with their families yet still advance their high-powered careers.[44]

3. A Manager's Work Is Characterized by Fragmentation, Brevity, & Variety Only about a tenth of the managerial activities observed by Mintzberg took more than an hour; about half were completed in under 9 minutes. Phone calls averaged 6 minutes, informal meetings 10 minutes, and desk-work sessions 15 minutes. "When free time appeared," wrote Mintzberg, "ever-present subordinates quickly usurped it."

No wonder the executive's work time has been characterized as "the interrupt-driven day" and that many managers—such as the late Mary Kay Ash, head of the Mary Kay Cosmetics company—get up as early as 5 A.M. so that they will have a quiet period in which to work undisturbed.[45] No wonder that finding balance between work and family lives is an ongoing concern and that many managers—such as Dawn Lepore, executive V.P. of discount broker Charles Schwab & Co.—have become "much less tolerant of activities that aren't a good use of my time" and so have become better delegators.[46]

It is clear from Mintzberg's work that *time and task management* are major challenges for every manager. The Practical Action box on the next page, "Getting Your Work Done," offers some suggestions along this line, as does the box at the end of this chapter (page 28), "Getting Control of Your Time: Dealing with the Information Deluge in College & in Your Career."

Three Types of Managerial Roles

Three Types of Managerial Roles: Interpersonal, Informational, & Decisional From his observations and other research, Mintzberg concluded that managers play three broad types of roles or "organized sets of behavior": *interpersonal, informational,* and *decisional.*

1. Interpersonal Roles—Figurehead, Leader, and Liaison In their *interpersonal roles,* managers interact with people inside and outside their work units. The three interpersonal roles include *figurehead, leader,* and *liaison* activities.

Practical Action

Getting Your Work Done: Don't Procrastinate, & Keep Your Eye on the Big Picture

Do you procrastinate about getting your work done? Most people do—and in fact the problem has worsened over the years: Today about 26% of Americans think of themselves as chronic procrastinators, up from 5% in 1978. The reason is that there are too many tempting diversions.[47] Ultimately, of course, putting off addressing important problems can lead you to feel completely overwhelmed.

Then there is Chris Peters. Peters is a vice president of Microsoft, a company famous for its killer workdays, but he's known for keeping reasonable hours. How does he do it? Like other high achievers, he's able to get more work done in shorter time because he stays focused on things he *has* to do instead of unimportant things he might be doing.[48]

Stars like Peters keep their eye on the big picture. They "have this grasp of what the bottom line is, what 'the critical path' is, and they stay there rather than getting pulled off it all the time," says Carnegie Mellon professor Robert E. Kelley.[49] Stars keep their priorities straight by seeing projects through the eyes of the customers or the co-workers who depend on them.

Says star manager Brian Graham, who sits out routine meetings and relies on co-workers to keep him informed, "The key for me is to know what not to do, and to always be looking for the path of quickest resolution."[50] Finally, stars avoid multitasking, which is an attempt to defy the brain's natural inability to concentrate on two things at once.[51] Successful CEOs do not multitask," says time-management guru Stephanie Winston, who advises people to turn off their instant messaging. "They concentrate intensely on one thing at a time."[52]

According to one survey, nearly two in three full-time U.S. employees said their workloads had increased during the past 12–24 months.[53] As a manager, how are you going to deal with this workload problem? College students already wrestle with this problem. Clearly, if you can come to grips with this beast now, you'll have developed some skills that can save your life in your career. Some strategies are given in the box ("Taking Something Practical Away from This Chapter") at the end of this chapter.

---

2. Informational Roles—Monitor, Disseminator, and Spokesperson The most important part of a manager's job, Mintzberg believed, is information handling, because accurate information is vital for making intelligent decisions. In their three *informational roles*—as *monitor, disseminator*, and *spokesperson*—managers receive and communicate information with other people inside and outside the organization.

3. Decisional Roles—Entrepreneur, Disturbance Handler, Resource Allocator, and Negotiator In their *decisional roles*, managers use information to make decisions to solve problems or take advantage of opportunities. The four decision-making roles are *entrepreneur, disturbance handler, resource allocator*, and *negotiator*.

These roles are summarized on the next page. *(See Table 1.1.)*

Did anyone say a manager's job is easy? Certainly it's not for people who want to sit on the sidelines of life. Above all else, managers are *doers*. ●

Doer. Frederick Smith, founder and CEO of FedEx, is an example of a doer. Given a low grade on a graduate-school paper on ideas for an overnight delivery service, he used his family's money to create the company.

table I.I

THREE TYPES OF MANAGERIAL ROLES: INTERPERSONAL, INFORMATIONAL, AND DECISIONAL

Broad Managerial Roles	Types of Roles	Description
Interpersonal Managerial Roles	Figurehead role	In your *figurehead role,* you show visitors around your company, attend employee birthday parties, and present ethical guidelines to your subordinates. In other words, you perform symbolic tasks that represent your organization.
	Leadership role	In your role of *leader,* you are responsible for the actions of your subordinates, since their successes and failures reflect on you. Your leadership is expressed in your decisions about training, motivating, and disciplining people.
	Liaison role	In your *liaison* role, you must act like a politician, working with other people outside your work unit and organization to develop alliances that will help you achieve your organization's goals.
Informational Managerial Roles	Monitor role	As a *monitor,* you should be constantly alert for useful information, whether gathered from newspaper stories about the competition or gathered from snippets of conversation with subordinates you meet in the hallway.
	Disseminator role	Workers complain they never know what's going on? That probably means their supervisor failed in the role of *disseminator.* Managers need to constantly disseminate important information to employees, as via e-mail and meetings.
	Spokesperson role	You are expected, of course, to be a diplomat, to put the best face on the activities of your work unit or organization to people outside it. This is the informational role of *spokesperson.*
Decisional Managerial Roles	Entrepreneur role	A good manager is expected to be an *entrepreneur,* to initiate and encourage change and innovation.
	Disturbance handler role	Unforeseen problems—from product defects to international currency crises—require you be a *disturbance handler,* fixing problems.
	Resource allocator role	Because you'll never have enough time, money, and so on, you'll need to be a resource *allocator,* setting priorities about use of resources.
	Negotiator role	To be a manager is to be a continual *negotiator,* working with others inside and outside the organization to accomplish your goals.

1.6 THE ENTREPRENEURIAL SPIRIT

Do I have what it takes to be an entrepreneur?	**major question?** 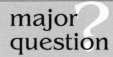

THE BIG PICTURE

Entrepreneurship, a necessary attribute of business, means taking risks to create a new enterprise. It is expressed through two kinds of innovators, the entrepreneur and the intrapreneur.

Like many colleges, Harvard offers every freshman a copy of the class directory, known as the "facebook," that shows photographs of all members of the class along with their names, birth dates, hometowns, and high schools. Harvard administrators had planned to put the facebook online, but in early 2004 a psychology student and programming hobbyist named Mark Zuckerberg beat them to it.

Zuckerberg had already tried some other projects, including Coursematch, which allowed Harvard students to find out who was enrolled in a particular class, and Facemash, which enabled students to rate student pictures for attractiveness. A version of the latter site was online a bare 4 hours when Zuckerberg's Internet access was revoked by administration officials and he was charged with breaching security—an offense for which he escaped with a warning. Later, at the invitation of some fellow students, he was invited to help write the code for a "social networking" site, modeled after Friendster and Tribe.net, to be called Harvard Connection. Meanwhile he continued to work on his own projects.

Entrepreneur. Mark Zuckerberg, shown at the Palo Alto, California, headquarters of FaceBook, has become one of today's most watched techno entrepreneurs. Most people, even young people, prefer the security of a job with a paycheck rather than the risks of starting a business. Which life would you prefer?

During a weeklong semester break, Zuckerberg stayed in his dorm room creating a Web site, and on February 4, 2004, Thefacebook.com went up. Within 24 hours it had between 1,200 and 1,500 registrants. Facebook allowed anyone with a Harvard e-mail address to join and to create a profile, consisting of a photograph and personal information. A search box helped users call up other profiles. Unlike Friendster and MySpace, social sites that are open to anyone, Facebook's members had a physical location, professors, and classes in common. That is, the site was not so much an on-line community as a directory that reinforces a physical community.

"By luck or design," says one account, "Zuckerberg had tapped into a powerful yearning: the desire of hundreds of ambitious and impressionable young people to establish themselves and make friends in an unfamiliar environment. . . . The site quickly became a platform for self-promotion, a place to boast and preen and vie for others' attention as much as for their companionship."[54] By the end of June 2004, the site had expanded to 40 schools and had 150,000 registered users. Zuckerberg and two friends who had pioneered Facebook then moved to Palo Alto, California, where later they began to meet with venture capitalists to expand the site. Today Facebook has about 40 million members and is growing at the rate of 3%–4% compounded weekly.[55]

Entrepreneurship Defined: Taking Risks in Pursuit of Opportunity

Facebook is one of the many small outfits in the United States that is one of the primary drivers of the nation's economy. Indeed, according to the Small Business Administration, small outfits create some 75% of all new jobs, represent 99.7% of all employers, and employ 50% of the private workforce.[56] Most small businesses originate with people like Zuckerberg. He and his partners are the entrepreneurs, the people with the idea, the risk takers.

So is Chip Conley, who has achieved success in the offbeat but expanding business of "boutique" hotels, each of which, unlike Hiltons and Hyatts, has its own one-of-a-kind charm. Conley likes magazines because they provide inspired themes for the hotels he buys and renovates. For instance, he says the Nob Hill Lambourne in San Francisco, which is oriented toward health-conscious travelers, resembles the magazine *Men's Health;* the hotel offers algae shakes, vitamins instead of chocolates on the pillows, and an on-call psychologist. The Hotel Rex, modeled on *The New Yorker,* features a book-lined cocktail lounge, old leather furniture, and poetry readings.[57]

The most successful entrepreneurs become wealthy and make the covers of business magazines: Fred Smith of Federal Express, Debbie Fields of Mrs. Fields' Cookies, Anita Roddick of The Body Shop, Michael Dell of Dell Computers. Failed entrepreneurs may benefit from the experience to live to fight another day—as did Henry Ford, twice bankrupt before achieving success with Ford Motor Co.

What Entrepreneurship Is *Entrepreneurship* is the process of taking risks to try to create a new enterprise. There are two types of entrepreneurship:

- **The entrepreneur.** An *entrepreneur* is someone who sees a new opportunity for a product or service and launches a business to try to realize it. Most entrepreneurs run small businesses with fewer than 100 employees.

- **The intrapreneur.** An *intrapreneur* is someone who works inside an existing organization who sees an opportunity for a product or service and mobilizes the organization's resources to try to realize it. This person might be a researcher or a scientist but could also be a manager who sees an opportunity to create a new venture that could be profitable.

Example

Example of an Intrapreneur: Art Fry & 3M's Post-it Notes

One of the most famous instances of intrapreneurship occurred at 3M Corp., a company famous for pumping out new products, when 3M employee Art Fry conceived of Post-it Notes, those bright-colored "sticky notes" that people use to post messages on walls and mark books. The company had invented an experimental adhesive for which it could find no use. Meanwhile, when attending church, Fry found that the bits of paper he used to mark hymns in his hymnbook kept slipping out. It dawned on him that 3M's experimental glue could provide adhesive-backed paper that would stick for a long time but could be easily removed without damaging the book.

Coming up with the product was only the first step. Market surveys were negative. Office-supply distributors thought the notion useless. Fry thereupon started giving samples to executives and secretaries at 3M, who began using the sticky paper and soon were hooked. Later Fry used the same approach with other executives and secretaries throughout the United States. After 12 years, the orders began to flow, and Post-its became a winning product for 3M.[58]

Your Call

What companies are you aware of that do their own in-house research and development of products?

How Do Entrepreneurs & Managers Differ? While the entrepreneur is not necessarily an inventor, he or she "always searches for change, responds to it, and exploits it as an opportunity," Peter Drucker pointed out.[59] How does this differ from being a manager?

Being an entrepreneur is what it takes to *start* a business; being a manager is what it takes to *grow or maintain* a business. As an entrepreneur/intrapreneur, you initiate new goods or services; as a manager you coordinate the resources to produce the goods or services.

The examples of success we mentioned above—Chip Conley, Fred Smith, Debbie Fields, Anita Roddick, Michael Dell—are actually *both* entrepreneurs and effective managers. Some people, however, find they like the start-up part but hate the management part. For example, Stephen Wozniak, entrepreneurial co-founder with Steve Jobs of Apple Computer, abandoned the computer industry completely and went back to college. Jobs, by contrast, went on to launch another business, Pixar, which among other things became the animation factory that made the movies *Toy Story* and *Finding Nemo*.

Entrepreneurial companies have been called "gazelles" for the two attributes that make them successful: *speed and agility.* "Gazelles have mastered the art of the quick," says Alan Webber, founding editor of *Fast Company* magazine. "They have internal approaches and fast decision-making approaches that let them move with maximum agility in a fast-changing business environment."[60]

Is this the kind of smart, innovative world you'd like to be a part of? Most people prefer the security of a job and a paycheck. Indeed, even young people—those ages 25–34—who might be expected to be attracted to the entrepreneurial life are about 40% less likely to be self-employed than their parents, according to the Bureau of Labor Statistics.[61]

Up and away. Gary Ream, president and partner of Woodward Camp, transformed this aging gymnastics camp in central Pennsylvania into an extreme-sports summer retreat. First he offered BMX lessons, then coached in-line skaters and skateboarders, then began hosting competitions, which attracted the attention of sports TV channel ESPN and generated further publicity. What is your passion that you might turn into a business?

Entrepreneurs do seem to have psychological characteristics that are different from managers, as follows:[62]

- **Characteristic of both—high need for achievement.** Both entrepreneurs and managers have a high need for achievement. However, entrepreneurs certainly seem to be motivated to pursue moderately difficult goals through their own efforts in order to realize their ideas and, they hope, financial rewards. Managers, by contrast, are more motivated by promotions and organizational rewards of power and perks.

- **Also characteristic of both—belief in personal control of destiny.** If you believe "I am the captain of my fate, the master of my soul," you have what is known as *internal locus of control,* the belief that you control your own destiny, that external forces will have little influence. (External locus of control means the reverse—you believe you don't control your destiny, that external forces do.) Both entrepreneurs and managers like to think they have personal control over their lives.

- **Characteristic of both, but especially of entrepreneurs—high energy level and action orientation.** Rising to the top in an organization probably requires that a manager put in long hours. For entrepreneurs, however, creating a new enterprise may require an extraordinary investment of time and energy. In addition, while some managers may feel a sense of urgency, entrepreneurs are especially apt to be impatient and to want to get things done as quickly as possible, making them particularly action oriented.

- **Characteristic of both, but especially of entrepreneurs—high tolerance for ambiguity.** Every manager needs to be able to make decisions based on ambiguous—that is, unclear or incomplete—information. However, entrepreneurs must have more tolerance for ambiguity because they are trying to do things they haven't done before.

- **More characteristic of entrepreneurs than managers—self-confidence and tolerance for risk.** Managers must believe in themselves and be willing to make decisions; however, this statement applies even more to entrepreneurs. Precisely because they are willing to take risks in the pursuit of new opportunities—indeed, even risk personal financial failure—entrepreneurs need the confidence to act decisively.

Test Your Knowledge:
Characteristics of Successful Entrepreneurs

PepsiCo's Indra Nooyi. Are entrepreneurs and managers really two different breeds? India-born Nooyi, CEO of PepsiCo, has taken the lead in attempting to move the company away from fast food and sodas into more healthy foods.

Of course, not all entrepreneurs have this kind of faith in themselves. So-called *necessity* entrepreneurs are people such as laid-off corporate workers, discharged military people, immigrants, and divorced homemakers who suddenly must earn a living and are simply trying to replace lost income and are hoping a job comes along. These make up about 11% of entrepreneurs. However, so-called *opportunity* entrepreneurs—the other 89%—are those who start their own business out of a burning desire rather than because they lost a job. Unlike necessity types, they tend to be more ambitious and to start firms that can lead to high-growth businesses.[63]

Which do you think you would be happier doing—being an entrepreneur or being a manager? ●

1.7 THE SKILLS STAR MANAGERS NEED

> To be a terrific manager, what skills should I cultivate?
>
> **major question?**

THE BIG PICTURE

Good managers need to work on developing three principal skills. The first is *technical,* the ability to perform a specific job. The second is *conceptual,* the ability to think analytically. The third is *human,* the ability to interact well with people.

CEO Judy McGrath once broke her wrist during a food fight at an MTV staff party. Is this the kind of beyond-the-call-of-duty activity that's required to have the right management stuff? Let's see what the "right stuff" might be.

In the mid-1970s, researcher **Robert Katz** found that through education and experience managers acquire three principal skills—*technical, conceptual,* and *human.*[64]

1. Technical Skills—The Ability to Perform a Specific Job

McGrath clearly has acquired the job-specific knowledge needed to function in the world of television and digital entertainment (as opposed to another industry—say, tax law, engineering, or restaurant work). Indeed, she has a college degree in English literature from Cedar Crest College and previously worked as a copy chief at *Glamour* magazine and as a senior writer at *Mademoiselle.*

Technical skills consist of the **job-specific knowledge needed to perform well in a specialized field.** Having the requisite technical skills seems to be most important at the lower levels of management—that is, among first-line managers.

2. Conceptual Skills—The Ability to Think Analytically

McGrath also has the "big picture" knowledge to keep up with her job. Although she tries to get home every night at a sane hour to see her 13-year-old daughter and stay-at-home husband, she lugs a bagful of scripts and tapes and exchanges Blackberry messages with executives well past midnight. She networks constantly with film, TV, and music industry executives and stars but also reads widely, everything from *US Weekly* to novels such as Samuel Beckett's *Malone Dies.* "Judy was the only person I ever worked with who knew as much about great literature as what was going on between East Coast and West Coast rappers," says a former MTV executive. "I always thought her intuitive appreciation of storytelling and characters was an enormous secret weapon."[65]

Conceptual skills consist of the **ability to think analytically, to visualize an organization as a whole and understand how the parts work together.** Conceptual skills are particularly important for top managers, who must deal with problems that are ambiguous but that could have far-reaching consequences.

3. Human Skills—The Ability to Interact Well with People

This may well be the most difficult set of skills to master. **Human skills** consist of the **ability to work well in cooperation with other people to get things done.** Often these are thought of as "soft skills." These skills—the ability to motivate, to inspire trust, to communicate with others—are necessary for managers of all levels. But because

MTV in New York City. The sprawl of the MTV empire includes multiple online communities for various geographical locations, shops such as this one in the Big Apple, and, of course, TV channels. MTV CEO Judy McGrath seems to have the three skills— technical, conceptual, and human— necessary to be a terrific manager for such an entertainment complex. Which skill do you think you need to work on the most? (Human skills are the most difficult to master.)

of the range of people, tasks, and problems in an organization, developing your human-interacting skills may turn out to be an ongoing, lifelong effort.

McGrath "is known for her skillful management of talent and the chaos that comes with a creative enterprise," reports a *BusinessWeek* article. "Judy's ability to concentrate on people" is intense, says an MTV executive. She tries to listen to everyone, from interns to senior vice-presidents, and then offer advice. As a result, she gets a lot of credit for fostering a company culture of inclusiveness, making it a better place for creativity and risk taking. "There is less testosterone," says her former boss. "It's not the system of the old Hollywood moguls where they are throwing chairs at each other. It's about listening and accepting ideas wherever and whoever they come from."[66]

The Most Valued Traits in Managers

McGrath embodies the qualities sought in star managers, especially top managers. "The style for running a company is different from what it used to be," says a top executive recruiter of CEOs. "Companies don't want dictators, kings, or emperors."[67] Instead of someone who gives orders, they want executives who ask probing questions and force the people beneath them to think and find the right answers.

Among the chief skills companies seek in top managers are the following:

- The ability to motivate and engage others.
- The ability to communicate.
- Work experience outside the United States.
- High energy levels to meet the demands of global travel and a 24/7 world.[68]

Let's see how you can begin to acquire these and other qualities for success. ●

Taking Something Practical Away from this Chapter

Getting Control of Your Time: Dealing with the Information Deluge in College & in Your Career

One great problem most college students face—and that all managers face—is how to manage their time. This first box describes skills that will benefit you in college and later in your career.

"I've managed to ratchet my schedule down so I can have an outside life," says Doug Shoemaker, a San Francisco architect who tries to be home by 6:00 every night. "I'm a highly organized guy, I really focus on tasks, and I get them done."[69]

Professionals and managers all have to deal with this central problem: how not to surrender their lives to their jobs. The place to start, however, is in college.

If you can learn to manage time while you're still a student, you'll find it will pay off not only in higher grades and more free time but also in more efficient information-handling skills that will serve you well as a manager later on.

Developing Study Habits: Finding Your "Prime Study Time"
Each of us has a different energy cycle. The trick is to use it effectively. That way your hours of best performance will coincide with your heaviest academic demands. For example, if your energy level is high during the evenings, you should plan to do your studying then.

Make a Study Schedule

First make a master schedule that shows all your regular obligations—especially classes and work—for the entire school term. Then insert the times during which you plan to study. Next write in major academic events, such as term paper due dates and when exams will take place. At the beginning of every week, schedule your study sessions. Write in the specific tasks you plan to accomplish during each session.

Find Some Good Places to Study

Studying means first of all avoiding distractions. Avoid studying in places that are associated with other activities, particularly comfortable ones, such as lying in bed or sitting at a kitchen table.

Avoid Time Wasters, but Reward Your Studying

While clearly you need to learn to avoid distractions so that you can study, you must also give yourself frequent rewards so that you will indeed be *motivated* to study. You should study with the notion that, after you finish, you will give yourself a reward. The reward need not be elaborate. It could be a walk, a snack, or some similar treat.

Improving Your Memory Ability

Memorizing is, of course, one of the principal requirements of staying in college. And it's a great help for success in life afterward.

Beyond getting rid of distractions, there are certain techniques you can adopt to enhance your memory.

Space Your Studying, Rather Than Cramming

Cramming—making a frantic, last-minute attempt to memorize massive amounts of material—is probably the least effective means of absorbing information. Indeed, it may actually tire you out and make you even more anxious before the test. Research shows that it is best to space out your studying of a subject on successive days. This is preferable to trying to do it all during the same number of hours on 1 day.[70] It is repetition that helps move information into your long-term memory bank.

Review Information Repeatedly—Even "Overlearn" It

By repeatedly reviewing information—"rehearsing"—you can improve both your retention and your understanding of it.[71] Overlearning can improve your recall substantially. Overlearning is continuing to repeatedly review material even after you appear to have absorbed it.

Use Memorizing Tricks

There are several ways to organize information so that you can retain it better. The exhibit opposite shows how to establish associations between items you want to remember. *(See Exhibit I.I.)*

How to Improve Your Reading Ability: The SQ3R Method

SQ3R Stands for *Survey, Question, Read, Recite, and Review*[72]

The strategy here is to break a reading assignment into small segments and master each before moving on. The five steps of the SQ3R method are as follows:

Survey the Chapter before You Read It

Get an overview of the chapter or other reading assignment before you begin reading it. If you have a sense what the material is about before you begin reading it, you can predict where it is going. Many textbooks offer some "preview"-type material—a list of

- **Mental and physical imagery:** Use your visual and other senses to construct a personal image of what you want to remember. Indeed, it helps to make the image humorous, action-filled, sexual, bizarre, or outrageous in order to establish a personal connection. Example: To remember the name of the 21st president of the United States, Chester Arthur, you might visualize an author writing the number "21" on a wooden chest. This mental image helps you associate <u>chest</u> (Chester), <u>author</u> (Arthur), and <u>21</u> (21st president).
- **Acronyms and acrostics:** An acronym is a word created from the first letters of items in a list. For instance, Roy G. Biv helps you remember the colors of the rainbow in order: <u>r</u>ed, <u>o</u>range, <u>y</u>ellow, <u>g</u>reen, <u>b</u>lue, <u>i</u>ndigo, <u>v</u>iolet. An acrostic is a phrase or sentence created from the first letters of items in a list. For example, *Every Good Boy Does Fine* helps you remember that the order of musical notes on the stave is E-G-B-D-F.
- **Location:** Location memory occurs when you associate a concept with a place or imaginary place. For example, you could learn the parts of a computer system by imagining a walk across campus. Each building you pass could be associated with a part of the computer system.
- **Word games:** Jingles and rhymes are devices frequently used by advertisers to get people to remember their products. You may recall the spelling rule "*I* before *E* except after *C* or when sounded like *A* as in *neighbor* or *weigh*." You can also use narrative methods, such as making up a story.

Exhibit I.I **SOME MEMORIZING TRICKS**

objectives or an outline of topic headings at the beginning of the chapter. Other books offer a summary at the end of the chapter. This book offers "The Big Picture" at the beginning of each section. It also offers a Summary at the end of each chapter. The strategy for reading this book is presented on page I.

Question the Segment in the Chapter before You Read It

This step is easy to do, and the point, again, is to get involved in the material. After surveying the entire chapter, go to the first segment—section, subsection, or even paragraph, depending on the level of difficulty and density of information. Look at the topic heading of that segment. In your mind, restate the heading as a question.

After you have formulated the question, go to steps 3 and 4 (read and recite). Then proceed to the next segment and restate the heading here as a question. For instance, consider the section heading in this chapter that reads "What Managers Do: The Four Principal Functions." You could ask yourself, What *are* the four functions of a manager? For the heading in Chapter 2 "Two Overarching Perspectives about Management & Four Practical Reasons for Studying Them," ask What *are* the types of management perspectives, and what are reasons for studying them?

Read the Segment about Which You Asked the Question

Now read the segment you asked the question about. Read with purpose, to answer the question you formulated. Underline or color-mark sentences you think are important, if they help you answer the question. Read this portion of the text more than once, if necessary, until you can answer the question. In addition, determine whether the segment covers any other significant questions, and formulate answers to these, too. After you have read the segment, proceed to step 4. (Perhaps you can see where this is all leading. If you read in terms of questions and answers, you will be better prepared when you see exam questions about the material later.)

Recite the Main Points of the Segment

Recite means "say aloud." Thus, you should speak out loud (or softly) the answer to the principal question about the segment and any other main points. Make notes on the principal ideas, so you can look them over later. Now that you have actively studied the first segment, move on to the second segment and do steps 2–4 for it. Continue doing this through the rest of the segments until you have finished the chapter.

Review the Entire Chapter by Repeating Questions

After you have read the chapter, go back through it and review the main points. Then, without looking at the book, test your memory by repeating the questions.

Clearly the SQ3R method takes longer than simply reading with a rapidly moving color marker or underlining pencil. However, the technique is far more effective because it requires your *involvement and understanding.* This is the key to all effective learning.

Learning from Lectures

Does attending lectures really make a difference? Research shows that students with grades of B or above were more apt to have better class attendance than students with grades of C− or below.[73]

Regardless of the strengths of the lecturer, here are some tips for getting more out of lectures.

Take Effective Notes by Listening Actively

Research shows that good test performance is related to good note taking.[74] And good note taking requires that you *listen actively*—that is, participate in the lecture process. Here are some ways to take good lecture notes:

- **Read ahead** and **anticipate the lecturer:** Try to anticipate what the instructor is going to say, based on your previous reading. Having background knowledge makes learning more efficient.

- **Listen for signal words:** Instructors use key phrases such as "The most important point is . . . ," "There are four reasons for . . . ," "The chief reason . . . ," "Of special importance . . . ," "Consequently. . . ." When you hear such signal phrases, mark your notes with an asterisk (*), or write *Imp* (for "Important").

- **Take notes in your own words:** Instead of just being a stenographer, try to restate the lecturer's thoughts in your own words. This makes you pay attention to the lecture and organize it in a way that is meaningful to you. In addition, don't try to write everything down. Just get the key points.

- **Ask questions:** By asking questions during the lecture, you participate in it and increase your understanding. Although many students are shy about asking questions, most professors welcome them.

Becoming an Effective Test Taker

Besides having knowledge of the subject matter, you can acquire certain skills that will help during the test-taking process. Some suggestions:[75]

Review Your Notes Regularly

Most students, according to one study, do take good notes, but they don't use them effectively. That is, they wait to review their notes until just before final exams, when the notes have lost much of their meaning.[76] Make it a point to review your notes regularly, such as the afternoon after the lecture or once or twice a week. We cannot emphasize enough how important this kind of reviewing is.

Reviewing: Study Information That Is Emphasized & Enumerated

Because you won't always know whether an exam will be an objective test or an essay test, you need to prepare for both. Here are some general tips.

- **Review material that is emphasized:** In the lectures, this consists of any topics your instructor pointed out as being significant or important. It also includes anything he or she spent a good deal of time discussing or specifically advised you to study. In the textbook, pay attention to key terms (often emphasized in *italic* or **boldface** type), their definitions, and their examples. In addition, of course, material that has a good many pages given over to it should be considered important.

- **Review material that is enumerated:** Pay attention to any numbered lists, both in your lectures and in your notes. Enumerations often provide the basis for essay and multiple-choice questions.

- **Review other tests:** Look over past quizzes, as well as the discussion questions or review questions provided at the end of chapters in many textbooks.

Prepare by Doing Final Reviews & Budgeting Your Test Time

Learn how to make your energy and time work for you. Whether you have studied methodically or must cram for an exam, here are some tips:

- **Review your notes:** Spend the night before the test reviewing your notes. Then go to bed without interfering with the material you have absorbed (as by watching television). Get up early the next morning, and review your notes again.

- **Find a good test-taking spot:** Make sure you arrive at the exam with any pencils or other materials you need. Get to the classroom early, or at least on time, and find a quiet spot. If you don't have a watch, sit where you can see a clock. Again review your notes. Avoid talking with others, so as not to interfere with the information you have learned or to increase your anxiety.

- **Read the test directions:** Many students don't do this and end up losing points because they didn't

understand precisely what was required of them. Also, listen to any verbal directions or hints your instructor gives you before the test.

- **Budget your time:** Here is an important test strategy: Before you start, read through the entire test and figure out how much time you can spend on each section. There is a reason for budgeting your time: you would hate to find you have only a few minutes left and a long essay still to be written. Write the number of minutes allowed for each section on the test booklet or scratch sheet and stick to the schedule. The way you budget your time should correspond to how confident you feel about answering the questions.

Objective Tests: Answer Easy Questions & Eliminate Options

Some suggestions for taking objective tests, such as multiple-choice, true/false, or fill-in, are as follows:

- **Answer the easy questions first:** Don't waste time stewing over difficult questions. Do the easy ones first, and come back to the hard ones later. (Put a check mark opposite those you're not sure about.) Your unconscious mind may have solved them in the meantime, or later items may provide you with the extra information you need.

- **Answer all questions:** Unless the instructor says you will be penalized for wrong answers, try to answer all questions. If you have time, review all the questions and make sure you have written the responses correctly.

- **Eliminate the options:** Cross out answers you know are incorrect. Be sure to read all the possible answers, especially when the first answer is correct. (After all, other answers could also be correct, so that "All of the above" may be the right choice.) Be alert that subsequent questions may provide information pertinent to earlier questions. Pay attention to options that are long and detailed, since answers that are more detailed and specific are likely to be correct. If two answers have the opposite meaning, one of the two is probably correct.

Essay Tests: First Anticipate Answers & Prepare an Outline

Because time is limited, your instructor is likely to ask only a few essay questions during the exam. The key to success is to try to anticipate beforehand what the questions might be and memorize an outline for an answer. Here are the specific suggestions:

- **Anticipate 10 probable essay questions:** Use the principles we discussed above of reviewing lecture and textbook material that is *emphasized* and *enumerated.* You will then be in a position to identify 10 essay questions your instructor may ask. Write out these questions.

- **Prepare and memorize informal essay answers:** For each question, list the main points that need to be discussed. Put supporting information in parentheses. Circle the key words in each main point and below the question put the first letter of the key word. Make up catch phrases, using acronyms, acrostics, or word games, so that you can memorize these key words. Test yourself until you can recall the key words the letters stand for and the main points the key words represent.

Key Terms Used in This Chapter

collaborative computing 11
competitive advantage 8
conceptual skills 27
controlling 14
databases 11
decisional roles 21
e-business 11
e-commerce 11
e-mail 11
effective 5
efficient 5
entrepreneur 25
entrepreneurship 25

first-line managers 17
four management functions 13
functional manager 17
general manager 17
human skills 27
informational roles 21
innovation 8
internal locus of control 26
Internet 11
interpersonal roles 20
intrapreneur 25
knowledge management 11
leading 14

management 4
management process 13
middle managers 16
organization 4
organizing 14
planning 13
project management
  software 11
technical skills 27
telecommute 11
top managers 16
videoconferencing 11

Summary

1.1 Management: What It Is, What Its Benefits Are

Management is defined as the pursuit of organizational goals *efficiently,* meaning to use resources wisely and cost-effectively, and *effectively,* meaning to achieve results, to make the right decisions, and to successfully carry them out to achieve the organization's goals.

1.2 Six Challenges to Being a Star Manager

The six challenges are (1) managing for competitive advantage, which means an organization must stay ahead in four areas—being responsive to customers, innovating new products or services offering better quality, being more

efficient; (2) managing for diversity among different genders, ages, races, and ethnicities; (3) managing for globalization, the expanding universe; (4) managing for computers and telecommunications—information technology; (5) managing for right and wrong, or ethical standards; and (6) managing for your own happiness and life goals.

1.3 What Managers Do: The Four Principal Functions

The four management functions are represented by the abbreviation *POLC:* (1) *planning*—setting goals and deciding how to achieve them; (2) *organizing*—arranging tasks, people, and other resources to accomplish the work; (3) *leading*—motivating, directing, and otherwise influencing people to work hard to achieve the organization's goals; and (4) *controlling*—monitoring performance, comparing it with goals, and taking corrective action as needed.

1.4 Pyramid Power: Levels & Areas of Management

Within an organization, there are managers at three levels: (1) *top managers* make long-term decisions about the overall direction of the organization and establish the objectives, policies, and strategies for it; (2) *middle managers* implement the policies and plans of their superiors and supervise and coordinate the activities of the managers below them; and (3) *first-line managers* make short-term operating decisions, directing the daily tasks of nonmanagement personnel. There are three types of organizations: (1) *for-profit*—formed to make money by offering products or services; (2) *nonprofit*—to offer services to some, but not to make a profit; and (3) *mutual-benefit*—voluntary collections of members created to advance members' interests.

1.5 Roles Managers Must Play Successfully

The Mintzberg study shows that, first, a manager relies more on verbal than on written communication; second, managers work long hours at an intense pace; and, third, a manager's work is characterized by fragmentation, brevity, and variety. Mintzberg concluded that managers play three broad roles: (1) *interpersonal*—figurehead, leader, and liaison; (2) *informational*—monitor, disseminator, and spokesperson; and (3) *decisional*—entrepreneur, disturbance handler, resource allocator, and negotiator.

1.6 The Entrepreneurial Spirit

Entrepreneurship, a necessary attribute of business, is the process of taking risks to create a new enterprise. Two types are (1) the *entrepreneur*, who sees a new opportunity for a product or service and launches a business to realize it; and (2) the *intrapreneur*, working inside an existing organization, who sees an opportunity for a product or service and mobilizes the organization's resources to realize it. Entrepreneurs start businesses, managers grow or maintain them. Both (but especially entrepreneurs) have a high need for achievement, high energy level and action orientation, and tolerance for ambiguity. Entrepreneurs are more self-confident and have higher tolerance for risk.

1.7 The Skills Star Managers Need

The three skills that star managers cultivate are (1) *technical*, consisting of job-specific knowledge needed to perform well in a specialized field; (2) *conceptual*, consisting of the ability to think analytically, to visualize an organization as a whole, and to understand how the parts work together; and (3) *human*, consisting of the ability to work well in cooperation with other people in order to get things done.

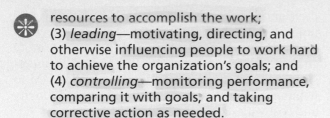

Management in Action

General Motors CEO Rick Wagoner Faces an Overwhelming Managerial Challenge

From his office on the 39th floor of General Motors' headquarters complex, chairman and CEO Rick Wagoner has a killer view. He can see for miles, across the Detroit River to Canada and south to the Ohio coastline of Lake Erie. This time of year, the sky is gray, the river is icing up, and the plainspoken Wagoner, 54, is giving an economic forecast that's as chilly as the heartland below.

He expects yet another tough year in 2008 for the beleaguered automaker. "We have some fairly severe headwinds: the weaker economy, high commodity and steel prices, and energy prices," he told *Fortune* in a rare interview. "Frankly, more headwinds, especially from the first two, than I would have hoped. We're going to be in soupy water for a while."

The season always seems to be winter for GM. Yet for the first time in years, signs of warming are emerging. Wagoner is feeling good about the automaker's progress, especially in the troubled heart of its business: making and selling cars in North America. GM's latest new-car launches—Buick Enclave, Cadillac CTS, Chevrolet Malibu—are getting enthusiastic reviews and generating strong sales. . . .

The new products are giving GM a much-needed image boost in the marketplace, while Wagoner has been making huge cuts in costs on the factory floor. By slashing both the hourly and salaried workforces, boosting productivity, and reducing health-care costs, he has cut $9 billion (or 22%) out of GM's fixed operating costs. And following years of patient negotiation, he reached a historic agreement with the United Auto Workers to push responsibility for retiree health care off GM's books, a burden that has been adding about $1,400 to the cost of every car and truck GM builds in North America. Once the health-care trust, called a voluntary employees' beneficiary association, or VEBA, is fully funded (GM's contribution: $29.5 billion), the company will have no more responsibility for it. Analysts expect the new union contract to produce as much as $4 billion in annual savings beginning in 2010.

Does all this add up to a long-overdue turnaround in GM's financial health? Well, just as GM started getting its house in order, the ground underneath it began to shake. Analysts expect that a slowing economy will reduce sales of cars and light trucks in the United States, which gives GM very little room to improve revenues in the short term. At the same time, the home-mortgage crisis has battered what had been one of GM's most moneymaking assets, the 49% stake it owns in General Motors Acceptance Corp. (GMAC), which issues home loans in its Residential Capital unit (ResCap). And GM's realization that it would be unable to make use of $38.3 billion in deferred-tax assets it carried on its books caused the company in November to charge off the entire amount in a single stroke. There was no cash involved, but it sent investors a signal that GM would not be producing significant profits in the next couple of years. The stock got hammered. . . .

The bureaucrat-in-chief, who has been CEO since 2000, hasn't been afraid to change the status quo. "A lot of success in this business," says Wagoner, "is having a big plan and implementing it better than the next guy." Three years ago Wagoner put his big plan into operation when he personally took charge of product development, manufacturing, and marketing and sales for North America. His

decision to put his reputation—and perhaps his tenure as CEO—on the line finally put some steel behind GM's repeated promises to become more competitive. By setting a few clear and easily understood performance targets, Wagoner has led GM to within a neck of catching up in labor productivity and cost with its No. 1 competitor, Toyota. . . .

Wagoner's biggest piece of unfinished business is to restart the growth of revenues from selling cars and trucks in the United States GM's market share in North America fell from 28.4% in 2000 to 23.7% in 2007, leaving in its wake bloated inventories, revenue-depleting rebates, and other sales incentives to move the stalled merchandise off the lots. But a host of indicators suggest that improvement, while slow, is underway. . . .

In Wagoner's fifth year as CEO, he could see that GM was heading for a cliff. Looking at the results of a dismal first quarter 2005, in which North American operations piled up $1.3 billion in losses, Wagoner decided, as he put it, "to hop in there myself." Though he had more than enough to do as chairman and CEO, Wagoner saw a crucial moment to make major changes in the company's most entrenched, tradition-bound operations—those in the United States. "As gas prices rocketed up, it was pretty clear we were going to be selling into a different world, and that was a world where profitability was going to be harder to come by," he said. "The other thing was, we had had a view for some time that we would be able to outrun the health-care cost. But between the pressures on the margins due to the mix shift [to smaller vehicles], and the unrelenting pressure in the annual inflation of health-care costs, it became clear we had to do something more fundamental."

In June 2005, Wagoner laid out his agenda for North America at GM's annual meeting. His four goals were so simple and direct—build great cars and trucks, revitalize sales and marketing, cut costs, and fix health care—that they made one wonder what GM had been doing for the preceding 97 years. His move practically escaped notice amid all the focus on GM's credit ratings (downgraded to junk). Wagoner was perceived as another unimaginative, risk-averse GM executive unwilling to rock the boat. Yet the onetime Duke basketball player (a hot new Corvette model was code-named Blue Devil in his honor) has a history of quietly exceeding expectations. While he may not be as inspirational as Lee Iacocca or Carlos Ghosn, he's methodical and stubborn, thinks strategically, and inspires loyalty among his subordinates. "Rick is a driver," says one of them. "He doesn't let up. He's not confrontational, but he keeps it all going." . . .

"With Rick's announcement, the focus became very crisp, the goals became very sharp, and the emphasis on execution became a necessity," says Troy Clarke, the engineer who succeeded Wagoner as head of North America in 2006. "If I ask anybody in the company, 'What are you doing with the turnaround strategy?' they feed it back to me—snap—just like that. There are four things we're working on. If you are not working on one of the four, you really need to go to your boss and get some help." . . .

If Wagoner has learned anything, it's to be bold and then be patient. "The moral to the story is that there's very little that you can't accomplish, but a lot of these things take time. Which isn't an excuse but is a statement that you'd better get on the path, because these things don't turn on a dime." If GM can just stay on the path through the next patch of bad weather, we may finally be able to tell the comeback story the world's been waiting for.

For Discussion

1. Which of the six managerial challenges discussed in this chapter did Rick Wagoner face upon becoming CEO of General Motors? Discuss.

2. Using Figure 1.1 as a guide, describe which functions of management were displayed by Wagoner.

3. Which of the three types of managerial roles did Wagoner display?

4. To what extent did Wagoner display an entrepreneurial orientation while trying to turn around GM? Explain.

5. How would you evaluate Wagoner's technical, conceptual, and human skills? Discuss your rationale.

Source: Excerpted from Alex Taylor III, "Gentlemen, Start Your Turnaround," *Fortune*, January 21, 2008, pp. 71–78.

Self-Assessment

Can You Pass the CEO Test?

Objectives

1. To assess whether or not you have "it" at this time to be a CEO.

2. To assess whether or not you want to be a CEO.

3. To see what seems to be expected of a CEO.

Introduction

The Chief Executive Officer of a company is the person in charge, the top star. This person has tremendous power and, consequently, experiences incredible pressures. Not everyone is cut out to be a CEO or aspires to be one. Many people would not want the stress and expectations for greatness that come with the job.

Instructions

Take the following quiz at **www.mbajungle.com/ monthlysurvey/ceotest.cfm** to "test" whether you have "it." Leading a successful company requires a combination of talents and skills that few people seem to have—some people have it, some don't. Here's your chance to find out where you stand.

Accompanying the quiz is an article by John Scaizi for the MBA Jungle Online magazine. Read it; then take the test and see if you are a potential rising star. Once you have completed the test and have submitted your responses, ask yourself the following questions and be prepared to discuss them.

Questions for Discussion

1. Do you want to be a CEO? Explain.

2. Do you want to climb the corporate ladder to become a star?

3. At what level in the organization do you think you would be comfortable?

4. What are the ethics behind #7, #8, #11, # 15, and #16?

5. How would you describe what it takes to be a CEO?

To Delay or Not to Delay?

You have been hired by a vice president of a national company to create an employee attitude survey, to administer it to all employees, and to interpret the results. You have known this vice president for over 10 years and have worked for her on several occasions. She trusts and likes you, and you trust and like her. You have completed your work and now are ready to present the findings and your interpretations to the vice president's management team. The vice president has told you that she wants your honest interpretation of the results, because she is planning to make changes based on the results. Based on this discussion, your report clearly identifies several strengths and weaknesses that need to be addressed. For example, employees feel that they are working too hard and that management does not care about providing good customer service. At the meeting you will be presenting the results and your interpretations to a group of 15 managers. You also have known most of these managers for at least 5 years.

You show up for the presentation armed with slides, handouts, and specific recommendations. Your slides are loaded on the computer, and most of the participants have arrived. They are drinking coffee and telling you how excited they are about hearing your presentation. You also are excited to share your insights. Ten minutes before the presentation is set to begin, the vice president takes you out of the meeting room and says she wants to talk with you about your presentation. The two of you go to another office, and she closes the door. She then tells you that her boss's boss decided to come to the presentation unannounced. She feels that he is coming to the presentation solely looking for negative information in your report. He does not like the vice president and wants to replace her with one of his friends. If you present your results as planned, it will provide this individual with the information he needs to create serious problems for the vice president. Knowing this, the vice president asks you to find some way to postpone your presentation. You have 10 minutes to decide what to do.

Solving the Dilemma

What would you do?

1. Deliver the presentation as planned.
2. Give the presentation but skip over the negative results.
3. Go back to the meeting room and announce that your spouse has had an accident at home and you must leave immediately. You tell the group that you just received this message and that you will contact the vice president to schedule a new meeting.
4. Invent other options. Discuss.

Management Theory
Essential Background for the Successful Manager

Major Questions You Should Be Able to Answer

2.1 Evolving Viewpoints: How We Got to Today's Management Outlook
Major Question: What's the payoff in studying different management perspectives, both yesterday's and today's?

2.2 Classical Viewpoint: Scientific & Administrative Management
Major Question: If the name of the game is to manage work more efficiently, what can the classical viewpoint teach me?

2.3 Behavioral Viewpoint: Behaviorism, Human Relations, & Behavioral Science
Major Question: To understand how people are motivated to achieve, what can I learn from the behavioral viewpoint?

2.4 Quantitative Viewpoints: Management Science & Operations Research
Major Question: If the manager's job is to solve problems, how might the two quantitative approaches help?

2.5 Systems Viewpoint
Major Question: How can the exceptional manager be helped by the systems viewpoint?

2.6 Contingency Viewpoint
Major Question: In the end, is there one best way to manage in all situations?

2.7 Quality-Management Viewpoint
Major Question: Can the quality-management viewpoint offer guidelines for true managerial success?

2.8 The Learning Organization in an Era of Accelerated Change
Major Question: Organizations must learn or perish. How do I build a learning organization?

Evidence-Based Management: An Attitude of Wisdom

"These days, there aren't any hot, new trends, just a lot of repackaged ones from the past," writes *Wall Street Journal* columnist Carol Hymowitz.[1] "Executives have been treated to an overdose of management guides that mostly haven't delivered what they promised. Many bosses have adopted them all, regardless of their company's business model, balance sheet, competition, employee bench strength, or any other unique qualities. They have become copycat managers, trying to find a one-stop, fix-it-all answer to their various problems."

How will you know whether the next "fix-it-all" book to hit the business bestseller list is simply a recycling of old ideas? The answer is: You have to have studied history—the subject of this chapter.

Is the practice of management an art or a science? Certainly it *can* be an art. Lots of top executives have no actual training in management—July McGrath, CEO of MTV Networks, for instance, whom we discussed in Chapter 1, has a background in English and journalism, not business. Great managers, like great painters or actors, are those who have the right mix of intuition, judgment, and experience.

But management is also a science. That is, rather than being performed in a seat-of-the-pants, trial-and-error, make-it-up-as-you-go-along kind of way—which can lead to some truly horrendous mistakes—management can be approached deliberately, rationally, systematically. That's what the scientific method is, after all—a logical process, embodying four steps: (1) You observe events and gather facts. (2) You pose a possible solution or explanation based on those facts. (3) You make a prediction of future events. (4) You test the prediction under systematic conditions.

The process of scientific reasoning underlies what is known as evidence-based management. *Evidence-based management* means translating principles based on best evidence into organizational practice, bringing rationality to the decision-making process.[2] Evidence-based management derives from evidence-based medicine, embracing what Stanford business scholars Jeffrey Pfeffer and Robert Sutton call *an attitude of wisdom*. This is a mind-set that, first, is willing to set aside belief and conventional wisdom and to act on the facts and, second, has an unrelenting commitment to gathering information necessary to make informed decisions and to keeping pace with new evidence to update practices.[3]

"The way a good doctor or a good manager works," Sutton says, "is to act with knowledge while doubting what you know. So if a patient goes to a doctor, you hope the doctor would do two things: first look at the literature and make the best decision given what's available. Then actually track the progress of the treatment and see what unexpected side effects you're having and what things are working."[4]

Evidence-based management is based on three truths:

- **There are few really new ideas:** Most supposedly new ideas are old, wrong, or both.

- **True is better than new:** Effective organizations and managers are more interested in what is true than in what is new.

- **Doing well usually dominates:** Organizations that do simple, obvious, and even seemingly trivial things well will dominate competitors who search for "silver bullets and instant magic."

For Discussion

Do you think managers are often driven by fads, by what they've read in the latest book or heard in the latest management seminar? Have you ever heard of a manager taking an experimental approach, as in trying out a new idea with an open mind to see what happens? How could you profit by taking an evidence-based approach to the ideas we will discuss in this chapter?

forecast

What's Ahead in This Chapter

This chapter gives you a short overview of the three principal *historical* perspectives or viewpoints on management—*classical, behavioral,* and *quantitative.* It then describes the three principal *contemporary* viewpoints—*systems, contingency,* and *quality-management.* Finally, we consider the concept of *learning organizations.*

THE BIG PICTURE

After studying theory, managers may learn the value of practicing evidence-based management, bringing rationality to the decision-making process. This chapter describes two principal theoretical perspectives—the *historical* and the *contemporary.* Studying management theory provides understanding of the present, a guide to action, a source of new ideas, clues to the meaning of your managers' decisions, and clues to the meaning of outside events.

"The best way to predict the future is to create it," Peter Drucker said. The purpose of this book is, to the extent possible, to give you the tools to create your own future as a manager.

Who is **Peter Drucker**? "He was the creator and inventor of modern management," says management guru Tom Peters. "In the early 1950s, nobody had a tool kit to manage these incredibly complex organizations that had gone out of control. Drucker was the first person to give us a handbook for that."[5]

An Austrian trained in economics and international law, Drucker came to the United States in 1937, where he worked as a correspondent for British newspapers and later became a college professor. In 1954, he published his famous text, *The Practice of Management,* in which he proposed that management was one of the major social innovations of the 20th century and that it should be treated as a profession, like medicine or law. In this and other books, he introduced several ideas that now underlie the organization and practice of management—that workers should be treated as assets, that the corporation could be considered a human community, that there is "no business without a customer," that institutionalized management practices were preferable to charismatic, cult leaders. Many ideas that you will encounter in this book—decentralization, management by objectives, knowledge workers—are directly traceable to Drucker's pen. "Without his analysis," says one writer, "it's almost impossible to imagine the rise of dispersed, globe-spanning corporations."[6]

Evidence-Based Management

Evidence-based management, described in the Manager's Toolbox, while not invented by Drucker, is very much in the spirit of his rational approach to management. As mentioned, *evidence-based management* **means translating principles based on best evidence into organizational practice, bringing rationality to the decision-making process.** As its two principal proponents, Stanford business scholars **Jeffrey Pfeffer and Robert Sutton,** put it, evidence-based management is based on the belief that "facing the hard facts about what works and what doesn't, understanding the dangerous half-truths that constitute so much conventional wisdom about management, and rejecting the total nonsense that too often passes for sound advice will help organizations perform better."[7] Learning to make managerial decisions based on evidence is the approach we hope you will learn to take after studying many other approaches—the perspectives described in this chapter.

Two Overarching Perspectives about Management

In this chapter, we describe two overarching perspectives about management:

- **Historical.** The *historical perspective* includes three viewpoints—*classical, behavioral,* and *quantitative.*
- **Contemporary.** The *contemporary perspective* also includes three viewpoints—*systems, contingency,* and *quality-management.*

Five Practical Reasons for Studying This Chapter

"Theory," say business professors Clayton Christensen and Michael Raynor, "often gets a bum rap among managers because it's associated with the word 'theoretical,' which connotes 'impractical.' But it shouldn't."[8] After all, what could be more practical than studying different approaches to see which work best?

Indeed, there are five good reasons for studying theoretical perspectives:

1. **Understanding of the present.** "Sound theories help us interpret the present, to understand what is happening and why," say Christensen and Raynor.[9] Understanding history will help you understand why some practices are still favored, whether for right or wrong reasons.

2. **Guide to action.** Good theories help us make predictions and enable you to develop a set of principles that will guide your actions.

3. **Source of new ideas.** It can also provide new ideas that may be useful to you when you come up against new situations.

4. **Clues to meaning of your managers' decisions.** It can help you understand your firm's focus, where the top managers are "coming from."

5. **Clues to meaning of outside events.** Finally, it may allow you to understand events outside the organization that could affect it or you. ●

Example

Is the Traditional Hierarchy the Only Way to Organize a Company? How Understanding Theory Can Help You

If Management 1.0 is what we're used to now, with its traditional pyramid hierarchy, what would Management 2.0 look like? What if, as management thinker Gary Hamel suggests, Management 2.0 looked a lot like Web 2.0 as represented in Wikipedia, YouTube, and other online communities?[10] Could the traditional hierarchy of boxes with lines actually become a corporate straitjacket?

That's what Lars Kolind, CEO of Danish digital hearing-aid producer Oticon, thought. In the early 1990s, he took Oticon's organization chart and simply threw it away. "He unilaterally abolished the old pyramid," says one account. In the new "spaghetti organization," as it came to be called, there was "no formal organization, no departments, no functions, no paper, no permanent desks."[11] All employees worked at mobile workstations, all desks were on wheels, and everybody worked on projects that were always subject to reorganization. Why such deliberate disorganization? Because if you want to have a company that is fast, agile, and innovative, as CEO Kolind did, you might want to have a flexible organizational structure that allows for fast reaction time. And it worked. By 1993, Oticon achieved the greatest profits since it was founded in 1904.

Your Call

Kolind says that the spaghetti organization structure has four characteristics: a much broader job definition, less formal structure, more open and informal physical layouts to facilitate communications, and management based on values.[12] Do you think a spaghetti organization could be applied to a factory with hundreds or thousands of employees, such as a Ford assembly plant?

2.2 CLASSICAL VIEWPOINT: SCIENTIFIC & ADMINISTRATIVE MANAGEMENT

major question

If the name of the game is to manage work more efficiently, what can the classical viewpoint teach me?

THE BIG PICTURE

The *three historical management viewpoints* we will describe include (1) the classical, described in this section; (2) the behavioral; and (3) the quantitative. The classical viewpoint, which emphasized ways to manage work more efficiently, had two approaches: (a) scientific management and (b) administrative management. *Scientific management*, pioneered by Frederick W. Taylor and Frank and Lillian Gilbreth, emphasized the scientific study of work methods to improve the productivity of individual workers. *Administrative management*, pioneered by Henri Fayol and Max Weber, was concerned with managing the total organization.

Bet you've never heard of a "therblig," although it may describe some physical motions you perform from time to time—perhaps when you have to wash dishes. A made-up word you won't find in most dictionaries, *therblig* was coined by Frank Gilbreth and is, in fact, "Gilbreth" spelled backward, with the "t" and the "h" reversed. It refers to 1 of 17 basic motions. By identifying the therbligs in a job, as in the tasks of a bricklayer (which he had once been), Frank and his wife, Lillian, were able to eliminate motions while simultaneously reducing fatigue.

The Gilbreths were a husband-and-wife team of industrial engineers who were pioneers in one of the classical approaches to management, part of the historical perspective. As we mentioned, there are *three historical management viewpoints* or approaches. *(See Figure 2.1, opposite page.)* They are

- Classical
- Behavioral
- Quantitative

In this section, we describe the classical perspective of management, which originated during the early 1900s. **The *classical viewpoint*, which emphasized finding ways to manage work more efficiently, had two branches—*scientific* and *administrative*—** each of which is identified with particular pioneering theorists. In general, classical management assumes that *people are rational*. Let's compare the two approaches.

Scientific Management: Pioneered by Taylor & the Gilbreths

The problem for which scientific management emerged as a solution was this: In the expansive days of the early 20th century, labor was in such short supply that managers were hard pressed to raise the productivity of workers. *Scientific management emphasized the scientific study of work methods to improve the productivity of individual workers.* Two of its chief proponents were **Frederick W. Taylor** and the team of **Frank and Lillian Gilbreth.**

Frederick Taylor & the Four Principles of Scientific Management No doubt there are some days when you haven't studied, or worked, as efficiently as you could. This could be called "underachieving," or "loafing," or what Taylor called it—*soldiering,*

① **Classical Viewpoint**
Emphasis on ways to manage work more efficiently

② **Behavioral Viewpoint**
Emphasis on importance of understanding human behavior and motivating and encouraging employees toward achievement

③ **Quantitative Viewpoint**
Applies quantitative techniques to management

Scientific management
Emphasized scientific study of work methods to improve productivity of individual workers

Proponents:
Frederick W. Taylor

Frank and Lillian Gilbreth

Early behaviorists

Proponents:
Hugo Munsterberg

Mary Parker Follet

Elton Mayo

Management science
Focuses on using mathematics to aid in problem solving and decision making

Administrative management
Concerned with managing the total organization

Proponents:
Henri Fayol

Max Weber

Human relations movement
Proposed better human relations could increase worker productivity

Proponents:
Abraham Maslow

Douglas McGregor

Operations management
Focuses on managing the production and delivery of an organization's products or services more effectively

Behavioral science approach
Relies on scientific research for developing theory to provide practical management tools

figure 2.1

THE HISTORICAL PERSPECTIVE

Three viewpoints are shown.

deliberately working at less than full capacity. Known as "the father of scientific management," Taylor was an American engineer from Philadelphia who believed that managers could eliminate soldiering by applying four principles of science:

1. Evaluate a task by scientifically studying each part of the task (not use old rule-of-thumb methods).
2. Carefully select workers with the right abilities for the task.
3. Give workers the training and incentives to do the task with the proper work methods.
4. Use scientific principles to plan the work methods and ease the way for workers to do their jobs.

Taylor based his system on *motion studies,* in which he broke down each worker's job at a steel company, say, into basic physical motions and then trained workers to use the methods of their best-performing co-workers. In addition, he suggested employers institute a *differential rate system,* in which more efficient workers earned higher wages.

Frederick W. Taylor. Called the father of scientific management, Taylor published *The Principles of Scientific Management* in 1911.

Lillian and Frank Gilbreth. These industrial engineers pioneered time and motion studies. If you're an athlete, you can appreciate how small changes can make you efficient.

Why Taylor Is Important: Although "Taylorism" met considerable resistance from employees fearing that working harder would lead to lost jobs except for the highly productive few, Taylor believed that by raising production both labor and management could increase profits to the point where they no longer would have to quarrel over them. If used correctly, the principles of scientific management can enhance productivity, and such innovations as motion studies and differential pay are still used today.

Frank & Lillian Gilbreth & Industrial Engineering   As mentioned, Frank and Lillian Gilbreth were a husband-and-wife team of industrial engineers who lectured at Purdue University in the early 1900s. Their experiences in raising 12 children—to whom they applied some of their ideas about improving efficiency (such as printing the Morse Code on the back of the bathroom door so that family members could learn it while doing other things)—later were popularized in a book, two movies, and a TV sitcom, *Cheaper by the Dozen.* The Gilbreths expanded on Taylor's motion studies—for instance, by using movie cameras to film workers at work in order to isolate the parts of a job.

Lillian Gilbreth, who received a PhD in psychology, was the first woman to be a major contributor to management science.

Administrative Management: Pioneered by Fayol & Weber

Scientific management is concerned with the jobs of individuals. *Administrative management* **is concerned with managing the total organization.** Among the pioneering theorists were **Henri Fayol** and **Max Weber.**

Henri Fayol & the Functions of Management   Fayol was not the first to investigate management behavior, but he was the first to systematize it. A French engineer and industrialist, he became known to American business when his most important work, *General and Industrial Management,* was translated into English in 1930.

Why Fayol Is Important: Fayol was the first to identify the major functions of management (p. 13)—planning, organizing, leading, and controlling, as well as coordinating—the first four of which you'll recognize as the functions providing the framework for this and most other management books.

Max Weber & the Rationality of Bureaucracy   In our time, the word "bureaucracy" has come to have negative associations: impersonality, inflexibility, red tape, a molasseslike response to problems. But to German sociologist Max Weber, a *bureaucracy* was a rational, efficient, ideal organization based on principles of logic. After all, in Weber's Germany in the late 19th century, many people were in positions of authority (particularly in the government) not because of their abilities but because of their social status. The result, Weber wrote, was that they didn't perform effectively.

A better-performing organization, he felt, should have five positive bureaucratic features:

1. A well-defined hierarchy of authority.
2. Formal rules and procedures.
3. A clear division of labor.
4. Impersonality.
5. Careers based on merit.

Why Weber Is Important: Weber's work was not translated into English until 1947, but it came to have an important influence on the structure of large corporations, such as the Coca-Cola Company.

The Problem with the Classical Viewpoint: Too Mechanistic

A flaw in the classical viewpoint is that it is mechanistic: It tends to view humans as cogs within a machine, not taking into account the importance of human needs. Behavioral theory addressed this problem, as we explain next.

Why the Classical Viewpoint Is Important: The essence of the classical viewpoint was that work activity was amenable to a rational approach, that through the application of scientific methods, time and motion studies, and job specialization it was possible to boost productivity. Indeed, these concepts are still in use today, the results visible to you every time you visit McDonald's or Pizza Hut. The classical viewpoint also led to such innovations as management by objectives and goal setting, as we explain elsewhere. ●

Scientific management. Car makers have broken down automobile manufacturing into its constituent tasks. This reflects the contributions of the school of scientific management. Is there anything wrong with this approach? How could it be improved?

2.3. BEHAVIORAL VIEWPOINT: BEHAVIORISM, HUMAN RELATIONS, & BEHAVIORAL SCIENCE

major question ?

To understand how people are motivated to achieve, what can I learn from the behavioral viewpoint?

THE BIG PICTURE

The second of the three historical management perspectives was the *behavioral* viewpoint, which emphasized the importance of understanding human behavior and of motivating employees toward achievement. The behavioral viewpoint developed over three phases: (1) *Early behaviorism* was pioneered by Hugo Munsterberg, Mary Parker Follett, and Elton Mayo. (2) The *human relations movement* was pioneered by Abraham Maslow (who proposed a hierarchy of needs) and Douglas McGregor (who proposed a Theory X and Theory Y view to explain managers' attitudes toward workers). (3) The *behavioral science approach* relied on scientific research for developing theories about behavior useful to managers.

The **behavioral viewpoint emphasized the importance of understanding human behavior and of motivating employees toward achievement.** The behavioral viewpoint developed over three phases: (1) early behaviorism, (2) the human relations movement, and (3) behavioral science.

Early Behaviorism: Pioneered by Munsterberg, Follett, & Mayo

The three people who pioneered behavioral theory were **Hugo Munsterberg, Mary Parker Follett,** and **Elton Mayo.**

Mary Parker Follett. She proposed that managers and employees should work together cooperatively.

Hugo Munsterberg & the First Application of Psychology to Industry

Called "the father of industrial psychology," German-born Hugo Munsterberg had a PhD in psychology and a medical degree and joined the faculty at Harvard University in 1892. Munsterberg suggested that psychologists could contribute to industry in three ways. They could:

1. Study jobs and determine which people are best suited to specific jobs.
2. Identify the psychological conditions under which employees do their best work.
3. Devise management strategies to influence employees to follow management's interests.

Why Munsterberg Is Important: His ideas led to the field of *industrial psychology,* the study of human behavior in workplaces, which is still taught in colleges today.

Mary Parker Follett & Power Sharing among Employees & Managers

A Massachusetts social worker and social philosopher, Mary Parker Follett was lauded on her death in 1933 as "one of the most important women America has yet produced in the fields of civics and sociology." Instead of following the usual hierarchical arrangement of managers as order givers and employees as order takers,

Follett thought organizations should become more democratic, with managers and employees working cooperatively.

The following ideas were among her most important:

1. Organizations should be operated as "communities," with managers and subordinates working together in harmony.

2. Conflicts should be resolved by having managers and workers talk over differences and find solutions that would satisfy both parties—a process she called *integration*.

3. The work process should be under the control of workers with the relevant knowledge, rather than of managers, who should act as facilitators.

Why Follett Is Important: With these and other ideas, Follett anticipated some of today's concepts of "self-managed teams," "worker empowerment," and "interdepartmental teams"—that is, members of different departments working together on joint projects.

Elton Mayo & the Supposed "Hawthorne Effect" Do you think workers would be more productive if they thought they were receiving special attention? This was the conclusion drawn by a Harvard research group in the late 1920s.

Conducted by Elton Mayo and his associates at Western Electric's Hawthorne (Chicago) plant, what came to be called the *Hawthorne studies* began with an investigation into whether workplace lighting level affected worker productivity. (This was the type of study that Taylor or the Gilbreths might have done.) In later experiments, other variables were altered, such as wage levels, rest periods, and length of workday. Worker performance varied but tended to increase over time, leading Mayo and his colleagues to hypothesize what came to be known as the *Hawthorne effect*—namely, that employees worked harder if they received added attention, if they thought that managers cared about their welfare and that supervisors paid special attention to them.

Hawthorne effect. Western Electric's Hawthorne plant, where Elton Mayo and his team conducted their studies in the 1920s. Do you think you'd perform better in a robotlike job if you thought your supervisor cared about you and paid more attention to you?

Why the Hawthorne Studies Are Important: Ultimately, the Hawthorne studies were faulted for being poorly designed and not having enough empirical data to support the conclusions. Nevertheless, they succeeded in drawing attention to the importance of "social man" (social beings) and how managers using good human relations could improve worker productivity. This in turn led to the so-called human relations movement in the 1950s and 1960s.

The Human Relations Movement: Pioneered by Maslow & McGregor

The two theorists who contributed most to the *human relations movement*—**which proposed that better human relations could increase worker productivity**—were Abraham Maslow and Douglas McGregor.

Abraham Maslow & the Hierarchy of Needs

What motivates you to perform: Food? Security? Love? Recognition? Self-fulfillment? Probably all of these, Abraham Maslow would say, although some needs must be satisfied before others. The chairman of the psychology department at Brandeis University and one of the earliest researchers to study motivation, in 1943 Maslow proposed his famous *hierarchy of human needs:* physiological, safety, love, esteem, and self-actualization[13] (as we discuss in detail in Chapter 12, where we explain why Maslow is important).

Douglas McGregor & Theory X versus Theory Y

Having been for a time a college president (at Antioch College in Ohio), Douglas McGregor came to realize that it was not enough for managers to try to be liked; they also needed to be aware of their attitudes toward employees.[14] Basically, McGregor suggested in a 1960 book, these attitudes could be either "X" or "Y."

Theory X represents a pessimistic, negative view of workers. In this view, workers are considered to be irresponsible, to be resistant to change, to lack ambition, to hate work, and to want to be led rather than to lead.

Theory Y? Debra Stark (third from left) built her Concord, Massachusetts–based Debra's Natural Gourmet store into a $2.5 million business by assigning each of her 26 employees, whom she calls "co-workers," a management role, such as monitoring product turnover. Each quarter, Stark distributes 20% of her after-tax profits among everyone, divided according to not only hours worked and salary level but also "how I see they're interacting with customers, each other, and me."

Theory Y represents the outlook of human relations proponents—an optimistic, positive view of workers. In this view, workers are considered to be capable of accepting responsibility, self-direction, and self-control and of being imaginative and creative.

Why Theory X/Theory Y Is Important: The principal contribution offered by the Theory X/Theory Y perspective is that it can help managers avoid falling into the trap of the *self-fulfilling prophecy*. This is the idea that if a manager expects a subordinate to act in a certain way, the worker may, in fact, very well act that way, thereby confirming the manager's expectations: The prophecy that the manager made is fulfilled.

The Behavioral Science Approach

The human relations movement was a necessary correction to the sterile approach used within scientific management, but its optimism came to be considered too simplistic for practical use. More recently, the human relations view has been superseded by the behavioral science approach to management. *Behavioral science* relies on scientific research for developing theories about human behavior that can be used to provide practical tools for managers. The disciplines of behavioral science include psychology, sociology, anthropology, and economics. ●

Example

Application of Behavioral Science Approach: Which Is Better—Competition or Cooperation?

A widely held assumption among American managers is that "competition brings out the best in people." From an economic standpoint, business survival depends on staying ahead of the competition. But from an interpersonal standpoint, critics contend competition has been overemphasized, primarily at the expense of cooperation.[15]

One strong advocate of greater emphasis on cooperation, Alfie Kahn, reviewed the evidence and found two reasons for what he sees as competition's failure.

First, he said, "success often depends on sharing resources efficiently, and this is nearly impossible when people have to work against one another." Competition makes people suspicious and hostile toward each other. Cooperation, by contrast, "takes advantage of all the skills represented in a group as well as the mysterious process by which that group becomes more than the sum of its parts."

Second, Kahn says, competition does not promote excellence, "because trying to do well and trying to beat others simply are two different things." Kahn points out the example of children in class who wave their arms to get the teacher's attention, but when they are finally recognized they then seem befuddled and ask the teacher to repeat the question—because they were more focused on beating their classmates than on the subject matter.[16]

What does the behavioral science research suggest about the question of cooperation versus competition? One team of researchers reviewed 122 studies encompassing a wide variety of subjects and settings and came up with three conclusions: (1) Cooperation is superior to competition in promoting achievement and productivity. (2) Cooperation is superior to individualistic efforts in promoting achievement and productivity. (3) Cooperation without intergroup competition promotes higher achievement and productivity than cooperation with intergroup competition.[17]

Your Call

What kind of office layout do you think would encourage more cooperation—a system of private offices or an open-office configuration with desks scattered about in a small area with no partitions?

2.4 QUANTITATIVE VIEWPOINTS: MANAGEMENT SCIENCE & OPERATIONS RESEARCH

major question?

If the manager's job is to solve problems, how might the two quantitative approaches help?

THE BIG PICTURE

The third and last category under historical perspectives consists of *quantitative viewpoints*, which emphasize the application to management of quantitative techniques, such as statistics and computer simulations. Two approaches of quantitative management are *management science* and *operations management*.

During the air war known as the Battle of Britain in World War II, a relative few Royal Air Force fighter pilots and planes were able to successfully resist the overwhelming might of the German military machine. How did they do it? Military planners drew on mathematics and statistics to determine how to most effectively allocate use of their limited aircraft.

When the Americans entered the war in 1941, they used the British model to form *operations research (OR)* teams to determine how to deploy troops, submarines, and other military personnel and equipment most effectively. For example, OR techniques were used to establish the optimum pattern that search planes should fly to try to locate enemy ships.

After the war, businesses also began using these techniques. One group of former officers, who came to be called the Whiz Kids, used statistical techniques at Ford Motor Co. to make better management decisions. Later Whiz Kid Robert McNamara, who had become Ford's president, was appointed Secretary of Defense and introduced similar statistical techniques and cost-benefit analyses throughout the Department of Defense. Since then, OR techniques have evolved into **quantitative management, the application to management of quantitative techniques, such as statistics and computer simulations. Two branches of quantitative management are *management science* and *operations management*.**

FedEx. What management tools do you use to schedule employees and aircraft to deal with wide variations in package volume—such as December 23 versus December 26?

Management Science: Using Mathematics to Solve Management Problems

How would you go about deciding how to assign utility repair crews during a blackout? Or how many package sorters you needed and at which times for an overnight delivery service such as FedEx or UPS? You would probably use the tools of management science.

Management science is not the same as Taylor's scientific management. **Management science focuses on using mathematics to aid in problem solving and decision making.** Sometimes management science is called *operations research.*

Why Management Science Is Important: Management science stresses the use of rational, science-based techniques and mathematical models to improve decision making and strategic planning.

Example

Management Science: Renting Hotel Rooms at Half the Price

"Anyone who spends more than a few nights in hotels each year should join a half-price hotel program," says travel writer Ed Perkinson.[18] "Like airlines, hotels use a yield-management system to set prices," says another travel writer, Robert Belsky. "The goal is to maximize occupancy when business is weak and hike rates when business is strong. Filling rooms in lean times means off-season deals at resorts, half-price weekends at downtown hotels that cater to business travelers, and cheap rooms in the summer at hotels booked with conventions the rest of the year."[19]

All it takes for the hotels to work out a half-price program is to do some management science–style math. Research shows that 80% occupancy is the standard for profitability. If the hotel is booked beyond that, half-price members don't get their discount; lower than 80%, they do. (There may be blackout periods for some days.)

Your Call

What other industries do you think might use this kind of discount system, and how might it work?

Operations Management: Helping Organizations Deliver Products or Services More Effectively

How does Costco decide when to reorder supplies? How does JetBlue decide which planes are to fly where and when? Managers use the techniques of operations management. A less sophisticated version of management science, *operations management* focuses on **managing the production and delivery of an organization's products or services more effectively.** It is concerned with work scheduling, production planning, facilities location and design, and decisions about the optimum levels of inventory a company should maintain.

Why Operations Management Is Important: Through the rational management of resources and distribution of goods and services, operations management helps ensure that business operations are efficient and effective. ●

Example

Operations Management: Can a Car Maker's "Lean Management" Production Techniques Be Applied to a Hospital?

Over the years, Toyota Motor Corp. has developed a variety of production techniques that draw in part on operations research.[20]

First, it emphasizes the smoothest possible *flow of work.* To accomplish this, managers perform *value stream mapping,* identifying the many steps in a production process and eliminating unnecessary ones. They also perform *mistake proofing* or *root-cause analysis,* using teamwork to examine problems and fix them as soon as they appear. In addition, the car maker helped pioneer the *just-in-time* approach to obtaining supplies from vendors only as they are needed in the factory. All such techniques now come under the term "lean management."

However, doctors and nurses don't think of themselves as assembly-line workers. Can lean management be used to improve hospital patient flow? Actually, it

can. At Allegheny General in Pittsburgh, for example, its two intensive-care units had been averaging 5.5 infections per 1,000 patient days, and in a 12-month period 37 patients had 49 infections and 51% died. The medical staff in the two units applied the Toyota "root-cause analysis" system to investigating every new infection as soon as it occurred. They concluded that an intravenous line inserted into an artery near the groin had a particularly high rate of infection. Now the hospital makes a continuous effort to replace these lines with lower-risk ones in the arm or near the collarbone.[21]

Your Call

If "lean management" can be applied at automakers and hospitals, could it be applied in higher education to educate students better? How?

THE BIG PICTURE

Three contemporary management perspectives are (1) the *systems*, (2) the *contingency*, and (3) the *quality-management* viewpoints. The *systems viewpoint* sees organizations as a system, either open or closed, with inputs, outputs, transformation processes, and feedback. The *contingency viewpoint* emphasizes that a manager's approach should vary according to the individual and environmental situation. The *quality-management viewpoint* has two traditional approaches: *quality control*, the strategy for minimizing errors by managing each stage of production, and *quality assurance*, which focuses on the performance of workers, urging employees to strive for zero defects. A third quality approach is the movement of *total quality management (TQM)*, a comprehensive approach dedicated to continuous quality improvement, training, and customer satisfaction.

Being of a presumably practical turn of mind, could you run an organization or a department according to the theories you've just learned? Probably not. The reason: People are complicated. To be an exceptional manager, you need to learn to deal with individual differences in a variety of settings.

Thus, to the historical perspective on management (classical, behavioral, and quantitative viewpoints), let us now add the *contemporary perspective*, which consists of three viewpoints. *(See Figure 2.2 below.)* These consist of:

- Systems
- Contingency
- Quality-management

In this section, we discuss the systems viewpoint.

The Systems Viewpoint Regards the organization as systems of interrelated parts that operate together to achieve a common purpose	**The Contingency Viewpoint** Emphasizes that a manager's approach should vary according to—i.e., be contingent on—the individual and environmental situation	**The Quality-Management Viewpoint** Three approaches
Quality control Strategy for minimizing errors by managing each state of production *Proponent:* Walter Shewart	**Quality assurance** Focuses on the performance of workers, urging employees to strive for "zero defects"	**Total quality management** Comprehensive approach dedicated to continuous quality improvement, training, and customer satisfaction *Proponents:* W. Edwards Deming Joseph M. Juran

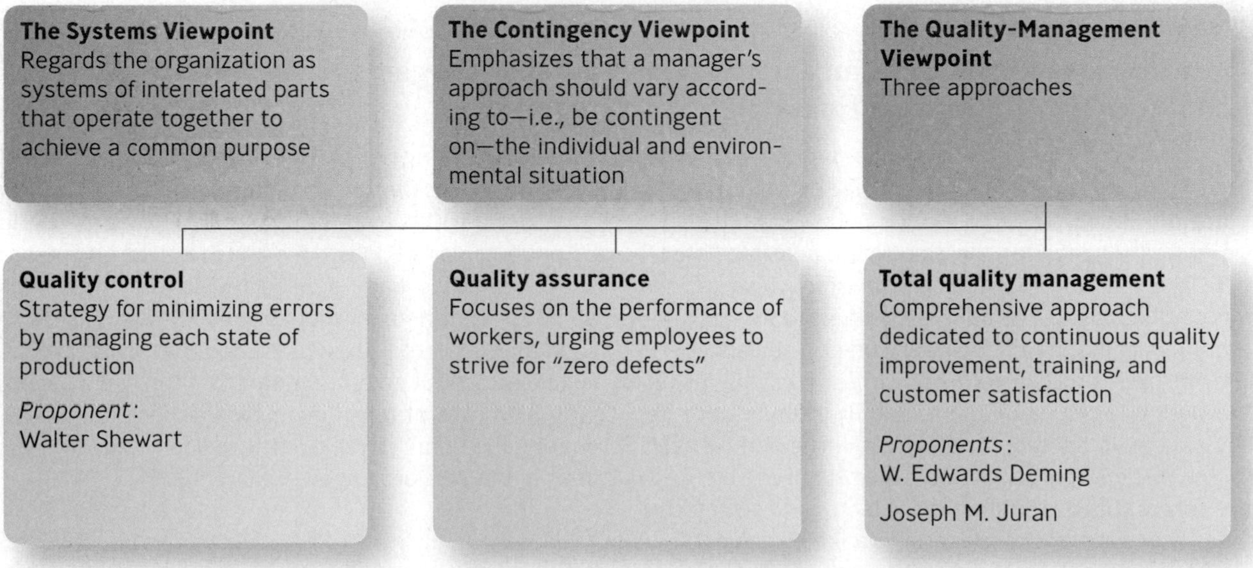

figure 2.2

THE CONTEMPORARY PERSPECTIVE

Three viewpoints

The Systems Viewpoint

The 52 bones in the foot. The monarchy of Great Britain. A weather storm front. Each of these is a system. **A *system* is a set of interrelated parts that operate together to achieve a common purpose.** Even though a system may not work very well—as in the inefficient way the Russian government collects taxes, for example—it is nevertheless still a system.

The *systems viewpoint* regards the organization as a system of interrelated parts. By adopting this point of view, you can look at your organization both as (1) a collection of *subsystems—parts making up the whole system*—and (2) a part of the larger environment. A college, for example, is made up of a collection of academic departments, support staffs, students, and the like. But it also exists as a system within the environment of education, having to be responsive to parents, alumni, legislators, nearby townspeople, and so on.

The Four Parts of a System

The vocabulary of the systems perspective is useful because it gives you a way of understanding many different kinds of organizations. The four parts of a system are defined as follows:

1. ***Inputs* are the people, money, information, equipment, and materials required to produce an organization's goods or services.** Whatever goes into a system is an input.

2. ***Outputs* are the products, services, profits, losses, employee satisfaction or discontent, and the like that are produced by the organization.** Whatever comes out of the system is an output.

3. ***Transformation processes* are the organization's capabilities in management and technology that are applied to converting inputs into outputs.** The main activity of the organization is to transform inputs into outputs.

4. ***Feedback* is information about the reaction of the environment to the outputs that affects the inputs.** Are the customers buying or not buying the product? That information is feedback.

The four parts of a system are illustrated below. *(See Figure 2.3.)*

figure 2.3

THE FOUR PARTS OF A SYSTEM

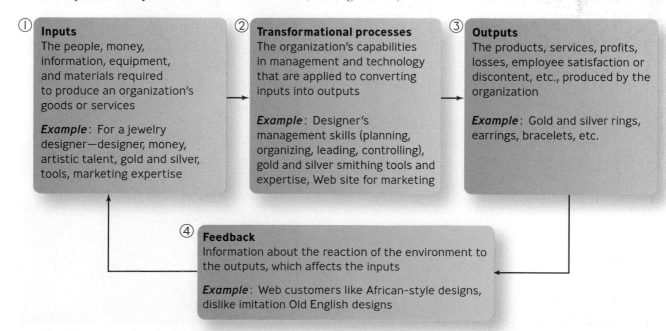

① **Inputs**
The people, money, information, equipment, and materials required to produce an organization's goods or services

Example: For a jewelry designer—designer, money, artistic talent, gold and silver, tools, marketing expertise

② **Transformational processes**
The organization's capabilities in management and technology that are applied to converting inputs into outputs

Example: Designer's management skills (planning, organizing, leading, controlling), gold and silver smithing tools and expertise, Web site for marketing

③ **Outputs**
The products, services, profits, losses, employee satisfaction or discontent, etc., produced by the organization

Example: Gold and silver rings, earrings, bracelets, etc.

④ **Feedback**
Information about the reaction of the environment to the outputs, which affects the inputs

Example: Web customers like African-style designs, dislike imitation Old English designs

Closed system. The Apple Newton Messagepad, a personal digital assistant released in 1993 and killed in 1998, probably failed because it was developed as a closed system, with inadequate feedback from consumers before launch. It was panned for being too expensive, too large, and having faulty handwriting recognition. (It still survives because of the efforts of Newton enthusiasts, not Apple.)

Open & Closed Systems Nearly all organizations are, at least to some degree, open systems rather than closed systems. An *open system* **continually interacts with its environment.** A *closed system* **has little interaction with its environment;** that is, it receives very little feedback from the outside. The classical management viewpoint often considered an organization a closed system. So does the management science perspective, which simplifies organizations for purposes of analysis. However, any organization that ignores feedback from the environment opens itself up to possibly spectacular failures.

Open system. Levi's confronted sinking sales arising from its closed system of market research. It now is actively trying to be an open-system company. Do you think a company that loses touch with its market can regain it?

Why the Systems Viewpoint—Particularly the Concept of Open Systems—Is Important: The history of management is full of accounts of organizations whose services or products failed because they weren't open enough systems and didn't have sufficient feedback. One of the most famous gaffes was the introduction of the 1959 Edsel by the Ford Motor Co. despite mixed reactions about the car's eccentric styling from customers given a preview of the vehicle. The concept of open systems, which stresses feedback from multiple environmental factors, both inside and outside the organization, attempts to ensure a continuous learning process in order to correct old mistakes and avoid new ones. ●

Example

Open & Closed Systems: How Do You Keep Up with Fashion Fads?

Are generations really different? However fuzzy the notion of what a "generation" is, we have been accustomed to hearing them labeled: the Baby Boomers (born between 1945 and 1962), then Generation X (born 1963 to 1978), and now Generation Y (born 1979 to 1994). Generation Y—also tagged the Echo Boomers and the Millennium Generation—consists of 60 million people. While this is not as huge as the 72 million Baby Boomers, it is a great deal larger than the 17 million in Gen X, and no marketer can afford to ignore a demographic bulge of this size. But how to discover what's cool and what's not to this generation?[22]

Having grown up with the Internet, Gen Yers are accustomed to high-speed information, research shows, which has made fashions faster changing, with young consumers inclined to switch brand loyalties in a millisecond. For a long time, Tommy Hilfiger stayed ahead of the style curve. "When Hilfiger's distinctive logo-laden shirts and jackets started showing up on urban rappers in the early '90s," says a *Business-Week* account, "the company started sending researchers into music clubs to see how this influential group wore the styles. It bolstered its traditional mass-media ads with unusual promotions. . . . Knowing its customers' passion for computer games, it sponsored a Nintendo competition and installed Nintendo terminals in its stores." By having constant feedback—an open system—with young consumers, Hilfiger was rewarded: Its jeans became the No. 1 brand in this age group.[23] Indeed, designers like Hilfiger, Nike, and DKNY have even refused to crack down on the pirating of their logos for T-shirts and baseball hats in the inner cities in order to maintain the "got to be cool" presence of their brands.[24]

By contrast, Levi Strauss and Co., a veritable icon of Baby Boomer youth, was jolted awake in 1997 when its market share slid, and the company's researchers found the brand was losing popularity among teens. "We all got older, and as a consequence, we lost touch with teenagers," said David Spangler, director of market research. Levi's thereupon opened up its relatively closed system by instituting ongoing teen panels to keep tabs on emerging trends. Generation Y "is a generation that must be reckoned with," said Spangler. "They are going to take over the country."

As Levi's has struggled to regain its luster, it has recently been hit by another threat: private-label jeans, in which retailers like Wal-Mart, Macy's, Target, and JC Penney create brands of their own, cutting out the middleman. Wal-Mart, for instance, introduced an in-house brand, called Metro 7, that competes against Levi's low-priced Signature jeans. On the other side are high-end jeans designers such as True Religion, Rock & Republic, Citizens of Humanity, and 7 for All Mankind, which produce "premium," or $100-plus, jeans that are sold in luxury stores.[25]

Your Call

Whereas in 1975 private labels and private brands were 25% of the apparel market, by 2010 they are expected to be over 60%. Still, consumers who prefer national brands, such as Levi's, outspend other shoppers by nearly 3 to 1 in department stores.[26] What would you recommend Levi's do to broaden its feedback system and respond to changing business conditions?

2.6 CONTINGENCY VIEWPOINT

major question

In the end, is there one best way to manage in all situations?

THE BIG PICTURE

The second viewpoint in the contemporary perspective, the contingency viewpoint, emphasizes that a manager's approach should vary according to the individual and environmental situation.

The classical viewpoints advanced by Taylor and Fayol assumed that their approaches had universal applications—that they were "the one best way" to manage organizations. The contingency viewpoint began to develop when managers discovered that under some circumstances better results could be achieved by breaking the one-best-way rule.

Example

The Contingency Viewpoint: When Does Using Data-Mining Software to Build Business Make Sense?

Most managers believe that technology increases productivity, a notion that Taylor and the Gilbreths might subscribe to. But does it always? Consider the use of data-mining software to increase business.

Gary Loveman, a former Harvard Business School professor, is now CEO of gambling giant Harrah's Entertainment, which owns or manages 50 casinos. Over the past 8 years, he has helped to build Harrah's into the world's largest gaming company. He has done this not by courting high rollers, as other gambling casinos do, but by, as one article describes it, "looking for frequent shoppers—the teachers, doctors, and accountants who walk through the doors to play the odds, again and again and again."[27]

The means of building business from this customer base, Loveman explained in a famous paper (and later book), "Diamonds in the Data Mine," was through the use of data-mining software, a computer-assisted process of sifting through and analyzing vast amounts of data in order to extract meaning and discover new knowledge.[28] Loveman identified its best customers through its Total Rewards incentive program and taught them to respond to the casino's marketing efforts in a way that added to their individual value.

But does data mining always boost productivity? New software enables companies to make faster sales by identifying and mining electronic networks of personal contacts. They allow people to get introductions to people they don't know, based on mathematical formulas that analyze tidbits of data in electronic calendars, phone logs, sales records, company databases, and the like.

Such software might seem a beneficial business-networking tool. However, the potential downside, one writer points out, is that a world "in which salespeople are using higher-powered electronic networking tools would inevitably be a world in which more pushy people engage in more intrusive behavior."[29] Such aggressive relationship mining might well backfire by angering and humiliating the very people you are trying to reach, like the endless "robocalls" that political candidates send to prospective voters at election time.

Indeed, this has already happened in pharmaceutical sales, where drug sales representatives have computerized dossiers showing which physicians are prescribing what drugs and used that knowledge to pressure a doctor to write more prescriptions for a brand-name drug or fewer orders for a competitor's drug. Now many doctors are in revolt against this intrusive data gathering and the resulting overzealous sales practices.[30]

Your Call

Should you or should you not adopt data-mining tools in a future business? What would be the answer, according to the contingency viewpoint?

The *contingency viewpoint* emphasizes that a manager's approach should vary according to—that is, be contingent on—the individual and the environmental situation.

A manager subscribing to the Gilbreth approach might try to get workers to build a better mousetrap, say, by simplifying the steps. A manager of the Theory X/Theory Y persuasion might try to use motivational techniques to boost worker productivity. But the manager following the contingency viewpoint would simply ask, "What method is the best to use under these particular circumstances?"

Why the Contingency Viewpoint Is Important: The contingency viewpoint would seem to be the most practical of the viewpoints discussed so far because it addresses problems on a case-by-case basis and varies the solution accordingly. ●

Practical Action

Mindfulness Over Mindlessness: Learning to Take a Contingency Point of View

"Be flexible." Isn't that what we're told?

Throughout your career, you will have to constantly make choices about how to solve various problems—which tools to apply, including the theories described in this chapter. However, one barrier to being flexible Is *mindlessness*. Instead we need to adopt the frame of mind that Harvard psychology professor Ellen Langer has called *mindfulness,* a form of active engagement.[31]

We've all experienced mindlessness. We misplace our keys. We write checks in January with the previous year's date. Mindlessness is characterized by the three following attributes.

Mindlessness #1: Entrapment in Old Categories

An avid tennis player, Langer says that at a tennis camp she, like all other students, was taught *exactly* how to hold her racquet and toss the ball when making a serve. But later, when watching a top tennis championship, she observed that none of the top players served the way she was taught and all served slightly differently.[32]

The significance: There is no one right way of doing things. In a conditional, or mindful, way of teaching, an instructor doesn't say, "This is THE answer," but rather, "This is ONE answer." Thus, all information—even in the hard sciences and mathematics, where it may seem as though there is just one correct answer—should be regarded with open-mindedness, because there may be exceptions. That is, you should act as though the information is true only for certain uses or under certain circumstances.

Mindlessness #2: Automatic Behavior

Langer tells of the time she used a new credit card in a department store. Noticing that Langer hadn't signed the card yet, the cashier returned it to her to sign the back. After passing the credit card through the imprinting machine, the clerk handed her the credit card receipt to sign, which Langer did. Then, says Langer, the cashier "held the form next to the newly signed card to see if the signatures matched."[33]

In automatic behavior, we take in and use limited signals from the world around us without letting other signals penetrate as well. By contrast, mindfulness is being open to new information—including that not specifically assigned to you. Mindfulness requires you to engage more fully in whatever it is you're doing.

Mindlessness #3: Acting from a Single Perspective

Most people, says Langer, typically assume that other peoples' motives and intentions are the same as theirs. For example, she says, "If I am out running and see someone walking briskly, I assume she is trying to exercise and would run if only she could," when actually she may only be trying to get her exercise from walking.

For most situations, many interpretations are possible. "Every idea, person, or object is potentially simultaneously many things depending on the perspective from which it is viewed," says Langer.[34] Trying out different perspectives gives you *more choices in how to respond;* a single perspective that produces an automatic reaction reduces your options.

Developing mindfulness means consciously adapting: Being open to novelty. Being alert to distinctions. Being sensitive to different contexts. Being aware of multiple perspectives. Being oriented in the present.

2.7 QUALITY-MANAGEMENT VIEWPOINT

major question? Can the quality-management viewpoint offer guidelines for true managerial success?

THE BIG PICTURE

The quality-management viewpoint, the third category under contemporary perspectives, consists of *quality control, quality assurance,* and especially the movement of *total quality management (TQM),* dedicated to continuous quality improvement, training, and customer satisfaction.

At one time in the 20th century, word got around among buyers of American cars that one shouldn't buy a "Monday car" or a "Friday car"—cars built on the days when absenteeism and hangovers were highest among dissatisfied autoworkers. The reason, supposedly, was that, despite the efforts of quantitative management, the cars produced on those days were the most shoddily made of what were coming to look like generally shoddy products.

The energy crisis of the 1970s showed different possibilities, as Americans began to buy more fuel-efficient cars made in Japan. Consumers found they could not only drive farther on a gallon of gas but that the cars were better made and needed repair less often. Eventually American car manufacturers began to adopt Japanese methods, leading to such slogans as "At Ford, Quality Is Job One." Today the average American car lasts 8 or 9 years compared to 5 or 6 just 20 years ago.[35]

Although not a "theory" as such, the *quality-management viewpoint, which includes quality control, quality assurance, and total quality management,* deserves to be considered because of the impact of this kind of thinking on contemporary management perspectives.

Quality Control & Quality Assurance

Quality **refers to the total ability of a product or service to meet customer needs.** Quality is seen as one of the most important ways of adding value to products and services, thereby distinguishing them from those of competitors. Two traditional strategies for ensuring quality are quality control and quality assurance.

Quality Control *Quality control* **is defined as the strategy for minimizing errors by managing each stage of production.** Quality control techniques were developed in the 1930s at Bell Telephone Labs by **Walter Shewart,** who used statistical sampling to locate errors by testing just some (rather than all) of the items in a particular production run.

Quality Assurance Developed in the 1960s, *quality assurance* **focuses on the performance of workers, urging employees to strive for "zero defects."** Quality assurance has been less successful because often employees have no control over the design of the work process.

Total Quality Management: Creating an Organization Dedicated to Continuous Improvement

In the years after World War II, the imprint "Made in Japan" on a product almost guaranteed that it was cheap and flimsy. That began to change with the arrival in Japan of two Americans, **W. Edwards Deming** and **Joseph M. Juran.**

TQM pioneer. W. Edwards Deming (right), shown with Kenzo Sasaoka, president of Yokogawa Hewlett-Packard, in Japan, 1982.

W. Edwards Deming   Desperate to rebuild its war-devastated economy, Japan eagerly received mathematician W. Edwards Deming's lectures on "good management." Deming believed that quality stemmed from "constancy of purpose"—steady focus on an organization's mission—along with statistical measurement and reduction of variations in production processes. However, he also emphasized the human side, saying that managers should stress teamwork, try to be helpful rather than simply give orders, and make employees feel comfortable about asking questions.

In addition, Deming proposed his so-called 85–15 rule—namely, when things go wrong, there is an 85% chance that the system is at fault, only a 15% chance that the individual worker is at fault. (The "system" would include not only machinery and equipment but also management and rules.) Most of the time, Deming thought, managers erroneously blamed individuals when the failure was really in the system.

Joseph M. Juran   Another pioneer with Deming in Japan's quality revolution was Joseph M. Juran, who defined quality as "fitness for use." By this he meant that a product or service should satisfy a customer's real needs. Thus, the best way to focus a company's efforts, Juran suggested, was to concentrate on the real needs of customers.

TQM: What It Is   From the work of Deming and Juran has come the strategic commitment to quality known as total quality management. *Total quality management (TQM)* **is a comprehensive approach—led by top management and supported throughout the organization—dedicated to continuous quality improvement, training, and customer satisfaction.**
The four components of TQM are as follows:

1. **Make continuous improvement a priority.** TQM companies are never satisfied. They make small, incremental improvements an everyday priority in all areas of the organization. By improving everything a little bit of the time all the time, the company can achieve long-term quality, efficiency, and customer satisfaction.

2. **Get every employee involved.** To build teamwork and trust, TQM companies see that every employee is involved in the continuous improvement process. This requires that workers must be trained and empowered to find and solve problems. The goal is to build teamwork, trust, and mutual respect.

3. **Listen to and learn from customers and employees.** TQM companies pay attention to their customers, the people who use their products or services. In addition, employees within the companies listen and learn from other employees, those outside their own work areas.

4. **Use accurate standards to identify and eliminate problems.** TQM organizations are always alert to how competitors do things better, then try to improve on them—a process known as benchmarking. Using these standards, they apply statistical measurements to their own processes to identify problems.

Why Total Quality Management Is Important: The total quality management viewpoint emphasizes infusing concepts of quality throughout the total organization in a way that will deliver quality products and services to customers. The adoption of TQM helped American companies deal with global competion. ●

2.8. THE LEARNING ORGANIZATION IN AN ERA OF ACCELERATED CHANGE

THE BIG PICTURE

Learning organizations actively create, acquire, and transfer knowledge within themselves and are able to modify their behavior to reflect new knowledge. There are three ways you as a manager can help build a learning organization.

Ultimately, the lesson we need to take from the theories, perspectives, and viewpoints we have described is this: We need to keep on learning. Organizations are the same way: Like people, they must continually learn new things or face obsolescence. A key challenge for managers, therefore, is to establish a culture that will enhance their employees' ability to learn—to build so-called learning organizations.

Learning organizations, says Massachusetts Institute of Technology professor **Peter Senge,** who coined the term, are places "where people continually expand their capacity to create the results they truly desire, where new and expansive patterns of thinking are nurtured, where collective aspiration is set free, and where people are continually learning how to learn together."[36]

The Learning Organization: Handling Knowledge & Modifying Behavior

More formally, a *learning organization* is an organization that actively creates, acquires, and transfers knowledge within itself and is able to modify its behavior to reflect new knowledge.[37] Note the three parts:

1. **Creating and acquiring knowledge.** In learning organizations, managers try to actively infuse their organizations with new ideas and information, which are the prerequisites for learning. They acquire such knowledge by constantly scanning their external environments, by not being afraid to hire new talent and expertise when needed, and by devoting significant resources to training and developing their employees.

2. **Transferring knowledge.** Managers actively work at transferring knowledge throughout the organization, reducing barriers to sharing information and ideas among employees. Electronic Data Systems (EDS), for instance, practically invented the information-technology services industry, but by 1996 it was slipping behind competitors—missing the onset of the Internet wave, for example. When a new CEO, Dick Brown, took the reins in 1999, he changed the culture from "fix the problem yourself" to sharing information internally.[38]

3. **Modifying behavior.** Learning organizations are nothing if not results oriented. Thus, managers encourage employees to use the new knowledge obtained to change their behavior to help further the organization's goals.[39]

Why Organizations Need to Be Learning Organizations: Living with Accelerated Change

Just as you as an individual will have to confront the challenges we mentioned in Chapter 1—globalization, information technology, diversity, and so on—so will organizations. The challenges posed by competition from a globalized marketplace and from the Internet and e-business revolution have led to unprecedented accelerated change, forcing organizations to be faster and more efficient.

Among some of the consequences of this fast-paced world:

1. **The rise of virtual organizations.** "Strip away the highfalutin' talk," says one industry observer, "and at bottom the Internet is a tool that dramatically lowers the cost of communication. That means it can radically alter any industry or activity that depends heavily on the flow of information."[40] One consequence of this is the **virtual organization, an organization whose members are geographically apart, usually working with e-mail, collaborative computing, and other computer connections,** while often appearing to customers and others to be a single, unified organization with a real physical location.[41]

2. **The rise of boundaryless organizations.** Computer connections and virtual organization have given rise to the concept of boundaryless organization. The opposite of a bureaucracy, with its numerous barriers and divisions, a **boundaryless organization is a fluid, highly adaptive organization whose members, linked by information technology, come together to collaborate on common tasks; the collaborators may include competitors, suppliers, and customers.** This means that the form of the business is ever-changing, and business relationships are informal.[42]

3. **The imperative for speed and innovation.** "Speed is emerging as the ultimate competitive weapon," says a *BusinessWeek* article. "Some of the world's most successful companies are proving to be expert at spotting new opportunities, marshaling their forces, and bringing to market new products or services in a flash. That goes for launching whole new ventures, too."[43] Speed is being driven by a new innovation imperative. "Competition is more intense than ever," the article continues, "because of the rise of the Asian powerhouses and the spread of disruptive new Internet technologies and business models."

4. **The increasing importance of knowledge workers. A knowledge worker is someone whose occupation is principally concerned with generating or interpreting information, as opposed to manual labor.** Knowledge workers add value to the organization by using their brains rather than the sweat of their brows, and as such they are the most common type of worker in 21st-century organizations. Because of globalization and information technology, the United States no longer has an advantage in knowledge workers. Indeed, because of the advancement of China, India, Russia, and Brazil; the offshoring of sophisticated jobs; the decrease in math and science skills among today's younger Americans; and other factors, the U.S. may be in danger of slipping behind.

5. **An appreciation for the importance of human capital. Human capital is the economic or productive potential of employee knowledge, experience, and actions.**[44] Thinking about people as human capital has an obvious basis: "Attracting, retaining, and developing great people is sometimes the only way our organizations can keep up with the competition across the street or around the globe," says Susan Meisinger, president and CEO of the Society for Human Resource Management. "Research has shown that highly educated, knowledgeable workers—*the most in demand*—are the hardest to find and easiest to lose."[45]

6. **An appreciation for the importance of social capital. Social capital is the economic or productive potential of strong, trusting, and cooperative relationships.**[46] Among aspects of social capital are goodwill, mutual

respect, cooperation, trust, and teamwork. Relationships within a company are important: In one survey, 77% of the women and 63% of the men rated "good relationship with boss" extremely important, outranking such matters as good equipment, easy commute, and flexible hours.[47]

7. **New emphasis on evidence-based management.** Is it such a radical idea to base decisions on the latest and best knowledge of what actually works? Wouldn't you think this would be the way medicine operates? In fact, say Jeffrey Pfeffer and Robert Sutton, most doctors rely on "obsolete knowledge gained in school, long-standing but never proven traditions, patterns gleaned from experience, the methods they believe in and are most skilled in applying, and information from hordes of vendors with products and services."[48] Business decision makers operate much the same way. Challenging this is a push for the use of evidence-based management in business. We continue the discussion about evidence-based management in Chapter 6.

How to Build a Learning Organization: Three Roles Managers Play

To create a learning organization, managers must perform three key functions or roles: (1) *build a commitment to learning,* (2) *work to generate ideas with impact,* and (3) *work to generalize ideas with impact.*[49]

1. **You can build a commitment to learning.** To instill in your employees an intellectual and emotional commitment to the idea of learning, you as a manager need to lead the way by investing in it, publicly promoting it, creating rewards and symbols of it, and performing other similar activities. For example, Mark Pigott, chairman of PACCAR, Inc., which makes Kenworth and Peterbilt trucks, accomplished this by looking at other kinds of businesses and learning from their success. By focusing intently on how to improve quality, PACCAR can charge up to 10% more then competitors for its trucks.[50]

2. **You can work to generate ideas with impact.** As a manager, you need to try to generate ideas with impact—that is, ideas that add value for customers, employees, and shareholders—by increasing employee competence through training, experimenting with new ideas, and engaging in other leadership activities.

   Soon after Dick Brown became new CEO of EDS, he saw that the company had to be reinvented as a cool brand to make people feel good about working there. His marketing director decided to launch a new campaign at the biggest media event of all: the Super Bowl. EDS ran an ad showing rugged cowboys riding herd on 10,000 cats. The message: "We ride herd on complexity."

3. **You can work to generalize ideas with impact.** Besides generating ideas with impact, you can also generalize them—that is, reduce the barriers to learning among employees and within your organization. You can create a climate that reduces conflict, increases communication, promotes teamwork, rewards risk taking, reduces the fear of failure, and increases cooperation. In other words, you can create a psychologically safe and comforting environment that increases the sharing of successes, failures, and best practices. ●

administrative management 44
behavioral science 49
behavioral viewpoint 46
boundaryless organization 61
classical viewpoint 42
closed system 54
contemporary perspective 41
contingency viewpoint 57
evidence-based management 40
feedback 53
historical perspective 41
human capital 61

human relations
  movement 48
inputs 53
knowledge worker 61
learning organization 60
management science 50
open system 54
operations management 51
outputs 53
quality 58
quality assurance 58
quality control 58

quality-management viewpoint 58
quantitative management 50
scientific management 42
social capital 61
subsystems 53
system 53
systems viewpoint 53
total quality management
  (TQM) 59
transformation processes 53
virtual organization 61

Summary

2.1 Evolving Viewpoints: How We Got to Today's Management

A rational approach to management is evidence-based management, which means translating principles based on best evidence into organizational practice, bringing rationality to the decision-making process. The two overarching perspectives on management are (1) the historical perspective, which includes three viewpoints—classical, behavioral, and quantitative; and (2) the contemporary perspective, which includes three other viewpoints—systems, contingency, and quality-management. There are five practical reasons for studying theoretical perspectives: They provide (1) understanding of the present, (2) a guide to action, (3) a source of new ideas, (4) clues to the meaning of your managers' decisions, and (5) clues to the meaning of outside ideas.

2.2 Classical Viewpoint: Scientific & Administrative Management

The first of the historical perspectives is the classical viewpoint, which emphasized finding ways to manage work more efficiently. It had two branches: (1) Scientific management emphasized the scientific study of work methods to improve productivity by individual

workers. It was pioneered by Frederick W. Taylor, who offered four principles of science that could be applied to management, and by Frank and Lillian Gilbreth, who refined motion studies that broke job tasks into physical motions. (2) Administrative management was concerned with managing the total organization. Among its pioneers were Henri Fayol, who identified the major functions of management (planning, organizing, leading, controlling), and Max Weber who identified five positive bureaucratic features in a well-performing organization. The classical viewpoint showed that work activity was amenable to a rational approach, but it has been criticized as being too mechanistic, viewing humans as cogs in a machine.

2.3 Behavioral Viewpoint: Behaviorism, Human Relations, & Behavioral Science

The second of the historical perspectives, the behavioral viewpoint emphasized the importance of understanding human behavior and of motivating employees toward achievement. It developed over three phases: (1) early behaviorism (2) the human relations movement, and (3) the behavioral science approach. Early behaviorism had three pioneers: (a) Hugo

Munsterberg suggested that psychologists could contribute to industry by studying jobs, identifying the psychological conditions for employees to do their best work. (b) Mary Parker Follett thought organizations should be democratic, with employees and managers working together. (c) Elton Mayo hypothesized a so-called Hawthorne effect, suggesting that employees worked harder if they received added attention from managers. The human relations movement suggested that better human relations could increase worker productivity. Among its pioneers were (a) Abraham Maslow, who proposed a hierarchy of human needs, and (b) Douglas McGregor, who proposed a Theory X (managers have pessimistic view of workers) and Theory Y (managers have positive view of workers). The behavioral science approach relied on scientific research for developing theories about human behavior that can be used to provide practical tools for managers.

2.4 Quantitative Viewpoints: Management Science & Operations Research
The third of the historical perspectives, quantitative viewpoints emphasized the application to management of quantitative techniques. Two approaches are (1) management science, which focuses on using mathematics to aid in problem solving and decision making; and (2) operations management, which focuses on managing the production and delivery of an organization's products or services more effectively.

2.5 Systems Viewpoint
We turn from the study of the historical perspective to the contemporary perspective, which includes three viewpoints: (1) systems, (2) contingency, and (3) quality-management. The systems viewpoint regards the organization as a system of interrelated parts or collection of subsystems that operate together to achieve a common purpose. A system has four parts: inputs, outputs, transformational processes, and feedback. A system can be open, continually interacting with the environment, or closed, having little such interaction.

2.6 Contingency Viewpoint
The second viewpoint in the contemporary perspective, the contingency viewpoint emphasizes that a manager's approach should vary according to the individual and the environmental situation.

2.7 Quality-Management Viewpoint
The third category in the contemporary perspective, the quality-management viewpoint is concerned with quality (the total ability of a product or service to meet customer needs) and has three aspects: (1) Quality control is the strategy for minimizing errors by managing each stage of production. (2) Quality assurance focuses on the performance of workers, urging employees to strive for "zero defects." (3) Total quality management (TQM) is a comprehensive approach dedicated to continuous quality improvement, training, and customer satisfaction. TQM has four components: (a) make continuous improvement a priority; (b) get every employee involved; (c) listen to and learn from customers and employees; and (d) use accurate standards to identify and eliminate problems.

2.8 The Learning Organization in an Era of Accelerated Change
A learning organization is one that actively creates, acquires, and transfers knowledge within itself and is able to modify its behavior to reflect new knowledge. Seven reasons why organizations need to become learning organizations are (1) the rise of virtual organizations, with members connected by electronic networks; (2) the rise of fluid, adaptive, boundaryless organizations; (3) the imperative for speed and innovation; (4) the increasing importance of knowledge workers, those principally concerned with generating or interpreting information; (5) an appreciation for the importance of human capital, the economic or productive potential of employees; (6) an appreciation for the importance of social capital, the economic or productive potential of strong and cooperative relationships; and (7) new emphasis on evidence-based management, in which managers face hard facts about

what works and what doesn't. Three roles that managers must perform to build a learning organization are to (1) build a commitment to learning, (2) work to generate ideas with impact, and (3) work to generalize ideas with impact.

Management in Action

Travelocity & H&R Block Make Decisions Based on Results from Customers' Written Feedback

A couple of years ago, Travelocity decided it had to get to know its customers better.

A company team spent several months poring over some 10,000 customer surveys, trying to figure out what people liked and didn't like about Travelocity. "As you can imagine, it was a very challenging process," says Don Hill, director of customer advocacy.

That was only the tip of the iceberg. To keep up with customers, Mr. Hill figured, his team would need to track and analyze 30,000 survey responses, 50,000 e-mails, and notes from half a million calls to the company's service centers—every month.

The solution? Travelocity turned to software maker Attensity Corp., whose products quickly analyze documents and pull out vital information. Using the software, Travelocity pinpointed critical customer concerns and came up with fixes. For instance, Travelocity found that some clients held the company accountable when airlines cancelled flights. Now Travelocity is trying to help customers plan itineraries that are less likely to get hit with cancellations. It's also developing better methods to help customers whose flights are cancelled.

Over the past few years, many big organizations have found themselves facing the same problem as Travelocity. They have access to treasure troves of customer intelligence—everything from surveys to e-mails to online reviews—but can't sift through them effectively. Employees don't have the time to read each document individually, and traditional database programs are designed to handle numerical data, not words.

That's where software like Attensity's comes in. These programs—known as text analytics—can scrutinize text documents, quickly identify crucial terms and concepts, and put all the information in an easily searchable form.

U.S. security agencies have been the biggest users of these technologies in the wake of 9/11. But a growing number of corporations are now discovering that text analytics can help them identify market trends and customer patterns, spot fraud and security threats, and highlight problems with products.

For instance, auto makers search through customer complaints, accident reports, and insurance claims to quickly identify defects in their cars. One car company was getting positive feedback about one of its models in surveys and customer e-mails. But software analysis showed that customers were burying a complaint in their notes: There was an annoying squeaking sound in the back passenger area. The auto maker fixed the problem before it hurt the company's reputation.

How does text analytics work? The software—programmed with dictionaries and a knowledge of grammar—starts by identifying the different components in sentences, such as nouns and verbs, and subjects and objects. Using that information, it determines the major themes in each sentence and paragraph, as well as the overall document, and then figures out the relationships between them. Finally, the software stores all that information in a database, where users can search by key terms. A company might check to see how customers regarded its Web site's "ease of use," for instance. . . .

"The market has changed. Customers can get what they want, and they are more vocal about what they like," says John Griggs, director of customer experience at H&R Block Inc., of Kansas City, Missouri.

H&R Block plunged into text analytics two years ago, when it faced stiff competition for its do-it-yourself online tax-preparation service.

As a first step, H&R Block wanted to understand why some customers were willing to recommend the service to friends and others weren't. With much of its business compressed into the weeks around tax time, the company needed to respond quickly to promote features or services that were popular—or fix problems that were turning off clients.

H&R Block turned to Clarabridge Inc., of Reston, Virginia, for software that analyzes surveys, customer e-mails, and notes from calls to H&R Block service centers, providing early-morning reports on some 10,000 customer contacts from the previous day. Mr. Griggs says it used to take 67 hours to review 1,500 customer surveys by hand. Clarabridge's software can do it in 30 minutes.

H&R Block zeroed in on customers' problems with the online filing process, which might make them hesitant to recommend the service. For example, customers were confused about the 2006 Telephone Excise Tax Refund. More than 160 million filers were eligible to request it, but H&R Block discovered that many clients didn't realize they qualified. The company quickly altered its online forms, clarifying who was eligible and helping customers maximize their refunds. . . .

For Discussion

1. Is the use of text analytics more reflective of managerial art or managerial science? Explain your rationale.

2. To what extent are the managerial practices being used at Travelocity and H&R Block consistent with principles associated with management science and operations management techniques? Discuss.

3. Use Figure 2.3 to analyze how H&R Block's use of text analytics follows a systems viewpoint.

4. How is the use of text analytics consistent with both a contingency and quality-management viewpoint? Explain your rationale.

5. What are the dangers of using text analytics to make managerial decisions? Discuss.

Source: Excerpted from Scott Morrison, "So Many, Many Words," *The Wall Street Journal*, January 28, 2008, p. R6. Copyright ©2008 by Dow Jones & Company, Inc. Reproduced with permission of Dow Jones & Company, Inc. via Copyright Clearance Center.

Self-Assessment

What Is Your Level of Self-Esteem?

Objectives

1. To get to know yourself a bit better.
2. To help you assess your self-esteem.

Introduction

Self-esteem, confidence, self-worth, and self-belief are all important aspects of being a manager in any organizational structure. However, the need for strong self-esteem is especially vital today because organizations demand that a manager manage people not as appendages of machines (as in Scientific Management) but as individuals who possess skills, knowledge, and self-will. Managers used to operate from a very strong position of centralized power and authority. However, in our modern organizational settings power is shared, and knowledge is to some extent "where you find it." To manage effectively in this situation, managers need strong self-esteem.

Instructions

To assess your self-esteem, answer the following questions. For each item, indicate the extent to which you agree or disagree by using the following scale. Remember, there are no right or wrong answers.

1 = strongly disagree
2 = disagree
3 = neither agree nor disagree
4 = agree
5 = strongly agree

1. I generally feel as competent as my peers.	1 2 3 4 5
2. I usually feel I can achieve whatever I want.	1 2 3 4 5
3. Whatever happens to me is mostly in my control.	1 2 3 4 5
4. I rarely worry about how things will work out.	1 2 3 4 5
5. I am confident that I can deal with most situations.	1 2 3 4 5
6. I rarely doubt my ability to solve problems.	1 2 3 4 5
7. I rarely feel guilty for asking others to do things.	1 2 3 4 5
8. I am rarely upset by criticism.	1 2 3 4 5
9. Even when I fail, I still do not doubt my basic ability.	1 2 3 4 5
10. I am very optimis tic about my future.	1 2 3 4 5
11. I feel that I have quite a lot to offer an employer.	1 2 3 4 5
12. I rarely dwell for very long on personal setbacks.	1 2 3 4 5
13. I am always comfortable in disagreeing with my boss.	1 2 3 4 5
14. I rarely feel that I would like to be somebody else.	1 2 3 4 5

TOTAL SCORE_____

Arbitrary Norms

High Self-esteem = 56−70
Moderate Self-esteem = 29−55
Low Self-esteem = 14−28

Questions for Discussion

1. Do you agree with the assessment? Why or why not?
2. How might you go about improving your self-esteem?
3. Can you survive today without having relatively good confidence in yourself?

Ethical Dilemma

Should Medical Devices Be Used as an Aid in Marketing Products?

[Magnetic resonance imaging (MRI)] technology has been used since the 1980s to detect injury or disease in patients suffering from symptoms such as seizures, paralysis, or severe headaches. But in just the past few years, manufacturers have developed stronger MRI magnets and more sophisticated software that can sort through a flood of subtle signals the scans collect.

. . . Imaging technology has leaped far beyond its roots of looking for lumps and shadows. Psychiatrists are now studying the mental activities of patients suffering from depression and other emotional ills. Basic researchers are rolling thousands of healthy subjects . . . into MRI machines in order to explore the very essence of the mind, asking them to think, decide, feel, and learn inside the scanners. Pharma companies hope the new "functional" MRI (fMRI) technology will enhance drug development. Law enforcement experts hope it could become a more accurate lie detector. Even our most private tastes and impulses are under scrutiny as so-called neuromarketing takes off.

. . . Unlike other brain-scanning technologies such as positron emission tomography (PET), which exposes patients to radiation, fMRI simply tracks the response in the brain tissue to magnetic fields. It's noninvasive and believed to be harmless. That means even very young children can be scanned— and scanned repeatedly as they grow older.

. . . One intriguing, yet controversial use of fMRI is probing consumer preferences—a technique sometimes called *neuromarketing*. At California Institute of Technology, researcher Stephen R. Quartz is using fMRI to explore how the brain perceives a cool product vs. an uncool one. Among portable MP3 players, "the [Apple] iPod is by far the market leader. What about that gives us a different signal in the brain?" he asks. Quartz also has formed a company that will offer services to Hollywood studios, imaging the brains of test audiences as they view movie trailers to see which generate the most brain buzz.

Solving the Dilemma

You are part of a committee on medical ethics organized to vote on whether fMRI should be used in capacities other than medicine—i.e., law enforcement and consumer marketing. How would you vote?

1. Absolutely not. It is wrong to use medical technology in any capacity other than healing.

2. Absolutely not. I don't think anyone should be able to peek into my own private thoughts and preferences.

3. Yes, but only if the brain scan data are made public. Such data could be of scientific interest and could be used to combat social issues such as racism and terrorism. This kind of data would also be extremely useful for law enforcement, because it would help determine what really went on in the mind of a criminal.

4. Invent other options. Discuss.

Source: From Joan C. O'Hamilton, "Journey to the Center of the Mind: Functional MRI Is Yielding a Clearer Picture of What Thoughts Look Like," *BusinessWeek,* April 19, 2004, pp. 78–80. Reprinted with permission.

The Manager's Changing Work Environment & Ethical Responsibilities

Doing the Right Thing

Treating Employees Right: Toward a More Open Workplace

Some companies are "toxic organizations," Stanford University business professor Jeffrey Pfeffer's name for firms with high turnover and low productivity. "Companies that manage people right will outperform companies that don't by 30% to 40%," says Pfeffer. "If you don't believe me, look at the numbers."[1]

The author of *The Human Equation: Building Profits by Putting People First*, Pfeffer says that employees' loyalty to employers isn't dead but that toxic companies drive people away.[2] Companies such as Costco, Starbucks, and The Men's Wearhouse have had lower turnover—and hence lower replacement and training costs—than their competitors for a reason: They have bent over backward to create workplaces that make people want to stay.

Here are some ways that companies keep their employees:

- **Being generous with personal and team recognition.** CompuWorks, a Pittsfield, Massachusetts, computer systems-integration company, cultivates employee loyalty by piling on personal and team recognition, as in giving the Wizard of the Week award to the employee who goes beyond the call of duty. It also operates the Time Bank, into which every month 10 hours of free time is "deposited" for each employee to use as he or she wishes. Training is given in how to read financial statements and in how to chart billable hours and watch cash-flow levels. Regular bonuses are given based on company profits.[3]

- **Occasionally backing employees over clients.** Sometimes, despite the mantra that "the customer is always right," companies will even side with employees against clients. For example, The Benjamin Group, a California public relations agency, has fired clients who have been arrogant and hard to work with. This reflects management theories that troublesome customers are often less profitable and less loyal and so aren't worth the extra effort.[4]

- **Use of "open-book management."** One way of challenging traditional military-style management and of empowering employees and increasing earnings is through "open-book management," *Inc.* magazine editor John Case's term for a company's being completely open with employees about its financial status, projections, costs, expenses, and even salaries.[5] This approach "means training employees in how the company is run," says one account. "It means asking for employee input and acting on it. It means rewarding employees with bonuses when the goals they create are met."[6]

By learning the key numbers, employees are able to use their heads instead of just doing their jobs and going home. "Whether or not you have equity ownership, open-book management helps employees to feel, think, and act like owners," says Gary T. Brown, director of human resources for Springfield ReManufacturing Corp., a rebuilder of truck engines in Springfield, Missouri. "True open-book management means asking employees what the goals should be."[7]

For Discussion In tomorrow's highly diverse workforce, with people representing many different ethnicities, ages, and abilities, taking care of employees will be one of the biggest challenges a manager will face. Could you work for an old-style company that did not feature some of the approaches mentioned above—even if it gave you a shot at getting into higher management?

forecast

What's Ahead in This Chapter

This chapter sets the stage for understanding the new world in which managers must operate and the responsibilities they will have. We begin by describing the community of stakeholders that managers have to deal with—first the internal stakeholders (of employees, owners, and directors), then the external stakeholders in two kinds of environments (task and general). We then consider the ethical and social responsibilities required in being a manager, as well as the new diversified workforce and the barriers and approaches to managing diversity.

3.1 THE COMMUNITY OF STAKEHOLDERS INSIDE THE ORGANIZATION

major question? Stockholders are only one group of stakeholders. Who are stakeholders important to me inside the organization?

THE BIG PICTURE

Managers operate in two organizational environments—internal and external—both made up of stakeholders, the people whose interests are affected by the organization. The first, or internal, environment consists of employees, owners, and the board of directors.

Costco. In the war of big-box stores, is Costco or Wal-Mart better for everyone involved?

Which company is better—Wal-Mart Stores (1.6 million employees) or rival warehouse club Costco Wholesale (132,000)? And why?

The difference in the way the two companies treat their employees is dramatic. Wal-Mart pays an hourly wage, currently $10.74 on average, that is similar to that of competitors such as Target or Kmart. Costco pays non-supervisory wages that range between $11.00 and $19.50 an hour. At Costco 96% of eligible workers are covered by company health insurance (higher than the 80% average at large U.S. companies). Wal-Mart says fewer than 10% of its employees lack health insurance; employees can purchase family coverage for $14–$21 a month, although the deductible is $2,000—a lot for someone earning less than $20,000 a year. Wal-Mart's low-wage policy has forced rivals, such as Safeway, to reduce benefits for their workers in order to stay competitive. Costco's wages have enabled its employees to buy homes and take vacation trips. Finally, Wal-Mart has reportedly locked out workers overnight, hired illegal immigrants to mop its floors, and been slapped with a big discrimination suit.[8]

Yet *Fortune* named Wal-Mart to the No. 1 or No. 2 spot on its annual "Most Admired Companies" list in the years 2000–2005. (It dropped to No. 12 and No. 19 in 2006 and 2007, respectively, whereas Costco moved up to No. 15 and No. 18 in those years.) Is this because Wal-Mart's low prices probably save consumers $20 billion a year? Because it generates 3.5 cents for each dollar on sales compared with Costco's 1.7 cents?

"Where you stand on Wal-Mart," says one account, "seems to depend on where you sit. If you're a consumer, Wal-Mart is good for you. If you're a wage earner, there's a good chance it's bad. If you're a Wal-Mart shareholder, you want the company to grow. If you're a citizen, you probably don't want it growing in your backyard."[9]

How you feel about Costco may also vary with where you sit. "From the perspective of investors," says one stock analyst, "Costco's benefits are overly generous. Public companies need to care for shareholders first." Responds Costco president and chief executive Jim Sinegal, "I happen to believe that in order to reward the shareholder in the long term, you have to please your customers and workers."[10]

The differences may be seen in annual employee turnover—at least 50%, perhaps 70%, for Wal-Mart, 24% for Costco.[11] It's been calculated that a 10% reduction in employee turnover can yield a 20% savings on labor costs. Thus, whereas Wal-Mart's labor costs amount to 12% of its annual sales, Costco's are only 7%. On a per-store basis, Wal-Mart's Sam's Club generates only half the sales of the average Costco store (in part because Costco attracts higher-income shoppers and because it charges a yearly membership fee, spending no money on advertising). Still, the more favorable employee benefits lead to a less favorable stock price for Costco compared with Wal-Mart.

Which should a company favor, its employees or its owners (stockholders)? Henry Ford, founder of Ford Motor Co., thought he could serve both. In 1914, he announced workers in his factories would receive $5 a day—a major boost over then-prevailing wages. The reason: He recognized that his promise to build a car affordable to the masses would be hypocritical if he didn't pay his own workers enough to buy it themselves.[12]

Internal & External Stakeholders

Should a company be principally responsible to just its stockholders? Perhaps we need a broader term to indicate all those with a stake in an organization. That term, appropriately, is *stakeholders*—**the people whose interests are affected by an organization's activities.**

Managers operate in two organizational environments, both made up of various stakeholders. *(See Figure 3.1.)* As we describe in the rest of this section, the two environments are these:

- Internal stakeholders
- External stakeholders

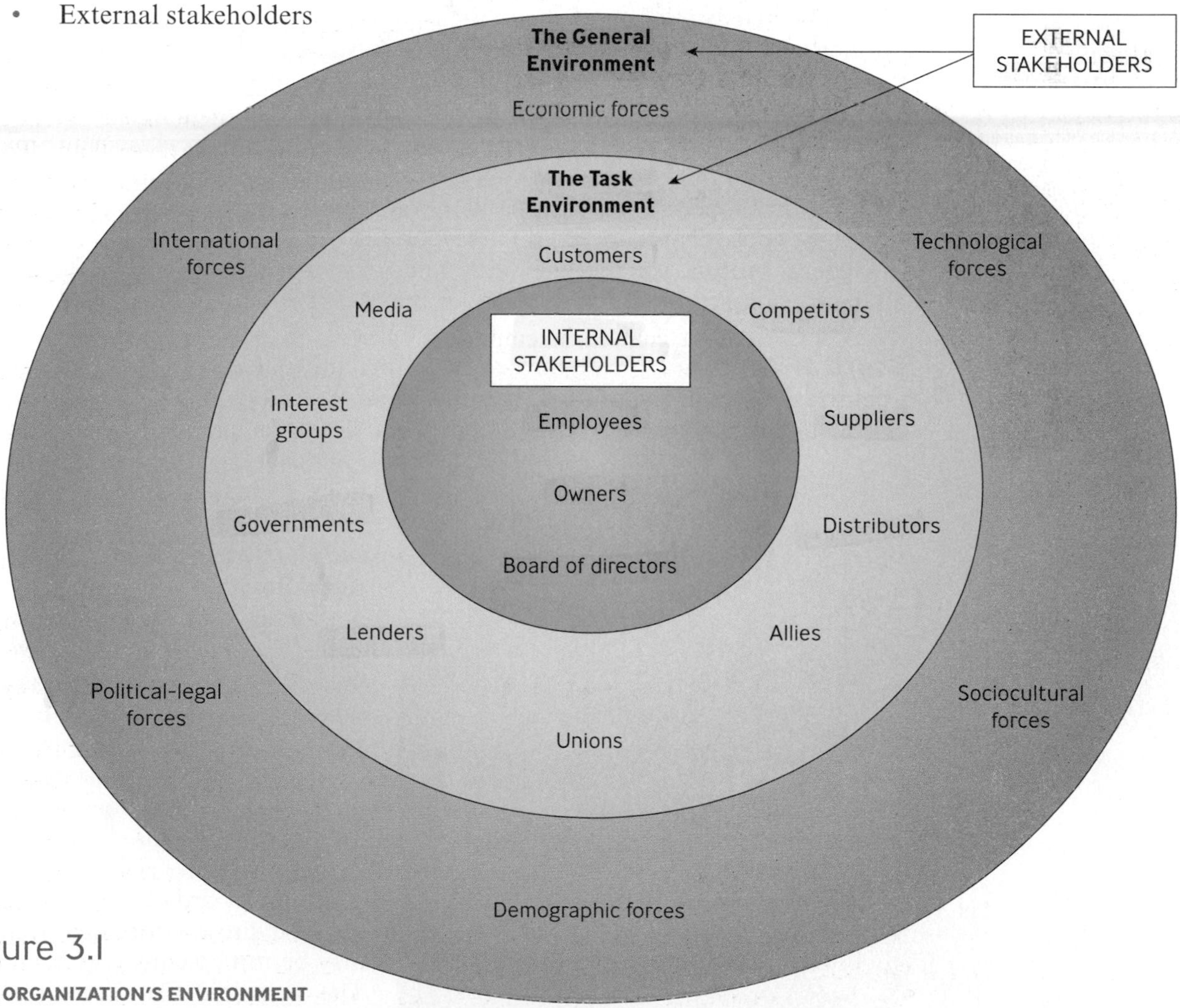

figure 3.1

THE ORGANIZATION'S ENVIRONMENT

The two main groups are internal and external stakeholders

Internal Stakeholders

Whether small or large, the organization to which you belong has people in it that have an important stake in how it performs. These ***internal stakeholders* consist of employees, owners, and the board of directors, if any.** Let us consider each in turn.

Employees As a manager, could you run your part of the organization if you and your employees were constantly in conflict? Labor history, of course, is full of accounts of just that. But such conflict may lower the performance of the organization, thereby hurting everyone's stake. In many of today's forward-looking organizations, employees are considered "the talent"—the most important resource.

For instance, at Trilogy Software in Austin, Texas, workers aren't really considered "employees." "They're all shareholders," says former U.S. Labor Secretary Robert Reich in an article about cutting-edge kinds of companies. "They're all managers. They're all partners. That's how [Joe] Liemandt, Trilogy's CEO, has chosen to run his company—and that's what makes it successful."[13]

Owners The *owners* **of an organization consist of all those who can claim it as their legal property,** such as Wal-Mart's stockholders. In the for-profit world, if you're running a one-person graphic design firm, the owner is just you—you're what is known as a sole proprietorship. If you're in an Internet startup with your brother-in-law, you're both owners—you're a partnership. If you're a member of a family running a car dealership, you're all owners—you're investors in a privately owned company. If you work for a company that is more than half owned by its employees (such as Food Giant, United Airlines, or W. L. Gore Associates, maker of Gore-Tex fabric), you are one of the joint owners—you're part of an Employee Stock Ownership Plan (ESOP).[14] And if you've bought a few shares of stock in a company whose shares are listed for sale on the New York Stock Exchange, such as General Motors, you're one of thousands of owners—you're a stockholder. In all these examples, of course, the goal of the owners is to make a profit.

Board of Directors Who hires the chief executive of a for-profit or nonprofit organization? In a corporation, it is the *board of directors,* whose members are elected by the stockholders to see that the company is being run according to their interests. In nonprofit organizations, such as universities or hospitals, the board may be called the *board of trustees* or *board of regents.* Board members are very important in setting the organization's overall strategic goals and in approving the major decisions and salaries of top management.

Not all firms have a board of directors. A lawyer, for instance, may operate as a sole proprietor, making all her own decisions. A large corporation might have eight or so members on its board of directors. Some of these directors (inside directors) may be top executives of the firm. The rest (outside directors) are elected from outside the firm. ●

Employee ownership. Zachary's Chicago Pizza, based in Oakland, California, uses a device known as an Employee Stock Ownership Plan, in which employees buy company stock in order to become owners. Although the idea was conceived over 50 years ago, there are only about 11,500 ESOPs today out of hundreds of thousands of businesses. Why do you suppose more companies aren't owned by their employees?

3.2 THE COMMUNITY OF STAKEHOLDERS OUTSIDE THE ORGANIZATION

> Who are stakeholders important to me outside the organization?
>
> major question?

THE BIG PICTURE

The external environment of stakeholders consists of the task environment and the general environment. The task environment consists of customers, competitors, suppliers, distributors, strategic allies, employee associations, local communities, financial institutions, government regulators, special-interest groups, and the mass media. The general environment consists of economic, technological, sociocultural, demographic, political-legal, and international forces.

In the first section we described the environment inside the organization. Here let's consider the environment outside it, which consists of **external stakeholders— people or groups in the organization's external environment that are affected by it.** This environment consists of:

- The task environment.
- The general environment.

The Task Environment

The *task environment* **consists of 11 groups that present you with daily tasks to handle: customers, competitors, suppliers, distributors, strategic allies, employee organizations, local communities, financial institutions, government regulators, special-interest groups, and mass media.**

I. Customers The first law of business, we've said, is *take care of the customer.* ***Customers* are those who pay to use an organization's goods or services.** Customers may be the focus not only of for-profit organizations but also nonprofit ones.

2. Competitors Is there any line of work you could enter in which there would *not* be *competitors*—**people or organizations that compete for customers or resources,** such as talented employees or raw materials? Every organization has to be actively aware of its competitors. Florist shops and delicatessens must be aware that customers can buy the same products at Safeway or Kroger.

3. Suppliers A *supplier* **is a person or an organization that provides supplies—that is, raw materials, services, equipment, labor, or energy—to other organizations.** Suppliers in turn have their own suppliers: The publisher of this book buys the paper on which it is printed from a paper merchant, who in turn is supplied by several paper mills, who in turn are supplied wood for wood pulp by logging companies with forests in the United States or Canada.

Take care of the customer. Apple manufactures and sells its personal computers not only over the Internet but also through its own stores. Does doing so give the company a competitive advantage over Internet sellers of PCs, such as Dell?

Example

Taking Care of Customers: Amazon.com Obsesses about "the Customer Experience"

What do Wall Street investors care about? Short-term profits. And profits are what Dell Computer tried to deliver when it scrimped on customer service. So did eBay when it saddled its most dedicated sellers with new costs. "Eventually," says *New York Times* business writer Joe Nocera, "those short-sighted decisions caught up with both companies."[15]

By contrast, Amazon.com founder and CEO Jeff Bezos is "obsessed," in his words, with what he calls "the customer experience." Customers "care about having the lowest prices, having vast selection, so they have choice, and getting the products . . . fast," Bezos said in 2007. "And the reason I'm so obsessed with these drivers of the customer experience is that I believe that the success we have had over the past 12 years has been driven exclusively by that customer experience."[16]

Thus, the company has easy-to-use online technology, money-losing (in Wall Street's view) 2-day free shipping on all packages for an annual fee of just $79, and a customer-service phone number that you can actually find. It also is willing to correct mistakes that it didn't make, as when it replaced, for free, a $500 PlayStation 3 Christmas present that Nocera had ordered for his son, which disappeared on arriving at his apartment building—and it saw to it that the replacement arrived on Christmas Eve.

Your Call

Spending huge sums of money on "frills" such as free shipping has depressed Amazon's profits from time to time, but in 2007 the company grew about 35% and its profitability was up around 6%. Other companies also bend over backward to take care of their customers. Can you think of others—and can you find out if they are profitable?

4. Distributors   A *distributor* **is a person or an organization that helps another organization sell its goods and services to customers.** Publishers of magazines, for instance, don't sell directly to newsstands; rather, they go through a distributor, or wholesaler. Tickets to Green Day, Evanescence, or other artists' performances might be sold to you directly by the concert hall, but they are also sold through such distributors as TicketMaster and Blockbuster Video.

Distributors can be quite important because in some industries (such as movie theaters and magazines) there is not a lot of competition, and the distributor has a lot of power over the ultimate price of the product. However, the rise in popularity of the Internet has allowed manufacturers of personal computers, for example, to cut out the "middleman"—the distributor—and to sell to customers directly.

5. Strategic Allies   Companies, and even nonprofit organizations, frequently link up with other organizations (even competing ones) in order to realize strategic advantages. The term *strategic allies* **describes the relationship of two organizations who join forces to achieve advantages neither can perform as well alone.**

With their worldwide reservation systems and slick marketing, big companies—Hilton, Hyatt, Marriott, Starwood, and so on—dominate the high-end business-center hotels. But in many cities, there are still independents—such as The Rittenhouse in Philadelphia, The Hay-Adams in Washington, DC, and The Adolphus in Dallas—that compete with the chains by promoting their prestigious locations, grand architecture, rich history, and personalized service. Recently, however, high-end independents have become affiliated with chains as strategic allies because chains can buy supplies for less and they have more far-reaching sales channels. The 97-year-old U.S. Grant in downtown San Diego, for example, joined Starwood's Luxury Collection in 2005 to gain "worldwide exposure," according to a hotel spokesman.[17]

6. Employee Organizations: Unions & Associations   As a rule of thumb, labor unions (such as the United Auto Workers or the Teamsters Union) tend to represent hourly workers; professional associations (such as the National Education

Association or the Newspaper Guild) tend to represent salaried workers. Nevertheless, during a labor dispute, the salary-earning reporters in the Newspaper Guild might well picket in sympathy with the wage-earning circulation-truck drivers in the Teamsters Union.

In recent years, the percentage of the labor force represented by unions has steadily declined (from 35% in the 1950s to 12.1% in 2007).[18] Moreover, union agendas have changed. Strikes and violence are pretty much out. Benefits, stock ownership, and campaigns for "living-wage" ordinances are in.[19]

7. Local Communities   Local communities are obviously important stakeholders, as becomes evident not only when a big organization arrives but also when it leaves, sending government officials scrambling to find new industry to replace it. Schools and municipal governments rely on the organization for their tax base. Families and merchants depend on its employee payroll for their livelihoods. In addition, everyone from the United Way to the Little League may rely on it for some financial support.[20]

Example

Local Communities as Stakeholders: Automakers' Impact on Indiana & Arkansas Towns

Anderson, Indiana, once had so many General Motors manufacturing plants that it had to stagger work schedules so that the streets would not be jammed with cars when the workday ended. Today there is not a single GM plant left, and Anderson's population has dropped from 70,000 to 58,000 people. Guide Corp., a tail-lamp factory, also closed in 2006, which means the town will probably lose another 400 families.[21] Even so, the town is still dependent on GM. About 10,000 GM retirees plus surviving spouses and other family members receive health and pension checks, which in turn support local restaurants, shopping centers, doctor's offices, and hospitals.

For Anderson's mayor, Kevin Smith, the dependence on retiree income is a major concern. "We realize those retiree pensions will not be here in the coming years," he said. "That's why it's important that we are involved in new job creation that will employ the younger people now, too, and keep them in our community."[22]

While industrial states like Indiana and Michigan continue to lose manufacturing jobs as U.S. automakers struggle to survive, other towns, particularly in the South, are benefiting from Asian and European auto companies looking for skilled workers. For example, Osceola, Arkansas, a town of 9,000 on the west bank of the Mississippi, induced Denso Corp., an affiliate of Toyota Motor Corp., to locate a new plant in town for producing air-conditioning and heating systems. Denso was particularly persuaded by Osceola's efforts to improve local education by creating a charter school. "We got the strong feeling that in Osceola education was being integrated with industry," says Denso plant manager Jerry McGuire.[23]

Your Call

If you ran a company that was owned by your family (not publicly owned) and that had been in the same town for three generations, employing local townspeople, would you feel a sense of responsibility to the town if you were faced with the opportunity to move to a cheaper location? What about if you ran a publicly owned company?

8. Financial Institutions   Want to launch a small start-up company? As Visa, MasterCard, and Discover continue to flood mailboxes with credit-card offers, some entrepreneurs have found it convenient to use multiple cards to fund new enterprises. Joe Liemandt of Trilogy Software charged up 22 cards to finance his startup.

Established companies also often need loans to tide them over when revenues are down or to finance expansion, but they rely for assistance on lenders such as commercial banks, investment banks, and insurance companies.

9. Government Regulators   The preceding groups are external stakeholders in your organization since they are clearly affected by its activities. But why would *government regulators*—**regulatory agencies that establish ground rules**

Government as stakeholder. Santa Fe, New Mexico, which depends largely on state government and tourism, is an expensive place to live. To help lower-paid workers, the city council voted to raise the minimum wage to $9.50 an hour, but some small business owners believe that's too high. In what ways does your local government affect business in your area?

Special interests. Farmworkers in San Francisco in 2005 urge people of goodwill to boycott Gallo Wines. Protestors and special-interest groups are among the external stakeholders managers must consider when making decisions.

under which organizations may operate—be considered stakeholders?

We are talking here about an alphabet soup of agencies, boards, and commissions that have the legal authority to prescribe or proscribe the conditions under which you may conduct business. To these may be added local and state regulators on the one hand and foreign governments and international agencies (such as the World Trade Organization, which oversees international trade and standardization efforts) on the other.

Such government regulators can be said to be stakeholders because not only do they affect the activities of your organization, they are in turn affected by it. The Federal Aviation Agency (FAA), for example, specifies how far planes must stay apart to prevent midair collisions. But when the airlines want to add more flights on certain routes, the FAA may have to add more flight controllers and radar equipment, since those are the agency's responsibility.

10. Special-Interest Groups   In late 2007, it was reported, "Gap has begun an effort to rebuild its reputation after a damaging child-labor scandal in India, announcing a package of measures . . . intended to tighten its commitment to eradicating the exploitation of children in the manufacture of its goods." [24] Any organization can become the target of special-interest groups, as the San Francisco–based apparel maker was by Save the Children and other organizations dedicated to outlawing child labor following the appearance of photos in a British newspaper showing children making clothes for Gap in an Indian sweatshop.

Special-interest groups **are groups whose members try to influence specific issues,** some of which may affect your organization. Examples are Mothers Against Drunk Driving, the National Organization for Women, and the National Rifle Association. Special-interest groups may try to exert political influence, as in contributing funds to lawmakers' election campaigns or in launching letter-writing efforts to officials. Or they may organize picketing and *boycotts*—holding back their patronage—of certain companies, as some African American groups did in recent years to protest reports of racism at Texaco and at Denny's restaurants. [25]

11. Mass Media   On March 24, 1989, when the tanker *Exxon Valdez* ran aground in Prince William Sound, it dumped 11 million gallons of North Slope crude oil into the water, blackening 1,500 miles of magnificent Gulf of Alaska coastline. This was not only one of the nation's worst environmental disasters, but for the Exxon Corporation it was also the start of a gigantic public-relations nightmare that never seemed to end. Even 19 years later, the news media were running prominent stories on the effects of the incident, once again bringing it to public attention. [26]

Exxon's troubles were not the fault of the press. But no manager can afford to ignore the power of the mass media—print, radio, TV, and the Internet—to rapidly and widely disseminate news both bad and good. Thus, most companies, universities, hospitals, and even government agencies have a public-relations person or department to communicate effectively with the press. In addition, top-level executives often receive special instruction on how to best deal with the media.

The General Environment

Beyond the task environment is the *general environment, or macroenvironment,* **which includes six forces: economic, technological, sociocultural, demographic, political-legal, and international.**

You may be able to control some forces in the task environment, but you can't control those in the general environment. Nevertheless, they can profoundly affect your organization's task environment without your knowing it, springing nasty surprises on you. Clearly, then, as a manager you need to keep your eye on the far horizon because these forces of the general environment can affect long-term plans and decisions.

I. Economic Forces *Economic forces* **consist of the general economic conditions and trends—unemployment, inflation, interest rates, economic growth—that may affect an organization's performance.** These are forces in your nation and region and even the world over which you and your organization probably have no control.

Are banks' interest rates going up in the United States? Then it will cost you more to borrow money to open new stores or build new plants. Is your region's unemployment rate rising? Then maybe you'll have more job applicants to hire from, yet you'll also have fewer customers with money to spend. Are natural resources getting scarce in an important area of supply? Then your company will need to pay more for them or switch to alternative sources.

One indicator that managers often pay attention to is productivity growth. Rising productivity leads to rising profits, lower inflation, and higher stock prices. In recent times, companies have been using information technology to cut costs, resulting in productivity growing at an annual rate of 3% in 2004. (However, it slumped to 1.8% in 2007.)[27]

2. Technological Forces *Technological forces* **are new developments in methods for transforming resources into goods or services.** For example, think what the U.S. would have been like if the elevator, air-conditioning, the combustion engine, and the airplane had not been invented. No doubt changes in computer and communications technology—especially the influence of the Internet—will continue to be powerful technological forces during your managerial career. But other technological currents may affect you as well.

For example, biotechnology may well turn health and medicine upside down in the coming decades. Researchers can already clone animals, and some reports say they are close to doing the same with humans.

3. Sociocultural Forces "I have one client who has tattoos of all kinds of stuff on her body," says Doug, owner of Doug's Tattoos in Oakland, California. "There's no theme to it. She has favorite cartoon names, her children's and grandchildren's names—just anything she likes at the time."[28]

Some day, of course, our descendants will view these customs as old-fogyish and quaint. That's how it is with sociocultural changes. *Sociocultural forces* **are influences and trends originating in a country's, a society's, or a culture's human relationships and values that may affect an organization.**

Entire industries have been rocked when the culture underwent a lifestyle change that affected their product or service. The interest in health and fitness, for instance, led to a decline in sales of cigarettes, whiskey, red meat, and eggs. And it led to a boost in sales of athletic shoes, spandex clothing, and Nautilus

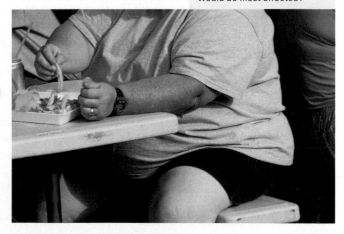

Sociocultural forces. The U.S. obesity rate is one of those sociocultural forces capable of altering entire industries. Which ones do you think would be most affected?

and other exercise machines. Low-carbohydrate, high-protein diets like the Atkins and the South Beach diets triggered a rise in chicken, pork, and beef sales, but then led to an oversupply and consequent dip in prices as consumers turned to a more balanced eating approach.[29] More recently, with more attention focused on the American epidemic of obesity, Mississippi restaurant owners were startled to learn of proposed state legislation that would have prohibited them from serving obese patrons.[30]

4. Demographic Forces *Demographics* derives from the ancient Greek word for "people"—*demos*—and deals with statistics relating to human populations. Age, gender, race, sexual orientation, occupation, income, family size, and the like are known as demographic characteristics when they are used to express measurements of certain groups. ***Demographic forces* are influences on an organization arising from changes in the characteristics of a population, such as age, gender, or ethnic origin.**

During the next 40 years, the United States is expected to undergo some great demographic changes. For instance, more babies are currently being born, the largest number of children born in 45 years—and dramatically exceeding birth rates in Europe. The birthrate is up for all racial and ethnic groups, but the increase for Hispanics is the largest.[31] By 2050, it's predicted, the U.S. population will soar to 438 million (from 303 million today), and the Hispanic population will triple, to 29% of the population, the increase being driven primarily by immigration.[32] Whites who are not Hispanic, now two-thirds of the population, will become a minority, their share dropping to 47%. The proportion of children and elderly who depend on others will rise to 72 per 100 from 59 per 100 in 2005. The foreign-born share of the workforce will increase to 23% from 15% in 2005.

5. Political-Legal Forces *Political-legal forces* **are changes in the way politics shape laws and laws shape the opportunities for and threats to an organization.** In the United States, whatever political view tends to be dominant at the moment may be reflected in how the government handles antitrust issues, in which one company tends to monopolize a particular industry. Should Microsoft, for instance, be allowed to dominate the market for personal-computer operating systems?

As for legal forces, some countries have more fully developed legal systems than others. And some countries have more lawyers per capita. (The United States has an estimated 25% of the world's lawyers, according to University of Wisconsin law professor Marc Galanter—not the 70% figure repeated for years by some conservative political figures.)[33] American companies may be more willing to use the legal system to advance their interests, as in suing competitors to gain competitive advantage. But they must also watch that others don't do the same to them.

6. International Forces *International forces* **are changes in the economic, political, legal, and technological global system that may affect an organization.** This category represents a huge grab bag of influences. How does the economic integration of the European Union create threats and opportunities for American companies? U.S. companies that do significant business in Europe are subject to regulation by the European Union. For instance, in a 3-year antitrust case, the EU ruled that Microsoft Corp. had abusively wielded its Windows and Office software monopoly, fined it the equivalent of $735 million, and ordered it to reduce practices that gave Microsoft an advantage in hooking up its products to Windows, limiting competition.[34] We consider global concerns in Chapter 4.

How well Americans can handle international forces depends a lot on their training. The American Council on Education says there is a "dangerous" shortage of experts in non-European cultures and languages. The council urges that schools teach a wider variety of languages and that instruction begin as early as kindergarten, since waiting until students are in college to begin instruction in more obscure languages hinders their ability to become fluent speakers.[35] ●

Test Your Knowledge:
Macroenvironmental Forces

3.3 THE ETHICAL RESPONSIBILITIES REQUIRED OF YOU AS A MANAGER

> What does the successful manager need to know about ethics and values?
>
> major question?

THE BIG PICTURE

Managers need to be aware of what constitutes ethics, values, the four approaches to ethical dilemmas, and how organizations can promote ethics.

"It's a tough issue, choosing between being a law-abiding person and losing your job," says lawyer Gloria Allred, who represented a woman fired for complaining about running her boss's office football pool.[36] Imagine having to choose between *economic performance* and *social performance*, which in business is what most ethical conflicts are about.[37] This is known as an ***ethical dilemma*, a situation in which you have to decide whether to pursue a course of action that may benefit you or your organization but that is unethical or even illegal.**

Defining Ethics & Values

Seventy-three percent of American employees working full time say they have observed ethical misconduct at work, and 36% have been "distracted" by it.[38] Most of us assume we know what "ethics" and "values" mean, but do we? Let's consider them.

Test Your Knowledge:
Ethics

Ethics *Ethics* **are the standards of right and wrong that influence behavior.** These standards may vary among countries and among cultures. ***Ethical behavior* is behavior that is accepted as "right" as opposed to "wrong" according to those standards.**

What are the differences among a tip, a gratuity, a gift, a donation, a commission, a consulting fee, a kickback, a bribe? Regardless of the amount of money involved, each one may be intended to reward the recipient for providing you with better service, either anticipated or performed. What should be the expectations of a medical society that accepts $700,000 from three pharmaceutical companies to be used for dinner lectures to brief doctors on the latest news about high blood pressure? What if the main point of these briefings is to expand the concept of

Higher self. If you worked for a drug company, would you think it's acceptable to give a medical society several thousand dollars to use on dinner lectures to inform doctors about high blood pressure and how your company's products can treat the condition? Would your perspective change if you were a patient with high blood pressure?

high blood pressure, increasing the pool of people taking blood-pressure medications?[39]

Values Ethical dilemmas often take place because of an organization's *value system,* **the pattern of values within an organization.** *Values* **are the relatively permanent and deeply held underlying beliefs and attitudes that help determine a person's behavior,** such as the belief that "Fairness means hiring according to ability, not family background." Values and value systems are the underpinnings for ethics and ethical behavior.

Organizations may have two important value systems that can conflict: (1) the value system stressing financial performance versus (2) the value system stressing cohesion and solidarity in employee relationships.[40]

Four Approaches to Deciding Ethical Dilemmas

How do alternative values guide people's decisions about ethical behavior? Here are four approaches, which may be taken as guidelines:

I. The Utilitarian Approach: For the Greatest Good
Ethical behavior in the *utilitarian approach* **is guided by what will result in the greatest good for the greatest number of people.** Managers often take the utilitarian approach, using financial performance—such as efficiency and profit—as the best definition of what constitutes "the greatest good for the greatest number."[41]

Thus, a utilitarian "cost-benefit" analysis might show that in the short run the firing of thousands of employees may improve a company's bottom line and provide immediate benefits for the stockholders. The drawback of this approach, however, is that it may result in damage to workforce morale and the loss of employees with experience and skills—actions not so readily measurable in dollars.

2. The Individual Approach: For Your Greatest Self-Interest Long Term, Which Will Help Others
Ethical behavior in the *individual approach* **is guided by what will result in the individual's best *long-term* interests, which ultimately are in everyone's self-interest.** The assumption here is that you will act ethically in the short run to avoid others harming you in the long run.

The flaw here, however, is that one person's short-term self-gain may *not,* in fact, be good for everyone in the long term. After all, the manager of an agribusiness that puts chemical fertilizers on the crops every year will always benefit, but the fishing industries downstream could ultimately suffer if chemical runoff reduces the number of fish. Indeed, this is one reason why Puget Sound Chinook, or king salmon, are now threatened with extinction in the Pacific Northwest.[42]

3. The Moral-Rights Approach: Respecting Fundamental Rights Shared by Everyone
Ethical behavior in the *moral-rights approach* **is guided by respect for the fundamental rights of human beings,** such as those expressed in the U.S. Constitution's Bill of Rights. We would all tend to agree that denying people the right to life, liberty, privacy, health and safety, and due process is unethical. Thus, most of us would have no difficulty condemning the situation of immigrants illegally brought into the United States and then effectively enslaved—as when made to work 7 days a week as maids.

The difficulty, however, is when rights are in conflict, such as employer and employee rights. Should employees on the job have a guarantee of privacy? Actually, it is legal for employers to listen to business phone calls and monitor all non-spoken personal communications.[43]

4. The Justice Approach: Respecting Impartial Standards of Fairness

Ethical behavior in the *justice approach* **is guided by respect for impartial standards of fairness and equity.** One consideration here is whether an organization's policies—such as those governing promotions or sexual harassment cases—are administered impartially and fairly regardless of gender, age, sexual orientation, and the like.

Fairness can often be a hot issue. For instance, many employees are loudly resentful when a corporation's CEO is paid a salary and bonuses worth hundreds of times more than what they receive—even when the company performs poorly—and when fired is then given a "golden parachute," or extravagant package of separation pay and benefits.

Enron, SarbOx, & Ethical Training

Their names have been repeatedly carved in headlines since 2001. Here's Dennis Kozlowski, former CEO of manufacturing conglomerate Tyco International, now serving time for grand larceny, conspiracy, securities fraud, and falsifying business records associated with looting $600 million to finance a lavish lifestyle. There's Bernard Ebbers, former head of WorldCom, who received 25 years in jail for engineering the largest corporate fraud in U.S. history. Eighty-two-year-old John Rigas, former chair and CEO of Adelphia, was found guilty of 18 counts of conspiracy and bank fraud and is serving 15 years in prison. Jeffrey Skilling, former CEO for Enron, the Houston-based energy giant, found guilty of many similar kinds of crimes, is serving a sentence of 24 years. Bringing up the rear is Refco ex–finance chief Robert Trosten, who in 2008 pleaded guilty to fraud and conspiracy charges for helping hide hundreds of millions of debt, for which he could get as much as 85 years in prison.[44]

Was this frenzy of white-collar crime an anomaly over which we can now breathe a sigh of relief? Unfortunately, probably not. Still, there is now a great deal more public and corporate awareness.

Public Outrage & the Sarbanes–Oxley Reform Act   The various forms of deceit practiced by top-level managers generated a great deal of public outrage, not only among the employees and shareholders who suffered great harm (most Enron workers and investors, for example, lost everything) but also among federal regulators and politicians. As a result, Congress passed the *Sarbanes–Oxley Act of 2002,* **often shortened to** *SarbOx* **or** *SOX*, **which establishes requirements for proper financial record keeping for public companies and penalties for noncompliance.**

Administered by the Securities and Exchange Commission, SarbOx requires a company's chief executive officer and chief financial officer to personally certify the organization's financial reports, prohibits them from taking personal loans or lines of credit, and makes them reimburse the organization for bonuses and stock options when required by restatement of corporate profits. It also requires the company to have established procedures and guidelines for audit committees. Penalties can be as much as 25 years in prison.[45]

How Do People Learn Ethics? Kohlberg's Theories   American business history is permeated with occasional corporate scandals, from railroad tycoons trying to corner the gold market (the 1872 Credit Mobilier scandal) to style mavens found to be lying to the government (Martha Stewart in 2004). Legislation such as SarbOx can't head off all such behavior. No wonder that now many colleges and universities have required more education in ethics.

"Schools bear some responsibility for the behavior of executives," says Fred J. Evans, dean of the College of Business and Economics at California State University at Northridge. "If you're making systematic errors in the [business] world, you have to go back to the schools and ask, 'What are you teaching?'"[46] There may be a ways to go, however: A 2006 survey of 50,000 undergraduates found that 26% of business majors admitted to serious cheating on exams, and 54% admitted to cheating on written assignments.[47]

Of course, most students' levels of moral development are established by personalities and upbringing long before they get to college, with some being more advanced than others. One psychologist, **Laurence Kohlberg,** has proposed three levels of personal moral development—preconventional, conventional, and postconventional.[48]

- **Level 1, preconventional—follows rules.** People who have achieved this level tend to follow rules and to obey authority to avoid unpleasant consequences. Managers of the Level 1 sort tend to be autocratic or coercive, expecting employees to be obedient for obedience's sake.

- **Level 2, conventional—follows expectations of others.** People whose moral development has reached this level are conformist but not slavish, generally adhering to the expectations of others in their lives. Level 2 managers lead by encouragement and cooperation and are more group and team oriented. Most managers are at this level.

- **Level 3, postconventional—guided by internal values.** The farthest along in moral development, Level 3 managers are independent souls who follow their own values and standards, focusing on the needs of their employees and trying to lead by empowering those working for them. Only about a fifth of American managers reach this level.

Self-Assessment:
Assessing Your Ethical
Decision-Making Skills

What level of development do you think you've reached?

How Organizations Can Promote Ethics

There are three ways an organization may foster high ethical standards:

Manager's Hot Seat:
Ethics: Let's Make a
Fourth-Quarter Deal

1. Support by Top Managers of a Strong Ethical Climate   The "tone at the top is critical—and it's always monkey see, monkey do," says Martha Clark Goss, VP and chief financial officer for consulting firm Booze Allen & Hamilton. At her firm, she says, "we have the sunshine rule, which asks employees to consider how they would feel if they had to stand in front of partners [that is, top managers] and explain a particular business expense. It's a good rule, but only a guideline. People almost always follow the example of the senior partners."[49]

If top executives "wink at the problem" or "look the other way" in ethical matters, so will employees farther down the organization.

2. Ethics Codes & Training Programs   A *code of ethics* consists of a formal written set of ethical standards guiding an organization's actions. Most codes offer guidance on how to treat customers, suppliers, competitors, and other stakeholders. The purpose is to clearly state top management's expectations for all employees. As you might expect, most codes prohibit bribes, kickbacks, misappropriation of corporate assets, conflicts of interest, and "cooking the books"—making false accounting statements and other records. Other areas frequently covered in ethics codes are political contributions, workforce diversity, and confidentiality of corporate information.[50]

In addition, according to a 2005 Society for Human Resource Management Weekly Survey, 32% of human resources professionals indicated that their organizations offered ethics training.[51] The approaches vary, but one way is to use a case approach to present employees with ethical dilemmas. By clarifying expectations, this kind of training may reduce unethical behavior.[52]

3. Rewarding Ethical Behavior: Protecting Whistleblowers

It's not enough to simply punish bad behavior; managers must also reward good ethical behavior, as in encouraging (or at least not discouraging) whistle-blowers.

A *whistleblower* **is an employee who reports organizational misconduct to the public,** such as health and safety matters, waste, corruption, or overcharging of customers. For instance, the law that created the Occupational Safety and Health Administration allows workers to report unsafe conditions, such as "exposure to toxic chemicals; the use of dangerous machines, which can crush fingers; the use of contaminated needles, which expose workers to the AIDS virus; and the strain of repetitive hand motion, whether at a computer keyboard or in a meat-packing plant."[53]

The law prohibits employers from firing employees who report workplace hazards, although one study found that about two-thirds of those who complained lost their jobs anyway.[54] Another study found that in cases involving 230 large public company frauds in which employee whistleblowers were identified, 82% of the informants "alleged they were fired, quit under duress, or had significantly altered responsibilities as a result of bringing the fraud to light."[55] In some cases, whistleblowers may receive a reward; the IRS, for instance, is authorized to pay tipsters rewards as high as 30% in cases involving large amounts of money.[56]

Public employees don't get the same break as everyone else. In 2006, the U.S. Supreme Court restricted the free-speech rights of the nation's 21 million government workers, ruling that the First Amendment to the Constitution does not protect them from being punished for reporting official misconduct.[57] ●

[handwritten note: whistleblower (tattle-tale) may or may not be rewarded. likelyhood is that he will be punished by employer]

Manager's Hot Seat:
Whistleblowing: Code Red or Red Ink?

Whistleblower. Sherron Watkins, a former vice president of Enron, is sworn in alongside Jeffrey Skilling, former CEO, before testifying at a U.S. Congressional hearing. Watkins testified about her attempts to warn top managers of her fears that the company would "implode" because of irregular accounting practices. Close to half of all whistleblowers are fired; given this fact, what would it take for you to become a whistleblower?

3.4 THE SOCIAL RESPONSIBILITIES REQUIRED OF YOU AS A MANAGER

THE BIG PICTURE

Managers need to be aware of the viewpoints supporting and opposing social responsibility and whether being and doing good pays off financially for the organization.

If ethical responsibility is about being a good individual citizen, social responsibility is about being a good organizational citizen. More formally, *social responsibility* **is a manager's duty to take actions that will benefit the interests of society as well as of the organization.** When generalized beyond the individual to the organization, social responsibility is called *corporate social responsibility (CSR),* **the notion that corporations are expected to go above and beyond following the law and making a profit.**

According to University of Georgia business scholar **Archie B. Carroll,** CSR rests at the top of a pyramid of a corporation's obligations, right up there with economic, legal, and ethical obligations. That is, while some people might hold that a company's first duty is to make a profit, Carroll suggests the responsibilities of organizations in the global economy should take the following priorities: (1) be a good global corporate citizen, (2) be ethical, (3) obey the law, and (4) be profitable—in that order.[58]

Example

Corporate Social Responsibility: Unilever's Strategy for the 21st Century

Unilever, a $52 billion Dutch-British rival to Procter & Gamble, now focuses not just on selling more soap but also on making the world a better place by helping to fight poverty, water scarcity, and the effects of climate change. The company operates a free community laundry in a São Paulo slum, finances eco-friendly "drip" irrigation, recycles waste at a toothpaste factory, helps women in remote Indian villages start micro-enterprises, and is reducing carbon dioxide emissions at its factories.

The reasons are not just for PR. "Some 40% of the company's sales and most of its growth now take place in developing nations," says *BusinessWeek.* Moreover, "As environmental regulations grow tighter around the world, Unilever must invest in green technologies or its leadership in packaged foods, soaps, and other goods could be imperiled."[59]

Your Call

Clearly social responsibility may have benefits beyond the acts of selflessness themselves. Can you think of any highly profitable and legal businesses that *do not* practice any kind of social responsibility?

Is Social Responsibility Worthwhile? Opposing & Supporting Viewpoints

In the old days of cutthroat capitalism, social responsibility was hardly thought of. A company's most important goal was to make money pretty much any way it could, and the consequences be damned. Today for-profit enterprises generally make a point of "putting something back" into society as well as taking something out.

Not everyone, however, agrees with these new priorities. Let's consider the two viewpoints.

Against Social Responsibility "Few trends could so thoroughly undermine the very foundations of our free society," argues free-market economist Milton Friedman, "as the acceptance by corporate officials of social responsibility other than to make as much money for their stockholders as possible."[60]

Friedman represents the view that, as he says, "The social responsibility of business is to make profits." That is, unless a company focuses on maximizing profits, it will become distracted and fail to provide goods and services, benefit the stockholders, create jobs, and expand economic growth—the real social justification for the firm's existence.

This view would presumably support the efforts of companies to set up headquarters in name only in offshore Caribbean tax havens (while keeping their actual headquarters in the U.S.) in order to minimize their tax burden.

For Social Responsibility "A large corporation these days not only may engage in social responsibility," says famed economist Paul Samuelson, "it had damned well better to try to do so."[61] That is, a company must be concerned for society's welfare as well as for corporate profits.

Beyond the fact of ethical obligation, the rationale for this view is that since businesses create problems (environmental pollution, for example), they should help solve them. Moreover, they often have the resources to solve problems in ways that the nonprofit sector does not. Finally, being socially responsible gives businesses a favorable public image that can help head off government regulation.

The Idea of Blended Value: Measuring Both Economic & Social Benefits

Jeb Emerson, a former social worker who became a lecturer at the Stanford Graduate School of Business, has gained some attention by asking, What if we did not judge business organizations on profits alone? According to Emerson, "We tend to categorize value as economic or social. You either work for a nonprofit that creates social value or you work for a for-profit that creates economic value."[62] In actuality, however, for-profits create social value: They create jobs (which lead to stable family units), they create products that improve people's lives, and they pay taxes that help build local communities. Conversely, nonprofits contribute economic value, because they also create jobs and they consume goods and services. (Nonprofits represent 7% of the gross domestic product.)

The notion of *blended value,* **then, is that all investments are understood to operate simultaneously in both economic and social realms.** "There is no 'trade off' between the two, but rather a concurrent pursuit of value—both social and financial," Emerson says. "The two operate together, in concert, at all times. They cannot be separated and considered as two distinct propositions, but are one and the same."[63]

Sorry Sears. Sometimes even major companies are obstructionist. In the most serious ethical breach in its history, Sears, Roebuck and Co. was discovered in 1999 to have secretly violated federal law for a decade. It even, suggested U.S. Justice Department lawyers, may have put its illegal practice in its procedures manual. Sears allegedly used unenforceable agreements to collect debts that legally no longer existed with some bankrupt credit-card holders. "The company's 111 years old," said the relatively new CEO at the time, Arthur Martinez, "and I'm the guy in the chair when we plead guilty to a criminal offense. Wonderful."

Economic and social value (which includes environmental value) may well be all part of a piece, as Emerson proposes. The problem, of course, is that financial performance can be measured by numbers ("econometrics"), whereas measuring social performance is more difficult. However, just as society has been grappling with measuring environmental impacts for only the last 5–10 years, so it may take another 5–50 years to learn how to adequately track and report social value, Emerson believes. "There is increasing pressure on companies to understand, quantify, and measure their social impact," he says. "It's inevitable. Successful companies will be savvy about how understanding the full value proposition can create wider opportunity."

Social conscience. Bonnie Nixon-Gardner was only a middle-level manager at Hewlett-Packard, but in 2005 she was successful in spurring the company to enforce anti-sweatshop policies in low-wage countries to which they outsource products. Coercing a Chinese supplier to foot the bill for earplugs so that workers could be protected from excessive machine noise took six trips and much personal effort—would you be willing to do the same?

Two Types of Social Responsibility: Sustainability & Philanthropy

In 2006, some major stories hit the news media that probably raised the consciousness of a number of Americans about two significant issues linked to business and social responsibility—sustainability and philanthropy.

Sustainability: The Business of Green Several companies—General Electric, Wal-Mart, Toyota, and others—launched "green marketing" campaigns promoting environmentally friendly causes, products, or stores.[64] In addition, an apparently changing climate, bringing increased damage from hurricanes, floods, and fires throughout the United States and the world, also brought the issue of "being green" to increased prominence. Former U.S. Vice President Al Gore's documentary film *An Inconvenient Truth,* along with his book by the same name, further popularized the concepts of global warming and the idea of sustainability as a business model.[65]

Our economic system has brought prosperity, but it has also led to unsustainable business practices because it has assumed that natural resources are limitless, which they are not. ***Sustainability* is defined as economic development that meets the needs of the present without compromising the ability of future generations to meet their own needs.**[66] G.E., which once polluted the Hudson River with PCBs from the transformers it manufactured, has been especially proactively green, promising to invest $1.5 billion a year in research in cleaner technologies. In part this is simply good business, because it enhances the efficiency of the products it sells.[67] But companies that have adopted an active pro-green stance have been able to avoid unfavorable publicity. ExxonMobil, for example, came under fire from shareholders and environmentalists in 2005 because it challenged the theory of global warming and wanted to drill in the Arctic National Wildlife Refuge. By contrast, BP (formerly British Petroleum), which has promoted a carbon-balanced world, did not.[68]

Practical Action

Going Green: How Businesses & Individuals Can Fight Global Warming

"When Wal-Mart became the largest retailer in the world," says Adam Werbach, "they didn't understand the responsibility that came with it, or the attention they'd get by being that symbol. But now they've reinvented what is possible. Whether you love or hate Wal-Mart, it has done more for sustainability than any environmental organization I've ever worked for."[69]

What makes this remark especially interesting is that not only is Werbach a former head of the Sierra Club, the environmental organization, whose members tend to revile Wal-Mart, but that Werbach's San Francisco environmental consulting firm, Act Now Productions, took on Wal-Mart as a client. Why? Because, Werbach says, the challenge gave him the opportunity to implement change on a scale few environmentalists will ever experience. Because of Wal-Mart's size, even the most incremental improvements it makes can result in enormous benefits. "They've made vast engineering changes inside the company," Wehrbach reports, "and doing things like reducing packaging sizes, and enclosing the cheese displays to save electricity. When you're the largest buyer of electricity in the country, that's a big deal."

Global warming is "unequivocal" and will bring "irreversible changes" without immediate action, the United Nations Intergovernmental Panel on Climate Change (IPCC) reported in 2007.[70] The IPCC argues that we can save the planet by investing heavily in alternative energy technology that already exists. A 2007 report by energy experts at McKinsey & Company, a consulting firm, says that as much as a 28% reduction in greenhouse gases can be accomplished from steps that would more than pay for themselves in lower energy bills.[71] Small businesses, for instance, report savings of 20%–30% by making energy-saving moves.[72]

There are a number of things that individuals and businesses can do to attempt to fight global warming, although the problem is complicated and intractable and needs a great deal more research.[73]

Increase Recycling
Increasing the recycle rate in the United States from 30% to 60% would save the equivalent of 315 million barrels of oil each year. (See **www.earth911.org** for tips on recycling.) Old computers and other electronics can be recycled or donated. (See **www.eiae.org**.)[74]

Install Energy-Saving Lightbulbs
Compact fluorescent bulbs (CFLs) cost more than regular incandescent bulbs, but they last up to 10 times longer, produce 90% less heat, and also produce fewer emissions. They are also cheaper over the long term: Replacing 30 incandescent bulbs with CFLs can save more than $1,000 over the life of the bulbs.[75]

Buy Energy Star Products
Energy Star appliances meet strict energy-efficiency guidelines. (See **www.energystar.gov.**) If every home replaced its TVs, DVD players, VCRs, and telephones with these models, it would be the equivalent of taking 3 million cars off the road.[76]

Convert to Green Energy
More than half of all retail power customers in the United States can now run their homes on renewable energy—electricity produced by wind, solar, and geothermal power; hydropower; and various plant materials—simply by asking their local utility. The cost is about $5 a month more for a typical residential user.[77] Wind energy, incidentally, now generates more than 1% of U.S. electricity.[78] (See **www.eere.energy.gov/greenpower.**)

Store Documents Digitally
Encouraging employees and customers to save documents digitally and not print out millions of paper copies can reduce waste and reduce operating budgets.[79] (See **www.greenbiz.com** and **www.greenerworldmedia.com.**)

Philanthropy: "Not Dying Rich" "He who dies rich dies thus disgraced," 19th-century steel magnate Andrew Carnegie is supposed to have said, after he turned his interests from making money to *philanthropy,* **making charitable donations to benefit humankind.** Carnegie became well known as a supporter of free libraries.

More recently, Bill Gates of Microsoft, the richest person in the world, made headlines when he announced that in 2008 he would step down from day-to-day oversight of the company he co-founded in order to focus on his $29 billion philanthropy, the Bill and Melinda Gates Foundation, which has pledged to spend billions on health, education, and overcoming poverty.[80] This news was closely followed by the announcement of the second-richest man in the world, investor Warren Buffet, chairman of Berkshire Hathaway, that he would channel $31 billion to the Gates Foundation to help in finding cures for the globe's most fatal diseases.[81]

Companies practice philanthropy, too. For example, Google made a pledge to investors when it went public to reserve 1% of its profit and equity to "make the world a better place." Its philanthropic organization benefits groups ranging from those fighting disease to those developing a commercial plug-in, electricity-powered car.[82] But even ordinary individuals can become philanthropists of a sort. Mona Purdy, an Illinois hairdresser, noticed while vacationing in Guatemala that many children coated their feet with tar in order to be able to run in a local race. So she went home and established the nonprofit Share Your Shoes, which collects shoes and sends them around the world. "I always thought I was too busy to help others," she says. "Then I started this and found myself wondering where I'd been all my life."[83]

How Does Being Good Pay Off?

From a hard-headed manager's point of view, does ethical behavior and high social responsibility pay off financially? Here's what some of the research shows.[84]

Effect on Customers According to one survey, 88% of the respondents said they were more apt to buy from companies that are socially responsible than from companies that are not.[85] Another survey of 2,037 adults found that 72% would prefer to purchase products and services from a company with ethical business practices and higher prices compared with 18% who would prefer to purchase from a company with questionable business practices and lower prices.[86]

Effect on Job Applicants & Employee Retention Ethics can affect the quality of people who apply to work in an organization. One online survey of 1,020 people indicated that 83% rated a company's record of business ethics as "very important" when deciding whether to accept a job offer; only 2% rated it as "unimportant."[87] A National Business Ethics Survey found that 79% of employees said their firms' concern for ethics was a key reason they remained.[88]

Effect on Sales Growth The announcement of a company's conviction for illegal activity has been shown to diminish sales growth for several years.[89] One survey found that 80% of people said they decide to buy a firm's goods or services partly on their perception of its ethics.[90]

Effect on Company Efficiency One survey found that 71% of employees who saw honesty applied rarely or never in their organization had seen misconduct in the past year, compared with 52% who saw honesty applied only occasionally and 25% who saw it frequently.[91]

Effect on Company Revenue Unethical behavior in the form of employee fraud costs U.S. organizations around $652 billion a year, according to the Association of Certified Fraud Examiners.[92] Employee fraud, which is twice as common as consumer fraud (such as credit card fraud and identity theft), costs employers about 20% of every dollar earned.[93]

Effect on Stock Price One survey found that 74% of people polled said their perception of a firm's honesty directly affected their decision about whether to buy its stock.[94] Earlier research found that investments in unethical firms earn abnormally negative returns for long periods of time.[95]

Effect on Profits Studies suggest that profitability is enhanced by a reputation for honesty and corporate citizenship.[96]

Ethical behavior and social responsibility are more than just admirable ways of operating. They give an organization a clear competitive advantage. ●

3.5 THE NEW DIVERSIFIED WORKFORCE

What trends in workplace diversity should managers be aware of?

major question?

THE BIG PICTURE

One of today's most important management challenges is working with stakeholders of all sorts who vary widely in diversity—in age, gender, race, religion, ethnicity, sexual orientation, capabilities, and socioeconomic background. Managers should also be aware of the differences between internal and external dimensions of diversity and barriers to diversity.

We are a changing people. Three random examples:

- **Race:** The percentage of non-Hispanic whites in the United States has dropped from 76% in 1950 to 67% in 2005.[97]

- **Religion:** A 2008 survey finds that 44% of adult Americans say their religious or secular affiliation or belief changed from that of their childhood.[98]

- **Pregnancy/work patterns:** Another 2008 study finds that more American women (67%) are working longer into pregnancy and returning to work faster than they did four decades ago (44%).[99]

As the country becomes more nonwhite, more secular, more single, more working parent, and so on, it also becomes diverse. In the view of Scott E. Page, professor of complex systems, political science, and economics at the University of Michigan, diversity and variety in staffing produces organizational strength.[100] "Diverse groups of people bring to organizations more and different ways of seeing a problem," he told an interviewer, "and, thus, faster/better ways of solving it. . . . There's certainly a lot of evidence that people's identity groups—ethnic, racial, sexual, age—matter when it comes to diversity in thinking."[101]

Diversity may have its benefits, but it can also be an important management challenge. Let's consider this.

How to Think about Diversity: Which Differences Are Important?

Diversity **represents all the ways people are unlike and alike—the differences and similarities in age, gender, race, religion, ethnicity, sexual orientation, capabilities, and socioeconomic background.** Note here that diversity is not synonymous with differences. Rather, it encompasses both differences and similarities. This means that as a manager you need to manage both simultaneously.

To help distinguish the important ways in which people differ, diversity experts Lee Gardenswartz and Anita Rowe have identified a "diversity wheel" consisting of four layers of diversity: (1) personality, (2) internal dimensions, (3) external dimensions, and (4) organizational dimensions. *(See Figure 3.2, next page.)*

Let's consider these four layers:

Personality At the center of the diversity wheel is personality. It is at the center because *personality* **is defined as the stable physical and mental characteristics responsible for a person's identity.** We cover the dimension of personality in Chapter 11.

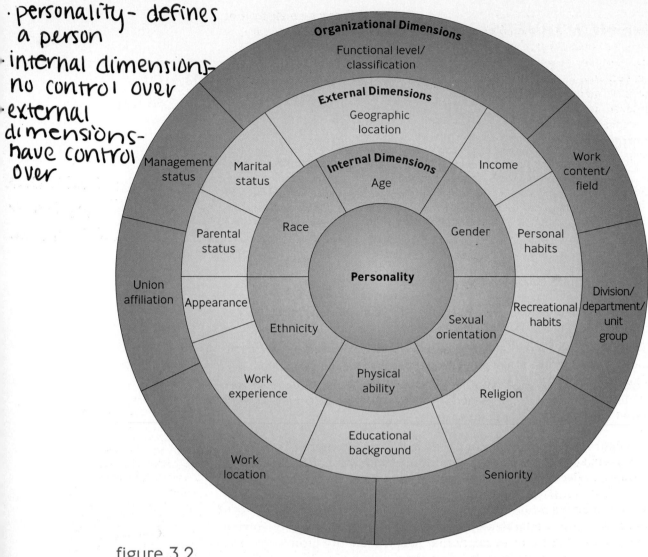

· personality - defines a person
· internal dimensions - no control over
· external dimensions - have control over

figure 3.2

THE DIVERSITY WHEEL

Four layers of diversity

Source: From L. Gardenswartz and A. Rowe, *Diverse Teams at Work: Capitalizing on the Power of Diversity,* 1994, p. 33. Reprinted with permission of The McGraw-Hill Companies.

Internal Dimensions ***Internal dimensions of diversity*** **are those human differences that exert a powerful, sustained effect throughout every stage of our lives:** gender, age, ethnicity, race, sexual orientation, physical abilities.[102] These are referred to as the *primary* dimensions of diversity because they are not within our control for the most part. Yet they strongly influence our attitudes and expectations and assumptions about other people, which in turn influence our own behavior.

What characterizes internal dimensions of diversity is that they are visible and salient in people. And precisely because these characteristics are so visible, they may be associated with certain stereotypes—for example, that black people work in menial jobs. For instance, an African American female middle manager reports that, while on vacation and sitting by the pool at a resort, she was approached by a 50ish white male who "demanded that I get him extra towels. I said, 'Excuse me?' He then said, 'Oh, you don't work here,' with no shred of embarrassment or apology in his voice."[103]

External Dimensions *External dimensions of diversity* include an element of choice; they consist of the personal characteristics that people acquire, discard, or modify throughout their lives: educational background, marital status, parental status, religion, income, geographic location, work experience, recreational habits, appearance, personal habits. They are referred to as the *secondary* dimensions of diversity because we have a greater ability to influence or control them than we do internal dimensions.

These external dimensions also exert a significant influence on our perceptions, behavior, and attitudes. If you are not a believer in the Muslim religion, for example, you may not perceive the importance of some of its practices—as with some managers at Atlanta-based Argenbright Security Inc., who sent seven Muslim female employees home for wearing Islamic head scarves at their security jobs at Dulles International Airport. Because wearing head scarves in no way affected their job performance, the company had to reimburse the women for back pay and other relief in a settlement negotiated with the Equal Employment Opportunity Commission.[104]

[handwritten note: example: cannot unempoly individuals for being muslim + covering their heads]

Organizational Dimensions Organizational dimensions include management status, union affiliation, work location, seniority, work content, and division or department.

Trends in Workforce Diversity

How is the U.S. workforce apt to become more diverse in the 21st century? Let's examine five categories on the internal dimension—*age, gender, race/ethnicity, sexual orientation, and physical/mental abilities*—and one category on the external dimension, *educational level*.

Age: More Older People in the Workforce
The most significant demographic event, management philosopher Peter Drucker suggested, "is that in the developed countries the number and proportion of younger people is rapidly shrinking. . . . Those shrinking numbers of younger people will have to both drive their economies and help support much larger numbers of older people."[105] In Europe and Japan, births are not keeping pace with deaths. Italy, for example, could drop from 60 million to 20 million by the end of the 21st century. Even China is faced with a nationwide aging gap, which means the country may face a shortage of cheap labor.[106]

The United States, suggested Drucker, is the only developed economy to have enough young people, and that is only because immigrants to the United States still have large families. Even so, the median age of the American worker is predicted to reach 41.4 by 2012, up from 34.3 in 1980.[107]

Diversity enriches. A diverse population in a company can provide ideas, experience, and points of view that strengthen the business culture. What has been your experience, if any, with a diverse workplace?

Gender: More Women Working
Since the 1960s, women have been flooding into the workplace in great numbers, with about 75% of women ages 25–54 in the workforce, up from about 40% in the late 1950s.[108] (For men in the same age range, participation is about 90%.) Although women's participation in the labor force has declined a bit (in part because of delayed motherhood), today females hold half of all management and professional jobs. In addition, more and more businesses are owned by women—about 30% of all U.S. nonfarm companies.[109]

Traditionally, however, women have earned roughly the same pay as men only in jobs paying $25,000–$30,000 a year. The farther up the pay scale and the higher

African American success.
Police chief Annetta Nunn, the first woman African American police chief of Birmingham, Alabama, at a press conference. Nunn broke through a glass ceiling of a different sort, taking over the police operations in 2003 for a city known for its racial discrimination only a few decades earlier.

the education level, the wider the earnings gap. Thus, for every dollar a man earns, a woman cashier earns 93 cents, an administrative assistant 93 cents, and a registered nurse 88 cents. But for a woman physician or surgeon, it is 59 cents, a woman lawyer or judge 69 cents, a woman college professor 75 cents, and a woman psychologist 83   The obstacles to women's progress are known as the *glass ceiling*—**the metaphor for an invisible barrier preventing women and minorities from being promoted to top executive jobs.** For instance, according to the Association of Executive Search Consultants, 56% of 357 global senior executives report their companies have one or no women among their top executives.[111] At Fortune 500 companies in 2006, females accounted for only 15.6% of corporate-officer positions.[112]

What factors are holding women back? Three that are mentioned are negative stereotypes, lack of mentors, and limited experience in line or general management.[113] For women who have become vice president or higher in Fortune 1000 companies, four strategies were identified as critical to their success: consistently exceeding performance expectations, developing a style with which male managers are comfortable, seeking out difficult or challenging assignments, and having influential mentors.[114]

Interestingly, however, several studies have suggested that female managers outshine their male counterparts on almost every measure, from motivating others to fostering communication to producing high-quality work to goal-setting to mentoring employees.[115] Indeed, one study, by Catalyst, an advocacy group for women in business, found that companies with more women executives have better financial performance.[116] We discuss this further in a later chapter.

Race & Ethnicity: More People of Color in the Workforce
By 2020, people of color are expected to make up 37% of the U.S. adult workforce (Hispanic/Latino 17%, African Americans 13%, Asian Americans 6%, and Native Americans 0.8%).[117] Unfortunately, three trends show that American businesses need to do a lot better by this population.

First, people of color, too, have hit the glass ceiling. For example, African Americans held only 11.3% and Hispanics only 10.9% of all managerial and professional jobs in 2001.[118]

Second, minorities tend to earn less than whites. Median household income in 2006 was $32,000 for African Americans and $37,800 for Hispanics. It was $50,700 for whites. (Asians had the highest median income, at $64,200.)[119]

Third, their chances of success have been hurt by perceived discrimination, as shown, for example, by a study of 200 black managers and 139 Hispanic employees.[120] African Americans also have been found to receive lower performance ratings than whites have.[121] Another study found 44 black managers experienced slower rates of promotion compared with 890 white managers.[122] No wonder the turnover rate is 40% higher for black than for white executives.[123]

Recently employers have had to become aware of another wrinkle in ethnic and race relations—namely, whether the labor they are hiring is legal. Illegal immigrants make up 1 in 20 workers, according to a 2006 Pew Hispanic Center study.[124] They account for nearly 1 in 4 farm workers, 1 in 6 maids and housekeepers, 1 in 7 in construction, and 1 in 8 in food preparation. Companies such as Georgia carpet maker Mohawk Industries depend substantially on immigrants from Mexico and other Latin American countries, many of whom are illegal.[125]

Sexual Orientation: Gays & Lesbians Become More Visible
Gays and lesbians make up, by some estimates, up to 6% of the U.S. population. Between a quarter and two-thirds report being discriminated against at work (with negative

attitudes directed toward them held more by men than by women).[126] One 2003 study found that 41% of gay employees said they had been harassed, pressured to quit, or denied a promotion because of their sexual orientation.[127] Homosexual workers report higher levels of stress compared with heterosexual workers, and one source of this may be the fact that in many states homosexuality is still a legitimate legal basis for firing an employee. Finally, gay and bisexual male workers were found to earn 11%–27% less than equally qualified heterosexual counterparts.[128]

How important is the issue of sexual preference? Once again, if managers are concerned about hiring and keeping workplace talent, they shouldn't ignore the motivation and productivity of 6% of the workforce. Many employers are recognizing this: 430 of the top 500 U.S. companies now offer policies prohibiting discrimination based on sexual preference, and more than half offer domestic partner benefits for same-sex couples.[129]

People with Differing Physical & Mental Abilities   One out of six Americans has a physical or mental disability, according to the U.S. Department of Labor. Since 1992 we have had the ***Americans with Disabilities Act,* which prohibits discrimination against the disabled** and requires organizations to reasonably accommodate an individual's disabilities.

Even so, disabled people have difficulty finding work. Although two-thirds of people with disabilities want to work, roughly two-thirds are unemployed. (Among blind adults, for example, about 70% are out of work.)[130] Here, too, is a talent pool that managers will no doubt find themselves tapping into in the coming years.

Educational Levels: Mismatches between Education & Workforce Needs   Two important mismatches between education and workplace are these:

- **College graduates may be in jobs for which they are overqualified.** About 27% of people working have a college degree. But some are ***underemployed—* working at jobs that require less education than they have**—such as tending bar, managing video stores, or other jobs that someone with less education could do.

  During the period 2000–2004, one national survey of 2,350 college graduates found that 18% were underemployed.[131] It is estimated that for the workforce in general, whether college educated or not, about a quarter is underemployed, a condition associated with higher absenteeism, arrest rates, and unmarried parenthood and with lower motivation, job involvement, and psychological well-being.[132]

- **High-school dropouts and others may not have the literacy skills needed for many jobs.** A recent study by the U.S. Department of Education found that, in the nation's largest 100 public school districts, 31% of students were dropping out or failing to graduate.[133] In addition, literacy has dropped at every level of education between 1992 and 2003.[134] If, as has been alleged, more than two-thirds of the American workforce reads below ninth-grade level, that is a real problem for employers, because about 70% of the on-the-job reading materials are written at or above that level.[135]

Disability. Everyone recognizes the wheelchair as signifying that a person is disabled, but other disabilities are not easily identified—and may not invite understanding. Do you think that mental disabilities, for example, should be accommodated in employment? If you were subject to mood swings, would you think that would prevent you from doing your job effectively?

Self-Assessment: Appreciating & Valuing Diversity

Barriers to Diversity

Some barriers are erected by diverse people themselves. In the main, however, most barriers are put in their paths by organizations.[136] When we speak of "the organization's barriers," we are, of course, referring to the *people* in the organization—especially those who may have been there for a while—who are resistant to making it more diverse.

Resistance to change in general is an attitude that all managers come up against from time to time, and resistance to diversity is simply one variation. It may be expressed in the following six ways.

I. Stereotypes & Prejudices *Ethnocentrism* **is the belief that one's native country, culture, language, abilities, or behavior is superior to those of another culture.** (An example is embodied in the title of the Wesley Snipes/Woody Harrelson movie about urban basketball hustlers: *White Men Can't Jump.*) When differences are viewed as being weaknesses—which is what many stereotypes and prejudices ultimately come down to—this may be expressed as a concern that diversity hiring will lead to a sacrifice in competence and quality.

2. Fear of Reverse Discrimination Some employees are afraid that attempts to achieve greater diversity in their organization will result in reverse discrimination—that more black or Asian employees will be promoted to fire captain or police lieutenant, for example, over the heads of supposedly more qualified whites.

3. Resistance to Diversity Program Priorities Some companies such as 3M offer special classes teaching tolerance for diversity, seminars in how to get along.[137] Some employees may see diversity programs as distracting them from the organization's "real work." In addition, they may be resentful of diversity-promoting policies that are reinforced through special criteria in the organization's performance appraisals and reward systems.

4. Unsupportive Social Atmosphere Diverse employees may be excluded from office camaraderie and social events.

5. Lack of Support for Family Demands In most families (63%, according to the Bureau of Labor Statistics), both parents work; in 29.5% only the father works, and in 4.5% only the mother works. But more and more women are moving back and forth between being at-home mothers and in the workforce, as economic circumstances dictate.[138] Yet in a great many households, it is still women who primarily take care of children, as well as other domestic chores. When organizations aren't supportive in offering flexibility in hours and job responsibilities, these

Global diversity vision. Johnson & Johnson publishes this expression of the health products company's desire "to become the employer of choice" in its employment policies.

OUR GLOBAL DIVERSITY VISION

Johnson & Johnson's Credo sets forth our responsibilities to our employees. It recognizes their dignity and merit, their individuality, and the requirement for equal opportunity in employment, development and advancement for those qualified. From these principles, modified over the years, Johnson & Johnson has fostered and encouraged the development of a diverse workforce - a workforce for the future. ▼ While we can point with pride to a commitment to diversity deeply rooted in our value system, we recognize that our employees, customers and communities, then, were far different from those of today. However, our commitment to these core stakeholders as they have evolved and as Johnson & Johnson has evolved is as strong as ever. ▼ Today's customers and employees come from all over the world and represent different ages, cultures, genders, races and physical capabilities. Through their life experiences, they provide a diversity of thought and perspective that must be reflected in our corporate culture.

Our global diversity vision is to become
  THE EMPLOYER OF CHOICE
  IN A DYNAMIC GLOBAL ENVIRONMENT.

To achieve this vision, we must build a workforce that is increasingly skilled, diverse, motivated and committed to dynamic leadership. This workforce should reflect our diverse customer base and be knowledgeable of the markets we serve. ▼ Being the Employer of Choice in a Dynamic Global Environment means embracing the differences and similarities of all our employees and prospective employees. It also means the execution of innovative diversity and marketing initiatives to ensure our ability to recruit, develop, retain and promote exceptional talent from an array of backgrounds and geographies, while continuing our pursuit of excellence. ▼ Our goal is to ensure our ability to meet the demands of a changing world with a vision worthy of our values and our commitment to be the leader in health care across the globe. When we achieve our vision, diversity becomes one of our most important competitive advantages.

Johnson & Johnson

women may find it difficult to work evenings and weekends or to take overnight business trips.

6. Lack of Support for Career-Building Steps Organizations may not provide diverse employees with the types of work assignments that will help qualify them for positions in senior management. In addition, organizations may fail to provide the kind of informal training or mentoring that will help them learn the political savvy to do networking and other activities required to get ahead. ●

Manager's Hot Seat:
Diversity: Mediating Morality

Key Terms Used in This Chapter

Americans with Disabilities Act 95
blended value 87
code of ethics 84
competitors 75
corporate social responsibility (CSR) 86
customers 75
demographic forces 80
distributor 76
diversity 91
ethnocentrism 96
economic forces 79
ethical behavior 81
ethical dilemma 81
ethics 81
external dimensions of diversity 93

external stakeholders 75
general environment 79
glass ceiling 94
government regulators 77
individual approach 82
internal dimensions of diversity 92
internal stakeholders 74
international forces 80
justice approach 83
macroenvironment 79
moral-rights approach 82
owners 74
personality 91
philanthropy 89
political-legal forces 80

Sarbanes–Oxley Act of 2002 83
social responsibility 86
sociocultural forces 79
special-interest groups 78
stakeholders 73
strategic allies 76
supplier 75
sustainability 88
task environment 75
technological forces 79
underemployed 95
utilitarian approach 82
value system 82
values 82
whistleblower 85

Summary

 3.1 The Community of Stakeholders Inside the Organization
Managers operate in two organizational environments—internal and external—both made up of stakeholders, the people whose interests are affected by the organization's activities. The first, or internal, environment, includes employees, owners, and the board of directors.

 3.2 The Community of Stakeholders Outside the Organization
The external environment of stakeholders consists of the task environment and the general environment.

The task environment consists of 11 groups that present the manager with

daily tasks to deal with. (1) Customers pay to use an organization's goods and services. (2) Competitors compete for customers or resources. (3) Suppliers provide supplies—raw materials, services, equipment, labor, or energy—to other organizations. (4) Distributors help another organization sell its goods and services to customers. (5) Strategic allies join forces to achieve advantages neither organization can perform as well alone. (6) Employee organizations are labor unions and employee associations. (7) Local communities are residents, com-panies, governments, and nonprofit entities that depend on the organization's taxes, payroll, and charitable contributions.

(8) Financial institutions are commercial banks, investment banks, and insurance companies that deal with the organization. (9) Government regulators are regulatory agencies that establish the ground rules under which the organization operates. (10) Special-interest groups are groups whose members try to influence specific issues that may affect the organization. (11) The mass media are print, radio, TV, and Internet sources that affect the organization's public relations.

The general environment includes six forces. (1) Economic forces consist of general economic conditions and trends—unemployment, inflation, interest rates, economic growth—that may affect an organization's performance. (2) Technological forces are new developments in methods for transforming resources into goods and services. (3) Sociocultural forces are influences and trends originating in a country, society, or culture's human relationships and values that may affect an organization. (4) Demographic forces are influences on an organization arising from changes in the characteristics of a population, such as age, gender, and ethnic origin. (5) Political-legal forces are changes in the way politics shapes laws and laws shape the opportunities for and threats to an organization. (6) International forces are changes in the economic, political, legal, and technological global system that may affect an organization.

3.3 The Ethical Responsibilities Required of You as a Manager

Ethics are the standards of right and wrong that influence behavior. Ethical behavior is behavior that is accepted as "right" as opposed to "wrong" according to those standards.

Ethical dilemmas often take place because of an organization's value system. Values are the relatively permanent and deeply held underlying beliefs and attitudes that help determine a person's behavior.

There are four approaches to deciding ethical dilemmas. (1) Utilitarian—ethical behavior is guided by what will result in the greatest good for the greatest number of people. (2) Individual—ethical behavior is guided by what will result in the individual's best long-term interests, which ultimately is in everyone's self-interest. (3) Moral-rights—ethical behavior is guided by respect for the fundamental rights of human beings, such as those expressed in the U.S. Constitution's Bill of Rights. (4) Justice—ethical behavior is guided by respect for the impartial standards of fairness and equity.

Public outrage over white-collar crime (Enron, Tyco) led to the creation of the Sarbanes–Oxley Act of 2002 (SarbOx), which establishes requirements for proper financial record keeping for public companies and penalties for noncompliance.

Laurence Kohlberg proposed three levels of personal moral development: (1) preconventional level of moral development—people tend to follow rules and to obey authority; (2) conventional level—people are conformist, generally adhering to the expectations of others; and (3) postconventional level—people are guided by internal values.

There are three ways an organization may foster high ethical standards. (1) Top managers must support a strong ethical climate. (2) The organization may have a code of ethics, which consists of a formal written set of ethical standards. (3) An organization must reward ethical behavior, as in not discouraging whistleblowers, employees who report organizational misconduct to the public.

3.4 The Social Responsibilities Required of You as a Manager

Social responsibility is a manager's duty to take actions that will benefit the interests of society as well as of the organization.

The idea of social responsibility has opposing and supporting viewpoints. The opposing viewpoint is that the social responsibility of business is to make profits. The supporting viewpoint is that since business creates some problems (such as pollution) it should help solve them.

It has been proposed that business organizations not be judged on profits alone—that there is blended value, in which all investments are understood to operate simultaneously in both economic and social realms.

Two types of social responsibility are (1) sustainability, defined as economic development that meets the needs of the present without compromising the ability of future generations to meet their own needs, and (2) philanthropy, making charitable donations to benefit humankind.

Positive ethical behavior and social responsibility can pay off in the form of customer goodwill, better quality of job applicants and retained employees, enhanced sales growth, less employee misconduct and fraud, better stock price, and enhanced profits.

3.5 The New Diversified Workforce

Diversity represents all the ways people are alike and unlike—the differences and similarities in age, gender, race, religion, ethnicity, sexual orientation, capabilities, and socioeconomic background.

There are two dimensions of diversity: (1) Internal dimensions of diversity are those human differences that exert a powerful, sustained effect throughout every stage of our lives: gender, ethnicity, race, physical abilities, age, and sexual orientation. (2) External dimensions of diversity consist of the personal characteristics that people acquire, discard, or modify throughout their lives: personal habits, educational background, religion, income, marital status, and the like.

There are five categories in the internal dimension and one category in the external dimension in which the U.S. workforce is becoming more diverse: (1) age, (2) gender, (3) race and ethnicity, (4) sexual orientation, (5) disabilities, and (6) educational level.

There are six ways in which employees and managers may express resistance to diversity: (1) Some express stereotypes and prejudices based on ethnocentrism, the belief that one's native country, culture, language, abilities, or behavior is superior to those of another country. (2) Some employees are afraid of reverse discrimination. (3) Some employees see diversity programs as distracting them from the organization's supposed "real work." (4) Diverse employees may experience an unsupportive social atmosphere. (5) Organizations may not be supportive of flexible hours and other matters that can help employees cope with family demands. (6) Organizations may show lack of support for career-building steps for diverse employees.

Management in Action

Safety Inspectors Blow the Whistle on Mechanical Problems with Airplanes

After mechanics at Northwest Airlines went out on strike on August 20, 2005, Federal Aviation Administration safety inspector Mark Lund began to see troubling signs. One replacement mechanic didn't know how to test an engine. Another couldn't close a cabin door. Many did not seem properly trained. In Lund's view, their inexperience resulted in dangerous mistakes. One DC-10, for example, had a broken lavatory duct that allowed human waste to spill onto vital navigation equipment. The leak developed during a flight from Amsterdam to Minneapolis. Northwest planned to let the plane continue on to Honolulu with the perilous and putrid problem unfixed—until one of Lund's fellow safety inspectors in Minneapolis intervened.

Just two days after the strike began, Lund fired off a "safety recommendation for accident prevention" letter to his supervisors and to FAA headquarters in Washington. It was the loudest alarm he had the authority to ring. Claiming that "a situation exists that jeopardizes life," Lund proposed cutting back on Northwest's flight schedule until mechanics and inspectors could do their job "without error." But instead of taking harsh action against the airline, the agency punished him. On August 29, Lund's supervisors confiscated the badge that gave him access to Northwest's facilities and gave him a desk job. That happened to be the same day the airline sent a letter to the FAA complaining about Lund's allegedly disruptive and unprofessional conduct. The FAA says it treated Lund fairly.

As the airline escalated its war against Lund, he counterattacked. Going over the heads of multiple layers of FAA managers, Lund faxed his safety recommendation to Mark Dayton, then the Democratic senator for Northwest's home state of Minnesota. Dayton, in turn, brought the matter to the attention of the Inspector General for the Transportation Department, which oversees the FAA.

In the two years after Lund blew the whistle on the unaddressed problems he perceived at Northwest, he says, the FAA made his life uncomfortable. Now Lund is returning the favor. On September 27, 2007, the Inspector General released a report on the episode that lambasted the FAA for its treatment of Lund, who held on to his job despite what he claims was an effort to fire him. At the request of the Inspector General, the agency is now in the process of modifying the procedures it uses to review safety allegations raised by inspectors. The FAA is bracing for more scrutiny on this issue. In March [2008], the House aviation subcommittee plans to hold a hearing on an alleged incident of retaliation involving an inspector for Southwest Airlines.

The "FAA's handling of [Lund's] safety concerns appeared to focus on discounting the validity of the complaints," the Inspector General's office wrote in its report. "A potential negative consequence of FAA's handling of this safety recommendation is that the other inspectors may be discouraged from bringing safety issues to FAA's attention."

Lund's story shines a spotlight on a conflict that most passengers have no idea exists: the one between safety inspectors and airlines. The inspectors are the on-the-ground cops who ensure that engines fire up properly, that the wing flaps function, and that all of the other complex machinery in an aircraft is in good working order. They have broad discretion to halt and delay flights—power that often rankles the thinly stretched, financially strapped carriers. When an inspector launches a formal investigation into an apparent safety violation at a passenger airline, something that happened more than 200 times [in 2007], it often triggers costly repairs. And when the bill exceeds $50,000, the FAA must issue a press release alerting the world to the problem.

The airlines sometimes fight back. Executives meet constantly with local FAA officials on a wide variety of issues and occasionally lodge informal complaints against tough inspectors. From time to time, the carriers bring their concerns directly to the agency's top official: the FAA administrator. "If the airline feels uncomfortable, management will call the FAA administrator," says Linda Goodrich, a former inspector who is now vice-president of the Professional Airways Systems Specialists (PASS) union, which represents inspectors and played no role in Lund's dispute with the agency. "The FAA administrator will immediately demand to know what we are doing to them. You can imagine an inspector trying to do his work when his local management is so fearful of the airline.". . .

Several safety inspectors interviewed by *BusinessWeek* said the pressure not to impose big expenses on the carriers increased after the September 11 terrorist attacks, which threw the airline industry into an economic tailspin. They said that this led to a decrease in the reporting of safety violations. In the six-year period following September 11, 2001, the number of so-called enforcement investigation reports (EIRs) filed for the six biggest airlines fell by 62%, to 1,480, compared with the prior six-year period, according to FAA data reviewed by *BusinessWeek*. The number of domestic passengers grew by about 42% during this same period. . . .

There's little doubt that Lund rubs some people the wrong way. He knows the agency's thick rule book almost by heart, and he interprets it strictly. "Mark stands up and speaks the truth," says fellow inspector Mike Gonzales, who works in Scottsdale, Arizona. "Some people, including even his colleagues, don't like him for that." Another colleague called him "dogmatic" and "hard to like." Before joining the FAA in 1990 Lund worked as an aircraft electrician for the U.S. Navy and as maintenance director for a small airline in Minneapolis. He makes no apologies for his sometimes abrasive personality. "I'm here to keep the public safe," says Lund, who is an official in the local PASS union. If a concern arises, "I'll stop the airplane, and I'll watch every step.". . .

Lund claims that most of the airline's complaints arose when he delayed planes. In 1993 Lund prevented five DC-10s from taking off because Northwest had not repaired passenger-seat defects that would cause them to come apart in a crash. "The paperwork had been signed off, but we found that they had not been repaired properly," Lund told *BusinessWeek*. He claims that Northwest pressured his bosses, who in turn told him to return to the office and assured him that the airline would fix the problem. "I'm sure they took care of it," he said. "But we have no verification."

While inspecting a Northwest 747 in 1994, Lund discovered that when its oxygen masks dropped in an emergency they were dangling two feet above the head of a typical passenger. That made the masks useless. He stopped the airplane until the problem was fixed. "The carrier went ballistic," said a Northwest Airlines

FAA inspector with direct knowledge of the matter. Northwest declined to comment on these incidents. . . .

Lund was also given orders he found unpalatable, according to co-workers. Once, a manager forced him to revise a report to edit out a reference to a minor safety problem. "When he refused, they issued a letter of warning and then a letter of reprimand," says one inspector with direct knowledge of the matter. That put Lund on the edge of dismissal. "They didn't want any more problems with the carrier and they didn't want any problems with Mark," this inspector says. The FAA did not comment on accusations that it attempted to dismiss Lund.

Vindication from the IG's [Inspector General's] office took nearly two years. As the IG recommended, the FAA is creating a new procedure to review concerns raised by inspectors. It will require independent agency staffers—from outside the inspector's direct line of supervision—to investigate disputes between inspectors and airlines. Lund says he now has less conflict with Northwest and FAA supervisors than before. The report "reaffirms to me to keep going, to keep doing what I'm doing," says Lund.

For Discussion

1. Which internal and external stakeholders are positively and negatively affected by the behavior of safety inspectors?

2. Which of the six general environmental forces are influencing Northwest's behavior toward Mark Lund? Discuss.

3. Use the four approaches to deciding ethical dilemmas to evaluate whether Northwest and the FAA are treating Mr. Lund ethically.

4. How might the FAA promote ethics within the airline industry?

5. To what extent did Northwest and the FAA act in a socially responsible manner? Explain.

Source: Excerpted from Stanley Holmes, "Airline Safety: A Whistleblower's Tale," *BusinessWeek*, February 11, 2008, pp. 48–52.

Self-Assessment

What Is Your Guiding Ethical Principle?

Objectives

1. To understand your ethical approach.
2. To understand that there are different ways to perceive ethics in the workplace.

Introduction

Over the centuries human beings have grappled with defining ethics and behaving ethically. Many different principles have evolved to deal with ethics from different perspectives. None is better or worse than the other—they are simply perspectives. You may choose one to be your guiding principle while your friend follows another. This is also true of companies and their employees. For example, Johnson & Johnson has a valued reputation for being very ethical and socially responsible, whereas actions by companies like Ford and Arthur Andersen have placed a large question mark on their ethical conduct and social responsibility.

Instructions

Rank each of the following principles in order from 1 (my most important guiding principle) to 3 (least relevant to my ethical principles).

1. *Utilitarianism:* The greatest good for the greatest number, or any view that holds that actions and policies should be evaluated on the basis of benefits and costs they will impose on society.

   Violation? The Ford Motor Company knew of the problems with its tires 6 years before they became known in the United States, but this was information from Europe, and U.S. law did not require that the company report it if it did not happen here.

2. *Rights Theory:* A right is an individual's entitlement or claim to something. A person has a right when he or she is entitled to act in a certain way or is entitled to have others act in a certain way toward him or her. It can be a legal right, a moral right, or a human right.

   Violation? Many stockholders at Microsoft want the company to adopt the "U.S. Business Principles for Human Rights of Workers in China," a statement supported by other companies such as Levi Strauss and Reebok. Microsoft management did not agree, arguing that its own principles and code of ethics covered the important points and that the statement principles were too broad and vague. Other companies also thought that American companies should not promote human rights in China because they would be abandoning a position of political neutrality.

3. *Justice as Fairness:* A principle that aims to protect those least able to protect themselves.

   Examples: Companies should establish strong affirmative action plans to redress the wrongs of discrimination; or, if a company introduces pay cuts, the workers paid the least should receive the smallest pay cut and those who are paid the most should get the largest pay cut.

Questions for Discussion

1. What are the pros and cons of your primary ethical principle in terms of advancing up the corporate ladder? Discuss.

2. Why do you think ethical principles are important in the workplace? Explain.

3. Which of the previous three principles would you want the company that you work for to adopt? Why?

4. In such a competitive world, how ethical can any company really be?

Developed by Anne C. Cowden, PhD, Laura P. Hartman, and Joseph R. DesJardins, *Business Ethics: Decision-Making for Personal Integrity and Social Responsibility* (Burr Ridge, IL: McGraw-Hill, 2008). See Chapter 3 for a detailed discussion for each approach.

Ethical Dilemma

Should Job Applicants Reveal Their Chronic Illnesses to Potential Employers?

You've just graduated from college and are excited to begin job hunting. You have many exciting prospects, but there is one thing holding you back—you were recently diagnosed with scleroderma. This chronic connective tissue disease is progressive and typically kills patients within 10 years. Your doctor is positive about your prognosis; however, you have already experienced some of the effects, such as swelling and stiffening in your fingers. Federal disability laws bar employers from asking about an applicant's health. However, the U.S. Supreme Court ruled that a company can refuse to hire an applicant whose medical condition might adversely affect the performance of a specific job function.

Solving the Dilemma

Knowing a company might be reluctant to hire you based on your condition, what would you do?

1. Don't immediately mention your disease during the interview. Instead, play up your abilities, experience, and enthusiasm for the job. If you get hired, you can explain your illness and make up for missed work owing to medical appointments and flare-ups by working on weekends.

2. Bring up your disease right away. You don't have to provide vivid details about your symptoms, but it is important for your employer to know you have a chronic disease and how it will affect you.

3. Don't mention your disease at all. If you get the job and have a flare-up and need to take sick days, it is your business.

4. Invent other options. Discuss.

Source: Based on Joann S. Lublin, "Should Job Hunters Reveal Chronic Illness? The Pros and Cons," *The Wall Street Journal*, January 13, 2004, p. B1.

Global Management
Managing across Borders

Major Questions You Should Be Able to Answer

4.1 Globalization: The Collapse of Time & Distance
Major Question: What three important developments of globalization will probably affect me?

4.2 You & International Management
Major Question: Why learn about international management, and what characterizes the successful international manager?

4.3 Why & How Companies Expand Internationally
Major Question: Why do companies expand internationally, and how do they do it?

4.4 The World of Free Trade: Regional Economic Cooperation
Major Question: What are barriers to free trade, and what major organizations and trading blocs promote trade?

4.5 The Importance of Understanding Cultural Differences
Major Question: What are the principal areas of cultural differences?

Learning to Be a Success Abroad: How Do You Become a World Citizen?

Whether you travel abroad on your own or on a work assignment for your company, there are several ways to make your experience enhance your career success.

- **Learn how not to be an "ugly American":** Americans "are seen throughout the world as an arrogant people, totally self-absorbed and loud," says Keith Reinhard, former head of advertising conglomerate DDB Worldwide, who is leading an effort to reverse that through a nonprofit group called Business for Diplomatic Action (BDA), from which many suggestions here are drawn.[1] A survey conducted by DDB in more than 100 countries found that respondents repeatedly mentioned "arrogant," "loud," and "uninterested in the world" when asked their perceptions of Americans.[2] Some sample advice for Americans traveling abroad is: Be patient, be quiet, listen at least as much as you talk, don't use slang, and don't talk about wealth and status.[3]

- **Be global in your focus, but think local.** Study up on your host country's local customs and try to meet new people who might help you in the future. For example, Bill Roedy, President of MTV Networks International, spent time hanging out with Arab rappers and meeting the mayor of Mecca before trying to sign a contract that would launch MTV Arabia.[4] His efforts helped seal the deal.

- **Learn what's appropriate behavior:** Before you go, spend some time learning about patterns of interpersonal communication. In Japan, for instance, it is considered rude to look directly into the eye for more than a few seconds. In Greece the hand-waving gesture commonly used in America is considered an insult. In Afghanistan, a man does not ask another man about his wife.[5]

  Learn rituals of respect, including exchange of business cards. Understand that shaking hands is always permissible, but social kissing may not be. Dress professionally. For women, this means no heavy makeup, no flashy jewelry, no short skirts or sleeveless blouses (particularly in Islamic countries). In some countries, casual dressing is a sign of disrespect. Don't use first names and nicknames with fellow employees overseas, especially in countries with strict social strata.[6]

- **Know your field:** If you know your field and behave with courtesy and assurance, you will be well received around the world. Indra Nooyi successfully uses this advice in her role as CEO of PepsiCo. She's cosmopolitan, well educated, and is respected by people around the globe.[7]

- **Become at least minimally skilled in the language:** Whatever foreign country you're in, at the very least you should learn a few key phrases, such as "hello," "please," and "thank you," in your host country's language. Successful international managers have learned there is no adequate substitute for knowing the local language.[8]

For Discussion Have you done much traveling? What tricks have you discovered to make it more satisfying?

forecast

What's Ahead in This Chapter

This chapter covers the importance of globalization—the rise of the global village, of one big market, of both worldwide megafirms and minifirms. We also describe the characteristics of the successful international manager and why and how companies expand internationally. We describe the barriers to free trade and the major organizations promoting trade. Finally, we discuss some of the cultural differences you may encounter if you become an international manager.

4.1. GLOBALIZATION: THE COLLAPSE OF TIME & DISTANCE

major question? What three important developments of globalization will probably affect me?

THE BIG PICTURE

Globalization, the trend of the world economy toward becoming a more interdependent system, is reflected in three developments: the rise of the "global village" and e-commerce, the trend of the world's becoming one big market, and the rise of both megafirms and Internet-enabled minifirms worldwide.

"You don't have to be big to be global," says Sonia Seye, who runs Hair Universal, a busy Los Angeles salon that specializes in braiding hair and turning multicolored hair extensions into fashionable coifs. With dreams of expanding her business, she launched a search in India for a supplier of human-hair extensions (which come from Hindu temples, where women shave their heads in offerings to the gods).

Seye spent 6 months researching suppliers online, peppering prospects by e-mail and checking them out with the Indian consulate, and then flew to India, where she met her final candidates. By buying direct, instead of going through middlemen, she halved her hair-extension costs, and thus is able to undercut the prices of rival salons. The trip to India has more than paid for itself.[9]

Can you visualize yourself operating like this? Like Seye, you are living in a world being rapidly changed by *globalization—the trend of the world economy toward becoming a more interdependent system.* Time and distance, which have been under assault for 150 years, have now virtually collapsed, as reflected in three important developments we shall discuss.[10]

1. The rise of the "global village" and electronic commerce.
2. The world's becoming one market instead of many national ones.
3. The rise of both megafirms and Internet-enabled minifirms worldwide.

The Rise of the "Global Village" & Electronic Commerce

The hallmark of great civilizations has been their great systems of communications. In the beginning, communications was based on transportation: the Roman Empire had its network of roads, as did other ancient civilizations, such as the Incas. Later the great European powers had their farflung navies. In the 19th century, the United States and Canada unified North America by building transcontinental railroads. Later the airplane reduced travel time between continents.

From Transportation to Communication Transportation began to yield to the electronic exchange of information. Beginning in 1844, the telegraph ended the short existence of the Pony Express and, beginning in 1876, found itself in competition with the telephone. The amplifying vacuum tube, invented in 1906, led to commercial radio. Television came into being in England in 1925. During the 1950s and 1960s, as television exploded throughout the world, communications philosopher Marshall McLuhan posed the notion of a "global village," where we all share our hopes, dreams, and fears in a "worldpool" of information. **The *global village* refers to the "shrinking" of time and space as air travel and the**

electronic media have made it easier for the people of the globe to communicate with one another.

Then the world became even faster and smaller. Fifteen years ago, cell phones, pagers, fax, and voice-mail links barely existed. When AT&T launched the first cellular communications system in 1983, it predicted fewer than a million users by 2000. By the end of 1993, however, there were more than 16 million cellular phone subscribers in the United States.[11] As of early 2007, about 2.8 billion cell phones were in use worldwide, and 1.6 million new ones entered into usage every day.[12]

The Net, the Web, & the World   Then came the Internet, the worldwide computer-linked "network of networks," for which there were an estimated 1.11 billion users throughout the world in 2007.[13] The Net might have remained the province of academicians had it not been for the contributions of Tim Berners-Lee, who came up with the coding system, linkages, and addressing scheme that debuted in 1991 as the World Wide Web. "He took a powerful communications system [the Internet] that only the elite could use," says one writer, "and turned it into a mass medium."[14]

The arrival of the Web quickly led to *e-commerce,* **or electronic commerce, the buying and selling of products and services through computer networks.** Total U.S. e-commerce sales were expected to top $136 billion in 2007.[15]

Example

Worldwide E-Commerce: Amazon.com

amazon.com.

Courtesy of Amazon.com.

In 1994, Jeffrey Bezos left a successful career on Wall Street with a plan to exploit the potential for electronic retailing on the World Wide Web by launching an on-line bookstore called Amazon.com.

Bezos realized that no bookstore with four walls could possibly stock the more than 2.5 million books that are now active and in print. Moreover, he saw that an online bookstore wouldn't have to make the same investment in retail clerks, store real estate, or warehouse space (in the beginning, Amazon.com ordered books from the publisher *after* Amazon took an order), so it could pass savings along to customers in the form of discounts. In addition, he appreciated that there would be opportunities to obtain demographic information about customers in order to offer personalized services, such as books of interest to them. Finally, Bezos saw that there could be a good deal of online interaction:

customers could post reviews of books they read and could reach authors by e-mail to provide feedback.

Amazon.com sold its first book in July 1995 and by the end of 1998 had served 6.2 million customers in more than 100 countries. Later the firm began expanding into nonbook areas, such as online retailing of music CDs, toys, electronics, drugs, cosmetics, pet supplies, and technologies for planned digital media services. In early 2008, it reported 2007 net sales rose 39%, to $14.84 billion, from a year earlier.[17]

Your Call

Can you think of any highly specialized worldwide medium-sized or small business that the invention of the Internet made possible? Could you see yourself launching a similar business?

One Big World Market: The Global Economy

"We are seeing the results of things started in 1988 and 1989," said Rosabeth Moss Kantor of the Harvard Business School a decade later.[16] It was in the late 1980s when the Berlin Wall came down, signaling the beginning of the end of communism in Eastern Europe. It was also when countries of the Pacific Rim began to open their economies to foreign investors. Finally, the trend toward governments deregulating their economies began sweeping the globe. These three events set up conditions by which goods, people, and money could move more freely throughout the world—a global economy. **The *global economy* refers to the increasing**

"Oh, same old thing." The cell phone represents a boon to less-developed countries because this kind of telephone infrastructure does not entail the costly process of installing miles of telephone poles and land lines.

tendency of the economies of the world to interact with one another as one market instead of many national markets.

The economies of the world have never been more entangled. As Kevin Maney writes in *USA Today,* "They're tied together by instantaneous information arriving via everything from currency trading databases to Web sites to CNN broadcasts. Capital—the money used to build businesses—moves globally and moves in a matter of keystrokes."[18]

Positive Effects Is a global economy really good for the United States? "Ultimately, the medium- to long-term benefits of globalization are positive for everybody," says the CEO of Infosys Technologies in India. "Let me give you an example. As our industry has increased economic activity in India, it's becoming a bigger market for American exports . . . Today you can't find any soft drinks in India except Coke or Pepsi."[19] Even in states such as Ohio, which has lost many manufacturing jobs to other countries, some U.S. businesses have benefited. Ohio companies exported $39.4 billion in goods in 2007.[20]

Negative Effects However, global economic interdependency can also be dangerous. Financial crises throughout the world, beginning in 1997, resulted in vast surplus funds from global investments flowing into the United States and being invested badly in a housing-and-credit bubble that has now burst (the so-called subprime mortgages meltdown), hurting many people.[21]

Another negative effect is the movement, or outsourcing (discussed in Section 4.3), of formerly well-paying jobs overseas as companies seek cheaper labor costs. Two decades ago, the loss was in American manufacturing jobs; more recently, many service jobs have moved offshore. Part of the reason for this, as Microsoft's Bill Gates has observed, is that "American high schools are obsolete . . . Until we design them to meet the needs of the 21st century, we will keep limiting—even ruining—the lives of millions of Americans every year."[22] In the competition with low-wage countries (India, China, and Asia), Americans are falling behind in the skills required to excel.

But the global economy isn't going to go away just because we don't like some of its destabilizing aspects. "The process is irreversible, if only because of the information technology and communications revolutions," says Claude Smadja, managing director of the World Economic Forum in Switzerland. "The problem also is that, contrary to some illusions, one cannot pick and choose in the package. . . . The new globality means a tremendous emphasis on speed, flexibility, versatility, and permanent change—in some respects, insecurity."[23]

Cross-Border Business: The Rise of Both Megamergers & Minifirms Worldwide

The global market driven by electronic information "forces things to get bigger and smaller at the same time," suggests technology philosopher Nicholas Negroponte. "And that's so ironic, when things want to do both but not stay in the middle. There will be an increasing absence of things that aren't either very local or very global."[24]

If Negroponte is correct, this means we will see more and more of two opposite kinds of businesses: mergers of huge companies into even larger companies, and small, fast-moving start-up companies.

Megamergers Operating Worldwide AOL + Time Warner. Glaxo Wellcome + SmithKline Beecham. Verizon + MCI. SBC + AT&T. Home Depot + Hughes. Walt Disney + Pixar. Nokia + Siemens.

The last 10 years have been megamerger time, "corporations on steroids," in one writer's phrase.[25] Oil, telecommunications, automobiles, financial services, and pharmaceuticals, for instance, aren't suited to being midsize, let alone small and local, so companies in these industries are trying to become bigger and cross-border. The means for doing so is to merge with other big companies. In automobiles, for instance, Porsche targeted Volkswagen to ensure that rivals did not get their hands on it; VW in turn targeted Swedish truckmaker Scania.[26]

Megamerger? A Porsche + Volkswagen merger has long been rumored, and Porsche recently increased its ownership stake in VW to about 31%. Later it said it made the move to protect VW from a foreign takeover but was not interested in a merger. Do you think we will see more auto company mergers?

Minifirms Operating Worldwide The Internet and the World Wide Web allow almost anyone to be global, which Kevin Maney points out has two important results:

1. Small Companies Can Get Started More Easily Because anyone can put goods or services on a Web site and sell worldwide, this wipes out the former competitive advantages of distribution and scope that large companies used to have.

2. Small Companies Can Maneuver Faster Little companies can change direction faster, which gives them an advantage in terms of time and distance over large companies. ●

Example

Small Companies That Get Started More Easily & Can Maneuver Faster: Bay-Traders

Many small firms have come from nowhere to collapse time and distance. For instance, so-called Bay-traders make a living selling things on eBay, the online auction company. Bay-traders find they get higher prices at Internet auctions than at swap meets or collectibles shows because bidding generates excitement and because the Internet's worldwide reach makes multiple bids more likely.

Judi Henderson-Townsand's Oakland, California, company, Mannequin Madness, began when, while working in marketing for a failing dot-com firm, she saw an online ad from a window dresser offering 50 mannequins. After purchasing the entire inventory, she started renting mannequins and later, after buying more from department stores, started selling them to special-event planners, retail stores, and artists.

Henderson-Townsand claims that the Internet, including eBay, has been by far her greatest marketing resource because it allows the firm to reach customers who could never be reached otherwise.[27]

Your Call

Do you have an idea for some uncommon products you might sell on eBay? What would they be?

major question ? Why learn about international management, and what characterizes the successful international manager?

THE BIG PICTURE

Studying international management prepares you to work with foreign customers or suppliers, for a foreign firm in the United States or for a U.S. firm overseas. Successful international managers aren't ethnocentric or polycentric but geocentric.

Part of the action. If "all of the action in business is international," as one expert says, what role do you think you might play in it? Do you think cultural bias against women in some foreign countries contributes to the low percentage of U.S. female executives working abroad?

Can you see yourself working overseas? It can definitely be an advantage to your career. "There are fewer borders," says Paul McDonald, executive director of recruitment firm Robert Half Management Resources. "Anyone with international experience will have a leg up, higher salary, and be more marketable."[28]

Julie Androshick spent 2 years teaching in Samoa, and then worked as a journalist and as an analyst for consulting company McKinsey & Company. Now based in New York, she says working abroad expanded her worldview, gave her the courage to pursue long-shot jobs, and made her a more loyal employee.[29] After graduating from Northwestern University, Nate Linkon found a job in marketing with InfoSys Technologies, the Indian software giant, in Bangalore.[30] Scott Stapleton, formerly of Oakland, California, also took a marketing job with InfoSys in India. "The job blends practical work experience with life in a developing country," says Stapleton, adding that it's "a rare opportunity to actually witness globalization."[31]

Foreign experience demonstrates independence, resourcefulness, and entrepreneurship, according to management recruiters. "You are interested in that person who can move quickly and is nimble and has an inquiring mind," says one. People who have worked and supported themselves overseas, she says, tend to be adaptive and inquisitive—valuable skills in today's workplace.[32]

Why Learn about International Management?

International management is management that oversees the conduct of operations in or with organizations in foreign countries, whether it's through a multinational corporation or a multinational organization.

- **A *multinational corporation*, or multinational enterprise, is a business firm with operations in several countries.** Our publisher, McGraw-Hill, is one such "multinational" (see the 17 foreign cities listed on our book's title page). In terms of revenue, the real behemoths in multinational corporations include the American firms Wal-Mart, ExxonMobil, General Motors, Chevron, ConocoPhillips, General Electric, and Ford Motor Co. The largest foreign companies are BP (Britain), Royal Dutch/Shell (Netherlands/Britain), DaimlerChrysler (Germany/USA), and Toyota (Japan).

- **A *multinational organization* is a nonprofit organization with operations in several countries.** Examples are the World Health Organization, the International Red Cross, the Church of Latter Day Saints.

Even if in the coming years you never travel to the wider world outside North America—an unlikely proposition, we think—the world will assuredly come to you. That, in a nutshell, is why you need to learn about international management.

More specifically, consider yourself in the following situations:

Practical Action

Being a Star Road Warrior

Since business travelers who fly 100,000-plus miles a year are no longer a rare breed, should you prepare for the possibility of joining them?

As we discussed, globalization has collapsed time and distance. Managers must be prepared to work for organizations that operate not only countrywide but worldwide. To stay connected with colleagues, employees, clients, and suppliers, you may have to travel a lot.

Business travel can have its rewards. Many people enjoy going to different cities, meeting new people, encountering new cultures. In one survey, people who took business trips of five nights or more said that being on the road provided certain escapes, as from their everyday workplace (35% of those polled), putting out work "fires" (20%), frequent meetings (12%), and co-worker distractions (11%).[33]

Business travelers have learned the following three lessons.

Lesson I: Frequent Travel May Be Needed Because Personal Encounters Are Essential

"There is no substitute for face time," says a *Business-Week* article.[34] Yes, technologies such as smartphones, e-mail, and videoconferencing make it easier to connect with others—superficially, at least. "But," says an investment banker, "in a global world you have to get in front of your employees, spend time with your clients, and show commitment when it comes to joint ventures, mergers, and alliances. The key is thoughtful travel—traveling when necessary."[35]

Lesson 2: Travel May Be Global, but Understanding Must Be Local

Being a road warrior is all about making bets with one's time, calculating the strategy of where to be when. Thus, world-traveling executives must do their homework to know cultures, organizations, and holders of power. "Cull information on the individuals and companies you're visiting," says one expert. "Follow the news relating to the region. If possible try to read a few books about the history and culture of the lands you will visit. . . . Learn a few words too."[36]

Lesson 3: Frequent Travel Requires Frequent Adjustments

How do you cope if you travel all the time? Some people pack their own bags. Others keep complete wardrobes in major cities. Lisa Bergson has a detailed packing list that "comprises everything, from voltage adaptors to herbal teas to foot spray." She has also developed a "day-by-day wardrobe chart for every trip of a week or more, attempting to leverage every item and still look chic."[37] Some parents who have no one to care for their children while they're on the road bring their kids along with them, taking advantage of such childcare enterprises as ChildrenFirst (Boston) and Family & Child Care Referral Agency (Washington, DC), which specialize in childcare for business travelers.[38]

You May Deal with Foreign Customers or Partners While working for a U.S. company you may have to deal with foreign customers. Or you may have to work with a foreign company in some sort of joint venture. The people you're dealing with may be outside the United States or visitors to it. Either way you would hate to blow a deal—and maybe all future deals—because you were ignorant of some cultural aspects you could have known about.

Examples are legion.[39] One American executive inadvertently insulted or embarrassed Thai businessmen by starting gatherings talking about business. "That's a no-no," he says. "I quickly figured out that I was creating problems by talking business before eating lunch and by initiating the talks."

You May Deal with Foreign Suppliers While working for an American company you may have to purchase important components, raw materials, or services from a foreign supplier. And you never know where foreign practices may diverge from what you're accustomed to.

It is estimated, for example, that North America's share of software developer jobs will decline from 23% in early 2007 to 18% in 2010, with nearly all these jobs being moved outside the United States—to places such as India, New Zealand, and Eastern Europe. Many U.S. software companies—Microsoft, IBM, Oracle, Motorola,

Working for a foreign firm. If you thought you might work for a foreign firm, either at home or overseas, what should you be doing now to prepare for it?

Novell, Hewlett-Packard, and Texas Instruments—have opened offices in India to take advantage of high-quality labor.[40]

You May Work for a Foreign Firm in the United States You may sometime take a job with a foreign firm doing business in the United States, such as an electronics, pharmaceutical, or car company. And you'll have to deal with managers above and below you whose outlook is different from yours. For instance, Japanese companies, with their emphasis on correctness and face saving, operate in significantly different ways from American companies.

Sometimes it is even hard to know that an ostensibly U.S. company actually has foreign ownership. For example, many American book publishers (though not McGraw-Hill) are British or German owned.

You May Work for an American Firm Outside the United States—or for a Foreign One You might easily find yourself working abroad in the foreign operation of a U.S. company. Most big American corporations have overseas subsidiaries or divisions. On the other hand, you might also well work for a foreign firm in a foreign country, such as a big Indian company in Bangalore or Mumbai.

The Successful International Manager: Geocentric, Not Ethnocentric or Polycentric

Maybe you don't really care that you don't have much understanding of the foreign culture you're dealing with. "What's the point?" you may think. "The main thing is to get the job done." Certainly there are international firms with managers who have this perspective. They are called *ethnocentric,* one of three primary attitudes among international managers, the other two being *polycentric* and *geocentric.*[41]

Ethnocentric Managers—"We Know Best" What do foreign executives fluent in English think when they hear Americans using an endless array of baseball, basketball, and football phrases (such as "out of left field" or "Hail Mary pass")[42] *Ethnocentric managers* **believe that their native country, culture, language, and behavior are superior to all others.** Ethnocentric managers tend to believe that they can export the managers and practices of their home countries to anywhere in the world and that they will be more capable and reliable. Often the ethnocentric viewpoint is less attributable to prejudice than it is to ignorance, since such managers obviously know more about their home environment than the foreign environment. Ethnocentrism might also be called *parochialism*—**that is, a narrow view in which people see things solely through their own perspective.**

Is ethnocentrism bad for business? It seems so. A survey of 918 companies with home offices in the United States, Japan, and Europe found that ethnocentric policies were linked to such problems as recruiting difficulties, high turnover rates, and lawsuits over personnel policies.[43]

Polycentric Managers—"They Know Best" *Polycentric managers* **take the view that native managers in the foreign offices best understand native personnel and practices, and so the home office should leave them alone.** Thus, the attitude of polycentric managers is nearly the opposite of that of ethnocentric managers.

Geocentric Managers—"What's Best Is What's Effective, Regardless of Origin" *Geocentric managers* **accept that there are differences and similarities between home and foreign personnel and practices and that they should use whatever techniques are most effective.** Clearly, being an ethno- or polycentric manager takes less work. But the payoff for being a geocentric manager can be far greater. ●

4.3 WHY & HOW COMPANIES EXPAND INTERNATIONALLY

> Why do companies expand internationally, and how do they do it?
>
> major question?

THE BIG PICTURE

Multinationals expand to take advantage of availability of supplies, new markets, lower labor costs, access to finance capital, or avoidance of tariffs and import quotas. Five ways they do so are by global outsourcing; importing, exporting, and countertrading; licensing and franchising; joint ventures; and wholly-owned subsidiaries.

Who makes Apple's iPod, with its 451 parts? Not Apple, but a number of Asian companies. The hard drive, for instance, is made by a Japanese company, which in turn outsources to the Philippines and China; the chips are made in Taiwan.[44] Who makes the furniture sold by Ethan Allen, that most American of names, evoking Ethan Allen and the Green Mountain Boys? About half is made overseas, by suppliers in China, the Philippines, Indonesia, and Vietnam.[45] With a goal of boosting sales by 5%–7%, where is consumer-products giant Procter & Gamble going to seek additional consumers? One area is Mexico, where poor consumers at small, rudimentary markets will buy a single-use P&G shampoo packet for the rock-bottom price of about 19 cents.[46] There are many reasons why American companies are going global. Let us consider why and how they are expanding beyond U.S. borders.

Why Companies Expand Internationally

Many a company has made the deliberate decision to restrict selling its product or service to just its own country. Is anything wrong with that?

The answer is: It depends. It would probably have been a serious mistake for NEC, Sony, or Hitachi to have limited their markets solely to Japan during the 1990s, a time when the country was in an economic slump and Japanese consumers weren't consuming. During that same period, however, some American banks might have been better off not making loans abroad, when the U.S. economy was booming but foreign economies were not. Going international or not going international—it can be risky either way.

Why, then, do companies expand internationally? There are at least five reasons, all of which have to do with making or saving money.

I. Availability of Supplies   Antique and art dealers, mining companies, banana growers, sellers of hard woods—all have to go where their basic supplies or raw materials are located. For years oil companies, for example, have expanded their activities outside the United States in seeking cheaper or more plentiful sources of oil.

2. New Markets   Elsewhere in this book (Chapter 6) we discuss the *product life cycle*, the natural rise and fall in the sales life of a product. Sometimes a company will find, as cigarette makers have, that the demand for their product has declined domestically but that they can still make money overseas. Or sometimes a company

U.S. export. Popular entertainment is a major U.S. export, as was this Tom Hanks film *The Da Vinci Code* to South Korea. Are there any negatives to sending American popular culture overseas?

톰 행크스
다빈치 코드
THE DA VINCI CODE

will steal a march on its competitors by aggressively expanding into foreign markets, as did Coca-Cola over PepsiCo under the leadership of legendary CEO Robert Goizueta. U.S. exports to emerging markets have increased 338% over the past 20 years.[47]

3. Lower Labor Costs   The decline in manufacturing jobs in the United States is directly attributable to the fact that American companies have found it cheaper to do their manufacturing outside the States. For example, the rationale for using *maquiladoras*—**manufacturing plants allowed to operate in Mexico with special privileges in return for employing Mexican citizens**—is that they provide less expensive labor for assembling everything from appliances to cars. However, even professional or service kinds of jobs may be shipped overseas. As mentioned, some makers of software applications programs are taking care of their programming needs by sending their jobs to India.

4. Access to Finance Capital   Companies may be enticed into going abroad by the prospects of capital being put up by foreign companies. Or sometimes a foreign government will offer a subsidy in hopes of attracting a company that will create jobs, as Ireland did in the 1970s for Lotus sports-car maker John DeLorean.

5. Avoidance of Tariffs & Import Quotas   Countries place tariffs (fees) on imported goods or impose import quotas—limitations on the numbers of products allowed in—for the purpose of protecting their own domestic industries. For example, Japan imposes tariffs on agricultural products, such as rice, imported from the United States. To avoid these penalties, a company might create a subsidiary to produce the product in the foreign country. General Electric and Whirlpool, for example, have foreign subsidiaries to produce appliances overseas.

How Companies Expand Internationally

Most companies don't start out to be multinationals. Generally, they edge their way into international business, making minimal investments and taking minimal risks, as shown in the drawing below. *(See Figure 4.1.)*

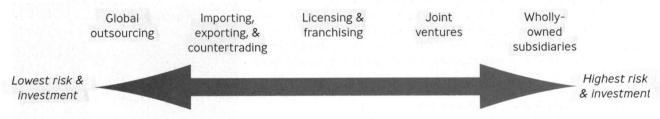

| Global outsourcing | Importing, exporting, & countertrading | Licensing & franchising | Joint ventures | Wholly-owned subsidiaries |

Lowest risk & investment   *Highest risk & investment*

figure 4.1

FIVE WAYS OF EXPANDING INTERNATIONALLY

These range from lowest risk and investment *(left)* to highest risk and investment *(right)*.

Let's consider these five ways.

1. Global Outsourcing   A common practice of many companies, *outsourcing* is **defined as using suppliers outside the company to provide goods and services.** For example, airlines are increasingly farming out aircraft maintenance to other companies.[48] Management philosopher Peter Drucker believes that in the near future organizations may be outsourcing all work that is "support"—such as information systems—rather than revenue producing.

Global outsourcing (or simply *global sourcing* or *offshoring*) extends this technique outside the United States **Global outsourcing is defined as using suppliers outside the United States to provide labor, goods, or services.** The reason may be that the foreign supplier has resources not available in the United States, such as Italian marble. Or the supplier may have special expertise, as do Pakistani weavers. Or—more likely these days—the supplier's labor is cheaper than American labor. As a manager, your first business trip outside the United States might be to inspect the production lines of one of your outsourcing suppliers.

2. Importing, Exporting, & Countertrading When *importing*, **a company buys goods outside the country and resells them domestically.** Nothing might seem to be more American than Jeep Wranglers, but they are made not only in the United States but also in Canada, from which they are imported and made available for sale in the United States. Many of the products we use are imported, ranging from Heineken beer (Netherlands) to Texaco gasoline (Saudi Arabia) to Honda snowblowers (Japan).

Practical Action

Global Outsourcing: Which Jobs Are Likely to Fall Victim to Offshoring?

Will there be any good jobs left for new college graduates?

Americans are rightly concerned about the changing jobs picture, brought about in part by offshoring of work to low-wage countries such as China, India, the Philippines, and Ireland. Few of the 2.8 million factory jobs that were lost between 2001 and 2004, for instance, have been replaced, forcing many workers to accept lower-paying alternatives, such as jobs in retail and health care, which pay on average 21% less than manufacturing jobs.[49] Now the same trend— global outsourcing—is happening with white-collar jobs.[50] Forrester Research estimates that 3.4 million service jobs will have moved offshore between 2000 and 2015.[51]

Offshoring Is Not the Only Job Killer
Offshoring is not the only culprit in doing away with many U.S. jobs. Much more important are productivity gains—increased output per existing worker through use of labor-saving technology, procurement efficiencies, and extended work hours. Every one percentage point of annual productivity growth, it's estimated, eliminates about 1.3 million jobs. Another factor is employers' hiring of temporary instead of permanent workers to save on health care and retirement benefit costs.[52]

Does Global Outsourcing Actually Benefit the United States?
Some people argue that the threat posed by offshoring has been vastly overstated. "More high-end service jobs seem to have washed onshore than off over the past several years," says economist Gene Epstein.[53] From 2002 to 2006, service jobs in fields supposedly threatened by offshoring grew by 7.7%, compared to 4.5% for all service jobs. Moreover, the 3.4 million service jobs that Forrester Research estimates will be lost over 15 years amount to only half the jobs created and lost in a single *3-month period*.

Supporters of free trade argue that jobs shipped offshore—even infotech and biotech jobs—generate returns to the United States "The money paid to foreign producers," says University of California at Berkeley business professor Hal Varian, "whether businesses or workers, typically comes back home to buy domestic goods and services, thereby generating domestic employment."[54] The difficulty is the political problem: "when the dollars flow offshore," he says, "it is easy to identify those who are hurt. But when the dollars flow back, it is much more difficult to discern the beneficiaries."

Observed management philosopher Peter Drucker: "Nobody seems to realize that we import twice or three times as many jobs as we export. I'm talking about the jobs created by foreign companies coming into the U.S. The most obvious [importers] are foreign auto companies. . . . We are exporting low-skill, low-paying jobs but are importing high-skill, high-paying jobs."[55]

How Can You Prepare for an Offshored World?
What career fields are apt to be most susceptible to offshoring?

"I believe you should outsource everything for which there is no career track that could lead into senior management," said Drucker. An example, he said, is the job of total-quality-control specialist, a job that can be done overseas. Among the jobs predicted by Forrester Research to move offshore: office support, computer, business operations, architecture, legal, sales, and art and design.[56]

"As soon as a job becomes routine enough to describe in a spec sheet, it becomes vulnerable to outsourcing," says another writer. "Jobs like data entry, which are routine by nature, were the first among obvious candidates for outsourcing." But even "design and financial-analysis skills can, with time, become well-enough understood to be spelled out in a contract and signed away."[57]

Says Fred Levy, a Massachusetts Institute of Technology economist, "If you can describe a job precisely, or write rules for doing it, it's unlikely to survive. Either we'll program a computer to do it, or we'll teach a foreigner to do it."[58] If you're a programmer or in a similar at-risk job, Bill Mitchell, CEO of a software company, suggests that you should "specialize to the point that you offer greater productivity, or change careers." Another option is to innovate; Mitchell mentions a friend who developed new programming methods, "which allowed him to write certain specialized applications about eight times faster than his typical Bangalore competitor."[59] However, this advantage might not last for long.

Which Jobs Will Remain in the United States?

It is difficult to predict which jobs will remain at home, since even the Bureau of Labor Statistics often can't get it right. However, jobs that endure may share certain traits, listed below, regardless of the industry they serve:[60]

- **Face to face.** Some involve *face-to-face contact,* such as being a salesperson with a specific territory or an emergency room doctor.

- **Physical contact.** Other jobs involve *physical contact,* such as those of dentists, nurses, massage therapists, gardeners, and nursing-home aides.

- **Recognizing complex patterns.** Others involve the human ability to *recognize complex patterns,* which are hard to computerize, such as a physician's ability to diagnose an unusual disease (even if the X-rays are read by a radiologist in India). This also describes such high-end jobs as teaching first grade or selling a mansion to a millionaire or jobs that demand an intimate knowledge of the United States, such as marketing to American teenagers or lobbying Congress.[61]

Finally, the Association for Computing Machinery has found after a year of study that the effects of offshoring on technical jobs have been overstated; that is, although 2%–3% of information technology jobs are being offshored each year, this is offset by an annual 3% increase in technical jobs in the U.S.[62]

Survival Rules

For you, as a prospective manager, there are perhaps three ideas to take away from all this:

- **Teamwork and creativity.** "Jobs that persist are dynamic and creative and require the ability to team with others," says Jim Spohrer of the IBM Almaden Research Center in San Jose, California, which studies the business operations of IBM's corporate clients. "At its heart, a company is simply a group of teams that come together to create" products and services.[63]

- **Flexibility.** "Jobs used to change very little or not at all over the course of several generations," says Spohrer. "Now, they might change three or four times in a single lifetime." Flexibility—as in being willing to undergo retraining—thus becomes important. Fortunately, as Drucker pointed out, the United States is "the only country that has a very significant continuing education system. This doesn't exist anywhere else." The United States is also the only country, he said, in which it is easy for younger people to move from one area at work to another.[64]

- **Education.** The more education one has, the more one is apt to prevail during times of economic change. Men and women with 4 years of college, for instance, earn nearly 45% more on average than those with only a high school diploma.[65]

When *exporting,* **a company produces goods domestically and sells them outside the country.** One of the greatest U.S. exports is American pop culture, in the form of movies, CDs, and fashion. The United States is also a leader in exporting computers and other information technology.

Sometimes other countries may wish to import American goods but lack the currency to pay for them. In that case, the exporting U.S. company may resort to *countertrading—that is, bartering goods for goods.* When the Russian ruble plunged in value in 1998, some goods became a better medium of exchange than currency.

3. Licensing & Franchising Licensing and franchising are two aspects of the same thing, although licensing is used by manufacturing companies and franchising is used more frequently by service companies.

In *licensing,* **a company allows a foreign company to pay it a fee to make or distribute the first company's product or service.** For example, the Du Pont chemical company might license a company in Brazil to make Teflon, the nonstick substance that is found on some frying pans. Thus, Du Pont, the licensor, can make money without having to invest large sums to conduct business directly in a foreign company. Moreover, the Brazilian firm, the licensee, knows the local market better than Du Pont probably would.

Franchising **is a form of licensing in which a company allows a foreign company to pay it a fee and a share of the profit in return for using the first company's brand name and a package of materials and services.** For example, Burger King, Hertz, and Hilton Hotels, which are all well-known brands, might provide the use of their names plus their operating know-how (facility design, equipment, recipes, management systems) to companies in Greece in return for an upfront fee plus a percentage of the profits.

By now Americans traveling throughout the world have become accustomed to seeing so-called U.S. franchises everywhere: Popeye's Chicken & Biscuits in China, DKNY and The GAP stores in Turkey, Coca-Cola in Mexico, Intercontinental hotels in Hungary.

4. Joint Ventures *Strategic allies* (described in Chapter 3) are two organizations that have joined forces to realize strategic advantages that neither would have if operating alone. A U.S. firm may form a *joint venture,* **also known as a** *strategic alliance,* **with a foreign company to share the risks and rewards of starting a new enterprise together in a foreign country.** For instance, General Motors operates a joint venture in Canada with Suzuki Motor Corp. and an assembly plant called NUMMI in California with Toyota.

Sometimes a joint venture is the only way an American company can have a presence in a certain country, whose laws may forbid foreigners from ownership.

General Motors found that the best way to do business in the new nation of Namibia (after it became independent of South African control) was to ship GM vehicles to a plant in that country. The Namibians, who wanted to be producers, not just consumers, then converted them from U.S.-style left-hand drive to right-hand drive, as required in parts of Africa.

5. Wholly-Owned Subsidiaries A *wholly-owned subsidiary* **is a foreign subsidiary that is totally owned and controlled by an organization.** The foreign subsidiary may be an existing company that is purchased outright. **A** *greenfield venture* **is a foreign subsidiary that the owning organization has built from scratch.**

General Motors owns Adam Opel AG in Germany, Vauxhall Motor Cars Ltd. in the United Kingdom, Holden's in Australia, and half of Saab Automobile AB in Sweden. ●

Jaguar. A number of formerly British-owned carmakers have gone over to foreign ownership. Jaguar and Land Rover became subsidiaries of Ford, but then in 2008 were sold to Tata of India. Do you think the American companies General Motors and Ford could ever wind up under foreign ownership?

4.4 THE WORLD OF FREE TRADE: REGIONAL ECONOMIC COOPERATION

major question? What are barriers to free trade, and what major organizations and trading blocs promote trade?

THE BIG PICTURE

Barriers to free trade are tariffs, import quotas, and embargoes. Organizations promoting international trade are the World Trade Organization, the World Bank, and the International Monetary Fund. Major trading blocs are NAFTA, the EU, APEC, and Mercosur.

If you live in the United States, you see foreign products on a daily basis—cars, appliances, clothes, foods, beers, wines, and so on. Based on what you see every day, which countries would you think are our most important trading partners? China? Japan? Germany? England? South Korea?

These five countries do indeed appear among the top leading U.S. trading partners (measured in terms of imports and exports added together). Interestingly, however, our No. 1 and No. 3 trading partners are our immediate neighbors—Canada and Mexico, whose products may not be quite so visible. (The top 10 countries, ranked in order, are Canada, China, Mexico, Japan, Germany, United Kingdom, South Korea, Taiwan, Saudi Arabia, and France.)[66]

Let's begin to consider *free trade,* **the movement of goods and services among nations without political or economic obstruction.**

Quite contained. Container-ships full of imports from China have benefited the American poor disproportionately, with cheap goods in discount stores, for instance, offsetting recent increased disparities in U.S. income. Could Americans' objections to globalization be misplaced?

Barriers to International Trade

Countries often use *trade protectionism*—**the use of government regulations to limit the import of goods and services**—to protect their domestic industries against foreign competition. The justification they often use is that this saves jobs. Actually, protectionism is not considered beneficial, mainly because of what it does to the overall trading atmosphere.

The three devices by which countries try to exert protectionism consist of *tariffs, import quotas,* and *embargoes.*

I. Tariffs A *tariff* **is a trade barrier in the form of a customs duty, or tax, levied mainly on imports.** At one time, for instance, to protect the American shoe industry, the United States imposed a tariff on Italian shoes.

Actually, there are two types of tariffs: One is designed simply to raise money for the government (revenue tariff). The other, which concerns us more, is to raise the price of imported goods to make the prices of domestic products more competitive (protective tariff). For example, in 2001 President George W. Bush called for tariffs on imported steel, following influxes in imported foreign steel in the previous 2 years. Although the tariffs gave the U.S. domestic steel industry a chance to regroup and better compete with foreign steelmakers, the tariffs were lifted after the World Trade Organization (discussed below) ruled in 2003 that they were illegal.[67]

2. Import Quotas An *import quota* is a trade barrier in the form of a limit on the numbers of a product that can be imported. Its intent is to protect domestic industry by restricting the availability of foreign products.

Effective January 2005, China agreed (as a condition of being allowed into the World Trade Organization) to cancel car import quotas, which it had used to protect its domestic car manufacturing industry against imported vehicles from the United States, Japan, and Germany.[68]

Quotas are designed to prevent *dumping,* **the practice of a foreign company's exporting products abroad at a lower price than the price in the home market—or even below the costs of production—in order to drive down the price of the domestic product.**

3. Embargoes Ever had a Cuban cigar? They're difficult for Americans to get, since they're embargoed. **An *embargo* is a complete ban on the import or export of certain products.** It has been years since anyone was allowed to import Cuban cigars and sugar into the United States or for an American firm to do business in Cuba. The U.S. government also tries to embargo the export of certain supercomputers and other high-tech equipment with possible military uses to countries such as China.

Organizations Promoting International Trade

In the 1920s, the institution of tariff barriers did not so much protect jobs as depress the demand for goods and services, thereby leading to the loss of jobs anyway—and the massive unemployment of the Great Depression of the 1930s.[69] As a result of this lesson, after World War II the advanced nations of the world began to realize that if all countries could freely exchange the products that each could produce most efficiently, this would lead to lower prices all around. Thus began the removal of barriers to free trade.

The three principal organizations designed to facilitate international trade are the *World Trade Organization,* the *World Bank,* and the *International Monetary Fund.*

I. The World Trade Organization (WTO) Consisting of 151 member countries, the ***World Trade Organization (WTO)* is designed to monitor and enforce trade agreements.** The agreements are based on the *General Agreement on Tariffs and Trade (GATT),* an international accord first signed by 23 nations in 1947, which helped to reduce worldwide tariffs and other barriers. Out of GATT came a series of "rounds," or negotiations, that resulted in the lowering of barriers; for instance, the Uruguay Round, implemented in 1996, cut tariffs by one-third. The current round of negotiations, the Doha Round, which began in Doha, Qatar, is aimed at helping the world's poor by, among other things, reducing trade barriers.

Founded in 1995 and headquartered in Geneva, Switzerland, WTO succeeded GATT as the world forum for trade negotiations and has the formal legal structure for deciding trade disputes. WTO also encompasses areas not previously covered by GATT, such as services and intellectual property rights. A particularly interesting area of responsibility covers telecommunications—cell phones, pagers, data transmission, satellite communications, and the like—with half of the WTO members agreeing in 1998 to open their markets to foreign telecommunications companies.[70]

2. The World Bank The World Bank was founded after World War II to help European countries rebuild. Today the purpose of the ***World Bank* is to provide low-interest loans to developing nations for improving transportation, education,**

health, and telecommunications. The bank has 185 member nations, with most contributions coming from Britain, the United States, Japan, and Germany.[71]

In recent years, the World Bank has been the target of demonstrations in Seattle, Washington, DC, Ottawa, and elsewhere. Some protestors believe it finances projects that could damage the ecosystem, such as the Three Gorges Dam on China's Yangtze River. Others complain it supports countries that permit low-paying sweatshops or that suppress religious freedom. Still others think it has dragged its feet on getting affordable AIDS drugs to less-developed countries in Africa. Many of the same protests were leveled against the International Monetary Fund, discussed next. The World Bank has responded by trying to support projects that are not harmful to the environment and that are aimed at helping lift people out of poverty.

3. The International Monetary Fund   Founded in 1945 and now affiliated with the United Nations, the International Monetary Fund is the second pillar supporting the international financial community. Consisting of 185 member nations, **the *International Monetary Fund (IMF)* is designed to assist in smoothing the flow of money between nations.** The IMF operates as a last-resort lender that makes short-term loans to countries suffering from unfavorable balance of payments (roughly the difference between money coming into a country and money leaving the country, because of imports, exports, and other matters).

For example, during the late 1990s' "Asian crisis," the value of Thailand's currency dropped until at the end of 1997 it was worth half what it was at the start of the year. This affected Thailand's *exchange rate,* **the rate at which one country's currency can be exchanged for another country's currency.** Because Thailand owed other countries, they, too, were affected: Indonesia's currency dropped 70% and South Korea's 45%. In response to pleas for help, the IMF loaned Asian countries billions of dollars—$57 billion to South Korea alone in 1997.

Major Trading Blocs: NAFTA, EU, APEC, & Mercosur

A *trading bloc,* **also known as an *economic community,* is a group of nations within a geographical region that have agreed to remove trade barriers with one another.** The five major trading blocs are the *NAFTA nations,* the *European Union,* the *APEC countries,* the *Mercosur,* and *CAFTA.*

1. NAFTA—the Three Countries of the North American Free Trade Agreement   Formed in 1994, **the *North American Free Trade Agreement (NAFTA)* is a trading bloc consisting of the United States, Canada, and Mexico,** encompassing 435 million people. The agreement is supposed to eliminate 99% of the tariffs and quotas among these countries, allowing for freer flow of goods, services, and capital in North America. Since 1994, trade with Canada and Mexico now accounts for one-third of the U.S. total, up from one-quarter in 1989.

Is NAFTA a job killer, as some have complained? In Mexico, it has failed to generate substantial job growth and has hurt hundreds of thousands of subsistence farmers, so that illegal immigration to the United States continues to grow. As for the United States, nearly 525,000 workers, mostly in manufacturing, have been certified by the U.S. government as having lost their jobs or had their hours or wages reduced because of NAFTA's shifting of jobs south of the border. It also spurred a U.S. trade deficit—$74 billion with Mexico and $65 billion with Canada in 2007.[72] However, supporters insist NAFTA ultimately will result in more jobs and a higher standard of living among all trading partners.

2. The EU—the 27 Countries of the European Union   Formed in 1957, the *European Union (EU)* consists of **27 trading partners in Europe**, covering 455 million consumers.

Nearly all internal trade barriers have been eliminated (including movement of labor between countries), making the EU a union of borderless neighbors and the world's largest free market.

By 2002, such national symbols as the franc, the mark, the lira, the peseta, and the guilder had been replaced with the EU currency, the euro. There has even been speculation that someday the euro could replace the U.S. dollar as the dominant world currency.[73]

3. APEC—21 Countries of the Pacific Rim   The *Asia-Pacific Economic Cooperation (APEC)* **is a group of 21 Pacific Rim countries whose purpose is to improve economic and political ties**. Most countries with a coastline on the Pacific Ocean are members of the organization, although there are a number of exceptions. Among the 21 members are the United States, Canada, and China. Since the founding in 1989, APEC members have worked to reduce tariffs and other trade barriers across the Asia-Pacific region. APEC member countries are highlighted below.

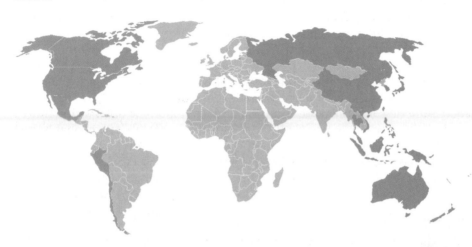

4. Mercosur—Ten Countries of Latin America   The *Mercosur* is the largest trade bloc in Latin America and has four core members—Argentina, Brazil, Paraguay, and Uruguay, with Venezuela scheduled to become a full member upon ratification by other countries—and five associate members: Bolivia, Chile, Colombia, Ecuador, and Peru. Besides reducing tariffs by 75%, Mercosur nations are striving for full economic integration, and the alliance is also negotiating trade agreements with NAFTA, the EU, and Japan.

5. CAFTA—Seven Countries of Central America   The newest trade agreement you may hear about is *CAFTA—the Central America Free Trade Agreement—*which **involves the United States and Costa Rica, the Dominican Republic, El Salvador, Guatemala, Honduras, and Nicaragua and which is aimed at reducing tariffs and other barriers to free trade.**[74]

Most Favored Nation Trading Status

Besides joining together in trade blocs, countries will also extend special, "most favored nation" trading privileges to one another. *Most favored nation* **trading status describes a condition in which a country grants other countries favorable trading treatment such as the reduction of import duties.** The purpose is to promote stronger and more stable ties between companies in the two countries. ●

4.5 THE IMPORTANCE OF UNDERSTANDING CULTURAL DIFFERENCES

major question

What are the principal areas of cultural differences?

THE BIG PICTURE

Managers trying to understand other cultures need to understand four basic cultural perceptions embodied in language, nonverbal communication, time orientation, and religion.

When President George W. Bush and Crown Prince Abdullah of Saudi Arabia met in Crawford, Texas, in 2005, they did something not usually done in the United States: They walked hand in hand. Men holding hands may raise eyebrows among most Americans, but it is common in the Middle East and does not carry any sexual connotation. "Holding hands is the warmest expression of affection between men," says one Lebanese sociologist. "It's a sign of solidarity and kinship."[75]

In Hong Kong, an American journalist riding in an elevator said hi to a Chinese colleague. She responded, "You've gained weight." Three other Chinese co-workers told him the same thing, a remark that in the United States would be regarded as tactless and offensive. "In China, such an intimate observation from a colleague isn't necessarily an insult," the journalist wrote. "It's probably just friendliness."[76]

Such are the kinds of cultural differences American managers are going to have to get used to. In the Arab world, which has historically been segregated by sex, men spend a lot of time together, and so holding hands, kissing cheeks, and long handshakes are meant to express devotion and equality in status. In China, people draw different lines between personal and work spaces, so that, for example, it is permissible for office colleagues to inquire about the size of your apartment and your salary and to give assessments of you wardrobe and your muscle tone.

Friendship, In the Arab world, not touching another man in greeting may be taken as a sign of distain. Do you have a problem with men touching or holding hands?

The Importance of National Culture

A nation's *culture* **is the shared set of beliefs, values, knowledge, and patterns of behavior common to a group of people.** We begin learning our culture starting at an early age through everyday interaction with people around us. This is why, from the outside looking in, a nation's culture can seem so intangible and perplexing. As cultural anthropologist Edward T. Hall puts it, "Since much of culture operates outside our awareness, frequently we don't even know what we know.... We unconsciously learn what to notice and what not to notice, how to divide time and space, how to walk and talk and use our bodies, how to behave as men or women, how to relate to other people, how to handle responsibility...."[77] Indeed, says Hall, what we think of as "mind" is really internalized culture.

And because a culture is made up of so many nuances, this is why visitors to another culture may experience culture shock—the feelings of discomfort and disorientation associated with being in an unfamiliar culture. According to anthropologists, culture shock involves anxiety and doubt caused by an overload of unfamiliar expectations and social cues.[78]

Cultural Dimensions: The Hofstede & GLOBE Project Models

Misunderstandings and miscommunications often arise in international business relationships because people don't understand the expectations of the other side. A person from North America, Great Britain, Scandinavia, Germany, or Switzerland, for example, comes from a **low-context culture in which shared meanings are primarily derived from written and spoken words.** Someone from China, Korea, Japan, Vietnam, Mexico, or many Arab cultures, on the other hand, comes from a **high-context culture in which people rely heavily on situational cues for meaning when communicating with others,** relying on nonverbal cues as to another person's official position, status, or family connections.

One way to avoid cultural collisions is to have an understanding of various cultural dimensions, as expressed in the Hofstede model and the GLOBE project.

Hofstede's Model of Four Cultural Dimensions

Thirty years ago Dutch researcher and IBM psychologist **Geert Hofstede** collected data from 116,000 IBM employees in 53 countries and proposed his *Hofstede model of four cultural dimensions,* **which identified four dimensions along which national cultures can be placed: (1) individualism/collectivism, (2) power distance, (3) uncertainty avoidance, and (4) masculinity/femininity.**[79]

- **Individualism/collectivism—how loosely or tightly are people socially bonded?** The United States, Australia, Sweden, France, Canada, and Great Britain have high individualistic values. *Individualism* indicates a preference for a loosely knit social framework in which people are expected to take care of themselves. Costa Rica, Thailand, Mexico, China, Guatemala, and Ecuador have high collectivist values. *Collectivism* indicates a preference for a tightly knit social framework in which people and organizations are expected to look after each other.

- **Power distance—how much do people accept inequality in power?** *Power distance* refers to the degree to which people accept inequality in social situations. *High power distance,* such as occurs in Mexico, India, Thailand, Panama, and the Philippines, means that people accept inequality in power among people, institutions, and organizations. *Low power distance,* such as occurs in Sweden, Germany, Israel, and Australia, means that people expect equality in power.

- **Uncertainty avoidance—how strongly do people desire certainty?** This dimension is about being comfortable with risk and uncertainty. Countries such as Japan, France, Greece, Portugal, and Costa Rica are very high in *uncertainty avoidance,* which expresses people's intolerance for uncertainty and risk. *High uncertainty avoidance* means people feel uncomfortable with uncertainty and support beliefs that promise certainty and conformity. Countries such as Sweden, India, the United States, Singapore, and Jamaica are very low on this dimension. *Low uncertainty avoidance* means that people have high tolerance for the uncertain and ambiguous.

- **Masculinity/femininity—how much do people embrace stereotypical male or female traits?** *Masculinity* expresses how much people value performance-oriented masculine traits, such as achievement, assertiveness, and material success. Countries with strong masculine preferences are Japan, Mexico, Austria, and Germany. *Femininity* expresses how much people embrace relationship-oriented feminine traits, such as cooperation and group decision making. Sweden, Norway, Thailand, Denmark, Costa Rica, and France are high on this cultural dimension.

Group Exercise:
Applying Hofstede's Cultural Values

Test Your Knowledge:
Hofstede's Model of Culture

In general, the United States ranked very high on individualism, relatively low on power distance, low on uncertainty avoidance, and moderately high on masculinity.

The GLOBE Project's Nine Cultural Dimensions   Started in 1993 by University of Pennsylvania professor **Robert J. House, the *GLOBE project* is a massive and ongoing cross-cultural investigation of nine cultural dimensions involved in leadership and organizational processes.**[80] (GLOBE stands for Global Leadership and Organizational Behavior Effectiveness.) GLOBE has evolved into a network of more than 150 scholars from 62 societies, and most of the researchers are native to the particular cultures they study. The nine cultural dimensions are as follows:

- **Power distance—how much unequal distribution of power should there be in organizations and society?** *Power distance* expresses the degree to which a society's members expect power to be unequally shared.

- **Uncertainty avoidance—how much should people rely on social norms and rules to avoid uncertainty?** *Uncertainty avoidance* expresses the extent to which a society relies on social norms and procedures to alleviate the unpredictability of future events.

- **Institutional collectivism—how much should leaders encourage and reward loyalty to the social unit?** *Institutional collectivism,* or *individualism/collectivism,* expresses the extent to which individuals should be encouraged and rewarded for loyalty to the social group as opposed to the pursuit of individual goals.

- **In-group collectivism—how much pride and loyalty should people have for their family or organization?** In contrast to individualism, *in-group collectivism* expresses the extent to which people should take pride in being members of their family, circle of close friends, and their work organization.

- **Gender egalitarianism—how much should society maximize gender role differences?** *Gender egalitarianism* expresses the extent to which a society should minimize gender discrimination and role inequalities.

- **Assertiveness—how confrontational and dominant should individuals be in social relationships?** *Assertiveness* represents the extent to which a society expects people to be confrontational and competitive as opposed to tender and modest.

- **Future orientation—how much should people delay gratification by planning and saving for the future?** *Future orientation* expresses the extent to which a society encourages investment in the future, as by planning and saving.

- **Performance orientation—how much should individuals be rewarded for improvement and excellence?** *Performance orientation* expresses the extent to which society encourages and rewards its members for performance improvement and excellence.

- **Humane orientation—how much should society encourage and reward people for being kind, fair, friendly, and generous?** *Humane orientation* represents the degree to which individuals are encouraged to be altruistic, caring, kind, generous, and fair.

Data from 18,000 managers yielded the country profiles shown on the next page. *(See Table 4.1.)*

table 4.1

COUNTRIES RANKING HIGHEST AND LOWEST ON THE GLOBE CULTURAL DIMENSIONS

Dimension	Highest	Lowest
Power distance	Morocco, Argentina, Thailand, Spain, Russia	Denmark, Netherlands, South Africa (black sample), Israel, Costa Rica
Uncertainty avoidance	Switzerland, Sweden, Germany (former West), Denmark, Austria	Russia, Hungary, Bolivia, Greece, Venezuela
Institutional collectivism	Sweden, South Korea, Japan, Singapore, Denmark	Greece, Hungary, Germany (former East), Argentina, Italy
In-group collectivism	Iran, India, Morocco, China, Egypt	Denmark, Sweden, New Zealand, Netherlands, Finland
Gender egalitarianism	Hungary, Poland, Slovenia, Denmark, Sweden	South Korea, Egypt, Morocco, India, China
Assertiveness	Germany (former East), Austria, Greece, United States, Spain	Sweden, New Zealand, Switzerland, Japan, Kuwait
Future orientation	Singapore, Switzerland, Netherlands, Canada (English speaking), Denmark	Russia, Argentina, Poland, Italy, Kuwait
Performance orientation	Singapore, Hong Kong, New Zealand, Taiwan, United States	Russia, Argentina, Greece, Venezuela, Italy
Human orientation	Philippines, Ireland, Malaysia, Egypt, Indonesia	Germany (former West), Spain, France, Singapore, Brazil

Source: Adapted from M. Javidan and R. J. House, "Cultural Acumen for the Global Manager: Lessons from Project GLOBE," *Organizational Dynamics,* Spring 2001, pp. 289–305.

The GLOBE dimensions show a great deal of cultural diversity around the world, but they also show how cultural patterns vary. For example, the U.S. managerial sample scored high on assertiveness and performance orientation—which is why Americans are widely perceived as being pushy and hardworking. Switzerland's high scores on uncertainty avoidance and future orientation help explain its centuries of political neutrality and world-renowned banking industry. Singapore is known as a great place to do business because it is clean and safe and its people are well educated and hardworking—no surprise, considering the country's high scores on social collectivism, future orientation, and performance orientation. By contrast, Russia's low scores on future orientation and performance orientation could foreshadow a slower-than-hoped-for transition from a centrally planned economy to free-enterprise capitalism. The practical lesson to draw from all this: *Knowing the cultural tendencies of foreign business partners and competitors can give you a strategic competitive advantage.*

GLOBE researchers also set out to find which, if any, attributes of leadership were universally liked or disliked, the results of which are shown on the next page. *(See Table 4.2.)* Throughout the world, visionary and inspirational leaders who are good team builders generally do the best; self-centered leaders seen as loners or face-savers received a poor reception.

table 4.2

LEADERSHIP ATTRIBUTES UNIVERSALLY LIKED AND DISLIKED ACROSS 62 NATIONS

Universally Positive Leader Attributes	Universally Negative Leader Attributes
Trustworthy	Loner
Just	Asocial
Honest	Noncooperative
Foresight	Irritable
Plans ahead	Nonexplicit
Encouraging	Egocentric
Positive	Ruthless
Dynamic	Dictatorial
Motive arouser	
Confidence builder	
Motivational	
Dependable	
Intelligent	
Decisive	
Effective bargainer	
Win-win problem solver	
Administrative skilled	
Communicative	
Informed	
Coordinator	
Team builder	
Excellence oriented	

Source: Excerpted and adapted from P. W. Dorfman, P. J. Hanges, and F. C. Brodbeck, "Leadership and Cultural Variation: The Identification of Culturally Endorsed Leadership Profiles," in R. J. House, P. J. Hanges, M. Javidan, P. W. Dorfman, and V. Gupta, eds. *Culture, Leadership, and Organizations: The GLOBE Study of 62 Societies,* (Thousand Oaks, CA: Sage, 2004), Tables 21.2 and 21.3, pp. 677–678.

Other Cultural Variations: Language, Interpersonal Space, Time Orientation, & Religion

How do you go about bridging cross-cultural gaps? It begins with understanding. Let's consider variations in four basic culture areas: (1) *language*, (2) *interpersonal space*, (3) *time orientation*, and (4) *religion*.

Note, however, that such cultural differences are to be viewed as *tendencies* rather than absolutes. We all need to be aware that the *individuals* we are dealing with may be exceptions to the cultural rules. After all, there *are* talkative and aggressive Japanese, just as there are quiet and deferential Americans, stereotypes notwithstanding.[81]

1. Language   More than 3,000 different languages are spoken throughout the world. However, even if you are operating in the English language, there are nuances between cultures that can lead to misperceptions. For instance, in Asia, a "yes" answer to a question "simply means the question is understood," says one well-traveled writer. "It's the beginning of negotiations."[82]

In communicating across cultures you have three options: (a) You can speak your own language. (The average American believes that about half the world can speak English, when actually it's about 20%.)[83] (b) You can use a translator. (If you do, try to get one that will be loyal to you rather than to your overseas host.) (c) You can learn the local language—by far the best option (as reflected in the *USA Today* headline: "U.S. Firms Becoming Tongue-Tied. Global Trade Requires Foreign Language Skills").[84]

2. Interpersonal Space   People of different cultures have different ideas about what is acceptable interpersonal space—that is, how close or far away one should be when communicating with another person. For instance, the people of North America and northern Europe tend to conduct business conversations at a range of 3–4 feet. For people in Latin American and Asian cultures, the range is about 1 foot. For Arabs, it is even closer.

This can lead to cross-cultural misunderstandings. "Arabs tend to get very close and breathe on you," says anthropologist Hall. "The American on the receiving end can't identify all the sources of his discomfort but feels that the Arab is pushy. The Arab comes close, the American backs up. The Arab follows, because he can only interact at certain distances."[85] However, once the American understands that Arabs handle interpersonal space differently and that "breathing on people is a form of communication," says Hall, the situation can sometimes be redefined so that the American feels more comfortable.

3. Time Orientation   Time orientation is different in many cultures. Anthropologist Hall makes a useful distinction between monochronic time and polychronic time:

- **Monochronic time.** This kind of time is standard American business practice. That is, **monochronic time is a preference for doing one thing at a time.** In this perception, time is viewed as being limited, precisely segmented, and schedule driven. This perception of time prevails, for example, when you schedule a meeting with someone and then give the visitor your undivided attention during the allotted time.[86]

  Indeed, you probably practice monochronic time when you're in a job interview. You work hard at listening to what the interviewer says. You may well take careful notes. You certainly don't answer your cell phone or gaze repeatedly out the window.

- **Polychronic time.** This outlook on time is the kind that prevails in Mediterranean, Latin American, and especially Arab cultures. ***Polychronic time is a preference for doing more than one thing at a time.*** Here time is viewed as being flexible and multidimensional.

  This perception of time prevails when you visit a Latin American client, find yourself sitting in the waiting room for 45 minutes, and then find in the meeting that the client is dealing with three other people at the same time. (The American variant these days is referred to as "multitasking," as when you talk on the phone while simultaneously watching television and doing a crossword puzzle.)

  As a manager, you will probably have to reset your mental clock when doing business across cultures.

Test Your Knowledge:
International Cultural Diversity

Example

Cultural Differences in Time: Peru Strives for Punctuality

Hora peruana, or Peruvian time, which usually means being an hour late, is considered by most citizens of Peru to be an endearing national trait. However, Peruvian officials believe that constant lateness reflects a negative attitude toward work and hurts national productivity. Professors, for instance, show up for class an hour after it has begun.

It's a "horrible, dreadful, harmful custom," President Alan Garcia said in a nationally televised event to kick off *La Hora sin Demora*—Time without Delay. The campaign, launched in March 2007, aims at asking schools, businesses, and government institutions to stop tolerating tardiness. A technology consultant from London applauded the campaign, saying that "a lot of Latin American countries lose business" owing to lateness. Although the new effort offers no penalties for being late or rewards for compliance, it hopes to shame latecomers into mending their ways.[87]

"There is a general tendency toward a different way of timekeeping that dominates in most of Latin America,"

says Robert Levine, a professor of psychology at California State University in Fresno. The author of *A Geography of Time,* Levine theorizes that different cultures mark time in varying "tempos"—some define events by the clock and others allow events to run their natural courses. Peruvian officials are "taking people who have been living on what we might call 'event time,' and asking them to switch to 'clock time,'" Levine says.[88]

Garcia's campaign did not get off to a good start. An invitation to the 11:00 A.M. ceremony was delivered by messenger to the Associated Press at 1:30 P.M.—after the event had ended.

Your Call

An Associated Press poll found the United States to be an impatient nation, with Americans getting antsy after 5 minutes on hold on the phone and 15 minutes maximum in a Department of Motor Vehicles line.[89] If you were trying to start a manufacturing business in Peru, what would you do to adjust?

4. Religion Are you a Protestant doing business in a predominantly Catholic country? Or a Muslim in a Buddhist country? How, then, does religion influence the work-related values of the people you're dealing with?

A study of 484 international students at a Midwestern university uncovered wide variations in the work-related values for different religious affiliations.[90] For example, among Catholics, the primary work-related value was found to be consideration. For Protestants, it was employer effectiveness; for Buddhists, social responsibility; for Muslims, continuity. There was, in fact, virtually *no agreement* among religions as to what is the most important work-related value. This led the researchers to conclude: "Employers might be wise to consider the impact that religious differences (and more broadly, cultural factors) appear to have on the values of employee groups."

Current Followers of the Major World Religions	
Christianity	2.1 billion
Islam	1.5 billion
Hinduism	900 million
Buddhism	376 million
Judaism	14 million
Chinese traditional religions	394 million

U.S. Managers on Foreign Assignments: Why Do They Fail?

There are about 300,000 U.S. managers known as *expatriates*—**people living or working in a foreign country**—who are working outside American borders. This number is expected to grow. For example, a survey of 390 companies by the U.S. State Department revealed that 29% had planned to send more people abroad in 2007 than the year before.[91] Supporting expatriate businesspeople and their families overseas is not cheap. "The tab for sending an executive who earns $160,000 in the U.S., plus a spouse and two children, to India for two years is about $900,000," says one expert.[92] Are the employers getting their money's worth? Probably not.

One study of about 750 companies (U.S., European, and Japanese) asked expatriates and their managers to evaluate their experiences. They found that 10%–20% of all U.S. managers sent abroad returned early because of job dissatisfaction or adjustment difficulties. Of those who stayed for the length of their assignments, about one-third did not perform to their superiors' expectations and one-fourth

Who made this car? Could you become an American manager in Japan but drive a Japanese car made in the United States? Unlikely, but possible. Still, Japanese car-makers build cars in the United States, such as this 2008 Toyota Camry, just as Buick builds cars in China: Both plants are located close to their markets.

left the company, often to join a competitor—a turnover rate double that of managers who did not go abroad.[93] Unfortunately, problems continue when expatriates return home, according to a recent study by Pricewaterhouse Coopers. Results indicated that 25% of repatriated employees quit their jobs within 1 year. Organizations can help reduce this turnover by communicating with employees throughout the international assignment and by providing at least 6 months' notice of when employees will return home.[94]

If you were to go abroad as a manager, what are the survival skills or outlook you will need? Perhaps the bottom line is revealed in a study of 72 human resource managers who were asked to identify the most important success factors in a foreign assignment: Nearly 35% said the secret was *cultural adaptability:* patience, flexibility, and tolerance for others' beliefs.[95] ●

Manager's Hot Seat:
Cultural Differences: Let's Break a Deal

Key Terms Used in This Chapter

Asia-Pacific Economic Cooperation (APEC) 121
Central America Free Trade Agreement (CAFTA) 121
countertrading 117
culture 122
dumping 119
e-commerce 107
embargo 119
ethnocentric managers 112
European Union (EU) 121
exchange rate 120
expatriates 129
exporting 116
franchising 117
free trade 118
geocentric managers 112

global economy 107
global outsourcing 115
global village 106
globalization 106
GLOBE project 124
greenfield venture 117
high-context culture 123
Hofstede model of four cultural dimensions 123
import quota 119
importing 115
International Monetary Fund (IMF) 120
joint venture 117
licensing 117
low-context culture 123
maquiladoras 114

Mercosur 121
monochronic time 127
most favored nation 121
multinational corporation 110
multinational organization 110
North American Free Trade Agreement (NAFTA) 120
outsourcing 114
parochialism 112
polycentric managers 112
polychronic time 128
tariff 118
trade protectionism 118
trading bloc 120
wholly-owned subsidiary 117
World Bank 119
World Trade Organization (WTO) 119

Summary

4.1 Globalization: The Collapse of Time & Distance

Globalization is the trend of the world economy toward becoming more interdependent. Globalization is reflected in three developments: (1) the rise of the global village and e-commerce; (2) the trend of the world's becoming one big market; and (3) the rise of both megafirms and Internet-enabled minifirms.

The rise of the "global village" refers to the "shrinking" of time and space as air travel and the electronic media have made global communication easier. The Internet and the Web have led to e-commerce, the buying and selling of products through computer networks.

The global economy is the increasing tendency of the economies of nations to interact with one another as one market.

The rise of cross-border business has led to megamergers, as giant firms have joined forces, and of minifirms, small companies in which managers can use the Internet and other technologies to get enterprises started more easily and to maneuver faster.

4.2 You & International Management

Studying international management prepares you to work with foreign customers or partners, with foreign suppliers, for a foreign firm in the United States, or for a U.S. firm overseas. International management is management that oversees the conduct of operations in or with organizations in foreign countries.

The successful international manager is not ethnocentric or polycentric but geocentric. Ethnocentric managers believe that their native country, culture, language, and behavior are superior to all others. Polycentric managers take the view that native managers in the foreign offices best understand native personnel and practices. Geocentric managers accept that there are differences and similarities between home and foreign personnel and practices, and they should use whatever techniques are most effective.

4.3 Why & How Companies Expand Internationally

Companies expand internationally for at least five reasons. They seek (1) cheaper or more plentiful supplies, (2) new markets, (3) lower labor costs, (4) access to finance capital, and (5) avoidance of tariffs on imported goods or import quotas.

There are five ways in which companies expand internationally. (1) They engage in global outsourcing, using suppliers outside the company and the United States to provide goods and services. (2) They engage in importing, exporting, and countertrading (bartering for goods). (3) They engage in licensing (allow a foreign company to pay a fee to make or distribute the company's product) and franchising (allow a foreign company to pay a fee and a share of the profit in return for using the first company's brand name). (4) They engage in joint ventures, a strategic alliance to share the risks and rewards of starting a new enterprise together in a foreign country. (5) They become wholly-owned subsidiaries, or foreign subsidiaries that are totally owned and controlled by an organization.

4.4 The World of Free Trade: Regional Economic Cooperation

Free trade is the movement of goods and services among nations without political or economic obstructions.

Countries often use trade protectionism—the use of government regulations to limit the import of goods and services—to protect their domestic industries against foreign competition. Three barriers to free trade are tariffs, import quotas, and embargoes. (1) A tariff is a trade barrier in the form of a customs duty, or tax, levied mainly on imports. (2) An import quota is a trade barrier in the form of a limit on the numbers of a product that can be imported. (3) An embargo is a complete ban on the import or export of certain products.

Three principal organizations exist that are designed to facilitate international trade. (1) The World Trade Organization is designed to monitor and enforce trade agreements. (2) The World Bank is designed to provide low-interest loans to developing nations for improving transportation, education, health, and telecommunications. (3) The International Monetary Fund is designed to assist in smoothing the flow of money between nations.

A trading bloc is a group of nations within a geographical region that have agreed to remove trade barriers. There are five major trading blocs: (1) North American Free Trade Agreement (NAFTA; U.S., Canada, and Mexico); (2) European Union (EU; 25 trading partners in Europe); (3) Asia-Pacific Economic Cooperation (APEC; 21 Pacific Rim countries); (4) Mercosur (Argentina, Brazil, Paraguay, and Uruguay; and (5) the Central America Free Trade Agreement (CAFTA; the United States and six Central American countries).

Besides joining together in trade blocs, countries also extend special, "most favored nation" trading privileges—that is, grant other countries favorable trading treatment such as the reduction of import duties.

4.5 The Importance of Understanding Cultural Differences

Misunderstandings and miscommunications often arise because one person doesn't understand the expectations of a person from another culture. In low-context cultures, shared meanings are primarily derived from written and spoken words. In high-context cultures, people rely heavily on situational cues for meaning when communicating with others.

Geert Hofstede proposed the Hofstede model of four cultural dimensions, which identified four dimensions along which national cultures can be placed: (1) individualism/collectivism, (2) power distance, (3) uncertainty avoidance, and (4) masculinity/femininity.

Robert House and others created the GLOBE (for Global Leadership and Organizational Behavior Effectiveness) Project, a massive and ongoing cross-cultural investigation of nine cultural dimensions involved in leadership and organizational processes: (1) power distance, (2) uncertainty avoidance, (3) institutional collectivism, (4) in-group collectivism, (5) gender egalitarianism, (6) assertiveness, (7) future orientation, (8) performance orientation, and (9) humane orientation.

A nation's culture is the shared set of beliefs, values, knowledge, and patterns of behavior common to a group of people. Visitors to another culture may experience culture shock—feelings of discomfort and disorientation. Managers trying to understand other cultures need to understand four basic cultural perceptions embodied in (1) language, (2) interpersonal space, (3) time orientation, and (4) religion.

Regarding language, when you are trying to communicate across cultures you have three options: Speak your own language (if others can understand you), use a translator, or learn the local language.

Interpersonal space involves how close or far away one should be when communicating with another person, with Americans being comfortable at 3–4 feet but people in other countries often wanting to be closer.

Time orientation of a culture may be either monochronic (preference for doing one thing at a time) or polychronic (preference for doing more than one thing at a time).

Managers need to consider the effect of religious differences. In order of size (population), the major world religions are Christianity, Islam, Hinduism, Buddhism, Judaism, and Chinese traditional religion.

Management in Action

IBM Expands Its Global Service Operations

When Rogerio Oliveira strolls through the vast IBM service delivery center in Hortolandia, Brazil, the contrast between the old and new IBM is stark. What was once a factory for mainframes is now crowded with hundreds of Brazilians on a different sort of assembly line. Their output is information, and they sit in rows of cubicles that stretch the length of a football field under a soaring, metal-trussed roof. A few years ago, the factory work performed here was just for Brazilian customers. Today, 100 clients for the facility's services, which range from software programming to financial accounting, come from 40 countries, including Canada, Mexico, South Africa, and the United States.

Oliveira, a 35-year IBM veteran and general manager for Latin America, stands at the heart of IBM's effort to transform itself into what it calls a "globally integrated enterprise." IBM has talked about its new global vision for two years. But only recently have managers like Oliveira turned that vision into a practical and solidly profitable business.

This is not the IBM of the 20th century, when Big Blue defined what it meant to be a multinational. Back then, its subsidiaries in 160 countries behaved like mini-IBMs—essentially, standalone operations serving their local customers. But replicating itself became too costly for IBM. So now the company is reorganizing around the principle that it will perform work for customers where the jobs can best be done—tapping the right talent at the right price.

That philosophy has produced a monumental shift in how IBM operates. In the past three years, the company has hired some 90,000 people in low-cost countries including Brazil, China, and India. These people, working in so-called global service delivery centers, provide a wide array of services for clients. The work goes beyond software programming to include data center operations, help-desk call centers, financial accounting, and benefits management. Initially, cheap labor was the big attraction of this move, with pay in India 70% to 80% lower than in the United States But these days, tapping the abundant talent pools—and new ideas—in emerging markets such as India and China is important as well.

Many of those global service employees report both to local supervisors and to managers thousands of miles away....

But there's still plenty of work to be done before IBM, with 375,000 people on six continents, is a smooth-running global machine. Says Chief Executive Samuel J. Palmisano: "The big issues for us are: Where do you put them? How do you retain them? How do you develop them? How do you move work to them or them to work?"

Palmisano began this journey almost three years ago. After getting the top job in 2003, he focused on innovation in high-end computers, chips, and software, and rapid expansion in emerging markets and services such as back-office information processing. Yet Palmisano's rise coincided with that of a handful of aggressive Indian tech services companies, which, thanks to their low-cost labor force, were able to undercut IBM's pricing. . . .

Cost-cutting alone wouldn't do the job: Palmisano had to transform how service work was done. He assigned Robert W. Moffat Jr., 51, a longtime IBMer, to the task. Moffat had already wrung $5 billion of annual costs out of IBM's manufacturing supply chain. For decades, IBM factories had focused primarily on one product and one geographic market. But by 2005 they made any number of products for a wide range of locales, so IBM was able to operate fewer plants and keep them running at higher capacity.

Moffat figured that the same approach could be taken with services. His team surveyed countries for costs, available talent, educational pipelines, languages spoken, proximity to markets, and political stability. They used this information to choose locations where IBM would serve clients anywhere around the world. Moffat set up finance and administration back-office centers, for example, in Bangalore, Buenos Aires, Krakow, Shanghai, and Tulsa....

Moffat and his colleagues also have used their manufacturing experience to keep track of IBM's far-flung employees. Just as every component used in an IBM computer is described in detail on inventory and planning documents, new databases contain profiles of employees that list their capabilities and their up-to-the-minute availability. Yet while a computer part doesn't change over time, people do. So the databases can be continuously updated by employees and their managers as employees gain skills and experience.

Before, project managers assembled teams largely made up of people they had worked with. But as IBM expanded around the globe, managers found it harder to pull teams together. Now project managers post detailed requests in one of the databases called Professional Marketplace that lists more than 170,000 employees along with their skills, pay rate, and availability. Other managers monitor the database and serve as matchmakers between jobs and people. The databases have shaved 20% from the average time it takes to assemble a team and have saved IBM $500 million overall.

By sifting through several personnel databases with sophisticated software, IBM's top managers can quantify the skills they have on hand worldwide and compare them with projections of what people they'll need in 6 to 9 months. When they spot a coming shortfall, managers coordinate with colleagues in other countries to recruit or train people....

IBM Brazil is a true microcosm of the enterprise. In 5 years the workforce has grown from 4,000 to 13,000 people, many of them based in Hortolandia, Brazil's Silicon Valley, about a 90-minute drive from São Paulo. Employees fly the national flags of their clients on their cubicles. Walk down the aisles and you'll hear English, French, Portuguese, and Spanish spoken. Salaries are about half of what IBM pays in the United States for similar work.

While most of the management team in Brazil is local, IBM mixes in people from other countries to hasten the global integration process. One such "assignee" is American Robert Payne, a 22-year IBM executive who runs part of the tech services organization in Brazil. Payne, 48, immerses himself in the cultures of the countries where he's assigned. He learned Japanese for his Tokyo gig. When he arrived in Brazil 3 years ago, he promised to conduct all of his meetings in Portuguese within 9 months. And he did....

Payne and other senior executives know that operating globally requires a great deal of hands-on management. In the old days at IBM, projects often were born and died within a single office building in New York State. These days, they're broken into pieces and farmed out to small teams worldwide. . . .

One of the major challenges in this setup is the difficulty of communicating by e-mail or even videoconferencing when programmers have never met one another. Strangers don't readily share knowledge. "A big problem is trust," says Dirk Wittkopp, director of IBM's Boeblingen lab. "It works better if you can go out to dinner with somebody and have a beer. But we can't put people on planes to visit each other all the time."

So Big Blue is trying to bridge the gap with software that borrows heavily from social networking. A new program called Beehive is essentially a corporate version of Facebook. IBM employees create profiles and post photos, list their interests, and comment about company events or happenings in their private lives.

For Discussion

1. Which of the recommendations listed in the Manager's Toolbox were used by Robert Payne? Explain.

2. Based on material contained in this chapter, why do you believe IBM is trying to create a "globally integrated enterprise"? Discuss.

3. To what extent is IBM following an ethnocentric, polycentric, and geocentric approach? Provide examples to support your conclusions.

4. What role is technology playing in IBM's efforts to create a global workforce? Explain.

5. What are the most important lessons to be learned about global management from this case? Discuss.

Source: From Steve Hamm, "International Isn't Just IBM's First Name," *BusinessWeek,* January 28, 2008, pp. 36–40. Reprinted with permission.

Self-Assessment

How Well Are You Suited to Becoming a Global Manager?

Objectives

1. To see if you are ready to be a global manager.
2. To help you assess your comfort level with other cultures.

Introduction

As our business world becomes increasingly globalized, U.S. companies need more managers to work in other countries. This usually means vast adjustments for the manager and her or his family during this job assignment. Flexibility is critical as is the ability to adjust to new ways, new people, new foods, different nonverbal communication, a new language, and a host of other new things.

Before agreeing to such an assignment, you need to know more about yourself and how you function in such situations.

Instructions

Are you prepared to be a global manager? Rate the extent to which you agree with each of the following 14 items by circling your response on the rating scale shown below. If you do not have direct experience with a particular situation (for example, working with people from other cultures), respond by circling how you *think* you would feel.

1 = Very strongly disagree
2 = Strongly disagree
3 = Disagree
4 = Neither agree nor disagree
5 = Agree
6 = Strongly agree
7 = Very strongly agree

1. When working with people from other cultures, I work hard to understand their perspectives.	1	2	3	4	5	6	7
2. I have a solid understanding of my organization's products and services.	1	2	3	4	5	6	7
3. I am willing to take a stand on issues.	1	2	3	4	5	6	7
4. I have a special talent for dealing with people.	1	2	3	4	5	6	7
5. I can be depended on to tell the truth regardless of circumstances.	1	2	3	4	5	6	7
6. I am good at identifying the most important part of a complex problem or issue.	1	2	3	4	5	6	7
7. I clearly demonstrate commitment to seeing the organization succeed.	1	2	3	4	5	6	7
8. I take personal as well as business risks.	1	2	3	4	5	6	7
9. I have changed as a result of feedback from others.	1	2	3	4	5	6	7
10. I enjoy the challenge of working in countries other than my own.	1	2	3	4	5	6	7
11. I take advantage of opportunities to do new things.	1	2	3	4	5	6	7
12. I find criticism hard to take.	1	2	3	4	5	6	7
13. I seek feedback even when others are reluctant to give it.	1	2	3	4	5	6	7
14. I don't get so invested in things that I cannot change when something doesn't work.	1	2	3	4	5	6	7

Interpretation

This exercise assesses factors associated with being a successful global manager. These factors include general intelligence, business knowledge, interpersonal skills, commitment, courage, cross-cultural competencies, and the ability to learn from experience.

Total your scores, which will fall between 14 and 98. The higher your score, the greater your potential for success as an international manager.

Arbitrary Norms

High Potential for Success	70–98
Moderate Potential for Success	40–69
Low Potential for Success	39 and below

Questions for Discussion

1. What do the results suggest about your preparedness to be a global manager? Do you agree with these results?

2. How comfortable would you be going to another country at this time in your life?

3. How have your experiences as a citizen of a very diverse nation helped you to understand the other cultures of the world?

4. How might you improve your preparedness to one day assume an international position? Explain.

Modified and adapted from G. M. Spreitzer, M. W. McCall Jr., and J. D. Mahoney, "Early Identification of International Executive Potential," *Journal of Applied Psychology*, February 1997, pp. 6–29.

Chiquita Brands International Discloses Payments to Colombian Terrorists

Assume that you are on a grand jury in the United States and you are debating whether to file charges against Roderick Hills, former head of Chiquita Brands International Inc.'s audit committee and former chairman of the Securities and Exchange Commission.

The case involves payments that the company made to a violent Colombian group that has been determined to be a terrorist group by the U.S. government. Mr. Hills was in charge of the company's audit committee during the time of the payments. The facts of the case indicate that "a paramilitary organization had threatened to kidnap or kill employees on the banana farms of Chiquita's Colombian subsidiary, Banadex, and Chiquita was concerned that its employees could be harmed if it cut the payments immediately." Mr. Hills and other executives viewed the expense payments as "security payments" that were saving employees' lives. "Lawyers familiar with the case say Mr. Hills and Mr. Olson [former general counsel] believe senior Justice Department officials understood this and were deferring any demand to stop the payments to the United Self-Defense Forces, known by its Spanish abbreviation AUC. Chiquita ultimately paid $1.7 million over seven years." Chiquita never hid the payments from its accountants or Ernst & Young, its auditor.

Solving the Dilemma

What would you do given the current situation?

1. Charge Mr. Hills. He knew that it was against U.S. policy to have dealings with terrorist organizations.

2. Fine the company $25 million. The company should have folded its operations in Colombia rather than make payments to a terrorist organization.

3. Don't charge Mr. Hills. He was trying to protect his employees' lives and he fully disclosed the company's actions to U.S. authorities.

4. Invent other options.

Source: Based on L. P. Cohen, "Chiquita Under the Gun," *The Wall Street Journal*, August 2, 2007, pp. A1, A9.

Planning
The Foundation of Successful Management

Major Questions You Should Be Able to Answer

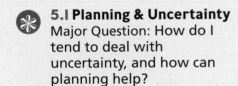 **5.1 Planning & Uncertainty**
Major Question: How do I tend to deal with uncertainty, and how can planning help?

5.2 Fundamentals of Planning
Major Question: What are mission and vision statements, and what are three types of planning and goals?

5.3 Promoting Goal Setting: Management by Objectives & SMART Goals
Major Question: What is MBO and how can it be implemented, and what are SMART goals?

5.4 The Planning/Control Cycle
Major Question: How does the planning/control cycle help keep a manager's plans headed in the right direction?

5.5 Project Planning
Major Question: What is project planning, why is it important, and what is the project life cycle?

Planning Different Career Paths: "It's a Career, Not a Job"

The purpose of planning is to help deal with uncertainty, both for the organization and for your individual career.

Do you have a sense of where you're going? No doubt what you're looking for is something about which you can say, "It's not just a job, it's a career." Your *career path* is the sequence of jobs and occupations you follow during your career.

Michael J. Driver has suggested there are different possible career paths, among them the *linear career, the steady-state career,* and the *spiral career.*[1]

- **The linear career: climbing the stairs.** The *linear career* resembles the traditional view of climbing the stairs in an organization's hierarchy. That is, you move up the organization in a series of jobs—generally in just one functional area, such as finance—each of which entails more responsibility and requires more skills.

  Of course, it's possible that a linear career will *plateau.* That is, you'll rise to a certain level and then remain there; there will be no further promotions. Career plateaus actually happen a lot and need not signify disgrace; they happen even to very successful managers.

  Another possibility, of course, is the *declining career,* in which a person reaches a certain level and then after a time begins descending back to the lower levels. This could come about, for instance, because technology changes the industry you're in.

- **The steady-state career: staying put.** The *steady-state career* is almost the opposite of a linear career: You discover early in life that you're comfortable with a certain occupation and you stay with it. Or you accept a promotion for a while, decide you don't like the responsibility, and take a step down.

This kind of career is actually fairly commonplace: Sales representatives, computer programmers, or physicians, for example, may decide they are happy being "hands-on" professionals rather than managers.

- **The spiral career: holding different jobs that build on one another.** The *spiral career* is, like the linear career, upwardly mobile. However, on this career path, you would have a number of jobs that are fundamentally different yet still build on one another, giving you more general experience and the skills to advance in rank and status.

  Of course, it's possible that you might (like some salespeople, actors, chefs, or construction workers) favor a variant called the *transitory career.* That is, you're the kind of person who doesn't want the responsibility that comes with promotion. You're a free spirit who likes the variety of experience that comes with continually shifting sideways from job to job or place to place (or you're afraid of making the commitment to doing any one thing).

  A variant is what is known as "portfolio careers" or "slash careers," in which a person puts together a portfolio of careers comprising multiple part-time jobs that, when combined, are equivalent to a full-time position, such as pilates instructor/art dealer, attorney/minister, teacher/dancer/puppeteer.[2] And then, of course, there are those who change their professions entirely, perhaps by switching departments within their companies or by going back to school and retraining for something else.[3]

For Discussion   What kind of career path do you think you're apt to follow? How are you planning for it?

forecast

What's Ahead in This Chapter

In this chapter, we describe planning, the first of the four management functions. We consider the benefits of planning and how it helps you deal with uncertainty. We deal with the fundamentals of planning, including the mission and vision statements and the three types of planning—strategic, tactical, and operational. We consider goals and action plans, management by objectives (MBO), SMART goals, and the planning/control cycle. We then consider project planning.

> **major question ?**
>
> How do I tend to deal with uncertainty, and how can planning help?

THE BIG PICTURE

Planning, the first of four functions in the management process, involves setting goals and deciding how to achieve them. Planning helps you check your progress, coordinate activities, think ahead, and cope with uncertainty. Uncertainty is of three types—state, effect, and response. Organizations respond to uncertainty in various ways.

What is known as the *management process,* you'll recall (from Chapter 1, p. 13), involves the four management functions of *planning, organizing, leading,* and *controlling,* which form four of the part divisions of this book. In this and the next two chapters we discuss *planning,* **which we previously defined as setting goals and deciding how to achieve them.** Another definition: *Planning* **is coping with uncertainty by formulating future courses of action to achieve specified results.**[4] When you make a plan, you make a blueprint for action that describes what you need to do to realize your goals.

Planning & Strategic Management

Planning, which we discuss in this chapter, is used in conjunction with strategic management, as we describe in Chapter 6. As we will see, strategic management is a process that involves managers from all parts of the organization—top managers, middle managers, and first-line managers—in the formulation, implementation, and execution of strategies and strategic goals to advance the purposes of the organization. Thus, planning covers not only strategic planning (done by top managers) but also tactical planning (done by middle managers) and operational planning (done by first-line managers). Planning and strategic management derive from an organization's mission and vision about itself, as we describe in the next few pages. *(See Figure 5.1.)*

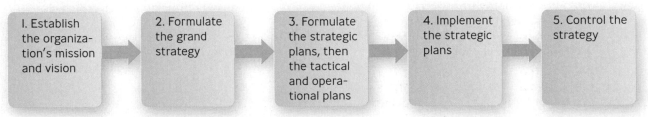

| I. Establish the organization's mission and vision | 2. Formulate the grand strategy | 3. Formulate the strategic plans, then the tactical and operational plans | 4. Implement the strategic plans | 5. Control the strategy |

figure 5.I

PLANNING AND STRATEGIC MANAGEMENT

The details of planning and strategic management are explained in Chapters 5 and 6.

Why Not Plan?

On the face of it, planning would seem to be a good idea—otherwise we would not be devoting three chapters to the subject. But there are two cautions to be aware of:

I. Planning Requires You to Set Aside the Time to Do It Time-starved managers may be quite resentful when superiors order them to prepare a 5-year plan for their work unit.

"What?" they may grouse. "They expect me to do that and *still* find time to meet this year's goals?" Somehow, though, that time for planning must be found. Otherwise, managers are mainly just reacting to events.

Planning means that you must involve the subordinates you manage to determine resources, opportunities, and goals. During the process, you may need to go outside the work unit for information about products, competitors, markets, and the like.

2. You May Have to Make Some Decisions without a Lot of Time to Plan In our time of Internet connections and speedy-access computer databases, can't nearly anyone lay hands on facts quickly to make an intelligent decision? Not always. A competitor may quickly enter your market with a highly desirable product. A change in buying habits may occur. A consumer boycott may suddenly surface. An important supplier may let you down. The caliber of employees you need may not be immediately available at the salary level you're willing to pay. And in any one of these you won't have the time to plan a decision based on all the facts.

Nevertheless, a plan need not be perfect to be executable. While you shouldn't shoot from the hip in making decisions, often you may have to "go with what you've got" and make a decision based on a plan that is perhaps only three-quarters complete.

How Planning Helps You: Four Benefits

You can always hope you'll luck out or muddle through the next time a hurricane, earthquake, tornado, or other natural disaster strikes your area. Or you can plan for it by stocking up on flashlight batteries and canned food. Which is better? The same consideration applies when you're a manager. Some day, after you've dealt with some crisis, you will be very happy that you had a plan for handling it. The benefits of planning are fourfold:

I. Planning Helps You Check on Your Progress The preprinted score card that golfers use when playing 18 holes of golf isn't blank. For each hole, the card lists the standard number of strokes ("par"), such as three or five, that a good player should take to hit the ball from the tee to the cup. The score card is the plan for the game, with objectives for each hole. After you play the hole, you write your own score in a blank space. At the end of the 18 holes, you add all your scores to see how you performed compared to the standard for the course.

What's the score? Like a golf score card, planning helps you check on your progress.

How well is your work going in an organization? You won't know unless you have some way of checking your progress. That's why, like a golfer, you need to have some expectations of what you're supposed to do—in other words, a plan.

2. Planning Helps You Coordinate Activities "The right hand doesn't know what the left hand is doing!"

We may hear that expression used, for example, when a crisis occurs and an organization's public relations department, legal department, and CEO's office all give the press separate, contradictory statements. Obviously, such an embarrassment can be avoided if the organization has a plan for dealing with the media during emergencies. A plan defines the responsibilities of various departments and coordinates their activities for the achievement of common goals—such as, at minimum, making an organization not look confused and disorganized.

3. Planning Helps You Think Ahead   Robert Nardelli, CEO of Chrysler, is making big plans to help the company overcome its poor financial performance over the last few years. He intends to expand international sales by increasing the amount of development work done at engineering centers in China, Mexico, India, and Eastern Europe. Looking into the future to try to plan for what might be the next big change in automotive products, he also plans to create a new engineering group that will focus on creating hybrids and electric cars.[5]

Similarly, as we describe under product life cycle (Chapter 6), the service or product with which you're engaged will probably at some point reach maturity, and sales will begin to falter. Thus, you need to look ahead, beyond your present phase of work, to try to be sure you'll be one of the quick rather than one of the dead.

4. Above All, Planning Helps You Cope with Uncertainty   You don't care for unpleasant surprises? Most people don't. (Pleasant surprises, of course, are invariably welcome.) That's why trying to plan for unpleasant contingencies is necessary (as we'll describe in Chapter 6). Planning helps you deal with uncertainty.

How Organizations Respond to Uncertainty

How do you personally respond to uncertainty? Do you react slowly? conservatively? proactively? Do you watch to see what others do? Organizations act in similar ways.

Four Basic Strategy Types   Scholars **Raymond E. Miles** and **Charles C. Snow** suggest that organizations adopt one of four approaches when responding to uncertainty in their environment. They become *Defenders, Prospectors, Analyzers,* or *Reactors.*[6]

Defenders—"Let's Stick with What We Do Best, Avoid Other Involvements"   Whenever you hear an organization's leader say that "We're sticking with the basics" or "We're getting back to our core business," that's the hallmark of a Defender organization. *Defenders* **are expert at producing and selling narrowly defined products or services.** Often they are old-line successful enterprises—such as Harley-Davidson motorcycles or Brooks Brothers clothiers—with a narrow focus. They do not tend to seek opportunities outside their present markets. They devote most of their attention to making refinements in their existing operations.

Prospectors—"Let's Create Our Own Opportunities, Not Wait for Them to Happen"   A company described as "aggressive" is often a Prospector organization. *Prospectors* **focus on developing new products or services and in seeking out new markets, rather than waiting for things to happen.** Like 19th-century gold miners, these companies are "prospecting" for new ways of doing things.

Edgy alternative. Using big black cans adorned with neon-colored claw marks, the high-caffeine, high-sugar Monster Energy drinks from Hansen Natural Corporation are positioned to compete as alternatives to Red Bull in the fast-growing energy drink market. What strategy type is being followed here?

The continual product and market innovation has a price: Such companies may suffer a loss of efficiency. Nevertheless, their focus on change can put fear in the hearts of competitors.

Analyzers—"Let Others Take the Risks of Innovating, & We'll Imitate What Works Best" Analyzers take a "me too" response to the world. By and large, you won't find them called "trendsetters." Rather, **Analyzers let other organizations take the risks of product development and marketing and then imitate (or perhaps slightly improve on) what seems to work best.**

Reactors—"Let's Wait Until There's a Crisis, Then We'll React" Whereas the Prospector is aggressive and proactive, the Reactor is the opposite—passive and reactive. **Reactors make adjustments only when finally forced to by environmental pressures.** In the worst cases, they are so incapable of responding fast enough that they suffer massive sales losses and are even driven out of business. Kmart, for instance, failed to respond to Wal-Mart's development of its distribution and inventory management competencies, resulting in stalled growth and a significant reduction in market share. Kmart's core business never recovered from this reactive strategy.[7]

The Adaptive Cycle Miles and Snow also introduced the idea of the *adaptive cycle,* which portrays businesses as continuously cycling through decisions about three kinds of business problems: (1) *entrepreneurial* (selecting and making adjustments of products and markets), (2) *engineering* (producing and delivering the products), and (3) *administrative* (establishing roles, relationships, and organizational processes).

Thus, a business that makes decisions in the entrepreneurial area that take it in the direction of being a Prospector will in a short time also begin making Prospector-oriented decisions in the engineering area, then the administrative area, and then even more so in the entrepreneurial area, and so on. Thus, as one scholar points out, "With enough cycles and insight, a given business becomes a very good, comprehensively aligned Prospector, Analyzer, or Defender. If a business lacks insight, or if it fails to take advantage of alignment opportunities afforded by the adaptive cycle, it will be an incongruent, poorly performing Reactor."[8] ●

What are mission and vision statements, and what are three types of planning and goals?

THE BIG PICTURE

Planning consists of translating an organization's mission into objectives. The organization's purpose is expressed as a mission statement, and what it becomes is expressed as a vision statement. From these are derived strategic planning, then tactical planning, then operational planning.

"Everyone wants a clear reason to get up in the morning," writes journalist Dick Leider. "As humans we hunger for meaning and purpose in our lives."[9]

And what is that purpose? "Life never lacks purpose," says Leider. "Purpose is innate—but it is up to each of us individually to discover or rediscover it."

An organization has a purpose, too—a mission. And managers must have an idea of where they want the organization to go—a vision. The approach to planning can be summarized in the following diagram, which shows how an organization's mission becomes translated into objectives. *(See Figure 5.2.)*

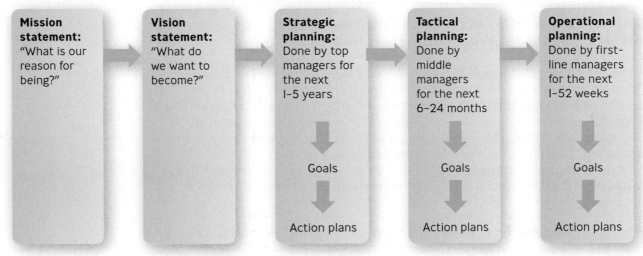

Mission statement:
"What is our reason for being?"

Vision statement:
"What do we want to become?"

Strategic planning:
Done by top managers for the next 1–5 years
↓
Goals
↓
Action plans

Tactical planning:
Done by middle managers for the next 6–24 months
↓
Goals
↓
Action plans

Operational planning:
Done by first-line managers for the next 1–52 weeks
↓
Goals
↓
Action plans

figure 5.2

MAKING PLANS

An organization's reason for being is expressed in a *mission statement.* What the organization wishes to become is expressed in a *vision statement.* From these are derived *strategic planning,* then *tactical planning,* and finally *operational planning.* The purpose of each kind of planning is to specify *goals* and *action plans* for accomplishing those goals.

Mission & Vision Statements

The planning process begins with two attributes: a mission statement (which answers the question "What is our reason for being?") and a vision statement (which answers the question "What do we want to become?").

The Mission Statement—"What Is Our Reason for Being?" An organization's *mission* is its purpose or reason for being. Determining the mission is the responsibility of top management and the board of directors. It is up to them to formulate a *mission statement*, which expresses the purpose of the organization.

"Only a clear definition of the mission and purpose of the organization makes possible clear and realistic . . . objectives," said Peter Drucker.[10] Whether the organization is for-profit or nonprofit, the mission statement identifies the goods or services the organization provides and will provide, and the reasons for providing them (to make a profit or to achieve humanitarian goals, for example).

Intel's mission statement:

Do a great job for our customers, employees, and stockholders by being the preeminent building block supplier to the worldwide Internet economy.

Example

Mission Statements for Small & Large Firms: Nest Fresh Eggs & Amazon.Com

Mission statements answer the question, "What is our reason for being?" or "Why are we here?"

Here is the mission statement for a small firm, Nest Fresh Eggs, a Colorado-based family business that produces eggs from free-range hens: "Nest Fresh Eggs' mission is to remain profitable by producing or purchasing premium cage-free and natural eggs to supply supermarkets and restaurants in its markets, providing those customers with excellent service and product and by being an environmentally responsible corporate citizen by using recyclable packaging and donating to targeted charities."[11]

Here is the mission statement for a large firm, Amazon.com: "[Our mission is to] use the Internet to offer products that educate, inform, and inspire. We decided to build an online store that would be customer friendly and easy to navigate and would offer the broadest possible selection."[12] Another part of the mission: "We believe that a fundamental measure of our success will be the shareholder value we create over the *long term*. This value will be a direct result of our ability to extend and solidify our current market leadership position. . . . Market leadership can translate directly to higher revenue, higher profitability. . . ."[13]

Your Call

Do you think either of these mission statements could be adapted to different companies offering different products or services? Give an example.

The Vision Statement—"What Do We Want to Become?" A *vision* is a long-term goal describing "what" an organization wants to become. It is a clear sense of the future and the actions needed to get there. "[A] vision should describe what's happening to the world you compete in and what you want to do about it," says one *Fortune* article. "It should guide decisions."[14]

Before Roger Enrico moved up to CEO of PepsiCo, the company thrived on "big-idea, renegade thinking," according to one report.[15] The problem was that the culture of autonomous business units led to decentralized control and managers who "were ricocheting off each other in search of their next promotion, or chasing new restaurant chains or joint ventures in far-flung parts of the world." Because Enrico had a clear sense of the future and the actions needed to get there—that is, a vision—he recentralized control and offered managers compensation schemes to encourage them to get their present jobs done rather than look for the next one.

After formulating a mission statement, top managers need to develop a *vision statement*, which expresses what the organization should become, where it wants to go strategically.[16]

Example

Vision Statements for Small & Large Firms: Nest Fresh Eggs & Amazon.Com

amazon.com.

Courtesy of Amazon.com.

Vision statements answer the question, "What do we want to become?" or "Where do we want to go?"

Here is Nest Fresh Eggs' small-firm vision statement: "Nest Fresh Eggs' vision is to influence the way the public views egg production in the U.S., to make it more economically feasible to reduce the number of hens in battery-caged facilities and/or to decrease cage density, and to create opportunities for small farmers to continue farming."[17]

Amazon.com started out selling books, but its vision goes far beyond books: "Our vision is to be earth's most customer-centric company; to build a place where people can come to find and discover anything they might want to buy online."[18]

Your Call

Do you think these vision statements meet *Fortune*'s criterion of describing "what's happening in the world you compete in and what you want to do about it. It should guide decisions"?

Three Types of Planning for Three Levels of Management: Strategic, Tactical, & Operational

Inspiring, clearly stated mission statements and vision statements provide the focal point of the entire planning process. Then three things happen:

- *Strategic planning by top management.* Using their mission and vision statements, top managers do *strategic planning*—**they determine what the organization's long-term goals should be for the next 1–5 years with the resources they expect to have available.** "Strategic planning requires visionary and directional thinking," says one authority.[19] It should communicate not only general goals about growth and profits but also ways to achieve them.

- *Tactical planning by middle management.* The strategic priorities and policies are then passed down to middle managers, who must do *tactical planning*—**that is, they determine what contributions their departments or similar work units can make with their given resources during the next 6–24 months.**

- *Operational planning by first-line management.* Middle managers then pass these plans along to first-line managers to do *operational planning*—**that is, they determine how to accomplish specific tasks with available resources within the next 1–52 weeks.**

The kinds of managers are described further in the figure on the page opposite. *(See Figure 5.3.)*

It is one thing to formulate a vision statement, however, and another to find concrete methods to manage and measure the performance that makes the vision a reality. One survey found that 73% of organizations said they had a clearly articulated strategic direction, but only 44% of them said they were able to communicate it well to the employees who must implement it.[20]

Goals, Action Plans, & Operating Plans

Whatever its type—strategic, tactical, or operational—the purpose of planning is to set a *goal* and then to formulate an *action plan*.

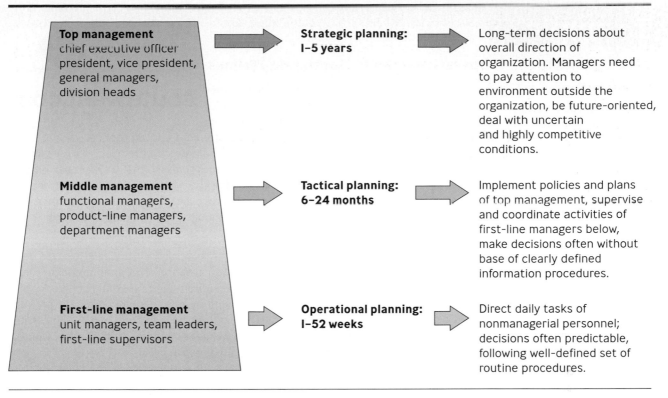

figure 5.3

THREE LEVELS OF MANAGEMENT, THREE TYPES OF PLANNING
Each type of planning has different time horizons, although the times overlap because the plans are somewhat elastic.

Goals   A *goal,* also known as an *objective,* is a specific commitment to achieve a measurable result within a stated period of time.

As with planning, goals are of the same three types—strategic, tactical, and operational. Also, like planning, goals are arranged in a hierarchy known as a *means-end chain* because in the chain of management (operational, tactical, strategic) the accomplishment of low-level goals is the means leading to the accomplishment of high-level goals or ends.

- *Strategic goals* are set by and for top management and focus on objectives for the organization as a whole.
- *Tactical goals* are set by and for middle managers and focus on the actions needed to achieve strategic goals.
- *Operational goals* are set by and for first-line managers and are concerned with short-term matters associated with realizing tactical goals.

The Action Plan & the Operating Plan   The goal should be followed by an *action plan,* which defines the course of action needed to achieve the stated goal, such as a marketing plan or sales plan. The *operating plan,* which is typically designed for a 1-year period, defines how you will conduct your business based on the action plan; it identifies clear targets such as revenues, cash flow, and market share.

Example

Strategic, Tactical, & Operational Goals: Southwest Airlines

Courtesy of Southwest Airlines.

Strategic Goals

The goal of top managers of Dallas-based Southwest Airlines is to ensure that the airline is highly profitable, following the general strategy of (a) keeping costs and fares down and (b) offering a superior on-time arrival record. One of the most important strategic decisions Southwest made was to fly just one type of airplane—Boeing 737s. (The fleet has 523 jets.) Thus, it is able to hold down training, maintenance, and operating expenses.[21] As of this writing, the airline is achieving its strategic goals: By the end of 2007, it had made money for 35 consecutive years. It has continually lowered its costs, and it leads the industry in on-time performance.[22] Another strategic decision was to create a strong corporate culture that, according to one former CEO, allows people to "feel like they're using their brains, they're using their creativity, they're allowed to be themselves and have a sense of humor, and they understand what the mission of the company is."[23]

Tactical Goals

Cutting costs and keeping fares low is a key tactical goal for Southwest's middle managers. For example, the organization cut costs in its maintenance program by doing more work on a plane when it's in for a check instead of bringing it in three different times. In addition, it gets more use out of its planes every day by limiting the turnaround time between flights to 20 minutes, compared to up to an hour for other airlines. Southwest also usually flies to less-congested airports, thus saving time and money by avoiding traffic. There is just one class of seating, doing away with the distinction between coach and first class. Even the boarding passes are reusable, being made of plastic. Finally, the airline saves by not feeding passengers: it serves mostly peanuts, no in-flight meals.

How do you make arrival times more reliable? To achieve this second tactical goal, middle managers did away with guaranteed seat reservations before ticketing, so that no-shows won't complicate (and therefore delay) the boarding process. (It changed that policy in 2007 to ensure that passengers paying extra for "business select" fares would be placed at the front of the line.)[24] In addition, as mentioned, the airline is religious about turning planes around in exactly 20 minutes, so that on-time departures are more apt to produce on-time arrivals. Although the airline is unionized, turnaround is helped by looser work rules, so that workers can pitch in to do tasks outside their normal jobs. "If you saw something that needed to be done," said one former employee, "and you thought you could do it, you did."[25]

Operational Goals

Consider how Southwest's first-line managers can enhance productivity in the unloading, refueling, and cleaning of arriving planes. "One example [of productivity] customers mention all the time," said former chairman Herb Kelleher, "is if you look out the window when the airplane is taxiing toward the jetway, you see our ground crews charging before the airplane has even come to rest. Customers tell me that with other airlines nobody moves until the airplane has turned off its engines."[26]

First-line managers also make sure that seat assignments (boarding passes) are not given out until an hour before the plane is due to leave to make sure that the maximum number of passengers will be on hand to fill the seats available.

Your Call

Southwest has inspired a host of low-fare imitators, such as JetBlue and AirTran, and it was expected to be the only one of the 10 largest U.S. airlines in 2008 that would not lose money.[27] Early in that year, however, the Federal Aviation Administration proposed to fine the airline $10.2 million—the largest in aviation history—for failing to immediately ground 46 aging planes in the 2 previous years to inspect them for fuselage cracks and for continuing to fly them after acknowledging the event. A congressional committee cited chronic problems in Southwest's oversight of inspection programs and a "cozy relationship" between maintenance officials and FAA inspectors (one of whom had been less than rigorous in enforcing FAA rules).[28] Southwest has since addressed the problem. Do you think this incident points to any flaws in the airline's goal setting?

Types of Plans: Standing Plans & Single-Use Plans

Plans are of two types—*standing plans* and *single-use plans. (See Table 5.1.)*

Plan	Description
Standing plan	For activities that occur repeatedly over a period of time
• Policy	Outlines general response to a designated problem or situation
• Procedure	Outlines response to particular problems or circumstances
• Rule	Designates specific required action
Single-use plan	For activities not likely to be repeated in the future
• Program	Encompasses a range of projects or activities
• Project	Has less scope and complexity than a program

table 5.1

STANDING PLANS AND SINGLE-USE PLANS

There are three types of standing plans and two types of single-use plans.

Standing Plans: Policies, Procedures, & Rules *Standing plans* **are plans developed for activities that occur repeatedly over a period of time.** Standing plans consist of policies, procedures, and rules.

- **A** *policy* **is a standing plan that outlines the general response to a designated problem or situation.** Example: "This workplace does not condone swearing." This policy is a broad statement that gives managers a general idea about what is allowable for employees who use bad language, but gives no specifics.

- **A** *procedure* **(or** *standard operating procedure***) is a standing plan that outlines the response to particular problems or circumstances.** Example: McDonald's specifies exactly how a hamburger should be dressed, including the order in which the mustard, ketchup, and pickles are applied.

- **A** *rule* **is a standing plan that designates specific required action.** Example: "No smoking is allowed anywhere in the building." This allows no room for interpretation.

Single-Use Plans: Programs & Projects *Single-use plans* **are plans developed for activities that are not likely to be repeated in the future.** Such plans can be programs or projects.

- **A** *program* **is a single-use plan encompassing a range of projects or activities.** Example: The U.S. government space *program* has several projects, including the *Challenger* project and the Hubble Telescope project.

- **A** *project* **is a single-use plan of less scope and complexity than a program.** Example: The space shuttle *Discovery* is one project in the government's space program. ●

5.3 PROMOTING GOAL SETTING: MANAGEMENT BY OBJECTIVES & SMART GOALS

major question? What is MBO and how can it be implemented, and what are SMART goals?

THE BIG PICTURE

A technique for setting goals, management by objectives (MBO) is a four-step process for motivating employees. Goals should be SMART—Specific, Measurable, Attainable, Results-oriented, and have Target dates.

Do you perform better when you set goals or when you don't? What about when you set difficult goals rather than easy ones?

Research shows that if goals are made more difficult ("increase study time 30%"), people may achieve them less often than they would easy goals ("increase study time 5%"), but they nevertheless perform at a higher level. People also do better when the objectives are specific ("increase study time 10 hours a week") rather than general ("do more studying this semester").[29]

These are the kinds of matters addressed in the activity known as *management by objectives.* First suggested by **Peter Drucker** in 1954, MBO has spread largely because of the appeal of its emphasis on converting general objectives into specific ones for all members of an organization.[30]

What Is MBO? The Four-Step Process for Motivating Employees

Management by objectives (MBO) **is a four-step process in which (1) managers and employees jointly set objectives for the employee, (2) managers develop action plans, (3) managers and employees periodically review the employee's performance, and (4) the manager makes a performance appraisal and rewards the employee according to results.** The purpose of MBO is to *motivate* rather than control subordinates. Let's consider the four steps.

1. Jointly Set Objectives   You sit down with your manager and the two of you jointly set objectives for you to attain. Later you do the same with each of your own subordinates. Joint manager/subordinate participation is important to the program. It's probably best if the objectives aren't simply imposed from above ("Here are the objectives I want you to meet"). Managers also should not simply approve the employee's objectives ("Whatever you aim for is okay with me"). It's necessary to have back-and-forth negotiation to make the objectives practicable. One result of joint participation, research shows, is that it impels people to set more difficult goals—to raise the level of their aspirations—which may have a positive effect on their performance.[31] The objectives should be expressed in writing and should be SMART, as we'll explain. There are three types of objectives, shown on the page opposite. *(See Table 5.2.)*

2. Develop Action Plan   Once objectives are set, managers at each level should prepare an action plan for attaining them. Action plans may be prepared for both individuals and for work units, such as departments.

table 5.2

THREE TYPES OF OBJECTIVES
USED IN MBO

Improvement Objectives

Purpose Express performance to be accomplished in a specific way for a specific area
Examples "Increase sport-utility sales by 10%." "Reduce food spoilage by 15%."

Personal development objectives

Purpose Express personal goals to be realized
Examples "Attend 5 days of leadership training." "Learn basics of Microsoft Office software by June 1."

Maintenance objectives

Purpose Express the intention to maintain performance at previously established levels
Examples "Continue to meet the increased sales goals specified last quarter." "Produce another 60,000 cases of wine this month."

3. Periodically Review Performance   You and your manager should meet reasonably often—either informally as needed or formally every 3 months—to review progress, as should you and your subordinates. Indeed, frequent communication is necessary so that everyone will know how well he or she is doing in meeting the objectives.

During each meeting, managers should give employees feedback, and objectives should be updated or revised as necessary to reflect new realities. If you were managing a painting or landscaping business, for example, changes in the weather, loss of key employees, or a financial downturn affecting customer spending could force you to reconsider your objectives.

4. Give Performance Appraisal & Rewards, If Any   At the end of 6 or 12 months, you and your subordinate should meet to discuss results, comparing performance with initial objectives. *Deal with results,* not personalities, emotional issues, or excuses.

Because the purpose of MBO is to *motivate* employees, performance that meets the objectives should be rewarded—with compliments, raises, bonuses, promotions, or other suitable benefits. Failure can be addressed by redefining the objectives for the next 6- or 12-month period, or even by taking stronger measures, such as demotion. Basically, however, MBO is viewed as being a learning process. After step 4, the MBO cycle begins anew.[32]

Cascading Objectives: MBO from the Top Down

For MBO to be successful, three things have to happen:

1. Top Management Must Be Committed   "When top-management commitment [to MBO] was high," said one review, "the average gain in productivity was 56%. When commitment was low, the average gain in productivity was only 6%."[33]

2. It Must Be Applied Organizationwide   The program has to be put in place throughout the entire organization. That is, it cannot be applied in just some divisions and departments; it has to be done in all of them.

Setting Objectives: Wal-Mart's CEO Lays Out an Agenda for Change

Earlier (Chapter 3, Practical Action box) we described how Wal-Mart Stores enlisted the former head of the Sierra Club to help the giant retailer achieve sustainability. Tired of criticism of its business practices, Wal-Mart took this action as one of several initiatives to show that it is a leader in areas where it was once thought to be a laggard.

In a January 2008 speech, Wal-Mart CEO H. Lee Scott Jr. laid out new environmental, health, and ethical goals.[34] Besides continuing to promote energy-saving products at low prices in its stores, such as fluorescent light bulbs, Scott said the company would focus on additional products that use a large amount of energy, like air-conditioners, microwave ovens, and televisions, working with suppliers to make such products 25% more energy efficient within 3 years.

On health care, Scott said Wal-Mart would apply its legendary cost-cutting

Environmental objective: Saving energy by selling fluorescent light bulbs.

skills to helping other companies deliver health care for their employees. By working with major American employers to help them manage and pay prescription drug claims (an expensive task now handled by companies called pharmacy benefit managers), Wal-Mart hoped to save companies $100 million in 2008.

Scott also said Wal-Mart was committed to creating a more socially and environmentally conscious network of suppliers around the world, pressing suppliers in China, for instance, to comply with that country's environmental regulations. He also urged other major retailers to join a global network of retailers and consumer goods companies that is developing socially conscious manufacturing standards.

Your Call

How do the objectives outlined by CEO Scott reflect the criteria for MBO and SMART goals?

3. Objectives Must "Cascade" MBO works by *cascading* **objectives down through the organization; that is, objectives are structured in a *unified hierarchy*, becoming more specific at lower levels of the organization.** Top managers set general *organizational* objectives, which are translated into *divisional* objectives, which are translated into *departmental* objectives. The hierarchy ends in *individual* objectives set by each employee.

Setting SMART Goals

Anyone can define goals. But the five characteristics of a good goal are represented by the acronym SMART. **A *SMART goal* is one that is *S*pecific, *M*easurable, *A*ttainable, *R*esults-oriented, and has *T*arget dates.**

Specific Goals should be stated in *specific* rather than vague terms. The goal that "As many planes as possible should arrive on time" is too general. The goal that "Ninety percent of planes should arrive within 15 minutes of the scheduled arrival time" is specific.

Measurable Whenever possible, goals should be *measurable*, or quantifiable (as in "90% of planes should arrive within 15 minutes . . ."). That is, there should be some way to measure the degree to which a goal has been reached.

Of course, some goals—such as those concerned with improving quality—are not precisely quantifiable. In that case, something on the order of "Improve the quality of customer relations by instituting 10 follow-up telephone calls every week" will do. You can certainly quantify how many follow-up phone calls were made.

Attainable   Goals should be challenging, of course, but above all they should be realistic and *attainable*. It may be best to set goals that are quite ambitious so as to challenge people to meet high standards. Always, however, the goals should be achievable within the scope of the time, equipment, and financial support available. *(See Figure 5.4.)*

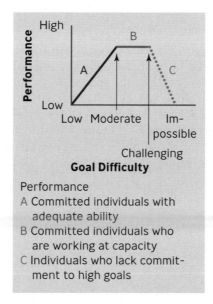

figure 5.4

RELATIONSHIP BETWEEN GOAL DIFFICULTY AND PERFORMANCE

Source: Adapted from E. A. Locke and G. P. Latham, *A Theory of Goal Setting and Task Performance* (Englewood Cliffs, NJ: Prentice Hall, 1990).

If too easy (as in "half the flights should arrive on time"), goals won't impel people to make much effort. If impossible ("all flights must arrive on time, regardless of weather"), employees won't even bother trying. Or they will try and continually fail, which will end up hurting morale.

Results-Oriented   Only a few goals should be chosen—say, five for any work unit. And they should be *results-oriented*—they should support the organization's vision.

In writing out the goals, start with the word "To" and follow it with action-oriented verbs—"complete," "acquire," "increase" ("to decrease by 10% the time to get passengers settled in their seats before departure").

Some verbs should not be used in your goal statement because they imply activities—the tactics used to accomplish goals (such as having baggage handlers waiting). For example, you should not use "to develop," "to conduct," "to implement."

Target Dates   Goals should specify the *target dates* or deadline dates when they are to be attained. For example, it's unrealistic to expect an airline to improve its on-time arrivals by 10% overnight. However, you could set a target date—3 to 6 months away, say—by which this goal is to be achieved. That allows enough time for lower-level managers and employees to revamp their systems and work habits and gives them a clear time frame in which they know what they are expected to do. ●

Group Exercise:
Using SMART Goals to Plan a Student Organization

5.4 THE PLANNING/CONTROL CYCLE

THE BIG PICTURE

The four-step planning/control cycle helps you keep in control, to make sure you're headed in the right direction.

Once you've made plans, how do you stay in control to make sure you're headed in the right direction? Actually, there is a continuous feedback loop known as the planning/control cycle. (The "organizing" and "leading" steps within the Planning-Organizing-Leading-Controlling sequence are implied here.) **The *planning/control cycle* has two planning steps (1 and 2) and two control steps (3 and 4), as follows: (1) Make the plan. (2) Carry out the plan. (3) Control the direction by comparing results with the plan. (4) Control the direction by taking corrective action in two ways— namely, (a) by correcting deviations in the plan being carried out, or (b) by improving future plans.** *(See Figure 5.5.)*

figure 5.5

THE PLANNING/CONTROL CYCLE

This describes a constant feedback loop designed to ensure plans stay headed in the right direction.

Source: From Robert Kreitner, *Management* 8th edition, Copyright © 2001 South-Western, a part of Cengage Learning, Inc. Reproduced with permission. www.cengage.com/permissions

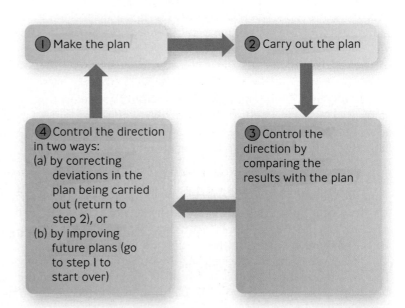

The Two Planning Steps

1. Make the plan
2. Carry out the plan

The Two Control Steps

4. Control the direction in two ways:
   (a) by correcting deviations in the plan being carried out (return to step 2), or
   (b) by improving future plans (go to step 1 to start over)

3. Control the direction by comparing the results with the plan

Test Your Knowledge:
Elements of Planning Process

The planning/control cycle loop exists for each level of planning—strategic, tactical, and operational. The corrective action in step 4 of the cycle (a) can get a project back on track before it's too late or (b) if it's too late, can provide data for improving future plans. ●

The Planning/Control Cycle: Apple Keeps Its Products Secret to Generate Buzz[35]

Most electronics and computer makers talk about their products well in advance of releasing them in order to give big customers and users a chance to prepare for them. Not Apple Inc., maker of the iPhone, iPod Touch, and MacBook Air and *Fortune*'s No. I Most Admired Company for 2008, as well as No. I among *Fortune* 500 companies for total return to shareholders over the past IO years. Secrecy is a big part of the company's marketing strategy. (Even when founder and CEO Steve Jobs was operated on for cancer, it was kept secret.) And the planning/control cycle figures closely in how well it is accomplished.

Step I: The Plan

About 60% of all personal computers are bought by corporate customers and other big technology purchasers. Because of the hefty investment involved, these customers favor suppliers that let them see major product plans a year in advance. However, Steve Jobs has determined that he favors selling technology directly to consumers rather than to corporate buyers and chief technology officers. By keeping a new product secret, Apple stimulates a great deal of public curiosity. "There's a great deal of mystery and speculation about what it will be," says one seasoned marketing executive. "That's created a marketing aura for them." Such was the plan, for example, when Apple and Hewlett-Packard made a deal to repackage Apple's iPod digital music player and sell it under the H-P label.

Step 2: Carrying Out the Plan

Following its plan to keep new products secret to generate marketing buzz, Apple often didn't tell H-P about new iPod models until the day before they were introduced to the public. It also insisted that H-P work on iPods under tight security, even though Apple's versions were already displayed on store shelves. The same has been true with other Apple products, with employees being sworn to secrecy for years. When, for example, the company decided to open its own chain of retail stores, an exact replica of a 6,000-square-foot store was built entirely inside a sealed-off warehouse away from Apple's main Cupertino, California, headquarters. When Apple decided to switch to Intel microprocessors, engineers worked on the project for 5 years under hush-hush conditions to adapt the Macintosh operating system to Intel chips.

Step 3: Comparing Results

The use of mystery "helps Apple attract crowds at its retail stores and generally garner much more visibility than its relatively modest advertising budget would suggest," says a *Wall Street Journal* story. "While new wares from Dell Inc. or H-P rarely get front-page treatment, Mr. Jobs has repeatedly appeared on the covers of *Time, Newsweek,* and *Fortune* showing off a new iPod or Macintosh computer." Secrecy has been a particular boon to Apple's fastest-growing product line, the iPod. Consumers have shown their willingness to abandon their old iPods in favor of newer ones that Apple unveils with great publicity and fanfare. On the negative side, Hewlett-Packard decided to terminate its iPod partnership with Apple, in part because of the secrecy issue.

Step 4: Taking Corrective Action

Leaks have occurred, and Apple has learned that secrecy requires strong measures. Thus, Apple has fired and later sued employees who leaked news about unannounced products. It has even sued Web sites that have published gossip about Apple products. The company also assigns different departments dissimilar code names for the same product, so it can more easily track where leaks come from. Employees are outfitted with special electronic badges that grant them access only to specific areas within the fortress-like Apple corporate headquarters.

Your Call

Can you think of a more effective way to generate consumer interest in a forthcoming product than just keeping it secret? What kind of planning/control cycle issues would it raise?

major
question?

What is project planning, why is it important, and what is the project life cyle?

THE BIG PICTURE

Project planning, designed to prepare single-use plans called projects, consists of a four-stage project life cycle: definition, planning, execution, and closing.

Manager's Hot Seat:
Project Management:
Steering the Committee

***Project planning** is the preparation of single-use plans, or projects.* Planning is followed by ***project management**, achieving a set of goals through planning, scheduling, and maintaining progress of the activities that comprise the project.*[36] The purpose of project planning and project management is to lower the risk of uncertainty in the execution of a project. As we will see, the heart of project planning is the four-stage project life cycle.

Why care about project planning? Because more and more, this is becoming the fastest way of getting things done. Technology has sped everything up, including the process of getting a new product or service to market.[37] The age of terrorism has also changed the way strategic planners must look at their companies' futures.[38] To complete specific projects quickly, companies will now draw together people with different skills to work together on a temporary basis, then disband once the job is done. Since project management works outside an organization's usual chain of command, project managers need to be adept at people skills, able to communicate, motivate, and negotiate (as we discuss in later chapters).

Project management has long been a standard way of operating for movie production companies, which will pull together a talented team of people to make a film, then disband when the picture is "wrapped." It's also a familiar approach for professional sports teams, construction companies, and even some types of legal teams. However, it is just beginning to be employed by other for-profit organizations, such as manufacturers and insurance companies, as well as nonprofit organizations, such as those in health care and education.

An example of project planning is the ***skunkworks**, the term given to a project team whose members are separated from the normal operation of an organization and asked to produce a new, innovative product.*

Example

Project Planning: Skunkworks Operate Outside the Rules

In the old *Li'l Abner* comic strip about hillbillies, the Skonk Works was the site of the bootleg brewing operation for moonshine (called Kickapoo Joy Juice). In a skunkworks, says futurist Alvin Toffler, "a team is handed a loosely specified problem or goal, given resources, and allowed to operate outside the normal company rules. The skunkworks group thus ignores both the cubbyholes and the official channels—that is,

the specialization and hierarchy of the existing corporate bureaucracy."[39]

In the 1960s through 1980s, Clarence "Kelly" Johnson managed Lockheed Aircraft's super-secret Advanced Development Projects Division facility—known as the Skunk Works—in Burbank, California, where under strict security some of the nation's most sophisticated aircraft, including the superfast Mach 3

SR-71 Blackbird, were developed. Among Johnson's basic operating rules were "The Skunk Works manager must be delegated practically complete control of his program in all respects" and "There must be a minimum number of reports required, but important work must be recorded thoroughly."

The computer industry has been particularly creative in employing the concept of the skunkworks. Racing to catch up with Apple Computer, which had been launched in 1976, International Business Machines launched its own version of the microcomputer, the IBM Personal Computer In 1981.[40] To get its PC to market quickly (it took only 12 months), it decided to abandon its traditional slow, methodical development process and instead gave the development of the PC to a nearly autonomous group in Boca Raton, Florida, whose members were reviewed quarterly by corporate headquarters but otherwise permitted to operate as they wished.

Google, the Mountain View, California, search-engine company, has extended the notion of skunkworks from protected place to protected idea. Google's managers keep a "Top 100" priorities list (which actually now numbers 240 items). An "S" next to the project stands for "skunkworks" and protects it from premature ideas and criticism.[41]

The skunkworks idea can also be applied to eliminating bad bets in the innovation process. Eli Lilly, the pharmaceutical company, launched an autonomous experimental unit called Chorus, which, according to one description, "looks for the most likely [drug candidate] winners in a portfolio of molecules (most of which are destined to fail), recommending only the strongest candidates for costly late-stage development."[42]

Your Call

"All big companies have trouble coming up with the Next Big Thing," says Gerard Mooney, director of corporate strategy at IBM.[43] The problem has been labeled the "innovator's dilemma": big companies cater to their best customers by focusing on advanced and more expensive products, leaving low-end products to startups, which eventually eat into the core markets of the large companies.[44] One possible contributor is that as big-company projects get more complicated, the veteran managers in charge of them stop learning from their experience, so the projects become delayed and over budget.[45] However, innovative big companies—Amazon, Apple, General Electric, Procter & Gamble—work hard at making their own luck. One trait they all have in common: courage.[46] Do you think it's possible to build courage into project planning?

The Project Life Cycle: The Predictable Evolution of a Project

Being a project manager is a challenging job if for no other reason than that you have to be attentive both to the big picture *and* to the details. Let us therefore look at the big picture—the four-stage project life cycle that any project goes through, whether it's developing an online magazine or staging an AIDS in Africa music benefit.

The *project life cycle* **has four stages from start to finish: definition, planning, execution, and closing.** *(See Figure 5.6, below.)* As we will see, the graph of the rise

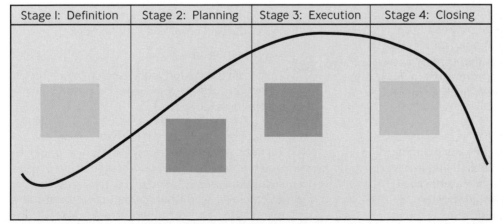

figure 5.6

THE PROJECT LIFE CYCLE

Source: Adapted from J. W. Weiss and R. K. Wysocki, *5-Phase Project Management* (Reading, MA: Addison-Wesley, 1992) and J. K. Pinto and O. P. Kharbanda, *Successful Project Manager: Leading Your Team to Success* (New York: Van Nostrand Reinhold, 1995), pp. 17–21.

and fall of the *project* life cycle resembles that for the *product* life cycle, which we discuss in Chapter 6.

Stage I: Definition   In the *definition* stage, you look at the big picture. You state the problem, look at the assumptions and risks, identify the project's goals and objectives, and determine the budget and schedule. You may also write a project proposal.

Stage 2: Planning   In the *planning* stage, you consider the details needed to make the big picture happen. You identify the facilities and equipment, the people and their duties, and the schedule and coordination efforts needed.

Staying on track. In between an organization's mission statement and an operational action plan there are plenty of opportunities for slips, miscommunications, and errors. If you were leading this meeting in the first stage of a project life cycle, what would be your initial words after "Good morning"?

Stage 3: Execution   The *execution* stage is the actual work stage. You define the management style and establish the control tools. You will need to monitor progress, review the project schedule, issue change orders, and prepare status reports to the "client" (boss or customer) for whom the work is being done. Larry Bossidy, former CEO of AlliedSignal, believes many managers don't give execution the attention required to make a company's strategy really deliver results. We discuss his ideas at length in Chapter 6.

Your main focus is to complete the project on time and under budget while trying to meet the client's expectations.

Example

Project Life Cycle: Writing a Research Paper

An example of a project is the approach recommended for producing a research paper.

Stage I: Definition

In the definition stage, you concentrate on picking a topic. That is, you set a deadline for when you will have decided on the topic, by which time you will have picked three alternative topics that are important to the instructor and interesting to you. You next refine the three proposed topics into three questions that your paper will be designed to answer. You then check the topic ideas with your instructor to see if he or she considers them satisfactory in importance and in scope.

Stage 2: Planning

When writing a term paper, in your planning stage you do initial research online and in the library to see if there is enough material available to you so that you can adequately research your paper. You then develop a rough outline so that you know the direction your paper will take.

Stage 3: Execution

When you're developing a research paper, the execution stage is the longest and most labor-intensive stage. This is when you do extensive research, sort your research notes, revise the outline to reflect changes suggested by your research, write a first draft, and then write and proofread your final draft.

Stage 4: Closing

The closing stage for your research paper occurs when you hand in your paper to your "client"— your instructor.

Your Call

Perhaps you've hurriedly written a paper in which you simply skipped stages I and 2. How successful was it? Would you try doing this for an employer who wanted you to investigate new markets for a product? Why or why not?

D

↓

P

↓

E

↓

C

Stage 4: Closing

The *closing* stage occurs when the project is accepted by the client. This stage can be abrupt but could be gradual, as when you're required to install deliverables (such as a complete computer system) and carry out training.

You may also be required to write a report about the project in which you document everything that happened.

The Importance of Project Deadlines

There's no question that college is a pressure cooker for many students. The reason, of course, is the seemingly never-ending deadlines. But consider: Would you do all the course work you're doing—and realize the education you're getting—if you *didn't* have deadlines?

As we saw under the "T" in SMART ("has Target date"), deadlines are as essential to project planning as they are to your college career. Because the whole purpose of a planned project is to deliver to a client specified results within a specified period of time, deadlines become a great motivator, both for you and for the people working for you.

It's possible, of course, to let deadlines mislead you into focusing too much on immediate results and thereby ignore project planning—just as students will focus too much on preparing for a test in one course while neglecting others. In general, however, deadlines can help you keep your eye on the "big picture" while simultaneously paying attention to the details that will help you realize the big picture. Deadlines can help concentrate the mind, so that you make quick decisions rather than put them off.

Deadlines help you ignore extraneous matters (such as cleaning up a messy desk) in favor of focusing on what's important—achieving the project on time and on budget. Deadlines provide a mechanism for giving ourselves feedback. ●

Practical Action

How to Achieve Your Important Goals: Don't Keep Every Option Open

We've all been told that "It's important to keep your options open." But should we?

"You don't even know how a camera's burst-mode flash works, but you persuade yourself to pay for the extra feature just in case," writes a journalist about this phenomenon. "You no longer have anything in common with someone who keeps calling you, but you hate to just zap the relationship. Your child is exhausted from after-school soccer, ballet, and Chinese lessons, but you won't let her drop the piano lessons. They could come in handy."[47]

The natural reluctance to close any door is pointed out by Dan Ariely, a behavioral economist at the Massachusetts Institute of Technology and author of *Predictably Irrational: The Hidden Forces That Shape Our Decisions*.[48] In that book, he describes experiments involving hundreds of MIT students who showed that they could not bear to let go of their options—even though it was bad strategy. The experiments involved playing a computer game in which students had 100 mouse clicks to look for money behind three doors on the screen and were paid real cash each time they found it.

To earn the most money, a student would quickly find out that the best strategy was to check out the three doors and settle on the one with the highest rewards. But when students stayed out of a room, the door would start shrinking and eventually disappear. Researchers found that most students would waste clicks by rushing back to reopen doors, even though they lost money by doing so—and they continued to frantically keep all their doors open even when they were fined for switching.

Were the students just trying to "keep their options open"? Ariely doesn't think so. The real motivation, he suggests, is fear of loss. "Closing a door on an option is experienced as a loss, and people are willing to pay a price to avoid the emotion of loss," he says.

Obviously, this lesson has some practical payoffs for all of us who are overscheduled and overworked and need all the help we can get to stay focused on our important goals. The next time you are considering adding a class, switching majors, or pursuing another career or you are wondering whether to continue a personal relationship that no longer benefits you, think about the advantages of . . . just saying no.

Key Terms Used in This Chapter

Summary

5.1 Planning & Uncertainty

Planning is defined as setting goals and deciding how to achieve them. It is also defined as coping with uncertainty by formulating future courses of action to achieve specified results.

Planning has four benefits. It helps you (1) check your progress, (2) coordinate activities, (3) think ahead, and (4) cope with uncertainty.

Organizations respond to uncertainty in one of four ways. (1) Defenders are expert at producing and selling narrowly defined products or services. (2) Prospectors focus on developing new products or services and in seeking out new markets, rather than waiting for things to happen. (3) Analyzers let other organizations take the risks of product development and marketing and then imitate what seems to work best. (4) Reactors make adjustments only when finally forced to by environmental pressures.

5.2 Fundamentals of Planning

An organization's reason for being is expressed in a mission statement. What the organization wishes to become—and the actions needed to get there—are expressed in a vision statement.

From these are derived strategic planning, then tactical planning, then operational planning. In strategic planning, managers determine what the organization's long-term goals should be for the next 1–5 years. In tactical planning, managers determine what contributions their work units can make during the next 6–24 months. In operational planning, they determine how to accomplish specific tasks within the next 1–52 weeks.

Whatever its type, the purpose of planning is to achieve a goal or objective, a specific commitment to achieve a measurable result within a stated period of time.

Strategic goals are set by and for top management and focus on objectives for the organization as a whole. Tactical goals are set by and for middle managers and focus on the actions needed to achieve strategic goals. Operational goals are set by and for first-line managers and are concerned with short-term matters associated with realizing tactical goals.

The goal should be followed by an action plan, which defines the course of action needed to achieve the stated goal. The operating plan, which is typically designed for a 1-year period, defines how you will conduct your business based on the action plan; it identifies clear targets such as revenues, cash flow, and market share.

Plans may be either standing plans, developed for activities that occur repeatedly over a period of time, or single-use plans, developed for activities that are not likely to be repeated in the future. There are three types of standing plans: (1) A policy is a standing plan that outlines the general response to a designated problem or situation. (2) A procedure outlines the response to particular problems or circumstances. (3) A rule designates specific required action. There are two types of single-use plans: (1) A program encompasses a range of projects or activities. (2) A project is a single-use plan of less scope and complexity.

5.3 Promoting Goal Setting: Management by Objectives & Smart Goals

Management by objectives (MBO) is a four-step process in which (1) managers and employees jointly set objectives for the employee, (2) managers develop action plans, (3) managers and employees periodically review the employee's performance, and (4) the manager makes a performance appraisal and rewards the employee according to results. The purpose of MBO is to motivate rather than control subordinates.

For MBO to be successful three things have to happen. (1) The commitment of top management is essential. (2) The program must be applied organizationwide. (3) Objectives must cascade—becoming more specific at lower levels of the organization.

The five characteristics of a good goal are represented by the acronym SMART. A SMART goal is one that is Specific, Measurable, Attainable, Results oriented, and has Target dates.

5.4 The Planning/Control Cycle

Once plans are made, managers must stay in control using the planning/control cycle, which has two planning steps (1 and 2) and two control steps (3 and 4), as follows: (1) Make the plan. (2) Carry out the plan. (3) Control the direction by comparing results with the plan. (4) Control the direction by taking corrective action in two ways—namely, (a) by correcting deviations in the plan being carried out, or (b) by improving future plans.

5.5 Project Planning

Project planning is the preparation of single-use plans, or projects. Project management achieves a set of goals through planning, scheduling, and maintaining progress of the activities. An example of project planning is the skunkworks.

A project evolves through a project life cycle involving four stages: (1) Definition—a project manager looks at the big picture, stating the problem, identifying the project's goals and objectives, and determining the budget and schedule. (2) Planning—managers consider the details needed to make the big picture happen, such as identifying equipment, people, and coordination efforts needed. (3) Execution—managers define the management style and establish the control tools, then ensure the work is being done on time and under budget. (4) Closing—the project is accepted by the client.

Deadlines are essential to project planning because they become great motivators both for the manager and for subordinates.

Management in Action

How Does Apple Plan for Its Technological Innovations?

Apple scoffs at the notion of a target market. It doesn't even conduct focus groups. "You can't ask people what they want if it's around the next corner," says Steve Jobs, Apple's CEO and co-founder.

At Apple, new-product development starts in the gut and gets hatched in rolling conversations that go something like this: What do we hate? (Our cell phones.) What do we have the technology to make?

(A cell phone with a Mac inside.) What would we like to own? (You guessed it, an iPhone.) "One of the keys to Apple is that we build products that really turn us on," says Jobs.

With that simple formula, Apple not only has upstaged the likes of Microsoft but has set the gold standard for corporate America with an entirely new business model: creating a brand, morphing it, and reincarnating it to thrive in a disruptive age. Now, just seven years after it unveiled the first iPod, fully half of Apple's revenues come from music and iPods. Interest in the iPod and iPhone has rubbed off on the Mac, whose sales growth outpaces the industry's. Apple has demonstrated how to create real, breathtaking growth by dreaming up products so new and ingenious that they have upended one industry after another: consumer electronics, the record industry, the movie industry, video and music production.

In the process the company that ranks as the new No. 1 among America's Most Admired Companies has become a roaring financial success. . . .

Here there is no such thing as hedging your bets. "One traditional management philosophy that's taught in many business schools is diversification. Well, that's not us," says [chief operating officer Tim] Cook. "We are the anti-business school." Apple's philosophy goes like this: Too many companies spread themselves thin, making a profusion of products to defuse risk, so they get mired in the mediocre. Apple's approach is to put every resource it has behind just a few products and make them exceedingly well. Apple is brutal about culling past hits: The company dropped its most popular iPod, the Mini, on the day it introduced the Nano (a better product, higher margins—why dilute your resources?). . . .

Here is what Steve Jobs had to say in an interview with Fortune *editor Betsy Morris:*

On the Birth of the iPhone

We all had cell phones. We just hated them, they were so awful to use. The software was terrible. The hardware wasn't very good. We talked to our friends, and they all hated their cell phones too. Everybody seemed to hate their phones. And we saw that these things really could become much more powerful and interesting to license. It's a huge market. I mean a billion phones get shipped every year, and that's almost an order of magnitude greater than the number of music players. It's four times the number of PCs that ship every year.

It was a great challenge. Let's make a great phone that we fall in love with. Nobody had ever

thought about putting operating systems as sophisticated as OS X inside a phone, so that was a real question. We had a big debate inside the company whether we could do that or not. And that was one where I had to adjudicate it and just say, "We're going to do it. Let's try." The smartest software guys were saying they can do it, so let's give them a shot. And they did.

On Apple's Focus

People think focus means saying yes to the thing you've got to focus on. But that's not what it means at all. It means saying no to the hundred other good ideas that there are. You have to pick carefully. I'm actually as proud of many of the things we haven't done as the things we have done. The clearest example was when we were pressured for years to do a PDA, and I realized one day that 90% of the people who use a PDA only take information out of it on the road. They don't put information into it. Pretty soon cell phones are going to do that, so the PDA market's going to get reduced to a fraction of its current size. So we decided not to get into it. If we had gotten into it, we wouldn't have had the resources to do the iPod. . . .

On His Marathon Monday Meetings

When you hire really good people you have to give them a piece of the business and let them run with it. That doesn't mean I don't get to kibitz a lot. But the reason you're hiring them is because you're going to give them the reins. I want [them] making as good or better decisions than I would. So the way to do that is to have them know everything, not just in their part of the business, but in every part of the business. So what we do every Monday is we review the whole business. We look at what we sold the week before. We look at every single product under development—products we're having trouble with, products where the demand is larger than we can make. All the stuff in development, we review. And we do it every single week. We don't have a lot of process at Apple, but that's one of the few things we do just to all stay on the same page.

On Catching Tech's Next Wave

Things happen fairly slowly, you know. They do. These waves of technology, you can see them way before they happen, and you just have to choose wisely which ones you're going to surf. If you choose unwisely, then you can waste a lot of energy, but if you choose wisely it actually unfolds fairly slowly. It takes years. One of our biggest insights [years ago] was that we didn't want to get into any business where we didn't own or control the primary technology because you'll get your head handed to you. We realized that for almost all future consumer electronics, the primary technology was going to be software. And we were pretty good at software. We could do the operating system software. We could write applications on the Mac or even PC. We could write the software in the device, like you might put in an iPod or an iPhone or something. And we could write the back-end software that runs on a cloud, like iTunes. So we could write all these different kinds of software and tweed it all together and make it work seamlessly. And you ask yourself, What other companies can do that? It's a pretty short list. . . .

On Managing Through the [2008] Economic Downturn

We've had one of these before, when the dot-com bubble burst. What I told our company was that we were just going to invest our way through the downturn, that we weren't going to lay off people, that we'd taken a tremendous amount of effort to get them into Apple in the first place—the last thing we were going to do is lay them off. And we were going to keep funding. In fact we were going to up our R&D budget so that we would be ahead of our competitors when the downturn was over. And that's exactly what we did. And it worked. And that's exactly what we'll do this time.

For Discussion

1. What is your evaluation of the planning process used by Apple? Discuss.
2. Which of the four basic strategy types were used by Apple? Explain your rationale.
3. What do you think about Steve Jobs's approach to product development?
4. Using Figure 5.4, describe the extent to which Apple is using the planning/control cycle.
5. What did you learn about planning based on this case? Explain.

Source: Excerpted from Betsy Morris, "What Makes Apple Golden," *Fortune*, March 17, 2008, pp. 68–74.

Self-Assessment

Holland Personality Types & You: Matching Your Personality to the Right Work Environment & Occupation

Objectives

1. To understand the need to plan for your career.
2. To try to match your personality with an occupation.

Introduction

What do you want to be when you grow up? Some people seem to know early in life. Others come to a realization in college. Still others may be forced to such awareness by a crisis in later life, such as being dismissed from a job. Of course, most of us make some sort of plans for our careers. But in doing so we may not always be knowledgeable about how to match our personalities with the choices available.

Instructions

There are four parts to this exercise.

First, select a number from the list of six personality types.

Second, match that choice with the personality you think that type would have.

Third, select the work environment you think would be best for that personality type and personality.

Fourth, based on the preceding three choices, select which occupation would fit best. (For example, if you selected #1, C, and f, the best fit for an occupation would be artist, musical conductor, and other related occupations.)

Try to connect each of the four parts and then check the key to see if your pairings are correct. After that, go through the list again, identifying what you think your personality type is, what your personality is, the work environment you like or think you would like best, and then the occupation that you would or do like best. See if there is an alignment by using the scoring guidelines and interpretation shown below; if there is such an alignment, this suggests you may be on your way to a successful career.

Personality Type

1. Artistic
2. Conventional

3. Realistic

4. Enterprising

5. Social

6. Investigative

Personality

A. Prefers to work with things; is present-oriented, athletic, and mechanical.

B. Is analytical, a problem solver, scientific, and original.

C. Relies on feelings and imagination, is expressive, is intuitive, and values esthetics.

D. Sensitive to needs of others, enjoys interpersonal gatherings, and values educational and social issues.

E. Adventurous, has leadership qualities, persuasive, and values political and economic matters.

F. Structured, accurate, detail-oriented, and loyal follower.

Work Environments

a. Technical/mechanical and industrial.

b. Traditional and rewards conformity and dependability.

c. Cooperative and rewards personal growth.

d. Managerial role in organizations and rewards monetary gains and achievements.

e. Rewards high academic achievement and uses technical abilities to complete tasks.

f. Unstructured and allows nonconformity and rewards creativity.

Occupations

7. Chemist/biological scientist, computer analyst, and emergency medical technician.

8. Lawyer, flight attendant, sales representative, reporter.

9. Accountant, bank teller, medical record technician.

10. Cook, drywall installer, auto mechanic.

11. Artist/commercial artist, musical director, architect, writer/editor.

12. Teacher, clergy, nurse, counselor, librarian.

Scoring Guidelines & Interpretation

Scoring is as follows:

1-C-f-11

2-F-b-9

3-A-a-10

4-E-d-8

5-D-c-12

6-B-e-7

The purpose of this type of exercise is to see how personality type, personality, work environment, and occupation can best fit together. When the elements mesh, you will usually feel more competent and more satisfied with your work conditions and occupation. When these elements or factors are mismatched, one can be very frustrated, feel incompetent, or not be good at one's job.

If you wish to know more about career planning, you can avail yourself of a much more in-depth planning process at **www.soice.state.nc.us/sociss/planning/jh-types.htm.**

Questions for Discussion

1. Does your assessment suggest that your career choice is best for your personality type? How do you feel about this assessment?

2. What do you think the management challenges are for those who are mismatched in their work? Explain.

3. Can you see and describe yourself more clearly in terms of personality type, personality, work environment, and occupation given the results of your scoring? Explain.

Developed by Anne C. Cowden, PhD, based on the information provided by the Web site **www.soice.state.nc.us/sociss/planning/jh-types.htm.**

Should Wal-Mart Drop Its Lawsuit Against a Former Employee?

Fifty-two-year-old Deborah Shank was left permanently brain damaged and wheelchair bound after a traffic accident with a semitrailer truck. The trucking company settled a lawsuit with the Shanks for $700,000. After paying medical expenses and legal fees, the Shanks were left with $417,000.

Mrs. Shank, who now lives in a nursing home and needs constant assistance with the most basic tasks, needs this money for her future care. Unfortunately, the insurance company of her former employer, Wal-Mart, is suing the Shanks for the $470,000 it has spent on Deborah's care. They are able to do this because of a small clause in Wal-Mart's health plan. The clause states that the company "reserves the right to recoup the medical expenses it paid for someone's treatment if the person also collects damages in an injury suit."

Solving the Dilemma

As the CEO of Wal-Mart, what would you do about this case?

1. Although you're sorry about this tragic situation, you would stay the course with the lawsuit. You need to protect shareholders' interests and the interests of all your employees. After all, Deborah Shank had also agreed to the health care plan.

2. Drop the lawsuit. This poor woman needs the money more than the insurance company does.

3. Gather input from an impartial source by sending the case to a mediator.

4. Invent other options.

Source: This case was based on V. Fuhrmans, "Accident Victims Face Grab for Legal Winnings," *The Wall Street Journal*, November 20, 2007, pp. A1, A16.

Strategic Management
How Star Managers Realize a Grand Design

Major Questions You Should Be Able to Answer

6.1 The Dynamics of Strategic Planning
Major Question: Am I really managing if I don't have a strategy?

6.2 The Strategic-Management Process
Major Question: What's the five-step recipe for the strategic-management process?

6.3 Establishing the Grand Strategy
Major Question: How can SWOT and forecasting help me establish my strategy?

6.4 Formulating Strategy
Major Question: How can three techniques—Porter's competitive forces, competitive strategies, and the product life cycle—help me formulate strategy?

6.5 Implementing & Controlling Strategy: Execution
Major Question: How does effective execution help managers during the strategic-management process?

How Successful Managers Stay Successful: Seeing Beyond the Latest Management Fads

"How can we build organizations that are as nimble as change itself—not only operationally, but strategically?" asks famed management professor Gary Hamel.[1]

Unfortunately, the way many people deal with the uncertainty of change is by succumbing to fads, or short-lived enthusiasms, suggests University of Delaware sociologist Joel Best, author of *Flavor of the Month: Why Smart People Fall for Fads*.[2] A fad, he says, "is seen as the way of the future, a genuine innovation that will help solve a big problem. . . . A lot of the attraction of a fad is that if you embrace it early, then you feel that you're ahead of other people, that you're hipper and maybe smarter than they are."[3]

That the field of management has its fads is evident in the constant production of business books touting the newest cure-all. Still, some ideas that started out as management fads survive. Why? Because they've been found to actually work. And one of those that has been found to work is *strategic planning*, as we describe in this chapter.

Two lessons of successful managers:

- **Lesson 1—In an era of management fads, strategic planning is still tops.** Every year, Bain & Company, a global business consulting firm, prepares a "Management Tools and Trends" survey of the use of and satisfaction with the most popular management tools. The 2007 survey found that the most widely used management tool in 2006 was the same as that used 6 and even 8 years earlier—namely, *strategic planning*, favored by 88% of the senior managers surveyed. The use of *mission and vision statements* also continued to be

popular, favored by 79%.[4] Strategic planning is concerned with developing a comprehensive program for long-term success. Mission statements describe the organization's purpose and vision statements describe its intended long-term goal. Successful managers know how to use all of these.

- **Lesson 2—Managers must be willing to make large, painful decisions to suddenly alter strategy.** Another lesson is that in a world of rapid and discontinuous change, managers must always be prepared to make large, painful decisions and radically alter their business design—the very basis of how the company makes money. Because of fast-spreading world conditions such as the threat of products becoming commodities, rapidly increasing productivity, and global overcapacity, managers must be able to make difficult decisions: "exiting businesses, firing people, admitting you were wrong (or at least not omniscient)," as writer Geoffrey Colvin puts it. "So the future will demand ever more people with the golden trait, the fortitude to accept and even seek psychic pain.[5]

For Discussion   Earlier we described the importance of practicing *evidence-based management*, with managers "seeing the truth as a moving target," always facing the hard facts, avoiding falling prey to half-truths, and being willing to admit when they're wrong and change their ways."[6] Do you think you would have this mind-set when thinking about the overall direction of your organization or work unit?

forecast

What's Ahead in This Chapter

We describe strategic management and strategic planning and why they're important. We go through the five steps in the strategic-management process. Then we show how grand strategy is developed, using two strategic-planning tools—SWOT analysis and forecasting. Next we show how strategy is formulated, using such techniques as Porter's four competitive strategies, product life cycles, single-product versus diversification strategies, and competitive intelligence. Finally, we show how strategy is carried out and controlled.

6.I THE DYNAMICS OF STRATEGIC PLANNING

Am I really managing if I don't have a strategy?

THE BIG PICTURE

This section distinguishes among strategy, strategic management, and strategic planning. We describe three reasons why strategic management and strategic planning are important and how they may work for both large and small firms.

Brian Allman, 17, saw a simple vending machine for sale at Sam's Club and bought it for $425. With that he started a small vending-machine business, Bear Snax Vending, stocking the machine and four others he added later with popular candy such as Skittles, M&Ms, and Snickers. His route includes small to mid-size businesses, such as banks.[7]

Did Allman have a big-picture vision for his business, incorporating it in a **business plan, a document that outlines a proposed firm's goals, the strategy for achieving them, and the standards for measuring success?** Apparently not. But that's often the case with entrepreneurs, even those far older than 17. One study found that 41% of *Inc.* magazine's 1989 list of fastest-growing private firms didn't have a business plan and 26% had only rudimentary plans.[8] A follow-up study by *Inc.* in 2002 found the percentage without a plan remained much the same. However, other evidence suggests that firms with formal business plans are more apt to survive. For instance, Scott Shane of Western Reserve University examined research of 396 entrepreneurs in Sweden and found that a greater number of firms that failed never had a formal business plan.[9]

Strategic planning. In 1997, brewer Anheuser Busch, maker of Budweiser and Busch, developed a strategic plan, called "100% Share of Mind," that offered beer distributors financial incentives if they did not distribute rival brands. Anheuser benefited; its share of the U.S. beer market grew. But no strategic plan lasts forever. In the fast-changing alcoholic-beverage industry, distributors with flattening sales began to chafe at carrying only Anheuser products. Some decided to begin selling rival beers, such as Pennsylvania's Yuengling Black & Tan lager. Anheuser's market share was reduced. What kind of strategic plan should it adopt now?

Business plans embody a firm's strategy. In this section, we do the following:

- Define strategy and strategic management.
- Explain why strategic planning is important.
- Describe the three key principles that underlie strategic positioning.
- Discuss strategic management in large versus small firms.

Strategy, Strategic Management, & Strategic Planning

Every organization needs to have a "big picture" about where it's going and how to get there. These are matters of strategy, strategic management, and strategic planning.

Strategy   A *strategy* **is a large-scale action plan that sets the direction for an organization.** It represents an "educated guess" about what must be done in the long term for the survival or the prosperity of the organization or its principal parts. We hear the word expressed in terms like "Budweiser's ultimate strategy . . ." or "Visa's overseas strategy . . ." or *financial strategy, marketing strategy,* and *human resource strategy.*

An example of a strategy is "Find out what customers want, then provide it to them as cheaply and quickly as possible" (the strategy of Wal-Mart). However, strategy is not something that can be decided on just once. Because of fast-changing conditions, it needs to be revisited from time to time, whether every year or every 5 years.

Strategic Management   In the late 1940s, most large U.S. companies were organized around a single idea or product line. By the 1970s, Fortune 500 companies were operating in more than one industry and had expanded overseas. It became apparent that to stay focused and efficient, companies had to begin taking a strategic-management approach.

Strategic management **is a process that involves managers from all parts of the organization in the formulation and the implementation of strategies and strategic goals.** This definition doesn't mean that managers at the top dictate ideas to be followed by people lower down. Indeed, precisely because middle managers are the ones who will be asked to understand and implement the strategies, they should also help to formulate them. The steps in this process are covered in Section 6.2.

Strategic Planning   *Strategic planning,* as we stated in Chapter 5, determines not only the organization's long-term goals for the next 1–5 years regarding growth and profits but also the ways the organization should achieve them.

As one consultant put it, "Simply put, strategic planning determines where an organization is going over the next year or more, how it's going to get there and how it'll know if it got there or not."[10]

Why Strategic Management & Strategic Planning Are Important

There are three reasons why an organization should adopt strategic management and strategic planning: They can (1) provide *direction and momentum,* (2) *encourage new ideas,* and above all (3) *develop a sustainable competitive advantage.*[11] Let's consider these three matters.

I. Providing Direction & Momentum Some executives are unable even to articulate what their strategy is.[12] Others are so preoccupied with day-to-day pressures that their organizations can lose momentum. But strategic planning can help people focus on the most critical problems, choices, and opportunities. If everyone is involved in the process, that can also help create teamwork, promote learning, and build commitment across the organization.

Unless a strategic plan is in place, managers may well focus on just whatever is in front of them, the usual run-of-the-mill problems—until they get an unpleasant jolt when a competitor moves out in front because it has been able to take a long-range view of things and act more quickly. Recently this surprise has been happening over and over as companies have been confronted by some digital or Internet trend that emerged as a threat—as Amazon.com was to Barnes & Noble; as digital cameras were to Kodak's film business; as Google News, blogs, and citizen media were to newspapers.[13]

But there are many other instances in which a big company didn't take competitors seriously (as Sears didn't Wal-Mart, IBM didn't Microsoft, and GM didn't Toyota). "We were five years late in recognizing that [microbreweries] were going to take as much market as they did," says August Busch III, CEO of massive brewer Anheuser-Busch, "and five years late in recognizing we should have joined them."[14]

Of course, a poor plan can send an organization in the wrong direction. Bad planning usually results from faulty assumptions about the future, poor assessment of an organization's capabilities, ineffective group dynamics, and information overload.[15]

2. Encouraging New Ideas Some people object that planning can foster rigidity, that it creates blinders that block out peripheral vision and reduces creative thinking and action. "Setting oneself on a predetermined course in unknown waters," says one critic, "is the perfect way to sail straight into an iceberg."[16]

Actually, far from being a straitjacket for new ideas, strategic planning can help encourage them by stressing the importance of innovation in achieving long-range success. Gary Hamel says that companies such as Apple have been successful because they have been able to unleash the spirit of "strategy innovation." Strategy innovation, he says, is the ability to reinvent the basis of competition

Upscale convenience. Most U.S. convenience stores carry basic necessities, along with candy and slushy drinks. Famima!! represents a different idea, one already successful in Japan—stores catering to people whose household incomes top $80,000. The stores offer not only diapers and dog food but also such luxuries as French stationery, artisanal teas, and organic oatmeal. The first 30 stores opened in the Los Angeles area, but the chain hopes to add 220 more nationwide by 2009. Do you think the concept will work?

within existing industries—"bold new business models that put incumbents on the defensive."[17]

Some successful innovators are companies creating new wealth in the grocery business, where Starbucks Coffee, Trader Joe's, Petco, ConAgra, and Wal-Mart, for example, have developed entirely new product categories and retailing concepts. For instance, Starbucks is launching a new brew called Pike Place Roast to confirm its role as a "coffee innovator." Starbucks' current strategy is to bring more innovations to this industry in the next 12 months than it has over the last 5 years.[18]

3. Developing a Sustainable Competitive Advantage   Strategic management provides a sustainable *competitive advantage,* which, you'll recall (from Chapter 1), is the ability of an organization to produce goods or services more effectively than its competitors do, thereby outperforming them. Sustainable competitive advantage occurs when an organization is able to get and stay ahead in four areas: (1) in being responsive to customers, (2) in innovating, (3) in quality, and (4) in effectiveness.

Example

Developing Competitive Advantage: Staples Simplifies Its Shopping Experience

Staples practically invented the office-retail store to supply small and medium-sized businesses, when it launched its first one in 1986. By the early 2000s, however, the field had become crowded with competitors and Staples' sales were falling off. Market research found that shoppers expected stores to carry everything but wanted helpful sales people to help them with hassle-free shopping. From this was born the tag line "Staples: That was easy."

But then Staples did something more than just create a new marketing message: it took a year to give its stores a major makeover, removing 800 superfluous items from inventory (such as Britney Spears backpacks), adding larger signs, removing office chairs from the rafters to the floor so customers could try them out, and retraining sales people ("sales associates") to walk shoppers to the correct aisle. Then they launched the new tag line, along with the iconic object, the "Easy Button."

Many marketers believe that if they just pronounce an advertising message long and loud enough, customers will come to believe it. In Staples' case, however, it is more likely that changing the customer experience within the stores did more. After 7 years of the rebranding effort, Staples became the leader in office retail. In 2007, its profit was up 7% over the year before, and it was ahead of its major competitors Office Depot and Office Max in revenues.[19]

Your Call

What other competitive retail industries can you think of where the Staples model could be extended for competitive advantage?

What Is an Effective Strategy? Three Principles

Harvard Business School professor **Michael Porter** "is the single most important strategist working today, and maybe of all time," raves Kevin Coyne of consulting firm McKinsey & Co.[20]

Is this high praise deserved? Certainly Porter's status as a leading authority on competitive strategy is unchallenged. The Strategic Management Society, for instance, voted him the most influential living strategist. We will refer to him repeatedly in this chapter.

According to Porter, *strategic positioning* **attempts to achieve sustainable competitive advantage by preserving what is distinctive about a company.** "It means," he says, "performing *different* activities from rivals, or performing *similar* activities in different ways."[21]

Three key principles underlie strategic positioning:[22]

I. Strategy Is the Creation of a Unique & Valuable Position
Strategic position emerges from three sources:

- **Few needs, many customers.** Strategic position can be derived from serving the few needs of many customers. Example: Jiffy Lube provides only lubricants, but it provides them to all kinds of people with all kinds of motor vehicles.

- **Broad needs, few customers.** A strategic position may be based on serving the broad needs of just a few customers. Example: Bessemer Trust targets only very high wealth clients.

- **Broad needs, many customers.** Strategy may be oriented toward serving the broad needs of many customers. Example: Carmike Cinemas operates only in cities with populations of fewer than 200,000 people.

2. Strategy Requires Trade-offs in Competing
As a glance at the choices above shows, some strategies are incompatible. Thus, a company has to choose not only what strategy to follow but what strategy *not* to follow. Example: Neutrogena soap, points out Porter, is positioned more as a medicinal product than as a cleansing agent. In achieving this narrow positioning, the company gives up sales based on deodorizing, gives up large volume, and accordingly gives up some manufacturing efficiencies.

3. Strategy Involves Creating a "Fit" among Activities
"Fit" has to do with the ways a company's activities interact and reinforce one another. Example: A mutual fund such as Vanguard Group follows a low-cost strategy and aligns all its activities accordingly, distributing funds directly to consumers and minimizing portfolio turnover. However, when Continental Lite tried to match some but not all of Southwest Airlines' activities, it was not successful because it didn't apply Southwest's whole interlocking system.

Does Strategic Management Work for Small as Well as Large Firms?

You would expect that a large organization, with its thousands of employees and even larger realm of "stakeholders," would benefit from strategic management and planning. After all, how can a huge company such as Ford Motor Co. run without some sort of grand design?

But what about smaller companies, which account for more than half of total employment and the bulk of employment growth in recent years? One analysis of several studies found that strategic planning was appropriate not just for large firms—companies with fewer than 100 employees could benefit as well, although the improvement in financial performance was small. Nevertheless, the researchers concluded, "it may be that the small improvement in performance is not worth the effort involved in strategic planning unless a firm is in a very competitive industry where small differences in performance may affect the firm's survival potential."[23] ●

6.2 THE STRATEGIC-MANAGEMENT PROCESS

What's the five-step recipe for the strategic-management process?

major question?

THE BIG PICTURE

The strategic-management process has five steps: Establish the mission and the vision, establish the grand strategy, formulate the strategic plans, carry out those plans, and maintain strategic control. In addition, all the steps may be affected by feedback that enables the taking of constructive action.

When is a good time to begin the strategic-management process? Often it's touched off by some crisis.

Procter & Gamble was compelled to do serious soul searching in 2000 after it lost $50 billion in stock market valuation in 6 months. Executives for P&G decided that they needed to develop a strategy that focused on innovation. For Dell, the crisis came in 2007, when it observed significant losses in sales and market share to Hewlett-Packard Co. and Apple Inc. Founder Michael Dell, who replaced Kevin Rollins as CEO, stated he planned to follow a strategy that focused on improving manufacturing and the company's supply chain.[24]

Example

Crisis Leading to the Strategic-Management Process: JetBlue Weathers an Ice Storm

Founded in 1998, JetBlue started out as a low-fare airline, promising fares up to 65% lower than competitors along with, in one description, "creature comforts like assigned seating, leather upholstery, and satellite TV on individual screens in every seat."[25] The formula was an immediate hit, and by 2007 JetBlue had grown from 6 daily flights and 300 employees to 575 daily flights to 52 destinations and 9,300 employees.

Then in 2005, the founder, David Neeleman, decided to depart from the low-cost model of Southwest Airlines–style carriers and to imitate more traditional airlines. He added different kinds of aircraft, increased routes and airports, and built a $25 million training center in anticipation of expanding the workforce to 30,000 by 2010. "These moves," says one analysis, "increased the airline's costs while drawing it into

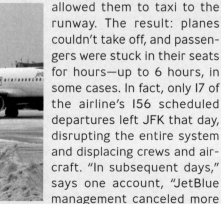

competition with a greater number of rivals, which in turn made it harder for JetBlue to raise fares."[26] JetBlue lost $20 million in 2005 and $1 million in 2006.

Then the Valentine's Day crisis happened. On February 14, 2007, an ice storm settled on JetBlue's New York hub at John F. Kennedy International Airport, preventing planes from taking off. Having acted on forecasters' prediction that the ice would change to rain, JetBlue had continued to load flights and allowed them to taxi to the runway. The result: planes couldn't take off, and passengers were stuck in their seats for hours—up to 6 hours, in some cases. In fact, only 17 of the airline's 156 scheduled departures left JFK that day, disrupting the entire system and displacing crews and aircraft. "In subsequent days," says one account, "JetBlue management canceled more and more flights, angering thousands of passengers, until finally, on February 20, normal operations resumed."[27]

The storm incident cost the carrier around $30 million, according to Neeleman.[28] In addition, he apologized publicly to over 131,000 customers affected by the cancellations and delays and offered different levels of compensation (such as a full refund and voucher for a free roundtrip flight to passengers stuck on a plane for more than 3 hours). Neeleman also announced a Customer Bill of Rights, which offered specific kinds of compensation for various types of delays and overbooking resulting in passengers getting bumped.

What did the incident show? Principally that the airline had grown too fast and didn't have enough people to handle all the passengers trying to rebook flights or to schedule crews during the disruptions. For instance, JetBlue's reservations system relied on a dispersed workforce that included many agents working flexible hours from home—"a low-cost solution that works well until thousands of passengers need to rebook at once," points out one author.[29] The company set a goal of doubling the number of agents who could access the company's reservations system. It also created a database to track crew locations and contact information, and initiated cross-training so that 900 employees working near JFK would be available during any future operational crisis.

Your Call

Is JetBlue's strategy really sound? Since its startup, says one analyst, "not a single competitor has matched its effort to provide actual comfort in coach class."[30] Can the airline keep its fares low, its comforts relatively high, and still have enough staff and arrangements to avoid another Valentine's Day massacre?

The Five Steps of the Strategic-Management Process

The strategic-management process has five steps, plus a feedback loop, as shown below. *(See Figure 6.1.)* Let's consider these five steps.

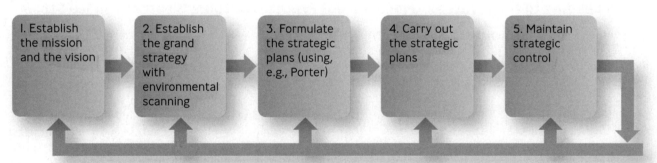

Feedback: Revise actions, if necessary, based on feedback

figure 6.1

THE STRATEGIC-MANAGEMENT PROCESS

The process has five steps.

Step I: Establish the Mission & the Vision   We discussed mission and vision in Chapter 5. If you were called on to write a mission statement and a vision statement, how would you go about it?

Characteristics of a Good Mission Statement   The *mission*, you'll recall, is the organization's purpose or reason for being, and it is expressed in a *mission statement.*

For example, the mission statement of McGraw-Hill, publisher of this book, is as follows:

> *To serve the worldwide need for knowledge at a fair profit by gathering, evaluating, producing, and distributing valuable information in a way that benefits our customers, employees, authors, investors, and our society.*

Characteristics of a Good Vision Statement   An organization's vision, you'll recall, is its long-term goal describing what it wants to become. It is expressed in a *vision statement,* which describes its long-term direction and strategic intent. For example, Walt Disney's original vision for Disneyland went in part like this:

Family business. Do small, family-owned businesses need a vision statement? If yes, what should be the one for Sylvia's soul food restaurant, the landmark Harlem eatery? If no, why not?

> *Disneyland will be something of a fair, an exhibition, a playground, a community center, a museum of living facts, and a showplace of beauty and magic. It will be filled with the accomplishments, the joys and hopes of the world we live in. And it will remind us and show us how to make those wonders part of our own lives.*[31]

Although a vision can be short, it should be positive and inspiring, and it should stretch the organization and its employees to achieve a desired future state that appears beyond its reach. Consider Google, for example. Google's vision is "to organize the world's information and make it universally accessible and useful." Google CEO Eric Schmidt estimated that it may take 300 years to achieve the company's vision. Doing so will require Google to have strategic patience and to develop a grand strategy that is broad in focus.[32]

Guidelines for constructing powerful mission statements and vision statements are shown below. *(See Table 6.1.)* "Visions that have these properties challenge and inspire people in the organization and help align their energies in a

Group Exercise:
Investigating Corporate Mission & Vision Statements

table 6.1

MISSION STATEMENTS AND VISION STATEMENTS

Mission statements: Does your company's mission statement answer these questions?

1. Who are our customers?	5. What is our commitment to economic objectives?	8. What are our public responsibilities, and what image do we wish to project?
2. What are our major products or services?	6. What are our basic beliefs, values, aspirations, and philosophical priorities?	9. What is our attitude toward our employees?
3. In what geographical areas do we compete?	7. What are our major strengths and competitive advantages?	
4. What is our basic technology?		

Vision statements: Does your company's vision statement answer "yes" to these questions?

1. Is it appropriate for the organization and for the times?	3. Does it clarify purpose and direction?	6. Does it reflect the uniqueness of the organization, its distinctive competence, what it stands for, what it's able to achieve?
2. Does it set standards of excellence and reflect high ideals?	4. Does it inspire enthusiasm and encourage commitment?	
	5. Is it well articulated and easily understood?	7. Is it ambitious?

Sources: F. R. David, "How Companies Define Their Mission," *Long Range Planning,* February 1989, pp. 90–97; and B. Nanus, *Visionary Leadership: Creating a Compelling Sense of Direction for Your Organization* (San Francisco: Jossey-Bass, 1992), pp. 28–29.

common direction," says Burt Nanus of the University of Southern California's School of Business Administration. "They prevent people from being overwhelmed by immediate problems because they help distinguish what is truly important from what is merely interesting."[33]

Step 2: Establish the Grand Strategy   The next step is to translate the broad mission and vision statements into a *grand strategy,* **which, after an assessment of current organizational performance, then explains how the organization's mission is to be accomplished.[34] Three common grand strategies are growth, stability, and defensive.**

The first part of the process of developing a grand strategy, then, is to make a rigorous analysis of the organization's present situation to determine *where it is presently headed.* The second part is to determine where it *should be headed in the future.*

Let's consider the three common grand strategies.

1. The Growth Strategy   A *growth strategy* **is a grand strategy that involves expansion—as in sales revenues, market share, number of employees, or number of customers or (for nonprofits) clients served.**

2. The Stability Strategy   A *stability strategy* **is a grand strategy that involves little or no significant change.**

3. The Defensive Strategy   A *defensive strategy* or a *retrenchment strategy,* **is a grand strategy that involves reduction in the organization's efforts.**

Examples of the three strategies are shown in the table below. *(See Table 6.2.)*

table 6.2

HOW COMPANIES CAN IMPLEMENT GRAND STRATEGIES

Growth strategy

- It can improve an existing product or service to attract more buyers.
- It can increase its promotion and marketing efforts to try to expand its market share.
- It can expand its operations, as in taking over distribution or manufacturing previously handled by someone else.
- It can expand into new products or services.
- It can acquire similar or complementary businesses.
- It can merge with another company to form a larger company.

Stability strategy

- It can go for a no-change strategy (if, for example, it has found that too-fast growth leads to foul-ups with orders and customer complaints).
- It can go for a little-change strategy (if, for example, the company has been growing at breakneck speed and feels it needs a period of consolidation).

Defensive strategy

- It can reduce costs, as by freezing hiring or tightening expenses.
- It can sell off (liquidate) assets—land, buildings, inventories, and the like.
- It can gradually phase out product lines or services.
- It can divest part of its business, as in selling off entire divisions or subsidiaries.
- It can declare bankruptcy.
- It can attempt a turnaround—do some retrenching, with a view toward restoring profitability.

How do you establish a grand strategy? Among the strategic-planning tools and techniques used are (1) *SWOT analysis* and (2) *forecasting,* as we describe in Section 6.3.

Step 3: Formulate Strategic Plans   The grand strategy must then be translated into more specific *strategic plans,* which determine what the organization's long-term goals should be for the next 1–5 years. These should communicate not only the organization's general goals about growth and profits but also information about how these goals will be achieved. Moreover, like all goals, they should be SMART— Specific, Measurable, Attainable, Results-oriented, and specifying Target dates (Chapter 5).

Strategy formulation is the process of choosing among different strategies and altering them to best fit the organization's needs. Because the process is so important, formulating strategic plans is a time-consuming process. Among the techniques used to formulate strategy are *Porter's competitive forces and strategies* and *product life cycles,* which we describe in Section 6.4.

Honest growth strategy. One growth strategy that Coca-Cola is employing is scouting for small, entrepreneurial beverage brands to add to its lineup. In 2008, Coke invested $40 million for a 40% interest in the trendy tea company Honest Tea, which makes low-calorie, organic teas and juices, such as Honest Ade. Do you think Coke's strategy of expanding into better-for-you and noncarbonated products is on the right track?

Step 4: Carry Out the Strategic Plans   Putting strategic plans into effect is *strategy implementation.* Strategic planning isn't effective, of course, unless it can be translated into lower-level plans. This means that top managers need to check on possible roadblocks within the organization's structure and culture and see if the right people and control systems are available to execute the plans.[35]

Often implementation means overcoming resistance by people who feel the plans threaten their influence or livelihood. This is particularly the case when the plans must be implemented rapidly, since delay is the easiest kind of resistance there is (all kinds of excuses are usually available to justify delays). Thus, top managers can't just announce the plans; they have to actively sell them to middle and supervisory managers.

Step 5: Maintain Strategic Control: The Feedback Loop   *Strategic control* **consists of monitoring the execution of strategy and making adjustments, if necessary.** To keep strategic plans on track, managers need control systems to monitor progress and take corrective action—early and rapidly—when things start to go awry. Corrective action constitutes a feedback loop in which a problem requires that managers return to an earlier step to rethink policies, redo budgets, or revise personnel arrangements. To keep a strategic plan on track, suggests Bryan Barry, you need to do the following:[36]

- **Engage people.** You need to actively engage people in clarifying what your group hopes to accomplish and how you will accomplish it.

- **Keep it simple.** Keep your planning simple, unless there's a good reason to make it more complex.

- **Stay focused.** Stay focused on the important things.

- **Keep moving.** Keep moving toward your vision of the future, adjusting your plans as you learn what works.

To see how good you think you'd be, see the Self-Assessment, "Core Skills Required in Strategic Planning," at the end of this chapter.

Now, in Section 6.3, let us consider some of the tools used for Step 2, establishing a grand strategy—SWOT and forecasting. ●

Practical Action

How to Streamline Meetings

"Beware of designing a planning process that requires 40 hours of meetings if your staff or board cannot realistically make the time commitment," advises Bryan W. Barry. "Frustration and failure can result. Effective strategic planning can be done in 10 to 15 hours of meeting time, with good preparation between meetings."[37]

Meetings certainly have their uses. Apple's Steve Jobs, as we mentioned at the end of Chapter 5, is renowned for holding marathon Monday meetings. The reason they take so much time, he says, is that Apple hires really good people, and "I want [them] making good or better decisions than I would. So the way to do that is have them know everything, not just in their part of the business but in every part of the business. So what we do every Monday is we review the whole business."[38] Economics professor Tyler Cowen points out that meetings also help attendees determine where everyone stands in the pecking order. "Who speaks? Who finds it necessary to praise whom?" People can also develop a sense of ownership in the decisions made in meetings, which can motivate them to turn those decisions into action.[39]

Still, if you're not in a position to call meetings but have to attend them regularly, it is frustrating to have to be a victim of a poorly run meeting. In one survey, 50% of workers at big companies said they had attended a meeting where at least one participant fell asleep.[40] (At smaller companies, where it is harder to hide, the figure was 26%.) Problem meetings can result from a lack of focus, nobody watching the clock, and no leader to keep the meeting on track.[41] Patrick Lencioni, author of *Death by Meeting,* believes one reason meetings are so ineffective is that top executives discourage conflict.[42] But that tactic backfires, he says, because it makes meetings boring and ignores crucial issues.[43]

As a participant, you can always pull an off-track conversation back by saying, for example, "We were discussing the 2009 budget, but now we seem to be discussing the shortfalls of last year." Or you can try making a summary of a series of comments to prevent others from covering the same ground again. If you're constantly exposed to ineffective meetings, you can also offer your assistance to the meeting leader in creating an agenda, with time frames attached for each item, suggests productivity specialist Odette Pollar. She adds: "Your approach, timing, and tone of voice are important. You must avoid appearing to tell the person what to do."[44]

If you're leading meetings, here are some good ways to streamline them:[45]

Eliminate Unnecessary Meetings & Meeting Attendance
Don't call a meeting if the same result can be accomplished in some other way: phone call, e-mail, memo, one-on-one visit, and so on. Invite only people who need to attend, and let them know they need stay for only those parts of the meeting that concern them. Hold the meeting in a place where distractions will be minimal. Consider using telephone conferencing or videoconferencing.

Distribute an Action Agenda in Advance
Do your homework about the issues. Prepare a list of meeting objectives, topics to be covered and the number of minutes allowed for discussion, and information participants should bring. Organize the topics with the most important ones first. Distribute this agenda a day or more in advance, if possible. For informal meetings, phone conversations, and one-on-one appointments, make a list of items to cover.

Stay in Control of the Meeting
Start on time and stay within the time frame of the agenda items. (Coffee breaks, lunchtime, or quitting time provide built-in limits.) Announce politely at the start of the meeting that you value everyone's time and so you will intervene if discussion becomes off-point, rambling, or unintelligible. Reserve judgments and conclusions until after discussion so that everyone will feel free to give their input. Don't allow a few members to monopolize the discussion. Encourage silent members to participate. Try to reach a decision or make an assignment for every item. Use two notepads or pieces of paper, one for general notes, the other for tasks and assignments. Summarize the highlights at the end of the meeting. Map out a timetable for actions to be taken.

Do Follow-Up
After the meeting, type up tasks and assignments for distribution. Set a date for a follow-up meeting to assess progress.

For more about running meetings, go to Effective-Meetings.com (***www.effectivemeetings.com***).

6.3 ESTABLISHING THE GRAND STRATEGY

How can SWOT and forecasting help me establish my strategy?

major question?

THE BIG PICTURE

To develop a grand strategy, you need to gather data and make projections, using the tools of SWOT analysis and forecasting.

The first part in developing a grand strategy, Step 2 of the five-step strategic management process, is intelligence gathering—internally and externally. The next part is to make some projections.

Two kinds of strategic-planning tools and techniques are (1) *SWOT analysis* and (2) *forecasting*—trend analysis and contingency planning.

SWOT Analysis

The starting point in establishing a grand strategy is **environmental scanning, careful monitoring of an organization's internal and external environments to detect early signs of opportunities and threats that may influence the firm's plans.** The process for doing such scanning is **SWOT analysis—also known as *a situational analysis*—which is a search for the Strengths, Weaknesses, Opportunities, and Threats affecting the organization.** A SWOT analysis should provide you with a realistic understanding of your organization in relation to its internal and external environments so you can better formulate strategy in pursuit of its mission. *(See Figure 6.2.)*

Test Your Knowledge:
SWOT Analysis

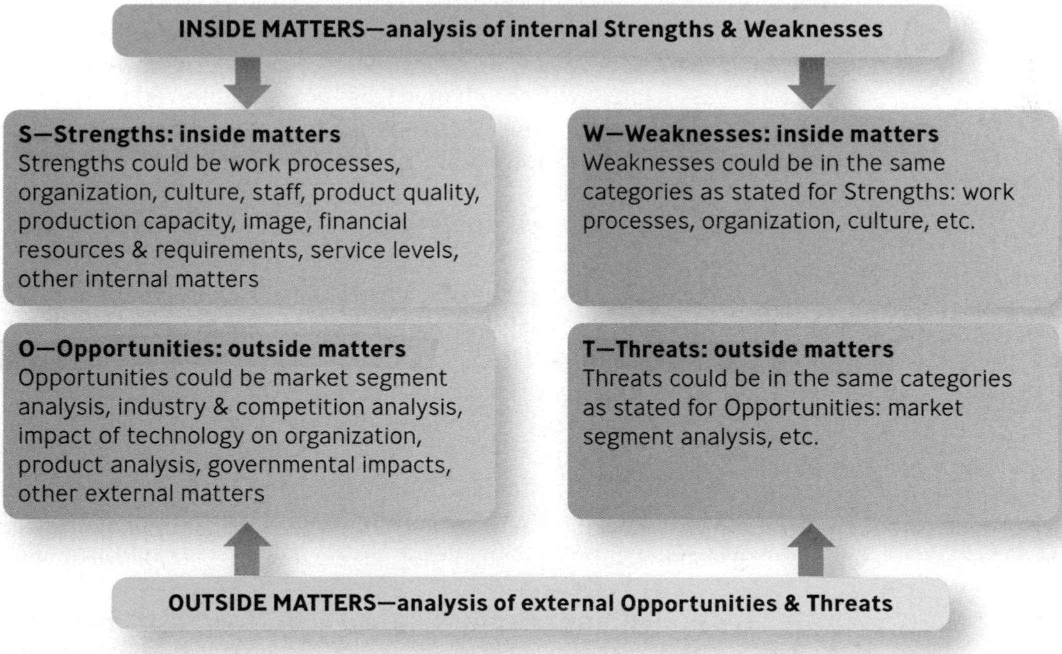

INSIDE MATTERS—analysis of internal Strengths & Weaknesses

S—Strengths: inside matters
Strengths could be work processes, organization, culture, staff, product quality, production capacity, image, financial resources & requirements, service levels, other internal matters

W—Weaknesses: inside matters
Weaknesses could be in the same categories as stated for Strengths: work processes, organization, culture, etc.

O—Opportunities: outside matters
Opportunities could be market segment analysis, industry & competition analysis, impact of technology on organization, product analysis, governmental impacts, other external matters

T—Threats: outside matters
Threats could be in the same categories as stated for Opportunities: market segment analysis, etc.

OUTSIDE MATTERS—analysis of external Opportunities & Threats

figure 6.2

SWOT ANALYSIS

SWOT stands for Strengths, Weaknesses, Opportunities, Threats.

table 6.3

SWOT CHARACTERISTICS THAT MIGHT APPLY TO A COLLEGE

Internal strengths

- Faculty teaching and research abilities
- High-ability students
- Loyal alumni
- Strong interdisciplinary programs

Internal weaknesses

- Limited programs in business
- High teaching loads
- Insufficient racial diversity
- Lack of high-technology infrastructure

External opportunities

- Growth in many local skilled jobs
- Many firms donating equipment to the college
- Local minority population increasing
- High school students take college classes

External threats

- Depressed state and national economy
- High school enrollments in decline
- Increased competition from other colleges
- Funding from all sources at risk

The SWOT analysis is divided into two parts: inside matters and outside matters—that is, an analysis of *internal strengths and weaknesses* and an analysis of *external opportunities and threats.* The table at left gives examples of SWOT characteristics that might apply to a college. *(See Table. 6.3.)*

Inside Matters: Analysis of Internal Strengths & Weaknesses Does your organization have a skilled workforce? a superior reputation? strong financing? These are examples of *organizational strengths*—**the skills and capabilities that give the organization special competencies and competitive advantages in executing strategies in pursuit of its mission.**

Or does your organization have obsolete technology? outdated facilities? a shaky marketing operation? These are examples of *organizational weaknesses*—**the drawbacks that hinder an organization in executing strategies in pursuit of its mission.**

Outside Matters: Analysis of External Opportunities & Threats Is your organization fortunate to have weak rivals? emerging markets? a booming economy? These are instances of *organizational opportunities*—**environmental factors that the organization may exploit for competitive advantage.**

Alternatively, is your organization having to deal with new regulations? a shortage of resources? substitute products? These are some possible *organizational threats*—**environmental factors that hinder an organization's achieving a competitive advantage.**

Forecasting: Predicting the Future

Once they've analyzed their organization's Strengths, Weaknesses, Opportunities, and Threats, planners need to do forecasting for making long-term strategy. **A *forecast* is a vision or projection of the future.**

Lots of people make predictions, of course—and often they are wrong. In the 1950s, the head of IBM, Thomas J. Watson, estimated that the demand for computers would never exceed more than five for the entire world. In the late 1990s, many computer experts predicted power outages, water problems, transportation disruptions, bank shutdowns, and far worse because of computer glitches (the "Y2K bug") associated with the change from year 1999 to 2000.

Of course, the farther into the future one makes a prediction, the more difficult it is to be accurate, especially in matters of technology. Yet forecasting is a necessary part of planning.

Two types of forecasting are *trend analysis* and *contingency planning.*

Trend Analysis A *trend analysis* is **a hypothetical extension of a past series of events into the future.** The basic assumption is that the picture of the present can be projected into the future. This is not a bad assumption, if you have enough historical data, but it is always subject to surprises. And if your data are unreliable, they will produce erroneous trend projections.

An example of trend analysis is a time-series forecast, which predicts future data based on patterns of historical data. Time-series forecasts are used to predict long-term trends, cyclic patterns (as in the up-and-down nature of the business cycle), and seasonal variations (as in Christmas sales versus summer sales).

Contingency Planning: Predicting Alternative Futures *Contingency planning*—**also known** as *scenario planning* **and** *scenario analysis*—**is the creation of alternative hypothetical but equally likely future conditions.** The scenarios present alternative combinations of different factors—different economic pictures, different strategies by competitors, different budgets, and so on.

SWOT Analysis: How Would You Analyze Starbucks Coffee?

Is Starbucks Corp. beginning to decline? Certainly investors worry that the world's largest chain of coffee shops may have hit its peak. Its stock value was nearly halved in 2007, and it has gone through a corporate shakeup that resulted in chairman and founder Howard Schultz taking back the reins as CEO. If you were a top manager, what would be the kinds of things you would identify in a SWOT analysis?[46]

First, the internal *Strengths:* In 15 years, the company went from $250 million to $24 billion in market capitalization. No small part of the company's success is based on the loyalty of its staff—Starbucks calls them "partners," most of whom are young (average age: 26) and 85% of whom have some education beyond high school. Because the company offers above-average pay for food service, health insurance for all, stock options, and channels such as e-mail for employee feedback, partners feel quite involved with the company, and turnover is half the industry average. Employees receive painstaking training in the art of making a high-quality cup of coffee, handling coffee beans and equipment, and dealing with customers. Starbucks has been breaking into new markets, opening retail stores throughout the country and the world (nearly 15,000 locations).

Second, the internal *Weaknesses:* The company may have been growing too fast, adding locations so quickly that the new stores are taking business from the old ones, slowing same-store sales growth. In addition, Starbucks lost sales in 2007 after it raised prices 9 cents a cup, causing some customers to go elsewhere. The company's moves in creating new beverages and (less profitable) breakfast sandwiches and salads have not created much excitement. Its attempt to expand its brand has also had mixed results; although its strategy of selling music has been a hit with customers, the films it has

promoted have had only minimal box-office success. Although the company prided itself on being built on word-of-mouth advertising, its weakening sales in 2007 caused it to begin a campaign of TV advertising. Founder Howard Schultz lamented that the chain might have commoditized its brand, removing itself from its original roots in the local culture and making itself more vulnerable to outside competition from fast-food chains.

Third, the external *Opportunities:* Other chains—Boston Chicken, Rainforest Café, Planet Hollywood—have found the restaurant business tough sledding and were done in because they couldn't get customers to return after the novelty wore off, but many Starbucks customers are extremely loyal. Starbucks is also fortunate to have numerous overseas opportunities in Asia and Europe.

Fourth, the external *Threats:* Despite Starbucks' rapid expansion, about 57% of the nation's coffeehouses are still mom and pops, and during 2000 to 2005 their number grew 40%, at a time when Starbucks tripled. Starbucks is often more expensive than local coffeehouses, and it offers a very limited food menu. Equally important, two national chains, McDonald's and Dunkin' Donuts, have entered the market. McDonald's plans to add coffee bars and a line of espresso drinks in thousands of its U.S. stores, and to sell them more cheaply than Starbucks. Dunkin' Donuts is also planning to cut into Starbucks' customer base.

Your Call

Some analysts believe that Starbucks needs to get away from its high-tech, corporate look and get back to its hip neighborhood coffeehouse roots, embedding itself in the local culture, making the retail presence less cookie-cutter, and refocusing on the luxury coffee experience. Do you agree? What would you advise Starbucks to do?

Fuel proof. Locking in the price of jet fuel with long-term contracts with suppliers, a form of contingency planning, has put low-cost airlines such as Southwest in a competitive position with rivals in controlling costs.

Example

Contingency Planning: Southwest Airlines Uses Hedging to Hold Down Price of Aviation Fuel

In early 2008, when the price of crude oil hit all-time highs ($100 a barrel), the cost of jet fuel threatened to take a big bite out of airline profits. Aviation fuel makes up as much as 15% of an airline's operating costs, the second biggest expense after labor.[47]

Most airlines use a technique known as *hedging* to hold down the price of jet fuel, but Southwest Airlines is particularly good at it, having decided to enter fuel hedge transactions "back when oil prices were so low that oil was cheaper than water," as one observer whimsically put it.[48] In this form of contingency planning, airlines hedge the rise of fuel prices in the futures market by locking in contracts that allow them to buy fuel at a fixed price. Compared to traditional carriers, Southwest has been in a better position to buy favorable futures contracts because of its financial strengths: It avoids expensive labor contracts, operates only one type of aircraft, and flies high-traffic routes.[49]

In the 2008 world of $100-plus-a-barrel oil, for instance, Southwest had 70% of its fuel hedged at $51 a barrel. For 2010, it has 30% of its fuel hedged at $63 a barrel. These prices are way below what other major airlines get. (United Airlines, for instance, had only 15% of its fuel hedged, and at between $91 and $101 per barrel.)

Your Call

Is hedging like playing poker—like being a riverboat gambler? "You have to have foresight, wisdom, and some courage to hedge," says Tammy Romo, Southwest's treasurer.[50] But if oil consumption will grow by more than 40% over the next quarter century and fuel prices stay high, what do you think airlines will have to do? (Hint: increase revenues, decrease costs, consolidate or liquidate assets.)[51]

Because the scenarios try to peer far into the future—perhaps 5 or more years—they are necessarily written in rather general terms. Nevertheless, the great value of contingency planning is that it not only equips an organization to prepare for emergencies and uncertainty, it also gets managers thinking strategically. ●

6.4 FORMULATING STRATEGY

How can three techniques—Porter's competitive forces, competitive strategies, and the product life cycle—help me formulate strategy?

major question?

THE BIG PICTURE
Strategy formulation makes use of several concepts. Here we discuss Porter's five competitive forces, four competitive strategies, the four-stage product life cycle, diversification and synergy, and competitive intelligence.

After the grand strategy has been determined (Step 2 in the strategic-management process), it's time to turn to strategy formulation (Step 3). Examples of techniques that can be used to formulate strategy are *Porter's five competitive forces, Porter's four competitive strategies, the product life cycle, diversification and synergy,* and *competitive intelligence.*

Porter's Five Competitive Forces

What determines competitiveness within a particular industry? After studying several kinds of businesses, strategic management expert Michael Porter suggested in his **Porter's model for industry analysis** that business-level strategies originate in **five primary competitive forces in the firm's environment: (1) threats of new entrants, (2) bargaining power of suppliers, (3) bargaining power of buyers, (4) threats of substitute products or services, and (5) rivalry among competitors.**[52]

I. Threats of New Entrants New competitors can affect an industry almost overnight, taking away customers from existing organizations. Example: Kraft Macaroni & Cheese is a venerable, well-known brand but is threatened from the low end by store brands, such as Wal-Mart's brand, and from the high end by Annie's Creamy Macaroni and Cheese with Real Aged Wisconsin Cheddar.[53]

2. Bargaining Power of Suppliers Some companies are readily able to switch suppliers in order to get components or services, but others are not. Example: Clark Foam of Laguna Niguel, California, supplied nearly 90% of the foam cores used domestically to make custom surfboards. When it suddenly closed shop in late 2005, blaming government agencies for trying to shut it down, many independent board shapers and small retailers found they couldn't afford to get foam from outside the country. On the other hand, Surftech in Santa Cruz, California, was one of the few board manufacturers to use resin instead of foam, and so it saw a spike in sales.[54]

3. Bargaining Power of Buyers Customers who buy a lot of products or services from an organization have more bargaining power than those who don't. Customers who use the Internet to shop around are also better able to negotiate a better price. Example: Buying a car used to be pretty much a local activity, but now potential car buyers can use the Net to scout a range of offerings within a 100-mile or larger radius, giving them the power to force down the asking price of any one particular seller. (Amazon.com recently introduced TextBuyIt, a program that lets shoppers compare prices and buy things simply by making a few quick taps on their cell phones.)[55]

4. Threats of Substitute Products or Services

Again, particularly because of the Internet, an organization is in a better position to switch to other products or services when circumstances threaten their usual channels. Example: Oil companies might worry that Brazil is close to becoming energy self-sufficient because it is able to meet its growing demand for vehicle fuel by substituting ethanol derived from sugar cane for petroleum.[56]

5. Rivalry among Competitors

The preceding four forces influence the fifth force, rivalry among competitors. Think of the wild competition among makers and sellers of portable electronics, ranging from cell phones to MP3 audio players to videogame systems. Once again, the Internet has intensified rivalries among all kinds of organizations.

Test Your Knowledge:
Porter's Five Forces

An organization should do a good SWOT analysis that examines these five competitive forces, Porter felt. Then it was in a position to formulate effective strategy, using what he identified as four competitive strategies, as we discuss next.

Porter's Four Competitive Strategies

Porter's four competitive strategies (also called *four generic strategies*) are (1) cost-leadership, (2) differentiation, (3) cost-focus, and (4) focused-differentiation.[57] The first two strategies focus on *wide* markets, the last two on *narrow* markets. *(See Figure 6.3.)* Time Warner, which produces lots of media and publications, serves wide markets around the world. Your neighborhood video store serves a narrow market of just local customers.

figure 6.3

PORTER'S FOUR COMPETITIVE STRATEGIES

	Type of market targeted	
Strategy	Wide	Narrow
I. Cost-leadership	✓	
2. Differentiation	✓	
3. Cost-focus		✓
4. Focused-differentiation		✓

Let's look at these four strategies.

I. Cost-Leadership Strategy: Keeping Costs & Prices Low for a Wide Market   The *cost-leadership strategy* is to keep the costs, and hence prices, of a product or service below those of competitors and to target a wide market.

This puts the pressure on R&D managers to develop products or services that can be created cheaply, production managers to reduce production costs, and marketing managers to reach a wide variety of customers as inexpensively as possible.

Firms implementing the cost-leadership strategy include computer maker Dell, watch maker Timex, hardware retailer Home Depot, and pen maker Bic.

2. Differentiation Strategy: Offering Unique & Superior Value for a Wide Market   The *differentiation strategy* is to offer products or services that are of unique and superior value compared to those of competitors but to target a wide market.

Because products are expensive, managers may have to spend more on R&D, marketing, and customer service. This is the strategy followed by Ritz-Carlton hotels and the makers of Lexus automobiles.

The strategy is also pursued by companies trying to create *brands* to differentiate themselves from competitors. Although Pepsi may cost only cents more than a supermarket's own house brand of cola, PepsiCo spends millions on ads.

3. Cost-Focus Strategy: Keeping Costs & Prices Low for a Narrow Market

The *cost-focus strategy* **is to keep the costs, and hence prices, of a product or service below those of competitors and to target a narrow market.**

This is a strategy you often see executed with low-end products sold in discount stores, such as low-cost beer or cigarettes, or with regional gas stations, such as the Terrible Herbst or Rotten Robbie chains in parts of the West.

Needless to say, the pressure on managers to keep costs down is even more intense than it is with those in cost-leadership companies.

4. Focused-Differentiation Strategy: Offering Unique & Superior Value for a Narrow Market

The *focused-differentiation strategy* **is to offer products or services that are of unique and superior value compared to those of competitors and to target a narrow market.**

Some luxury cars are so expensive—Rolls-Royce, Ferrari, Lamborghini—that only a few car buyers can afford them. Other companies following the strategy are jeweler Cartier and shirtmaker Turnbull & Asser. Yet focused-differentiation products need not be expensive. The publisher Chelsea Green has found success with niche books, such as *The Straw Bale House*.

Focused differentiation. The world's largest cruise ship, the 1,112-foot-long, 15-deck *Freedom of the Seas*, features such amenities as a skating rink, rock-climbing facilities, basketball, a surfing pool, a miniature golf course, a three-story-high dining room, and lavish lodging quarters. Clearly, there's something here for everyone—if you can afford it.

The Product Life Cycle: Different Stages Require Different Strategies

In Chapter 5, we described a *project* life cycle. A *product* life cycle has a similar curve (although the end is usually not quite so abrupt). **A *product life cycle* is a model that graphs the four stages that a product or a service goes through during the "life" of its marketability: (1) introduction, (2) growth, (3) maturity, and (4) decline.** *(See Figure 6.4.)*

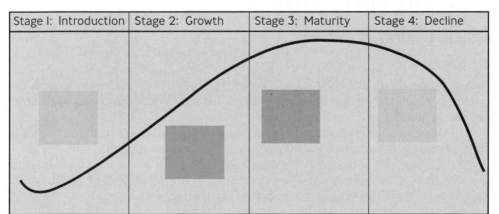

Stage 1: Introduction	Stage 2: Growth	Stage 3: Maturity	Stage 4: Decline

figure 6.4

THE PRODUCT LIFE CYCLE

Managers can use this cycle to create strategies appropriate to each stage.

Some products, such as faddish toys or collectibles (for example, Beanie Babies), may have a life cycle of only months or a year or so. Others, such as a shopping center, may have a life cycle equivalent to a human generation (about 30 years) before they begin to decline and need to be redesigned for fresh appeal and modern sensibilities.

For you as a manager it's useful to know about the concept of product life cycle because different strategies—such as those advanced by Michael Porter—can be used to support different products or services in different stages of the cycle. Let's look at these stages.

Stage 1: Introduction—Getting the Product to Market   The *introduction stage* is the stage in the product life cycle in which a new product is introduced into the marketplace.

This is the stage that is heavy on start-up costs for production, marketing, and distribution. Managers have to concentrate on building inventory and staff without loss of quality. With sales usually low during this period, the product is probably losing the company money. There is also the huge risk that the product may be rejected.

During the introduction stage, one should, to use a military analogy, follow a strategy of infiltration. A differentiation or a focus (cost-focus or focused-differentiation) strategy may be appropriate.

Stage 2: Growth—Demand Increases   The *growth stage,* which is the most profitable stage, is the period in which customer demand increases, the product's sales grow, and (later) competitors may enter the market.

At the start, the product may have the marketplace to itself and demand for it may be high. Managers need to worry about getting sufficient product into the distribution pipeline, maintaining quality, and expanding the sales and distribution effort. This phase may go on for years. But all the while, competitors will be scrambling to enter the market.

During the growth stage, managers would advance their attack, probably continuing Stage 1 differentiation or focus strategies.

Stage 3: Maturity—Growth Slows   The *maturity stage* is the period in which the product starts to fall out of favor and sales and profits begin to fall off.

In this phase, sales start to decline as competition makes inroads. At this point, managers need to concentrate on reducing costs and instituting efficiencies to maintain the product's profitability. Sometimes they can extend the life of the product by tinkering with its various features.

During the maturity stage, managers would become more defensive, perhaps using a cost-leadership or focus strategy.

Stage 4: Decline—Withdrawing from the Market   The *decline stage* is the period in which the product falls out of favor and the organization withdraws from the marketplace.

In this stage, the product falls out of favor, and managers sound the bugle for retreat, scaling down relevant inventory, supplies, and personnel.

While this phase may mean withdrawal of support for the old product, it doesn't necessarily mean a complete shutdown for the organization. Much of the same expertise will be required to support new products.

The Product Life Cycle: The Rise & Fall of the Divx Disk

First came the VCR, perhaps the most popular consumer-electronics medium in a generation. Then in the early 1990s came the DVD (short for digital video disk), principally backed by Warner Home Video and designed to replace the VCR. The DVD was just beginning to sell when along came a new rival, the Divx disk.

In stage 1, introduction, the Divx, backed by the huge electronics chain of Circuit City Stores (along with a Hollywood law firm), was launched in 1997 as a competitor to both the VCR and the DVD. The key idea behind Divx was that it would allow consumers to buy a movie-on-a-disk as for the price of renting a VCR tape.

In stage 2, growth, demand for Divx began to grow, threatening the growth of DVDs. Consumers could buy a disk with a movie on it for the price of a video rental, then have 48 hours in which to view it. After that they could choose between simply throwing the disk away (since further viewings were not possible without further payment) or paying an extra $15—billed by Divx directly to their credit card. This credit card fee authorized the company's central computer, through a modem connection to the customer's home computer, to grant outright ownership for unlimited viewing, thereby obviating further rental fees at video stores.

In stage 3, maturity, DVD backers, led by Warner Home Video, began to fight back. They were able to take advantage of four external factors. First, only 750 of some 10,000 electronics stores nationwide agreed to carry Divx, most not wishing to boost the revenues of rival Circuit City. Second, only three manufacturers agreed to make Divx players, mainly because they didn't wish to offend the mammoth retailer. Third, video stores realized that Divx would cut their rentals in half, so they started offering DVD rentals instead. Fourth, DVD backers were successful in forming an alliance among Hollywood movie studios, which began making more and more movies available on DVD, allowing Toshiba, Sony, and other DVD hardware manufacturers to slash their prices.

In stage 4, decline, after losing $375 million, Circuit City announced it was discontinuing the Divx.

Your Call

In a more recent disk war, the DVD was succeeded by a new high-definition technology, Toshiba's HD-DVD, backed by Microsoft, Sanyo, NEC, and movie studios like New Line and Universal. A rival high-definition technology, Blu-ray, was supported by Apple, Panasonic, Philips, Samsung, Sharp, Pioneer, Dell, and movie studios like Sony, 20th Century Fox, and Disney. Ultimately, in early 2008, the contest was won by Blu-ray, as Toshiba dropped the HD-DVD.[58] Today regular DVDs still dominate most video sales, although they slipped about 3% in 2007.[59] How long do you think it will take for DVDs to reach stages 3 and 4 in the product life cycle?

Single-Product Strategy versus Diversification Strategy

You might begin to see why, with the birth-to-death stages of the product life cycle, a company needs to think about whether to have a *single-product strategy* or a *diversification strategy*. After all, if you have only one product to sell, what do you do if that product fails?

What stage in the life cycle? This shopping center clearly has seen better days. Do you think a shopping center could be built that would last 100 years?

The Single-Product Strategy: Focused but Vulnerable In a *single-product strategy,* **a company makes and sells only one product within its market.** This is the kind of strategy you see all the time as you drive past the small retail businesses in a small town: there may be one shop that sells only flowers, one that sells only security systems, and so on. It's also a strategy used by some bigger companies. For instance, Indian Motorcycle Company, which was once a worthy rival to Harley-Davidson, sold only motorcycles.

The single-product strategy has both positives and negatives:

- **The benefit—focus.** Making just one product allows you to focus your manufacturing and marketing efforts just on that product. This means that your company can become savvy about repairing defects, upgrading production lines, scouting the competition, and doing highly focused advertising and sales. See's Candies, for instance, is a San Francisco–based chain of 200 stores throughout the West that specializes in making boxed chocolates—something it does so well that when it was acquired by Berkshire Hathaway, its corporate owner chose not to tamper with success and runs it with a "hands-off" policy.

- **The risk—vulnerability.** The risk, of course, is that if you do *not* focus on all aspects of the business, if a rival gets the jump on you, or if an act of God intervenes (for a florist, roses suffer a blight right before Mother's Day), your entire business may go under. For instance, in 2003, Gilroy, California–based Indian Motorcycle went bankrupt a second time (it went under in 1953, too) because it was unable to focus on meeting its projected production targets.[60]

The Diversification Strategy: Operating Different Businesses to Spread the Risk   The obvious answer to the risks of a single-product strategy is *diversification,* **operating several businesses in order to spread the risk.** You see this at the small retailer level when you drive past a store that sells gas *and* food *and* souvenirs *and* rents videotape and DVD movies. Big companies do it, too: all the major entertainment/media companies, such as Disney, Time Warner, and Sony, run different divisions specializing in television, music, publishing, and the like (a divisional structure we explain further in Chapter 8).

There are two kinds of diversification—*unrelated* and *related.*

Unrelated Diversification: Independent Business Lines   If you operate a small shop that sells flowers on one side and computers on the other, you are exercising a strategy of *unrelated diversification*—**operating several businesses under one ownership that are not related to one another.** This has been a common big-company strategy in the recent past. General Electric, for instance, which began by making lighting products, diversified into such unrelated areas as plastics, broadcasting, and financial services (a so-called conglomerate structure that we discuss in Chapter 8).

Related Diversification: Related Business Lines   In some parts of the world you have to do all your grocery shopping in separate stores—the butcher, the baker, the green grocer, and so on. In most U.S. grocery stores, all these businesses appear under the same roof, an example of the strategy of *related diversification,* **in which an organization under one ownership operates separate businesses that are related to one another.** The famous British raincoat maker Burberry, for instance, started by making and marketing outerwear clothing but since then has expanded into related business lines, including accessories such as umbrellas, children's clothing, and even fragrances, which it sells in its own stores.

Related diversification has three advantages:

- **Reduced risk—because more than one product.** Unlike Indian Motorcycles, Burberry is able to reduce its risks. During seasons when rainwear sales are slow, for instance, Burberry's economic risk is reduced by sales of other product lines.

- **Management efficiencies—administration spread over several businesses.** Whatever the business, it usually has certain obligatory administrative costs—accounting, legal, taxes, and so on. Burberry need not have separate versions of these for each business line. Rather, it can actually save money by using the same administrative services for all its businesses.

- **Synergy—the sum is greater than the parts.** When a company has special strengths in one business, it can apply those to its other related businesses—as PepsiCo, for instance, can do in marketing not only Pepsi Cola but also 7-Up and Mountain Dew. This is an example of *synergy*—**the economic value of separate, related businesses under one ownership and management is greater together than the businesses are worth separately.**

Competitive Intelligence

Regardless of the kind of diversification (or lack of) a company may have, if it is to survive it must keep track of what its competitors are doing—what is known as competitive intelligence. Practicing *competitive intelligence* **means gaining information about one's competitors' activities so that you can anticipate their moves and react appropriately.** If you are a manager, one of your worst nightmares is that a competitor will come out with a service or product—whether it's boutique beer to a major brewer or mountain bikes to a major bicycle maker—that will revolutionize the market and force you to try to play catch-up, if indeed that's even possible.

Gaining competitive intelligence isn't always easy, but there are several avenues—and, surprisingly, most of them are public sources—including the following:

- **The public prints and advertising.** A product may be worked on in secret for several years, but at some point it becomes subject to announcement— through a press release, advertising piece, news leak, or the like. Much of this is available free through the Internet or by subscription to certain specialized databases, such as Nexus, which contains hundreds of thousands of news stories.

- **Investor information.** Information about new products and services may also be available through the reports filed with the Securities and Exchange Commission and through corporate annual reports.

- **Informal sources.** People in the consumer electronics industry every year look forward to major trade shows, such as the International Consumer Electronics Show in Las Vegas, when companies roll out their new products. At such times, people also engage in industry-gossip conversation to find out about future directions. Finally, salespeople and marketers, who are out calling on corporate clients, may return with tidbits of information about what competitors are doing. ●

major question ?

How does effective execution help managers during the strategic management process?

THE BIG PICTURE

Strategic implementation is closely aligned with strategic control. Execution is a process that helps align these two phases of the strategic-management process.

Stage 1 of the strategic-management process was establishing the mission and the vision. Stage 2 was establishing the grand strategy. Stage 3 was formulating the strategic plans. Now we come to the last two stages—4, strategic implementation, and 5, strategic control.

Execution: Getting Things Done

Larry Bossidy, former CEO of AlliedSignal (later Honeywell), and **Ram Charan,** a business advisor to senior executives, are authors of *Execution: The Discipline of Getting Things Done.*[61] ***Execution,* they say, is not simply tactics, it is a central part of any company's strategy; it consists of using questioning, analysis, and follow-through in order to mesh strategy with reality, align people with goals, and achieve results promised.** As we will discuss, execution consists of linking the three core processes of any business—the people process, the strategy, and the operating plan—together to get things done on time.

    Many executives appear to have an aversion to execution, which they associate with tactics—with the tedium of doing, as opposed to visioning, and which they hand off to subordinates. But, Bossidy and Charan point out, this notion can be a fatal flaw. "There's an enormous difference between leading an organization and presiding over it," they write. "The leader who boasts of her hands-off style or puts her faith in empowerment is not dealing with the issues of the day. . . . Leading for execution is not about micromanaging. . . . Leaders who excel at execution immerse themselves in the substance of execution and even some of the key details. They use their knowledge of the business to constantly probe and question. They bring weaknesses to light and rally their people to correct them."[62]

Execution. Located in Mountain View, California, Google was rated the No. 1 company on Fortune's 2008 list of "Best Companies to Work For." With the stock soaring, many employees have become millionaires. What other measures would you evaluate to see if Google is truly successful?

How important is execution to organizational success in today's global economy? A recent survey of 769 global CEOs from 40 countries revealed that "excellence in execution" was their most important concern—more important than profit growth, customer loyalty, stimulating innovation, and finding qualified employees.[63]

Bossidy and Charan outline how organizations and managers can improve the ability to execute. Effective execution requires managers to build a foundation for execution within three core processes found in any business: people, strategy, and operations.[64]

The Three Core Processes of Business

A company's overall ability to execute is a function of effectively executing in terms of its people processes, strategic processes, and operational processes. Because all work ultimately entails some form of human interaction, effort, or involvement, Bossidy and Charan believe that the people process is the most important.

The First Core Process: People "If you don't get the people process right," say Bossidy and Charan, "you will never fulfill the potential of your business." But today most organizations focus on evaluating the jobs people are doing at present, rather than considering which individuals can handle the jobs of the future. An effective leader tries to evaluate talent by linking people to particular strategic milestones, developing future leaders, dealing with nonperformers, and transforming the mission and operations of the human resource department.

The Second Core Process: Strategy In most organizations, the strategies developed fail to consider the "how" of execution. According to the authors, a good strategic plan addresses nine questions. *(See Table 6.4.)* In considering whether the organization can execute the strategy, a leader must take a realistic and critical view of its capabilities and competencies. If it does not have the talent

1. What is the assessment of the external environment?	
2. How well do you understand the existing customers and markets?	
3. What is the best way to grow the business profitably, and what are the obstacles to growth?	
4. Who is the competition?	
5. Can the business execute the strategy?	
6. Are the short term and long term balanced?	
7. What are the important milestones for executing the plan?	
8. What are the critical issues facing the business?	
9. How will the business make money on a sustainable basis?	

table 6.4

QUESTIONS A STRONG STRATEGIC PLAN MUST ADDRESS

Source: From *Execution* by Larry Bossidy and Ram Charan, Copyright © 2002 by Larry Bossidy and Ram Charan. Used by permission of Crown Business, a division of Random House, Inc.

in finance, sales, and manufacturing to accomplish the vision, the chances of success are drastically reduced.

The Third Core Process: Operations   The strategy process defines where an organization wants to go, and the people process defines who's going to get it done. The third core process, operations, or the operating plan, provides the path for people to follow. The operating plan, as we described in Chapter 5, should address all the major activities in which the company will engage—marketing, production, sales, revenue, and so on—and then define short-term objectives for these activities, to provide targets for people to aim at.

Building a Foundation of Execution

The foundation of execution is based on leadership (discussed in Chapter 14) and organizational culture (discussed in Chapter 8). Bossidy and Charan propose that there are seven essential types of leader behaviors that are needed to fuel the engine of execution. Managers are advised to engage in the following behaviors:

Know Your People & Your Business   In companies that don't execute, leaders are usually out of touch with the day-to-day realities. Bossidy and Charan insist leaders must engage intensely and personally with their organization's people and its businesses; they cannot rely on second-hand knowledge through other people's observations, assessments, and recommendations.

Insist on Realism   Many people want to avoid or shade reality, hiding mistakes or avoiding confrontations. Making realism a priority begins with the leaders being realistic themselves, and making sure realism is the goal of all dialogues in the organization.

Set Clear Goals & Priorities   Leaders who execute focus on a very few clear priorities that everyone can grasp.

Follow Through   Failing to follow through is a major cause of poor execution. "How many meetings have you attended where people left without firm conclusions about who would do what and when?" Bossidy and Charan ask. Accountability and follow-up are important.

Reward the Doers   If people are to produce specific results, they must be rewarded accordingly, making sure that top performers are rewarded far better than ordinary performers.

Expand People's Capabilities   Coaching is an important part of the executive's job, providing useful and specific feedback that can improve performance.

Know Yourself   Leaders must develop "emotional fortitude" based on honest self-assessments. Four core qualities are authenticity, self-awareness, self-mastery, and humility.

Organizational culture is a system of shared beliefs and values within an organization that guides the behavior of its members. In this context, effective execution will not occur unless the culture supports an emphasis on getting quality work done in a timely manner. Chapter 8 presents 11 ways managers can attempt to create an execution-oriented culture.[65]

Key Terms Used in This Chapter

business plan 168
competitive intelligence 189
contingency planning 180
cost-focus strategy 185
cost-leadership strategy 184
decline stage 186
defensive strategy 176
differentiation strategy 184
diversification 188
environmental scanning 179
execution 190
focused-differentiation
  strategy 185
forecast 180
grand strategy 176

growth stage 186
growth strategy 176
introduction stage 186
maturity stage 186
organizational
  opportunities 180
organizational strengths 180
organizational threats 180
organizational weaknesses 180
Porter's four competitive
  strategies 184
Porter's model for industry
  analysis 183
product life cycle 185
related diversification 188

scenario analysis 180
single-product
  strategy 187
stability strategy 176
strategic control 177
strategic management 169
strategic positioning 171
strategy 169
strategy formulation 177
strategy implementation 177
SWOT analysis 179
synergy 189
trend analysis 180
unrelated diversification 188

Summary

6.1 The Dynamics of Strategic Planning
Every organization needs to have a "big picture" about where it's going and how to get there, which involves strategy, strategic management, and strategic planning. A strategy is a large-scale action plan that sets the direction for an organization. Strategic management involves managers from all parts of the organization in the formulation and implementation of strategies and strategic goals. Strategic planning determines the organization's long-term goals and ways to achieve them.

Three reasons why an organization should adopt strategic management and strategic planning: they can (1) provide direction and momentum, (2) encourage new ideas, and (3) develop a sustainable competitive advantage. Sustainable competitive advantage occurs when an organization is able to get and stay ahead in four areas: (1) in being responsive to customers, (2) in innovating, (3) in quality, and (4) in effectiveness.

Strategic positioning attempts to achieve sustainable competitive advantage

by preserving what is distinctive about a company. Three key principles underlie strategic positioning: (1) Strategy is the creation of a unique and valuable position. (2) Strategy requires trade-offs in competing. (3) Strategy involves creating a "fit" among a company's activities.

6.2 The Strategic Management Process
The strategic management process has five steps plus a feedback loop.

Step 1 is to establish the mission statement and the vision statement. The mission statement expresses the organization's purpose. The vision statement describes the organization's long-term direction and strategic intent.

Step 2 is to translate the broad mission and vision statements into a grand strategy that explains how the organization's mission is to be accomplished. Three common grand strategies are (1) a growth strategy, which involves expansion—as in sales revenues; (2) a stability strategy, which involves little or no significant change; and (3) a defensive strategy, which involves reduction in the organization's efforts.

Step 3 is strategy formulation, the translation of the grand strategy into more specific strategic plans, choosing among different strategies and altering them to best fit the organization's needs.

Step 4 is strategy implementation—putting strategic plans into effect. Step 5 is strategic control, monitoring the execution of strategy and making adjustments.

Corrective action constitutes a feedback loop in which a problem requires that managers return to an earlier step to rethink policies, budgets, or personnel arrangements.

6.3 Establishing the Grand Strategy

To develop a grand strategy (Step 2 above), you need to gather data and make projections. This starts with environmental scanning, careful monitoring of a firm's internal and external environments to detect opportunities and threats.

The process for doing such scanning is called SWOT analysis, a search for the Strengths, Weaknesses, Opportunities, and Threats affecting the organization. Organizational strengths are the skills and capabilities that give the organization special competencies and competitive advantages. Organizational weaknesses are the drawbacks that hinder an organization in executing strategies. Organizational opportunities are environmental factors that the organization may exploit for competitive advantage. Organizational threats are environmental factors that hinder an organization's achieving a competitive advantage.

Another tool for developing a grand strategy is forecasting—creating a vision or projection of the future. Two types of forecasting are (1) trend analysis, a hypothetical extension of a past series of events into the future; and (2) contingency planning, the creation of alternative hypothetical but equally likely future conditions.

6.4 Formulating Strategy

Strategy formulation (Step 3 in the strategic-management process) makes use of several concepts, including (1) Porter's five competitive forces, (2) Porter's four competitive strategies, and (3) product life cycles.

Porter's model for industry analysis suggests that business-level strategies originate in five primary competitive forces in the firm's environment: (1) threats of new entrants, (2) bargaining power of suppliers, (3) bargaining power of buyers, (4) threats of substitute products or services, and (5) rivalry among competitors.

Porter's four competitive strategies are as follows: (1) The cost-leadership strategy is to keep the costs, and hence the prices, of a product or service below those of competitors and to target a wide market. (2) The differentiation strategy is to offer products or services that are of unique and superior value compared to those of competitors but to target a wide market. (3) The cost-focus strategy is to keep the costs and hence prices of a product or service below those of competitors and to target a narrow market. (4) The focused-differentiation strategy is to offer products or services that are of unique and superior value compared to those of competitors and to target a narrow market.

A product life cycle is a model of the four stages a product or service goes through: (1) introduction—a new product is introduced into the marketplace and is heavy on start-up costs for production, marketing, and distribution; (2) growth—customer demand increases, the product's sales grow, and later competitors may enter the market; (3) maturity—the product starts to fall out of favor and sales and profits fall off; (4) decline—the product falls out of favor, and the organization withdraws from the marketplace.

Companies needed to choose whether to have a single-product strategy, making and selling only one product within their market, or a diversification strategy, operating several businesses to spread the risk. There are two kinds of diversification: unrelated diversification consists of operating several businesses that are not related to each other; related diversification consists of operating separate businesses that are related to each other, which may reduce risk, produce management efficiencies, and produce synergy or the sum being greater than the parts.

Companies must practice competitive intelligence, gaining information about competitors to try to anticipate their moves, using advertising, news stories, investor information, and informal sources.

 ### 6.5 Implementing & Controlling Strategy: Execution

The last two stages of the strategic-management process are 4, strategic implementation, and 5, strategic control.

Execution, say Larry Bossidy and Ram Charan, is not simply tactics, it is a central part of any company's strategy; it consists of using questioning, analysis, and follow-through to mesh strategy with reality, align people with goals, and achieve results promised.

Three core processes of execution are people, strategy, and operations. (1) You have to evaluate talent by linking people to particular strategic milestones, developing future leaders, dealing with nonperformers, and transforming the mission and operations of the human resource department. (2) In considering whether the organization can execute the strategy, a leader must take a realistic and critical view of its capabilities and competencies. (3) The third core process, operations, or the operating plan, provides the path for people to follow. The operating plan should address all the major activities in which the company will engage and then define short-term objectives for these activities, to provide targets for people to aim at.

Management in Action

Walgreen Pursues New Growth Strategy

Walgreen Co. thrived for decades by opening stores faster than its competitors—a new location pops up every 16 hours—and by pushing out more prescriptions per year than any other chain.

But facing pressure from rivals, a weak economy and cracks in the health system, Walgreen is changing its time-tested formula. Instead of simply bottling pills, it is refashioning itself into a broad health-care provider.

On [March 17, 2008], the Deerfield, Illinois–based company announced plans to buy I-trax Inc. and Whole Health Management, two companies that run a total of 350 health centers at corporate offices. The centers offer services from treating simple illnesses to counseling patients on managing diabetes.

Walgreen expects to open more pharmacies at work sites and to attract employees, their family members, and retirees to its stores. The acquired companies will form part of Walgreen's new health and wellness division and will include Take Care Health Clinics, which operate 136 clinics inside Walgreen stores.

"This is only the beginning of our presence in this sector," Walgreen Chief Executive Jeffrey Rein said in a conference call with analysts. In the United States, there are more than 7,600 office sites with 1,000 or more employees that could support a health-care center, he said.

In the last few years, Walgreen has begun making bolder moves. It has dropped its longtime aversion to acquisitions and snapped up specialty pharmacies that are experts in infertility, cancer, AIDS, and other conditions that are expensive to treat. It is opening pharmacies in hospitals and assisted-living facilities. Last year, it quadrupled the number of pharmacists certified to give flu shots and other immunizations.

Investors, though, aren't sure it is taking the right approach. In October [2007], Walgreen reported its first quarterly earnings decline in nearly a decade, hurt by lower generic-drug reimbursements, and higher store and advertising expenses. Investors were rattled by the rare wobble from Walgreen's normally steady business. Since then, its stock price has dropped nearly 22%. . . .

Meanwhile, two of Walgreen's big rivals, Wal-Mart Stores Inc. and CVS Caremark Corp., are expanding in what they consider a big growth area: the business of managing employer drug-benefit programs.

At a January [2008] meeting with store managers, Wal-Mart Chief Executive Lee Scott signaled that the giant discounter plans to expand health-care cost-cutting initiatives. Among other things, Mr. Scott said the retailer is initiating a pilot program to help "select employers . . . manage how they process and pay prescription claims."

Wal-Mart wouldn't name the companies, and details were sketchy. But Mr. Scott said that by eliminating unnecessary costs, he believes Wal-Mart can save employers more than $100 million this year alone.

CVS has staked its business on the future success of pharmacy-benefit managers, or PBMs, purchasing Caremark last year in a landmark deal. PBMs provide prescription-drug coverage to workers at most U.S. companies, striking deals with retail pharmacies for lower prices and collecting rebates from drug manufacturers. CVS Caremark executives say the combined company will be able to lower employer costs and simplify patient access to prescriptions.

But Mr. Rein, Walgreen's chief executive, has said his drugstore chain doesn't plan to pursue buying a major PBM. "Our relationships with employers and health plans will grow because of our independence from major PBMs," he said. . . .

Walgreen has its own, smaller PBM, but it doesn't play a major role in its new strategy. In the past, Mr. Rein has questioned whether PBMs, which depend heavily on rebates from drug companies, will survive in the long run.

"We believe that the services provided by PBMs are essential to the functioning of the health-care system and will always be needed," said Eileen Howard Dunn, a spokeswoman for CVS Caremark. "Healthy PBMs don't have an overreliance on rebates."

While Walgreen shares have fallen, CVS Caremark shares have risen 17% in the last 52 weeks. . . .

"What folks are missing is that multiple strategies are able to win in such a big area," Gregory Wasson, Walgreen's president, said in an interview. "It's easy to see something big and tangible. CVS has had its shareholders gain value. Ours is a winning strategy. People may not have realized the value yet."

Meanwhile, the business of health care is getting trickier. U.S. prescription sales grew just 3.8% [in 2007], to $286.5 billion, marking the slowest growth rate since 1961, according to a report released . . . by market-research firm IMS Health.

Walgreen has responded to the shifting environment in part by expanding into specialty pharmacy, where drug sales are growing much faster than the overall prescription market.

Specialty pharmacy, a $60 billion business, is increasing 15% to 20% a year, Walgreen says. It also is highly profitable. Many of the newest drugs can't be produced in pill form, and must instead be infused into the patient's bloodstream or injected by an experienced technician.

In September [2007], Walgreen completed its $850 million purchase of OptionCare, which specializes in infusion drugs, such as certain cancer treatments. It was the largest deal in Walgreen's 107-year history, and it made Walgreen the nation's largest independent specialty-pharmacy company.

Although the gross profit margin for specialty drugs is lower on a percentage basis, the profit dollars per prescription are much greater, because specialty drugs are so much more expensive than traditional medicines. Some specialty drugs can cost $1,000 or more per prescription, compared with $75 for the average prescription in 2006, according to the National Association of Chain Drug Stores, a trade group.

Walgreen executives envision bringing together its Take Care clinics, specialty operations, and workplace centers, using electronic prescriptions and medical records, to cover a range of needs.

Patients might visit a Walgreen-owned clinic in their office building, for example, and then pick up a prescription at a Walgreen pharmacy at work or on the way home.

"The real opportunity is to begin to connect the dots," says Mr. Wasson, Walgreen's president.

For Discussion

1. Based on Michael Porter's discussion of the characteristics of an effective strategy, does Walgreen have a good growth strategy? Explain.

2. To what extent is Walgreen following the five steps of the strategic management process?

3. Conduct an environmental scan or SWOT analysis of Walgreen's current reality and recommend whether Walgreen's current strategy is poised to succeed.

4. To what extent will Porter's five competitive forces help or hurt Walgreen's growth strategy? Discuss.

5. What is the greatest take-away from this case in terms of strategic management?

Source: Excerpted from Amy Merrick, "How Walgreen Changed Its Prescription for Growth," *The Wall Street Journal*, March 19, 2008, pp. B1, B2. Copyright © 2008 by Dow Jones & Company, Inc. Reproduced with permission of Dow Jones & Company, Inc. via Copyright Clearance Center.

Self-Assessment

Core Skills Required in Strategic Planning

Objectives

1. To assess if you have the skills to be in strategic planning.
2. To see what you think are the important core skill areas in strategic planning.

Introduction

Strategic planning became important as a method of managing the increasing velocity of change. The business environment no longer evolves at a manageable pace but increasingly through a process Charles Handy calls "discontinuous change"—change that radically alters how we think, work, and often behave. The computer, for instance, has completely changed how we communicate, research, write, and work. To meet this challenge, companies have strategic planners and others knowledgeable about their organizations, culture, and environment to shape strategy. Individuals must develop knowledge about their own abilities so that they formulate their own kind of strategic planning.

Instructions

To see whether you have the required skills needed to be a strategic planner, truthfully and thoughtfully assess your ability level for the following list of 12 skills. Rate each skill by using a five-point scale in which 1 = exceptional, 2 = very high, 3 = high, 4 = low, and 5 = very low.

I. Ability to synthesize		I	2	3	4	5
2. Analytical skills		I	2	3	4	5
3. Computer skills		I	2	3	4	5
4. Decisiveness		I	2	3	4	5
5. Interpersonal skills		I	2	3	4	5
6. Listening skills		I	2	3	4	5
7. Persuasiveness		I	2	3	4	5
8. Problem-solving skills		I	2	3	4	5
9. Research skills		I	2	3	4	5
10. Team skills		I	2	3	4	5
II. Verbal skills		I	2	3	4	5
12. Written skills		I	2	3	4	5

Scoring & Interpretation

According to research conducted at the Ohio State University College of Business, the core required skills for the 12 skills above rate as follows:

Ability to synthesize:	2
Analytical skills:	1
Computer skills:	3
Decisiveness:	3
Interpersonal skills:	1
Listening skills:	2
Persuasiveness:	2
Problem-solving skills:	3

Research skills: 3
Team skills: 2
Verbal skills: 2
Written skills: 3

If you scored mostly 4s and 5s, strategic planning is probably not for you.

If you scored near the "perfect" score, it may be a possible career path.

If you scored all 1s and 2s, you might do extremely well at this type of work and might want to look into it more.

Questions for Discussion

1. Based on your results, do you think you would like to make a career out of strategic planning? Why or why not?

2. What appeals or does not appeal to you about this career? Explain.

3. How might you enhance your strategic skills? Discuss.

Developed by Anne C. Cowden, PhD.

Ethical Dilemma

Should Companies Stockpile the Avian-Influenza Drug Tamiflu?

In 2005, Procter & Gamble asked its company doctors whether P&G should try to secure a private stash of the avian-influenza drug Tamiflu for its staff of 25,000 in Asia. A year later they were still debating the question.

"How ethical would it be if we were holding supplies that the general public didn't have access to but badly needed?" asked Shivanand Priolkar, the company's medical leader for southern Asia. He even worried that "people could come to know you have a life-saving medicine and you could make yourself a target."

Here the tensions are between a company's obligations to its employees and shareholders and its responsibility to the community. "We always believe we support the communities in which we operate," said P&G's Dr. Shivanand. Stockpiling Tamiflu "would take supplies out of the system."

Solving the Dilemma

Suppose you were on a committee at P&G that was considering the issue of stockpiling Tamiflu. What would you recommend?

1. Even though the Avian flu has not killed many people to date, your most important responsibilities are to your employees and shareholders. Stockpile the drug for your employees.

2. Don't worry about the situation because the avian flu has not mutated to a form that is transmissible to humans. A pandemic is very unlikely.

3. Develop stockpiles of the drug in remote areas where you have operations, like Vietnam. Employees in these areas are more likely to get the flu and they are less likely to have access to top-notch health care.

4. Invent other options. Discuss.

Source: Excerpted from Cris Prystay, Murray Hiebert, and Kate Linebaugh, "Companies Face Ethical Issues Over Tamiflu," *The Wall Street Journal*, January 16, 2006, pp. B1, B3.

Individual & Group Decision Making

How Managers Make Things Happen

Major Questions You Should Be Able to Answer

7.1 The Nature of Decision Making
Major Question: How do I decide to decide?

7.2 Two Kinds of Decision Making: Rational & Nonrational
Major Question: How do people know when they're being logical or illogical?

7.3 Evidence-Based Decision Making & Analytics
Major Question: How can I improve my decision making using evidence-based management and business analytics?

7.4 Making Ethical Decisions
Major Question: What guidelines can I follow to be sure that decisions I make are not just lawful but ethical?

7.5 Group Decision Making: How to Work with Others
Major Question: How do I work with others to make things happen?

7.6 How to Overcome Barriers to Decision Making
Major Question: Trying to be rational isn't always easy. What are the barriers?

How Exceptional Managers Check to See If Their Decisions Might Be Biased

The biggest part of a manager's job is making decisions—and quite often they are wrong. Some questions you might ask next time you're poised to make a decision:

- **"Am I being too cocky?" The overconfidence bias.** If you're making a decision in an area in which you have considerable experience or expertise, you're less likely to be overconfident. Interestingly, however, you're more apt to be overconfident when dealing with questions on subjects you're unfamiliar with or questions with moderate to extreme difficulty.[1]

  Recommendation: When dealing with unfamiliar or difficult matters, think how your impending decision might go wrong. Afterward pay close attention to the consequences of your decision.

- **"Am I considering the actual evidence, or am I wedded to my prior beliefs?" The prior-hypothesis bias.** Do you tend to have strong beliefs? When confronted with a choice, decision makers with strong prior beliefs tend to make their decision based on their beliefs—even if evidence shows those beliefs are wrong. This is known as the *prior-hypothesis bias.*[2]

  Recommendation: Although it's always more comforting to look for evidence to support your prior beliefs, you need to be tough-minded and weigh the evidence.

- **"Are events really connected, or are they just chance?" The ignoring-randomness bias.** Is a rise in sales in athletic shoes because of your company's advertising campaign or because it's the start of the school year? Many managers don't understand the laws of randomness.

  Recommendation: Don't attribute trends or connections to a single, random event.

- **"Is there enough data on which to make a decision?" The unrepresentative sample bias.** If all the secretaries in your office say they prefer dairy creamer to real cream in their coffee, is that enough data on which to launch an ad campaign trumpeting the superiority of dairy creamer? It might if you polled 3,000 secretaries, but 3 or even 30 is too small a sample.

  Recommendation: You need to be attuned to the importance of sample size.

- **"Looking back, did I (or others) really know enough then to have made a better decision?" The 20-20 hindsight bias.** Once managers know what the consequences of a decision are, they may begin to think they could have predicted it. They may remember the facts as being a lot clearer than they actually were.[3]

  Recommendation: Try to keep in mind that hindsight does not equal foresight.

For Discussion "Facing the hard facts about what works and what doesn't," how able do you think you are to make the tough decisions that effective managers have to make?

forecast

What's Ahead in This Chapter

We describe decision making and types of decisions, and we describe the range of decision-making conditions. Next we distinguish between rational and nonrational decision making, and we describe five nonrational models. We then consider evidence-based decision making and the use of analytics. We discuss four steps in practical decision making. We follow with a discussion of group decision making, including participative management and group problem-solving techniques. We conclude by considering how individuals respond to decision situations and four common decision-making biases.

7.I THE NATURE OF DECISION MAKING

How do I decide to decide?

THE BIG PICTURE

Decision making, the process of identifying and choosing alternative courses of action, may be programmed or nonprogrammed. Decision-making conditions range from certainty to risky to uncertainty to confusion.

Ben Swett—former Vassar English major, University of Chicago MBA, TV comedy writer, and Quaker Oats executive—started windowbox.com in 1997 after failing in the seemingly simple task of growing a plant on his balcony in Los Angeles. His mission: to run an online organization that satisfied the needs of urban gardeners, as well as to contribute to the social good.

Selling plants to patio and balcony gardeners, it turns out, is an extremely seasonal business. About half of Swett's annual sales occur at three times: Valentine's Day, Mother's Day, and the 2 weeks before Christmas. What kinds of decisions do Swett and his managers have to make to scale up and down for such a volatile business?[4]

Decision Making Defined

A *decision* is a choice made from among available alternatives. For example, should your college offer (if it currently does not) computer-based distance learning to better serve students who work odd hours or are homebound and can't easily get to lectures on campus? That question is a decision that the college administrators must make.

Decision making **is the process of identifying and choosing alternative courses of action.** For example, the college could offer distance learning by televising the lectures of a single professor into several classrooms or to community centers off campus. Or it could offer distance learning interactively over the Internet. It could offer distance learning only for certain subjects (business and education, say) or for selected courses in all majors. It could offer distance learning only during the summer or only during the evenings. It could charge extra for such courses. It could offer them for credit to high school students or to students attending other colleges. Identifying and sorting out these alternatives is the process of decision making.

Success. Tom Brady, quarterback for the Boston-based New England Patriots, warming up on the sidelines. One of pro football's most successful players, Brady has led his team to three Super Bowl victories. As the leader of his team, a quarterback must make many decisions about what is the right way to success. Brady maintains a standard of excellence both on and off the field. If you were a quarterback, what would you do differently?

General Decision-Making Styles: Directive, Analytical, Conceptual, Behavioral

Do men and women differ in the way they make decisions? Do they, for example, differ in risk propensity? *Risk propensity* **is the willingness to gamble or to undertake risk for the possibility of gaining an increased payoff.**

Perhaps another name for this is competitiveness. And research does seem to show that, as one scholar summarized it, "Even in tasks where they do well, women seem to shy away from competition, whereas men seem to enjoy it too much."[5] In an experiment involving winning small amounts of money in number-memorizing tournaments, men were avid competitors and were eager to continue, partly from overconfidence regardless of their success in earlier rounds, and they rated their abilities more highly than the women rated theirs. Most women declined to compete, even when they had done the best in earlier rounds.[6]

This brings us to the subject of decision-making style. **A *decision-making style* reflects the combination of how an individual perceives and responds to information.** A team of researchers developed a model of decision-making styles based on the idea that styles vary along two different dimensions: value orientation and tolerance for ambiguity.[7]

Value orientation reflects the extent to which a person focuses on either task and technical concerns or people and social concerns when making decisions. Some people, for instance, are very task focused at work and do not pay much attention to people issues, whereas others are just the opposite.

The second dimension pertains to a person's *tolerance for ambiguity*. This individual difference indicates the extent to which a person has a high need for structure or control in his or her life. Some people desire a lot of structure in their lives (a low tolerance for ambiguity) and find ambiguous situations stressful and psychologically uncomfortable. In contrast, others do not have a high need for structure and can thrive in uncertain situations (a high tolerance for ambiguity). Ambiguous situations can energize people with a high tolerance for ambiguity.

When the dimensions of value orientation and tolerance for ambiguity are combined, they form four styles of decision making: *directive, analytical, conceptual,* and *behavioral. (See Figure 7.1.)*

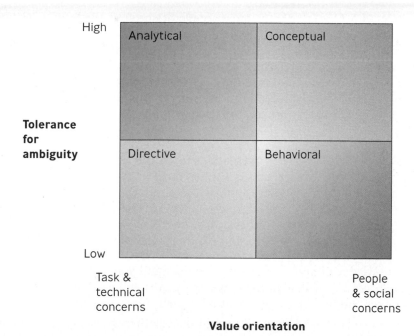

figure 7.1

DECISION-MAKING STYLES

I. Directive People with a directive style have a low tolerance for ambiguity and are oriented toward task and technical concerns in making decisions. They are efficient, logical, practical, and systematic in their approach to solving problems.

People with this style are action oriented and decisive and like to focus on facts. In their pursuit of speed and results, however, these individuals tend to be autocratic, to exercise power and control, and to focus on the short run.

These, er, guys are CEOs?
Herb Kelleher, left, in surgical garb and Gary Kelley, dressed as Edna Turnblad, the mom from *Hairspray*, at a staff Halloween party. They are the former and present CEOs of Southwest Airlines, which was founded in 1971 on the premise of getting passengers to their destinations on time at the lowest possible fares and making sure they had a good time doing it. What kind of decision-making styles would you expect these executives to have?

2. Analytical This style has a much higher tolerance for ambiguity and is characterized by the tendency to overanalyze a situation. People with this style like to consider more information and alternatives than managers following the directive style.

Analytic individuals are careful decision makers who take longer to make decisions but who also respond well to new or uncertain situations.

3. Conceptual People with a conceptual style have a high tolerance for ambiguity and tend to focus on the people or social aspects of a work situation. They take a broad perspective to problem solving and like to consider many options and future possibilities.

Conceptual types adopt a long-term perspective and rely on intuition and discussions with others to acquire information. They also are willing to take risks and are good at finding creative solutions to problems. However, a conceptual style can foster an indecisive approach to decision making.

4. Behavioral This style is the most people oriented of the four styles. People with this style work well with others and enjoy social interactions in which opinions are openly exchanged. Behavioral types are supportive, receptive to suggestions, show warmth, and prefer verbal to written information.

Although they like to hold meetings, people with this style have a tendency to avoid conflict and to be concerned about others. This can lead behavioral types to adopt a wishy-washy approach to decision making and to have a hard time saying no.

Which Style Do You Have? Research shows that very few people have only one dominant decision-making style. Rather, most managers have characteristics that fall into two or three styles. Studies also show that decision-making styles vary across occupations, job level, and countries.[8] There is not a best decision-making style that applies to all situations.

You can use knowledge of decision-making styles in three ways:

- Knowledge of styles helps you to understand yourself. Awareness of your style assists you in identifying your strengths and weaknesses as a decision maker and facilitates the potential for self-improvement.

- You can increase your ability to influence others by being aware of styles. For example, if you are dealing with an analytical person, you should provide as much information as possible to support your ideas.

- Knowledge of styles gives you an awareness of how people can take the same information and yet arrive at different decisions by using a variety of decision-making strategies. Different decision-making styles represent one likely source of interpersonal conflict at work.

Self-Assessment:
Your Preferred Decision-Making Style

To get a sense of your own decision-making style, see the Self-Assessment at the end of this chapter. ●

7.2 TWO KINDS OF DECISION MAKING: RATIONAL & NONRATIONAL

How do people know when they're being logical or illogical?

THE BIG PICTURE

Decision making may be rational, but often it is nonrational. Four steps in making a rational decision are (1) identify the problem or opportunity, (2) think up alternative solutions, (3) evaluate alternatives and select a solution, and (4) implement and evaluate the solution chosen. Two examples of nonrational models are satisficing and incremental.

Why do engineers design products such as DVD remote controls with 52 buttons, devices ultimately useful only to other engineers? Why do professional investors and bankers turn out to be as prone to risk as amateurs, as evidenced by the 2008 subprime-mortgage crisis, in which housing loans were made to borrowers who were truly not good candidates? Why do some managers have trouble convincing their employees to adopt new processes? The answer may be what's known as *the curse of knowledge.* As one writer put it about engineers, for example, "People who design products are experts cursed by their knowledge, and they can't imagine what it's like to be as ignorant as the rest of us."[9] In other words, as our knowledge and expertise grow, we may be less and less able to see things from an outsider's perspective—hence, we are often apt to make irrational decisions.

Let us look at the two approaches managers may take to making decisions: They may follow a *rational model* or various kinds of *nonrational models.*

Rational Decision Making: Managers Should Make Logical & Optimal Decisions

The *rational model of decision making,* also called the *classical model,* explains how managers *should* make decisions; it assumes managers will make logical decisions that will be the optimum in furthering the organization's best interests.

Typically there are four stages associated with rational decision making. *(See Figure 7.2.)*

figure 7.2

THE FOUR STEPS IN RATIONAL DECISION MAKING

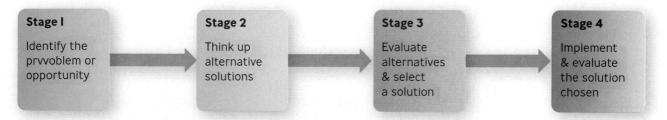

Stage 1
Identify the prvvoblem or opportunity

Stage 2
Think up alternative solutions

Stage 3
Evaluate alternatives & select a solution

Stage 4
Implement & evaluate the solution chosen

Stage I: Identify the Problem or Opportunity—Determining the Actual versus the Desirable

As a manager, you'll probably find no shortage of *problems,* or difficulties that inhibit the achievement of goals. Customer complaints. Supplier breakdowns. Staff turnover. Sales shortfalls. Competitor innovations.

However, you'll also often find *opportunities—situations that present possibilities for exceeding existing goals.* It's the farsighted manager, however, who can look past the steady stream of daily problems and seize the moment to actually do *better* than the goals he or she is expected to achieve. When a competitor's top salesperson unexpectedly quits, that creates an opportunity for your company to hire that person away to promote your product more vigorously in that sales territory.

Whether you're confronted with a problem or an opportunity, the decision you're called on to make is how to make *improvements—*how to change conditions from the present to the desirable. This is a matter of *diagnosis—***analyzing the underlying causes.**

Example

What Do Billionaire Warren Buffett & Female Investors Have in Common? Making a Correct Diagnosis

"Warren Buffett Invests Like a Girl," reads the headline over an article by LouAnn DiCosmo.[10] Is that a good thing? Buffett is the renowned billionaire investor known as the "Oracle of Omaha" who heads the financial juggernaut Berkshire Hathaway. His investment decisions are so successful that $1,000 invested with him in 1956 was worth $27.6 million at the end of 2006.[11] So, does he really invest like a girl?

As it turns out, Buffett and female investors have something in common: "Women trade much less often than men, do a lot more research, and tend to base their investment decisions on considerations other than just numbers," according to one account.[12] Men, says DiCosmo, tend to be "frazzled, frenetic day traders, with their ties askew, hair on end, and eyes bleary. Patience and good decision making help set women apart here." As a result, according to a study cited by DiCosmo, women's portfolios on average gain 1.4% more than men's, and single women's portfolios do 2.3% better than single men's.[13] As for the fabled Buffett, his approach is to use basic arithmetic to analyze several file-cabinet drawers of annual reports and other readily available company financial documents and to look for a record of "high returns on equity capital, low debt, and a consistent, predictable business with sustainable advantages—like Coca-Cola's soft-drink franchise."[14] In other words, he takes pains to make a correct diagnosis before making a decision.

Your Call

When preparing to make decisions—especially financial decisions—do you spend a lot of time trying to make a correct diagnosis, doing deep research (as women investors are said to do), or do you chase "hot" tips and make snap judgments (as men reportedly do)?

Stage 2: Think Up Alternative Solutions—Both the Obvious & the Creative

Employees burning with bright ideas are an employer's greatest competitive resource. "Creativity precedes innovation, which is its physical expression," says *Fortune* magazine writer Alan Farnham. "It's the source of all intellectual property."[15]

After you've identified the problem or opportunity and diagnosed its causes, you need to come up with alternative solutions.

Stage 3: Evaluate Alternatives & Select a Solution—Ethics, Feasibility, & Effectiveness

In this stage, you need to evaluate each alternative not only according to cost and quality but also according to the following questions: (1) Is it *ethical*? (If it isn't, don't give it a second look.) (2) Is it *feasible*? (If time is short, costs are high, technology unavailable, or customers resistant, for example, it is not.) (3) Is it ultimately *effective*? (If the decision is merely "good enough" but not optimal in the long run, you might reconsider.)

Stage 4: Implement & Evaluate the Solution Chosen

With some decisions, implementation is usually straightforward (though not necessarily easy—firing employees who steal may be an obvious decision but it can still be emotionally draining). With other decisions, implementation can be quite difficult; when one company acquires another, for instance, it may take months to consolidate the departments, accounting systems, inventories, and so on.

Successful Implementation   For implementation to be successful, you need to do two things:

- **Plan carefully.** Especially if reversing an action will be difficult, you need to make careful plans for implementation. Some decisions may require written plans.
- **Be sensitive to those affected.** You need to consider how the people affected may feel about the change—inconvenienced, insecure, even fearful, all of which can trigger resistance. This is why it helps to give employees and customers latitude during a changeover in business practices or working arrangements.

Example

Faulty Implementation: Customer Service Is Often "Just Talk"

"My claim to fame, the only thing I've ever been really good at, is returning people's phone calls every single day," says Mark Powers. No doubt it is that kind of customer service that is the reason why Excelsior Roofing of San Francisco, founded by Powers's grandfather over 100 years ago, is still in business.[16]

"Executives talk about the importance of responding to customers' needs with top-notch customer service," writes *Wall Street Journal* columnist Carol Hymowitz. "But often it's just talk."[17]

The problem with faulty customer service, however, is that sometimes the company may be the last to hear about it, but a great many other potential customers may hear of it by word of mouth. One study found that only 6% of shoppers who experienced a problem with a retailer contacted the company. However, 31% went on to tell friends, family, and colleagues what had happened. Indeed, if 100 people have a bad experience, a retailer stands to lose between 32

and 36 current or potential customers, according to the study.[18]

Consultants working for one large telecommunications company encourage customer service reps at one call center to share their problems and successes with each other and bring in customers to report their positive and negative experiences with the call center. To encourage customer reps to "step inside the shoes of customers," the consultants also presented a weekly award of a pair of baby shoes to the employee who solved the most customer problems.[19]

Your Call

We're all accustomed to pumping our own gas and doing our own banking through ATMs. Now retailers are moving toward self-service checkout lanes, as is done by Fresh & Easy grocery stores, and airlines toward self-check-in kiosks.[20]

What do you think the self-serve trend means for customer service?

Evaluation One "law" in economics is the Law of Unintended Consequences—things happen that weren't foreseen. For this reason, you need to follow up and evaluate the results of the decision.

What should you do if the action is not working? Some possibilities:

- **Give it more time.** You need to make sure employees, customers, and so on have had enough time to get used to the new action.

- **Change it slightly.** Maybe the action was correct, but it just needs "tweaking"—a small change of some sort.

- **Try another alternative.** If Plan A doesn't seem to be working, maybe you want to scrap it for another alternative.

- **Start over.** If no alternative seems workable, you need to go back to the drawing board—to Stage 1 of the decision-making process.

What's Wrong with the Rational Model?

The rational model is *prescriptive,* describing how managers ought to make decisions. It doesn't describe how managers *actually* make decisions. Indeed, the rational model makes some highly desirable assumptions—that managers have complete information, are able to make an unemotional analysis, and are able to make the best decision for the organization. *(See Table 7.1.)*

table 7.1

ASSUMPTIONS OF THE RATIONAL MODEL

- **Complete information, no uncertainty:** You should obtain complete, error-free information about all alternative courses of action and the consequences that would follow from each choice.

- **Logical, unemotional analysis:** Having no prejudices or emotional blind spots, you are able to logically evaluate the alternatives, ranking them from best to worst according to your personal preferences.

- **Best decision for the organization:** Confident of the best future course of action, you coolly choose the alternative that you believe will most benefit the organization.

Example

Evaluation: The Boeing 787 Dreamliner, a Bet-the-Company Decision

The airline industry is one of the most volatile around, and Boeing Co., the Chicago-headquartered aerospace giant, has been through some rough boom-and-bust cycles. In 1997, for instance, production problems shut down two assembly lines and cost the company $2.5 billion.

Then, at a time when Boeing was losing business to its European rival Airbus, the company was wracked by scandals involving Pentagon contracts, and rising fuel costs were dramatically impacting the commercial airline industry, Boeing management made a bold decision: It would build a new medium-sized commercial jet, the 787 Dreamliner, its first new aircraft in 10 years, that would fly faster than the competition and would consume 20% less fuel than similar-sized planes. To achieve this, the 787 would feature more fuel-efficient engines and the fuselage would be built from plastic composite materials instead of aluminum. This would cut down on structural fatigue and corrosion, thereby reducing the number of inspections necessary and increasing the number of flights possible. "A light, strong plane is the big payoff for the huge technical risk Boeing is taking in crafting parts out of composites," said aerospace reporter Stanley Holmes.[21]

However, in mid-2006, as the scheduled 2008 delivery date neared, the company was encountering bad news. The fuselage section had failed in testing, and engineers had discovered worrisome bubbles in its skin. The carbon-fiber wing was too heavy, adding to the plane's overall weight. To hold costs down, Boeing had outsourced about 70% of the production to major suppliers acting as risk-sharing partners and playing a greater role in design and manufacturing. In return for investing more upfront and taking on a share of the development costs, suppliers were given major sections of the airplane to build.[22] By late 2007, however, it was apparent that suppliers were struggling to meet the exacting

technological demands and deadlines and their software programs were having trouble communicating with each other. In October, Boeing announced it would no longer meet its May 2008 target date, and was postponing its first delivery to October or November of that year.[23] In early 2008, the company said the poor quality of outsourced work and the unprecedented amount of coordination among suppliers caused Boeing to shift much of the work back to its Everett, Washington, assembly plant, adding to delays. It said it was working to try to begin deliveries of the 787 to customers not in late 2008 but in the first quarter of 2009.[24] In April, it changed the scheduled delivery date once again—to the third quarter of 2009.[25]

Your Call

By now you, the reader, may be in a position to know whether Boeing made its 2009 deadline and how much it had to pay in financial penalties to the customers it had lined up. Did the company's huge bet on the Dreamliner pay off? How would you evaluate Boeing's decisions?

Nonrational Decision Making: Managers Find It Difficult to Make Optimal Decisions

Nonrational models of decision making **explain how managers make decisions; they assume that decision making is nearly always uncertain and risky, making it difficult for managers to make optimal decisions.** The nonrational models are *descriptive* rather than prescriptive: They describe how managers *actually* make decisions rather than how they should. Three nonrational models are (1) *satisficing,* (2) *incremental,* and (3) *intuition.*

I. Bounded Rationality & the Satisficing Model: "Satisfactory Is Good Enough"   During the 1950s, economist **Herbert Simon**—who later received the Nobel Prize—began to study how managers actually make decisions. From his research he proposed that managers could not act truly logically because their rationality was bounded by so many restrictions.[26] Called *bounded rationality,* **the concept suggests that the ability of decision makers to be rational is limited by numerous constraints,** such as complexity, time and money, and their cognitive capacity, values, skills, habits, and unconscious reflexes. *(See Figure 7.3.)*

- **Complexity:**
The problems that need solving are often exceedingly complex, beyond understanding.

- **Time and money constraints:**
There is not enough time and money to gather all relevant information.

- **Different cognitive capacity, values, skills, habits, and unconscious reflexes:**
Managers aren't all built the same way, of course, and all have personal limitations and biases that affect their judgment.

- **Imperfect information:**
Managers have imperfect, fragmentary information about the alternatives and their consequences.

- **Information overload:**
There is too much information for one person to process.

- **Different priorities:**
Some data are considered more important, so certain facts are ignored.

- **Conflicting goals:**
Other managers, including colleagues, have conflicting goals.

figure 7.3

SOME HINDRANCES TO PERFECTLY RATIONAL DECISION MAKING

Because of such constraints, managers don't make an exhaustive search for the best alternative. Instead, they follow what Simon calls the ***satisficing model—*** **that is, managers seek alternatives until they find one that is satisfactory, not optimal.** Once a Motorola-led consortium called Irridium developed a clunky satellite-linked mobile phone that weighed 1 pound, could not be used inside buildings or moving cars, and cost $3,000. Instead of waiting to improve the technology, Irridium tried to market the mobile phone, a clear and costly example of satisficing.

While looking for a solution that is merely "satisficing" might seem to be a weakness, it may well outweigh any advantages gained from delaying making a decision until all information is in and all alternatives weighed. However, making snap decisions can also backfire.

Nonrational decision making? This renovated McDonald's in Hacienda Heights, California, with its ever-expanding Asian population, was designed with the help of experts in feng shui, the Chinese art of creating harmonious surroundings. Walls are curved, ceiling and floor tiles are placed at distinctive angles, and doors swing open and shut in opposite directions, all in the name of keeping luck within the restaurant. Are these good nonrational decisions?

2. The Incremental Model: "The Least That Will Solve the Problem" Another nonrational decision-making model is the ***incremental model,*** **in which managers take small, short-term steps to alleviate a problem,** rather than steps that will accomplish a long-term solution. Of course, over time a series of short-term steps may move toward a long-term solution. However, the temporary steps may also impede a beneficial long-term solution.

3. The Intuition Model: "It Just Feels Right" Despite the lack of supporting marketing research, Bob Lutz, then president of Chrysler Corporation, ordered the development of the Dodge Viper, a "muscle car" that became very popular. "It was this subconscious, visceral feeling," he said about his decision later. "And it just felt right."[27]

"Going with your gut," or ***intuition,*** **is making a choice without the use of conscious thought or logical inference.** Intuition that stems from *expertise*—a person's explicit and tacit knowledge about a person, situation, object, or decision opportunity—is known as a *holistic hunch.*

Intuition based on feelings—the involuntary emotional response to those same matters—is known as *automated experience*. It is important to try to develop your intuitive skills because they are as important as rational analysis in many decisions. Some suggestions appear below. *(See Table 7.2.)*

table 7.2

GUIDELINES FOR DEVELOPING INTUITIVE AWARENESS

Recommendation	Description
1. Open up the closet	To what extent do you experience intuition; trust your feelings; count on intuitive judgments; suppress hunches; covertly rely upon gut feel.
2. Don't mix up your I's	Instinct, Insight, and Intuition are not synonymous; practice distinguishing between your instincts, your insights, and your intuitions.
3. Elicit good feedback	Seek feedback on your intuitive judgments; build confidence in your gut feel; create a learning environment in which you can develop better intuitive awareness.
4. Get a feel for your batting average	Benchmark your intuitions; get a sense of how reliable hunches are; ask yourself how your intuitive judgment might be improved.
5. Use imagery	Use imagery rather than words; literally visualize potential future scenarios that take your gut feelings into account.
6. Play devil's advocate	Test out intuitive judgments; raise objections to them; generate counter-arguments; probe how robust gut feel is when challenged.
7. Capture and validate your intuitions	Create the inner state to give your intuitive mind the freedom to roam; capture your creative intuitions; log them before they are censored by rational analysis.

Source: E. Sadler-Smith and E. Shefy, "The Intuitive Executive: Understanding and Applying Gut Feel in Decision Making," *Academy of Management Executive,* November 2004, p. 88. Copyright © 2004 by Academy of Management. Reproduced with permission of Academy of Management via Copyright Clearance Center.

As a model for making decisions, intuition has at least two benefits. (1) It can speed up decision making, useful when deadlines are tight.[28] (2) It can be helpful to managers when resources are limited. A drawback, however, is that it can be difficult to convince others that your hunch makes sense. In addition, intuition is subject to the same biases as those that affect rational decision making, as we discuss in Section 7.6.[29] Still, we believe that intuition and rationality are complementary and that managers should develop the courage to use intuition when making decisions.[30] ●

Manager's Hot Seat:
Office Romance: Groping For Answers

major question?

How can I improve my decision making using evidence-based management and business analytics?

THE BIG PICTURE

Evidence-based decision making, which depends on an "attitude of wisdom," rests on three truths. This section describes seven principles for implementing evidence-based management. We also describe why it is hard to bring this approach to bear on one's decision making. Finally, we describe analytics and its three key attributes.

It was the jet that Boeing *didn't* build that avoided what could have been possibly the worst disaster in the company's history and gave the aircraft builder the opportunity to go in a new direction.

In late 2002, Boeing was desperately trying to figure out what kind of passenger airliner to build that would allow the company to effectively compete with its European rival Airbus. In October, Boeing executives met with several global airline representatives in Seattle. A Boeing manager drew a graph on a whiteboard, with axes representing cruising range and passenger numbers. Then he asked airline representatives to locate their ideal position on the graph. "The distribution of the data," reports *Time,* "favored efficiency over speed—the exact opposite of what Boeing was thinking. Two months later, Boeing ditched plans for a high-speed, high-cost jetliner to embark on a new program"—what became the massive attempt to build the 787 Dreamliner.[31]

Evidence-Based Decision Making

"Too many companies and too many leaders are more interested in just copying others, doing what they've always done, and making decisions based on beliefs in what ought to work rather than what actually works," say Stanford professors **Jeffrey Pfeffer** and **Robert Sutton.** "They fail to face the hard facts and use the best evidence to help navigate the competitive environment."[32] This is what Boeing narrowly averted in that Seattle conference, when it was getting ready to spend billions of dollars trying to outcompete Airbus by building a faster aircraft. Companies that use evidence-based management—the translation of principles based on best evidence into organizational practice—routinely trump the competition, Pfeffer and Sutton suggest.

Seven Implementation Principles Pfeffer and Sutton identify seven implementation principles to help companies that are committed to doing what it takes to profit from evidence-based management:[33]

- **Treat your organization as an unfinished prototype.** Leaders need to think and act as if their organization is an unfinished prototype that won't be ruined by dangerous new ideas or impossible to change because of employee or management resistance. Example: The products home-shopping network QVC sells are selected through a process of constant experimentation, punctuated by evidence-based analysis as to why some sell and some don't.

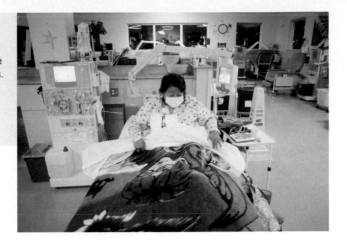

Evidence-based decisions. The staff at DaVita kidney dialysis centers try to evaluate evidence before making patient decisions. Would you expect a "just the facts" approach to be normal in business (and medical) organizations or unusual?

- **No brag, just facts.** This slogan is an antidote for assertions made with complete disregard for whether they correspond to facts. Example: Hewlett-Packard CEO Carly Fiorina bragged to the press about HP's merger with Compaq but failed to consider facts about consumer dissatisfaction with Compaq products until after the merger. Other companies, such as DaVita, which operates dialysis centers, take pains to evaluate data before making decisions.

- **See yourself and your organization as outsiders do.** Most managers are afflicted with "rampant optimism," with inflated views of their own talents and prospects for success, which causes them to downplay risks and continue on a path despite evidence things are not working. "Having a blunt friend, mentor, or counselor," Pfeffer and Sutton suggest, "can help you see and act on better evidence."

- **Evidence-based management is not just for senior executives.** The best organizations are those in which everyone, not just the top managers, is guided by the responsibility to gather and act on quantitative and qualitative data and share results with others.

- **Like everything else, you still need to sell it.** "Unfortunately, new and exciting ideas grab attention even when they are vastly inferior to old ideas," the Stanford authors say. "Vivid, juicy stories and case studies sell better than detailed, rigorous, and admittedly dull data—no matter how wrong the stories or how right the data." To sell an evidence-based approach, you may have to identify a preferred practice based on solid if unexciting evidence, then use vivid stories to grab management attention.

- **If all else fails, slow the spread of bad practice.** Because many managers and employees face pressures to do things that are known to be ineffective, it may be necessary for you to practice "evidence-based misbehavior"—that is, ignore orders you know to be wrong or delay their implementation.

- **The best diagnostic question: what happens when people fail?** "Failure hurts, it is embarrassing, and we would rather live without it," the authors write. "Yet there is no learning without failure.... If you look at how the most effective systems in the world are managed, a hallmark is that when something goes wrong, people face the hard facts, learn what happened and why, and keep using those facts to make the system better." From the U.S. civil aviation system, which rigorously examines airplane accidents, near misses, and equipment problems, to Intel's Andy Grove's willingness to learn from mistakes, evidence-based management makes the point that failure is a great teacher. This means, however, that the organization must "forgive and remember" people who make mistakes, not be trapped by preconceived notions, and confront the best evidence and hard facts.

What Makes It Hard to Be Evidence Based Despite your best intentions, it's hard to bring the best evidence to bear on your decisions. Among the reasons:[34] (1) There's too much evidence. (2) There's not enough *good* evidence. (3) The evidence doesn't quite apply. (4) People are trying to mislead you. (5) *You* are trying to mislead you. (6) The side effects outweigh the cure. (Example: Despite the belief that social promotion in school is a bad idea—that is, that schools shouldn't advance children to the next grade when they haven't mastered the material—the side effect is skyrocketing costs because it crowds schools with older students, and angrier students, demanding more resources.) (7) Stories are more persuasive, anyway.

In Praise of Analytics

Perhaps the purest application of evidence-based management is the use of *analytics,* or *business analytics,* **the term used for sophisticated forms of business data analysis.** One example of analytics is portfolio analysis, in which an investment advisor evaluates the risks of various stocks. Another example is the time-series forecast, which predicts future data based on patterns of historical data.

Some leaders and firms have become exceptional practitioners of analytics. Elsewhere (Chapter 2) we mentioned Harrah's Gary Loveman, whose famous paper and book *Diamonds in the Data Mine* explained how data-mining software was used to analyze vast amounts of casino customer data to target profitable patrons.[35] Others are Marriott International, which through its Total Hotel Optimization program has used quantitative data to establish the optimal price for hotel rooms, evaluate use of conference facilities and catering, and develop systems to optimize offerings to frequent customers.[36]

Example

Use of Analytics: The Oakland A's Play "Moneyball"

As one of the poorest teams in Major League Baseball, with the sixth-lowest payroll ($41 million in 2002, compared with the New York Yankees' $126 million), how did the Oakland Athletics win so many games? That was the question writer Michael Lewis set out to investigate, and he provides answers in *Moneyball: The Art of Winning an Unfair Game.*[37]

Clearly, the A's couldn't afford superstar talent by competing on the open market for it. Thus, the organization had to find players who could contribute in ways that other clubs didn't value as much, and then minimize the risk in their investment by using players in

unconventional ways to maximize their value. Avoiding the use of traditional baseball statistics, the California club found, for example, that better indicators of success lay in on-base percentage and slugging percentage, and that avoiding an out was more important than getting a hit.

Armed with an unprecedented seven first-round draft picks for the 2002 season, the A's crunched the numbers and concentrated primarily on college players (rather than veteran professionals), taking 25 college players with their first 28 picks. Despite the low budget for player salaries, the analytics paid off, and the A's have won as many as 102 games a season and emerged as a perennial playoff team.[38]

Since the Athletics' success, other professional sports franchises have also applied analytics to their payrolls, including, in the NFL, the New England Patriots, winners of three Super Bowls in 4 years.[39]

Your Call

Executives and personnel people in other lines of work are often like the old baseball traditionalists, relying on résumé, degree, years of experience, and even looks in evaluating job applicants. What other, more quantifiable measures might be used instead?

Thomas H. Davenport and others at Babson College's Working Knowledge Research Center studied 32 organizations that made a commitment to quantitative, fact-based analysis and found three key attributes among analytics competitors.[40]

I. Use of Modeling: Going beyond Simple Descriptive Statistics

Companies such as Capital One look well beyond basic statistics, using data mining and predictive modeling to identify potential and most profitable customers. *Predictive modeling* **is a data mining technique used to predict future behavior and anticipate the consequences of change.** Thus, Capital One conducts more than 30,000 experiments a year, with different interest rates, incentives, direct-mail packaging, and other variables to evaluate which customers are most apt to sign up for credit cards and will pay back their debt.

2. Having Multiple Applications, Not Just One

UPS (formerly United Parcel Service) applies analytics not only to tracking the movement of packages but also to examining usage patterns to try to identify potential customer defections so that salespeople can make contact and solve problems. Analytics competitors "don't gain advantage from one killer app [application], but rather from multiple applications supporting many parts of the business," says Davenport.

3. Support from the Top

"A companywide embrace of analytics impels changes in culture, processes, behavior, and skills for many employees," says Davenport. "And so, like any major transition, it requires leadership from executives at the very top who have a passion for the quantitative approach." ●

Are the customers browned off? Big Brown, or UPS, uses analytics for more than one application—not only to track package deliveries but also to determine if customers are defecting.

7.4 MAKING ETHICAL DECISIONS

major question?   What guidelines can I follow to be sure that decisions I make are not just lawful but ethical?

THE BIG PICTURE

A graph known as a decision tree can help one make ethical decisions. In addition, one should be aware of "the magnificent seven" general moral principles for managers.

For kinder capitalism. Bill Gates, former chairman of Microsoft, has called for "creative capitalism" that uses market forces to address poor-country needs. Would you agree with him that the rate of improvement in technology, health care, and education for the bottom third of the world's people has been unsatisfactory?

The ethical behavior of businesspeople has become of increasing concern in recent years, brought about by a number of events. First were the business scandals of the early 2000s, from Enron to WorldCom, producing photos of handcuffed executives. "The supposedly 'independent' auditors, directors, accountants, and stock market advisers and accountants were all tarnished," wrote Mortimer Zuckerman, editor-in-chief of *U.S. News & World Report,* "the engine of the people's involvement, the mutual fund industry, was shown to be permeated by rip-off artists rigging the system for the benefit of insiders and the rich."[41] Then, reports came back of sweetheart deals and gross abuses by civilian contractors working in Iraq war zones. In 2007, it became apparent that banks and others in the financial industry had forsaken sound business judgment—including ethical judgments—by making mortgage loans (subprime loans) to essentially unqualified buyers, which led to a wave of housing foreclosures and helped push the country into a recession. Through it all, voices were being raised that American capitalism was not doing enough to help the poorer nations in the world. "We have to find a way to make the aspects of capitalism that serve wealthier people serve poorer people as well," said Microsoft's Bill Gates in 2008. Companies in wealthier countries, he urged, should focus on "a twin mission: making profits and also improving lives for those who don't fully benefit from market forces."[42]

All these concerns have forced the subject of right-minded decision making to the top of the agenda in many organizations. Indeed, many companies now have an ***ethics officer, someone trained about matters of ethics in the workplace, particularly about resolving ethical dilemmas.*** More and more companies are also creating values statements to guide employees as to what constitutes desirable business behavior.[43] As a result of this raised consciousness, managers now must try to make sure their decisions are not just lawful but also ethical, a subject discussed in detail in Chapter 3.

Road Map to Ethical Decision Making: A Decision Tree

One of the greatest pressures—if not *the* greatest pressure—on top executives is to maximize shareholder value, to deliver the greatest return on investment to the owners of their company. But is a decision that is beneficial to shareholders yet harmful to employees—such as forcing them to contribute more to their health benefits, as IBM has done—unethical? Harvard Business School professor Constance Bagley suggests that what is needed is a decision tree to help with ethical decisions.[44] **A *decision tree* is a graph of decisions and their possible consequences; it is used to create a plan to reach a goal.** Decision trees are used to aid in making decisions. Bagley's ethical decision tree is shown on the next page. *(See Figure 7.4.)*

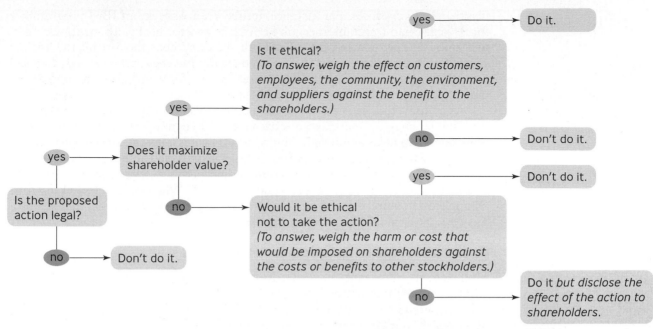

Source: Reprinted by permission of *Harvard Business Review*. Exhibit from "The Ethical Leader's Decision Tree," by C. E. Bagley, February 2003. Copyright © 2003 by the Harvard Business School Publishing Corporation; all rights reserved.

figure 7.4

THE ETHICAL DECISION TREE: WHAT'S THE RIGHT THING TO DO?

When confronted with any proposed action for which a decision is required, a manager should ask the following questions:

1. **Is the Proposed Action Legal?** This may seem an obvious question. But, Bagley observes, "recent [2002–2003] corporate shenanigans suggest that some managers need to be reminded: If the action isn't legal, don't do it."

2. **If "Yes," Does the Proposed Action Maximize Shareholder Value?** If the action is legal, one must next ask whether it will profit the shareholders. If the answer is "yes," should you do it? Not necessarily.

3. **If "Yes," Is the Proposed Action Ethical?** As Bagley, points out, though directors and top managers may believe they are bound by corporate law to always maximize shareholder value, the courts and many state legislatures have held they are not. Rather, their main obligation is to manage "for the best interests of the corporation," which includes the larger community.

   Thus, says Bagley, building a profitable-but-polluting plant in a country overseas may benefit the shareholders but be bad for that country—and for the corporation's relations with that nation. Ethically, then, managers should add pollution-control equipment.

4. **If "No," Would It Be Ethical *Not* to Take the Proposed Action?** If the action would not directly benefit shareholders, might it still be ethical to go ahead with it?

   Not building the overseas plant might be harmful to other stakeholders, such as employees or customers. Thus, the ethical conclusion might be to build the plant with pollution-control equipment but to disclose the effects of the decision to shareholders.

Applying the Ethical Decision Tree

When IBM raised the amount of the contribution it required of its retirees to continue their health benefits, in order to save the company money, was that an ethical decision? Certainly it created a positive impact on shareholder value. However, at the same time it hurt employees, some of whom were not able to easily pay for

Self-Assessment:
Assessing Your Ethical Decision-Making Skills

Group Exercise:
Applying the Ethical Decision-Making Tree

health-related expenses. For instance, retiree Fran Asbeck, an IBM programmer for 32 years, had to get another job in order to pay for his health insurance. "I'm just going to have to work until I'm in the box and hear the dirt hit the lid," he says.[45] Retirees realize that IBM is covered legally, but they feel betrayed. "We feel that IBM has a social contract with the retirees . . . for which they are now reneging," says a former IBM employee in Vermont.[46]

As a basic guideline to making good ethical decisions on behalf of a corporation, Bagley suggests that directors, managers, and employees need to follow their own individual ideas about right and wrong. There is a lesson, she suggests, in the response of the pension fund manager who, when asked whether she would invest in a company doing business in a country that permits slavery, responded, "Do you mean me, personally, or as a fund manager?" When people feel entitled or compelled to compromise their own personal ethics to advance the interests of a business, "it is an invitation to mischief."[47]

Manager's Hot Seat:
Ethics: Let's Make a Fourth-Quarter Deal

General Moral Principles for Managers

Management consultant and writer Kent Hodgson suggests there are no absolute ethical answers for managerial decision makers. Rather, the goal for managers, he believes, should be to rely on moral principles so that their decisions are *principled, appropriate,* and *defensible.*[48] Accordingly, Hodgson has put forth what he calls "the magnificent seven" general moral principles for managers. *(See Table 7.3.)* ●

table 7.3

THE MAGNIFICENT SEVEN: GENERAL MORAL PRINCIPLES FOR MANAGERS

1. **Dignity of human life: The lives of people are to be respected.** Human beings, by the fact of their existence, have value and dignity. We may not act in ways that directly intend to harm or kill an innocent person. Human beings have a right to live; we have an obligation to respect that right to life. Human life is to be preserved and treated as sacred.
2. **Autonomy: All persons are intrinsically valuable and have the right to self-determination.** We should act in ways that demonstrate each person's worth, dignity, and right to free choice. We have a right to act in ways that assert our own worth and legitimate needs. We should not use others as mere "things" or only as means to an end. Each person has an equal right to basic human liberty, compatible with a similar liberty for others.
3. **Honesty: The truth should be told to those who have a right to know it.** Honesty is also known as integrity, truth telling, and honor. One should speak and act so as to reflect the reality of the situation. Speaking and acting should mirror the way things really are. There are times when others have the right to hear the truth from us; there are times when they do not.
4. **Loyalty: Promises, contracts, and commitments should be honored.** Loyalty includes fidelity, promise keeping, keeping the public trust, good citizenship, excellence in quality of work, reliability, commitment, and honoring just laws and policies.
5. **Fairness: People should be treated justly.** One has the right to be treated fairly, impartially, and equitably. One has the obligation to treat others fairly and justly. All have the right to the necessities of life—especially those in deep need and the helpless. Justice includes equal, impartial, unbiased treatment. Fairness tolerates diversity and accepts differences in people and their ideas.
6. **Humaneness.** There are two parts: (1) **Our actions ought to accomplish good,** and (2) **we should avoid doing evil.** We should do good to others and to ourselves. We should have concern for the well-being of others; usually, we show this concern in the form of compassion, giving, kindness, serving, and caring.
7. **The common good: Actions should accomplish the "greatest good for the greatest number" of people.** One should act and speak in ways that benefit the welfare of the largest number of people, while trying to protect the rights of individuals.

Source: From Kent Hodgson, *A Rock and a Hard Place: How to Make Ethical Business Decisions When the Choices Are Tough,* AMACOM, 1992, pp. 69–73. Reprinted with permission of the author.

7.5 GROUP DECISION MAKING: HOW TO WORK WITH OTHERS

How do I work with others to make things happen?

THE BIG PICTURE

Group decision making has five potential advantages and four potential dis-advantages. There are a number of characteristics of groups that a manager should be aware of, as well as participative management and group problem-solving techniques.

The movies celebrate the lone heroes who, like Clint Eastwood, make their own moves, call their own shots. Most managers, however, work with groups and teams (as we discuss in Chapter 13). Although groups don't make as high-quality decisions as the best individual acting alone, research suggests that groups make better decisions than *most* individuals acting alone.[49] Thus, to be an effective manager, you need to learn about decision making in groups.

Advantages & Disadvantages of Group Decision Making

Because you may often have a choice as to whether to make a decision by yourself or to consult with others, you need to understand the advantages and disadvantages of group-aided decision making.

Group Exercise:
Stranded in the Desert: An Exercise in Decision-Making

Advantages   Using a group to make a decision offers five possible advantages.[50] For these benefits to happen, however, the group must be made up of diverse participants, not just people who all think the same way.

- **Greater pool of knowledge.** When several people are making the decision, there is a greater pool of information from which to draw. If one person doesn't have the pertinent knowledge and experience, someone else might.

- **Different perspectives.** Because different people have different perspectives—marketing, production, legal, and so on—they see the problem from different angles.

- **Intellectual stimulation.** A group of people can brainstorm or otherwise bring greater intellectual stimulation and creativity to the decision-making process than is usually possible with one person acting alone.

- **Better understanding of decision rationale.** If you participate in making a decision, you are more apt to understand the reasoning behind the decision, including the pros and cons leading up to the final step.

- **Deeper commitment to the decision.** If you've been part of the group that has bought into the final decision, you're more apt to be committed to seeing that the course of action is successfully implemented.

Disadvantages   The disadvantages of group-aided decision making spring from problems in how members interact.[51]

- **A few people dominate or intimidate.** Sometimes a handful of people will talk the longest and the loudest, and the rest of the group will simply

Different perspectives or groupthink? A diversified team can offer differing points of view, as well as a greater pool of knowledge and intellectual stimulation. Or it can offer groupthink and satisficing. What has been your experience as to the value of decision making in the groups you've been in?

give in. Or one individual, such as a strong leader, will exert disproportional influence, sometimes by intimidation. This cuts down on the variety of ideas.

- **Groupthink.** *Groupthink* **occurs when group members strive to agree for the sake of unanimity and thus avoid accurately assessing the decision situation.** Here the positive team spirit of the group actually works against sound judgment.

- **Satisficing.** Because most people would just as soon cut short a meeting, the tendency is to seek a decision that is "good enough" rather than to push on in pursuit of other possible solutions. Satisficing can occur because groups have limited time, lack the right kind of information, or are unable to handle large amounts of information.[52]

- **Goal displacement.** Although the primary task of the meeting may be to solve a particular problem, other considerations may rise to the fore, such as rivals trying to win an argument. *Goal displacement* **occurs when the primary goal is subsumed by a secondary goal.**

What Managers Need to Know about Groups & Decision Making

If you're a manager deliberating whether to call a meeting for group input, there are four characteristics of groups to be aware of:

I. They Are Less Efficient Groups take longer to make decisions. Thus, if time is of the essence, you may want to make the decision by yourself. Faced with time pressures or the serious effect of a decision, groups use less information and fewer communication channels, which increases the probability of a bad decision.[53]

2. Their Size Affects Decision Quality The larger the group, the lower the quality of the decision.[54]

3. They May Be Too Confident Groups are more confident about their judgments and choices than individuals are. This, of course, can be a liability because it can lead to groupthink.

4. Knowledge Counts Decision-making accuracy is higher when group members know a good deal about the relevant issues. It is also higher when a group leader has the ability to weight members' opinions.[55] Depending on whether group members know or don't know one another, the kind of knowledge also counts. For example, people who are familiar with one another tend to make better decisions when members have a lot of unique information. However, people who aren't familiar with one another tend to make better decisions when the members have common knowledge.[56]

Remember that individual decisions are not *necessarily* better than group decisions. As we said at the outset, although groups don't make as high-quality decisions as the *best* individual acting alone, groups generally make better decisions than *most* individuals acting alone. Some guidelines to using groups are presented on the next page. *(See Table 7.4.)*

1. **When it can increase quality:** If additional information would increase the quality of the decision, managers should involve those people who can provide the needed information. Thus, if a type of decision occurs frequently, such as deciding on promotions or who qualifes for a loan, groups should be used because they tend to produce more consistent decisions than individuals do.

2. **When it can increase acceptance:** If acceptance within the organization is important, managers need to involve those individuals whose acceptance and commitment are imporant.

3. **When it can increase development:** If people can be developed through their participation, managers may want to involve those whose development is most important.

Participative Management: Involving Employees in Decision Making

"Only the most productive companies are going to win," says former General Electric CEO Jack Welch about competition in the world economy. "If you can't sell a top-quality product at the world's lowest price, you're going to be out of the game. In that environment, 6% annual improvement may not be good enough anymore; you may need 8% to 9%."[57]

What Is PM?   One technique that has been touted for meeting this productivity challenge is *participative management (PM)*, **the process of involving employees in (a) setting goals, (b) making decisions, (c) solving problems, and (d) making changes in the organization.**[58] Employees themselves seem to want to participate more in management: in one nationwide survey of 2,408 workers, two-thirds expressed the desire for more influence or decision-making power in their jobs.[59] Thus, participative management is predicted to increase motivation, innovation, and performance because it helps employees fulfill three basic needs: autonomy, meaningfulness of work, and interpersonal contact.[60]

Is PM Really Effective?   Does participative management really work? Certainly it can increase employee job involvement, organizational commitment, and creativity, and it can lower role conflict and ambiguity.[61] Yet it has been shown that, although participation has a significant effect on job performance and job satisfaction, that effect is small—a finding that calls into question the practicality of using PM at all.[62]

So what's a manager to do? In our opinion, PM is not a quick-fix solution for low productivity and motivation. Yet it can probably be effective in certain situations, assuming that managers and employees interact constructively—that is, have the kind of relationship that fosters cooperation and respect rather than competition and defensiveness.[63]

Although participative management doesn't work in all situations, it can be effective if certain factors are present, such as supportive managers and employee trust. *(See Table 7.5, next page.)*

Group Problem-Solving Techniques: Reaching for Consensus

Using groups to make decisions generally requires that they reach a *consensus,* **which occurs when members are able to express their opinions and reach agreement to support the final decision.** More specifically, consensus is reached "when all

table 7.4

WHEN A GROUP CAN HELP IN DECISION MAKING: THREE PRACTICAL GUIDELINES

The guidelines may help you as a manager decide whether to include people in a decision-making process and, if so, which people.

Source: Derived from George P. Huber, *Managerial Decision Making* (Glenview, IL: Scott Foresman, 1980), p. 149.

table 7.5

FACTORS THAT CAN HELP
MAKE PARTICIPATIVE
MANAGEMENT WORK

- **Top management is continually involved:** Implementing PM must be monitored and managed by top management.

- **Middle and supervisory managers are supportive:** These managers tend to resist PM because it reduces their authority. Thus, it's important to gain the support and commitment of managers in these ranks.

- **Employees trust managers:** PM is unlikely to succeed when employees don't trust management.

- **Employees are ready:** PM is more effective when employees are properly trained, prepared, and interested in participating.

- **Employees don't work in interdependent jobs:** Interdependent employees generally don't have a broad understanding of the entire production process, so their PM contribution may actually be counterproductive.

- **PM is implemented with TQM:** A study of Fortune 1000 firms during three different years found employee involvement was more effective when it was implemented as part of a broader total quality management (TQM) program.

Sources: P. E. Tesluk, J. L. Farr, J. E. Matheieu, and R. J. Vance, "Generalization of Employee Involvement Training to the Job Setting: Individual and Situational Effects," *Personnel Psychology,* Autumn 1995, pp. 607–632; R. Rodgers, J. E. Hunter, and D. L. Rogers, "Influence of Top Management Commitment on Management Program Success," *Journal of Applied Psychology,* February 1993, pp. 151–155; and S. A. Mohrman, E. E. Lawler III, and G. E. Ledford Jr., "Organizational Effectiveness and the Impact of Employee Involvement and TQM Programs: Do Employee Involvement and TQM Programs Work?" *Journal for Quality and Participation,* January/February 1996, pp. 6–10.

Toward consensus. Working to achieve cooperation in a group can tell you a lot about yourself. How well do you handle the negotiation process? What do you do when you're disappointed in a result achieved by consensus?

members can say they either agree with the decision or have had their 'day in court' and were unable to convince the others of their viewpoint," says one expert in decision making. "In the final analysis, everyone agrees to support the outcome."[64] This does not mean, however, that group members agree with the decision, only that they are willing to work toward its success.

One management expert offers the following dos and don'ts for achieving consensus.[65]

- **Dos:** Use active listening skills. Involve as many members as possible. Seek out the reasons behind arguments. Dig for the facts.

- **Don'ts:** Avoid log rolling and horse trading ("I'll support your pet project if you'll support mine"). Avoid making an agreement simply to keep relations amicable and not rock the boat. Finally, don't try to achieve consensus by putting questions to a vote; this will only split the group into winners and losers, perhaps creating bad feelings among the latter.

More Group Problem-Solving Techniques

Decision-making experts have developed several group problem-solving techniques to aid in problem solving. Two we will discuss here are (1) *brainstorming* and (2) *computer-aided decision making.*

I. Brainstorming: For Increasing Creativity *Brainstorming* **is a technique used to help groups generate multiple ideas and alternatives for solving problems.**[66] Developed by advertising executive A. F. Osborn, the technique consists in having members of a group meet and review a problem to be solved. Individual members are then asked to silently generate ideas or solutions, which are then collected (preferably without identifying their contributors) and written on a board or flip chart. A second session is then used to critique and evaluate the alternatives. A modern-day variation is *electronic brainstorming,* **sometimes called** *brainwriting,* **in which members of a group come together over a computer network to generate ideas and alternatives.**[67]

Some rules for brainstorming suggested by IDEO, a product design company, are shown below. *(See Table 7.6.)*

table 7.6
SEVEN RULES FOR BRAINSTORMING

1. **Defer judgment.** Don't criticize during the initial stage of idea generation. Avoid phrases such as "we've never done it that way," "it won't work," "it's too expensive," and "our manager will never agree."

2. **Build on the ideas of others.** Encourage participants to extend others' ideas by avoiding "buts" and using "ands."

3. **Encourage wild ideas.** Encourage out-of-the-box thinking. The wilder and more outrageous the ideas, the better.

4. **Go for quantity over quality.** Participants should try to generate and write down as many new ideas as possible. Focusing on quantity encourages people to think beyond their favorite ideas.

5. **Be visual.** Use different colored pens (e.g., red, purple, blue) to write on big sheets of flip-chart paper, white boards, or poster boards that are put on the wall.

6. **Stay focused on the topic.** A facilitator should be used for keeping the discussion on target.

7. **One conversation at a time.** The ground rules are that no one interrupts another person, no dismissing of someone's ideas, no disrespect, and no rudeness.

Source: R. Kreitner and A. Kinicki, *Organizational Behavior,* 8th ed., 2008, pp. 355–356. These recommendations and descriptions were derived from B. Nussbaum, "The Power of Design," *BusinessWeek,* May 17, 2004, pp. 86–94. Reprinted with permission of The McGraw-Hill Companies.

The benefit of brainstorming is that it is an effective technique for encouraging the expression of as many useful new ideas or alternatives as possible. For example, Mark Hurd, CEO of Hewlett-Packard, engages in brainstorming with his top nine executives to generate ideas for how to increase sales in emerging markets.[68] That said, brainstorming also can waste time generating a lot of unproductive ideas, and it is not appropriate for evaluating alternatives or selecting solutions.

2. Computer-Aided Decision Making As in nearly every other aspect of business life, computers have entered the area of decision making, where they are useful not only in collecting information more quickly but also in reducing roadblocks to group consensus.

The two types of computer-aided decision-making systems are *chauffeur driven* and *group driven,* as follows:[69]

- **Chauffeur-driven systems—for push-button consensus.** *Chauffeur-driven computer-aided decision-making systems* ask participants to answer predetermined questions on electronic keypads or dials. These have been used as polling devices, for instance, with audiences on live television shows such as *Who Wants to Be a Millionaire,* allowing responses to be computer-tabulated almost instantly.

- **Group-driven systems—for anonymous networking.** A *group-driven computer-aided decision system* involves a meeting within a room of participants who express their ideas anonymously on a computer network. Instead of talking with one another, participants type their comments, reactions, or evaluations on their individual computer keyboards. The input is projected on a large screen at the front of the room for all to see. Because participation is anonymous and no one person is able to dominate the meeting on the basis of status or personality, everyone feels free to participate, and the roadblocks to consensus are accordingly reduced.

Compared to traditional brainstorming, group-driven systems have been shown to produce greater quality and quantity of ideas for large groups of people, although there is no advantage with groups of 4–6 people.[70] The technique also produces more ideas as group size increases from 5 to 10 members.

Computer-aided decision making has been found to produce greater quality and quantity of ideas than either traditional brainstorming or the nominal group technique for both small and large groups of people.[71] However, other research reveals that the use of online chat groups led to decreased group effectiveness and member satisfaction and increased time to complete tasks compared with face-to-face groups.[72] ●

Traditional group work. This photo shows the kind of traditional arrangement we expect of groups—colleagues are seated close together in clusters to better focus on their particular projects. Do you think you'd rather work in this type of arrangement than in one that is more individually based? Why or why not?

7.6 HOW TO OVERCOME BARRIERS TO DECISION MAKING

> **Trying to be rational isn't always easy. What are the barriers?**
>

THE BIG PICTURE

Responses to a decision situation may take the form of four ineffective reactions or three effective reactions. Managers should be aware of four common decision-making biases.

Do your moods influence your decisions? Do you, for instance, spend more when you're sad and self-absorbed? That's what one experiment found: When researchers exposed student participants to a sadness-inducing video clip about the death of a boy's mentor, the students were inclined to offer more money for a product (a sporty-looking water bottle) than were other subjects who had watched a neutral clip.[73]

Not just the moods themselves but your expectations about how happy or unhappy you think future outcomes will make you perhaps also can influence your decisions. It seems that people expect certain life events to have a much greater emotional effect than in fact they do, according to Harvard University psychologist Daniel Gilbert, who has studied individual emotional barometers in decision making. College professors, for example, expect to be quite happy if they are given tenure and quite unhappy if they aren't. However, Gilbert found those who received tenure were happy but not as happy as they themselves had predicted, whereas those denied tenure did not become very unhappy.

The expectation about the level of euphoria or disappointment was also found to be true of big-jackpot lottery winners and of people being tested for HIV infection. That is, people are often right when they describe what outcome will make them feel good or bad, but they are often wrong when asked to predict how strongly they will feel that way and how long the feeling will last. "Even severe life events have a negative impact on people's sense of well-being and satisfaction for no more than three months," says one report, "after which their feelings at least go back to normal."[74]

Perhaps knowing that you have this "immune system" of the mind, which blunts bad feelings and smoothes out euphoric ones, can help make it easier for you to make difficult decisions.

How Do Individuals Respond to a Decision Situation? Ineffective & Effective Responses

What is your typical response when you're suddenly confronted with a challenge in the form of a problem or an opportunity? There are perhaps four ineffective reactions and three effective ones.[75]

Four Ineffective Reactions There are four defective problem-recognition and problem-solving approaches that act as barriers when you must make an important decision in a situation of conflict:

1. Relaxed Avoidance—"There's no point in doing anything; nothing bad's going to happen" In *relaxed avoidance,* **a manager decides to take no action in the belief that there will be no great negative consequences.** This condition, then, is a form of complacency: You either don't see or you disregard the signs of danger (or of opportunity).

Relaxed avoidance was vividly demonstrated in 2007, the year of the subprime mortgage meltdown (when banks made cheap housing loans to a lot of unqualified buyers, precipitating a huge financial crisis and drying up of credit). During the summer, a lot of smart people in denial said not to worry, that the mortgage mess would be "contained." They included many bank presidents and even Ben Bernanke, chairman of the Federal Reserve.[76]

2. Relaxed Change—"Why not just take the easiest way out?" In *relaxed change,* a manager realizes that complete inaction will have negative consequences but opts for the first available alternative that involves low risk. This is, of course, a form of "satisficing"; the manager avoids exploring a variety of alternatives in order to make the best decision.

For example, if you go to the college career center, sign up for one job interview, and are offered and accept a job based on that single interview, you may have no basis for comparison to know that you made the right choice.

3. Defensive Avoidance—"There's no reason for me to explore other solution alternatives" In *defensive avoidance,* a manager can't find a good solution and follows by (a) procrastinating, (b) passing the buck, or (c) denying the risk of any negative consequences. This is a posture of resignation and a denial of responsibility for taking action. By procrastinating, you put off making a decision ("I'll get to this later").[77] In passing the buck, you let someone else take the consequences of making the decision ("Let George do it"). In denying the risk that there will be any negative consequences, you are engaging in rationalizing ("How bad could it be?").

An example of defensive avoidance often occurs in firms with high turnover. Although some executives try to stop high performers from exiting by offering raises or promotions, others react defensively, telling themselves that the person leaving is not a big loss. "It's psychologically threatening to those who are staying to acknowledge there's a reason some people are leaving," says the CEO of a corporate-psychology consulting company, "so executives often dismiss them as untalented or even deny that an exodus is occurring."[78] He mentions one financial-services company whose executives insisted turnover was low when in fact 50% of hundreds of new employees quit within years.

4. Panic—"This is so stressful, I've got to do something—anything—to get rid of the problem" This reaction is especially apt to occur in crisis situations. In *panic,* a manager is so frantic to get rid of the problem that he or she can't deal with the situation realistically. This is the kind of situation in which the manager has completely forgotten the idea of behaving with "grace under pressure," of staying cool and calm. Troubled by anxiety, irritability, sleeplessness, and even physical illness, if you're experiencing this reaction, your judgment may be so clouded that you won't be able to accept help in dealing with the problem or to realistically evaluate the alternatives.

Panic can even be life-threatening. When in 1999 a jetliner skidded off the runway at Little Rock National Airport, passenger Clark Brewster and a flight attendant tried repeatedly to open an exit door that would not budge. "About that time I hear someone say the word 'Fire!'" Brewster said. "The flight attendant bends down and says, 'Please pray with me.'" Fortunately, cooler, quicker-thinking individuals were able to find another way out.[79]

Three Effective Reactions: Deciding to Decide In *deciding to decide,* a manager agrees that he or she must decide what to do about a problem or opportunity and take effective decision-making steps. Three ways to help you decide whether to decide are to evaluate the following:[80]

1. Importance—"How high priority is this situation?" You need to determine how much priority to give the decision situation. If it's a threat, how extensive might prospective losses or damage be? If it's an opportunity, how beneficial might the possible gains be?

2. Credibility—"How believable is the information about the situation?" You need to evaluate how much is known about the possible threat or opportunity. Is the source of the information trustworthy? Is there credible evidence?

3. Urgency—"How quickly must I act on the information about the situation?" Is the threat immediate? Will the window of opportunity stay open long? Can actions to address the situation be done gradually?

Example

Deciding to Decide: How Should MTV Networks React to the Broadband Internet?

By the summer of 2006, old-media companies had become aware of the staggering implications of the arrival of the broadband Internet. Disney's ABC Network, for instance, had agreed to provide hit shows for downloading to Apple's iTunes, Facebook had jumped to 5.5 million users, and YouTube was launched. However, MTV Networks, owned by Viacom and its cantankerous founder, Sumner Redstone, found itself lagging. "MTV Networks, which for years had been the arbiter of youth culture, seemed to be squandering its birthright," wrote *Newsweek*. "Even as its core audience was embracing the Internet as the next entertainment medium, MTV could not shake its old-media image."[81] How does Redstone decide how to decide?

The first decision—*Should this be considered a high-priority matter?*—became apparent when Redstone observed the aggressive moves being made by his competition. And indeed Viacom went on a buying spree itself to bolster MTV Networks' digital presence, making $200 million in acquisitions, including Atom Entertainment, with its AtomFilms.com and the gaming sites Shockwave.com and AddictingGames.com.

The second decision—*How believable is the information?*—was reinforced when one important deal eluded MTV's grasp, the hot brand known as MySpace, described as the "it" site of social networking, was snatched away by rival Rupert Murdoch's News Corp. Redstone blamed the loss on his longtime lieutenant, Viacom CEO Tom Freston.

The answer to the final decision—*How quickly should this information be acted on?*—became obvious when Redstone fired Freston and hired a new CEO, Philippe Dauman, with the simple mandate: Make MTV digitally cool, but don't do it by making any extravagant acquisitions (which could repeat the mistake made by old-media company Time Warner when it merged with AOL, a colossal failure). A principal result is that MTV Networks promoted a digital impresario named Mika Salmi, who reports to MTV CEO Judy McGrath (whom we described in Chapter I). MTV and its related brands now have more than 300 Internet sites, including some 30 media-rich broadband sites featuring video, music, and lots of interactivity (examples: Pimp My Ride, AddictingGames.com).

Your Call

After deciding that the threat to MTV Networks is serious, real, and immediate, how would you have tried to reshape MTV's business strategy, if you were in charge?

Six Common Decision-Making Biases: Rules of Thumb, or "Heuristics"

If someone asked you to explain the basis on which you make decisions, could you even say? Perhaps, after some thought, you might come up with some "rules of thumb." Scholars call them *heuristics* (pronounced "hyur-*ris*-tiks")—**strategies that simplify the process of making decisions.**

Despite the fact that people use such rules of thumb all the time, that doesn't mean they're reliable. Indeed, some are real barriers to high-quality decision making. Among those that tend to bias how decision makers process information are (1) *availability,* (2) *confirmation,* (3) *representativeness,* (4) *sunk cost,* (5) *anchoring and adjustment,* and (6) *escalation of commitment.*[82]

1. The Availability Bias: Using Only the Information Available   If you had a perfect on-time work attendance record for 9 months but then were late for work 4 days during the last 2 months because of traffic, shouldn't your boss take into account your entire attendance history when considering you for a raise? Yet managers tend to give more weight to more recent behavior. This is because of the ***availability bias*— managers use information readily available from memory to make judgments.**

The bias, of course, is that readily available information may not present a complete picture of a situation. The availability bias may be stoked by the news media, which tends to favor news that is unusual or dramatic. Thus, for example, because of the efforts of interest groups or celebrities, more news coverage may be given to AIDS or to breast cancer than to heart disease, leading people to think the former are the bigger killers when in fact the latter is the biggest killer.

2. The Confirmation Bias: Seeking Information to Support One's Point of View   The ***confirmation bias* is when people seek information to support their point of view and discount data that do not.** Though this bias would seem obvious, people practice it all the time.

3. The Representativeness Bias: Faulty Generalizing from a Small Sample or a Single Event   As a form of financial planning, playing state lotteries leaves something to be desired. When, for instance, in a recent year the New York jackpot reached $70 million, a New Yorker's chance of winning was 1 in 12,913,588.[83] (A person would have a greater chance of being struck by lightning.) Nevertheless, millions of people buy lottery tickets because they read or hear about a handful of fellow citizens who have been the fortunate recipients of enormous winnings. This is an example of the ***representativeness bias,* the tendency to generalize from a small sample or a single event.**

The bias here is that just because something happens once, that doesn't mean it is representative—that it will happen again or will happen to you. For example, just because you hired an extraordinary sales representative from a particular university, that doesn't mean that same university will provide an equally qualified candidate next time. Yet managers make this kind of hiring decision all the time.

4. The Sunk Cost Bias: Money Already Spent Seems to Justify Continuing   The ***sunk cost bias* or *sunk cost fallacy,* is when managers add up all the money already spent on a project and conclude it is too costly to simply abandon it.**

· Most people have an aversion to "wasting" money. Especially if large sums have already been spent, they may continue to push on with an iffy-looking project so as to justify the money already sunk into it. The sunk cost bias is sometimes called the "Concorde" effect, referring to the fact that the French and British governments continued to invest in the Concorde supersonic jetliner even when it was evident there was no economic justification for the aircraft.

5. The Anchoring & Adjustment Bias: Being Influenced by an Initial Figure   Managers will often give their employees a standard percentage raise in salary, basing the decision on whatever the workers made the preceding year. They may do this even though the raise may be completely out of alignment with what other companies are paying for the same skills. This is an instance of the ***anchoring and adjustment bias,* the tendency to make decisions based on an initial figure.**

The bias is that the initial figure may be irrelevant to market realities. This phenomenon is sometimes seen in real estate sales. A homeowner may at first list his or her house at an extremely high (but perhaps randomly chosen) selling price. The seller is then unwilling later to come down substantially to match the kind of buying offers that reflect what the marketplace thinks the house is really worth.

6. The Escalation of Commitment Bias: Feeling Overly Invested in a Decision

If you really hate to admit you're wrong, you need to be aware of the *escalation of commitment bias,* **whereby decision makers increase their commitment to a project despite negative information about it.** History is full of examples of heads of state who escalated their commitment to an original decision in the face of overwhelming evidence that it was producing detrimental consequences. A noteworthy example was President Lyndon B. Johnson's pressing on of the Vietnam War despite mounting casualties abroad and political upheavals at home.

The bias is that what was originally made as perhaps a rational decision may continue to be supported for irrational reasons—pride, ego, the spending of enormous sums of money, and being "loss averse." Indeed, scholars have advanced what is known as the *prospect theory,* which suggests that decision makers find the notion of an actual loss more painful than giving up the possibility of a gain.[84] We saw a variant of this when we described the tendency of investors to hold on to their losers but cash in their winners.

Example

Avoiding Escalation of Commitment: L.L. Bean CEO Is Glad to Reverse Big Decision, Even at a Cost of $500,000

Most executives, like most people, tend to stick with their initial decisions because they hate to admit they were wrong, or simply because it is the path of least resistance, according to management experts. Indeed, they say, top executives are even less likely to reverse themselves because their position seems to require projecting self-assurance. This is the kind of mind-set that can lead to escalation of commitment.

Thus, Christopher McCormick, chief executive of outdoor-clothing retailer L.L. Bean, is unusual for being more concerned about making the best decision rather than being bothered about appearing wishy-washy. This makes him very much in the spirit of evidence-based decision making.

In the fall of 2004, L.L. Bean began building a call center near Waterville, Maine. A few months later, mobile-phone carrier T-Mobile USA said it would build its own call center next door, one that would house 700 or more employees. McCormick immediately ordered construction on the Bean center halted, even though

$500,000 beyond the land cost had already been spent on it. A few weeks later, the company announced it would abandon the Waterville site entirely and would open a new call center about 55 miles away.

What circumstances led to this evaluation? McCormick worried that Waterville, population 16,000, didn't have enough workers to supply both companies or that employees would prefer year-round employment with T-Mobile to seasonal employment with Bean.

Your Call

Even though thousands of dollars had already been spent on the Waterville center, McCormick says he had no reservations about his decision. He said he also wanted to send a signal to other Bean executives. "I want my people to consider all the options," he said. "I don't want them to be a champion of one point of view."[85] Do you think you're capable of making such a momentous decision?

Practical Action

How Exceptional Managers Make Decisions

"Failure is a great teacher." That was one of the life lessons expressed by one CEO who has had to make thousands of decisions during his career.[86] Failure is always a possibility, but that possibility can't stop one from making decisions. And you can probably always learn from the result.

"When Should I Make a Decision & When Should I Delay?"

Often you want to stay open-minded before making a decision. But sometimes that can just be a cover for procrastination. (After all, *not* making a decision is in itself a kind of decision.) How do you know when you're keeping an open mind or are procrastinating? Here are some questions to consider:[87]

Understanding: "Do I have a reasonable grasp of the problem?"

Comfort level about outcome: "Would I be satisfied if I chose one of the existing alternatives?"

Future possible alternatives: "Would it be unlikely that I could come up with a better alternative if I had more time?"

Seizing the opportunity: "Could the best alternatives disappear if I wait?"

If you can answer "yes" to those questions, you almost certainly should decide now, not wait.

"Are There Guidelines for Making Tough Choices?"

"On a daily and weekly basis we can be faced with making hundreds of decisions," says management consultant Odette Pollar. "Most of them are small, but the larger ones where more is at stake can be truly painful." Here are some ways she suggests making decision making easier:[88]

Decide in a timely fashion: "Rarely does waiting significantly improve the quality of the decision," says Pollar. In fact, delay can result in greater unpleasantness in loss of money, time, and peace of mind.

Don't agonize over minor decisions: Postponing decisions about small problems can mean that they simply turn into large ones later.

Separate outcome from process: Does a bad outcome mean you made a bad decision? Not necessarily. The main thing is to go through a well-reasoned process of choosing among alternatives, which increases the chances of success. But even then you can't be sure there will always be a positive outcome.

Learn when to stop gathering facts: "Gather enough information to make a sound decision," suggests Pollar, "but not all the possible information." Taking extra time may mean you'll miss a window of opportunity.

When overwhelmed, narrow your choices: Sometimes there are many good alternatives, and you need to simplify decision making by eliminating some options.

Key Terms Used in This Chapter

analytics 214
anchoring and adjustment bias 228
availability bias 228
bounded rationality 209
brainstorming 223
confirmation bias 228
consensus 221
deciding to decide 226
decision 202
decision making 202
decision-making style 203
decision tree 216

defensive avoidance 226
diagnosis 206
electronic brainstorming 223
escalation of commitment bias 229
ethics officer 216
goal displacement 220
groupthink 220
heuristics 227
intuition 210
incremental model 210
nonrational models of decision making 209
opportunities 206

panic 226
participative management (PM) 221
predictive modeling 215
problems 205
rational model of decision making 205
relaxed avoidance 225
relaxed change 226
representativeness bias 228
risk propensity 202
satisficing model 210
sunk cost bias 228

7.1 The Nature of Decision Making

A decision is a choice made from among available alternatives. Decision making is the process of identifying and choosing alternative courses of action.

A decision-making style reflects the combination of how an individual perceives and responds to information. Decision-making styles may tend to have a value orientation, which reflects the extent to which a person focuses on either task or technical concerns versus people and social concerns when making decisions. Decision-making styles may also reflect a person's tolerance for ambiguity, the extent to which a person has a high or low need for structure or control in his or her life. When the dimensions of value orientation and tolerance for ambiguity are combined, they form four styles of decision making: directive, analytical, conceptual, and behavioral.

7.2 Two Kinds of Decision Making: Rational & Nonrational

Two models managers follow in making decisions are rational and nonrational.

In the rational model, there are four steps in making a decision: Stage 1 is identifying the problem or opportunity. A problem is a difficulty that inhibits the achievement of goals. An opportunity is a situation that presents possibilities for exceeding existing goals. This is a matter of diagnosis—analyzing the underlying causes. Stage 2 is thinking up alternative solutions. Stage 3 is evaluating the alternatives and selecting a solution. Alternatives should be evaluated according to cost, quality, ethics, feasibility, and effectiveness. Stage 4 is implementing and evaluating the solution chosen.

The rational model of decision making assumes managers will make logical decisions that will be the optimum in furthering the organization's best interests. The rational model is prescriptive, describing how managers ought to make decisions.

Nonrational models of decision making assume that decision making is nearly always uncertain and risky, making it difficult for managers to make optimum decisions. Three nonrational models are satisficing, incremental, and intuition. (1) Satisficing falls under the concept of bounded rationality—that is, that the ability of decision makers to be rational is limited by enormous constraints, such as time and money. These constraints force managers to make decisions according to the satisficing model—that is, managers seek alternatives until they find one that is satisfactory, not optimal. (2) In the incremental model, managers take small, short-term steps to alleviate a problem rather than steps that will accomplish a long-term solution. (3) Intuition is making choices without the use of conscious thought or logical inference. The sources of intuition are expertise and feelings.

7.3 Evidence-Based Decision Making & Analytics

Evidence-based management means translating principles based on best evidence into organizational practice. It is intended to bring rationality to the decision-making process.

Scholars Jeffrey Pfeffer and Robert Sutton identify seven implementation principles to help companies that are committed to doing what it takes to profit from evidence-based management: (1) treat your organization as an unfinished prototype; (2) "no brag, just facts"; (3) see yourself and your organization as outsiders do; (4) have everyone, not just top executives, be guided by the responsibility to gather and act on quantitative and qualitative data; (5) you may need to use vivid stories to sell unexciting evidence to others in the company; (6) at the very least, you should slow the spread of bad practices; and (7) you should learn from failure by using the facts to make things better.

Applying the best evidence to your decisions is difficult, for seven reasons: (1) There's too much evidence. (2) There's not enough *good* evidence. (3) The evidence doesn't quite apply. (4) People are trying to mislead you. (5) *You* are trying to mislead you. (6) The side effects outweigh the cure. (7) Stories are more persuasive, anyway.

Perhaps the purest application of evidence-based management is the use of analytics, or business analytics, the term used for sophisticated forms of business data analysis. Among organizations that have made a commitment to quantitative, fact-based analysis, scholars have found three key attributes: (1) They go beyond simple descriptive statistics and use data mining and predictive modeling to identify potential and most profitable customers. (2) Analytics competitors don't gain advantage from one principal application but rather from multiple applications supporting many parts of the business. (3) A companywide embrace of analytics impels changes in culture, processes, behavior, and skills for many employees, and so requires the support of top executives.

 ### 7.4 Making Ethical Decisions

Corporate corruption has made ethics in decision making once again important. Many companies have an ethics officer to resolve ethical dilemmas, and more companies are creating values statements to guide employees as to desirable business behavior.

To help make ethical decisions, a decision tree—a graph of decisions and their possible consequences—may be helpful. Managers should ask whether a proposed action is legal and, if it is intended to maximize shareholder value, whether it is ethical—and whether it would be ethical *not* to take the proposed action.

A goal for managers should be to rely on moral principles so that their decisions are principled, appropriate, and defensible, in accordance with "the magnificent seven" general moral principles for managers.

7.5 Group Decision Making: How to Work with Others

Groups make better decisions than most individuals acting alone, though not as good as the best individual acting alone.

Using a group to make a decision offers five possible advantages: (1) a greater pool of knowledge; (2) different perspectives; (3) intellectual stimulation; (4) better understanding of the reasoning behind the decision; and (5) deeper commitment to the decision. It also has four disadvantages: (1) a few people may dominate or intimidate; (2) it will produce groupthink, when group members strive for agreement among themselves for the sake of unanimity and so avoid accurately assessing the decision situation; (3) satisficing; and (4) goal displacement, when the primary goal is subsumed to a secondary goal.

Some characteristics of groups to be aware of are (1) groups are less efficient, (2) their size affects decision quality, (3) they may be too confident, and (4) knowledge counts—decision-making accuracy is higher when group members know a lot about the issues.

Participative management (PM) is the process of involving employees in setting goals, making decisions, solving problems, and making changes in the organization. PM can increase employee job involvement, organizational commitment, and creativity and can lower role conflict and ambiguity.

Using groups to make decisions generally requires that they reach a consensus, which occurs when members are able to express their opinions and reach agreement to support the final decision.

Two problem-solving techniques aid in problem solving. (1) Brainstorming is a technique used to help groups generate multiple ideas and alternatives for solving problems. A variant is electronic brainstorming, in which group members use a computer network to generate ideas. (2) In computer-aided decision making, chauffeur-driven systems may be used, which ask participants to answer predetermined questions on electronic keypads or dials, or group-driven systems may be used, in which participants in a room express their ideas anonymously on a computer network.

7.6 How to Overcome Barriers to Decision Making

When confronted with a challenge in the form of a problem or an opportunity, individuals may respond in perhaps four ineffective ways and three effective ones.

The ineffective reactions are as follows: (1) In relaxed avoidance, a manager decides to take no action in the belief that there will be no great negative consequences. (2) In relaxed change, a manager realizes that complete inaction will have negative consequences but opts for the first available alternative that involves low risk. (3) In defensive avoidance, a manager can't find a good solution and follows by procrastinating, passing the buck, or denying the risk of any negative consequences. (4) In panic, a manager is so frantic to get rid of the problem that he or she can't deal with the situation realistically.

The effective reactions consist of deciding to decide—that is, a manager agrees that he or she must decide what to do about a problem or opportunity and take effective decision-making steps. Three ways to help a manager decide whether to decide are to evaluate (1) importance—how high priority the situation is; (2) credibility—how believable the information about the situation is; and (3) urgency—how quickly the manager must act on the information about the situation.

Heuristics are rules of thumb or strategies that simplify the process of making decisions. Some heuristics or barriers that tend to bias how decision makers process information are availability, confirmation representativeness, sunk cost anchoring and adjustment, and escalation of commitment. (1) The availability bias means that managers use information readily available from memory to make judgments. (2) The confirmation bias means people seek information to support their own point of view and discount data that do not. (3) The representativeness bias is the tendency to generalize from a small sample or a single event. (4) The sunk cost bias is when managers add up all the money already spent on a project and conclude that it is too costly to simply abandon it. (5) The anchoring and adjustment bias is the tendency to make decisions based on an initial figure or number. (6) The escalation of commitment bias describes when decision makers increase their commitment to a project despite negative information about it. An example is the prospect theory, which suggests that decision makers find the notion of an actual loss more painful than giving up the possibility of a gain.

Management in Action

Does the Use of Analytics Produce Better Decisions?

Business today is awash in data and data crunchers, but only certain companies have transformed this technology from a supporting tool into a strategic weapon. Their ability to collect, analyze and act on data is the essence of their competitive advantage and the source of their superior performance.

A prime example is Anheuser-Busch Companies Inc., brewer of many of the world's best-selling beers, based in St. Louis. It has made a science out of monitoring the metrics that allow it to understand when, where, and why consumers buy beer—insights that have allowed the company to post double-digit profit gains for 20 straight quarters.

The core of the company's competitive capability is BudNet, a real-time network capable of gathering data on dozens of key performance indicators which the company's distributors report as they review shelves and product positioning in the field. Analysts at corporate HQ regularly analyze and mine the data for decision support.

What's more, Anheuser-Busch combines the figures it gleans from its distributors' information systems with other key data, such as U.S. Census figures on the ethnic and economic makeup of neighborhoods, allowing the company to design local promotions that match their markets to a tee.

Recently, Anheuser-Busch was the first to identify an important shift in customer purchasing preferences toward more healthy beverages, information the company harnessed to successfully capture the low-carb beer market.

Granted, organizations have been gathering massive amounts of data on customers' buying habits and the efficiency of their operational processes for decades. But Anheuser-Busch is one of a new breed of data-driven companies that has taken analytics to a new level.

"Firms like Anheuser-Busch are outsmarting and outmaneuvering the competition because they have made information analysis and management a distinctive capability, one that is fundamental to their formula for doing business," observes Paul F. Nunes, an executive research fellow at the Accenture Institute for High Performance Business in Wellesley, Mass.

Accenture's continuing research into the components of high performance proves that information can indeed be power. The global management consultancy, technology services, and outsourcing company recently surveyed 450 executives in 370 companies spread across 35 countries and 19 industries. The company identified a strong link between extensive and sophisticated use of analytics and sustained high performance.

Of the respondents, high-performance companies—businesses that Accenture research has identified on the basis of their ability to substantially and consistently outperform their competitors over the long term, over economic and industry cycles and through generations of leadership—were five times more likely than low performers to single out analytics as critical to their competitive edge.

"It's not about better number crunching, it's about reinventing a company's core value algorithm to embrace analytics and make it part of the company's distinctive capability," notes Jeanne Harris, a director of Accenture's Institute for High Performance Business who spearheaded the survey. "This focus consistently distinguishes the market leaders from the also-rans."

In addition, Accenture has identified three categories of companies that win on analytics.

"Some were born that way," Ms. Harris explains. Prime examples include Internet giants such as Google, the dominant search-engine company; Amazon, the leading online retailer; and Netflix, the pioneering online DVD rental company. Such companies were built from the ground up on new ways of capturing and analyzing data. "They correctly view their algorithms as a key weapon in their competitive arsenal."

Other companies, such as Procter & Gamble and General Electric, have a "long and proud history" of using analytics to drive high performance, Ms. Harris continues.

Finally, there are the companies that have come to embrace analytics, either as part of a turnaround strategy or a plan to dramatically change their market position. "These are the companies that have transformed themselves by harnessing technology to drive results and pull away from the competition," she says.

In line with this, Accenture has pinpointed the three approaches companies can choose from to join the ranks of analytics juggernauts.

Put simply, organizations can, first, leverage analytics to add value to their offer in the form of service improvements, such as better or more timely delivery of goods and services; second, they can develop and deliver more personalized services to their customers; or third, they can expand their participation in the value chain.

Cemex S.A., a global supplier of cement and building solutions headquartered in Monterrey, Mexico, grew from a regional player to a world leader by using analytics to deliver its products to its customers on time and on their terms.

A deep understanding of its customers—which the company gained by meticulously gathering data about its customers' needs—allowed it to identify a crucial and unmet demand: quick delivery.

Ready-mix concrete is perishable and begins to set when a truck is loaded. Cemex found that, on average, it took three hours from the receipt of a contractor's order to the delivery of the concrete. These delays were costly to contractors, whose crews were at a standstill until the concrete arrived.

To complicate matters, Mexico, like other developing countries, is plagued by traffic congestion in its major cities, making it hard for a company to accurately plan deliveries.

Cemex determined that it could charge a premium to time-pressed contractors—as well as reduce costs by decreasing the amount of concrete that hardened en route—if they could reduce delivery times.

To accomplish this, Cemex again turned to analytics, this time to collect data and study the techniques and technologies used by couriers, delivery firms, police, and paramedics.

Based on this research, Cemex devised a strategy to cut response times by equipping its concrete-mixing trucks in Mexico with global-positioning satellite locators and Web-based vehicle dispatch technology. Using these systems to reconfigure its business processes allowed the company to deliver cement to its customers within a 20-minute window, boosting both productivity and customer loyalty.

For Discussion

1. Which of the four steps associated with the rational model of decision making are most likely to be affected by the use of analytics? Discuss your rationale.

2. Which of the seven evidence-based decision-making implementation principles were used by Anheuser-Busch and Cemex? Provide examples to support your conclusions.

3. Would the use of analytics lead to more or less ethical decisions? Explain.

4. Why don't more companies rely on evidence-based management?

Source: Excerpted from Peggy Anne Salz, "Intelligent Use of Information Is a Powerful Corporate Tool," *The Wall Street Journal*, April 27, 2006, p. A10. Copyright © 2007 by Dow Jones & Company, Inc. Reproduced with permission of Dow Jones & Company, Inc. via Copyright Clearance Center.

Self-Assessment

What Is Your Decision-Making Style?

Objectives

1. To assess your decision-making style.
2. To consider the implications of your decision-making style.

Introduction

This chapter discussed a model of decision-making styles. Decision-making styles are thought to vary according to a person's tolerance for ambiguity and value orientation. In turn, the combination of these two dimensions results in four different decision-making styles (see Figure 7.1). This exercise gives you the opportunity to assess your decision-making style.

Instructions

Following are nine items that pertain to decision making. Read each statement and select the option that best represents your feelings about the issue. Remember, there are no right or wrong answers.

1. I enjoy jobs that
   a. are technical and well defined.
   b. have considerable variety.
   c. allow independent action.
   d. involve people.

2. In my job, I look for
   a. practical results.
   b. the best solutions.
   c. new approaches or ideas.
   d. a good working environment.

3. When faced with solving a problem, I
   a. rely on proven approaches.
   b. apply careful analysis.
   c. look for creative approaches.
   d. rely on my feelings.

4. When using information, I prefer
   a. specific facts.
   b. accurate and complete data.
   c. broad coverage of many options.
   d. limited data that are easily understood.

5. I am especially good at
   a. remembering dates and facts.
   b. solving difficult problems.
   c. seeing many possibilities.
   d. interacting with others.

6. When time is important, I
   a. decide and act quickly.
   b. follow plans and priorities.
   c. refuse to be pressured.
   d. seek guidance and support.

7. I work well with those who are
   a. energetic and ambitious.
   b. self-confident.
   c. open-minded.
   d. polite and trusting.

8. Others consider me
   a. aggressive.
   b. disciplined.
   c. imaginative.
   d. supportive.

9. My decisions typically are
   a. realistic and direct.
   b. systematic or abstract.
   c. broad and flexible.
   d. sensitive to the needs of others.

Scoring & Interpretation

Score the exercise by giving yourself one point for every time you selected an A, one point for every B, and so on. Add up your scores for each letter. Your highest score represents your dominant decision-making style. If your highest score was A, you have a directive style; B = analytical; C = conceptual; and D = behavioral. See the related material in this chapter for a thorough description of these four styles.

Questions

1. What are your highest- and lowest-rated styles?
2. Do the results accurately reflect your self-perceptions? Explain.

3. What are the advantages and disadvantages of your style? Discuss.
4. Which of the other decision-making styles is least consistent with your style? How might you work more effectively with someone who has this style? Discuss.

Adapted from A. J. Rowe, J. D. Boulgarides, and M. R. McGrath, *Managerial Decision Making* (Chicago: SRA, 1984).

Ethical Dilemma

Should the Principal of Westwood High Allow an Exception to the Graduation Dress Code?

This dilemma involves a situation faced by Helen Riddle, the principal of Westwood High School in Mesa, Arizona. Westwood High has 225 Native American students, including 112 from the Salt River Pima-Maricopa Indian Community, most of which lies within the boundaries of the Mesa Unified School District. Districtwide there are 452 Native American high school students, 149 of whom are from the Salt River Reservation.

Here is the situation: Native American students asked the principal if they could be allowed to wear eagle feathers during their graduation ceremony. Although this may seem like a reasonable request given these students' customs and traditions, Westwood High had a rule stating that, according to a newspaper report, "students were only allowed to wear a traditional cap and gown for graduation, with no other adornments or clothing, including military uniforms. The rules were based on past practice and tradition at schools, not school board policy."

Advocates for the Native American students argued that students should be allowed to wear the eagle feathers because they represent a significant achievement in the lives of those individuals. In contrast, one school board member opposed the exception to the rule because "it would open the door for other students wanting to display symbols of their own culture or background."

Solving the Dilemma

What would you do if you were the principal of Westwood High?

1. Allow the Native American students to wear the eagle feathers now and in the future. This shows an appreciation for diversity.
2. Do not allow the Native American students to wear the eagle feathers because it violates an existing rule. Allowing an exception opens the door for additional requests about changing the dress code. How will you defend one exception over another?
3. Allow the students to wear the eagle feathers only in this year's ceremony, then form a committee to review the dress code requirements.
4. Invent other options. Discuss.

Souce: Excerpted from J. Kelley, "Westwood Students Get OK for Eagle Feathers," *The Mesa Republic*, May 25, 2006, p. 15.

Organizational Culture, Structure, & Design

Building Blocks of the Organization

Major Questions You Should Be Able to Answer

8.1 What Kind of Organizational Culture Will You Be Operating In?
Major Question: How do I find out about an organization's "social glue," its normal way of doing business?

8.2 Developing High-Performance Cultures
Major Question: What can be done to an organization's culture to increase its economic performance?

8.3 What Is an Organization?
Major Question: How are for-profit, nonprofit, and mutual-benefit organizations structured?

8.4 The Major Elements of an Organization
Major Question: When I join an organization, what seven elements should I look for?

8.5 Basic Types of Organizational Structures
Major Question: How would one describe the seven organizational structures?

8.6 Contingency Design: Factors in Creating the Best Structure
Major Question: What factors affect the design of an organization's structure?

toolbox

When Should You Delegate & When Not? How Managers Get More Done

All managers must learn how to delegate—to assign management authority and responsibilities to people lower in the company hierarchy. But failure to delegate can happen even with high-powered executives, including those you might least suspect—such as the president of Harvard University. Dr. Neil L. Rudenstine, who became president of Harvard in 1991, initially became so exhausted from overwork that he had to stay home for 2 weeks to recover. The incident sent a message that his future survival would depend on his ability to set priorities and delegate responsibility.[1]

"To do more in a day, you must do less—not do everything faster," says Oakland, California, productivity expert Odette Pollar.[2] If as a manager you find yourself often behind, always taking work home, doing your subordinates' work for them, and constantly having employees seeking your approval before they can act, you're clearly not delegating well. How do you decide when to delegate and when not to? Here are some guidelines:[3]

- **Delegate routine and technical matters:** Always try to delegate routine tasks and routine paperwork. When there are technical matters, let the experts handle them.

- **Delegate tasks that help your subordinates grow:** Let your employees solve their own problems whenever possible. Let them try new things so they will grow in their jobs.

- **Don't delegate confidential and personnel matters:** Any tasks that are confidential or

that involve the evaluation, discipline, or counseling of subordinates should never be handed off to someone else.

- **Don't delegate emergencies:** By definition, an emergency is a crisis for which there is little time for solution, and you should handle this yourself.

- **Don't delegate special tasks that your boss asked you to do—unless you have his or her permission:** If your supervisor entrusts you with a special assignment, such as attending a particular meeting, don't delegate it unless you have permission to do so.

- **Match the tasks delegated to your subordinates' skills and abilities:** While recognizing that delegation involves some risk, make your assignments appropriate to the training, talent, skills, and motivation of your employees.

For Discussion There are many reasons why managers fail to delegate.[4] An excessive need for perfection. A belief that only they should handle "special," "difficult," or "unusual" problems or clients. A wish to keep the parts of a job that are fun. A fear that others will think them lazy. A reluctance to let employees lower down in the hierarchy take risks. A worry that subordinates won't deliver. A concern that the subordinates will do a better job and show them up. Are any of these reasons why you might not be very good at delegating? What are some others?

forecast

What's Ahead in This Chapter

In this chapter, we consider organizational cultures and why they are important. We then consider the three types of organizations and seven basic characteristics of an organization. We next discuss seven types of organizational structures. Finally, we look at five factors that should be considered when one is designing the structure of an organization.

8.1 WHAT KIND OF ORGANIZATIONAL CULTURE WILL YOU BE OPERATING IN?

major question?	How do I find out about an organization's "social glue," its normal way of doing business?

THE BIG PICTURE

The study of organizing, the second of the four functions in the management process, begins with a study of organizational culture, which exists on three levels. An organizational culture has four functions.

Want to get ahead in the workplace but hate the idea of "office politics"?

Probably you can't achieve the first without mastering the second. Although hard work and talent can take you a long way, "there is a point in everyone's career where politics becomes more important," says management professor Kathleen Kelley Reardon. You have to know the political climate of the company you work for, says Reardon, who is author of *The Secret Handshake* and *It's All Politics.*[5] "Don't be the last person to understand how people get promoted, how they get noticed, how certain projects come to attention. Don't be quick to trust. If you don't understand the political machinations, you're going to fail much more often."[6]

A great part of learning to negotiate the politics—that is, the different behavioral and psychological characteristics—of a particular office means learning to understand the organization's *culture.* The culture consists not only of the slightly quirky personalities you encounter but also all of an organization's normal way of doing business.

What Is an Organizational Culture?

According to scholar **Edgar Schein,** *organizational culture,* **sometimes called** *corporate culture,* **is a system of shared beliefs and values that develops within an organization and guides the behavior of its members.**[7] This is the "social glue" that binds members of the organization together. Just as a human being has a personality—fun-loving, warm, uptight, competitive, or whatever—so an organization has a "personality," too, and that is its culture.

Culture can vary considerably, with different organizations having differing emphases on risk taking, treatment of employees, teamwork, rules and regulations,

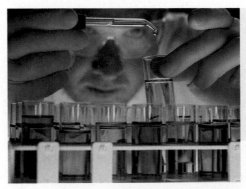

Culture of risk. At Connecticut pharmaceutical company, Pfizer pharmacy, drug discover is a high-risk, costly endeavor in which hundreds of scientists screen thousands of chemicals against specific disease targets, but 96% of these compounds are ultimately found to be unworkable. The culture, then, is one of managing failure and disappointment, of helping drug researchers live for small victories.

conflict and criticism, and rewards. And the sources of these characteristics also vary. They may represent the strong views of the founders, of the reward systems that have been instituted, of the effects of competitors, and so on.[8]

Four Types of Organizational Culture: Clan, Adhocracy, Market, & Hierarchy

According to one common methodology known as the *competing values framework,* organizational cultures can be classified into four types: (1) *clan,* (2) *adhocracy,* (3) *market,* and (4) *hierarchy.*[9]

I. Clan Culture: An Employee-Focused Culture Valuing Flexibility, Not Stability
A *clan culture* **has an internal focus and values flexibility rather than stability and control.** Like a family-type organization, it encourages collaboration among employees, striving to encourage cohesion through consensus and job satisfaction and to increase commitment through employee involvement. Clan organizations devote considerable resources to hiring and developing their employees, and they view customers as partners. Southwest Airlines is a good example of a company with a clan culture.

2. Adhocracy Culture: A Risk-Taking Culture Valuing Flexibility
An *adhocracy culture* **has an external focus and values flexibility.** This type of culture attempts to create innovative products by being adaptable, creative, and quick to respond to changes in the marketplace. Employees are encouraged to take risks and experiment with new ways of getting things done. Adhocracy cultures are well suited for start-up companies, those in industries undergoing constant change, and those in mature industries that are in need of innovation to enhance growth. W. L. Gore is an example of a company with an adhocracy culture.

3. Market Culture: A Competitive Culture Valuing Profits Over Employee Satisfaction
A *market culture* **has a strong external focus and values stability and control.** Because market cultures are focused on the external environment and driven by competition and a strong desire to deliver results, customers, productivity, and profits take precedence over employee development and satisfaction. Employees are expected to work hard, react fast, and deliver quality work on time; those who deliver results are rewarded. Merrill Lynch is an example of a company with a market culture.

4. Hierarchy Culture: A Structured Culture Valuing Stability & Effectiveness
A *hierarchy culture* **has an internal focus and values stability and control over flexibility.** Companies with this kind of culture are apt to have a formalized, structured work environment aimed at achieving effectiveness through a variety of control mechanisms that measure efficiency, timeliness, and reliability in the creation and delivery of products. Dell Computer is an example of a company with a hierarchical structure.

The Three Levels of Organizational Culture

Organizational culture appears as three layers: (1) *observable artifacts,* (2) *espoused values,* and (3) *basic assumptions.*[10] Each level varies in terms of outward visibility and resistance to change, and each level influences another level.

Level I: Observable Artifacts—Physical Manifestations of Culture
At the most visible level, organizational culture is expressed in *observable artifacts*—physical manifestations such as manner of dress, awards, myths and stories about the company, rituals and ceremonies, and decorations, as well as visible behavior exhibited by managers and employees. Department store retailer JCPenney Co. is

Self-Assessment:
Corporate culture assessment scale

HP founders. David Packard (left) and William Hewlett created a close-knit organizational culture that gave a lot of responsibility to employees and fostered innovation within the company.

Example

Corporate Cultures: The Different "Personalities" of Organizations

Organizational cultures are nearly as varied as human personalities. Do any of the following instances seem to fit the types of organizational cultures just described?

Valero Energy Corp. was named the third best company to work for in America in 2006 by *Fortune* magazine. "We truly do put our employees first," says chairman Bill Greehey. "We've never had a layoff in our company's history. We offer the best salaries and the best benefits, and we give stock options down to the lowest level in the company. . . . Everyone is treated equally with equal respect, and no one is ever talked down to. . . . The caring attitude is truly a part of our corporate culture, and it is something that we not only preach but we live every day."[11]

At Connecticut-based Pfizer Pharmaceuticals, drug discovery is a high-risk, costly endeavor in which hundreds of scientists screen thousands of chemicals against specific disease targets, but 96% of these compounds are ultimately found to be unworkable. The culture, then, is one of managing failure and disappointment, of helping drug researchers live for the small victories. Thus, says one account, "when a researcher publishes a paper, or when a lab gets some positive results on a new therapy, it's trumpeted throughout the organization."[12]

When Robert Nardelli (now head of Chrysler Corp.) became CEO of Home Depot in 2001, he decided to make some changes to the culture, to grow the business. He reduced store managers' autonomy and centralized the purchasing function. He also created common performance metrics that were used during Monday morning conference calls with his top 15 executives. Once a year he conducted an 8-day planning session, which was followed by quarterly business reviews. High performers were rewarded, those who failed to make their goals were fired.[13]

The preceding are examples of clan, adhocracy, and market cultures, in that order.

Your Call

Not all cultures work well. For instance, the corporate culture at failed Houston energy trader Enron was said to have made it a "very arrogant place, with a feeling of invincibility," according to whistleblower Sherron Watkins.[14] New York book publisher HarperCollins was accused in one employee lawsuit of encouraging "a culture of gossip, back-stabbing, negative leaks, and hostility."[15] Some Wall Street firms, such as Citigroup Inc. and Merrill Lynch & Co., are reported to have such a strong perform-or-die culture—in which executives are pushed to maximize profits and are quickly fired if they fail to deliver—that it is difficult to find talent to promote from within when chief executives leave.[16] Sometimes a company will do a corporate overhaul in an attempt to improve its performance, but the actual results may turn out otherwise. This reportedly happened with Intel, the Santa Clara, California, computer chip giant, which cut its workforce in 2006, letting go many managers skilled at people development. In the aftermath, employees complained that Intel lost what made it such a celebrated place to work, including being "a place that prizes fresh ideas, frank talk, and employee engagement."[17] What kinds of cultures would these seem to be?

---

trying to revamp itself from a traditional, hierarchical culture into one that is more informal and flexible by, for example, allowing such observable artifacts as business-casual dress on weekdays and jeans on Fridays.[18]

Level 2: Espoused Values—Explicitly Stated Values & Norms *Espoused values* **are the explicitly stated values and norms preferred by an organization,** as may be put forth by the firm's founder or top managers. For example, the founders of technology company Hewlett-Packard stressed the "HP Way," a collegial, egalitarian culture that gave as much authority and job security to employees as possible. Although managers may hope the values they espouse will directly influence employee behavior, employees don't always "walk the talk," frequently being more influenced by *enacted values,* **which represent the values and norms actually exhibited in the organization.** Thus, for example, an international corporation hung signs throughout the hallways of its headquarters proclaiming that "trust" was one of its driving principles (espoused value), yet had a policy of searching employees' belongings each time they entered or exited the building (enacted value).[19]

Level 3: Basic Assumptions—Core Values of the Organization *Basic assumptions,* which are not observable, represent the core values of an organization's culture—those that are taken for granted and, as a result, are highly resistant to change. Robert Nardelli encountered this kind of resistance as the new CEO of Home Depot, when he dismantled a culture in which store managers were allowed wide latitude in making decisions. Faced with a new, highly centralized culture that stressed uniformity, managers complained they spent more time filling out forms than serving customers, and many were so demoralized that they quit.[20]

Group Exercise:
Exploring Organizational Culture

How Employees Learn Culture: Symbols, Stories, Heroes, & Rites & Rituals

Culture is transmitted to employees in several ways, most often through such devices as (1) *symbols,* (2) *stories,* (3) *heroes,* and (4) *rites and rituals.*[21]

I. Symbols A *symbol* **is an object, act, quality, or event that conveys meaning to others.** In an organization, symbols convey its most important values. For instance, 3M has a trophy known as the Gold Step award, which is presented every year to employees whose new products achieve significant revenue levels.

2. Stories A *story* **is a narrative based on true events, which is repeated—and sometimes embellished upon—to emphasize a particular value.** Stories are oral histories that are told and retold by members about incidents in the organization's history.

An example is the one told at Ritz-Carlton hotels, in which a beach attendant busily stacking chairs for an evening event was asked by a guest to leave out two chairs, because the guest wanted to return to the beach that evening with his girlfriend and propose marriage. "Although the beach attendant was going off duty," according to one account of the story, "he didn't just leave two chairs on the beach; he put on a tuxedo and brought flowers, champagne, and candles. He met the couple when they arrived at the beach later that evening. He escorted them to the chairs, presented the flowers, lit the candles, and served the champagne." The point: The story of the beach attendant's above-and-beyond-the-call-of-duty efforts expresses the Ritz-Carlton dedication to bending over backward to serve customer needs.[22]

3. Heroes A *hero* **is a person whose accomplishments embody the values of the organization.** The accomplishments of heroes, past and present, are put forth to motivate other employees to do the right thing. The Ritz-Carlton beach attendant is an example of one such hero.

4. Rites & Rituals *Rites and rituals* **are the activities and ceremonies, planned and unplanned, that celebrate important occasions and accomplishments in the organization's life.** Military units and sports teams have long known the value of ceremonies handing out decorations and awards, but many companies have rites and rituals as well. Mary Kay, Inc., for instance, annually hosts five back-to-back conventions attended by 50,000 independent beauty consultants to recognize and reward its top producers for outstanding achievements in sales and recruiting. The founder, the late Mary Kay Ash, would personally present the best salespeople with jewelry, trips, and pink Cadillacs—items still awarded today.[23]

The Importance of Culture

Culture can powerfully shape an organization's long-term success.

"If employees know what their company stands for, if they know what standards they are to uphold, then they are much more likely to make decisions that will support those standards," write management experts Terrence Deal and Alan Kennedy. "They are also more likely to feel as if they are an important part of the organization.

figure 8.1

**FOUR FUNCTIONS OF
ORGANIZATIONAL CULTURE**

Source: Adapted from discussion
in L. Smircich, "Concepts of
Culture and Organizational
Analysis," *Administrative Science
Quarterly,* September 1983,
pp. 339–358. Copyright © 1983
Johnson Graduate School of
Management, Cornell University.
Reprinted with permission.

They are motivated because life in the company has meaning for them."[24] Much the same thing could be said for employees in nonprofit organizations.

An organization's culture has four functions.[25] *(See Figure 8.1, above.)*

I. It Gives Members an Organizational Identity   At Southwest Airlines, for instance, top executives constantly reinforce the company's message that workers should be treated like customers, and they continually celebrate employees whose contributions go beyond the call of duty.[26]

2. It Facilitates Collective Commitment   Consider 3M, one of whose corporate values is to be "a company that employees are proud to be part of." This collective commitment results in a turnover rate of less than 3% among salaried personnel. "I'm a 27-year 3Mer because, quite frankly, there's no reason to leave," says one manager. "I've had great opportunities to do different jobs and to grow a career. It's just a great company."[27]

3. It Promotes Social-System Stability   The more effectively conflict and change are managed within an organization and the more that employees perceive the work environment to be positive and reinforcing, the more stable the social system within the organization. At 3M, social stability is encouraged by promoting from within, by hiring capable college graduates in a timely manner, and by providing displaced workers 6 months to find new jobs.

4. It Shapes Behavior by Helping Employees Make Sense of Their Surroundings   The culture helps employees understand why the organization does what it does and how it intends to accomplish its long-term goals. 3M sets expectations for innovation, for example, by having an internship and co-op program, which provides 30% of the company's new college hires.

Sometimes culture can be strong enough to take the place of structure; that is, the expectations of the culture replace formal rules and regulations. In these cases, the sense of orderliness and predictability that employees look to for guidance are provided by the culture rather than by a rule book. ●

8.2 DEVELOPING HIGH-PERFORMANCE CULTURES

What can be done to an organization's culture to increase its economic performance?

major question?

THE BIG PICTURE

Three perspectives have been suggested to explain why an organization's culture can enhance the firm's economic performance: strength, fit, and adaptive. There are many ways in which a particular culture can become embedded in an organization, 11 of which are described here.

What does a company do when the growth of its most successful product starts slowing down? This was the situation that confronted financial software maker Intuit Inc., as we shall see. How successfully an organization reacts depends on its culture.

Cultures for Enhancing Economic Performance: Three Perspectives

What types of organizational culture can increase an organization's economic performance in terms of increasing competitiveness and profitability? Three perspectives have been proposed: (1) strength, (2) fit, and (3) adaptive.

I. The Strength Perspective: Success Results When a Firm Has a Strong Culture The *strength perspective* **assumes that the strength of a corporate culture is related to a firm's long-term financial performance.** A culture is said to be "strong" when employees adhere to the organization's values because they believe in its purpose. A culture is said to be "weak" when employees are forced to adhere to the organization's values through extensive procedures and bureaucracies. The strength perspective embraces the point of view that strong cultures create goal alignment, employee motivation, and the appropriate structure and controls needed to improve organizational performance.[28]

The downside of a strong culture, critics believe, is that such financial success can so reinforce cultural norms that managers and employees become arrogant, inwardly focused, and resistant to change, with top managers becoming blinded to the need for new strategic plans. Example: A case could be made that the strong cultures of American auto makers for many years made them resistant to the need to make radical adjustments.

2. The Fit Perspective: Success Results When Culture Fits with the Firm's Business Context The *fit perspective* **assumes that an organization's culture must align, or fit, with its business or strategic context.** A "correct" fit is expected to foster higher financial performance.

Example: Prior to the arrival of Carleton Fiorina, Hewlett-Packard's "HP Way" culture from 1957 to the early 1990s pushed authority as far down as possible in the organization and created an environment that emphasized integrity, respect for individuals, teamwork, innovation, and an emphasis on customers and community improvement. This fit perspective was a key contributor to HP's success—until the high-technology industry began to change in the late 1990s.[29]

3. The Adaptive Perspective: Success Results When Culture Helps the Firm Adapt
The *adaptive perspective* assumes that the most effective cultures help organizations anticipate and adapt to environmental changes.

Which Perspective Is Accurate? An investigation of 207 companies from 22 industries during the years 1977–1988 partly supported the strength and fit perspectives. However, findings were completely consistent with the adaptive perspective. Long-term financial performance was highest for organizations with an adaptive culture.[30]

Example

Intuit Demonstrates an Adaptive Culture

Intuit Inc. of Mountain View, California, is well known as the maker of finance software, such as TurboTax, QuickBooks, and Quicken. In 2003, however, the company's culture began to change, especially at Quicken, where sales had begun to stall as online banking reduced the need for software for managing personal finances. Peter Karpas, who was then in charge of Quicken Solutions Group, began spurring his staff to think of innovative ideas beyond just simply improving their core software program. He identified several people who had "that entrepreneurial spark," then challenged them to "Find something that excites you, go forward, and answer these questions."

One of them was engineering manager Dan Robinson, father to a son, Zane, who had been born in 2000 with a rare genetic disorder that required open heart surgery, an operation on his stomach, and other treatment. For 6 months, Robinson and his wife were so overwhelmed that they paid little attention to the medical bills arriving almost daily. "When Robinson finally sat down with the file box of papers he had accumulated," says a *BusinessWeek* account, "among them were a $100,000 bill for Zane's heart surgery that had not been sent to his insurance company, threatening letters about charges he had never received, and dozens of 'explanation of benefits'

statements from his insurer that he couldn't match to any bills."[31]

To keep track of everything, Robinson thereupon sat down and wrote a software program. In doing so, he came to the realization that there were probably many other people with health problems who needed something like it. In the fall of 2003, he pitched his idea to Karpas. Robinson and a partner, Kate Welker, were given time and resources to visit dozens of people to see how they handled their health care bills and statements. They found that people would spend hours to get even a few dollars out of their insurers, and they wanted some way to assert control over their medical paperwork.

Eventually Medical Expense Manager was born, and it was quickly adopted by a select group of people dealing with serious medical matters. So far it is only a modest money maker by Intuit's standards, but the company is convinced that it could revolutionize health care.

Your Call
Do you think most organizations are capable of being adaptable under changing circumstances? What does it take to implant a culture of adaptability within an organization?

Eleven Ways Cultures Become Embedded in Organizations

Those who found a business, and the managers who follow them, essentially use a teaching process to embed the values, beliefs, expectations, behaviors, and business philosophy that constitute the organization's culture. Among the mechanisms used are the following.[32]

I. Formal Statements   The first way to embed preferred culture is through the use of formal statements of organizational philosophy, mission, vision, values, as well as materials used for recruiting, selecting, and socializing employees. Example: Wal-Mart founder Sam Walton stated that three basic values represented the core of the retailer's culture: (1) respect for the individual, (2) service to customers, and (3) striving for excellence.[33]

2. Slogans & Sayings   The desirable corporate culture can be expressed in language, slogans, sayings, and acronyms. Example: Robert Mittelstaedt, Dean of the W.P. Carey School of Business at Arizona State University, promotes his goal of having a world-class university through the slogan "top-of-mind business school." This slogan encourages instructors to engage in activities that promote quality education and research.

3. Stories, Legends, & Myths   A highly valued resource at The Associates is time. To reinforce the importance of not wasting time, many stories circulate about senior managers missing planes or being locked out of meetings because they were late.[34]

4. Leader Reactions to Crises   How top managers respond to critical incidents and organizational crises sends a clear cultural message. Example: Canadian Dov Charney got into the clothing business as a college student, when he would buy thousands of T-shirts at Kmart, then import them via a U-Haul truck into Canada. Then he dropped out of college, borrowed $10,000 from his father, and moved to South Carolina to manufacture clothes—just at a time when the rest of the garment industry found it was cheaper to make clothing overseas. Charney filed for bankruptcy but then moved his company to California, determined to make it work. "I knew I could do it differently, and I knew I could turn it around," he said. "Passion" is the key to success. "When you believe in what you're doing, that's the first thing. And you have to be resilient, because people are going to try to knock you down." Today his company, American Apparel, has over 6,700 employees. And it does something other garment makers have abandoned: it makes all its clothing in the United States.[35]

5. Role Modeling, Training, & Coaching   Triage Consulting Group, a health care financial consulting firm in California, places a high value on superior performance at achieving measurable goals. New employees are immediately prepared for this culture with a 4-day orientation in Triage's culture and methods, followed by 15 training modules scheduled in 6-week intervals. After less than a year, the best performers are ready to begin managing their own projects, furthering their career development. Performance evaluations take place four times a year, further reinforcing the drive for results.[36]

6. Physical Design Intel originally had all its people work in uniform cubicles, consistent with the value it placed on equality. (Top managers don't have reserved parking spaces either.) However, the cubicle arrangement conflicted with the value Intel places on innovation, so the company is experimenting with open-seating arrangements combined with small conference rooms. Not only are open-seating arrangements thought to encourage collaboration, they also can reduce noise because employees can see when their activities are annoying to people nearby. Intel hopes that this environment will better support creative thinking.[37]

7. Rewards, Titles, Promotions, & Bonuses At Triage Consulting Group, employees at the same level of their career earn the same pay, but employees are eligible for merit bonuses, again reinforcing the culture of achievement. The awarding of merit bonuses is partly based on co-workers' votes for who contributed most to the company's success, and the employees who received the most votes are recognized each year at the company's "State of Triage" meeting.[38]

8. Organizational Goals & Performance Criteria Many organizations establish organizational goals and criteria for recruiting, selecting, developing, promoting, dismissing, and retiring people, all of which reinforce the desired organizational culture. Example: PepsiCo sets challenging goals that reinforce a culture aimed at high performance.

9. Measurable & Controllable Activities There are a number of activities, processes, or outcomes that an organization's leaders can pay attention to, measure, and control that can foster a certain culture. Example: ExxonMobil's credo is "efficiency in everything we do," so that managers make a concerted effort to measure, control, and reward cost efficiency. As a result, the company is famous for delivering consistent returns, regardless of whether the price of oil is up or down.[39]

I0. Organizational Structure The hierarchical structure found in most traditional organizations is more likely to reinforce a culture oriented toward control and authority compared to the flatter organization that eliminates management layers in favor of giving employees more power. Example: The hierarchical structure of a railroad provides a much different culture from that of the former "spaghetti" organization of Danish hearing-aid maker Oticon, described in Chapter 2.

II. Organizational Systems & Procedures Companies are increasingly using electronic networks to increase collaboration among employees, to increase innovation, quality, and efficiency. For example, Serena Software Inc., a California-based company with 800 employees located in 29 offices across 14 countries, encouraged its employees to sign up for Facebook for free and to use the network as a vehicle for getting to know each other. In contrast to using a public site for networking, Dow Chemical launched its own internal social network to create relationships among current, past, and temporary employees.[40] ●

> How are for-profit, nonprofit, and mutual-benefit organizations structured?
>
> major question?

THE BIG PICTURE

The organizational structure of the three types of organizations—for-profit, nonprofit, and mutual-benefit—may be expressed vertically or horizontally on an organization chart.

According to **Chester I. Barnard's** classic definition, **an *organization* is a system of consciously coordinated activities or forces of two or more people.**[41] By this definition, a crew of two coordinating their activities to operate a tuna fishing boat is just as much an organization as the entire StarKist Tuna Co.—assuming the two fishers are catching tuna for a living and not just for fun.

The Organization: Three Types

As we stated in Chapter 1, there are three types of organizations classified according to the three different purposes for which they are formed:[42]

- **For-profit organizations.** These are formed to make money, or profits, by offering products or services.
- **Nonprofit organizations.** These are formed to offer services to some clients, not to make a profit (examples: hospitals, colleges).
- **Mutual-benefit organizations.** These are voluntary collectives whose purpose is to advance members' interests (examples: unions, trade associations).

Clearly, you might have an occupation (such as auditor or police officer) that is equally employable in any one of these three sectors. As a manager, however, you would be principally required to focus on different goals—making profits, delivering public services, or satisfying member needs—depending on the type of organization.

Hybrid. By 2030, some experts say, 72% of fleet vehicles and 85% of new cars will be hybrid electric vehicles. This 2008 Toyota Prius hybrid is the most fuel-efficient car sold in the United States. Are some types of organizations better able to respond to change than others? Why didn't American automakers foresee changes in the price of gasoline?

The Organization Chart

Whatever the size or type of organization, it can be represented in an organization chart. **An *organization chart* is a box-and-lines illustration showing the formal lines of authority and the organization's**

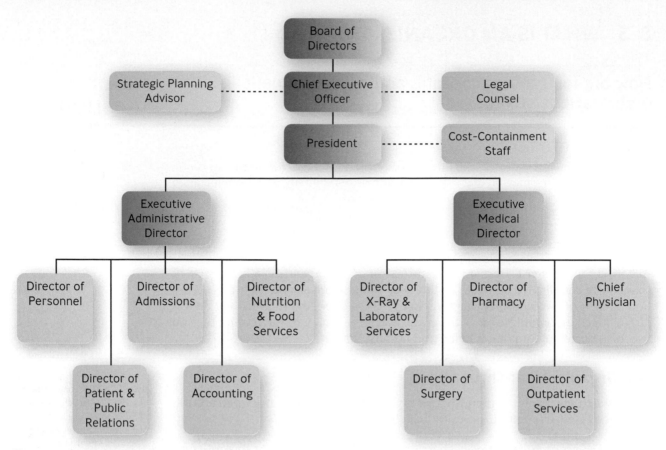

figure 8.2

ORGANIZATION CHART

Example for a hospital

official positions or work specializations. This is the family-tree-like pattern of boxes and lines posted on workplace walls and given to new hires. *(See Figure 8.2, above.)*

Two kinds of information that organization charts reveal about organizational structure are (1) the *vertical hierarchy of authority*—who reports to whom, and (2) the *horizontal specialization*—who specializes in what work.

The Vertical Hierarchy of Authority: Who Reports to Whom   A glance up and down an organization chart shows the *vertical hierarchy,* the chain of command. A formal vertical hierarchy also shows the official communication network—who talks to whom. In a simple two-person organization, the owner might communicate with just a secretary or an assistant. In a complex organization, the president talks principally to the vice presidents, who in turn talk to the assistant vice presidents, and so on.

The Horizontal Specialization: Who Specializes in What Work   A glance to the left and right on the line of an organization chart shows the *horizontal specialization,* the different jobs or work specialization. The husband-and-wife partners in a two-person desktop-publishing firm might agree that one is the "outside person," handling sales, client relations, and finances, and the other is the "inside person," handling production and research. A large firm might have vice presidents for each task—marketing, finance, and so on. ●

Mentoring: The New Rules

Who's going to help you learn the ropes in a new organization? Maybe you need a mentor.

If you can find an experienced employee to mentor you—to be your organizational sponsor and help you understand and navigate the organization's culture and structure—it can be a great asset to your career. Indeed, mentoring may be especially useful for female and minority managers, for whom there may be fewer role models within their particular organizations. One survey of 4,561 respondents from 42 countries found that 46% felt that coaching or mentoring had a great impact and 45% a moderate impact on their career success.[43]

What's the best advice about acquiring a mentor? Here are some of the new rules.[44]

Choose Anyone You Can Learn From, Not Just Someone Higher Up

It used to be thought that a mentor should be a seasoned manager higher up in the organization. But a mentor can also be a peer—someone at your own level inside the organization.

Choose More Than One Mentor

It might be nice to have a single mentor who can give you lots of one-on-one attention. But everyone's busy, so look around and see if there are two or three people who might be helpful to you. "Diversify your mentor portfolio," goes one piece of advice.

Pick Your Mentors, Don't Wait to Be Picked

Don't wait for organizational veterans to select you to be their protégé. It's up to you to make the first move, to be assertive in a nice way.

Mentoring. Think you could succeed in a new job with a new organization without the help of mentors? Did mentors help you find your way in college?

Do a Self-Assessment

Before you begin contacting people to be mentors, assess where you want to go and what skills and knowledge you need to get there, so that you'll know the kind of help you need.

Look for Someone Different from You

It used to be thought the mentor and mentee should have a lot in common, as in personal chemistry or personal style. But someone who is different from you will challenge you and help you be more objective.

Investigate Your Prospects

Before approaching prospective mentors, call their administrative assistants, explain your plans, and ask what their bosses are like to work with. Find out the best time to approach them.

Show Your Prospective Mentor How You Can Be Helpful

"Mentoring is a two-way street," says Anne Hayden, senior vice president of Metropolitan Life insurance company. "The person being mentored gets help, advice, and coaching, and the person doing the mentoring generally gets extra effort—someone very committed to working on special projects or on assignments that maybe don't fall within the boxes on the organizational chart."[45]

Agree on How Your Mentoring Relationship Will Work

In your first meeting, set the ground rules for how frequently you will meet and the type of contact, such as whether it will be in the office, over lunch, or at the gym. A minimum of one meeting a month is recommended, and in between the two of you should keep in touch by phone and e-mail.

When I join an organization, what seven elements should I look for?

THE BIG PICTURE

Seven basic elements or features of an organization are described in this section.

Whether for-profit, nonprofit, or mutual-benefit, organizations have a number of elements in common. We discuss four proposed by an organizational psychologist, and then describe three others that most authorities agree on.

Common Elements of Organizations: Four Proposed by Edgar Schein

Organizational psychologist **Edgar Schein** proposed the four common elements of (1) *common purpose,* (2) *coordinated effort,* (3) *division of labor,* and (4) *hierarchy of authority.*[46] Let's consider these.

I. Common Purpose: The Means for Unifying Members   An organization without purpose soon begins to drift and become disorganized. **The *common purpose* unifies employees or members and gives everyone an understanding of the organization's reason for being.**

2. Coordinated Effort: Working Together for Common Purpose   The common purpose is realized through *coordinated effort,* **the coordination of individual efforts into a group or organization-wide effort.** Although it's true that individuals can make a difference, they cannot do everything by themselves.

3. Division of Labor: Work Specialization for Greater Efficiency   *Division of labor,* **also known as *work specialization,* is the arrangement of having discrete parts of a task done by different people.** Even a two-person crew operating a fishing boat probably has some work specialization—one steers the boat, the other works the nets. With division of labor, an organization can parcel out the entire complex work effort to be performed by specialists, resulting in greater efficiency.

4. Hierarchy of Authority: The Chain of Command   The *hierarchy of authority,* or *chain of command,* **is a control mechanism for making sure the right people do the right things at the right time.** If coordinated effort is to be achieved, some people—namely, managers—need to have more authority, or the right to direct the work of others. Even in member-owned organizations, some people have more authority than others, although their peers may have granted it to them.

In addition, authority is most effective when arranged in a hierarchy. Without tiers or ranks of authority, a lone manager would have to confer with everyone in his or her domain, making it difficult to get things done. Even in newer organizations that flatten the hierarchy, there still exists more than one level of management.

Finally, a principle stressed by early management scholars was that of *unity of command,* **in which an employee should report to no more than one manager** in order to avoid conflicting priorities and demands. Today, however, with advances in computer technology and networks, there are circumstances in which it makes sense for a person to communicate with more than one manager (as is true, for instance, with the organizational structure known as the matrix structure, as we'll describe).

Test Your Knowledge:
Allocating Authority

Common Elements of Organizations: Three More That Most Authorities Agree On

To Schein's four common elements we may add three others that most authorities agree on: (5) *span of control,* (6) *authority, responsibility, and delegation,* and (7) *centralization versus decentralization of authority.*

5. Span of Control: Narrow (or Tall) versus Wide (or Flat)

The *span of control, or span of management,* refers to the number of people reporting directly to a given manager.[47] There are two kinds of spans of control, narrow (or tall) and wide (or flat).

Narrow Span of Control   This means a manager has a limited number of people reporting—three vice presidents reporting to a president, for example, instead of nine vice presidents. An organization is said to be *tall* when there are many levels with narrow spans of control.

Wide Span of Control   This means a manager has several people reporting—a first-line supervisor may have 40 or more subordinates, if little hands-on supervision is required, as is the case in some assembly-line workplaces. An organization is said to be *flat* when there are only a few levels with wide spans of control.

Historically, spans of about 7 to 10 subordinates were considered best, but there is no consensus as to what is ideal. In general, when managers must be closely involved with their subordinates, as when the management duties are complex, they are advised to have a narrow span of control. This is why presidents tend to have only a handful of vice presidents reporting to them. By contrast, first-line supervisors directing subordinates with similar work tasks may have a wide span of control.

The recent emphasis on lean management staffs and more efficiency has meant that spans of control need to be as wide as possible while still providing adequate supervision. Wider spans also fit in with the trend toward allowing workers greater autonomy in decision making. Research in Europe suggests that a manager can oversee 30 or more employees when aided by technology to communicate and help monitor performance.[48]

6. Authority, Responsibility, & Delegation: Line versus Staff Positions

Male sea lions have to battle other males to attain authority over the herd. In human organizations, however, authority is related to the management authority in the organization; it has nothing to do with the manager's fighting ability or personal characteristics. With authority goes *accountability, responsibility,* and the ability to *delegate* one's authority.

Accountability   **Authority refers to the rights inherent in a managerial position to make decisions, give orders, and utilize resources.** (Authority is distinguished from *power,* which, as we discuss in Chapter 14, is the extent to which a person is able to influence others so they respond to orders.) In the military, of course, orders are given with the expectation that they will be obeyed, disobedience making one liable to a dishonorable discharge or imprisonment. In civilian organizations, disobeying orders may lead to less dire consequences (demotion or firing), but subordinates are still expected to accept that a higher-level manager has a legitimate right to issue orders.

Authority means *accountability*—**managers must report and justify work results to the managers above them.** Being accountable means you have the responsibility for performing assigned tasks.

Responsibility   With more authority comes more responsibility. **Responsibility is the obligation you have to perform the tasks assigned to you.** A car assembly-line worker has little authority but also little responsibility: just install those windshields over and over. A manager, however, has greater responsibilities.

It is a sign of faulty job design when managers are given too much authority and not enough responsibility, in which case they may become abusive to subordinates and capricious in exerting authority.[49] Conversely, managers may not be given enough authority, so the job becomes difficult.

Span of control. Do you think you could supervise 30 employees or more? Do you think it depends on the kind of work they do?

Delegation ***Delegation* is the process of assigning managerial authority and responsibility to managers and employees lower in the hierarchy.** To be more efficient, most managers are expected to delegate as much of their work as possible. However, a business entrepreneur may fall into the common trap of perfection, believing, as one writer puts it, that "you are the only person who can handle a given situation, work with a special client, design a program."[50] But a surprising number of managers fail to realize that delegation is an important part of their job.

Regarding authority and responsibility, the organization chart distinguishes between two positions, *line* and *staff. (See Figure 8.3.)*

figure 8.3

LINE AND STAFF

Line have solid lines, staff have dotted lines.

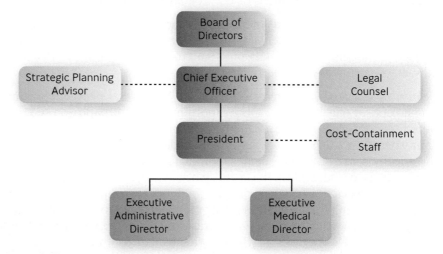

Line Position ***Line managers* have authority to make decisions and usually have people reporting to them.** Examples: the president, the vice presidents, the director of personnel, and the head of accounting. Line positions are indicated on the organization chart by a *solid line* (usually a vertical line).

Staff Position ***Staff personnel* have authority functions; they provide advice, recommendations, and research to line managers** (examples: specialists such as legal counsels and special advisors for mergers and acquisitions or strategic planning). Staff positions are indicated on the organization chart by a *dotted line* (usually a horizontal line).

7. Centralization versus Decentralization of Authority
Who makes the important decisions in an organization? That is what the question of centralization versus decentralization of authority is concerned with.

Centralized Authority **With *centralized authority,* important decisions are made by higher-level managers.** Very small companies tend to be the most centralized, although nearly all organizations have at least some authority concentrated at the top of the hierarchy. Kmart and McDonald's are examples of companies using this kind of authority.

An advantage in using centralized authority is that there is less duplication of work, because fewer employees perform the same task; rather, the task is often performed by a department of specialists. Another advantage of centralization is that procedures are uniform and thus easier to control; all purchasing, for example, may have to be put out to competitive bids.

Decentralized Authority **With *decentralized authority,* important decisions are made by middle-level and supervisory-level managers.** Here, obviously, power has been delegated throughout the organization. Among the companies using decentralized authority are General Motors and Harley-Davidson.

An advantage in having decentralized authority is that managers are encouraged to solve their own problems rather than to buck the decision to a higher level. In addition, decisions are made more quickly, which increases the organization's flexibility and efficiency. ●

8.5 BASIC TYPES OF ORGANIZATIONAL STRUCTURES

> How would one describe the seven organizational structures?
>
> **major question?**

THE BIG PICTURE

Seven types of organizational structures are simple, functional, divisional, matrix, team-based, network, and modular.

Culture and structure are often intertwined. When in 1997 the Federal Railroad Administration (FRA) sent inspectors to Union Pacific's headquarters in Omaha, Nebraska, to examine why the railroad had had a series of fatal accidents, they learned that the company had a top-down, military-style hierarchy and culture that seemed to discourage teamwork and communication. The antiquated style of management had its roots in the days when railroads' executive ranks were filled with combat-hardened former Civil War officers. "When something happened," said a railroad vice president explaining the attitude of leading by fear, "you pulled out your gun and shot the guy in charge of the territory." Said the head of the FRA of Union Pacific's dysfunctional working arrangements, "They were separated from each other in a way that almost guaranteed problems."[51]

We may categorize the arrangements of organizations into seven types of structures: (1) *simple*, (2) *functional*, (3) *divisional*, (4) *matrix*, (5) *team-based*, (6) *network*, and (7) *modular*.

I. The Simple Structure: For the Small Firm

The first organizational form is the simple structure. This is the form often found in a firm's very early, entrepreneurial stages, when the organization is apt to reflect the desires and personality of the owner or founder. **An organization with a *simple structure* has authority centralized in a single person, a flat hierarchy, few rules, and low work specialization.** *(See Figure 8.4, at right.)*

There are hundreds of thousands of organizations that are arranged according to a simple structure—for instance, small mom 'n' pop firms running landscaping, construction, insurance sales, and similar businesses. Some of these firms, of course, grow into larger organizations with different kinds of structures. Both Hewlett-Packard and Apple Computer began as two-man garage startups that later became large.

2. The Functional Structure: Grouping by Similar Work Specialties

The second organizational form is the functional structure. **In a *functional structure*, people with similar occupational specialties are put together in formal groups.** This is a quite commonplace structure, seen in all kinds of organizations, for-profit and nonprofit. *(See Figure 8.5, next page.)*

A manufacturing firm, for example, will often group people with similar work skills in a Marketing Department, others in a Production Department, others in Finance, and so on. A nonprofit educational institution might group employees according to work specialty under Faculty, Admissions, Maintenance, and so forth.

Small firm. What type of organizational structure is best suited to a local floral shop? Should the number of employees influence the decision?

figure 8.4

SIMPLE STRUCTURE: AN EXAMPLE

There is only one hierarchical level of management beneath the owner.

figure 8.5

FUNCTIONAL STRUCTURE: TWO EXAMPLES

This shows the functional structure for a business and for a hospital.

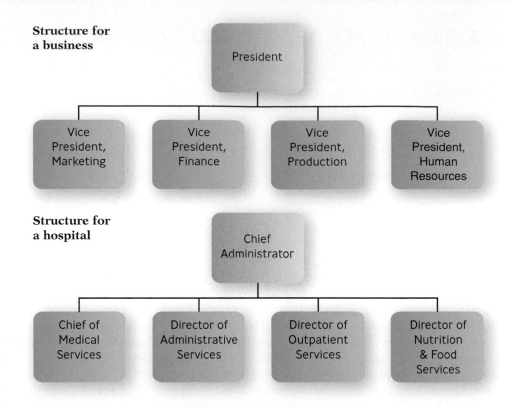

Structure for a business

President

- Vice President, Marketing
- Vice President, Finance
- Vice President, Production
- Vice President, Human Resources

Structure for a hospital

Chief Administrator

- Chief of Medical Services
- Director of Administrative Services
- Director of Outpatient Services
- Director of Nutrition & Food Services

3. The Divisional Structure: Grouping by Similarity of Purpose

The third organizational form is the divisional structure. **In a *divisional structure*, people with diverse occupational specialties are put together in formal groups by similar products or services, customers or clients, or geographic regions.** *(See Figure 8.6, opposite page.)*

Product Divisions: Grouping by Similar Products or Services *Product divisions* **group activities around similar products or services.** For instance, the media giant Time Warner has different divisions for magazines, movies, recordings, cable television, and so on. The Warner Bros. part of the empire alone has divisions spanning movies and television, a broadcast network, retail stores, theaters, amusement parks, and music.

Customer Divisions: Grouping by Common Customers or Clients *Customer divisions* **tend to group activities around common customers or clients.** For instance, Ford Motor Co. has separate divisions for passenger-car dealers, for large trucking customers, and for farm products customers. A savings and loan might be structured with divisions for making consumer loans, mortgage loans, business loans, and agricultural loans.

Geographic Divisions: Grouping by Regional Location *Geographic divisions* **group activities around defined regional locations.** This arrangement is frequently used by government agencies. The Federal Reserve Bank, for instance, has 12 separate districts around the United States. The Internal Revenue Service also has several districts.

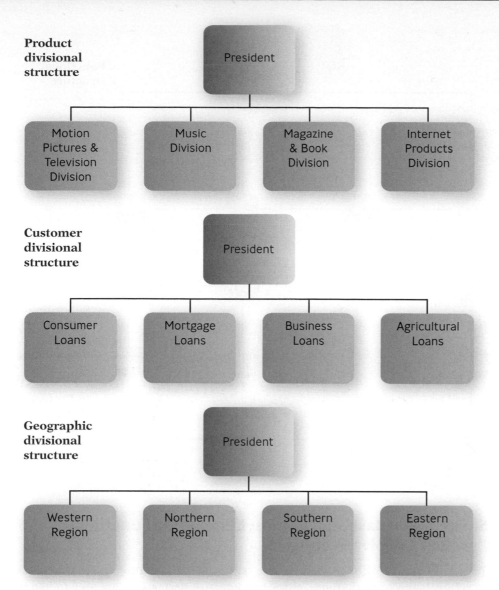

Product divisional structure

President

- Motion Pictures & Television Division
- Music Division
- Magazine & Book Division
- Internet Products Division

Customer divisional structure

President

- Consumer Loans
- Mortgage Loans
- Business Loans
- Agricultural Loans

Geographic divisional structure

President

- Western Region
- Northern Region
- Southern Region
- Eastern Region

figure 8.6

DIVISIONAL STRUCTURE: THREE EXAMPLES

This shows product, customer, and geographic divisions.

4. The Matrix Structure: A Grid of Functional & Divisional for Two Chains of Command

The fourth organizational form is the matrix structure. **In a *matrix structure,* an organization combines functional and divisional chains of command in a grid so that there are two command structures—vertical and horizontal.** The functional structure usually doesn't change—it is the organization's normal departments or divisions, such as Finance, Marketing, Production, and Research & Development. The divisional structure may vary—as by product, brand, customer, or geographic region. *(See Figure 8.7, next page.)*

For example, the functional structure might be the departments of Engineering, Finance, Production, and Marketing, each headed by a vice president. Thus, the reporting arrangement is vertical. The divisional structure might be by product (the new models of Taurus, Mustang, Explorer, and Expedition, for example), each headed by a project manager. This reporting arrangement is horizontal. Thus, a marketing person, say, would report to *both* the Vice President of Marketing *and* to the Project Manager for the Ford Mustang. Indeed, Ford Motor Co. used the matrix approach to create the Taurus and a newer version of the Mustang.

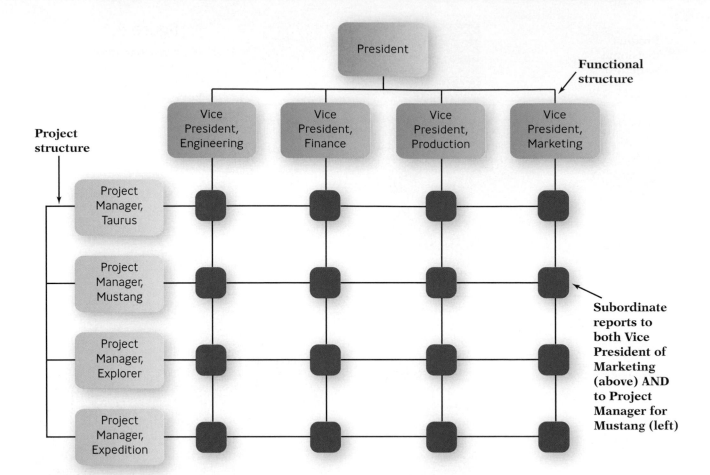

President

Functional structure

Vice President, Engineering

Vice President, Finance

Vice President, Production

Vice President, Marketing

Project structure

Project Manager, Taurus

Project Manager, Mustang

Project Manager, Explorer

Project Manager, Expedition

Subordinate reports to both Vice President of Marketing (above) AND to Project Manager for Mustang (left)

figure 8.7

MATRIX STRUCTURE

An example of an arrangement that Ford might use.

5. The Team-Based Structure: Eliminating Functional Barriers to Solve Problems

The fifth organizational form is the team-based structure. **In a *team-based structure,* teams or workgroups, either temporary or permanent, are used to improve horizontal relations and solve problems throughout the organization.**[52] When managers from different functional divisions are brought together in teams—known as cross-functional teams—to solve particular problems, the barriers between the divisions break down. The focus on narrow divisional interests yields to a common interest in solving the problems that brought them together. Yet team members still have their full-time functional work responsibilities and still formally report to their own managers above them in the functional-division hierarchy. *(See Figure 8.8, opposite page.)*

6. The Network Structure: Connecting a Central Core to Outside Firms by Computer Connections

In the sixth organizational form, *network structure,* **the organization has a central core that is linked to outside independent firms by computer connections, which are used to operate as if all were a single organization.** *(See Figure 8.9, opposite page.)* Corporations using this structure are sometimes called *virtual corporations* or *virtual organizations,* as we mentioned in Chapter 2.[53] Another term used is the *hollow corporation* or *hollow organization,* in which the company retains important core processes critical to its performance (such as design or marketing) and

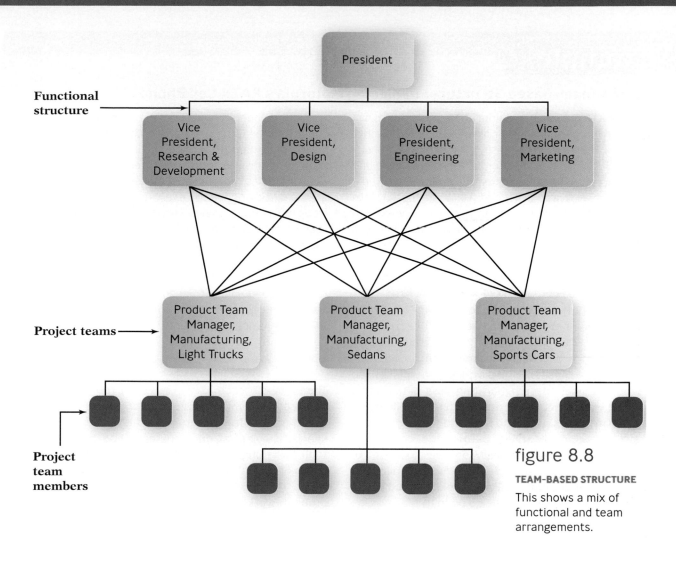

Functional structure →

President

Vice President, Research & Development

Vice President, Design

Vice President, Engineering

Vice President, Marketing

Project teams →

Product Team Manager, Manufacturing, Light Trucks

Product Team Manager, Manufacturing, Sedans

Product Team Manager, Manufacturing, Sports Cars

Project team members →

figure 8.8

TEAM-BASED STRUCTURE

This shows a mix of functional and team arrangements.

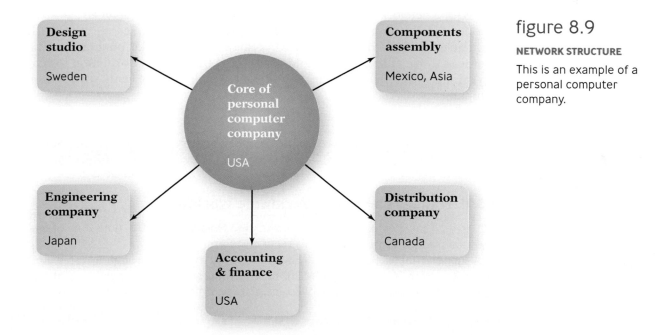

Design studio

Sweden

Components assembly

Mexico, Asia

Core of personal computer company

USA

Engineering company

Japan

Accounting & finance

USA

Distribution company

Canada

figure 8.9

NETWORK STRUCTURE

This is an example of a personal computer company.

Example

Use of a Team-Based Structure: Designing Motorola's RAZR Cell Phone

In early 2003, the mood was grim at Motorola, which had watched rival cell phone maker Nokia leap to No. I worldwide in market share on the basis of its "candy bar" phone designs. But engineers in Motorola's concept-phone unit had a vision for something different, having produced a mock-up of what was described as "an impossibly thin phone—at ten millimeters . . . half the girth of a typical flip-flop" cell phone.[54] Engineer Roger Jellicoe was told to pull a team together and produce the thinnest phone ever released—and to do it within a year in order to make a splash by handing it out as a high-end niche product to celebrities at the February 2004 Academy Awards.

Eventually the team grew to as many as 20 engineers, who met daily in a conference room in Motorola's Libertyville, Illinois, office, to deliberate over how to cram a checklist of components—antenna, speaker, keypad, camera, display, light source, and so on—into minimal space. Operating as a skunkworks that kept the project secret even from their colleagues, the team members used materials and techniques that Motorola had never tried before and threw out accepted models of what a cell phone was supposed to look and feel like. "In short," says a *Fortune* account, "the team that created the RAZR broke the mold, and in the process rejuvenated the company."

As engineers worked on the components, industrial designer Chris Arnholt worked on the look, rendering designs onto a page and then letting another designer translate them into three-dimensional computer graphics, which model makers could use to craft plastic mock-ups. Nearly every activity came down to a trade-off of functionality versus thinness, which eventually led to two compromises: the phone exceeded the original targeted size by about an eighth of an inch and the team missed the February 2004 deadline.

When the RAZR was finally unveiled in a splashy presentation in July, it became an instant hit. And the company realized that the product it had designed to be a high-priced, high-end jewel had mass market appeal.

Your Call

The team approach, known as *concurrent engineering* or *integrated product development,* has been found to speed up the design of new products because all the specialists meet at once, instead of separately doing their own thing, then handing off the result to the next group of specialists. Can you think of circumstances in which the old-fashioned nonteam approach would probably work better?

outsources most other processes (such as human resources, warehousing, or distribution), thereby seeming to "hollow out" the organization.[55]

With a network structure, an organization can become a *boundaryless organization,* as we described in Chapter 2, operating with extensive, even worldwide operations, yet its basic core can remain small, thus keeping payrolls and overhead down. The glue that holds everything together is information technology, along with strategic alliances and contractual arrangements with supplier companies.

Example

Network Structure: MySQL Manages a Virtual Worldwide Workforce

MySQL (pronounced "my S-Q-L") is a $40 million software maker that employs 320 workers in 25 countries, 70% of whom work from home. Although Thomas Basil, MySQL's director of support, operates from his basement home office in Baltimore, he keeps his clocks set

7 hours ahead to Helsinki time, the time zone of many of his team members.

Employees stay in touch through Internet Relay Chat (IRC), which acts as a companywide chatroom, as well as Skype, which allows them to make free voice calls over the Internet—"and just as important," adds writer Josh Hyatt, "to keep themselves from perishing in what can quickly intensify into . . . e-mail storms."[56] As Basil says, "Voice is more personal than text and more helpful in building real understanding."

A virtual, boundaryless company like MySQL operates differently from a traditional company, with managers learning to evaluate people and give feedback differently. "Productivity is measured strictly by output; mushy factors like charisma don't pertain in cyberspace," says Hyatt. "The company has developed software called Worklog, which requires employees to check off tasks as they finish them." As might be expected, the company hires strictly for skill, not "the ability to play nicely with others."

Your Call

Many people like the social interaction that comes with working in a physical office with other people. Others, however, are turned off by the "office politics" and time-wasting activities that seem to be a necessary concomitant and welcome the opportunity to do task-oriented work in a makeshift home office, occasionally having to cope with loneliness and restlessness. Which would you favor?

7. The Modular Structure: Outsourcing Pieces of a Product to Outside Firms

The seventh organizational form differs from the sixth in that it is oriented around outsourcing certain *pieces of a product* rather than outsourcing certain *processes* (such as human resources or warehousing) of an organization. In a **modular structure, a firm assembles product chunks, or modules, provided by outside contractors.** One article compares this form of organization to "a collection of Lego bricks that can snap together."[57] ●

Self-Assessment: Identify Your Preferred Organizational Structure

Example

Modular Structure: Bombardier Builds a Snap-Together Business Jet[58]

Bombardier (pronounced "bom-*bar*-dee-ay"), whose main factory is located in Wichita, Kansas, makes an eight-passenger business jet called the Continental, so named because it can fly across the United States without refueling. The aircraft is designed into a dozen large modules, which are manufactured by a mix of both internal Bombardier divisions and outside contractors around the world. The cockpit and forward fuselage, for instance, are built by Bombardier Montreal. The center section is built in Belfast, the wing by Mitsubishi in Japan, the stabilizers and rear fuselage by Aerospace Industrial Development in Taiwan, the landing gear by Messier-Dowty in Canada, and the tailcone by Hawker de Havilland in Australia. The engines are provided by General Electric and the avionics gear by Rockwell Collins, both companies in the U.S.A. The 12 modules are shipped to Wichita, where the parts are snapped together in just 4 days.

Bombardier. A regional vice president of sales for Bombardier, David Dixon, poses in front of a Bombardier luxury aircraft, built using the modular structure of organization.

Your Call

Could you envision building automobiles, bicycles, and computers using a modular approach? What other products?

8.6 CONTINGENCY DESIGN: FACTORS IN CREATING THE BEST STRUCTURE

major question? What factors affect the design of an organization's structure?

THE BIG PICTURE

Five factors affecting an organization's structure are whether its environment is mechanistic or organic, whether its environment stresses differentiation or integration, and size, technology, and life cycle.

What is the optimal size for an organization? How big is too big?

"The real growth and innovation in this country," said famed management consultant Peter F. Drucker, "has been in medium-size companies that employ between 200 and 4,000 workers." Despite the informality, smaller than 200 is not necessarily better. "If you are in a small company, you are running all out," Drucker pointed out. "You have neither the time nor the energy to devote to anything but yesterday's crisis." A medium-size company, by contrast, "has the resources to devote to new products and markets, and it's still small enough to be flexible and to move fast. And these companies now have what they once lacked—they've learned how to manage."[59]

When managers are considering what organizational arrangements to choose from, size is one of several factors, or *contingencies,* to consider. Recall from Chapter 2 that the *contingency approach* to management emphasizes that a manager's approach should vary according to—that is, be contingent on—the individual and environmental situation. Thus, the manager following the contingency approach simply asks, "What method is the best to use under these particular circumstances?" **The process of fitting the organization to its environment is called** ***contingency design.***

Managers taking a contingency approach must consider the following factors in designing the best kind of structure for their particular organization at that particular time:

1. *Environment—mechanistic versus organic*
2. *Environment—differentiation versus integration*
3. *Size*
4. *Technology*
5. *Life cycle*

I. The Environment: Mechanistic versus Organic Organizations—the Burns & Stalker Model

"Here every job is broken down into the smallest of steps, and the whole process is automated," wrote *BusinessWeek* correspondent Kathleen Deveny, reporting about a day she spent working in a McDonald's restaurant. "Anyone could do this, I think."[60]

Actually, Deveny found that she fell behind in, say, bagging French fries, but it was certainly the intention of McDonald's guiding genius Ray Kroc that, in fact, nearly anyone *should* be able to do this—and that a Big Mac should taste the same anywhere. Thus, for example, procedure dictates that a hamburger is always dressed the same way: first the mustard, then the ketchup, then two pickles.

McDonald's is a hugely successful example of what British behavioral scientists **Tom Burns** and **G. M. Stalker** call a *mechanistic organization,* as opposed to an *organic organization.*[61] *(See Table 8.1.)*

Could anyone do this?
McDonald's follows the model of a mechanistic organization.

table 8.1

MECHANISTIC VERSUS ORGANIC ORGANIZATIONS

Mechanistic Organizations	Organic Organizations
Centralized hierarchy of authority	Decentralized hierarchy of authority
Many rules and procedures	Few rules and procedures
Specialized tasks	Shared tasks
Formalized communication	Informal communication
Few teams or task forces	Many teams or task forces
Narrow span of control, taller structures	Wider span of control, flatter structures

Mechanistic Organizations: When Rigidity & Uniformity Work Best

In a *mechanistic organization,* **authority is centralized, tasks and rules are clearly specified, and employees are closely supervised.** Mechanistic organizations, then, are bureaucratic, with rigid rules and top-down communication. This kind of structure is effective at McDonald's because the market demands uniform product quality, cleanliness, and fast service.

In general, mechanistic design works best when an organization is operating in a stable environment. Yet new companies that have gone through a rough-and-tumble start-up period may decide to change their structures so that they are more mechanistic, with clear lines of authority.

Organic Organizations: When Looseness & Flexibility Work Best

In an *organic organization,* **authority is decentralized, there are fewer rules and procedures, and networks of employees are encouraged to cooperate and respond quickly to unexpected tasks.** Tom Peters and Robert Waterman called this kind of organization a "loose" structure.[62]

Organic organizations are sometimes termed "adhocracies" because they operate on an ad hoc basis, improvising as they go along. As you might expect, information-technology companies such as Motorola favor the organic arrangement because they constantly have to adjust to technological change—yet so do companies that need to respond to fast-changing consumer tastes, such as clothing retailer The Worth Collection, which operates as a virtual company offering high-end women's clothing through direct selling in people's homes.[63]

Test Your Knowledge:
Mechanistic vs. Organic Organizational Structure

2. The Environment: Differentiation versus Integration— the Lawrence & Lorsch Model

Burns and Stalker's ideas were extended in the United States by Harvard University researchers **Paul R. Lawrence** and **Jay W. Lorsch.**[64] Instead of a *mechanistic-organic dimension,* however, they proposed a *differentiation-integration* dimension—forces that impelled the parts of an organization to move apart or to come together. The stability of the environment confronting the parts of the organization, according to Lawrence and Lorsch, determines the degree of differentiation or integration that is appropriate.

Differentiation: When Forces Push the Organization Apart *Differentiation* **is the tendency of the parts of an organization to disperse and fragment.** The more subunits into which an organization breaks down, the more highly differentiated it is.

This impulse toward dispersal arises because of technical specialization and division of labor. As a result, specialists behave in specific, delimited ways, without coordinating with other parts of the organization. For example, a company producing dental floss, deodorants, and other personal-care products might have different product divisions, each with its own production facility and sales staff—a quite differentiated organization.

Integration: When Forces Pull the Organization Together *Integration* **is the tendency of the parts of an organization to draw together to achieve a common purpose.** In a highly integrated organization, the specialists work together to achieve a common goal. The means for achieving this are a formal chain of command, standardization of rules and procedures, and use of cross-functional teams and computer networks so that there is frequent communication and coordination of the parts.

3. Size: The Larger the Organization, the More Mechanistic

Organizational size **is usually measured by the number of full-time employees.** In general, research shows that larger organizations—those with 2,000 or more full-time employees (or the equivalent workload in a mix of full- and part-timers)—tend to have more rules, regulations, and procedures and more job specialization, as well as greater decentralization. That is, larger firms tend to be more mechanistic.[65] Small organizations tend to be more informal, to have fewer rules and regulations, and to have less work specialization. In other words, small firms tend to be more organic.

Economists have long extolled the virtues of economies of scale, suggesting that "bigger is better" because the per-unit cost of production decreases as the organization grows. Opponents, however, contend that "small is beautiful," because large organizations tend to breed apathy, alienation, absenteeism, and turnover. Indeed, nowadays the thinking is that bigger is not always better. In the 1960s, companies often favored a form of organization known as the *conglomerate,* **in which a large company would do business in different, quite unrelated areas.** Thus, companies such as ITT, Textron, and Tyco bought up businesses as disparate as hotels, food, and machine tools. Today management consultants and business schools are promulgating the idea of "core competencies," in which companies are supposed to focus only on businesses that best fit their skills and distribution channels. As a result, Tyco has sold off its electronics and health care businesses and is emphasizing its product roster of safety equipment, valves, and controls.[66] Similarly, the Dutch company Philips, maker of everything from lightbulbs and toothbrushes to TVs and X-ray machines, is selling off some divisions and narrowing its focus to consumer technology, lighting, and health care.[67]

According to Tom Peters and Robert Waterman, most top-performing organizations keep their division size between $50 million and $100 million, "with a maximum of 1,000 or so employees each. Moreover, they grant their divisions extraordinary independence—and give them the functions and resources to exploit."[68] For example, Parker Hannifin, maker of industrial valves, auto parts, and programmable motion controls, among many other products, has 100 autonomous divisions, with 263 plants in 46 countries. Each division operates only a few plants in order to keep the company non-union and the managers close to

Conglomerate. Philips, the Dutch conglomerate, is getting out of some product lines and is now concentrating on consumer technology, lighting, and health care. Do you see any natural fit among these businesses?

their customers. "Whenever we get more than 200 people in a plant," says chairman Patrick Parker, "we like to move 50 miles down the road and start another."[69]

4. Technology: Small-Batch, Large-Batch, or Continuous-Process—the Woodward Model

Technology has an important influence on organizational design. **Technology consists of all the tools and ideas for transforming materials, data, or labor (inputs) into goods or services (outputs).** A hand-cranked ice-cream-making machine, for instance, is the technology that, with your muscle power, transforms cream, ice, sugar, and flavoring into ice cream. This book, the classroom, the blackboard, the instructor's lectures, and so on are the technologies that deliver an education about management.

In a study of 100 manufacturing firms in England, **Joan Woodward** classified firms according to three forms of technology in increasing levels of complexity: *small-batch, large-batch,* and *continuous process.*[70]

Small-Batch Technology: Custom-Made Products Made by Organic Organizations In *small-batch technology,* **often the least complex technology, goods are custom-made to customer specifications in small quantities.** The one-of-a-kind portrait painting, the Saville Row bespoke suit, the *Columbia* space shuttle, the personal stationery you had designed and printed just for you are all examples.

Small-batch organizations, Woodward found, tend to be informal and flexible—that is, organic.

Large-Batch Technology: Mass-Produced Products Made by Mechanized Organizations *Large-batch technology* **is mass-production, assembly-line technology.** Large volumes of finished products are made by combining easily available component parts. The clothes you buy at Macy's, Kenmore washers and dryers, Toyota automobiles, and most of the products we purchase on a daily basis fall into this category.

Large-batch organizations tend to have a higher level of specialization and to be more bureaucratic, according to Woodward.

Continuous-Process: Highly Routinized Products Made by Organic Organizations *Continuous-process technology* **is highly routinized technology in which machines do all the work.** Examples of this kind of technology are found in petroleum refineries, vodka distilleries, nuclear power plants, and steel mills, in which human operators mainly read dials and repair machine breakdowns.

Successful continuous-process organizations, Woodward found, tend to be more organic than mechanistic—less rigid and formal.

5. Life Cycle: Four Stages in the Life of an Organization

Like the four stages of a *project* life cycle (described in Chapter 5) and of a *product* life cycle (Chapter 6), organizations, too, have a life cycle. **The four-stage *organizational life cycle* has a natural sequence of stages: birth, youth, midlife, and maturity.** In general, as an organization moves through these stages, it becomes not only larger but also more mechanistic, specialized, decentralized, and bureaucratic. Each stage offers different managerial challenges and different organizational design issues.[71]

Stage I. The Birth Stage—Nonbureaucratic   The *birth stage* **is the nonbureaucratic stage, the stage in which the organization is created.** Here there are no written rules and little if any supporting staff beyond perhaps a secretary.

The founder may be a lone entrepreneur, such as Michael Dell, who began Dell Computers by selling microcomputers out of his University of Texas college dorm room. Or the founders may be pals who got together, as did Apple Computer founders Steven Jobs and Stephen Wozniak, who built the first computer in Wozniak's parents' Palo Alto, California, garage, using the proceeds from the sale of an old Volkswagen.

Stage 2. The Youth Stage—Prebureaucratic   In the *youth stage,* **the organization is in a prebureaucratic stage, a stage of growth and expansion.**

Now the company has a product that is making headway in the marketplace, people are being added to the payroll (most clerical rather than professional), and some division of labor and setting of rules are being instituted.

For Apple Computer, this stage occurred during the years 1978–1981, with the establishment of the Apple II product line.

Stage 3. The Midlife Stage—Bureaucratic   In the *midlife stage,* **the organization becomes bureaucratic, a period of growth evolving into stability.**

Now the organization has a formalized bureaucratic structure, staffs of specialists, decentralization of functional divisions, and many rules.

In the 1980s, Apple Computer became a large company with many of these attributes. In 1983, Pepsi-Cola marketer John Scully was hired as a professional manager. Jobs became chairman; Wozniak left.

Stage 4. The Maturity Stage—Very Bureaucratic   In the *maturity stage,* **the organization becomes very bureaucratic, large, and mechanistic.** The danger at this point is lack of flexibility and innovation.

After Jobs was fired in a boardroom struggle in 1985, Apple entered a period in which it seemed to lose its way, having trouble developing successful products and getting them to market. Scully, who emphasized the wrong technology (a "personal data assistant" called Newton, which failed to establish a following) was followed by two more CEOs who were unable to arrest the company's declining market share.

In 1997, Jobs was brought back as a "temporary" chairman, and Apple's fortunes began to revive.

Group Exercise:
Designing an Organization

Employees who were present during birth and youth stages may long for the good old days of informality and fewer rules as the organization moves toward more formalized and bureaucratic structures. Whereas clearly some organizations jump the gun and institute such structures before they are appropriate, some expanding companies in effect never grow up, holding on to the prebureaucratic way of life for too long, hindering their ability to deliver goods or services efficiently in relation to their size. ●

Key Terms Used in This Chapter

Summary

8.1 What Kind of Organizational Culture Will You Be Operating In?

Organizational culture is a system of shared beliefs and values that develops within an organization and guides the behavior of its members. Four types of culture are (1) clan, which has an internal focus and values flexibility; (2) adhocracy, which has an external focus and values flexibility; (3) market, which has a strong external focus and values stability and control; and (4) hierarchy, which has an internal focus and values stability and control.

Organizational culture appears as three layers. Level 1 is observable artifacts, the physical manifestations of culture. Level 2 is espoused values, explicitly stated values and norms preferred by an organization, although employees are frequently influenced by enacted values, which represent the values and norms actually exhibited in the organization.

Level 3 consists of basic assumptions, the core values of the organization.

Culture is transmitted to employees in symbols, stories, heroes, and rites and rituals. A symbol is an object, act, quality, or event that conveys meaning to others. A story is a narrative based on true events, which is repeated—and sometimes embellished on—to emphasize a particular value. A hero is a person whose accomplishments embody the values of the organization. Rites and rituals are the activities and ceremonies, planned and unplanned, that celebrate important occasions and accomplishments in the organization's life.

Culture, which can powerfully shape an organization's success over the long term, has four functions. (1) It gives members an organizational identity. (2) It facilitates collective commitment. (3) It promotes social-system stability. (4) It shapes behavior by helping employees make sense of their surroundings.

8.2 Developing High-Performance Cultures

What types of organizational culture can increase an organization's competitiveness and profitability? Three perspectives have been proposed: (1) The strength perspective assumes that the strength of a corporate culture is related to a firm's long-term financial performance; (2) the fit perspective assumes that an organization's culture must align, or fit, with its business or strategic context; and (3) the adaptive perspective assumes that the most effective cultures help organizations anticipate and adapt to environmental changes.

Among the mechanisms managers use to embed a culture in an organization are: (1) formal statements; (2) slogans and sayings; (3) stories, legends, and myths; (4) leader reactions to crises; (5) role modeling, training, and coaching; (6) physical design; (7) rewards, titles, promotions, and bonuses; (8) organizational goals and performance criteria; (9) measurable and controllable activities; (10) organizational structure; and (11) organizational systems and procedures.

8.3 What Is an Organization?

An organization is a system of consciously coordinated activities or forces of two or more people. There are three types of organizations classified according to the three different purposes for which they are formed: for-profit, nonprofit, and mutual-benefit.

Whatever the size of organization, it can be represented in an organization chart, a boxes-and-lines illustration showing the formal lines of authority and the organization's official positions or division of labor. Two kinds of information that organizations reveal about organizational structure are (1) the vertical hierarchy of authority—who reports to whom, and (2) the horizontal specialization—who specializes in what work.

8.4 The Major Elements of an Organization

Organizations have seven elements: (1) common purpose, which unifies employees or members and gives everyone an understanding of the organization's reason for being; (2) coordinated effort, the coordination of individual efforts into a group or organization-wide effort; (3) division of labor, having discrete parts of a task done by different people; (4) hierarchy of authority, a control mechanism for making sure the right people do the right things at the right time; (5) span of control, which refers to the number of people reporting directly to a given manager; (6) authority and accountability, responsibility, and delegation. Authority refers to the rights inherent in a managerial position to make decisions, give orders, and utilize resources. Accountability means that managers must report and justify work results to the managers above them. Responsibility is the obligation you have to perform the tasks assigned to you. Delegation is the process of assigning managerial authority and responsibility to managers and employees lower in the hierarchy. Regarding authority and responsibility, the organization chart distinguishes between two positions, line and staff. Line managers have authority to make decisions and usually have people reporting to them. Staff personnel have advisory functions; they provide advice, recommendations, and research to line managers. (7) Centralization versus decentralization of authority. With centralized authority, important decisions are made by higher-level managers. With decentralized authority, important decisions are made by middle-level and supervisory-level managers.

8.5 Basic Types of Organizational Structures

Organizations may be arranged into seven types of structures. (1) In a simple structure, authority is centralized in a single person; this structure has a flat hierarchy, few rules, and low work specialization. (2) In a functional structure, people with similar occupational specialties are put together in formal groups. (3) In a divisional structure, people with diverse occupational specialties are put together in formal groups by similar products or services, customers or clients, or geographic regions. (4) In a matrix structure, an organization combines functional and divisional chains of command in grids so that there are two command structures—vertical and horizontal. (5) In a team-based structure, teams or workgroups are used to improve horizontal relations and solve problems throughout the organization. (6) In a network structure, the organization has a central core that is linked to outside independent firms by computer connections, which are used to operate as if all were a single organization. (7) In a modular structure, a firm assembles product chunks, or modules, provided by outside contractors.

⊗ 8.6 Contingency Design: Factors in Creating the Best Structure

The process of fitting the organization to its environment is called contingency design. Managers taking a contingency approach must consider five factors in designing the best kind of structure for their organization at that particular time.

(1) An organization may be either mechanistic or organic. In a mechanistic organization, authority is centralized, tasks and rules are clearly specified, and employees are closely supervised. In an organic organization, authority is decentralized, there are fewer rules and procedures, and networks of employees are encouraged to cooperate and respond quickly to unexpected tasks.

(2) An organization may also be characterized by differentiation or integration. Differentiation is the tendency of the parts of an organization to disperse and fragment. Integration is the tendency of the parts of an organization to draw together to achieve a common purpose.

(3) Organizational size is usually measured by the number of full-time employees. Larger organizations tend to have more rules, regulations, job specialization, and decentralization. Smaller organizations tend to be more informal, have fewer rules, and have less work specialization.

(4) Technology consists of all the tools and ideas for transforming materials, data or labor (inputs) into goods or services (outputs). Firms may be classified according to three forms of technology in increasing levels of complexity. In small-batch technology, often the least complex technology, goods are custom-made to customer specifications in small quantities. Large-batch technology is mass-production, assembly-line technology. Continuous-process technology is highly routinized technology in which machines do all the work.

(5) The four-stage organizational life cycle has a natural sequence of stages: birth, youth, midlife, and maturity. The birth stage is the nonbureaucratic stage, the stage in which the organization is created. The youth stage is the prebureaucratic stage, a stage of growth and expansion. In the midlife stage, the organization becomes bureaucratic, a period of growth evolving into stability. In the maturity stage, the organization becomes very bureaucratic, large, and mechanistic. The danger at this point is lack of flexibility and innovation.

Management in Action

Japan's Fuji & Marine Insurance Co.'s CEO Is Trying to Change the Organizational Culture

Bijan Khosrowshahi, the Iranian-American chief executive of Japan's Fuji Fire and Marine Insurance Co., is seldom without his interpreter and a wireless headset that pipes translations directly into his ear.

Mr. Khosrowshahi, an English-speaking insurance-industry veteran who took over Fuji in 2004, says this seamless system for communicating with his Japanese-speaking employees helps him blend into the company even as he works to change it. . . .

But Fuji is a domestic firm in a long-protected and famously slow-moving industry. So Mr. Khosrowshahi is moving slower, inspiring change rather than mandating it, and encouraging Fuji employees to take more initiative.

Fuji staffers say he is having an impact. Fuji's net premiums written—an insurer's equivalent of sales revenue—rose 0.2% to 296.6 billion yen, or $2.81 billion, in the fiscal year ended March 31 [2008], the first increase in four years. Fuji expects net premiums written to drop again this fiscal year, amid a nationwide fall in car and housing sales that's pummeling auto and homeowners' polices.

The company is aggressively promoting female managers—it has 21, up from one in 2004. And it regularly asks rank-and-file employees for new-product ideas. Both are unusual practices in Japan. . . .

At 46, Mr. Khosrowshahi is younger than many subordinates—a shock for a company that long awarded promotions by seniority. Mr. Khosrowshahi immigrated to the U.S. from Iran when he was 15. From 1997 to 2004, he ran AIG operations in Turkey and South Korea, experiences he says made him comfortable in foreign cultures. Insiders at 6,500-strong Fuji were skeptical. . . .

Mr. Khosrowshahi read up on Mr. Ghosn's turnaround of Nissan and started studying Japanese. He retained Japanese as the company's main language—even in the executive suite—and hired people to translate documents into English for his own use. But he did shake up some longtime company practices. He changed reporting lines so more managers talked directly to him. Then he forbade participants from reading prepared reports word-for-word in meetings, as had been customary.

Mr. Khosrowshahi considered importing several AIG executives, then chose not to. "I decided I cannot change the company" by bringing in outsiders, he says. "It has to be done with Fuji people."

To assess talent, he grilled about 40 senior managers on the details of their jobs, discussing issues from reinsurance schemes to the chances of getting business from Toyota Motor Corp.

Katsuhiko Saka, then head of Fuji's claims department, noticed a difference from prior managers. "Japanese presidents don't ask for details," he says. Mr. Saka says he felt Mr. Khosrowshahi was testing how well managers knew their jobs, and their willingness to change. He was later promoted to managing executive officer and head of sales. Mr. Khosrowshahi says he could evaluate staff without speaking Japanese. "It's not just language," he says. "Results, energy level, body language—it fills in the gaps for other things." After a year, he trimmed the executive team to 11 from 19, replacing some veterans with promising insiders.

Executives grumbled about submitting reports ahead of meetings so they could be translated into English. Some chose to write in their own imperfect English. But Mr. Khosrowshahi didn't let up, scheduling many meetings where managers had to make presentations, Mr. Nishida says.

Some male managers complained privately about Mr. Khosrowshahi's push to promote women, Mr. Nishida says. Others requested not to have new female hires assigned to their sections. . . .

Mr. Khosrowshahi is prodding managers to identify solutions as well as problems, and urging employees to take more initiative. Early on, he solicited volunteers to develop new-product ideas. Yasunobu Aoki, a branch manager who led one volunteer team, says he raised his hand out of curiosity; another member of his team was ordered to volunteer by his boss.

Mr. Aoki's team was asked to create a new auto-insurance policy. It focused on a higher-priced policy that would offer speedy claim updates and free introductions to lawyers. When Mr. Aoki presented the plan to a Fuji committee including Mr. Khosrowshahi, he was taken aback by their tough questions. . . .

Mr. Khosrowshahi also worked on boosting morale, scheduling lunches with employees, and launching a training program with Tokyo's Hitotsubashi University. To commemorate Fuji's improved earnings last year, he gave each of its employees 10,000 yen, or around $95, accompanied by thank-you notes in envelopes decorated with his caricature.

Hiroko Ikeno, an office worker who was a member of Mr. Aoki's team, says Mr. Khosrowshahi is so popular that some colleagues have taped his photo to their PCs.

Fuji executives say they are now accustomed to communicating with Mr. Khosrowshahi through interpreters, and explaining themselves. In a recent sales strategy meeting, the pace of discussion was rapid. Mr. Khosrowshahi quizzed Mr. Saka, the sales chief, and three other executives—one via teleconference from Tokyo—on rivals' financial results. The interpreter repeated Mr. Khosrowshahi's English questions to the group in Japanese. She murmured a simultaneous translation of the answers into a microphone on her headset, which was transmitted to the CEO's earpiece. Occasionally, Mr. Khosrowshahi asked a question in Japanese.

Mr. Nishida, who grew up in a Japanese business culture that reveres modesty, says he has been urged by Mr. Khosrowshahi to "become a tiger." He says work is more fun, "but there's more tension too."

For Discussion

1. Why is Mr. Khosrowshahi trying to change the culture and structure at Fuji Fire and Marine Insurance Co.? Explain.
2. Using the competing values framework as a point of reference, how would you describe the current organizational culture? What type of culture is desired by Mr. Khosrowshahi to meet his goals? Discuss.
3. Which of the 11 ways to embed organizational culture is Mr. Khosrowshahi using to change the company's culture? Provide examples to support your conclusions.

4. Does Mr. Khosrowshahi want to create more of a mechanistic or organic organization? Explain.

5. What is the most important lesson from this case? Discuss.

Source: Excerpted from Phred Dvorak, "Outsider CEO Translates a New Message in Japan," *The Wall Street Journal,* March 28, 2008. Copyright © 2008 by Dow Jones & Company, Inc. Reproduced with permission of Dow Jones & Company, Inc. via Copyright Clearance Center.

Self-Assessment

Is Your Organization a Learning Organization?

Objectives

1. To gain familiarity with the characteristics of learning organizations.
2. To identify whether your organization is a learning organization.

Introduction

As we learned in Chapter 2, a learning organization is one that actively creates, acquires, and transfers new knowledge. Learning organizations are places in which new ideas and patterns of thinking are nurtured and in which people are allowed to continually expand their abilities to achieve desired results. Most importantly, a learning organization is a place in which the organization and individuals in it are continually learning in order to achieve its goals. The purpose of this exercise is to identify whether the organization in which you work is a learning organization.

Instructions

The following survey was created to assess the extent to which an organization follows the principles of a learning organization. If you are currently working, you should answer the questions in regard to this organization. If you are not currently working but have worked in the past, use a past job in completing the survey. If you have never had a job, you can use your school as a reference or use an organization you might be familiar with. For example, you might interview your parents to determine the extent to which the organization they work for follows the principles of a learning organization. Read each statement and use the following scale to indicate which answer most closely matches your response: 1 = strongly disagree; 2 = disagree; 3 = neither agree nor disagree; 4 = agree; 5 = strongly agree.

1. Management uses rewards, praise, and recognition to get what they want done.	1	2	3	4	5
2. The company promotes teamwork.	1	2	3	4	5
3. People are recognized and rewarded on the basis of what they do rather than *who* they know.	1	2	3	4	5
4. I see more examples of optimistic attitudes/behaviors rather than negative and cynical ones.	1	2	3	4	5
5. I have a clear picture of the organization's vision and my role in helping to accomplish it.	1	2	3	4	5
6. This organization relies more on team-based solutions than individual ones.	1	2	3	4	5
7. This organization tends to look at the big picture rather than analyzing problems from a narrow perspective.	1	2	3	4	5
8. People have an open mind when working with others.	1	2	3	4	5
9. This company looks for the root cause of a problem rather than a "quick fix."	1	2	3	4	5
10. I have the skills and knowledge to continuously improve the way I do my job.	1	2	3	4	5

Total _____

Scoring

To get your score, add up the numbers that correspond to your responses. The range will be from 10 to 50. Comparative norms for learning organizations are as follows:

Total score of 10–23 = low learning organization
Total score of 24–36 = moderate learning organization
Total score of 37–50 = high learning organization

Ethical Dilemma

When Your Brother-in-Law Is Bending the Rules

Assume you are the purchasing manager for a small, family-run homebuilding firm. Your brother-in-law works in the framing department and your sister is the company's chief financial officer (CFO). The firm has a policy that employees can do small home-building jobs (projects valued at less than $2,000) on the side and can purchase their building supplies for these projects through the company. This policy allows employees to make some extra cash while purchasing materials at much discounted rates.

Because of your role, you are aware of all side projects taking place and the dollar amount of materials purchased through the company for these projects. You recently noticed that your brother-in-law has been purchasing raw materials that you suspect will exceed the $2,000 threshold—he purchased $3,000 worth of materials for one project and $1,500 for another.

You approved both of the purchases even though you suspect that he is doing projects that are valued at around $5,000–$8,000. These types of projects are not permitted as side jobs because the company itself does work in this price range. You sense that your brother-in-law's behavior is OK because your sister also knows about these purchases, given her role as CFO.

Solving the Dilemma

Your brother-in-law just submitted a purchase request for materials valued at $10,000 for side jobs. What should you do?

1. Approve the purchase. It's not your job to police your brother-in-law, and your sister is aware of what he's doing.

2. Call your sister and express your concern about what your brother-in-law is doing. Let her deal with any potential ethical breaches.

3. Contact your brother-in-law and ask him if he is abiding by the company policy of not doing side jobs valued at over $2,000. If he says yes, approve the purchases.

4. Go to the CEO and let him know about the details of your brother-in-law's purchases. The CEO can then do whatever he thinks is best.

5. Invent other options.

Human Resource Management
Getting the Right People for Managerial Success

Major Questions You Should Be Able to Answer

9.1 Strategic Human Resource Management
Major Question: How do star managers view the role of people in their organization's success?

9.2 The Legal Requirements of Human Resource Management
Major Question: To avoid exposure to legal liabilities, what areas of the law do I need to be aware of?

9.3 Recruitment & Selection: Putting the Right People into the Right Jobs
Major Question: How can I reduce mistakes in hiring and find great people who might work for me?

9.4 Orientation, Training, & Development
Major Question: Once people are hired, what's the best way to see that they do what they're supposed to do?

9.5 Performance Appraisal
Major Question: How can I assess employees' performance more accurately and give more effective feedback?

9.6 Managing an Effective Workforce: Compensation & Benefits
Major Question: What are the various forms of compensation?

9.7 Managing Promotions, Transfers, Disciplining, & Dismissals
Major Question: What are some guidelines for handling promotions, transfers, disciplining, and dismissals?

How to Stand Out in a New Job: Fitting into an Organization in the First 60 Days

"As an ambitious 22-year-old readying to enter the corporate world, how can I quickly distinguish myself as a winner?"asked Dain Zaitz of Corvallis, Oregon.

"Once you are in the real world—and it doesn't make any difference if you are 22 or 62, starting your first job or your fifth," answered *BusinessWeek* columnists Jack and Suzy Welch, "the way to look great and get ahead is to overdeliver."[1]

Overdelivering means doing more than what is asked of you—not just doing the report your boss requests, for example, but doing the extra research to provide him or her with something truly impressive.

Among other things you should do in the first three months:[2]

- **Get to know some people and listen to what they have to say.** During the first 2 weeks, get to know a few people and try to have lunch with them. Find out how the organization works, how people interact with the boss, what the corporate culture encourages and discourages. Your role here is to listen, rather than to slather on the charm. Realize that you have a lot to learn.

- **Be aware of the power of first impressions.** Within 3 minutes of meeting someone new, people form an opinion about where the future of the relationship is headed, according to one study.[3] (Actually, first impressions can be formed in as little as 1/20th of a second, according to a study of human reactions to Web pages.)[4]

Roger Ailes, CEO of Fox News and former top Republican strategist, points out that 7 seconds is all the time people need to start making up their minds about you, so this is the period in which to make a good first impression. "When meeting someone for the first time, concentrate on one thing: your energy level," Ailes says. Amp it up. "If you don't demonstrate energetic attitude on your first day, you're already screwing up."[5]

Note: If you feel you've blown it in trying to make a positive first impression on someone, don't be too distressed. What's key, research shows, is making sure you have other chances to meet that person again so that you can show different sides of yourself.[6]

- **Make it easy for others to give you feedback.** Ask your boss, co-workers, and subordinates to give you feedback about how you're doing. Be prepared to take unpleasant news gracefully.[7]

  At the end of 30 days, have a "How am I doing?" meeting with your boss.

- **Overdeliver.** Because performance reviews for new-hires generally take place at 60 to 90 days, you need to have accomplished enough—and preferably something big—to show your boss your potential. In other words, do as the Welches suggest: overdeliver.

For Discussion How does the foregoing advice square with your past experiences in starting a new job? Are there things you wish you could have done differently?

forecast

What's Ahead in This Chapter

This chapter considers human resource (HR) management—planning for, attracting, developing, and retaining an effective workforce. We consider how this subject fits in with the overall company strategy, how to evaluate current and future employee needs, and how to recruit and select qualified people. We discuss orientation, training, and development; how to assess employee performance and give feedback; and what HR laws managers should be aware of. Finally, we consider how to manage compensation and benefits, promotions and discipline, and workplace performance problems.

9.1 STRATEGIC HUMAN RESOURCE MANAGEMENT

How do star managers view the role of people in their organization's success?

THE BIG PICTURE

Human resource management consists of the activities managers perform to plan for, attract, develop, and retain an effective workforce. Planning the human resources needed consists of understanding current employee needs and predicting future employee needs.

How do you get hired by one of the companies on *Fortune* magazine's annual "100 Best Companies to Work For" list—companies such as Google, Wegmans Food Markets, Genentech, and Starbucks on the 2008 list?[8] You try to get to know someone in the company, suggests one guide; you play up volunteer work on your résumé, you get ready to interview and interview and interview, and you do extensive research on the company (far more than just online research, as by talking to customers).[9]

And what kinds of things does an employee of a *Fortune* "Best" company get? At Google, the Mountain View, California, search engine company, which was ranked no. 1 in 2007 and 2008, you're entitled to eat in 1 of 11 free gourmet cafeterias, as well as to visit free snack rooms that contain various cereals, candy, nuts, fresh fruit, and other snacks. You can bring your dog to work, get haircuts onsite, work out at the gym, attend subsidized exercise classes, study Mandarin or other languages, have your laundry done free, or consult five onsite doctors for a checkup, free of charge. The company has also launched numerous compensation incentives, special bonuses, and founders' awards that can run into millions of dollars.[10]

The reason for this exceptional treatment? "Happy people are more productive," says CEO Eric Schmidt.[11] That productivity has made Google an earnings powerhouse; in early 2008, for example, it reported a 30% jump in net income for its first quarter.[12] Google has discovered, in other words, that its biggest competitive advantage lies in its human resources—its *people.*

Human Resource Management: Managing an Organization's Most Important Resource

Human resource (HR) management **consists of the activities managers perform to plan for, attract, develop, and retain an effective workforce.** Whether it's McKenzie looking for entry-level business consultants, the U.S. Navy trying to fill its ranks, or churches trying to reverse the declining number of priests and ministers, all organizations must deal with staffing.

The fact that the old Personnel Department is now called the Human Resources Department is not just a cosmetic change. It is intended to suggest the importance of staffing to a company's success. Although talking about people as "resources" might seem to downgrade them to the same level as financial resources and material resources, in fact people are an organization's most important resource. Indeed, companies such as South San Francisco biotechnology firm Genentech (No. 1 on the 2006 *Fortune* magazine Best Companies list), supermarket chain Wegmans Food Markets (No. 1 in 2005), jam maker J. M. Smucker (No. 1 in 2004), stockbroker Edward Jones (No. 1 in 2003 and 2002), and box retailer The Container Store (No. 1 in 2001 and 2000) have discovered that putting employees first has been the foundation for their success. "If you're not thinking all the time about making every person valuable, you don't have a chance," says former General Electric head Jack Welch. "What's the alternative? Wasted minds? Uninvolved people? A labor force that's angry or bored? That doesn't make sense!"[13]

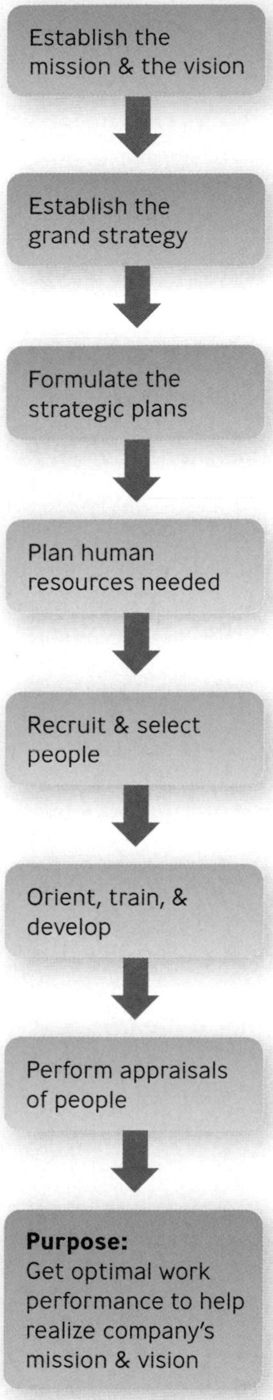

Human Resources as Part of Strategic Planning At many companies, human resources has become part of the strategic-planning process. Thus, HR departments deal not only with employee paperwork and legal accountability—a very important area, as we describe in Section 9.2—but also with helping to support the organization's overall strategy.

For example, is it important, as Wegmans' owners think, to have loyal, innovative, smart, passionate employees who will give their best to promote customer satisfaction (the grocery chain's mission)? Who, then, should be recruited? How should they be trained? What's the best way to evaluate and reward their performance? The answers to these questions should be consistent with the firm's strategic mission. The purpose of the strategic human resource process, then—shown in the yellow-orange shaded boxes at right—is to get the optimal work performance that will help the company's mission and goals.[14] *(See Figure 9.1.)*

Two concepts important in this view of human resource management, which we mentioned in Chapter 2, are *human capital* and *social capital.*

Human Capital: Potential of Employee Knowledge & Actions *Human capital,* you'll recall, is the economic or productive potential of employee knowledge and actions.[15] A present or future employee with the right combination of knowledge, skills, and motivation to excel represents human capital with the potential to give the organization a competitive advantage. Why is human capital important? "We are living in a time," says one team of human resource management authors, "when a new economic paradigm—characterized by speed, innovation, short cycle times, quality, and customer satisfaction—is highlighting the importance of intangible assets, such as brand recognition, knowledge, innovation, and particularly human capital."[16]

Social Capital: Potential of Strong & Cooperative Relationships *Social capital,* we said, is the economic or productive potential of strong, trusting, and cooperative relationships.[17] Relationships do matter. For instance, the brothers running family-owned J. M. Smucker follow a simple code of conduct set forth by their father: "Listen with your full attention, look for the good in others, have a sense of humor, and say thank you for a job well done."[18] (The company's voluntary employee turnover rate is a mere 3%.)

Planning the Human Resources Needed

When a building contractor, looking to hire someone for a few hours to dig ditches, drives by a group of idle day laborers standing on a street corner, is that a form of HR planning? Certainly it shows the contractor's awareness that a pool of laborers usually can be found in that spot. But what if the builder needs a lot of people with specialized training—to give him or her the competitive advantage that the strategic planning process demands?

figure 9.1

THE STRATEGIC HUMAN RESOURCE MANAGEMENT PROCESS

Establish the mission & the vision

Establish the grand strategy

Formulate the strategic plans

Plan human resources needed

Recruit & select people

Orient, train, & develop

Perform appraisals of people

Purpose: Get optimal work performance to help realize company's mission & vision

Big Brown. A UPS driver's problems of driving in a big city—traffic, double parking, addressees not at home—are different from those of driving in rural areas, where there may be long stretches of boredom. Specialists in job analysis can interview drivers about their problems in order to write job descriptions that allow for varying circumstances.

Here we are concerned with something more than simply hiring people on an "as needed" basis. ***Strategic human resource planning* consists of developing a systematic, comprehensive strategy for (a) understanding current employee needs and (b) predicting future employee needs.** Let's consider these two parts.

Understanding Current Employee Needs   To plan for the future, you must understand the present—what today's staffing picture looks like. This requires that you (or a trained specialist) do, first, a *job analysis* and from that write a *job description* and a *job specification.*[19]

- **Job analysis.** The purpose of ***job analysis* is to determine, by observation and analysis, the basic elements of a job.** Specialists who do this interview job occupants about what they do, observe the flow of work, and learn how results are accomplished. For example, United Parcel Service has specialists who ride with the couriers and time how long it takes to deliver a load of packages and note what problems are encountered (traffic jams, vicious dogs, recipients not home, and so on).

- **Job description and job specification.** Once the fundamentals of a job are understood, then you can write a ***job description,* which summarizes what the holder of the job does and how and why he or she does it.** Next you can write a ***job specification,* which describes the minimum qualifications a person must have to perform the job successfully.**

This process can produce some surprises. Jobs that might seem to require a college degree, for example, might not after all. Thus, the process of writing job analyses, descriptions, and specifications can help you avoid hiring people who are overqualified (and presumably more expensive) or underqualified (and thus not as productive) for a particular job.

In addition, by entering a job description and specification with their attendant characteristics into a database, an organization can do computer-searching for candidates by matching keywords (nouns) on their résumés with the keywords describing the job. A position in desktop publishing, for instance, might be described by the kinds of software programs with which applicants should be familiar: *Adobe Illustrator, Adobe PageMaker, Adobe Photoshop, InDesign, QuarkXPress, Acrobat Distiller.*

Predicting Future Employee Needs Job descriptions change, of course: auto mechanics, for instance, now have to know how computer chips work in cars. (A C-class Mercedes may have 153 processors onboard.) And new jobs are created: who could have visualized the position of "e-commerce accountant" 10 years ago, for example?

As you might expect, predicting future employee needs means you have to become knowledgeable about the *staffing the organization might need* and the *likely sources for that staffing:*

- **The staffing the organization might need.** You could assume your organization won't change much. In that case, you can fairly easily predict that jobs will periodically become unoccupied (because of retirement, resignations, and so on) and that you'll need to pay the same salaries and meet the same criteria about minority hiring to fill them.

  Better, however, to assume the organization will change. Thus, you need to understand the organization's vision and strategic plan so that the proper people can be hired to meet the future strategies and work.

- **The likely sources for staffing.** You can recruit employees from either inside or outside the organization. In looking at those inside, you need to consider which employees are motivated, trainable, and promotable and what kind of training your organization might have to do. A device for organizing this kind of information is a **human resource inventory, a report listing your organization's employees by name, education, training, languages, and other important information.**

  In looking outside, you need to consider the availability of talent in your industry's and geographical area's labor pool, the training of people graduating from various schools, and such factors as what kind of people are moving into your area. The U.S. Bureau of Labor Statistics and the U.S. Census Bureau issue reports on such matters. ●

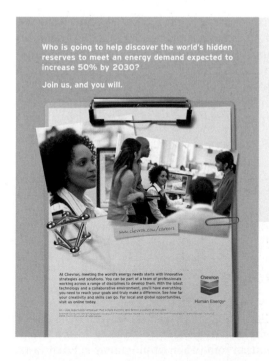

One way to attract potential employees. This Chevron ad serves two purposes: encouraging people to get involved in the energy crisis discussion and appealing to socially responsible engineers, scientists, and strategists looking to work for a company with an active social conscience. A Web site included in the ad shows additional close-ups of each component of the ad collage and a link to Chevron's careers portal.

major question?

To avoid exposure to legal liabilities, what areas of the law do I need to be aware of?

THE BIG PICTURE

Four areas of human resource law any manager needs to be aware of are labor relations, compensation and benefits, health and safety, and equal employment opportunity.

Whatever your organization's human resource strategy, in the United States (and in U.S. divisions overseas) it has to operate within the environment of American law. Four areas you need to be aware of are as follows. Some important laws are summarized in the table opposite. *(See Table 9.1, opposite page.)*

I. Labor Relations

The earliest laws affecting employee welfare had to do with unions, and they can still have important effects. Legislation passed in 1935 (the Wagner Act) resulted in the ***National Labor Relations Board,* which enforces procedures whereby employees may vote to have a union and for collective bargaining.** *Collective bargaining consists of negotiations between management and employees about disputes over compensation, benefits, working conditions, and job security.*

A 1947 law (the Taft-Hartley Act) allows the President of the United States to prevent or end a strike that threatens national security.

2. Compensation & Benefits

The Social Security Act in 1935 established the U.S. retirement system. The passage of the ***Fair Labor Standards Act* of 1938 established minimum living standards for workers engaged in interstate commerce, including provision of a federal minimum wage** (currently $6.55 an hour, to increase to $7.25 on July 24, 2009) and a maximum workweek (now 40 hours, after which overtime must be paid), along with banning products from child labor.[20] Salaried executive, administrative, and professional employees are exempt from overtime rules.

3. Health & Safety

From miners risking tunnel cave-ins to cotton mill workers breathing lint, industry has always had dirty, dangerous jobs. Beginning with the Occupational Safety and Health Act (OSHA) of 1970, there has grown a body of law requiring organizations to provide employees with nonhazardous working conditions. Later laws extended health coverage.

4. Equal Employment Opportunity

The effort to reduce discrimination in employment based on racial, ethnic, and religious bigotry and gender stereotypes began with Title VII of the Civil Rights Act of 1964. This established the ***Equal Employment Opportunity (EEO) Commission,* whose job it is to enforce antidiscrimination and other employment-related laws.**

table 9.1

SOME IMPORTANT RECENT U.S. FEDERAL LAWS AND REGULATIONS PROTECTING EMPLOYEES

Year	Law or regulation	Provisions
Labor relations		
1974	Privacy Act	Gives employees legal right to examine letters of reference concerning them
1986	Immigration Reform & Control Act	Requires employers to verify the eligibility for employment of all their new hires (including U.S. citizens)
1988	Polygraph Protection Act	Limits employer's ability to use lie detectors
1988	Worker Adjustment & Retraining Notification Act	Requires organizations with 100 or more employees to give 60 days' notice for mass layoffs or plant closings
2003	Sarbanes-Oxley Act	Prohibits employers from demoting or firing employees who raise accusations of fraud to a federal agency
Compensation and benefits		
1974	Employee Retirement Income Security Act (ERISA)	Sets rules for managing pension plans; provides federal insurance to cover bankrupt plans
1993	Family & Medical Leave Act	Requires employers to provide 12 weeks of unpaid leave for medical and family reasons, including for childbirth, adoption, or family emergency
1996	Health Insurance Portability & Accountability Act (HIPPA)	Allows employees to switch health insurance plans when changing jobs and receive new coverage regardless of preexisting health conditions; prohibits group plans from dropping ill employees
2007	Fair Minimum Wage Act	Increases federal minimum wage to $7.25 per hour on July 24, 2009
Health and safety		
1970	Occupational Safety & Health Act (OSHA)	Establishes minimum health and safety standards in organizations
1985	Consolidated Omnibus Budget Reconciliation Act (COBRA)	Requires an extension of health insurance benefits after termination
Equal employment opportunity		
1963	Equal Pay Act	Requires men and women be paid equally for performing equal work
1964, amended 1972	Civil Rights Act, Title VII	Prohibits discrimination on basis of race, color, religion, national origin, or sex
1967, amended 1978 and 1986	Age Discrimination in Employment Act (ADEA)	Prohibits discrimination in employees over 40 years old; restricts mandatory retirement
1978	Pregnancy Discrimination Act	Broadens discrimination to cover pregnancy, childbirth, and related medical conditions; protects job security during maternity leave

table 9.1 *(Continued)*

Year	Law or regulation	Provisions
1990	Americans with Disabilities Act (ADA)	Prohibits discrimination against essentially qualified employees with physical or mental disabilities or chronic illness; requires "reasonable accommodation" be provided so they can perform duties
1991	Civil Rights Act	Amends and clarifies Title VII, ADA, and other laws; permits suits against employers for punitive damages in cases of intentional discrimination

Title VII applies to all organizations or their agents engaged in an industry affecting interstate commerce that employs 15 or more employees. Contractors who wish to do business with the U.S. government (such as most colleges and universities, which receive federal funds) must be in compliance with various executive orders issued by the President covering antidiscrimination. Later laws prevented discrimination against older workers and people with physical and mental disabilities.[21]

Three important concepts covered by EEO laws are *discrimination, affirmative action,* and *sexual harassment.*

Manager's Hot Seat:
Diversity in Hiring: Candidate Conundrum

Discrimination   *Discrimination* **occurs when people are hired or promoted—or denied hiring or promotion—for reasons not relevant to the job,** such as skin color or eye shape, gender, religion, national origin, and the like. A fine point to be made here is that, although the law prohibits discrimination in all aspects of employment, it does not require an employer to extend *preferential treatment* because of race, color, religion, and so on.

When an organization is found to have been practicing discrimination, the people discriminated against may sue for back pay and punitive damages. In 2007, federal job discrimination complaints filed by workers against private employers shot up 9%, the largest annual increase since the early 1990s.[22] Racial harassment cases filed with the Equal Employment Opportunity Commission (EEOC) increased 24% in that year.[23] Pregnancy bias complaints to the EEOC also increased 14% in 2007, up from 40% from a decade ago.[24] Earlier, in 2005, the Bureau of Labor Statistics found pay discrepancies in many areas, with black men earning 74% and Hispanic men earning 58% of the wages of white men, and women overall earning 77% of men's wages.[25]

Test Your Knowledge:
Comparing Affirmative Action, Valuing Diversity, and Managing Diversity

Affirmative Action   *Affirmative action* **focuses on achieving equality of opportunity within an organization.** It tries to make up for past discrimination in employment by actively finding, hiring, and developing the talents of people from groups traditionally discriminated against. Steps include active recruitment, elimination of prejudicial questions in interviews, and establishment of minority hiring goals. It's important to note that EEO laws *do not* allow use of hiring quotas.[26]

Affirmative action has created tremendous opportunities for women and minorities, but it has been resisted more by some white males who see it as working against their interests.[27] Affirmative action plans are more successful when employees view them as being fair and equitable and when whites are not prejudiced against people of color.[28] In addition, research shows that women and minorities hired on the basis of affirmative action felt stigmatized as unqualified and incompetent and experienced lower job satisfaction and more stress than employees supposedly selected on the basis of merit.[29]

Sexual Harassment *Sexual harassment* consists of unwanted sexual attention that creates an adverse work environment. This means obscene gestures, sex-stereotyped jokes, sexually oriented posters and graffiti, suggestive remarks, unwanted dating pressure, physical nonsexual contact, unwanted touching, sexual propositions, threatening punishment unless sexual favors are given, obscene phone calls, and similar verbal or physical actions of a sexual nature.[30] The harassment may be by a member of the opposite sex or a member of the same sex, by a manager, by a co-worker, or by an outsider.[31] If the harasser is a manager or an agent of the organization, the organization itself can be sued, even if it had no knowledge of the situation.[32]

Sexual harassment. If this woman is unaware of the men ogling her legs, does that make their behavior acceptable? Or does it still contribute to an offensive work environment?

There are two types of sexual harassment:

- **Quid pro quo—tangible economic injury.** In the *quid pro quo* type, the person to whom the unwanted sexual attention is directed is put in the position of jeopardizing being hired for a job or obtaining job benefits or opportunities unless he or she implicitly or explicitly acquiesces.

- **Hostile environment—offensive work environment.** In the *hostile environment* type, the person being sexually harassed doesn't risk economic harm but experiences an offensive or intimidating work environment. In 2007, according to one survey, 38% of women said they heard sexual innuendo, wisecracks, or taunts at the office, up from 22% in 2006.[33] Another growing problem is bullying on the job, experienced by 37% of workers, male as well as female.[34]

Manager's Hot Seat:
Office Romance: Groping for Answers

The table at left shows some guidelines for preventing sexual harassment. *(See Table 9.2.)* ●

table 9.2

GUIDELINES FOR PREVENTING SEXUAL HARASSMENT

- Don't do uninvited touching, hugging, or patting of someone's body.

- Don't request or suggest sexual favors for rewards related to work or promotion.

- Don't make suggestive jokes of a sexual nature, demeaning remarks, slurs, or obscene gestures or sounds.

- Don't create sexual pictures or displays or written notes of a sexual nature.

- Don't laugh at others' sexually harassing words or behaviors.

Source: Adapted from U.S. Equal Employment Opportunity Commission, "Sexual Harassment," March 29, 2006, www.eeoc.gov/types/sexual_harassment.html (accessed August 12, 2008); and CCH Inc., "Business Owners' Tool Kit," © 2006 CCH Inc., www.toolkit.cch.com/tools/sxhrst_m.asp (accessed August 12, 2008).

9.3 RECRUITMENT & SELECTION: PUTTING THE RIGHT PEOPLE INTO THE RIGHT JOBS

major question? How can I reduce mistakes in hiring and find great people who might work for me?

THE BIG PICTURE
Qualified applicants for jobs may be recruited from inside or outside the organization. The task of choosing the best person is enhanced by such tools as reviewing candidates' application forms, résumés, and references; doing interviews, either structured or unstructured; and screening with ability, personality, performance, and other kinds of employment tests.

"Hiring great people is brutally hard," write *BusinessWeek* columnists Jack (former General Electric CEO) and Suzy Welch. "New managers are lucky to get it right half the time. And even executives with decades of experience will tell you that they make the right calls 75% of the time at best."[35]

However difficult it may be, it's important to try to get hiring right. "We're essentially in an innovation economy where good people come up with really good ideas," says one CEO. "Companies want to hit home runs with the next greatest product, and the imperative is making sure you have great people to do that."[36]

Recruitment: How to Attract Qualified Applicants

At some time nearly every organization has to think about how to find the right kind of people. **Recruiting is the process of locating and attracting qualified applicants for jobs open in the organization.** The word "qualified" is important: You want to find people whose skills, abilities, and characteristics are best suited to your organization. Recruiting is of two types: *internal* and *external*.

I. Internal Recruiting: Hiring from the Inside *Internal recruiting* means **making people already employed by the organization aware of job openings.** Indeed, most vacant positions in organizations are filled through internal recruitment, mainly through *job posting,* **placing information about job vacancies and qualifications on bulletin boards, in newsletters, and on the organization's intranet.**

2. External Recruiting: Hiring from the Outside *External recruiting* means **attracting job applicants from outside the organization.** Notices of job vacancies are placed through newspapers, employment agencies, executive recruiting firms, union hiring halls, college job-placement offices, technical training schools, and word of mouth through professional associations. Many organizations—and not just high-technology companies—are advertising job openings on the Internet.

Both methods have advantages and disadvantages. *(See Table 9.3, opposite page.)*

table 9.3

INTERNAL AND EXTERNAL RECRUITING: ADVANTAGES AND DISADVANTAGES

Internal recruiting

Advantages	Disadvantages
1. Employees tend to be inspired to greater effort and loyalty. Morale is enhanced because they realize that working hard and staying put can result in more opportunities.	1. Internal recruitment restricts the competition for positions and limits the pool of fresh talent and fresh viewpoints.
2. The whole process of advertising, interviewing, and so on is cheaper.	2. It may encourage employees to assume that longevity and seniority will automatically result in promotion.
3. There are fewer risks. Internal candidates are already known and are familiar with the organization.	3. Whenever a job is filled, it creates a vacancy elsewhere in the organization.

External recruiting

Advantages	Disadvantages
1. Applicants may have specialized knowledge and experience.	1. The recruitment process is more expensive and takes longer.
2. Applicants may have fresh viewpoints.	2. The risks are higher because the persons hired are less well known.

Which External Recruiting Methods Work Best?   In general, the most effective sources are employee referrals, say human resource professionals, because, to protect their own reputations, employees are fairly careful about whom they recommend, and they know the qualifications of both the job and the prospective employee."[37] Other effective ways of finding good job candidates are e-recruitment tools, such as "dot-jobs" Web sites; membership directories for associations and trade groups; social networking sites; and industry-specific blogs, forums, newsgroups, or listserves.[38]

Realistic Job Previews   Often an organization will put on its best face to try to attract the best outside candidates—and then wonder why the new hires leave when the job doesn't turn out to be as rosy as promised.

A better approach is to present what's known as a ***realistic job preview***, **which gives a candidate a picture of both positive and negative features of the job and the organization before he or she is hired.**[39] People with realistic expectations tend to quit less frequently and be more satisfied than those with unrealistic expectations.

Test Your Knowledge:
Recruitment Sources

Selection: How to Choose the Best Person for the Job

Whether the recruitment process turns up a handful of job applicants or thousands, now you turn to the ***selection process,*** **the screening of job applicants to hire**

the best candidate. Essentially this becomes an exercise in *prediction:* how well will the candidate perform the job and how long will he or she stay?

Three types of selection tools are *background information, interviewing,* and *employment tests.*

I. Background Information: Application Forms, Résumés, & Reference Checks

Application forms and résumés provide basic background information about job applicants, such as citizenship, education, work history, and certifications.

Unfortunately, a lot of résumé information consists of mild puffery and even outrageous fairy tales. InfoLink Screening Services, which does background checks, reported that 14% of the tens of thousands of applicants it had screened had lied about their education.[40] Vermont-based ResumeDoctor.com, a résumé-writing service, surveyed 1,133 résumés that had been uploaded to its site and found that nearly 42.7% had at least one inaccuracy and 12.6% had two or more factual errors.[41] A 2003 survey by the Society of Human Resource Management found that 44% of 2.6 million respondents said they had misstated their work experience on their résumés.[42] And Background Information Services, a pre-employment screening company in Cleveland, found 56% of résumés contained falsehoods of some kind.[43]

Lying about education is the most prevalent distortion (such as pretending to hold a degree or an advanced degree). RadioShack CEO David Edmondson achieved some notoriety in 2006 and had to resign after a newspaper discovered he had falsely claimed on his résumé to hold degrees in psychology and theology.[44] In 2007, it came out that the foundation that runs online encyclopedia Wikipedia had neglected to do a basic background check before hiring Carolyn Doran as its chief operating officer; she had been convicted of drunken driving and fleeing a car accident.[45] Automatic Data Processing of Roseland, New Jersey, which has studied employee background verification, reported that 41% of education records showed a difference between the information provided by an applicant and that provided by the educational institution.[46]

Another common fabrication includes creative attempts to cover gaps in employment history (although there are straightforward ways of dealing with this, such as highlighting length of service instead of employment dates).[47] People also lie about their ages for fear of seeming to be too experienced (hence expensive) or too old.[48] As you might expect, people also embellish their salary histories, job titles, and achievements on projects.[49] And, in a time of rising numbers of illegal (undocumented) workers, it becomes incumbent on human resource officers to also verify U.S. citizenship.[50] Yet another difficulty for HR departments is applicants' increasing use of video résumés, which could expose the organization to a possible failure-to-hire claim on grounds of discrimination if the applicant belongs to a "protected class"—a minority individual or older person, for example.[51]

References are also a problem. Many employers don't give honest assessments of former employees, for two reasons: (1) They fear that if they say anything negative, they can be sued by the former employee. (2) They fear if they say anything positive, and the job candidate doesn't pan out, they can be sued by the new employer.[52]

2. Interviewing: Unstructured, Situational, & Behavioral-Description

Interviewing, the most commonly used employee-selection technique, may take place face to face, by videoconferencing, or—as is increasingly the case—via the

Practical Action

Applying for a Job? Here Are Some Mistakes to Avoid

There are several mistakes that job candidates often make in initial interviews. Here are some tips:[53]

Be Prepared—Very Prepared

Can you pronounce the name of the company you're interviewing with? Of the person/people interviewing you? Do you understand the company and the position you're interviewing for? Do you know the company's competition? How about your own job strengths and weaknesses? What do you need to improve on to move ahead?

Go online and read the company's Web site. Search for any news articles written about the firm. Call the company and ask about pronunciation. Take time to practice questions and answers so you'll sound confident.

Dress Right & Pay Attention to Your Attitude

Is the company dress code "business casual"? That doesn't mean you should dress that way (or the way you dress on campus) for the interview.

Dress professionally for the interview. Be aware of your attitude as soon as you enter the building. Be on time. (Time your commute by doing a test run a day or so before the interview.) If unforeseeable circumstances arise and cause you to be late, call to inform your interviewer. Be polite to the receptionist, and greet everyone who greets you. Turn off your cellphone ringer.

Don't Get Too Personal with the Interviewer

Don't be overfriendly and share too much, especially in the initial interview. Although the interviewer will try to make you feel comfortable, you should focus on the position and practice your answers. Rehearse questions to ask the interviewer, such as the challenges for the position in the future. Don't make negative comments about your old company. Rather, figure out the positives and convey what you learned and gained from your experience.

Be Aware That Your Background Will Be Checked

Because it seems to be getting harder to distinguish honest job applicants from dishonest ones, companies now routinely check résumés or hire companies that do so. Ninety-six percent of employers conduct background checks, according to one study.[54] And here's something to think about if you are a MySpace, Facebook, YouTube enthusiast or blogger: employers now frequently use search engines such as Google or Yahoo as a way to do continuous and stealthy background checks on prospective employees, effectively making an end run around discrimination laws.[55]

Internet.[56] (However, face-to-face interviews have been found to be perceived as more fair and to lead to higher job acceptance intentions than were videoconferencing and telephone interviews.)[57] To help eliminate bias, interviews can be designed, conducted, and evaluated by a committee of three or more people. The most commonly used employee-selection technique, interviewing, takes three forms.[58]

- **Unstructured interview.** Like an ordinary conversation, an **_unstructured interview_ involves asking probing questions to find out what the applicant is like.** There is no fixed set of questions asked of all applicants and no systematic scoring procedure. As a result, the unstructured interview has been criticized as being overly subjective and apt to be influenced by the biases of the interviewer. Equally important, nowadays it is susceptible to legal attack, because some questions may infringe on non-job-related matters such as privacy, diversity, or disability.[59] However, compared with the structured interview method, the unstructured interview has been found to provide a more accurate assessment of an applicant's job-related personality traits.[60]

Practical Action

The Right Way to Conduct an Interview

Because hiring people who later have to be let go is such an expensive proposition, companies are now putting a great deal of emphasis on effective interviewing. Although this is a subject worth exploring further, here are some minimal suggestions:[61]

Before the Interview: Define Your Needs & Review Applicant's Résumé

Write out what skills, traits, and qualities the job requires. "Looking to hire somebody is like going to the supermarket," says one HR manager. "You need to have a list and know what you need."[62]

Look at the applicant's résumé or application form to determine relevant experience, gaps, and discrepancies.

Write Out Interview Questions

You should ask each candidate the same set of questions, so that you can compare their answers. (This helps keep you out of legal trouble, too.) In general, the questions should be designed to elicit the following types of information.

- **Does the applicant have the knowledge to do the job?** Examples: "Give an example where you came up with a creative solution." "How do you do research on the Internet?"

- **Can the applicant handle difficult situations?** Examples: "Tell me about a time when you dealt with an irate customer. How did you handle the situation and what was the outcome?"

- **Is the applicant willing to cope with the job's demands?** Examples: "How do you feel about making unpopular decisions?" "Are you willing to travel 30% of the time?"

- **Will the applicant fit in with the organization's culture?** Examples: "How would your last supervisor describe you?" "How much leeway did they give you in your previous job in charging travel expenses?"

Follow a Three-Scene Interview Scenario

The interview itself may follow a three-scene script.

- **Scene I: The first 3 minutes—small talk and "compatibility" test.** The first scene is really a "compatibility test." It takes about 3 minutes and consists of exchanging small talk, giving you a chance to establish rapport and judge how well the candidate makes a first impression.

  Note: As many as four out of five hiring decisions are made within the first 10 minutes of an interview, according to some research. Thus, be aware that if you are immediately impressed with a candidate, you may spend more time talking than listening—perhaps trying to sell the candidate on the job rather than screen his or her qualifications.[63]

- **Scene 2: The next 15–60 minutes—asking questions and listening to the applicant's "story."** In the next scene, you ask the questions you wrote out (and answer those the candidate directs to you). Allow the interviewee to do 70%–80% of the talking.

  Take notes to remember important points. Don't ignore your "gut feelings." Intuition plays a role in hiring decisions. (But be careful you don't react to people as stereotypes.)

- **Scene 3: The final I–2 minutes—closing the interview and setting up the next steps.** In the final minute, you listen to see whether the candidate expresses interest in taking the job.

After the Interview

Write a short report making some sort of quantitative score of the candidate's qualifications. Indicate your reasons for your decision.

Check the applicant's references before inviting him or her to a second interview.

- **Structured interview type 1—the situational interview. The *structured interview* involves asking each applicant the same questions and comparing their responses to a standardized set of answers.**

  In one type of structured interview, the ***situational interview,*** **the interviewer focuses on hypothetical situations.** Example: "What would you do if you saw two of your people arguing loudly in the work area?" The idea here is to find out if the applicant can handle difficult situations that may arise on the job.

- **Structured interview type 2—the behavioral-description interview.** In the second type of structured interview, the *behavioral-description interview,* **the interviewer explores what applicants have actually done in the past.** Example: "What was the best idea you ever sold to a supervisor, teacher, peer, or subordinate?" This question (asked by the U.S. Army of college students applying for its officer training program) is designed to assess the applicant's ability to influence others.

Group Exercise:
Practicing Your Interview Skills

3. Employment Tests: Ability, Personality, Performance, & Others

It used to be that employment selection tests consisted of paper-and-pencil, performance, and physical-ability tests. Now, however, *employment tests* **are legally considered to consist of any procedure used in the employment selection decision process.** Thus, even application forms, interviews, and educational and experience requirements are now considered tests.[64]

Probably the three most common employment tests are the following.

- **Ability tests.** *Ability tests* measure physical abilities, strength and stamina, mechanical ability, mental abilities, and clerical abilities. Telephone operators, for instance, need to be tested for hearing, and assembly-line workers for manual dexterity. Intelligence tests are also catching on as ways to predict future executive performance.[65]

- **Performance tests.** *Performance tests* or *skills tests* measure performance on actual job tasks, as when computer programmers take a test on a particular programming language such as C++ or middle managers work on a small project. Some companies have an *assessment center,* **in which management candidates participate in activities for a few days while being assessed by evaluators.**[66]

- **Personality tests.** *Personality tests* measure such personality traits as adjustment, energy, sociability, independence, and need for achievement. One of the most famous such tests, in existence for 60-plus years, is the 93-question Myers-Briggs Type Indicator, with about 2.5 million tests given each year throughout the world. Myers-Briggs endures, observers say, "because it does a good job of pointing up differences between people, offers individuals a revealing glimpse of themselves, and is a valuable asset in team-building, improving communication, and resolving personality-conflict."[67] Southwest Airlines, for instance, has found Myers-Briggs helps build trust in developing teams.[68] Hewlett-Packard uses a personality test to see if employees are temperamentally suited to working alone at home—that is, telecommuting—and can handle limited supervision.[69] At Children's Healthcare of Atlanta, personality tests are used to find employees who will be "nice people"—those with "the qualities of being nurturing, kind, and warm-hearted," in the words of a human resources vice president.[70]

    Myers-Briggs and other personality tests should be used with caution because of the difficulty of measuring personality characteristics and of making a legal defense if the results are challenged.[71]

Other Tests The list of employment testing techniques has grown to include— in appropriate cases—drug testing, polygraph (lie detectors), genetic screening, and even (a questionable technique) handwriting analysis.[72] (Human resource professionals need to be aware, incidentally, that there are a variety of products available on the Internet to help employees beat a company's drug tests.)[73]

Example

Personality Tests: A Sporting-Goods Chain Uses a Web-Based Test to Screen Job Applicants

About 30% of American companies, from tiny independents to giant General Motors, use personality tests, according to one 2003 survey.[74] At Finish Line, a nationwide chain of sporting-goods stores, store managers use the results of Web-based personality tests developed by Unicru, of Beaverton, Oregon, to screen applicants for jobs as retail sales clerks. Candidates may apply through Unicru's kiosks or computer phones, which are installed in the stores. One Finish Line store in Chicago screens as many as 70 applicants a week during the store's pre-holiday season.

Unicru's computer scores test takers according to how strongly they agree or disagree (on a four-point scale) with statements such as "You do not fake being polite" and "You love to listen to people talk about themselves." High scores on attributes such as sociability and initiative reward applicants with a "green" rating that allows them to move on to an interview with a human manager. Scores in the middle earn a "yellow," and a lesser chance of landing a job; low-scoring "reds" are out of luck.

"The kinds of people who do well," says Unicru psychologist David Scarborough, " . . . obviously have to have good self-control. They have to be patient. They have to enjoy helping people. All those characteristics are quite measurable."[75] Finish Line says that Unicru's system has reduced turnover by 24%.

Your Call

There are, by some estimates, around 2,500 cognitive and personality employment tests on the market, and it's important that employers match the right test for the right purpose.[76] Moreover, tests aren't supposed to have a disparate impact on a protected class of people, such as certain racial or ethnic groups.[77] What questions would you want to ask about a personality test before you submitted yourself to it?

Test Your Knowledge:
Reliability and Validity

With any kind of test, an important legal consideration is the test's ***reliability—*** **the degree to which a test measures the same thing consistently**—so that an individual's score remains about the same over time, assuming the characteristics being measured also remain the same.

Another legal consideration is the test's ***validity—*** **the test measures what it purports to measure and is free of bias.** If a test is supposed to predict performance, then the individual's actual performance should reflect his or her score on the test. Using an invalid test to hire people can lead to poor selection decisions. It can also create legal problems if the test is ever challenged in a court of law. ●

Lie detectors. Defense contractors and other security-minded companies are apt to require polygraph testing. Would you object to taking such a test?

9.4 ORIENTATION, TRAINING, & DEVELOPMENT

> Once people are hired, what's the best way to see that they do what they're supposed to do?
>
> major question**?**

THE BIG PICTURE

Three ways newcomers are helped to perform their jobs are through *orientation,* to fit them into the job and organization; *training,* to upgrade the skills of technical and operational employees; and *development,* to upgrade the skills of professionals and managers.

In muckraker Upton Sinclair's 1906 novel *The Jungle,* "employers barely paused when a worker swooned from overwork or fell into a rendering tank," writes columnist Sue Shellenbarger. "They just got another warm body to replace him."[78]

That's hardly the case anymore. Now when a hire is made, companies often resort to what is known as "onboarding," rolling out a welcome by assigning "buddies," providing detailed orientations, even sending goody baskets, so as to bring rookies up to speed quickly and give them a fast introduction to company culture.[79] This is because, as we said, the emphasis is on "human capital." Only a third to half of most companies' stock-market value is accounted for by hard assets such as property, plant, and equipment, according to a Brookings Institution report. Most of a firm's value is in such attributes as patents, processes, and—important to this discussion—employee or customer satisfaction.[80] The means for helping employees perform their jobs are *orientation, training,* and *development.*

Orientation: Helping Newcomers Learn the Ropes

The finalist candidate is offered the job, has accepted it, and has started work. Now he or she must begin, in that old sailor's phrase, to "learn the ropes." This is the start of ***orientation,* helping the newcomer fit smoothly into the job and the organization.**

Helping New Employees Get Comfortable: The First 6 Months   "How well will I get along with other employees?" "What if I screw up on a project?" Coming into a new job can produce a lot of uncertainty and anxiety. In part this is because, depending on the job, a new hire can accomplish only 60% as much in the first 3 months as an experienced worker, according to MCI Communications.[81]

The first 6 months on a job can be critical to how one performs over the long haul, because that's when the psychological patterns are established. Thus, employers have discovered that it's far better to give newcomers a helping hand than to let them learn possibly inappropriate behavior that will be hard to undo later.[82]

The Desirable Characteristics of Orientation
Like Orientation Week for new college students, the initial socialization period is designed to give new employees the information they need to be effective. In a large organization, orientation may be a formal, established process. In a small organization, it may be so informal that employees find themselves having to make most of the effort themselves.

Group training. In large companies, orientation and on-going training are often conducted in group sessions led by a presenter while the employees follow along. Do you see any problems with this approach?

Following orientation, the employee should emerge with information about three matters (much of which he or she may have acquired during the job-application process):

- **The job routine.** At minimum, the new employee needs to have learned what is required in the job for which he or she was hired, how the work will be evaluated, and who the immediate co-workers and managers are. This is basic.

- **The organization's mission and operations.** Certainly all managers need to know what the organization is about—its purpose, products or services, operations, and history. And it's now understood that low-level employees perform better if they, too, have this knowledge.

- **The organization's work rules and employee benefits.** A public utility's HR department may have a brochure explaining formalized work rules, overtime requirements, grievance procedures, and elaborate employee benefits. A technology startup may be so fluid that many of these matters will have not been established yet. Even so, there are matters of law (such as those pertaining to sexual harassment) affecting work operations that every employee should be made aware of.

Training & Development: Helping People Perform Better

Which business strategy offers the highest returns: (1) downsizing; (2) total quality management, which focuses on work methods and process control; or (3) employee involvement, which focuses on upgrading workers' skills and knowledge? According to a study of 216 big firms, the winner is employee involvement, which had an average return on investment of 19.1% (versus 15.4% for downsizing and 15% for TQM).[83]

In hiring, you always try to get people whose qualifications match the requirements of the job. Quite often, however, there are gaps in what new employees need to know. These gaps are filled by training. The training process involves five steps, as shown below. *(See Figure 9.2.)*

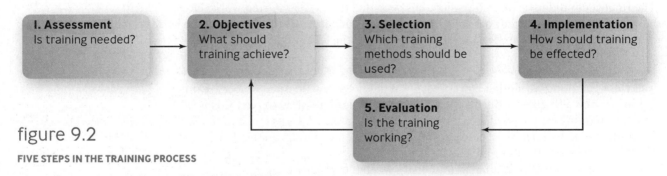

figure 9.2

FIVE STEPS IN THE TRAINING PROCESS

HR professionals distinguish between *training* and *development.*

- **Training—upgrading skills of technical and operational employees.** Electronics technicians, data processors, computer network administrators, and X-ray technicians, among many others, need to be schooled in new knowledge as the requirements of their fields change. *Training,* then, refers to educating technical and operational employees in how to better do their current jobs.

- **Development—upgrading skills of professionals and managers.** Accountants, nurses, lawyers, and managers of all levels need to be continually educated in how to do their jobs better not just today but also tomorrow. *Development* refers to educating professionals and managers in the skills they need to do their jobs in the future.

Typical areas for which employee training and development are given are customer service, safety, leadership, computer skills, quality initiatives, communications, human relations, ethics, diversity, and sexual harassment.[84]

The Different Types of Training or Development   There are all kinds of training and development methods, and their effectiveness depends on whether what is being taught are facts or skills. If people are to learn *facts*—such as work rules or legal matters—lectures, videotapes, and workbooks are effective. If people are to learn *skills*—such as improving interpersonal relations or using new tools—then techniques such as discussion, role playing, and practice work better.

Another way to categorize training methods is to distinguish on-the-job from off-the-job methods. *On-the-job training* takes place in the work setting while employees are performing job-related tasks. Four major training methods are coaching, training positions, job rotation, and planned work activities. *Off-the-job training* consists of classroom programs, videotapes, workbooks, and the like. Lots of off-the-job training consists of **computer-assisted instruction (CAI), in which computers are used to provide additional help or to reduce instructional time.**

Example

Off-the-Job Training: Getting Ahead through E-Learning

College students, of course, have already discovered e-learning (electronic learning). Several score million other people are also taking short-term, practical courses related to their careers, mostly at business schools and continuing-education institutions around the country.

Outside of education, in other U.S. organizations, e-learning has also become a well-established fact. Although instructor-led classrooms are still the dominant training method, at 65% of total student hours in 2007 (up from 62% a year earlier), online self-study e-learning and virtual classrooms made up 30% (up from 29%).[85] The benefits of e-learning, of course, are that no transportation is needed and you can follow a flexible schedule and often work at your own pace. However, there are some drawbacks. "The one thing e-learning boosters don't want to talk about is the simple fact that very few people ever actually finish an e-learning course when it involves a technically complex or

Off-the-job training. How does receiving feedback from an instructor affect your retention of knowledge?

lengthy subject such as software training or programming," says corporate trainer Roland Van Liew. "People perform the complex process of assimilating information best in socially interactive environments."[86]

Because of the lack of classroom interaction between students and teachers in online education, both must assume more responsibility. "If students do not receive adequate teacher feedback and reinforcement," points out one writer, "they will not always know whether they possess an accurate knowledge of the subject matter."[87]

Your Call

Neuroscientists are finding out that the human brain is a "social animal" that needs interaction with others.[88] How do you think this fact relates to e-learning? Do you think you learn better in a classroom rather then online?

What If No One Shows Up?   Many employers offer employee training, whether internal or external, or funding to attend seminars. But research has shown that a surprisingly high percentage of employees simply don't know about it. For instance, while 92% of employers in one survey offered funding to attend seminars and trade shows, only 28% of employees were aware the funding existed.[89] Clearly, then, employers need to find out whether the training offered fits with the majority of employee development goals. ●

Test Your Knowledge:
Training Methods

How can I assess employees' performance more accurately and give more effective feedback?

THE BIG PICTURE

Performance appraisal, assessing employee performance and providing them feedback, may be objective or subjective. Appraisals may be by peers, subordinates, customers, oneself. Feedback may be formal or informal.

Every student sooner or later discovers that professors grade on different standards—some harder, some easier, some in the middle. "The workplace is often no different," points out one writer. "Some managers are hard raters of performance, some easy, and some in the middle."[90] Indeed, one study of 5,970 employees reporting to two managers found that the majority got inconsistent ratings.[91] Just as some students may worry that classmates with superior political skills may gain unfair advantage in the grading system, so employees are similarly concerned—and they may be right to be so.[92]

Performance appraisals need to be fair and accurate not just because it's right but also because it's essential to effective **performance management, the continuous cycle of improving job performance through goal setting, feedback and coaching, and rewards and positive reinforcement.** The purpose of performance management is to focus employees on attaining goals that are tied to the organization's strategic goals and vision, and to evaluate how successful they were in accomplishing those goals. We describe goal-setting theory, rewards, and reinforcement in later chapters. Here let us consider performance appraisal.

Defining Performance Appraisal

Performance appraisal **consists of (1) assessing an employee's performance and (2) providing him or her with feedback.** Thus, this management task has two purposes: First, performance appraisal helps employees understand how they are doing in relation to objectives and standards; here you must *judge* the employee. Second, it helps in their training and personal development; here you must *counsel* the employee.[93]

Appraisals are of two general types—objective and subjective.

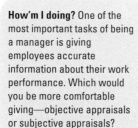

How'm I doing? One of the most important tasks of being a manager is giving employees accurate information about their work performance. Which would you be more comfortable giving—objective appraisals or subjective appraisals?

I. Objective Appraisals *Objective appraisals,* **also called** *results appraisals,* **are based on facts and are often numerical.** In these kinds of appraisals, you would keep track of such matters as the numbers of products the employee sold in a month, customer complaints filed against an employee, miles of freight hauled, and the like.

There are two good reasons for having objective appraisals:

- **They measure results.** It doesn't matter if two appliance salespeople have completely different personal traits (one is formal, reserved, and patient; the other informal, gregarious, and impatient) if each sells the same number of washers and dryers. Human resource professionals point out that, just as in business we measure sales, profits, shareholder value, and other so-called metrics, so it's important to measure employee performance, benefit costs, and the like as an aid to strategy.[94]

- **They are harder to challenge legally.** Not being as subject to personal bias, objective appraisals are harder for employees to challenge on legal grounds, such as for age, gender, or racial discrimination.

We discussed an objective approach in Chapter 5 under *management by objectives,* which can encourage employees to feel empowered to adopt behavior that will produce specific results. MBO, you'll recall, is a four-step process in which (1) managers and employees jointly set objectives for the employee, (2) managers develop action plans, (3) managers and employees periodically review the employee's performance, and (4) the manager makes a performance appraisal and rewards the employee according to results. For example, an objective for a copier service technician might be to increase the number of service calls 15% during the next 3 months.

2. Subjective Appraisals   Few employees can be adequately measured just by objective appraisals—hence the need for *subjective appraisals,* **which are based on a manager's perceptions of an employee's (1) traits or (2) behaviors.**

Test Your Knowledge:
Appraisal Methods

- **Trait appraisals.** *Trait appraisals* are ratings of such subjective attributes as "attitude," "initiative," and "leadership." Trait evaluations may be easy to create and use, but their validity is questionable because the evaluator's personal bias can affect the ratings.
- **Behavioral appraisals.** Behavioral appraisals measure specific, observable aspects of performance—being on time for work, for instance—although making the evaluation is still somewhat subjective. An example is the *behaviorally anchored rating scale (BARS),* **which rates employee gradations in performance according to scales of specific behaviors.** For example, a five-point BARS rating scale about attendance might go from "Always early for work and has equipment ready to fully assume duties" to "Frequently late and often does not have equipment ready for going to work," with gradations in between.

Who Should Make Performance Appraisals?

As you might expect, most performance appraisals are done by managers. However, to add different perspectives, sometimes appraisal information is provided by other people knowledgeable about particular employees.

Peers, Subordinates, Customers, & Self   Among additional sources of information are co-workers and subordinates, customers and clients, and the employees themselves.

- **Peers and subordinates.** Co-workers, colleagues, and subordinates may well see different aspects of your performance. Such information can be useful for development, although it probably shouldn't be used for evaluation. (Many managers will resist soliciting such information about themselves, of course, fearing negative appraisals.)
- **Customers and clients.** Some organizations, such as restaurants and hotels, ask customers and clients for their appraisals of employees. Publishers ask authors to judge how well they are doing in handling the editing, production, and marketing of their books. Automobile dealerships may send follow-up questionnaires to car buyers.
- **Self-appraisals.** How would you rate your own performance in a job, knowing that it would go into your personnel file? Probably the bias would be toward the favorable. Nevertheless, *self-appraisals* help employees

become involved in the whole evaluation process and may make them more receptive to feedback about areas needing improvement.

360-Degree Assessment: Appraisal by Everybody   We said that performance appraisals may be done by peers, subordinates, customers, and oneself. Sometimes all these may be used in a technique called 360-degree assessment.

In a "theater in the round," the actors in a dramatic play are watched by an audience on all sides of them—360 degrees. Similarly, as a worker, you have many people watching you from all sides. Thus has arisen the idea of the ***360-degree assessment,* or *360-degree feedback appraisal,* in which employees are appraised not only by their managerial superiors but also by peers, subordinates, and sometimes clients,** thus providing several perspectives.

Typically, an employee chooses between 6 and 12 other people to make evaluations, who then fill out anonymous forms, the results of which are tabulated by computer. The employee then goes over the results with his or her manager and together they put into place a long-term plan for performance goals.

There are advantages and disadvantages to incorporating 360-degree feedback into the performance appraisal process. Recent research found that "improvement is most likely to occur when feedback indicates that change is necessary, recipients have a positive feedback orientation, perceive a need to change their behavior, react positively to feedback, believe change is feasible, set appropriate goals to regulate their behavior, and take actions that lead to skill and performance improvement."[95] At the heart of the process is the matter of *trust.* "Trust determines how much an individual is willing to contribute for an employer," says one expert. "Using 360 confidentially, for developmental purposes, builds trust; using it to trigger pay and personnel decisions puts trust at risk."[96]

Test Your Knowledge:
Potential Errors in the Rating Process

Example

The 360-Degree Assessment: How Can It Be Compromised?

The 360-degree assessment can be very effective for performance improvement, career development, and even training. Texas computer maker Dell Inc., for instance, realized that it needed to nurture its talent in order to achieve better performance. Accordingly, it designed an in-house training program taught primarily by Dell's own top executives, chairman Michael Dell and CEO Kevin Rollins, who submitted to 360-degree assessments in the hope of inspiring the executives beneath them to do the same. "Pay," says one report, "is now determined in part by how well a manager does at nurturing people."[97]

There are many ways, however, in which 360-degree assessments can become disasters. In one health care organization, the vice president of human resources was rated by his staff as being a strong, positive, effective leader, but his boss, the corporate senior vice president, did not rate him as being very effective. At a meeting to review the 360-degree assessment, the HR manager

asked to discuss the differences in perceptions, but his boss said, "Obviously, everyone else is right and I am wrong. So, we'll just go along with what others have said"—thereby destroying the opportunity to give constructive feedback or coaching to the HR VP.

In another case, a manager confronted specific employees about their 360 assessments, effectively compromising the integrity of the process. In a third case, a sales organization executed an effective assessment and feedback, but, as one writer says, "there was no accountability for development plans, there was no follow-up after the initial feedback meetings, and no training was offered or provided for clearly identified weaknesses in a majority of the sales people."[98]

Your Call

If you were the recipient of a 360-degree assessment, what kind of steps would you like to see taken to ensure that you could trust the process?

Forced Ranking: Grading on a Curve

To increase performance, as many as a quarter of Fortune 500 companies (such as General Electric, Ford, Cisco, and Intel) have instituted performance review systems known as forced ranking (or "rank and yank") systems.[99] **In *forced ranking performance review systems,* all employees within a business unit are ranked against one another and grades are distributed along some sort of bell curve**—just like students being graded in a college course. Top performers (such as the top 20%) are rewarded with bonuses and promotions, the worst performers (such as the bottom 20%) are rehabilitated or dismissed. For instance, every year 10% of GE's managers are assigned the bottom grade, and if they don't improve, they are asked to leave the company.

Proponents of forced ranking say it encourages managers to identify and remove poor performers and also structures a predetermined compensation curve, which enables them to reward top performers. If, however, the system is imposed on an organization overnight without preparation, by pitting employees against one another, it can produce shocks to morale, productivity, and loyalty. There may also be legal ramifications, as when employees filed class-action lawsuits alleging that the forced-ranking methods had a disparate effect on particular groups of employees.[100]

Effective Performance Feedback

The whole point of performance appraisal, of course, is to stimulate better job performance. But, says Lawrence Bossidy (introduced in Chapter 7), the typical appraisal is often three pages long and filled with vague, uncommunicative language and is useless to ensure that improvement happens.[101] Bossidy recommends an appraisal take up half a page and cover just three topics: what the boss likes about your performance, what you can improve, and how you and your boss are going to make sure that improvement happens.

To help increase employee performance, a manager can use two kinds of appraisals—formal and informal.

I. Formal Appraisals *Formal appraisals* **are conducted at specific times throughout the year and are based on performance measures that have been established in advance.** An emergency medical technician might be evaluated twice a year by his or her manager, using objective performance measures such as work attendance time sheets and more subjective measures such as a BARS to indicate the employee's willingness to follow emergency procedures and doctors' and nurses' orders.

As part of the appraisal, the manager should give the employee feedback, describing how he or she is performing well and not so well and giving examples. Managers are sometimes advised to keep diaries about specific incidents so they won't have to rely on their memories (and so that their evaluations will be more lawsuit-resistant). Facts should always be used rather than impressions.

2. Informal Appraisals Formal appraisals are the equivalent of a student receiving a grade on a midterm test and a grade on a final test—weeks may go by in which you are unaware of how well you're doing in the course. Informal appraisals are the equivalent of occasional unscheduled pop quizzes and short papers or drop-in visits to the professor's office to talk about your work—you have more frequent feedback about your performance. *Informal appraisals* **are conducted on an unscheduled basis and consist of less rigorous indications of employee performance.**

You may not feel comfortable about critiquing your employees' performance, especially when you have to convey criticism rather than praise. Nevertheless, giving performance feedback is one of the most important parts of the manager's job. Some suggestions for improvement appear at right. *(See Table 9.4.)* ●

table 9.4

HOW TO GIVE PERFORMANCE FEEDBACK TO EMPLOYEES

Think of yourself as a coach, as though you were managing a team of athletes.

- *Take a problem-solving approach, avoid criticism, and treat employees with respect.* Recall the worst boss you ever worked for. How did you react to his or her method of giving feedback? Avoid criticism that might be taken personally.

  Example: Don't say "You're picking up that bag of cement wrong" (which criticizes by using the word "wrong"). Say "Instead of bending at the waist, a good way to pick up something heavy is to bend your knees. That'll help save your back."

- *Be specific in describing the employee's present performance and in the improvement you desire.* Describe your subordinate's current performance in specific terms and concentrate on outcomes that are within his or her ability to improve.

  Example: Don't say "You're always late turning in your sales reports." Say "Instead of making calls on Thursday afternoon, why don't you take some of the time to do your sales reports so they'll be ready on Friday along with those of the other sales reps."

- *Get the employee's input.* In determining causes for a problem, listen to the employee and get his or her help in crafting a solution.

  Example: Don't say "You've got to learn to get here at 9:00 every day." Say "What changes do you think could be made so that your station is covered when people start calling at 9:00?"

✖ 9.6 MANAGING AN EFFECTIVE WORKFORCE: COMPENSATION & BENEFITS

major question?	What are the various forms of compensation?

THE BIG PICTURE

Managers must manage for compensation—which includes wages or salaries, incentives, and benefits.

Do we work only for a paycheck? Many people do, of course. But money is only one form of compensation.

Compensation **has three parts: (1) wages or salaries, (2) incentives, and (3) benefits.** In different organizations one part may take on more importance than another. For instance, in some nonprofit organizations (education, government), salaries may not be large, but health and retirement benefits may outweigh that fact. In a high-technology startup, the salary and benefits may actually be somewhat humble, but the promise of a large payoff in incentives, such as stock options or bonuses, may be quite attractive. Let's consider these three parts briefly. (We expand on them in Chapter 12 when we discuss ways to motivate employees.)

Wages or Salaries

Base pay **consists of the basic wage or salary paid employees in exchange for doing their jobs.** The basic compensation is determined by all kinds of economic factors: the prevailing pay levels in a particular industry and location, what competitors are paying, whether the jobs are unionized, if the jobs are hazardous, what the individual's level is in the organization, and how much experience he or she has.

Incentives

To induce employees to be more productive or to attract and retain top performers, many organizations offer incentives, such as commissions, bonuses, profit-sharing plans, and stock options. We discuss these in detail in Chapter 12.

Stock options. Companies like to offer favored employees stock options rather than higher salaries as benefits. Not only do employees place a high value on options, but companies can issue as many as they want without hurting corporate profits because, under present accounting rules, they don't have to count the options' value as an expense.

How to Make Incentive Pay Plans Meet Company Goals: Communicate Them to Employees[102]

There are many incentive compensation plans, ranging from cash awards and gifts to profit sharing and stock ownership, as we discuss in detail in Chapter 12.

Here let's ask the question: Do they work?

A survey of 139 companies, more than a third of them in the Fortune 500, found that 72% had variable pay plans. But only 22% said their plans had helped them achieve all their business objectives, and 28% said their plans had achieved none of them.

What explains the difference? Good plan design is important but so is good communication and oversight.

According to Ken Abosch, a consultant at Chicago-based Hewett Associates, which conducted the survey, often plans fail to deliver on their intended goals because employees aren't told enough about them and aren't kept up to date on the progress of the plans. Eighty-nine percent of companies that regularly communicated with their employees said their incentive plans met their goals, compared with only 57% of companies that did not discuss them with their employees.

Five keys to a successful incentive-pay plan are the following, according to Abosch:

- **Simplicity.** Does the plan pass the simplicity test? As Abosch puts it, "Can you explain it on an elevator ride?"
- **Clear goals.** Are the goals clear? Are the goals fully supported by management?
- **Realistic goals.** Are the goals realistic—that is, neither too difficult nor too easy to achieve?
- **Consistency with present goals.** Is the plan in line with the organization's present goals? Company goals change. "There are very few organizations that have the same business objective for five to seven years," points out Abosch.
- **Regular communication.** Do managers regularly communicate with employees about the plan? "People want a scorecard," Abosch says.

Benefits

Benefits, or *fringe benefits,* are additional nonmonetary forms of compensation designed to enrich the lives of all employees in the organization, which are paid all or in part by the organization. Examples are many: health insurance, dental insurance, life insurance, disability protection, retirement plans, holidays off, accumulated sick days and vacation days, recreation options, country club or health club memberships, family leave, discounts on company merchandise, counseling, credit unions, legal advice, and education reimbursement. For top executives, there may be "golden parachutes," generous severance pay for those who might be let go in the event the company is taken over by another company.

Benefits are no small part of an organization's costs. According to the U.S. Chamber of Commerce, employee benefit costs were 44% of payroll costs in 2006, with medical benefit costs constituting the largest part.[103] ●

Communication is everything. The questions human resource managers need to keep in mind are: What good does it do a company to have attractive incentive plans if employees don't understand them? Will an employee exert the extra effort in pursuit of rewards if he or she doesn't know what the rewards are?

9.7 MANAGING PROMOTIONS, TRANSFERS, DISCIPLINING, & DISMISSALS

What are some guidelines for handling promotions, transfers, disciplining, and dismissals?

THE BIG PICTURE

As a manager, you'll have to manage employee replacement actions, as by promoting, transferring, demoting, laying off, or firing.

American society, points out George Washington University sociologist Amitai Etzioni, can be depicted by the term "pluralism within unity." Unlike Europeans, who have great difficulty accepting the idea of diversity—of Turkish-Germans, Algerian-Frenchmen, or Romanian-Austrians, for example—in the United States we pretty much take it for granted that hyphenated Americans can be good workers and citizens.[104]

Indeed, our sense of inclusiveness seems to be gradually growing to embrace not only ethnic and racial diversity but also both genders and different ages, religions, sexual orientation, and physical and mental abilities.[105] And there's more, as roles continue to change. Now more men seek paternity leaves, working parents want flexible hours, employees want to telecommute from home, and questions of "work-life balance" are receiving greater priority. What this shows is that as a manager you may have quite a complex workforce.

Among the major—and most difficult—decisions you will make as a manager are those about employee movement within an organization: whom should you promote? transfer? discipline? fire? All these matters go under the heading of *employee replacement*. And, incidentally, any time you need to deal with replacing an employee in a job, that's a time to reconsider the job description to see how it might be made more effective for the next person to occupy it.

You'll have to deal with replacement whenever an employee quits, retires, becomes seriously ill, or dies. Or you may initiate the replacement action by promoting, transferring, demoting, laying off, or firing.[106]

Promotion: Moving Upward

Promotion—moving an employee to a higher-level position—is the most obvious way to recognize that person's superior performance (apart from giving raises and bonuses). Three concerns are these:

Fairness It's important that promotion be *fair*. The step upward must be deserved. It shouldn't be for reasons of nepotism, cronyism, or other kind of favoritism.

Nondiscrimination The promotion cannot discriminate on the basis of race, ethnicity, gender, age, or physical ability.

Others' Resentments   If someone is promoted, someone else may be resentful about being passed over. As a manager, you may need to counsel the people left behind about their performance and their opportunities in the future.

Transfer: Moving Sideways

Transfer is movement of an employee to a different job with *similar responsibility.* It may or may not mean a change in geographical location (which might be part of a promotion as well).

There are four principal reasons why employees might be transferred: (1) to solve organizational problems by using their skills at another location; (2) to broaden their experience in being assigned to a different position; (3) to retain their interest and motivation by being presented with a new challenge; or (4) to solve some employee problems, such as personal differences with their bosses.

Disciplining & Demotion: The Threat of Moving Downward

Poorly performing employees may be given a warning or a reprimand and then disciplined. That is, they may be temporarily removed from their jobs, as when a police officer is placed on suspension or administrative leave—removed from his or her regular job in the field and perhaps given a paperwork job or told to stay away from work.

Alternatively, an employee may be demoted—that is, have his or her current responsibilities, pay, and perquisites taken away, as when a middle manager is demoted to a first-line manager. (Sometimes this may occur when a company is downsized, resulting in fewer higher-level management positions.)

Dismissal: Moving Out of the Organization

Dismissals are of three sorts:

Layoffs   The phrase being *laid off* tends to suggest that a person has been dismissed *temporarily*—as when a car maker doesn't have enough orders to justify keeping its production employees—and may be recalled later when economic conditions improve.

Manager's Hot Seat:
Personal Disclosure:
Confession Coincidence

Downsizings   A *downsizing* is a *permanent* dismissal; there is no rehiring later. An auto maker discontinuing a line of cars or on the path to bankruptcy might permanently let go of its production employees.

Firings   The phrase being *fired,* with all its euphemisms and synonyms—being "terminated," "separated," "let go," "canned"—tends to mean that a person was dismissed *permanently "for cause"*: absenteeism, sloppy work habits, failure to perform satisfactorily, breaking the law, and the like.

It used to be that managers could use their discretion about dismissals. Today, however, because of the changing legal climate, steps must be taken to avoid employees suing for "wrongful termination." That is, an employer has to carefully *document* the reasons for dismissals.

The Practical Action box on the next page offers some suggestions for handling dismissals. ●

Practical Action

The Right Way to Handle a Dismissal

"Employment at will" is the governing principle of employment in the great majority of states, which means that anyone can be dismissed at any time for any reason at all—or for no reason. Exceptions are whistleblowers and people with employment contracts. Civil-rights laws also prohibit organizations' dismissing people for their gender, skin color, or physical or mental disability.[107]

Four suggestions for handling a dismissal follow.

Give the Employee a Chance First

If you're dealing with someone who has a problem with absenteeism, alcohol/drug dependency, or the like, articulate to that employee what's wrong with his or her performance, then set up a plan for improvement (which might include counseling). Or if you're dealing with an employee who has a bad cultural or personality fit with the company—a buttoned-down, by-the-book style, say, that's at odds with your flexible, fast-moving organization—have a conversation and give the employee time to find a job elsewhere.[108]

Don't Delay the Dismissal, & Make Sure It's Completely Defensible

If improvements aren't forthcoming, don't carry the employee along because you feel sorry for him or her. Your first duty is to the performance of the organization. Make sure, however, that you've *documented* all the steps taken in advance of the dismissal. Also be sure that they follow the law and all important organizational policies.[109]

Be Aware How Devastating a Dismissal Can Be—Both to the Individual & to Those Remaining

To the person being let go, the event can be as much of a blow as a divorce or a death in the family. Dismissals can also adversely affect those remaining with the company. This is what psychiatrist Manfred Kets de Vries calls *layoff survivor sickness,* which is characterized by anger, depression, fear, guilt, risk aversion, distrust, vulnerability, powerlessness, and loss of motivation. Indeed, a 5-year study by Cigna and the American Management Association found an enormous increase in medical claims, particularly for stress-related illnesses, not only among those dismissed but among continuing employees as well.[110]

Offer Assistance in Finding Another Job

Dismissing a long-standing employee with only a few weeks of severance pay not only hurts the person let go but will also hurt the organization itself, as word gets back to the employees who remain, as well as to outsiders who might be prospective employees. Knowledgeable employers offer assistance in finding another job.

"The best demonstration that a company's values are real," says management scholar Rosabeth Moss Kanter, "is to act on them today even for people who will not be around tomorrow. A company, like a society, can be judged by how it treats its most vulnerable. . . . Bad treatment of departing employees can destroy the commitment of those who stay."[111]

Key Terms Used in This Chapter

360-degree assessment 296

affirmative action 282

assessment center 289

base pay 298

behavioral-description interview 289

behaviorally anchored rating scale (BARS) 295

benefits 299

collective bargaining 280

compensation 298

computer-assisted instruction (CAI) 293

development 292

discrimination 282

employment tests 289

Equal Employment Opportunity (EEO) Commission 280

external recruiting 284

Fair Labor Standards Act 280

forced ranking performance review systems 297

formal appraisals 297

human resource inventory 279

human resource (HR) management 276

informal appraisals 297

internal recruiting 284

job analysis 278

job description 278

job posting 284

job specification 278

National Labor Relations Board 280

objective appraisals 294

orientation 291

performance appraisal 294

Summary

9.1 Strategic Human Resource Management

Human resource management consists of the activities managers perform to plan for, attract, develop, and retain an effective workforce. The purpose of the strategic human resource management process is to get the optimal work performance that will help realize the company's mission and vision.

Two concepts important to human resource management are (1) human capital, the economic or productive potential of employee knowledge, and (2) social capital, the economic or productive potential of strong, trusting, and cooperative relationships.

Strategic human resource planning consists of developing a systematic, comprehensive strategy for (a) understanding current employee needs and (b) predicting future employee needs.

Understanding current employee needs requires first doing a job analysis to determine, by observation and analysis, the basic elements of a job. Then a job description can be written, which summarizes what the holder of the job does and how and why he or she does it. Next comes the job specification, which describes the minimum qualifications a person must have to perform the job successfully.

Predicting employee needs means a manager needs to become knowledgeable about the staffing an organization might need and the likely sources of staffing, perhaps using a human resource inventory to organize this information.

9.2 The Legal Requirements of Human Resource Management

Four areas of human resource law that any manager needs to be aware of are as follows: (1) Labor relations are dictated in part by the National Labor Relations Board, which enforces procedures whereby employees may vote to have a union and for collective bargaining. Collective bargaining consists of negotiations between management and employees about disputes over compensation, benefits, working conditions, and job security. (2) Compensation and benefits are covered by the Social Security Act of 1935 and the Fair Labor Standards Act, which established minimum wage and overtime pay regulations. (3) Health and safety are covered by the Occupational Safety and Health Act of 1970, among other laws. (4) Equal employment opportunity is covered by the Equal Employment Opportunity (EEO) Commission, whose job it is to enforce antidiscrimination and other employment-related laws. Three important concepts covered by EEO are (a) discrimination, which occurs when people are hired or promoted—or denied hiring or promotion—for reasons not relevant to the job, such as skin color or national origin; (b) affirmative action, which focuses on achieving equality of opportunity within an organization; and (c) sexual harassment, which consists of unwanted sexual attention that creates an adverse work environment and which may be of two types—the quid pro quo type, which may cause direct economic injury, and the hostile environment type, in which the person being harassed experiences an offensive work environment.

9.3 Recruitment & Selection: Putting the Right People into the Right Jobs

Recruiting is the process of locating and attracting qualified applicants for jobs open in the organization. (1) Internal recruiting means making people already employed by the organization aware of job openings. (2) External recruiting means attracting job applicants from outside the organization. A useful approach with external recruitment is the realistic job preview, which gives a candidate a picture of both positive and negative features of the job and organization before he or she is hired.

The selection process is the screening of job applicants to hire the best candidates. Three types of selection tools are background information, interviewing, and employment tests. (1) Background information is ascertained through application forms, résumés, and reference checks. (2) Interviewing takes three forms. (a) The unstructured interview involves asking probing questions to find out what the applicant is like. (b) The structured interview involves asking each applicant the same questions and comparing their responses to a standardized set of answers. The first type of structured interview is the situational interview, in which the interview focuses on hypothetical situations. (c) The second type of structured interview is the behavioral-description interview, in which the interviewer explores what applicants have actually done in the past. (3) Employment tests are legally considered to consist of any procedure used in the employment selection decision process, but the three most common tests are ability tests, personality tests, and performance tests. Some companies have assessment centers, in which management candidates participate in activities for a few days while being assessed in performance tests by evaluators. Other tests include drug testing, polygraphs, and genetic screening. With any kind of test, an important legal consideration is the test's reliability, the degree to which a test measures the same thing consistently, and validity, whether the test measures what it purports to measure and is free of bias.

9.4 Orientation, Training, & Development
Three ways in which newcomers are helped to perform their jobs are through orientation, training, and development. (1) Orientation consists of helping the newcomer fit smoothly into the job and organization. Following orientation, the employee should emerge with information about the job routine, the organization's mission and operations, and the organization's work rules and employee benefits. (2) Training must be distinguished from development. Training refers to educating technical and operational employees in how to better do their current jobs. (3) Development is the term describing educating professionals and managers in the skills they need to do their jobs in the future. Both training and development may be effected through on-the-job training methods and off-the-job training methods.

9.5 Performance Appraisal
Performance appraisal consists of assessing an employee's performance and providing him or her with feedback. Appraisals are of two general types—objective and subjective. Two good reasons for having objective appraisals are that they measure results and they are harder to challenge legally. (1) Objective appraisals are based on facts and are often numerical. An example is management by objectives. (2) Subjective appraisals are based on a manager's perceptions of an employee's traits or behaviors. Trait appraisals are ratings of subjective attributes such as attitude and leadership. Behavioral appraisals measure specific, observable aspects of performance. An example is the behaviorally anchored rating scale (BARS), which rates employee gradations in performance according to scales of specific behaviors.

Most performance appraisals are made by managers, but they may also be made by co-workers and subordinates, customers and clients, and employees themselves (self-appraisals). Sometimes all of these may be used, in a technique called the 360-degree assessment, in which employees are appraised not only by their managerial superiors but also by their peers, subordinates, and sometimes clients. In another evaluation technique, forced ranking performance review systems, all employees within a business unit are ranked against one another, and grades are distributed along some sort of bell curve.

Effective performance feedback can be effected in two ways: (1) Formal appraisals are conducted at specific times throughout the year and are based on performance measures that have been established in advance. (2) Informal appraisals are conducted on an unscheduled basis and consist of less rigorous indications of employee performance.

 9.6 Managing an Effective Workforce: Compensation & Benefits
Compensation has three parts: wages or salaries, incentives, and benefits. (1) In the category of wages or salaries, the concept of base pay consists of the basic wage or salary paid employees in exchange for doing their jobs. (2) Incentives include commissions, bonuses, profit-sharing plans, and stock options. (3) Benefits are additional nonmonetary forms of compensation, such as health insurance, retirement plans, and family leave.

 9.7 Managing Promotions, Transfers, Disciplining, & Dismissals
Managers must manage promotions, transfers, disciplining, and dismissals. (1) In considering promotions, managers must be concerned about fairness, nondiscrimination, and other employees' resentment. (2) Transfers, or moving employees to a different job with similar responsibility, may take place in order to solve organizational problems, broaden managers' experience, retain managers' interest and motivation, and solve some employee problems. (3) Poor-performing employees may need to be disciplined or demoted. (4) Dismissals may consist of layoffs, downsizings, or firings.

Management in Action

How Should Managers Fire Good Workers Who Don't Fit?

Valerie Frederickson, a human-resources consultant in Silicon Valley, had a delicate problem: Her office administrator was smart and well-spoken, but after two months on the job, she didn't seem to like the work. "We needed to have her do things like data entry and clean the refrigerator, and she wanted to plan events for us," Ms. Frederickson says.

So Ms. Frederickson decided to let the administrator go—gently. She gave the woman a small amount of severance pay, helped her get a new job and assured her that the firing wasn't personal. "I told her, 'I like you a lot, and I think of you like a little sister, but I don't want you working here any more,'" Ms. Frederickson recalls.

That humane approach to firing may seem like common sense. But human-resources professionals say that figuring out how to handle employees who aren't fitting into the workplace is one of the trickiest tasks a manager can face.

Employers are well-schooled in how to eliminate jobs or fire poor performers. Yet they often don't know what to do with people who are doing their work passably, or even better, but aren't suited for the job, for reasons ranging from personal chemistry to mismatched skills.

In that gray area, employers often fumble, either keeping people on because they don't know what else to do, or seeking evidence of poor performance—even when that isn't the real issue. Badly handled firings can damage workplace morale, traumatize the employee, and end up in court, says Maureen Clark, a human-resources consultant in Menlo Park, Calif., who is asked often to investigate when things go wrong.

Employers need a graceful way to say, "It's not working; it's not your fault; let's figure out how to get you somewhere else," Ms. Clark says.

U.S. employers generally can fire employees not protected by a labor contract without a reason. In practice, however, courts often act to protect employees, faulting companies for firing longtime workers or those who have had good performance reviews. Judges also scrutinize disputed firings to ensure there was no race, gender, or other discrimination, employment attorneys say.

At the same time, increasing job mobility and changing skill requirements are producing more personnel problems that "don't fit in the box," says Rhoma Young, a human-resources consultant in Oakland, Calif.

In one case Ms. Young is investigating for a high-technology concern, the company shifted an engineer out of a programming position where he was doing well and into a job with more responsibility that required communication skills he lacked. The stress, combined with pressure from management, led the engineer to take several months of disability leave, and eventually the situation cost him his job. Now, he is threatening to sue.

Employment attorneys and human-resources consultants say companies can stay out of trouble by following some guidelines when thinking of firing a worker who doesn't fit in.

Managers should make sure they understand the problem—and be certain that the employee does, too. Sometimes bosses haven't properly explained what they want, or what the job requires, Ms. Young says.

Marlene Muraco, an attorney at labor-law specialist Littler Mendelson in San Jose, Calif., suggests considering options other than termination, such as training, a different post or another boss.

At Banco Popular North America, a unit of Puerto Rico's Popular Inc., human-resources chief Jeannette Frett says managers are instructed to tell employees who aren't fitting in exactly where they aren't meeting expectations and to offer training to fix the problem before considering dismissal. That has been important, because jobs at the bank have changed a lot in the past few years, as Banco Popular has snapped up other lenders—along with their staff—and has pushed its bankers to market the bank's services more aggressively.

If an employee must be fired, be honest and nice, experts say. Ms. Frett says Banco Popular gives employees it is letting go as much notice as possible, and sometimes it offers outplacement counseling or severance pay. "They walk out with their dignity and respect," Ms. Frett says.

Ms. Clark, the human-resources consultant, advises clients to specify in employee handbooks that the company will offer support to workers who are fired because they don't fit in.

One of those clients, the chief executive of public relations firm McGrath/Power in Silicon Valley, used the clause a few years ago when he fired a new account executive. Jonathan Bloom says the executive wasn't as experienced as he had hoped, and he felt that she was disturbing other employees by gossiping a lot. The company gave her a small severance payment and agreed with her about how to describe the dismissal.

"The more honest you are, the smoother the process tends to go," Mr. Bloom says.

Managers should remember that employees who aren't fitting in well are often unhappy themselves and may agree that they would be better off elsewhere, says Ms. Frederickson, the recruiter who fired her office administrator. "You want them to admit it is a bad fit and get out of there," she says.

Ms. Frederickson should know: She was fired years ago from a human-resources firm, largely because she didn't get along with her boss. She started her own firm later and competes with her former employer.

For Discussion

1. How might companies inadvertently discriminate when firing good employees who don't fit? Explain.

2. How can an employer use its recruitment and selection process to minimize the problem of hiring people who don't fit? Provide specific recommendations.

3. How can companies revise their performance appraisal procedures and processes to reduce the problem of employing people who don't fit? Discuss your recommendations.

4. Why is it hard for managers to fire employees who don't fit in? What can be done to overcome these causes? Explain.

Source: Excerpted from Phred Dvorak, "Firing Good Workers Who Are a Bad Fit," *The Wall Street Journal,* May 1, 2006, p. B5. Copyright © 2006 by Dow Jones & Company, Inc. Reproduced with permission of Dow Jones & Company, Inc. via Copyright Clearance Center.

Self-Assessment

HR 101: An Overview

Objectives

1. To learn that there is more to HR than recruitment and hiring.

2. To assess your skills and determine if a career in HR is right for you.

Introduction

Your chosen career should optimally be based on your interests. The HR field, for example, offers many different career paths that require many different skills. The purpose of this exercise is to help you become familiar with the different career paths available to an HR professional and to see which path best fits your interests. This experience may help you decide if an HR career is right for you.

Among the professionals in the HR field are the following:

The HR generalist: HR generalists take on many different roles, whether negotiating a company's employee benefits package or interviewing a candidate for a director-level position. An HR generalist is supposed to be flexible and able to change gears at a moment's notice.

Compensation professional: Compensation professionals, who are very much in demand, design reward systems that attract, retain, and motivate employees. The job requires not only good technical skills but good people skills as well, a rare combination. It also requires a great deal of number crunching, creativity, and ingenuity, because a compensation package that might work for one employee might not work for another.

HRIS professional: HRIS stands for Human Resource Information Systems. With technology now such a key part of human resources, HRIS products help companies manage their personnel. Because the information systems are now so sophisticated, there is great demand for experienced HRIS professionals, who must be very detail oriented and, of course, enjoy working with computers. Such professionals are involved in product selection, systems customization, implementation, and ongoing administration.

Benefits professional: This individual is responsible for designing and implementing benefits plans. The job requires strong technical and communication skills.

Training and development professional: This individual is responsible for building environments that foster learning and management and leadership development. People in this field may be involved in distance learning programs as well as on-site, computer-based training programs.

Organizational development professional: Organizational development professionals work with top management to make sure that the organizational design sticks to the company's mission, vision, and goals. Besides doing some training and development, an OD professional must be able to embrace change and work long hours.

Instructions

Ask yourself the following questions and circle whether the statement applies to you. Once you have answered all of the questions, use the interpretation guidelines to analyze your responses and determine if a career in HR is right for you.

1.	Do I enjoy changing gears on a moment's notice?	Yes	No
2.	Am I open to learning about areas in which I currently have no expertise?	Yes	No
3.	Am I comfortable leaving a project unfinished to handle emergency situations?	Yes	No
4.	Do I consider myself fairly flexible?	Yes	No
5.	Am I good at creatively solving problems when resources and instructions are scarce?	Yes	No
6.	Do I have an aptitude for numbers?	Yes	No
7.	Am I comfortable seeing other people's salaries?	Yes	No
8.	Do I have strong communication skills?	Yes	No
9.	Do I have strong computer skills?	Yes	No
10.	Am I comfortable working at a computer all day?	Yes	No
11.	Am I well organized?	Yes	No
12.	Am I detail oriented?	Yes	No
13.	Am I comfortable constantly reworking projects I thought were already done?	Yes	No

		Yes	No
14.	Am I willing to pay for and donate my free time to professional certifications?	Yes	No
15.	Am I good at taking complex ideas and making them understandable to the average person?	Yes	No
16.	Am I good at expressing my ideas and getting people to go along with them?	Yes	No
17.	Am I a creative person with strong computer skills?	Yes	No
18.	Am I comfortable in front of an audience?	Yes	No
19.	Am I comfortable working one very long project instead of lots of small projects?	Yes	No
20.	Am I passionate about learning and about teaching others?	Yes	No
21.	Can I handle change? Can I handle it well?	Yes	No
22.	Do I enjoy pulling together pieces of a puzzle?	Yes	No
23.	Do I perform well in times of stress?	Yes	No
24.	Am I a big-picture person?	Yes	No

Interpretation

If you answered "yes" to three or more of questions 1–4 (which apply to the HR generalist), three or more of questions 5–8 (compensation professional), three or more of questions 9–12 (HRIS professional), three or more of questions 13–16 (benefits professional), three or more of questions 17–20 (training and development professional), and three or more of questions 21–24 (organizational development professional), then you are well suited for the field of HR.

If you answered "no" to most of the previous 24 questions, the field of HR may not be right for you. (However, since this is only a small sampling of the many aspects of this field, there may still be a place for you in HR.)

Questions for Discussion

1. To what extent did the results fit your interests? Explain.

2. Look at the top two areas of HR for which you tested as being best suited. Look over the descriptions of these fields. What skills do you need to have to be successful? Describe.

3. Even if you do not pursue a career in HR, which skills do you feel you should continue to develop? Explain.

Adapted from R.C. Matuson, "HR 101: An Overview, Parts I and II," *Monster HR, www.monster.com,* June 2002.

Ethical Dilemma

More Companies Want the FBI to Screen Employees for Terrorist Connections

A wide range of industry groups, from trucking associations to sporting-event organizers, are trying to gain access to the FBI's closely guarded data on suspected terrorists and criminals in an effort to screen their own employees.

The American Trucking Association, for one, is lobbying Congress to give it authority to go directly to the Federal Bureau of Investigation with names and fingerprints of drivers, loading-dock workers, and job applicants of its member companies. . . .

Fueling this push is the supposition that, next time around, terrorists may attack something besides an airplane. But allowing companies to tap into FBI intelligence banks opens a can of worms both for the government and civil liberties advocates. Unions protest that employers could use the system to find old skeletons in people's closets and use them as a pretext for dismissal. . . .

Giving an industry access to the FBI lists typically requires an act of Congress or a new federal regulation. Some industries, such as banking, airlines, and nuclear power plants, already have such access. . . .

Of particular interest to this latest round of companies are the FBI's watch lists of suspected terrorists, including people who may have infiltrated the American workplace years ago as "sleeper" agents. One of these lists, from the State Department, contains 64,000 names from around the world. The FBI keeps its own list and won't say how many people are on it. . . .

Although terrorists typically are trained to avoid detection, at least a few of the Sept. 11 hijackers were on watchlists because their names had popped up in connection with prior attacks: Mohamed Atta had been flagged by the Customs Service, and Khalid al-Midhar was on a CIA list.

FBI background checks should turn up anybody with, among other things, an arrest record, criminal conviction, or protective order filed against them. Not all this information is readily accessible to those outside the agency, and companies are concerned about missing such information in a check on their own. . . .

But truckers and others who want FBI background checks say the pros outweigh the cons. Tony Chrestman, president of the trucking unit of Ruan Transportation Management Systems, says: "Previously, I would never have thought about anyone taking one of our loads of propane and running it into a building. There's got to be improvements to background checks."

Solving the Dilemma

What would you do if you were evaluating the trucking industry's desire for FBI background checks?

1. Allow the trucking industry to obtain FBI background checks.
2. Not allow the trucking industry access to FBI records because such information might adversely affect employment conditions for potential and existing employees.
3. Allow the trucking industry to obtain limited information (that is, only information pertaining to terrorism) about people.
4. Invent other options. Explain.

Source: Excerpted from Ana Davis, "Companies Want the FBI to Screen Employees for Suspected Terrorists," *The Wall Street Journal*, February 6, 2002, pp. B1, B4. Copyright © 2002 by Dow Jones & Company, Inc. Reproduced with permisssion of Dow Jones & Company, Inc. via Copyright Clearance Center.

Organizational Change & Innovation

Lifelong Challenges for the Exceptional Manager

Major Questions You Should Be Able to Answer

10.1 The Nature of Change in Organizations
Major Question: Since change is always with us, what should I understand about it?

10.2 Organization Development: What It Is, What It Can Do
Major Question: What are the uses of OD, and how effective is it?

10.3 Promoting Innovation within the Organization
Major Question: What do I need to know to encourage innovation?

10.4 The Threat of Change: Managing Employee Fear & Resistance
Major Question: How are employees threatened by change, and how can I help them adjust?

Managing for Innovation & Change Takes a Careful Hand

"What I try to do is go out and grab lightning every day."

That's the way Terry Fadem, head of business development at DuPont Co., describes the company's never-ending search for tomorrow's breakthroughs.[1]

Managing for innovation and change takes a careful hand. "Even when their jobs depend on adopting and inventing new maneuvers," says columnist Carol Hymowitz, "most workers hold fast to old ones. The majority either are overwhelmed when asked to do things differently or become entrenched, clinging harder to the past. . . ."[2]

Because the revolution in technology is inflicting what Tom Peters calls Discontinuous Times, or "a brawl with no rules," dealing with change is an ongoing challenge for every manager.[3] "The one constant factor in business today is we live in a perpetual hurricane season," says Mellon Bank Corp. Vice Chairman Martin McGuinn. "A leader's job is less about getting through the current storm and more about enabling people to navigate the ongoing series of storms."[4]

Some ways to deal with change and innovation:[5]

- **Allow room for failure.** "If somebody has an idea, don't stomp on it," says a psychologist and developer of ideas at Intuit, the software company famous for TurboTax and QuickBooks. "It's more important to get the stupidest idea out there and build on it than not to have it in the first place."[6] At Intuit, failure is very much an option as long as one learns from it.

- **Give one consistent explanation for the change.** When a company is undergoing change, myriad rumors will fly and employees will be uneasy; you and the managers who report to you need to give one consistent explanation. In McGuinn's case, the explanation for overhauling Mellon Bank's retail division was "We want to be the best retailer in financial services."

- **Look for opportunities in unconventional ways.** Most "new" products and services are really knockoffs or marginal variations of the things already on the market and hence are doomed to failure, says Robert Cooper, professor of marketing at Ontario's McMaster University. This doesn't mean, of course, that there isn't room for leveraging existing products with utterly unoriginal ideas. But most people are blinded by the limits of conventional wisdom and their own experience and fail to see huge potential markets in unconventional concepts. Try this advice from a Yale entrepreneurship instructor: Write down every hassle you encounter during the day. "At the end of the month, you will have 20 business ideas," he says, "and some of them will work."[7]

- **Have the courage to follow your ideas.** This may be the hardest job of all—trying to convince others that your ideas for change are feasible, especially if the ideas are radical. This may mean working to gain allies within the organization, standing up to intimidating competitors inside and out, and perhaps being prepared to follow a lonely course for a long time.[8]

- **Allow grieving, then move on.** Managers overseeing change need to give long-term employees a chance to grieve over the loss of the old ways, says McGuinn, who found that staffers were more willing to change after they had a chance to vent their fears.

For Discussion If you were going to instill a climate of innovation in a company you worked for, what kinds of things would you do?

forecast

What's Ahead in This Chapter

In this chapter, we consider the nature of change in organizations, including the two types of change—reactive and proactive—and the forces for change originating outside and inside the organization. We describe the four areas in which change is often needed: people, technology, structure, and strategy. We then discuss organizational development, a set of techniques for implementing planned change. We next discuss how to promote innovation within an organization. Finally, we explore the threat of change and how you can manage employee fear and resistance.

Since change is always with us, what should I
understand about it?

THE BIG PICTURE

Two types of change are reactive and proactive. Forces for change may consist of forces
outside the organization—demographic characteristics, market changes, technological
advancements, and social and political pressures. Or they may be forces inside the
organization—employee problems and managers' behavior. Four areas in which change
is often needed are people, technology, structure, and strategy.

People are generally uncomfortable about change, even change in apparently minor
matters. Philosopher Eric Hoffer told how as a younger man he spent a good part
of one year as an agricultural worker picking peas, starting in southern California in
January and working his way northward. He picked the last of the peas in June,
then moved to another area where, for the first time, he was required to pick string
beans. "I still remember," he wrote, "how hesitant I was that first morning as I was
about to address myself to the string bean vines. Would I be able to pick string
beans? Even the change from peas to string beans had in it elements of fear."[9]

If small changes can cause uneasiness, large changes can cause considerable
stress. And as a manager, you will no doubt have to deal with both.

Fundamental Change: What Will You Be Called On to Deal With?

"It is hard to predict, especially the future," physicist Niels Bohr is supposed to
have quipped.

But it is possible to identify and prepare for *the future that has already happened*,
in the words of management theorist Peter Drucker, by looking at some of the fundamental changes that are happening now.[10] Declining population in developed
countries. More diversity in the workforce. The ascent of knowledge work. Increased
globalization. Awareness of global warming and need for sustainability. The rise of
business-to-business (B2B) technology. Digital long-distance networks. The increase
in data storage. The capturing of customer-specific information. The customization
of mass goods. Sales in the form of auctions instead of fixed prices.[11]

Beyond these overarching trends there are also some supertrends shaping the
future of business:[12]

I. The Marketplace Is Becoming More Segmented & Moving Toward More
Niche Products
In the recent past, managers could think in terms of mass
markets—mass communication, mass behavior, and mass values. Now we have "de-
massification," with customer groups becoming segmented into smaller and more
specialized groups responding to more narrowly targeted commercial messages. "Our
culture and economy are increasingly shifting away from a focus on a relatively small
number of hits (mainstream products and markets) . . . and moving toward a huge
number of niches," says Chris Anderson in *The Long Tail*. "In an era without the
constraints of physical shelf space and other bottlenecks of distribution, narrowly
targeted goods and services can be as economically attractive as mainstream fare."[13]
Or, as the book's subtitle states, "the future of business is selling less of more."

Example: In the Internet Age, retailers like Amazon.com and Apple Computer are not constrained by physical shelf space and can offer consumers a much

wider variety of products, yet small sales, one or two rather than millions of items at a time, can produce big profits.

2. There Are More Competitors Offering Targeted Products, Requiring Faster Speed-to-Market

Companies offering a broad range of products or services are now experiencing intense pressure from competitors offering specialized solutions—and beating them to the punch by devising novel speed-to-market strategies. Indeed, "Speed is emerging as the ultimate competitive weapon," says one report. "Some of the world's most successful companies are proving to be expert at spotting new opportunities, marshaling their forces, and bringing to market new products or services in a flash."[14]

Example: Virgin Group Ltd., headed by Sir Richard Branson, is known mainly for its music and airline businesses, but it has entered several new businesses one after the other—mobile phones, credit cards, hotels, games, trains, even space travel—and very quickly. Virgin Comics, aimed at India's multibillion-dollar comics market, went from idea to public announcement in less than 11 months.

3. Some Traditional Companies May Not Survive Radically Innovative Change

In *The Innovator's Dilemma: When New Technologies Cause Great Firms to Fail,* Clayton Carlson, a Harvard Business School professor, argues that when successful companies are confronted with a giant technological leap that transforms their markets, all choices are bad ones. Indeed, he thinks, it's very difficult for an existing successful company to take full advantage of a technological breakthrough such as digitalization—what he calls "disruptive innovation." Instead, he argues that such a company should set up an entirely separate organization that can operate much like a startup.[15]

Example: Eastman Kodak found its sales hit $14 billion in 1999 and dropped to $13.3 billion in 2003 as digital cameras began to take their toll on the chemical-based film business. The company quit making big investments in film and shifted its resources to digital cameras and accessories, digital health-imaging technologies, and inkjet printing and liquid displays. After a $3.4 billion restructuring, it finished 2007 with a jump in profit.[16]

Rising to the challenge. "Faster times demand faster technology," says Kodak's electronic billboard on the New York Marriott Marquis hotel, indicating that the company is inventing innovating solutions to the digital revolution. Do you think this once-traditional company can survive radically innovative change?

4. China, India, & Other Offshore Suppliers Are Changing the Way We Work

As we said in Chapter 2, globalization and outsourcing are transforming whole industries and changing the way we work. China, India, Mexico, the Philippines, and other countries offer workers and even professionals willing to work twice as hard for half the pay, giving American businesses substantial labor savings. These developing nations also, says *BusinessWeek,* offer "enormous gains in efficiency, productivity, quality, and revenues that can be achieved by fully leveraging offshore talent."[17] While unquestionably some American jobs are lost, others become more productive, with some engineers and salespeople, for example, being liberated from routine tasks so that they can spend more time innovating and dealing with customers.

Example: Querétaro is not a place you would probably go for spring break, but it is rapidly becoming known for something not normally associated with Mexico: aircraft construction. American aircraft makers from Bombardier to Cessna Aircraft to Hawker Beechcraft have various kinds of subassembly work here, where wages are lower but skill levels are not.[18] But if some manufacturing jobs have moved cross-border, so have many customers for American products. Houston-based SolArt, which offers energy management software and services to

U.S. airlines, found opportunities to expand abroad, and now has new clients such as Singapore Airlines. [19] As often as not, however, overseas firms now look to the United States for talented workers, especially in technology and finance, as has been the case with information-technology companies in Ireland.[20]

5. Knowledge, Not Information, Is Becoming the New Competitive Advantage "Information is rapidly becoming a profitless commodity, and knowledge is becoming the new competitive advantage," says San Diego management consultant Karl Albrecht.[21] That is, as information technology does more of the work formerly done by humans, even in high-tech areas (such as sorting data for relevance), many low-level employees previously thought of as knowledge workers are now being recognized as "data workers," who contribute very little added value to the processing of information. Unlike routine information handling, knowledge work is analytic and involves problem solving and abstract reasoning—exactly the kind of thing required of skillful managers, professionals, salespeople, and financial analysts. As futurists Alvin and Heidi Toffler suggest, knowledge work drives the future and creates wealth.[22]

Example: Many *back-office* systems and functions, those the customer does not see, such as inventory management and accounts payable, are rapidly being outsourced, although even some tasks of software engineers and other technical experts are also being sent overseas.

Clearly, we are all in for an interesting ride.

Two Types of Change: Reactive versus Proactive

As a manager, you will typically have to deal with two types of change: *reactive* and *proactive*.

I. Reactive Change: Responding to Unanticipated Problems & Opportunities When managers talk about "putting out fires," they are talking about *reactive change*, **making changes in response to problems or opportunities as they arise.** When you have to respond to surprises, there is usually less time to get all the information and resources you need to adequately manage the change, and serious mistakes may be made. Nevertheless, some of the best stories in business concern the intelligent management of unanticipated calamities.

Example

Reactive Change: The Print Media Deal with Changing Reader Habits

Crises can happen quickly and without warning, and many companies have shown they don't deal with them well, as happened with Exxon's handling of the 1989 *Exxon Valdez* oil spill in the Gulf of Alaska, Coca-Cola's reactions to the 1999 illness in Europe attributed to bottlers in Belgium and France, and Bausch & Lomb's delay in 2006 in withdrawing a contaminated contact lens cleaner. (You can find out about these mishaps through an online search.)

However, some crises happen gradually, giving companies plenty of time, one would think, to come up with an appropriate solution strategy. One that is happening today is the crisis in print media, especially newspapers and magazines, brought about by the ascendancy of the Internet. According to the 2008 annual *State of the Media* report by the Project for Excellence in Journalism, traditional mainstream news media—newspapers, magazines, TV, and radio news—are losing money.[23] The reasons: (1) Consumers still like the media, but they prefer to get their information from free sources, and the mainstream media don't know how to get online customers to pay. (Only *The Wall Street Journal* has been successful in charging for online viewing of the news.) (2) In addition to losing circulation (a drop of 2.5% nationally in 2007), newspapers are also losing advertising (about a 7% decline since 2005) to digital media.

No wonder the 90-year-old Madison, Wisconsin, daily *The Capital Times* stopped putting out a print version and instead publishes its daily report on the Web. (It also continues to produce two print products, a free weekly entertainment and a news weekly, delivered in a rival cross-town paper.)[24] In the future, technology forecasters and journalism researchers predict, we won't use newspapers or TV programs for our news. Rather, says one account, "we'll be more likely to find a news story through a link emailed from a friend, in a blog post, or from a syndicated news feed. . . . The next decade will also see the spread of powerful portable devices as easy to read and navigate as a print newspaper."[25]

Your Call

Newspapers seem to have lost control of their essential product—well-researched and written information prepared by trained observers (something bloggers and citizen-journalism Web sites generally can't offer)—when they agreed to let themselves be put online for free, on the theory that it would promote interest in the printed paper. Publishers have mainly reacted to the loss of circulation and advertising by pruning staffs and reducing news coverage—thereby putting at risk the very thing they have to sell. How do you think newspapers *should* have reacted to the Internet threat, and is it too late for them to change?

2. Proactive Change: Managing Anticipated Problems & Opportunities

In contrast to reactive change, *proactive change* or planned change involves making carefully thought-out changes in anticipation of possible or expected problems or opportunities.[26]

Example

Proactive Change: Being Ahead of the Curve with Natural Beef

The high-desert cattle ranch, 180 miles southeast of Denver in Colorado's San Luis Valley, is the home of Coleman Natural Foods, founded by Mel Coleman Sr. in 1979 on the ranch of his ancestors, who had moved there in 1875. Coleman sold "natural" beef back when most shoppers were unaware of the term. On a sales trip in the 1980s, Coleman would pitch grocers that his cows were not given antibiotics and growth hormones like those of the big producers, but were fed a vegetarian diet.

It took Coleman years to win converts, says a *New York Times* story, "not only among retailers but also among consumers and government regulators. Now, paradoxically, natural and organic meats have become so popular that even the big conventional meat producers are getting into the business, and Coleman is left in the unexpected position of scrambling for shelf space."[27]

The word "natural" can signify many things—that the animals were not given hormones or antibiotics, not fed rendered animal by-products, or were raised entirely out of doors—or it can mean nothing at all. "Organic," however, means the meat adheres to more stringent standards—no use of antibiotics, growth hormones, or parasite-killing chemicals and animals were given feed grown without pesticides or chemical fertilizers.[28] Regardless, shoppers have learned to pay a premium, as much as 50% more, particularly for organic beef. Indeed, organic meat is now the fastest-growing segment of the organic food business. The Coleman ranch is now run by Mel Coleman Jr., but his father's legacy lives on. "Mel Sr. was one of the pioneers to develop a truly natural meat company," says an admirer.

Your Call

Most instances of proactive change involve technology companies, symbolized by Apple's willingness to make sharp turns in direction—to be a "cross-boundary disrupter," in one observer's phrase.[29] In 2007, Apple dropped "Computer" from its name, signaling a move beyond computers—the Apple I, Apple II, Macintosh, and so on—into products intended for what it calls "the digital lifestyle," as represented by the iPod and the iPhone. Can you think of other examples of proactive change?

The Forces for Change: Outside & Inside the Organization

How do managers know when their organizations need to change? The answers aren't clear-cut, but you can get clues by monitoring the forces for change—both outside and inside the organization. *(See Figure 10.1, next page.)*

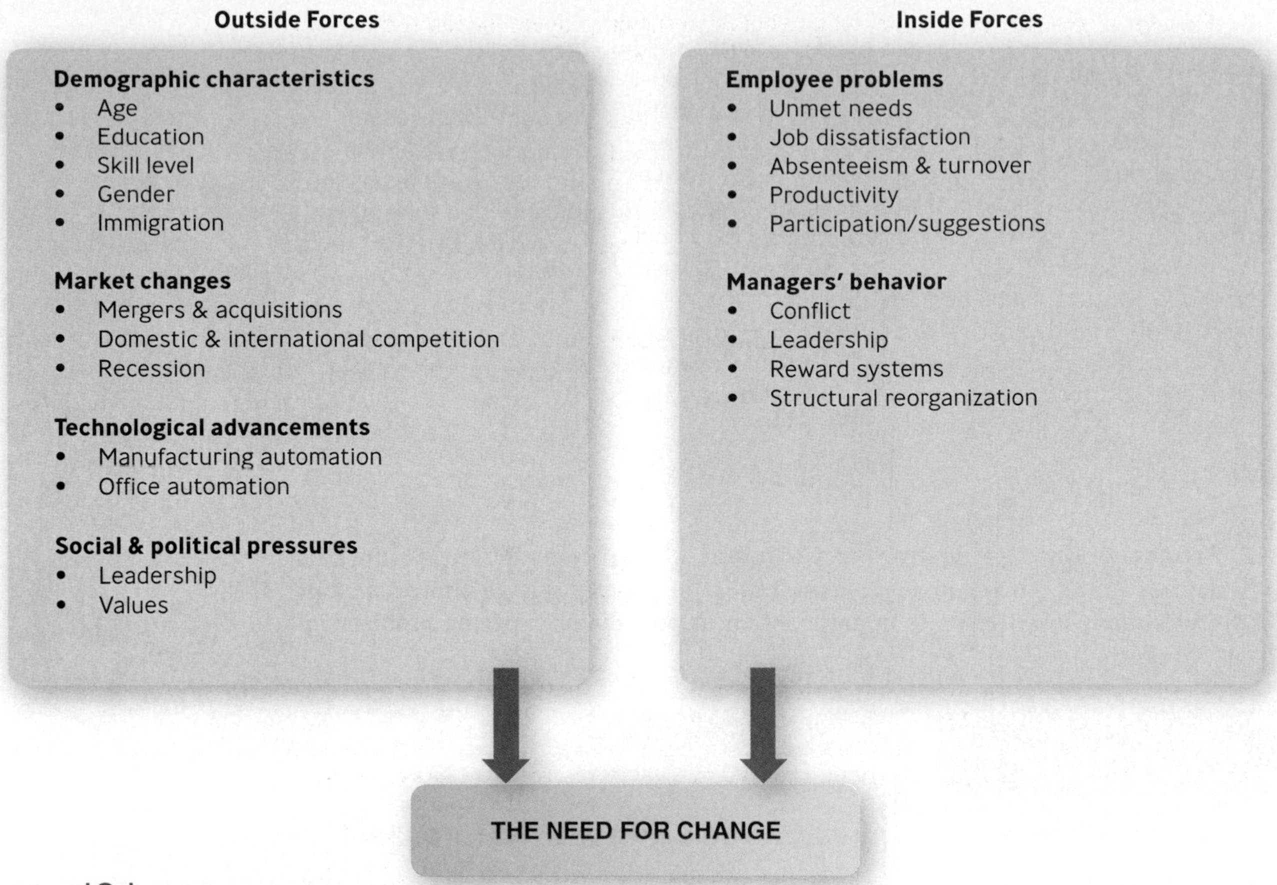

Outside Forces

Demographic characteristics
- Age
- Education
- Skill level
- Gender
- Immigration

Market changes
- Mergers & acquisitions
- Domestic & international competition
- Recession

Technological advancements
- Manufacturing automation
- Office automation

Social & political pressures
- Leadership
- Values

Inside Forces

Employee problems
- Unmet needs
- Job dissatisfaction
- Absenteeism & turnover
- Productivity
- Participation/suggestions

Managers' behavior
- Conflict
- Leadership
- Reward systems
- Structural reorganization

THE NEED FOR CHANGE

figure 10.1

FORCES FOR CHANGE OUTSIDE AND INSIDE THE ORGANIZATION

Forces Originating Outside the Organization External forces consist of four types, as follows.

1. Demographic Characteristics Earlier we discussed the demographic changes occurring in the U.S. workforce. We've pointed out that the workforce is now more diverse, and organizations need to effectively manage this diversity.

2. Market Changes As discussed in Chapter 4, the global economy is forcing companies to change the way they do business, with U.S. companies forging new partnerships and alliances with employees, suppliers, and competitors. This force has led Nokia to lose 13% market share in the United States because Nokia has been slow to collaborate with AT&T and Verizon, the dominant U.S. wireless carriers.[30]

3. Technological Advancements Information technology may be one of the greatest forces for productivity in our lifetime. But it can also create headaches.

4. Social & Political Pressures Social events can create great pressures. Changing drinking habits, for example, have led to a rise in wine sales and a decline in whiskey sales.

Forces Originating Inside the Organization Internal forces affecting organizations may be subtle, such as low job satisfaction, or more dramatic, such as constant labor-management conflict. Internal forces may be of the two following types.

Test Your Knowledge:
Macroenvironmental Forces

1. Employee Problems Is there a gap between the employees' needs and desires and the organization's needs and desires? Job dissatisfaction—as expressed through high absenteeism and turnover—can be a major signal of the need for change. Organizations may respond by addressing job design, reducing employees' role conflicts, and dealing with work overload, to mention a few matters.

For instance, when Martin McGuinn was reorganizing the retail division of Mellon Bank, many of the employees who were upset over expanded banking hours were appeased when they were given more freedom to arrange their own schedules.

2. Managers' Behavior Excessive conflict between managers and employees may be another indicator that change is needed. Perhaps there is a personality conflict, so that an employee transfer may be needed. Or perhaps some interpersonal training is required.

Phil Dusenberry, chairman of ad agency BBDO, says that he used to have a gentle way of letting people down because he didn't want to hurt their feelings. Often, however, this would simply confuse people. "They'd go off thinking that I liked their work even if I didn't," he says. "Over time I realized that dealing in terms of black and white wasn't a bad thing. I became much more direct."[31]

Areas in Which Change Is Often Needed: People, Technology, Structure, & Strategy

Change can involve any part of the organization. However, the four areas in which change is most apt to be needed are *people, technology, structure,* and *strategy.*

1. Changing People Even in a two-person organization, people changes may be required. The changes may take the following forms:

- **Perceptions.** Employees might feel they are underpaid for what they do. Managers might be able to show that pay and benefits are comparable or superior to those offered by competitors.

- **Attitudes.** In old-line manufacturing industries, employees may feel that it is the nature of things that they should be in an adversarial relationship with their managers. It may be up to management to try to change the culture and the attitudes by using educational techniques to show why the old labor wars should become a thing of the past.

- **Performance.** Should an organization pay the people who contract to wash its windows by the hour? by the window? or by the total job? Will one method cause them to work fast and sloppily but cost less? Will one cause them to do pristine windows but cost too much? It's often a major challenge to find incentives to improve people's performance.

- **Skills.** Altering or improving skill levels is often an ongoing challenge, particularly these days, when new forms of technology can change an organization's way of doing business, as we describe next.

2. Changing Technology Technology is a major area of change for many organizations. *Technology* **is not just computer technology; it is any machine or process that enables an organization to gain a competitive advantage in changing materials used to produce a finished product.** Breweries, for example, used to make beer by letting malted cereal grain flavored with hops brew slowly by fermentation; nowadays, the process is often sped up by the direct injection of carbonation (from carbon dioxide) into the process.

Cell phone power. Camera phones have become commonplace, but the cell phone is still evolving—and rapidly. In South Korea, where cell phones operate at broadband speeds, young commuters on the subway are forsaking print matter and occupying themselves with cell phone news services, videos, and music downloads, as well as e-mail and phone calls. Cell phones there can double as credit cards: a consumer can point his or her phone at an infrared terminal on a store counter, which sends credit card information straight to the card company. In the future, cell phones might also take the place of ID cards such as driver's licenses. When cell phones and accompanying text-messaging features are joined to advanced search engines and huge databases the technology will no doubt stand several industries on their heads. Which ones do you think these might be?

Example

Changing Technology: Web 2.0 Could Radically Alter How Business Is Done

Futurist Paul Saffo, director of the think tank Institute for the Future in Menlo Park, California, says that new technologies lead to new products. The invention of television, for example, led to TV dinners and TV trays. The invention of the iPod led to the selling of music singles—something that hadn't happened since the 45 rpm record. "Each time it gets cheaper to do something," says Saffo, "you get more players. It's irreversibly more complex."[32]

Thus, the original World Wide Web has led to what is known as Web 2.0, a second generation of Internet-based services that lets people collaborate and share information online in a new way.[33] Among the results are social networking sites (MySpace, Facebook) photo-sharing sites (Flickr), and wikis (group-editable Web pages, such as the reference source Wikipedia), which all demand active participation and social interaction. Web 2.0 services have also come into the business world, with wikis, for example, being used by the Walt Disney Co. and other firms to enhance collaboration. Other companies are using social networking services such as LinkedIn Corp to gain sales leads and hiring prospects. The "mobile Web," involving wireless communication and mobile gadgets (Blackberrys, digital-music players), will change commerce, allowing wireless shopping.[34] "In essence," says a *BusinessWeek* article, "these services are coalescing into one giant computer that anyone with access to an Internet-connected PC can use, from anywhere in the world."[35]

A significant structural result of Web 2.0 will be a further assault on conventional reporting arrangements, already being transformed by globalization and outsourcing. That is, the new freeform technologies will help to further flatten clear lines of authority between managers and employees and to reduce organizational boundaries between the company and its partners and customers.

Your Call

What possibilities do you see for applying the social networking services, photo-sharing sites, blogs, and wikis you are familiar with as a college student to business uses?

3. Changing Structure   When one organization acquires another, the structure often changes—perhaps from a divisional structure, say, to a matrix structure. The recent trend is toward "flattening the hierarchy," eliminating several middle layers of management, and to using work teams linked by electronic networks.

4. Changing Strategy   Shifts in the marketplace often may lead organizations to have to change their strategy. As a result of the sudden rise in popularity of the Netscape Navigator Web browser, Microsoft Corp. found itself having to shift from a PC-based strategy to an Internet strategy. ●

IO.2 ORGANIZATION DEVELOPMENT: WHAT IT IS, WHAT IT CAN DO

What are the uses of OD, and how effective is it?

major question?

THE BIG PICTURE

Organization development (OD) is a set of techniques for implementing change, such as managing conflict, revitalizing organizations, and adapting to mergers. OD has three steps: diagnosis, intervention, and evaluation. Four factors have been found to make OD programs effective.

Organization development (OD) **is a set of techniques for implementing planned change to make people and organizations more effective.** Note the inclusion of people in this definition. OD focuses specifically on people in the change process. Often OD is put into practice by a person known as a *change agent,* **a consultant with a background in behavioral sciences who can be a catalyst in helping organizations deal with old problems in new ways.**

What Can OD Be Used For?

OD can be used to address the following three matters:

I. Managing Conflict   Conflict is inherent in most organizations. Sometimes an OD expert in the guise of an executive coach will be brought in to help advise an executive on how to improve relationships with others in the organization.

For instance, David Hitz and Michael Malcolm, two cofounders of Network Appliance, a data-storage firm in Sunnyvale, California, were feuding with each other. The problem: Malcolm couldn't stick to his decisions, which drove Hitz crazy. An organization behavior specialist began working with the warring executives in separate sessions to solve the problem.

2. Revitalizing Organizations   Information technology is wreaking such change that nearly all organizations these days are placed in the position of having to adopt new behaviors in order to resist decline. OD can help by opening communication, fostering innovation, and dealing with stress.

3. Adapting to Mergers   Mergers and acquisitions are associated with increased anxiety, stress, absenteeism, turnover, and decreased productivity.[36] What is the organizational fit between two disparate organizations, such as Chrysler and DaimlerBenz? OD experts can help integrate two firms with varying cultures, products, and procedures.

How OD Works

Like physicians, OD managers and consultants follow a medical-like model. (Or, to use our more current formulation, they follow the rules of evidence-based management.) They approach the organization as if it were a sick patient, using *diagnosis, intervention,* and *evaluation*—"diagnosing" its ills, "prescribing" treatment or intervention, and "monitoring" or evaluating progress. If the evaluation shows that the procedure is not working effectively, the conclusions drawn are

figure 10.2

THE OD PROCESS

Sources: Adapted from W. L. French and C. H. Bell Jr., *Organization Development: Behavioral Interventions for Organizational Improvement* (Englewood Cliffs, NJ: Prentice-Hall, 1978); and E. G. Huse and T. G. Cummings, *Organizational Development and Change,* 3rd ed. (St. Paul: West, 1985).

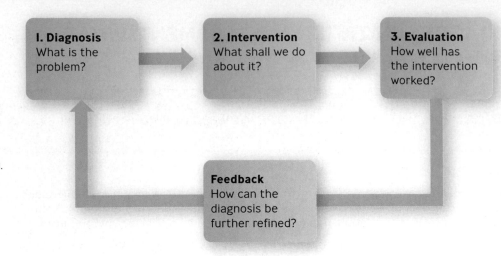

then applied (see feedback loop) to refining the diagnosis, and the process starts again. *(See Figure 10.2, above.)*

1. Diagnosis: What Is the Problem?   To carry out the diagnosis, OD consultants or managers use some combination of questionnaires, surveys, interviews, meetings, records, and direct observation to ascertain people's attitudes and to identify problem areas.

2. Intervention: What Shall We Do about It?   "Treatment" or *intervention* is **the attempt to correct the diagnosed problems.** Often this is done using the services of an OD consultant who works in conjunction with management teams. Some OD activities for implementing planned change are communicating survey results to employees to engage them in constructive problem solving, observing employee communication patterns and teaching them skills to improve them, helping group members learn to function as a team, stimulating better cohesiveness among several work groups, and improving work technology or organizational design.

3. Evaluation: How Well Has the Intervention Worked?   An OD program needs objective evaluation to see if it has done any good. Answers may lie in hard data about absenteeism, turnover, grievances, and profitability, which should be compared with earlier statistics. The change agent can use questionnaires, surveys, interviews, and the like to assess changes in employee attitudes.

Example

Organization Development: Patagonia Tries to Become Greener[37]

Founded by an environmentalist in 1979, apparel company Patagonia sells outdoor clothing and gear and has long been a strong supporter of the environmental movement. In fact, its mission statement is "Build the best product, cause no unnecessary harm, use business to inspire and implement solutions to the environmental crisis." However, as customers have become more eco-aware, the company has been getting more questions about how "green" the origins and handling of its products are. The approach Patagonia took resembles the steps in organization development:

Diagnosis—*"What is the problem?"* Forced to examine how green it actually is, Patagonia sent employees in May 2007 to track the "environmental footprint" of five products, from design studio to raw-materials stage to U.S. distribution center. The investigators visited yarn spinners in Thailand, a footwear factory in China, and a fiber manufacturer in North Carolina. The good news: they learned that transporting products took surprisingly little energy, because most were shipped by sea, which represented less than 1% of the total energy use in the supply chain. The bad news:

manufacturing took more energy than was expected and sometimes produced ecologically unfriendly by-products, such as possibly toxic PFOA (perfluorooctanoic acid), found in Patagonia parkas.

Intervention—*"What shall we do about it?"* The company believed that using PFOA-free materials might sacrifice performance, so it continued to use PFOA-containing water-repellant membranes and coatings while searching for alternatives. By fall 2008, membranes were to have been replaced by polyester and polyurethane. However, no satisfactory substitute has been found for the existing coatings.

Evaluation—*"How well has the intervention worked?"* Not finding a PFOA substitute for the coatings is not ecologically satisfying, but the company insists on maintaining quality. "We don't want to sacrifice quality for environmental reasons," says Jill Dumain, Patagonia's director of environmental analysis. "If a garment is thrown away sooner due to a lack of durability, we haven't solved any environmental problem." In addition, the findings are of limited value, because only the primary materials were traced, and no packaging was evaluated. Patagonia has posted the results of its investigation of IO products online under the heading "the Footprint Chronicles" at **http://www .patagonia.com/web/us/footprint/index.jsp.**

Your Call

Do you think every company should take an organization-development approach to the environmental quality of its products and services? Do you feel putting production information in the public domain and available to competitors is risky? Or do the benefits of openness outweigh the costs, because it could spur others to action?

The Effectiveness of OD

Among organizations that have practiced organization development are American Airlines, B.F. Goodrich, General Electric, Honeywell, ITT, Polaroid, Procter & Gamble, Prudential, Texas Instruments, and Westinghouse Canada—companies covering a variety of industries.

Research has found that OD is most apt to be successful under the following circumstances.

I. Multiple Interventions OD success stories tend to use multiple interventions. Goal setting, feedback, recognition and rewards, training, participation, and challenging job design have had good results in improving performance and satisfaction.[38] Combined interventions have been found to work better than single interventions.[39]

2. Management Support OD is more likely to succeed when top managers give the OD program their support and are truly committed to the change process and the desired goals of the change program.[40] Also, the expectations for change were not unrealistic.[41]

3. Goals Geared to Both Short- & Long-Term Results Change programs are more successful when they are oriented toward achieving both short-term and long-term results. Managers should not engage in organizational change for the sake of change. Change efforts should produce positive results.[42]

4. OD Is Affected by Culture OD effectiveness is affected by cross-cultural considerations. Thus, an OD intervention that worked in one country should not be blindly applied to a similar situation in another country.[43] ●

Team building. One technique for implementing change is team building. Teams are often diverse in gender, age, ethnicity, and educational background and experience. Would you prefer to work with a highly diverse team of people?

THE BIG PICTURE

Innovation may be a product innovation or a process innovation, an incremental innovation or a radical innovation. Four characteristics of innovation are that it is uncertain, people closest to it know the most about it, it may be controversial, and it may be complex. Three ways to encourage innovation are by providing the organizational culture, the resources, and the reward system. To make innovation happen, you need to recognize problems and opportunities, gain allies, and overcome employee resistance.

Innovation, as we've said earlier in the book, is the activity of creating new ideas and converting them into useful applications—specifically new goods and services. The spirit of innovation is essential to keeping an organization vital and in maintaining a competitive advantage. Otherwise, the innovation will come from your competitors, forcing you to scramble to catch up—if you can.

Self-Assessment:
Assessing Your Creativity
Quotient

Succeeding at Innovation

American companies constantly put forth ads touting the spirit of innovation, but how well are they actually doing? Ironically, a survey of 4,559 corporate managers in 36 industries found that U.S. executives thought their own companies gave innovation or creativity short shrift—only 4% felt their organizations could be respected for their leadership in this area.[44]

Why Are U.S. Firms Lagging? Scholars Larry Selden and Ian MacMillan argue that firms are focusing their innovation efforts in the wrong way: "Companies are pouring money into their insular R&D [research and development] labs, instead of working to understand what the customer wants and then using the understanding to drive innovation."[45]

Cynthia Barton Rabe, a former innovation strategist for Intel, suggests that too much knowledge and experience can actually kill innovation. "When we become expert," she says, "we often trade our 'what if' flights of fancy for the grounded reality of 'what is,'" thereby limiting our approaches to challenges.[46] This may be the "curse of knowledge" we mentioned in Chapter 7.[47]

Jack and Suzy Welch say that organizations must create an innovation mindset or culture in order to effectively innovate. (Recall our discussion about culture in Chapter 8.) They encourage managers to involve employees from all levels in the organization in the innovation process and to reward those who bring new ideas forward.[48]

Picking Many People's Brains: The Open-Source Idea Innovation can happen by design or by accident, and it need not come about because of a for-profit orientation. For instance, the computer operating system Linux was written by Finnish programmer Linus Torvalds, who then put his work in the public domain. It is now a free, "open-source" operating system created by hundreds of programmers around the world who contribute to its source code, its underlying instructions available to anyone.[49]

Some companies have extended the open source idea by taking a Linux-style approach that taps masses of people for inspiration. Tim O'Reilly, founder of computer publisher O'Reilly Media, believes, according to one report, that "creativity is no longer about which companies have the most visionary executives, but who has the most compelling 'architecture of participation.' That is, which companies make it easy, interesting, and rewarding for a wide range of contributors to offer ideas, solve problems, and improve products?"[50] Padmasree Warrior, Motorola's chief technology officer, in pursuit of a follow-up success story to the best-selling RAZR cell phone, oversees a Web-based system called Innovate, in which 25,000 Motorola engineers are encouraged to blog new ideas nonstop. "I'm a firm believer in the idea that the future belongs to the genius of the collaborative innovator," she says.[51] (Unfortunately, Motorola's mobile-devices unit was so battered by the onslaught of its rival BlackBerry, from Research In Motion, that it began bleeding money, and the company was ultimately forced to sell it off.)[52]

Linus Torvalds, innovator. In 1991, computer programmer Torvalds, then a graduate student in Finland, posted his free Linux operating system on the Internet. Linux is a free version of Unix, and its continual improvements result from the efforts of tens of thousands of volunteer programmers. Can you think of any other innovations that occurred that did not come about because of a for-profit orientation?

The Culture of Innovation   As we will see, a big part of what makes innovation happen is a country and a corporation's culture. Unlike most Europeans, who abhor "precariousness," or the absence of security, Americans as a whole seem to be more comfortable with taking risks. As one writer puts it, "Risk, movement, and personal ambition are fundamental. . . . The United States is about the endless possibility of self-invention through hard work. It is inseparable from change."[53] It is not an accident that so many risk-averse countries that have tried to generate Silicon Valley–style entrepreneurial magic through government-sponsored technical havens—Malaysia with its Multimedia Supercorridor, Dubai with its Internet City, Singapore with its Singapore One—have been unsuccessful.[54]

Types of Innovation: Product or Process, Incremental or Radical

Innovations may be of the following two types.

Product versus Process Innovations   As a manager, you may need to improve your organization's product or service itself; this is generally a technological innovation. Or you may need to improve the process by which the product or service is created, manufactured, or distributed; this is generally a managerial innovation.

More formally, a ***product innovation*** **is a change in the appearance or the performance of a product or a service or the creation of a new one. A** ***process innovation*** **is a change in the way a product or service is conceived, manufactured, or disseminated.**

Today, says an article about the world's most innovative companies, "innovation is about much more than new products. It is about reinventing business processes and building entirely new markets that meet untapped customer needs."[55]

Incremental versus Radical Innovations   An innovation may be small or large. The difference is in modifying versus replacing existing products or services. That is, you might have ***incremental innovations*—the creation of products, services, or technologies that modify existing ones.** Or you might have ***radical innovations*—the creation of products, services, or technologies that replace existing ones.**

Test Your Knowledge:
Technological Change

Practical Action

What Makes a Startup?

Many startups don't begin with radical ideas. According to Amar V. Bhidé, author of *The Origin and Evolution of New Businesses,* successful entrepreneurs start out by making "a small modification in what somebody else is doing."[56] One has only to think of how the notion of disposability has been extended to so many products—phone cards, DVDs, even cell phones.[57]

Most entrepreneurs, he explains, see a small niche opportunity—one in which the company he or she is working for is already involved, or a supplier or customer is involved. "And the person jumps in with very little preparation and analysis," he says, "but with direct firsthand knowledge of the profitability of that opportunity—and pretty much does what somebody else is already doing, but does it better and faster."

And "better and faster" seems to be the main difference. Such entrepreneurs don't have anything in the way of technology or concept that differentiates them from other businesses. "They just work harder, hustle for customers, and know that the opportunity may not last for more than six or eight months," says Bhidé. "But they expect to make a reasonable return on those six to eight months. And along the way they'll figure out something else that will keep the business going."

Another quality of entrepreneurs is "a tolerance for ambiguity," Bhidé says. They are willing to jump into things when it's hard to even imagine what the possible outcomes will be, going ahead in the absence of information, very much capital—or even a very novel idea.

An example of a startup fitting these criteria is Netflix, which rents DVD movies by mail to customers ordering online. This concept does not seem very innovative. The wrinkle, however, which struck founder Reed Hastings when he was charged $40 for returning a movie late to a video rental outfit, is that for a $19.95 monthly subscription, customers can keep three films out at a time. "If you rent five or six a month," says one California retired engineer, "you're ahead compared to what you pay at Blockbuster." (In 1 month, he watched more than 40 movies.) Another differentiating feature: when you rate the movie you rented, Netflix will recommend other movies you might enjoy that you might not have heard of.[58]

Think you'd like to start up a startup yourself and make yourself rich? Before you do, you might want to read *The Illusions of Entrepreneurship* by Case Western professor Scott Shane.[59] Shane says that the average new venture will fail within 5 years and that even successful founders earn less than they would as employees—35% less over 10 years. The biggest myth, he says, is that entrepreneurs believe "the growth and performance of their startups depends more on their entrepreneurial talent than on the businesses they choose." Over the past 20 years, he found, about 4% of all the startups in the computer and office equipment industry made *Inc.* magazine's Inc. 500 list of America's fastest-growing companies. But only about 0.005% of startups in the hotel and motel industries made that list, and 0.007% of startups in eating and drinking establishments. "So that means the odds that you make the Inc. 500 are 840 times higher if you start a computer company than if you start a hotel or motel."[60]

Four Characteristics of Innovation

According to Harvard management scholar Rosabeth Moss Kanter, innovation has four characteristics:[61]

1. Innovating Is an Uncertain Business Being an innovator means being like the first driver in a line of cars in a snowstorm: You're dealing with the unknown while the less adventurous souls behind you may be carping about your performance. When you're innovating, progress is difficult to predict, and the ultimate success of your endeavor is always somewhat in doubt.

2. People Closest to the Innovation Know the Most about It, at Least Initially Innovation is knowledge-intensive. The people closest to the development of the idea know the most about it, at least in the early stages. Consequently, it is often difficult for outsiders—such as co-workers or managers who are removed from the process—to understand and appreciate it. This leads to characteristic 3.

3. Innovation May Be Controversial
Whoever is doing the innovating is using the organization's people and funds for that purpose. Since there is always competition for resources, others in the organization may take issue with the way they are being used here—especially since the innovation has not yet shown positive results.

4. Innovation Can Be Complex Because It May Cross Organizational Boundaries
An innovation may involve more than one department or business unit. This, of course, increases the complexity of the process. Thus, you as a manager need to understand not only how the process of innovation works in general but also how it requires special handling to make it successful within different parts of the organization. Shepherding an innovation, therefore, may require you to draw on your finest communication skills—especially because of characteristic 2 above.

Celebrating Failure: Cultural & Other Factors Encouraging Innovation

Innovation doesn't happen as a matter of course. Organizations have to develop ways to make it happen—over and over. Three ways to do so are by providing (1) the right organizational *culture,* (2) the appropriate *resources,* and (3) the correct *reward system.*

I. Culture: Is Innovation Viewed as a Benefit or a Boondoggle?
Although much of American culture seems oriented toward punishing failure, an organizational culture that doesn't just allow but *celebrates* failure is vital toward fostering innovation. Pharmaceutical company Eli Lilly, for example, is said to have "long had a culture that looks at failure as an inevitable part of discovery and encourages scientists to take risks."[62] Most new ideas will fail. Only a few will be successful. But if an organization doesn't encourage this kind of risk taking—if people tend to view experimentation as a boondoggle—that organization won't become a superstar in innovation.

An organizational culture, as we said in Chapter 8, is the "social glue," or system of shared beliefs and values, that binds members together. The top 10 companies with cultures that strongly encourage innovation, according to *Business Week,* are Apple, Google, 3M, Toyota, General Electric, Microsoft, Procter & Gamble, 3M, Walt Disney, and IBM.[63]

2. Resources: Do Managers Put Money Where Their Mouths Are?
An organization's managers may say they encourage innovation, but if they balk at the expense, they aren't putting their money where their mouths are. Innovation doesn't come cheap. Its costs can be measured in all kinds of ways: dollars, time, energy, and focus. For instance, an organization's research and development (R&D) department may need to hire top scientists, whose salaries may be high.

Of course, because there is always competition within an organization for resources, innovation may simply be given short shrift because other concerns seem so urgent—even within a company with a culture encouraging experimentation. But the risk of downgrading innovation in favor of more immediate concerns is that a company may "miss the next wave"—the next big trend, whatever that is.

3. Rewards: Is Experimentation Reinforced in Ways That Matter? Top-performing salespeople are often rewarded with all kinds of incentives, such as commissions, bonuses, and perks. Are R&D people rewarded the same way? Every year Monsanto Corp., for instance, presents a $50,000 award to the scientist or scientists who developed the largest commercial breakthrough.

The converse is also important: People should not be punished when their attempts to innovate don't work out, or else they won't attempt new things in the future. By the nature of experimentation, the end result can't be foreseen. Top managers at 3M, for instance, recognize that three-fifths of the new ideas suggested each year fail in the marketplace. Only when people attempting an innovation are acting half-heartedly, sloppily, or otherwise incompetently should sanctions be used such as the withholding of raises and promotions.

Example

Achieving Success by Celebrating Failure: 3M's Culture of Innovation

Courtesy of 3M Company.

In Chapter 3 we mentioned 3M's Art Fry, inventor of Post-it Notes, as an example of an intrapreneur. But 3M is also famous for having a culture of innovation that celebrates taking chances—which means achieving success by celebrating failure.

Only with 20-20 hindsight can people see that a policy of celebrating failure can lead to success. No one can know, when setting out on a new course, whether the effort will yield positive results, and usually, in fact, most such experiments *are* failures. But the *attempts* must be encouraged, or innovation will never happen.

For many years, 3M built innovation into its culture. Mistakes were allowed, destructive criticism was forbidden, experimentation was encouraged, and divisions and individuals were allowed to operate with a good deal of autonomy. 3M set goals decreeing that 25%–30% of annual sales must come from products that were only 5 years old or less. Investment in research and development was almost double the rate of that of the average American company. In addition, 3M employees were permitted to spend 15% of their time pursuing personal research interests that were not related to current company projects, knowing that if their ideas weren't successful, they would be encouraged to pursue other paths. The result was a culture that produced a string of hit products: masking tape, Scotchgard, optical films for coating liquid-crystal display screens.[64]

That culture changed when a former General Electric executive, James McNerney, took over in 2001 as 3M's CEO and instituted a system known as Six Sigma (discussed in Chapter 16). "Efficiency programs such as Six Sigma are designed to identify problems in work processes—and then use rigorous measurement to reduce variation and eliminate defects," says one account. "When these types of initiatives become ingrained in a company's culture, as they did at 3M, creativity can easily get squelched. After all, a breakthrough innovation is something that challenges existing procedures and norms."[65] By 2007, McNerney was gone, and his successor, George Buckley, was struggling to balance efficiency with innovation, which had declined. By early 2008, 3M had climbed back to No. 19 on *Fortune*'s "Most Admired Companies" list (and No. 3 in the medical and other precision equipment industry).[66]

Your Call

Stanford University organizational behavior scholar Jerker Denrell believes that there is too much study of successes and not enough of failures, although it's very likely that firms pursuing risky strategies tend to achieve either a very high or very low performance whereas firms pursuing conservative strategies always achieve an average performance.[67] But while risk taking can lead to either spectacular success or disastrous failure, looking only at successes will show a positive correlation between success and risk taking. Do you think this is true?

How You Can Foster Innovation: Three Steps

If you're going to not just survive but *prevail* as a manager, you need to know how to make innovation happen within an organization. Here we offer three steps for doing so. *(See Figure 10.3.)*

I. Recognize problems & opportunities & devise solutions → 2. Gain allies by communicating your vision → 3. Overcome employee resistance, & empower & reward them to achieve progress

figure 10.3

THREE STEPS FOR FOSTERING INNOVATION

Source: Adapted from eight steps in K. M. Bartol and D. C. Martin, *Management 3E,* McGraw-Hill/Irwin, 1998, pp. 360–363. Reprinted with permission of The McGraw-Hill Companies.

I. Recognize Problems & Opportunities & Devise Solutions   Change may be needed because you recognize a *problem* or recognize an *opportunity.*

- **Recognizing a problem—find a "better way."** Problems, whether competitive threat or employee turnover, tend to seize our attention.

  Sometimes problems lead to new business ideas. When Nevada real estate agents Barbara and Marshall Zucker watched the Las Vegas foreclosure rate skyrocket 169% from 2006 to 2007, they also noticed that 40% of all home sales were foreclosed properties. So in 2008 they bought a 24-seat Ford bus, named it the Vegas Foreclosure Express, and began offering prospective buyers tours of repossessed homes, offering 10-minute views of each property.[68]

- **Recognizing an opportunity.** Recognition of opportunities may come from long-term employees who regularly expose themselves to new ideas ("technological gate-keepers" in one phrase).[69] Ideas originating at the grassroots level of an organization may be a particularly fruitful source of innovation.[70]

2. Gain Allies by Communicating Your Vision   Once you've decided how you're going to handle the problem or opportunity, you need to start developing and communicating your vision. You need to create a picture of the future and paint in broad strokes how your innovation will be of benefit. That is, you need to start persuading others inside—and perhaps outside—the organization to support you. Having hard data helps. Others will be more persuaded, for example, if you can demonstrate that a similar idea has been successful in another industry. Or if you can take current trends (such as sales or demographics) and project them into the future.

But a great deal of innovation comes about precisely because the future has no resemblance to the past. Thus, you may have to use your imagination to paint the brightest picture you can of the possible payoffs of your innovation.

3. Overcome Employee Resistance, & Empower & Reward Them to Achieve Progress   Once you've persuaded and gotten the blessing of your managerial superiors, then you need to do the same with the people reporting to you. It's possible, of course, that the idea for innovation came from them and that you already have their support.

Alternatively, you may have to overcome their resistance. Then you'll need to remove obstacles that limit them in executing the vision, such as having to get management to sign off on all aspects of a project. Finally, you'll need to hand out periodic rewards—recognition, celebrations, bonuses—for tasks accomplished. And the rewards should not be withheld until the end of the project, which may be many months away, but given out for the successful accomplishment of short-term phases in order to provide constant encouragement. ●

10.4 THE THREAT OF CHANGE: MANAGING EMPLOYEE FEAR & RESISTANCE

major question How are employees threatened by change, and how can I help them adjust?

THE BIG PICTURE

This section discusses the degree to which employees fear change, from least threatening to most threatening. It also describes Lewin's three-stage change model: unfreezing, changing, and refreezing. Finally, it describes Kotter's eight steps for leading organizational change, which correspond to Lewin's three stages.

As a manager, particularly one working for an American organization, you may be pressured to provide short-term, quick-fix solutions. But when applied to organizational problems, this approach usually doesn't work: quick-fix solutions have little staying power.

What, then, are effective ways to manage organizational change and employees' fear and resistance to it? In this section, we discuss the following:

- The extent to which employees fear change and reasons why employees resist change.
- Lewin's change model.
- Kotter's eight stages for leading organizational change.

The Degree to Which Employees Fear Change: From Least Threatening to Most Threatening

Whether organizational change is administrative or technological, the degree to which employees feel threatened by it in general depends on whether the change is *adaptive, innovative,* or *radically innovative.*[71]

Least Threatening: Adaptive Change *Adaptive change* **is reintroduction of a familiar practice**—the implementation of a kind of change that has already been experienced within the same organization. This form of change is lowest in complexity, cost, and uncertainty. Because it is familiar, it is the least threatening to employees and thus will create the least resistance.

For example, during annual inventory week, a department store may ask its employees to work 12 hours a day instead of the usual 8. During tax-preparation time, the store's accounting department may imitate this same change in work hours. Although accounting employees are in a different department from stockroom and sales employees, it's expected they wouldn't be terribly upset by the temporary change in hours since they've seen it in effect elsewhere in the store.

Somewhat Threatening: Innovative Change *Innovative change* **is the introduction of a practice that is new to the organization.** This form of change involves moderate complexity, cost, and uncertainty. It is therefore apt to trigger some fear and resistance among employees.

For example, should a department store decide to adopt a new practice of competitors by staying open 24 hours a day, requiring employees to work flexible schedules, it may be felt as moderately threatening.

Very Threatening: Radically Innovative Change *Radically innovative change involves introducing a practice that is new to the industry.* Because it is the most complex, costly, and uncertain, it will be felt as extremely threatening to managers' confidence and employees' job security and may well tear at the fabric of the organization.[72]

For example, a department store converting some of its operations to e-commerce—selling its goods on the Internet—may encounter anxiety among its staff, especially those fearing being left behind.

Manager's Hot Seat:
Change: More Pain Than Gain?

Ten Reasons Employees Resist Change Whether changes are adaptive, innovative, or radically innovative, employees may resist them for all kinds of reasons. Ten of the leading ones are as follows.[73]

Self-Assessment:
Assessing Your Flexibility

- **Individual's predisposition toward change.** How people react to change depends a lot on how they learned to handle change and ambiguity as children. One person's parents may have been patient, flexible, and understanding, and from the time the child was weaned she may have learned there were positive compensations for the loss of immediate gratification. Thus, she will associate making changes with love and approval. Another person's parents may have been unreasonable and unyielding, forcing him to do things (piano lessons, for example) that he didn't want to do. Thus, he will be distrustful of making changes because he will associate them with demands for compliance.[74]

- **Surprise and fear of the unknown.** When radically different changes are introduced without warning—for example, without any official announcements—the office rumor mill will go into high gear and affected employees will become fearful of the implications of the changes. Harvard business scholar Rosabeth Moss Kanter recommends that in such cases a transition manager should be appointed who is charged with keeping all relevant parties adequately informed.[75]

- **Climate of mistrust.** Trust involves reciprocal faith in others' intentions and behavior. Mistrust encourages secrecy, which causes deeper mistrust, putting even well-conceived changes at risk of failure. Managers who trust their employees make the change process an open, honest, and participative affair. Employees who trust their managers are more apt to expend extra effort and take chances with something different.

- **Fear of failure.** Intimidating changes on the job can cause employees to doubt their capabilities. Self-doubt erodes self-confidence and cripples personal growth and development.

- **Loss of status or job security.** Administrative and technological changes that threaten to alter power bases or eliminate jobs—as often happens during corporate restructurings that threaten middle-management jobs—generally trigger strong resistance.

- **Peer pressure.** Even people who are not themselves directly affected by impending changes may actively resist in order to protect the interests of their friends and co-workers.

- **Disruption of cultural traditions or group relationships.** Whenever individuals are transferred, promoted, or reassigned, it can disrupt existing cultural and group relationships. Traditionally, for example, Sony Corp. promoted insiders to new positions; when an outsider, Howard Stringer, was named as the next chairman and CEO and six corporate officers were asked to resign, creating a majority board of foreigners, the former CEO, Nobuyuki Idei, worried the moves might engender strong employee resistance.[76]

- **Personality conflicts.** Just as a friend can get away with telling us something we would resent hearing from an adversary, the personalities of change agents can breed resistance.

Group Exercise:
Overcoming Resistance to Change

- **Lack of tact or poor timing.** Introducing changes in an insensitive manner or at an awkward time can create employee resistance. Employees are more apt to accept changes when managers effectively explain their value, as, for example, in demonstrating their strategic purpose to the organization.

- **Nonreinforcing reward systems.** Employees are likely to resist when they can't see any positive rewards from proposed changes, as, for example, when one is asked to work longer hours without additional compensation.

To gauge how adaptable you're apt to be to organizational change, complete the Self-Assessment at the end of this chapter.

Lewin's Change Model: Unfreezing, Changing, & Refreezing

Most theories of organizational change originated with the landmark work of social psychologist **Kurt Lewin.** Lewin developed a model with three stages—*unfreezing, changing,* and *refreezing*—to explain how to initiate, manage, and stabilize planned change.[77]

1. "Unfreezing": Creating the Motivation to Change
In the *unfreezing stage,* managers try to instill in employees the motivation to change, encouraging them to let go of attitudes and behaviors that are resistant to innovation. For this "unfreezing" to take place, employees need to become dissatisfied with the old way of doing things. Managers also need to reduce the barriers to change during this stage.

2. "Changing": Learning New Ways of Doing Things
In the *changing stage,* employees need to be given the tools for change: new information, new perspectives, new models of behavior. Managers can help here by providing benchmarking results, role models, mentors, experts, and training. It's advisable, experts say, to convey the idea that change is a continuous learning process, not just a one-time event.[78]

3. "Refreezing": Making the New Ways Normal
In the *refreezing stage,* employees need to be helped to integrate the changed attitudes and behavior into their normal ways of doing things. Managers can assist by encouraging employees to exhibit the new change and then, through additional coaching and modeling, by reinforcing the employees in the desired change. *(See Table 10.1.)*

One technique used in Stage 1, to help unfreeze organizations, is **benchmarking, a process by which a company compares its performance with that of high-performing organizations.**[79] Professional sports teams do this all the time, but so do other kinds of organizations, including nonprofit ones.

For example, one company discovered that its costs to develop a computer system were twice those of competitors and that the time to get a new product to market was four times longer. These data were ultimately used to unfreeze employees' attitudes and motivate people to change the organization's internal processes in order to remain competitive.[80]

Kotter's Eight Steps for Leading Organizational Change

An expert in leadership and change management, **John Kotter** believes that, to be successful, organizational change needs to follow eight steps to avoid the eight common errors senior management usually commits.[81] *(See Table 10.2, opposite page.)* These correspond with Lewin's unfreezing-changing-refreezing steps.

Steps 1–4 represent unfreezing: establish a sense of urgency, create the guiding coalition, develop a vision and strategy, and communicate the change vision.

Steps 5–7 represent the changing stage: empower broad-based action, generate short-term wins, and consolidate gains and produce more change.

table 10.1

SIX METHODS FOR MANAGING EMPLOYEE RESISTANCE TO CHANGE

I.	Education and communication
2.	Participation and involvement
3.	Facilitation and support
4.	Negotiation and rewards
5.	Manipulation and cooptation
6.	Explicit and implicit coercion

Source: Adapted from J. P. Kotter and L. A. Schlesinger, "Choosing Strategies for Change," *Harvard Business Review,* March–April 1979, pp. 106–114.

Step	Description
1. Establish a sense of urgency.	Unfreeze the organization by creating a compelling reason for why change is needed.
2. Create the guiding coalition.	Create a cross-functional, cross-level group of people with enough power to lead the change.
3. Develop a vision and a strategy.	Create a vision and a strategic plan to guide the change process.
4. Communicate the change vision.	Create and implement a communication strategy that consistently communicates the new vision and strategic plan.
5. Empower broad-based action.	Eliminate barriers to change, and use target elements of change to transform the organization. Encourage risk taking and creative problem solving.
6. Generate short-term wins.	Plan for and create short-term "wins" or improvements. Recognize and reward people who contribute to the wins.
7. Consolidate gains and produce more change.	The guiding coalition uses credibility from short-term wins to create more change. Additional people are brought into the change process as change cascades throughout the organization. Attempts are made to reinvigorate the change process.
8. Anchor new approaches in the culture.	Reinforce the changes by highlighting connections between new behaviors and processes and organizational success. Develop methods to ensure leadership development and succession.

table 10.2

STEPS TO LEADING ORGANIZATIONAL CHANGE

Source: Reprinted by permission of Harvard Business School. Excerpt from *Leading Change* by J.P. Kotter, 1996. Copyright © 1996 by the Harvard Business School Publishing Corporation; all rights reserved.

Step 8, corresponding to refreezing, is to anchor new approaches in the organization's culture.

The value of Kotter's steps is that they provide specific recommendations about behaviors that managers need to exhibit to successfully lead organizational change. It is important to remember that Kotter's research reveals that it is ineffective to skip steps and that successful organizational change is 70%–90% leadership and only 10%–30% management. Senior managers are thus advised to focus on leading rather than on managing change.[82] ●

Lookalikes. One key to the success of Southwest Airlines is that all the planes in its fleet have been the same type, Boeing 737s, which saves on maintenance and training costs. As Southwest expands from being a short-haul, low-fare carrier to running long-haul flights as well, it has needed to add new-generation 737s, which can travel longer distances than the older planes did. Southwest still offers no-frills service—no seat assignments and snacks instead of meals—and competes principally on fare price. In evolving from short routes to long ones, should the company expect to have to undergo any of the steps in Lewin's change model—unfreezing, changing, and refreezing?

Summary

 10.1 The Nature of Change in Organizations
Among supertrends shaping the future of business: (1) The marketplace is becoming more segmented and moving toward more niche products. (2) There are more competitors offering targeted products, requiring faster speed-to-market. (3) Some traditional companies may not survive radically innovative change. (4) China, India, and other offshore suppliers are changing the way we work. (5) Knowledge, not information, is becoming the new competitive advantage.

Two types of change are reactive and proactive. Reactive change is making changes in response to problems or opportunities as they arise. Proactive change involves making carefully thought-out changes in anticipation of possible or expected problems or opportunities.

Forces for change may consist of forces outside the organization or inside it. (1) External forces consist of four types: demographic characteristics, market changes, technological advancements, and social and political pressures. (2) Internal forces may be of two types: employee problems and managers' behavior.

Four areas in which change is most apt to be needed are people, technology, structure, and strategy. (1) People changes may require changes in perceptions, attitudes, performance, or skills. (2) Technology is any machine or process that enables an organization to gain a competitive advantage in changing materials used to produce a finished product. (3) Changing structure may happen when one organization acquires another. (4) Changing strategy may occur because of changes in the marketplace.

 10.2 Organization Development: What It Is, What It Can Do
Organization development (OD) is a set of techniques for implementing planned change to make people and organizations more effective. Often OD is put into practice by a change agent, a consultant with a background in behavioral sciences who can be a catalyst in helping organizations deal with old problems in new ways. OD can be used to manage conflict, revitalize organizations, and adapt to mergers.

The OD process follows a three-step process: (1) Diagnosis attempts to ascertain the problem. (2) Intervention is the attempt to correct the diagnosed problems. (3) Evaluation attempts to find out how well the intervention worked.

Four factors that make OD work successfully are (1) multiple interventions are used; (2) top managers give the OD program their support; (3) goals are geared to both short- and long-term results; and (4) OD is affected by culture.

 10.3 Promoting Innovation within the Organization
Innovations may be a product innovation or a process innovation. A product innovation is a change in the appearance or performance of a product or service or the creation of a new one. A process innovation is a change in the way a product or service is conceived, manufactured, or disseminated. Innovations may also be an incremental innovation or a radical innovation. An incremental innovation is the creation of a product, service, or technology that modifies an existing one. A radical

innovation is the creation of a product, service, or technology that replaces an existing one.

Four characteristics of innovation are that (1) it is an uncertain business; (2) people closest to the innovation know the most about it, at least initially; (3) it may be controversial; and (4) it can be complex because it may cross organizational boundaries.

Innovation doesn't happen as a matter of course. Three ways to make it happen are to provide the right organizational culture, so that it is viewed as a benefit rather than as a boondoggle; to provide the resources; and to provide the rewards, so that experimentation is reinforced in ways that matter. Three steps for fostering innovation are as follows. (1) Recognize problems and opportunities and devise solutions. (2) Gain allies by communicating your vision. (3) Overcome employee resistance and empower and reward them to achieve progress.

 ### 10.4 The Threat of Change: Managing Employee Fear & Resistance

The degree to which employees feel threatened by change depends on whether the change is adaptive, innovative, or radically innovative. Adaptive change, the least threatening, is reintroduction of a familiar practice. Innovative change is the introduction of a practice that is new to the organization. Radically innovative change, the most threatening, involves introducing a practice that is new to the industry.

Ten reasons employees resist change are as follows: (1) individuals' predisposition toward change; (2) surprise and fear of the unknown; (3) climate of mistrust; (4) fear of failure; (5) loss of status or job security; (6) peer pressure; (7) disruption of cultural traditions or group relationships; (8) personality conflicts; (9) lack of tact or poor timing; and (10) nonreinforcing reward systems.

Kurt Lewin's change model has three stages—unfreezing, changing, and refreezing—to explain how to initiate, manage, and stabilize planned change. (1) In the unfreezing stage, managers try to instill in employees the motivation to change. One technique used is benchmarking, a process by which a company compares its performance with that of high-performing organizations. (2) In the changing stage, employees need to be given the tools for change, such as new information. (3) In the refreezing stage, employees need to be helped to integrate the changed attitudes and behavior into their normal behavior.

In a model corresponding with Lewin's, John Kotter's suggests an organization needs to follow eight steps to avoid the eight common errors senior management usually commits. The first four represent unfreezing: establish a sense of urgency, create the guiding coalition, develop a vision and strategy, and communicate the change vision. The next three steps represent the changing stage: empower broad-based action, generate short-term wins, and consolidate gains and produce more change. The last step, corresponding to refreezing, is to anchor new approaches in the organization's culture.

Management in Action

Companies Try to Change Employees' Behavior Toward Using Car Pooling, Mass Transit, Shuttles, & Buses

For years, in-house transportation gurus at companies across the country have been obsessing about how to cajole employees out of their cars. They've handed out mass-transit passes, ordered fleets of luxury coaches, reserved premium parking spots for van pools, and filled locker rooms with toiletries and towels for those who bike to work. They've educated workers about the evils of not only the SUV but the SOV (single-occupancy vehicle). And they've appealed to the corporate drudge's quest for happiness, brandishing research showing that those who travel to work alone in cars are the most miserable commuters of all.

Nothing, however, has done as much for their cause as today's record prices for petrol. Employees who once sneered at the "bus people" or "bike freaks" are clamoring to sign up for all manner of company-subsidized transportation programs. "Every time gas prices rise, I get more and more employees who are taking our car pools or van pools or shuttle buses," says Schering-Plough's transportation chief Sheila Gist. This new golden age has Gist in overdrive, scheduling new routes for what has become Schering's own in-house transit system. In the past year alone, Gist says, ridership is up by as much as 40%. Companies are big on breaking the car addiction because doing so raises productivity, amps morale, and delivers much lusted-after green cred.

The surge in oil prices has accelerated the trend. So have new corporate tax deductions for employer-subsidized transportation. Consider what's happening at insurer Safeco. When the company moved to Seattle last year, it installed commuting concierges to help employees figure out how best to use the company's vouchers for mass transit, shuttles, car pools, and ferries. Free rentals from Zipcar await those who need to run errands during the day. Safeco also encourages its staff to skip the commute altogether by offering free phone and broadband service for their home offices, as well as a furniture stipend with which to decorate. Today [in 2008], 90% of employees are out of their cars, up from 50% in 2006. The company is aiming for zero-car status. Says Safeco transportation analyst Brady Clark: "We're still working on that 10%."

Some companies can't meet the demand fast enough. After Microsoft rolled out a new shuttle-bus service last fall, employees immediately howled for more routes. The plush, Wi-Fi-equipped coaches have become so wildly popular—strategy chief Craig Mundie is a big fan—that when word leaked recently that Microsoft was adding to the service, a group of Microserfs hacked into the reservation system and filled up the new routes before they were even announced. Employee Bryan Keller used to commute alone in his 20-mpg Honda Pilot. "I've regained two hours of my day," he says. Using Microsoft's online "carbon calculator," Keller estimates he's saved $150 on gas and dropped 1,000 pounds of CO_2 from his carbon footprint since he began using the service in October [2007].

For Discussion

1. Which of the forces for change are causing organizations such as Safeco and Microsoft to try and change employees' views about driving to work? Explain.

2. Thinking more broadly, will the price of gasoline create incremental or radical innovation for organizations? What type of industries will be most affected?

3. How did Safeco and Microsoft try to reduce employees' resistance to their work travel programs? Describe.

4. To what extent would Safeco and Microsoft's travel programs increase productivity? Explain.

Source: From Michelle Conlin, "Suddenly, It's Cool to Take the Bus," *BusinessWeek,* May 5, 2008, p. 24. Reprinted with permission.

Self-Assessment

How Adaptable Are You?

Objectives

1. To assess your adaptability.
2. To examine how being adaptable can help you cope with organizational change.

Introduction

Ultimately all organizational change passes through an organization's people. People who adapt more easily are better suited to cope with organizational changes and so they clearly are important assets to any organization. The purpose of this exercise is to determine your adaptability.

Instructions

Read the following statements. Using the scale provided, circle the number that indicates the extent to which you agree or disagree with each statement:

1 = strongly disagree
2 = disagree
3 = neither agree nor disagree
4 = agree
5 = strongly agree

1.	In emergency situations, I react with clear, focused thinking and maintain emotional control in order to step up to the necessary actions.	1	2	3	4	5
2.	In stressful circumstances, I don't overreact to unexpected news. I keep calm, focused, and manage frustration well.	1	2	3	4	5
3.	I solve problems creatively by turning them inside out and upside down looking for new approaches to solving them that others may have missed.	1	2	3	4	5
4.	I easily change gears in response to uncertain or unexpected events, effectively adjusting my priorities, plans, goals, and actions.	1	2	3	4	5
5.	I enjoy learning new ways to do my work and I do what is necessary to keep my knowledge and skills current.	1	2	3	4	5
6.	I adjust easily to changes in my workplace by participating in assignments or training that prepares me for these changes.	1	2	3	4	5
7.	I am flexible and open-minded with others. I listen and consider others' viewpoints, adjusting my own when necessary.	1	2	3	4	5
8.	I am open to both negative and positive feedback. I work well in teams.	1	2	3	4	5
9.	I take action to learn and understand the values of other groups, organizations, or cultures. I adjust my own behavior to show respect for different customs.	1	2	3	4	5
10.	I adjust easily to differing environmental states such as extreme heat, humidity, cold, or dirtiness.	1	2	3	4	5
11.	I frequently push myself to complete strenuous or demanding tasks.	1	2	3	4	5
Total						_____

Interpretation

When you are done, add up your responses to get your total score to see how adaptable you are. Arbitrary norms for adaptability:

11–24 = Low adaptability

25–39 = Moderate adaptability

40–55 = High adaptability

Questions for Discussion

1. Were you surprised by your results? Why or why not?

2. Look at the areas where your score was the lowest. What are some skills you can work on or gain to increase your adaptability? Describe and explain.

3. What are some ways being adaptable can improve the way you handle change? Discuss.

Adapted from S. Arad, M. A. Donovan, K. E. Plamondon, and E. D. Pulakos, "Adaptability in the Workplace: Development of Taxonomy of Adaptive Performance," *Journal of Applied Psychology*, August 2000, pp. 612–624.

Should Drug Salespeople Be Allowed to Give Doctors Free Drug Samples & Gifts?

For years, they've been the standard freebies that drug companies have offered in an attempt to get doctors to prescribe their medications: expensive dinners, golf outings, trips to ski resorts, and drug samples. . . .

This week, 11 current and former sales executives from TAP Pharmaceutical Products—a leading drug company—go on trial, accused of conspiring to pay kickbacks to doctors, hospitals, and other customers. The charges focus on efforts to get doctors to prescribe Lupron, the company's prostate cancer drug, as well as Prevacid, its heartburn drug. . . .

Doctors approached by the 11 TAP employees were offered gifts including trips to swanky golf and ski resorts and "educational grants," used to pay for cocktail parties, office Christmas parties and travel, according to prosecutors. Defense lawyers say the sales executives were simply doing their jobs. "As far as I can tell, this is the first time there has ever been a prosecution under the health care statute in which salespeople are being charged with a crime [for things] that they thought were completely within their job descriptions," says Roal Martine, a Chicago attorney who represents Carey Smith, a former TAP executive.

Solving the Dilemma

What is your feeling about drug salespeople giving doctors free drug samples and trips and/or "educational grants" as a way to get doctors to prescribe their products?

1. There is nothing wrong with this practice. Giving drug samples and gifts is simply another form of advertising.

2. Although this practice amounts to bribery, the doctors should not take the gifts. But I think it is all right for doctors to take only free drug samples. Doctors who take trips and "educational grants" for cocktail parties should be punished.

3. The salespeople and TAP should be punished. This practice drives up the costs of drugs, which ultimately are passed along to consumers.

4. Because guidelines established by the American Medical Association are vague, the TAP employees should not be punished. We need clear guidelines that include real penalties for not following them.

Source: Excerpted from D. Lavoie, "Drug Firm Sales Reps Go on Trial," *San Francisco Chronicle,* April 13, 2004, pp. C1, C5.

Managing Individual Differences & Behavior

Supervising People as People

Major Questions You Should Be Able to Answer

 11.1 Personality & Individual Behavior
Major Question: In the hiring process, do employers care about one's personality and individual traits?

 11.2 Values, Attitudes, & Behavior
Major Question: How do the hidden aspects of individuals— their values and attitudes— affect employee behavior?

 11.3 Work-Related Attitudes & Behaviors Managers Need to Deal With
Major Question: Is it important for managers to pay attention to employee attitudes?

 11.4 Perception & Individual Behavior
Major Question: What are the distortions in perception that can cloud one's judgment?

 11.5 Understanding Stress & Individual Behavior
Major Question: What causes workplace stress, and how can it be reduced?

Managing Gen Y: What's Different about Today's Generation of Younger Workers

Are the Gen Yers (the 75 million so-called Millennials, born between 1977 and 1994) really so different from earlier generations (the 78 million Boomers, born 1946–1964, and 49 million Gen Xers, 1965–1976)? Does this new crop of twentysomethings—perhaps you're in this group—now beginning to enter the workplace need to be managed in different ways? Experts say the answer to both questions is yes.[1]

Some major characteristics of Millennials are as follows: (1) They are extremely independent, because many were raised as day care or latchkey kids by two working parents or by a divorced, single parent, and so they have been left alone to make their own decisions. (2) They are tech-savvy, used to cell phones and the Internet as means of communication and accustomed to a faster pace of life. (3) They are racially and ethnically diverse. (4) They are confident, feel optimistic about the future, and believe they can do it all. In the workplace, these translate into a skepticism about rules, policies, and procedures; a requirement for more autonomy; and a need for constant stimulation. What Gen Yers are looking for in the workplace is not only a good income and good relationships with their bosses and co-workers but also challenging daily work, the opportunity for growth, the chance to show off skills and be recognized for their accomplishments, casual dress environment, and flexible schedules for social and personal time.

What should leaders do in managing this group? Here are some suggestions.

- **Allow them independent decision making and expression:** Gen Yers are impatient, skeptical, and blunt and expressive, but they are used to adapting and making decisions. Show appreciation for their individuality and let them participate in decision making.

- **Train them and mentor them:** As the most education-oriented generation in history, Millennials are strongly attracted to education and training, the best kind not being classroom training but forms of independent learning. At the same time, they should be given the chance to create long-term bonds with mentors.

- **Give them constant feedback and recognition:** Gen Yers need to know they are making an impact and need to be recognized for their workplace contributions. Thus, supervisors should show them how their work contributes to the bottom line. This generation revels in, even craves, constant praise, so managers should provide rewards in the form of praise, flextime, and extra responsibility.

- **Provide them with access to technology:** To attract and retain Generation Y employees, companies need to provide the newest and best technology.

- **Create customized career paths:** Gen Yers would most like to be self-employed, but few are able to do it because of high start-up costs. Employers can reinforce the sense of control that this generation desires by providing them with a realistic account of their progress and their future within the organization.

For Discussion   As a worker, you might hope to be led by someone who would follow the above suggestions. But suppose your boss is of the old "tough guy" school and doesn't manage this way. In a difficult job market, would you stick it out? How would you try to let your supervisor know how you would prefer to be managed?

forecast

What's Ahead in This Chapter

This first of five chapters on leadership discusses how to manage for individual differences and behaviors. We describe personality and individual behavior; values, attitudes, and behavior; and specific work-related attitudes and behaviors managers need to be aware of. We next discuss distortions in perception, which can affect managerial judgment. Finally, we consider what stress does to individuals.

THE BIG PICTURE

Personality consists of stable psychological and behavioral attributes that give you your identity. We describe five personality dimensions and five personality traits that managers need to be aware of to understand workplace behavior.

Self-Assessment:
Career Planning Based on Brain Dominance and Thinking Styles Inventory

In this and the next four chapters we discuss the third management function (after planning and organizing)—namely, leading. *Leading,* as we said in Chapter 1, is defined as *motivating, directing, and otherwise influencing people to work hard to achieve the organization's goals.*

How would you describe yourself? Are you outgoing? aggressive? sociable? tense? passive? lazy? quiet? Whatever the combination of traits, which result from the interaction of your genes and your environment, they constitute your personality. More formally, *personality* **consists of the stable psychological traits and behavioral attributes that give a person his or her identity.**[2] As a manager, you need to understand personality attributes because they affect how people perceive and act within the organization.

The Big Five Personality Dimensions

In recent years, the many personality dimensions have been distilled into a list of factors known as the Big Five.[3] The *Big Five personality dimensions* **are (1) extroversion, (2) agreeableness, (3) conscientiousness, (4) emotional stability, and (5) openness to experience.**

- **Extroversion.** How outgoing, talkative, sociable, and assertive a person is.
  - **Agreeableness.** How trusting, good-natured, cooperative, and soft-hearted one is.
  - **Conscientiousness.** How dependable, responsible, achievement-oriented, and persistent one is.
  - **Emotional stability.** How relaxed, secure, and unworried one is.
  - **Openness to experience.** How intellectual, imaginative, curious, and broad-minded one is.

Assertive and sociable. Does it take a certain kind of personality to be a good salesperson? Have you ever known people who were quiet, unassuming, even shy but who were nevertheless very persistent and persuasive—that is, good salespeople?

Standardized personality tests are used to score people on each dimension to draw a person's personality profile that is supposedly as unique as his or her fingerprints. For example, if you scored low on the first trait, extroversion, you would presumably be prone to shy and withdrawn behavior. If you scored low on emotional stability, you supposedly would be nervous, tense, angry, and worried.

Do Personality Tests Work for the Workplace? As a manager, you would want to know if the Big Five model in particular and personality testing in general can help predict behavior in the workplace. Is a personality test helpful in predicting a match between personality and job performance? Two findings:

- **Extroversion—the outgoing personality.** As might be expected, extroversion (an outgoing personality) has been associated with success for managers and salespeople. Also, extroversion is a stronger predictor of job performance than agreeableness, across all professions, according to researchers. "It appears that being courteous, trusting, straightforward, and soft-hearted [that is, agreeableness] has a smaller impact on job performance," conclude the researchers, "than being talkative, active, and assertive [that is, extroversion]."[4]

- **Conscientiousness—the dependable personality.** Conscientiousness (strong work ethic) has been found to have the strongest positive correlation with job performance and training performance. According to researchers, "those individuals who exhibit traits associated with a strong sense of purpose, obligation, and persistence generally perform better than those who do not."[5]

The table below presents tips to help managers avoid abuses and discrimination lawsuits when using personality and psychological testing for employment decisions.[6] *(See Table 11.1.)*

table 11.1

CAUTIONS ABOUT USING PERSONALITY TESTS IN THE WORKPLACE

• *Use professionals.* Rely on reputable, licensed psychologists for selecting and overseeing the administration, scoring, and interpretation of personality and psychological tests. This is particularly important, since not every psychologist is expert at these kinds of tests.	• *Don't hire on the basis of personality test results alone.* Supplement any personality test data with information from reference checks, personal interviews, ability tests, and job performance records. Also avoid hiring people on the basis of specified personality profiles. As a case in point, there is no distinct "managerial personality."	• *Be alert for gender, racial, and ethnic bias.* Regularly assess any possible adverse impact of personality tests on the hiring of women and minorities. This is truly a matter of great importance, since you don't want to find your company (or yourself) embroiled in a lawsuit at some point downstream.	• *Graphology tests don't work, but integrity tests do.* Personality traits and aptitudes cannot be inferred from samples of people's penmanship, as proponents of graphology tests claim. However, dishonest job applicants can often be screened by integrity tests, since dishonest people are reportedly unable to fake conscientiousness, even on a paper-and-pencil test.

The Proactive Personality   A person who scores well on the Big Five dimension of conscientiousness is probably a good worker. He or she may also be a *proactive personality,* **someone who is more apt to take initiative and persevere to influence the environment.**[7] People of this sort identify opportunities and act on them, which makes them associated not only with success—individual, team, and organizational— but also with entrepreneurship.

Five Traits Important in Organizations

Five of the most important personality traits that managers need to be aware of to understand workplace behavior are (1) *locus of control,* (2) *self-efficacy,* (3) *self-esteem,* (4) *self-monitoring,* and (5) *emotional intelligence.*

I. Locus of Control: "I Am/Am Not the Captain of My Fate"   As we discussed briefly in Chapter 3, **locus of control indicates how much people believe they control their fate through their own efforts.** If you have an *internal locus of control,* you believe you control your own destiny. If you have an *external locus of control,* you believe external forces control you.

Research shows internals and externals have important workplace differences. Internals exhibit less anxiety, greater work motivation, and stronger expectations that effort leads to performance. They also obtain higher salaries.[8]

These findings have two important implications for managers:

- **Expect different degrees of structure and compliance for each type.** Employees with internal locus of control will probably resist close managerial supervision. Hence, they should probably be placed in jobs requiring high initiative and lower compliance. By contrast, employees with external locus of control might do better in highly structured jobs requiring greater compliance.

- **Employ different reward systems for each type.** Since internals seem to have a greater belief that their actions have a direct effect on the consequences of that action, internals likely would prefer and respond more productively to incentives such as merit pay or sales commissions. (We discuss incentive compensation systems in Chapter 12.)

2. Self-Efficacy: "I Can/Can't Do This Task"   A related trait is **self-efficacy, belief in one's personal ability to do a task.** Unlike locus of control, this characteristic isn't about how much fate controls events (as in believing whether getting a high grade in a course is determined by you or by outside factors, such as the grade curve or trick questions). Rather, it's about your personal belief that you have what it takes to succeed. (Erik Weihenmayer, 35, is blind but also a self-described "unrealistic optimist," who was the first blind climber to scale Mt. Everest.)[9]

Have you noticed that those who are confident about their ability tend to succeed, whereas those preoccupied with failure tend not to? Indeed, high expectations of self-efficacy have been linked with all kinds of positives: not only success in varied physical and mental tasks but also reduced anxiety and increased tolerance for pain.[10] One study found that the sales performance of life-insurance agents was much better among those with high self-efficacy.[11] Low self-efficacy is associated with **learned helplessness, the debilitating lack of faith in one's ability to control one's environment.**[12]

Among the implications for managers:

- **Assign jobs accordingly.** Complex, challenging, and autonomous jobs tend to enhance people's perceptions of their self-efficacy. Boring, tedious jobs generally do the opposite.

- **Develop self-efficacy.** Self-efficacy is a quality that can be nurtured. Employees with low self-efficacy need lots of constructive pointers and positive feedback.[13] Goal difficulty needs to match individuals' perceived self-efficacy, but goals can be made more challenging as performance improves.[14] Small successes need to be rewarded. Employees' expectations can be improved through guided experiences, mentoring, and role modeling.[15]

3. Self-Esteem: "I Like/Dislike Myself"

How worthwhile, capable, and acceptable do you think you are? The answer to this question is an indicator of your *self-esteem,* **the extent to which people like or dislike themselves, their overall self-evaluation.**[16] Research offers some interesting insights about how high or low self-esteem can affect people and organizations.

- **People with high self-esteem.** Compared to people with low self-esteem, people with high self-esteem are more apt to handle failure better, to emphasize the positive, to take more risks, and to choose more unconventional jobs.[17] However, when faced with pressure situations, high-self-esteem people have been found to become egotistical and boastful.[18] Some have even been associated with aggressive and violent behavior.

- **People with low self-esteem.** Conversely, low-self-esteem people confronted with failure have been found to have focused on their weaknesses and to have had primarily negative thoughts. Moreover, they are more dependent on others and are more apt to be influenced by them and to be less likely to take independent positions.

Can self-esteem be improved? According to one study, "low self-esteem can be raised more by having the person think of *desirable* characteristics *possessed* rather than of undesirable characteristics from which he or she is free."[19] Some ways in which managers can build employee self-esteem are shown below. *(See Table 11.2.)*

table 11.2

SOME WAYS THAT MANAGERS CAN BOOST EMPLOYEE SELF-ESTEEM

- Reinforce employees' positive attributes and skills.

- Provide positive feedback whenever possible.

- Break larger projects into smaller tasks and projects.

- Express confidence in employees' abilities to complete their tasks.

- Provide coaching whenever employees are seen to be struggling to complete tasks.

4. Self-Monitoring: "I'm Fairly Able/Unable to Adapt My Behavior to Others"

As you're rushing to an important meeting, you are stopped by a co-worker, who starts to discuss a personal problem. You need to break away, so you glance at your watch.

(a) Does your co-worker Get It? Seeing you look at your watch, he says, "Sorry, I see you're busy. Catch you later." Or (b) does he Not Get It? He keeps talking, until you say "I'm late for a big meeting" and start walking away.

The two scenarios show the difference between a high self-monitor and a low self-monitor. *Self-monitoring* **is the extent to which people are able to observe their own behavior and adapt it to external situations.** Of course, we would all like to think we are high in self-monitoring—able to regulate our "expressive self-presentation for the sake of desired public appearances," as some experts write, "and thus be highly responsive to social and interpersonal cues" of others.[20] But whereas some high self-monitors are criticized for being chameleons, always able to adapt their self-presentation to their surroundings, low self-monitors are often criticized for being on their own planet and insensitive to others. Instead, their behavior may reflect their own inner states, including their attitudes and feelings.

It might be expected that people in top management are more apt to be high self-monitors able to play different roles—even contradictory roles—to suit different situations. Research shows a positive relationship between high self-monitoring and career success. Among 139 MBA graduates who were tracked for 5 years, high self-monitors enjoyed more internal and external promotions than did their low self-monitoring classmates.[21] Other research has found that managerial success (in terms of speed of promotions) was tied to political savvy (knowing how to socialize, network, and engage in organizational politics).[22]

Self-Assessment:
Assessing Your Emotional Intelligence

5. Emotional Intelligence: "I'm Pretty Good/Not Good at Empathizing with Others & Being Self-Motivated"

Daniel Goleman is co-chairman of the Consortium for Research on Emotional Intelligence in Organizations at Rutgers University and author of the popular 1995 book *Emotional Intelligence.* In 1998, he argued that the most important attribute in a leader is **emotional intelligence, the ability to cope, empathize with others, and be self-motivated.**[23] "When I compared star performers with average ones in senior leadership positions," Goleman wrote, "nearly 90% of the difference in their profiles was attributable to emotional intelligence factors rather than cognitive abilities."[24] The traits of emotional intelligence are (1) self-awareness, (2) self-management, (3) social awareness, and (4) relationship management. *(See Table 11.3.)*

table 11.3

THE TRAITS OF EMOTIONAL INTELLIGENCE

1. *Self-awareness.* The most essential trait. This is the ability to read your own emotions and gauge your moods accurately, so you know how you're affecting others.

2. *Self-management.* This is the ability to control your emotions and act with honesty and integrity in reliable and adaptable ways. You can leave occasional bad moods outside the office.

3. *Social awareness.* This includes empathy, allowing you to show others that you care, and organizational intuition, so you keenly understand how your emotions and actions affect others.

4. *Relationship management.* This is the ability to communicate clearly and convincingly, disarm conflicts, and build strong personal bonds.

Sources: Adapted from D. Goleman, R. Boyatzis, and A. McKee, "Primal Leadership: The Hidden Driver of Great Performance," *Harvard Business Review,* December 2001, p. 49; and *Primal Leadership: Realizing the Power of Emotional Intelligence* (Boston: Harvard Business School Press, 2002), p. 39. Copyright © 2001 and 2002 by the Harvard Business School Publishing Corporation. Reprinted with permission; all rights reserved.

Is there any way to raise your own emotional intelligence, to sharpen your social skills? Yes and no. Parts of emotional intelligence represent stable traits that are not readily changed. In contrast, other aspects of emotional intelligence, such as using empathy, can be developed. Awareness about your level of emotional intelligence is the first step in improving this trait. The Self-Assessment at the end of this chapter can be used for this purpose. The next step would be to learn more about those aspects of emotional intelligence in which you feel improvement is needed. For example, you might improve your skills at using empathy by finding articles on the topic and then trying to implement the proposed recommendations. One such article suggests that empathy in communications is enhanced by trying to (1) understand how others feel about what they are communicating and (2) gaining appreciation of what people want from an exchange.[25]

Preliminary evidence suggests that emotional intelligence can land you a job. A simulated interview process indicated that interviewers' assessments of an applicant's emotional intelligence were positively associated with their impression of the application.[26] However, given the difficulty of measuring emotional intelligence, further research is needed on this new leadership trait.[27] ●

Self-Assessment:
Assessing Your Empathy Skills

> How do the hidden aspects of individuals—their values and attitudes—affect employee behavior?

major question?

THE BIG PICTURE

Organizational behavior (OB) considers how to better understand and manage people at work. In this section, we discuss individual values and attitudes and how they affect people's actions and judgments.

If you look at a company's annual report or at a brochure from its corporate communications department, you are apt to be given a picture of its *formal aspects:* Goals. Policies. Hierarchy. Structure. Could you exert effective leadership if the formal aspects were all you knew about the company? What about the *informal aspects?* Values. Attitudes. Personalities. Perceptions. Conflicts. Culture. Clearly, you need to know about these hidden, "messy" characteristics as well. *(See Figure 11.1, at right.)*

Organizational Behavior: Trying to Explain & Predict Workplace Behavior

The informal aspects are the focus of the interdisciplinary field known as ***organizational behavior (OB), which is dedicated to better understanding and management of people at work.*** In particular, OB tries to help managers not only *explain* workplace behavior but also to *predict* it, so that they can better lead and motivate their employees to perform productively. OB looks at two areas:

*   **Individual behavior.** This is the subject of this chapter. We discuss such individual attributes as values, attitudes, personality, perception, and learning.
*   **Group behavior.** This is the subject of later chapters, particularly Chapter 13, where we discuss norms, roles, and teams.

Let us begin by considering individual values, attitudes, and behavior.

Values: What Are Your Consistent Beliefs & Feelings about *All* Things?

***Values** are abstract ideals that guide one's thinking and behavior across all situations.*[28] Lifelong behavior patterns are dictated by values that are fairly well set by the time people are in their early teens. After that, however, one's values can be reshaped by significant life-altering events, such as having a child, undergoing a business failure, or surviving the death of a loved one, a war, or a serious health threat.

From a manager's point of view, it's helpful to know that values are those concepts, principles, things, people, or activities for which a person is willing to work hard—even make sacrifices for. Compensation, recognition, and status are common values in the workplace.[29] However, according to a survey by the Society for Human Resource Management, employees are more interested in striking a

figure II.I

FORMAL AND INFORMAL ASPECTS OF AN ORGANIZATION

Group Exercise:
What Do You Value?

balance between work and family life rather than just earning a paycheck.[30] For instance, 60% of working mothers say part-time work would be their ideal work situation.[31]

Attitudes: What Are Your Consistent Beliefs & Feelings about *Specific* Things?

Values are abstract ideals—global beliefs and feelings—that are directed toward all objects, people, or events. Values tend to be consistent both over time and over related situations. By contrast, attitudes are beliefs and feelings that are directed toward *specific* objects, people, or events. More formally, an **attitude is defined as a learned predisposition toward a given object.**[32] It is important for you to understand the components of attitudes because attitudes directly influence our behavior.[33]

Example: If you dislike your present job, will you be happier if you change to a different job? Not necessarily. It depends on your attitude. In one study, researchers found that the attitudes of 5,000 middle-aged male employees toward their jobs were very stable over a 5-year period. Men with positive attitudes tended to stay positive, those with negative attitudes tended to stay negative. More revealingly, even those who changed jobs or occupations generally expressed the same attitudes they had previously.[34]

table II.4

EXAMPLES OF THE THREE COMPONENTS OF ATTITUDES

The Three Components of Attitudes: Affective, Cognitive, & Behavioral Attitudes have three components.[35] *(See Table 11.4.)*

Affective	"I hate people who talk on cell phones in restaurants." "I hate putting on a suit for work." "I really like working from home." "I like commuting by train because I have time to myself." "I don't like working in office cubicles because they don't have doors and so there's no privacy."
Cognitive	"I can't appoint Herschel because creative people don't make good administrators." "The tallest building in the world is in Chicago." (Actually, it's in Taiwan.)
Behavioral	"I intend to fill out my expense report tomorrow." "I'm going to turn over a new leaf at New Year's and stop eating junk food." "I'm going to try to avoid John because he's a Democrat." "I'm never going to talk to George because he's a Republican."

- The affective component—"I feel." The *affective component of an attitude* consists of the feelings or emotions one has about a situation.

- The cognitive component—"I believe." The *cognitive component of an attitude* consists of the beliefs and knowledge one has about a situation.

- The behavioral component—"I intend." The *behavioral component of an attitude,* also known as the *intentional component,* refers to how one intends or expects to behave toward a situation.

All three components are often manifested at any given time. For example, if you call a corporation and get one of those telephone-tree menus ("For customer service, press 1 . . .") that never seems to connect you to a human being, you might be so irritated that you would say:

"I hate being given the run-around." [*affective component—your feelings*]

"That company doesn't know how to take care of customers." [*cognitive component—your perceptions*]

"I'll never call them again." [*behavioral component—your intentions*]

When Attitudes & Reality Collide: Consistency & Cognitive Dissonance   One of the last things you want, probably, is to be accused of hypocrisy—to be criticized for saying one thing and doing another. Like most people, you no doubt want to maintain consistency between your attitudes and your behavior.

But what if a strongly held attitude bumps up against a harsh reality that contradicts it? Suppose you're extremely concerned about getting AIDS, which you believe you might get from contact with body fluids, including blood. Then you're in a life-threatening auto accident in a third-world country and require surgery and blood transfusions—including transfusions of blood from (possibly AIDS-infected) strangers in a blood bank. Do you reject the blood to remain consistent with your beliefs about getting AIDS?

In 1957, social psychologist **Leon Festinger** proposed the term *cognitive dissonance* **to describe the psychological discomfort a person experiences between his or her cognitive attitude and incompatible behavior.**[36] Because people are uncomfortable with inconsistency, Festinger theorized, they will seek to reduce the "dissonance" or tension of the inconsistency. How they deal with the discomfort, he suggested, depends on three factors:

- **Importance.** How important are the elements creating the dissonance? Most people can put up with some ambiguities in life. For example, many drivers don't think obeying speed limits is very important, even though they profess to be law-abiding citizens. People eat greasy foods even though they know that ultimately they may contribute to heart disease.

- **Control.** How much control does one have over the matters that create dissonance? A juror may not like the idea of voting the death penalty but believe that he or she has no choice but to follow the law in the case. A taxpayer may object to his taxes being spent on, say, special-interest corporate welfare for a particular company but not feel that he or she can withhold taxes.

- **Rewards.** What rewards are at stake in the dissonance? You're apt to cling to old ideas in the face of new evidence if you have a lot invested emotionally or financially in those ideas. If you're a police officer who worked 20 years to prove a particular suspect guilty of murder, you're not apt to be very accepting of contradictory evidence after all that time.

Among the main ways to reduce cognitive dissonance are the following. *(See Table 11.5, next page.)*

- **Change your attitude and/or behavior.** This would seem to be the most obvious, even rational, response to take when confronted with cognitive dissonance.

- **Belittle the importance of the inconsistent behavior.** This happens all the time.

- **Find consonant elements that outweigh the dissonant ones.** This kind of rationalizing goes on quite often, as when employees are confronted with ethical dilemmas but fear losing their jobs.

Behavior: How Values & Attitudes Affect People's Actions & Judgments

Values (global) and attitudes (specific) are generally in harmony, but not always. For example, a manager may put a positive *value* on helpful behavior (global) yet may have a negative *attitude* toward helping an unethical co-worker (specific). Together, however, values and attitudes influence people's workplace *behavior*—**their actions and judgments.** ●

Leon Festinger. In 1957, the psychologist and his associates penetrated a cult whose members predicted that most people on earth would perish in a cataclysmic event except for a handful that would be rescued by aliens in a flying saucer. Festinger found himself standing with cult members on a hilltop awaiting the event, which, of course, did not happen. Later he proposed the term *cognitive dissonance* to explain how they rationalized the failure of their prophecy. Have you observed people employing this mechanism when the sure-fire thing they predicted did not occur?

table II.5

EXAMPLES OF WAYS TO REDUCE COGNITIVE DISSONANCE

Technique	Examples
Change attitude and/or behavior	Gregory Withow once belonged to the White Aryan Resistance and other racist groups. He preached hatred and bashed Japanese tourists in San Francisco. Then he met Sylvia, who rejected his white-supremacist ideas. As he grew to love her, he found himself caught between his ideas and her disapproval. To decrease this cognitive dissonance, he renounced his old racist beliefs and changed his behavior, even becoming a spokesperson for the antiracist Anti-Defamation League.
Belittle importance of the inconsistent behavior	All cigarette smokers are repeatedly exposed to information that smoking is hazardous to health. But many belittle the habit as not being as risky as the antismoking messages suggest. ("My grandmother smokes, and she's in her 80s.")
Find consonant elements that outweigh dissonant ones	Ethics professor Sissela Bok says students may justify cheating on an exam by saying "I don't usually do this, but here I really have to do it." As one MIT graduate student said, students see cheating take place and "feel they have to. People get used to it, even though they know it's not right."

Sources: R. Plotnik, *Introduction to Psychology,* 3rd ed. (Pacific Grove, CA: Brooks/Cole, 1993), p. 602; S. Bok, cited in E. Venant, "A Nation of Cheaters," *San Francisco Chronicle,* January 7, 1992, p. D3, reprinted from *Los Angeles Times;* A. Dobrzeniecki, quoted in D. Butler, "MIT Students Guilty of Cheating," *Boston Globe,* March 2, 1991, p. 25.

Example

How Values & Attitudes Affect Behavior: IBM Uses an "Innovation Jam" to Move Beyond Incremental Improvements to Catalytic Innovations

As a manager, would you think most employees would agree that innovation is beneficial—that the original Silicon Valley firms prospered because they were constantly creating new products and services? Employees may have the *value,* then, that innovation is good—that it leads to productivity and profitability.

However, for a particularly successful product within your company, your employees might have the *attitude* that radical innovation is unnecessary. If the product is so successful, they may feel, why mess with it? Why not just make incremental improvements?

IBM found that the company's current reputation for constant incremental innovation hadn't inspired investors, resulting in its stock price remaining flat for 3 years. Recent earnings had come through cost-cutting, not the leaps in growth propelled by new business. Accordingly, CEO Samuel J. Palmisano decided to create what he called an "Innovation Jam," pulling together thousands of people—clients, consultants, and employees' family members, as well as IBM workers—in the

online equivalent of a town meeting. His hope, according to one account, is that "The opinions of some 100,000 minds will lead to catalytic innovations so powerful they will transform industries, alter human behavior, and lead to new businesses for IBM."[37] IBM wouldn't own any ideas emerging from the two 72-hour "open source" sessions; they could be used by anyone.

IBM's 2006 Innovation Jam brought together more than 150,000 people from 104 countries and 67 companies. As a result, 10 new IBM businesses were launched with seed investment totaling $100 million.[38] In 2007, for the fifteenth consecutive year, IBM racked up more U.S. patents than any other company in the world—3,125 in all, or 60 patents a week.[39]

Your Call

The Innovation Jam certainly provides new ideas and furthers IBM's image as a forward-thinking global competitor. Do you think this kind of transformative event could be adopted to a different kind of company (such as Sears), to change employee values and attitudes?

II.3 WORK-RELATED ATTITUDES & BEHAVIORS MANAGERS NEED TO DEAL WITH

major question?

Is it important for managers to pay attention to employee attitudes?

THE BIG PICTURE

Attitudes are important because they affect behavior. Managers need to be alert to work-related attitudes having to do with job satisfaction, job involvement, and organizational commitment. Among the types of employee behavior they should attend to are their on-the-job performance and productivity, absenteeism and turnover, organizational citizenship behaviors, and counterproductive work behaviors.

"Keep the employees happy."

It's true that attitudes are important, the reason being that *attitudes affect behavior.* But is keeping employees happy all that managers need to know to get results? We discuss motivation for performance in the next chapter. Here let us consider what managers need to know about work-related attitudes and behaviors.

Work-Related Attitudes: Job Satisfaction, Job Involvement, & Organizational Commitment

Employees will gripe about almost anything. About working in cubicles instead of offices. About not having enough help. About the mediocre cafeteria food. About managers "who don't know anything." They may also say some good things. About the great retirement plan. About flex time. About a product beating competing products. About how cool Manager X is.

Three types of attitudes managers are particularly interested in are (1) *job satisfaction,* (2) *job involvement,* and (3) *organizational commitment.*

1. Job Satisfaction: How Much Do You Like or Dislike Your Job? **Job satisfaction is the extent to which you feel positively or negatively about various aspects of your work.** Most people don't like everything about their jobs. Their overall satisfaction depends on how they feel about several components, such as *work, pay, promotions, co-workers, and supervision.*[40] Among the key correlates of job satisfaction are stronger motivation, job involvement, organizational commitment, and life satisfaction and less absenteeism, tardiness, turnover, and perceived stress.[41]

Many middle managers are dissatisfied with their jobs, feeling overworked and underappreciated, especially during economic downturns, when companies cut staff and managers work longer hours for small pay increases and little recognition.[42] But what is the relationship between job satisfaction and job performance—does more satisfaction cause better performance or does better performance cause more satisfaction? This is a subject of much debate among management scholars.[43] One comprehensive study found that (1) job satisfaction and performance are moderately related, meaning that employee job satisfaction is a key work attitude managers should consider when trying to increase performance; but (2) the relationship between satisfaction and performance is complex and it seems that both variables influence each other through a host of individual differences and work-environment characteristics.[44]

2. Job Involvement: How Much Do You Identify with Your Work? *Job involvement* **is the extent to which you identify or are personally involved with your job.** Many people, of course, work simply to put bread on the table; they have no interest in excelling at their jobs. More fortunate are those who actively participate in their jobs and consider their work performance important to their self-worth.

Analysis of nearly 28,000 individuals from 87 different studies demonstrates that job involvement is moderately correlated with job satisfaction.[45] Thus, managers are encouraged to foster satisfying work environments to fuel employees' job involvement.[46]

3. Organizational Commitment *Organizational commitment* **reflects the extent to which an employee identifies with an organization and is committed to its goals.** For instance, some managers question whether mothers with children can be fully committed to their jobs, although one survey found that only 4% of more than 2,612 women said that their bosses think that they are not as committed to their jobs because they have children.[47] Research shows a strong positive relationship between organizational commitment and job satisfaction and a moderate association with job performance.[48] Thus, managers are advised to increase job satisfaction to elicit higher levels of commitment. In turn, higher commitment can facilitate higher performance.[49]

Important Workplace Behaviors

Why, as a manager, do you need to learn how to manage individual differences? The answer, as you might expect, is so that you can influence employees to do their best work. Among the types of behavior are (1) performance and productivity, (2) absenteeism and turnover, (3) organizational citizenship behaviors, and (4) counterproductive work behaviors.

1. Evaluating Behavior When Employees Are Working: Performance & Productivity Every job has certain expectations, but in some jobs performance and productivity are easier to define than in others. How many contacts should a telemarketing sales rep make in a day? How many sales should he or she close? Often a job of this nature will have a history of accomplishments (from what previous job holders have attained) so that it is possible to quantify performance behavior.

However, an advertising agency account executive handling major clients such as a carmaker or a beverage manufacturer may go months before landing this kind of big account. Or a researcher in a pharmaceutical company may take years to develop a promising new prescription drug.

In short, the method of evaluating performance must match the job being done.

2. Evaluating Behavior When Employees Are Not Working: Absenteeism & Turnover Should you be suspicious of every instance of *absenteeism*—when an employee doesn't show up for work? Of course, some absences—illness, death in the family, or jury duty, for example—are legitimate. Such no-show behavior is to be expected from time to time. However, absenteeism is related to job dissatisfaction.[50]

Performance monitors. These British Airways customer service reps are being monitored by software that keeps track not only of ticket sales and customer-complaint resolutions but also of the amount of time spent on breaks and personal phone calls. In tracking employee effectiveness, the technology can count incentive dollars tied to performance and immediately direct them into employee paychecks. Do you think these incentive calculators are justified or do you think they intrude too much on employee privacy?

Absenteeism may be a precursor to *turnover,* **when employees leave their jobs.** Every organization experiences some turnover, as employees leave for reasons of family, better job prospects, or retirement. However, except in low-skill industries, a continual revolving door of new employees is usually not a good sign, since replacement and training is expensive.[51] For instance, one study found the direct and indirect costs of recruiting and training a new mid-level manager—along with lost business to competitors, lost technical knowledge, decreased morale among remaining employees, and the like—came to $64,000.[52] Another study found it costs nearly $108,000 to replace a key worker or a manager.[53]

3. Evaluating Behavior That Exceeds Work Roles: Organizational Citizenship Behaviors

Organizational citizenship behaviors **are those employee behaviors that are not directly part of employees' job descriptions—that exceed their work-role requirements.** Examples, according to one description, include "such gestures as constructive statements about the department, expression of personal interest in the work of others, suggestions for improvement, training new people, respect for the spirit as well as the letter of housekeeping rules, care for organizational property, and punctuality and attendance well beyond standard or enforceable levels."[54] Several studies reveal a significant and moderately positive correlation between organizational citizenship behaviors and job satisfaction and performance.[55]

4. Evaluating Behavior That Harms the Organization: Counterproductive Work Behaviors

The flip side of organizational citizenship behaviors would seem to be what are called *counterproductive work behaviors (CWB),* **types of behavior that harm employees and the organization as a whole.** Such behaviors may include absenteeism and tardiness, drug and alcohol abuse, and disciplinary problems but also extend beyond them to more serious acts such as accidents, sabotage, sexual harassment, violence, theft, and white-collar crime.[56]

A fairly common kind of CWB, for example, is the bullying, harassment, or unfair treatment of subordinates, co-workers, and even customers. Indeed, in one survey of U.S. employees, 45% said they had had a boss who was abusive.[57] Such behavior is especially toxic to the organization because when employees are intimidated, humiliated, or undermined by an abusive manager they say they are more likely to quit their jobs or to retaliate with CWB aimed at that manager or their fellow workers.[58] The problem has become so bad that legislators in 13 states have introduced antibullying legislation.[59] Further, newspaper stories about mass shootings by disgruntled or mentally ill employees (or students, as at Virginia Tech) have made organizations more aware that erratic behavior has to be spotted and dealt with early. Pitney Bowes, for instance, set up a hotline that employees may call anonymously to report any such concerns, and it has trained managers in identifying signs of troubling behavior.[60]

Clearly, if an employee engages in some kind of CWB, the organization needs to respond quickly and appropriately, defining the specific behaviors that are unacceptable and the requirements for acceptable behavior.[61] It is more desirable, however, to take preventive measures. One way is to screen for CWB during the hiring process. For instance, it's been found that applicants scoring higher on cognitive ability (intelligence) tests are less likely to be involved in violence and property damage after they are hired.[62] Employees are also less likely to engage in CWB if they have satisfying jobs that offer autonomy or that don't require them to supervise too many people.[63] ●

major question ? What are the distortions in perception that can cloud one's judgment?

THE BIG PICTURE

Perception, a four-step process, can be skewed by four types of distortion: selective perception, stereotyping, the halo effect, and causal attribution. We also consider the self-fulfilling prophecy, which can affect our judgment as well.

If you were a smoker, which warning on a cigarette pack would make you think more about quitting? "Smoking seriously harms you and others around you." A blunt " Smoking kills." Or a stark graphic image showing decaying teeth.

This is the kind of decision public health authorities in various countries are wrestling with. (And a Canadian Cancer Society study in 2000 found that 58% of smokers who saw graphic images thought twice about the health effects of smoking.)[64] These officials, in other words, are trying to decide how *perception* might influence behavior.

The Four Steps in the Perceptual Process

figure II.2

THE FOUR STEPS IN THE
PERCEPTUAL PROCESS

Perception **is the process of interpreting and understanding one's environment.** The process of perception is complex, but it can be boiled down to four steps. *(See Figure 11.2.)*

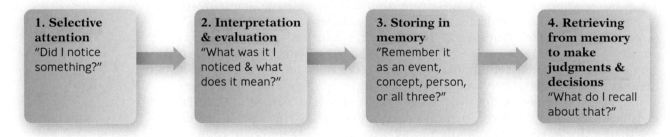

1. Selective attention
"Did I notice something?"

2. Interpretation & evaluation
"What was it I noticed & what does it mean?"

3. Storing in memory
"Remember it as an event, concept, person, or all three?"

4. Retrieving from memory to make judgments & decisions
"What do I recall about that?"

Group Exercise:
Win, Lose, or Schema

In this book, we are less concerned about the theoretical steps in perception than in how perception is distorted, since this has considerable bearing on the manager's judgment and job. In any one of the four stages of the perception process there is the possibility for misunderstandings or errors in judgment. Perceptual errors can lead to mistakes that can be damaging to yourself, other people, and your organization.

Four Distortions in Perception

Although there are other types of distortion in perception, we will describe the following: (1) *selective perception,* (2) *stereotyping,* (3) the *halo effect,* and (4) *causal attribution.*

I. Selective Perception: "I Don't Want to Hear about That"   Are there topics that you find especially uncomfortable—your own death, say, or child molestation, or cheating in college—so that you tune out these subjects when people bring them up? For example, many people avoid making a will because they find it too awful to think about their future earthly nonexistence. *Selective perception* **is the tendency to filter out information that is discomforting, that seems irrelevant, or that contradicts one's beliefs.**

One classic study found that when executives were asked to determine the key problem in a complex business case, they identified the problem as falling within their particular functional areas of work—they evidently filtered out information about other areas. That is, human resource managers said the principal problem was a people issue, marketing executives said it was a sales issue, and production people said it was a manufacturing issue.[65] This shows how managers can distort problem solving through selective perception.

2. Stereotyping: "Those Sorts of People Are Pretty Much the Same"   If you're a tall African American man, do people make remarks about basketball players? If you're of Irish descent, do people believe you drink a lot? If you're Jewish, do people think you're money-oriented? If you're a woman, do people think you're automatically nurturing? All these are stereotypes. *Stereotyping* **is the tendency to attribute to an individual the characteristics one believes are typical of the group to which that individual belongs.**[66]

Group Exercise:
*Do Stereotypes
Unconsciously Influence
the Perception Process?*

Principal areas of stereotyping that should be of concern to you as a manager are (1) *sex-role stereotypes,* (2) *age stereotypes,* and (3) *race/ethnicity stereotypes.*

- **Sex-role stereotypes.** A *sex-role stereotype* is the belief that differing traits and abilities make males and females particularly well suited to different roles.

     A classic study found that women were viewed "as relatively less competent, less independent, less objective, and less logical than men; men are perceived as lacking interpersonal sensitivity, warmth, and expressiveness in comparison to women." Moreover, the study found, "stereotypically masculine traits are more often perceived to be desirable than are stereotypically feminine characteristics."[67]

     Although research shows that men and women do not differ in such a stereotypical manner, the stereotypes still persist.[68] And, unfortunately, promotional decisions may still be affected by sex-role stereotyping. A study of a multinational Fortune 500 company, for example, revealed that men received more favorable evaluations than women in spite of controlling for age, education, organizational tenure, salary grade, and type of job.[69]

- **Age stereotypes.** *Age stereotypes* tend to depict older workers as less involved in their work, less satisfied, less motivated, and less committed than younger workers. But in fact research shows that as employees' age increases, so does their job involvement and satisfaction, work motivation, and organizational commitment.[70]

     Stereotypes also depict older workers as being less creative and more accident prone; however, this is not borne out.[71] Finally, the stereotype that older workers have higher absenteeism is not supported by the research; if anything, managers should focus more attention on absenteeism among younger rather than older workers.[72]

     Because the median age of Americans is currently 36.7 years—the oldest in our history—it seems clear that managers will probably be dealing with an older workforce.[73] Moreover, by 2030, about one-fifth of the population will be over age 65, but many, whether by choice or by necessity, will continue working.[74] World-famous heart surgeon Michael DeBakey, for instance, who was born in 1908, continued to work into his late nineties.[75]

- **Race/ethnicity stereotypes.** *Race/ethnicity stereotypes* don't bear repeating here, but it is noteworthy that there are not a lot of Hispanic and African American managers in the United States. For example, Hispanics and Latinos held only 17% of managerial and professional jobs and blacks only 27%, compared with 35.5% for whites and 47.3% for Asians.[76]

3. The Halo Effect: "One Trait Tells Me All I Need to Know" Do you think physically attractive people have more desirable traits than unattractive people—that they are happier, kinder, more successful, more socially skilled, more sensitive, more interesting, independent, exciting, sexually warm, even smarter and nicer? All of these traits have been attributed to attractive people.[77] This situation is an example of the ***halo effect, in which we form an impression of an individual based on a single trait.*** (The phenomenon is also called the *horn-and-halo effect,* because not only can a single positive trait be generalized into an array of positive traits but the reverse is also true.)

Example

The Halo Effect: Are Attractive Men & Women Paid More Than Ordinary People?

Are attractive employees paid more than ordinary (or unattractive) people for the same work? Two economists, Markus Mobius of Harvard and Tanya Rosenblat of Wesleyan University, decided to look into that question.[78]

Students were recruited to play the roles of both applicants and employers for a job that involved solving mazes. To determine how attractive applicants were, a separate panel of students was shown their photographs and asked to rate them on a beauty scale. After applicants solved mazes, employers considered the prospective employees under different circumstances. They examined (1) only an applicant's résumé, which listed age, sex, university, graduation date, job experience, and activities and hobbies; (2) the résumé and a photograph; (3) the résumé and a telephone interview; (4) the résumé, a telephone interview, and a photograph; and (5) the résumé, a telephone interview, and a face-to-face interview. The employers used the interview information to form their own estimates of the number of mazes the subjects would solve during their 15-minute jobs, and the subjects then solved the mazes as best they could.

The economists found some interesting results: (1) Although beautiful people are no better than ordinary people at solving mazes, they are more self-confident about their abilities. "Being good looking," says one article about the study, "seems to be strongly associated with self-confidence, a trait that is apparently attractive to employers."[79] (2) When employers looked only at résumés, physical appearance had no effect on their judgments, as you might expect. With all of the other treatments, employers showed higher estimates for beautiful people's productivity—especially when they had face-to-face interviews but even with telephone-only interviews, the result, apparently, of the effect of self-confidence that came across on the phone. (3) Good-looking people are good communicators, which also contributes to employers' positive perceptions. In sum, "Employers (wrongly) expect good-looking workers to perform better than their less-attractive counterparts under both visual and oral interaction," said the researchers, "even after controlling for individual worker characteristics and worker confidence."

Your Call

Are you yourself influenced in your judgment of people by how attractive they are? Do you think as a manager you could look beyond people's physical appearances to be a good judge of their competence?

Handsomely compensated. Attractive employees are generally paid better than unattractive ones are. Why do you think that is? Do you think it's inevitable?

As if we needed additional proof that life is unfair, it has been shown that attractive people generally are treated better than unattractive people. Teachers have higher expectations of them in terms of academic achievement.[80] Potential employers are more apt to view them favorably.[81] Attractive employees are generally paid higher salaries than unattractive ones are.[82] Clearly, however, if a manager fails to look at *all* an individual's traits, he or she has no right to complain if that employee doesn't work out.

4. Causal Attributions

Causal attribution is the activity of inferring causes for observed behavior. Rightly or wrongly, we constantly formulate cause-and-effect explanations for our own and others' behavior. Attributional statements such as the following are common: "Joe drinks too much because he has no willpower; but I need a couple of drinks after work because I'm under a lot of pressure." Even though our causal attributions tend to be self-serving and are often invalid, it's important to understand how people formulate attributions because they profoundly affect organizational behavior. For example, a supervisor who attributes an employee's poor performance to a lack of effort might reprimand that person. However, training might be deemed necessary if the supervisor attributes the poor performance to a lack of ability.

As a manager, you need to be alert to two attributional tendencies that can distort one's interpretation of observed behavior—the *fundamental attribution bias* and the *self-serving bias.*

- **Fundamental attribution bias.** In the *fundamental attribution bias,* people attribute another person's behavior to his or her personal characteristics rather than to situational factors.

  Example: A study of manufacturing employees found that top managers attributed the cause of industrial back pain to individuals, whereas workers attributed it to the environment.[83]

- **Self-serving bias.** In the *self-serving bias,* people tend to take more personal responsibility for success than for failure.

  Example: The way students typically analyze their performance on exams shows self-serving bias, with "A" students likely to attribute their grade to high ability or hard work and "D" students blaming factors such as bad luck, unclear lectures, and unfair testing.[84] Another example: Disgraced Enron CEO Ken Lay asserted that his company failed not because of his doings but because it was the victim of "a real conspiracy"—

by *The Wall Street Journal;* by one-time chief financial officer Andrew Fastow, who testified for the government; and by short-sellers, investors who bet that Enron's shares would fall.[85]

The Self-Fulfilling Prophecy, or Pygmalion Effect

The *self-fulfilling prophecy,* also known as the *Pygmalion* ("pig-*mail*-yun") *effect,* describes the phenomenon in which people's expectations of themselves or others lead them to behave in ways that make those expectations come true.

Expectations are important. An example is a waiter who expects some poorly dressed customers to be stingy tippers, who therefore gives them poor service and so gets the result he or she expected—a much lower tip than usual. Research has shown that by raising managers' expectations for individuals performing a wide variety of tasks, higher levels of achievement and productivity can be achieved.[86] The lesson for you as a manager is that when you expect employees to perform badly, they probably will, and when you expect them to perform well, they probably will. (In the G. B. Shaw play *Pygmalion,* a speech coach bets he can get a lower-class girl to change her accent and her demeanor so that she can pass herself off as a duchess. In 6 months, she successfully "passes" in high society, having become a woman of sensitivity and taste.) ●

Practical Action

How Can Managers Harness the Pygmalion Effect to Lead Employees?

Does the self-fulfilling prophecy really work? Research in a variety of industries and occupations shows that the effect can be quite strong. [87]

At Microsoft Corp., employees routinely put in 75-hour weeks, especially when trying to meet shipping deadlines for new products. Because Microsoft prides itself on trying to meet its deadlines, positive group-level expectations help create and reinforce an organizational culture of high expectancy for success. This process then excites people about working for the organization, thereby reducing turnover.[88]

This shows the Pygmalion effect at work—that is, managerial expectations powerfully influence employee behavior and performance. Managers can harness this effect by building a hierarchical framework that reinforces positive performance expectations throughout the organization. The foundation of this framework is employee self-expectations. In turn, positive self-expectations improve interpersonal expectations by encouraging people to work toward common goals. This cooperation enhances group-level productivity and promotes positive performance expectations within the work group.

How to Create a Pygmalion Effect

Because positive self-expectations are the foundation for creating an organizationwide Pygmalion effect, let us consider how managers can create positive performance expectations. This task may be accomplished using various combinations of the following:

1. Recognize that everyone has the potential to increase his or her performance.
2. Instill confidence in your staff.
3. Set high performance goals.
4. Positively reinforce employees for a job well done.
5. Provide constructive feedback when necessary.
6. Help employees advance through the organization.
7. Introduce new employees as if they have outstanding potential.
8. Become aware of your personal prejudices and nonverbal messages that may discourage others.
9. Encourage employees to visualize the successful execution of tasks.
10. Help employees master key skills and tasks.[89]

11.5 UNDERSTANDING STRESS & INDIVIDUAL BEHAVIOR

What causes workplace stress, and how can it be reduced?

major question?

THE BIG PICTURE

Stress is what people feel when enduring extraordinary demands or opportunities and are not sure how to handle them. There are six sources of stress: individual differences, individual task, individual role, group, organizational, and nonwork demands. We describe some consequences of stress and three ways to reduce it in the organization.

Although most workers are satisfied with their jobs, 24% say their work is "very stressful," and 43% say it is "moderately stressful."[90] A study by one health plan of 46,000 people working for six large employers found that the employers paid nearly 8% a year of total health care for treatment of what employees characterized as out-of-control stress. Such workers, who suffered from a variety of stress-related illnesses, such as migraines, back pain, and gastrointestinal disorders, had 46% higher health costs.[91] The American Institute of Stress estimates that workplace stress costs the U.S. economy over $300 billion a year in health care, missed work, and stress-reduction treatment.[92]

Work stress can also, as you might guess, put managers at risk. Researchers who interviewed 800 hospital heart-attack patients over a 5-year period found that managers run twice the normal risk of heart attack the week after they have had to fire someone or face a high-pressure deadline.[93]

Workplace stress is negatively related to positive emotions, job satisfaction, organizational commitment, and job performance and positively associated with alcohol and illicit drug use, overeating, and turnover.[94] Indeed, historically researchers have generally believed that there is an *inverted U-shaped relationship* between stress and performance. That is, low levels of stress lead to low performance (because people are not "charged up" to perform), but high levels of stress also lead to an energy-sapping fight-or-flight response that produces low performance. Optimal performance, according to this hypothesis, results when people are subjected to moderate levels of stress.

What Is Stress?

Stress is the tension people feel when they are facing or enduring extraordinary demands, constraints, or opportunities and are uncertain about their ability to handle them effectively.[95] Stress is the feeling of tension and pressure; **the source of stress is called a *stressor*.**

Stress has both physical and emotional components. Physically, according to Canadian researcher Hans Selye, considered the father of the modern concept of stress, stress is "the nonspecific response of the body to any demand made upon it."[96] Emotionally, stress has been defined as the feeling of being overwhelmed, "the perception that events or circumstances have challenged, or exceeded, a person's ability to cope."[97]

Stressors can be *hassles,* or simple irritants, such as misplacing or losing things, concerns about one's physical appearance,

Trading frenzy. Many jobs are stressful, but some are more stressful than others, such as those of traders on the floor of the New York Stock Exchange. What occupations do you think are the most stress-inducing?

and having too many things to do.[98] Or they can be *crises,* such as sudden occasions of overwhelming terror—a horrible auto accident, an incident of childhood abuse. Or they can be *strong stressors,* which can dramatically strain a person's ability to adapt—extreme physical discomfort, such as chronic severe back pain.

Stressors can be both *negative* and *positive.* That is, one can understand that being fired or being divorced can be a great source of stress but so can being promoted or getting married. As Selye writes, "It is immaterial whether the agent or the situation we face is pleasant or unpleasant; all that counts is the intensity of the demand for adjustment and adaptation."[99] In addition, Selye distinguished between bad stress (what he called "distress"), in which the result of the stressor can be anxiety and illness, and good stress ("eustress"), which can stimulate a person to better coping and adaptation, such as performing well on a test. In this discussion, however, we are mainly concerned with how stress negatively affects people and their performance.

The Sources of Job-Related Stress

There are six sources of stress on the job: (1) *demands created by individual differences,* (2) *individual task demands,* (3) *individual role demands,* (4) *group demands,* (5) *organizational demands,* and (6) *nonwork demands.*

1. Demands Created by Individual Differences: The Stress Created by Genetic or Personality Characteristics

Self-Assessment:
The Type A Scale

Some people are born worriers, those with a gene mutation (known as BDNF) that Yale researchers identify with people who chronically obsess over negative thoughts.[100] Others are impatient, hurried, deadline-ridden, competitive types with the personality characteristic known as **Type A behavior pattern, meaning they are involved in a chronic, determined struggle to accomplish more in less time.**[101] Type A behavior has been associated with increased performance in the work of professors, students, and life insurance brokers.[102] However, it also has been associated with greater cardiovascular activity and higher blood pressure, as well as to heart disease, especially for individuals who showed strong feelings of anger, hostility, and aggression.[103]

2. Individual Task Demands: The Stress Created by the Job Itself

Some occupations are more stressful than others. Being a retail store manager, for instance, can be quite stressful for some people.[104] But being a home-based blogger, paid on a piecework basis to generate news and comment, may mean working long hours to the point of exhaustion.[105]

Low-level jobs can be more stressful than high-level jobs because employees often have less control over their lives and thus have less work satisfaction. Being a high-speed data processor or doing telemarketing sales, for instance, can be quite stressful.

There is also considerable stress caused by worries over the prospective loss of a job. Recent surveys indicate that employees frequently worry about being laid off.[106] Job security is an important stressor to manage because it can result in reduced job satisfaction, organizational commitment, and performance.[107]

3. Individual Role Demands: The Stress Created by Others' Expectations of You

Roles are sets of behaviors that people expect of occupants of a position.[108] Stress may come about because of *role overload, role conflict,* and *role ambiguity.*

- **Role overload.** Role overload occurs when others' expectations exceed one's ability. Example: If you as a student are carrying a full course load plus working two-thirds time plus trying to have a social life, you know what role overload is—and what stress is. Similar things happen to managers and workers.

- **Role conflict.** Role conflict occurs when one feels torn by the different expectations of important people in one's life. Example: Your supervisor says the company needs you to stay late to meet an important deadline, but your family expects you to be present for your child's birthday party.

- **Role ambiguity.** Role ambiguity occurs when others' expectations are unknown. Example: You find your job description and the criteria for promotion vague, a complaint often voiced by newcomers to an organization.

4. Group Demands: The Stress Created by Co-workers & Managers Even if you don't particularly care for the work you do but like the people you work with, that can be a great source of satisfaction and prevent stress. When people don't get along, that can be a great stressor. Alternatively, even if you have stress under control, a co-worker's stress might bother you, diminishing productivity.[109]

In addition, managers can create stress for employees in a number of ways: Exhibiting inconsistent behaviors. Failing to provide support. Showing lack of concern. Providing inadequate direction. Creating a demanding, high-productivity environment. Focusing on negatives while ignoring good performance.[110] People who have bad managers are five times more likely to have stress-induced headaches, upset stomachs, and loss of sleep.[111]

5. Organizational Demands: The Stress Created by the Environment & Culture The physical environments of some jobs are great sources of stress: poultry processing, asbestos removal, coal mining, fire fighting, police work, ambulance driving, and so on. Even white-collar work can take place in a stressful environment, with poor lighting, too much noise, improper placement of furniture, and no privacy.[112]

An organizational culture that promotes high-pressure work demands on employees will fuel the stress response.[113] The pace of information technology certainly adds to the stress. "For example," says Michael Patsalos-Fox, chairman of the Americas region for consulting firm McKinsey & Company, "you used to have media companies and you used to have telecom [telecommunications] companies, right? . . . The problem is that they are encroaching on each other. The onset of a lot of technologies is blurring the boundary between industries that were quite separate, creating opportunities for industries to attack each other."[114] Such rapidly changing technologies and financial pressures are what keep top executives up at night.

Research shows preliminary support for the idea that organizational stress can be reduced by participatory management.[115]

6. Nonwork Demands: The Stresses Created by Forces Outside the Organization As anyone knows who has had to cope with money problems, divorce, support of elderly relatives, or other serious nonwork concerns, the stresses outside one's work life can have a significant effect on work. And people with lower incomes, education level, and work status are particularly apt to have higher stress.[116] But even people with ordinary lives can find the stress of coping with family life rugged going.

Test Your Knowledge:
Types, Causes, and
Management of Stress

The Consequences of Stress

Positive stress is constructive and can energize you, increasing your effort, creativity, and performance. Negative stress is destructive, resulting in poorer-quality work, dissatisfaction, errors, absenteeism, and turnover.

De-stressing. Experts say that exercise can be a tremendous stress reliever. Many companies maintain physical-fitness centers not only as an employee perk but also because they realize that exercise helps to improve stamina and endurance while reducing tension.

Self-Assessment:
What is Your Communication
Style Under Stress?

Manager's Hot Seat:
Personal Disclosure:
Confession Coincidence

Symptoms of Stress Negative stress reveals itself in three kinds of symptoms:

- **Physiological signs.** Lesser physiological signs are sweaty palms, restlessness, backaches, headaches, upset stomach, and nausea. More serious signs are hypertension and heart attacks.

- **Psychological signs.** Psychological symptoms include boredom, irritability, nervousness, anger, anxiety, hostility, and depression.

- **Behavioral signs.** Behavioral symptoms include sleeplessness, changes in eating habits, and increased smoking/ alcohol/drug abuse. Stress may be revealed through reduced performance and job satisfaction.

Burnout "When you keep investing more energy and the return remains low, that's when you burn out," suggests Michael Staver, founder of an executive training company.[117]

Burnout **is a state of emotional, mental, and even physical exhaustion,** expressed as listlessness, indifference, or frustration. Clearly, the greatest consequence of negative stress for the organization is reduced productivity. Overstressed employees are apt to call in sick, miss deadlines, take longer lunch breaks, and show indifference to performance. However, some may put in great numbers of hours at work without getting as much accomplished as previously.[118]

Mental health experts estimate that 10% of the workforce suffers from depression or high levels of stress that may ultimately affect job performance. In addition, researchers estimate that in a recent year stress caused 11% of employee absenteeism.[119]

Alcohol & Other Drug Abuse Have an employee who's often late? Who frequently calls in sick on Mondays? Who is somewhat sloppy? Maybe he or she is afflicted with *alcoholism,* a chronic, progressive, and potentially fatal disease characterized by a growing compulsion to drink. Alcoholics come from every social class, from students to college professors to priests to airline pilots. Alcoholism may not interfere with a person's job in an obvious way until it shows up in absenteeism, accidents, slipshod work, or significant use of a company's medical benefits.

Alcohol is the most common drug of abuse, but the misuse of others may also affect a person's productivity—legal drugs such as tranquilizers or illegal drugs such as marijuana, Ecstasy, cocaine, or heroin. Although workplace drug use seems to have declined over the past 15 years, 8.2% of full-time workers aged 18 to 64 were found to have used illicit drugs during the years 2002–2004.[120]

If you as a manager think you might be dealing with an employee with a substance-abuse problem, it's suggested you not try to make accusations but firmly point out that productivity is suffering and that it's up to the subordinate to do something about it. While not doing any counseling yourself, you can try steering the employee to the Human Resources Department, which may have an employee assistance program that may help employees overcome personal problems affecting their job performance.

Incidentally, although many people swear by 12-step programs, such as that offered by Alcoholics Anonymous, an examination of several studies found that such programs were no more and no less successful than any other interventions in reducing alcohol dependence and alcohol-related problems.[121]

Reducing Stressors in the Organization

There are all kinds of *buffers,* **or administrative changes, that managers can make to reduce the stressors that lead to employee burnout.** Examples: Extra staff or equipment at peak periods. Increased freedom to make decisions. Recognition for accomplishments. Time off for rest or personal development. Assignment to a new position.[122] Three- to 5-day employee retreats at offsite locations for relaxation and team-building activities. Sabbatical leave programs to replenish employees' energy and desire to work.[123]

Some general organizational strategies for reducing unhealthy stressors are the following:[124]

- **Rollout employee assistance programs.** *Employee assistance programs (EAPs)* **include a host of programs aimed at helping employees to cope with stress, burnout, substance abuse, health-related problems, family and marital issues, and any general problem that negatively influences job performance.**

- **Recommend a holistic wellness approach.** A *holistic wellness program* **focuses on self-responsibility, nutritional awareness, relaxation techniques, physical fitness, and environmental awareness.** This approach goes beyond stress reduction by encouraging employees to strive, in one definition, for "a harmonious and productive balance of physical, mental, and social well-being brought about by the acceptance of one's personal responsibility for developing and adhering to a health promotion program."[125]

- **Create a supportive environment.** Job stress often results because employees work under poor supervision and lack freedom. Wherever possible, it's better to keep the organizational environment less formal, more personal, and more supportive of employees.[126]

- **Make jobs interesting.** Stress also results when jobs are routinized and boring. Better to try to structure jobs so that they allow employees some freedom.

- **Make career counseling available.** Companies such as IBM make career planning available, which reduces the stress that comes when employees don't know what their career options are and where they're headed. ●

Key Terms Used in This Chapter

Summary

 11.1 Personality & Individual Behavior

Personality consists of the stable psychological traits and behavioral attributes that give a person his or her identity. There are five personality dimensions and five personality traits that managers need to be aware of to understand workplace behavior.

The Big Five personality dimensions are extroversion, agreeableness, conscientiousness, emotional stability, and openness to experience. Extroversion, an outgoing personality, is associated with success for managers and salespeople. Conscientiousness, or a dependable personality, is correlated with successful job performance. A person who scores well on conscientiousness may be a proactive personality, someone who is more apt to take initiative and persevere to influence the environment.

There are five personality traits that managers need to be aware of in order to understand workplace behavior. (1) Locus of control indicates how much people believe they control their fate through their own efforts. (2) Self-efficacy is the belief in one's personal ability to do a task. Low self-efficacy is associated with learned helplessness, the debilitating lack of faith in one's ability to control one's environment. (3) Self-esteem is the extent to which people like or dislike themselves. (4) Self-monitoring is the extent to which people are able to observe their own behavior and adapt it to external situations. (5) Emotional intelligence indicates the ability to cope, empathize with others, and be self-motivated.

 11.2 Values, Attitudes, & Behavior

Organizational behavior (OB) is dedicated to better understanding and managing people at work. OB looks at two areas:

individual behavior (discussed in this chapter) and group behavior (discussed in later chapters).

Values must be distinguished from attitudes and from behavior. (1) Values are abstract ideals that guide one's thinking and behavior across all situations. (2) Attitudes are defined as learned predispositions toward a given object. Attitudes have three components. The affective component consists of the feelings or emotions one has about a situation. The cognitive component consists of the beliefs and knowledge one has about a situation. The behavioral component refers to how one intends or expects to behave toward a situation. When attitudes and reality collide, the result may be cognitive dissonance, the psychological discomfort a person experiences between his or her cognitive attitude and incompatible behavior. Cognitive dissonance depends on three factors: importance, control, and rewards. The ways to reduce cognitive dissonance are to change your attitude and/or your behavior, belittle the importance of the inconsistent behavior, or find consonant elements that outweigh the dissonant ones. (3) Together, values and attitudes influence people's workplace behavior—their actions and judgments.

 11.3 Work-Related Attitudes & Behaviors Managers Need to Deal With

Managers need to be alert to work-related attitudes having to do with (1) job satisfaction, the extent to which you feel positively or negatively about various aspects of your work; (2) job involvement, the extent to which you identify or are personally involved with your job; and (3) organizational commitment, reflecting the extent to which an employee identifies

The Big Five personality dimensions are extroversion, agreeableness, → neuroticism conscientiousness, emotional stability, and

with an organization and is committed to its goals.

Among the types of behavior that managers need to influence are (1) performance and productivity; (2) absenteeism, when an employee doesn't show up for work, and turnover, when employees leave their jobs; (3) organizational citizenship behaviors, those employee behaviors that are not directly part of employees' job descriptions—that exceed their work-role requirements; and (4) counterproductive work behaviors, behaviors that harm employees and the organization as a whole.

II.4 Perception & Individual Behavior

Perception is the process of interpreting and understanding one's environment. The process can be boiled down to four steps: selective attention, interpretation and evaluation, storing in memory, and retrieving from memory to make judgments and decisions. Perceptual errors can lead to mistakes that affect management.

Four types of distortion in perception are (1) selective perception, the tendency to filter out information that is discomforting, that seems irrelevant, or that contradicts one's beliefs; (2) stereotyping, the tendency to attribute to an individual the characteristics one believes are typical of the group to which that individual belongs; (3) the halo effect, the forming of an impression of an individual based on a single trait; and (4) causal attribution, the activity of inferring causes for observed behavior. Two attributional tendencies that can distort one's interpretation of observed behavior are the fundamental attribution bias, in which people attribute another person's behavior to his or her personal characteristics rather than to situational factors, and the self-serving bias, in which people tend to take more personal responsibility for success than for failure.

The self-fulfilling prophecy (Pygmalion effect) describes the phenomenon in which people's expectations of themselves or others leads them to behave in ways that make those expectations come true.

II.5 Understanding Stress & Individual Behavior

Stress is the tension people feel when they are facing or enduring extraordinary demands, constraints, or opportunities and are uncertain about their ability to handle them effectively. Stress is the feeling of tension and pressure; the source of stress is called a stressor.

There are six sources of stress on the job: (1) Demands created by individual differences may arise from a Type A behavior pattern, meaning people have the personality characteristic that involves them in a chronic, determined struggle to accomplish more in less time. (2) Individual task demands are the stresses created by the job itself. (3) Individual role demands are the stresses created by other people's expectations of you. Roles are sets of behaviors that people expect of occupants of a position. Stress may come about because of role overload, role conflict, or role ambiguity. (4) Group demands are the stresses created by co-workers and managers. (5) Organizational demands are the stresses created by the environment and culture of the organization. (6) Nonwork demands are the stresses created by forces outside the organization, such as money problems or divorce.

Positive stress can be constructive. Negative stress can result in poor-quality work; such stress is revealed through physiological, psychological, or behavioral signs. One sign is burnout, a state of emotional, mental, and even physical exhaustion. Stress can lead to alcohol and other drug abuse.

There are buffers, or administrative changes, that managers can make to reduce the stressors that lead to employee burnout, such as adding extra staff or giving employees more power to make decisions. Some general organizational strategies for reducing unhealthy stressors are to roll out employee assistance programs, recommend a holistic wellness approach, create a supportive environment, make jobs interesting, and make career counseling available.

Management in Action

The Problem with Working for a Yes Man

Susan Loring remembers working for a yes man. "Oh God, I'm so glad I'm not there anymore," she moans.

It wasn't just the overabundance of work. Her boss reported to the company founder, who shared with him lots of new ideas that required major changes to projects well under way. Then, the moment of untruth always came for her yes man: He never pointed to the merits of the old plan or the flaws in the new one. The yes man caved. "What a wonderful idea!" Ms. Loring recalls him saying. "We'll have it for you on Monday."

Whenever she said "no" to her boss, she was told she didn't get either "it" or "the big picture." And there was always someone willing to bend to her yes man, making her look worse. "So you give up. You turn into the worst thing possible, which is a yes man's yes man," she says.

Her yes man became a founder favorite while Ms. Loring "had a stomachache every day getting ready for work."

Yes men, defined as stooges, flunkies, and pushovers, are so full of follow that they can't lead. They head up the corporate ladder because their agreeability is in direct proportion to their lust for power. Yes men create a make-work marathon, darting goals and work-life imbalance. They render their staffers as goose chasers, wasting time if not company money. Everyone gets tired working for the yes man, longing for a can't-do spirit.

The problem is you can't say "no" to a yes man. Having rarely uttered it, they don't value the currency of a "no." This is not about the get-lost "no," but even the most well reasoned, softly peddled, bad-for-the-bottom-line "no." No matter how deftly delivered, a "no" to a yes man is transformed into one of corporate America's most career-limiting charges: You're not a team player. . . .

This would be amusing if human yessers didn't seem even more satirical. One middle manager at an insurance company has a yes-man supervisor who tells his boss, "I was thinking the same thing myself." That was said when his boss's boss wanted a group that worked on compliance to do a task better done by accounting. "It made absolutely no sense," she says.

Similarly, Linda Shoemaker, a former sales manager, had a boss who would say, " 'No' is not in my vocabulary!" And she routinely got sent on make-work missions, like reorganizing the office files. Near the end of three weeks, her boss told her it needed to be done differently, even though she had checked with her twice. It was deflating, to put it mildly.

Working for yes men, notes Robert Sutton, a professor of management science at Stanford University, "just s---s." Because a yes man can't filter out extraneous tasks the way good leaders can, he says, his staffers are "cognitively overloaded and condemned to do many things, almost all of them badly."

Innovation also takes a hit. "In an organization where innovation happens, very often people ignore orders and don't do what they're told," he says.

To avoid pointless tasks that a yes man has greenlighted, says Prof. Sutton, you can try to reason with facts. Or you can implement the best of bad alternatives, which may actually cost the company less than full compliance: "You say you're going to do it and you do it slowly and incompetently," he says.

That maneuver can make the boss's interest in the request fade fast, he says. . . .

Lee Folger, a former salesman, is a recovered yesser. He used to yes his clients constantly only to discover that on a few occasions, he couldn't deliver on promises. The failures torched his credibility.

So after he learned his lesson, instead of yes, he'd say, "I'm just not sure we can meet your expectations."

It's better managing but he misses seeing the satisfaction, even the romance, in the other person's eyes. "It's like a wonderful, romantic dinner—and someone stops the record."

For Discussion

1. Have you ever worked for a yes man? What was it like?

2. How would you describe Susan Loring's work attitudes while working in her previous job? Explain.

3. How does the perception process explain the behavior of yes men?

4. To what extent would a yes man likely possess the Big Five personality dimensions? Explain your rationale.

5. How can employees combat the stress of working for a yes man? Discuss.

Source: Excerpted from Jared Sandberg, "How Do You Say 'No' to a Yes Man? Often Unsuccessfully," *The Wall Street Journal*, July 25, 2006, p. B1. Copyright © 2006 by Dow Jones & Company, Inc. Reproduced with permission of Dow Jones & Company, Inc. via Copyright Clearance Center.

What Is Your Emotional Intelligence Score?

Objectives

1. To help you assess your emotional intelligence.
2. To expand your knowledge of the new interpretations of intelligence.

Introduction

Employers have long been guided by one dimension of our personality, our intelligence quotient (IQ). However, a number of researchers and observers of human behavior have been examining components of intelligence that include emotions. Your Emotional Intelligence (EI) includes your abilities to motivate yourself and persist even when you are frustrated, to control your impulses and delay gratification, to regulate your mood and keep distress from overwhelming your thinking ability, to empathize with others, and to hope. The recognition of the emotional dimension to intelligence is vital today in a world of constant change and increased stress. Having a sense of your own EI is fundamental to being successful. The purpose of this exercise is to determine your own EI.

Instructions

Use this scale to indicate the extent to which you agree or disagree with each statement below.

1 = strongly disagree
2 = disagree
3 = neither agree nor disagree
4 = agree
5 = strongly agree

1.	I am usually aware—from moment to moment—of my feelings as they change.	1 2 3 4 5
2.	I think before I act.	1 2 3 4 5
3.	I am impatient when I want something.	1 2 3 4 5
4.	I bounce back quickly from life's setbacks.	1 2 3 4 5
5.	I can pick up subtle social cues that indicate others' needs or wants.	1 2 3 4 5
6.	I'm very good at handling myself in social situations.	1 2 3 4 5
7.	I'm persistent in going after the things I want.	1 2 3 4 5
8.	When people share their problems with me, I'm good at putting myself in their shoes.	1 2 3 4 5
9.	When I'm in a bad mood, I make a strong effort to get out of it.	1 2 3 4 5
10.	I can find common ground and build rapport with people from all walks of life.	1 2 3 4 5

Scoring & Interpretation

This questionnaire taps the five basic dimensions of EI: self-awareness (items 1 and 9), self-management (2, 4), self-motivation (3, 7), empathy (5, 8), and social skills (6, 10). Compute your total EI score by adding your responses to all 10 statements. Your total score will fall between 10 and 50. While no definite cutoff scores are available, scores of 40 or higher indicate a high EI. Scores of 20 or less suggest a relatively low EI.

Emotional intelligence is a collection of abilities and competencies that have an effect on a person's capacity to succeed in dealing with demands and pressures. People with high EI have the capacity to correctly perceive, evaluate, articulate, and manage emotions and feelings.

EI may be most predictive of performance in jobs such as sales or management, in which achievement is based as much on interpersonal skills as on technical ability. People with low EI are likely to have trouble managing others, making successful sales presentations, and functioning on teams.

Questions for Discussion

1. Did the results surprise you? Why or why not?

2. Look at the three items on which your score was lowest. What are some skills or attitudes you can work on to improve your EI? Explain.

3. Do you think your EI would help or hinder you when working in a team?

Based on D. Goleman, *Emotional Intelligence: Why It Can Matter More Than IQ* (New York: Bantam, 1995).

Ethical Dilemma

Should the "Fake Bad Scale" Be Used in Injury Lawsuits?

A test designed to expose fakers is roiling the field of personal-injury law, distressing plaintiffs and strengthening the hand of employers and insurers.

Proponents hail the true-or-false test as a valid way to identify people feigning pain, psychological symptoms, or other ills to collect a payout. In hundreds of cases, expert witnesses have testified that the test provided evidence that plaintiffs were lying about their injuries, just as suggested by the test's colorful name: the Fake Bad Scale.

Use of the scale surged last year after publishers of one of the world's most venerable personality tests, the Minnesota Multiphasic Personality Inventory, endorsed the Fake Bad Scale and made it an official subset of the MMPI. The Fake Bad Scale has been used by 75% of neuropsychologists, who regularly appear in court as expert witnesses, according to a survey by St. Louis University.

But now some psychologists say the test is branding as liars too many people who have genuine symptoms. Some say it discriminates against women, too. In May [2008], an American Psychological Association panel said there appeared to be a lack of good research supporting the test.

In two Florida court cases [in 2007], state judges, before allowing the test to be cited, held special hearings on whether it was valid enough to be used as courtroom evidence. Both judges ended up barring it.

"Virtually everyone is a malingerer according to this scale," says a leading critic, James Butcher, a retired University of Minnesota psychologist who has published research faulting the Fake Bad Scale. "This is great for insurance companies, but not great for people."

The test asks a person to answer true or false to 43 statements, such as "My sleep is fitful and disturbed" and "I have nightmares every few nights." Someone who suffers from, say, post-traumatic stress disorder might legitimately answer "true" to these questions. But doing so would earn the test-taker two points toward the total of 23 or so that marks a person as a possible malingerer.

Other test statements are "I have very few headaches" and "I have few or no pains." These are false, someone who has chronic headaches would say. Again, those replies would incur two more points toward a possible assessment as a malingerer. About a third of the questions relate to physical symptoms; there are questions about stress, sleep disturbance, and low energy. There is also a batch of questions related to denial of bad behavior. For instance, those who answer false to "I do not always tell the truth" get a point toward malingering. . . .

[The test] recently figured in the case of Steven Thompson, a onetime truck driver in Iraq for the KBR unit of Halliburton Inc. He said he hadn't been able to hold a job since returning to the United States in 2004. Two doctors concluded Mr. Thompson had "chronic" and "fairly severe" post-traumatic stress disorder. He filed a disability claim that was denied by the insurer of Halliburton's since-sold KBR unit.

Mr. Thompson appealed to the U.S. Labor Department, which has jurisdiction in such cases. He testified that memories of attacks on his convoys, seeing dead bodies, and smelling burning flesh led to nightmares and sleeping problems that left him too irritable and difficult to work with to hold a job.

A psychiatrist hired by the defense, John D. Griffith of Houston, concluded Mr. Thompson was exaggerating his symptoms, and cited his score of 32 on the Fake Bad Scale. A Labor Department administrative law judge denied Mr. Thompson's claim, citing the test results along with inconsistencies in his testimony. Mr. Thompson is appealing. . . .

Solving the Dilemma

How would you have ruled if you were the administrative law judge in Mr. Thompson's case?

1. I would deny the claim. The test results show that Mr. Thompson is a malingerer who is most likely lying about his condition. He just wants to be paid for doing nothing.

2. I would grant the claim based on conclusions reached by the American Psychological Association (APA). The APA questioned the validity of the survey and it thus should not be used to determine whether someone is lying.

3. I don't believe that you can determine whether someone is lying based on answers to questions about physical symptoms. Approve the claim.

4. Although more research is needed to support the accuracy of the test, I would deny the claim because Mr. Thompson scored 32 and there were inconsistencies in his testimony.

5. Invent other options.

Source: Excerpted from David Armstrong, "Malingerer Test Roils Personal-Injury Law," *The Wall Street Journal*, March 5, 2008, p. A1, A13. Copyright © 2008 Dow Jones & Company, Inc. Reproduced with permission of Dow Jones & Company, Inc. via Copyright Clearance Center.

Motivating Employees
Achieving Superior Performance in the Workplace

Major Questions You Should Be Able to Answer

12.1 Motivating for Performance
Major Question: What's the motivation for studying motivation?

12.2 Content Perspectives on Employee Motivation
Major Question: What kinds of needs motivate employees?

12.3 Process Perspectives on Employee Motivation
Major Question: Is a good reward good enough? How do other factors affect motivation?

12.4 Job Design Perspectives on Motivation
Major Question: What's the best way to design jobs—adapt people to work or work to people?

12.5 Reinforcement Perspectives on Motivation
Major Question: What are the types of incentives I might use to influence employee behavior?

12.6 Using Compensation & Other Rewards to Motivate
Major Question: How can I use compensation and other rewards to motivate people?

Managing for Motivation: Keeping Employees Invested in Their Jobs

"Get a life!" everyone says. But what, exactly, is a "life," anyway?

As more and more people have begun asking this question, it has spilled over into organizational life. The result has been a new category of work rewards and incentives called *work-life benefits.*

As one definition has it, work-life benefits are programs "used by employers to increase productivity and commitment by removing certain barriers that make it hard for people to strike a balance between their work and personal lives."[1] Examples are nonsalary incentives such as flexible work arrangements, tuition assistance, and paid time off for education and community service.

In managing for motivation, the subject of this chapter, you need to be thinking about employees not as "human capital" or "capital assets" but as people who are *investors:* they are investing their time, energy, and intelligence—their lives—in your organization, for which they deserve a return that makes sense to them.

To keep your employees invested in their jobs and performing well for the company, it helps for you to know what the Gallup Organization discovered in surveying 80,000 managers and 1 million workers over 25 years.[2] Gallup found that in the best workplaces employees gave strong "yes" answers to the following 12 questions:

- Do I know what's expected of me?
- Do I have the right materials and equipment I need to do my work right?
- Do I have the opportunity to do what I do best every day?
- In the last 7 days, have I received recognition or praise for good work?

- Does my supervisor, or someone at work, seem to care about me as a person?
- Is there someone at work who encourages my development?
- Does my opinion seem to count?
- Does the mission of my company make me feel like my work is important?
- Are my co-workers committed to doing quality work?
- Do I have a best friend at work?
- In the last 6 months, have I talked with someone about my progress?
- Have I had opportunities to learn and grow?

The best managers, Gallup says, meet with workers individually at least every 3 months, not just once or twice a year. In doing so, they not only discuss performance but also try to find out what employees want to accomplish and how the manager can help. In addition, good managers focus on strengths, rather than weaknesses, allowing employees to devote time to what they do best.

Even before *Fortune* magazine began publishing its annual list of "The 100 Best Companies to Work For," managers had been concerned about trying to motivate their employees. The best organizations, according to a project leader who helps with the *Fortune* list, keep their employees an average of 6 years, as opposed to the nationwide average of 3.6 years. They accomplish this by pushing for employees at all levels to feel involved in the company's success.[3]

For Discussion Which 3 of the 12 questions listed above are most important to you? Which do you think are most important to most employees?

forecast

What's Ahead in This Chapter

This chapter discusses how to motivate people to perform well. We consider motivation from four perspectives: content (covering theories by Maslow, Alderfer, McClelland, and Herzberg); process (covering equity, expectancy, and goal-setting theories); job design; and reinforcement. Finally, we apply these perspectives to compensation and other rewards for motivating performance.

THE BIG PICTURE

Motivation is defined as the psychological processes that arouse and direct people's goal-directed behavior. The model of how it works is that people have certain needs that motivate them to perform specific behaviors for which they receive rewards, both extrinsic and intrinsic, that feed back and satisfy the original need. The three major perspectives on motivation are need-based, process, and reinforcement.

What would make you rise a half hour earlier than usual to ensure you got to work on time—and to perform your best once there?

A nice office? A new leased car? Help with college tuition? Bringing your dog to work? Onsite laundry, gym, or childcare? Free lunch? Achievement awards? Really nice bosses?

Believe it or not, these are among the perks available to some lucky employees—and not just high-level managers.[4] Especially when employment rates are high, companies are desperate to attract, retain, and motivate key people. But even in tough economic times, there are always industries and occupations in which employers feel they need to bend over backward to retain their human capital.

Motivation: What It Is, Why It's Important

Why do people do the things they do? The answer is this: they are mainly motivated to fulfill their wants, their needs.

What Is Motivation & How Does It Work?   *Motivation* **may be defined as the psychological processes that arouse and direct goal-directed behavior.**[5] Motivation is difficult to understand because you can't actually see it or know it in another person; it must be *inferred* from one's behavior. Nevertheless, it's imperative that you as a manager understand the process of motivation if you are to guide employees in accomplishing your organization's objectives.

The way motivation works actually is complex. However, in a simple model of motivation, people have certain *needs* that *motivate* them to perform specific *behaviors* for which they receive *rewards* that *feed back* and satisfy the original need. *(See Figure 12.1.)*

figure 12.1

A SIMPLE MODEL OF MOTIVATION

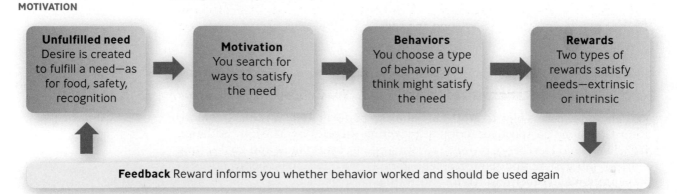

| **Unfulfilled need** Desire is created to fulfill a need—as for food, safety, recognition | **Motivation** You search for ways to satisfy the need | **Behaviors** You choose a type of behavior you think might satisfy the need | **Rewards** Two types of rewards satisfy needs—extrinsic or intrinsic |

Feedback Reward informs you whether behavior worked and should be used again

For example, you find you are hungry (need), which impels you to seek food (motive). You make a sandwich and eat it (behavior), which provides satisfaction (reward) and informs you (feedback loop) that sandwiches will reduce hunger and so should be used in the future. Or as an hourly worker you desire more money (need), which impels you (motivates you) to work more hours (behavior), which provides you with more money (reward) and informs you (feedback loop) that working more hours will fulfill your need for more money in the future.

Rewards (as well as motivation itself) are of two types—*extrinsic* and *intrinsic*.[6] Managers can use both to encourage better work performance.

- **Extrinsic rewards—satisfaction in the payoff from others.** An *extrinsic reward* **is the payoff, such as money, a person receives from others for performing a particular task.** An extrinsic reward is an external reward; the payoff comes from pleasing others.

  Example: In performing your job as a maker of custom sailboats, you get your principal satisfaction from receiving the great amount of money buyers pay you for a boat—an extrinsic reward.

- **Intrinsic rewards—satisfaction in performing the task itself. An *intrinsic reward* is the satisfaction, such as a feeling of accomplishment, a person receives from performing the particular task itself.** An intrinsic reward is an internal reward; the payoff comes from pleasing yourself.

  Example: Jenny Balaze left her post in Ernst & Young LLC's Washington, DC, office to spend 12 weeks in Buenos Aires as a volunteer providing free accounting services to a small publishing firm. It was among "the best three months of my life," says the 27-year-old business advisory services manager.[7]

Group Exercise:
What Rewards Motivate Student Achievement?

Why Is Motivation Important? It seems obvious that organizations would want to motivate their employees to be more productive. Actually, though, there are five reasons why you as a manager will find knowledge of motivation important.[8] In order of importance, you want to motivate people to . . .

1. *Join your organization.* You need to instill in talented prospective workers the desire to come to work for you.

2. *Stay with your organization.* Whether you are in good economic times or bad, you always want to be able to retain good people.

3. *Show up for work at your organization.* In many organizations, absenteeism and lateness are tremendous problems.[9]

4. *Perform better for your organization.* Some employees do just enough to avoid being fired.[10] But what you really want is employees who will give you high productivity.

5. *Do extra for your organization.* You hope your employees will perform extra tasks above and beyond the call of duty (be organizational "good citizens").

The Four Major Perspectives on Motivation: Overview

There is no theory accepted by everyone as to what motivates people. In this chapter, therefore, we present the four principal perspectives. From these, you may be able to select what ideas seem most workable to you. The four perspectives on motivation are (1) *content,* (2) *process,* (3) *job design,* and (4) *reinforcement,* as described in the following four main sections. ●

12.2 CONTENT PERSPECTIVES ON EMPLOYEE MOTIVATION

major question?   What kinds of needs motivate employees?

THE BIG PICTURE

Content perspectives are theories emphasizing the needs that motivate people. Needs are defined as physiological or psychological deficiencies that arouse behavior. The content perspective includes four theories: Maslow's hierarchy of needs, Alderfer's ERG theory, McClelland's acquired needs theory, and Herzberg's two-factor theory.

Content perspectives, also known as *need-based perspectives,* are theories that emphasize the needs that motivate people. Content theorists ask, "What kind of needs motivate employees in the workplace?" *Needs* are defined as physiological or psychological deficiencies that arouse behavior. They can be strong or weak, and, because they are influenced by environmental factors, they can vary over time and from place to place.

In addition to McGregor's Theory X/Theory Y (see Chapter 2), content perspectives include four theories:

- Maslow's hierarchy of needs theory
- Alderfer's ERG Theory
- McClelland's acquired needs theory
- Herzberg's two-factor theory

Maslow's Hierarchy of Needs Theory: Five Levels

In 1943, Brandeis University psychology professor **Abraham Maslow,** one of the first researchers to study motivation, put forth his *hierarchy of needs theory,* **which proposes that people are motivated by five levels of needs: (1) physiological, (2) safety, (3) love, (4) esteem, and (5) self-actualization.**[11]

Self-actualization. No one has to engage in volunteerism, as this teacher is doing with a young girl at a Garden Grove, California, after-school reading program. But for some people, according to Maslow's theory, it represents the kind of realization of the best life has to offer—after other needs are satisfied. What activity or experience within your lifetime would represent self-fulfillment for you, the best that would realize your potential?

The Five Levels of Needs In proposing this hierarchy of five needs, ranging from basic to highest level, Maslow suggested that needs are never completely satisfied. That is, our actions are aimed at fulfilling the "deprived" needs, the needs that remain unsatisfied at any point in time. Thus, for example, once you have achieved security, which is the second most basic need, you will then seek to fulfill the third most basic need—belongingness.

In order of ascendance, from bottom to top, the five levels of needs are as follows. *(See Figure 12.2.)*

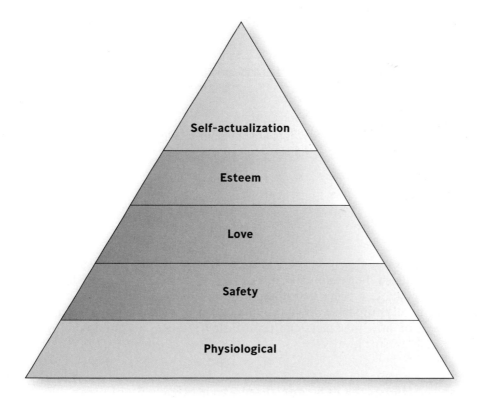

figure 12.2

MASLOW'S HIERARCHY OF NEEDS

1. Physiological Needs These are the most basic human physical needs, in which one is concerned with having food, clothing, shelter, and comfort and with self-preservation.

2. Safety Needs These needs are concerned with physical safety and emotional security, so that a person is concerned with avoiding violence and threats.

3. Love Needs Once basic needs and security are taken care of, people look for love, friendship, and affection.

4. Esteem Needs After they meet their social needs, people focus on such matters as self-respect, status, reputation, recognition, and self-confidence.

5. Self-Actualization Needs The highest level of need, self-actualization is self-fulfillment—the need to develop one's fullest potential, to become the best one is capable of being.

Example

Higher-Level Needs: One Man Finds a Way to Measure Integrity

Software engineer Firinn Taisdeal of Walnut Creek, California, designed a social event database, now called LinkUp Central, that offers its 19,000 San Francisco Bay–area members 12,000 events per year, from rock climbing to theater, for $5 a month. But he discovered early on that events were being ruined and hosts disappointed by people who didn't show up. "Flakes," he calls them.

So he modified the database to chart patterns of flakiness—an accountability system. Thus, if a person RSVPs for events but doesn't show up 50% of the time, his or her "reliability threshold" goes down. With some events, such as restaurant dinners, guests can sign up only if they have a reliability index of 50% or more. "By changing their behavior over time," says one report, "people can improve their ratings."[12]

Driven to raise the level of integrity in the culture, Taisdeal is an example of a "cultural creative," a term coined by sociologists Paul Ray and Sherry Ruth Anderson to describe people who long to create deep and meaningful change in their lives and in the world.[13] Another name for people like Taisdeal is "tempered radical," the term that Stanford organizational behavior professor Debra Meyerson uses to describe people who work to strike a balance between what they believe in and what the system expects.[14] In this way, they fulfill their safety needs while also striving to fulfill their self-actualization needs.

Your Call

What kind of higher-level needs do you think you could fulfill through your work?

Research does not clearly support Maslow's theory, although it remains popular among managers. For example, Chip Conley, CEO and founder of Joie de Vivre Hospitality, wrote a book describing how he used Maslow's theory to save his boutique hotel company with 40 locations from going bankrupt. Chip is a strong proponent of how managers can use Maslow's theory to build employee, customer, and investor loyalty.[15]

Using the Hierarchy of Needs Theory to Motivate Employees　For managers, the importance of Maslow's contribution is that he showed that workers have needs beyond that of just earning a paycheck. To the extent the organization permits, managers should first try to meet employees' level 1 and level 2 needs, of course, so that employees won't be preoccupied with them. Then, however, they need to give employees a chance to fulfill their higher-level needs in ways that also advance the goals of the organization.

Alderfer's ERG Theory: Existence, Relatedness, & Growth

Developed by **Clayton Alderfer** in the late 1960s, ***ERG theory* assumes that three basic needs influence behavior—existence, relatedness, and growth,** represented by the letters E, R, and G.

The Three Kinds of Needs　Unlike Maslow's theory, ERG theory suggests that behavior is motivated by three needs, not five, and that more than one need may be activated at a time rather than activated in a stair-step hierarchy. From lowest to highest level, the three needs are as follows:

1. E—Existence Needs   Existence needs are the desire for physiological and material well-being.

2. R—Relatedness Needs   Relatedness needs are the desire to have meaningful relationships with people who are significant to us.

3. G—Growth Needs   Growth needs are the desire to grow as human beings and to use our abilities to their fullest potential.

Alderfer also held that if our higher-level needs (such as Growth needs) are frustrated, we will then seek more intensely to fulfill our lower-level needs (such as Existence needs). This is called the *frustration-regression component*.[16]

Using the ERG Theory to Motivate Employees   The frustration-regression component of ERG theory certainly has some applicability to the workplace. For example, if you work as a bill collector making difficult phone calls and having no contact with co-workers, you might lobby your boss for better pay and benefits. Also ERG theory is consistent with the finding that individual and cultural differences influence our need states. It's clear, for instance, that people are motivated by different needs at different times in their lives, which suggests that managers should customize their reward and recognition programs to meet employees' varying needs.

McClelland's Acquired Needs Theory: Achievement, Affiliation, & Power

David McClelland, a well-known psychologist, investigated the needs for affiliation and power and as a consequence proposed the **acquired needs theory, which states that three needs—achievement, affiliation, and power—are major motives determining people's behavior in the workplace.**[17] McClelland believes that we are not born with our needs; rather we learn them from the culture—from our life experiences.

The Three Needs   Managers are encouraged to recognize three needs in themselves and others and to attempt to create work environments that are responsive to them. The three needs, one of which tends to be dominant in each of us, are as follows. *(See Figure 12.3, at right.)*

- **Need for achievement—"I need to excel at tasks."** This is the desire to excel, to do something better or more efficiently, to solve problems, to achieve excellence in challenging tasks.

- **Need for affiliation—"I need close relationships."** This is the desire for friendly and warm relations with other people.

- **Need for power—"I need to control others."** This is the desire to be responsible for other people, to influence their behavior or to control them.[18]

McClelland identifies two forms of the need for power.

The negative kind is the need for *personal power,* as expressed in the desire to dominate others, and involves manipulating people for one's own gratification.

The positive kind, characteristic of top managers and leaders, is the desire for *institutional power,* as expressed in the need to solve problems that further organizational goals.

figure 12.3

MCCLELLAND'S THREE NEEDS

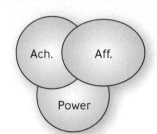

A "well-balanced" individual: achievement, affiliation, and power are of equal size

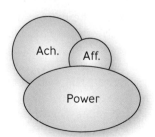

A "control freak" individual: achievement is normal, but affiliation is small and power is large

Using Acquired Needs Theory to Motivate Employees McClelland associates the three needs with different sets of work preferences, as follows:[19]

- **Need for achievement.** If you (or an employee) are happy with accomplishment of a task being its own reward, don't mind or even prefer working alone, and are willing to take moderate risks, then you probably have a *high need for achievement.* That being the case, you (or your employee) would probably prefer doing the kind of work that offers feedback on performance, challenging but achievable goals, and individual responsibility for results. People high in need for achievement tend to advance in technical fields requiring creativity and individual skills.[20]

- **Need for power.** If you, like most effective managers, have a *high need for power,* that means you enjoy being in control of people and events and being recognized for this responsibility. Accordingly, your preference would probably be for work that allows you to control or have an effect on people and be publicly recognized for your accomplishments.

- **Need for affiliation.** If you tend to seek social approval and satisfying personal relationships, you may have a *high need for affiliation.* In that case, you may not be the most efficient manager because at times you will have to make decisions that will make people resent you. Instead, you will tend to prefer work, such as sales, that provides for personal relationships and social approval.

Example

Acquired Needs Theory: The Need for Power of an Ad Agency CEO

In their book *The 100-Mile Walk: A Father and Son on a Quest to Find the Essence of Leadership,* Sander A. Flaum and his son, Jonathan, describe the generational values that divide them.[21] Sander, 69, became CEO of health care ad agency Robert A. Becker Euro RSCG in New York, a $1.7 billion business with 975 employees. Jonathan, 38, started his own public/corporate relations firm, WriteMind Communications, in Asheville, North Carolina, and hires people by the project. Sander learned to be diligent and loyal and to put work ahead of family, which led to his divorce. Jonathan grew up to be self-reliant, skeptical, and determined to balance work and family.

When the two decided to coauthor a book on leadership, they arranged to walk a combined total of 100 miles together in various places, from New York City to pre–Hurricane Katrina New Orleans, during which they talked about their views of the workplace. The book offers a comparison of their outlooks. Sander's view: "Show company loyalty." Jonathan's view: "Move on if recognition and growth opportunities are absent." Sander: "Young people in India and China are not talking about work/life balance or . . . worrying about how to spend more time at home." Jonathan: "Work without adequate time for intimate connection and personal time has long-term degenerative effects." Sander: "I think you should be attuned to the knowledge that, at any time, every competitor of yours is out to recruit your best people, steal your ideas, take over your customers, and reinvent and improve your products." Jonathan: "Paranoia works . . . sometimes. But it robs us of fully enjoying those times when everything is just fine."

Your Call

In acquired needs theory, Sander would seem to embody the need for power. What needs do you think Jonathan embodies?

Herzberg's Two-Factor Theory: From Dissatisfying Factors to Satisfying Factors

Frederick Herzberg arrived at his needs-based theory as a result of a landmark study of 203 accountants and engineers, who were interviewed to determine the factors responsible for job satisfaction and dissatisfaction.[22] Job satisfaction was more frequently associated with achievement, recognition, characteristics of the work, responsibility, and advancement. Job dissatisfaction was more often associated with working conditions, pay and security, company policies, supervisors, and interpersonal relationships. The result was Herzberg's *two-factor theory,* **which proposed that work satisfaction and dissatisfaction arise from two different factors—work satisfaction from** *motivating factors* **and work dissatisfaction from** *hygiene factors*.

Group Exercise:
What Motivates You?

Hygiene Factors versus Motivating Factors   In Herzberg's theory, the hygiene factors are the lower-level needs, the motivating factors are the higher-level needs. The two areas are separated by a zone in which employees are neither satisfied nor dissatisfied. *(See Figure 12.4, below.)*

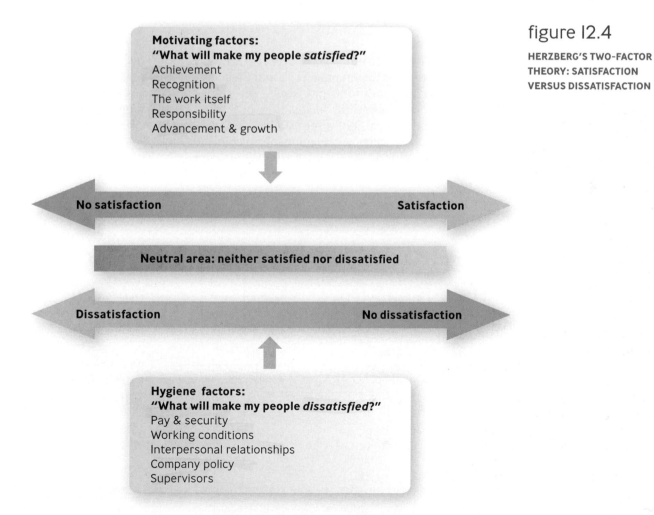

figure 12.4

HERZBERG'S TWO-FACTOR THEORY: SATISFACTION VERSUS DISSATISFACTION

- **Hygiene factors—"Why are my people dissatisfied?"** The lower-level needs, *hygiene factors,* are factors associated with job *dissatisfaction*—such as salary, working conditions, interpersonal relationships, and company policy—all of which affect the job *context* in which people work.

  An example of a hygiene factor is the temperature in a factory that's not air-conditioned during the summer. Installing air-conditioning will remove a cause of job dissatisfaction. It will not, however, spur factory workers' motivation and make them greatly satisfied in their work. Because motivating factors are absent, workers become, in Herzberg's view, merely neutral in their attitudes toward work—neither dissatisfied nor satisfied.

- **Motivating factors—"What will make my people satisfied?"** The higher-level needs, *motivating factors,* or simply *motivators,* are factors associated with job *satisfaction*—such as achievement, recognition, responsibility, and advancement—all of which affect the job content or the rewards of work performance. Motivating factors—challenges, opportunities, recognition—must be instituted, Herzberg believed, to spur superior work performance.

  An example of a motivating factor would be to give factory workers more control over their work. For example, instead of repeating a single task over and over, a worker might join with other workers in a team in which each one does several tasks. This is the approach that Swedish automaker Volvo has taken in building cars.

Using Two-Factor Theory to Motivate Employees The basic lesson of Herzberg's research is that managers should first eliminate dissatisfaction, making sure that working conditions, pay levels, and company policies are reasonable. They should then concentrate on spurring motivation by providing opportunities for achievement, recognition, responsibility, and personal growth. All these relate to job design and enrichment—creating jobs that include motivating factors—topics we take up in Section 12.4.

The four needs theories are compared below. *(See Figure 12.5.)* ●

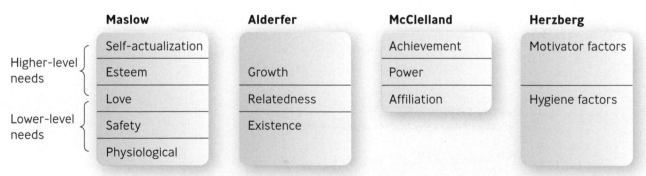

figure 12.5

A COMPARISON OF NEEDS THEORIES: MASLOW, ALDERFER, McCLELLAND, AND HERZBERG
McClelland has no classification for lower-level needs.

> Is a good reward good enough? How do other factors affect motivation?
>
> major
> question?

THE BIG PICTURE

Process perspectives, which are concerned with the thought processes by which people decide how to act, have three viewpoints: equity theory, expectancy theory, and goal-setting theory.

Process perspectives **are concerned with the thought processes by which people decide how to act**—how employees choose behavior to meet their needs. Whereas need-based perspectives simply try to understand employee needs, process perspectives go further and try to understand why employees have different needs, what behaviors they select to satisfy them, and how they decide if their choices were successful.

In this section we discuss three process perspectives on motivation:

- Equity theory
- Expectancy theory
- Goal-setting theory

Equity Theory: How Fairly Do You Think You're Being Treated in Relation to Others?

Fairness—or, perhaps equally important, the *perception* of fairness—can be a big issue in organizations. For example, if, as a salesperson for Best Buy, you received a 10% bonus for doubling your sales, would that be enough? What if other Best Buy salespeople received 15%?

Equity theory **focuses on employee perceptions as to how fairly they think they are being treated compared to others.** Developed by psychologist **J. Stacy Adams,** equity theory is based on the idea that employees are motivated to see fairness in the rewards they expect for task performance.[23] Employees are motivated to resolve feelings of injustice. How, for example, might employees respond to knowing that the average pay for CEOs is greater than 180 times the average worker's pay? How about the fact that women make about 20% less than men for comparable work?[24] Some experts suggest that this imbalance is partly responsible for the more than $50 billion a year in employee theft.[25]

The Elements of Equity Theory: Comparing Your Inputs & Outputs with Those of Others The key elements in equity theory are *inputs, outputs (rewards),* and *comparisons. (See Figure 12.6, next page.)*

- **Inputs—"What do you think you're putting into the job?"** The inputs that people perceive they give to an organization are their time, effort, training, experience, intelligence, creativity, seniority, status, and so on.
- **Outputs or rewards—"What do you think you're getting out of the job?"** The outputs are the rewards that people receive from an organization:

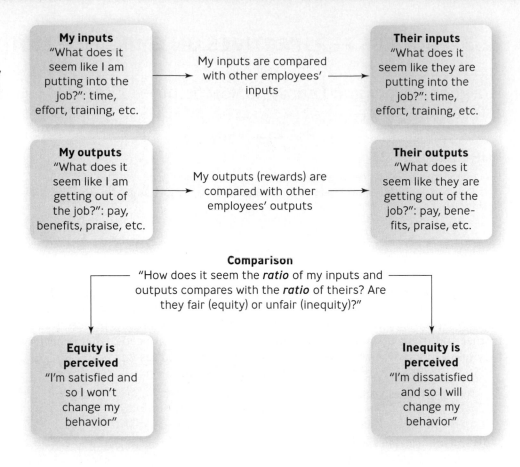

My inputs
"What does it seem like I am putting into the job?": time, effort, training, etc.

My inputs are compared with other employees' inputs

Their inputs
"What does it seem like they are putting into the job?": time, effort, training, etc.

My outputs
"What does it seem like I am getting out of the job?": pay, benefits, praise, etc.

My outputs (rewards) are compared with other employees' outputs

Their outputs
"What does it seem like they are getting out of the job?": pay, benefits, praise, etc.

Comparison
"How does it seem the *ratio* of my inputs and outputs compares with the *ratio* of theirs? Are they fair (equity) or unfair (inequity)?"

Equity is perceived
"I'm satisfied and so I won't change my behavior"

Inequity is perceived
"I'm dissatisfied and so I will change my behavior"

pay, benefits, praise, recognition, bonuses, promotions, status perquisites (corner office with a view, say, or private parking space), and so on.

- **Comparison—"How do you think your ratio of inputs and rewards compares with those of others?"** Equity theory suggests that people compare the *ratio* of their own outcomes to inputs against the *ratio* of someone else's outcomes to inputs. When employees compare the ratio of their inputs and outputs (rewards) with those of others—whether co-workers within the organization or even other people in similar jobs outside it—they then make a judgment about fairness. Either they perceive there is *equity*—they are satisfied with the ratio and so they don't change their behavior. Or they perceive there is *inequity*—they feel resentful and act to change the inequity.

To get a sense of your own reaction to equity differences, see the Self-Assessment at the end of this chapter.

Using Equity Theory to Motivate Employees Adams suggests that employees who feel they are being underrewarded will respond to the perceived inequity in one or more negative ways, as by reducing their inputs, trying to change the outputs or rewards they receive, distorting the inequity, changing the object of comparison, or leaving the situation. *(See Table 12.1, opposite page.)*

By contrast, employees who think they are treated fairly are more likely to support organizational change, more apt to cooperate in group settings, and less apt to turn to arbitration and the courts to remedy real or imagined wrongs.

table 12.1

SOME WAYS EMPLOYEES TRY
TO REDUCE INEQUITY

- **They will reduce their inputs:** They will do less work, take long breaks, call in "sick" on Mondays, leave early on Fridays, and so on.

- **They will try to change the outputs or rewards they receive:** They will lobby the boss for a raise, or they will pilfer company equipment.

- **They will distort the inequity:** They will exaggerate how hard they work so they can complain they're not paid what they're worth.

- **They will change the object of comparison:** They may compare themselves to another person instead of the original one.

- **They will leave the situation:** They will quit, transfer, or shift to another reference group.

Three practical lessons that can be drawn from equity theory are as follows.

1. Employee Perceptions Are What Count   Probably the most important result of research on equity theory is this: no matter how fair managers think the organization's policies, procedures, and reward system are, each employee's *perception* of those factors is what counts.

2. Employee Participation Helps   Managers benefit by allowing employees to participate in important decisions. For example, employees are more satisfied with their performance appraisal when they have a "voice" during their appraisal review.[26]

3. Having an Appeal Process Helps   When employees are able to appeal decisions affecting their welfare, it promotes the belief that management treats them fairly. Perceptions of fair treatment promote job satisfaction, commitment, and citizenship behavior and reduce absenteeism and turnover.[27]

Expectancy Theory: How Much Do You Want & How Likely Are You to Get It?

Introduced by **Victor Vroom**, *expectancy theory* **suggests that people are motivated by two things: (1) how much they want something and (2) how likely they think they are to get it.**[28] In other words, assuming they have choices, people will make the choice that promises them the greatest reward if they think they can get it.

The Three Elements: Expectancy, Instrumentality, Valence   What determines how willing you (or an employee) are to work hard at tasks important to the success of the organization? The answer, says Vroom, is: You will do what you *can* do when you *want* to.

Your motivation, according to expectancy theory, involves the relationship between your *effort,* your *performance,* and the desirability of the *outcomes* (such as pay or recognition) of your performance. These relationships, which are shown in the

How much do you want? Would a well-appointed office represent the tangible realization of managerial success for you? How likely do you think you are to get it? The answers to these questions represent your important motivations, according to expectancy theory.

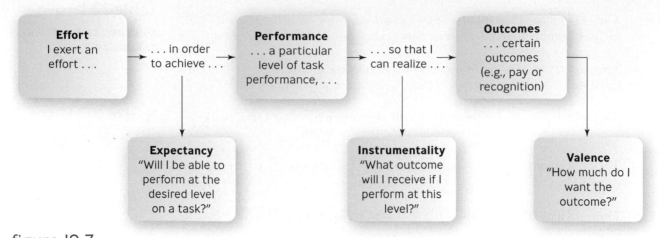

figure 12.7

EXPECTANCY THEORY: THE
MAJOR ELEMENTS

accompanying drawing, are affected by the three elements of *expectancy, instrumentality,* and *valence.* *(See Figure 12.7, above.)*

1. Expectancy—"Will I be able to perform at the desired level on a task?" **Expectancy** **is the belief that a particular level of effort will lead to a particular level of performance.** *This is called the* effort-to-performance expectancy.

Example: If you believe that putting in more hours working at Best Buy selling videogame machines will result in higher sales, then you have high effort-to-performance expectancy. That is, you believe that your efforts will matter. You think you have the ability, the product knowledge, and so on so that putting in extra hours of selling can probably raise your sales of videogame machines.

2. Instrumentality—"What outcome will I receive if I perform at this level?" **Instrumentality** **is the expectation that successful performance of the task will lead to the outcome desired.** This is called the *performance-to-reward expectancy.*

Example: If you believe that making higher sales will cause Best Buy to give you a bonus, then you have high performance-to-reward expectancy. You believe *if* you can achieve your goals, the outcome will be worthwhile. This element is independent of the previous one—you might decide you don't have the ability to make the extra sales, but if you did, you'll be rewarded. (Lately, because of the public's concern about the quality of the educational system in the United States, school boards and politicians are implementing programs that tie teachers' pay to performance.)[29]

3. Valence—"How much do I want the outcome?" **Valence** **is value, the importance a worker assigns to the possible outcome or reward.**

Example: If you assign a lot of importance or a high value to Best Buy's prospective bonus or pay raise, then your valence is said to be high.

For your motivation to be high, you must be high on all three elements—expectancy, instrumentality, and valence. If any element is low, you will not be motivated. Your effort-to-performance expectancy might be low, for instance, because you doubt making an effort will make a difference (because retail selling has too much competition from Internet sellers). Or your performance-to-reward expectancy might be low because you don't think Best Buy is going to give you a bonus for being a star at selling. Or your valence might be low because you don't think the bonus or raise is going to be high enough to justify working evenings and weekends.

Using Expectancy Theory to Motivate Employees The principal problem with the expectancy theory is that it is complex. Even so, the underlying logic is understandable, and research seems to show that managers are not following its principles.[30]

When attempting to motivate employees, managers should ask the following questions:

- **What rewards do your employees value?** As a manager, you need to get to know your employees and determine what rewards (outcomes) they value, such as pay raises or recognition.

- **What are the job objectives and the performance level you desire?** You need to clearly define the performance objectives and determine what performance level or behavior you want so that you can tell your employees what they need to do to attain the rewards.

- **Are the rewards linked to performance?** You want to reward high performance, of course. If high-performing employees aren't rewarded, they may leave or slow down and affect the performance of other employees. Thus, employees must be aware that X level of performance within Y period of time will result in Z kinds of rewards.[31]

- **Do employees believe you will deliver the right rewards for the right performance?** Your credibility is on the line here. Your employees must believe that you have the power, the ability, and the will to give them the rewards you promise for the performance you are requesting.

Champion. For athletes, such as Chicago Blackhawks hockey star Patrick Kane, voted outstanding rookie for 2008, performance seems easily measured by a simple outcome—whether you win or not. Do you think performance can be as clearly measured in the business world?

Example

Use of Expectancy Theory: Tying Teacher Pay to Student Achievement in the Denver Public Schools

The concept of instrumentality can be seen in practice by considering the debate over pay-for-performance compensation for teachers. Many educational and political leaders have been promoting the idea of providing financial rewards to teachers for improving the achievement of students, as a way to improve both student achievement and teacher quality in public schools.

A landmark 4-year study sponsored jointly by the Denver public schools and the Denver Classroom Teachers Association of a pay-for-performance program found that linking teacher compensation to student achievement can trigger fundamental improvements in school systems.[32] In the pilot program, which was implemented in 13% of the district schools, teachers developed two annual objectives for the achievement of their students that required the approval of the principal. Teachers received additional compensation if they met their objectives. The study found that students whose teachers had excellent objectives achieved higher scores, on average, than other students. The findings held true at elementary, middle, and high school levels. When the Denver program was rolled out citywide in 2006, the criteria by which teachers were allowed to earn more were extended to include teachers who agreed to work in struggling schools or teach hard-to-staff subjects such as math. Salary bumps ranged from $342 to $9,600 a year.[33]

Similar programs have been initiated in other states and cities, including California, Florida, Kentucky, Louisiana, and Minnesota and Chicago, Houston, and Nashville.[34] Previous pay-for-performance programs have been unsuccessful because they were based on the belief that compensation is the primary incentive for teachers to perform at high levels or they were designed to punish teachers who were labeled as underperforming. The study referred to above notes that for the program to work, school districts need to align and improve the quality of the curriculum, instructional delivery, and supervision and training. In addition, districts need to be sure they have high-quality assessments that can measure student progress based on what teachers are being asked to teach.

Your Call

Do you think a pay-for-performance program can work if it is simply imposed on teachers without the teachers' collaboration? What about pay-for-performance for students, as is now being tried in a number of places (such as a seven-state program that pays high school students $100 for each passing grade on advanced placement college prep exams)?[35]

Goal-Setting Theory: Objectives Should Be Specific & Challenging but Achievable

Self-Assessment:
Assessing How Personality Type Impacts Your Goal-Setting Skills

Goal-setting theory **suggests that employees can be motivated by goals that are specific and challenging but achievable.** According to psychologists **Edwin Locke** and **Gary Latham,** who developed the theory, it is natural for people to set and strive for goals; however, the goal-setting process is useful only if people *understand* and *accept* the goals. Thus, the best way to motivate performance is to set the right objectives in the right ways.[36]

The benefits of setting goals is that a manager can tailor rewards to the needs of individual employees, clarify what is expected of them, provide regular reinforcement, and maintain equity.

Three Elements of Goal-Setting Theory A *goal* is defined as an objective that a person is trying to accomplish through his or her efforts. To result in high motivation and performance, according to goal-setting theory, goals must be *specific, challenging,* and *achievable.*

1. Goals Should Be Specific Goals such as "Sell as many cars as you can" or "Be nicer to customers" are too vague and therefore have no effect on motivation. Instead, goals need to be specific—usually meaning *quantitative.* As a manager, for example, you may be asked to boost the revenues of your unit by 25% and to cut absenteeism by 10%, all specific targets.

2. Goals Should Be Challenging Goal theory suggests you not set goals that a lot of people can reach, since this is not very motivational. Rather you should set goals that are challenging, which will impel people to focus their attention in the right place and to apply more effort or inputs toward their jobs—in other words, motivate them toward higher performance.

Small business. Do employees in small businesses, such as this worker in a bakery, need the same kind of motivational goals as employees in large corporations? Is setting goals in small businesses, where there's apt to be less specialization, more or less difficult than in large organizations?

3. Goals Should Be Achievable Goals can't be unattainable, of course. You might ask data-entry clerks to enter 25% more names and addresses an hour into a database, but if they don't have touch-typing skills, that goal won't be attainable. Thus, managers need to make sure employees have additional training, if necessary, to achieve difficult goals.

Using Goal-Setting Theory to Motivate Employees In addition, when developing employee goals, you need to follow the recommendation made in Chapter 5 that goals should be SMART—that is, Specific, Measurable, Attainable, Results-oriented, and have Target dates. It is also important to make sure that employees have the abilities and resources to accomplish their goals.

Finally, make sure that you give feedback so that employees know of their progress—and don't forget to reward people for doing what they set out to do. ●

> What's the best way to design jobs—adapt people to work or work to people?

THE BIG PICTURE

Job design, the division of an organization's work among employees, applies motivational theories to jobs to increase performance and satisfaction. The traditional approach to job design is to fit people to the jobs; the modern way is to fit the jobs to the people, using job enrichment and approaches that are based on Herzberg's landmark two-factor theory, discussed earlier in this chapter. The job characteristics model offers five job attributes for better work outcomes.

Job design is (1) the division of an organization's work among its employees and (2) the application of motivational theories to jobs to increase satisfaction and performance. There are two different approaches to job design, one traditional, one modern, that can be taken in deciding how to design jobs. The traditional way is *fitting people to jobs;* the modern way is *fitting jobs to people.*[37]

Fitting people to jobs is based on the assumption that people will gradually adapt to any work situation. Even so, jobs must still be tailored so that nearly anyone can do them. This is the approach often taken with assembly-line jobs and jobs involving routine tasks. For managers the main challenge becomes *"How can we make the worker most compatible with the work?"*

One technique is *job simplification,* the process of reducing the number of tasks a worker performs. When a job is stripped down to its simplest elements, it enables a worker to focus on doing more of the same task, thus increasing employee efficiency and productivity. This may be especially useful, for instance, in designing jobs for mentally disadvantaged workers, such as those run by Goodwill Industries. However, research shows that simplified, repetitive jobs lead to job dissatisfaction, poor mental health, and a low sense of accomplishment and personal growth.[38]

Fitting Jobs to People

Fitting jobs to people is based on the assumption that people are underutilized at work and that they want more variety, challenges, and responsibility. This philosophy, an outgrowth of Herzberg's theory, is one of the reasons for the popularity of work teams in the United States. The main challenge for managers is *"How can we make the work most compatible with the worker so as to produce both high performance and high job satisfaction?"* Two techniques for this type of job design include (1) *job enlargement* and (2) *job enrichment.*

Job Enlargement: Putting More Variety into a Job   The opposite of job simplification, *job enlargement* consists of increasing the number of tasks in a job to increase variety and motivation. For instance, the job of installing television picture tubes could be enlarged to include installation of the circuit boards.

Although proponents claim job enlargement can improve employee satisfaction, motivation, and quality of production, research suggests job enlargement by itself won't have a significant and lasting positive effect on job performance. After all, working at two boring tasks instead of one doesn't add up to a challenging job. Instead, job enlargement is just one tool of many that should be considered in job design.[39]

Job Enrichment: Putting More Responsibility & Other Motivating Factors into a Job   Job enrichment is the practical application of Frederick Herzberg's two-factor motivator-hygiene theory of job satisfaction.[40] Specifically, *job enrichment* **consists of building into a job such motivating factors as responsibility, achievement, recognition, stimulating work, and advancement.**

However, instead of the job-enlargement technique of simply giving employees additional tasks of similar difficulty (known as *horizontal loading*), with job enrichment employees are given more responsibility (known as *vertical loading*). Thus, employees take on chores that would normally be performed by their supervisors. For example, one department store authorized thousands of its sales clerks to handle functions normally reserved for store managers, such as handling merchandise-return problems and approving customers' checks.[41]

The Job Characteristics Model: Five Job Attributes for Better Work Outcomes

Developed by researchers **J. Richard Hackman** and **Greg Oldham,** the job characteristics model of design is an outgrowth of job enrichment.[42] The *job characteristics model* **consists of (a) five core job characteristics that affect (b) three critical psychological states of an employee that in turn affect (c) work outcomes—the employee's motivation, performance, and satisfaction.** The model is illustrated below. *(See Figure 12.8.)*

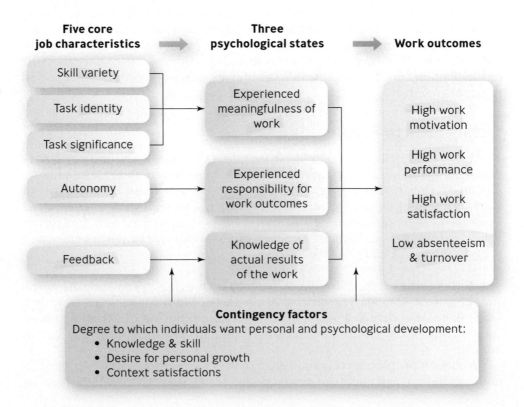

figure 12.8

THE JOB CHARACTERISTICS MODEL

Source: From J. Richard Hackman and Greg R. Oldham, *Work Redesign,* 1st edition © 1980. Reproduced by permission of Pearson Education, Inc., Upper Saddle River, New Jersey.

Five Job Characteristics   The five core job characteristics are as follows.

1. Skill Variety—"How Many Different Skills Does Your Job Require?"   *Skill variety* describes the extent to which a job requires a person to use a wide range of different skills and abilities.

Example: The skill variety required by a rocket scientist is higher than that for a short-order cook.

2. Task Identity—"How Many Different Tasks Are Required to Complete the Work?"   *Task identity* describes the extent to which a job requires a worker to perform all the tasks needed to complete the job from beginning to end.

Example: The task identity for a craftsperson who goes through all the steps to build a hand-made acoustic guitar is higher than it is for an assembly-line worker who just installs windshields on cars.

3. Task Significance—"How Many Other People Are Affected by Your Job?"   *Task significance* describes the extent to which a job affects the lives of other people, whether inside or outside the organization.

Example: A technician who is responsible for keeping a hospital's electronic equipment in working order has higher task significance than does a person wiping down cars in a carwash.

4. Autonomy—"How Much Discretion Does Your Job Give You?"   *Autonomy* describes the extent to which a job allows an employee to make choices about scheduling different tasks and deciding how to perform them.

Example: College-textbook salespeople have lots of leeway in planning which campuses and professors to call on. Thus, they have higher autonomy than do toll-takers on a bridge, whose actions are determined by the flow of vehicles.

Skill variety. Being an airline pilot—or jewelry designer, building contractor, physician, or orchestra conductor— requires a greater number of skills than, say, driving a truck. Do highly skilled employees typically make good managers? What skills do airline pilots have that would make them effective managers in other kinds of work?

5. Feedback—"How Much Do You Find Out How Well You're Doing?" *Feedback* describes the extent to which workers receive clear, direct information about how well they are performing the job.

Example: Professional basketball players receive immediate feedback on how many of their shots are going into the basket. Engineers working on new weapons systems may go years before learning how effective their performance has been.

How the Model Works According to the job characteristics model, these five core characteristics affect a worker's motivation because they affect three critical psychological states: *meaningfulness of work, responsibility for results,* and *knowledge of results.* (Refer to Figure 12.8 again.) In turn, these positive psychological states fuel *high motivation, high performance, high satisfaction,* and *low absenteeism and turnover.*

One other element—shown at the bottom of Figure 12.8– needs to be discussed: *contingency factors.* This refers to the degree to which a person wants personal and psychological development. Job design works when employees are motivated; to be so, they must have three attributes: (1) necessary knowledge and skill, (2) desire for personal growth, and (3) context satisfactions—that is, the right physical working conditions, pay, and supervision.

Job design works. A recent meta-analysis of 259 studies involving 219,625 people showed that job design was positively associated with employee performance, job satisfaction, organizational commitment, and physical and psychological well-being. Job design also was associated with lower absenteeism and intentions to quit.[43]

Applying the Job Characteristics Model There are three major steps to follow when applying the model.

- **Diagnose the work environment to see whether a problem exists.** Hackman and Oldham developed a self-report instrument for managers to use called the *job diagnostic survey.* This will indicate whether an individual's so-called motivating potential score (MPS)—the amount of internal work motivation associated with a specific job—is high or low.

- **Determine whether job redesign is appropriate.** If a person's MPS score is low, an attempt should be made to determine which of the core job characteristics is causing the problem. You should next decide whether job redesign is appropriate for a given group of employees. Job design is most likely to work in a participative environment in which employees have the necessary knowledge and skills.

- **Consider how to redesign the job.** Here you try to increase those core job characteristics that are lower than national norms.

Example: Employers want to save on health costs by helping employees with diabetes, heart disease, and similar chronic conditions avoid emergency room visits and hospital admissions. However, since primary care doctors, who could help patients manage their conditions (as by reminding diabetics to monitor their blood-glucose levels daily), are paid less than physicians in other specialties, the system has turned such doctors "into little chipmunks on a wheel, pumping out patients every five minutes," as one observer described it.[44] The solution? Redesign the job by rewarding primary care doctors for spending more time with patients. ●

12.5 REINFORCEMENT PERSPECTIVES ON MOTIVATION

> **What are the types of incentives I might use to influence employee behavior?**   *major question?*

THE BIG PICTURE

Reinforcement theory suggests behavior will be repeated if it has positive consequences and won't be if it has negative consequences. There are four types of reinforcement: positive reinforcement, negative reinforcement, extinction, and punishment. This section also describes how to use some reinforcement techniques to modify employee behavior.

Reinforcement evades the issue of people's needs and thinking processes in relation to motivation, as we described under the need-based and process perspectives. Instead, the reinforcement perspective, which was pioneered by **Edward L. Thorndike** and **B. F. Skinner,** is concerned with how the consequences of a certain behavior affect that behavior in the future.[45]

Skinner was the father of *operant conditioning,* the process of controlling behavior by manipulating its consequences. Operant conditioning rests on Thorndike's *law of effect,* which states that behavior that results in a pleasant outcome is likely to be repeated and behavior that results in unpleasant outcomes is not likely to be repeated.

From these underpinnings has come **reinforcement theory, which attempts to explain behavior change by suggesting that behavior with positive consequences tends to be repeated, whereas behavior with negative consequences tends not to be repeated.** The use of reinforcement theory to change human behavior is called *behavior modification.*

Test Your Knowledge:
Reinforcement Theory

The Four Types of Reinforcement: Positive, Negative, Extinction, & Punishment

Reinforcement **is anything that causes a given behavior to be repeated or inhibited,** whether praising a child for cleaning his or her room or scolding a child for leaving a tricycle in the driveway. There are four types of reinforcement: (1) *positive reinforcement,* (2) *negative reinforcement,* (3) *extinction,* and (4) *punishment. (See Figure 12.9, next page.)*

Positive Reinforcement: Giving Rewards   *Positive reinforcement* **is the use of positive consequences to encourage desirable behavior.**

Example: A supervisor who's asked an insurance salesperson to sell more policies might reward successful performance by saying, "It's great that you exceeded your quota, and you'll get a bonus for it. Maybe next time you'll sell even more and will become a member of the Circle of 100 Top Sellers and win a trip to Paris as well." Note the rewards: praise, more money, recognition, awards. Presumably this will *strengthen* the behavior and the sales rep will work even harder in the coming months.

Negative Reinforcement: Avoiding Unpleasantness   *Negative reinforcement* **is the removal of unpleasant consequences following a desired behavior.**

Example: A supervisor who has been nagging a salesperson might say, "Well, so you exceeded your quota" and stop the nagging. Note the neutral statement;

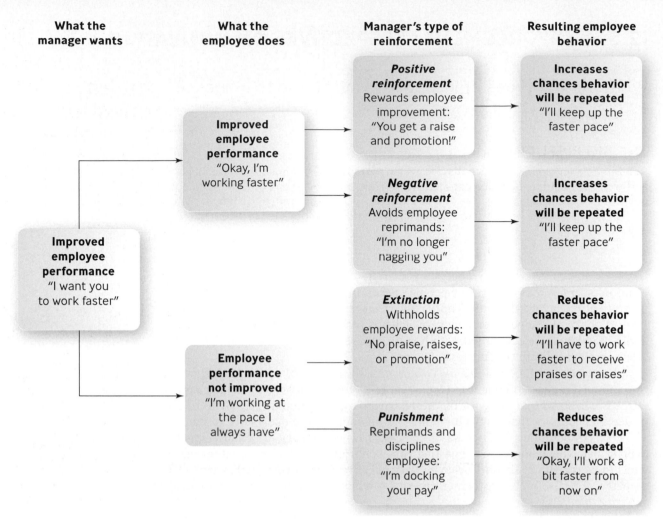

What the manager wants	What the employee does	Manager's type of reinforcement	Resulting employee behavior

Improved employee performance "I want you to work faster"

Improved employee performance "Okay, I'm working faster"

Employee performance not improved "I'm working at the pace I always have"

Positive reinforcement Rewards employee improvement: "You get a raise and promotion!"

Negative reinforcement Avoids employee reprimands: "I'm no longer nagging you"

Extinction Withholds employee rewards: "No praise, raises, or promotion"

Punishment Reprimands and disciplines employee: "I'm docking your pay"

Increases chances behavior will be repeated "I'll keep up the faster pace"

Increases chances behavior will be repeated "I'll keep up the faster pace"

Reduces chances behavior will be repeated "I'll have to work faster to receive praises or raises"

Reduces chances behavior will be repeated "Okay, I'll work a bit faster from now on"

figure 12.9

FOUR TYPES OF REINFORCEMENT

These are different ways of changing employee behavior.

there is no praise but also no longer any negative statements. This could cause the sales rep to *maintain* his or her existing behavior.

Extinction: Withholding Rewards *Extinction* **is the withholding or withdrawal of positive rewards for desirable behavior, so that the behavior is less likely to occur in the future.**

Example: A supervisor might tell a successful salesperson, "I know you exceeded your quota, but now that our company has been taken over by another firm, we're not giving out bonuses any more." Presumably this will *weaken* the salesperson's efforts to perform better in the future.

Punishment: Applying Negative Consequences *Punishment* **is the application of negative consequences to stop or change undesirable behavior.**

Example: A supervisor might tell an unsuccessful salesperson who's been lazy about making calls to clients and so didn't make quota, "Well, if this keeps up, you'll probably be let go." This could *inhibit* the salesperson from being so lackadaisical about making calls to clients.

Using Reinforcement to Motivate Employees

The following are some guidelines for using two types of reinforcement—positive reinforcement and punishment.

Positive Reinforcement   There are several aspects of positive reinforcement, which should definitely be part of your toolkit of managerial skills:

- **Reward only desirable behavior.** You should give rewards to your employees only when they show *desirable* behavior. Thus, for example, you should give praise to employees not for showing up for work on time (an expected part of any job) but for showing up early.

- **Give rewards as soon as possible.** You should give a reward as soon as possible after the desirable behavior appears. Thus, you should give praise to an early-arriving employee as soon as he or she arrives, not later in the week.

- **Be clear about what behavior is desired.** Clear communication is everything. You should tell employees exactly what kinds of work behaviors are desirable and you should tell everyone exactly what they must do to earn rewards.

- **Have different rewards and recognize individual differences.** Recognizing that different people respond to different kinds of rewards, you should have different rewards available. Thus, you might give a word of praise verbally to one person, shoot a line or two by e-mail to another person, or send a hand-scrawled note to another.

Punishment. Does getting a wallet-busting parking ticket change your behavior? What if it happens several times? Yet consider also other, presumably stronger forms of governmental punishment that are supposed to act as deterrents to bad behavior. Does the possibility of the death punishment really deter homicides? Why or why not?

Punishment   Unquestionably there will be times when you'll need to threaten or administer an unpleasant consequence to stop an employee's undesirable behavior. Sometimes it's best to address a problem by combining punishment with positive reinforcement. Some suggestions for using punishment are as follows.

- **Punish only undesirable behavior.** You should give punishment only when employees show frequent *undesirable* behavior. Otherwise, employees may come to view you negatively as a tyrannical boss. Thus, for example, you should reprimand employees who show up, say, a half hour late for work but not 5 or 10 minutes late.

- **Give reprimands or disciplinary actions as soon as possible.** You should mete out punishment as soon as possible after the undesirable behavior occurs. Thus, you should give a reprimand to a late-arriving employee as soon as he or she arrives.

- **Be clear about what behavior is undesirable.** Tell employees exactly what kinds of work behaviors are undesirable and make any disciplinary action or reprimand match the behavior. A manager should not, for example, dock an hourly employee's pay if he or she is only 5 or 10 minutes late for work.

- **Administer punishment in private.** You would hate to have your boss chew you out in front of your subordinates, and the people who report to you also shouldn't be reprimanded in public, which would lead only to resentments that may have nothing to do with an employee's infractions.

- **Combine punishment and positive reinforcement.** If you're reprimanding an employee, be sure to also say what he or she is doing right and state what rewards the employee might be eligible for. For example, while reprimanding someone for being late, say that a perfect attendance record over the next few months will put that employee in line for a raise or promotion. ●

Test Your Knowledge:
Reinforcing Performance

THE BIG PICTURE

Compensation, the main motivator of performance, includes pay for performance, bonuses, profit sharing, gain sharing, stock options, and pay for knowledge. Other nonmonetary incentives address needs that aren't being met, such as work-life balance, growth in skills, and commitment.

"In the past, people could see the fruits of their labor immediately: a chair made or a ball bearing produced," writes *Wall Street Journal* columnist Jared Sandberg. However, in the information age, when so much of a person's time is spent looking into a computer screen and working on partial tasks seemingly unconnected to something whole, "it can be hard to find gratification from work that is largely invisible."[46] As work becomes more invisible and intangible, more team-based rather than individual-based, it also becomes harder to measure, harder to define its successful accomplishment—and harder to motivate employees to perform well at it.

No wonder there is now so much interest in the field of ***employee engagement, defined as a heightened emotional connection that an employee feels for his or her organization, which influences him or her to exert greater discretionary effort in his or her work.***[47] Reportedly only 20%–30% of employees in a typical organization are actively engaged and willing to give their best efforts.[48] Yet one 3-year study of 40 multinationals found that companies with high engagement scores had profit margins that were 3.44% higher than those of low-engagement companies.[49]

Perhaps the first thing that comes to mind when you think about motivating performance is compensation—how much money you or your employees can make. But consider how motivation worked for software engineer Firinn Taisdeal, mentioned previously. In 2003, he walked away from a job just before a historic public offering that probably would have made him rich. Why? Because the people he worked with repelled him. "They were not just greedy," he says. "They had no integrity."[50] Or consider Mary Morse, another software engineer, who turned down several offers from other Silicon Valley firms, at least one of which would have made her wealthy, in order to stay with the computer-aided design firm Autodesk. The reason? She liked her bosses.[51]

Morse in particular demonstrates the truth of a Gallup Organization poll that found that most workers rate having a caring boss higher than they value monetary benefits.[52] Clearly, then, motivating doesn't just involve dollars.

Motivation & Compensation

Most people are paid an hourly wage or a weekly or monthly salary. Both of these are easy for organizations to administer, of course. But by itself a wage or a salary gives an employee little incentive to work hard. Incentive compensation plans try to do so, although no single plan will boost the performance of all employees.

Motivation as a small business owner. Susan Brown of Golden, Colorado, had dreamed of opening her own business since she was a child. However, she invented the Boppy, a simple pillow stuffed with foam, almost accidentally, when her daughter's day care center asked parents to bring in pillows to prop up infants who couldn't sit up on their own. Today the Boppy Co. has annual sales of $15 million to $25 million. For some people, like Brown, the only way to merge motivation and compensation is to own and manage their own business. What factors or incentives motivate you to work hard?

Characteristics of the Best Incentive Compensation Plans   In accordance with most of the theories of motivation we described earlier, for incentive plans to work, certain criteria are advisable, as follows. (1) Rewards must be linked to performance and be measurable. (2) The rewards must satisfy individual needs. (3) The rewards must be agreed on by manager and employees. (4) The rewards must be believable, and achievable by employees.

Popular Incentive Compensation Plans   How would you like to be rewarded for your efforts? Some of the most well-known incentive compensation plans are *pay for performance, bonuses, profit sharing, gainsharing, stock options,* and *pay for knowledge.*

- **Pay for performance.** Also known as *merit pay,* ***pay for performance* bases pay on one's results.** Thus, different salaried employees might get different pay raises and other rewards (such as promotions) depending on their overall job performance.[53]

    Examples: One standard pay-for-performance plan, already mentioned, is payment according to a ***piece rate,* in which employees are paid according to how much output they produce,** as is often used with farmworkers picking fruit and vegetables. Another is the ***sales commission, in which sales representatives are paid a percentage of the earnings the company made from their sales,*** so that the more they sell, the more they are paid. We discussed teacher pay for performance under expectancy theory. A good deal of the criticism of excessive executive pay is that it has not been tied to company performance.[54]

- **Bonuses.** *Bonuses* **are cash awards given to employees who achieve specific performance objectives.**

    Example: Nieman Marcus, the department store, pays its salespeople a percentage of the earnings from the goods they sell.

    Unfortunately, the documents that most companies file (proxy documents to the Securities and Exchange Commission) to explain what specific targets executives had to meet to earn their bonuses are not very clear, being couched mainly in legalese.[55]

- **Profit sharing.** *Profit sharing* **is the distribution to employees of a percentage of the company's profits.**

  Example: In one T-shirt and sweatshirt manufacturing company, 10% of pretax profits are distributed to employees every month, and more is given out at the end of the year. Distributions are apportioned according to such criteria as performance, attendance, and lateness for individual employees.

- **Gainsharing.** *Gainsharing* **is the distribution of savings or "gains" to groups of employees who reduced costs and increased measurable productivity.**

  Example: There are different types of gainsharing plans, but in one known as the *Scanlon plan,* developed in the 1920s by a steel-industry union leader named Joseph Scanlon, a portion of any cost savings, usually 75%, are distributed back to employees; the company keeps the other 25%.[56]

- **Stock options.** With *stock options,* **certain employees are given the right to buy stock at a future date for a discounted price.** The motivator here is that employees holding stock options will supposedly work hard to make the company's stock rise so that they can obtain it at a cheaper price. By giving stock options to all employees who work 20 or more hours a week, Starbucks Corp. has been able to hold its annual turnover rate to 60%—in an industry (fast food and restaurants) in which 300% is not unheard of.[57] (The use of stock options has been criticized recently because many companies allowed "backdating"—permitting their executives to buy company stock at low purchase prices from previous days or weeks. As one writer points out, this is sort of like being able to make a fortune by betting on a Kentucky Derby whose outcome you've known for some time.)[58]

- **Pay for knowledge.** Also known as *skill-based pay,* ***pay for knowledge*** **ties employee pay to the number of job-relevant skills or academic degrees they earn.**

  Example: The teaching profession is a time-honored instance of this incentive, in which elementary and secondary teachers are encouraged to increase their salaries by earning further college credit. However, firms such as FedEx also have pay-for-knowledge plans.

Nonmonetary Ways of Motivating Employees

Employees who can behave autonomously, solve problems, and take the initiative are apt to be the very ones who will leave if they find their own needs aren't being met—namely:

- **The need for work-life balance.** A PricewaterhouseCoopers survey of 2,500 university students in 11 countries found that 57% named as their primary career goal "attaining a balance between personal life and career."[59] A 25-year study of values in the United States found that "employees have become less convinced that work should be an important part of one's life or that working hard makes me a better person."[60] Gen Yers in particular are apt to seek out firms that emphasize work-life balance.[61]

- **The need to expand skills.** Having watched their parents undergo downsizing, younger workers in particular are apt to view a job as a way of gaining skills that will enable them to earn a decent living in the future.

- **The need to matter.** Workers now want to be with an organization that allows them to feel they matter. They want to commit to their profession or fellow team members rather than have to profess a blind loyalty to the corporation.

There is a whole class of nonmonetary incentives to attract, retain, and motivate employees. The foremost example is the *flexible workplace*—including part-time work, flextime, compressed workweek, job sharing, and telecommuting, as described in the box below.

Practical Action

The Flexible Workplace

With so many two-paycheck families, single parents, and other diverse kinds of employees in the workforce, many employers now recognize the idea of a *flexible workplace* as a way of recruiting, retaining, and motivating employees. Among the types of alternative work schedules available:

Part-Time Work—Less Than 40 hours
Part-time work is any work done on a schedule less than the standard 40-hour workweek. Some part-time workers—so-called temporary workers or contingency workers—actually want to work 40 hours or more, but can't find full-time jobs. Others, however, work part time by choice. Today an organization can hire not only part-time clerical help, for instance, but also part-time programmers, market researchers, lawyers, even part-time top executives.

Flextime—Flexible Working Hours
Flextime, or flexible time, consists of flexible working hours, or any schedule that gives one some choices in working hours. If, for example, an organization's normal working hours are 9 A.M. to 5 P.M., a flextime worker might be allowed to start and finish an hour earlier or an hour later—for instance, to work from 8 A.M. to 4 P.M. The main requirement is that the employee be at work during certain core hours, to be available for meetings, consultations, and so on. By offering flextime hours, organizations can attract and keep employees with special requirements such as the need to take care for children or elderly parents. It also benefits employees who wish to avoid commuting during rush hour.

Compressed Workweek—40 Hours in Four Days
In a compressed workweek, employees perform a full-time job in less than 5 days of standard 8- (or 9-) hour shifts. The most common variation is a 40-hour week performed in 4 days of 10 hours each, which gives employees three (instead of two) consecutive days off. The benefits are that organizations can offer employees more leisure time and reduced wear and tear and expense from commuting. The disadvantages are possible scheduling problems, unavailability of an employee to co-workers and customers, and fatigue from long workdays.

Job Sharing—Two People Split the Same Job
In job sharing, two people divide one full-time job. Usually, each person works a half day, although there can be other arrangements (working alternate days or alternate weeks, for example). As with a compressed workweek, job sharing provides employees with more personal or leisure time. The disadvantage is that it can result in communication problems with co-workers or customers.

Telecommuting & Other Work-at-Home Schedules
There have always been some employees who have had special full-time or part-time arrangements whereby they are allowed to work at home, keeping in touch with their employers and co-workers by mail and phone. The fax machine, the personal computer, the Internet, and overnight-delivery services have now made work-at-home arrangements much more feasible.

Working at home with telecommunications between office and home is called telecommuting. The advantages to employers are increased productivity because telecommuters experience less distraction at home and can work flexible hours.

Other incentives can be expressed simply as *treat employees well,* some examples of which follow.

Thoughtfulness: The Value of Being Nice   A study by Walker Information, an Indianapolis-based research firm, found that employers spend too little time showing workers they matter, as manifested in lack of communication and lack of interest in new ideas and contributions.[62] A majority of employees feel underappreciated, according to a 1999 survey. Forty percent of employees who rated their boss's performance as poor said they were likely to look for a new job; only 11% of those who rated it excellent said they would.[63] "Being nice" to employees means, for example, reducing criticism, becoming more effusive in your praise, and writing thank-you notes to employees for exceptional performance.[64]

The No. 1 reason people quit their jobs, it's believed, is their dissatisfaction with their supervisors, not their paychecks. Thus, industrial psychologist B. Lynn Ware suggests that if you learn valued employees are disgruntled, you should discuss it with them.[65] Employers can promote personal relationships, which most employees are concerned about on the job, by offering breaks or other opportunities in which people can mix and socialize.

Work-Life Benefits   Work-life benefits, according to Kathie Lingle, are programs "used by employers to increase productivity and commitment by removing certain barriers that make it hard for people to strike a balance between their work and personal lives."[66]

Lingle, who is national work-life director for KPMG, an accounting and consulting firm, emphasizes that work-life benefits "are not a reward, but a way of getting work done." After all, some employees are low performers simply because of a lack of life-work balance, with great demands at home. "If you only give these 'rewards' to existing high performers," says Lingle, "you're cutting people off who could, with some support, be high performers." Nevertheless, handing out extra time off can be used to reward performance and prevent burnout.[67]

Besides alternative scheduling, work-life benefits include helping employees with daycare costs or even establishing on-site centers; domestic-partner benefits; job-protected leave for new parents; and provision of technology such as mobile phones and laptops to enable parents to work at home.[68]

Surroundings   The cubicle, according to new research, is stifling the creativity and morale of many workers, and the bias of modern-day office designers for open spaces and neutral colors is leading to employee complaints that their workplaces are too noisy or too bland.

"There is no such thing as something that works for everybody," says Alan Hedge, a professor of environmental analysis at Cornell University.[69] An 8-foot-by-8-foot cubicle may not be a good visual trigger for human brains, and companies wanting to improve creativity and productivity may need to think about giving office employees better things to look at.[70]

Skill-Building & Educational Opportunities   Learning opportunities can take two forms. Managers can see that workers are matched with co-workers from whom they can learn, allowing them, for instance, to "shadow" workers in other jobs or be in interdepartmental task forces. There can also be tuition reimbursement for part-time study at a college or university.[71]

Cubicle culture. It might be too difficult to design a setup in which everyone has an office with a view. But would it be possible to design a layout in which everyone has a private office? Do you think it would better motivate employees?

Sabbaticals Intel and Apple understand that in a climate of 80-hour weeks people need to recharge themselves. But even McDonald's offers sabbaticals to longtime employees, giving a month to a year of paid time off in which to travel, learn, and pursue personal projects. The aim, of course, is to enable employees to recharge themselves but also, it is hoped, to cement their loyalty to the organization.[72] ●

Key Terms Used in This Chapter

12.1 Motivating for Performance

Motivation is defined as the psychological processes that arouse and direct goal–directed behavior. In a simple model of motivation, people have certain needs that motivate them to perform specific behaviors for which they receive rewards that feed back and satisfy the original need. Rewards are of two types: (1) An extrinsic reward is the payoff, such as money, a person receives from others for performing a particular task. (2) An intrinsic reward is the satisfaction, such as a feeling of accomplishment, that a person receives from performing the particular task itself.

As a manager, you want to motivate people to do things that will benefit your organization—join it, stay with it, show up for work at it, perform better for it, and do extra for it.

Four major perspectives on motivation are (1) content, (2) process, (3) job design, and (4) reinforcement.

12.2 Content Perspectives on Employee Motivation

Content perspectives or need-based perspectives emphasize the needs that motivate people. Needs are defined as physiological or psychological deficiencies that arouse behavior. Besides the McGregor Theory X/Theory Y (Chapter 1), need-based perspectives include (1) the hierarchy of needs theory, (2) the ERG theory, (3) the acquired needs theory, and (4) the two-factor theory.

The hierarchy of needs theory proposes that people are motivated by five levels of need: physiological, safety, love, esteem, and self-actualization needs.

ERG theory assumes that three basic needs influence behavior—existence, relatedness, and growth.

The acquired needs theory states that three needs—achievement, affiliation, and power—are major motives determining people's behavior in the workplace.

The two-factor theory proposes that work satisfaction and dissatisfaction arise from two different factors—work satisfaction from so-called motivating factors, and work dissatisfaction from so-called hygiene factors. Hygiene factors, the lower-level needs, are factors associated with job dissatisfaction—such as salary and working conditions—which affect the environment in which people work. Motivating factors, the higher-level needs, are factors associated with job satisfaction—such as achievement and advancement—which affect the rewards of work performance.

12.3 Process Perspectives on Employee Motivation

Process perspectives are concerned with the thought processes by which people decide how to act. Three process perspectives on motivation are (1) equity theory, (2) expectancy theory, and (3) goal-setting theory.

Equity theory focuses on employee perceptions as to how fairly they think they are being treated compared to others. The key elements in equity theory are inputs, outputs (rewards), and comparisons. (1) With inputs, employees consider what they are putting into the job in time, effort, and so on. (2) With outputs or rewards, employees consider what they think they're getting out of the job in terms of pay, praise, and so on. (3) With comparison, employees compare the ratio of their own outcomes to inputs against the ratio of someone else's outcomes to inputs. Three practical lessons of equity theory are that employee perceptions are what count, employee participation helps, and having an appeal process helps.

Expectancy theory suggests that people are motivated by how much they want something and how likely they think they are to get it. The three elements affecting motivation are expectancy, instrumentality, and valence. (1) Expectancy is the belief that a particular level of effort will lead to a particular level of performance. (2) Instrumentality is the expectation that successful performance of the task will lead to the outcome desired. (3) Valence is the value, the importance a worker assigns to the possible outcome or reward. When attempting to motivate employees, according to the logic of expectancy theory, managers should ascertain what rewards employees value, what job objectives and performance level they desire, whether there are rewards linked to performance, and whether employees believe managers will deliver the right rewards for the right performance.

Goal-setting theory suggests that employees can be motivated by goals that are specific and challenging but achievable. In addition, the theory suggests that goals should be set jointly with the employee, be measurable, and have a target date for accomplishment and that employees should receive feedback and rewards.

 12.4 Job Design Perspectives on Motivation
Job design is, first, the division of an organization's work among its employees and, second, the application of motivational theories to jobs to increase satisfaction and performance. Two approaches to job design are fitting people to jobs (the traditional approach) and fitting jobs to people.

Fitting jobs to people assumes people are underutilized and want more variety. Two techniques for this type of job design include (1) job enlargement, increasing the number of tasks in a job to increase variety and motivation, and (2) job enrichment, building into a job such motivating factors as responsibility, achievement, recognition, stimulating work, and advancement.

An outgrowth of job enrichment is the job characteristics model, which consists of (a) five core job characteristics that affect (b) three critical psychological states of an employee that in turn affect (c) work outcomes—the employee's motivation, performance, and satisfaction. The five core job characteristics are (1) skill variety—how many different skills a job requires; (2) task identity—how many different tasks are required to complete the work; (3) task significance—how many other people are affected by the job; (4) autonomy—how much discretion the job allows the worker; and (5) feedback—how much employees find out how well

they're doing. These five characteristics affect three critical psychological states: meaningfulness of work, responsibility for results, and knowledge of results. Three major steps to follow when applying the job characteristics model are (1) diagnose the work environment to see if a problem exists, (2) determine whether job redesign is appropriate, and (3) consider how to redesign the job.

 12.5 Reinforcement Perspectives on Motivation
Reinforcement theory attempts to explain behavior change by suggesting that behavior with positive consequences tends to be repeated whereas behavior with negative consequences tends not to be repeated. Reinforcement is anything that causes a given behavior to be repeated or inhibited.

There are four types of reinforcement. (1) Positive reinforcement is the use of positive consequences to encourage desirable behavior. (2) Negative reinforcement is the removal of unpleasant consequences followed by a desired behavior. (3) Extinction is the withholding or withdrawal of positive rewards for desirable behavior, so that the behavior is less likely to occur in the future. (4) Punishment is the application of negative consequences to stop or change undesirable behavior.

In using positive reinforcement to motivate employees, managers should reward only desirable behavior, give rewards as soon as possible, be clear about what behavior is desired, and have different rewards and recognize individual differences. In using punishment, managers should punish only undesirable behavior, give reprimands or disciplinary actions as soon as possible, be clear about what behavior is undesirable, administer punishment in private, and combine punishment and positive reinforcement.

12.6 Using Compensation & Other Rewards to Motivate
Compensation is only one form of motivator. For incentive compensation plans for work, rewards must be linked to

performance and be measurable; they must satisfy individual needs; they must be agreed on by manager and employee; and they must be perceived as being equitable, believable, and achievable by employees.

Popular incentive compensation plans are the following. (1) Pay for performance bases pay on one's results. One kind is payment according to piece rate, in which employees are paid according to how much output they produce. Another is the sales commission, in which sales representatives are paid a percentage of the earnings the company made from their sales. (2) Bonuses are cash awards given to employees who achieve specific performance objectives. (3) Profit sharing is the distribution to employees of a percentage of the company's profits. (4) Gainsharing is the distribution of savings or "gains" to groups of employees who reduced costs and increased measurable productivity. (5) Stock options allow certain employees to buy stock at a future date for a discounted price. (6) Pay for knowledge ties employee pay to the number of job-relevant skills or academic degrees they earn.

There are also nonmonetary ways of compensating employees. Some employees will leave because they feel the need for work-life balance, the need to expand their skills, and the need to matter. To retain such employees, nonmonetary incentives have been introduced, such as the flexible workplace. Other incentives that keep employees from leaving are thoughtfulness by employees' managers, work-life benefits such as daycare, attractive surroundings, skill-building and educational opportunities, and work sabbaticals.

Management in Action

Sue Nokes Motivates Employees with a Variety of Techniques

This isn't just any suit: It's Sue Nokes. She's the flashy, feisty spark plug of a woman who runs sales and customer service at T-Mobile USA, the fast-growing $17 billion subsidiary of Deutsche Telekom. In that capacity she's in charge of more than 15,000 employees around the U.S. . . .

Though T-Mobile is ranked fourth, with 11% of the U.S. market, behind Verizon, AT&T, and Sprint Nextel, since the end of 2002 it has gained more than five share points, according to Mark Cardwell of Sanford C. Bernstein. Even more impressive, within two years of Nokes's arrival in 2002, the company catapulted to the top of J.D. Power's rankings of customer care in the wireless industry. It has now won the biannual title six times in a row. . . .

That's a huge turnaround from 2002, when T-Mobile ranked dead last according to internal surveys. (J.D. Power started its national wireless surveys in 2003.) Dotson, who had just been named CEO, reached out to Nokes, then at Wal-Mart.com, telling her that the company's customer organization needed a complete overhaul. Before committing to the job, Nokes visited a few call centers and was horrified by what she saw. Absenteeism averaged 12% daily; turnover was a staggering 100%-plus annually. The company used "neighborhood seating," a common technique at call centers in which employees don't have desks but instead drag their stuff from cubicle to cubicle. "I asked [managers], 'Are you losing any good people?' They said, 'Yeah,'" Nokes says. "I said, 'Anybody feeling bad about that?'" . . .

Although Nokes loves to talk, she actually spends much of her day listening. In a focus group in the Menaul [call center in Albuquerque], dressed in a natty black jacket with white trim, tons of gold jewelry, and funky black-and-white-checked glasses to match, Nokes, 52, says what she says at virtually every such meeting (after, that is, making a bunch of wisecracks about her weight, age, and declining mental functions). "I have two questions: What's going well, and what's broken?"

One rep suggests a feature that lets customers turn off incoming text messages so that they don't have to be charged; another, Sergio Juardo, wonders why T-Mobile.com has no web page in Spanish. Nokes listens carefully, seemingly unfazed by the fact that Juardo's cheek is painted with the words I HEART SUE NOKES. In the focus groups and in the larger town hall meetings, Nokes is brutally honest, telling the group, for instance, that the company erred by not adding enough service reps to support T-Mobile's new pay-as-you-go service. Responding to a complaint that it's too time-consuming to log in to the system, she tells employees that a quick fix is impossible given the company's other technological priorities. "It's important that we build an environment where you can tell me my baby is ugly," Nokes says, her hard A's revealing her Midwestern roots. "And when you ask what's wrong, you'd better fix some stuff." . . .

Connecting to everyday workers was particularly important when Nokes landed at Wal-Mart .com, working for then-CEO Jeanne Jackson to build a customer-service organization nearly from scratch. "Sue, to me, is the world's perfect executive," says Jackson, now with MSP Capital. "You don't have to go to sleep at night worrying about her decisions. And on the other hand she makes you feel like a brilliant boss—not by sucking up but by giving you honest feedback." Jackson recalls Nokes "reading me the riot act" one day. "I was spending most of my time with the engineering staff, and she said [I needed to] get out there and show my face to call-center employees. She was absolutely right.". . .

Nokes quickly gave workers their own seats and asked for $17 million to bring salaries up to the 50th percentile. She also overhauled the training process (reps now go through 132 hours of training and team meetings each year) and began hiring based more on attitude than experience. She also created a standard set of metrics to measure reps on, tracking call quality, attendance, and schedule reliability along with the speed of the call resolution. "I will never hold you accountable for things that don't matter to your customer or to fellow employees," Nokes tells her Albuquerque acolytes before explaining—in her own inimitable way—what she's looking for. Absenteeism ("pimping your peers," she calls it) is bad. Solving problems in one phone call (one-call resolution, or OCR), she says, is critical. "We have frigged up [our customers'] day," she says. "They need to go to the john and do other things."

To motivate employees in what has long been considered a dead-end job, Nokes promised when she joined that 80% of promotions would eventually go to existing employees. By August 2007 that number had hit 82%. Her team also created a new "rewards and recognition system" in which high performers—using the new metrics—were rewarded with trips to Las Vegas or Hawaii and prizes. Today absenteeism is at 3% annually and attrition is at 42%. Employee satisfaction—at 80%—is the highest it's ever been.

For Discussion

1. How has Sue Nokes used recommendations derived from content perspectives of motivation to motivate employees? Discuss.

2. To what extent is Nokes changing hygiene factors and motivating factors to provide a positive work environment? Provide examples to support your conclusions.

3. To what extent are Nokes's actions consistent with both equity and expectancy theory? Explain.

4. What are the key lessons learned from this case? Discuss.

Source: From Jennifer Reingold, "Behind T-Mobile's Customer Service Success," *Fortune*, October 1, 2007, pp. 55–58. Copyright © 2007 Time Inc. All rights reserved.

Self-Assessment

What Is Your Reaction to Equity Differences?

Objectives

1. Assess your reaction to equity differences.
2. Gain more insight into yourself.

Introduction

Have you ever noticed that certain people scream "No fair!" whenever they perceive something as unequal? Have you also noticed that other people don't seem bothered by inequity at all? According to researchers, when given the same amount of inequity, people respond differently depending on their individual equity sensitivity. There are varying degrees of equity sensitivity:

Benevolents are individuals who prefer their outcome/input ratios to be less than the others being compared. These are people who don't mind being underrewarded.

Equity Sensitives are individuals who prefer outcome/input ratios to be equal. These people are concerned with obtaining rewards that they perceive to be fair in relation to what others are receiving.

Entitleds are individuals who prefer that their outcome/input ratios go above those of the others being compared. These people aren't worried by inequities and actually prefer situations in which they see themselves as overrewarded.

The purpose of this exercise is to assess your equity sensitivity.

Instructions

The five statements below ask what you would like your relationship to be within any organization. For each question, *divide* 10 points between the two answers (A and B) *by giving the most points to the answer that is most like you and the fewest points to the answer least like you.* You can give an equal number of points to A and B. You can make use of zeros if you like. Just be sure to use all 10 points on each question. (For instance, if statement A is completely appropriate and B is not at all appropriate, give A 10 points and B zero points. If A is somewhat appropriate and B is not completely appropriate, give A 7 points and B 3 points.) Place your points next to each letter.

In any organization where I might work . . .

1. It would be more important for me to:
   A. Get from the organization _____
   B. Give to the organization _____

2. It would be more important for me to:
   A. Help others _____
   B. Watch out for my own good _____

3. I would be more concerned about:
   A. What I received from the organization _____
   B. What I contributed to the organization _____

4. The hard work I would do should:
   A. Benefit the organization _____
   B. Benefit me _____

5. My personal philosophy in dealing with the organization would be:
   A. If you don't look out for yourself, nobody else will _____
   B. It's better to give than to receive _____

Calculate your total score by adding the points you allocated to the following items: 1B, 2A, 3B, 4A, and 5B. Total score = _____

Analysis & Interpretation

Your total will be between 0 and 50. If you scored less than 29, you are an Entitled; if your score was between 29 and 32, you are Equity Sensitive; and if your score was above 32, you are a Benevolent.

Questions for Discussion

1. To what extent are the results consistent with your self-perception? Explain.

2. Using the survey items as a foundation, how should managers try to motivate Benevolents, Equity Sensitives, and Entitleds? Discuss in detail.

From R. C. Huseman, J. D. Hatfield, and E. W. Miles, "Test for Individual Perceptions of Job Equity: Some Preliminary Findings," *Perceptual and Motor Skills* 62 (1985), pp 1055–1064. Copyright © 1985 by Ammons Scientific, Ltd. Reproduced with permission of Ammons Scientific, Ltd. via Copyright Clearance Center.

Ethical Dilemma

How Would You Handle a Confrontation between an Employee & a Customer?

Mala Amarsingh, a JetBlue Airways Corp. attendant, was standing in the Las Vegas airport in June [2007], waiting to hitch a ride to New York to start her shift. An intoxicated female passenger approached her, started cursing, threatened to beat her up, and then spit in her face. The flight attendant says she lost her cool, cursed back at the passenger, and later was terminated by the airline for "inappropriate behavior." JetBlue won't comment about personnel matters, but says "customers traveling today are more frustrated by delays and perceived service lapses."

Ms. Amarsingh thinks "uniformed flight attendants are walking targets for passenger frustrations," which "absolutely" have gotten worse in her more than 6 years in the job.

Assume that you are the vice president of JetBlue and that you just became aware of the situation involving Ms. Amarsingh. What would you do?

1. Do nothing. Ms. Amarsingh's behavior violated corporate policy about the treatment of customers and she deserved to be fired. Changing the decision would set a bad precedent for other employees.

2. Acknowledge that the employee's behavior violates corporate policy, but hire her back given the

extenuating circumstances. Provide Ms. Amarsingh with back pay for any lost time.

3. The customer committed assault and battery by purposely spitting in Ms. Amarsingh's face. Hire the employee back and use company resources to sue the customer. This would send a clear message that you care about your employees and that JetBlue will not allow its employees to be assaulted.

4. Invent other options.

Source: Excerpted from Susan Carey, "Cranky Skies: Fliers Behave Badly Again As 9/11 Era Fades," *The Wall Street Journal,* September 12, 2007, p. A16. Copyright © 2007 by Dow Jones & Company, Inc. Reproduced with permission of Dow Jones & Company, Inc. via Copyright Clearance Center.

Groups & Teams
Increasing Cooperation, Reducing Conflict

Major Questions You Should Be Able to Answer

13.1 Groups versus Teams
Major Question: How is one collection of workers different from any other?

13.2 Stages of Group & Team Development
Major Question: How does a group evolve into a team?

13.3 Building Effective Teams
Major Question: How can I as a manager build an effective team?

13.4 Managing Conflict
Major Question: Since conflict is a part of life, what should a manager know about it in order to deal successfully with it?

Reaching Across Time & Space: The Challenge of Managing Virtual Teams

Once upon a time, managers subscribed to the so-called Fifty-Foot Rule—namely, "If people are more than 50 feet apart, they are not likely to collaborate." That is no longer true in today's era of virtual teams. Virtual teams (also known as geographically dispersed teams) are groups of people who use information technology—computers and telecommunications—to collaborate across space, time, and organizational boundaries.[1]

As technology has made it easier for workers to function from remote places, it has posed challenges for managers. Following are some suggestions for managing virtual workers, whether they are working a few miles away at home or on the other side of the world:[2]

- **Take baby steps and manage by results.** When trying out virtual arrangements with new employees, take it slow. Let them show they can handle the challenge. Focus on what's accomplished, not whether an employee is working from her patio or at 10 P.M. Set interim deadlines on projects and stick to them.

- **State expectations.** Nip problems in the bud by letting virtual workers know what you expect from them. With home-based workers, for example, go over the terms of your virtual arrangement—whether, for example, you want them to carry an office cell phone—and tell them if there are specific ways you want the job done.

- **Write it down.** Record directions, project changes, and updates in writing, by sending an e-mail or fax or by using Web-based services that allow for sharing calendars and tracking projects. Keep all communications in a shared database, so that a historical document of the group's work is available for new team members to study.

- **Communicate, but be considerate.** Team members should know what times are appropriate to call one another (think time zones here) and what days (considering cultural, family, or work schedules) are off limits. Make sure everyone is reachable during normal business hours, as via phone, e-mail, fax, or chat.

- **Be aware of cultural differences.** Even if everyone on a global team speaks English, be aware that others may not understand slang, culturally narrow expressions, and American humor. Encourage everyone to slow down their speech. Realize that team members from China and India, say, may have difficulty saying no or may fall silent in order to save face. At bottom, building global and virtual teams is all about building trust—being respectful and doing what you say you're going to do. Handle serious conflicts face to face whenever possible.

- **Meet regularly.** Human contact still matters. If possible, launch the team with a face-to-face meeting. When possible, schedule periodic and regular meetings where all team members can discuss current projects and telecommuters can catch up on office gossip. Fly out-of-towners in at least quarterly, so they can develop working friendships with your in-office staff.

For Discussion What do you feel might be the greatest difficulties of always working online with numerous people that you never see? How would you try to avoid or solve these difficulties?

forecast

What's Ahead in This Chapter

In this chapter, we consider groups versus teams and discuss different kinds of teams. We describe how groups evolve into teams and discuss how managers can build effective teams. We also consider the nature of conflict, both good and bad.

✳ 13.1 GROUPS VERSUS TEAMS

major question? How is one collection of workers different from any other?

THE BIG PICTURE

Teamwork promises to be a cornerstone of future management. A team is different from a group. A group typically is management-directed, a team self-directed. Groups may be formal, created to do productive work, or informal, created for friendship. Work teams, which engage in collective work requiring coordinated effort, may be organized according to four basic purposes: advice, production, project, and action. Two types of teams are quality circles and self-managed teams.

How well do American sports teams fare on the world stage? The answer: Not well, if the year 2006—the last big year for world contests in soccer, baseball, and basketball—is any indicator. Consider soccer: The U.S. team failed to muster one victory at the World Cup. In baseball, the U.S. team was defeated by Mexico, Korea, and Canada at the World Baseball Classic and did not even make it to the semifinals. And in basketball, a sport invented by Americans, the U.S. men's team came in third (behind Spain and Greece) at the Basketball World Championship.[3] Will U.S. teams do better next time around (2010, 2009, and 2010, respectively)? That depends on how well they learn the lessons of 2006.

Take the basketball team, which despite having such NBA stars as Dwyane Wade and LeBron James nevertheless lost to Greece 101–95 in the semifinals. Team USA players had been together for more than a year, but, says one account, "the lack of experience—and familiarity with each other—was glaringly obvious against a Greek squad that has been together three years."[4] But perhaps there was more to it than that. "Our best male athletes have regressed as team players—as *teammates,*" writes Michael Sokolove. "A couple of decades of free agency and lavish salaries freed the players from the grips of owners but also unbound them from one another. . . . If our greatest young athletes don't care enough about one another to commit to effort and team play, that can't be a good thing."[5]

More Teamwork: The Change Today's Employees Need to Make

As far back as 20 years ago, management philosopher Peter Drucker predicted that future organizations would not only be flatter and information-based but also organized around teamwork—and that has certainly come to pass.[6] "You lead today by building teams and placing others first," says General Electric CEO Jeffrey Immelt. "It's not about you."[7] "We have this mythology in America about the lone genius," echoes Tom Kelley, general manager of Ideo, a Palo Alto, California, multidisciplinary industrial design company that helped create the Apple mouse, first laptop computer, and soft-handled Gripper toothbrush for Oral-B. "We love to personify things. But Michelangelo didn't paint the Sistine Chapel alone, and Edison didn't invent the light bulb alone."[8]

There are many reasons why teamwork is now the cornerstone of progressive management, as the table opposite shows. *(See Table 13.1.)* Regardless, when you take a job in an organization, the chances are you won't be working as a lone genius or even as a lone wolf. You'll be working with others in situations demanding teamwork.

table 13.1

WHY TEAMWORK IS IMPORTANT

The improvements	Example
Increased productivity	At one GE factory, teamwork resulted in a workforce that was 20% more productive than comparable GE workforces elsewhere.
Increased speed	Guidant Corp., maker of life-saving medical devices, halved the time it took to get products to market.
Reduced costs	Boeing used teamwork to develop the 777 at costs far less than normal.
Improved quality	Westinghouse used teamwork to improve quality performance in its truck and trailer division and within its electronic components division.
Reduced destructive internal competition	Men's Wearhouse fired a salesman who wasn't sharing walk-in customer traffic, and total clothing sales volume among all salespeople increased significantly.
Improved workplace cohesiveness	Cisco Systems told executives they would gain or lose 30% of their bonuses based on how well they worked with peers and in 3 years had record profits.

Groups & Teams: How Do They Differ?

Aren't a group of people and a team of people the same thing? By and large, no. One is a collection of people, the other a powerful unit of collective performance. One is typically management-directed, the other self-directed.

Consider the differences.

What a Group Is: Collection of People Performing as Individuals A *group* **is defined as two or more freely interacting individuals who share collective norms, share collective goals, and have a common identity.**[9] A group is different from a crowd, a transitory collection of people who don't interact with one another, such as a crowd gathering on a sidewalk to watch a fire. And it is different from an organization, such as a labor union, which is so large that members also don't interact.[10]

An example of a work group would be a collection of, say, 10 employees meeting to exchange information about various companies' policies on wages and hours.

What a Team Is: Collection of People with Common Commitment McKinsey & Company management consultants Jon R. Katzenbach and Douglas K. Smith say it is a mistake to use the terms *group* and *team* interchangeably. Successful teams, they say, tend to take on a life of their own. Thus, a *team* **is defined as a small group of people with complementary skills who are committed to a common purpose, performance goals, and approach for which they hold themselves mutually accountable.**[11] "The essence of a team is common commitment," say Katzenbach and Smith. "Without it, groups perform as individuals; with it, they become a powerful unit of collective performance."[12]

An example of a team would be a collection of 2–10 employees who are studying industry pay scales with the goal of making recommendations for adjusting pay grades within their own company.

Formal versus Informal Groups

Groups may be either formal or informal.

- **Formal groups—created to do productive work. A *formal group* is a group established to do something productive for the organization and is headed by a leader.** A formal group may be a division, a department, a work group, or a committee. It may be permanent or temporary. In general, people are assigned to them according to their skills and the organization's requirements.

- **Informal groups—created for friendship. An *informal group* is a group formed by people seeking friendship and has no officially appointed leader, although a leader may emerge from the membership.** An informal group may be simply a collection of friends who hang out with one another, such as those who take coffee breaks together, or it may be as organized as a prayer breakfast, a bowling team, a service club, or other voluntary organization.

What's important for you as a manager to know is that informal groups can advance or undercut the plans of formal groups. The formal organization may make efforts, say, to speed up the plant assembly line or to institute workplace reforms. But these attempts may be sabotaged through the informal networks of workers who meet and gossip over lunch pails and after-work beers.[13]

However, interestingly, informal groups can also be highly productive—even more so than formal groups.

Example

Informal Groups & Informal Learning: Getting Workers to Share Their Know-How with One Another

As a manager, what would you think if you saw employees making brief conversation near the lunchroom coffeepot? "The assumption was made that this was chitchat, talking about their golf game," said a training director at the Siemens Power Transmission and Distribution plant in Wendell, North Carolina, where managers worried about workers gathering so often in the cafeteria. "But there was a whole lot of work activity."[14]

And indeed a 2-year study by the Center for Workplace Development found that 70% of workplace learning is informal.[15] As a result of the study conclusions, Siemens managers alerted supervisors about the informal meetings and even placed overhead projectors and empty pads of paper in the lunchroom to facilitate the exchange of information.

What about when employees are in far-flung places and can't gather in a cafeteria? "Sales reps are out in the field and they're kind of on islands," pointed out an executive at ExactTarget, an Indianapolis-based software firm. "It's a challenge to keep everyone connected."[16] So what was the company to do when the 75 reps started overwhelming the sales-support staff with questions about product details and client information? To ease the strain, ExactTarget leveraged the knowledge of its sales force by creating a Web site on which the reps could post and answer questions in an informal peer-to-peer learning setting.

Talking it out. Ever worked in a job in which you got a lot of informal training through conversations over coffee?

Your Call
Ever heard of Second Life, the multiplayer online role-playing game that is also described as a "3-D Internet" and a "virtual social world"? Could this or other "social media" be used to foster informal workplace collaboration? How would this work? (Hint: Companies such as IBM and PA Consulting Group are already using Second Life for collaboration with employees and customers and for hiring real-life employees.)[17]

Work Teams for Four Purposes: Advice, Production, Project, & Action

The names given to different kinds of teams can be bewildering. We have identified some important ones *below*. *(See Table 13.2.)*

table 13.2

VARIOUS TYPES OF TEAMS

These teams are not mutually exclusive. Work teams, for instance, may also be self-managed, cross-functional, or virtual.

Cross-functional team	Members composed of people from different departments, such as sales and production, pursuing a common objective
Problem-solving team	Knowledgeable workers who meet as a temporary team to solve a specific problem and then disband *parallel*
Quality circle	Volunteers of workers and supervisors who meet intermittently to discuss workplace and quality-related problems
Self-managed team	Workers are trained to do all or most of the jobs in a work unit, have no direct supervisor, and do their own day-to-day supervision
Top-management team	Members consist of the CEO, president, and top department heads and work to help the organization achieve its mission and goals *management*
Virtual team	Members interact by computer network to collaborate on projects *within-type*
Work team	Members engage in collective work requiring coordinated effort; purpose of team is advice, production, project, or action *(see text discussion)*

You will probably benefit most by understanding the various types of work teams distinguished according to their purpose. Work teams, which engage in collective work requiring coordinated effort, are of four types, which may be identified according to their basic purpose: *advice, production, project,* or *action*.[18]

1. Advice Teams *Advice teams* are created to broaden the information base for managerial decisions. Examples are committees, review panels, advisory councils, employee involvement groups, and quality circles (as we'll discuss).

2. Production Teams *Production teams* are responsible for performing day-to-day operations. Examples are mining teams, flight-attendant crews, maintenance crews, assembly teams, data processing groups, and manufacturing crews.

3. Project Teams *Project teams* work to do creative problem solving, often by applying the specialized knowledge of members of a *cross-functional team*, **which is staffed with specialists pursuing a common objective.** Examples are task forces, research groups, planning teams, architect teams, engineering teams, and development teams.

4. Action Teams *Action teams* work to accomplish tasks that require people with (1) specialized training and (2) a high degree of coordination, as on a baseball team, with specialized athletes acting in coordination. Examples are hospital surgery teams, airline cockpit crews, mountain-climbing expeditions, police SWAT teams, and labor contract negotiating teams.

Self-Managed Teams: Workers with Own Administrative Oversight

To give you an idea of how teams work, consider self-managed teams. These kinds of teams have emerged out of *quality circles,* **which consist of small groups of volunteers or workers and supervisors who meet intermittently to discuss workplace- and quality-related problems.** Typically a group of 10–12 people will meet for 60–90 minutes once or twice a month, with management listening to presentations and the important payoff for members usually being the chance for meaningful participation and skills training.[19]

In many places, such as the Texas Instruments electronics factory in Malaysia, the quality circles have evolved into a system made up almost entirely of self-managed teams, with routine activities formerly performed by supervisors now performed by team members. "Self-managed" does not, however, mean simply turning workers loose to do their own thing. *Self-managed teams* **are defined as groups of workers who are given administrative oversight for their task domains.** Administrative oversight involves delegated activities such as planning, scheduling, monitoring, and staffing. Nearly 70% of *Fortune* 1000 companies have created self-managed work teams.[20]

Self-managed teams are an outgrowth of a blend of behavioral science and management practice.[21] The goal has been to increase productivity and employee quality of work life. The traditional clear-cut distinction between manager and managed is being blurred as nonmanagerial employees are delegated greater authority and granted increased autonomy.

In creating self-managed teams, both technical and organizational redesign are necessary. Self-managed teams may require special technology. Volvo's team-based auto assembly plant, for example, relies on portable assembly platforms rather than traditional assembly lines. Structural redesign of the organization must take place because self-managed teams are an integral part of the organization, not patched onto it, as is the case with quality circles. Personnel and reward systems need to be adapted to encourage teamwork. Staffing decisions may shift from management to team members who hire their own co-workers. Individual bonuses must give way to team bonuses. Supervisory development workshops are needed to teach managers to be facilitators rather than order givers.[22] Finally, extensive team training is required to help team members learn more about technical details, the business as a whole, and how to be team players.[23] ●

Team building. The team ethic at Hong Kong–based Cathay Pacific has helped the multinational airline provide excellent service that pleases both passengers and shareholders. Here Cathay trainees get practice handling unruly passengers and putting on their best face. Do you think there are better ways to get this training?

13.2 STAGES OF GROUP & TEAM DEVELOPMENT

How does a group evolve into a team?

major question?

THE BIG PICTURE

Groups may evolve into teams by going through five stages of development: forming, storming, norming, performing, and adjourning.

Elsewhere in this book we have described how products and organizations go through stages of development. Groups and teams go through the same thing. One theory proposes five stages of development: *forming, storming, norming, performing, adjourning.*[24] *(See Figure 13.1.)* Let us consider these stages in which groups may evolve into teams—bearing in mind that the stages aren't necessarily of the same duration or intensity.

figure 13.1

FIVE STAGES OF GROUP AND TEAM DEVELOPMENT

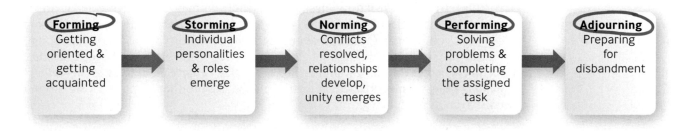

| **Forming** | **Storming** | **Norming** | **Performing** | **Adjourning** |
| Getting oriented & getting acquainted | Individual personalities & roles emerge | Conflicts resolved, relationships develop, unity emerges | Solving problems & completing the assigned task | Preparing for disbandment |

Stage I: Forming—"Why Are We Here?"

The first stage, ***forming, is the process of getting oriented and getting acquainted.*** This stage is characterized by a high degree of uncertainty as members try to break the ice and figure out who is in charge and what the group's goals are. For example, if you were to become part of a team that is to work on a class project, the question for you as an individual would be "How do I fit in here?" For the group, the question is "Why are we here?"[25]

At this point, mutual trust is low, and there is a good deal of holding back to see who takes charge and how. If the formal leader (such as the class instructor or a supervisor) does not assert his or her authority, an emergent leader will eventually step in to fill the group's need for leadership and direction.

What the Leader Should Do Leaders typically mistake this honeymoon period as a mandate for permanent control, but later problems may force a leadership change. During this stage, leaders should allow time for people to become acquainted and socialize.

Stage 2: Storming—"Why Are We Fighting Over Who Does What & Who's in Charge?"

The second stage, ***storming, is characterized by the emergence of individual personalities and roles and conflicts within the group.*** For you as an individual, the question is "What's my role here?" For the group, the issue is "Why are we fighting over who does

Manager's Hot Seat:
Working in Teams: Cross-functional Dysfunction

what and who's in charge?" This stage may be of short duration or painfully long, depending on the goal clarity and the commitment and maturity of the members.

This is a time of testing. Individuals test the leader's policies and assumptions as they try to determine how they fit into the power structure.[26] Subgroups take shape, and subtle forms of rebellion, such as procrastination, occur. Many groups stall in stage 2 because power politics may erupt into open rebellion.

What the Leader Should Do   In this stage, the leader should encourage members to suggest ideas, voice disagreements, and work through their conflicts about tasks and goals.

Stage 3: Norming—"Can We Agree on Roles & Work as a Team?"

In the third stage, *norming,* **conflicts are resolved, close relationships develop, and unity and harmony emerge.** For individuals, the main issue is "What do the others expect me to do?" For the group, the issue is "Can we agree on roles and work as a team?" Note, then, that the *group* may now evolve into a *team.*

Teams set guidelines related to what members will do together and how they will do it. The teams consider such matters as attendance at meetings, being late, and missing assignments as well as how members treat one another.

Groups that make it through stage 2 generally do so because a respected member other than the leader challenges the group to resolve its power struggles so something can be accomplished. Questions about authority are resolved through unemotional, matter-of-fact group discussion. A feeling of team spirit is experienced because members believe they have found their proper roles. *Group cohesiveness,* **a "we feeling" binding group members together,** is the principal by-product of stage 3. (We discuss cohesiveness next, in Section 13.3.)

What the Leader Should Do   This stage generally does not last long. Here the leader should emphasize unity and help identify team goals and values.

Stage 4: Performing—"Can We Do the Job Properly?"

In *performing,* **members concentrate on solving problems and completing the assigned task.** For individuals, the question here is "How can I best perform my role?" For the group/team, the issue is "Can we do the job properly?"

What the Leader Should Do   During this stage, the leader should allow members the empowerment they need to work on tasks.

Stage 5: Adjourning—"Can We Help Members Transition Out?"

In the final stage, *adjourning,* **members prepare for disbandment.** Having worked so hard to get along and get something done, many members feel a compelling sense of loss. For the individual, the question now is "What's next?" For the team, the issue is "Can we help members transition out?"

What the Leader Should Do   The leader can help ease the transition by rituals celebrating "the end" and "new beginnings." Parties, award ceremonies, graduations, or mock funerals can provide the needed punctuation at the end of a significant teamwork project. The leader can emphasize valuable lessons learned in group dynamics to prepare everyone for future group and team efforts. ●

❖ 13.3 BUILDING EFFECTIVE TEAMS

> How can I as a manager build an effective team?
>
> major question?

THE BIG PICTURE

Two types of change are reactive and proactive. Forces for change may consist of forces outside the organization—demographic characteristics, market changes, technological advancements, and social and political pressures. Or they may be forces inside the organization—employee problems and managers' behavior.

Within an organization, you may hear managers loosely (and incorrectly) use the word *team* to describe any collection of people that have been pulled together. But because traditional managers are often reluctant to give up control, no thought is given to providing the "team" (really just a group) with training and support. That is, no attempt is made to sharpen communication skills, reward innovation, or encourage independence without group members running away and losing control.[27]

Thus, as a manager, the first thing you have to realize is that building a high-performance team is going to require some work. But the payoff will be a stronger, better-performing work unit.

The considerations in building a group into an effective team are (1) *performance goals and feedback,* (2) *motivation through mutual accountability,* (3) *size,* (4) *roles,* (5) *norms,* (6) *cohesiveness,* and (7) *groupthink.*

I. Performance Goals & Feedback

As an individual, you no doubt prefer to have measurable goals and to have feedback about your performance. The same is true with teams. Teams are not just collections of individuals. They are individuals organized for a collective purpose. That purpose needs to be defined in terms of specific, measurable performance goals with continual feedback to tell team members how well they are doing.

An obvious example are the teams you see on television at Indianapolis or Daytona Beach during automobile racing. When the driver guides the race car off the track to make a pit stop, a team of people swarm over the wall and quickly jack up the car to change tires, refuel the tank, and clean the windshield—all operating in a matter of seconds. The performance goals are to have the car back on the track as quickly as possible. The number of seconds of elapsed time—and the driver's place among competitors once back in the race—tells them how well they are doing.

2. Motivation through Mutual Accountability

Do you work harder when you're alone or when you're in a group? When clear performance goals exist, when the work is considered meaningful, when members believe their efforts matter, and when they don't feel they are being exploited by others, this kind of culture supports teamwork.[28] Being mutually accountable to other members of the team rather than to a supervisor makes members feel mutual trust and commitment—a key part in motivating members for team effort. To bring about this team culture, managers often allow teams to do the hiring of new members.

Cooperation and collaboration. Army of Two represents a trend in cooperative video games in which people are invited to play collaboratively, allowing them to make individual moves but also work together to reach common goals. Is this a valuable teamwork business tool?

3. Size: Small Teams or Large Teams?

Size, which is often determined by the team's purpose, can be important in affecting members' commitment and performance. Whereas in some flat-organization structures groups may consist of 30 or more employees, teams seem to range in size from 2–16 people, with those of 5–12 generally being the most workable and 5–6 considered optimal.[29] A survey of 400 workplace team members in the United States found that the average team consisted of 10 members, with 8 being the most common size.[30]

Small and large teams have different characteristics, although the number of members is, to be sure, somewhat arbitrary.[31]

Small Teams: 2–9 Members for Better Interaction & Morale   Teams with 9 or fewer members have two advantages:

- **Better interaction.** Members are better able to interact, share information, ask questions of one another, and coordinate activities than are those in larger teams. In particular, teams with five or fewer offer more opportunity for personal discussion and participation.
- **Better morale.** They are better able to see the worth of their individual contributions and thus are more highly committed and satisfied. Members are less apt to feel inhibited in participating. Team leaders are subject to fewer demands and are able to be more informal.[32]

However, small teams also have some disadvantages:

- **Fewer resources.** With fewer hands, there will be fewer resources—less knowledge, experience, skills, and abilities to apply to the team's tasks.
- **Possibly less innovation.** A group that's too small may show less creativity and boldness because of the effect of peer pressure.
- **Unfair work distribution.** Because of fewer resources and less specialization, there may be an uneven distribution of the work among members.

Large Teams: 10–16 Members for More Resources & Division of Labor
Teams with 10–16 members have different advantages over small teams. (Again, the numbers are somewhat arbitrary.)

- **More resources.** Larger teams have more resources to draw on: more knowledge, experience, skills, abilities, and perhaps time. These will give them more leverage to help them realize the team's goals.
- **Division of labor.** In addition, a large team can take advantage of *division of labor,* in which the work is divided into particular tasks that are assigned to particular workers.

Yet bigness has its disadvantages:

- **Less interaction.** With more members, there is less interaction, sharing of information, and coordinating of activities. Leaders may be more formal and autocratic, since members in teams this size are apt to be more tolerant of autocratic leadership. The larger size may also lead to the formation of cliques.
- **Lower morale.** Because people are less able to see the worth of their individual contributions, they show less commitment and satisfaction and more turnover and absenteeism. They also express more disagreements and turf struggles and make more demands on leaders.

- **Social loafing.** The larger the size, the more likely performance is to drop, owing to the phenomenon known as *social loafing,* **the tendency of people to exert less effort when working in groups than when working alone.**[33] (Today social loafers are more apt to be known as *sliders*—high achievers who have "checked out," in the words of *BusinessWeek* columnists Jack and Suzy Welch, and who have to be dealt with "before they begin to suck the team into their negative energy field and drag it down.")[34]

Example

Team Size: And the Magic Number Is . . .

The subject of team size has become a topic of fascination, according to two scholars, because "in the past decade, research on team effectiveness has burgeoned as teams have become increasingly common in organizations of all kinds."[35] What's the right number of people for a team? Various companies have various rules. At Amazon.com, there is a "two-pizza rule"—namely, if a team can't be fed by two pizzas, it's too large.[36] Other companies have their own ideal sizes: Titeflex, 6–10 people; EDS, 8–12; Johnsonville Foods, 12; Volvo, 20. Microsoft Corp. felt the optimal size for a software-development team was 8.[37]

J. Richard Hackman, Harvard professor of social and organizational psychology, thinks there should be no more than 6—the maximum he will allow for students forming project groups.[38] In 1970, Hackman and colleague Neil Vidmar set out to discover the perfect size, asking various teams large and small whether their number was too large or too small for the task.[39] The optimal number: 4.6.

Size is not the only consideration, however. For instance, says Wharton management professor Katherine J. Klein, the nature of the team's task is key because it defines the type of skills you are looking for and the type of coordination necessary.[40]

Your Call

What's been your experience, if any, with team size? At what point does adding members begin to hurt a team's performance as people become less motivated and group coordination becomes more difficult?

4. Roles: How Team Members Are Expected to Behave

A *role* **is a socially determined expectation of how an individual should behave in a specific position.** As a team member, your role is to play a part in helping the team reach its goals. Members develop their roles based on the expectations of the team, of the organization, and of themselves, and they may do different things. You, for instance, might be a team leader. Others might do some of the work tasks. Still others might communicate with other teams.

Two types of team roles are task and maintenance.[41]

Group Exercise:
Identifying Task and Maintenance Roles within Groups

Task Roles: Getting the Work Done   A *task role,* **or** *task-oriented role,* **consists of behavior that concentrates on getting the team's tasks done.** Task roles keep the team on track and get the work done. If you stand up in a team meeting and say, "What is the real issue here? We don't seem to be getting anywhere," you are performing a task role.

Examples: Coordinators, who pull together ideas and suggestions; orienters, who keep teams headed toward their stated goals; initiators, who suggest new goals or ideas; and energizers, who prod people to move along or accomplish more are all playing task roles.

Self-Assessment:
Team Roles Preference Scale

E
SS
H
C

Maintenance Roles: Keeping the Team Together A *maintenance role,* or *relationship-oriented role,* consists of behavior that fosters constructive relationships among team members. Maintenance roles focus on keeping team members. If someone at a team meeting says, "Let's hear from those who oppose this plan," he or she is playing a maintenance role.

Examples: Encouragers, who foster group solidarity by praising various viewpoints; standard setters, who evaluate the quality of group processes; harmonizers, who mediate conflict through reconciliation or humor; and compromisers, who help resolve conflict by meeting others "halfway."

5. Norms: Unwritten Rules for Team Members

Norms are more encompassing than roles. *Norms* **are general guidelines or rules of behavior that most group or team members follow.** Norms point up the boundaries between acceptable and unacceptable behavior.[42] Although norms are typically unwritten and seldom discussed openly, they have a powerful influence on group and organizational behavior.[43]

Example

Team Norms: A Steelmaker Treats Workers Like Owners

When the electrical grid at Nucor Corp.'s steelmaking plant in Hickman, Arkansas, failed, electricians drove or flew in from other Nucor plants as far away as Alabama and North Carolina. No supervisor asked them to do so, nor was there any direct financial incentive for them to blow their weekends to help out. The electricians were following team norms. They came because, as a *BusinessWeek* article states, "Nucor's flattened hierarchy and emphasis on pushing power to the front line lead its employees to adopt the mindset of owner-operators."[44]

Nucor's close-knit culture is the outgrowth of former CEO F. Kenneth Iverson's insight that employees would make extraordinary efforts if they were treated with respect, given real power, and rewarded richly. Instead of following the typical command-and-control model typical of most American businesses in recent decades, Nucor executives motivate their front-line people by "talking to them, listening to them, taking a risk on their ideas, and accepting the occasional failure," says *BusinessWeek.*

Good work is rewarded—production of defect-free steel can triple a worker's pay—but bad work is penalized, with employees losing bonuses they normally would have made. Executive pay is tied to team building, with bonuses tied not just to the performance of a particular plant but to the entire corporation's performance. There is not only healthy competition among facilities and shifts but also cooperation and idea-sharing. The result: Nucor was named the top steel manufacturer in 2008 by American Metal Market for producing the most steel in the United States.[45] *BusinessWeek* ranked it first in its annual list of top-performing companies in 2005 and No. 4 in 2007.[46]

Your Call

Can you think of any kind of businesses in which Nucor's model for strengthening team norms would not work very well? Could American manufacturing companies, automakers, and certain airlines make a comeback if their work and pay rules were made to copy Nucor's?

Why Norms Are Enforced: Four Reasons Norms tend to be enforced by group or team members for four reasons:[47]

- **To help the group survive—"Don't do anything that will hurt us."** Norms are enforced to help the group, team, or organization survive.

Special norms. Enterprise Rent-A-Car, the largest and most prosperous car-rental company in the United States (more than Hertz and Avis), operates on the principle that "If you take care of your customers and employees, the bottom line will take care of itself." In one survey, 80% of customers said they were "completely satisfied" with their Enterprise rental—which *Fortune* magazine calls "an extraordinary score."

Example: The manager of your team or group might compliment you because you've made sure it has the right emergency equipment.

- **To clarify role expectations—"You have to go along to get along."** Norms are also enforced to help clarify or simplify role expectations.

  Example: At one time, new members of Congress wanting to buck the system by which important committee appointments were given to those with the most seniority were advised to "go along to get along"—go along with the rules in order to get along in their congressional careers.

- **To help individuals avoid embarrassing situations—"Don't call attention to yourself."** Norms are enforced to help group or team members avoid embarrassing themselves.

  Examples: You might be ridiculed by fellow team members for dominating the discussion during a report to top management ("Be a team player, not a show-off"). Or you might be told not to discuss religion or politics with customers, whose views might differ from yours.

- **To emphasize the group's important values and identity—"We're known for being special."** Finally, norms are enforced to emphasize the group, team, or organization's central values or to enhance its unique identity.

  Examples: Nordstrom's department store chain emphasizes the great lengths to which it goes in customer service. Every year a college gives an award to the instructor whom students vote best teacher.

6. Cohesiveness: The Importance of Togetherness

Another important characteristic of teams is *cohesiveness,* **the tendency of a group or team to stick together.** This is the familiar sense of togetherness or "we-ness" you feel, for example, when you're a member of a volleyball team, a fraternity or a sorority, or a company's sales force.[48]

Managers can stimulate cohesiveness by allowing people on work teams to pick their own teammates, allowing off-the-job social events, and urging team members to recognize and appreciate each other's contributions to the team goal.[49] Cohesiveness is also achieved by keeping teams small, making sure performance standards are clear and accepted, and following the tips in the following table. *(See Table 13.3, next page.)*

table 13.3

WAYS TO BUILD COLLABORATIVE TEAMS: EIGHT FACTORS THAT LEAD TO SUCCESS

1. **Investing in signature relationship practices.** Executives can encourage collaborative behavior by making highly visible investments—in facilities with open floor plans to foster communication, for example—that demonstrate their commitment to collaboration.

2. **Modeling collaborative behavior.** At companies where the senior executives demonstrate highly collaborative behavior themselves, teams collaborate well.

3. **Creating a "gift culture."** Mentoring and coaching—especially on an informal basis—help people build the networks they need to work across corporate boundaries.

4. **Ensuring the requisite skills.** Human resources departments that teach employees how to build relationships, communicate well, and resolve conflicts creatively can have a major impact on team collaboration.

5. **Supporting a strong sense of community.** When people feel a sense of community, they are more comfortable reaching out to others and more likely to share knowledge.

6. **Assigning team leaders that are both task- and relationship-oriented.** The debate has traditionally focused on whether a task or a relationship orientation creates better leadership, but in fact both are key to successfully leading a team. Typically, leaning more heavily on a task orientation at the outset of a project and shifting toward a relationship orientation once the work is in full swing works best.

7. **Building on heritage relationships.** When too many team members are strangers, people may be reluctant to share knowledge. The best practice is to put at least a few people who know one another on the team.

8. **Understanding role clarity and task ambiguity.** Cooperation increases when the roles of individual team members are sharply defined yet the team is given latitude on how to achieve the task.

Source: Reprinted by permission of *Harvard Business Review.* Exhibit from "Eight Ways to Build Collaborative Teams," by L. Gratton and T. J. Erickson, November 2007. Copyright © 2007 by the Harvard Business School Publishing Corporation; all rights reserved.

7. Groupthink: When Peer Pressure Discourages "Thinking Outside the Box"

Cohesiveness isn't always good. An undesirable by-product that may occur, according to psychologist **Irvin Janis,** is *groupthink*—**a cohesive group's blind unwillingness to consider alternatives.** In this phenomenon, group or team members are friendly and tight-knit, but they are unable to think "outside the box." Their "strivings for unanimity override their motivation to realistically appraise alternative courses of action," said Janis.[50]

Example: The Senate Intelligence Committee said groupthink was a major factor in the U.S. invasion of Iraq because too many people in the government had tended to think alike and therefore failed to challenge basic assumptions about Iraq's weapons capability.[51]

It cannot be said, however, that group opinion is always risky. Indeed, financial writer James Surowiecki, author of *The Wisdom of Crowds,* argues that "Under the right circumstances, groups are remarkably intelligent, and are often smarter than the smartest people in them."[52] As evidence, he cites how groups have been used to predict the election of the president of the United States, find lost submarines, and correct the spread on a sporting event.

Symptoms of Groupthink   How do you know that you're in a group or team that is suffering from groupthink? Some symptoms:[53]

- **Invulnerability, inherent morality, and stereotyping of opposition.** Because of feelings of invulnerability, group members have the illusion that nothing can go wrong, breeding excessive optimism and risk taking. Members may also be so assured of the rightness of their actions that they ignore the ethical implications of their decisions. These beliefs are helped along by stereotyped views of the opposition, which leads the group to underestimate its opponents.

- **Rationalization and self-censorship.** Rationalizing protects the pet assumptions underlying the group's decisions from critical questions. Self-censorship also stifles critical debate. It is especially hard to argue with success, of course. But if enough key people, such as outside analysts, had challenged the energy giant Enron when it seemed to be flying high, it might not have led to the largest bankruptcy in corporate history.

- **Illusion of unanimity, peer pressure, and mindguards.** The illusion of unanimity is another way of saying that silence by a member is interpreted to mean consent. But if people do disagree, peer pressure leads other members to question the loyalty of the dissenters. In addition, in a groupthink situation there may exist people who might be called *mindguards*—self-appointed protectors against adverse information.

- **Groupthink versus "the wisdom of crowds."** Groupthink is characterized by a pressure to conform that often leads members with different ideas to censor themselves—the opposite of collective wisdom, says James Surowiecki, in which "each person in the group is offering his or her best independent forecast. It's not at all about compromise or consensus."[54]

The Results of Groupthink: Decision-Making Defects   Groups with a moderate amount of cohesiveness tend to produce better decisions than groups with low or high cohesiveness. Members of highly cohesive groups victimized by groupthink make the poorest decisions—even though they show they express great confidence in those decisions.[55]

Among the decision-making defects that can arise from groupthink are the following.

- **Reduction in alternative ideas.** The principal casualty of groupthink is a shrinking universe of ideas. Decisions are made based on few alternatives. Once preferred alternatives are decided on, they are not reexamined, and, of course, rejected alternatives are not reexamined.

- **Limiting of other information.** When a groupthink group has made its decision, others' opinions, even those of experts, are rejected. If new information is considered at all, it is biased toward ideas that fit the group's preconceptions. Thus, no contingency plans are made in case the decision turns out to be faulty.

Groupthink: Is Dell a "One-Trick Pony"?[56]

Dell Inc. became a success story through one core idea: becoming a lean, mean, direct sales machine. Using the slogan "Direct from Dell," it made personal computers cheaply by being super-efficient in acquiring and assembling their components (supply chain management) and selling them directly to consumers via the Internet.

In 2006, however, sales began to decline as competitors stepped up their efforts and markets shifted away from some of Dell's key advantages. Instead of adapting, however, Dell stuck to its old way of doing things, cutting costs to the point that, critics say, they compromised customer service and possibly product quality. Said a rival, "They're a one-trick pony. It was a great trick for over 10 years, but the rest of us have figured it out and Dell hasn't plowed any of its profits into creating a new trick." Even back in 2003, Dell revealed the limits of its business model. "There are some organizations where people think they're a hero if they invent a new thing," said then-CEO Kevin Rollins. "Being a hero at Dell means saving money."

The depth of groupthink at Dell was revealed in the extent to which new ideas were discouraged. Says one former manager, "You had to be very confident and thick-skinned to stay on an issue that wasn't popular. A lot of red flags got waved—but only once." Adds Geoffrey Moore, author of *Dealing with Darwin: How Great Companies Innovate at Every Phase of Their Evolution,* "Dell's culture is not inspirational or aspirational. This is when they need to be imaginative, but [Dell's] culture only wants to talk about execution."[57] Recently, one analyst voted Dell "the worst stock for 2008," primarily because of the company's overdependence on U.S. sales, increased competition, and—noteworthy for this example—a lack of innovative products.[58]

Your Call

The primacy of groups and teamwork "is so ingrained that we seldom stop to think about it anymore," says an *Inc. Magazine* writer. However, he adds, "In many cases, individuals do *much* better on their own. Our bias toward groups is counterproductive."[59] If you were chairman Michael Dell, who originally founded the company in his University of Texas dorm room, what would you do to break the groupthink culture at Dell?

Preventing Groupthink: Making Criticism & Other Perspectives Permissible Janis believes it is easier to prevent groupthink than to cure it. As preventive measures, he suggests the following:

- **Allow criticism.** Each member of a team or group should be told to be a critical evaluator, able to actively voice objections and doubts. Subgroups within the group should be allowed to discuss and debate ideas. Once a consensus has been reached, everyone should be encouraged to rethink his or her position to check for flaws.

Fighting groupthink. For a long time, the Coca-Cola Co. had a culture of politeness and consensus that kept it from developing new products, at a time when consumers were flocking to a new breed of coffees, juices, and teas. Now the company is developing new beverages, such as the coffee-flavored Coca-Cola Blak. Do you think Coke can move beyond groupthink and "me-too" products to become cutting edge?

- **Allow other perspectives.** Outside experts should be used to introduce fresh perspectives. Different groups with different leaders should explore the same policy questions. Top-level executives should not use policy committees to rubber-stamp decisions that have already been made. When major alternatives are discussed, someone should be made devil's advocate to try to uncover all negative factors. ●

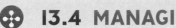

13.4 MANAGING CONFLICT

Since conflict is a part of life, what should a manager know about it in order to deal successfully with it?

THE BIG PICTURE

Conflict, an enduring feature of the workplace, is a process in which one party perceives that its interests are being opposed or negatively affected by another party. Conflict can be negative (bad) or functional (good). Indeed, either too much or too little conflict can affect performance. This section identifies seven sources of conflict in organizations and also describes four ways to stimulate constructive conflict.

"I've fired many employees through the years," writes a manager to an advice columnist, "but right now I've got a guy who scares me. Maybe there's been one too many postal shootings, but I'm afraid this guy could turn violent."[60]

Firings, of course, generate strong emotions and can easily trigger outbursts, though dismissed workers seldom "go postal"—become violent and start shooting people. Indeed, U.S. workplace homicides actually declined between 1993 and 2002. (About 16 workers are murdered on the job every week, but few are by enraged co-workers or former co-workers; about 82% of workplace homicides occur during the course of a robbery or other crime.)[61] Nevertheless, employee dismissals—along with increased workloads, pressure-cooker deadlines, demands for higher productivity, and other kinds of stress—are among the sources of that enduring feature of the workplace: conflict.

The Nature of Conflict: Disagreement Is Normal

Mention the term *conflict* and many people envision shouting and fighting. But as a manager, during a typical workday you will encounter more subtle, nonviolent types of conflict: opposition, criticism, arguments. Thus, a definition of conflict seems fairly mild: *Conflict* **is a process in which one party perceives that its interests are being opposed or negatively affected by another party.**[62] Conflict is simply disagreement, a perfectly normal state of affairs. Conflicts may take many forms: between individuals, between an individual and a group, between groups, within a group, and between an organization and its environment. (To see what your own conflict-management style is, see the Self-Assessment at the end of this chapter.)

While all of us might wish to live lives free of conflict, it is now recognized that certain kinds of conflict can actually be beneficial.[63] Let us therefore distinguish between *negative conflict* (bad) and *constructive conflict* (good).

- **Negative conflict—bad for organizations.** From the standpoint of the organization, *negative conflict* **is conflict that hinders the organization's performance or threatens its interests.** As a manager, you need to do what you can to remove negative conflict, sometimes called *dysfunctional conflict.*

- **Constructive conflict—good for organizations.** The good kind of conflict is *constructive conflict,* **which benefits the main purposes of the organization and serves its interests.**[64] There are some situations in which this kind of conflict—also called *functional conflict* or *cooperative conflict*—is considered advantageous.

Negative & Positive Conflict: Do Nasty Bosses Get Better Performance?

In the film *The Devil Wears Prada,* Meryl Streep stars as a fear-inspiring fashion-magazine editor who keeps her new assistant quivering with dread. Is the portrait real? Says Liz Lange, a maternity-clothes designer, who was herself an editorial assistant, "If you happen to be working for the wrong editor, you could find yourself doing their kid's homework or being yelled at, or crying in the bathroom."[65] Unfortunately, this kind of tyranny is very common, with 37% of American workers reporting they had been bullied at work, according to a Zogby International survey.[66]

Does such negative conflict get results? Surprisingly, often it does. One study of 373 randomly chosen employees found that, although some reacted to abusive bosses by doing little or nothing, others performed better—in part, it's speculated, to make themselves look good and others look worse.[67] Yet other research shows that abuse flows downhill, and when supervisors feel they have been unjustly treated, they may vent their resentment by abusing those who report to them. Subordinates generally cope either through avoidance or, less commonly, through confrontation, and are in any case less inclined to feel committed to their organizations, to speak unfavorably about their companies to outsiders, and to seek jobs elsewhere.[68]

When Stanford organizational psychologist Robert Sutton published a short essay in which he urged more civility in organizations by steady application of what he calls "the no-jerk rule" (although he used a far stronger word than "jerk"), he elicited more e-mails than he had received on any other subject, showing the topic had touched a nerve.[69] Jerks may be everywhere, he says, but "the key is to make explicit to everyone involved in hiring decisions that candidates who have strong skills but who show signs they will belittle and disrespect others cannot be hired under any circumstances." In addition, "Insults, put-downs, nasty teasing, and rude interruptions [should be] dealt with as soon as possible, preferably by the most respected and powerful members" of the company.[70]

Your Call

Have you ever worked for jerks (otherwise known, as Sutton puts it, as "tyrants, bullies, boors, destructive narcissists, and psychologically abusive people")? How did you respond to them?

Can Too Little or Too Much Conflict Affect Performance?

It's tempting to think that a conflict-free work group is a happy work group, as indeed it may be. But is it a productive group? In the 1970s, social scientists specializing

On Strike. *Grey's Anatomy* actor Patrick Dempsey pickets in support of TV and film writers on strike in 2007 over revenue sharing from Internet reuse of their material. What principal issues do you think lead to too much conflict in the workplace?

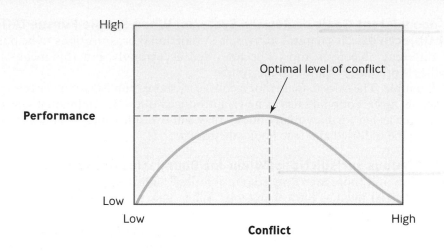

figure 13.2

THE RELATIONSHIP BETWEEN LEVEL OF CONFLICT AND LEVEL OF PERFORMANCE

Too little conflict or too much conflict causes performance to suffer.

in organizational behavior introduced the revolutionary idea that organizations could suffer from *too little* conflict.

- **Too little conflict—indolence.** Work groups, departments, or organizations that experience too little conflict tend to be plagued by apathy, lack of creativity, indecision, and missed deadlines. The result is that organizational performance suffers.

- **Too much conflict—warfare.** Excessive conflict, on the other hand, can erode organizational performance because of political infighting, dissatisfaction, lack of teamwork, and turnover. Workplace aggression and violence are manifestations of excessive conflict.[71]

Thus, it seems that a moderate level of conflict can induce creativity and initiative, thereby raising performance, as shown in the diagram above. *(See Figure 13.2.)* As might be expected, however, the idea as to what constitutes "moderate" will vary among managers.

Seven Causes of Conflict

There are a variety of sources of conflict—so-called conflict triggers. Seven of the principal ones are listed below. By understanding these, you'll be better able to take charge and manage the conflicts rather than letting the conflicts take you by surprise and manage you.

1. Competition for Scarce Resources: When Two Parties Need the Same Things Within organizations there is often a scarcity of needed resources—for example, funds, office space, equipment, employees, and money for raises. When resources are scarce, being a manager becomes more difficult and conflict more likely.[72]

Example: There are lots of computer software glitches but not enough programmers to fix them.

2. Time Pressure: When People Believe There Aren't Enough Hours to Do the Work Setting a deadline is a useful way of inducing people to perform. Or it can be a source of resentment, rage, and conflict if employees think their manager has unrealistic expectations.

Example: If you're in the business of marketing Christmas items to department stores and gift shops, it's imperative that you have your product ready for those important trade shows at which store buyers will appear. But the product-ready deadline for Marketing may be completely unworkable for your company's Production Department, leading to angry conflict.

Manager's Hot Seat:
Partnership: The Unbalancing Act

3. Inconsistent Goals or Reward Systems: When People Pursue Different Objectives

It's natural for people in functional organizations to be pursuing different objectives and to be rewarded accordingly, but this means that conflict is practically built into the system.

Example: The sales manager for a college textbook publisher may be rewarded for achieving exceptional sales of newly introduced titles. But individual salespeople are rewarded for how many books they sell overall, which means they may promote the old tried and true books they know.

4. Ambiguous Jurisdictions: When Job Boundaries Are Unclear

"That's not my job and those aren't my responsibilities." "Those resources belong to me because I need them as part of my job." When task responsibilities are unclear, that can often lead to conflict.

Examples: Is the bartender or the waiter supposed to put the lime in the gin and tonic and the celery in the Bloody Mary? Is management or the union in charge of certain work rules? Is Marketing or Research & Development supposed to be setting up focus groups to explore ideas for new products?

5. Status Differences: When There Are Inconsistencies in Power & Influence

It can happen that people who are lower in status according to the organization chart actually have disproportionate power over those theoretically above them, which can lead to conflicts.

Examples: If a restaurant patron complains his or her steak is not rare enough, the chef is the one who cooked it, but the waiter—who is usually lower in status—is the one who gave the chef the order. Airlines could not hold their schedules without flight crews and ground crews working a certain amount of overtime. But during labor disputes, pilots, flight attendants, and mechanics may simply refuse managers' requests to work the extra hours.

Test Your Knowledge:
Styles of Handling Conflict

6. Personality Clashes: When Individual Differences Can't Be Resolved

Personality, values, attitudes, and experience can be so disparate that sometimes the only way to resolve individual differences—personality clashes—is to separate two people.

Example: Are you easygoing, but she's tense and driven? Does he always shade the facts, while you're a stickler for the truth? If you're basically Ms. Straight Arrow and he's Mr. Slippery, do you think you could adapt your personality to fit his? Maybe you should ask for a transfer.

Group Exercise:
Assessing the Effectiveness of Conflict-Handling Styles

7. Communication Failures: When People Misperceive & Misunderstand

The need for clear communication is a never-ending, ongoing process. Even under the best of circumstances, people misunderstand others, leading to conflict.

Example: Hewlett-Packard hired a consulting firm to explore acquisition of the computer maker Compaq, and at a crucial directors' meeting the consultant gave HP board members a document about the two companies to discuss. However, an important board member, Walter Hewlett, son of one of the founders, wasn't there. He was playing his cello somewhere—at an annual event he had appeared in for the past 3 years—and had assumed the board would accommodate him, as it had in the past. But the board plowed ahead, believing Hewlett wouldn't miss such an important session. This turned out to be a crucial misstep for HP management.[73] The miscommunication ultimately led to a major battle between Hewlett and top HP officers, including CEO Carleton Fiorina. Heirs of the company's founders, which owned 18% of the stock, were upset at the personal tone Fiorina took in painting Hewlett as a musician and academic who flip-flopped over board decisions.

Self-Assessment:
What Is Your Preferred Conflict-Handling Style?

Practical Action

Dealing with Disagreements: Five Conflict-Handling Styles

(Competing)

Even if you're at the top of your game as a manager, working with groups and teams of people will now and then put you in the middle of disagreements, sometimes even destructive conflict. How can you deal with it?

There are five conflict-handling styles, or techniques, a manager can use for handling disagreements with individuals, as follows.[74] Which style are you most likely to use, based on your experience?

Avoiding—"Maybe the Problem Will Go Away"
Avoiding involves ignoring or suppressing a conflict. Avoidance is appropriate for trivial issues, when emotions are high and a cooling-off period is needed, or when the cost of confrontation outweighs the benefits of resolving the conflict. It is not appropriate for difficult or worsening problems.

The benefit of this approach is that it buys time in unfolding and ambiguous situations. The weakness is that it provides only a temporary fix and sidesteps the underlying problem.

Accommodating—"Let's Do It Your Way"
An accommodating manager is also known as a "smoothing" or "obliging" manager. *Accommodating* is allowing the desires of the other party to prevail. As one writer describes it, "An obliging [accommodating] person neglects his or her own concern to satisfy the concern of the other party."[75] Accommodating may be an appropriate conflict-handling strategy when it's possible to eventually get something in return or when the issue isn't important to you. It's not appropriate for complex or worsening problems.

The advantage of accommodating is that it encourages cooperation. The weakness is that once again it's only a temporary fix that fails to confront the underlying problem.

Forcing—"You Have to Do It My Way"
Also known as "dominating," *forcing* is simply ordering an outcome, when a manager relies on his or her formal authority and power to resolve a conflict. Forcing is appropriate when an unpopular solution must be implemented and when it's not important that others be committed to your viewpoint.

The advantage of forcing is speed: it can get results quickly. The disadvantage is that in the end it doesn't resolve personal conflict—if anything, it aggravates it by breeding hurt feelings and resentment.

Compromising—"Let's Split the Difference"
In *compromising*, both parties give up something in order to gain something. Compromise is appropriate when both sides have opposite goals or possess equal power. But compromise isn't workable when it is used so often that it doesn't achieve results—for example, continual failure to meet production deadlines.

The benefit of compromise is that it is a democratic process that seems to have no losers. However, since so many people approach compromise situations with a win-lose attitude, they may be disappointed and feel cheated.

(Integrating)

Collaborating—"Let's Cooperate to Reach a Win-Win Solution That Benefits Both of Us"
Collaborating strives to devise solutions that benefit both parties. Collaboration is appropriate for complex issues plagued by misunderstanding. It is inappropriate for resolving conflicts rooted in opposing value systems.

The strength of collaborating is its longer-lasting impact because it deals with the underlying problem, not just its symptoms. Its weakness is that it's very time consuming. Nevertheless, collaboration is usually the best approach for dealing with groups and teams of people.

How to Stimulate Constructive Conflict

As a manager you are being paid not just to manage conflict but even to create some, where it's constructive and appropriate, in order to stimulate performance. Constructive conflict, if carefully monitored, can be very productive under a number of circumstances: when your work group seems afflicted with inertia and apathy, resulting in low performance. When there's a lack of new ideas and resistance to change. When there seem to be a lot of yes-men and yes-women (expressing groupthink) in the work unit. When there's high employee turnover. When managers seem unduly concerned with peace, cooperation, compromise, consensus, and their own popularity rather than in achieving work objectives.

Manager's Hot Seat:
Negotiation: Thawing the Salary Freeze

Top employee. Companies frequently stimulate constructive competition among employees to produce better performance. Top salespeople, for instance, may be rewarded with a trip to a Mexican resort. Do you think you would do well in a company that makes you compete with others to produce higher results?

The following four devices are used to stimulate constructive conflict:

1. Spur Competition among Employees Competition is, of course, a form of conflict, but competition is often healthy in spurring people to produce higher results. Thus, a company will often put its salespeople in competition with each other by offering bonuses and awards for achievement—a trip to a Caribbean resort, say, for the top performer of the year.

2. Change the Organization's Culture & Procedures Competition may also be established by making deliberate and highly publicized moves to change the corporate culture—by announcing to employees that the organization is now going to be more innovative and reward original thinking and unorthodox ideas. Procedures, such as paperwork sign-off processes, can also be revamped. Results can be reinforced in visible ways through announcements of bonuses, raises, and promotions.

3. Bring in Outsiders for New Perspectives Without "new blood," organizations can become inbred and resistant to change. This is why managers often bring in outsiders—people from a different unit of the organization, new hires from competing companies, or consultants. With their different backgrounds, attitudes, or management styles, these outsiders can bring a new perspective and can shake things up.

4. Use Programmed Conflict: Devil's Advocacy & the Dialectic Method
Programmed conflict is designed to elicit different opinions without inciting people's personal feelings.[76]

Sometimes decision-making groups become so bogged down in details and procedures that nothing of substance gets done. The idea here is to get people, through role playing, to defend or criticize ideas based on relevant facts rather than on personal feelings and preferences.

The method for getting people to engage in this debate of ideas is to do disciplined role-playing, for which two proven methods are available: *devil's advocacy* and the *dialectic method*.

These two methods work as follows:

- **Devil's advocacy—role-playing criticism to test whether a proposal is workable.** *Devil's advocacy* **is the process of assigning someone to play the role of critic** to voice possible objections to a proposal and thereby generate critical thinking and reality testing.[77]

  Periodically role-playing devil's advocate has a beneficial side effect in that it is good training for developing analytical and communicative skills. However, it's a good idea to rotate the job so no one person develops a negative reputation.

- **The dialectic method—role-playing two sides of a proposal to test whether it is workable.** Requiring a bit more skill training than devil's advocacy

Use of the Dialectic Method: How Anheuser-Busch Debates Important Moves

When the corporate policy committee of Anheuser-Busch is considering a major move—such as whether to make a big capital expenditure or get into or out of a business—it sometimes assigns two, even three, groups of people to make the case for each side of the question. Each team is knowledgeable about the subject, and each has the same information. Sometimes an opponent of the project is asked to argue for it—and vice versa.

The exercise may produce a final decision that represents a synthesis of the opposing views. "We end up with decisions and alternatives we hadn't thought of," says Pat Stokes, who heads the company's beer empire. "You become a lot more anticipatory, better able to see what might happen, because you have thought through the process."[79]

Your Call

What kind of specific business move can you think of in which it would be helpful to apply the dialectic method?

does, the *dialectic method* **is the process of having two people or groups play opposing roles in a debate in order to better understand a proposal.** After the structured debate, managers are better able to make a decision.[78]

Whatever kind of organization you work for, you'll always benefit from knowing how to manage conflict. ●

Key Terms Used in This Chapter

adjourning 412
cohesiveness 417
conflict 421
constructive conflict 421
cross-functional team 410
devil's advocacy 426
dialectic method 427
division of labor 414
formal group 408

forming 411
group 407
group cohesiveness 412
groupthink 418
informal group 408
maintenance role 416
negative conflict 421
norming 412
norms 416

performing 412
programmed conflict 426
quality circles 410
role 415
self-managed teams 410
social loafing 415
storming 411
task role 415
team 407

Summary

13.1 Groups versus Teams

Groups and teams are different—a group is typically management-directed, a team self-directed. A group is defined as two or more freely interacting individuals who share collective norms, share collective goals, and have a common identity. A team is defined as a small group of people with complementary skills who are committed to a common purpose, performance goals, and approach for which they hold themselves mutually accountable.

Groups may be either formal, established to do something productive for the organization and headed by a leader, or informal, formed by people seeking friendship with no officially appointed leader.

Teams are of various types, but one of the most important is the work team, which engages in collective work requiring coordinated effort. Work teams may be of four types, identified according to their basic purpose: advice, production, project, and action. A project team may also be a cross-functional team, staffed with specialists pursuing a common objective.

Two types of teams worth knowing about are quality circles, consisting of small groups of volunteers or workers and supervisors who meet intermittently to discuss workplace and quality-related problems, and self-managed teams, defined as groups of workers given administrative oversight for their task domains.

13.2 Stages of Group & Team Development

A group may evolve into a team through five stages. (1) Forming is the process of getting oriented and getting acquainted. (2) Storming is characterized by the emergence of individual personalities and roles and conflicts within the group. (3) In norming, conflicts are resolved, close relationships develop, and unity and harmony emerge. (4) In performing, members concentrate on solving problems and completing the assigned task. (5) In adjourning, members prepare for disbandment.

13.3 Building Effective Teams

There are seven considerations managers must take into account in building a group into an effective team.

(1) They must establish measurable goals and have feedback about members' performance.

(2) They must motivate members by making them mutually accountable to one another.

(3) They must consider what size is optimal. Teams with nine or fewer members have better interaction and morale, yet they also have fewer resources, are possibly less innovative, and may have work unevenly distributed among members. Teams of 10–16 members have more resources, and can take advantage of division of labor, yet they may be characterized by less interaction, lower morale, and social loafing.

(4) They must consider the role each team member must play. A role is defined as the socially determined expectation of how an individual should behave in a specific position. Two types of team roles are task and maintenance. A task role consists of behavior that concentrates on getting the team's tasks done. A maintenance role consists of behavior that fosters constructive relationships among team members.

(5) They must consider team norms, the general guidelines or rules of behavior that most group or team members follow. Norms tend to be enforced by group or team members for four reasons: to help the group survive, to clarify role expectations, to help individuals avoid embarrassing situations, and to emphasize the group's important values and identity.

(6) They must consider the team's cohesiveness, the tendency of a group or team to stick together.

(7) They must be aware of groupthink, a cohesive group's blind unwillingness to consider alternatives. Symptoms of groupthink are feelings of invulnerability, certainty of the rightness of their actions, and stereotyped views of the opposition; rationalization and self-censorship; and illusion of unanimity, peer pressure, and the appearance of self-appointed protectors against adverse information. The results of groupthink can be reduction in alternative ideas and limiting of other information. Two ways to prevent groupthink are to allow criticism and to allow other perspectives.

13.4 Managing Conflict

Conflict is a process in which one party perceives that its interests are being opposed or negatively affected by another party. Conflict can be negative. However, constructive, or functional, conflict benefits the main purposes of the organization and serves its interests. Too little conflict can lead to indolence; too much conflict can lead to warfare.

Seven causes of conflict are (1) competition for scarce resources, (2) time pressure, (3) inconsistent goals or reward systems, (4) ambiguous jurisdictions, (5) status differences, (6) personality clashes, and (7) communication failures.

Four devices for stimulating constructive conflict are (1) spurring competition among employees, (2) changing the organization's culture and procedures, (3) bringing in outsiders for new perspectives, and (4) using programmed conflict to elicit different opinions without inciting people's personal feelings. Two methods used in programmed conflict are (1) devil's advocacy, in which someone is assigned to play the role of critic to voice possible objections to a proposal, and (2) the dialectic method, in which two people or groups play opposing roles in a debate in order to better understand a proposal.

Management in Action

Teams Are the Foundation of Financial Growth for ICU Medical Inc.

American corporations love teamwork. But few companies are as smitten as ICU Medical Inc.

At the San Clemente, California, maker of medical devices, any worker can form a team to tackle any project. Team members set meetings, assign tasks, and create deadlines themselves. Chief Executive George Lopez says he's never vetoed a team decision, even when he disagreed with it. These teams have altered production processes and set up a 401(k) plan, among other changes. . . .

Most big companies assign teams for projects. ICU, which has around 1,480 employees, is unusual in that it allows workers to initiate the teams. . . .

Dr. Lopez, an internist, founded ICU in 1984. By the early 1990s, the company had about $10 million in annual revenue and was preparing for a public offering. Demand for the company's Clave product, used in connecting a patient's IV systems, was skyrocketing; Dr. Lopez needed to figure out how to ramp up production.

ICU had fewer than 100 employees but was expanding rapidly. Handling the booming growth and demand "was an overwhelming task for one entrepreneur CEO," says Dr. Lopez, 59 years old. He was still making most decisions himself, often sleeping at the office.

Then, he had an epiphany watching his son play hockey. The opposing team had a star, but his son's team ganged up on him and won. "The team was better than one player," says Dr. Lopez. He decided to delegate power by letting employees form teams, hoping it would help him spread out the decision-making and encourage input from people closest to the problems.

Some executives hated the idea; his chief financial officer quit. Putting the new system in place, Dr. Lopez told employees to form teams to come up with ways to boost production. It didn't work. With no leaders, and no rules, "nothing was getting done, except people were spending a lot of time talking," he says.

After about a year and a half, he decided teams should elect leaders, which brought a vast improvement. In 1995 he hired Jim Reitz, now the human-resources director, who helped him create a structure with a minimum of bureaucracy. They developed core values—"take risks"—and so-called rules of engagement—"challenge the issue, not the person." At the same time, ICU started paying teams rewards based on a percentage of the cumulative salaries of their members.

It worked. Employees embraced teams. Today 12 to 15 teams finish projects each quarter, often meeting once a week or so. The typical team has five to seven members, and the company allots $75,000 quarterly to reward those that succeed.

Teams have propelled changes over the objections of top executives. Dr. Lopez, worried about the cost, didn't want to institute a 401(k) plan, but acquiesced after a team recommended one. He now concedes the plan has helped in retaining employees.

Dr. Lopez can veto team decisions but says he hasn't yet. For teams to work, employees need to feel they have authority, he says. A veto would "really have to be worth it," Dr. Lopez says. The team would have to be putting the company "on a pathway to destruction."

So far, that hasn't happened. ICU's revenue grew 28% last year to $201.6 million, though the company projects that revenue will decline this year. Its stock has climbed more than sixfold in the past decade. . . .

At ICU, team members don't get a break from their regular jobs. Serving on teams is technically voluntary but some employees with special expertise are "requested" to join. "It's above and beyond your job," says business-applications manager Colleen Wilder, who has served on many teams in the 10 years at ICU. "You still have to get your job done."

The rewards can create tension. Ms. Wilder once balked at sharing a reward with co-workers she thought had joined a team solely for the money. She proposed dividing the money based on what tasks team members performed. "I said, 'You did nothing, and I propose you get nothing,'" she says. The team agreed.

The payment system has been changed to peg the size of the reward to the importance of the project. "People started thinking, 'We created a whole new product for the company and these guys painted the lunch room, and they're getting the same amount of money that we are?'" Mr. Reitz says. He encourages employees to question whether teams really met their goals, or whether a project is significant enough to merit high reward levels.

Over the years, ICU has instituted more rules to help teams function smoothly. A group of employees created a 25-page handbook that concretely spells out team operations—for instance, listing eight items for "What should we do at the first meeting?"—and addresses frequently asked questions. Teams must post notes of each meeting to the company intranet, where any employee can offer feedback. . . .

For Discussion

1. What type of team is being used at ICU? Explain.

2. To what extent are the teams self-managing?

3. Which of the seven techniques for building effective teams have been instituted at ICU Medical? Provide supporting evidence.

4. Rewards have created tensions at ICU Medical. What is your evaluation of how the company has handled the rewarding of teams and team members?

5. Which of the five conflict handling styles were used to resolve conflict about team rewards?

Source: Excerpted from Erin White, "How a Company Made Everyone a Team Player," *The Wall Street Journal*, August 13, 2007. Copyright © 2007 by Dow Jones & Company, Inc. Reproduced with permission of Dow Jones & Company, Inc. via Copyright Clearance Center.

Self-Assessment

What Is Your Conflict-Management Style?

Objectives

1. To assess your conflict-management style.
2. To gain insight on how you manage conflict.

Introduction

Have you ever had a professor whose viewpoints were in conflict with your own? Have you worked in a group with someone who seems to disagree just to cause conflict? How did you react in that situation? In this chapter, you learned that there are five different ways of handling conflict: (1) *avoiding*—this approach is seen in people who wish to suppress conflict or back down from it altogether; (2) *accommodating*—this approach is seen in people who place the other party's interests above their own; (3) *forcing*—this approach is seen when people rely on their authority to solve conflict; (4) *compromising*—this approach is seen in people who are willing to give up something in order to reach a solution; and (5) *collaboration*—this approach is seen in people who desire a win-win situation, striving to address concerns and desires of all the parties involved in the conflict. The purpose of this exercise is to determine your conflict handling style.

Instructions

Read each of the statements below and use the following scale to indicate how often you rely on each tactic.

1 = very rarely
2 = rarely
3 = sometimes
4 = fairly often
5 = very often

1. I work to come out victorious no matter what.	1 *2* 3 4 5
2. I try to put the needs of others above my own.	1 2 *3* 4 5
3. I look for a mutually satisfactory solution.	1 2 3 4 *5*
4. I try to get involved in conflicts.	1 *2* 3 4 5
5. I strive to investigate and understand the issues involved in the conflict.	1 2 3 4 *5*
6. I never back away from a good argument.	1 2 *3* 4 5

7.	I strive to foster harmony.	1 2 3 ~~4~~ 5
8.	I negotiate to get a portion of what I propose.	1 2 3 ~~4~~ 5
9.	I avoid open discussion of controversial subjects.	1 ~~2~~ 3 4 5
10.	When I am trying to resolve disagreements, I openly share information.	1 2 3 4 ~~5~~
11.	I would rather win than compromise.	~~1~~ 2 3 4 5
12.	I work through conflict by accepting suggestions of others.	1 2 ~~3~~ 4 5
13.	I look for a middle ground to resolve disagreements.	1 2 3 4 ~~5~~
14.	I keep my true opinions to myself to avoid hard feelings.	~~1~~ 2 3 4 5
15.	I encourage the open sharing of concerns and issues.	1 2 3 4 ~~5~~
16.	I am reluctant to admit I am wrong.	1 2 ~~3~~ 4 5
17.	I try to save others from embarrassment in a disagreement.	1 2 ~~3~~ 4 5
18.	I stress the advantages of give and take.	1 2 3 ~~4~~ 5
19.	I give in early on rather than argue about a point.	1 ~~2~~ 3 4 5
20.	I state my position and stress that it is the only correct point of view.	~~1~~ 2 3 4 5

Scoring & Interpretation

Enter your responses, item by item, in the five categories below. Add your responses to get your total for each of the five conflict handling styles. Your primary conflict-handling style will be the area where you scored the highest. Your back-up conflict-handling style will be your second highest score.

Avoiding		Accommodating		Forcing		Compromising		Collaborating	
Item	Score	Item	Score	Item	Score	Item	Score	Item	Score
4.	2	2.	3	1.	2	3.	5	5.	5
9.	2	7.	4	6.	3	8.	4	10.	5
14.	1	12.	3	11.	1	13.	5	15.	5
19.	2	17.	3	16.	3	18.	4	20.	1
Total =	7	Total =	13	Total =	9	Total =	18	Total =	16

Questions for Discussion

1. Were you surprised by the results? Why or why not? Explain.

2. Were the scores for your primary and back-up conflict-handling styles relatively similar, or was there a large gap? What does this imply? Discuss.

3. Is your conflict-handling style one that can be used in many different conflict scenarios? Explain.

4. What are some skills you can work on to become more effective at handling conflict? Describe and explain.

The survey was developed using conflict-handling styles defined by K. W. Thomas, "Conflict and Conflict Management," in M. Dunnette ed., *Handbook of Industrial and Organizational Psychology* (Chicago: Rand McNally, 1976), pp. 889–935.

When Employees Smoke Marijuana Socially: A Manager's Quandary

You are a supervisor at a telephone call center and have very positive relationships with members of your work team and your manager. A friend of yours, Christina, is also a supervisor, and her younger brother, Blake, is a member of her work team.

Christina invites you to her birthday party at her home, and you happily agree to attend. During the party, you walk out to the backyard to get some fresh air and notice that Blake and several other employees of your company are smoking marijuana. You have been told on several occasions by members of your own work team that these same individuals have used marijuana at other social events.

Blake and his friends are not part of your work team, and you never noticed any of them being impaired at work.

Solving the Dilemma

As a supervisor, what would you do?

1. Report the drug users and the incident to the company's human resources department.

2. Mind your own business. The employees are not on your team and don't appear to be impaired at work.

3. Talk to your boss and get her opinion about what should be done.

4. Invent other options. Discuss.

Power, Influence, & Leadership

From Becoming a Manager to Becoming a Leader

Major Questions You Should Be Able to Answer

14.1 The Nature of Leadership: Wielding Influence
Major Question: I don't want to be just a manager; I want to be a leader. What's the difference between the two?

14.2 Trait Approaches: Do Leaders Have Distinctive Personality Characteristics?
Major Question: What does it take to be a successful leader?

14.3 Behavioral Approaches: Do Leaders Show Distinctive Patterns of Behavior?
Major Question: Do effective leaders behave in similar ways?

14.4 Contingency Approaches: Does Leadership Vary with the Situation?
Major Question: How might effective leadership vary according to the situation at hand?

14.5 The Full-Range Model: Uses of Transactional & Transformational Leadership
Major Question: What does it take to truly inspire people to perform beyond their normal levels?

14.6 Four Additional Perspectives
Major Question: If there are many ways to be a leader, which one would describe me best?

Advancing Your Career: Staying Ahead in the Workplace of Tomorrow

Someday maybe you can afford to have a *personal career coach*—the kind long used by sports and entertainment figures and now adopted in the upper ranks of business. These individuals "combine executive coaching and career consulting with marketing and negotiations," says one account. "They plot career strategy, help build networks of business contacts, . . . and shape their clients' images."[1]

One such career coach is Richard L. Knowdell, president of Career Research and Testing in San Jose, California. He offers the following strategies for staying ahead in the workplace of tomorrow.[2]

- **Take charge of your career, and avoid misconceptions:** Because you, not others, are in charge of your career, and it's an ongoing process, you should develop a career plan and base your choices on that plan. When considering a new job or industry, find out how that world *really* works, not what it's reputed to be. When considering a company you might want to work for, find out its corporate "style" or culture by talking to its employees.

- **Develop new capacities:** "Being good at several things will be more advantageous in

the long run than being excellent at one narrow specialty," says Knowdell. "A complex world will not only demand *specialized knowledge* but also *general and flexible skills.*"

- **Anticipate and adapt to, even embrace, changes:** Learn to analyze, anticipate, and adapt to new circumstances in the world and in your own life. For instance, as technology changes the rules, *embrace* the new rules.

- **Keep learning:** "You can take a one- or two-day course in a new subject," says Knowdell, "just to get an idea of whether you want to use those specific skills and to see if you would be good at it. Then, if there is a match, you could seek out an extended course."

- **Develop your people and communications skills:** No matter how much communication technology takes over the workplace, there will always be a strong need for effectiveness in interpersonal relationships. In particular, learn to listen well.

For Discussion Which of these five rules do you think is most important—and why?

forecast

What's Ahead in This Chapter

Are there differences between managers and leaders? This chapter considers this question. We discuss the sources of a leader's power and how leaders use persuasion to influence people. We then consider the following approaches to leadership: trait, behavioral, contingency, full-range, and four additional perspectives.

THE BIG PICTURE

Being a manager and being a leader are not the same. A leader is able to influence employees to voluntarily pursue the organization's goals. Leadership is needed for organizational change. We describe five sources of power leaders may draw on. Leaders use the power of persuasion or influence to get others to follow them. Five approaches to leadership are described in the next five sections.

Leadership. What is it? Is it a skill anyone can develop?

Leadership **is the ability to influence employees to voluntarily pursue organizational goals.**[3] In an effective organization, leadership is present at all levels, say Tom Peters and Nancy Austin in *A Passion for Excellence,* and it represents the sum of many things. Leadership, they say, "means vision, cheerleading, enthusiasm, love, trust, verve, passion, obsession, consistency, the use of symbols, paying attention as illustrated by the content of one's calendar, out-and-out drama (and the management thereof), creating heroes at all levels, coaching, effectively wandering around, and numerous other things."[4]

Managers & Leaders: Not Always the Same

You see the words "manager" and "leader" used interchangeably all the time. However, as one leadership expert has said, "leaders manage and managers lead, but the two activities are not synonymous."[5]

Retired Harvard Business School professor **John Kotter** suggests that one is not better than the other, that in fact they are complementary systems of action. The difference is that . . .

- *Management* is about coping with *complexity,*
- *Leadership* is about coping with *change.*[6]

Let's consider these differences.

Being a Manager: Coping with Complexity Management is necessary because complex organizations, especially the large ones that so much dominate the economic landscape, tend to become chaotic unless there is good management.

According to Kotter, companies manage complexity in three ways:

- **Determining what needs to be done—planning and budgeting.** Companies manage complexity first by *planning and budgeting*—setting targets or goals for the future, establishing steps for achieving them, and allocating resources to accomplish them.
- **Creating arrangements of people to accomplish an agenda—organizing and staffing.** Management achieves its plan by *organizing and staffing,* Kotter says—creating the organizational structure and hiring qualified individuals to fill the necessary jobs, then devising systems of implementation.

- **Ensuring people do their jobs—<u>controlling and problem solving</u>.** Management ensures the plan is accomplished by *controlling and problem solving,* says Kotter. That is, managers monitor results versus the plan in some detail by means of reports, meetings, and other tools. They then plan and organize to solve problems as they arise.

Being a Leader: Coping with Change   As the business world has become more competitive and volatile, doing things the same way as last year (or doing it 5% better) is no longer a formula for success. More changes are required for survival—hence the need for leadership.

Leadership copes with change in three ways:

- **Determining what needs to be done—<u>setting a direction</u>.** Instead of dealing with complexity through planning and budgeting, leaders strive for constructive change by *setting a direction.* That is, they develop a vision for the future, along with strategies for realizing the changes.

- **Creating arrangements of people to accomplish an agenda—<u>aligning people</u>.** Instead of organizing and staffing, leaders are concerned with *aligning people,* Kotter says. That is, they communicate the new direction to people in the company who can understand the vision and build coalitions that will realize it.

- **Ensuring people do their jobs—<u>motivating and inspiring</u>.** Instead of controlling and problem solving, leaders try to achieve their vision by *motivating and inspiring.* That is, they appeal to "basic but often untapped human needs, values, and emotions," says Kotter, to keep people moving in the right direction, despite obstacles to change.

Do Kotter's ideas describe real leaders in the real business world? Certainly many participants in a seminar convened by *Harvard Business Review* appeared to agree. "The primary task of leadership is to communicate the vision and the values of an organization," Frederick Smith, chairman and CEO of FedEx, told the group. "Second, leaders must win support for the vision and values they articulate. And third, leaders have to reinforce the vision and the values."[7]

Group Exercise:
What Is Your Motivation to Lead?

Do You Have What It Takes to Be a Leader?   Managers have legitimate power (as we'll describe) that derives from the formal authority of the positions to which they have been appointed. This power allows managers to hire and fire, reward and punish. Managers plan, organize, and control, but they don't necessarily have the characteristics to be leaders.

Whereas management is a process that lots of people are able to learn, leadership is more visionary. As we've said, leaders inspire others, provide emotional support, and try to get employees to rally around a common goal. Leaders also play a role in creating a vision and strategic plan for an organization, which managers are then charged with implementing.

Do you have what it takes to be a leader? To learn more about the skills required and to assess your own leadership ability, try the Self-Assessment at the end of this chapter.

Amazing Amazon. Jeffrey Bezos, founder and CEO of online retailer Amazon.com, has done nearly everything Kotter suggests. For instance, Bezos's "culture of divine discontent" permits employees to plunge ahead with new ideas even though they know that most will probably fail.

Five Sources of Power

To really understand leadership, we need to understand the concept of power and authority. *Authority* is the right to perform or command; it comes with the job.

In contrast, *power* is the extent to which a person is able to influence others so they respond to orders.

People who pursue *personalized power*—**power directed at helping oneself**—as a way of enhancing their own selfish ends may give the word power a bad name. However, there is another kind of power, *socialized power*—**power directed at helping others.**[8] This is the kind of power you hear in expressions such as "My goal is to have a powerful impact on my community."

Within organizations there are typically five sources of power leaders may draw on: *legitimate, reward, coercive, expert,* and *referent.*

1. Legitimate Power: Influencing Behavior Because of One's Formal Position *Legitimate power,* **which all managers have, is power that results from managers' formal positions within the organization.** All managers have legitimate power over their employees, deriving from their position, whether it's a construction supervisor, ad account supervisor, sales manager, or CEO. This power may be exerted both positively or negatively—as praise or as criticism, for example.

2. Reward Power: Influencing Behavior by Promising or Giving Rewards *Reward power,* **which all managers have, is power that results from managers' authority to reward their subordinates.** Rewards can range from praise to pay raises, from recognition to promotions.

Example: "Talking to people effectively is all about being encouraging," says Andrea Wong, president and CEO of Lifetime Network and Entertainment Services. She tries to use praise to reward positive behavior. "When I have something bad to say to someone, it's always hard because I'm always thinking of the best way to say it."[9]

3. Coercive Power: Influencing Behavior by Threatening or Giving Punishment *Coercive power,* **which all managers have, results from managers' authority to punish their subordinates.** Punishment can range from verbal or written reprimands to demotions to terminations. In some lines of work, fines and suspensions may be used. Coercive power has to be used judiciously, of course, since a manager who is seen as being constantly negative will produce a lot of resentment among employees. But there have been many leaders who have risen to the top of major corporations—such as Disney's Michael Eisner, Miramax's Harvey Weinstein, and Hewlett-Packard's Carly Fiorina—who have been abrasive and intimidating.[10]

4. Expert Power: Influencing Behavior Because of One's Expertise *Expert power* **is power resulting from one's specialized information or expertise.** Expertise, or special knowledge, can be mundane, such as knowing the work schedules and assignments of the people who report to you. Or it can be sophisticated, such as having computer or medical knowledge. Secretaries may have expert power because, for example, they have been in a job a long time and know all the necessary contacts. CEOs may have expert power because they have strategic knowledge not shared by many others.

5. Referent Power: Influencing Behavior Because of One's Personal Attraction *Referent power* **is power deriving from one's personal attraction.** As we will see later in this chapter (under the discussion of transformational leadership), this kind of power characterizes strong, visionary leaders who are able to persuade their followers by dint of their personality, attitudes, or background. Referent power may be associated with managers, but it is more likely to be characteristic of leaders.

Test Your Knowledge:
Sources of Power

A Strong Leader: Andy Grove, Former CEO of Intel Corp.

Symbolic of his ability to reinvent himself, Andy Grove has had three different names in his life. Born in 1936 as a Hungarian Jew, he was known as Andras Istvan Grof until 1944, when the Nazis invaded Hungary, at which point his mother changed his name to the Slavic Andras Malesevics. The following year, when the communists arrived, he changed back to Andras Grof. Nauseated by Communism, he escaped and arrived in the U.S. in 1957, where he enrolled at City College of New York and changed his name to Andrew Stephen Grove.

In 1968, with a PhD in chemical engineering, Grove joined two engineering colleagues in starting Intel Corporation in Mountain View, California, where at age 32 he found himself in the role of leader in a manufacturing startup. It was then that he began to teach himself about management. "Grove succeeded where others didn't," says historian Richard Tedlow, "in part, by approaching management as a discipline unto itself. There's a real urgency in his efforts to school himself: He never lost his Hungarian refugee's apprehension of the risk of imminent failure."[11]

By 1983, Intel was a $1.1 billion maker of memory chips and Grove had become its president. But something was about to happen that would reinforce in him a lesson he would later write about in his book *Only the Paranoid Survive*—namely, that in business you often don't see the cliff until you've already walked off it.[12] In the mid-1980s, Intel woke up to find that Japanese companies had mastered the industry it had invented and were turning memory chips into a commodity, so that in a single year Intel profits plunged from $198 million to $2 million.

A key to Grove's leadership was that he seemed to be one of the original practitioners of what we in this text have described as

"evidence-based management." His management style was "direct and confrontational," says *BusinessWeek*. "His shouts echoed down company halls."[13] Adds Tedlow, "At Intel he fostered a culture in which 'knowledge power' would trump 'position power.' Anyone could challenge anyone else's idea, so long as it was about the idea and not the person—and so long as you were ready for the demand 'Prove it.' That required data. Without data, an idea was only a story—a representation of reality and thus subject to distortion."[14]

It was at that point that Grove made the painful decision to abandon Intel-the-memory-chip-company, firing some 8,000 people, and to stake its future on the microprocessor. The personal computer was just coming into being, and once IBM chose to base its PCs on Intel's processor chip, the former memory company started a successful 11-year run. In 1986, it took a chance when launching the Intel 386 microprocessor to license it not just to IBM but to other computer makers as well. With the success of Microsoft's smash-hit Windows 3.0, designed to work on 386-chip machines, Intel began a compound annual growth rate of nearly 30%.

Andy Grove is celebrated as a leader because, as Tedlow says, he "was willing to let go of his instincts—since they could be wrong—and view himself as a student might: from outside, peering down with the wide-angle, disinterested perspective of the observer. . . . It is the singular ability to inhabit both roles at once—subject and object, actor and audience, master and student—that sets Grove apart."

Your Call

Which of the five sources of leadership power do you think Grove represents? Do you think you could follow Grove's example?

Leadership & Influence: Using Persuasion to Get Your Way at Work

Steve Harrison, CEO of a career management firm, was escorting Ray, his newly hired chief operating officer, to meet people at a branch office. After greeting the receptionist and starting to lead Ray past her into the interior offices, Harrison felt himself being pulled back. He watches as Ray stuck out his hand, smiled, and said, "Good morning, Melissa, I'm Ray. I'm new here. It's so great to meet you!" He then launched into a dialogue with Melissa, to her obvious delight. Afterward, Harrison asked Ray, "What was that all about?" "It's called the two-minute schmooze," Ray replied. "Our receptionists meet or talk by phone to more people critical to our company in one day than you or I will ever meet in the course of a year.[15]

Ray would probably be considered a leader because of his ability to *influence* others—to get them to follow his wishes. There are nine tactics for trying to influence others, but some work better than others. In one pair of studies, employees were asked in effect, "How do you get your boss, coworker, or subordinate to do something you want?" The nine answers—ranked from most used to least used tactics—were as follows.[16]

1. Rational Persuasion   Trying to convince someone by using reason, logic, or facts.
>Example: "You know, all the cutting-edge companies use this approach."

2. Inspirational Appeals   Trying to build enthusiasm or confidence by appealing to others' emotions, ideals, or values.
>Example: "If we do this as a goodwill gesture, customers will love us."

3. Consultation   Getting others to participate in a decision or change.
>Example: "Wonder if I could get your thoughts about this matter."

4. Ingratiating Tactics   Acting humble or friendly or making someone feel good or feel important before making a request.
>Example: "I hate to impose on your time, knowing how busy you are, but you're the only one who can help me."

5. Personal Appeals   Referring to friendship and loyalty when making a request.
>Example: "We've known each other a long time, and I'm sure I can count on you."

6. Exchange Tactics   Reminding someone of past favors or offering to trade favors.
>Example: "Since I backed you at last month's meeting, maybe you could help me this time around."

7. Coalition Tactics   Getting others to support your effort to persuade someone.
>Example: "Everyone in the department thinks this is a great idea."

8. Pressure Tactics   Using demands, threats, or intimidation to gain compliance.
>Example: "If this doesn't happen, you'd better think about cleaning out your desk."

Group Exercise:
The Effects of Abusing Power

9. Legitimating Tactics   Basing a request on one's authority or right, organizational rules or policies, or express or implied support from superiors.
>Example: "This has been green-lighted at the highest levels."

These influence tactics are considered *generic* because they are applied in all directions—up, down, and sideways within the organization. The first five influence tactics are considered "soft" tactics because they are considered friendlier than the last four "hard," or pressure, tactics. As it happens, research shows that of the three possible responses to an influence tactic—enthusiastic commitment, grudging compliance, and outright resistance—commitment is most apt to result when the tactics used are consultation, strong rational persuasion, and inspirational appeals.[17]

Knowing this, do you think you have what it takes to be a leader? To answer this, you need to understand what factors produce people of leadership character. We consider these in the rest of the chapter.

Self-Assessment:
Do You Have What it Takes to Be a Leader?

Five Approaches to Leadership

The next five sections describe five principal approaches or perspectives on leadership, which have been refined by research. They are (1) *trait,* (2) *behavioral,* (3) *contingency,* (4) *full-range,* and (5) *four additional. (See Table 14.1.)* ●

table 14.1

FIVE APPROACHES TO LEADERSHIP

1. **Trait approaches**
   - *Kouzes & Posner's five traits*—honest, competent, forward-looking, inspiring, intelligent
   - *Gender studies*—motivating others, fostering communication, producing high-quality work, and so on
   - *Leadership lessons from the GLOBE project*—visionary and inspirational charismatic leaders who are good team builders are best worldwide

2. **Behavioral approaches**
   - *Michigan model*—two leadership styles: job-centered and employee-centered
   - *Ohio State model*—two dimensions: initiating-structure behavior and consideration behavior

3. **Contingency approaches**
   - *Fiedler's contingency model*—task-oriented style and relationship-oriented style—*and three dimensions of control:* leader-member, task structure, position power
   - *House's path-goal revised leadership model*—clarifying paths for subordinates' goals, and employee characteristics and environmental factors that affect leadership behaviors
   - *Hersey & Blanchard's situational leadership model*—adjusting leadership style to employee readiness

4. **Full-range approach**
   - *Transactional leadership*—clarify employee roles and tasks, and provide rewards and punishments
   - *Transformational leadership*—transform employees to pursue organizational goals over self-interests, using inspirational motivation, idealized influence, individualized consideration, intellectual stimulation

5. **Four additional perspectives**
   - *Leader-member exchange (LMX) model*—leaders have different sorts of relationships with different subordinates
   - *Shared leadership*—mutual influence process in which people share responsibility for leading
   - *Greenleaf's servant leadership model*—providing service to others, not oneself
   - *E-Leadership*—using information technology for one-to-one, one-to-many, and between group and collective interactions

14.2 TRAIT APPROACHES: DO LEADERS HAVE DISTINCTIVE PERSONALITY CHARACTERISTICS?

major question? What does it take to be a successful leader?

THE BIG PICTURE

Trait approaches attempt to identify distinctive characteristics that account for the effectiveness of leaders. We describe (1) the trait perspective expressed by Kouzes and Posner, (2) some results of gender studies, and (3) leadership lessons from the GLOBE project.

Consider two high-powered leaders of the late 20th century. Each "personifies the word 'stubborn,'" says a *Fortune* magazine account. Both "are piercingly analytical thinkers who combine hands-on technical smarts with take-no-prisoners business savvy. Both absolutely hate to lose."[18]

Who are they? They are two of the most successful former CEOs in American business—Bill Gates of Microsoft and Andy Grove of Intel. Do they have distinctive personality traits that might teach us something about leadership? Perhaps they do. They would seem to embody the traits of (1) dominance, (2) intelligence, (3) self-confidence, (4) high energy, and (5) task-relevant knowledge.

These are the five traits that researcher **Ralph Stogdill** in 1948 concluded were typical of successful leaders.[19] Stogdill is one of many contributors to *trait approaches to leadership,* **which attempt to identify distinctive characteristics that account for the effectiveness of leaders.**[20]

Is Trait Theory Useful?

Traits play a central role in how we perceive leaders, and they ultimately affect leadership effectiveness. On the basis of past studies, we can suggest a list of positive traits that are important for leaders to have, as shown below.[21] *(See Table 14.2.)* If assuming a leadership role interests you, you might wish to cultivate these traits for your future success, using personality tests to evaluate your strengths and weaknesses in preparing (perhaps with the aid of an executive coach) a personal development plan.[22]

table 14.2

KEY POSITIVE LEADERSHIP TRAITS

Intelligence	Sociability
Self-confidence	Problem-solving skills
Determination	Extraversion
Honesty/integrity	Conscientiousness

Source: R. Kreitner and A. Kinicki, *Organizational Behavior,* 8th ed. (New York: McGraw-Hill/Irwin, 2008), p. 470.

Two ways in which organizations may apply trait theory are as follows:

Use Personality & Trait Assessments   Organizations may include personality and trait assessments into their selection and promotion processes (being careful to use valid measures of leadership traits).

Use Management Development Programs   To enhance employee leadership traits, organizations may send targeted employees to management development programs that include management classes, coaching sessions, trait assessments, and the like.[23]

Kouzes & Posner's Research: Is Honesty the Top Leadership Trait?

During the 1980s, **James Kouzes** and **Barry Posner** surveyed more than 7,500 managers throughout the United States as to what personal traits they looked for and admired in their superiors.[24] The respondents suggested that a credible leader should have five traits. He or she should be (1) honest, (2) competent, (3) forward-looking, (4) inspiring, and (5) intelligent. The first trait, honesty, was considered particularly important, being selected by 87% of the respondents, suggesting that people want their leaders to be ethical.

Although this research does reveal the traits preferred by employees, it has not, however, been able to predict which people might be successful leaders.

Gender Studies: Do Women Have Traits That Make Them Better Leaders?

WOMEN ASPIRE TO BE CHIEF AS MUCH AS MEN DO, declared the headline in *The Wall Street Journal.* A study by a New York research firm found that 55% of women and 57% of men aspire to be CEO, challenging the notion that more women aren't at the top because they don't want to be there.[25] And, in fact, it's possible that women may have traits that make them better managers—indeed, better leaders—than men.

The Evidence on Women Executives   A number of management studies conducted in the United States for companies ranging from high-tech to manufacturing to consumer services were reviewed by *BusinessWeek.*[26] By and large, the magazine reports, the studies showed that "women executives, when rated by their peers, underlings, and bosses, score higher than their male counterparts on a wide variety of measures—from producing high-quality work to goal-setting to mentoring employees." Researchers accidentally stumbled on these findings about gender differences while compiling hundreds of routine performance evaluations and analyzing the results. In one study of 425 high-level executives, women won higher ratings on 42 of the 52 skills measured.[27]

What are the desirable traits in which women excel? Among those traits mentioned are teamwork and partnering, being more collaborative, seeking less personal glory, being motivated less by self-interest than in what they can do for the company, being more stable, and being less turf-conscious. Women were also found to be better at producing quality work, recognizing trends, and generating new ideas and acting on them. A gender comparison of skills is summarized on the next page. *(See Table 14.3.)*

table 14.3

WHERE FEMALE EXECUTIVES DO BETTER: A SCORECARD

The check mark denotes which group scored higher on the respective studies. The asterisk indicates that in one study women's and men's scores in these categories were statistically even.

Skill	Men	Women
Motivating others		✓✓✓✓
Fostering communication		✓✓✓✓*
Producing high-quality work		✓✓✓✓
Strategic planning	✓✓	✓✓*
Listening to others		✓✓✓✓
Analyzing issues	✓✓	✓✓*

Source: Data from Hagberg Consulting Group, Management Research Group, Lawrence A. Pfaff, Personnel Decisions International Inc., and Advanced Teamware Inc., in table in R. Sharpe, "As Leaders, Women Rule," *BusinessWeek,* November 20, 2000, p. 75.

The Lack of Women at the Top   Why, then, aren't more women in positions of leadership? Males and females disagree about this issue. A team of researchers asked this question of 461 executive women holding titles of vice president or higher in Fortune 100 companies and all the male Fortune 100 CEOs. CEOs believed that women are not in senior leadership positions because (1) they lack significant general management experience and (2) women have not been in the executive talent pool long enough to get selected. Women, by contrast, believed that (1) male stereotyping and (2) exclusion from important informal networks are the biggest barriers to promotability.[28]

There are three additional possible explanations. First, as we suggested earlier in the book, there are many women who, though hard working, simply aren't willing to compete as hard as most men are or are not willing to make the required personal sacrifices.[29] (As Jamie Gorelick, former vice chair of Fannie Mae but also mother of two children ages 10 and 15, said when declining to be considered for CEO: "I just don't want that pace in my life.")[30] Second, women have a tendency to be overly modest and to give credit to others rather than taking it for themselves, which can undermine opportunities for promotions and raises.[31] Third, women are more likely than their male counterparts to have access to a supportive mentor.[32]

Group Exercise:
What Kind of Leader Do You Prefer?

Leadership Lessons from the GLOBE Project

Project GLOBE (Global Leadership and Organizational Behavior Effectiveness), you'll recall from Chapter 4, is a massive and ongoing attempt to develop an empirically based theory to "describe, understand, and predict the impact of specific cultural variables on leadership and organizational processes and the effectiveness of these processes."[33] Surveying 17,000 middle managers working for 951 organizations across 62 countries, the researchers determined that certain attributes of leadership were universally liked or disliked. *(See Table 14.4.)* Visionary and inspirational *charismatic leaders* who are good team builders generally do the best. *Self-centered leaders* seen as loners or face-savers generally receive a poor reception worldwide. ●

table 14.4

LESSONS FROM GLOBE: LEADERSHIP ATTRIBUTES UNIVERSALLY LIKED AND DISLIKED ACROSS 62 NATIONS

Universally positive leader attributes	Universally negative leader attributes
Trustworthy	Loner
Just	Asocial
Honest	Noncooperative
Foresight	Irritable
Plans ahead	Nonexplicit
Encouraging	Egocentric
Positive	Ruthless
Dynamic	Dictatorial
Motive arouser	
Confidence builder	
Motivational	
Dependable	
Intelligent	
Decisive	
Effective bargainer	
Win-win problem solver	
Administrative skilled	
Communicative	
Informed	
Coordinator	
Team builder	
Excellence oriented	

Source: Excerpted and adapted from P. W. Dorfman, P. J. Hanges, and F. C. Brodbeck, "Leadership and Cultural Variation: The Identification of Culturally Endorsed Leadership Profiles," in R. J. House, P. J. Hanges, M. Javidan, P. W. Dorfman, and V. Gupta eds., *Culture, Leadership and Organizations: The GLOBE Study of 62 Societies* (Thousand Oaks, CA: Sage, 2004), Tables 21.2 and 21.3 , pp. 677–678.

14.3 BEHAVIORAL APPROACHES: DO LEADERS SHOW DISTINCTIVE PATTERNS OF BEHAVIOR?

major question ?

Do effective leaders behave in similar ways?

THE BIG PICTURE

Behavioral leadership approaches try to determine the distinctive styles used by effective leaders. Two models we describe are the University of Michigan model and the Ohio State model.

Printing press. What kind of leadership behavior is appropriate for directing these kinds of workers?

Maybe what's important to know about leaders is not their *personality traits* but rather their *patterns of behavior* or *leadership styles*. This is the line of thought pursued by those interested in **behavioral leadership approaches, which attempt to determine the distinctive styles used by effective leaders.** By *leadership styles,* we mean the combination of traits, skills, and behaviors that leaders use when interacting with others.

What all models of leadership behavior have in common is the consideration of *task orientation versus people orientation.* Two classic studies came out of the universities of Michigan and Ohio State.

The University of Michigan Leadership Model

In the late 1940s, researchers at the University of Michigan came up with what came to be known as the **University of Michigan Leadership Model.** A team led by **Rensis Likert** began studying the effects of leader behavior on job performance, interviewing numerous managers and subordinates.[34] The investigators identified two forms of leadership styles: *job-centered* and *employee-centered.*

Job-Centered Behavior—"I'm Concerned More with the Needs of the Job" In *job-centered behavior,* managers paid more attention to the job and work procedures. Thus, their principal concerns were with achieving production efficiency, keeping costs down, and meeting schedules.

Employee-Centered Behavior—"I'm Concerned More with the Needs of Employees" In *employee-centered behavior,* managers paid more attention to employee satisfaction and making work groups cohesive. By concentrating on subordinates' needs they hoped to build effective work groups with high-performance goals.

The Ohio State Leadership Model

A second approach to leadership research was begun in 1945 at Ohio State University under **Ralph Stogdill** (mentioned in the last section). Hundreds of dimensions of leadership behavior were studied, resulting in what came to be known as the **Ohio State Leadership Model**.[35] From surveys of leadership behavior, two major dimensions of leader behavior were identified, as follows.

Initiating Structure—"What Do I Do to Get the Job Done?" *Initiating structure* is leadership behavior that organizes and defines what group members should be doing. It consists of the efforts the leader makes to get things organized and get the job done. This is much the same as Likert's "job-centered behavior."

Consideration—"What Do I Do to Show Consideration for My Employees?" *Consideration* is leadership behavior that expresses concern for employees by establishing a warm, friendly, supportive climate. This behavior, which resembles Likert's "employee-centered behavior," is sensitive to subordinates' ideas and feelings and establishes mutual trust.

All in all, one management expert concluded from the Michigan and Ohio studies that effective leaders (1) tend to have supportive or employee-centered relationships with employees, (2) use group rather than individual methods of supervision, and (3) set high-performance goals.[36] ●

Practical Action

Transition Problems on Your Way Up: How to Avoid the Pitfalls

Before you can become a good leader you need to become a good manager. Making the leap from individual contributor to a manager of several employees is one of the most difficult in peoples' careers.

Although corporations and managements may make noises about training and mentoring support, newly promoted managers may not see any of this and may simply be expected to know what to do. And, as managers move up the ladder, they may encounter other problems that they have not anticipated. How can you avoid some pitfalls as you make your ascent? Some suggestions:[37]

- **Have realistic expectations.** New managers often focus on the rights and privileges of their new jobs and underestimate the duties and obligations.

- **Don't forget to manage upward and sideways as well as downward.** You not only need to manage your subordinates but also the perceptions of your peers and your own managers above you.

- **Stay in touch with managers in other departments.** In addition, you need to have good relationships with managers in other departments—and be perceptive about their needs and priorities—since they have resources you need to get your job

done. Don't make the mistake of thinking your own department is the center of the universe.

- **Think about what kind of manager or leader you want to be.** Make a list of all your previous bosses and their good and bad attributes. This may produce a list of dos and don'ts that can serve you well.

- **Get guidance from other managers.** You may not get advice on how to manage from your own manager, who may have promoted you to help reduce his or her workload, not add to it by expecting some coaching. If this is the case, don't be shy about consulting other managers as well as people in professional organizations.

- **Resist isolation.** If you're promoted beyond supervisor of a small team and you have to manage hundreds rather than dozens, or thousands rather than hundreds, you may find the biggest surprise is isolation. The way to stay in touch is to talk daily with your senior managers, perhaps have "town meetings" with staffers several times a year, and employ "management by walking around"—bringing teams together to talk.

14.4 CONTINGENCY APPROACHES: DOES LEADERSHIP VARY WITH THE SITUATION?

major question? How might effective leadership vary according to the situation at hand?

THE BIG PICTURE

Effective leadership behavior depends on the situation at hand, say believers in the three contingency approaches: Fiedler's contingency leadership model, House's path–goal leadership model, and Hersey and Blanchard's situational leadership model.

Perhaps leadership is not characterized by universally important traits or behaviors. Perhaps there is no one best style that will work in all situations. This is the point of view of proponents of the ***contingency approach* to leadership, who believe that effective leadership behavior depends on the situation at hand.** That is, as situations change, different styles become appropriate.

Let's consider three contingency approaches: (1) the *contingency leadership model* by Fiedler, (2) the *path–goal leadership model* by House, and (3) the *situational leadership model* by Hersey and Blanchard.

I. The Contingency Leadership Model: Fiedler's Approach

The oldest model of the contingency approach to leadership was developed by **Fred Fiedler** and his associates in 1951.[38] **The *contingency leadership model* determines if a leader's style is (1) task-oriented or (2) relationship-oriented and if that style is effective for the situation at hand.** Fiedler's work was based on 80 studies conducted over 30 years.

Two Leadership Orientations: Tasks versus Relationships

Are you task-oriented or relationship-oriented? That is, are you more concerned with task accomplishment or with people?

To find out, you or your employees would fill out a questionnaire (known as the least preferred co-worker, or LPC, scale), in which you think of the co-worker you least enjoyed working with and rate him or her according to an eight-point scale of 16 pairs of opposite characteristics (such as friendly/unfriendly, tense/relaxed, efficient/inefficient). The higher the score, the more the relationship-oriented the respondent; the lower the score, the more task-oriented.

The Three Dimensions of Situational Control

Once the leadership orientation is known, then you determine *situational control*—how much control and influence a leader has in the immediate work environment.

There are three dimensions of situational control: *leader–member relations, task structure,* and *position power.*

- **Leader–member relations—"Do my subordinates accept me as a leader?"** This dimension, the most important component of situational control, reflects the extent to which a leader has or doesn't have the support, loyalty, and trust of the work group.

- **Task structure—"Do my subordinates perform unambiguous, easily understood tasks?"** This dimension refers to the extent to which tasks are routine, unambiguous, and

Tile style. Do successful entrepreneurs or small-business managers need to be task-oriented, relationship-oriented, or both? What style of leadership model would best suit a small tile manufacturing business in which employees need to work with a great deal of independence?

easily understood. The more structured the jobs, the more influence a leader has.

- **Position power—"Do I have power to reward and punish?"** This dimension refers to how much power a leader has to make work assignments and reward and punish. More power equals more control and influence.

For each dimension, the amount of control can be *high* —the leader's decisions will produce predictable results because he or she has the ability to influence work outcomes. Or it can be *low*—he or she doesn't have that kind of predictability or influence. By combining the three different dimensions with different high/low ratings, we have eight different leadership situations.

Which Style Is Most Effective?   Neither leadership style is effective all the time, Fiedler's research concludes, although each is right in certain situations.

- **When task-oriented style is best.** The task-oriented style works best in either *high-control* or *low-control* situations.

  Example of *high-control* situation (leader decisions produce predictable results because he or she can influence work outcomes): Suppose you were supervising parking-control officers ticketing cars parked illegally in expired meter zones, bus zones, and the like. You have (1) high leader-member relations because your subordinates are highly supportive of you and (2) high task structure because their jobs are clearly defined. (3) You have high position control because you have complete authority to evaluate their performance and dole out punishment and rewards. Thus, a task-oriented style would be best.

  Example of *low-control* situation (leader decisions can't produce predictable results because he or she can't really influence outcomes): Suppose you were a high school principal trying to clean up graffiti on your private-school campus, helped only by students you can find after school. You might have (1) low leader-member relations because many people might not see the need for the goal. (2) The task structure might also be low because people might see many different ways to achieve the goal. And (3) your position power would be low because the committee is voluntary and people are free to leave. In this low-control situation, a task-oriented style would also be best.

- **When relationship-oriented style is best.** The relationship-oriented style works best in situations of *moderate control*.

  Example: Suppose you were working in a government job supervising a group of firefighters fighting wildfires. You might have (1) low leader-member relations if you were promoted over others in the group but (2) high task structure, because the job is fairly well defined. (3) You might have low position power, because the rigidity of the civil-service job prohibits you from doing much in the way of rewarding and punishing. Thus, in this moderate-control situation, relationship-oriented leadership would be most effective.

Test Your Knowledge:
Fiedler's Contingency Model of Leadership

What do you do if your leadership orientation does not match the situation? Then, says Fiedler, it's better to try to move leaders into suitable situations rather than try to alter their personalities to fit the situations.[39]

2. The Path–Goal Leadership Model: House's Approach

A second contingency approach, advanced by **Robert House** in the 1970s and revised by him in 1996, is the ***path–goal leadership model*, which holds that the effective leader makes available to followers desirable rewards in the workplace and increases their motivation by clarifying the *paths,* or behavior, that will help them achieve those *goals* and providing them with support.** A successful leader thus helps followers by tying meaningful rewards to goal accomplishment, reducing barriers,

figure 14.1

GENERAL REPRESENTATION
OF HOUSE'S REVISED
PATH–GOAL THEORY

and providing support, so as to increase "the number and kinds of personal pay-offs to subordinates for work-goal attainment."[40]

Numerous studies testing various predictions from House's original path–goal theory provided mixed results.[41] As a consequence, he proposed a new model, a graphical version, shown below. *(See Figure 14.1.)*

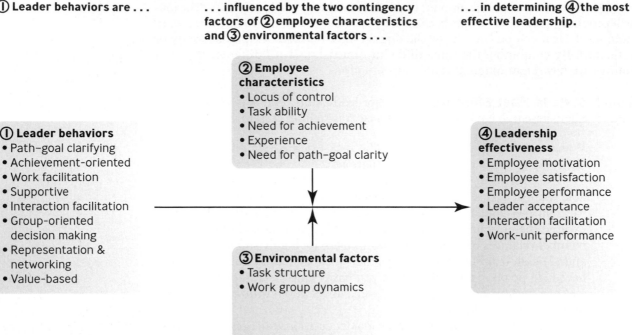

① **Leader behaviors are . . .**   **. . . influenced by the two contingency factors of ② employee characteristics and ③ environmental factors . . .**   **. . . in determining ④ the most effective leadership.**

① Leader behaviors
- Path–goal clarifying
- Achievement-oriented
- Work facilitation
- Supportive
- Interaction facilitation
- Group-oriented decision making
- Representation & networking
- Value-based

② Employee characteristics
- Locus of control
- Task ability
- Need for achievement
- Experience
- Need for path–goal clarity

③ Environmental factors
- Task structure
- Work group dynamics

④ Leadership effectiveness
- Employee motivation
- Employee satisfaction
- Employee performance
- Leader acceptance
- Interaction facilitation
- Work-unit performance

What Determines Leadership Effectiveness: Employee Characteristics & Environmental Factors Affect Leader Behavior   As the drawing indicates, two contingency factors, or variables—*employee characteristics* and *environmental factors*—cause some *leadership behaviors* to be more effective than others.

- **Employee characteristics.** Five employee characteristics are locus of control (described in Chapter 11), task ability, need for achievement, experience, and need for path–goal clarity.

- **Environmental factors.** Two environmental factors are task structure (independent versus interdependent tasks) and work group dynamics.

- **Leader behaviors.** Originally House proposed that there were four leader behaviors, or leadership styles—*directive* ("Here's what's expected of you and here's how to do it"), *supportive* ("I want things to be pleasant, since everyone's about equal here"), *participative* ("I want your suggestions in order to help me make decisions"), and *achievement-oriented* ("I'm confident you can accomplish the following great things"). The revised theory expands the number of leader behaviors from four to eight. *(See Table 14.5, opposite.)*

Thus, for example, employees with an internal locus of control are more likely to prefer achievement-oriented leadership or group-oriented decision making (formerly participative) leadership because they believe they have control over the work environment. The same is true for employees with high task ability and experience.

Employees with an external locus of control, however, tend to view the environment as uncontrollable, so they prefer the structure provided by supportive or path–goal clarifying (formerly directive) leadership. The same is probably true of inexperienced employees.

table 14.5

EIGHT LEADERSHIP STYLES OF THE REVISED PATH–GOAL THEORY

Style of leader behaviors	Description of behavior toward employees
1. Path–goal clarifying ("Here's what's expected of you and here's how to do it")	Clarify performance goals. Provide guidance on how employees can complete tasks. Clarify performance standards and expectations. Use positive and negative rewards contingent on performance.
2. Achievement-oriented ("I'm confident you can accomplish the following great things")	Set challenging goals. Emphasize excellence. Demonstrate confidence in employee abilities.
3. Work facilitation ("Here's the goal, and here's what I can do to help you achieve it")	Plan, schedule, organize, and coordinate work. Provide mentoring, coaching, counseling, and feedback to assist employees in developing their skills. Eliminate roadblocks. Provide resources. Empower employees to take actions and make decisions.
4. Supportive ("I want things to be pleasant, since everyone's about equal here")	Treat as equals. Show concern for well-being and needs. Be friendly and approachable.
5. Interaction facilitation ("Let's see how we can all work together to accomplish our goals")	Emphasize collaboration and teamwork. Encourage close employee relationships and sharing of minority opinions. Facilitate communication, resolve disputes.
6. Group-oriented decision making ("I want your suggestions in order to help me make decisions")	Pose problems rather than solutions to work group. Encourage members to participate in decision making. Provide necessary information to the group for analysis. Involve knowledgeable employees in decision making.
7. Representation & networking ("I've got a great bunch of people working for me whom you'll probably want to meet")	Present work group in positive light to others. Maintain positive relationships with influential others. Participate in organization-wide social functions and ceremonies. Do unconditional favors for others.
8. Value-based ("We're destined to accomplish great things")	Establish a vision, display passion for it, and support its accomplishment. Communicate high performance expectations and confidence in others' abilities to meet their goals. Give frequent positive feedback. Demonstrate self-confidence.

Source: Adapted from R. J. House, "Path–Goal Theory of Leadership: Lessons, Legacy, and a Reformulated Theory," *Leadership Quarterly,* Autumn 1996, pp. 323–352.

Besides expanding the styles of leader behavior from four to eight, House's revision of his theory also puts more emphasis on the need for leaders to foster intrinsic motivation through empowerment. Finally, his revised theory stresses the concept of shared leadership, the idea that employees do not have to be supervisors or managers to engage in leader behavior but rather may share leadership among all employees of the organization.

Does the Revised Path–Goal Theory Work? There have not been enough direct tests of House's revised path–goal theory using appropriate research methods and statistical procedures to draw overall conclusions. Research on transformational leadership, however, which is discussed in Section 14.5, is supportive of the revised model.[42]

Although further research is needed on the new model, it offers two important implications for managers:

*   *Use more than one leadership style.* Effective leaders possess and use more than one style of leadership. Thus, you are encouraged to study the eight

Test Your Knowledge:
Path–Goal Theory

Cranium's grand poo-bah and chief noodler. Richard Tait (left), responsible for business operations and marketing for the 14-person, Seattle-based game company Cranium, takes the unorthodox title of grand poo-bah. Whit Alexander, who focuses on product development, editorial content, and manufacturing, is called chief noodler. In devising the board game Cranium, the two entrepreneurs decided to adopt the acronym CHIFF—for "clever, high quality, innovative, friendly, and fun"—as the criterion by which all decisions would be guided. "Our survival and success will come from optimizing fun, focus, passion, and profits," says Tait. Which one of the eight path–goal leadership styles would you expect to find dominating this organization?

styles offered in path–goal theory so that you can try new leader behaviors when a situation calls for them.

- **Modify leadership style to fit employee and task characteristics.** A small set of employee characteristics (ability, experience, and need for independence) and environmental factors (task characteristics of autonomy, variety, and significance) are relevant contingency factors, and managers should modify their leadership style to fit them.[43]

3. The Situational Leadership Theory Model: Hersey & Blanchard's Approach

A third contingency approach has been proposed by management writers **Paul Hersey** and **Kenneth Blanchard.**[44] **In their *situational leadership theory,* leadership behavior reflects how leaders should adjust their leadership style according to the readiness of the followers.** The model suggests that managers should be flexible in choosing a leadership behavior style and be sensitive to the readiness level of their employees. ***Readiness* is defined as the extent to which a follower possesses the ability and willingness to complete a task.** Subordinates with high readiness (with high ability, skills, and willingness to work) require a different leadership style than do those with low readiness (low ability, training, and willingness).

The appropriate leadership style is found by cross-referencing follower readiness (low–high) with one of four leaderships styles. *(See Figure 14.2, opposite.)*

How the Situational Leadership Model Works   Let's see what the illustration means.

- **Leadership styles—relationship behavior plus task behavior.** The upper part of the drawing shows the leadership style, which is based on the combination of relationship behavior (vertical axis) and task behavior (horizontal axis).

   Relationship behavior is the extent to which leaders maintain personal relationships with their followers, as in providing support and keeping communication open.

   Task behavior is the extent to which leaders organize and explain the role of their followers, which is achieved by explaining what subordinates are to do and how tasks are to be accomplished.

- **Four leadership styles—telling, selling, participating, delegating.** The bell-shaped curve indicates when each of the four leadership styles—telling (S1), selling (S2), participating (S3), and delegating (S4)—should be used.

- **When a leadership style should be used—depends on the readiness of the followers.** How do you know which leadership style to employ? You need to have an understanding of the *readiness* of your followers, as represented by the scale at the bottom of the drawing, where R1 represents low readiness and R4 represents high readiness.

   Let's consider which leadership style to apply when.

   Telling represents the guiding and directing of performance. This leadership style works best for followers with a low level of readiness—that is, subordinates are neither willing nor able to take responsibility.

   Selling is explaining decisions and persuading others to follow a course of action. Because it offers both direction and support, this leadership style is most suitable for followers who are unable but willing to assume task responsibility.

   Participating involves encouraging followers to solve problems on their own. Because it shares decision making, this leadership style encourages subordinates in performing tasks. Thus, it is most appropriate for followers whose readiness is in the moderate to high range.

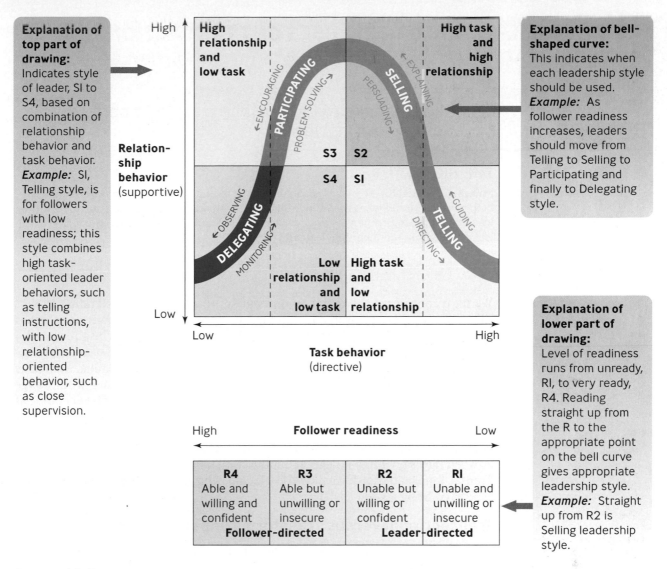

Explanation of top part of drawing: Indicates style of leader, SI to S4, based on combination of relationship behavior and task behavior. *Example:* SI, Telling style, is for followers with low readiness; this style combines high task-oriented leader behaviors, such as telling instructions, with low relationship-oriented behavior, such as close supervision.

Explanation of bell-shaped curve: This indicates when each leadership style should be used. *Example:* As follower readiness increases, leaders should move from Telling to Selling to Participating and finally to Delegating style.

Explanation of lower part of drawing: Level of readiness runs from unready, RI, to very ready, R4. Reading straight up from the R to the appropriate point on the bell curve gives appropriate leadership style. *Example:* Straight up from R2 is Selling leadership style.

figure 14.2

HERSEY AND BLANCHARD'S SITUATIONAL LEADERSHIP MODEL

Source: From P. Hersey, K. H. Blanchard, and D. E. Johnson, *Management of Organizational Behavior: Leading Human Resources,* 8e. Copyright © 2006 Reprinted with permission of the Center for Leadership Studies, Inc. Escondido, CA 92025. All rights reserved.

Delegating is providing subordinates with little support or direction. As such, the leader's role is to observe and monitor. This leadership style is best for followers who have a high level of readiness, both able and willing to perform tasks.

Does the Hersey-Blanchard Model Work?   The situational leadership model is widely used as a training tool, but it is not strongly supported by scientific research. For instance, a study of 459 salespeople found that leadership effectiveness was not attributable to the predicted interaction between follower readiness and leadership style.[45] This is consistent with another study, in which 57 chief nurse executives were found not to delegate in accordance with situational leadership theory.[46] Researchers also have concluded that the self-assessment instrument used to measure leadership style and follower readiness is inaccurate.[47] In sum, managers should exercise discretion when using prescriptions from this model. ●

14.5 THE FULL-RANGE MODEL: USES OF TRANSACTIONAL & TRANSFORMATIONAL LEADERSHIP

THE BIG PICTURE

Full-range leadership describes leadership along a range of styles, with the most effective being transactional/transformational leaders. Four key behaviors of transformational leaders in affecting employees are they inspire motivation, inspire trust, encourage excellence, and stimulate them intellectually.

We have considered the major traditional approaches to understanding leadership—the trait, behavioral, and contingency approaches. But newer approaches seem to offer something more by trying to determine what factors inspire and motivate people to perform beyond their normal levels.

One recent approach proposed by **Bernard Bass and Bruce Avolio,** known as *full-range leadership,* **suggests that leadership behavior varies along a full range of leadership styles, from take-no-responsibility (*laissez-faire*) "leadership" at one extreme, through transactional leadership, to transformational leadership at the other extreme.**[48] Not taking responsibility can hardly be considered leadership (although it often seems to be manifested by CEOs whose companies got in trouble, as when they say "I had no idea about the criminal behavior of my subordinates"). Transactional and transformational leadership behaviors, however, are both positive aspects of being a good leader.

Transactional versus Transformational Leaders

Plans, budgets, schedules. Would you expect management in the construction field to focus more on the nonpeople aspects of work?

India-born Indra Nooyi, chairman and CEO of PepsiCo Inc., is able to be both a transactional and a transformational leader. Let us consider the differences.

Transactional Leadership As a manager, your power stems from your ability to provide rewards (and threaten reprimands) in exchange for your subordinates' doing the work. When you do this, you are performing *transactional leadership*, focusing on clarifying employees' roles and task requirements and providing rewards and punishments contingent on performance. Transactional leadership also encompasses the fundamental managerial activities of setting goals and monitoring progress toward their achievement.[49]

"You give the team of people a set of objectives and goals and get them all to buy into it, and they can move mountains," says Nooyi, who was ranked No. 5 on *Forbes* magazine's 2007 list of the world's most powerful women.[50] Under her leadership, PepsiCo has turned in impressive earnings despite rising costs "through a combination of new products, productivity improvements, higher prices, and packaging tweaks," says a *Fortune* article.[51]

We shouldn't think of a transactional leader as being a mediocre leader—indeed, competent transactional leaders are badly needed. But transactional leaders are best in stable situations. What's needed in rapidly changing situations, as is often the case in many organizations today, is a transformational leader.

Transformational Leadership *Transformational leadership* **transforms employees to pursue organizational goals over self-interests.** Transformational leaders, in one description, "engender trust, seek to develop leadership in others, exhibit self-sacrifice, and serve as moral agents, focusing themselves and followers on objectives that transcend the more immediate needs of the work group."[52] Whereas transactional leaders try to get people to do *ordinary* things, transformational leaders encourage their people to do *exceptional* things—significantly higher levels of intrinsic motivation, trust, commitment, and loyalty—that can produce significant organizational change and results.

Transformational leaders are influenced by two factors:

- **Individual characteristics.** The personalities of such leaders tend to be more extroverted, agreeable, and proactive than nontransformational leaders. (Female leaders tend to use transformational leadership more than male leaders do.)[53]

- **Organizational culture.** Adaptive, flexible organizational cultures are more likely than are rigid, bureaucratic cultures to foster transformational leadership.

The Best Leaders Are Both Transactional & Transformational

It's important to note that transactional leadership is an essential *prerequisite* to effective leadership, and the best leaders learn to display both transactional and transformational styles of leadership to some degree. Indeed, research suggests that transformational leadership leads to superior performance when it "augments" or adds to transactional leadership.[54]

This is apparent in the case of PepsiCo CEO Nooyi. One of her "most stunning talents is the art of suasian," says one writer. "She can rouse an audience and rally them around something as mind-numbing as a new companywide software installation. Her new motto, 'Performance With Purpose,' is both a means of 'herding the organization' and of presenting PepsiCo globally."[55] Most important is her vision for moving the company beyond what it calls "fun for you foods" (soda pop and salty snacks) and into "better for you" foods, and into tackling issues like obesity and sustainability. Nooyi, says Howard Schultz, CEO of Starbucks, which has a joint-venture partnership with PepsiCo, was "way ahead of her competitors in moving the company toward healthier products. She pushed for PepsiCo to buy Quaker Oats and Tropicana, and . . . PepsiCo removed trans fats from its products well before most other companies did."[56]

Four Key Behaviors of Transformational Leaders

Whereas transactional leaders are dispassionate, transformational leaders excite passion, inspiring and empowering people to look beyond their own interests to

Sir Branson. One of today's most flamboyant businessmen, Britain's Richard Branson is shown here announcing new service for his virgin Atlantic airline. Branson left school at 16 to start a 1960s counterculture magazine. By 2006, he was heading a $5 billion-plus empire—the Virgin Group—that includes airlines, entertainment companies, car dealerships, railroads, bridal gowns, soft drinks, financial services, and a space tourism company. Knighted in 2000—which entitles him to be called "Sir"—Branson, who is dyslexic, says he is not for scrutinizing spreadsheets and plotting strategies based on estimates of market share. "In the end," he says, "it is your own gut and your own experience of running businesses." Do you think charismatic business leaders like Sir Branson are able to be more successful than more conventional and conservative managers?

the interests of the organization. They appeal to their followers' self-concepts—their values and personal identity—to create changes in their goals, values, needs, beliefs, and aspirations.

Transformational leaders have four key kinds of behavior that affect followers.[57]

1. Inspirational Motivation: "Let Me Share a Vision That Transcends Us All" Transformational leaders have *charisma* ("kar-*riz*-muh"), **a form of interpersonal attraction that inspires acceptance and support.** Charismatic leadership (once viewed as a category of its own but now considered part of transformational leadership) inspires motivation by offering an agenda, a grand design, an ultimate goal—in short, a *vision,* "a realistic, credible, attractive future" for the organization, as leadership expert Burt Nanus calls it. The right vision unleashes human potential, says Nanus, because it serves as a beacon of hope and common purpose. It does so by attracting commitment, energizing workers, creating meaning in their lives, establishing a standard of excellence, promoting high ideals, and bridging the divide between the organization's problems and its goals and aspirations.[58]

Examples: Civil rights leader Martin Luther King Jr. had a vision—a "dream," as he put it—of racial equality. United Farm Workers leader Cesar Chavez had a vision of better working conditions and pay for agricultural workers. Candy Lightner, founder of Mothers Against Drunk Driving, had a vision of getting rid of alcohol-related car crashes. Apple Computer's Steve Jobs had a vision of developing an "insanely great" desktop computer.

2. Idealized Influence: "We Are Here to Do the Right Thing" Transformational leaders are able to inspire trust in their followers because they express their integrity by being consistent, single-minded, and persistent in pursuit of their goal. Not only do they display high ethical standards and act as models of desirable values, but they are also able to make sacrifices for the good of the group.[59]

Examples: In 1982, when seven people died consuming cyanide-laced Tylenol capsules, Johnson & Johnson CEO James Burke retained consumer confidence by his actions in taking the drug off the market. Anita Roddick of The Body Shop cosmetics company was a model for her beliefs in fair trade, environmental awareness, animal protection, and respect for human rights.

3. Individualized Consideration: "You Have the Opportunity Here to Grow & Excel" Transformational leaders don't just express concern for subordinates' well-being. They actively encourage them to grow and to excel by giving them challenging work, more responsibility, empowerment, and one-on-one mentoring.

Example: When Indra Nooyi was chosen over her friend Mike White to lead PepsiCo, she went to great lengths to keep him on. "I treat Mike as my partner," she says. "He could easily have been CEO." At meetings, she always makes sure he is seated at her right.[60]

4. Intellectual Stimulation: "Let Me Describe the Great Challenges We Can Conquer Together" These leaders are gifted at communicating the organization's strengths, weaknesses, opportunities, and threats so that subordinates develop a new sense of purpose. Employees become less apt to view problems as insurmountable or "that's not my department." Instead they learn to view them as personal challenges that they are responsible for overcoming, to question the status quo, and to seek creative solutions.

Example: Nooyi is intent on balancing profit motive with making healthier foods, having minimal negative impact on the environment, and taking care of PepsiCo's workforce. "Companies today are bigger than many economies," she says. "We are little republics. . . . If companies don't do [responsible] things, who is going to?"

Implications of Transformational Leadership for Managers

The research shows that transformational leadership yields several positive results. For example, it is positively associated with (1) measures of organizational effectiveness;[61] (2) measures of leadership effectiveness and employee job satisfaction;[62] (3) more employee identification with their leaders and with their immediate work groups;[63] and (4) higher levels of intrinsic motivation, group cohesion, work engagement, and setting of goals consistent with those of the leader.[64]

Besides the fact that, as we mentioned, the best leaders are *both* transactional and transformational, there are three important implications of transformational leadership for managers, as follows.

1. It Can Improve Results for Both Individuals & Groups You can use the four types of transformational behavior just described to improve results for individuals—such as job satisfaction, organizational commitment, and performance. You can also use them to improve outcomes for groups—an important matter in today's organization, where people tend not to work in isolation but in collaboration with others.

2. It Can Be Used to Train Employees at Any Level Not just top managers but employees at any level can be trained to be more transactional and transformational.[65] This kind of leadership training among employees should be based on an overall corporate philosophy that constitutes the foundation of leadership development.

3. It Can Be Used by Both Ethical & Unethical Leaders Ethical transformational leaders help employees to enhance their self-concepts. Unethical leaders may select or produce obedient, dependent, and compliant followers. To better ensure positive results from transformational leadership, top managers should do the following:[66]

- **Employ a code of ethics.** The company should create and enforce a clearly stated code of ethics.
- **Choose the right people.** Recruit, select, and promote people who display ethical behavior.
- **Make performance expectations reflect employee treatment.** Develop performance expectations around the treatment of employees; these expectations can be assessed in the performance-appraisal process.
- **Emphasize value of diversity.** Train employees to value diversity.
- **Reward high moral conduct.** Identify, reward, and publicly praise employees who exemplify high moral conduct. ●

THE BIG PICTURE

We consider four other kinds of leadership. The *leader–member exchange model* emphasizes that leaders have different sorts of relationships with different subordinates. In *shared leadership,* people share responsibility for leading with others. In *servant leadership,* leaders provide service to employees and the organization. *E-leadership* involves leader interactions with others via information technology.

Four additional kinds of leadership deserve discussion: (1) *leader–member exchange (LMX) model of leadership,* (2) *shared leadership,* (3) *servant leadership,* and (4) *e-leadership.*

Leader–Member Exchange (LMX) Leadership

Proposed by **George Graen and Fred Dansereau,** the *leader–member exchange (LMX) model of leadership* **emphasizes that leaders have different sorts of relationships with different subordinates.**[67] Unlike other models we've described, which focus on the behaviors or traits of leaders or followers, the LMX model looks at the quality of relationships between managers and subordinates. Also, unlike other models, which presuppose stable relationships between leaders and followers, the LMX model assumes each manager-subordinate relationship is unique (what behavioral scientists call a "vertical dyad").

In-Group Exchange versus Out-Group Exchange The unique relationship, which supposedly results from the leader's attempt to delegate and assign work roles, can produce two types of leader–member exchange interactions:[68]

- **In-group exchange.** In the *in-group exchange,* the relationship between leader and follower becomes a partnership characterized by mutual trust, respect and liking, and a sense of common fates. Subordinates may receive special assignments and may also receive special privileges.

- **Out-group exchange.** In the *out-group exchange,* leaders are characterized as overseers who fail to create a sense of mutual trust, respect, or common fate. Subordinates receive less of the manager's time and attention than those in in-group exchange relationships.

Self-Assessment:
Assessing Your
Leader–Member
Exchange

Is the LMX Model Useful? It is not clear why a leader selects particular subordinates to be part of the in-group, but presumably the choice is made for reasons of compatibility and competence. Certainly, however, a positive (that is, in-group) leader–member exchange is positively associated with goal commitment, trust between managers and employees, work climate, satisfaction with leadership, and—important to any employer—job performance and job satisfaction.[69] The type of leader–member exchange also was found to predict not only turnover among nurses and computer analysts but also career outcomes, such as promotability, salary level, and receipt of bonuses, over a 7-year period.[70]

Shared Leadership

Which is better—leadership in a single chain of command or shared leadership responsibility among two or more individuals? Perhaps, it's suggested, shared leadership is more optimal.[71] **Shared leadership is a simultaneous, ongoing, mutual influence process in which people share responsibility for leading.** It is based on the idea that people need to share information and collaborate to get things done. This kind of leadership is most likely to be needed when people work in teams, are involved in complex projects, or are doing knowledge work   work requiring voluntary contributions of intellectual capital by skilled professionals.[72] Researchers are beginning to explore the process of shared leadership, and the results are promising. For example, shared leadership in teams has been found to be positively associated with group cohesion, group citizenship, and group effectiveness.[73]

Example

Shared Leadership: Tech Companies Spread the Power

All kinds of organizations are run with shared leadership. The famed Mayo Clinic, for example, which employs more than 42,000 employees in various hospitals and clinics, relies on shared leadership to provide high-quality health care and customer service.[74] For a while, Ford Motor Company was run by three individuals at the top.[75] At Google, cofounders Sergey Brin, President, Technology, and Larry Page, President, Products, are part of a triumvirate with Eric Schmidt, Chief Executive Officer.[76]

The fastest-growing Web site on the planet, with 110 million "friends," is MySpace.com. The founders, Tom Anderson and Chris DeWolfe, who live in Los Angeles, created the site, according to *Fortune,* "to promote local acts and connect fans and friends . . . who connected friends . . . who connected friends. . . . The two had a friendship based on business, then they—quite literally—founded a business based on friendship." When News Corp. CEO Rupert Murdoch offered $580 million for MySpace's parent company, they accepted the deal but remained on as the top executives, with DeWolfe as CEO and Anderson as President. DeWolfe is the business brain, the smart person with the compelling vision; Anderson is the "soul" of the enterprise, the one who understands the users.[77]

Your Call

If you were leading a business with a friend of yours, which role do you think would suit you best—the "business brain" or the "soul"?

Servant Leadership: Meeting the Goals of Followers & the Organization, Not of Oneself

The term *servant leadership,* coined in 1970 by **Robert Greenleaf,** reflects not only his one-time background as a management researcher for AT&T but also his views as a lifelong philosopher and devout Quaker.[78] **Servant leaders focus on providing increased service to others—meeting the goals of both followers and the organization—rather than to themselves.**

Former UCLA coach John Wooden, described as "a humble, giving person who wants nothing in return but to see other people succeed," is one such example. Wooden led the university's men's basketball teams to 10 national championships.[79] Wal-Mart's Sam Walton believed that leadership consisted of providing employees with the products, training, and support needed to serve customers and then standing back and letting them do their jobs.[80] Max De Pree, former chairman of furniture maker Herman Miller Inc., promoted a "covenant" with his employees. Leaders, he wrote, should give employees "space so that we can both give and receive such beautiful things as ideas, openness, dignity, joy, healing, and inclusion."[81] Starbucks CEO Howard Schultz is also cited as being one of the foremost practitioners of servant-style leadership. Schultz has made sure his employees have health insurance and work in a positive environment and as a result Starbucks has a strong brand following.[82]

Servant leadership is not a quick-fix approach to leadership. Rather, it is a long-term, transformational approach to life and work. Ten characteristics of the servant leader are shown below. *(See Table 14.6.)* One can hardly go wrong by trying to adopt these characteristics.

table 14.6

TEN CHARACTERISTICS OF THE SERVANT LEADER

1. Focus on listening.
2. Ability to empathize with others' feelings.
3. Focus on healing suffering.
4. Self-awareness of strengths and weaknesses.
5. Use of persuasion rather than positional authority to influence others.
6. Broad-based conceptual thinking.
7. Ability to foresee future outcomes.
8. Belief they are stewards of their employees and resources.
9. Commitment to the growth of people.
10. Drive to build community within and outside the organization.

Source: From L. C. Spears, "Introduction: Servant-Leadership and the Greenleaf Legacy," in L. C. Spears, ed., *Reflections on Leadership: How Robert K. Greenleaf's Theory of Servant-Leadership Influenced Today's Top Management,* John Wiley & Sons, 1995, pp. 1–14. Reprinted with permission of John Wiley & Sons, Inc.

E-Leadership: Managing for Global Networks

The Internet and other forms of advanced information technology have led to new possible ways for interacting within and between organizations (e-business) and with customers and suppliers (e-commerce). Leadership within the context of this electronic technology, called *e-leadership,* **can involve one-to-one, one-to-many, within-group and between-group and collective interactions via information technology.**[83]

An e-leader doesn't have to be a tech guru, but he or she does have to know enough about information technology to overhaul traditional corporate structures. E-leaders, says one writer, "have a global mind-set that recognizes that the Internet is opening new markets and recharging existing ones. They don't bother fighting mere battles with competitors because they're too busy creating businesses that will surround and destroy them."[84] Harvard Business School professor D. Quinn Mills, author of *E-Leadership,* suggests that individual companies will be replaced by much broader global networks that a single CEO will not be able to manage. Thus, while 20th-century management emphasized competition, he says, future organizations will run on knowledge sharing and open exchange.[85]

These observations suggest that e-leadership means having to deal with quite a number of responsibilities, some of which are listed in the table below. Some of these responsibilities are developing business opportunities through cooperative relationships, restructuring a company into global networks, decentralizing the company's organization, and energizing the staff.[86] *(See Table 14.7.)* ●

table 14.7

SIX SECRETS OF SUCCESSFUL E-LEADERS

These tips are offered by Don MacRae, president of the Lachlan Group, Toronto.

1. **Create the future rather than a better status quo.** No matter how successful your business is now, it can be wiped out overnight by the swiftness of the Internet economy. Pay attention to new possibilities rather than simply reacting to today's problems.

2. **Create a "teachable vision."** When Steve Jobs started Apple Computer, his teachable vision was to develop a computer that was as simple to use as a bicycle. Think about how your organization needs to act differently in order to stay at the top of your industry. Have the best and brightest stars in your company investigate how your traditional markets are shifting and what new opportunities might be up for grabs.

3. **Follow a strategy your customers set, not you.** Get over your love affair with your own products and services. What matters most is whether your customers love them. Talk to them about their needs and how you could serve them better. Let them set corporate direction.

4. **Foster a collaborative culture.** E-leaders don't give orders from the top. They let teams form organically in their organizations and encourage people to question the way things are done. Be open to unorthodox strategies.

5. **Think globally.** Technology allows you to build ties with customers, suppliers, and strategic partners all over the world. Don't neglect the opportunity. Be disciplined about finding the best places to do business and seeing opportunities where they exist.

6. **Thrive on information.** This means all kinds of information: overnight sales figures, customer-satisfaction scores, employee turnover, on-time delivery rates, canceled orders, and so on. Technology allows e-leaders to track their companies by every conceivable detail. Without taking a 360-degree view of what's going on in your business—and adjusting your strategy accordingly—you can forget about leading for much longer.

Source: Adapted from D. MacRae, *BusinessWeek online,* September 6, 2001, www.businessweek.com/technology/content/sep2001/tc2001096_619.htm, accessed August 15, 2004.

Key Terms Used in This Chapter

behavioral leadership approaches 446
charisma 456
coercive power 438
contingency approach 448
contingency leadership model 448
e-leadership 460
expert power 438
full-range leadership 454

leader–member exchange (LMX) model of leadership 458
leadership 436
legitimate power 438
path–goal leadership model 449
personalized power 438
readiness 452
referent power 438

reward power 438
servant leaders 459
shared leadership 459
situational leadership theory 452
socialized power 438
trait approaches to leadership 442
transactional leadership 454
transformational leadership 455

14.1 The Nature of Leadership: Wielding Influence

Leadership is the ability to influence employees to voluntarily pursue organizational goals. Being a manager and being a leader are not the same. Management is about coping with complexity, whereas leadership is about coping with change. Companies manage complexity by planning and budgeting, organizing and staffing, and controlling and problem solving. Leadership copes with change by setting a direction, aligning people to accomplish an agenda, and motivating and inspiring people.

To understand leadership, we must understand authority and power. Authority is the right to perform or command; it comes with the manager's job. Power is the extent to which a person is able to influence others so they respond to orders. People may pursue personalized power, power directed at helping oneself, or, better, they may pursue socialized power, power directed at helping others.

Within an organization there are typically five sources of power leaders may draw on; all managers have the first three. (1) Legitimate power is power that results from managers' formal positions within the organization. (2) Reward power is power that results from managers' authority to reward their subordinates. (3) Coercive power results from managers' authority to punish their subordinates. (4) Expert power is power resulting from one's specialized information or expertise. (5) Referent power is power deriving from one's personal attraction.

There are nine influence tactics for trying to get others to do something you want, ranging from most used to least used tactics as follows: rational persuasion, inspirational appeals, consultation, ingratiating tactics, personal appeals, exchange tactics, coalition tactics, pressure tactics, and legitimating tactics.

Four principal approaches or perspectives on leadership, as discussed in the rest of the chapter, are (1) trait, (2) behavioral, (3) contingency, and (4) emerging.

 14.2 Trait Approaches: Do Leaders Have Distinctive Personality Characteristics?

Trait approaches to leadership attempt to identify distinctive characteristics that account for the effectiveness of leaders. Representatives of this approach are Kouzes and Posner, gender studies, and leadership lessons from the GLOBE project. (1) Kouzes and Posner identified five traits of leaders. A leader should be honest, competent, forward-looking, inspiring, and intelligent. (2) Women may rate higher than men do on producing high-quality work, goal setting, mentoring employees, and other measures. Women excel in such traits as teamwork and partnering, being more collaborative, seeking less personal glory, being motivated less by self-interest than company interest, being more stable, and being less turf-conscious. (3) Project GLOBE surveyed 17,000 middle managers in 62 countries and determined that visionary and inspirational charismatic leaders who are good team builders do best.

 14.3 Behavioral Approaches: Do Leaders Show Distinctive Patterns of Behavior?

Behavioral leadership approaches try to determine the distinctive styles used by effective leaders. Leadership style means the combination of traits, skills, and behaviors that leaders use when interacting with others. We described some important models of leadership behavior.

In the University of Michigan Leadership Model, researchers identified two forms of leadership styles. In job-centered behavior, managers paid more attention to the job and work procedures. In employee-centered behavior, managers paid more attention to employee satisfaction and making work groups cohesive.

In the Ohio State Leadership Model, researchers identified two major dimensions of leader behavior: Initiating structure organizes and defines what group members should be doing. Consideration is leadership behavior that expresses concern for employees by establishing a supportive climate.

One expert concludes from the Michigan and Ohio studies that effective leaders tend to have supportive relationships with employees, use group rather than individual methods of supervision, and set high performance goals.

14.4 Contingency Approaches: Does Leadership Vary with the Situation?

Proponents of the contingency approach to leadership believe that effective leadership behavior depends on the situation at hand—that as situations change, different styles become effective. Three contingency approaches are described.

The Fiedler contingency leadership model determines if a leader's style is task-oriented or relationship-oriented and if that style is effective for the situation at hand. Once it is determined whether a leader is more oriented toward tasks or toward people, then it's necessary to determine how much control and influence a leader has in the immediate work environment. The three dimensions of situational control are leader–member relations, which reflects the extent to which a leader has the support of the work group; the task structure, which reflects the extent to which tasks are routine and easily understood; and position power, which reflects how much power a leader has to reward and punish and make work assignments. For each dimension, the leader's control may be high or low. A task-oriented style has been found to work best in either high-control or low-control situations; the relationship-oriented style is best in situations of moderate control.

The House path–goal leadership model, in its revised form, holds that the effective leader clarifies paths through which subordinates can achieve goals and provides them with support. Two variables, employee characteristics and environmental factors, cause one or more leadership behaviors—which House expanded to eight from his original four—to be more effective than others.

Hersey and Blanchard's situational leadership theory suggests that leadership behavior reflects how leaders should adjust their leadership style according to the readiness of the followers. Readiness is defined as the extent to which a follower possesses the ability and willingness to complete a task. The appropriate leadership style is found by cross-referencing follower readiness (low to high) with one of four leadership styles: telling, selling, participating, delegating.

14.5 The Full-Range Model: Uses of Transactional & Transformational Leadership

Full-range leadership describes leadership along a range of styles, with the most effective being transactional/transformational leaders. Transactional leadership focuses on clarifying employees' roles and task requirements and providing rewards and punishments contingent on performance. Transformational leadership transforms employees to pursue goals over self-interests. Transformational leaders are influenced by two factors: (1) Their personalities tend to be more extroverted, agreeable, and proactive. (2) Organizational cultures are more apt to be adaptive and flexible.

The best leaders are both transactional and transformational. Four key behaviors of transformational leaders in affecting employees are they inspire motivation, inspire trust, encourage excellence, and stimulate them intellectually.

Transformational leadership has three implications. (1) It can improve results for both individuals and groups. (2) It can be used to train employees at any level. (3) It can be used by both ethical or unethical leaders.

14.6 Four Additional Perspectives

Four additional kinds of leadership are (1) leader–membership exchange model, (2) shared leadership, (3) servant leadership, and (4) e-leadership.

The leader–member exchange (LMX) model of leadership emphasizes that leaders have different sorts of relationships with different subordinates.

Shared leadership is a simultaneous, ongoing, mutual influence process in which people share responsibility for leading. It is based on the idea that people need to share information and collaborate to get things done.

Servant leaders focus on providing increased service to others—meeting the goals of both followers and the organization—rather than to themselves.

E-leadership involves leader interactions with others via the Internet and other forms of advanced information technology, which have made possible new ways for interacting within and between organizations (e-business) and with customers and suppliers (e-commerce). E-leadership can involve one-to-one, one-to-many, within-group and between-group and collective interactions via information technology.

Management in Action

Vikram Pandit Faces Big Challenges at Citigroup

Four months into his tenure as Citigroup Inc.'s chief executive, Vikram Pandit faces mounting pressure to show that a detail-obsessed ex-professor can turn around one of the world's largest and most troubled banks.

Even executives who praise his cautious, deliberative approach express concern Mr. Pandit is taking too long to make decisions. He has earned high marks for quickly addressing the most pressing financial issues. Still, executives and investors alike complain that Mr. Pandit hasn't articulated his vision for the company. Some executives also say they are stuck in holding patterns awaiting instructions from his team on decisions that previously wouldn't have attracted such high-level attention.

"At a time like this, you really want people marching shoulder-to-shoulder with you," says Sanford Weill, the former CEO who engineered the 1998 merger that created the Citigroup behemoth that Mr. Pandit is still wrestling with today. Mr. Weill, who supports Mr. Pandit, has urged him to use the bully pulpit of his job to boost morale and reassure investors.

"The leader needs to relate to the people," says Mr. Weill. "They need to know who they're following."

Some of Mr. Pandit's biggest changes have stirred controversy. For instance, an executive shakeup in late March resulted in a complex new chain of command: Some executives now have two or more bosses, sometimes located thousands of miles apart.

"Where does the decision-making lie?" Sallie Krawcheck, who runs Citigroup's wealth-management business, asked Mr. Pandit at a meeting of top executives, according to people familiar with the matter. She expressed concern that the new structure could cause "paralysis." . . .

The CEO strongly defends his analytical approach to fixing the company. Because Citigroup—a mammoth firm of some 370,000 employees spread across more than 100 countries—has so many problems, there is no room for making poorly informed snap decisions, Mr. Pandit said in an interview.

"The more patience people have, the better off they're going to be at seeing the true value of this company," he says. "It's probably going to take some time.". . .

He has supporters within the firm. "I will take substance over form any day of the week," says James Forese, a senior capital-markets executive at Citigroup. "I will take judgment over charisma any day of the week.". . .

Asked about his vision for the company, Mr. Pandit says first it needs to fix the little things. "Only after we get those foundations right do we earn the right to talk about vision," he says.

His late-March management restructuring isn't the first time Citigroup has grappled with chain of command for the sprawling enterprise. A scandal in Japan in 2004, which temporarily cost the bank its private-banking license there, was blamed in part on a lack of clarity in reporting lines to the New York headquarters.

In this latest management reorganization, after Ms. Krawcheck and other senior executives raised concerns about the blurry reporting lines, Citigroup executives clarified who would be responsible for what.

Mr. Pandit is busy clamping down on expenses big and small. Late last year, he reinstated an annual ritual of weeding out the worst-performing 5% of the staff. Citigroup has also begun charging lower-level employees to use the investment bank's coveted box seats at sporting events when big shots aren't occupying them. . . .

Despite being ambitious, Mr. Pandit resists the celebrity status that can accompany success on Wall Street. He skips gabfests like the World Economic

Forum in Davos and sometimes rides the subway instead of using Citigroup's fleet of on-call cars. . . .

To get his arms more fully around the company he now led, Mr. Pandit late last year enrolled himself in a crash course with Ajay Banga, who at the time ran Citigroup's international consumer group. Mr. Pandit spent hours grilling him about the Japanese consumer-finance unit, which was reeling from customer defaults.

Citigroup executives say they have learned to expect interrogations like this when Mr. Pandit shows up. "What are you doing with the shareholders' money?" is a typical starting point, they say.

Yet some worry that the CEO's fixation on details is slowing decisions. Shortly after taking over, he convened a group of top investment bankers to consider ways to reorganize their businesses to reduce overlap. They spent a month brainstorming and came back with ideas, but "nothing happened," says one executive, who felt Mr. Pandit was happy to explore things on a theoretical level but hesitant to implement them. Today [May 2008], four months after that meeting, Citigroup is now preparing to reorganize the unit along the lines originally proposed, according to people familiar with the situation. The goal will be to knock down long-standing barriers between corporate and investment bankers.

Similarly, at a February [2008] meeting in Turkey, a Citigroup employee wanted to know when staffers would no longer "have to go to New York" for approval of every decision.

"It's going to take some time because we have to be diligent," Mr. Pandit responded politely.

"I don't want this to be based only on intuition.". . .

For Discussion

1. How many of the five sources of power is Vikram Pandit using? Explain.
2. Which of the eight influence tactics is Pandit using?
3. Which different leadership traits and styles does Pandit display? Cite examples and discuss.
4. To what extent is Pandit using the full-range model of leadership? Explain.
5. Is Pandit exhibiting any negative leadership traits, styles, or behaviors? Discuss.

Source: Excerpted from David Enrich, "Citigroup's Pandit Faces Test as Pressure on Bank Grows," *The Wall Street Journal*, May 6, 2008, pp. A1, A20. Copyright © 2008 by Dow Jones & Company, Inc. Reproduced with permission of Dow Jones & Company, Inc. via Copyright Clearance Center.

Self-Assessment

Do You Have What It Takes to Be a Leader?

Objectives

1. To learn more about the skills required for being a leader.
2. To assess your own leadership ability.

Introduction

Managers cope with complexity: They look at what needs to be done (planning and budgeting), pull together the people needed to get the job done together (organizing and staffing), and ensure that people do their jobs (controlling and problem solving). Leaders, however, cope with change: They look at what needs to be done by setting a direction rather than planning and budgeting, pull people together to do the job through alignment rather than organizing and staffing, and ensure people do their jobs through motivation and inspiration instead of controlling and problem solving. The purpose of this exercise is to assess your skills and determine if you have what it takes to be a leader.

Instructions

Read each of the following statements, and circle the number that best represents your self-perceptions, where 1 = strongly disagree, 2 = disagree, 3 = neither agree nor disagree, 4 = agree, 5 = strongly agree. There is no right or wrong answer.

1. I can separate my personal life from work/school.	1 2 3 4 **5**
2. I'm honest with myself.	1 2 3 4 **5**
3. I communicate my ideas clearly.	1 2 3 4 **5**
4. I regularly prioritize what I need to get done.	1 2 3 4 **5**
5. I am on time for meetings/classes.	1 2 3 4 **5**
6. I am positive and upbeat.	1 2 3 4 **5**
7. I am solution oriented rather than problem oriented.	1 2 3 4 **5**
8. I take responsibility for my actions.	1 2 3 4 **5**
9. I do not blame others for my mistakes.	1 2 3 4 **5**
10. When working in a group, I work with members to solve and prevent problems.	1 2 3 4 **5**
11. I don't have to redo things because my work is thorough and complete.	1 2 3 **4** 5
12. I do not procrastinate on projects/tasks.	1 2 3 **4** 5
13. I do not get distracted when working on projects/tasks.	1 2 3 **4** 5
14. I work well in a group.	1 2 3 **4** 5
15. I am people oriented, not just results oriented.	1 2 3 4 **5**
16. I listen to others beyond just the words being spoken.	1 2 3 **4** 5
17. When working in a group, I am more concerned with the group's success than my own.	1 2 **3 4 5**
18. I adjust well to different communication styles.	1 2 3 4 **5**
19. I praise others when they are doing a good job.	1 2 3 4 **5**
20. I work at getting ahead, but within appropriate boundaries.	1 2 3 4 **5**
	Total **95**

Scoring & Interpretation

Compute your score by adding the responses for all 20 items. The questions in this survey were designed to give you feedback on your skills in the following areas: (1) personal stability, (2) productivity, (3) self-management, (4) communication, (5) boundary setting, (6) work quality, (7) teamwork. All of these skills are found in good managers, and they represent necessary skills for leaders.

Arbitrary norms for leadership skills:

Excellent leadership skills (95–100) ✳
Good leadership skills (85–90)
Moderate leadership skills (75–80)

Low leadership skills (65–70)

Poor leadership skills (60 and below)

Questions for Discussion

1. Were you surprised by your results? Why or why not?

2. Look at the five questions where you scored the lowest. What can you do to improve or develop your skills represented by these items? Explain.

3. Does the content in the five lowest areas relate to Table 14.2? If it does, can you identify additional ways you can improve these traits? Describe and explain .

Questions for this survey were adapted from Interlink Training and Coaching, "The Leadership Assessment Tool," *www.interlinktc.com/assessment.html*. Interlink Training and Coaching, 3655 W. Anthem Way, Box 315, Anthem, AZ 85086.

Ethical Dilemma

Covering for a Laid-Off Friend

You manage a group of software developers for a large organization and several days ago had the difficult task of notifying a friend who works for the company that he is being laid off. Even though he has performed wonderfully in the past and you hate to see him go, your company lost a contract with a major client and thus his position has become obsolete.

The employee wants to build a house, and you're aware that he is 10 days away from closing on a loan for it. He has sold his previous home and now is living with his in-laws. He asks you for a favor: could you extend his employment just 10 more days so that he can qualify for his new home loan? Unfortunately, you don't have the authority to do so, and you tell him you can't help him.

He then tells you that the mortgage company will be calling sometime soon to get a verbal confirmation of his employment. The confirmation is an essential prerequisite if your friend is to obtain the loan for his new home. Would you, he asks, tell the mortgage company that he is still employed?

Solving the Dilemma

As a manager, what would you do?

1. Tell the mortgage company your friend is still employed by the company. Your friend needs a break, and you're confident that he'll find a job in the near future.

2. Refuse to lie. It is unethical to falsify information regarding employment.

3. Simply avoid the mortgage company's phone call.

4. Invent other options. Discuss.

Interpersonal & Organizational Communication
Mastering the Exchange of Information

Major Questions You Should Be Able to Answer

15.1 The Communication Process: What It Is, How It Works
Major Question: What do I need to know about the communication process to be an effective communicator?

15.2 Barriers to Communication
Major Question: What are the important barriers I need to be aware of, so I can improve my communication skills?

15.3 How Managers Fit into the Communication Process
Major Question: How can I use the different channels and patterns of communication to my advantage?

15.4 Communication in the Information Age
Major Question: How do contemporary managers use information technology to communicate more effectively?

15.5 Improving Communication Effectiveness
Major Question: How can I be a better listener, reader, writer, and speaker?

Communicating by Listening

The reason that people act subversively against their employers is that they can't or are afraid to communicate with their managers. Resistance may take the form of "malicious compliance" (following supervisors' instructions to the letter while ignoring the real goal), withholding crucial data, or sabotaging projects that reflect directly on the manager.

One bookstore employee sabotaged his nonlistening, always-angry boss by going through the store and discreetly pocketing any pens, pencils, even crayons, and then hiding them in a backroom cabinet. "My already preternaturally enraged boss," he reported later, "reached glorious heights of apoplexy."[1]

Effective communication begins with listening; paying attention to the words being spoken. "To begin with, listen to people as if you don't know the answer," suggests Meg Price, a Reno, Nevada, human resource professsional. "This means that you will ask more questions to try to understand the situation from the other person's perspective. When you think you've got it, make a statement to the speaker summarizing what you believe they have told you. Only when they agree that indeed you do 'get it' should you begin to offer potential solutions or answers."[2]

Of course, sometimes there are true disagreements, and no amount of listening is going to change that fact. Here, according to David Stiebel, author of *When Talking Makes Things Worse! Resolving Problems When Communication Fails,* is how to identify the nature of a dispute:

- If you only listened to the other person, would she feel satisfied and stop opposing you?
- If you succeed in explaining yourself, would you really change the other person's mind?
- If the other person explained himself more, would you change your mind?

When true disagreements occur, one person ultimately must be willing to change so that negotiations can begin.[3]

For Discussion   How good are you at listening? How good do you think most other people are? When someone else is talking, are you mainly thinking about your reply?

forecast

What's Ahead in This Chapter

This chapter describes the process of transferring information and understanding from one person to another. It also describes three communications barriers—physical, semantic, and personal. It shows how you can use different channels and patterns of communication, both formal and informal, to your advantage. It discusses how star managers use information technology to communicate more effectively. Finally, we talk about how to be a better listener, talker, writer, and reader.

major question ?

What do I need to know about the communication process to be an effective communicator?

THE BIG PICTURE

Communication is the transfer of information and understanding from one person to another. The process involves sender, message, and receiver; encoding and decoding; the medium; feedback; and dealing with "noise," or interference. Managers need to tailor their communication to the appropriate medium (rich or lean) for the appropriate situation.

"I get to work and turn on my computer [and buddy list] to let everyone know I am here," writes an employee who identifies himself as being in "high-tech communications." "Then I usually start getting IMed [receiving instant messages]. I sometimes have four or five instant messages going at once. Then I will take a phone call, and while I am in that conversation I will reply to my instant messages and then open my e-mail. I always have at least three things going at once. . . . That is how it is around here."[4]

Problems with communicating are a fact of human existence, as we just described in the Manager's Toolbox. That said, it is important to develop your communication skills, according to a recent survey of 636 human resource professionals. They rated interpersonal communication skills as the most important factor in advancing their careers.[5]

No wonder faulty communication has become such a problem in the workplace. According to one survey, executives say 14% of each 40-hour workweek is wasted because of poor communication between staff and managers.[6] That's the equivalent of 7 workweeks of lost productivity a year. Thus, there's a hard-headed argument for better communication: It can save money.

I hear you. Today some people can work almost anywhere, even more so as the cell phone has become a more versatile instrument permitting Internet and e-mail access, text messaging, and access to huge databases. Do you think our ability to work outside traditional offices because of today's technology will negatively affect the communication process and employee camaraderie?

Communication Defined: The Transfer of Information & Understanding

Communication—**the transfer of information and understanding from one person to another**—is an activity that you as a manager will have to do a lot of. Indeed, one study found that 81% of a manager's time in a typical workday is spent communicating.[7]

The fact that managers do a lot of communicating doesn't mean they're necessarily good at it—that is, that they are efficient or effective. You are an *efficient communicator* when you can transmit your message accurately in the least time. You are an *effective communicator* when your intended message is accurately understood by the other person. Thus, you may well be efficient in sending a group of people a reprimand by e-mail. But it may not be effective if it makes them angry so that they can't absorb its meaning.

From this, you can see why it's important to have an understanding of the communication process.

How the Communication Process Works

Communication has been said to be a process consisting of "a sender transmitting a message through media to a receiver who responds."[8] Let's look at these and other parts of the process.

Sender, Message, & Receiver The *sender* **is the person wanting to share information—called a** *message*—**and the** *receiver* **is the person for whom the message is intended,** as follows.

Sender → Message → Receiver

Encoding & Decoding Of course, the process isn't as simple as just sender/message/receiver. If you were an old-fashioned telegraph operator using Morse code to send a message over a telegraph line, you would first have to encode the message, and the receiver would have to decode it. But the same is true if you are sending the message by voice to another person in the same room, when you have to decide what language to speak in and what terms to use.

Encoding **is translating a message into understandable symbols or language.** *Decoding* **is interpreting and trying to make sense of the message.** Thus, the communication process is now

Sender **[Encoding]** → Message → **[Decoding]** Receiver

The Medium The means by which you as a communicator send a message is important, whether it is by typing an e-mail traveling over the Internet, by voice over a telephone line, or by hand-scrawled note. This is the *medium,* **the pathway by which a message travels:**

Sender [Encoding] → Message **[Medium]** Message → [Decoding] Receiver

Feedback "Flight 123, do you copy?" In the movies, that's what you hear the flight controller say when radioing the pilot of a troubled aircraft to see if he or she received ("copied") the previous message. And the pilot may radio back, "Roger, Houston, I copy." This is an example of *feedback*—**the receiver expresses his or her reaction to the sender's message.**

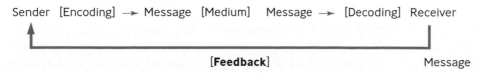

Sender [Encoding] → Message [Medium] Message → [Decoding] Receiver

[Feedback]   Message

Noise Unfortunately, the entire communication process can be disrupted at several different points by what is called *noise*—**any disturbance that interferes with the transmission of a message.** The noise can occur in the medium, of course, as when you have static in a radio transmission or fadeout on a cell phone or when there's loud music when you're trying to talk in a noisy restaurant. Or it can occur in the encoding or decoding, as when a pharmacist can't read a prescription because of a doctor's poor handwriting.[9]

Noise also occurs in *nonverbal communication* (discussed later in this chapter), as when our physical movements send a message that is different from the one we are speaking, or in *cross-cultural communication* (discussed in Chapter 4), as when we make assumptions about other people's messages based on our own culture instead of theirs. We discuss noise further in the next section.

The communication process is shown below. *(See Figure 15.1.)*

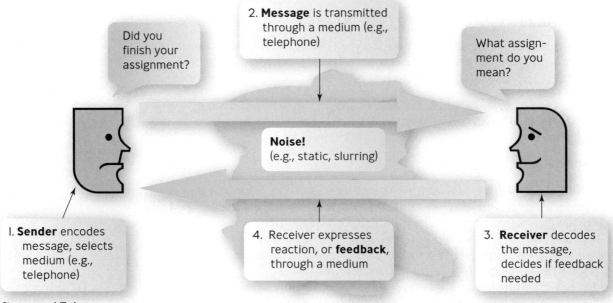

2. **Message** is transmitted through a medium (e.g., telephone)

Did you finish your assignment?

What assignment do you mean?

Noise! (e.g., static, slurring)

1. **Sender** encodes message, selects medium (e.g., telephone)

4. Receiver expresses reaction, or **feedback**, through a medium

3. **Receiver** decodes the message, decides if feedback needed

figure 15.1

THE COMMUNICATION PROCESS

"Noise" is not just noise or loud background sounds but any disturbance that interferes with transmission—static, fadeout, distracting facial expressions, uncomfortable meeting site, competing voices, and so on.

Selecting the Right Medium for Effective Communication

There are all kinds of communications tools available to managers, ranging from one-to-one face-to-face conversation all the way to use of the mass media. However, managers need to know how to use the right tool for the right condition—when to use e-mail, when to meet face to face, for example. Should you praise an employee by voicing a compliment, sending an e-mail, posting an announcement near the office coffee machine—or all three? How about when carrying out a reprimand?

Is a Medium Rich or Lean in Information? As a manager, you will have many media to choose from: conversations, meetings, speeches, the telephone, e-mail, memos, letters, bulletin boards, PowerPoint presentations, videoconferencing, printed publications, videos, and so on. Beyond these are the sophisticated communications possibilities of the mass media: public relations; advertising; news reports via print, radio, TV, the Internet.

Media richness **indicates how well a particular medium conveys information and promotes learning.** That is, the "richer" a medium is, the better it is at conveying information. The term *media richness* was proposed by respected organizational theorists Richard Daft and Robert Lengel as part of their contingency model for media selection.[10]

Ranging from high media richness to low media richness, types of media may be positioned along a continuum as follows:

High media richness
(Best for nonroutine,
ambiguous situations)

Low media richness
(Best for routine,
clear situations)

| Face-to-face presence | Video-conferencing | Telephone | Personal written media (e-mail, memos, letters) | Impersonal written media (newsletters, fliers, general reports) |

Face-to-face communication, also the most personal form of communication, is the richest. It allows the receiver of the message to observe multiple cues, such as body language and tone of voice. It allows the sender to get immediate feedback, to see how well the receiver comprehended the message. At the other end of the media richness scale, impersonal written media is just the reverse—only one cue and no feedback—making it low in richness.

Matching the Appropriate Medium to the Appropriate Situation   In general, follow these guidelines:

- **Rich medium—best for nonroutine situations and to avoid oversimplification.** A *rich* medium is more effective with nonroutine situations.

  Examples: In what way would you like to learn the facts from your boss of a nonroutine situation such as a major company reorganization, which might affect your job? Via a memo tacked on the bulletin board (a lean medium)? Or via face-to-face meeting or phone call (rich medium)?

  The danger of using a rich medium for routine matters (such as monthly sales reports) is that it results in information *overloading*—more information than necessary.

- **Lean medium—best for routine situations and to avoid overloading.** A *lean* medium is more effective with routine situations.

  Examples: In what manner would you as a sales manager like to get routine monthly sales reports from your 50 sales reps? Via time-consuming phone calls (somewhat rich medium)? Or via e-mails or written memos (somewhat lean medium)? The danger of using a lean medium for nonroutine manners (such as a company reorganization) is that it results in information *oversimplification*—it doesn't provide enough of the information the receiver needs and wants. ●

major question?

What are the important barriers I need to be aware of, so I can improve my communication skills?

THE BIG PICTURE

We describe three barriers to communication. Physical barriers include sound, time, and space. Semantic barriers include unclear use of words and jargon. Personal barriers include variations in communication skills, trustworthiness and credibility, stereotypes and prejudices, and faulty listening skills.

Stand up and give a speech to a group of co-workers? Connecticut businessman Robert Suhoza would prefer to be trampled by elephants, says a news story. "Make small talk at a cocktail party?" it goes on. "Just go ahead and shoot him. Introduce himself to a room full of strangers? Maybe he'll just come back some other time. . . . Even answering the phone seemed at times an insurmountable task: He knew he should pick up the receiver, but he was paralyzed by not knowing who was on the other end, or what the caller wanted."[11]

Suhoza is 53 years old, but all his life he has suffered from social phobia or social anxiety disorder. In this he has plenty of company: One in every eight Americans apparently meets the diagnostic criteria for social anxiety disorder at some point in their lives, making it the third most common psychiatric condition. More women suffer from it than men, although men are more likely to seek treatment.[12]

Social anxiety disorder is an example (though an extreme one) of a communication *barrier*—a barrier being anything interfering with accurate communication between two people. Some barriers may be thought of as happening within the communication process itself, as the table on the opposite page shows. *(See Table 15.1.)* It's more practical, however, to think of barriers as being of three types: (1) *physical barriers*, (2) *semantic barriers*, and (3) *personal barriers*.

Without walls. Supposedly businesses that have open floor plans with cubicles instead of private offices function better because people can more easily talk across the shoulder-high partitions. But do you think the absence of floor-to-ceiling physical barriers might, in fact, lead to other kinds of barriers—such as others' talking making it hard to hear while on the phone?

table 15.1

SOME BARRIERS THAT HAPPEN WITHIN THE COMMUNICATION PROCESS

All it takes is one blocked step in the communication process described in the text for communication to fail. Consider the following.

- **Sender barrier—no message gets sent.** Have you ever had an idea but were afraid to voice it because (like Robert Suhoza) you feared criticism? Then obviously no message got sent.

   But the barrier need not be for psychological reasons. Suppose as a new manager you simply didn't realize (because you weren't told) that supervising your subordinates' expense accounts was part of your responsibility. In that case, it may be understandable why you never call them to task about fudging their expense reports—why, in other words, no message got sent.

- **Encoding barrier—the message is not expressed correctly.** No doubt you've sometimes had difficulty trying to think of the correct word to express how you feel about something. If English is not your first language, perhaps, then you may have difficulty expressing to a supervisor, co-worker, or subordinate what it is you mean to say.

- **Medium barrier—the communication channel is blocked.** You never get through to someone because his or her phone always has a busy signal. The computer network is down and the e-mail message you sent doesn't go through. These are instances of the communication medium being blocked.

- **Decoding barrier—the recipient doesn't understand the message.** Your boss tells you to "lighten up" or "buckle down," but because English is not your first language, you don't understand what the messages mean. Or perhaps you're afraid to show your ignorance when someone is throwing computer terms at you and says that your computer connection has "a bandwidth problem."

- **Receiver barrier—no message gets received.** Because you were talking to a co-worker, you weren't listening when your supervisor announced today's work assignments, and so you have to ask him or her to repeat the announcement.

- **Feedback barrier—the recipient doesn't respond enough.** No doubt you've had the experience of giving someone street directions, but since they only nod their heads and don't repeat the directions back to you, you don't really know whether you were understood. The same thing can happen in many workplace circumstances.

1. Physical Barriers: Sound, Time, Space, & So On

Try shouting at someone on the far side of a construction site—at a distance of several yards over the roar of earth-moving machinery—and you know what physical barriers are. Other such barriers are time-zone differences, telephone-line static, and crashed computers. Office walls can be physical barriers, too, which is one reason for the trend toward open floor plans with cubicles instead of offices in many workplace settings.

2. Semantic Barriers: When Words Matter

When a supervisor tells you, "We need to get this done right away," what does it mean? Does "We" mean just you? You and your co-workers? Or you, your co-workers, and the boss? Does "right away" mean today, tomorrow, or next week? These are examples of semantic barriers. *Semantics* **is the study of the meaning of words.**

In addition, we may encounter semantic difficulties when dealing with other cultures (as we discussed in Chapter 4). When talking on the phone with Indians working in call centers in India, for example, we may find their pronunciation unusual. Perhaps that is because, according to one Indian speech-voice consultant, whereas "Americans think in English, we think in our mother tongue and translate it while speaking."[13] As our society becomes more technically oriented, semantic meaning becomes a problem because jargon develops. *Jargon* **is terminology specific to a particular profession or group.** (Example: "The HR VP wants the RFP to go out ASAP." Translation: "The Vice President of Human Resources wants the Request For Proposal to go out as soon as possible.") As a manager in a specialized field, you need to remember that what are ordinary terms for you may be mysteries to outsiders.[14]

Practical Action

Minding Your Manners: Workplace Etiquette Can Be Crucial to Your Career

Even when you're not talking, you're often communicating—nonverbally (as we discuss elsewhere in this chapter). Manners are a big part of this.

Consider: While at lunch with your business clients, do you eat your soup by swiping the spoon from 12 o'clock to 6 o'clock in the bowl? (It should be the reverse.) Do you order a glass of wine with your meal? (Best not to drink alcohol on someone else's clock.) Do you squeeze lemon into your ice tea with a client across the table? (Best not—you might squirt him or her in the eye.) Do you scratch your back with your fork?

We are talking about a form of communication known as *etiquette* or *manners*. Despite the informality (including not just dress-down Fridays but dress-down everydays) of many offices, managers need to learn business etiquette—manners, politeness, appropriate behavior—if they are to achieve career success. Etiquette is more than table manners; it is the expression of being considerate. If you have to take clients out to dinner a couple times a week, you'll be glad if you know which fork to use. MBA candidates at Daniels College of Business at the University of Denver are required to attend an etiquette dinner, and the Massachusetts Institute of Technology also runs a not-for-credit charm school. These and similar courses provide lessons in dining etiquette, pager protocol, cell phone politeness, and the like. "In climbing the slippery ladder of success," says the founder of an etiquette training firm, "people have to recognize that they will never get promoted if their bosses and customers don't see them as looking and acting the part."

Some matters to be aware of:[15]

- **Handshakes and social kisses.** With strangers, you're always safe with just doing a solid handshake: grasp the other's hand firmly at an angle, then give two or three pumps. Kisses on the cheek are never appropriate with strangers or at the start of job interviews. However, if you're dealing with someone that you know who is higher in rank, you should mirror the other, turning and presenting your right cheek (or both cheeks), if he or she takes the initiative.

- **Introductions.** When your boss is meeting your client, you should start with the person you want to honor—the client. ("Mr. Smith, I'd like you to meet my boss, Janet Jones. Jan, this is Horatio Smith, vice-president of Associated Success Inc.") Also, you should give some information about each person in order to get a conversation started. ("Jan is head of our Far West Division, and she just got back from a rock-climbing vacation.")

- **Thank-you notes.** When someone prepares an all-day or all-week program in which you've participated, send him or her a thank-you note. When the boss entertains you on her boat, send her a thank-you note. When a client gives you a plant tour, send him a note. And ALWAYS send a thank-you note after a job interview.

- **Dining tips and table manners.** Don't order the most expensive item. Don't start eating before your host. Avoid ordering food you think you might have difficulty handling properly because of splattering (such as soup or pasta). Know what to do with your bread. (Take the bread or roll, hold it over your plate—it's the plate on the left—break off a piece of it, and then put butter on it. If you drop a roll on the floor, don't pick it up; point it out to the waiter.) Don't kick your shoes off under the table. Turn off your cell phone so it won't beep. When you leave the table and plan to return, leave your napkin on your chair; when you're leaving for good, leave it on the table. In the U.S., you should keep your elbows off the table, and it's okay to keep your hands beneath it. In European countries, however, the reverse is considered polite.

For books on workplace etiquette, see *Emily Post's The Etiquette Advantage in Business* or *One Minute Manners: Mastering the Unwritten Rules of Business Success.*[16]

3. Personal Barriers: Individual Attributes That Hinder Communication

"Is it them or is it me?"

How often have you wondered, when someone has shown a surprising response to something you said, how the miscommunication happened? Let's examine nine personal barriers that contribute to miscommunication.[17]

Variable Skills in Communicating Effectively   As we all know, some people are simply better communicators than others. They have the speaking skills, the vocabulary, the facial expressions, the eye contact, the dramatic ability, the "gift of gab" to express themselves in a superior way. Conversely, other people don't have this quality. But better communication skills can be learned.

Variations in How Information Is Processed & Interpreted   Are you from a working-class or privileged background? Are you from a particular ethnic group? Are you better at math or at language? Are you from a chaotic household filled with alcoholism and fighting, which distracts you at work?

Because people use different frames of reference and experiences to interpret the world around them, they are selective about what things have meaning to them and what don't. All told, these differences affect what we say and what we think we hear.

Variations in Trustworthiness & Credibility   Without trust between you and the other person, communication is apt to be flawed. Instead of communicating, both of you will be concentrating on defensive tactics, not the meaning of the message being exchanged.[18] How will subordinates react to you as a manager if your predecessors in your job lied to them? They may give you the benefit of a doubt, but they may be waiting for the first opportunity to be confirmed in the belief that you will break their trust.

Oversized Egos   Our egos—our pride, our self-esteem, even arrogance—are a fifth barrier. Egos can cause political battles, turf wars, and the passionate pursuit of power, credit, and resources. Egos influence how we treat each other as well as how receptive we are to being influenced by others. Ever had someone take credit for an idea that was yours? Then you know how powerful ego feelings can be.

Faulty Listening Skills   When you go to a party, do people ever ask questions of you and about who you are and what you're doing? Or are they too ready to talk about themselves? And do they seem to be waiting for you to finish talking so that they can then resume saying what they want to say? (But here's a test: Do you actually *listen* when they're talking?)

Self-Assessment:
What Is Your Communication Style under Stress?

Tendency to Judge Others' Messages   Suppose another student in this class sees you reading this text and says, "I like the book we're reading." You might say, "I agree." Or you might say, "I disagree—it's boring." The point is that we all have a natural tendency, according to psychologist Carl Rogers, to judge others' statements from our own point of view (especially if we have strong feelings about the issue).[19]

Inability to Listen with Understanding   To really listen with understanding, you have to imagine yourself in the other person's shoes. Or, as Rogers and his co-author put it, you have to "see the expressed idea and attitude from the other person's point of view, to sense how it feels to him, to achieve his frame of reference in regard to the thing he is talking about."[20] When you listen with understanding, it makes you feel less defensive (even if the message is criticism) and improves your accuracy in perceiving the message.

Stereotypes & Prejudices   **A *stereotype* consists of oversimplified beliefs about a certain group of people.** There are, for instance, common stereotypes about old

Test Your Knowledge:
Barriers to Effective Communication

people, young people, males, and females. Wouldn't you hate to be categorized according to just a couple of exaggerated attributes—by your age and gender, for example? ("Young men are reckless." "Old women are scolds." Yes, *some* young men and *some* old women are this way, but it's unrealistic and unfair to tar every individual in these groups with the same brush.)

We consider matters of gender communication later in this chapter.

Nonverbal Communication   Do your gestures and facial expressions contradict your words? This is the sort of nonverbal communication that you may not even be aware of. We discuss this subject in more detail next.

Nonverbal Communication

Nonverbal communication **consists of messages sent outside of the written or spoken word.** Says one writer, it includes such factors as "use of time and space, distance between persons when conversing, use of color dress, walking behavior, standing, positioning, seating arrangement, office locations, and furnishings."[21] Nonverbal communication is responsible for perhaps as much as 60% of a message being communicated, according to some researchers.[22] Others estimate it as high as 90%.[23] Given the prevalence of nonverbal communication and its impact on organizational behavior (such as hiring decisions, perceptions of others, and getting one's ideas accepted by others), it is important that you become familiar with the various sources of nonverbal communication.[24] Indeed, this is particularly so when you are dealing with people of other cultures around the world, as we saw back in Chapter 4 (Section 4.5) in our discussion of cultural differences.

Seven ways in which nonverbal communication is expressed are through (1) *interpersonal space,* (2) *eye contact,* (3) *facial expressions,* (4) *body movements and gestures,* (5) *touch,* (6) *setting,* and (7) *time.*

Body language. Who's paying attention and who isn't? If you were a manager speaking at this meeting and you noticed the man at the end of the row looking out the window as you talked, would you continue to speak to those who seem attentive? Or would you try to adjust your remarks—and your own body language—to try to reach the man who is tuning you out?

1. Interpersonal Space   People of different cultures have different ideas about what is acceptable interpersonal space—that is, how close or far away one should be when communicating with another person. For instance, the people of North America and northern Europe tend to conduct business conversations at a range of 3–4 feet. For people in Latin American and Asian cultures, the range is about 1 foot. For Arabs, it is even closer.

This can lead to cross-cultural misunderstandings. "Arabs tend to get very close and breathe on you," says anthropologist Edward Hall. "The American on the receiving end can't identify all the sources of his discomfort but feels that the Arab is pushy. The Arab comes close, the American backs up. The Arab follows, because he can only interact at certain distances."[25] However, once the American understands that Arabs handle interpersonal space differently and that "breathing on people is a form of communication," says Hall, the situation may be redefined so that the American feels more comfortable.

Group Exercise:
Nonverbal Communication:
A Twist on Charades

2. Eye Contact   Eye contact serves four functions in communication: (1) It signals the beginning and end of a conversation; there is a tendency to look *away* from others when beginning to speak and to look *at* them when done. (2) It expresses emotion; for instance, most people tend to avoid eye contact when conveying bad news or negative feedback. (3) Gazing monitors feedback because it reflects interest and attention. (4) Depending on the culture, gazing also expresses the type of relationship between the people communicating. For instance, Westerners are taught at an early age to look at their parents when spoken to. However, Asians are taught to avoid eye contact with a parent or superior in order to show obedience and subservience.[26]

3. Facial Expressions Probably you're accustomed to thinking that smiling represents warmth, happiness, or friendship whereas frowning represents dissatisfaction or anger. But these interpretations of facial expressions don't apply across all cultures.[27] A smile, for example, doesn't convey the same emotions in different countries.

4. Body Movements & Gestures An example of a body movement is leaning forward; an example of a gesture is pointing. Open body positions, such as leaning backward, express openness, warmth, closeness, and availability for communication. Closed body positions, such as folding one's arms or crossing one's legs, represent defensiveness.

Some body movements and gestures are associated more with one sex than the other, according to communication researcher Judith Hall. For instance, women nod their heads and move their hands more than men do. Men exhibit large body shifts and foot and leg movements more than women do.[28]

We need to point out, however, that interpretations of body language are subjective, hence easily misinterpreted, and highly dependent on the context and cross-cultural differences.[29] You'll need to be careful when trying to interpret body movements, especially when you're operating in a different culture.

5. Touch Norms for touching vary significantly around the world. For example, as we noted in Chapter 4, in the Middle East it is normal for two males who are friends to walk together holding hands—not commonplace behavior in the U.S.

Men and women interpret touching differently, with women tending to do more touching during conversations than men do.[30] If women touch men, it is viewed as sexual; the same interpretation is made when men touch other men.[31] Yet even handshakes and embracing seem to be changing, with the male handshake now evolving into a range of more intimate gestures—"the one-armed hug, the manly shoulder bump, the A-frame clasp with handshake in the middle, the mutual back-slap," as one article puts it.[32]

6. Setting How do you feel when you visit someone who sits behind a big desk and is backlit by a window so her face is obscured? What does it say when someone comes out from behind his desk and invites you to sit with him on his office couch? The location of an office (such as corner office with window versus interior office with no window), its size, and the choice of furniture often expresses the accessibility of the person in it.

7. Time When your boss keeps you waiting 45 minutes for an appointment with him, how do you feel? When she simply grunts or makes one-syllable responses to your comments, what does this say about her interest in your concerns? As a manager yourself, you should always give the people who work for you adequate time. You should also talk with them frequently during your meetings with them so they will understand your interest.

The table on the next page gives some suggestions for better nonverbal communication skills. *(See Table 15.2.)*

Gender-Related Communication Differences

Men are eight times as likely as women to bargain over starting pay. Indeed, says one account, "Women often are less adroit at winning better salaries, assignments, and jobs—either because they don't ask or because they cave in when they do."[33] In other words, women need to hone their negotiation skills, or else they will fall behind.

Some possible general differences in communication between genders are summarized on the next page. *(See Table 15.3.)* Note, however, that these don't apply in all cases, which would constitute stereotyping.

table 15.2

TOWARD BETTER NONVERBAL COMMUNICATION SKILLS

You can practice these skills by watching TV with the sound off and interpreting people's emotions and interactions.

Do	Don't
Maintain eye contact	Look away from the speaker
Lean toward the speaker	Turn away from the speaker
Speak at a moderate rate	Speak too quickly or slowly
Speak in a quiet, reassuring tone	Speak in an unpleasant tone
Smile and show animation	Yawn excessively
Occasionally nod head in agreement	Close your eyes

Source: Adapted from W. D. St. John, "You Are What You Communicate," *Personnel Journal,* October 1985, p. 43.

How useful do you think these specific styles are in a managerial context? (Recall the discussion of men and women with reference to leadership in Chapter 14.)

Author Judith Tingley suggests that women and men should learn to "genderflex"—temporarily use communication behaviors typical of the other gender to increase the potential for influence.[34] For example, a female manager might use sports analogies to motivate a group of males.

Deborah Tannen, by contrast, recommends that everyone become aware of how differing linguistic styles affect our perceptions and judgments. For example, in a meeting, regardless of gender, "those who are comfortable speaking up in groups, who

table 15.3

COMMUNICATION DIFFERENCES

How do men and women differ?

Linguistic Characteristic	Men	Women
Taking credit	Greater use of "I" statements (e.g., "I did this" and "I did that"); more likely to boast about their achievements	Greater use of "We" statements (e.g., "We did this" and "We did that"); less likely to boast about their achievements
Displaying confidence	Less likely to indicate that they are uncertain about an issue	More likely to indicate a lack of certainty about an issue
Asking questions	Less likely to ask questions (e.g., asking for directions)	More likely to ask questions
Conversation rituals	Avoid making apologies because it puts them in a one-down position	More frequently say "I'm sorry"
Giving feedback	More direct and blunt	More tactful; tend to temper criticism with praise
Giving compliments	Stingy with praise	Pay more compliments than men do
Indirectness	Indirect when it comes to admitting fault or when they don't know something	Indirect when telling others what to do

Source: Derived from D. Tannen, "The Power of Talk: Who Gets Heard and Why," *Harvard Business Review,* September–October 1995; and D. Tannen, *You Just Don't Understand: Women and Men in Conversation* (New York: Ballantine Books, 1990).

Example

Do Female Executives Have an Edge in Business? Women & Communication

Women in business have the edge in two ways, says Chris Clarke, head of an executive search firm with offices in more than 40 countries. "There is increasing evidence," he says, "that women are superior at multitasking, which is needed to handle business complexities, and that they are better at relationships, which is important in developing effective teams."[35]

There is another way that women also have an edge, suggests a *BusinessWeek* article: instead of tightly controlling information, they are more willing to share it.[36] A representative of this viewpoint is Anu Shukla, who sold her Internet marketing company for $390 million and made 65 of her 85 employees millionaires. "It's better to overcommunicate," she says. As an example, she made it her policy to share information with all her employees rather than to impart it to selected employees on a need-to-know basis. In addition, she created what she called the "CEO lunch," in which she invited six to eight employees at a time to discuss the business with her.

Your Call

Anne Cummings, professor of business administration at the University of Minnesota at Duluth, suggests there are "masculine" and "feminine" styles in business, in which men tend to be more task-oriented and assertive and to take greater intellectual risks whereas women tend to be more relationship oriented and "democratic" and to be more efficient at solving problems.[37] (Of course, all this behavior operates on a continuum, and most people have a multitude of styles.) Do you think a woman can be successful by taking on the "masculine" style? Can a man be successful taking on the "feminine" style?

need little or no silence before raising their hands, or who speak out easily without waiting to be recognized are more apt to be heard," she says. "Those who refrain from talking until it's clear that the previous speaker is finished, who wait to be recognized, and who are inclined to link their comments to those of others will do fine at a meeting where everyone else is following the same rules but will have a hard time getting heard in a meeting with people whose styles are more like the first pattern."[38]

By now most male students and managers know they should avoid the use of masculine wording for jobs or roles that are occupied by both genders, using *police officer* instead of *policeman; supervisor* rather than *foreman.* (Conversely, secretaries, nurses, and babysitters should no longer be referred to as "she.") If you stay alert, it's fairly easy to avoid sentence constructions that are demeaning to women. (Instead of saying "he is," say "he or she is" or "they are.")

But, of course, there's more to effective managerial communication than that. Indeed, there are executive-training programs designed to teach men the value of emotion in relationships—the use of "soft skills" to communicate, build teams, and develop flexibility. "The nature of modern business requires what's more typical to the female mold of building consensus as opposed to the top-down male military model," says Millington F. McCoy, managing director of a New York executive search firm. One program given by London-based James R. Traeger helps participants break down the stereotype of the aggressive, controlling man who always wants to take charge and solve problems and to learn to listen and work in harmony.

Interestingly, although men hold 82% of the top corporate jobs, when they want the advice of an executive coach—a trained listener to help them with their goals and personal problems—they usually turn to a woman. And, in fact, females always want another female as a coach. As a result, 7 out of 10 graduates of Coach U, the largest training school for executive coaches, are women. Because good coaches, says Coach U's CEO Sandy Vilas (who is male), are intuitive communicators and have done a lot of personal development work, "that profile tends to fit women better." Says Susan Bloch, who heads an executive coaching practice, "When a man is asked to coach another, they have a tendency to compete. Man to man, they have to show each other how great they are."[39] ●

major question? How can I use the different channels and patterns of communication to my advantage?

THE BIG PICTURE

Formal communication channels follow the chain of command, which is of three types—vertical, horizontal, and external. Informal communication channels develop outside the organization's formal structure. One type is gossip and rumor. Another is management by wandering around, in which a manager talks to people across all lines of authority.

If you've ever had a low-level job in nearly any kind of organization, you know that there is generally a hierarchy of management between you and the organization's president, director, or CEO. If you had a suggestion that you wanted him or her to hear, you doubtless had to go up through management channels. That's formal communication. However, you may have run into that top manager in the elevator. Or in the restroom. Or in a line at the bank. You could have voiced your suggestion casually then. That's informal communication.

Formal Communication Channels: Up, Down, Sideways, & Outward

Formal communication channels **follow the chain of command and are recognized as official.** The organizational chart we described in Chapter 8 (page 250) indicates how official communications—memos, letters, reports, announcements—are supposed to be routed.

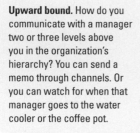

Upward bound. How do you communicate with a manager two or three levels above you in the organization's hierarchy? You can send a memo through channels. Or you can watch for when that manager goes to the water cooler or the coffee pot.

Formal communication is of three types: (1) *vertical*—meaning upward and downward, (2) *horizontal*—meaning laterally (sideways), and (3) *external*—meaning outside the organization.

I. Vertical Communication: Up & Down the Chain of Command

Vertical communication is the flow of messages up and down the hierarchy within the organization: bosses communicating with subordinates, subordinates communicating with bosses. As you might expect, the more management levels through which a message passes, the more it is prone to some distortion.

- **Downward communication—from top to bottom.** *Downward communication* **flows from a higher level to a lower level (or levels).** In small organizations, top-down communication may be delivered face to face. In larger organizations, it's delivered via meetings, e-mail, official memos, and company publications.

- **Upward communication—from bottom to top.** *Upward communication* **flows from a lower level to a higher level(s).** Often this type of communication is from a subordinate to his or her immediate manager, who in turn will relay it up to the next level, if necessary. Effective upward communication depends on an atmosphere of trust. No subordinate is going to want to be the bearer of bad news to a manager who is always negative and bad-tempered.

Types of downward and upward communication are shown below. *(See Table 15.4.)*

table 15.4

TYPES OF DOWNWARD AND UPWARD COMMUNICATION

Downward communication
Most downward communication involves one of the following kinds of information:

- Instructions related to particular job tasks. Example (supervisor to subordinate): "The store will close Monday for inventory. All employees are expected to participate."

- Explanations about the relationship between two or more tasks. Example: "While taking inventory, employees need to see what things are missing. Most of that might be attributable to shoplifting."

- Explanations of the organization's procedures and practices. Example: "Start counting things on the high shelves and work your way down."

- A manager's feedback about a subordinate's performance. Example: "It's best not to try to count too fast."

- Attempts to encourage a sense of mission and dedication to the organization's goals. Example: "By keeping tabs on our inventory, we can keep our prices down and maintain our reputation of giving good value."

Upward communication
Most upward communication involves the following kinds of information:

- Reports of progress on current projects. Example: "We shut down the store yesterday to take inventory."

- Reports of unsolved problems requiring help from people higher up. Example: "We can't make our merchandise count jibe with the stock reports."

- New developments affecting the work unit. Example: "Getting help from the other stores really speeded things up this year."

- Suggestions for improvements. Example: "The stores should loan each other staff every time they take inventory."

- Reports on employee attitudes and efficiency. Example: "The staff likes it when they go to another store and sometimes they pick up some new ways of doing things."

Sources: D. Katz and R. Kahn, *The Social Psychology of Organizations* (New York: Wiley, 1966); and E. Planty and W. Machaver, "Upward Communications: A Project in Executive Development," *Personnel* 28 (1952), pp. 304–318.

2. Horizontal Communication: Within & Between Work Units *Horizontal communication* **flows within and between work units; its main purpose is coordination.** As a manager, you will spend perhaps as much as a third of your time in this form of communication—consulting with colleagues and co-workers at the same level as you within the organization. In this kind of sideways communication, you will be sharing information, coordinating tasks, solving problems, resolving conflicts, and getting the support of your peers. Horizontal communication is encouraged through the use of committees, task forces, and matrix structures.

Horizontal communication can be impeded in three ways: (1) by specialization that makes people focus just on their jobs alone; (2) by rivalry between workers or work units, which prevents sharing of information; and (3) by lack of encouragement from management.[40]

3. External Communication: Outside the Organization *External communication* **flows between people inside and outside the organization.** These are other stakeholders: customers, suppliers, shareholders or other owners, and so on. Companies have given this kind of communication heightened importance, especially with customers or clients, who are the lifeblood of any company.

Informal Communication Channels

Informal communication channels **develop outside the formal structure and do not follow the chain of command**—they skip management levels and cut across lines of authority.

Two types of informal channels are (1) the *grapevine* and (2) *management by wandering around.*

The *grapevine* is the unofficial communication system of the informal organization, a network of gossip and rumor of what is called "employee language." Research shows that the grapevine is faster than formal channels, is about 75% accurate, and is used by employees to acquire the majority of their on-the-job information.[41]

***Management by wandering around (MBWA)* is the term used to describe a manager's literally wandering around his or her organization and talking with people across all lines of authority.**[42] Management by wandering around helps to reduce the problems of distortion that inevitably occur with formal communication flowing up a hierarchy. MBWA allows managers to listen to employees and learn about their problems as well as to express to employees what values and goals are important. ●

MBWA. Management by wandering around is sort of the reverse of employees exchanging informal views with top managers at the water cooler. That is, by wandering around the organization, top managers can stop and talk to nearly anyone—and thus perhaps learn things that might be screened out by the formal up-the-organization reporting process. If top managers can do MBWA, do you think mid-level managers can as well?

15.4 COMMUNICATION IN THE INFORMATION AGE

How do contemporary managers use information technology to communicate more effectively?

major question?

THE BIG PICTURE

We discuss seven communications tools of information technology: (1) the Internet and its associated intranets and extranets, (2) e-mail, (3) videoconferencing, (4) group support systems, (5) telecommuting, (6) handheld devices, and (7) blogs. We also discuss impediments to productivity: (1) misuse of technology, (2) fussing with computers, and (3) information overload.

As we discussed in Chapter 1, the use of computers and information technology is dramatically affecting many aspects of management and employee behavior. For example, many people feel that information technology enables them to multitask and get more things done in a shorter amount of time. However, research shows that people can't actually think about two tasks at the same time, and employees may be more productive if they can organize their time so that they aren't constantly switching between tasks.[43]

In addition to multitasking, researchers have uncovered another modern-day trend in communication—multicommunicating. *Multicommunicating* represents **"the use of technology to participate in several interactions at the same time."**[44] Examples would be answering e-mail messages during a lecture, and texting during a dinner conversation or while participating in a group conference call. As you probably know, multicommunicating has both positive and negative consequences. While it sometimes enables us to get more things done in a shorter amount of time, it also can create miscommunication and can foster stress and hurt feelings for those involved. Our advice is to multicommunicate with caution, and be aware that there are times and places when it is inappropriate.[45]

Communications Tools of Information Technology

The U.S. information and technology infrastructure is one of the best in the world. However, it falls behind Denmark, Sweden, and Switzerland (owing to weaknesses in education, government, and tax regulation), according to the World Economic Forum. Clearly work will have to be done if the United States is to continue to be the most innovative country in the world.[46] In this section we explore some of the more important aspects of information technology: (1) the Internet along with intranets and extranets, (2) e-mail, (3) videoconferencing, (4) group support systems, (5) telecommuting, (6) handheld devices, and (7) blogs.

I. The Internet, Intranets, & Extranets   The Internet, or more simply "the Net," is more than a computer network. As we said in Chapter 1, it is a network of computer networks. The Internet is a global network of independently operating but interconnected computers, linking hundreds of thousands of smaller networks around the world. The Internet connects everything from personal computers to supercomputers in organizations of all kinds.[47]

Two private uses of the Internet are as intranets and extranets.

- **Intranets. An *intranet* is nothing more than an organization's private Internet.** Intranets also have *firewalls* that block outside Internet users from accessing internal information. This is done to protect the privacy and confidentiality of company documents. The top four uses for intranets are information sharing, information publishing, e-mail, and document management.[48]

- **Extranets. An *extranet* is an extended intranet in that it connects internal employees with selected customers, suppliers, and other strategic partners.** Ford Motor Co., for instance, has an extranet that connects its dealers worldwide. Ford's extranet was set up to help support the sales and servicing of cars and to enhance customer satisfaction.

2. E-mail E-mail, short for *electronic mail,* uses the Internet to send computer-generated text and documents between people. E-mail has become a major communications medium because of four key benefits: (1) reduced cost of distributing information, (2) increased teamwork, (3) reduced paper costs, and (4) increased flexibility. On the other hand, it has three drawbacks: It can lead to (1) wasted time, as in having to deal with *spam,* **or unsolicited jokes and junk mail;** (2) information overload, as in dealing with all those e-mails crying out for responses; and (3) neglect of other media. *(See Table 15.5.)*

table 15.5

E-MAIL: BENEFITS, DRAWBACKS, AND TIPS FOR DOING BETTER

Benefits

- *Reduced cost of distributing information.* One software developer found that its telephone bill dropped by more than half after its employees and dealers were told to use e-mail instead of the phone.
- *Increased teamwork.* Users can send messages to colleagues anywhere, whether in the office or around the world.
- *Reduced paper costs.* E-mail reduces the costs and time associated with print duplication and paper distribution.
- *Increased flexibility.* Employees with portable computers, PDAs, and cell phones can access their e-mail from anywhere.

Drawbacks

- *Wasted time.* E-mail can distract employees from critical job duties. Employees now average nearly an hour a day managing their e-mail.
- *Information overload.* E-mail users tend to get too much information—in some cases, only 10 of 120 daily inbox messages may be worthwhile.
- *Neglect of other media.* Increased use of e-mail can be found to be associated with decreased face-to-face interactions and decreased overall organizational communication, with lessened cohesion.

Tips for better e-mail handling

- *Treat all e-mail as confidential.* Pretend every message is a postcard that can be read by anyone. (Supervisors may legally read employee e-mail.)
- *Be careful with jokes and informality.* Nonverbal language and other subtleties are lost, so jokes may be taken as insults or criticism.
- *Avoid sloppiness, but avoid criticizing others' sloppiness.* Avoid spelling and grammatical errors, but don't criticize errors in others' messages.
- *When replying, quote only the relevant portion.* Edit long e-mail messages you've received down to the relevant paragraph and put your response immediately following.
- *Not every topic belongs on e-mail.* Complicated topics may be better discussed on the phone or in person to avoid misunderstandings.

Sources: J. Yaukey, "E-Mail Out of Control for Many," *Reno Gazette-Journal,* May 7, 2001, p. IE; D. Halpern, "Dr. Manners on E-Mail Dos and Don'ts," *Monitor of Psychology,* April 2004, p. 5; and B. K. Williams and S. C. Sawyer, *Using Information Technology,* 7th ed. (New York: McGraw-Hill/Irwin, 2007), p. 91; and P. R. Brown, "Same Office, Different Planets," *The New York Times,* January, 26, 2008, p. 135.

3. Videoconferencing Also known as *teleconferencing, videoconferencing* uses video and audio links along with computers to enable people located at different locations to see, hear, and talk with one another. This enables people from many locations to conduct a meeting without having to travel. Video-conferencing can thus significantly reduce an organization's travel expenses.

Many organizations set up special videoconferencing rooms or booths with specially equipped television cameras. Some of the more sophisticated equipment is known as *telepresence technology*, **high-definition videoconference systems that simulate face-to-face meetings between users.** Whereas traditional videoconferencing systems can be set up in a conventional conference room, telepresence systems require a specially designed room with multiple cameras and high-definition video screens, simulating "the sensation of two groups of people at identical tables facing each other through windows," according to one report.[49]

Clearly, telepresence technology can be quite expensive. Other equipment enables people to attach small cameras and microphones to their desks or computer monitors. This enables employees to conduct long-distance meetings and training classes without leaving their office or cubicle.[50]

Videoconferencing. In this arrangement, three people in different locations can computer-conference— view and interact with one another— while studying a layout on-screen. Video-conferencing offers considerable savings in time and money over the cost of travel. Do you think you would feel inhibited working with people in this way?

4. Group Support Systems *Group support systems (GSSs)* **entail using state-of-the-art computer software and hardware to help people work better together.** They enable people to share information without the constraints of time and space. This is accomplished using computer networks to link people across a room or across the globe. Collaborative applications include messaging and e-mail systems, calendar management, videoconferencing, and electronic whiteboards. GSS applications have demonstrated increased productivity and cost savings. In addition, groups using GSSs during brainstorming experienced greater participation and influence quality, a greater quantity of ideas generated, and less domination by individual members than did groups meeting face to face.[51]

Organizations that use full-fledged GSSs have the ability to create virtual teams (described in Chapter 13), who tend to use Internet or intranet systems, collaborative software, and videoconferencing to communicate with team members anytime. It is important to keep in mind that modern-day information technology enables people to interact virtually, but it doesn't guarantee effective communications. Indeed, there is a host of unique communication problems associated with using information technology to operate virtually.[52]

5. Telecommuting *Telecommuting* involves doing work that is generally performed in the office away from the office, using a variety of information technologies. Employees typically receive and send work from home via phone and fax or by using a modem to link a home computer to an office computer. Among the benefits are (1) reduction of capital costs, because employees work at home; (2) increased flexibility and autonomy for workers; (3) competitive edge in recruiting hard-to-get employees; (4) increased job satisfaction and lower turnover; (5) increased productivity; and (6) ability to tap nontraditional labor pools (such as prison inmates and homebound disabled people).[53]

Manager's Hot Seat:
Virtual Workplace: Out of Office Reply

Telecommuting is more common for jobs that involve computer work, writing, and phone or brain work that requires concentration and limited interruptions. A report by the Reason Foundation, a California-based think tank, found that telecommuters presently outnumbered actual mass-transit commuters in 27 of the largest U.S. metropolitan areas, and that two-thirds of Fortune 1000 companies now have telecommuting programs.[54]

Although telecommuting represents an attempt to accommodate employee needs and desires, it requires adjustments and is not for everybody.[55] People who enjoy the social camaraderie of the office setting, for instance, probably won't like it. Others lack the self-motivation needed to work at home.[56]

6. Handheld Devices   Handheld devices such as personal digital assistants (PDAs) and smartphones offer users the portability to do work from any location. PDAs, for example, are used to track appointments, work spreadsheets, manage e-mail, organize photos, play games, and watch videos. Multimedia smartphones, which combine some of the capabilities of a personal computer with a handset, offer a wealth of gadgetry: text messaging, cameras, music players, videogames, e-mail access, digital-TV viewing, search tools, personal information management, GPS locators, Internet phone service, and even phones doubling as credit cards (which, among other things, can be used to pay for parking time on a new generation of wireless parking meters).[57] Some companies even provide training to their employees through their PDAs and cell phones.[58] For blue-collar workers in many occupations, cell phones and portable music players have had profound effects, allowing them to escape from the tedium or physical isolation of their jobs.[59]

7. Blogs   A *blog* **is an online journal in which people write whatever they want about any topic.** The benefits of blogs include the opportunity for people to discuss issues in a casual format, serving much like a chat group and thus providing managers with insights from a variety of employees and customers. Thus, managers such as Paul Otellini, CEO of Intel, who was one of the first executive bloggers, use blogs to discuss matters of importance.[60] Small businesses that can't afford a lot of marketing use blogs as an alternative.[61] Blogs also give people the opportunity to air their opinions, grievances, and creative ideas. In addition, blogs can be used to obtain feedback.

But blogs also have some drawbacks. One is the lack of legal and organizational guidelines about what can be posted online, resulting in some people being fired after posting information online (such as suggestive pictures or information about company finances). Another problem is that employees can use blogs to say unflattering things or leak confidential information about their employers. There is also the problem of believability: Can you trust what you read on blogs when, for example, bloggers are being paid to push products without disclosure?[62]

Workplace Problems: Impediments to Productivity

First the mainframe computer, then the desktop stand-alone personal computer, and then the networked computer were all brought into the workplace for one reason only: to improve productivity. But there are several ways in which information technology actively interferes with productivity. We consider (1) *misuse of technology,* (2) *fussing with computers,* and (3) *information overload.*

Manager's Hot Seat:
Privacy: Burned by the
Firewall

I. Misuse of Technology   Employees may look busy, as they stare into their computer screens with brows crinkled, but sometimes they are just hard at work playing video games. Or browsing online malls, or looking at their investments or pornography sites. One survey found the average U.S. worker fritters away 1.86 hours per 8-hour workday and that the biggest time killer was personal use of the Internet (52% said they wasted more time online than any other way).[63] A Houston funeral-services company discovered that 70% of the workers in its 125-person headquarters watched online videos about an hour a day.[64]

2. Fussing with Computers   Most computer users at some point have to get involved with making online connections work or experience the frustrations of untangling complications caused by spam, viruses, and other Internet deviltry. A Stanford study found that junk e-mail and computer maintenance take up a significant amount of time spent online each day. Indeed, people surveyed said they spent 14 minutes daily dealing with computer problems, which would add up to a total of 10 days a year.[65] Another difficulty is "featuritis," smart machines with too many bells and whistles and that require constant human supervision and correction.[66]

3. Information Overload   *Information overload* **occurs when the amount of information received exceeds a person's ability to handle or process it.** Clearly, information technology is a two-edged sword. Cell phones, pagers, and laptops may untether employees from the office, but these employees tend to work longer hours under more severe deadline pressure than do their tethered counterparts who stay at the office. Moreover, the devices that once promised to do away with irksome business travel by ushering in a new era of communications have done the opposite. They have created the office-in-a-bag that allows businesspeople to continue to work from airplane seats, hotel desks, and their own kitchen tables. The diminishing difference between work and leisure is what Motorola calls the "blurring of life segments."[67]

Makers of handheld devices claim that the combination of portability and multitasking features makes people more productive, but David Greenfield, director of the Center for Internet Studies, thinks this idea "is a scam and illusion," because multitasking can easily become "multislacking" and in fact may make us take more time to accomplish basic tasks.[68] Probably a better information-management strategy is to reduce your information load and increase your information-processing capacity. *(See Table 15.6.)* ●

table 15.6

INFORMATION MANAGEMENT STRATEGY

Reducing information load and increasing information-processing capacity

Reducing your information load

- *Preview and ignore messages.* When going through your e-mail, quickly glance at the subject line and immediately delete anything that looks like spam or (if you can) messages from people you don't know. Do the same with voice mail or phone slips.
- *Filter messages.* Many e-mail programs have message filtering, so that an urgent message from the boss, for example, will go to the top of your e-mail queue. Spam-killer software is available to help eliminate junk mail. Some executives put all "cc" e-mails in a special file and rarely read them.
- *Organize your e-mail inbox.* Set up a folder for e-mails you want to keep. Don't use your e-mail inbox for general storage.

Increasing your information-processing capacity

- *Use discipline.* Check e-mail only three times a day. Handle every message only once. When an e-mail message arrives, deal with it immediately—read it and then either respond to it, delete it, or file it away in a folder.
- *Get a unified messaging site.* It's possible to get one unified messaging site to which all your e-mails, faxes, and voice mails are delivered. Voice mails arrive as audio files that you can listen to, while e-mails are read to you over the phone by a virtual (robot) assistant.
- *Use your company address for work-related e-mails only.* Have personal messages go to a separate account.

Sources: C. Hymowitz, "Taking Time to Focus on the Big Picture Despite the Flood of Data," *The Wall Street Journal,* February 27, 2001, p. B1; R. Strauss, "You've Got Maelstrom," *The New York Times,* July 5, 2001, pp. D1, D9; C. Canabou, "A Message about Managing E-mail," *Fast Company,* August 2001, p. 38; C. Cavanagh, *Managing Your Email: Thinking Outside the Inbox* (New York: John Wiley & Sons, 2003); and J. Zaslow, "Hoarders vs. Deleters: How You Handle Your Email Inbox Says a Lot About You," *The Wall Street Journal,* August 10, 2006, p. D1.

15.5 IMPROVING COMMUNICATION EFFECTIVENESS

major
question? How can I be a better listener, reader, writer, and speaker?

THE BIG PICTURE

We describe how you can be a more effective listener, as in learning to concentrate on the content of a message. We also describe how to be an effective reader. We offer four tips for becoming a more effective writer. Finally, we discuss how to be an effective speaker, through three steps.

Self-Assessment:
Active Listening Skills
Inventory

The principal activities the typical manager does have to do with communication—listening, 40%; talking, 35%; reading, 16%; and writing, 9%.[69] Listening and speaking often take place in meetings (see the Practical Action box "How to Streamline Meetings" in Chapter 5), although they are not the only occasions. Human resource managers consider interpersonal communication skills the most important factor in advancing their careers, according to one survey.[70] Let's see how you can be more effective at the essential communication skills.

Being an Effective Listener

Is listening something you're good at? Then you're the exception. Generally, people comprehend only about 35% of a typical verbal message, experts say.[71] Two-thirds of all employees feel management isn't listening to them.[72] Interestingly, the average speaker communicates 125 words per minute, while we can process 500 words per minute. Poor listeners use this information-processing gap to daydream. They think about other things, thus missing the important parts of what's being communicated.[73] Good listeners know how to use these gaps effectively, mentally summarizing the speaker's remarks, weighing the evidence, and listening between the lines.

How do you become the kind of manager who others say is a good listener? Following are some suggestions (you can practice them in your college lectures and seminars).[74]

Understand me. What's the recipe for effective listening—for really finding out what someone has to say? Probably it is *listen, watch, write, think, question.* What do you do to fight flagging concentration if you're tired or bored? You suppress negative thoughts, ignore distractions about the speaker's style of delivery or body language, and encourage the speaker with eye contact, an interested expression, and an attentive posture. This will make you more involved and interested in the subject matter.

Concentrate on the Content of the Message Don't think about what you're going to say until the other person has finished talking.

- **Judge content, not delivery.** Don't tune out someone because of his or her accent, clothing, mannerisms, personality, or speaking style.

- **Ask questions, summarize remarks.** Good listening is hard work. Ask questions to make sure you understand. Recap what the speaker said.

- **Listen for ideas.** Don't get diverted by the details; try to concentrate on the main ideas.

- **Resist distractions, show interest.** Don't get distracted by things other people are doing, paperwork on your desk, things happening outside the window, television or radio, and the like. Show the speaker you're listening, periodically restating in your own words what you've heard.

490   PART 5 ✳ Leading

- **Give a fair hearing.** Don't shut out unfavorable information just because you hear a term—"Republican," "Democrat," "union," "big business," "affirmative action," "corporate welfare"—that suggests ideas you're not comfortable with. Try to correct for your biases.

Manager's Hot Seat:
Listening Skills: Yeah,
Whatever

Being an Effective Reader

Reading shares many of the same skills as listening. You need to concentrate on the content of the message, judge the content and not the delivery, and concentrate on the main ideas. But because managers usually have to do so much reading, you also need to learn to apply some other strategies.

Realize That Speed Reading Doesn't Work   Perhaps you've thought that somewhere along the line you could take a course on speed reading. By and large, however, speed reading isn't effective. Psychologists have found that speed reading or skimming may work well with easy or familiar reading material, but it can lead to problems with dense or unfamiliar material. For instance, in one study, when questioned about their reading of difficult material, average readers got half the questions right, while speed readers got only one in three.[75]

Learn to Streamline Reading   Management consultant and UCLA professor Kathryn Alesandrini offers a number of suggestions for streamlining your reading.[76]

- **Be savvy about periodicals and books.** Review your magazine and newspaper subscriptions and eliminate as many as possible. You can subscribe to just a few industry publications, scan and mark interesting material, later read what's marked, and pitch the rest. Read summaries and reviews that condense business books and articles.

- **Transfer your reading load.** With some material you can ask some of your employees to screen or scan it first, then post an action note on each item that needs additional reading by you. You can also ask your staff to read important books and summarize them in four or five pages.

- **Make internal memos and e-mail more efficient.** Ask others to tell you up front in their e-mails, memos, and reports what they want you to do. Instruct them to include a one-page executive summary of a long report. When you communicate with them, give them specific questions you want answered.

Speed-read this? Maybe you could—if it's easy or familiar material. But lots of things managers are required to read take patient study. How are you going to manage such reading day after day?

Do Top-Down Reading—SQ3R   "The key to better reading is to be a productive rather than a passive reader," writes Alesandrini. "You'll get more out of what you read if you literally produce meaningful connections between what you already know and what you're reading."[77] This leads to what she calls a "top-down" strategy for reading, a variant on the SQ3R (Survey, Question, Read, Recite, Review) method we discussed in the box at the end of Chapter 1.

The top-down system has five steps:

- **Rate reasons to read.** Rate your reasons for reading ("Why should I read this? Will reading it contribute to my goals?").

- **Question and predict answers.** Formulate specific questions you want the reading to answer. This will give you reasons for reading—to get answers to your questions.

- **Survey the big picture.** Survey the material to be read so you can get a sense of the whole. Take a few minutes to get an overview so that you'll be better able to read with purpose.
- **Skim for main ideas.** Skimming the material is similar to surveying, except it's on a smaller scale. You look for the essence of each subsection or paragraph.
- **Summarize.** Summarize as you skim. Verbally restate or write notes of the main points, using your own words. Visualize or sketch the main points. Answer your initial questions as you skim the material.

Being an Effective Writer

Writing is an essential management skill, all the more so because e-mail has replaced the telephone in so much of business communication. In addition, downsizing has eliminated the administrative assistants who used to edit and correct business correspondence, so even upper-level executives often write their own letters and e-mail now.[78] A lot of students, however, don't get enough practice in writing, which puts them at a career disadvantage. Taking a business writing class can be a real advantage. (Indeed, as a manager, you may have to identify employees who need writing training.)

Following are some tips for writing more effectively. These apply particularly to memos and reports but are also applicable to e-mail messages.

Don't Show Your Ignorance   E-mail correspondence and texting have made people more relaxed about spelling and grammar rules. While this is fine among friends, as a manager you'll need to create a more favorable impression in your writing. Besides using the spelling checkers and grammar checkers built in to most word processing programs, you should reread, indeed proofread, your writing before sending it on.

Understand Your Strategy before You Write   Following are three strategies for laying out your ideas in writing.

- **Most important to least important.** This is a good strategy when the action you want your reader to take is logical and not highly political.
- **Least controversial to most controversial.** This builds support gradually and is best used when the decision is controversial or your reader is attached to a particular solution other than the one you're proposing.
- **Negative to positive.** This strategy establishes a common ground with your reader and puts the positive argument last, which makes it stronger.[79]

Start with Your Purpose   Often people organize their messages backward, putting their real purpose last, points out Alesandrini. You should *start* your writing by telling your purpose and what you expect of the reader.

Write Simply, Concisely, & Directly   Keep your words simple and use short words, sentences, and phrases. Be direct instead of vague, and use the active voice rather than the passive. (Directness, active voice: "Please call a meeting for Wednesday." Vagueness, passive voice: "It is suggested that a meeting be called for Wednesday.")

Telegraph Your Writing with a Powerful Layout   Make your writing as easy to read as possible, using the tools of highlighting and white space.

- **Highlighting.** Highlighting consists of using **boldface** and *italics* to emphasize key concepts and introduce new concepts, and bullets—small circles or squares like the ones in the list you're reading—to emphasize list items. (Don't overuse any of these devices, or they'll lose their effect. And particularly don't use ALL CAPITAL LETTERS for emphasis, except rarely.)
- **White space.** White space, which consists of wide margins and a break between paragraphs, produces a page that is clean and attractive.[80]

Being an Effective Speaker

Speaking or talking covers a range of activities, from one-on-one conversations, to participating in meetings, to giving formal presentations. In terms of personal oral communication, most of the best advice comes under the heading of listening, since effective listening will dictate the appropriate talking you need to do.

However, the ability to talk to a room full of people—to make an oral presentation—is one of the greatest skills you can have. A study conducted by AT&T and Stanford University found that the top predictor of success and professional upward mobility is how much you enjoy public speaking and how effective you are at it.[81]

The biggest problem most people have with public speaking is controlling their nerves. Author and lecturer Gael Lindenfield suggests that you can prepare your nerves by practicing your speech until it's near perfect, visualizing yourself performing with brilliance, getting reassurance from a friend, and getting to the speaking site early and releasing physical tension by doing deep breathing. (And staying away from alcohol and caffeine pick-me-ups before your speech.)[82]

As for the content of the speech, some brief and valuable advice is offered by speechwriter Phil Theibert, who says a speech comprises just three simple rules: (1) Tell them what you're going to say. (2) Say it. (3) Tell them what you said.[83]

I. Tell Them What You're Going to Say The introduction should take 5%–15% of your speaking time, and it should prepare the audience for the rest of the speech. Avoid jokes and such phrases as "I'm honored to be with you here today . . ." Because everything in your speech should be relevant, try to go right to the point. For example:

"Good afternoon. The subject of identity theft may seem far removed from the concerns of most employees. But I intend to describe how our supposedly private credit, health, employment, and other records are vulnerable to theft by so-called identity thieves and how you can protect yourself."

2. Say It The main body of the speech takes up 75%–90% of your time. The most important thing to realize is that your audience won't remember more than a few points anyway. Thus, you need to decide which three or four points must be remembered.[84] Then cover them as succinctly as possible.

Be particularly attentive to transitions during the main body of the

Predictor for success. Enjoying public speaking and being good at it are the top predictors of success and upward mobility. Do you think you could develop these skills?

speech. Listening differs from reading in that the listener has only one chance to get your meaning. Thus, be sure you constantly provide your listeners with guidelines and transitional phrases so they can see where you're going. Example:

"There are five ways the security of your supposedly private files can be compromised. The first way is . . ."

3. Tell Them What You Said   The end might take 5%–10% of your time. Many professional speakers consider the conclusion to be as important as the introduction, so don't drop the ball here. You need a solid, strong, persuasive wrap-up.

Use some sort of signal phrase that cues your listeners that you are heading into your wind-up. Examples:

"Let's review the main points . . ."

"In conclusion, what CAN you do to protect against unauthorized invasion of your private files? I point out five main steps. One . . ."

Give some thought to the last thing you will say. It should be strongly upbeat, a call to action, a thought for the day, a little story, a quotation. Examples:

"I want to leave you with one last thought . . ."

"Finally, let me close by sharing something that happened to me . . ."

"As Albert Einstein said, 'Imagination is more important than knowledge.'"

Then say "Thank you" and stop talking. ●

Key Terms Used in This Chapter

Summary

 15.1 The Communication Process: What It Is, How It Works

Communication is the transfer of information and understanding from one person to another. The process involves sender, message, and receiver; encoding and decoding; the medium; feedback; and dealing with "noise." The sender is the person wanting to share information. The information is called a message. The receiver is the person for whom the message is intended. Encoding is translating a message into understandable symbols or language. Decoding is interpreting and trying to make sense of the message. The medium is the pathway by which a message travels. Feedback is the process in which a receiver expresses his or her reaction to the sender's message. The entire communication process can be disrupted at any point by noise, defined as any disturbance that interferes with the transmission of a message.

For effective communication, a manager must select the right medium. Media richness indicates how well a particular medium conveys information and promotes learning. The richer a medium is, the better it is at conveying information. Face-to-face presence is the richest; an advertising flyer would be one of the lowest. A rich medium is best for nonroutine situations and to avoid oversimplification. A lean medium is best for routine situations and to avoid overloading.

15.2 Barriers to Communication

Barriers to communication are of three types: (1) Physical barriers are exemplified by walls, background noise, and time-zone differences. (2) Semantics is the study of the meaning of words. Jargon, terminology specific to a particular profession or group, can be a semantic barrier. (3) Personal barriers are individual attributes that hinder communication. Nine such barriers are (a) variable skills in communicating effectively, (b) variations in frames of reference and experiences that affect how information is interpreted, (c) variations in trustworthiness and credibility, (d) oversized egos, (e) faulty listening skills, (f) tendency to judge others' messages, (g) inability to listen with understanding, (h) stereotypes (oversimplified beliefs about a certain group of people) and prejudices, and (i) nonverbal communication (messages sent outside of the written or spoken word, including body language).

Seven ways in which nonverbal communication is expressed are through (1) interpersonal space, (2) eye contact, (3) facial expressions, (4) body movements and gestures, (5) touch, (6) setting, and (7) time.

15.3 How Managers Fit into the Communication Process

Communication channels may be formal or informal.

Formal communication channels follow the chain of command and are recognized as official. Formal communication is of three types: (1) Vertical communication is the flow of messages up and down the organizational hierarchy. (2) Horizontal communication flows within and between work units; its main purpose is coordination. (3) External communication flows between people inside and outside the organization.

Informal communication channels develop outside the formal structure and do not follow the chain of command. Two aspects of informal channels are the grapevine and management by wandering around. (1) The grapevine is the unofficial communication system of the informal organization. The grapevine is faster than formal channels, is about 75% accurate, and is used by employees to acquire most on-the-job information. (2) In management by wandering around (MBWA), a manager literally wanders around his or her organization and talks with people across all lines of authority; this reduces distortion caused by formal communication.

15.4 Communication in the Information Age

A modern-day trend is multicommunicating, the use of technology to participate in several interactions at the same time. Contemporary managers use seven communications tools of information technology: (1) The Internet is a global network of independently operating but interconnected computers, linking smaller networks. Two private uses of the Internet are for intranets, organizations' private Internets, and for extranets, extended intranets that connect a company's internal employees with selected customers, suppliers, and other strategic partners. (2) E-mail, for electronic mail, uses the Internet to send computer-generated text and documents between people. E-mail has become a major communication medium because it reduces the cost of distributing information, increases teamwork, reduces paper costs, and increases flexibility. However, e-mail has three drawbacks: wasted time; information overload, in part because of spam, or unsolicited jokes and junk mail; and it leads people to neglect other media. (3) Videoconferencing uses video and audio links along with computers to enable people located at different locations to see, hear, and talk with one another. Telepresence technology consists of high-definition videoconference systems that simulate face-to-face meetings between users. (4) Group support systems entail using state-of-the-art computer software and hardware to help people work better together. (5) Telecommuting involves doing work that is generally performed in the office away from the office, using a variety of information technologies. (6) Handheld devices such as personal digital assistants and smartphones offer users the portability to work from any location. (7) Blogs are online journals in which people write whatever they want about any topic.

Three impediments to productivity of information technology are (1) the technology is misused, as for video games; (2) it requires a lot of fussing with, as in untangling complications caused by spam and viruses; and (3) it can produce information overload—the amount of information received exceeds a person's ability to handle or process it.

 I5.5 Improving Communication Effectiveness

To become a good listener, you should concentrate on the content of the message. You should judge content, not delivery; ask questions and summarize the speaker's remarks; listen for ideas; resist distractions and show interest; and give the speaker a fair hearing.

To become a good reader, you need to first realize that speed reading usually doesn't work. You should also be savvy about how you handle periodicals and books, transfer your reading load to some of your employees, and ask others to use e-mails and reports to tell you what they want you to do. A top-down reading system that's a variant on the SQ3R system (survey, question, read, recite, review) is also helpful.

To become an effective writer, you can follow several suggestions. Use spelling and grammar checkers in word processing software. Use three strategies for laying out your ideas in writing: go from most important topic to least important; go from least controversial topic to most controversial; and go from negative to positive. When organizing your message, start with your purpose. Write simply, concisely, and directly. Telegraph your writing through use of highlighting and white space.

To become an effective speaker, follow three simple rules. Tell people what you're going to say. Say it. Tell them what you said.

Management in Action

Effective Communication Takes Work

Executives know success in business depends on identifying and fixing problems before they become crises. It is the most basic rule in management: No matter how smart your strategies seem on paper, if you don't know how they're being executed and whether there are urgent problems, you won't be successful.

The higher executives climb, the less likely they are to know what is and isn't working at their companies. Many are surrounded by yes people who filter information; others dismiss or ignore bearers of bad news.

"I've heard so many executives tell employees to be candid and then jump down their throats if they bring up a problem or ask a critical question," says Yogesh Gupta, president and CEO of Fatwire, a software company that helps businesses manage their Web sites.

Mr. Gupta was determined not to do that when he was recruited to Fatwire from CA in August [2007]. Since then, he has spent hours talking with his 200 employees and seeking the advice of his nine senior managers—all but one of whom are veterans of the company. He has frequent private meetings with each member of the management team so they will feel freer to be candid with him. In that way, he can ask the important questions: What am I doing wrong? What would you do differently if you were running the company? What's the biggest thing getting in the way of you doing your job well?

Already, he learned from these talks that Fatwire should beef up its staff in marketing and in product development. Others have counseled him to improve Fatwire's customer-support processes. Every time he has gotten good advice privately, he has found a way to publicly praise the manager so others will come forward with suggestions.

"I know I have to say, 'You did the right thing to speak up' again and again, because employees fear they'll get blamed if they say anything negative," says Mr. Gupta. . . .

Executives at big companies who have many layers of management between themselves and front-line employees face the biggest challenge finding out how their strategies are actually working. Those who want accurate information must commit to spending time in the field—often and on their own—where they are away from handlers and can coax employees to be forthcoming about problems.

Kathleen Murphy, CEO of ING's U.S. Wealth Management unit, which sells a variety of products, from annuities to financial-planning services, oversees 3,000 employees. She holds town-hall meetings with large groups of employees but admits the sessions "are mostly for me to push my message out because people are less candid at big meetings." So, she also meets regularly with smaller groups of managers at all levels of her division. Once, when an operations group complained about a convoluted work process, she agreed the change they proposed was more efficient.

But she says she doesn't always act on what she hears, believing that executives have to filter out the inevitable complaints from the crucial information and ideas that create a productive and congenial workplace.

An upbeat executive, Ms. Murphy has teamwork in her DNA. She grew up negotiating with her five siblings for elbow room at the dinner table and played lots of sports. She says she has a "low tolerance" for people who are complainers. "There's a big difference between candor that stems from caring about doing things better and negative energy, which can be toxic," she says.

After reorganizing her division recently, Ms. Murphy sat through several meetings at which managers made suggestions and expressed their concerns. She encouraged everyone to voice their objections, but made her case that the changes would help them expand the business and better serve their customers.

They went through "a few rough sessions," she admits. But in the end, they found common ground. Her listening made all the difference. Now moving to a new building, she'll be next door to her customer-service staff.

For Discussion

1. What are Yogesh Gupta and Kathleen Murphy doing to reduce the "noise" in their communications? Discuss.

2. Which of the nine personal barriers to communication are being addressed by Gupta and Murphy? Explain your rationale.

3. How might Gupta and Murphy use the tools of information technology to enhance their communication effectiveness? Discuss.

4. What does this case teach you about effective communication? Explain.

Source: Excerpted from Carol Hymowitz, "Sometimes, Moving Up Makes It Harder to See What Goes on Below," *The Wall Street Journal*, October 15, 2007, p. B1. Copyright © 2007 by Dow Jones & Company, Inc. Reproduced with permission of Dow Jones & Company, Inc. via Copyright Clearance Center.

Self-Assessment

What Is Your Most Comfortable Learning Style?

Objectives

1. To learn about your visual, auditory, and kinesthetic learning/communication style.

2. To consider how knowledge about learning/communication styles can be used to enhance your communication effectiveness.

Introduction

The purpose of this exercise is to find out what your most prominent learning style is—that is, what forms of communication can you best learn from. You should find the information of value for understanding not only your own style but those of others. Knowing your own style should also allow you to be a much more effective learner.

Instructions

Read the following 36 statements and indicate the extent to which each statement is consistent with your behavior by using the following rating scale: 1 = almost never applies; 2 = applies once in a while; 3 = sometimes applies; 4 = often applies; 5 = almost always applies.

I. I take lots of notes.	1	2	3	4	5

2. When talking to others, I have the hardest time handling those who do not maintain good eye contact with me.　　　1　2　3　4　5

3. I make lists and notes because I remember things better when I write them down.　　　1　2　3　4　5

4. When reading a novel, I pay a lot of attention to passages picturing the clothing, scenery, setting, etc.　　　1　2　3　4　5

5. I need to write down directions so that I can remember them.　　　1　2　3　4　5

6. I need to see the person I am talking to in order to keep my attention focused on the subject.　　　1　2　3　4　5

7. When meeting a person for the first time, I initially notice the style of dress, visual characteristics, and neatness.　　　1　2　3　4　5

8. When I am at a party, one of the things I love to do is stand back and "people watch."　　　1　2　3　4　5

9. When recalling information, I can see it in my mind and remember where I saw it.　　　1　2　3　4　5

10. If I had to explain a new procedure or technique, I would prefer to write it out.　　　1　2　3　4　5

11. With free time I am most likely to watch television or read.　　　1　2　3　4　5

12. If my boss has a message for me, I am most comfortable when he or she sends a memo.　　　1　2　3　4　5

Total A (the minimum is 12 and the maximum is 60)　　　__48__

1. When I read, I read out loud or move my lips to hear the words in my head.　　　1　2　3　4　5

2. When talking to someone else, I have the hardest time handling those who do not talk back with me.　　　1　2　3　4　5

3. I do not take a lot of notes, but I still remember what was said. Taking notes distracts me from the speaker.　　　1　2　3　4　5

4. When reading a novel, I pay a lot of attention to passages involving conversations.　　　1　2　3　4　5

5. I like to talk to myself when solving a problem or writing.	1 2 3 **4** 5	
6. I can understand what a speaker says, even if I am not focused on the speaker.	1 **2** 3 4 5	
7. I remember things easier by repeating them again and again.	1 **2** 3 4 5	
8. When I am at a party, one of the things I love to do is have in-depth conversations about a subject that is important to me.	1 **2** 3 4 5	
9. I would rather receive information from the radio than a newspaper.	1 **2** 3 4 5	
10. If I had to explain a new procedure or technique, I would prefer telling about it.	1 2 3 **4** 5	
11. With free time I am most likely to listen to music.	1 2 3 **4** 5	
12. If my boss has a message for me, I am most comfortable when he or she calls on the phone.	1 2 **3** 4 5	

Total B (the minimum is 12 and the maximum is 60) ___**35**___

1. I am not good at reading or listening to directions.	1 **2** 3 4 5	
2. When talking to someone else, I have the hardest time handling those who do not show any kind of emotional support.	1 2 3 4 **5**	
3. I take notes and doodle, but I rarely go back and look at them.	1 **2** 3 4 5	
4. When reading a novel, I pay a lot of attention to passages revealing feelings, moods, action, drama, etc.	1 **2** 3 4 5	
5. When I am reading, I move my lips.	1 2 3 4 **5**	
6. I will exchange words and places and use my hands a lot when I can't remember the right thing to say.	1 2 3 4 **5**	
7. My desk appears disorganized.	**1** 2 3 4 5	
8. When I am at a party, one of the things I love to do is enjoy activities, such as dancing, games, and totally losing myself.	1 2 **3** 4 5	
9. I like to move around. I feel trapped when seated at a meeting or desk.	**1** 2 3 4 5	

(continued)

10. If I had to explain a new procedure or technique, I would prefer actually demonstrating it.	1 ~~2~~ 3 4 5
11. With free time, I am most likely to exercise.	1 2 3 4 ~~5~~
12. If my boss has a message for me, I am most comfortable when he or she talks to me in person.	1 2 3 4 ~~5~~
Total C (the minimum is 12 and the maximum is 60)	~~38~~

Scoring & Interpretation

Total A is your Visual Score _48_; Total B is your Auditory Score _35_; and Total C is your Kinesthetic Score _38_. The area in which you have your highest score represents your "dominant" learning style. You can learn from all three, but typically you learn best using one style. Communication effectiveness is increased when your dominant style is consistent with the communication style used by others. For example, if you are primarily kinesthetic and your boss gives you directions orally, you may have trouble communicating because you do not learn or process communication well by just being told something. You must consider not only how you communicate but also how the people you work with communicate.

Questions for Discussion

1. Do you agree with the assessment? Why or why not? Explain.

2. How valuable is it to know your learning style? Does it help explain why you did well in some learning situations and poorly in others? Describe and explain.

3. How important is it to know the learning style of those you work with? Explain.

Source: www.nwlink.com/~donclark/hrd/vak.html. Used by permission.

Ethical Dilemma

Should People Making False Statements in Blogs Be Prosecuted?

It bills itself as the world's "most prestigious college discussion board," giving a glimpse into law school admissions policies, post-graduate social networking, and the hiring practices of major law firms.

But the AutoAdmit site, widely used by law students for information on schools and firms, is also known as a venue for racist and sexist remarks and career-damaging rumors.

Now it's at the heart of a defamation lawsuit that legal experts say could test the anonymity of the Internet.

After facing lewd comments and threats by posters, two women at Yale Law School filed a suit on June 8 [2007] in U.S. District Court in New Haven, Connecticut, that includes subpoenas for 28 anonymous users of the site, which has generated more than 7 million posts since 2004.

According to court documents, a user on the site named "STANFORDtrol" began a thread in 2005 seeking to warn Yale students about one of the women in the suit, entitled "Stupid Bitch to Enter Yale Law." Another threatened to rape and sodomize her, the documents said.

The plaintiff, a respected Stanford University graduate identified only as "Doe I" in the lawsuit, learned of the Internet attack in the summer of 2005 before moving to Yale in Connecticut. The posts gradually became more menacing.

Some posts made false claims about her academic record and urged users to warn law firms, or accused her of bribing Yale officials to gain admission and of forming a lesbian relationship with a Yale administrator, the court papers said.

The plaintiff said she believes the harassing remarks, which lasted nearly two years, cost her an important summer internship. After interviewing with 16 firms, she received only four call-backs and ultimately had zero offers—a result considered unusual given her qualifications.

Another woman, identified as Doe II, endured similar attacks. The two, who say they suffered substantial "psychological and economic injury," also sued a former manager of the site because he refused to remove disparaging messages. The manager had cited free-speech protections.

Solving the Dilemma

What is your opinion about the issue of false, negative blogs?

1. The U.S. Constitution allows free speech, and people should be allowed to say whatever they want. Further, it is normal for people to have different perceptions about others. As such, it does not seem fair to prosecute someone who has a unique, negative perception about someone else.

2. The reputations of these two women were damaged by malicious, negative statements that were untrue. The individuals posting these statements should be punished, but not the AutoAdmit site. The site cannot police the accuracy of posted blogs.

3. Both the individuals making the malicious, negative statements and the blog site—AutoAdmit—should be punished. AutoAdmit should be held accountable because the women asked management of the site to remove untrue posts.

4. Invent other options.

Source: Copyright © 2007 Reuters. Reprinted with permission from Reuters. Reuters content is the intellectual property of Reuters or its third party content providers. Any copying, republication or redistribution of Reuters content is expressly prohibited without the prior written consent of Reuters. Reuters shall not be liable for any errors or delays in content, or for any action taken in reliance there on. Reuters and the Reuters Sphere Logo are registered trademarks of the Reuters group of companies around the world. For additional information about Reuters content and services, please visit Reuters website at www.reuters.com.

Control
Techniques for Enhancing Organizational Effectiveness

Major Questions You Should Be Able to Answer

16.1 Managing for Productivity
Major Question: How do managers influence productivity?

16.2 Control: When Managers Monitor Performance
Major Question: Why is control such an important managerial function?

16.3 The Balanced Scorecard, Strategy Maps, & Measurement Management
Major Question: How can three techniques—balanced scorecard, strategy maps, and measurement management—help me establish standards and measure performance?

16.4 Levels & Areas of Control
Major Question: How do successful companies implement controls?

16.5 Some Financial Tools for Control
Major Question: Financial performance is important to most organizations. What are the financial tools I need to know about?

16.6 Total Quality Management
Major Question: How do top companies improve the quality of their products or services?

16.7 Managing Control Effectively
Major Question: What are the keys to successful control, and what are the barriers to control success?

Improving Productivity: Going Beyond Control Techniques to Get the Best Results

How, as a manager, can you increase productivity—get better results with what you have to work with?

In this chapter we discuss control techniques for achieving better results. What are other ways for improving productivity? Following are some suggestions:[1]

- **Establish base points, set goals, and measure results.** To be able to tell whether your work unit is becoming more productive, you need to establish systems of measurement. You can start by establishing the base point, such as the number of customers served per day, quantity of products produced per hour, and the like. You can then set goals to establish new levels that you wish to attain, and institute systems of measurement with which to ascertain progress. Finally, you can measure the results and modify the goals or work processes as necessary.

- **Use new technology.** Clearly, this is a favorite way to enhance productivity. With a word processor, you can produce more typed pages than you can with a typewriter. With a computerized database, you can store and manipulate information better than you can using a box of file cards. Still, computerization is not a panacea; as we have seen, information technology also offers plenty of opportunities for simply wasting time.

- **Improve match between employees and jobs.** You can take steps to ensure the best fit between employees and their jobs, including improving employee selection, paying attention to training, redesigning jobs, and providing financial incentives that are tied to performance.

- **Encourage employee involvement and innovation.** Companies improve productivity by funding research and development (R&D) departments. As a manager, you can encourage your employees, who are closest to the work process, to come up with suggestions for improving their own operations. And, of course, you can give workers a bigger say in doing their jobs, allow employee flextime, and reward people for learning new skills and taking on additional responsibility.

- **Encourage employee diversity.** By hiring people who are diverse in gender, age, race, and ethnicity, you're more likely to have a workforce with different experience, outlooks, values, and skills. By melding their differences, a team can achieve results that exceed the previous standards.

- **Redesign the work process.** Some managers think productivity can be enhanced through cost cutting, but this is not always the case. It may be that the work process can be redesigned to eliminate inessential steps.

For Discussion Some observers think the pressure on managers to perform will be even more intense than before, because the world is undergoing a transformation on the scale of the industrial revolution 200 years ago as we move toward an information-based economy.[2] In what ways do you think you'll have to become a champion of adaptation?

forecast

What's Ahead in This Chapter

This final chapter explores the final management function—control. Controlling is monitoring performance, comparing it with goals, and taking corrective action as needed. In the first section, we discuss managing for *productivity,* defining what it is and explaining why it's important. We then discuss *controlling,* identify six reasons it's needed, explain the steps in the control process, and describe three types of control managers use. Next we discuss levels and areas of control. In the fifth section, we discuss financial tools for control—budgets, financial statements, ratio analysis, and audits. We then discuss total quality management (TQM), identifying its core principles and showing some TQM techniques. We conclude the chapter by describing the four keys to successful control and five barriers to successful control.

How do managers influence productivity?

THE BIG PICTURE

The purpose of a manager is to make decisions about the four management functions—planning, organizing, leading, and controlling—to get people to achieve productivity and realize results. Productivity is defined by the formula of outputs divided by inputs for a specified period of time. Productivity is important because it determines whether the organization will make a profit or even survive.

In Chapter 1, we pointed out that as a manager in the 21st century you will operate in a complex environment in which you will need to deal with six challenges—managing for (1) competitive advantage, (2) diversity, (3) globalization, (4) information technology, (5) ethical standards, and (6) your own happiness and life goals.

Within this dynamic world, you will draw on the practical and theoretical knowledge described in this book to make decisions about the four management functions of planning, organizing, leading, and controlling.

The purpose is to get the people reporting to you *to achieve productivity and realize results.*

This process is diagrammed below. *(See Figure 16.1.)*

figure 16.1

MANAGING FOR PRODUCTIVITY AND RESULTS

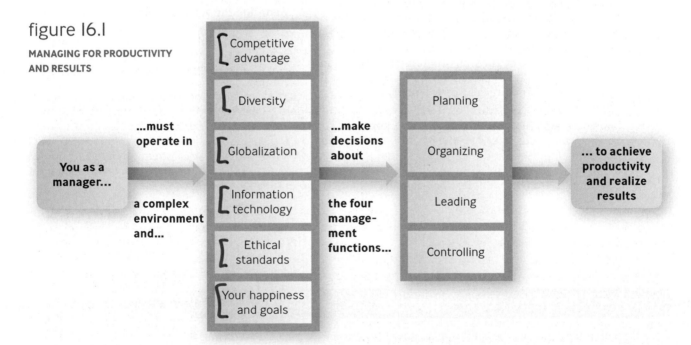

What Is Productivity?

Productivity can be applied at any level, whether for you as an individual, for the work unit you're managing, or for the organization you work for. Productivity is defined by the formula of *outputs divided by inputs* for a specified period of time.

Outputs are all the goods and services produced. Inputs are not only labor but also capital, materials, and energy. That is,

$$\text{productivity} = \frac{\text{outputs}}{\text{inputs}} \quad \text{or} \quad \frac{\text{goods} + \text{services}}{\text{labor} + \text{capital} + \text{materials} + \text{energy}}$$

What does this mean to you as a manager? It means that you can increase overall productivity by making substitutions or increasing the efficiency of any one element: labor, capital, materials, energy. For instance, you can increase the efficiency of labor by substituting capital in the form of equipment or machinery, as in employing a bulldozer instead of laborers with shovels to dig a hole.[3] Or you can increase the efficiency of materials inputs by expanding their uses, as when lumber mills discovered they could sell not only boards but also sawdust and wood chips for use in gardens. Or you can increase the efficiency of energy by putting solar panels on a factory roof so the organization won't have to buy so much electrical power from utility companies.

Why Increasing Productivity Is Important

"For a company and for a nation," said former General Electric CEO Jack Welch, "productivity is a matter of survival."[4]

Productivity is important to companies because ultimately it determines whether the organization will make a profit or even survive. But the productivity of the nation is important to us individually and collectively. The more goods and services that are produced and made easily available to us and for export, the higher our standard of living.

During the 1960s, productivity in the United States averaged a spectacular 2.9% a year, then sank to a disappointing 1.5% right up until 1995. Because the decline in productivity no longer allowed the improvement in wages and living standards that had benefited so many Americans in the 1960s, millions of people took second jobs or worked longer hours to keep from falling behind. From 1995 to 2000, however, during the longest economic boom in American history, the productivity rate jumped to 2.5% annually, as the total output of goods and services rose faster than the total hours needed to produce them. From the business cycle peak in the first quarter of 2001 to the end of 2007, productivity grew at an annual rate of 2.7%.[5]

Most economists seem to think the recent productivity growth is the result of organizations' huge investment in information technology—computers, the Internet, other telecommunications advances, and computer-guided production line improvements.[6] For example, it used to be thought that service industries are so labor-intensive that productivity improvements are hard to come by. But from 1995 to 2001, labor productivity in services grew at a 2.6% rate, outpacing the 2.3% for goods-producing sectors. The consensus among economists is that information technology played a major role.[7]

Productivity, argues William Lewis, founding director of the McKinsey Global Institute, is produced by product market competition. Although Japan's auto industry, for example, is the most productive in the world—because it is sharpened by bruising global competition—its food-processing industry, which is still dominated by mom-and-pop stores, is only 39% as productive as the U.S. industry (in which Wal-Mart and other retailers have bargained down prices, making wholesalers improve their own operations). As a result, Japanese consumers pay unnecessarily high prices for food.[8]

Maintaining productivity depends on *control.* Let's look at this. ●

Competing internationally for productivity. This oil tanker represents the continual competition among companies and among nations to achieve productivity—"a matter of survival," as GE's Jack Welch put it. Is the United States doing everything it could to be more productive? What about taking measures to reduce dependence on foreign oil?

THE BIG PICTURE

Controlling is monitoring performance, comparing it with goals, and taking corrective action. This section describes six reasons why control is needed and four steps in the control process.

Control is making something happen the way it was planned to happen. **Controlling is defined as monitoring performance, comparing it with goals, and taking corrective action as needed.** Controlling is the fourth management function, along with planning, organizing, and leading, and its purpose is plain: to make sure that performance meets objectives.

- **Planning** is setting goals and deciding how to achieve them.
- **Organizing** is arranging tasks, people, and other resources to accomplish the work.
- **Leading** is motivating people to work hard to achieve the organization's goals.
- **Controlling** is concerned with seeing that the right things happen at the right time in the right way.

All these functions affect one another and in turn affect an organization's productivity. *(See Figure 16.2.)*

figure 16.2

CONTROLLING FOR PRODUCTIVITY

What you as a manager do to get things done, with controlling shown in relation to the three other management functions. (These are not lockstep; all four functions happen concurrently.)

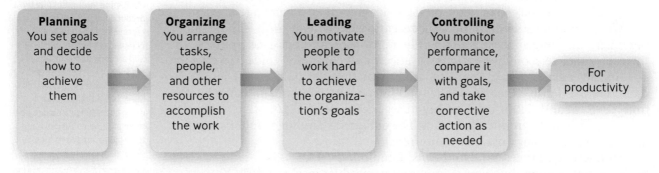

Why Is Control Needed?

There are six reasons why control is needed.

1. To Adapt to Change & Uncertainty Markets shift. Consumer tastes change. New competitors appear. Technologies are reborn. New materials are invented. Government regulations are altered. All organizations must deal with these kinds of environmental changes and uncertainties. Control systems can help managers anticipate, monitor, and react to these changes.[9]

Example: As is certainly apparent by now, the issue of global warming has created a lot of change and uncertainty for many industries. The restaurant industry in particular is feeling the pressure to become "greener," since restaurants are the retail world's largest energy user, with a restaurant using five times more energy per square foot than any other type of commercial building, according to Pacific Gas & Electric's Food Service Technology Center.[10] Nearly 80% that commercial food service spends annually for energy use is lost in inefficient food cooking, holding, and storage. In addition, a typical restaurant generates 100,000 pounds of garbage per location per year. Thus, restaurants are being asked to reduce their "carbon footprints" by instituting tighter controls on energy use.

2. To Discover Irregularities & Errors   Small problems can mushroom into big ones. Cost overruns, manufacturing defects, employee turnover, bookkeeping errors, and customer dissatisfaction are all matters that may be tolerable in the short run. But in the long run, they can bring about even the downfall of an organization.

Example: You might not even miss a dollar a month looted from your credit card account. But an Internet hacker who does this with thousands of customers can undermine the confidence of consumers using their credit cards to charge online purchases at Amazon.com, Priceline.com, and other Web retailers. Thus, a computer program that monitors Internet charge accounts for small, unexplained deductions can be a valuable control strategy.

3. To Reduce Costs, Increase Productivity, or Add Value   Control systems can reduce labor costs, eliminate waste, increase output, and increase product delivery cycles. In addition, controls can help add value to a product so that customers will be more inclined to choose them over rival products. For example, as we have discussed early in the book (and will again in this chapter), the use of quality controls among Japanese car manufacturers resulted in cars being produced that were perceived as being better built than American cars.

4. To Detect Opportunities   Hot-selling products. Competitive prices on materials. Changing population trends. New overseas markets. Controls can help alert managers to opportunities that might have otherwise gone unnoticed.

Example: A markdown on certain grocery-store items may result in a rush of customer demand for those products, signaling store management that similar items might also sell faster if they were reduced in price.

5. To Deal with Complexity   Does the right hand know what the left hand is doing? When a company becomes larger or when it merges with another company, it may find it has several product lines, materials-purchasing policies, customer bases, even workers from different cultures. Controls help managers coordinate these various elements.

Example: In recent years, Macy's Inc. has twice had to deal with complexity. In 2006, it pulled together several chains with different names—Marshall Field's, Robinsons-May, Kaufmann's, and other local stores—into one chain with one name, Macy's, and a much-promoted national strategy. But after losing money in 2007, CEO Terry Lundgren began altering course from a one-size-fits-all nationwide approach to a strategy that tailors the merchandise in local stores to cater to local tastes.[11]

6. To Decentralize Decision Making & Facilitate Teamwork Controls allow top management to decentralize decision making at lower levels within the organization and to encourage employees to work together in teams.

Example: At General Motors, former chairman Alfred Sloan set the level of return on investment he expected his divisions to achieve, enabling him to push decision-making authority down to lower levels while still maintaining authority over the sprawling GM organization.[12] Later GM used controls to facilitate the team approach in its joint venture with Toyota at its California plant.

The six reasons are summarized below. *(See Figure 16.3.)*

figure 16.3

SIX REASONS WHY CONTROL IS NEEDED

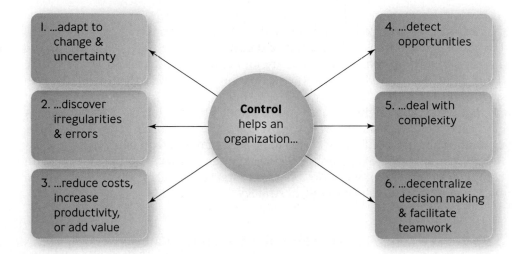

1. ...adapt to change & uncertainty
2. ...discover irregularities & errors
3. ...reduce costs, increase productivity, or add value

Control helps an organization...

4. ...detect opportunities
5. ...deal with complexity
6. ...decentralize decision making & facilitate teamwork

Steps in the Control Process

Control systems may be altered to fit specific situations, but generally they follow the same steps. The four *control process steps* **are (1) establish standards; (2) measure performance; (3) compare performance to standards; and (4) take corrective action, if necessary.** *(See Figure 16.4.)*

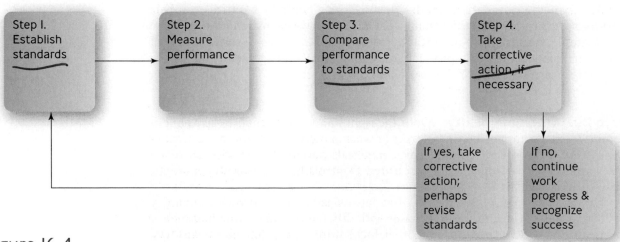

Step 1. Establish standards

Step 2. Measure performance

Step 3. Compare performance to standards

Step 4. Take corrective action, if necessary

If yes, take corrective action; perhaps revise standards

If no, continue work progress & recognize success

figure 16.4

STEPS IN THE CONTROL PROCESS

Let's consider these four steps.

I. Establish Standards: "What Is the Outcome We Want?"   A *control standard,* or *performance standard* or simply *standard,* **is the desired performance level for a given goal.** Standards may be narrow or broad, and they can be set for almost anything, although they are best measured when they can be made quantifiable. Nonprofit institutions might have standards for level of charitable contributions, number of students retained, or degree of legal compliance. For-profit organizations might have standards of financial performance, employee hiring, manufacturing defects, percentage increase in market share, percentage reduction in costs, number of customer complaints, and return on investment. More subjective standards, such as level of employee morale, can also be set, although they may have to be expressed more quantifiably as reduced absenteeism and sick days and increased job applications.

Example: UPS establishes certain standards for its drivers that set projections for the number of miles driven, deliveries, and pickups. Because conditions vary depending on whether routes are urban, suburban, or rural, the standards are different for different routes.[13]

One technique for establishing standards is to use *the balanced scorecard,* as we explain later in this chapter.

2. Measure Performance: "What Is the Actual Outcome We Got?"   The second step in the control process is to measure performance, such as by number of products sold, units produced, or cost per item sold. Less quantifiable activities, such as new products or patents created by a research scientist or scholarly writings produced by a college professor, may be measured by opinions expressed in peer reports.

Performance measures are usually obtained from three sources: (1) written reports, including computerized printouts; (2) oral reports, as in a salesperson's weekly recitation of accomplishments to the sales manager; and (3) personal observation, as when a manager takes a stroll of the factory floor to see what employees are doing.

Example: Every day, UPS managers look at a computer printout showing the miles, deliveries, and pickups a driver attained during his or her shift the previous day.

As we've hinted, measurement techniques can vary for different industries, as for manufacturing industries versus service industries. We discuss this further later in the chapter.

3. Compare Performance to Standards: "How Do the Desired & Actual Outcomes Differ?"   The third step in the control process is to compare measured performance against the standards established. Most managers are delighted with performance that exceeds standards, which becomes an occasion for handing out bonuses, promotions, and perhaps offices with a view. For performance that is below standards, they need to ask: Is the deviation from performance significant? The greater the difference between desired and actual performance, the greater the need for action.

How much deviation is acceptable? That depends on *the range of variation* built in to the standards in step 1. In voting for political candidates, for instance, there is supposed to be no range of variation; as the expression goes, "every vote counts" (although the 2000 U.S. Presidential election was an eye-opener for many people in this regard). In political polling, however, a range of 3%–4% error is considered an acceptable range of variation. In machining parts for the space shuttle, the range of variation may be a good deal less tolerant than when machining parts for a power lawnmower.

The range of variation is often incorporated in computer systems into a principle called management by exception. *Management by exception* **is a control principle that states that managers should be informed of a situation only if data show a significant deviation from standards.**

Example: UPS managers compare the printout of a driver's performance (miles driven and number of pickups and deliveries) with the standards that were set for his or her particular route. A range of variation may be allowed to take into account such matters as winter or summer driving or traffic conditions that slow productivity.

4. Take Corrective Action, If Necessary: "What Changes Should We Make to Obtain Desirable Outcomes?"
There are three possibilities here: (1) Make no changes. (2) Recognize and reinforce positive performance. (3) Take action to correct negative performance.

When performance meets or exceeds the standards set, managers should give rewards, ranging from giving a verbal "Job well done" to more substantial payoffs such as raises, bonuses, and promotions to reinforce good behavior.

When performance falls significantly short of the standard, managers should carefully examine the reasons why and take the appropriate action. Sometimes it may turn out the standards themselves were unrealistic, owing to changing conditions, in which case the standards need to be altered. Sometimes it may become apparent that employees haven't been given the resources for achieving the standards. And sometimes the employees may need more attention from management as a way of signaling that they have been insufficient in fulfilling their part of the job bargain.

Example: When a UPS driver fails to perform according to the standards set for him or her, a supervisor then rides along and gives suggestions for improvement. If drivers are unable to improve, they are warned, then suspended, and then dismissed. ●

Test Your Knowledge:
Categories of Managerial Control

Small business. How important is it for small businesses to implement all four steps of the control process? Do you think that employees in small companies—such as a restaurant—typically have more or less independence from managerial control than those in large companies do?

16.3 THE BALANCED SCORECARD, STRATEGY MAPS, & MEASUREMENT MANAGEMENT

How can three techniques—balanced scorecard, strategy maps, and measurement management—help me establish standards and measure performance?

major question?

THE BIG PICTURE

To establish standards, managers often use the balanced scorecard, which provides four indicators for progress. A visual representation of the balanced scorecard is the strategy map. Measurement management techniques help managers measure performance.

Wouldn't you, as a top manager, like to have displayed in easy-to-read graphics all the information on sales, orders, and the like assembled from data pulled in real-time from corporate software? The technology exists and it has a name: a *dashboard,* like the instrument panel in a car. "The dashboard puts me and more and more of our executives in real-time touch with the business," says Ivan Seidenberg, CEO at Verizon Communications. "The more eyes that see the results we're obtaining every day, the higher the quality of the decisions we can make."[14]

Throughout this book we have stressed the importance of *evidence-based management*—the use of real-world data rather than fads and hunches in making management decisions. When properly done, the dashboard is an example of the important tools that make this kind of management possible. Others are *the balanced scorecard, strategy maps,* and *measurement management,* techniques that even new managers will find useful.

The Balanced Scorecard

Robert Kaplan is a professor of accounting at the Harvard Business School. David Norton is founder and president of Renaissance Strategy Group, a Massachusetts consulting firm. Kaplan and Norton developed what they call the **balanced scorecard, which gives top managers a fast but comprehensive view of the organization via four indicators: (1) customer satisfaction, (2) internal processes, (3) innovation and improvement activities, and (4) financial measures.**

"Think of the balanced scorecard as the dials and indicators in an airplane cockpit," write Kaplan and Norton. For a pilot, "Reliance on one instrument can be fatal. Similarly, the complexity of managing an organization today requires that managers be able to view performance in several areas simultaneously."[15] It is not enough, say Kaplan and Norton, to simply measure financial performance, such as sales figures and return on investment. Operational matters, such as customer satisfaction, are equally important.

The Balanced Scorecard: Four "Perspectives"   The balanced scorecard establishes (a) *goals* and (b) *performance measures* according to four "perspectives" or areas—*financial, customer, internal business,* and *innovation and learning. (See Figure 16.5, next page.)*

1. Financial Perspective: "How Do We Look to Shareholders?"   Typical financial goals have to do with profitability, growth, and shareholder values. Financial

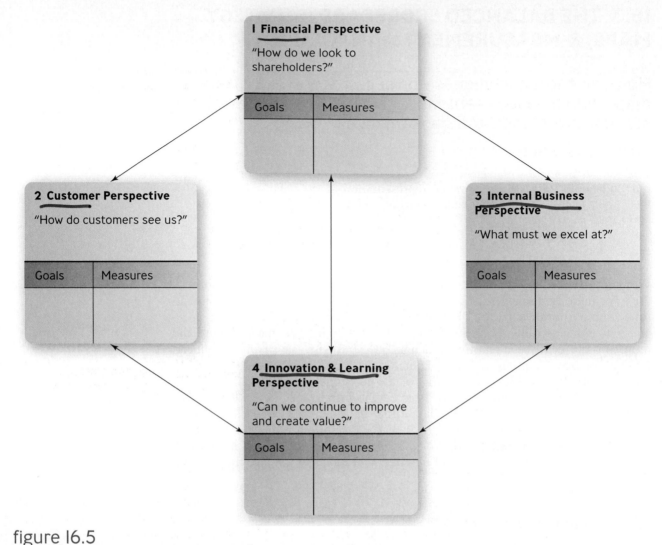

figure 16.5

THE BALANCED SCORECARD: FOUR PERSPECTIVES

Source: Reprinted by permission of *Harvard Business Review.* Exhibit from "The Balanced Scorecard—Measures That Drive Performance," by R. S. Kaplan and D. P. Norton, February 1992. Copyright © 1992 by the Harvard Business School Publishing Corporation; all rights reserved.

measures such as quarterly sales have been criticized as being short-sighted and not reflecting contemporary value-creating activities. Moreover, critics say that traditional financial measures don't improve customer satisfaction, quality, or employee motivation.

However, making improvements in just the other three operational "perspectives" we will discuss won't *necessarily* translate into financial success. Kaplan and Norton mention the case of an electronics company that made considerable improvements in manufacturing capabilities that did not result in increased profitability.

The hard truth is that "if improved [operational] performance fails to be reflected in the bottom line, executives should reexamine the basic assumptions of their strategy and mission," say Kaplan and Norton. "Not all long-term strategies are profitable strategies. . . . A failure to convert improved operational performance, as measured in the scorecard, into improved financial performance should send executives back to their drawing boards to rethink the company's strategy or its implementation plans."[16]

2. Customer Perspective: "How Do Customers See Us?"   Many organizations make taking care of the customer a high priority. The balanced scorecard translates the mission of customer service into specific measures of concerns that really matter to customers—time between placing an order and taking delivery, quality in terms of defect level, performance and service, and cost.

Examples of customer measures are mean-time response to a service call, customer report cards of price and quality compared to the competition, and third-party surveys (such as the J.D. Powers quality survey of automobiles).

3. Internal Business Perspective: "What Must We Excel At?"   This part translates what the company must do internally to meet its customers' expectations. These are business processes such as quality, employee skills, and productivity.

Top management's judgment about key internal processes must be linked to measures of employee actions at the lower levels, such as time to process customer orders, get materials from suppliers, produce products, and deliver them to customers. Computer information systems can help, for example, in identifying late deliveries, tracing the problem to a particular plant.

4. Innovation & Learning Perspective: "Can We Continue to Improve & Create Value?"   Learning and growth of employees is the foundation for innovation and creativity. Thus, the organization must create a culture that encourages rank-and-file employees to make suggestions and question the status quo and it must provide employees with the environment and resources needed to do their jobs. The company can use employee surveys and analysis of training data to measure the degree of learning and growth.

Group Exercise:

Applying the Balanced Scorecard

The Visual Balanced Scorecard: Strategy Maps

Since they devised the balanced scorecard, Kaplan and Norton have come up with an improvement called the strategy map.[17] **A *strategy map* is a visual representation of the four perspectives of the balanced scorecard that enables managers to communicate their goals so that everyone in the company can understand how their jobs are linked to the overall objectives of the organization.** As Kaplan and Norton state, "Strategy maps show the cause-and-effect links by which specific improvements create desired outcomes," such as objectives for revenue growth, targeted customer markets, the role of excellence and innovation in products, and so on. An example of a strategic map for a company such as Target is shown on the next page, with the goal of creating long-term value for the firm by increasing productivity growth and revenue growth. *(See Figure 16.6, next page.)* Measures and standards can be developed in each of the four operational areas—financial goals, customer goals, internal goals, and learning and growth goals—for the strategy.

Measurement Management

"You simply can't manage anything you can't measure," said Richard Quinn, then–vice president of quality at the Sears Merchandising Group.[18]

Is this really true? Concepts such as the balanced scorecard seem like good ideas, but how well do they actually work? John Lingle and William Schiemann, principals in a New Jersey consulting firm specializing in strategic assessment, decided to find out.[19]

In a survey of 203 executives in companies of varying size they identified the organizations as being of two types: *measurement-managed* and *non–measurement-managed.* The measurement-managed companies were those in which senior management reportedly agreed on measurable criteria for determining strategic

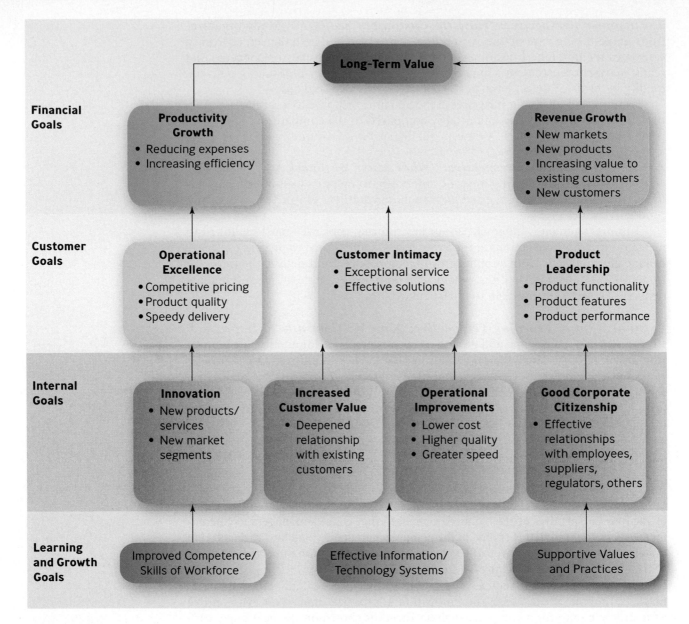

figure 16.6

THE STRATEGY MAP

This example might be used for a retail chain such as Target or Wal-Mart.

Source: T. S. Bateman and S. A. Snell, *Management: Leading & Collaborating in a Competitive World,* 7th ed. (Burr Ridge. IL: McGraw-Hill/Irwin, 2007), Fig. 4.3, p. 124. Adapted from R. Kaplan and D. Norton, "Plotting Success with Strategy Maps," *Optimize,* February 2004, http://www.optimizemag.com/article/showArticle.jhtml?articleId=18200733 (accessed September 18, 2006); and R. S. Kaplan and D. P. Norton, "Having Trouble with Your Strategy? Then Map It," *Harvard Business Review,* September–October 2000, pp. 167–176.

success, and management updated and reviewed semiannual performance measures in three or more of six primary performance areas. The six areas were financial performance, operating efficiency, customer satisfaction, employee performance, innovation/change, and community/environment. The results, concluded Lingle and Schiemann: "A higher percentage of measurement-managed companies were identified as industry leaders, as being financially in the top third of their industry, and as successfully managing their change effort." (The last indicator suggests that measurement-managed companies tend to anticipate the future and are likely to remain in a leadership position in a rapidly changing environment.) "Forget magic," they say. "Industry leaders we surveyed simply have a greater handle on the world around them."

Why Measurement-Managed Firms Succeed   Why do measurement managed companies outperform those that are less disciplined? The study's data point to four mechanisms that contribute to these companies' success:[20]

- **Top executives agree on strategy.** Most top executives in management-managed companies agreed on business strategy, whereas most of those in non–management-measured companies reported disagreement. Translating strategy into measurable objectives helps make them specific.

- **Communication is clear.** The clear message in turn is translated into good communication, which was characteristic of managed-measurement organizations and not of non–managed-measurement ones.

- **There is better focus and alignments.** Measurement-managed companies reported more frequently that unit (division or department) performance measures were linked to strategic company measures and that individual performance measures were linked to unit measures.

- **The organizational culture emphasizes teamwork and allows risk taking.** Managers in measurement-managed companies more frequently reported strong teamwork and cooperation among the management team and more willingness to take risks.

The Barriers to Effective Measurement   The four most frequent barriers to effective measurement, according to Lingle and Schiemann, are:

- **Objectives are fuzzy.** Company objectives are often precise in the financial and operational areas but not in areas of customer satisfaction, employee performance, and rate of change. Managers need to work at making "soft" objectives measurable.

- **Managers put too much trust in informal feedback systems.** Managers tend to overrate feedback mechanisms such as customer complaints or sales-force criticisms about products. But these mechanisms aren't necessarily accurate.

- **Employees resist new measurement systems.** Employees want to see how well measures work before they are willing to tie their financial futures to them. Measurement-managed companies tend to involve the workforce in developing measures.

- **Companies focus too much on measuring activities instead of results.** Too much concern with measurement that is not tied to fine-tuning the organization or spurring it on to achieve results is wasted effort.

Are There Areas That Can't Be Measured?   It's clear that some areas are easier to measure than others—manufacturing, for example, as opposed to services. We can understand how it is easier to measure the output of, say, a worker in a steel mill than that of a bellhop in a hotel or a professor in a classroom. Nevertheless, human resource professionals are trying to have a greater focus on employee productivity "metrics."[21] In establishing quantifiable goals for "hard to measure" jobs, managers should seek input from the employees involved, who are usually more familiar with the details of the jobs. ●

THE BIG PICTURE

This section describes three levels of control—strategic, tactical, and operational—and six areas of control: physical, human, informational, financial, structural (bureaucratic and decentralized), and cultural.

How are you going to apply the steps and types of control to your own management area? Let's look at this in three ways: First, you need to consider the *level* of management at which you operate—top, middle, or first level. Second, you need to consider the *areas* that you draw on for resources—physical, human, information, and/or financial. Finally, you need to consider the *style* or control philosophy—bureaucratic, market, or clan, as we will explain.

Levels of Control: Strategic, Tactical, & Operational

There are three levels of control, which correspond to the three principal managerial levels: *strategic* planning by top managers, *tactical* planning by middle managers, and *operational* planning by first-line (supervisory) managers.

1. Strategic Control by Top Managers *Strategic control* **is monitoring performance to ensure that strategic plans are being implemented and taking corrective action as needed.** Strategic control is mainly performed by top managers, those at the CEO and VP levels, who have an organization-wide perspective. Monitoring is accomplished by reports issued every 3, 6, 12, or more months, although more frequent reports may be requested if the organization is operating in an uncertain environment.

2. Tactical Control by Middle Managers *Tactical control* **is monitoring performance to ensure that tactical plans—those at the divisional or departmental level—are being implemented and taking corrective action as needed.** Tactical control is done mainly by middle managers, those with such titles as "division head," "plant manager," and "branch sales manager." Reporting is done on a weekly or monthly basis.

3. Operational Control by First-Level Managers *Operational control* **is monitoring performance to ensure that operational plans—day-to-day goals—are being implemented and taking corrective action as needed.** Operational control is done mainly by first-level managers, those with titles such as "department head," "team leader," or "supervisor." Reporting is done on a daily basis.

Considerable interaction occurs among the three levels, with lower-level managers providing information upward and upper-level managers checking on some of the more critical aspects of plan implementation below them.

Six Areas of Control

The six areas of organizational control are *physical, human, informational, financial, structural,* and *cultural.*

1. Physical Area The physical area includes buildings, equipment, and tangible products. Examples: There are equipment controls to monitor the use of computers, cars, and other machinery. There are inventory-management controls to keep track of how many products are in stock, how many will be needed, and what their delivery dates are from suppliers. There are quality controls to make sure that products are being built according to certain acceptable standards.

2. Human Resources Area The controls used to monitor employees include personality tests and drug testing for hiring, performance tests during training, performance evaluations to measure work productivity, and employee surveys to assess job satisfaction and leadership.

3. Informational Area Production schedules. Sales forecasts. Environmental impact statements. Analyses of competition. Public relations briefings. All these are controls on an organization's various information resources.

4. Financial Area Are bills being paid on time? How much money is owed by customers? How much money is owed to suppliers? Is there enough cash on hand to meet payroll obligations? What are the debt-repayment schedules? What is the advertising budget? Clearly, the organization's financial controls are important because they can affect the preceding three areas.

5. Structural Area How is the organization arranged from a hierarchical or structural standpoint?[22] Two examples are *bureaucratic control* and *decentralized control*.

- *Bureaucratic control* **is an approach to organizational control that is characterized by use of rules, regulations, and formal authority to guide performance.** This form of control attempts to elicit employee compliance, using strict rules, a rigid hierarchy, well-defined job descriptions, and administrative mechanisms such as budgets, performance appraisals, and compensation schemes (external rewards to get results). The foremost example of use of bureaucratic control is perhaps the traditional military organization.

  Bureaucratic control works well in organizations in which the tasks are explicit and certain. While rigid, it can be an effective means of ensuring that performance standards are being met. However, it may not be effective if people are looking for ways to stay out of trouble by simply following the rules, or if they try to beat the system by manipulating performance reports, or if they try to actively resist bureaucratic constraints.

- *Decentralized control* **is an approach to organizational control that is characterized by informal and organic structural arrangements,** the opposite of bureaucratic control. This form of control aims to get increased employee commitment, using the corporate culture, group norms, and workers taking responsibility for their performance. Decentralized control is found in companies with a relatively flat organization.

6. Cultural Area The cultural area is an informal method of control. It influences the work process and levels of performance through the set of norms that develop as a result of the values and beliefs that constitute an organization's culture. If an organization's culture values innovation and collaboration, then employees are likely to be evaluated on the basis of how much they engage in collaborative activities and enhance or create new products. The biotechnology company Genentech, ranked by *Fortune* in 2006 as the best U.S. company to work for (No. 2 in 2007, No. 5 in 2008), is a good example of an organization that promotes, measures, and rewards employee motivation. For instance, all scientists and engineers are encouraged to spend 20% of their workweek on pet projects. Genentech's tremendous revenue growth over the last decade is clearly driven by a set of cultural values, norms, and internal processes that reinforce creativity.[23] ●

Bureaucratic control. In businesses such as large railroads, tasks are explicit and certain, and employees are expected to perform them the same way each time. However, a small railroad, such as one line serving tourists, need not be bureaucratic.

16.5 SOME FINANCIAL TOOLS FOR CONTROL

THE BIG PICTURE
Financial controls are especially important. These include budgets, financial statements, ratio analysis, and audits.

As you might expect, one of the most important areas for control is in regard to money—financial performance. Just as you need to monitor your personal finances to ensure your survival and avoid catastrophe, so managers need to do likewise with an organization's finances. Whether your organization is for-profit or nonprofit, you need to be sure that revenues are covering costs.

There are a great many kinds of financial controls, but here let us look at the following: *budgets, financial statements, ratio analysis,* and *audits.* (Necessarily this is merely an overview of this topic; financial controls are covered in detail in other business courses.)

Budgets: Formal Financial Projections

A *budget* **is a formal financial projection.** It states an organization's planned activities for a given period of time in quantitative terms, such as dollars, hours, or number of products. Budgets are prepared not only for the organization as a whole but also for the divisions and departments within it. The point of a budget is to provide a yardstick against which managers can measure performance and make comparisons (as with other departments or previous years).

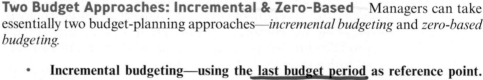

Two Budget Approaches: Incremental & Zero-Based Managers can take essentially two budget-planning approaches—*incremental budgeting* and *zero-based budgeting.*

Coca-Cola's fleet. The truck fleet represents a huge part of a beverage distributor's capital expenditures budget. What types of data would be needed to justify expansion of this delivery system?

- **Incremental budgeting—using the last budget period as reference point.** Incremental budgets are the traditional form of budget. *Incremental budgeting* **allocates increased or decreased funds to a department by using the last budget period as a reference point; only incremental changes in the budget request are reviewed.**

  One difficulty is that incremental budgets tend to lock departments into stable spending arrangements; they are not flexible in meeting environmental demands. Another difficulty is that a department may engage in many activities—some more important than others—but it's not easy to sort out how well managers performed at the various activities. Thus, the department activities and the yearly budget increases take on lives of their own.

- **Zero-based budgeting—starting over at each budget period.** Developed by the U.S. Department of Agriculture and later adopted by Texas Instruments, *zero-based budgeting (ZBB)* **forces each department to start from zero in projecting its funding needs for the coming budget period.** Thus, ZBB forces managers to reexamine their departments' activities and justify their need for funds for the coming budget period based on strategic plans for that period.

One difficulty with ZBB is that it requires managers to spend more time rationalizing the need for more funds.

Another difficulty is that it tends to work better in small work units or departments that are declining in resources.[24]

Fixed versus Variable Budgets   There are numerous kinds of budgets, and some examples are listed below. *(See Table 16.1.)* In general, however, budgets may be categorized as two types: *fixed* and *variable*.

table 16.1

EXAMPLES OF TYPES OF BUDGETS

Type of budget	Description
Cash or cashflow budget	Forecasts all sources of cash income and cash expenditures for daily, weekly, or monthly period
Capital expenditures budget	Anticipates investments in major assets such as land, buildings, and major equipment
Sales or revenue budget	Projects future sales, often by month, sales area, or product
Expense budget	Projects expenses (costs) for given activity for given period
Financial budget	Projects organization's source of cash and how it plans to spend it in the forthcoming period
Operating budget	Projects what an organization will create in goods or services, what financial resources are needed, and what income is expected
Nonmonetary budget	Deals with units other than dollars, such as hours of labor or office square footage

- **Fixed budgets—where resources are allocated on a single estimate of costs.** Also known as a *static budget,* a *fixed budget* allocates resources on the basis of a single estimate of costs. That is, there is only one set of expenses; the budget does not allow for adjustment over time. For example, you might have a budget of $50,000 for buying equipment in a given year—no matter how much you may need equipment exceeding that amount.

- **Variable budgets—where resources are varied in proportion with various levels of activity.** Also known as a *flexible budget,* a *variable budget* allows the allocation of resources to vary in proportion with various levels of activity. That is, the budget can be adjusted over time to accommodate pertinent changes in the environment. For example, you might have a budget that allows you to hire temporary workers or lease temporary equipment if production exceeds certain levels.

Financial Statements: Summarizing the Organization's Financial Status

A *financial statement* **is a summary of some aspect of an organization's financial status.** The information contained in such a statement is essential in helping managers maintain financial control over the organization.

There are two basic types of financial statements: the *balance sheet* and the *income statement.*

The Balance Sheet: Picture of Organization's Financial Worth for a Specific Point in Time
A *balance sheet* **summarizes an organization's overall financial worth—that is, assets and liabilities—at a specific point in time.**

Assets are the resources that an organization controls; they consist of current assets and fixed assets. *Current assets* are cash and other assets that are readily convertible to cash within 1 year's time. Examples are inventory, sales for which payment has not been received (accounts receivable), and U.S. Treasury bills or money market mutual funds. *Fixed assets* are property, buildings, equipment, and the like that have a useful life that exceeds 1 year but that are usually harder to convert to cash. *Liabilities* are claims, or debts, by suppliers, lenders, and other nonowners of the organization against a company's assets.

The Income Statement: Picture of Organization's Financial Results for a Specified Period of Time
The balance sheet depicts the organization's overall financial worth at a specific point in time. By contrast, the *income statement* **summarizes an organization's financial results—revenues and expenses—over a specified period of time,** such as a quarter or a year.

Revenues are assets resulting from the sale of goods and services. *Expenses* are the costs required to produce those goods and services. The difference between revenues and expenses, called the *bottom line,* represents the profits or losses incurred over the specified period of time.

Ratio Analysis: Indicators of an Organization's Financial Health

The bottom line may be the most important indicator of an organization's financial health, but it isn't the only one. Managers often use *ratio analysis*—**the practice of evaluating financial ratios**—to determine an organization's financial health.

Among the types of financial ratios are those used to calculate liquidity, debt management, asset management, and return. *Liquidity ratios* indicate how easily an organization's assets can be converted into cash (made liquid). *Debt management* ratios indicate the degree to which an organization can meet its long-term financial obligations. *Asset management* ratios indicate how effectively an organization is managing its assets, such as whether it has obsolete or excess inventory on hand. *Return ratios*—often called return on investment (ROI) or return on assets (ROA)—indicate how effective management is generating a return, or profits, on its assets.

Audits: External versus Internal

When you think of auditors, do you think of grim-faced accountants looking through a company's books to catch embezzlers and other cheats? That's one

Accountants at the Academy Awards? No, these are 2008 Oscar winners (from left) Daniel-Day Lewis, voted best actor (for his role in *There Will Be Blood*), Tilda Swinton, for best supporting actress (in *Michael Clayton*); Marion Cotillard, for best actress (in *La Vie en Rose*); and Javier Bardem, for best supporting actor (in *No Country for Old Men*). But every year since 1929 the secret ballots for Oscar nominees voted on by members of the Academy of Motion Picture Arts and Sciences have been tabulated by accountants from the firm now known as PricewaterhouseCoopers. The accounting firm takes this event very seriously; secrecy is tight, and there is no loose gossip around the office water cooler. Two accountants tally the votes, stuff the winners' names in the envelopes—the ones that will be handed to award presenters during the Academy Awards—and then memorize the winners' names, just in case the envelopes don't make it to the show. Accounting is an important business because investors depend on independent auditors to verify that a company's finances are what they are purported to be.

function of auditing, but besides verifying the accuracy and fairness of financial statements it also is intended to be a tool for management decision making. *Audits* **are formal verifications of an organization's financial and operational systems.**

Audits are of two types—*external* and *internal.*

External Audits—Financial Appraisals by Outside Financial Experts

An *external audit* **is a formal verification of an organization's financial accounts and statements by outside experts.** The auditors are certified public accountants (CPAs) who work for an accounting firm (such as PricewaterhouseCoopers) that is independent of the organization being audited. Their task is to verify that the organization, in preparing its financial statements and in determining its assets and liabilities, followed generally accepted accounting principles.

Internal Audits—Financial Appraisals by Inside Financial Experts

An *internal audit* **is a verification of an organization's financial accounts and statements by the organization's own professional staff.** Their jobs are the same as those of outside experts—to verify the accuracy of the organization's records and operating activities. Internal audits also help uncover inefficiencies and thus help managers evaluate the performance of their control systems. ●

16.6 TOTAL QUALITY MANAGEMENT

THE BIG PICTURE

Total quality management (TQM) is dedicated to continuous quality improvement, training, and customer satisfaction. Two core principles are people orientation and improvement orientation. Some techniques for improving quality are employee involvement, benchmarking, outsourcing, reduced cycle time, and statistical process control.

The Ritz-Carlton Hotel Co., LLC, a luxury chain of 70 hotels worldwide that is an independently operated division of Marriott International, puts a premium on doing things right. First-year managers and employees receive 250–310 hours of training. The president meets each employee at a new hotel to ensure he or she understands the Ritz-Carlton standards for service. The chain has also developed a database that records the preferences of more than 1 million customers, so that each hotel can anticipate guests' needs.[25]

Because of this diligence, the Ritz-Carlton has twice been the recipient (in 1992 and in 1999) of the Malcolm Baldrige National Quality Award. As we mentioned in Chapter 2, the Baldrige award was created by Congress in 1987 to be the most prestigious recognition of quality in the United States and is given annually to U.S. organizations in manufacturing, service, small business, health care, education, and nonprofit.[26]

The Baldrige award is an outgrowth of the realization among U.S. managers in the early 1980s that three-fourths of Americans were telling survey takers that the label "Made in America" no longer represented excellence—that they considered products made overseas, especially Japan, equal or superior in quality to U.S.-made products. As we saw in Chapter 2, much of the impetus for quality improvements in Japanese products came from American consultants W. Edwards Deming and Joseph M. Juran, whose work led to the strategic commitment to quality known as total quality management.

Deming Management: The Contributions of W. Edwards Deming to Improved Quality

Much of the impetus for quality improvement in Japanese products, as we saw in Chapter 2, came from American consultant **W. Edwards Deming** (along with Joseph Juran). Previously, Frederick Taylor's scientific management philosophy, designed to maximize worker productivity, had been widely instituted. But by the 1950s, scientific management had led to organizations that were rigid and unresponsive to both employees and customers. Deming's challenge, known as **Deming management, proposed ideas for making organizations more responsive, more democratic, and less wasteful.** These included the following principles:

I. Quality Should Be Aimed at the Needs of the Consumer "The consumer is the most important part of the production line," Deming wrote.[27] Thus, the efforts of individual workers in providing the product or service should be directed toward meeting the needs and expectations of the ultimate user.

2. Companies Should Aim at <u>Improving the System</u>, Not Blaming Workers Deming suggested that U.S. managers were more concerned with blaming problems on individual workers rather than on the organization's structure, culture, technology, work rules, and management—that is, "the system." By treating employees well, listening to their views and suggestions, Deming felt, managers could bring about improvements in products and services.

3. Improved Quality Leads to <u>Increased Market Share</u>, Increased Company Prospects, & <u>Increased Employment</u> When companies work to improve the quality of goods and services, they produce less waste, fewer delays, and are more efficient. Lower prices and superior quality lead to greater market share, which in turn leads to improved business prospect and consequently increased employment.

4. Quality Can Be Improved on the <u>Basis of Hard Data</u>, Using the PDCA Cycle Deming suggested that quality could be improved by acting on the basis of hard data. The process for doing this came to be known as the **PDCA cycle, a plan-do-check-act cycle using observed data for continuous improvement of operations.** *(See Figure 16.7.)*

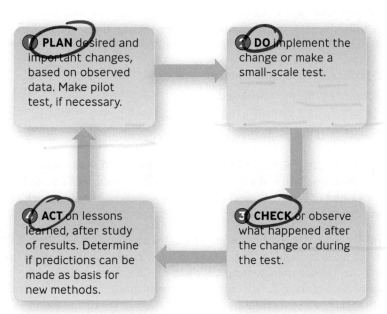

figure 16.7

THE PDCA CYCLE: PLAN-DO-CHECK-ACT

The four steps continuously follow each other, resulting in continuous improvement.

Source: From W. Edwards Deming, *Out of the Crisis,* Figure page 88; "Plan Do Check Act Cycle." Copyright © 2000 Massachusetts Institute of Technology, by permission of MIT Press.

Example

Initiating a Quality Fix: Crown Audio Redesigns Its Production Line to Eliminate Defective Products

Crown Audio, maker of high-tech audio equipment, found that the market requirements for more complex products were clashing with the need to produce those products cheaply, putting pressure on manufacturing operations. Indeed, the number of defective products requiring rework had become a $4 million headache.

The solution: Crown Audio completely shut down its production so as not to generate any more rework, and then analyzed and tested all the flawed products. Components were apportioned into groups based on their common problems, and then examined for defect reduction strategies before being put back through the production process. This exercise, says operations vice president Larry Coburn, also gave the company a pretty good handle on the parts of the process that needed changing. "When we started, we had months and sometimes close to a year of backlog that needed to be fixed and repaired," he says. "Now we are talking in terms of hours of rework in front of us."[28]

Your Call

A major part of the quality-improvement process at Crown Audio was dealing with "employee engagement,"

empowering production employees by providing them with real-time data on which to base their decisions. Now different lines and shifts brag about their first-pass production successes to each other. "Morale is everything in quality," Coburn says. "People want to do a good job, and we have to enable that." Do you think it's possible to raise employee morale and improve manufacturing quality without taking the drastic step of completely shutting down production lines to analyze every operation?

Core TQM Principles: Deliver Customer Value & Strive for Continuous Improvement

Total quality management (TQM) **is defined as a comprehensive approach—led by top management and supported throughout the organization—dedicated to continuous quality improvement, training, and customer satisfaction.**

In Chapter 2 we said there are four components to TQM:

1. Make continuous improvement a priority.
2. Get every employee involved.
3. Listen to and learn from customers and employees.
4. Use accurate standards to identify and eliminate problems.

These may be summarized as *two core principles of TQM*—namely, (1) *people orientation*—everyone involved with the organization should focus on delivering value to customers—and (2) *improvement orientation*—everyone should work on continuously improving the work processes.[29] Let's look at these further.

I. People Orientation—Focusing Everyone on Delivering Customer Value Organizations adopting TQM value people as their most important resource—both those who create a product or service and those who receive it. Thus, not only are employees given more decision-making power, so are suppliers and customers.

This people orientation operates under the following assumptions.

- **Delivering customer value is most important.** The purpose of TQM is to focus people, resources, and work processes to deliver products or services that create value for customers.

- **People will focus on quality if given empowerment.** TQM assumes that employees and suppliers will concentrate on making quality improvements if given the decision-making power to do so. Customers can also be a valuable part of the process if they are allowed to express choices.

- **TQM requires training, teamwork, and cross-functional efforts.** Employees and suppliers need to be well trained, and they must work in teams. Teamwork is considered important because many quality problems are spread across functional areas. For example, if car or cell phone design specialists conferred with marketing specialists (as well as customers and suppliers), they would find the real challenge of using a cell phone in a car is not talking on it but pushing 11 tiny buttons to call a phone number while driving 65 miles an hour.

2. Improvement Orientation—Focusing Everyone on Continuously Improving Work Processes Americans seem to like big schemes, grand designs, and crash programs. While these approaches certainly have their place, the lesson of the quality movement from overseas is that the way to success is through continuous small improvements. ***Continuous improvement* is defined as ongoing small, incremental improvements in all parts of an organization**—all products, services, functional areas, and work processes.[30]

This improvement orientation has the following assumptions.

- **It's less expensive to do it right the first time.** TQM assumes that it's better to do things right the first time than to do costly reworking. To be sure, there are many costs involved in creating quality products and services—training, equipment, and tools, for example. But they are less than the costs of dealing with poor quality—those stemming from lost customers, junked materials, time spent reworking, and frequent inspection, for example.[31]

- **It's better to do small improvements all the time.** This is the assumption that continuous improvement must be an everyday matter, that no improvement is too small, that there must be an ongoing effort to make things better a little bit at a time all the time.

- **Accurate standards must be followed to eliminate small variations.** TQM emphasizes the collection of accurate data throughout every stage of the work process. It also stresses the use of accurate standards (such as benchmarking, as we discuss) to evaluate progress and eliminate small variations, which are the source of many quality defects.

- **There must be strong commitment from top management.** Employees and suppliers won't focus on making small incremental improvements unless managers go beyond lip service to support high-quality work. In 2008, for instance, the president of Toyota, aiming to make his company the biggest car company in the world, issued a passionate plea to his employees to take responsibility for the quality of Toyota cars and trucks.[32]

Group Exercise:
Exploring Total Quality Management

Continuous improvement. In the 1980s, building contractor Fred Carl found restaurant-style commercial stoves impractical for his own home kitchen, so he designed his own, then opened a manufacturing plant in Greenwood, Mississippi, under the name Viking Range Corporation. From Toyota Viking borrowed Japanese manufacturing techniques grouped under the word "kaizen," which translates into "continuous improvement." Production is set up so that if there is a problem everyone on the line is instantly aware of it, and the problem is solved right on the plant floor—so that customers are continuously supplied with elegant yet dependable stoves like the one shown here.

Applying TQM to Services: The RATER Dimensions

Manufacturing industries provide tangible products (think jars of baby food), service industries provide intangible products (think childcare services). Manufactured products can be stored (such as dental floss in a warehouse); services generally need to be consumed immediately (such as dental hygiene services). Services tend to involve a good deal of people effort (although there is some automation, as with bank automated teller machines). Finally, services are generally provided at locations and times convenient for customers; that is, customers are much more involved in the delivery of services than they are in the delivery of manufactured products.

Perhaps you're beginning to see how judging the quality of services is a different animal from judging the quality of manufactured goods, because it comes down to meeting the customer's *satisfaction,* which may be a matter of *perception.* (After all, some hotel guests, restaurant diners, and supermarket patrons, for example, are more easily satisfied than others.)

How, then, can we measure the quality of a delivered service? For one, we can use the **_RATER scale,_** **which enables customers to rate the quality of a service along five dimensions**—*reliability, assurance, tangibles, empathy,* **and** *responsiveness* **(abbreviated** *RATER***)—each on a scale from 1 (for very poor) to 10 (for very good).**[33] The meanings of the RATER dimensions are as follows:

- **Reliability**—ability to perform the desired service dependably, accurately, and consistently.

- **Assurance**—employees' knowledge, courtesy, and ability to convey trust and confidence.

- **Tangibles**—physical facilities, equipment, appearance of personnel.

- **Empathy**—provision of caring, individualized attention to customers.

- **Responsiveness**—willingness to provide prompt service and help customers.

Practical Action

What's Makes a Service Company Successful?

With services now employing more than 75% of American workers, universities are bringing more research attention to what is being called "services science." This is a field that uses management, technology, mathematics, and engineering expertise to improve the performance of service businesses, such as retailing and health care.[34] For instance, Harvard Business School scholar Frances X. Frei has determined that a successful service business must make the right decisions about four core elements and balance them effectively:[35]

- **The offering.** Which service attributes, as informed by the needs of customers, does the company target for excellence and which does it target for inferior performance? Does a bank, for example, offer more convenient hours and friendlier tellers (excellence) but pay less attractive interest rates (inferior performance)?

- **The funding mechanism.** How should the company fund its services? Should it have the customer pay for them? This can be done either in a palatable way, as when Starbucks funds its stuffed-chair ambience by charging more for coffee, or in making savings in service features, as when Progressive Casualty Insurance cuts down on frauds and lawsuits by deploying its own representatives to the scene of an auto accident. Or should the company cover the cost of excellence with operational savings, as by spending now to save later or having the customer do the work? Call centers usually charge for customer support, but Intuit offers free support and has product-development people, as well as customer-service people, field calls so that subsequent developments in Intuit software are informed by direct knowledge of customer problems. Other companies, such as gas stations, save money by having customers pump their own gas.

- **The employee management system.** Service companies need to think about what makes their employees *able* to achieve excellence and what makes them reasonably *motivated* to achieve excellence. For instance, bank customers may expect employees to meet a lot of complex needs, but the employees aren't *able* to meet these needs because they haven't been trained. Or they aren't *motivated* to achieve excellence because the bank hasn't figured out how to screen in its hiring, as in hiring people for attitude first and training them later versus paying more to attract highly motivated people.
- **The customer management system.** Like employees, customers in a service business must also be "trained" as well, as the airlines have done with check-in. At Zipcar, the popular car-sharing service, the company keeps its costs low by depending on customers to clean, refuel, and return cars in time for the next user. In training customers, service companies need to determine which customers they're focusing on, what behaviors they want, and which techniques will most effectively influence customer behavior.

In integrating these four core features, service companies need to determine whether the decisions they make in one area are supported by those made in the other areas; whether the service model creates long-term value for customers, employees, and shareholders; and whether they are trying to be all things to all people or specific things to specific people.

Some TQM Techniques

Several techniques are available for improving quality. Here we describe *employee involvement, benchmarking, outsourcing, reduced cycle time,* and *statistical process control.*

Employee Involvement: Quality Circles, Self-Managed Teams, & Special-Purpose Teams As part of the TQM people orientation, employees (and often suppliers and customers) are given more decision-making power than is typical in non-TQM organizations. The reasoning here is that the people actually involved with the product or service are in the best position to detect opportunities for quality improvements.

Three means for implementing employee involvement are as follows.

- **Quality circles.** *Quality circles,* mentioned briefly in Chapter 13, consist of small groups of workers and supervisors who meet intermittently to discuss workplace and quality-related problems. A quality circle may consist of a group of 10–12 people meeting an hour or so once or twice a month, with management listening to presentations. Members of the quality circle attempt to identify and solve problems in production and quality in the work performed in their part of the company.

- **Self-managed teams.** *Self-managed teams,* also described in Chapter 13, are groups of workers who are given administrative oversight of activities such as planning, scheduling, monitoring, and staffing for their task domains. A common feature of self-managed teams is cross-functionalism— that is, a team is made up of technical specialists from different areas.

- **Special-purpose teams.** Quality circles and self-managed teams usually meet on a regular basis. Sometimes, however, an organization needs a *special-purpose team* to meet to solve a special or one-time problem. The team then disbands after the problem is solved. These teams are often cross-functional, drawing on members from different departments. American medicine, for instance, is moving toward a team-based approach for certain applications, involving multiple doctors as well as nurse practitioners and physician assistants.[36]

Benchmarking: Learning from the Best Performers We discussed benchmarking briefly in Chapter 10. As we stated there, *benchmarking* is a process by which a company compares its performance with that of high-performing organizations. For example, at Xerox Corp., generally thought to be the first American company to use benchmarking, it is defined as, in one description, "the continuous process of measuring products, services, and practices against the toughest competitors or those companies recognized as industry leaders."[37]

Example

Searching for "Best Practices": What Kind of Newspaper Ads Work Best?

Benchmarking is a search for "best practices" that can be applied to one's own business. Southwest Airlines, for instance, studied auto-racing pit crews to learn how to reduce the turnaround time of its aircraft at each scheduled stop. Toyota managers got the idea for just-in-time inventory deliveries by looking at how U.S. supermarkets replenish their shelves.

Sometimes companies go far afield in their search for best practices that might benefit them. QualPro Inc. of Knoxville, Tennessee, was able to use multivariable testing (MVT), a statistical technique that originated during World War II when the British were seeking ways to shoot down German bombers more effectively, to help AutoNation, a conglomeration of car dealers, test what combination of up to 30 factors made for more effective newspaper ads. Typically scientific experiments try to test one variable at a time while keeping all other factors constant. But one-at-a-time experiments can take a long time and miss instances involving multiple factors. QualPro tested numerous variables at the same time—for example, half-page versus full-page ads, or color ads versus black-and-white—to see the effect on dealer sales. "Some surprises popped out," says an account of the experiment. "A full-page ad was no more effective than a half-page one. The addition of color—a considerable expense—did not generate any extra sales."[38]

Your Call

Jeffrey Pfeffer and Robert Sutton, authors of a book on evidence-based management, worry that managers use benchmarking too casually ("GE does it? We should too!").[39] Are you aware of any instances in which a company simply picked up or copied a practice that turned out not to be useful?

Outsourcing: Let Outsiders Handle It *Outsourcing* (discussed in detail in Chapter 4) is the subcontracting of services and operations to an outside vendor. Usually this is done because the subcontractor vendor can do the job better or cheaper. Or, stated another way, when the services and operations are done in-house, they are not done as efficiently or are keeping personnel from doing more important things. For example, despite its well-known advertising campaign, "An American Revolution," Chevrolet outsources the engine for its Chevrolet Equinox to China, where it found it could get high-quality engines built at less cost.[40] And when IBM and other companies outsource components inexpensively for new integrated software systems, says one researcher, offshore programmers make information technology affordable to small and medium-size businesses and others who haven't yet joined the productivity boom.[41]

Outsourcing is also being done by many state and local governments, which, under the banner known as privatization, have subcontracted traditional government services such as fire protection, correctional services, and medical services.

The ISO 9000 Series: Meeting Standards of Independent Auditors If you're a sales representative for Du Pont, the American chemical company, how will your overseas clients know that your products have the quality they are expecting? If you're a purchasing agent for an Ohio-based tire company, how can you tell if the synthetic rubber you're buying overseas is adequate?

At one time, buyers and sellers simply had to rely on a supplier's past reputation or personal assurances. In 1979, the International Organization for Standardization (ISO), based in Geneva, Switzerland, created a set of quality standards known as the 9000 series—"a kind of Good Housekeeping seal of approval for global business," in one description.[42] **The *ISO 9000 series* consists of quality-control procedures companies must install—from purchasing to manufacturing to inventory to shipping—that can be audited by independent quality-control experts, or "registars."** The goal is to reduce flaws in manufacturing and improve productivity. Companies must document the procedures and train their employees to use them. For instance, DocBase Direct is a Web-delivered document and forms-management system that helps companies comply with key ISO management standards, such as traceable changes and easy reporting.

The ISO 9000 designation is now recognized by more than 100 countries around the world, and a quarter of the corporations around the globe insist that suppliers have ISO 9000 certification. "You close some expensive doors if you're not certified," says Bill Ekeler, general manager of Overland Products, a Nebraska tool-and-die-stamping firm.[43] In addition, because the ISO process forced him to analyze his company from the top down, he found ways to streamline manufacturing processes that improved his bottom line.

Reduced Cycle Time: Increasing the Speed of Work Processes   Another TQM technique is the emphasis on increasing the speed with which an organization's operations and processes can be performed. This is known as *reduced cycle time,* **or reduction in steps in a work process,** such as fewer authorization steps required to grant a contract to a supplier. The point is to improve the organization's performance by eliminating wasteful motions, barriers between departments, unnecessary procedural steps, and the like.

Statistical Process Control: Taking Periodic Random Samples   As the pages of this book were being printed, every now and then a press person would pull a few pages out of the press run and inspect them (under a bright light) to see that the consistency of the color and quality of the ink were holding up. This is an ongoing human visual check for quality control.

All kinds of products require periodic inspection during their manufacture: hamburger meat, breakfast cereal, flashlight batteries, wine, and so on. The tool often used for this is *statistical process control,* **a statistical technique that uses periodic random samples from production runs to see if quality is being maintained within a standard range of acceptability.** If quality is not acceptable, production is stopped to allow corrective measures.

Statistical process control is the technique that McDonald's uses, for example, to make sure that the quality of its burgers is always the same, no matter where in the world they are served. Companies such as Intel and Motorola use statistical process control to ensure the reliability and quality of their products.

Some statistical process control tools are shown on the next page. *(See Table 16.2.)* These are all graphical or visual aids to help control quality.

Six Sigma & Lean Six Sigma: Data-Driven Ways to Eliminate Defects   "The biggest problem with the management technique known as Six Sigma is this: It sounds too good to be true," says a *Fortune* writer. "How would your company like a 20% increase in profit margins within one year, followed by profitability over the long-term that is *ten times* what you're seeing now? How about a 4% (or greater) annual gain in market share?"[44]

What is this name, Six Sigma, which is probably Greek to you, and is it a path to management heaven? The name comes from *sigma,* the Greek letter that statisticians use to define a standard deviation. The higher the sigma, the fewer the

table 16.2 SOME STATISTICAL PROCESS CONTROL TOOLS

Flowchart	Graphical tool for representing the sequence of events required to complete a project and for laying out "what-if" scenarios. (See the appendix.)
Pareto analysis	Bar chart indicating which problem needs the most attention.
Cause-and-effect diagram	Also known as a *fishbone diagram;* a graphical mechanism for identifying potential causes of problems and tracing back to identify the root causes.
Control chart	Graphical aid showing data collected over time and the acceptable and unacceptable variations from the norm for repeated operations.
Histogram	Bar chart showing deviations from standard bell-shaped curve.
Scatter diagram	Diagram that plots relationships between two variables.
Run chart	Also called a *time series chart;* tracks the amount or frequency of a variable over time.

Sources: Adapted from L. R. Gomez-Mejia, D. B. Balkin, and R. L. Cardy, *Management: People, Performance, Change,* 3rd ed.(New York: McGraw-Hill/Irwin, 2008), p. 656; and R. Kreitner, *Management,* 8th ed. (Boston: Houghton Mifflin, 2001), pp. 541–543.

deviations from the norm—that is, the fewer the defects. Developed by Motorola in 1985 and since embraced by General Electric, Allied Signal, American Express, and other companies, **Six Sigma is a rigorous statistical analysis process that reduces defects in manufacturing and service-related processes.** By testing thousands of variables and eliminating guesswork, a company using the technique attempts to improve quality and reduce waste to the point where errors nearly vanish. In everything from product design to manufacturing to billing, the attainment of Six Sigma means there are no more than 3.4 defects per million products or procedures.

"Six Sigma gets people away from thinking that 96% is good, to thinking that 40,000 failures per million is bad," says a vice president of consulting firm A. T. Kearney.[45] Six Sigma means being 99.9997% perfect. By contrast, Three Sigma or Four Sigma means settling for 99% perfect—the equivalent of no electricity for 7 hours each month, two short or long landings per day at each major airport, or 5,000 incorrect surgical operations per week.[46]

Six Sigma may also be thought of as a philosophy—to reduce variation in your company's business and make customer-focused, data-driven decisions. The method preaches the use of Define, Measure, Analyze, Improve, and Control (DMAIC). Team leaders may be awarded a Six Sigma "black belt" for applying DMAIC.

More recently, companies are using an approach known as **lean Six Sigma, which focuses on problem solving and performance improvement—speed with excellence—of a well-defined project.**[47] Xerox Corp., for example, has focused on getting new products to customers faster, which has meant taking steps out of the design process without loss of quality. A high-end, $200,000 machine that can print 100 pages a minute traditionally has taken three to five cycles of design; removing just one of those cycles can shave up to a year off time to market.[48] The grocery chain Albertsons Inc. announced in 2004 that it was going to launch Six Sigma training to reduce customer dissatisfaction and waste to the lowest level possible.[49]

Six Sigma may not be a perfect process, since it cannot compensate for human error or control events outside a company. Still, it lets managers approach problems with the assumption that there's a data-oriented, tangible way to approach problem solving.[50] ●

16.7 MANAGING CONTROL EFFECTIVELY

THE BIG PICTURE

This section describes four keys to successful control and five barriers to successful control.

How do you as a manager make a control system successful, and how do you identify and deal with barriers to control? We consider these topics next.[51]

The Keys to Successful Control Systems

Successful control systems have a number of common characteristics: (1) They are strategic and results oriented. (2) They are timely, accurate, and objective. (3) They are realistic, positive, and understandable and they encourage self-control. (4) They are flexible.[52]

1. They Are <u>Strategic</u> & <u>Results</u> Oriented   Control systems support strategic plans and are concentrated on significant activities that will make a real difference to the organization. Thus, when managers are developing strategic plans for achieving strategic goals, that is the point at which they should pay attention to developing control standards that will measure how well the plans are being achieved.

Example: Global warming is now shifting the climate on a continental scale, changing the life cycle of animals and plants, scientists say, and surveys show more Americans feel guilty for not living greener.[53] A growing number of companies are discovering that embracing environmental safe practices is paying

One of 10 million trees. Established in 1986, Pro-Natura is a nongovernmental organization that specializes in sustainable development. The mission of the organization is to conserve biodiversity through integrated sustainable development projects adapted as models that can be replicated at regional levels.

off in savings of hundreds of millions of dollars. Thus, Sun Microsystems, the technology company, is aiming to reduce its greenhouse gas emissions by 20% by 2012 through a range of practices, such as using energy-saving technology in its computer chips or allowing thousands of its 18,000 employees to work at home.[54]

2. They Are Timely, Accurate, & Objective   Good control systems—like good information of any kind—should . . .

- **Be timely—meaning when needed.** The information should not necessarily be delivered quickly, but it should be delivered at an appropriate or specific time, such as every week or every month. And it certainly should be often enough to allow employees and managers to take corrective action for any deviations.

- **Be accurate—meaning correct.** Accuracy is paramount, if decision mistakes are to be avoided. Inaccurate sales figures may lead managers to mistakenly cut or increase sales promotion budgets. Inaccurate production costs may lead to faulty pricing of a product.

- **Be objective—meaning impartial.** Objectivity means control systems are impartial and fair. Although information can be inaccurate for all kinds of reasons (faulty communication, unknown data, and so on), information that is not objective is inaccurate for a special reason: It is biased or prejudiced. Control systems need to be considered unbiased for everyone involved so that they will be respected for their fundamental purpose— enhancing performance.

3. They Are Realistic, Positive, & Understandable & Encourage Self-Control   Control systems have to focus on working for the people who will have to live with them. Thus, they operate best when they are made acceptable to the organization's members who are guided by them. Thus, they should . . .

- **Be realistic.** They should incorporate realistic expectations. If employees feel performance results are too difficult, they are apt to ignore or sabotage the performance system.

- **Be positive.** They should emphasize development and improvement. They should avoid emphasizing punishment and reprimand.

- **Be understandable.** They should fit the people involved, be kept as simple as possible, and present data in understandable terms. They should avoid complicated computer printouts and statistics.

- **Encourage self-control.** They should encourage good communication and mutual participation. They should not be the basis for creating distrust between employees and managers.

4. They Are Flexible   Control systems must leave room for individual judgment, so that they can be modified when necessary to meet new requirements.

Barriers to Control Success

Among the several barriers to a successful control system are the following:[55]

I. Too Much Control   Some organizations, particularly bureaucratic ones, try to exert too much control. They may try to regulate employee behavior in everything from dress code to timing of coffee breaks. Allowing employees too little discretion for analysis and interpretation may lead to employee frustration—particularly among professionals, such as college professors and medical doctors. Their frustration may lead them to ignore or try to sabotage the control process.

2. Too Little Employee Participation   As highlighted by W. Edwards Deming, discussed elsewhere in the book (Chapter 12), employee participation can enhance productivity. Involving employees in both the planning and execution of control systems can bring legitimacy to the process and heighten employee morale.

3. Overemphasis on Means Instead of Ends   We said that control activities should be strategic and results oriented. They are not ends in themselves but the means to eliminating problems. Too much emphasis on accountability for weekly production quotas, for example, can lead production supervisors to push their workers and equipment too hard, resulting in absenteeism and machine breakdowns. Or it can lead to game playing—"beating the system"—as managers and employees manipulate data to seem to fulfill short-run goals instead of the organization's strategic plan.

4. Overemphasis on Paperwork   A specific kind of misdirection of effort is management emphasis on getting reports done, to the exclusion of other performance activity. Reports are not the be-all and end-all. Undue emphasis on reports can lead to too much focus on quantification of results and even to falsification of data.

Example: A research laboratory decided to use the number of patents the lab obtained as a measure of its effectiveness. The result was an increase in patents filed but a decrease in the number of successful research projects.[56]

5. Overemphasis on One Instead of Multiple Approaches   One control may not be enough. By having multiple control activities and information systems, an organization can have multiple performance indicators, thereby increasing accuracy and objectivity.

Example: An obvious strategic goal for gambling casinos is to prevent employee theft of the cash flowing through their hands. Thus, casinos control card dealers by three means. First, they require they have a dealer's license before they are hired. Second, they put them under constant scrutiny, using direct supervision by on-site pit bosses as well as observation by closed-circuit TV cameras and through overhead one-way mirrors. Third, they require detailed reports at the end of each shift so that transfer of cash and cash equivalents (such as gambling chips) can be audited.[57] ●

Temptation. Because legal gambling is a heavy cash business, casinos need to institute special controls against employee theft. One of them is the "eye in the sky" over card and craps tables.

Summary

 16.1 Managing for Productivity
A manager has to deal with six challenges— managing for competitive advantage, diversity, globalization, information technology, ethical standards, and his or her own happiness and life goals. The manager must make decisions about the four management functions— planning, organizing, leading, and controlling—to get people to achieve productivity and realize results. Productivity is defined by the formula of outputs divided by inputs for a specified period of time. Productivity is important because it determines whether the organization will make a profit or even survive. Productivity depends on control.

 16.2 Control: When Managers Monitor Performance
Controlling is defined as monitoring performance, comparing it with goals, and taking corrective action as needed. There are six reasons why control is needed: (1) to adapt to change and uncertainty; (2) to discover irregularities and errors; (3) to reduce costs, increase productivity, or add value; (4) to detect opportunities; (5) to deal with complexity; and (6) to decentralize decision making and facilitate teamwork.

There are four control process steps. (1) The first step is to set standards. A control standard is the desired performance level for a given goal. (2) The second step is to measure performance, based on written reports, oral reports, and personal observation. (3) The third step is to compare measured performance against the standards established. (4) The fourth step is to take corrective action, if necessary, if there is negative performance.

 16.3 The Balanced Scorecard, Strategy Maps, & Measurement Management
To establish standards, managers often use the balanced scorecard, which provides a fast but comprehensive view of the organization via four indicators: (1) financial measures, (2) customer satisfaction, (3) internal processes, and (4) innovation and improvement activities.

The strategy map, a visual representation of the four perspectives of the balanced scorecard—financial, customer, internal business, and innovation and learning—enables managers to communicate their goals so that everyone in the company can understand how their jobs are linked to the overall objectives of the organization.

Measurement-managed companies use measurable criteria for determining strategic success, and management updates and reviews three or more of six primary performance areas: financial performance, operating efficiency, customer satisfaction, employee performance, innovation/change, and community/environment. Four mechanisms that contribute to the success of such companies are top executives agree on strategy, communication is clear, there is better focus and alignments, and the organizational culture emphasizes teamwork and allows risk taking. Four barriers to effective measurement are objectives are fuzzy, managers put too much trust in informal feedback systems, employees resist new management systems, and companies focus too much on measuring activities instead of results.

Some areas are difficult to measure, such as those in service industries.

16.4 Levels & Areas of Control

In applying the steps and types of control, managers need to consider (1) the level of management at which they operate, (2) the areas they can draw on for resources, and (3) the style of control philosophy.

There are three levels of control, corresponding to the three principal managerial levels. (1) Strategic control, done by top managers, is monitoring performance to ensure that strategic plans are being implemented. (2) Tactical control, done by middle managers, is monitoring performance to ensure that tactical plans are being implemented. (3) Operational control, done by first-level or supervisory managers, is monitoring performance to ensure that day-to-day goals are being implemented.

Most organizations have six areas that they can draw on for resources. (1) The physical area includes buildings, equipment, and tangible products; these use equipment control, inventory-management control, and quality controls. (2) The human resources area uses personality tests, drug tests, performance tests, employee surveys, and the like as controls to monitor people. (3) The informational area uses production schedules, sales forecasts, environmental impact statements, and the like to monitor

the organization's various resources. (4) The financial area uses various kinds of financial controls, as we discuss in Section 16.5. (5) The structural area uses hierarchical or other arrangements such as bureaucratic control, which is characterized by use of rules, regulations, and formal authority to guide performance, or decentralized control, which is characterized by informal and organic structural arrangements. (6) The cultural area influences the work process and levels of performance through the set of norms that develop as a result of the values and beliefs that constitute an organization's culture.

16.5 Some Financial Tools for Control

Financial controls include (1) budgets, (2) financial statements, (3) ratio analysis, and (4) audits.

A budget is a formal financial projection. There are two budget-planning approaches, incremental and zero-based. (1) Incremental budgeting allocates increased or decreased funds to a department by using the last budget period as a reference point; only incremental changes in the budget request are reviewed. (2) Zero-based budgeting (ZBB) forces each department to start from zero in projecting the funding needs for the coming budget period. Whether incremental or zero-based, budgets are either fixed, which allocate resources on the basis of a single estimate of costs, or variable, which allow resource allocation to vary in proportion with various levels of activity.

A financial statement is a summary of some aspect of an organization's financial status. One type, the balance sheet, summarizes an organization's overall financial worth— assets and liabilities—at a specific point in time. The other type, the income statement, summarizes an organization's financial results—revenues and expenses—over a specified period of time.

Ratio analysis is the practice of evaluating financial ratios. Managers may use this tool to determine an organization's financial health, such as liquidity ratios, debt management ratios, or return ratios.

Audits are formal verifications of an organization's financial and operational systems. Audits are of two types. An external audit is formal verification of an organization's financial accounts and statements by outside experts. An internal audit is a verification of an organization's financial accounts and statements by the organization's own professional staff.

 16.6 Total Quality Management
Much of the impetus for quality improvement came from W. Edwards Deming, whose philosophy, known as Deming management, proposed ideas for making organizations more responsive, more democratic, and less wasteful. Among the principles of Deming management are (1) quality should be aimed at the needs of the consumer; (2) companies should aim at improving the system, not blaming workers; (3) improved quality leads to increased market share, increased company prospects, and increased employment; and (4) quality can be improved on the basis of hard data, using the PDCA, or plan-do-check-act, cycle.

Total quality management (TQM) is defined as a comprehensive approach—led by top management and supported throughout the organization—dedicated to continuous quality improvement, training, and customer satisfaction. The two core principles of TQM are people orientation and improvement orientation.

In the people orientation, everyone involved with the organization is asked to focus on delivering value to customers, focusing on quality. TQM requires training, teamwork, and cross-functional efforts.

In the improvement orientation, everyone involved with the organization is supposed to make ongoing small, incremental improvements in all parts of the organization. This orientation assumes

that it's less expensive to do things right the first time, to do small improvements all the time, and to follow accurate standards to eliminate small variations.

TQM can be applied to services using the RATER scale, which stands for reliability, assurance, tangibles, empathy, and responsiveness.

Several techniques are available for improving quality. (1) Employee involvement can be implemented through quality circles, self-managed teams, and special-purpose teams—teams that meet to solve a special or one-time problem. (2) Benchmarking is a process by which a company compares its performance with that of high-performing organizations. (3) Outsourcing is the subcontracting of services and operations to an outside vendor. (4) Reduced cycle time consists of reducing the number of steps in a work process. (5) Statistical process control is a statistical technique that uses periodic random samples from production runs to see if quality is being maintained within a standard range of acceptability.

 16.7 Managing Control Effectively
Successful control systems have four common characteristics: (1) They are strategic and results oriented. (2) They are timely, accurate, and objective. (3) They are realistic, positive, and understandable and they encourage self-control. (4) They are flexible.

Among the barriers to a successful control system are the following: (1) Organizations may exert too much control. (2) There may be too little employee participation. (3) The organization may overemphasize means instead of ends. (4) There may be an overemphasis on paperwork. (5) There may be an overemphasis on one approach instead of multiple approaches.

Management in Action

Dashboards Are Becoming a Key Control Technique for Enhancing Organizational Effectiveness

Since the advent of the mainframe in the 1950s, companies have dreamed of using computers to manage their businesses. But early efforts came up short, with technology that was too costly or too clunky. Now, thanks to the Net and dashboards, those dreams are starting to come true. Forrester

Research Inc. analyst Keith Gile estimates that 40% of the 2,000 largest companies use the technology. Some of the most prominent chief executives in the world are believers, from Steven A. Ballmer at Microsoft and Ivan G. Seidenberg at Verizon Communications to Robert L. Nardelli at Home Depot. . . .

The dashboard is the CEO's killer app, making the gritty details of a business that are often buried deep within a large organization accessible at a glance to senior executives. So powerful are the programs that they're beginning to change the nature of management, from an intuitive art into more of a science. Managers can see key changes in their businesses almost instantaneously—when salespeople falter or quality slides—and take quick, corrective action. At Verizon, Seidenberg and other executives can choose from among 300 metrics to put on their dashboards, from broadband sales to wireless subscriber defections. At General Electric Co., James P. Campbell, chief of the Consumer & Industrial division, which makes appliances and lighting products, tracks the number of orders coming in from each customer every day and compares that with targets. "I look at the digital dashboard the first thing in the morning so I have a quick global view of sales and service levels across the organization," says Campbell. "It's a key operational tool in our business." . . .

Still, dashboards have drawn some flak. Critics say CEOs can miss the big picture if they're glued to their computer screens. GE agrees with that point. While business unit chiefs such as Campbell are active dashboard users, CEO Jeffrey Immelt is not, since he focuses on issues such as broad strategy and dealmaking that the technology can't yet capture.

Other critics fear dashboards are an alluring but destructive force, the latest incarnation of Big Brother. The concern is that companies will use the technology to invade the privacy of workers and wield it as a whip to keep them in line. Even managers who use dashboards admit the tools can raise pressure on employees, create divisions in the office, and lead workers to hoard information.

One common concern is that dashboards can hurt morale. Consider the case of Little Earth Productions Inc., a Pittsburgh clothing manufacturer. The company uses NetSuite's tools to monitor the amount of business each salesperson has brought in and then displays it publicly. "You do feel bummed out sometimes if you are low on the list," says Ronisue Koller, a Little Earth salesperson. . . .

Still, most management experts think the rewards are well worth the risks. They caution that executives should roll out the systems slowly and avoid highlighting individual performance, at least at first. They also underscore the need for business leaders to spend time up-front figuring out which metrics are the most useful to track. But that's a question of how to use the technology, not whether to implement it. . . .

One big fan of dashboards is Microsoft Corp., which of course makes plenty of business software itself. Jeff Raikes, president of the Microsoft division that makes its Microsoft Office software, says that more than half of its employees use dashboards, including Ballmer and chief software architect William H. Gates III. "Every time I go to see Ballmer, it's an expectation that I bring my dashboard with me," says Raikes. Ballmer, he says, reviews the dashboards of his seven business heads during one-on-one meetings, zeroing in on such metrics as sales, customer satisfaction, and the status of key products under development.

As for Gates, Raikes says the Microsoft founder uses a dashboard during his "think week," when he leaves the office and reads more than 100 papers about the tech industry prepared by employees. "He uses the dashboard to track what he has read and the feedback and actions that should be taken," says Raikes.

Dashboards are a natural for monitoring operations. In manufacturing, GE execs use them to follow the production of everything from lightbulbs to dishwashers, making sure production lines are running smoothly. In the software business, Raikes uses his dashboard to track the progress of the upcoming version of Office. Shaygan Kheradpir, the chief information officer at Verizon, has on his dashboard what co-workers call the Wall of Shaygan, a replica of every single node on the telecom giant's network. All green is good. Yellow or red merits a click. Red means an outage somewhere. "It makes you move where you need to move," he says.

Dashboard technology can help keep customers happy, too. Before NetSuite, American Reporting's Porter says customer-service reps just answered the phone and had no place to store client requests. Now the company's entire customer-service team uses the software. As a result, customer-service managers can see who is responding to calls. And service reps have access to every repair ticket, making it easier to handle customer problems. "It allows us to compete against some of the bigger boys," says Porter.

American Reporting isn't the only small fry that's benefiting. Jerry Driggs, chief operating office of Little Earth, took four months last winter to move his business onto the NetSuite system. Little Earth sells funky eco-fashion products, such as a handbag made with recycled license plates. Today half of the company's 50 employees use the system to manage their production, sales, and financial operations. "Once you see it is so intuitive, you wonder how we ran the business before," says Driggs.

In fact, Driggs ran the business by the seat of his pants, and it showed. Because the company had no system to measure its production requirements or level of raw materials, much of which came from China, it took about six weeks to make and ship a handbag. And Little Earth constantly struggled with cash problems because Driggs would often buy more trim pieces and twist-knob closures than he needed. "You used to see dollars sitting on the shelves," he says. Now, using NetSuite, Driggs can monitor his purchase orders and inventory levels, and the system even alerts him when he is running low on closures and other parts. The result: Little Earth has slashed its shipping time to three days. "All of those things that used to drive us crazy are literally at our fingertips," says Driggs.

For Discussion

1. What are the pros and cons of using dashboards as a control technique? Explain.

2. How can the use of the balanced scorecard and strategy mapping be integrated within the dashboard technology? Discuss.

3. Which of the three levels of control can be provided through the use of dashboards? Provide examples to support your conclusions.

4. How can dashboards be used to improve quality and customer service? Explain.

Source: From Spencer E. Ante with Jena McGregor, "Giving the Boss the Big Picture," *BusinessWeek*, February 13, 2006, pp. 48–51. Reprinted with permission.

Self-Assessment

Do You Have Good Time-Management Skills?

Objectives

1. To determine how productive you are.
2. To discuss what time-management skills need developing.

Introduction

As we learned in this chapter, productivity is important to companies because it determines their profitability. For managers, productivity depends on effective time management, a skill involving planning and self-discipline that should be perfected in college. The purpose of this exercise is to evaluate your time-management skills.

Instructions

Read each question, and answer each one "Yes" or "No." Answer not as you feel you *should* but rather as you feel you *would* if you were being completely truthful.

1. I have a hard time saying "no." **NO**
2. I sometimes postpone a task so long that I'm embarrassed to do it. **No**
3. I feel like I'm always in a hurry. **NO**
4. I feel guilty when I play or goof off instead of studying. **Yes**
5. I tend to make excuses when I don't finish my work. **NO**
6. I often feel like I have too much to do. **Yes**
7. I work better under pressure. **Yes No**
8. I feel resentful when someone reminds me I haven't finished my work. **No**
9. I have difficulty deciding how to use my time. **No**
10. I generally put off semester projects until the week before they're due. **No**

Interpretation

Count the number of "No" responses. Your time-management skills may be characterized as follows:

9–10: Excellent
8–9: Good, but they could be improved in minor ways
6–8: Somewhat inadequate; you could benefit from training
4–6: Poor; you definitely need training
4 or less: Emergency! You know little about time management and need to pay immediate attention here

Questions for Discussion

1. Were you surprised by the results? Why or why not?

2. Many statements in the assessment represent procrastination, with good intentions being eclipsed by excuses and bad time management. Do you frequently procrastinate?

3. What are some ways you could improve your time-management skills? Discuss.

Source: www.ecu.edu/aretsci/cas/advising/TimeManagement .com © Thomas Harriot College of Arts & Sciences, Advising Center, East Carolina University, Greenville, NC.

Is Corporate Monitoring of Employee Behavior Outside of Work Going Too Far?

Attempting to cut health care costs and increase productivity, companies are increasingly trying to get employees to lose weight, stop smoking, and exercise. For example, Incentive Logic Inc. in Arizona "keeps track of points employees earn for everything from walking to passing health screenings and it lets employees redeem their points for iPods, plasma TVs or other items they want from its 3 million-item catalog."

Further, some companies claim that health care costs are higher for smokers and overweight employees than they are for nonsmokers and nonoverweight people. "In response to these higher costs, more employers are instituting bans on hiring smokers, even if they only smoke during off-duty hours, and/or are charging more for health insurance to smokers, overweight workers, and other categories of employees."

Right now, organizations are targeting and monitoring smokers and overweight employees, but other groups might be next. "Other groups that may be subject to such 'lifestyle' regulations include people with hypertension or high serum cholesterol levels, social drinkers, and sports enthusiasts."

What types of employee behavior outside of work should organizations monitor and reward/punish?

Solving the Dilemma

1. Organizations should stay out of our personal lives. If we want to overeat or smoke, that is our choice. Organizations should not be allowed to monitor weight and smoking behavior.

2. Organizations should monitor employees' weight and smoking behavior and reward/punish accordingly. After all, overweight people and smokers cost employers more in terms of health insurance and it's only fair that people pay for these increased costs in one way or another.

3. I'm okay with rewarding/punishing people who are overweight and smoke, but that is it. Organizations have no business tracking how much I drink and what type of sports or social activities I enjoy. If I want to go skydiving, it's my business, not the company's.

4. Invent other options.

Sources: Jane Larson, "Firm's Reward Program Gets Employees Moving," *The Arizona Republic,* May 24, 2008, p. D5; and "Off-Duty but on Your Mind," *Training,* April 2008, p. 11.

Major Question ?

What are some future management models, and what are six keys to personal managerial success?

THE BIG PICTURE

As we end the book, this section describes business guru Gary Hamel's thoughts on management innovation and leaves you with some life lessons to take away.

We have described a number of valuable principles in this book. Valuable, but not sacred, not chiseled in stone.

After all, during your lifetime you will have to deal with an onslaught of global competitors, from this and other countries, and they will be innovative, shrewd, and driven. Company cultures, structures, job designs, and forms of leadership are all changing. As a matter of our survival, therefore, today's principles of management wisdom will probably have to be rewritten.

Management Ideas Are Not Fixed but Are a Process: The Thoughts of Gary Hamel

"Over time," says Gary Hamel, co-founder of the Management Innovation Lab, "every great invention, management included, travels a road that leads from birth to maturity, and occasionally to senescence."[1] Ranked by *The Wall Street Journal* as today's most influential business thinker, Hamel holds that much of management theory is dated and doesn't fit the current realities of organizational life.[2] What we need to do, he suggests, is look at management as a *process,* and then make improvement and innovation systemic and ongoing—the very kind of *process innovation* that companies are used to applying to equipment and techniques to improve production or delivery methods. Stated another way, if managers now innovate by creating new products or new business strategies, why can't they be equally innovative in how they manage their companies? Hamel contends that management innovation is essential to future organizational success.

Are there any blueprints for this kind of change? In his 2007 book, *The Future of Management,* Hamel profiles three companies of vastly different types that challenged current management thinking and suggested that they represent future management models: retailer Whole Foods Market, industrial products manufacturer W. L. Gore (inventor of Gore-Tex), and Internet icon Google.

- **Whole Foods Market—empowering front-line employees in small teams.** At most retail companies, employees are hired by supervisors (not fellow employees), decisions about what products to order are made by someone high up at central headquarters, and the amounts of people's paychecks are kept secret. At Whole Foods, however, each individual store organizes itself into roughly eight teams, with compensation tied to team rather than individual performance and performance measurements and pay being open to all. Each team has the mission of improving the food for which it is responsible; is given wide flexibility in how it manages its responsibilities, hires and fires its members, and stocks its shelves; and is given a lot of power in how it responds to the changing tastes of local consumers. Indeed, Whole Food employees are given both the freedom to do the right thing for customers and the incentive to do the right thing for profits. The financial results of this business model: Whole Foods is the most profitable U.S. food retailer, when measured by profit per square foot; its stock price rose nearly 3,000% in the 15 years after 1992; and its same-store sales growth averaged 11% per year from 2002 to 2007, nearly triple the industry average.

- **W. L. Gore—allowing employees to pursue own ideas and challenge supervisors.** Gore also has small, self-managed teams, and individuals are given "dabble time" to pursue new ideas, which may eventually contribute to the firm's roster of products. Contrary to companies with traditional systems of management, Gore allows employees to push back against their managers, challenging the very notion of a management hierarchy. Employees also choose which teams to work on, and they can say no to requests. There are no management layers, no organization chart, few people have titles. Some employees gain the appellation "leader" by demonstrating a capacity to get things done and excelling at team building. Those who make a disproportionate contribution to team success over time attract followers. "We vote with our feet," says one employee. "If you call a meeting, and people show up, you're a leader."[3]

- **Google—embracing the 70-20-10 rule for applying company resources.** Google, the wildly successful search-engine company, also is structured in small teams in which, unlike in most companies, the team leadership is rotated among team members. Also unlike in other companies, employees in product development are encouraged to pursue their own ideas, following the 70-20-10 rule—namely, devote 70% of their resources to the firm's core business, 20% to services that might expand from that business, and 10% to fringe ideas. Thus, engineers will take a day or so every week to work on whatever they like. What prevents people from wasting time on crackpot ideas that go nowhere? First, there's all the horizontal communication with peers, which tends to kill off bad ideas and reinforce good ones. In addition, although employees can follow their passions, they won't get much in the way of Google resources until they've accumulated some positive user feedback. The point of all this: to give employees the freedom to innovate by using a carrot instead of a stick approach.

Do front-line employees really know better than top managers what's best for an organization? That's the assumption here. After all, they are the ones closest to the customers and most familiar with the products. While certainly managers will always be needed to maintain a firm's stability, employees organized in teams, Hamel suggests, are in a better position to innovate—to determine what products are needed and how time and money should be spent. They should also be inspired to pursue a passion rather than just profits. By balancing centralized control and front-line initiative as well as pursuit of a mission and pursuit of profits, companies might also, says Hamel, achieve competitive models that will be very hard to copy by more top-down companies such as those in China and India.

But what if you're not starting from scratch in a brand-new enterprise and cannot apply revolutionary ideas the way the founders of Whole Foods, Gore, and Google did? How do you get the ball rolling in a traditional, conventional company? Hamel believes that the answer can be found by identifying core beliefs that people have about the organization. You may recall from Chapter 8 that beliefs are the foundation of organizational culture. As such, Hamel is recommending that we need to examine the components of organizational culture that detract from the pursuit of management innovation. He suggests that these beliefs can be rooted out by repeatedly asking the right questions—namely,

1. Is this a belief worth challenging? Is it debilitating? Does it get in the way of an important organizational attribute that we'd like to strengthen?

2. Is this belief universally valid? Are there counterexamples? If so, what do we learn from those cases?

3. How does this belief serve the interests of its adherents? Are there people who draw reassurance or comfort from this belief?

4. Have our choices and assumptions conspired to make this belief self-fulfilling? Is this belief true simply because we have made it true—and, if so, can we imagine alternatives?[4]

In reciting Hamel's ideas, we certainly don't mean to imply that what you have read in the preceding pages represents old, useless thinking. To the contrary, research is replete with studies suggesting you have everything to gain by having a complete understanding of such traditional concepts as goal setting, job design, self-management, transformational leadership, and the host of other ideas we discussed. The bottom line is simply this: The world is changing and is changing fast, and it will demand your utmost flexibility and resilience.

What Should You Do? What Managerial Principles Can You Count On?

How, then, are you going to compete? Let us offer a few recommendations, pulled from our business experience, research, teaching, consulting, and reading, that can make you a "keeper" in an organization and help you be successful.

- **Find your passion and follow it.** "The mission matters," Hamel writes. "People change for what they care about." Employees aren't motivated much by the notion of "increasing shareholder value" (or if they are, the result may be an Enron-like environment, in which greed overwhelms higher-minded goals). Says Hamel, "A company must forever be on the way to *becoming* something more than it is right now." And the same should apply to you. Find something you love to do, and do it vigorously.

- **Encourage self-discovery, and be realistic.** To stay ahead of the pack, you need to develop self-awareness, have an active mind, and be willing to grow and change. Here's a life lesson: "Be brutally honest with yourself about what you know, and ask what skill you need to take the next step." This includes not just the tools of your trade—finance, technology, and so on—but most importantly people skills.

- **Every situation is different, so be flexible.** No principle, no theory will apply under all circumstances. Industries, cultures, supervisors, customers will vary. If you're the new kid in a new job, for instance, you should know that "culture is critical," suggests Angeli R. Rasbury in *Black Enterprise*. A life lesson: "Before you can begin to set goals, know the organization in which you're working. Learn how employees conduct business and view success, and how the company rewards achievement. An organization's culture defines its management and business guidelines."[5] Another life lesson: "Remove 'It's not my job' from your vocabulary."

- **Fine-tune your people skills.** The workplace is not an area where lone individuals make their silent contributions. Today we live and work in a team universe. If, as is the case with Whole Foods Market, getting and keeping a job depends on the reviews of your peers, with teammates voting on your fate, you can see that communication skills become ever more important. Recommendation: Get feedback on your interpersonal skills and develop a plan for improvement.

- **Learn how to develop leadership skills.** Every company should invest in the leadership development of its managers if it is to improve the quality of its future leaders. But you can also work to develop your own leadership skills. An example and a life lesson: "Leaders who wait for bad news to come to them are taking a major risk, so learn to seek it out—as by encouraging employees to bring you news of potential problems and thanking them for it, not punishing them for their candor."[6] You can also pick up news about problems, potential and actual, by practicing "management by walking around." Another life lesson: "If you set the bar high, even if you don't reach it, you end up in a pretty good place—that is, achieving a pretty high mark."

- **Treat people as if they matter, because they do.** If you treat employees and customers with dignity, they respond accordingly. The highly successful online shoe retailer Zappos, for instance, "is fanatical about great service," says the writer of a *Harvard Business Publishing* online blog, "not just satisfying customers, but amazing them," as in promising delivery in 4 days and delivering in 1. How? It's all in the hiring, which Zappos does with great intensity. After four weeks' training, new call-center employees are offered $1,000 on top of what they have earned to that point if they want to quit—the theory being that people who take the money "obviously don't have the commitment" that Zappos requires of its employees. (About 10% of the trainees take the offer.) The life lesson: "Companies don't engage emotionally with their customers—people do. If you want to create a memorable company, you have to fill your company with memorable people."[7]

- **Draw employees and peers into your management process.** The old top-down, command-and-control model of organization is moving toward a flattened, networked kind of structure. Managers now work more often with peers, where lines of authority aren't always clear or don't exist, so that one's persuasive powers become key.[8] Power has devolved to front-line employees who are closest to the customer and to small, focused, self-managed teams that have latitude to pursue new ideas. The life lesson: "The best organizations will be those whose employees have the power to innovate, not just follow orders from on high."[9]

- **Be flexible, keep your cool, and take yourself lightly.** Things aren't always going to work out your way, so flexibility is important. In addition, the more unflappable you appear in difficult circumstances, the more you'll be admired by your bosses and co-workers. Having a sense of humor helps, since there are enough people spreading gloom and doom in the workplace. Life lesson: "When you're less emotional, you're better able to assess a crisis and develop a workable solution."

We wish you the very best of luck. And we mean it!

Angelo Kinicki
Brian K. Williams

The Project Planner's Toolkit
Flowcharts, Gantt Charts, & Break-Even Analysis

 How can you use planning tools to enhance your performance and achieve utmost success?

major question?

THE BIG PICTURE

Three tools used in project planning, which was covered in Chapter 5, are flowcharts, Gantt charts, and break-even analysis.

Project planning may begin (in the definition stage) as a back-of-the-envelope kind of process, but the client will expect a good deal more for the time and money being invested. Fortunately, there are various planning and monitoring tools that give the planning and execution of projects more precision. Three tools in the planner's tool-kit are (1) flowcharts, (2) Gantt charts, and break-even analysis.

Tool #1: Flowcharts—for Showing Event Sequences & Alternate Decision Scenarios

A *flowchart* is a useful graphical tool for representing the sequence of events required to complete a project and for laying out "what-if" scenarios. Flowcharts have been used for decades by computer programmers and systems analysts to make a graphical "road map," as it were, of the flow of tasks required. These professionals use their own special symbols (indicating "input/output," "magnetic disk," and the like), but there is no need for you to make the process complicated. Generally, only three symbols are needed: (1) an oval for the "beginning" and "end," (2) a box for a major activity, and (3) a diamond for a "yes or no" decision. *(See Figure A.1, next page.)*

Computer programs such as Micrographix's ABC Flow Charter are available for constructing flowcharts. You can also use the drawing program in word processing programs such as Microsoft Word.

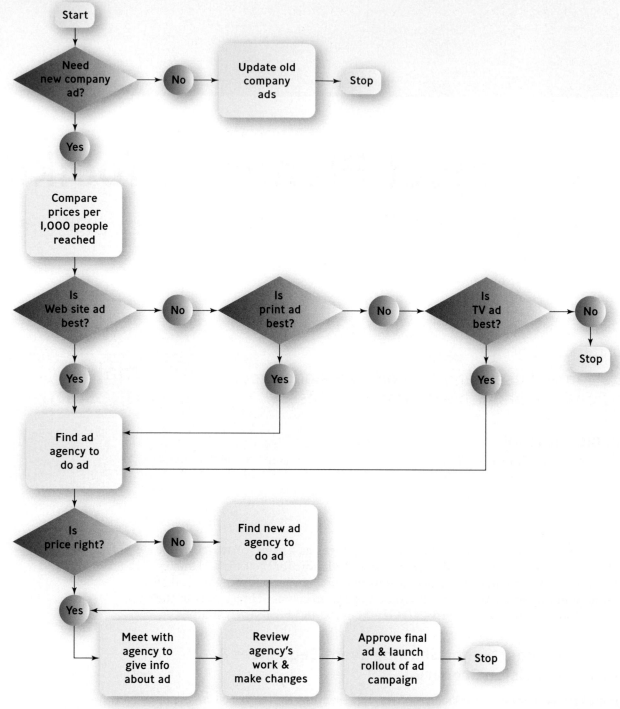

figure A.I

FLOWCHART: WEB SITE, PRINT, OR TELEVISION?

Example of a flowchart for improving a company's advertising

Benefits Flowcharts have two benefits:

- **Planning straightforward activities.** A flowchart can be quite helpful for planning ordinary activities—figuring out the best way to buy textbooks or a car, for example. It is also a straightforward way of indicating the sequence of events in, say, thinking out a new enterprise that you would then turn into a business plan.

- **Depicting alternate scenarios.** A flowchart is also useful for laying out "what-if" scenarios—as in if you answer "yes" to a decision question you should follow Plan A, if you answer "no" you should follow Plan B.

Limitations   Flowcharts have two limitations:

- **No time indication.** They don't show the amounts of time required to accomplish the various activities in a project. In building a house, the foundation might take only a couple of days, but the rough carpentry might take weeks. These time differences can't be represented graphically on a flowchart (although you could make a notation).
- **Not good for complex projects.** They aren't useful for showing projects consisting of several activities that must all be worked on at the same time. An example would be getting ready for football season's opening game, by which time the players have to be trained, the field readied, the programs printed, the band rehearsed, the ticket sellers recruited, and so on. These separate activities might each be represented on their own flowcharts, of course. But to try to express them all together all at once would produce a flowchart that would be unwieldy, even unworkable.

Tool #2: Gantt Charts—Visual Time Schedules for Work Tasks

We have mentioned how important deadlines are to making a project happen. Unlike a flowchart, a Gantt chart can graphically indicate deadlines.

The Gantt chart was developed by **Henry L. Gantt,** a member of the school of scientific management (discussed in Chapter 2). **A *Gantt chart* is a kind of time schedule—a specialized bar chart that shows the relationship between the kind of work tasks planned and their scheduled completion dates.** *(See Figure A.2, next page.)*

A number of software packages can help you create and modify Gantt charts on your computer. Examples are CA-SuperProject, Microsoft Project Manager, SureTrak Project Manager, and TurboProject Professional.

Benefits   There are three benefits to using a Gantt chart:

- **Express time lines visually.** Unlike flowcharts, Gantt charts allow you to indicate visually the time to be spent on each activity.
- **Compare proposed and actual progress.** A Gantt chart may be used to compare planned time to complete a task with actual time taken to complete it, so that you can see how far ahead or behind schedule you are for the entire project. This enables you to make adjustments so as to hold to the final target dates.
- **Simplicity.** There is nothing difficult about creating a Gantt chart. You express the time across the top and the tasks down along the left side. As Figure A.2 shows, you can make use of this device while still in college to help schedule and monitor the work you need to do to meet course requirements and deadlines (for papers, projects, tests).

Limitations   Gantt charts have two limitations:

- **Not useful for large, complex projects.** Although a Gantt chart can express the interrelations among the activities of relatively small projects, it becomes cumbersome and unwieldy when used for large, complex projects. More sophisticated management planning tools may be needed, such as PERT networks.
- **Time assumptions are subjective.** The time assumptions expressed may be purely subjective; there is no range between "optimistic" and "pessimistic" of the time needed to accomplish a given task.

Accomplished: ‖‖‖‖‖‖‖
Planned: \\\\\\\\\

Stage of development	Week 1	Week 2	Week 3	Week 4	Week 5
1. Examine competitors' Web sites	‖‖‖‖‖‖‖‖‖‖‖‖‖‖ ‖‖‖‖‖‖‖‖	‖‖‖‖‖‖‖‖			
2. Get information for your Web site	‖‖‖‖‖‖‖‖‖‖‖ ‖‖‖‖‖‖‖‖	‖‖‖‖‖‖‖‖‖‖‖‖ ‖‖‖‖‖‖‖‖			
3. Learn Web-authoring software		‖‖‖‖‖‖‖‖‖‖‖‖‖‖ ‖‖‖‖‖‖‖‖	‖‖‖‖‖‖‖‖‖‖‖‖‖‖ ‖‖‖‖‖‖‖‖		
4. Create (design) your Web site			\\\\\\\\\	\\\\\\\\\\\\\\\\\\ \\	\\\\\
5. "Publish" (put) Web site online					\\\\\\\\\\\\

figure A.2

GANTT CHART FOR DESIGNING A WEB SITE.

This shows the tasks accomplished and the time planned for remaining tasks to build a company Web site.

Tool #3: Break-Even Analysis—How Many Items Must You Sell to Turn a Profit?

figure A.3

BREAK-EVEN ANALYSIS

Break-even analysis **is a way of identifying how much revenue is needed to cover the total costs of developing and selling a product.** Let's walk through the computation of a break-even analysis, referring to the illustration. *(See Figure A.3.)* We assume

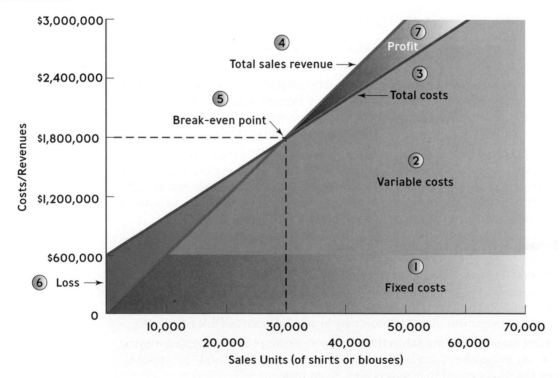

A4

① *Fixed costs (green area):* Once you start up a business, whether you sell anything or not, you'll have expenses that won't vary much, such as rent, insurance, taxes, and perhaps salaries. These are called *fixed costs,* **expenses that don't change regardless of your sales or output.** Fixed costs are a function of time—they are expenses you have to pay out on a regular basis, such as weekly, monthly, or yearly. Here the chart shows the fixed costs (green area) are $600,000 per year no matter how many sales units (of shirts or blouses) you sell.

② *Variable costs (blue area):* Now suppose you start producing and selling a product, such as blouses or shirts. At this point you'll be paying for materials, supplies, labor, sales commissions, and delivery expenses. These are called *variable costs,* **expenses that vary directly depending on the numbers of the product that you produce and sell.** (After all, making more shirts will cost you more in cloth, for example.) Variable costs, then, are a function of volume—they go up and down depending on the number of products you make or sell. Here the variable costs (blue area) are relatively small if you sell only a few thousand shirts but they go up tremendously if you sell, say, 70,000 shirts.

③ *Total costs (first right upward-sloping line—green plus blue area added together):* The sum of the fixed costs and the variable costs equals the total costs (the green and blue areas together). This is indicated by the line that slopes upward to the right from $600,000 to $3,000,000.

④ *Total sales revenue (second right upward-sloping line):* This is the total dollars received from the sale of however many units you sell. The sales revenue varies depending on the number of units you sell. Thus, for example, if you sell 30,000 shirts, you'll receive $1,800,000 in revenue. If you sell 40,000 shirts, you'll receive somewhat more than $2,400,000 in revenue.

⑤ *Break-even point (intersection of dashed lines):* Finding this point is the purpose of this whole exercise. **The** *break-even point* **is the amount of sales revenue at which there is no profit but also no loss to your company.** On the graph, this occurs where the "Total sales revenues" line crosses the "Total costs" line, as we've indicated here where the dashed lines meet. This means that you must sell 30,000 shirts and receive $1,800,000 in revenue in order to recoup your total costs (fixed plus variable). Important note: Here is where pricing the shirts becomes important. If you raise the price per shirt, you may be able to make the same amount of money (hit your break-even point) by selling fewer of them—but that may be harder to do because customers may resist buying at the higher price.

⑥ *Loss (red area):* If you fail to sell enough shirts at the right price (the break-even point), you will suffer a loss. *Loss* **means your total costs exceed your total sales revenue.** As the chart shows, here you are literally "in the red"—you've lost money.

⑦ *Profit (black area):* Here you are literally "in the black"—you've made money. All the shirts you sell beyond the break-even point constitute a profit. *Profit* **is the amount by which total revenue exceeds total costs.** The more shirts you sell, of course, the greater the profit.

    The kind of break-even analysis demonstrated here is known as the *graphic method.* The same thing can also be done algebraically.

you are an apparel manufacturer making shirts or blouses. Start in the lower-right corner of the diagram on the previous page and follow the circled numbers as you read the descriptions above.

Benefits   Break-even analysis has two benefits:

- **For doing future "what-if" alternate scenarios of costs, prices, and sales.** This tool allows you to vary the different possible costs, prices, and sales

Example

Break-Even Analysis: Why Do Airfares Vary So Much?

Why do some airlines charge four times more than others for a flight of the same distance?

There are several reasons, but break-even analysis enters into it.

United Airlines' average cost for flying a passenger 1 mile in 2003 was 11.7 cents, whereas Southwest's was 7.7 cents. Those are the break-even costs. What they charged beyond that was their profit.

Why the difference? One reason, according to a study by the U.S. Department of Transportation, is that Southwest's expenses are lower. United flies more long routes than short ones, so its costs are stretched out over more miles, making its costs for flying shorter routes higher than Southwest's.

Another factor affecting airfares is the type of passengers flying a particular route—whether they are high-fare-paying business travelers or more price-conscious leisure travelers. Business travelers often don't mind paying a lot (they are reimbursed by their companies), and those routes (such as Chicago to Cincinnati) tend to have more first-class seats, which drives up the average price. Flights to vacation spots (such as Las Vegas) usually have more low-price seats because people aren't willing to pay a lot for pleasure travel. Also, nonstop flight fares often cost more than flights with connections.

quantities to do rough "what-if" scenarios to determine possible pricing and sales goals. Since the numbers are interrelated, if you change one, the others will change also.

- **For analyzing the profitability of past projects.** While break-even analysis is usually used as a tool for future projects, it can also be used retroactively to find out whether the goal of profitability was really achieved, since costs may well have changed during the course of the project. In addition, you can use it to determine the impact of cutting costs once profits flow.

Limitations   Break-even analysis is not a cure-all.

- **It oversimplifies.** In the real world, things don't happen as neatly as this model implies. For instance, fixed and variable costs are not always so readily distinguishable. Or fixed costs may change as the number of sales units goes up. And not all customers may pay the same price (some may get discounts).

- **The assumptions may be faulty.** On paper, the formula may work perfectly for identifying a product's profitability. But what if customers find the prices too high? Or what if sales figures are outrageously optimistic? In the marketplace, your price and sales forecasts may really be only good guesses. ●

A6

chapter notes

CHAPTER I

1. R. E. Kelley, *How to Be a Star at Work: Nine Breakthrough Strategies You Need to Succeed* (New York: Times Books, 1999). See also J. Welch and S. Welch, "Chief Executive Officer-in-Chief," *BusinessWeek,* February 4, 2008, p. 88; S. Steckner, "Want to Move Ahead? Take a Look at Your Personality," *The Arizona Republic,* February 5, 2008, http://www.azcentral.com/arizonarepublic/business/articles/0203biz-azw-personality0204int . . . ; B. Groysberg, "How Star Women Build Portable Skills," *Harvard Business Review,* February 2008, pp. 74–81; and N. Anand and J. Conger, "Capabilities of the Consummate Networker," *Organizational Dynamics,* 2006, pp. 13–27.

2. "MTV Networks International and Corus Entertainment Expand Nickelodeon Content Partnership into Digital Space," *RedOrbit,* January 8, 2008, http://www.redorbit.com/news/technology/1208237/mtv_networks_international_and_corus_entertainment_expand_nickelodeon_content_partnership/index.html?source=r_technology (accessed January 21, 2008).

3. Judy McGrath, quoted in T. Lowry, "Can MTV Stay Cool?" *BusinessWeek,* February 20, 2006, pp. 50–60; M. Robichaux, "Finding Her Groove," *Broadcasting & Cable,* October 22, 2007, http://www.broadcastingcable.com/article/CA6492810.html?&display=Features&referral=SUPP&q=Judy+McGrath (accessed January 21, 2008).

4. M. P. Follett, quoted in J. F. Stoner and R. E. Freeman, *Management,* 5th ed. (Englewood Cliffs, NJ: Prentice Hall, 1992), p. 6.

5. The Gartner Group, cited in Don Oldenburg, Associated Press, "Tired of Automated Phone Menus? Press 1," *Reno Gazette-Journal,* March 15, 2004, p. 3E.

6. Scott Broetzmann, quoted in Oldenburg, 2004.

7. Richard Shapiro, quoted in W. C. Taylor, "Your Call Should Be Important to Us, but It's Not," *The New York Times,* February 26, 2006, sec. 3, p. 3; G. J. Carter, "How to Get a Human to Answer the Phone," *USA Weekend,* April 14–16, 2006, p. 4. See also the gethuman Web site at www.gethuman.com.

8. "At Customer Service, Hunt Is On for a Live Voice," *USA Today*, November 27, 2007, p. 11A.

9. Taylor, 2006.

10. G. Colvin, "Catch a Rising Star," *Fortune,* February 6, 2006, pp. 46–50.

11. "Usual Weekly Earnings of Wage and Salary Workers: Fourth Quarter 2007," *News,* Bureau of Labor Statistics, January 17, 2008, http://www.bls.gov/news.release/wkyeng.nr0.htm (accessed January 21, 2008).

12. J. Mouawad, "For Leading Exxon to Its Riches, $144,573 a Day," *The New York Times,* April 15, 2006, pp. A1, B4.

13. "Salary.com Survey Finds Median Pay for Small-Biz CEOs," *Birmingham Business Journal,* November 29, 2007, http://www.bizjournals.com/birmingham/stories/2007/11/26/daily23.html?ana=from_rss (accessed January 21, 2008).

14. O. Pollar, "Are You Sure You Want to Be a Manager?" *San Francisco Examiner,* October 4, 1998, p. J-3.

15. M. Csikszentmihalyi, *Flow: The Psychology of Optimal Experience* (New York: HarperCollins, 1990), and *Beyond Boredom and Anxiety* (San Francisco: Jossey-Bass, 1975), *Creativity: Flow and the Psychology of Discovery and Invention* (New York: Harper Perennial, 1996), *Finding Flow: The Psychology of Engagement with Everyday Life* (New York: Basic Books, 1998); and *Good Business. Leadership, Flow, and the Making of Meaning* (New York: Penguin Books, 2003).

16. B. Stelter, "Networks Show Five Percent Decline," *The New York Times,* October 16, 2007, http://tvdecoder.blogs.nytimes.com/2007/10/16/networks-show-five-percent-declines (accessed January 23, 2008).

17. T. Friend, "Don't Touch That Dial," *The New Yorker,* May 22, 2006, pp. 81–82.

18. R. Gover, "The Sound of Many Hands Zapping," *BusinessWeek,* May 22, 2006, p. 38.

19. S. Elliott and J. Bosman, "That New Show Starring . . . a Tube of Toothpaste," *The New York Times,* May 18, 2006, p. C10. See also N. A. Hira, "The Evolving Art of Outwitting TiVo," *Fortune,* May 15, 2006, p. 36.

20. J. Heilemann, "Cable's Niche Player," *Business 2.0,* May 2006, pp. 36–39.

21. U.S. Census Bureau, "U.S. Interim Projections by Age, Sex, Race, and Hispanic Origin," Table 1a, 2004; www.census.gov/ipc/www/usinterimproj (accessed May 16, 2006).

22. Statistics from Centers for Disease Control and Prevention, reported in M. Stobbe, "More Babies Born in U.S., Unlike Trend in Europe," *San Francisco Chronicle,* January 16, 2008, p. A8.

23. See, for instance, S. E. Page, *The Difference: How the Power of Diversity Creates Better Groups, Firms, Schools and Societies* (Princeton, NJ: Princeton University Press, 2007); C. Dreifus, "In Professor's Model, Diversity = Productivity," *The New York Times,* January 8, 2008, p. D2; and M. J. Pearsall, A. Ellis, and J. Evans, "Unlocking the Effects of Gender Faultlines on Team Creativity: Is Activation the Key?" *Journal of Applied Psychology,* January 2008, pp. 225–234.

24. S. McCartney, "Teaching Americans How to Behave Abroad," *The Wall Street Journal,* April 11, 2006, pp. D1, D4. See also J. Clark, "That 'Ugly American' Image Is Getting a Makeover Guide," *USA Today,* April 28, 2006, p. 9D.

25. T. L. Friedman, *The World Is Flat: A Brief History of the Twenty-first Century* (New York: Farrar, Straus and Giroux, 2005).

26. Michael M. Phillips, "More Work Is Outsourced to U.S. Than Away from It, Data Show," *The Wall Street Journal,* March 15, 2004, p. A2.

27. C. M Glasheen, N. Comiskey, and J. F. Gantz, *Worldwide Internet Usage and Commerce 2007–2010 Forecast: Internet Commerce Market Model Version 11.1,* April 2007, http://www.idc.com/getdoc.jsp?containerId=206420 (accessed February 18, 2008).

28. M. J. Mandel and R. D. Hof, "Rethinking the Internet," *BusinessWeek,* March 26, 2001, p. 118. See also B. Powell, "The New World Order," *Fortune,* May 14, 2001, pp. 134, 136.

29. See C. Graham, "In-Box Overload," *The Arizona Republic,* April 16, 2007, p. A14; and J. Vascellaro, "What's a Cellphone For?" *The Wall Street Journal,* March 26, 2007, p. R5.

30. J. Sandberg, "Down Over Moving Up: Some Bosses Find They Hate Their Jobs," *The Wall Street Journal,* July 27, 2005, p. B1. See also D. Jones, "Besides Being Lonely at the Top, It Can Be 'Disengaging' as Well," *USA Today,* June 21, 2005, pp. 1B, 2B.

31. S. Armour, "Management Loses Its Allure," *USA Today,* October 15, 1997, pp. 1B, 2B. See also J. Kornik, "With Leaders Like These . . . ," *Training,* December 2005, p. 10.

32. Pollar, 1998.

33. P. Drucker, reported in R. L. Knowdell, "A Model for Managers in the Future Workplace: Symphony Conductor," *The Futurist,* June–July 1998, p. 22.

34. S. E. Needleman, "What's in a Title? Ego Stroking, Chiefly," *The Wall Street Journal,* December 26, 2007, p. B7.

35. S. Spring, "Job Titles of the Future: Chief Travel Scientist," *Fast Company,* February–March, 1999, p. 68.

36. A. Thompson, "The Hardest Management Job, " *The Costco Connection,* August 2005, pp. 30–33.

37. "5-Year Winners," *Fast Company,* December 2007–January 2008, p. 115.

38. P. M. Blau and W. R. Scott, *Formal Organizations* (San Francisco: Chandler, 1962).

39. H. Mintzberg, *The Nature of Managerial Work* (New York: Harper & Row, 1973).

40. Mintzberg, 1973.

41. Ed Reilly, quoted in W. J. Holstein, "Attention-Juggling in the High-Tech Office," *The New York Times,* June 4, 2006, sec. 3, p. 9.

42. J. P. Kotter, "What Effective General Managers Really Do," *Harvard Business Review,* March–April 1999, pp. 145–159.

43. L. Stroh, quoted in A. Muoio, "Balancing Acts," *Fast Company,* February–March 1999, pp. 83–90.

44. S. MacDermid, Purdue University, and M. D. Lee, McGill University, 2-year study cited in R. W. Huppke, Associated Press, "Take This Job, and Love It," *San Francisco Chronicle,* January 28, 1999, p. B2.

45. A. Deutschman, "The CEO's Secret of Managing Time," *Fortune,* June 1, 1992, pp. 135–146.

46. D. G. Lepore, quoted in Muoio, 1999.

47. P. Steel, "The Nature of Procrastination: A Meta-Analytic and Theoretical Review of Quintessential Self-Regulatory Failure," *Psychological Bulletin,* January 2007, pp. 65–94. See also S. Borenstein, "Study: More Americans Doing Less," *San Francisco Chronicle,* January 12, 2007, p. A2.

48. H. Lancaster, "Managing Your Time in Real-World Chaos Takes Real Planning," *The Wall Street Journal,* August 19, 1997, p. B1.

49. R. E. Kelley, quoted in S. Shellenbarger, "You Don't Have to Be Chained to Your Desk to Be a Star Performer," *The Wall Street Journal,* August 12, 1998, p. B1.

50. B. Graham, quoted in Shellenbarger, 1998.

51. The use of magnetic resonance imaging to isolate the processing bottleneck in the brain and measure the efficiency loss of trying to handle more than one task simultaneously is described in P. E. Dux, J. Ivanoff, C. L. Asplund, and R. Marois, "Neuron Isolation of a Central Bottleneck of Information Processing with Time-Resolved fMRI," *Neuron,* December 21, 2006, pp. 1109–1120.

52. S. Winston, quoted in A. Fisher, "Get Organized at Work—Painlessly," *Fortune,* January 10, 2005, p. 30.

53. Survey by global management-consulting company Accenture Ltd., cited in S. E. Needleman, "How Organization Helps Make Most of a Workday," *The Wall Street Journal,* January 9, 2007, p. B7.

54. J. Cassidy, "Me Media," *The New Yorker,* May 15, 2006, pp. 50–59. See also A. Saracevic, "Facebook Will Protect You—Sort of," *San Francisco Chronicle,* May 9, 2006, p. C3; "Mark Zuckerberg," Wikipedia, http://en.wikipedia.org/wiki/Mark_Zuckerberg (accessed June 8, 2006); "Exclusive Interview with Mark Zuckerberg," Current Magazine— MSNBC.com, November 30, 2004, www.msnbc.com/id/6596533/site/newsweek (accessed June 8, 2006); V. Vara, "Facebook Gets Help from Its Friends," *The Wall Street Journal,* June 22, 2007, pp. B1, B2; E. Lee, "Making Amends," *San Francisco Chronicle,* September 12, 2006, pp. D1, D7; J. Swartz, "Tech Giants Poke Around Facebook," *USA Today,* October 3, 2007, pp. 1B, 2B; B. Stone, "In Facebook, Investing in a Theory," *The New York Times,* October 4, 2007, pp. C1, C2; E. Lee and R. Kim, "Microsoft's Big Bet," *San Francisco Chronicle,* October 25, 2007, pp. A1, A10; and R. Kim, "He's 23, Rich, and Seems Unfazed," *San Francisco Chronicle,* October 25, 2007, pp. C1, C6.

55. D. Farber, "Facebook Could Surpass 200 Million Users in a Year," *ZDNet,* September 9, 2007, http://blogs.zdnet.com/BTL/?p=6195 (accessed January 24, 2008).

56. S. Perman, "The Entrepreneurial Melting Pot," BusinessWeek Online, June 6, 2005; www.businessweek.com/smallbiz/content/jun2006/sb20060606_980_521.htm?chan=smallbiz_smallbiz+index+page_getting+started (accessed June 8, 2006). See also J. Mehring, "The Real Job Engines," *BusinessWeek SmallBiz,* Spring 2006, p. 42; and A. Weintraub, "Hot Growth," *BusinessWeek,* June 5, 2006, pp. 48–52.

57. N. Templin, "Boutique-Hotel Group Thrives on Quirks," *The Wall Street Journal,* March 1999, pp. B1, B9; and K. Howe, D. Tong, D. Armstrong, S. Corder, and C. Benson, "Joie de Vivre Hospitality—On the Record: Chip Conley," *San Francisco Chronicle,* August 7, 2005, p. E-1.

58. J. M. Higgins, "Innovate or Evaporate: Seven Secrets of Innovative Corporations," *The Futurist,* September–October 1995, pp. 42–43; K. Yakal, "Now You Can Use Your Post-It Notes Electronically," *Computer Shopper,* June 1997, p. 547; and "A Notable Idea," *Selling Power,* May 1998, p. 81.

59. P. F. Drucker, *Innovation and Entrepreneurship* (New York: Harper & Row, 1986), pp. 27–28.

60. A. M. Webber, "Danger: Toxic Company," *Fast Company,* November 1998, pp. 152–161.

61. Bureau of Labor Statistics, 1998.

62. D. C. McClelland, *The Achieving Society* (New York: Van Nostrand, 1961); D. C. McClelland, *Human Motivation* (Glenview, IL: Scott, Foresman, 1985); D. L. Sexton and N. Bowman, "The Entrepreneur: A Capable Executive and More," *Journal of Business Venturing* 1 (1985), pp. 129–140; D. Hisrich, "Entrepreneurship/Intrapreneurship," *American Psychologist,* February 1990, p. 218; T. Begley and D. P. Boyd, "Psychological Characteristics Associated with Performance in Entrepreneurial Firms and Smaller Businesses," *Journal of Business Venturing* 2 (1987), pp. 79–93; and C. R. Kuehl and P. A. Lambing, *Small Business: Planning and Management* (Fort Worth, TX: Dryden Press, 1990).

63. Global Entrepreneurship Monitor, 2002 study by London Business School and Babson College, reported in J. Bailey, "Desire—More Than Need—Builds a Business," *The Wall Street Journal,* May 21, 2002, p. B4.

64. R. L. Katz, "Skills of an Effective Administrator," *Harvard Business Review,* September–October, 1974, p. 94. Also see M. K. De Vries, "The Eight Roles Executives Play," *Organizational Dynamics,* 2007, pp. 28–44.

65. Sara Levinson, quoted in Lowry, 2006, p. 60.
66. Lowry, 2006, p. 55.
67. CEO recruiter, quoted in Colvin, 2006.
68. Colvin, 2006.
69. D. Shoemaker, quoted in I. DeBare, "The Incredible Growing Workweek," *San Francisco Chronicle,* February 12, 1999, pp. B1, B2.
70. E. B. Zechmeister and S. E. Nyberg, *Human Memory: An Introduction to Research and Theory* (Pacific Grove, CA: Brooks/Cole, 1982).
71. B. K. Bromage and R. E. Meyer, "Quantitative and Qualitative Effects of Repetition on Learning from Technical Text," *Journal of Educational Psychology,* 1982, vol. 78, pp. 271–278.
72. F. P. Robinson, *Effective Study,* 4th ed. (New York: Harper & Row, 1970).
73. H. C. Lindgren, The *Psychology of College Success: A Dynamic Approach* (New York: Wiley, 1969).
74. R. J. Palkovitz and R. K. Lore, "Note Taking and Note Review: Why Students Fail Questions Based on Lecture Material," *Teaching of Psychology, 7*(1980), pp. 159–161.
75. J. Langan and J. Nadell, *Doing Well in College: A Concise Guide to Reading, Writing, and Study Skills* (New York: McGraw-Hill, 1980), pp. 93–110.
76. Palkovitz and Lore, 1980, pp. 159–161.

CHAPTER 2

1. C. Hymowitz, "Executives Must Stop Jumping Fad to Fad and Learn to Manage," *The Wall Street Journal,* May 15, 2006, p. B1.
2. D. M. Rosseau, "Is There Such a Thing as 'Evidence-Based Management'?" *Academy of Management Review,* April 2006, pp. 256–269.
3. J. Pfeffer and R. I. Sutton, "Profiting from Evidence-Based Management," *Strategy & Leadership* 34, no. 2 (2006), pp. 35–42; and J. Pfeffer and R. I. Sutton, "Evidence-Based Management," *Harvard Business Review,* January 2006, pp. 63–74. Pfeffer and Sutton have also produced a book, *Hard Facts, Danger Half-Truths, and Total Nonsense* (Boston: Harvard Business School Press, 2006). For a discussion of this book, see Hymowitz, 2006.
4. R. I. Sutton, interviewed in "Asked & Answered: Prove It," *Stanford Magazine,* May/June 2006, http://www.stanfordalumni.org/news/magazine/2006/mayjun/dept/management.html (accessed January 28, 2008).
5. Tom Peters, quoted in J. A. Byrne, "The Man Who Invented Management," *BusinessWeek,* November 28, 2005, http://www.businessweek.com/magazine/content/05_48/b3961001.htm (accessed January 28, 2008).
6. Byrne, 2005. See also R. Karlgaard, "Peter Drucker on Leadership," *Forbes.com,* November 19, 2004, http://www.forbes.com/2004/11/19/cz_rk_1119drucker.html; B. J. Feder, "Peter F. Drucker, a Pioneer in Social and Management Theory, Is Dead at 95," *The New York Times,* November 12, 2005, http://www.nytimes.com/2005/11/12/business/12drucker.html; and P. Sullivan, "Management Visionary Peter Drucker Dies," *The Washington Post,* November 12, 2005, http://www.washingtonpost.com/wp-dyn/content/article/2005/11/11/AR2005111101938.html (all accessed January 28, 2008).
7. Pfeffer and Sutton, "Profiting from Evidence-Based Management," 2006.
8. C. M. Christensen and M. E. Raynor, "Why Hard-Nosed Executives Should Care about Management Theory," *Harvard Business Review,* September 2003, pp. 67–74.
9. Christensen and Raynor, 2003, p. 68.
10. G. Hamel, *The Future of Management* (Boston: Harvard Business School Press, 2007).
11. A. Webber, "The Best Organization Is No Organization," *USA Today,* March 6, 1997, p. 13A.
12. "The Leader as Naval Architect: Beyond the Spaghetti Organization," interview with Lars Kolind, *Wharton @ Work: e-Buzz,* July 2005; http://execed-web.wharton.upenn.edu/ebuzz/0507/fellows.html (accessed May 23, 2006). See also N. J. Foss, "Selective Intervention and Internal Hybrids: Interpreting and Learning from the Rise and Decline of the Oticon Spaghetti Organization," *Organization Science* 14(2003), pp. 331–349.
13. A. Maslow, "A Theory of Human Motivation," *Psychological Review,* July 1943, pp. 370–396.
14. D. McGregor, *The Human Side of Enterprise* (New York: McGraw-Hill, 1960).
15. See J. T. Delaney, "Workplace Cooperation: Current Problems, New Approaches," *Journal of Labor Research,* Winter 1996, pp. 45–61; H. Mintzberg, D. Dougherty, J. Jorgensen, and F. Westley, "Some Surprising Things About Collaboration— Knowing How People Connect Makes It Work Better," *Organizational Dynamics,* Spring 1996, pp. 60–71; R. Crow, "Institutionalized Competition and Its Effects on Teamwork," *Journal for Quality and Participation,* June 1995, pp. 46–54; K. G. Smith, S. J. Carroll, and S. J. Ashford, "Intra- and Interorganizational Cooperation: Toward a Research Agenda," *Academy of Management Journal,* February 1995, pp. 7–23; M. E. Haskins, J. Liedtka, and J. Rosenblum, "Beyond Teams: Toward an Ethic of Collaboration," *Organizational Dynamics,* Spring 1998, pp. 34–50; and C. C. Chen, X. P. Chen, and J. R. Meindl, "How Can Cooperation Be Fostered? The Cultural Effects of Individualism-Collectivism," *Academy of Management Review,* April 1998, pp. 285–304.
16. A. Kohn, "How to Succeed without Even Vying," *Psychology Today,* September 1986, pp. 27–28. Sports psychologists discuss "cooperative competition" in S. Sleek, "Competition: Who's the Real Opponent?" *APA Monitor,* July 1996, p. 8.
17. D. W. Johnson, G. Maruyama, R. Johnson, D. Nelson, and L. Skon, "Effects of Cooperative, Competitive, and Individualistic Goal Structures on Achievement: A Meta-Analysis," *Psychological Bulletin,* January 1981, pp. 56–57. An alternative interpretation of the foregoing study that emphasizes the influence of situational factors can be found in J. L. Cotton and M. S. Cook, "Meta-Analysis and the Effects of Various Reward Systems: Some Different Conclusions from Johnson et al.," *Psychological Bulletin,* July 1982, pp. 176–183. Also see A. E. Ortiz, D. W. Johnson, and R. T. Johnson, "The Effect of Positive Goal and Resource Interdependence on Individual Performance," *The Journal of Social Psychology,* April 1996, pp. 243–249; and S. L. Gaertner, J. F. Dovidio, M. C. Rust, J. A. Nier, B. S. Banker, C. M. Ward, G. R. Mottola, and M. Houlette, "Reducing Intergroup Bias: Elements of Intergroup Cooperation," *Journal of Personality and Social Psychology,* March 1999, pp. 388–402.
18. E. Perkins, "How to Book Hotel Rooms at Half the Price," *San Francisco Examiner,* December 13, 1998, p. T-2.
19. R. W. Belsky, "Being Hotel Savvy," *The Dollar Stretcher;* www.stretcher.com/stories/00/000515c.cfm (accessed March 25, 2004).
20. S. F. Brown, "Wresting New Wealth from the Supply Chain," *Fortune,* November 9, 1998, pp. 204[C]–204[Z]. See also M. Maynard, "Toyota Shows Big Three How It's Done," *The New York Times,* January 13, 2006, pp. C1, C4.
21. B. Wysocki Jr., "To Fix Health Care, Hospitals Take Tips from Factory Floor," *The Wall Street Journal,* April 9, 2004, pp. A1, A6.

22. For a description of Generation X characteristics, see N. A. Hira, "You Raised Them, Now Manage Them," *Fortune,* May 28, 2007, pp. 38–46.

23. J. Strasburg, "Shaking the Blues," *San Francisco Chronicle,* February 3, 2002, pp. GI, G3; N. Munk, "How Levi's Trashed a Great American Brand," *Fortune,* April l2, 1999, pp. 83–90; and E. Neuborne, K. Kerwin, and bureau reports, "Generation Y," *BusinessWeek,* February l5, 1999, pp. 80–88.

24. N. Klein, *No Logo: Taking Aim at the Brand Bullies* (New York: St. Martin's Press, 1999).

25. R. Jana, "Riding Hip Jeans into New Luxury Markets," *BusinessWeek,* January 22, 2007, http://www.businessweek.com/print/innovate/content/jan2007/id20070122_366747.htm (accessed January 28, 2008).

26. NPD Group retail analyst Marshal Cohen, cited in P. Sarkar, "Stores Boost Sales with Own Labels," *San Francisco Chronicle,* May 5, 2006, pp. DI, D6.

27. J. Schlosser, "Teacher's Bet," *Fortune,* March 8, 2004, pp. l58–164.

28. G. Loveman, "Diamonds in the Data Mine," *Harvard Business Review,* May 2003, pp. l09–113.

29. L. Walker, "Data-Mining Software Digs for Business Leads," *San Francisco Chronicle,* March 8, 2004, p. E6; reprinted from *Washington Post.*

30. S. Saul, "Doctors Object as Drug Makers Learn Who's Prescribing What," *The New York Times,* May 4, 2006, pp. AI, C4.

31. E. J. Langer, *Mindfulness* (Reading, MA: Addison-Wesley, 1989). See also D. J. Siegel, *The Mindful Brain: Reflection and Attunement in the Cultivation of Well-Being* (New York: W.W. Norton, 2007); and M. Landau, "When Doctors Negotiate Uncertainty," *Focus Online: News from Harvard Medical, Dental, and Public Health Schools,* May 4, 2007, http://focus.hms.harvard.edu/2007/050407/education.shtml (accessed February 20, 2008).

32. E. J. Langer, *The Power of Mindful Learning* (Reading, MA: Addison-Wesley, 1997), p. 4.

33. Langer, 1989, pp. l2–13.

34. Langer, 1989, p. 69.

35. P. Senge, *The Fifth Discipline* (New York: Doubleday, 1990), p. I.

36. R. Hodgetts, F. Luthans, and S. Lee, "New Paradigm Organizations: From Total Quality to Learning to World-Class," *Organizational Dynamics,* Winter 1994, pp. 5–19D; and A. Garvin, "Building a Learning Organization," *Harvard Business Review,* July/August 1993, pp. 78–91.

37. A. S. Miner and S. J. Mezias, "Ugly Duckling No More: Pasts and Futures of Organizational Learning Research," *Organization Science,* January–February 1996, pp. 88–99; and R. P. Mai, *Learning Partnerships: How Leading American Companies Implement Organizational Learning* (Chicago: Irwin, 1996).

38. B. Breen, "How EDS Got Its Groove Back," *Fast Company,* September 2001, p. 106.

39. D. M. Noer, *Breaking Free: A Prescription for Personal and Organizational Change* (San Francisco: Jossey-Bass, 1996); S. F. Slater, "Learning to Change," *Business Horizons,* November–December 1995, pp. 13–20; and D. Ulrich, T. Jick, and M. Von Glinow, "High-Impact Learning: Building and Diffusing Learning Capability," *Organizational Dynamics,* Autumn 1993, pp. 52–66.

40. M. J. Mandel and R. D. Hof, "Rethinking the Internet," *BusinessWeek,* March 26, 2001, p. 118.

41. Adapted from "Virtual Organization," Whatis.com; http://whatis.techtarget.com/definition/0,,sid9_gci213301,00.html (accessed June 12, 2006).

42. Adapted from "Boundaryless," *Encyclopedia of Small Business,* ed. K. Hillstrom and L. C. Hillstrom (Farmington Hills, MI: Thomson Gale, 2002, and Seattle, WA: eNotes. com, 2006) http://business.enotes.com/small-business-encyclopedia/boundaryless (accessed June 12, 2006). Regarding the impact of Web services on organizational boundaries, see R. D. Hof, "Web 2.0: The New Guy at Work," *BusinessWeek,* June 19, 2006, pp. 58–59.

43. S. Hamm, "Speed Demons," *BusinessWeek,* March 27, 2006, pp. 68–75. See also J. McGregor, "The World's Most Innovative Companies," *BusinessWeek,* April 24, 2006, pp. 63–74.

44. B. E. Becker, M. A. Huselid, and D. Ulrich, *The HR Scorecard: Linking People, Strategy, and Performance* (Boston: Harvard Business School Press, 2001), p. 4; and G. Gohlander, S. Snell, and A. Sherman, *Managing Human Resources,* 13th ed. (Mason, OH: South-Western Publishing, 2004).

45. S. Meisinger, "Taking the Measure of Human Capital," *HR Magazine,* January 2003, p. 10. See also R. J. Grossman, "Blind Investment," *HR Magazine,* January 2005, pp. 40–47; and *Unlocking the DNA of the Adaptable Workforce: The Global Human Capital Study 2008,* IBM Global Services, http://www.935.ibm.com/services/us/gbs/bus/html/2008ghcs.html (accessed February 20, 2008).

46. Inspired by P. S. Adler and S. Kwon, "Social Capital: Prospects for New Concept," *Academy of Management Review,* January 2002, pp. 17—40. See also R. A. Baaron and G. D. Markman, "Beyond Social Capital: How Social Skills Can Enhance Entrepreneurs' Success," *Academy of Management Executive,* February 2000, pp. 106–116; and L. Prusak and D. Cohen, "How to Invest in Social Capital," *BusinessWeek Online,* October 23, 2007, http://www.businessweek.com/managing/content/oct2007/ca20071023_070114.htm?chan=search (accessed February 20, 2008).

47. Data from "What Makes a Job Okay," *USA Today,* May 15, 2000, p. IB.

48. J. Pfeffer and R. I. Sutton, "Evidence-Based Management," *Harvard Business Review,* January 2006, pp. 63–74. See also D. M. Rousseau, "Is There Such a Thing as 'Evidence-Based Management'?" *Academy of Management Review,* April 2006, pp. 256–269.

49. J. Pfeffer and R. I. Sutton, "Profiting from Evidence-Based Management," *Strategy & Leadership* 34(2) (2006), pp. 35–42.

50. M. Arndt, "Built for the Long Haul," *BusinessWeek,* January 30, 2006, p. 66.

CHAPTER 3
----

1. J. Pfeffer, in A. M. Webber, "Danger: Toxic Company," *Fast Company,* November 1998, pp. 152–161.

2. J. Pfeffer, *The Human Equation: Building Profits by Putting People First* (Boston: Harvard Business School Press, 1996).

3. K. Carney, "How to Keep Staff in a Boom Economy," *Inc.,* November 1998, p. 110.

4. S. Shellenbarger, "More Firms Siding with Employees, Bid Bad Clients Farewell," *The Wall Street Journal*, February 16, 2000, p. BI; and P. J. Frost, *Toxic Emotions at Work: How Compassionate Managers Handle Pain and Conflict* (Boston: Harvard Business School Press, 2002), http://books.google.com/books?id = FOrQrRYw4vOC&pg = PAI77&lpg = PAI77&dq = %22 Benjamin+Group%22+clients&source = web&ots = AI3Hh7ZJrt&sig=_hwZC67n9mMF3OXT9zrmFdcML2c (accessed February 22, 2008).

5. J. Case, *Open-Book Management: The Coming Business Revolution* (New York: HarperBusiness, 1996).

6. C. Kleiman, "Companies Embracing 'Open-Book' Management," *San Jose Mercury News,* May 18, 1997, pp. PCI, PC2.

7. G. T. Brown, quoted in Kleiman, 1997.

8. A. Zimmerman, "Costco's Dilemma: Be Kind to Its Workers, or Wall Street?" *The Wall Street Journal*, March 26, 2004, pp. B1, B3; J. Flanigan, "Costco Sees Value in Higher Pay," *Los Angeles Times,* February 15, 2004, www.latimes.com/business/la-fi-flan15feb15,1,61048 (accessed March 29, 2008); and C. Frey, "Costco's Love of Labor: Employees' Well-being Key to Its Success," *Seattle Post-Intelligencer*, March 29, 2004, http://seattlepi.nwsource.com/business/166680_costco29.html (accessed March 29, 2008); S. Greenhouse, "How Costco Became the Anti-Wal-Mart," *The New York Times,* July 17, 2005, sec. 7, p. 1; C. Migden, "Wal-Mart Must Pay Its Share," *San Francisco Chronicle*, March 16, 2006, p. B9; and B. Saporito, "Restoring Wal-Mart," *Time*, November 12, 2007, pp. 46–52.

9. J. Useem, "Should We Admire Wal-Mart?" *Fortune*, March 8, 2004, pp. 118–120.

10. Zimmerman, 2004, p. B1.

11. "Store Wars: When Wal-Mart Comes to Town," *PBS*, February 24, 2007.

12. D. Leonhardt, "The Economics of Henry Ford May Be Passé," *The New York Times*, April 5, 2006, pp. C1, C12.

13. R. B. Reich, "The Company of the Future," *Fast Company*, November 1998, pp. 124–150.

14. For more on Employee Stock Ownership Plans (ESOPs), see I. DeBare, "Stock Plan Transfers Ownership to Employees," *San Francisco Chronicle*, May 15, 2006, pp. C1, C4; J. Raymond, "Unlikely Pioneers," *BusinessWeek SmallBiz*, Spring 2006, pp. 56–59; and W. C. Taylor, "These Workers Act Like Owners (Because They Are)," *The New York Times*, May 21, 2006, sec. 3, p. 5.

15. J. Nocera, "Put Buyers First? What a Concept," *The New York Times*, January 5, 2008, pp. B1, B9.

16. Jeff Bezos, quoted in Nocera, 2008, p. B9.

17. B. De Lollis and R. Yu, "Indie Hotels Cater to Elite Travelers," *USA Today*, January 29, 2008, p. 4B.

18. Bureau of Labor Statistics, U.S. Department of Labor, "Union Members in 2007," *Union Members Summary*, January 25, 2008, www.bls.gov/news.release/union2.nr0.htm (accessed February 25, 2008).

19. R. Pollin, "In Politics: Savvy Organizers Win 'Living Wage' Across U.S.," *San Jose Mercury News*, December 6, 1998, pp. 1P, 6P.

20. L. Atkinson and J. Galaskiewicz, "Stock Ownership and Company Contributions to Charity," *Administrative Science Quarterly* 33 (1988), pp. 82–100.

21. Associated Press, "Hundreds Could Leave Indiana for GM Jobs Elsewhere," Theindychannel.com, February 10, 2008, http://www.theindychannel.com/news/15266008/detail.html (accessed February 24, 2008).

22. J. M. Peters and M. Maynard, "Company Town Relies on G. M. Long After Plants Have Closed," *The New York Times*, February 20, 2006, pp. A1, A12.

23. N. Shirouzu, "As Detroit Slashes Car Jobs, Southern Towns Pick Up Slack," *The Wall Street Journal*, February 1, 2006, pp. A1, A12.

24. A. Gentleman, "Gap Vows to Combat Child Labor at Suppliers," *The New York Times*, November 16, 2007, p. C6.

25. For a discussion of how politically passionate consumers take aim at certain businesses, see R. S. Dunham, "Companies in the Crossfire," *BusinessWeek*, April 17, 2006, pp. 30–33.

26. See, for example, F. Barringer, "$92 Million More Is Sought for Exxon Valdez Cleanup," *The New York Times*, June 2, 2006, p. A13; and R. D'Oro, "Alaskans Await Ruling on Exxon *Valdez*," *Reno Gazette-Journal*, February 26, 2008, p. 5B.

27. S. Chandra, "U.S. Productivity Increases 1.8%, More Than Forecast," *Bloomberg.com,* February 6, 2008, http://www.bloomberg.com/apps/news?pid=20601087&refer=home&sid=ag2qO2Nt5HcY (accessed February 25, 2008).

28. Doug, quoted in C. Sutton, "Designing Women Show Off Their Marks," *San Francisco Examiner*, March 7, 1999, p. W-33.

29. M. Kabel, "Diet Trends Affect U.S. Meat Glut," *Reno Gazette-Journal*, May 16, 2006, p. 4D.

30. N. Hellmich, "Restaurants as Obesity Cops Doesn't Sit Well," *USA Today*, February 6, 2008, p. 9A.

31. Data analyzed by Associated Press from Centers for Disease Control and Prevention and from Population Reference Bureau, reported in M. Stobbe, "More Babies Born in U.S., Unlike Trend in Europe," *San Francisco Chronicle*, January 16, 2008, p. A8.

32. J. Passel and D'V. Cohn, *Immigration to Play Lead Role in Future U.S. Growth,* Pew Research Center, February 11, 2008, http://pewresearch.org/pubs/729/united-states-population-projections (accessed February 25, 2008).

33. M. Galanter, reported in W. Glaberson, "When the Verdict Is Just a Fantasy," *The New York Times*, June 6, 1999, sec. 4 pp. 1, 6.

34. D. Bass, "Microsoft Makes Changes to Ease EU Competition," *Boomberg.com*, February 21, 2008, http://www.bloomberg.com/apps/news?pid=20601087&sid=azE39eAmWCLU&refer=home (accessed February 25, 2008).

35. American Council on Education, reported by P. Wingert, "'F' in Global Competence," *Newsweek,* May 20, 2002, p. 11. See also D. J. Lynch, "U.S. Firms Becoming Tongue-Tied," *USA Today,* February 9, 2006, p. 6B; and "Execs Learning to Speak Second Language," *Reno Gazette-Journal*, May 5, 2006, p. 6D.

36. G. Allred, quoted in S. Armour, "Facing a Tough Choice: Your Ethics or Your Job," *USA Today*, September 21, 1998, p. B1.

37. L. T. Hosmer, *The Ethics of Management* (Homewood, IL: Irwin, 1987). See also S. Welch, "The Uh-Oh Feeling," *O Magazine,* November 2007, pp. 117–120. For more on money-and-ethics matters, see J. Fleming and L. Schwartz, *Isn't It Their Turn to Pick Up the Check?* (New York: Free Press, 2008).

38. Study by LRN, consultant on corporate ethics, cited in "Corporate Ethics Affect Employee Productivity," *HR Magazine,* July 2007, p. 16.

39. S. Saul, "Unease on Industry's Role in Hypertension Debate," *The New York Times*, May 20, 2006, pp. A1, B9; and C. Arnst, "Hey, You Don't Look So Good," *BusinessWeek*, May 8, 2006, pp. 30–32. For the results of a survey concerning doctors' ethics, see E. G. Campbell, S. Regan, R. L. Gruen, T. G. Ferris, S. R. Rao, P. D. Cleary, and D. Blumenthal, "Professionalism in Medicine: Results of a National Survey of Physicians," *Annals of Internal Medicine*, December 4, 2007, pp. 795–802.

40. B. Kabanoff, "Equity, Equality, Power, and Conflict," *Academy of Management Review,* April 1991, pp. 416–441.

41. D. Fritzsche and H. Baker, "Linking Management Behavior to Ethical Philosophy: An Empirical Investigation," *Academy of Management Journal*, March 1984, pp. 166–175.

42. Associated Press, "Pacific Salmon to Stay on Endangered List," May 28, 2004, http://msnbc.msn.com/id/5085081, and "Chemicals in Our Water Are Affecting Humans and Aquatic Life in Unanticipated Ways," *Science Daily*, February 21, 2008, http://www.sciencedaily.com/releases/2008/02/080216095740.htm (both accessed February 26, 2008).

43. J. Sandberg, "Monitoring of Workers Is Boss's Right but Why Not Include Top Brass," *The Wall Street Journal*, May 18, 2005, p. B1.

44. G. Morgenson, "The Big Winner, Again, Is 'Scandalot,'" *The New York Times*, January 1, 2006, sec. 3, pp. 1, 7; C. Said, "From White Collars to Prison Blues," *San Francisco Chronicle*, May 26, 2006, pp. D1, D6; G. Morgenson, "Are Enrons Bustin' Out All Over?" *The New York Times*, May 28, 2006, sec. 3, pp. 1, 8; K. Clark and M. Lavelle, "Guilty as Charged!" *U.S. News & World Report*, June 5, 2006, A. Sloan, "Laying Enron to Rest," *Newsweek*, June 5, 2006, pp. 25–30, pp. 44–45; M. Gimein, "The Skilling Trap," *BusinessWeek*, June 12, 2006, pp. 31–32. See also S. Labaton, "Four Years Later, Enron's Shadow Lingers as Change Comes Slowly," *The New York Times*, January 5, 2006, pp. C1, C4; J. H. Zamansky, "At the Least, Former Enron Chiefs Are Guilty of Moral Bankruptcy," *USA Today*, February 1, 2006, p. 11A; A. Shell, "Enron Verdicts Good for Investors," *USA Today*, May 30, 2006, p. 1B; K. Eichenwald and A. Barrionuevo, "Enron Shows Businesses Face Tough Tactics," *The New York Times,* May 27, 2006, pp. A1, B4; and D. Glovin, "Refco Ex-Finance Chief Trosten Pleads Guilty to Fraud," *Bloomberg.com*, February 20, 2008, http://www.bloomberg.com/apps/news?pid=20601087&sid=aBl5wsezRDT4&refer=home# (accessed February 26, 2008).

45. See D. R. Dalton and C. M. Dalton, "Sarbanes-Oxley Legislation and the Private Company: If Not a Marriage, Then Certainly an Engagement," *Journal of Business Strategy,* February 2005, pp. 7–8; E. Iwata, "CEOs Report Stricter Rules," *USA Today,* March 20, 2006, p. 1B; D. A. Moore, "SarbOx Doesn't Go Far Enough," *BusinessWeek*, April 17, 2006, p. 112; V. Anand and L. Arnold, "Sarbanes-Oxley Hurts Some Firms, Says GAO," *San Francisco Chronicle*, May 9, 2006, p. C3; J. H. Quigley, "Please Be Patient," *The Wall Street Journal,* May 25, 2006, p. A14; "SOX: No One-Size-Fits-All Solution to Dishonest Accounting," Knowledge@W.P.Carey, June 7, 2006, http://knowledge.wpcarey.asu.edu/index.cfm?fa=viewArticle&id=1259 (accessed June 23, 2006); "Research Supports Value of IT Consults in Post-SOX Age," Knowledge@W.P.Carey, June 7, 2006, http://knowledge.wpcarey.asu.edu/index.cfm?fa=view Article&id=1261 (accessed June 23, 2006); and W. Cienke, "Small Companies Also Can Benefit from Sarbanes-Oxley," *Small Business Times*, February 22, 2008, http://www.biztimes.com/news/2008/2/22/small-companies-also-can-benefit-from-sarbanes-oxley (accessed February 26, 2008).

46. F. J. Evans, quoted in C. S. Stewart, "A Question of Ethics: How to Teach Them?" *The New York Times*, March 21, 2004, sec. 3, p. 11.

47. Research by the Center for Academic Integrity, Kenan Institute for Ethics, Duke University, cited in H. Oh, "Biz Majors Get an F for Honesty," *BusinessWeek*, February 6, 2006, p. 14.

48. L. Kohlberg, "Moral Stages and Moralization: The Cognitive-Developmental Approach," in T. Lickona, ed., *Moral Development and Behavior: Theory, Research, and Social Issues* (New York: Holt, Rinehart and Winston, 1976), pp. 31–53; and J. W. Graham, "Leadership, Moral Development and Citizenship Behavior," *Business Ethics Quarterly*, January 1995, pp. 43–54. See also S. J. Reynolds and T. L. Ceranic, "The Effects of Moral Judgment and Moral Identity on Moral Behavior: An Empirical Examination of the Moral Individual," *Journal of Applied Psychology,* November 2007, pp. 1610–1624.

49. M. C. Gross, quoted in C. Hymowitz, "CEOs Set the Tone for How to Handle Questions of Ethics," *The Wall Street Journal*, December 22, 1998, p. B1.

50. A. Bennett, "Ethics Codes Spread Despite Criticism," *The Wall Street Journal*, July 15, 1988, p. 13.

51. Society for Human Resource Management Weekly Survey, 2005, cited in J. Thilmany, *HR Magazine*, September 2007, pp. 105–112.

52. T. R. Mitchell, D. Daniels, H. Hopper, J. George-Falvy, and G. R. Ferris, "Perceived Correlates of Illegal Behavior in Organizations," *Journal of Business Ethics*, April 1996, pp. 439–455. See also M. W., "Ethics Training Works," *Training,* November 2005, p. 15; L. Paine, R. Deshpandé, J. D. Margolis, and K. E. Bettcher, "Up to Code: Does Your Company's Conduct Meet World-Class Standards?" *Harvard Business Review*, December 1, 2005, pp. 122–135; and J. Brockner, "Why It's So Hard to Be Fair," *Harvard Business Review,* March 1, 2006, p. 122–132.

53. R. Pear, "Whistleblowers Likely to Get Stronger Federal Protections," *The New York Times*, March 15, 1999, pp. A1, A17.

54. Study by C. C. Masten, inspector general, U.S. Department of Labor, reported in Pear, 1999.

55. I. J. A. Dyck, A. Morse, and L. Zingales, "Who Blows the Whistle on Corporate Fraud?" AFA Chicago Meetings Paper, February 2007, http://ssrn.com/abstract=891482. See also "Fraud Study Says Whistleblowers Are the Most Common Means of Identifying Fraud, but This Comes at a High Personal Cost When Whistleblower Anonymity Is Not Maintained," *Fulcrum Inquiry*, February 2007, http://www.fulcruminquiry.com/Whistleblower_Fraud_Study.htm (both accessed February 26, 2008).

56. T. Herman, "Tipster Rewards Require Patience," *The Wall Street Journal*, December 26, 2007, p. D3.

57. L. Greenhouse, "Some Whistle-Blowers Lose Free-Speech Protections," *The New York Times*, May 31, 2006, p. A14; and D. G. Savage, "Ruling Limits Free Speech at Work," *San Francisco Chronicle*, May 31, 2006, p. A3, reprinted from *Los Angeles Times.* See also "Blow the Whistle, Loudly" [editorial], *The New York Times*, May 31, 2006, p. A22; and "Blow to Whistle-Blowers" [editorial], *San Francisco Chronicle*, June 2, 2006, p. B10.

58. A. B. Carroll, "Managing Ethically with Global Stakeholders: A Present and Future Challenge," *Academy of Management Executive,* May 2004, p. 118. Also see B. W. Husted and D. B. Allen, "Corporate Social Responsibility in the Multinational Enterprise: Strategic and Institutional Approaches," *Journal of International Business Studies,* November 2006, pp. 838–849.

59. P. Engardio, "Beyond the Green Corporation," *BusinessWeek,* January 29, 2007, pp. 50–64.

60. M. Friedman, *Capitalism and Freedom* (Chicago: University of Chicago Press, 1962). See also S. Gallagher, "A Strategic Response to Freidman's Critique of Business Ethics," *Journal of Business Strategy,* January 2005, pp. 55–60.

61. P. Samuelson, "Love that Corporation," *Mountain Bell Magazine,* Spring 1971.

62. Jed Emerson, quoted in C. Dahle, "60 Seconds with Jed Emerson," *Fast Company*, March 2004, p. 42.

63. J. Emerson, "The Nature of Returns: A Social Capital Markets Inquiry into Elements of Investment and the Blended Value Proposition," *Social Enterprise Series No. 17* (Boston: Harvard Business School Press, 2000), p. 36.

64. T. Howard, "Being Eco-Friendly Can Pay Economically," *USA Today*, August 15, 2005, p. 7B; D. Fonda, "G.E.'s Green Awakening," *Time Inside Business*, August 2005, pp. A10–A16; "The Business of Green" [special section], *The New York Times,* May 17, 2006, pp. E1–12.

65. A. Gore, *An Inconvenient Truth* (Emmaus, PA: Rodale, 2006). See also A. Gore and D. Blood, "For People and Planet," *The Wall Street Journal*, March 28, 2006, p. A20.

66. This definition of *sustainability* was developed in 1987 by the World Commission on Environment and Development.

67. M. L. Wald, "What's Kind to Nature Can Be Kind to Products," *The New York Times,* May 17, 2006, pp. E1, E5.

68. Wald, 2006, p. E5. See also J. Carroll, "Exxon Faces Pressure over Environment and Gay Rights," *San Francisco Chronicle,* May 31, 2006, p. C3.

69. Alan Werbach, quoted in B. Snider, "Werbach at Wal-Mart?" *San Francisco Chronicle Magazine,* January 6, 2008, pp. 14–21.

70. United Nations Intergovernmental Panel on Climate Change, Fourth Assessment Report, *Climate Change 2007: Synthesis Report, Summary for Policy Makers,* November 2007,

71. B. J. Creyts, A. Derkach, S. Nyquist, K. Ostrowski, and J. Stephenson, *Reducing U.S. Greenhouse Gas Emissions: How Much at What Cost?* U.S. Greenhouse Gas Abatement Mapping Initiative, Executive Report, December 2007, McKinsey & Company, www.mckinsey.com/clientservice/ccsi/pdf/US_ghg_final_report.pdf (accessed February 23, 2008). See also M. L. Wald, "Study Details How U.S. Could Cut 28% of Greenhouse Gases," *The New York Times,* November 30, 2007, p. C5.

72. Center for Small Business and the Environment, reported in E. Iwata, "Small Businesses Take Big Steps into Green Practices," *USA Today,* December 3, 2007, p. 4B.

73. See R. J. Samuelson, "Greenhouse Simplicities," *Newsweek,* August 27, 2007, p. 47. Also see R. Abrams, "Going Green Makes Good Business Sense," *Reno Gazette-Journal,* March 13, 2007, p. 6D; C. H. Deutsch, "For Suppliers, the Pressure Is On," *The New York Times,* November 7, 2007, pp. H1, H11; B. Feder, "Aiding the Environment, a Nanostep at a Time," *The New York Times,* November 7, 2007, p. H6; A. Martin, "If It's Fresh and Local, Is It Always Greener?" *The New York Times,* December 9, 2007, p. BU11; and J. Carlton, "Tech Aims to Green Up Its Act," *The Wall Street Journal,* January 7, 2008, p. B6.

74. J. Ramirez, "How to Live a Greener Life," *Newsweek,* April 16, 2007, p. 82.

75. D. Gross, "Edison's Dimming Bulbs," *Newsweek,* October 15, 2007, p. E22.

76. Ramirez, 2007.

77. D. Ransom, "Consider the Source," *The Wall Street Journal,* November 12, 2007, p. R4.

78. American Wind Energy Association, reported in P. Davidson, "Wind Power Growth Gusts Strongly in U.S.A. in 2007," *USA Today,* January 18, 2008, p. 3B.

79. Iwata, 2007.

80. J. Markoff and S. Lohr, "Gates to Reduce Microsoft Role as Era Changes," *The New York Times,* June 16, 2008, pp. A1, C8; and J. Guynn, "He's Opening Windows to Philanthropy," *San Francisco Chronicle,* June 18, 2006, pp. F1, F5.

81. T. L. O'Brien and S. Saul, "Buffet to Give Bulk of Fortune to Gates Charity," *The New York Times,* June 26, 2006, pp. A1, A15; and D. G. McNeil Jr. and R. Lyman, "Buffet's Billions Will Aid Fight Against Disease," *The New York Times,* June 27, 2006, pp. A1, C4.

82. H. Rubin, "Google's Searches Now Include Ways to Make a Better World," *The New York Times,* January 18, 2008, pp. C1, C5; and K. J. Delaney, "Google: From 'Don't Be Evil' to How to Do Good," *The Wall Street Journal,* January 18, 2008, pp. B1, B2.

83. A.-A. Jarvis, "Pulling Off an Impressive Feet," *Newsweek,* July 3–10, 2006, p. 64.

84. A. Fox, "Corporate Social Responsibility Pays Off," *HR Magazine,* August 2007, pp. 43–47. For an example of an advertising agency that profits from developing social-responsibility campaigns, see S. Kang, "Agency's Social Responsibility Focus," *The Wall Street Journal,* August 17, 2007, p. B3.

85. R. Gildea, "Consumer Survey Confirms Corporate Social Action Affects Buying Decisions," *Public Relations Quarterly,* Winter 1994, pp. 20–21.

86. Caravan survey from Opinion Research developed by LRN of 2,037 adults, reported in "Ethics vs. Price," *USA Today,* June 14, 2006, p. 1B.

87. Results can be found in "Tarnished Employment Brands Affect Recruiting," *HR Magazine,* November 2004, pp. 16, 20.

88. 2003 National Business Ethics Survey, cited in *The Hidden Costs of Unethical Behavior* (Los Angeles: Josephson Institute of Ethics, 2004), p. 3, www.josephsoninstitute.org/pdf/workplace-flier_0604.pdf (accessed June 23, 2006). See also D. Turban and G. Greening, "Corporate Social Performance and Organizational Attractiveness to Prospective Employees," *Academy of Management Journal,* 40 (1997), pp. 658–672.

89. M. Baucus and D. Baucus, "Paying the Piper: An Empirical Examination of Longer-Term Financial Consequences of Illegal Corporate Behavior," *Academy of Management Journal,* 40 (1997), pp. 129–151.

90. 2003 survey by Wirthlin Worldwide, cited in *The Hidden Costs of Unethical Behavior,* p. 2.

91. 2000 National Business Ethics Survey, cited in *The Hidden Costs of Unethical Behavior,* p. 3.

92. "ACFE's Highly-Anticipated Report to the Nation to Be Published in June," preview of *2006 ACFE Report to the Nation on Occupational Fraud & Abuse,* Association of Certified Fraud Examiners http://www.acfe.com/announcement-rttn-preview.asp (accessed June 23, 2006).

93. Ernst & Young survey 2002 and KPMG Fraud Survey 2003, both cited in *The Hidden Costs of Unethical Behavior,* p. 2.

94. 2003 survey by Wirthlin Worldwide, cited in *The Hidden Costs of Unethical Behavior,* p. 2.

95. D. M. Long and S. Rao, "The Wealth Effects of Unethical Business Behavior," *Journal of Economics and Finance,* Summer 1995, pp. 65–73.

96. A discussion of ethics and financial performance is provided by R. M. Fulmer, "The Challenge of Ethical Leadership," *Organizational Dynamics,* August 2004, pp. 307–317.

97. J. C. Day, National Population Projections, U.S. Census Bureau, Population Division and Housing and Household Economics Statistics Division, last revised January 18, 2001, http://www.census.gov/population/www/pop-profile/natproj.html; and U.S. Census Bureau, *Current Population Survey, March and Annual Social and Economic Supplements, 2005 and earlier* (Washington, DC: U.S. Government Printing Office, 2006), http://www.census.gov/population/socdemo/hh-fam/ms2.pdf (both accessed February 27, 2008).

98. Pew Forum on Religion & Public Life, *The U.S. Religious Landscape Survey* (Washington, DC: The Pew Research Center, 2008), http://religions.pewforum.org/reports (accessed February 27, 2008). See also N. Banerjee, "A Fluid Religious Life Is Seen in U.S., with Switches Common," *The New York Times,* February 26, 2008, pp. A1, A12.

99. T. D. Johnson, "Maternity Leave and Employment Patterns of First-Time Mothers, 1961–2003," *Current Population Reports,* February 2008, http://www.census.gov/Press-Release/www/releases/archives/employment_occupations/011536.html (accessed February 27, 2008). See also S. Roberts, "Shifts in Pregnancy and Work," *The New York Times,* February 26, 2008, p. A11.

100. S. E. Page, *The Difference: How the Power of Diversity Creates Better Groups, Firms, Schools and Societies* (Princeton, NJ: Princeton University Press, 2007).

101. S. E. Page, quoted in C. Dreifus, "In Professor's Model, Diversity = Productivity," *The New York Times,* January 8, 2008, p. D2. See also G. A. Van Kleef and C. Kl. W. De Dreu, "Bridging Faultlines by Valuing Diversity: Diversity Beliefs, Information

Elaboration, and Performance in Diverse Work Groups," *Journal of Applied Psychology,* September 2007, pp. 1189–1199.

102. M. Loden, *Implementing Diversity* (Chicago: Irwin, 1996), pp. 14–15.

103. H. Collingwood, "Who Handles a Diverse Work Force Best?" *Working Woman,* February 1996, p. 25.

104. See A. Karr, "Work Week: A Special News Report about Life on the Job—and Trends Taking Shape There," *The Wall Street Journal,* June 1, 1999, p. A1.

105. B. Schlender, "Peter Drucker Takes the Long View," *Fortune,* September 28, 1998, pp. 162–173.

106. H. W. French, "As China Ages, a Shortage of Cheap Labor Looms," *The New York Times*, June 30, 2006, pp. A1, A10. See also Stobbe, 2008.

107. M. Toossi, "Labor Force Projections to 2012: The Graying of the U.S. Workforce," *Monthly Labor Review,* February 2004, http://findarticles.com/p/articles/mi_m1153/is_2_127/ai_I15346590/pg_13 (accessed February 28, 2008). See also R. L. Wiener, "Age Discrimination and Disparate Impact on Employment," *Monitor on Psychology*, May 2007, p. 27; D. R. Avery, P. F. McKay, and D. C. Wilson, "Engaging the Aging Workforce: The Relationship between Perceived Age Similarity, Satisfaction with Coworkers, and Employee Engagement," *Journal of Applied Psychology,* November 2007, pp. 1542–1556; and E. White, "The New Recruits: Older Workers," *The Wall Street Journal*, January 14, 2008, p. B3.

108. E. Porter, "Stretched to Limit, Women Stall March to Work," *The New York Times*, March 2, 2006, pp. A1, C2.

109. I. DeBare, "A Female Success Story," *San Francisco Chronicle,* January 26, 2006, pp. C1, C2.

110. Study by Hilary Lips, Radford University, reported in B. Morris, "How Corporate America Is Betraying Women," *Fortune,* January 10, 2005, pp. 64–74.

111. Association of Executive Search Consultants, *BlueSteps 2007 Diversity Report*, cited in J. D. McCool, "Diversity Pledges Ring Hollow," *BusinessWeek.com*, February 5, 2008, http://www.businessweek.com/managing/content/feb2008/ca2008025_080192.htm?chan=search (accessed February 28, 2008).

112. These statistics were obtained from B. Fitzgerald, "Ms. Fortune 500: Less Women Are Corporate Officers," *The Star Ledger*, February 22, 2007, http://www.nj.com/business/ledger/index.ssf?/base/busines-5/I172123103202440.xml&c...; and "Women CEOs for Fortune 500 Companies," *CNNMoney.co*, http://money.cnn.com/magazines/fortune/fortune500/womenceos (both accessed February 28, 2008). Regarding gender stereotypes, see J. A. Segal, "Woman in the Moon," *HR Magazine*, August 2007, pp. 107–114.

113. For further discussion of various aspects of the glass ceiling, see also R. Morris, "To Get Ahead, Own the Store," *The New York Times,* November 18, 2004, p. C10; R. E. Herzlinger, "A Corporate Push—Against Women," *USA Today*, December 7, 2004, p. 13A; C. H. Deutsch, "Are Women Responsible for Their Own Low Pay?" *The New York Times*, February 27, 2005, sec. 3, p. 7; T. L. O'Brien, "Up the Down Staircase," *The New York Times*, March 19, 2006, sec. 3, pp. 1, 4; E. White, "Why Few Women Run Plants," *The Wall Street Journal*, May 1, 2006, pp. B1, B5; and R. Parloff, "The War Over Unconscious Bias," *Fortune*, October 1, 2007, http://money.cnn.com/magazines/fortune/fortune_archive/2007/10/15/100537276/index.htm (accessed February 28, 2008). See also K. Miner-Rubino and L. M. Cortina, "Beyond Targets: Consequences of Vicarious Exposure to Misogyny at Work," *Journal of Applied Psychology*, September 2007, pp. 1254–1269.

114. B. R. Ragins, B. Townsend, and M. Matttis, "Gender Gap in the Executive Suite: CEOs and Female Executives Report on Breaking the Glass Ceiling," *Academy of Management Review*, February 1998, pp. 28–42.

115. R. Sharpe, "As Leaders, Women Rule," *BusinessWeek*, November 20, 2000, pp. 75–84.

116. K. Wisul, "The Bottom Line on Women at the Top," *BusinessWeek,* January 26, 2004; http://www.businessweek.com/bwdaily/dnflash/jan2004/nf20040126_3378_db035.htm (accessed April 7, 2006).

117. U.S. Census Bureau, 2000 Census, cited in National Center for Public Policy and Higher Education, Policy Alert, "Income of U.S. Workforce Projected to Decline If Education Does Not Improve," November 2005, p. 2; http://www.highereducation.org/reports/pa_decline/pa_decline.pdf (accessed July 1, 2006).

118. "Worker Health Chartbook 2004," National Institute for Occupational Safety and Health, Table 1-3, NIOSH Publication No. 2004–146; http://www2.cdc.gov/nioshChartbook/imagedetail.asp?imgid=401 (accessed July 22, 2006).

119. "Household Income Rises, Poverty Rate Declines, Number of Uninsured Up," U.S. Census Bureau, August 28, 2007, http://www.census.gov/Press-Release/www/releases/archives/income_wealth/010583.html (accessed February 28, 2008).

120. J. I. Sanchez and P. Brock, "Outcomes of Perceived Discrimination among Hispanic Employees: Is Diversity Management a Luxury or a Necessity?" *Academy of Management Journal*, June 1996, pp. 704–719.

121. F. J. Milliken and L. L. Martins, "Searching for Common Threads: Understanding the Multiple Effects of Diversity in Organizational Groups," *Academy of Management Review*, April 1996, pp. 402–433.

122. Results can be found in E. H. James, "Race-Related Differences in Promotions and Support: Underlying Effects of Human and Social Capital," *Organization Science*, September–October 2000, pp. 493–508.

123. Results are reported in C. Daniels, "Young, Gifted, Black—and Out of Here," *Fortune*, May 2004, p. 48.

124. J. S. Passel, "The Size and Characteristics of the Unauthorized Migrant Population in the U.S.: Estimates Based on the March 2005 Current Population Survey," Research Report, Pew Hispanic Center, March 7, 2006; http://pewhispanic.org/files/reports/61.pdf (accessed July 1, 2006).

125. B. Grow, "A Body Blow to Illegal Labor?" *BusinessWeek*, March 27, 2006, pp. 86–87. See also E. Porter, "Who Will Work the Farms?" *The New York Times*, March 23, 2006, pp. C1, C4; A. Goodnough, "Crackdown on Workers Brings Dismay and Anxiety," *The New York Times*, April 22, 2006, p. A8; "Yes, the Law Can Be Enforced, but Will You Like the Result?" [editorial], *USA Today,* April 26, 2006, p. 12A; A. Bernstein, "Hiring Illegals: Inside the Deal Ahead," *BusinessWeek,* May 29, 2006, pp. 35–36; J. Deschenaux, "Anti-Illegal Immigration Law Still Stands," *HR Magazine*, January 2008, p. 24; and D. Cadrain, "More States Take on Immigration Reform," *HR Magazine*, January 2008, pp. 42–46.

126. B. E. Whitley, Jr., and M. E. Kite, "Sex Differences in Attitudes toward Homosexuality: A Comment on Oliver and Hyde (1993)," *Psychological Bulletin*, January 1995, pp. 146–154. For different studies producing different percentages, see S. M. Rogers and C. F. Turner, "Male-Male Sexual Contact in the U.S.A.: Findings from Five Sample Surveys, 1970–1990," *Journal of Sex Research* 28(1991), pp. 491–519; L. S. Doll, L. R. Petersen, C. R. White, E. S. Johnson, J. W. Ward, and the Blood Donor Study Group, "Homosexual and Nonhomosex-

ual Identified Men: A Behavioral Comparison, *Journal of Sex Research* 29(1992), pp. 1–14; J. Lever, D. E. Kanouse, W. H. Rogers, S. Carson, and R. Hertz, "Behavior Patterns and Sexual Identity of Bisexual Males," *Journal of Sex Research* 29(1992), pp. 141–167; J. Billy, K. Tanfer, W. R. Grady, and D. H. Kiepinger, "The Sexual Behavior of Men in the United States," *Family Planning Perspectives* 25(1993), pp. 52–60; E. Laumann, R. Michael, S. Michaels, and J. Gagnon, "Thermidor in the Sexual Revolution?" *National Review,* November 7, 1994, p. 18; and W. D. Mosher, A. Chandra, and J. Jones, "Sexual Behavior and Selected Health Measures: Men and Women 15–44 Years of Age, United States, 2002," *Advance Data from Vital and Health Statistics,* no. 362, September 15, 2005 (Hyattsville, MD: National Center for Health Statistics).

127. October 1, 2003, study by Harris Interactive Inc. and Witeck Combs Communications Inc., reported in C. Edwards, "Coming Out in Corporate America," *BusinessWeek*, December 15, 2003; www.businessweek.com:/print/magazine/content/03_50/b3862080.htm?bw (accessed April 7, 2006).

128. J. M. Croteau, "Research on the Work Experiences of Lesbian, Gay, and Bisexual People: An Integrative Review of Methodology and Findings," *Journal of Vocational Behavior,* April 1996, pp. 195–209; and L. Badgett, "The Wage Effects of Sexual Orientation Discrimination," *Industrial and Labor Relations Review,* July 1995, pp. 726–739. See also B. R. Ragins, R. Singh, and J. M. Cornwell, "Making the Invisible Visible: Fear and Disclosure of Sexual Orientation at Work," *Journal of Applied Psychology*, July 2007, pp. 1103–1118.

129. Human Rights Campaign survey, reported in I. DeBare, "Gay, Lesbian Workers Gradually Gain Benefits," *San Francisco Chronicle,* June 30, 2006, pp. D1, D2.

130. K. Springen, "A Boost for Braille," *Newsweek,* May 20, 2002, p. 13.

131. Survey by CollegeGrad.com, reported in "Underemployment Affects 18 Percent of Entry Level Job Seekers," September 9, 2004; http://www.collegegrad.com/press/underemployed.shtml (accessed July 2, 2006).

132. D. C. Feldman and W. H. Turnley, "Underemployment among Recent Business College Graduates," *Journal of Organizational Behavior,* November 1995, pp. 691–706.

133. P. Thomas and J. Date, "Students Dropping Out of High School Reaches Epidemic Levels," *ABCNews.com*, November 20, 2006, http://i.abcnews.com/US/story?id=2667532&page=1 (accessed February 28, 2008).

134. M. Schneider, "2003 National Assessment of Adult Literacy Results," National Center for Education Statistics, December 15, 2005, http://nces.ed.gov/whatsnew/commissioner/remarks2005/12_15_2005.asp. See also M. Kutner, E. Greenberg, Y. Jin, B. Boyle, Y.-c. Hsu, and E. Dunleavy, *Literacy in Everyday Life: Results from the 2003 National Assessment of Adult Literacy* (Washington, DC: National Center for Education Statistics, 2007).

135. T. L. Smith, "The Resource Center: Finding Solutions for Literacy," *HRFocus,* February 1995, p. 7. See also A. Bernstein, "The Time Bomb in the Workforce: Illiteracy," *BusinessWeek,* Febarury 25, 2002, p. 122.

136. M. Loden, 1996; E. E. Spragins, "Benchmark: The Diverse Work Force," *Inc.,* January 1993, p. 33; and A. M. Morrison, *The New Leaders: Guidelines on Leadership Diversity in America* (San Francisco: Jossey-Bass, 1992).

137. G. Dell'Orto, "Special Classes Help 3M Workers Learn How to Get Along," *San Francisco Chronicle*, June 2, 2000, p. B4.

138. S. Shellenbarger, "Please Send Chocolate: Moms Now Face Stress Moving In and Out of Work Force," *The Wall Street Journal,* May 9, 2002, p. D1. See also A. Bernstein, "Too Many Workers? Not for Long," *BusinessWeek,* May 20, 2002, pp. 126–130.

CHAPTER 4

1. K. Reinhard, quoted in S. McCartney, "Teaching Americans How to Behave Abroad," *The Wall Street Journal*, April 11, 2006, pp. D1, D4.

2. DDB Worldwide survey, cited in J. Clark, "That 'Ugly American' Image Is Getting a Makeover Guide," *USA Today*, April 28, 2006, p. 9D.

3. *World Citizens Guide*, Business for Diplomatic Action, May 2006, http://www.worldcitizensguide.org/index2.html (accessed March 3, 2008).

4. T. Lowry and F. Balfour, "It's All about the Face-to-Face," *BusinessWeek*, January 28, 2008, pp. 48, 50.

5. E. Schmitt, "A Man Does Not Ask a Man about His Wife," *The New York Times*, January 8, 2006, sec. 4, p. 7.

6. T. Rivas, "Name Game Hits a Global Roadblock," *The Wall Street Journal*, May 30, 2006, p. B5.

7. B. Morris, "The Pepsi Challenge: Can This Snack and Soda Giant Go Healthy?" *Fortune*, March 3, 2008, pp. 55–66.

8. L. Nardon and R. M. Steers, "The New Global Manager: Learning Cultures on the Fly," *Organizational Dynamics,* January–March 2008, pp. 47–59.

9. R. Richmond, "Entrepreneurs with Big Dreams Tap Global Market," *The Wall Street Journal*, April 17, 2007, p. B6.

10. See the related discussion in J. McGregor and S. Hamm, "Managing the Global Workforce," *BusinessWeek,* January 28, 2008, p. 34; C. Boles, "Last Call? Gates Pushes Globalism in Remarks," *The Wall Street Journal*, March 13, 2008, p. B3; and M. Herbst, "Guess Who's Getting the Most Work Visas," *BusinessWeek,* March 17, 2008, pp. 62, 64.

11. Cellular Telecommunications Industry Association, cited in A. Dunkin, "Smart, Useful—and They Won't Put a Sag in Your Suit," *BusinessWeek,* May 30, 1994, p. 141.

12. D. B. Britton and S. McGonegal, *The Digital Economy Fact Book*, 9th ed. (Washington, DC: The Progress & Freedom Foundation, 2007), p. 22, www.pff.org (accessed March 3, 2008).

13. Britton and McGonegal, 2007, p. 4.

14. See J. Quittner, "Tim Berners-Lee," *Time,* March 29, 1999, pp. 193–194.

15. "Quarterly Retail E-Commerce Sales, 4th Quarter 2007," *U.S. Census Bureau News,* February 15, 2008, http://www.census.gov/mrts/www/data/html/07Q4.html (accessed March 3, 2008).

16. R. M. Kantor, quoted in K. Maney, "Economy Embraces Truly Global Workplace," *USA Today,* December 31, 1998, pp. 1B, 2B.

17. "Amazon.com Announces Fourth Quarter Sales up 42% to $5.7 Billion; 2007 Free Cash Flow More Than Doubles, Surpassing $1 Billion for the First Time," Amazon.com, January 30, 2008, http://biz.yahoo.com/bw/080130/20080130006013.html (accessed March 3, 2008).

18. Maney, 1998.

19. Kris Gopalakrishnan, interviewed in R. M. Smith, "A Titan of Globalism," *Newsweek*, November 19, 2007, p. E26.

20. D. J. Lynch, "Some Ohio Firms Have Done Well Under NAFTA," *USA Today,* March 3, 2008, p. 2B.

21. "Is Global Finance Sector a Force for Good or Ill?" *The Wall Street Journal,* November 28, 2007, p. B9; and P. Krugman, "Don't Cry for Me, America," *The New York Times,* January 18, 2008, p. A23.

22. Bill Gates, quoted in T. L. Friedman, "U.S. Is Losing the Race to Flatten Globe," *Arizona Republic,* May 4, 2006, p. B9; reprinted from *The New York Times.*

23. C. Smadja, "Living Dangerously," *Time,* February 22, 1999, pp. 94–95. Globalization is a subject of intense debate. Some books on the subject are S. B. Berger and the MIT Industrial Performance Center, *How We Compete: What Companies Around the World Are Doing to Make It in Today's Global Economy* (New York: Currency/Doubleday, 2006); D. Cohen, *Globalization and Its Enemies,* J. B. Baker trans. (Cambridge, MA: MIT Press, 2006); J. Faux, *The Global Class War: How America's Bipartisan Elite Lost Our Future—and What It Will Take to Win It Back* (New York: John Wiley, 2006); J. A. Frieden, *Global Capitalism: Its Fall and Rise in the Twentieth Century* (New York: W. W. Norton, 2006); and B. C. Lynn, *End of the Line: The Rise and Coming Fall of the Global Corporation* (New York: Doubleday, 2006). For two antithetical views, see also J. Owens, "Embrace Globalism," *The Wall Street Journal,* April 17, 2006, p. A17; and D. Gross, "Invest Globally, Stagnate Locally," *The New York Times,* April 2, 2006, sec. 3, p. 3.

24. N. Negroponte, quoted in Maney, 1998.

25. A. Sloan, "In the Land of Giants," *Newsweek,* August 10, 1998, pp. 42–43. See also A. Rozens, "Record Year of Mergers Expected," *San Francisco Chronicle,* March 1, 2006, p. C5; D. K. Berman, "Blizzard of Deals Heralds New Era of Megamergers," *The Wall Street Journal,* June 27, 2006, pp. A1, A16.

26. M. Landler, "Porsche and VW: One Happy Family?" *The New York Times,* December 23, 2007, Business section, pp. 1, 8; and M. Moore, "Porsche Targets VW, Which Pursues Scania," Associated Press, March 3, 2008, http://ap.google.com/article/ALeqM5gPdxJfID4Tr7scxhOcMBvnDHpZtQD8V683L80 (accessed March 4, 2008). Not all mergers are beneficial. See, for example, S. McCartney, "Mergers Benefit Airlines; Shame about the Fliers," *The Wall Street Journal,* January 15, 2008, pp. D1, D4; and J. Bailey, "In the Math of Mergers, Airlines Fail," *The New York Times,* January 17, 2008, pp. C1, C12.

27. S. Weimer, "Mannequin Madness," California Materials Exchange, Integrated Waste Management Board, April 23, 2004, http://www.ciwmb.ca.gov/CalMAX/Creative/2003/Winter.htm (accessed July 4, 2006); I. DeBare, "New Lease on Life for Mannequins," *San Francisco Chronicle,* July 29, 2006, p. J2; S. L. Thomas, "Warehouse Visit Spawns Mannequin Madness," *East Bay Business Times,* February 24, 2006, http://eastbay.bizjournals.com/eastbay/stories/2006/02/27/smallb1.html (accessed July 4, 2006).

28. P. McDonald, quoted in M. L. Levin, "Global Experience Makes Candidates More Marketable," *The Wall Street Journal,* September 11, 2007, p. B6.

29. J. Androshick, quoted in H. Chura, "A Year Abroad (or 3) as a Career Move," *The New York Times,* February 25, 2006, p. B5.

30. T. Chea, "Americans Seek Opportunity in Bangalore," *Reno Gazette-Journal,* April 3, 2006, p. 3E.

31. S. Stapleton, quoted in R. Erlich, "Going Far in the East," *San Francisco Chronicle,* June 24, 2006, pp. C1, C2.

32. R. C. Carter, senior vice president for human resources at A&E Television Networks, quoted in Chura, 2006. For more about Americans working overseas, particularly in India, see J. S. Lublin, "Job Hopping Overseas Can Enhance a Career, but It Takes Fortitude," *The Wall Street Journal,* June 7, 2005, p. B1; N. Lakshman, "Subcontinental Drift," *BusinessWeek,* January 16, 2006, pp. 42–43; and R. J. Newman, "Coming and Going," *U.S. News & World Report,* January 23, 2006, pp. 50–52.

33. Survey by the Zimmerman Agency for Residence Inn by Marriott, in "Things You Love to Miss," *USA Today,* March 1, 1999, p. 1B.

34. Lowry and Balfour, 2008.

35. Paul Calello of Credit Suisse, quoted in Lowry and Balfour, 2008.

36. L. Bergson, "A Road Scholar's Bag of Tricks," *BusinessWeek,* September 29, 2003, http://www.businessweek.com/small-biz/content/sep2003/sb20030929_6259_sb002.htm?chan=search (accessed March 21, 2008).

37. Bergson, 2003.

38. R. E. Calem, "For Road Warriors, Child Care on the Go," *BusinessWeek,* July 18, 2000, http://www.businessweek.com/careers/content/jul2000/ca20000718_505.htm?chan=search (accessed March 21, 2008).

39. G. Stoller, "Doing Business Abroad? Simple Faux Pas Can Sink You," *USA Today,* August 24, 2007, pp. 1B, 2B.

40. Britton and McGonegal, 2007, p. 120.

41. D. A. Heenan and H. V. Perlmutter, *Multinational Organization Development* (Reading, MA: Addison-Wesley, 1979).

42. D. Jones, "Do Foreign Executives Balk at Sports Jargon?" *USA Today,* March 30, 2007, pp. 1B.2B.

43. R. Kopp, "International Human Resource Policies and Practices in Japanese, European, and United States Multinationals," *Human Resource Management,* Winter 1994, pp. 581–599.

44. H. R. Varian, "An iPod Has Global Value. Ask the (Many) Countries That Make It," *The New York Times*, June 28, 2007, p. C3.

45. W. J. Holstein, "Colonial Roots Have Spread Worldwide," *The New York Times,* June 16, 2007, p. B3.

46. E. Byron, "P&G's Global Target: Shelves of Tiny Stores," *The Wall Street Journal*, July 16, 2007, pp. A1, A10.

47. A, van Agtmael, "How Can U.S. Stay on Top of the World?" *USA Today,* March 7, 2007, p. II A.

48. S. McCartney, "Who's Inspecting Your Airplane?" *The Wall Street Journal,* March 3, 2004, pp. D1, D12.

49. Study of government data by Economic Policy Institute, Washington, DC, cited in R. Keil and L. Arnold, "New Jobs Created at Low End," *San Francisco Chronicle,* April 13, 2004, p. C5.

50. "Outsourcing Jobs: Is It Bad?" *BusinessWeek,* August 25, 2003, p. 36; "Where Are the Jobs?" *BusinessWeek,* March 22, 2004, p. 37.

51. Forrester Research, cited in G. Epstein, "Static Disrupts the Bangalore Connection," *Barron's Online*, September 10, 2007, http://online.barrons.com/article/SB118921200748221265.html (accessed March 6, 2008).

52. S. Zuckerman, "Some Jobs May Not Return," *San Francisco Chronicle,* February 22, 2004, pp. I-1, I-14; J. Madrick, "As Job Exports Rise, Some Economists Rethink the Mathematics of Free Trade," *The New York Times,* March 18, 2004, p. C2; J. C. Cooper, "The Price of Efficiency," *BusinessWeek,* March 22, 2004, pp. 38–42; and J. E. Hilsenrath, "Behind Outsourcing Debate: Surprisingly Few Hard Numbers," *The Wall Street Journal,* April 12, 2004, pp. A1, A7.

53. Epstein, 2007. See also D. Farrell, M. Laboissiere, R. Pascal, J. Rosenfeld, C. de Segundo, S. Stürze, and F. Umezawa, *The Emerging Global Labor Market,* June 2005, McKinsey Global Institute, San Francisco, http://www.mckinsey.com/mgi/publications/emerginggloballabormarket/index.asp (accessed March 6, 2008).

54. H. R. Varian, "With Free Trade, What Goes Abroad Usually Finds Its Way Back, to Everyone's Benefit," *The New York Times,* March 11, 2004, p. C2.

55. B. Schlender, "Peter Drucker Sets Us Straight," *Fortune,* January 12, 2004, pp. 115–118. See also P. Engardio, "The Future of Outsourcing," *BusinessWeek,* January 30, 2006, pp. 50–58; E. White, "Smaller Companies Join the Outsourcing Trend," *The Wall Street Journal,* May 8, 2006, p. B3; and

L. Buchanan, "The Thinking Man's Outsourcing," *Inc. Magazine,* May 2006, pp. 31–33.

56. Forrester Research, "Losing Our Edge? Estimated Number of High-Skilled U.S. Jobs Moving Offshore," reported in K. Madigan, "Yes: This Is No Longer About a Few Low-Wage or Manufacturing Jobs. Now One Out of Three Jobs Is At Risk," *BusinessWeek,* August 25, 2003, pp. 37–38.

57. J. Thottam, "Is Your Job Going Abroad?" *Time,* March 1, 2004, pp. 26–34.

58. F. Levy, quoted in D. Wessel, "The Future of Jobs: New Ones Arise, Wage Gap Widens," *The Wall Street Journal,* April 2, 2004, pp. Al, A5.

59. K. B. Mitchell, quoted in A. Fisher, "Think Globally, Save Your Job Locally," *Fortune,* February 23, 2004, p. 60.

60. For some caveats about offshoring, see M. Bolch, "Going Global," *Training,* January 2008, pp. 28–29; M. Weinstein, "On Target Offshore," *Training,* January 2008, pp. 34–36; and M. Bandyk, "Now Even Small Firms Can Go Global," *U.S. News & World Report,* March 10, 2008, p. 52.

61. A. M. Chaker, "Where the Jobs Are," *The Wall Street Journal,* March 18, 2004, pp. Dl, D3; J. Shinal, "Which Types of Jobs Will Be in Demand?" *San Francisco Chronicle,* March 25, 2004, pp. Cl, C4; and D. Wessel, "The Future of Jobs: New Ones Arise, Wage Gap Widens," *The Wall Street Journal,* April 2, 2004, pp. Al, A5.

62. Association for Computing Machinery, reported in C. Kirby, "Tech Jobs Still Plentiful in U.S.," *San Francisco Chronicle,* February 24, 2006, pp. Dl, D6.

63. J. Spohrer, quoted in Shinal, 2004.

64. Drucker, quoted in Schlender, 2004.

65. L. Uchitelle, "College Degree Still Pays, but It's Leveling Off," *The New York Times,* January 17, 2005, pp. Cl, C2.

66. U.S. Census Bureau, "Top Ten Countries with Which the U.S. Trades, for the Month of December 2007," http://www.census.gov/foreigni=trade/top/dst/current/balance.html (accessed March 8, 2008).

67. J. Ewinger, "Steel, Tariffs, and Politics Mix at U.S.-Canada Conference," *Cleveland Plain Dealer,* April 18, 2004; www.cleveland.com/news/plaindealer/index.ssf?/base/news/1082282265327050.xml (accessed April 18, 2006).

68. "China to Cancel Car Import Quota in 2005," *China Daily,* February 13, 2004; www.chinadaily.com.cn/english/doc/2004-02/13/ content_305954.htm (accessed April 18, 2006).

69. J. Bhagwati, *Protectionism* (Cambridge, MA: MIT Press, 1988).

70. "WTO Telecoms Deal Will Ring in the Changes on 5 February 1998," *World Trade Organization,* January 26, 1998.

71. M. Landler, "Britain Overtakes U.S. as Top World Bank Donor," *The New York Times,* December 15, 2007, http://www.nytimes.com/2007/12/15/world/15worldbank.html (accessed March 8, 2008).

72. D. Workman, "U.S. Global Trade Debt by Country," Suitel01.com, February 1, 2008, http://import-export. 101.com/article.cfm/us_global_trade_debt_by_country (accessed March 8, 2008).

73. See, for example, E. Papaioannou, R. Portes, and G. Siourounis, "Optimal Currency Shares in International Reserves: The Impact of the Euro and the Prospects for the Dollar," NBER Working Paper No. 12333, June 2006, National Bureau of Economic Research, http://papers.nber.org/papers/wl2333 (accessed March 8, 2008); and Associated Press, "Report: Greenspan Says Euro Could Replace U.S. Dollar as Reserve Currency of Choice," *International Herald Tribune,* September 17, 2007, http://www.iht.com/articles/ap/2007/09/17/ business/EU-FIN-MKT-Germany-Greenspan-Euro.php (accessed March 8, 2008).

74. See M. A. O'Grady, "One Year After CAFTA," *The Wall Street Journal,* February 26, 2007, p. A 18.

75. Samir Khalaf, quoted in H. M. Fattah, "Why Arab Men Hold Hands," *The New York Times,* May 1, 2005, sec. 4, p. 2.

76. G. A. Fowler, "In China's Offices, Foreign Colleagues Might Get an Earful," *The Wall Street Journal,* February 13, 2007, p. Dl.

77. "How Cultures Collide," *Psychology Today,* July 1976, p. 69.

78. See P. R. Harris and R. T. Moran, *Managing Cultural Differences,* 4th ed. (Houston: Gulf Publishing, 1996), pp. 223–228; and M. Hilling, "Avoid Expatriate Culture Shock," *HR Magazine,* July 1993, pp. 58–63.

79. For complete details, see G. Hofstede, *Culture's Consequences: International Differences in Work-Related Values,* abridged ed. (Newbury Park, CA: Sage, 1984); "The Interaction between National and Organizational Value Systems," *Journal of Management Studies,* July 1985, pp. 347–357; and "Management Scientists Are Human," *Management Science,* January 1994, pp. 4–13.

80. M. Javidan and R. J. House, "Cultural Acumen for the Global Manager: Lessons from Project GLOBE," *Organizational Dynamics,* Spring 2001, pp. 289–305; R. J. House, P. J. Hanges, M. Javidan, P. W. Dorfman, and V. Gupta, eds., *Culture, Leadership, and Organizations: The GLOBE Study of 62 Societies* (Thousand Oaks, CA: Sage, 2004); and M. Javidan, P. W. Dorfman, M. S. de Luque, and R. J. House, "In the Eye of the Beholder: Cross Cultural Lessons in Leadership from Project GLOBE," *Academy of Management Perspectives,* February 2006, pp. 67–90.

81. A discussion of Japanese stereotypes in America can be found in L. Smith, "Fear and Loathing of Japan," *Fortune,* February 26, 1990, pp. 50–57.

82. G. A. Michaelson, "Global Gold," *Success,* March 1996, p. 16. English is increasingly becoming the language of business and more and more is being taught in foreign business universities. See D. Carvajal, "English as Language of Global Education," *The New York Times,* April 11, 2007, p. A21. In U.S. institutions, enrollments in Arabic-language classes are skyrocketing, but there is a great shortage of teachers. See T. Yahalom, "Surge in Students Studying Arabic Outstrips Supply of Teachers," *USA Today,* September 5, 2007, p. 7D.

83. Harris Poll, National Foreign Language Center, reported in "Lingua Franca?" *USA Today,* February 23, 1999, p. IA.

84. D. J. Lynch, "U.S. Firms Becoming Tongue-Tied," *USA Today,* February 9, 2006, p. 6B.

85. "How Cultures Collide," 1976.

86. E. T. Hall, *The Hidden Dimension* (New York: Doubleday, 1966).

87. C. Salazar, "Time Is of the Essence in Peru's Punctuality Effort," *San Francisco Chronicle,* March 2, 2007, p. Al6.

88. Robert Levine, quoted in R. Vecchio, "Global Psyche: On Their Own Time," *Psychology Today,* July/August 2007, http://psychologytoday.com/articles/pto-20070723-000007.html (accessed March 10, 2008).

89. C. Woodward, "AP Poll Paints Portrait of Impatient American," *Reno Gazette-Journal,* May 29, 2006, pp. IC, 7C.

90. Results adapted from and value definitions quoted from S. R. Safranski and I.-W. Kwon, "Religious Groups and Management Value Systems," in R. N. Farner and E. G. McGoun, eds., *Advances in International Comparative Management,* vol. 3 (Greenwich, CT: JAI Press, 1988), pp. 171–183.

91. Data from D. Beck, "What Negotiating Tactics Reveal about Executives," www.careerjournal.com, February 11–17, 2002;

and L. Grensing-Pophal, "Expat Lifestyles Take a Hit," *HRMagazine*, March 2008, pp. 51-54.

92. Jacqui Hauser, vice president of consulting services for Cendant Mobility, a relocation-services firm, cited in P. Capell, "Employers Seek to Trim Pay for U.S. Expatriates," April 16, 2005, www.careerjournal.com.

93. J. S. Black and H. B. Gregersen, "The Way to Manage Expats," *Harvard Business Review*, March-April 1999, p. 53.

94. See A. Maingault, L. Albright, and V. Neal, "Policy Tips, Repatriation, Safe Harbor Rules," *HRMagazine*, March 2008, pp. 34-35.

95. S. Dallas, "Rule No. 1: Don't Diss the Locals," *BusinessWeek*, May 15, 1995, p. 8. Also see M. A. Shaffer, D. A. Harrison, H. Gregersen, J. S. Black, and L. A. Ferzandi, "You Can Take It with You: Individual Differences and Expatriate Effectiveness," *Journal of Applied Psychology*, January 2006, pp. 109-125.

CHAPTER 5

1. M. J. Driver, "Careers: A Review of Personnel and Organizational Research," in C. L. Cooper and I. Robertson, eds., *International Review of Industrial and Organizational Psychology* (New York: Wiley, 1988).

2. T. Gutner, "Doubling Up on Careers Suits More Workers," *The Wall Street Journal*, February 5, 2008, p. B4. See also M. Alboher, *One Person/Multiple Careers: A New Model for Work/Life Success* (New York: Warner Books, 2007).

3. E. White, "Profession Changes Take Time but May Be Worth Wait," *The Wall Street Journal*, November 27, 2007, p. B6.

4. R. Kreitner, *Management*, 7th ed. (Boston: Houghton Mifflin, 1998), p. 160.

5. J. Valcourt, "Chrysler Begins Overhaul in Engineering," *The Wall Street Journal*, February 19, 2008, p. A13.

6. R. E. Miles and C. C. Snow, *Organizational Strategy, Structure, and Process* (New York: McGraw-Hill, 1978).

7. See M. Olson, D. van Bever, and S. Verry, "When Growth Stalls," *Harvard Business Review*, March 2008, pp. 51-61.

8. D. C. Hambrick, "On the Staying Power of Defenders, Analyzers, and Prospectors," *Academy of Management Executive*, November 2003, pp. 115-118. For more about the four basic strategy types, see also D. J. Ketchen Jr., "Introduction: Raymond E. Miles and Charles C. Snow's *Organizational Strategy, Structure, and Process*," *Academy of Management Executive*, November 2003, pp. 95-96; D. J. Ketchen Jr., "An Interview with Raymond E. Miles and Charles C. Snow," *Academy of Management Executive*, November 2003, pp. 97-104; S. E. Brunk, "From Theory to Practice: Applying Miles and Snow's Ideas to Understand and Improve Firm Performance," *Academy of Management Executive*, November 2003, pp. 105-108; and S. Ghoshal, "Miles and Snow: Enduring Insights for Managers," *Academy of Management Executive*, November 2003, pp. 109-114.

9. D. Leider, "Purposeful Work," *Utne Reader*, July/August 1988, p. 52; excerpted from *On Purpose: A Journal about New Lifestyles & Workstyles*, Winter 1986.

10. P. F. Drucker, *The Practice of Management* (New York: Harper & Row, 1954), p. 122.

11. Web site, Nest Fresh Eggs, "Cyd's Nestfresh," mission statement, http://www.nestfresh.com/story.html#mission (accessed March 11, 2008).

12. P. de Jonge, "Riding the Wild, Perilous Waters of Amazon .com," *The New York Times Magazine*, March 14, 1999, pp. 36-41, 54, 68, 79-80.

13. Amazon.com 2006 Annual Report, reprinting letter from 1997 Annual Report, http://phx.corporate-ir.net/phoenix. zhtml?c=97664&p=irol-reportsAnnual (accessed March 11, 2008).

14. T. A. Stewart, "A Refreshing Change: Vision Statements That Make Sense," *Fortune*, September 30, 1996, pp. 195-196.

15. F. Gibney Jr., "Pepsi Gets Back in the Game," *Time*, April 26, 1999, pp. 38-40.

16. For application of vision to nonprofits, see A. Kilpatrick and L. Silverman, "The Power of Vision," *Strategy & Leadership*, February 2005, pp. 24-26.

17. Web site, Nest Fresh Eggs.

18. Amazon.com, AMZN Investor Relations, FAQs, http://phx .corporate-ir.net/phoenix.zhtml?c=97664&p=irol-faq#14296 (accessed March 11, 2008).

19. P. J. Below, G. L. Morrisey, and B. L. Acomb, *The Executive Guide to Strategic Planning* (San Francisco: Jossey-Bass, 1987), p. 2.

20. Survey conducted by the Society for Human Resource Management and the Balance Scorecard Collaborative, reported in J. Mullich, "Get in Line," *Workforce Management*, December 2003, pp. 43-44.

21. S. Khan and B. Hansen, "Routes, Type of Fliers Affect Range in Airfare Costs," *USA Today*, May 11, 1999, p. 9B; and B. De Lollis, "Southwest Plans Non-stop, Coast-to-Coast Flights," *USA Today*, May 8, 2002, p. 1B.

22. Hoover's, "Southwest Airlines Company Description," http:// www.hoovers.com/southwest-airlines/--ID__11377--/free-co-profile.xhtml (accessed March 13, 2008).

23. James Parker, quoted in W. J. Holstein, "At Southwest, the Culture Drives Success," *BusinessWeek.com*, February 21, 2008, http://www.businessweek.com/managing/content/ feb2008/ca20080221_179423.htm (accessed March 13, 2008). Parker is author of *Do the Right Thing: How Dedicated Employees Create Loyal Customers and Large Profits* (Philadelphia: Wharton School Publishing, 2008).

24. S. Stellin, "Now Boarding Business Class," *The New York Times*, February 26, 2008, p. C6.

25. Willie Wilson, quoted in J. Bailey, "On Some Flights, Millionaires Serve the Drinks," *The New York Times*, May 15, 2006, pp. A1, A16.

26. Herb Kelleher, quoted in "How Herb Keeps Southwest Hopping," *Money*, June 1999, pp. 61-62.

27. T. Maxon, "Airline Stocks Dive After Downgrades," *The Dallas Morning News*, March 13, 2008, http://www.dallasnews .com/sharedcontent/dws/bus/industries/airlines/stories/ DN-airstox_13bus.State.Edition1.b570d2.html (accessed March 13, 2008).

28. M. L. Wald, "F.A.A. Fines Southwest Air in Inspections," *The New York Times*, March 7, 2008, http://www.nytimes .com/2008/03/07/business/07air.html?fta=y; J. Bailey, "After Fine, Southwest Suspends 3 and Hires Specialist," *The New York Times*, March 12, 2008, http://www.nytimes .com/2008/03/12/business/12air.html; Reuters, "Southwest Grounds 41 Planes," *The New York Times*, March 12, 2008, http://www.nytimes.com/reuters/business/business-southwest-planes.html?_r=1&oref=slogin; J. Bailey, "New Inspections Ground 38 Southwest Jets," *The New York Times*, March 13, 2008, http://www.nytimes.com/2008/03/13/business/13air .html?em&ex=1205553600&en=3e70lf8b06cc4fdd&ei=5087%0A.

29. See E. A. Locke and G. P. Latham, "Building a Practically Useful Theory of Goal Setting and Task Motivation," *American Psychologist*, September 2002, pp. 705-717.

30. Drucker, 1954.

31. Lock and Latham, 2002.

32. The performance management process is discussed by H. Aguinis and C. Pierce, "Enhancing the Relevance of Organizational Behavior by Embracing Performance

Management Research," *Journal of Organizational Behavior,* January 2008, pp. 139–145.

33. R. Rodgers and J. E. Hunter, "Impact of Management by Objectives on Organizational Productivity," *Journal of Applied Psychology,* April 1991, pp. 322–336.

34. M. Barbaro, "Wal-Mart Sets Agenda of Change," *The New York Times,* January 24, 2008, p. C3; and K. Ohannessian, "CEO Lee Scott Speaks About Wal-Mart's New Strategies," *FastCompany.com,* January 24, 2008, http://blog.fastcompany.com/archives/2008/01/24/ceo_lee_scott_speaks_about_walmarts_new_strategies.html (accessed March 19, 2008).

35. Adapted from N. Wingield, "At Apple, Secrecy Complicates Life but Maintains Buzz," *The Wall Street Journal,* June 28, 2006, pp. A1, A11. See also A. L. Peneberg, "All Eyes on Apple," *Fast Company,* December 2007/January 2008, pp. 83–87, 133–136; "The World's 50 Most Innovative Companies," *Fast Company,* March 2008, p. 92; B. Morris, "What Makes Apple Golden," *Fortune,* March 17, 2008, pp. 68–74; and P. Ekind, "The Trouble with Steve," *Fortune,* March 17, 2008, pp. 88–98, 156–160.

36. TheFreeDictionary.com, 2004, http://encyclopedia.thefreedictionary.com/project%20management (accessed June 23, 2004).

37. R. Gandossy, "The Need for Speed," *Journal of Business Strategy,* January/February 2003, pp. 29–33. See also M. B. Lippitt, "Six Priorities That Make a Great Strategic Decision," *Journal of Business Strategy,* January/February 2003, pp. 21–24.

38. See P. B. Marren, "Business in the Age of Terrorism," *Journal of Business Strategy,* July/August 2002, pp. 19–23.

39. A. Toffler, *Powershift: Knowledge, Wealth, and Violence at the Edge of the 21st Century* (New York: Bantam Books, 1990), pp. 196–197.

40. M. Campbell-Kelly and W. Aspray, *Computer: A History of the Information Machine* (New York: Basic Books, 1996), pp. 253–256.

41. B. Elgin, "Google," *BusinessWeek,* May 3, 2004, pp. 82–90.

42. E. Bonabeau, N. Bodick, and R. W. Armstrong, "A More Rational Approach to New-Product Development," *Harvard Business Review,* March 2008, pp. 96–102.

43. Gerard M. Mooney, quoted in R. D. Hof, "Building an Idea Factory," *BusinessWeek,* October 11, 2004, pp. 194–200.

44. The phrase "innovator's dilemma" was coined by Clayton M. Christensen, in *The Innovator's Dilemma: When New Technologies Cause Great Firms to Fail* (Boston: Harvard Business School Press, 1997).

45. See K. Sengupta, T. K. Abdel-Hamid, and L. N. Van Wassenhove, "The Experience Trap," *Harvard Business Review,* February 2008, pp. 94–101. See also J. Rae-Dupree, "Eureka! It Really Takes Years of Hard Work," *The New York Times,* February 3, 2008, Business section, p. 4.

46. Hof, 2004.

47. J. Tierney, "The Advantages of Closing a Few Doors," *The New York Times,* February 26, 2008, pp. D1, D6.

48. D. Ariely, *Predictably Irrational: The Hidden Forces That Shape Our Decisions* (New York: HarperCollins, 2008).

CHAPTER 6

1. G. Hamel, "What Is Management's Moonshot?" *Management 2.0,* December 7, 2007, http://discussionleader.hbsp.com/hamel/2007/12/what_is_managements_moonshot.html (accessed March 28, 2008).

2. J. Best, *Flavor of the Month: Why Smart People Fall for Fads* (Berkeley: University of California Press, 2006).

3. J. Best, interviewed by A. Manser, "Flavor of the Month," UDaily, University of Delaware Web site, May 22, 2006, http://www.udel.edu/PR/UDaily/2006/may/jbest052206.html (accessed March 28, 2008).

4. D. Rigby and B. Bilodeau, "Bain's Global 2007 Management Tools and Trends Survey," *Strategy & Leadership,* http://www.emeraldinsight.com/Insight/viewContentItem.do;jsessionid=B7E2FBC8B9E00A7542C9CIEAF00AADDD?contentType=Article&contentId=1626431; and D. Rigby and B. Bilodeau, "Management Tools and Trends 2007," Bain & Company, http://www.bain.com/management_tools/home.asp (both accessed March 28, 2008).

5. G. Colvin, "The Most Valuable Quality in a Manager," *Fortune,* December 29, 1997, pp. 279–280.

6. J. Pfeffer and R. I. Sutton, "Profiting from Evidence-Based Management," *Strategy & Leadership* 34, no. 2 (2006), pp. 35–42.

7. J. Kellner, "17-Year-Old Entrepreneur Writes Own Business Plan," *Reno Gazette-Journal,* January 29, 2007, p. 8E.

8. Study by Amar Bhide, cited in K. K. Spors, "Do Start-Ups Really Need Formal Business Plans?" *The Wall Street Journal,* January 9, 2007, p. B9.

9. Study by S. Shane, cited in Spors, 2007.

10. C. McNamara, "Strategic Planning (in Nonprofit or For-Profit Organizations," Free Management Library, 1997–2008, http://www.managementhelp.org/plan_dec/str_plan/str_plan.htm (accessed March 28, 2008).

11. A. A. Thompson Jr. and A. J. Strickland III, *Strategic Management: Concepts and Cases,* 6th ed. (Homewood, IL: BPI/Irwin, 1992).

12. D. J. Collis and M. G. Rukstad, "Can You Say What Your Strategy Is?" *Harvard Business Review,* April 2008, pp. 82–90.

13. See G. Hamel, with B. Breen, *The Future of Management* (Boston: Harvard Business School Press, 2007), p. 191. For a discussion of the effect of the Web on newspapers, see E. Alterman, "Out of Print," *The New Yorker,* March 31, 2008, pp. 48–59.

14. A. Busch III, quoted in interview with G. Hamel, "Turning Your Business Upside Down," *Fortune,* June 23, 1997, pp. 87–88. See also D. Kesmodel, "Beer Distributors Want More Than One Best Bud," *The Wall Street Journal,* February 6, 2006, pp. B1, B2.

15. L. G. Hrebiniak, "Obstacles to Effective Strategy Implementation," *Organizational Dynamics,* February 2006, pp. 12–31.

16. H. Mintzberg, "The Strategy Concept II: Another Look at Why Organizations Need Strategies," *California Management Review,* 30, no. 1 (1987), pp. 25–32.

17. Hamel and Breen, 2007, p. 33.

18. M. Bartiromo, "Facetime: Howard Schultz on Reinventing Starbucks," *BusinessWeek,* April 21, 2008, pp. 19–20.

19. Adapted from M. Myser, "Marketing Made Easy," *Business 2.0,* June 2006, pp. 43–45. See also "Staples," wikinvest, March 2008, http://www.wikinvest.com/stock/Staples_(SPLS) (accessed March 28, 2008).

20. J. Surowiecki, "The Return of Michael Porter," *Fortune,* February 1, 1998, pp. 135–138.

21. M. E. Porter, "What Is Strategy?" *Harvard Business Review,* November–December 1996, pp. 61–78. Porter has updated his 1979 paper on competitive forces in M. E. Porter, "The Five Competitive Forces That Shape Strategy," *The Harvard Business Review,* January 2008, pp. 79–93.

22. Porter, 1996.

23. Byrne, 1998.

24. See A. Lafley and R. Charan, "The Consumer Is Boss," *Fortune,* March 17, 2008, pp. 121–126; and L. Lee and P. Burrows, "Is Dell Too Big for Michael Dell?" *BusinessWeek,* February 12, 2007, p. 33.

25. S. Carey and P. Prada, "Course Change: Why JetBlue Shuffled Top Rank," *The Wall Street Journal,* May 11, 2007, pp. B1, B2.

26. Carey and Prada, 2007.

27. J. Hanna, "HBS Cases: JetBlue's Valentine's Day Crisis," *Harvard Business School Working Knowledge,* March 31, 2008, http://hbswk.hbs.edu/item/5880.html (accessed March 31, 2008).

28. "Winter Storm Rattles JetBlue," *BusinessWeek,* February 20, 2007, http://www.businessweek.com/investor/content/feb2007/pi20070220_742628.htm?chan=search (accessed March 31, 2008).

29. Hanna, 2008.

30. T. Reed, "Is JetBlue Back?" TheStreet.com, February 5, 2008, http://www.thestreet.com/_more/s/is-jetblue-back/newsanalysis/transportation/10401822.html? (accessed March 31, 2008).

31. W. Disney, quoted in B. Nanus, *Visionary Leadership: Creating a Compelling Sense of Direction for Your Organization* (San Francisco: Jossey-Bass, 1992), p. 28; reprinted from B. Thomas, *Walt Disney: An American Tradition* (New York: Simon & Schuster, 1976), p. 247.

32. B. Iyer and T. Davenport, "Reverse Engineering Google's Innovation Machine," *Harvard Business Review*, April 2008, pp. 59–68.

33. Nanus, 1992, pp. 28–29.

34. R. Kreitner, *Management,* 7th ed. (Boston: Houghton Mifflin, 1998), p. 206. Also see S. Kapner, "How Fashion's VF Supercharges Its Brands," *Fortune,* April 14, 2008, pp. 108–110.

35. C. H. Roush Jr. and B. C. Ball Jr., "Controlling the Implementation of Strategy," *Managerial Planning,* November–December 1980, p. 4.

36. B. W. Barry, "A Beginner's Guide to Strategic Planning," *The Futurist,* April 1998, pp. 33–36 from B. W. Barry, *Strategic Planning Workbook for Nonprofit Organizations,* revised and updated (St. Paul, MN: Amherst H. Wilder Foundation, 1997).

37. Barry, 1998, p. 36.

38. Steve Jobs, interviewed by B. Morris, "What Makes Apple Golden," *Fortune,* March 17, 2008, pp. 72, 74.

39. T. Cowan, "In Favor of Face Time," *Forbes,* October 1, 2007, p. 30.

40. K. Maher, "Running Meetings," *The Wall Street Journal,* January 13, 2004, p. B6.

41. C. L. Romero, "Tedious Meetings Top Time-Waster," *Arizona Republic,* April 22, 2003, p. D2.

42. P. M. Lencioni, *Death by Meeting: A Leadership Fable . . . About Solving the Most Painful Problem in Business* (San Francisco: Jossey-Bass, 2004).

43. P. Lencioni, reported in D. Murphy, "Making Sense of Meetings," *San Francisco Chronicle,* April 3, 2004, p. 1C.

44. O. Pollar, "Questions on Peers, Time, and Meetings," *San Francisco Examiner,* June 27, 1999, p. J-3.

45. Winston, 1994, pp. 152–157, 163–164; G. English, "How About a Good Word for Meetings?" *Management Review,* June 1990, pp. 58–60; L. G. McDougle, "Conducting a Successful Meeting," *Personnel Journal,* January 1981; D. Batstone, "Right Reality: Most Meetings Stink . . . 5 Tips for Making Yours Useful," *The Wag,* December 21, 2005, http://www.rightreality.com/wag_items/issues/051221wag.html (accessed July 11, 2008); S. G. Rogelberg, D. J. Leach, P. B. Warr, and J. L. Burnfield, "'Not Another Meeting!' Are Meeting Time Demands Related to Employee Well-Being?" *Journal of Applied Psychology,* January 2006, pp. 86–96; and M. Linksky, "The Morning Meeting Ritual," *Harvard Management Communication Letter,* June 19, 2006, http://hbswk.hbs.edu/archive/5388.html (accessed May 11, 2008).

46. J. Adamy, "McDonald's Takes On a Weakened Starbucks," *The Wall Street Journal,* November 7, 2008, pp. A1, A10; J. Adamy, "At Starbucks, Too Many, Too Quick?" *The Wall Street Journal,* November 15, 2007, pp. B1, B2; "Price Rise at Starbucks Cuts Visits and Shares," *The New York Times,* November 16, 2007, p. C4; S. Kang, J. Adamy, and S. Vranica, "TV Culture Is Culture Shift for Starbucks," *The Wall Street Journal,* November 17, 2007, pp. A1, A7; T. Howard, "Battle Brews for Your Coffee-Drinking Habit," *USA Today,* December 20, 2007, p. 3B; T. Clark, "Don't Fear Starbucks," *Slate Magazine,* December 28, 2007, http://www.slate.com/id/2180301/ (accessed April 1, 2008); B. Helm and J. McGregor, "Howard Schultz's Grande Challenge," *BusinessWeek,* January 21, 2008, p. 28; and M. Vella, "How to Reenergize Starbucks," *BusinessWeek,* February 20, 2008, http://www.businessweek.com/innovate/content/feb2008/id20080220_372003.htm?chan=search (accessed April 1, 2008).

47. "'Commercial Jet Fuel Supply: Impact & Cost on the U.S. Airline Industry' Hearing Scheduled for Wednesday Morning," press release, U.S. House Committee on Transportation and Infrastructure, Washington, DC, February 14, 2006, http://www.house.gov/transportation/press/press2006/release5.html (accessed July 12, 2006).

48. J. C. Ogg, "Fuel Hedges Aren't Helping Southwest Shares," 14/7 Wall St., February 5, 2008, http://www.247wallst.com/2008/02/fuel-hedges-are.html (accessed April 1, 2008).

49. D. Levin, "Hedging Helps Low-Cost Airlines Hold Down Price of Aviation Fuel," *Detroit News,* March 18, 2004, www.detnews.com/2004/business/0403/18/c01-95805.htm (accessed June 7, 2006).

50. T. Romo, quoted in E. Roston, "Hedging Their Costs," *Time,* June 20, 2005, http://www.time.com/time/globalbusiness/article/0,9171,1074147,00.html (accessed July 12, 2006).

51. D. Grossman, "Oil Prices Put Business Travelers Over a Barrel," *USA Today,* March 31, 2008, http://www.usatoday.com/travel/columnist/grossman/2008-03-28-oil-prices-rising_N.htm (accessed April 2, 2008).

52. M. E. Porter, *Competitive Strategy* (New York: The Free Press, 1980). See also Porter, 2008.

53. Example from Michael J. Silverstein, *Treasure Hunt,* cited in M. Archer, "Author Finds 'Value Calculus' at Work," *USA Today,* June 12, 2006, p. 7B.

54. P. L. Brown, "Surfers in Turmoil with the Loss of a Major Supplier," *The New York Times,* December 30, 2006, p. A12; and M. Overfelt, "Rough Surf," *USA Today,* February 17, 2006, http://money.cnn.com/magazines/fsb/fsb_archive/2006/02/01/8368201/index.htm (accessed July 12, 2006).

55. "Amazon Lets Customers Text to Buy," *Reno Gazette-Journal,* April 2, 2008, p. 11A.

56. L. Rohter, "With Big Boost from Sugar Cane, Brazil Is Satisfying Its Fuel Needs," *The New York Times,* April 10, 2006, p. A1. See also R. Cohen, "Is Ethanol for Everybody?" *The New York Times,* January 10, 2008, http://www.nytimes.com/2008/01/10/opinion/10cohen.html (accessed April 2, 2008).

57. J. Greenberg, quoted in B. Horovitz, "Restoring the Golden-Arch Shine," *USA Today,* June 16, 1999, p. 3B.

58. S. McBride and Y. I. Kane, "As Toshiba Surrenders, What's Next for DVD's?" *The Wall Street Journal,* February 19, 2008,

pp. BI, B2; B. Barnes and M. Richtel, "Studios Are Trying to Stop DVD's from Fading to Black," *The New York Times,* February 25, 2008, pp. CI, C8; and P. Svensson, "Sony's Blu-ray Wins as Toshiba Drops HD DVD," *San Francisco Chronicle,* February 26, 2008, p. C3.

59. M. Snider, "DVD Feels First Sting of Slipping Sales," *USA Today,* January 7, 2008, p. ID.

60. "The End Again for Indian Motorcycle Corporation," *American Motorcycle Network,* September 22, 2003, www.american-motor.com/news.cfm?newsid=2236 (accessed May 20, 2006).

61. L. Bossidy and Ram Charan, with C. Burck, *Execution: The Discipline of Getting Things Done* (New York: Crown Business, 2002).

62. Bossidy and Charan, 2002, pp. 27–28.

63. Results can be found in "Wanted: Employees Who Get Things Done," *HR Magazine,* January 2008, p. 10.

64. Also see R. Kaplan and D. Norton, "Mastering the Management System," *Harvard Business Review,* January 2008, pp. 66–77.

65. Execution is also discussed by C. Montgomery, "Putting Leadership Back into Strategy," *Harvard Business Review,* January 2008, pp. 54–60; and J. Lorsch and R. Clark, "Leading from the Boardroom," *Harvard Business Review,* April 2008, pp. 105–III.

CHAPTER 7

1. M. H. Bazerman, *Judgment in Managerial Decision Making,* 7th ed. (New York: Wiley, 2008). See also D. E. Bell, H. Raiffa, and A. Tversky, eds., *Decision Making: Descriptive, Normative, and Prescriptive Interactions* (Cambridge: Cambridge University Press, 1988).

2. M. Easterby-Smith and M. A. Lyles, *The Blackwell Handbook of Organizational Learning and Knowledge Management* (Oxford: Blackwell Publishing, 2003).

3. B. Fischoff, "Hindsight ≠ Foresight: The Effect of Outcome Knowledge on Judgment under Uncertainty," *Journal of Experimental Psychology: Human Perception and Performance* I(1975), pp. 288–299.

4. P. Thomas, "Be Prepared for Surges of a Volatile Business," *The Wall Street Journal,* May II, 2004, p. B4; and "Windowbox.com: Making the World a Better Place; Ben Swett—Founder & CEO Biography," www.windowbox.com/contact/pr_benbio.html (accessed May 29, 2008).

5. Muriel Niederle, quoted in J. Tierney, "What Women Want," *The New York Times,* May 24, 2005, p. A25.

6. M. Niederle and L. Vesterlund, "Do Women Shy Away from Competition? Do Men Compete Too Much?" *Quarterly Journal of Economics,* August 2007, pp. 1067–1101.

7. The discussion of styles was based on material contained in A. J. Rowe and R. O. Mason, *Managing with Style: A Guide to Understanding, Assessing and Improving Decision Making* (San Francisco: Jossey-Bass, 1987), pp. I–17.

8. See Rowe and Mason, 1987; and M. J. Dollinger and W. Danis, "Preferred Decision-Making Styles: A Cross-Cultural Comparison," *Psychological Reports,* 1998, pp. 755–761 ; and K. R. Brousseau, M. J. Driver, G. Hourihan, and R. Larsson, "The Seasoned Executive's Decision-Making Style," *Harvard Business Review,* February 2006, p. III, http://custom.hbsp.com/custom/KORNFR0602F2006012769.pdf;jsessionid=BBCU302NQJFKOAKRGWCB5VQBKEOYIIPS (accessed July 16, 2008).

9. Chip Heath, quoted in J. Rae-Dupree, "Innovative Minds Don't Think Alike," *The New York Times,* December 30, 2007, business section, p. 3. C. Heath and D. Heath are co-authors of *Made to Stick: Why Some Ideas Survive and Others Die* (New York: Random House, 2007). For other writings pertaining to the curse of knowledge, see J. Fox, "Herd on the Street," *Time,* September I7, 2007, p. 59; D. Jones, "Even Good CEOs Pick the Wrong Direction," *USA Today,* November 7, 2007, pp. IB, 2B; F. Norris, "Bank Profits Had Whiff of Suspicion," *The New York Times,* November I6, 2007, pp. CI, C2; and P. L. Bernstein, "To Botch a Forecast, Rely on Past Experience," *The New York Times,* December 30, 2007, business section, p. 4.

10. L. DiCosmo, "Warren Buffett Invests Like a Girl," *The Motley Fool,* March 20, 2008, http://www.fool.com/investing/value/2008/03/20/warren-buffett-invests-like-a-girl.aspx (accessed April 9, 2008).

11. A. Markels, "Built to Make Billions?" *U.S. News & World Report,* August 6, 2007, pp. 51–52. See also A. Markels, "How to Make Money the Buffett Way," *U.S. News & World Report,* August 6, 2007, pp. 46–51.

12. D. Mitchell, "At Last, Buffett's Key to Success," *The New York Times,* April 5, 2008, p. B5. See also J. Clements, "He Invests, She Invests: Who Gets the Better Returns?" *The Wall Street Journal,* February 6, 2008, p. DI.

13. B. M. Barber and T. Odean, "Boys Will Be Boys: Gender, Overconfidence, and Common Stock Investment," *The Quarterly Journal of Economics,* February 2001, pp. 261–292, faculty.haas.berkeley.edu/odean/papers/gender/BoysWillBeBoys.pdf (accessed April 9, 2008).

14. Markels, "Built to Make Billions?" 2007.

15. A. Farnham, "Teaching Creativity Tricks to Buttoned-Down Executives," *Fortune,* January 10, 1994, pp. 94–100.

16. I. DeBare, "The Business May Change, but the Values Are the Same," *San Francisco Chronicle,* April 2, 2006, p. G5.

17. C. Hymowitz, "Everyone Likes to Laud Service to the Customer; Doing It Is the Problem," *The Wall Street Journal,* February 27, 2006, p. BI.

18. The Retail Customer Dissatisfaction Study 2006, conducted by the Jay H. Baker Retailing Initiative, Wharton, University of Pennsylvania, and the Verde Group, Toronto, reported in "Beware of Dissatisfied Customers: They Like to Blab," Knowledge@Wharton, http://knowledge.wharton.upenn.edu/index (accessed July I5, 2008).

19. Hymowitz, "Everyone Likes to Laud Service," 2006.

20. B. Kiviat, "The End of Customer Service," *Time,* March 24, 2008, p. 42.

21. S. Holmes, "The 787 Encounters Turbulence," *BusinessWeek,* June I9, 2006, pp. 38-40. See also S. Holmes, "Cleaning Up Boeing," *BusinessWeek,* March I3, 2006, pp. 63–68; and S. Holmes, "Boeing Straightens Up and Flies Right," *BusinessWeek,* May 8, 2006, pp. 69–70.

22. For a discussion of the strategy behind the Dreamliner, see C. Masters, "How Boeing Got Going," *Time,* September 10, 2007, pp. Global I–Global 6.

23. J. L. Lunsford, "Boeing, in Embarrassing Setback, Says 787 Dreamliner Will Be Delayed," *The Wall Street Journal,* October II, 2007, pp. AI, AI6.

24. R. Yu, "Boeing Again Delays Dreamliner's Debut," *USA Today,* January I7, 2008, p. 3B.

25. J. L. Lunsford, "Boeing Delays Dreamliner Delivery Again," *The Wall Street Journal,* April 10, 2008, p. B3.

26. H. A. Simon, *Administrative Behavior,* 3rd ed. (New York: Free Press, 1996); and H. A. Simon, "Making Management Decisions: The Role of Intuition and Emotion," *The Academy of Management Executive,* February 1987, pp. 57–63.

27. E. Sadler-Smith and E. Shefy, "The Intuitive Executive: Understanding and Applying 'Gut Feel' in Decision Making," *Academy of Management Executive,* February 2005, p. 20.

28. See E. Dane and M. G. Pratt, "Exploring Intuition and Its Role in Managerial Decision Making," *Academy of Management Review,* January 2007, pp. 33–54.

29. See D. Begley, "You Might Help a Teen Avoid Dumb Behavior by Nurturing Intuition," *The Wall Street Journal,* November 3, 2006, p. B1.

30. Courage and intuition are discussed by K. K. Reardon, "Courage as a Skill," *Harvard Business Review,* March 2007, pp. 51–56.

31. Masters, 2007.

32. J. Pfeffer and R. I. Sutton, "Profiting from Evidence-Based Management," *Strategy & Leadership,* 34, no. 2(2006), pp. 35–42; and J. Pfeffer and R. I. Sutton, "Evidence-Based Management," *Harvard Business Review,* January 2006, pp. 63–74. Pfeffer and Sutton have also produced a book, *Hard Facts, Dangerous Half-Truths, and Total Nonsense* (Cambridge, MA: Harvard Business School Press, 2006). For a discussion of the book, see C. Hymowitz, "Executives Must Stop Jumping Fad to Fad and Learn to Manage," *The Wall Street Journal,* May 15, 2006, p. B1.

33. Pfeffer and Sutton, "Profiting from Evidence-Based Management," 2006.

34. Pfeffer and Sutton, "Evidence-Based Management," 2006, pp. 66–67.

35. G. Loveman, "Diamonds in the Data Mine," *Harvard Business Review,* May 2003, pp. 109–113. See also T. Davenport, L. Prusak, and B. Strong, "Putting Ideas to Work," *The Wall Street Journal,* March 10, 2008, p. R11.

36. T. H. Davenport, "Competing on Analytics," *Harvard Business Review,* January 2006, pp. 99–107.

37. M. Lewis, *Moneyball: The Art of Winning an Unfair Game* (New York: W.W. Norton, 2004).

38. For comment on the Oakland A's and *Moneyball,* see J. Manuel, "Majoring in Moneyball," Baseball America Features, December 23, 2003, http://www.baseballamerica.com/today/features/031223collegemoneyball.html; J. Zasky, "Pay for Performance, Stupid," *Failure Magazine,* June 2003, http://failuremag.com/archives_business_sports_moneyball.html; R. Van Zandt, "Billy Beane's Perfect Draft: A Baseball Revolution?" BaseballEvolution.com, April 13, 2006, http://baseballevolution.com/guest/richard/rvzbeanel.html; and "Moneyball: The Art of Winning an Unfair Game," Wikipedia, July 12, 2006, http://en.wikipedia.org/wiki/Moneyball (all accessed July 14, 2008).

39. C. Price, *The Blueprint: How the New England Patriots Beat the System to Create the Last Great NFL Superpower* (New York: Thomas Dunne/St. Martin's Press, 2007).

40. Davenport, 2006.

41. M. B. Zuckerman, "Policing the Corporate Suites," *U.S. News & World Report,* January 19, 2004, p. 72.

42. Bill Gates, quoted in R. A. Guth, "Bill Gates Issues Call for Kinder Capitalism," *The Wall Street Journal,* January 24, 2008, pp. A1, A15. See also C. Boles, "Last Call? Gates Pushes Globalism in Remarks," *The Wall Street Journal,* March 13, 2008, p. B3.

43. C. McNamara, "Complete Guide to Ethics Management: An Ethics Toolkit for Managers," www.mapnp.org/library/ethics/ethxgde.htm (accessed May 29, 2008).

44. C. E. Bagley, "The Ethical Leader's Decision Tree," *Harvard Business Review,* February 2003, pp. 18–19.

45. A.-M. Cusac, "U.S. Companies Trick Retirees out of Health Benefits," *UNI In Depth,* September 4, 2001, www.union-network.org/uniindep.nsf/0/5449la47e00ad956cl256a2900282ebe?Open Document (accessed May 29, 2008).

46. J. Appleby, "More Companies Trim Retiree Health Benefits," *USATODAY.com,* January 14, 2004, www.usatoday.com/money/industries/health/2004-01-15-retiree_x.htm (accessed May 29, 2008).

47. Bagley, 2003, p. 19.

48. K. Hodgson, *A Rock and a Hard Place: How to Make Ethical Business Decisions When the Choices Are Tough* (New York: AMACOM, 1992), pp. 66–77.

49. G. W. Hill, "Group versus Individual Performance: Are $n + 1$ Heads Better Than I?" *Psychological Bulletin,* May 1982, pp. 517–539. Also see W.T.H. Koh, "Heterogeneous Expertise and Collective Decision-Making," *Social Choice and Welfare,* April 2008, pp. 457–473.

50. N. F. R. Maier, "Assets and Liabilities in Group Problem Solving: The Need for Integrative Function," *Psychological Review* 74(1967) pp. 239–249.

51. Maier, 1967.

52. Methods for increasing group consensus were investigated by R. L. Priem, D. A. Harrison, and N. K. Muir, "Structured Conflict and Consensus Outcomes in Group Decision Making," *Journal of Management,* December 22, 1995, pp. 691–710.

53. See D. L. Gladstein and N. P. Reilly, "Group Decision Making under Threat: The Tycoon Game," *Academy of Management Journal,* September 1985, pp. 613–627.

54. These conclusions were based on the following studies: J. H. Davis, "Some Compelling Intuitions about Group Consensus Decisions, Theoretical and Empirical Research, and Interpersonal Aggregation Phenomena: Selected Examples, 1950–1990," *Organizational Behavior and Human Decision Processes,* June 1992, pp. 3–38; and J. A. Sniezek, "Groups Under Uncertainty: An Examination of Confidence in Group Decision Making," *Organizational Behavior and Human Decision Processes,* June 1992, pp. 124–155.

55. Supporting results can be found in J. R. Hollenbeck, D. R. Ilgen, D. J. Sego, J. Hedlund, D. A. Major, and J. Phillips, "Multilevel Theory of Team Decision Making: Decision Performance in Teams Incorporating Distributed Expertise," *Journal of Applied Psychology,* April 1995, pp. 292–316.

56. See D. H. Gruenfeld, E. A. Mannix, K. Y. Williams, and M. A. Neale, "Group Composition and Decision Making: How Member Familiarity and Information Distribution Affect Process and Performance," *Organizational Behavior and Human Decision Processes,* July 1996, pp. 1–15.

57. "Jack Welch's Lessons for Success," *Fortune,* January 25, 1993, p. 86.

58. See D. Pojidaeff, "Human Productivity and Pride in Work: The Core Principles of Participative Management," *Journal for Quality and Participation,* December 1995, pp. 44–47; and N. A. Holland, "A Pathway to Global Competitiveness and Total Quality: Participative Management," *Journal for Quality and Participation,* September 1995, pp. 58–62.

59. Results are presented in J. T. Delaney, "Workplace Cooperation: Current Problems, New Approaches," *Journal of Labor Research,* Winter 1996, pp. 45–61.

60. For an extended discussion, see M. Sashkin, "Participative Management Is an Ethical Imperative," *Organizational Dynamics,* Spring 1984, pp. 4–22. Also see S. Meisinger, "Management Holds Key to Employee Engagement," *HR Magazine,* February 2008, p. 8.

61. Supporting results can be found in C. R. Leana, R. S. Ahlbrandt, and A. J. Murrell, "The Effects of Employee Involvement Programs on Unionized Workers' Attitudes, Perceptions, and Preferences in Decision Making," *Academy of Management Journal,* October 1992, pp. 861–873; and D. Plunkett, "The Creative Organization: An Empirical Investigation of the Importance of Participation in Decision Making," *Journal of Creative Behavior,* Second Quarter 1990, pp. 140–148. Results

pertaining to role conflict and ambiguity can be found in C. S. Smith and M. T. Brannick, "A Role Replication and Theoretical Extension," *Journal of Organizational Behavior,* March 1990, pp. 91–104.

62. See J. A. Wagner III, "Participation's Effects on Performance and Satisfaction: A Reconsideration of Research Evidence," *Academy of Management Review,* April 1994, pp. 312–330.

63. A thorough discussion of this issue is provided by W. A. Randolph, "Navigating the Journey to Empowerment," *Organizational Dynamics,* Spring 1995, pp. 19–32.

64. G. M. Parker, *Team Players and Teamwork: The New Competitive Business Strategy* (San Francisco: Jossey-Bass, 1990).

65. These recommendations were obtained from G. M. Parker, *Team Players and Teamwork.*

66. A. F. Osborn, *Applied Imagination: Principles and Procedures of Creative Thinking,* 3rd ed. (New York: Scribner's, 1979). For an example of how brainstorming works, see P. Croce, "Think Brighter," *FSB,* January 2006, p. 35.

67. W. H. Cooper, R. Brent Gallupe, S. Pallard, and J. Cadsby, "Some Liberating Effects of Anonymous Electronic Brainstorming," *Small Group Research,* April 1998, pp. 147–178.

68. These recommendations and descriptions were derived from B. Nussbaum, "The Power of Design," *BusinessWeek,* May 17, 2004, pp. 86–94.

69. A thorough description of computer-aided decision-making systems is provided by M. C. Er and A. C. Ng, "The Anonymity and Proximity Factors in Group Decision Support Systems," *Decision Support Systems,* May 1995, pp. 75–83; and A. LaPlante, "Brainstorming," *Forbes,* October 25, 1993, pp. 45–61.

70. Results can be found in J. S. Valacich and C. Schwenk, "Devils' Advocacy and Dialectical Inquiry Effects on Face-to-Face and Computer-Mediated Group Decision Making," *Organizational Behavior and Human Decision Processes,* August 1995, pp. 158–173; R. B. Gallupe, W. H. Cooper, M. Grise, and L. M. Bastianutti, "Blocking Electronic Brain-storms," *Journal of Applied Psychology,* February 1994, pp. 77–86; and A. R. Dennis and J. S. Valacich, "Computer Brainstorms: More Heads Are Better Than One," *Journal of Applied Psychology,* August 1993, pp. 531–537.

71. Supportive results can be found in S. S. Lam and J. Schaubroeck, "Improving Group Decisions by Better Polling Information: A Comparative Advantage of Group Decision Support Systems," *Journal of Applied Psychology,* August 2000, pp. 565–573; and I. Benbasat and J. Lim, "Information Technology Support for Debiasing Group Judgments: An Empirical Evaluation," *Organizational Behavior and Human Decision Processes,* September 2000, pp. 167–183.

72. B. B. Baltes, M. W. Dickson, M. P. Sherman, C. C. Bauer, and J. S. LaGanke, "Computer-Mediated Communication and Group Decision Making: A Meta-Analysis," *Organizational Behavior and Human Decision Processes,* January 2002, pp. 156–179.

73. C. E. Cryder, J. S. Lerner, J. J. Gross, and R. E. Dahl, "Misery Is Not Miserly: Sad and Self-Focused Individuals Spend More," *Psychological Science,* June 2008, in press. The study is reported in M. Jewell, "People Spend More When They Are Sad and Self-Absorbed," *San Francisco Chronicle,* February 8, 2008, p. C3.

74. A description of the work of Daniel Gilbert appears in P. J. Hilts, "In Forecasting Their Emotions, Most People Flunk Out," *The New York Times,* February 16, 1999, p. D2. See also D. Gilbert, *Stumbling on Happiness* (New York: Vintage, 2007).

75. D. D. Wheeler and I. L. Janis, *A Practical Guide for Making Decisions* (New York: Free Press, 1980), pp. 34–35; and I. L. Janis and L. Mann, *Decision Making: A Psychological Analysis of Conflict, Choice, and Commitment* (New York: The Free Press, 1977).

76. R. Beck, "The Difference a Year Made in Mortgage Mess," *San Francisco Chronicle,* December 26, 2007, p. D2.

77. P. Steel, "The Nature of Procrastination: A Meta-Analytic and Theoretical Review of Quintessential Self-Regulatory Failure," *Psychological Bulletin* 133(2007), pp. 65–94.

78. Gurnek Bains, CEO of YSC, London, quoted in C. Hymowitz, "Best Way to Save: Analyze Why Talent Is Going Out the Door," *The Wall Street Journal,* September 24, 2007, p. B1.

79. A. Levin and L. Parker, "Human, Mechanical Flaws Cut Off Path to Survival," *USA Today,* July 12, 1999, pp. 1A, 8A, 9A. Sometimes observers speak of a "fog of war," in which too much information or scattered information overwhelms decision-making abilities. See, for example, E. Lipson, "Hurricane Investigators See 'Fog of War' at White House," *The New York Times,* January 28, 2006, p. A8. Decision makers may also often be unable to discriminate between relevant and irrelevant alternatives, including extraneous considerations in their probability judgments. See M. R. Dougherty and A. Sprenger, "The Influence of Improper Sets of Information on Judgment: How Irrelevant Information Can Bias Judged Probability," *Journal of Experimental Psychology: General,* May 2006, pp. 262–281.

80. Wheeler and Janis, 1980.

81. Based on J. L. Roberts, "I Want My (Web) MTV," *Newsweek,* April 14, 2008, pp. E8–E11.

82. D. Kahnemann and A. Tversky, "Judgment under Uncertainty: Heuristics and Biases," *Science* 185(1974), pp. 1124–1131; A. Tversky and D. Kahneman, "Availability: A Heuristic for Judging Frequency and Probability," *Cognitive Psychology* 5(1975), pp. 207–232; A. Tversky and D. Kahneman, "The Belief in the Law of Numbers," *Psychological Bulletin* 76(1971), pp. 105–110; C. R. Schwenk, "Cognitive Simplification Processes in Strategic Decision Making," *Strategic Management Journal* 5(1984), pp. 111–128; K. McKean, "Decisions," *Discover,* June 1985, pp. 22–31; J. Rockner, "The Escalation of Commitment to a Failing Course of Action: Toward Theoretical Progress," *Academy of Management Review* 17(1980), pp. 39–61; D. R. Bobocel and J. P. Meyer, "Escalating Commitment to a Failing Course of Action: Separating the Roles of Choice and Justification," *Journal of Applied Psychology,* June 1994, pp. 360–363; B. M. Shaw, "The Escalation of Commitment to a Course of Action," *Academy of Management Review,* October 1981, pp. 577–587; and M. Useem and J. Useem, "Great Escapes," *Fortune,* June 27, 2005, pp. 97–102; K. Sengupta, T. Abdel-Hamid, and L. Van Wassenhove, "The Experience Trap," *Harvard Business Review,* February 2008, pp. 94–101; and M. Heilman and T. Okimoto, "Motherhood: A Potential Source of Bias in Employment Decisions," *Journal of Applied Psychology,* January 2008, pp. 189–198.

83. W. Goodman, "How Gambling Makes Strange Bedfellows," *The New York Times,* June 10, 1997, p. B3.

84. P. Slovic, "The Construction of a Preference," *American Psychologist* 50(1995), pp. 364–371; K. J. Dunegan, "Framing, Cognitive Roles, and Image Theory: Toward an Understanding of a Glass Half Full," *Journal of Applied Psychology* 78(1993), pp. 491–503; and K. F. E. Wong, M. Yik, and J. Y. Y. Kwong, "Understanding the Emotional Aspects of Escalation of Commitment: The Role of Negative Affect," *Journal of Applied Psychology,* March 2006, pp. 282–297.

85. S. Thurm, "Seldom-Used Executive Power: Reconsidering," *The Wall Street Journal,* February 6, 2006, p. B3.

86. David Dorfman, quoted in H. Lancaster, "How Life Lessons Have Helped a Successful Manager," *San Francisco Sunday*

Examiner & Chronicle, August 15, 1999, p. CL-33; reprinted from *The Wall Street Journal.*

87. J. S. Hammond, R. L. Keeney, and H. Raiffa, *Smart Choices: A Practical Guide to Making Better Decisions* (Boston: Harvard Business School Press, 1999).

88. O. Pollar, "Six Steps for Making Tough Choices," *San Francisco Examiner & Chronicle,* April 4, 1999, p. J-3.

CHAPTER 8

1. S. Stecklow, "Management 101," *The Wall Street Journal,* December 9, 1994, p. B1.

2. O. Pollar, "Don't Overlook the Importance of Delegating," *San Francisco Examiner,* August 8, 1999, p. J-3.

3. C. M. Avery, M. A. Walker, and E. O'Toole, *Teamwork Is an Individual Skill: Getting Your Work Done When Sharing Responsibility* (San Francisco: Berrett-Koehler, 2001); S. Gazda, "The Art of Delegating: Effective Delegation Enhances Employee Morale, Manager Productivity, and Organizational Success," *HR Magazine,* January 2002, pp. 75–79; R. Burns, *Making Delegation Happen: A Simple and Effective Guide to Implementing Successful Delegation* (St. Leonards, Australia: Allen & Unwin, 2002); D. M. Genett, *If You Want It Done Right, You Don't Have to Do It Yourself! The Power of Effective Delegation* (Sanger, CA: Quill Driver Books, 2003); R. Charan, "People Acumen," *Fast Company,* December 2007, http://www.fastcompany.com/articles/2007/12/ram-charan-acumen.html (accessed April 13, 2008).

4. E. Raudsepp, "Why Supervisors Don't Delegate," *Supervision,* May 1979, pp. 12–15; D. Anderson, "Supervisors and the Hesitate to Delegate Syndrome," *Supervision,* November 1992, pp. 9–11; O. Pollar, 1999; Avery et al., 2001; Burns, 2002; and Genett, 2003.

5. K. K. Reardon, *The Secret Handshake: Mastering the Politics of the Business Inner Circle* (New York: Doubleday, 2002) and *It's All Politics: Winning in a World Where Hard Work and Talent Aren't Enough* (New York: Currency/Random House, 2005).

6. K. K. Reardon, interviewed by J. Vishnevsky, "Ask the Expert: Kathleen Kelley Reardon," *U.S. News & World Report,* July 25, 2005, p. EE10. See also C. Bush, "Learn How to Work with Others," *Arizona Republic,* August 21, 2005, p. EC1.

7. E. H. Schein, "The Role of the Founder in Creating Organizational Culture," *Organizational Dynamics,* Summer 1983, pp. 13–28; E. H. Schein, *Organizational Culture and Leadership* (San Francisco: Jossey-Bass, 1985); and E. H. Schein, "Organizational Culture," *American Psychologist* 45(1990), pp. 109–119.

8. Reward systems are discussed in J. Kerr and J. W. Slocum, "Managing Corporate Culture through Reward Systems," *Academy of Management Executive,* November 2005, pp. 83–94.

9. A thorough description of the competing values framework is provided in K. S. Cameron, R. E. Quinn, J. Degraff, and A. V. Thakor, *Creating Values Leadership* (Northhampton, MA: Edward Elgar, 2006); and K. S. Cameron and R. E. Quinn, *Diagnosing and Changing Organizational Culture* (New York: Addison-Wesley, 1999).

10. E. H. Schein, *Organizational Culture and Leadership,* 2nd ed. (San Francisco: Jossey-Bass, 1992).

11. Bill Greehey, quoted in B. Leonard, "Taking Care of Their Own," *HR Magazine,* June 2006, pp. 113–114.

12. B. Breen, "The Thrill of Defeat," *Fast Company,* June 2004, pp. 76–81. A comprehensive article about companies that cultivate cultures that embrace failure and learn from it is

J. McGregor, "How Failure Breeds Success," *BusinessWeek,* July 10, 2006, pp. 42–52.

13. R. Charan, "Home Depot's Blueprint for Culture Change," *Harvard Business Review,* April 2006, pp. 61–71; and B. Grow, "Renovating Home Depot," *BusinessWeek,* March 6, 2006, pp. 50–58.

14. S. S. Watkins, in testimony before the Oversight and Investigations Subcommittee of the House Energy and Commerce Committee, U.S. Congress, February 14, 2002.

15. Defamation complaint filed in New York State Supreme Court by former employee Judith Regan of HarperCollins, reported in M. Rich, "In Complaint, a Portrait of a Company Marked by Rivalry," *The New York Times,* November 14, 2007, p. A18.

16. A. Lucchetti and M. Langley, "Amid Turmoil, a Shake-up at Citi: Perform-or-Die Culture Leaves Thin Talent Pool for Top Wall Street Jobs," *The Wall Street Journal,* November 5, 2007, pp. A1, A16.

17. E. Frauenheim, "Lost in the Shuffle," *Workforce Management,* January 14, 2008, pp. 1, 12–17.

18. E. Byron, "Call Me Mike!" *The Wall Street Journal,* March 27, 2006, p. B1.

19. P. Babcock, "Is Your Company Two-Faced?" *HR Magazine,* January 2004, p. 43.

20. C. Hymowitz, "New CEOs May Spur Resistance If They Try to Alter Firm's Culture," *The Wall Street Journal,* August 13, 2007, p. B1.

21. T. E. Deal and A. A. Kennedy, *Corporate Cultures: The Rites and Rituals of Corporate Life* (Reading, MA: Addison-Wesley, 1982), p. 22. See also T. E. Deal and A.A. Kennedy, *The New Corporate Cultures: Revitalizing the Workplace After Downsizing, Mergers, and Reengineering* (Cambridge, MA: Perseus, 2000).

22. C. Jarnagin and J. W. Slocum Jr., "Creating Corporate Cultures through Mythopoetic Leadership," *Organizational Dynamics* 36(2007), pp. 288–302.

23. A. Farnham, "Mary Kay's Lessons in Leadership," *Fortune,* September 20, 1993, pp. 68–77.

24. Deal and Kennedy, 1982.

25. Adapted from L. Smircich, "Concepts of Culture and Organizational Analysis," *Administrative Science Quarterly,* September 1983, pp. 339–358.

26. S. McCarney, "Airline Industry's Top-Rated Woman Keeps Southwest's Small-Fry Spirit Alive," *The Wall Street Journal,* November 30, 1996, pp. B1, B11.

27. D. Anfuso, "3M's Staffing Strategy Promotes Productivity and Pride," *Personnel Journal,* February 1995, pp. 28–34.

28. The strength perspective was promoted by T. E. Deal and A. A. Kennedy, 1982.

29. The HP Way is thoroughly discussed in J. Dong, "The Rise and Fall of the HP Way," *Palo Alto Weekly Online Edition,* April 10, 2002; http://www.paloaltoonline.com/weekly/morgue/2002/2002_04_10.hpway10.html (accessed August 4, 2008).

30. J. P. Kotter and J. L. Heskett, *Corporate Culture and Performance* (New York: Free Press, 1992).

31. S. Berfield, "Less Insult from Injury," *BusinessWeek,* August 14, 2006, pp. 62–63.

32. The mechanisms are based on material contained in E. H. Schein, "The Role of the Founder in Creating Organizational Culture," *Organizational Dynamics,* Summer 1983, pp. 13–28.

33. Wal-Mart's values are stated on its corporate Web site, "About Wal-Mart," http://www.walmart.com/catalog/cata-log.gsp?cat=131473#null (accessed August 7, 2008)

34. Jarnagin and Slocum, 2007.

35. J. Stossel and G. Silber, "Sexy Sweats without the Sweat-shop," ABC News, July 31, 2006; http://abcnews.go.com/2020/Business/story?id=2257111 (accessed August 7, 2008).

36. D. Moss, "Triage: Methodically Developing Its Employees," HRMagazine, July 2007, p 45.

37. D. Clark, "Why Silicon Valley Is Rethinking the Cubicle Office," The Wall Street Journal, October 15, 2007, http://online.wsj.com/article/SB119240097861658633.html?mod=hps_us_mostpop_viewed (accessed April 27, 2008).

38. Moss, 2007.

39. J. Ball, "Might Profit Maker," The Wall Street Journal, April 8, 2005, p. B1.

40. B. Robert, "Social Networking at the Office," Newsfactor.com, March 6, 2008, http://www.newsfactor.com/story.xhtml?story_id=020001U670NS&page=1 (accessed) May 16, 2008).

41. C. I. Barnard, The Functions of the Executive (Cambridge, MA: Harvard University Press, 1938), p. 73.

42. P. M. Blau and W. R. Scott, Formal Organizations (San Francisco: Chandler, 1962).

43. Development Dimension International (DDI) Global Leadership Forecast of 4,561 respondents from 42 countries, reported in "Mentoring Impact," USA Today, March 22, 2006, p. 1B.

44. M. Cottle, "Minding Your Mentors," The New York Times, March 7, 1999, sec. 3, p. 8; C. Dahle, "HP's Mentor Connection," Fast Company, November 1998, pp. 78-80; and I. Abbott, "If You Want to Be an Effective Mentor, Consider These Tips," San Francisco Examiner, October 18, 1998, p. J-3; D. A. Thomas, "The Truth about Mentoring Minorities—Race Matters," Harvard Business Review, April 2001, pp. 366-391; S. A. Mehta, "Best Companies for Minorities: Why Mentoring Works," Fortune, July 9, 2001, www.fortune.com/fortune/diversity/articles/0,15114,370475,00.html (accessed April 15, 2008); F. Warner, "Inside Intel's Mentoring Movement," Fast Company, April 2002, p. 116; B. Raabe and T. A. Beehr, "Formal Mentoring versus Supervisor and Coworker Relationships: Differences in Perceptions and Impact," Journal of Organizational Behavior 24(2003), pp. 271-293; and A. Fisher, "A New Kind of Mentor," Fortune, July 2004, www.fortune.com/fortune/annie/0,15704,368863,00.html (accessed April 15, 2008).

45. Anne Hayden, quoted in Cottle, 1999.

46. E. H. Schein, Organizational Psychology, 3rd ed. (Englewood Cliffs, NJ: Prentice-Hall, 1980).

47. For an overview of the span of control concept, see D. D. Van Fleet and A. G. Bedeian, "A History of the Span of Management," Academy of Management Review, July 1977, pp. 356-372.

48. Research by V. Smeets and F. Warzynski, Aarhus School of Business, Denmark, to be published in Labour Economics. Reported in G. Anders, "Overseeing More Employees—With Fewer Managers," The Wall Street Journal, March 24, 2008, p. B6.

49. T. A. Stewart, "CEOs See Clout Shifting," Fortune, November 6, 1989, p. 66.

50. Pollar, 1999.

51. D. Machalaba, "After Crippling Chaos, Union Pacific Can See the Proverbial Light," The Wall Street Journal, August 25, 1999, pp. A1, A8.

52. L. Grant, "New Jewel in the Crown," U.S. News & World Report, February 28, 1994, pp. 55-57; H. Rothman, "The Power of Empowerment," Nation's Business, June 1993, pp. 49-52; and J. Galbraith, Designing Complex Organizations (Reading, MA: Addison-Wesley, 1973).

53. "Virtual Organization," Whatis.com, http://whatis.techtarget.com/definition/0,,sid9_gci213301,00.html (accessed June 12, 2006). See also J. A. Byrne, "The Virtual Corporation," BusinessWeek, February 8, 1993, pp. 98-102; G. Lorenzoni and C. Baden-Fuller, "Creating a Strategic Center to Manage a Web of Partners," California Management Review, Spring 1995, pp. 146-163.

54. A. Lashinsky, "RAZR's Edge," Fortune, June 12, 2006, pp. 124-132.

55. N. Anand and R. L. Daft, "What Is the Right Organization Design?" Organizational Dynamics 36(2007), pp. 329-344.

56. J. Hyatt, "The Soul of a New Team," Fortune, June 12, 2006, pp. 134-143.

57. Anand and Daft, 2007, p. 336.

58. S. Siekman, "The Snap-Together Business Jet," Fortune, January 21, 2002, http://money.cnn.com/magazines/fortune/fortune_archive/2002/01/21/316585/index.htm (accessed April 16, 2008); and Anand and Daft, 2007, p. 336.

59. P. F. Drucker, quoted in J. A. Byrne, "Advice from the Dr. Spock of Business," BusinessWeek, September 28, 1987, p. 61.

60. K. Deveny, "Bag Those Fries, Squirt That Ketchup, Fry That Fish," BusinessWeek, October 13, 1986, p. 86.

61. T. Burns and G. M. Stalker, The Management of Innovation (London: Tavistock, 1961). See also W. D. Sine, H. Mitsuhashi, and D. A. Kirsch, "Revisiting Burns and Stalker: Formal Structure and New Venture Performance in Emerging Economic Sectors," Academy of Management Journal, February 2006, pp. 121-132.

62. T. J. Peters and R. H. Waterman, In Search of Excellence (New York: Harper & Row, 1982).

63. Inc.com, "Virtual Company Advice," 101 Great Ideas for Managing People from America's Most Innovative Small Companies, October 1999, http://www.inc.com/articles/1999/10/19238.html (accessed August 9, 2008); and M. Puente, "Direct Selling Brings It All Home," USA Today, October 27, 2003, http://www.usatoday.com/life/2003-10-27-home-shopping_x.htm (accessed August 9, 2008).

64. P. R. Lawrence and J. W. Lorsch, Organization and Environment (Homewood, IL: Irwin, 1967).

65. D. S. Pugh and D. J. Hickson, Organization Structure in Its Context: The Aston Program (Lexington, MA: D. C. Heath, 1976); and R. Z. Gooding and J. A. Wagner III, "A Meta-Analytic Review of the Relationship between Size and Performance: The Productivity and Efficiency of Organizations and Their Subunits," Administrative Science Quarterly, December 1985, pp. 462-481.

66. C. H. Deutsch, "In 2007, Some Giants Went Smaller," The New York Times, January 1, 2008, pp. C1, C5; and B. Hindo, "Solving Tyco's Identity Crisis," BusinessWeek, February 18, 2008, pp. 62-63.

67. A. Smith, "The Complex Task of Simplicity," Time, March 3, 2008, pp. Global 1-Global 4.

68. Peters and Waterman, 1982, pp. 272-273.

69. P. Parker, quoted in C. Palmeri, "A Process that Never Ends," Forbes, December 21, 1992, p. 55.

70. J. Woodward, Industrial Organization: Theory and Practice (London: Oxford University Press, 1965).

71. J. R. Kimberly, R. H. Miles, and associates, The Organizational Life Cycle (San Francisco: Jossey-Bass, 1980).

CHAPTER 9

1. J. Welch and S. Welch, "Dear Graduate. . . ," BusinessWeek, June 19, 2006, p. 100.

2. E. Holton, S. Naquin, and E. Holton, So You're New Again: How to Succeed When You Change Jobs (San Francisco:

Berrett-Koehler Publishers, 2001); M. Watkins, *The First 90 Days: Critical Success Strategies for New Leaders at All Levels* (Boston: Harvard Business School Press, 2003); J. S. Lublin, "How to Win Support from Colleagues at Your New Job," *The Wall Street Journal,* November 25, 2003, p. B1; J. Burke, "Dip, Before Diving, into That New Job," *Business-Week Online,* June 28, 2004, http://www.businessweek .com/bschools/content/jun2004/bs20040628_9967_ bs001.htm (accessed April 19, 2008); L. Wolgemuth, "Breaking Out of the First-Job Trap," *U.S. News & World Report,* March 24/March 31, 2008, pp. 56, 58.

3. M. Sunnafrank and A. Ramirez Jr., "At First Sight: Persistent Relational Effects of Get-Acquainted Conversations," *Journal of Social and Personal Relationships,* June 1, 2004, pp. 361–379. See also J. Zaslow, "First Impressions Get Faster," *The Wall Street Journal,* February 16, 2006, p. D4.

4. G. Lingaard, G. Fernandes, C. Dudek, and J. Brown, "Attention Web Designers: You Have 50 Milliseconds to Make a Good First Impression," *Behaviour & Information Technology,* March–April 2006, pp. 115–126.

5. R. Ailes, in "Your First Seven Seconds," *Fast Company,* June–July 1998, p. 184.

6. J. Denrell, "Why Most People Disapprove of Me: Experience Sampling in Impression Formation," *Psychological Review,* October 2005, pp. 951–978. See also M. Krakovsky, "Researcher Disputes Notion You Have Only One Chance to Make a Good Impression," *Stanford Report,* August 18, 2004, http://news-service.stanford.edu/news/2004/august18/ impressions-818.html (accessed April 19, 2008).

7. L. P. Frankel, in "Your First Impression," *Fast Company,* June–July 1998, p. 188.

8. R. Levering and M. Moskowitz, "The Rankings," *Fortune,* February 4, 2008, pp. 75–94.

9. A. Fisher, "How to Get Hired by a 'Best' Company," *Fortune,* February 4, 2008, p. 96.

10. A. Lashinsky, "The Perks of Being a Googler," *Fortune,* January 8, 2007, http://money.cnn.com/galeries/2007/fortune/0701/gallery.Google_perks (accessed April 19, 2008).

11. E. Schmidt, quoted in interview by A. Lashinsky, "Back2Back Champs," *Fortune,* February 4, 2008, p. 70.

12. S. Clifford, "A Web Shift in the Way Advertisers Seek Clicks," *The New York Times,* April 21, 2008, pp. C1, C9.

13. J. Welch, quoted in N. M. Tichy and S. Herman, *Control Your Destiny or Someone Else Will: How Jack Welch Is Making General Electric the World's Most Competitive Corporation* (New York: Doubleday, 1993), p. 251.

14. P. Capelli and A. Crocker-Hefter, "Distinctive Human Resources Are Firms' Core Competencies," *Organizational Dynamics,* Winter 1996, pp. 7–22.

15. G. Bollander, S. Snell, and A. Sherman, *Managing Human Resources,* 12th ed. (Cincinnati, OH: SouthWestern Publishing, 2001), pp. 13–15; and B. E. Becker, M. A. Huselid, and D. Ulrich, *The HR Scorecard: Linking People, Strategy, and Performance* (Boston: Harvard Business School Press, 2001), p. 4. See also D. Stamps, "Measuring Minds," *Training,* May 2000, pp. 76–85; C. A. Bartlett and S. Ghoshal, "Building Competitive Advantage through People," *MIT Sloan Management Review,* Winter 2002, pp. 34–41; and R. Rodriguez, "Meet the New Learning Executive," *HR Magazine,* April 2005, pp. 64–69.

16. B. E. Becker, M. A. Huselid, and D. Ulrich, *The HR Scorecard: Linking People, Strategy, and Performance* (Boston: Harvard Business School Press, 2001), p. 4.

17. Inspired by P. S. Adler and S. Kwon, "Social Capital: Prospects for New Concept," *Academy of Management Review,* January 2002, pp. 17–40. See also D. Lidsky, "Winning the Relationship Game," *Fast Company,* October 2004, pp. 113–115; J. Steinberg, "One Heart at a Time," *Fast Company,* November 2004, p. 49; K. H. Hammonds, "A Lever Long Enough to Move the World," *Fast Company,* January 2005, pp. 60–63; and A. C. Inkpen and E.W.K. Tsang, "Social Capital, Networks, and Knowledge Transfer," *Academy of Management Review,* January 2005, pp. 146–165.

18. R. Levering and M. Moskowitz, "The 100 Best Companies to Work For," *Fortune,* January 12, 2004, p. 68.

19. R. J. Mirabile, "The Power of Job Analysis," *Training,* April 1990, pp. 70–74; and S. F. Mona, "The Job Description," *Association Management,* February 1991, pp. 33–37.

20. S. Lau, J. Sweeney, and R. Halvorsen, "Minimum Wage, Record Retention, Major Change," *HR Magazine,* September 2007, p. 35.

21. See S. E. Needleman, "More Programs to Halt Bias Against Gays," *The Wall Street Journal,* November 26, 2007, p. B3. A countertrend to age discrimination may be the result of baby boomers retiring, bringing an overall shortfall in workers. See E. White, "The New Recruits: Older Workers," *The Wall Street Journal,* January 14, 2008, p. B3.

22. Associated Press, "Bias Cases by Workers Increase 9%," *The Wall Street Journal,* March 6, 2008, p. D6.

23. M. Bello, "Racial Harassment Cases Rise Sharply," *USA Today,* February 6, 2008, p. 3A.

24. S. Shellenbarger, "More Women Pursue Claims of Pregnancy Discrimination," *The Wall Street Journal,* March 27, 2008, p. D1.

25. Bureau of Labor Statistics, reported in C. Hymowitz, "On Diversity, America Isn't Putting Its Money Where Its Mouth Is," *The Wall Street Journal,* February 25, 2008, p. B1.

26. For a thorough discussion of affirmative action, see F. J. Crosby, A. Iyer, S. Clayton, and R. A. Downing, "Affirmative Action," *American Psychologist,* February 2003, pp. 93–115.

27. See H. J. Walker, H. S. Feild, W. F. Giles, J. B. Bernerth, and L. A. Jones-Farmer, "An Assessment of Attraction Toward Affirmative Action Organizations: Investigating the Role of Individual Differences," *Journal of Organizational Behavior,* May 2007, pp. 455–507.

28. E. H. James, A. P. Brief, J. Dietz, and R. R. Cohen, "Prejudice Matters: Understanding the Reactions of Whites to Affirmative Action Programs Targeted to Benefit Blacks," *Journal of Applied Psychology,* December 2001, pp. 1120–1128.

29. For a thorough review of relevant research, see M. E. Heilman, "Affirmative Action: Some Unintended Consequences for Working Women," in B. M. Staw and L. L. Cummings, eds., *Research in Organizational Behavior,* vol. 16 (Greenwich, CT: JAI Press, 1994), pp. 125–169.

30. M. Rotundo, D.-H. Nguyen, and P. R. Sackett, "A Meta-Analytic Review of Gender Differences in Perceptions of Sexual Harassment," *Journal of Applied Psychology,* October 2001, pp. 914–922.

31. Most research on sexual harassment has focused on harassment inside organizations. For a discussion of harassment beyond the boundaries of the organization, see H. J. Gettman and J. J. Gelfand, "When the Customer Shouldn't Be King: Antecedents and Consequences of Sexual Harassment by Clients and Customers," *Journal of Applied Psychology,* May 2007, pp. 757–770.

32. M. Maremont, "A Case Puts a Value on Touching and Fondling," *The Wall Street Journal,* May 25, 1999, pp. B1, B4; S. Armour, "More Men Say They Are Sexually Harassed at Work," *USA Today,* September 17, 2004, p. 1B; C. A. Pierce and H. Aguinis, "Legal Standards, Ethical Standards, and Responses to Social-Sexual Conduct at Work," *Journal of Organizational Behavior* 26 (2005), pp. 727–732; L. A. Baar,

"Harassment Case Proceeds Despite Failure to Report," *HR Magazine,* June 2005, p. 159; and S. Shellenbarger, "Supreme Court Takes on How Employers Handle Worker Harassment Complaints," *The Wall Street Journal,* April 13, 2006, p. D1.

33. Survey in 2007 by Novations Group, Boston, reported in D. Stead, "Is the Workplace Getting Raunchier?" *BusinessWeek,* March 17, 2008, p. 19.

34. Survey in 2007 by Zogby International, reported in T. Parker-Pope, "When the Bully Sits in the Next Cubicle," *The New York Times,* March 25, 2008, p. D5. See also J. A. Segal, "'I Did It, But. . . ,'" *HR Magazine,* March 2008, pp. 91–93.

35. J. Welch and S. Welch, "Hiring Wrong—and Right," *BusinessWeek,* January 29, 2007, p. 102.

36. Dave Lefkow, CEO of TalentSpark, quoted in C. Winkler, "Quality Check," *HR Magazine,* May 2007, pp. 93–98.

37. G. McWilliams, "The Best Way to Find a Job," *The Wall Street Journal,* December 6, 1999, pp. R16, R22. Respondents to the Society for Human Resource Management's *2007 E-Recruiting Survey* also reported that employee referrals generated the highest quality of job candidates and best return on investment for their organization. See T. Minton-Eversole, "E-Recruitment Comes of Age, Survey Says," *HR Magazine,* August 2007, p. 34. Also see D. G. Allen and R. V. Mahto, "Web-Based Recruitment: Effects of Information, Organizational Brand, and Attitudes Toward a Web Site on Applicant Attraction," *Journal of Applied Psychology,* November 2007, pp. 1696–1708.

38. Minton-Eversole, 2007. Also see D. Kirkpatrick, "Web 2.0 Gets Over Its Goofing-Off Phase," *Fortune,* March 31, 2008, pp. 32–34.

39. B. M. Meglino, A. S. DeNisi, S. A. Youngblood, and K. J. Williams, "Effects of Realistic Job Previews: A Comparison Using an Enhancement and a Reduction Preview," *Journal of Applied Psychology* 73 (1981), pp. 259–266.

40. Survey by InfoLink Screen Services, reported in H. B. Herring, "On Our Résumés, Couldn't We All Have Gone to Yale?" *The New York Times,* March 12, 2006, sec. 3, p. 2.

41. Survey by ResumeDoctor.com, reported in C. Soltis, "Eagle-Eyed Employers Scour Résumés for Little White Lies," *The Wall Street Journal,* March 21, 2006, p. B7.

42. Survey by Society of Human Resource Management, reported in M. Villano, "Served as King of England, Said the Résumé," *The New York Times,* March 19, 2006, sec. 3, p. 9.

43. Survey by Background Information Services, reported in Villano, 2006.

44. C. W. Nevius, "If You Like Fiction, Read the Job Resumes," *San Francisco Chronicle,* February 28, 2006, pp. B1, B2. See also D. Koeppel, "That Padded Résumé Won't Help Break Your Fall," *San Francisco Chronicle,* April 23, 2006, p. F5; reprinted from *The New York Times.*

45. B. Bergstein, "Ex-Wiki Exec's Criminal History," *San Francisco Chronicle,* December 27, 2007, pp. C1, C2.

46. Report by Automatic Data Processing, Roseland, NJ, cited in J. L. Seglin, "Lies Can Have a (Long) Life of Their Own," *The New York Times,* June 16, 2002, sec. 3, p. 4. See also S. Armour, "Security Checks Worry Workers," *USA Today,* June 19, 2004, p. 1B.

47. J. S. Lublin, "Job Hunters with Gaps in Their Résumés Need to Write Around Them," *The Wall Street Journal,* May 6, 2003, p. B1.

48. M. Conlin, "Don't Hedge Your Age," *BusinessWeek,* October 6, 2003, p. 14. See also C. Dahle, "A Nip and Tuck for the Résumé," *The New York Times,* April 17, 2005, sec. 3, p. 10.

49. S. McManis, "Little White-Collar Lies," *San Francisco Chronicle,* October 1, 1999, pp. B1, B3.

50. See E. Krell, "Unmasking Illegal Workers," *HR Magazine,* December 2007, pp. 49–52; and S. Berfield, "Illegals and Business: A Glimpse of the Future?" *BusinessWeek,* January 14, 2008, pp. 52–54.

51. See K. Gurchiek, "Video Résumés Spark Curiosity, Questions," *HR Magazine,* May 2007, pp. 28, 30–31; and J. McGregor, "Beware of That Video Résumé," *BusinessWeek,* June 11, 2007, p. 12. Recently "facial coding" experts have examined videos of CEOs such as Nike's Phil Knight and Oracle's Larry Ellison for clues about lying; see D. Jones, "It's Written All Over Their Faces," *USA Today,* February 25, 2008, pp. 1B, 2B.

52. References are even a problem in faculty hiring in universities. See D. M. Barden, "The Unreliability of References," *The Chronicle of Higher Education,* January 11, 2008, pp. C1, C4.

53. Based on P. Bathurst, "How to Avoid Those Fatal Interview Mistakes," *The Arizona Republic,* March 9, 2008, p. EC1.

54. Survey by Society for Human Resource Management, reported in J. Schramm, "Background Checking," *HR Magazine,* January 2005, p. 128.

55. M. Conlin, "You Are What You Post," *BusinessWeek,* March 27, 2006, pp. 52–53; A. Finder, "When a Risqué Online Persona Undermines a Chance for a Job," *The New York Times,* June 11, 2006, pp. A1, A24; and L. Nicita, "Fired Before You're Hired," *The Arizona Republic,* July 28, 2007, pp. E1, E5.

56. D. Stamps, "Cyberinterviews Combat Turnover," *Training,* August 1995, p. 16.

57. D. S. Chapman, K. L. Uggerslev, and J. Webster, "Applicant Reactions Face-to-Face and Technology-Mediated Interviews: A Field Investigation," *Journal of Applied Psychology* 88 (2003), pp. 944–953.

58. See J. Levashina and M. A. Campion, "Measuring Faking in the Employment Interview: Development and Validation of an Interview Faking Behavior Scale," *Journal of Applied Psychology,* November 2007, pp. 1638–1656.

59. E. D. Pursell, M. A. Campion, and S. R. Gaylord, "Structured Interviewing: Avoiding Selection Problems," *Personnel Journal,* November 1980.

60. M. C. Blackman, "Personality Judgment and the Utility of the Unstructured Employment Interview," *Basic and Applied Social Psychology* 24 (2002), pp. 241–250.

61. "Biggest Interviewing Mistakes," *USA Today,* November 19, 2001, p. 1B; D. Murphy, "Interviewers Just Don't Get the Importance of Failure," *San Francisco Chronicle,* May 19, 2002, pp. J1, J3B; Rosner, "Turning Your Job Interview into a Circus Isn't Always Bad," *San Francisco Chronicle,* June 2, 2002, p. J2; L. Adler, *Hire with Your Head: Using POWER Hiring to Build Great Teams,* 2nd ed. (New York: John Wiley, 2002); R. W. Wendover, *Smart Hiring: The Complete Guide to Finding and Hiring the Best Employees,* 3rd ed. (Naperville, IL: Sourcebooks, 2002); A. Arredondo, "Prepare Yourself for the Behavioral Interview," *The Arizona Republic,* March 2, 2008, p. EC1; K. Weirick, "The Perfect Interview," *HR Magazine,* April 2008, pp. 85–88; and AllBusiness.com, "Interviewing Skills Will Help Land the Right Employee for Your Firm," *San Francisco Chronicle,* April 91, 2008, p. C4. Some other articles useful for interviewees are C. Cadwell, "Making the Cover Letter Better," *San Francisco Chronicle,* January 13, 2008, p. H1, which describes how the introductory note accompanying your résumé can help lead to an interview; C. Binkley, "Tassels, Pantsuits, and Other Interview Don'ts," *The Wall Street Journal,* January 17, 2008, p. D8; and J. S. Lublin, "Notes to Interviewers Should Go Beyond a Simple Thank You," *The Wall Street Journal,* February 15, 2008, p. B1.

62. H. Lancaster, "Making a Good Hire Takes a Little Instinct and a Lot of Research," *The Wall Street Journal,* March 3, 1998, p. BI.

63. L. G. Otting, "Don't Rush to Judgment," *HR Magazine,* January 2004, pp. 95–98.

64. M. P. Cronin, "This Is a Test," *Inc.,* August 1993, pp. 64–68.

65. M. J. Frase, "Smart Selections," *HR Magazine,* December 2007, pp. 63–67.

66. For more about skills testing, see J. T. Arnold, "Getting Facts Fast," *HR Magazine,* February 2008, pp. 57–62.

67. D. P. Shuit, "At 60, Myers-Briggs Is Still Sorting Out and Identifying People's Types," *Workforce Management,* December 2003, pp. 72–74.

68. "Personality Assessment Soars at Southwest," *Training,* January 2008, p. 14.

69. "Out of Sight, Yes. Out of Mind, No," *BusinessWeek,* February 18, 2008, p. 60.

70. Senior vice president of human resources Linda Matzigkeit, quoted in M. Bolch, "Nice Work," *HR Magazine,* February 2008, pp. 78–81.

71. S. Adler, "Personality Tests for Salesforce Selection: Worth a Fresh Look," *Review of Business,* Summer/Fall 1994, pp. 27–31.

72. For a discussion of some of these tests, see P. Bathurst, "Pre-Job Tests Weed Out Imperfect Fits," *The Arizona Republic,* January 28, 207, p. ECI.

73. D. Cadrain, "Are Your Employee Drug Tests *Accurate?*" *HR Magazine,* January 2003, pp. 41–45.

74. Survey by Management Recruiters International, 2003, reported in L. Daniel, "Use Personality Tests Legally and Effectively," *Staffing,* April–June 2005, http://www.shrm.org/ema/sm/acrticles/2005/apriljune05cover.asp (accessed August 14, 2008).

75. B. Rose, "Critics Wary as More Jobs Hinge on Personality Tests," *Chicago Tribune,* October 31, 2004, p. 15.

76. S. Clifford, "The Science of Hiring," *Inc. Magazine,* August 2006, pp. 90–98.

77. V. Knight, "More Employers Are Using Personality Tests as Hiring Tools," *CareerJournal.com,* March 21, 2006; http://www.careerjournal.com/jobhunting/interviewing/20060321-knight.html (accessed August 14, 2008).

78. S. Shellenbarger, "Companies Are Finding It Really Pays to Be Nice to Employees," *The Wall Street Journal,* July 22, 1998, p. BI. For more about *The Jungle,* see C. Phelps, "How Should We Teach 'The Jungle'?" *The Chronicle of Higher Education,* March 3, 2006, pp. B10–BII.

79. R. Rigby, "Balloons and Buddies That Help New Recruits Fit In," *Financial Times,* March 17, 2008, http://us.ft.com/ft-gateway/superpage.ft?news_id=fto031720081550034310 (accessed April 24, 2008).

80. Brookings Institution, cited in Shellenbarger, 1998.

81. MCI Communications surveys, reported in Shellenbarger, 1998.

82. G. R. Jones, "Organizational Socialization as Information Processing Activity: A Life History Analysis," *Human Organization* 42, no. 4 (1983), pp. 314–320.

83. E. Lawler, reported in S. Ross, "Worker Involvement Pays Off," *San Francisco Examiner,* November 15, 1998, p. J-2. The 2007 *Global Workforce Study,* by consultancy Towers Perrin, found that only 21% of employees surveyed around the world are engaged in their work, meaning they are willing to go the extra mile to help their companies succeed. See Towers Perrin, *2007 Global Workforce Study: Key Facts and Figures,* www.towersperrin.com/tp/getwebcachedoc7.webc=HRS/USA/2007/200710/GWS_Fact_Sheet_draft_109_07_v5.pdf (accessed April 24, 2008). Also see S. Meisinger, "Management Hold Key to Employee Engagement," *HR Magazine,* February 2008, p. 8.

84. C. McNamara, "Employee Training and Development: Reasons and Benefits," Free Management Library, 1999; http://www.managementhelp.org/trng_dev/basics/reasons.htm (accessed August 14, 2008). See also "Training Top 125 2008," *Training,* February 2008, pp. 76–III.

85. "Training: 2007 Industry Report," *Training,* November/December 2007, pp. 8–24.

86. R. Van Liew, quoted in "E-Learning's Dirty Little Secret," *Training,* February 2006, p. 6. See also J. Gordon, "Seven Revelations about E-Learning," *Training,* April 2006, pp. 28–31.

87. B. Muirhead, "Looking at Net Colleges" [letter], *USA Today,* November 12, 1999, p. 14A.

88. For a discussion from a training standpoint of how the brain learns, see A. Fox, "The Brain at Work," *HR Magazine,* March 2008, pp. 37–42.

89. M. W., "What If You Held a Training Session and No One Showed Up?" *Training,* January 2006, p. 10.

90. J. Sammer, "Calibrating Consistency," *HR Magazine,* January 2008, pp. 73–75.

91. Study by Personnel Decisions International, reported in Sammer, 2008.

92. See D. C. Treadway, G. R. Ferris, A. B. Duke, G. L. Adams, and J. B. Thatcher, "The Moderating Role of Subordinate Political Skill on Supervisors' Impressions of Subordinate Ingratiation and Ratings of Subordinate Interpersonal Facilitation," *Journal of Applied Psychology,* May 2007, pp. 848–855.

93. L. B. Combings and D. P. Schwab, *Performance in Organizations: Determinants and Appraisal* (Glenview, IL: Scott Foresman, 1973).

94. D. J. Cohen, "HR Metrics: A Must," *HR Magazine,* February 2003, p. 136.

95. A meta-analysis of 24 360-degree feedback studies appears in J. W. Smither, M. London, and R. R. Reilly, "Does Performance Improve Following Multisource Feedback? A Theoretical Model, Meta-Analysis, and Review of Empirical Findings," *Personnel Psychology,* Spring 2005, p. 33.

96. D. E. Coates, "Don't Tie 360 Feedback to Pay," *Training,* September 1998, pp. 68–78. See also A. S. Wellner, "Everyone's a Critic," *Inc.,* July 2004, pp. 38, 41; and W. C. Byham, "Fixing the Instrument," *Training,* July 2004, p. 50.

97. "Dell: Home Schooled by the Brass," *BusinessWeek Online,* October 10, 2005; http://www.businessweek.com/magazine/content/05_41/b3954007.htm (accessed August 14, 2008).

98. C. S. Peck, "360-Degree Feedback: How to Avoid a Disaster," Workinfo.com, http://www.workinfo.com/free/downloads/71.htm (accessed August 14, 2008).

99. M. Boyle, "Performance Reviews: Perilous Curves Ahead," *Fortune,* May 15, 2001, www.fortune.com/fortune/subs/print/0,15935,374010,00.html (accessed June 6, 2008); C. M. Ellis, G. B. Moore, and A. M. Saunier, "Forced Ranking: Not So Fast," *Perspectives,* June 30, 2003, www.imakenews.com/eletra/mod_print_view.cfm?this_id=162170&u=sibson&issue_id=000034313 (accessed June 6, 2008); and A. Meisler, "Dead Man's Curve," *Workforce Management,* July 2003, pp. 45–49.

100. S. Scherreik, "Your Performance Review: Make It Perform," *BusinessWeek Online,* December 17, 2001, http://www.businessweek.com/magazine/content/01_51/b3762136.htm?chan=search (accessed August 14, 2008); and J. McGregor, "The Struggle to Measure Performance," *BusinessWeek Online,* January 9, 2006, http://www.businessweek.com/magazine/content/06_02/b3966060.htm?chan=search (accessed August 14, 2008). See also criticism of forced

ranking in J. Pfeffer and R. I. Sutton, *Hard Facts, Dangerous Half-Truths & Total Nonsense: Profiting from Evidence-Based Management* (Boston: Harvard Business School Press, 2006).

101. L. A. Bossidy, "What Your Leader Expects of You," *Harvard Business Review,* April 3, 2007, pp. 58–65.

102. Adapted from D. L. McClain, "Tricks for Motivating the Pay to Motivate the Ranks," *The New York Times,* November 15, 1998, sec. 3, p. 5.

103. *Employee Benefits Study, 2006* (Washington, DC: U.S. Chamber of Commerce, 2007).

104. A. Etzioni, "Americans Could Teach Austrians about Diversity," *USA Today,* February 14, 2000, p. 19A.

105. For some perspectives on racial diversity and perception, see S. Meisinger, "Diversity: More Than Just Representation," *HR Magazine,* January 2008, p. 8; "Promoting Positive Prejudice May Beat Damping Negative," *The Wall Street Journal,* January 1, 2008, p. B8; and S. Begley, "How Your Brain Looks at Race," *Newsweek,* March 3, 2008, pp. 26–27.

106. For a discussion of workplace discipline, see L. E. Atwater, J. F. Brett, and A. C. Charles, "The Delivery of Workplace Discipline: Lessons Learned," *Organizational Dynamics* 36 (2007), pp. 392–403.

107. A. Fisher, "Dumping Troublemakers, and Exiting Gracefully," *Fortune,* February 15, 1999, p. 174.

108. C. Hymowitz, "Why Managers Take Too Long to Fire Employees," *San Francisco Examiner,* February 21, 1999, p. J-2; reprinted from *The Wall Street Journal.*

109. For a discussion of the threat of litigation attending dismissals, see M. Orey, "Fear of Firing," *BusinessWeek,* April 23, 2007, pp. 52–62.

110. R. Moss Kanter, "Show Humanity When You Show Employees the Door," *The Wall Street Journal,* September 21, 1997, p. A22.

111. Moss Kanter, 1997.

CHAPTER 10

1. T. J. Fadem, quoted in O. Port and J. Carey, "Getting to 'Eureka!'" *BusinessWeek,* November 10, 1997, pp. 72–75.

2. C. Hymowitz, "Task of Managing in Workplace Takes a Careful Hand," *The Wall Street Journal,* July 1, 1997, p. B1.

3. T. Peters, "A Brawl with No Rules," *Forbes ASAP,* February 21, 2000, p. 155.

4. M. McGuinn, quoted in Hymowitz, 1997.

5. M. Weinstein, "Innovate or Die Trying," *Training Magazine,* May 2006, pp. 38–44; D. Hall, "The Customer Is Clueless," *BusinessWeek SmallBiz,* Spring 2006, p. 20; D. Brady, "Ideas That Bloom," *BusinessWeek SmallBiz,* Spring 2006, pp. 46–53; and P. Loewe and J. Dominiquini, "Overcoming the Barriers to Effective Innovation," *Strategy & Leadership* 34, no. 1 (2006), pp. 24–31.

6. Anthony Creed, quoted in D. Kirkpatrick, "Throw It at the Wall and See If It Sticks," *Fortune,* December 12, 2005, pp. 142–150.

7. Bruce Judson, quoted in J. M. Pethokoukis, "Bootstrapping Your Way into Business," *U.S. News & World Report,* March 27, 2006, p. 58. See also M. Bandyk, "Launching a Start-Up? Here's What Really Works," *U.S. News & World Report,* February 18, 2008, p. 58.

8. K. Stebbins, "Take a Risk," *Northern Nevada Healthy Living,* February 2008, p. 1.

9. E. Hoffer, *Ordeal of Change* (New York: Harper & Row, 1963).

10. P. Drucker, "The Future That Has Already Happened," *The Futurist,* November 1998, pp. 16–18.

11. Drucker, ibid.; J. C. Glenn, "Scanning the Global Situation and Prospects for the Future," *The Futurist,* January–February 2008, pp. 41–46; M. J. Cetron and O. Davies, "Trends Shaping Tomorrow's World: Forecasts and Implications for Business, Government, and Consumers (Part One), *The Futurist,* March–April 2008, pp. 35–52; and M. J. Cetron and O. Davies, "Trends Shaping Tomorrow's World: Forecasts and Implications for Business, Government, and Consumers (Part Two), *The Futurist,* May–June 2008, pp. 35–50.

12. Some of these trends are based on K. Albrecht, "Eight Supertrends Shaping the Future of Business," *The Futurist,* September–October 2006, pp. 25–29.

13. C. Anderson, quoted in A. T. Saracevic, "Economic Theories in 'The Long Tail' Don't Deserve Short Shrift," *San Francisco Chronicle,* July 16, 2006, pp. F1, F5. See also C. Anderson, *The Long Tail: Why the Future of Business Is Selling Less of More* (New York: Hyperion, 2006).

14. S. Hamm, "Speed Demons," *BusinessWeek,* March 27, 2006, pp. 68–75.

15. C. M. Christensen, *The Innovator's Dilemma: When New Technologies Cause Great Firms to Fail* (Boston, MA: Harvard Business School Press, 1997). See also F. Arner and R. Tiplady, "'No Excuse Not to Succeed,'" *BusinessWeek,* May 10, 2004, pp. 96–98.

16. W. M. Bulkeley, "Kodak's Move to Digital Shows Progress," *The Wall Street Journal,* November 2, 2007, p. B5; and B. Dobbins, "Kodak's Restructuring Clicks," *San Francisco Chronicle,* January 31, 2008, p. C5.

17. P. Engardio, "The Future of Outsourcing," *BusinessWeek,* January 30, 2006, pp. 50–58.

18. C. Hawley, "Mexico Takes on More Aircraft Construction," *USA Today,* April 7, 2008, p. 11A.

19. M. Bandyk, "Now Even Small Firms Can Go Global," *U.S. News & World Report,* March 10, 2008, p. 52.

20. L. T. LaCapra, "Ireland Taps U.S. to Fill Need for Skilled Workers," *The Wall Street Journal,* October 31, 2006, p. B4.

21. Albrecht, 2006. See also T. O'Driscoll, "Join the Webvolution," *Training,* February 2008, p. 24.

22. A. Toffler and H. Toffler, *Revolutionary Wealth* (New York: Alfred A. Knopf, 2006). Also see T. H. Davenport, L. Prusak, and B. Strong, "Putting Ideas to Work," *The Wall Street Journal,* March 10, 2008, p. R11.

23. Project for Excellence in Journalism, *The State of the News Media 2008: An Annual Report on American Journalism,* March 17, 2008, http://www.stateofthemedia.com/2008/narrative_overview_eight.php?cat=1&media=1 (accessed April 26, 2008). See also S. Sutel, "Circulation Declines at U.S. Newspapers; More Readers Go Online," *Reno Gazette-Journal,* November 6, 2007, p. 8A, 9A; S. Ellison, "Newspapers Try New Math on Circulation," *The Wall Street Journal,* November 6, 2007, p. B10; Associated Press, "Newspaper Publishers Bet on Growth Online in '08," *The Wall Street Journal,* December 6, 2007, p. B7; S. Stecklow, "Despite Woes, McClatchy Banks on Newspapers," *The Wall Street Journal,* December 26, 2007, pp. A1, A9; J. Garofoli, "The Audience Is There; It's Just Not Paying for News," *San Francisco Chronicle,* March 17, 2008, p. D3.

24. N. Cohen, "Reluctantly, a Daily Stops Its Presses, Living Online," *The New York Times,* April 28, 2008, pp. C1, C4.

25. M. Totty, "How We Get News," *The Wall Street Journal,* January 28, 2008, pp. R3, R4.

26. P. Robertson, D. Roberts, and J. Porras, "Dynamics of Planned Organizational Change: Assessing Empirical Support for a Theoretical Model," *Academy of Management Journal* 36, no. 3 (1993), pp. 619–634.

27. S. Moran, "The Range Gets Crowded for Natural Beef," *The New York Times,* June 10, 2006, pp. B1, B4.

28. M. Warner, "When It Comes to Meat, 'Natural' Is a Vague Term," *The New York Times,* June 10, 2006, p. B4.

29. Andy Grove of Intel, quoted in L. Berlin, "A Look at Apple through the Years: Never Afraid to Change Its Direction," *San Francisco Chronicle,* January 15, 2008, pp. C1, C2.

30. D. Kiley, "Nokia Starts Listening," *BusinessWeek,* May 5, 2008, p. 30.

31. P. Dusenberry, "The Challenges of Managing Creative People," *USA Today,* November 20, 1997, p. 4B.

32. R. D. Hof, "Online Extra: Trading in a Cloud of Electrons," *BusinessWeek Online,* May 20, 2004, www.businessweek .com/@@TUSaZYUQTmOUSwOA/magazine/content/04_19/ b388262l.htm (accessed June 8, 2006).

33. The term "Web 2" was popularized by Tim O'Reilly, CEO of O'Reilly Media Inc. See T. O'Reilly, "What Is Web 2.0," O'Reilly, September 30, 2005; http://www.oreillynet.com/pub/a/ oreilly/tim/news/2005/09/30/what-is-web-20.html (accessed August 22, 2008).

34. See W. E. Halal, "Technology's Promise: Highlights from the TechCast Project," *The Futurist,* November–December 2007, pp. 41 50; B. Charney, "Technological Gadgets Smarten Up," *The Wall Street Journal,* December 31, 2007, p. B3; L. Cauley, "Race Is On for Mobile Web's Pot of Gold," *USA Today,* January 10, 2008, pp. 1B, 2B; and M. Mangalindan, "How We Shop," *The Wall Street Journal,* January 28, 2008, p. R3.

35. R. D. Hof, "Web 2.0: The New Guy at Work," *BusinessWeek,* June 19, 2006, pp. 58–59.

36. M. Fugate, A. Kinicki, and C. L. Scheck, "Coping with an Organizational Merger over Four Stages," *Personnel Psychology,* Winter 2002, pp. 905–928.

37. Based on A. Walker, "Measuring Footprints," *Fast Company,* April 2008, pp. 59–60.

38. See "Change Management: The HR Strategic Imperative as a Business Partner," *Research Quarterly,* Fourth Quarter 2007, pp. 1–9; and D. A. Garvin, A. C. Edmondson, and F. Gino, "Is Yours a Learning Organization?" *Harvard Business Review,* March 2008, pp. 109–116.

39. W. G. Dyer, *Team Building: Current Issues and New Alternatives,* 3rd ed. (Reading, MA: Addison-Wesley, 1995).

40. See R. Rodgers, J. E. Hunter, and D. L. Rogers, "Influence of Top Management Commitment on Management Program Success," *Journal of Applied Psychology,* February 1993, pp. 151–155.

41. R. J. Schaffer and H. A. Thomson, "Successful Change Programs Begin with Results" *Harvard Business Review,* January–February 1992, pp. 80–89.

42. P. J. Robertson, D. R. Roberts, and J. I. Porras, "Dynamics of Planned Organizational Change: Assess Empirical Support for a Theoretical Model," *Academy of Management Journal,* June 1993, pp. 619–634.

43. C.-M. Lau and H.-Y. Ngo, "Organization Development and Firm Performance: A Comparison of Multinational and Local Firms," *Journal of International Business Studies,* First Quarter 2001, pp. 95–114.

44. Survey by Development Dimensions International Inc., 2005, reported in "The Big Picture: All Talk? Despite Management's Focus on Innovation, U.S. Executives Say Their Companies Give It Short Shrift," *BusinessWeek,* March 6, 2006, p. 13.

45. L. Selden and I. C. MacMillan, "Manage Customer-Centric Innovation—Systematically ," *Harvard Business Review,* April 2006, pp. 108–116.

46. C. B. Rabe, *The Innovation Killer: How What We Know Limits What We Can Imagine—and What Smart Companies Are Doing about It* (New York: Amacom, 2006).

47. See J. Rae-Dupree, "Innovative Minds Don't Think Alike," *The New York Times,* December 30, 2007, business section, p. 3.

48. J. Welch and S. Welch, "Finding Innovation Where It Lives," *BusinessWeek,* April 21, 2008, p. 84.

49. W. M. Bulkeley, "Can Linux Take Over the Desktop?" *The Wall Street Journal,* May 24, 2004, pp. R1, R4; and S. Hamm, "Software Shift," *BusinessWeek,* May 10, 2004, p. 90.

50. T. O'Reilly, quoted in W. C. Taylor, "Here's an Idea: Let Everyone Have Ideas," *The New York Times,* March 26, 2006, sec. 3, p. 3. See also R. E. Miles, G. Miles, and C. C. Snow, " Collaborative Entrepreneurship: A Business Model for Continuous Innova- tion," *Organizational Dynamics,* February 2006, pp. 1–11.

51. P. Warrior, cited in M. Lev-Ram, "Unwiring Motorola," *Business 2.0,* September 2006, pp. 103 –105.

52. B. Arends, "Does Break-Up Make Motorola a Good Buy?" *The Wall Street Journal,* March 26, 2008, http://online.wsj .com/article/SB120656389616066401.html (accessed April 29, 2008).

53. R. Cohen, "Vive La Dolce Vita," *The New York Times,* April 16, 2006, sec. 4, pp. 1, 4.

54. K. Maney, "Tech Start-ups Don't Grow on Trees Outside USA," *USA Today,* June 28, 2006, pp. 1B, 2B.

55. J. McGregor, "The World's Most Innovative Companies," *BusinessWeek,* April 24, 2006, pp. 63–74.

56. A. V. Bhidé, quoted in G. Gendron, "The Origin of the Entrepreneurial Species," *Inc.,* February 2000, pp. 105–114.

57. J. Yaukey, "Disposable Cell Phones Will Reach Retail Soon," *Reno Gazette-Journal,* October 22, 2001, p. 1E; and D. Pogue, "Cellphones for a Song, Just in Case," *The New York Times,* September 27, 2001, pp. D1, D7.

58. B. Evangelista, "Movies by Mail: Netflix.com Makes Renting DVDs Easy," *San Francisco Chronicle,* January 26, 2002, p. B1; V. Kopytoff, "Successful Netflix Faces Competition," *San Francisco Chronicle,* March 8, 2004, pp. E1, E4; and M. Boyle, "Reed Hastings," *Fortune,* May 28, 2007, pp. 30–31.

59. S. A. Shane, *The Illusions of Entrepreneurship: The Costly Myths That Entrepreneurs, Investors, and Policy Makers Live By* (New Haven, CT: Yale University Press, 2008).

60. Scott Shane, interviewed by J. Tozzi, "The Entrepreneurship Myth," *BusinessWeek,* January 23, 2008, http://www.businessweek.com/smallbiz/content/jan2008/sb20080123_ 809271.htm?chan=search (accessed April 29, 2008).

61. R. Moss Kanter, *The Change Masters* (New York: Simon & Schuster, 1983).

62. T. Kuczmarski, "Inspiring and Implementing the Innovation Mind-Set," *Planning Review,* September–October 1994, pp. 37–48; L. K. Gundry, J. R. Kickul, and C. W. Prather, "Building the Creative Organization," *Organizational Dynamics,* Spring 1994, pp. 22–36; and T. M. Burton, "By Learning from Failures, Lilly Keeps Drug Pipeline Full," *The Wall Street Journal,* April 21, 2004, pp. A1, A9.

63. "The World's 25 Most Innovative Companies," *BusinessWeek,* May 14, 2007, pp. 54–55.

64. J. C. Collins and J. I. Porris, *Built to Last: Successful Habits of Visionary Companies* (New York: HarperBusiness, 1994). See also T. J. Martin, "Ten Commandments for Managing Creative People," *Fortune,* January 16, 1995, pp. 135–136.

65. B. Hindo, "At 3M, a Struggle between Efficiency and Creativity," *BusinessWeek,* June 2007, pp. 8IN–14IN.

66. "America's Most Admired Companies: The List of Industry Stars," *Fortune,* March 17, 2008, pp. 77–84.

67. J. Denrell, "Vicarious Learning, Undersampling of Failure, and the Myths of Management," *Organizational Science,* May–June 2003, pp. 227–243.

68. J. Freese, "Magical Misery Tour," *Fortune Small Business,* May 2008, p. 29.

69. T. J. Allen and S. I. Cohen, "Information Flow in Research and Development Laboratories," *Administrative Science Quarterly,* March 1969, pp. 12–19.

70. Moss Kanter, 1983.

71. This three-way typology of change was adapted from discussion in P. C. Nutt, "Tactics of Implementation," *Academy of Management Journal,* June 1986, pp. 230–261.

72. Radical organizational change is discussed by T. E. Vollmann, *The Transformational Imperative* (Boston: Harvard Business School Press, 1996); and J. A. Neal and C. L. Tromley, "From Incremental Change to Retrofit: Creating High-Performance Work Systems," *Academy of Management Executive,* February 1995, pp. 42–53.

73. Adapted in part from J. D. Ford, L. W. Ford, and A. D'Amelio, "Resistance to Change: The Rest of the Story," *Academy of Management Review,* April 2008, pp. 362–377.

74. See "Vulnerability and Resilience," *American Psychologist,* January 1996, pp. 22–28. See also T. Kiefer, "Feeling Bad: Antecedents and Consequences of Negative Emotions in Ongoing Change," *Journal of Organizational Behavior,* December 2005, pp. 875–897.

75. See R. Moss Kanter, "Managing Traumatic Change: Avoiding the 'Unlucky 13,'" *Management Review,* May 1987, pp. 23–24.

76. Details of this example are provided by B. Schlender, "Inside the Shakeup at Sony," *Fortune,* April 4, 2005, pp. 94–104.

77. K. Lewin, *Field Theory in Social Science* (New York: Harper & Row, 1951).

78. The role of learning within organizational change is discussed by C. Hendry, "Understanding and Creating Whole Organizational Change through Learning Theory," *Human Relations,* May 1996, pp. 621–641; and D. Ready, "Mastering Leverage, Leading Change," *Executive Excellence,* March 1995, pp. 18–19.

79. C. Goldwasser, "Benchmarking: People Make the Process," *Management Review,* June 1995, p. 40; and *Cambridge Advanced Learner's Dictionary* (Cambridge: Cambridge University Press, 2004), http://dictionary.cambridge.org/define.asp?key=94109&dict=CALD (accessed July 5, 2004).

80. R. Kreitner and A. Kinicki, *Organizational Behavior,* 4th ed. (Burr Ridge, IL: Irwin/McGraw-Hill, 1998), p. 619.

81. These errors are discussed by J. P. Kotter, "Leading Change: The Eight Steps to Transformation," in J. A. Conger, G. M. Spreitzer, and E. E. Lawler III, eds., *The Leader's Change Handbook* (San Francisco: Jossey-Bass, 1999), pp. 87–99.

82. The type of leadership needed during organizational change is discussed by S. Furst and D. M. Cable, "Employee Resistance to Organizational Change: Managerial Influence Tactics and Leader-Member Exchange," *Journal of Applied Psychology,* March 2008, pp. 453–462; and D. M. Herold, D. B. Fedor, S. Caldwell, and Y. Liu, "The Effects of Transformational and Change Leadership on Employees' Commitment to a Change: A Multilevel Study," *Journal of Applied Psychology,* March 2008, pp. 346–357.

CHAPTER II

1. "Generation Y: The Millennials—Ready or Not, Here They Come," *NAS Insights,* 2006, http://72.14.253.104/search?q=cache:__bxYtpqltoJ:www.nasrecruitment.com/TalentTips/NASinsights/GenerationY.pdf+%E2%80%9CGeneration+Y:+The+Millennials,%E2%80%9D+NAS+Insights,+2006&hl=en&ct=clnk&cd=1&gl=us (accessed May 3, 2008); H. Dolezalek, "Boomer Reality," *Training,* May 2007, pp. 16–21;

N. A. Hira, "You Raised Them, Now Manage Them," *Fortune,* May 28, 2007, pp. 38–46; K. Tyler, "Generation Gaps," *HR Magazine,* January 2008, pp. 69–72; S. Kapuria, "Millennial Workforce: IT Risk or Benefit," posted March 19, 2008, http://www.symantec.com/enterprise/security_response/weblog/2008/03/millennial_workforce_it_risk_o.html (accessed May 3, 2008); P. Bathurst, "Boomers, Younger Employees Give and Take to Find Common Ground," *The Arizona Republic,* April 20, 2008, p. ECI; and P. Bathurst, "Millennials at Work," *The Arizona Republic,* May 4, 2008, p. ECI.

2. For a thorough discussion of personality psychology, see D. P. McAdams and J. L. Pals, "A New Big Five: Fundamental Principles for an Integrative Science of Personality," *American Psychologist,* April 2006, pp. 204–217.

3. The landmark report is J. M. Digman, "Personality Structure: Emergence of the Five-Factor Model," *Annual Review of Psychology* 41 (1990), pp. 417–440. Also see M. R. Barrick and M. K. Mount, "Autonomy as a Moderator of the Relationships between the Big Five Personality Dimensions and Job Performance," *Journal of Applied Psychology,* February 1993, pp. 111–118; C. Viswesvaran and D. S. Ones, "Measurement Error in 'Big Five Factors' Personality Assessment: Reliability Generalization across Studies and Measures," *Education and Psychological Measurement,* April 2000, pp. 224–235; and P. Sackett and F. Lievens, "Personnel Selection," *Annual Review of Psychology,* 2008, pp. 419–450.

4. M. R. Barrick and M. K. Mount, "The Big Five Personality Dimensions and Job Performance: A Meta-Analysis," *Personnel Psychology,* Spring 1991, pp. 1–26.

5. Barrick and Mount, 1991, p. 18; also see H. Moon, "The Two Faces of Conscientiousness: Duty and Achievement Striving in Escalation of Commitment Dilemmas," *Journal of Applied Psychology,* June 2001, pp. 533–540; and M. R. Barrick, G. L. Stewart, and M. Piotrowski, "Personality and Job Performance: Test of the Mediating Effects of Motivation among Sales Representatives," *Journal of Applied Psychology,* February 2002, pp. 43–51.

6. See F. P. Morgeson, M. A. Campion, R. L. Dipboye, J. R. Hollenbeck, K. Murphy, and N. Schmitt, "Reconsidering the Use of Personality Tests in Personnel Selection," *Personnel Psychology,* Autumn 2007, pp. 683–729; and D. Armstrong, "Malingerer Test Roils Personal-Injury Law," *The Wall Street Journal,* March 5, 2008, pp. A1, A13.

7. J. M. Crant, "Proactive Behavior in Organizations," *Journal of Management,* no. 3, 2000, pp. 439–441; and J. M. Crant, "The Proactive Personality Scale as a Predictor of Entrepreneurial Intentions," *Journal of Small Business Management,* July 1996, pp. 42–49.

8. For an overall view of research on locus of control, see P. E. Spector, "Behavior in Organizations as a Function of Employee's Locus of Control," *Psychological Bulletin,* May 1982, pp. 482–497; the relationship between locus of control and other dimensions of personality is examined by R. E. Johnson, C. C. Rosen, and P. E. Levy, "Getting to the Core of Core Self-Evaluation: A Review and Recommendations," *Journal of Organizational Behavior,* April 2008, pp. 391–413.

9. D. Sacks, "60 Seconds with Erik Weihenmayer," *Fast Company,* May 2004, p. 40.

10. See, for example, V. Gecas, "The Social Psychology of Self-Efficacy," in W. R. Scott and J. Blake, eds., *Annual Review of Sociology,* vol. 15 (Palo Alto, CA: Annual Reviews, 1989), pp. 291–316; and C. K. Stevens, A. G. Bavetta, and M. E. Gist, "Gender Differences in the Acquisition of Salary Negotiation Skills: The Role of Goals, Self-Efficacy, and Perceived Control," *Journal of Applied Psychology,* October 1993, pp. 723–735; and D. Eden and Y. Zuk, "Seasickness as a Self Fulfilling

Prophecy: Raising Self-Efficacy to Boost Performance at Sea," *Journal of Applied Psychology,* October 1995, pp. 628–635.

11. J. Barling and R. Beattle, "Self-Efficacy Beliefs and Sales Performance," *Journal of Organizational Behavior Management,* Spring 1983, pp. 41–51.

12. For more on learned helplessness, see M. J. Martinko and W. L. Gardner, "Learned Helplessness: An Alternative Explanation for Performance Deficits," *Academy of Management Review,* April 1982, pp. 195–204; and C. R. Campbell and M. J. Martinko, "An Integrative Attributional Perspective of Employment and Learned Helplessness: A Multimethod Field Study," *Journal of Management,* no. 2, 1998, pp. 173–200.

13. W. S. Silver, T. R. Mitchell, and M. E. Gist, "Response to Successful and Unsuccessful Performance: The Moderating Effect of Self-Efficacy on the Relationship between Training and Newcomer Adjustment," *Journal of Applied Psychology,* April 1995, pp. 211–225.

14. See J. V. Vancouver, K. M. More, and R. J. Yoder, "Self-Efficacy and Resource Allocation: Support for a Nonmonotonic, Discontinuous Model," *Journal of Applied Psychology,* January 2008, pp. 35–47.

15. The positive relationship between self-efficacy and readiness for retraining is documented in L. A. Hill and J. Elias, "Retraining Midcareer Managers: Career History and Self-Efficacy Beliefs," *Human Resource Management,* Summer 1990, pp. 197–217.

16. V. Gecas, "The Self-Concept," in R. H. Turner and J. F. Short Jr. eds., *Annual Review of Sociology*, vol. 8 (Palo Alto, CA: Annual Reviews, 1982); also see N. Branden, *Self-Esteem at Work: How Confident People Make Powerful Companies* (San Francisco: Jossey-Bass, 1998).

17. P. G. Dodgson and J. V. Wood, "Self-Esteem and the Cognitive Accessibility of Strengths and Weaknesses after Failure," *Journal of Personality and Social Psychology,* July 1998, pp. 178–197; and D. B. Fedor, J. M. Maslyn, W. D. Davis, and K. Mathieseon, "Performance Improvement Efforts in Response to Negative Feedback: The Roles of Source Power and Recipient Self-Esteem," *Journal of Management,* January–February 2001, pp. 79–97.

18. B. R. Schlenker, M. F. Weigold, and J. R. Hallam, "Self-Serving Attributions in Social Contest: Effects of Self-Esteem and Social Pressure," *Journal of Personality and Social Psychology,* May 1990, pp. 855–863; and P. Sellers, "Get Over Yourself," *Fortune,* April 2001, pp. 76–88.

19. J. W. McGuire and C. V. McGuire, "Enhancing Self-Esteem by Directed-Thinking Tasks: Cognitive and Affective Positivity Asymmetries," *Journal of Personality and Social Psychology,* June 1996, p. 1124.

20. M. Snyder and S. Gangestad, "On the Nature of Self-Monitoring: Matters of Assessment, Matters of Validity," *Journal of Personality and Social Psychology,* July 1986, p. 125.

21. Data from M. Kilduff and D. V. Day, "Do Chameleons Get Ahead? The Effects of Self-Monitoring on Managerial Careers," *Academy of Management Journal,* August 1994, pp. 1047–1060.

22. See F. Luthans, "Successful vs. Effective Managers," *Academy of Management Executive,* May 1988, pp. 127–132; also see W. H. Turnley and M. C. Bolino, "Achieving Desired Images While Avoiding Undesired Images: Exploring the Role of Self-Monitoring in Impression Management," *Journal of Applied Psychology,* April 2001, pp. 351–360.

23. D. Goleman, *Emotional Intelligence* (New York: Bantam, 1995).

24. D. Goleman, "What Makes a Leader," *Harvard Business Review,* November–December 1998, pp. 93–102.

25. See A. Chapman, "Empathy, Trust, Diffusing Conflict and Handling Complaints," *Businessballs.com,* http://www.businessballs.com/empathy.htm (accessed May 8, 2008).

26. S. Fox and P. E. Spector, "Relations of Emotional Intelligence, Practical Intelligence, General Intelligence, and Trait Affectivity with Interview Outcomes: It's Not All Just 'G,'" *Journal of Organizational Behavior,* March 2000, pp. 203–220.

27. See J. C. Rode, C. H. Mooney, M. L. Arthaud-Day, J. P. Near, T. T. Baldwin, R. S. Busin, and W. H. Bommer, "Emotional Intelligence and Individual Performance: Evidence of Direct and Moderated Effects," *Journal of Organizational Behavior,* May 2007, pp. 399–421; J. Mayer, R. Roberts, and S. Barsade, "Human Abilities: Emotional Intelligence," *Annual Review of Psychology,* January 2008, pp. 507–536; D. Eilerman, "The Significance of Emotional Engagement in Conflict Management," *Mediate.com,* January 2008, http://www.mediate.com/articles/eilermanD10.Cfm (accessed May 8, 2008).

28. See M. Rokeach, *Beliefs, Attitudes, and Values* (San Francisco: Jossey-Bass, 1968), p. 168.

29. M. Rokeach, *The Nature of Human Values* (New York: Free Press, 1973).

30. Survey by Society for Human Resource Management, reported in J. Herzlich, "Work/Life Balance Tops List," *The Arizona Republic,* January 6, 2008, p. EC1.

31. Pew Research Center, cited in K. Palmer, "The New Mommy Track," *U.S. News & World Report,* September 3, 2007, pp. 40–45.

32. M. Fishbein and I. Ajzen, *Belief, Attitude, Intention and Behavior: An Introduction to Theory and Research* (Reading, MA: Addison-Wesley Publishing, 1975), p. 6.

33. See M. Reid and A. Wood, "An Investigation into Blood Donation Intentions Among Non-Donors," *International Journal of Nonprofit and Voluntary Sector Marketing,* February 2008, pp. 31–43; and J. Ramsey, B. J. Punnett, and D. Greenidge, "A Social Psychological Account of Absenteeism in Barbados," *Human Resource Management Journal,* April 2008, pp. 97–117.

34. B. M. Shaw and J. Ross, "Stability in the Midst of Change: A Dispositional Approach to Job Attitudes," *Journal of Applied Psychology,* August 1985, pp. 469–480; see also J. Schaubroeck, D. C. Ganster, and B. Kemmerer, "Does Trait Affect Promote Job Attitude Stability?" *Journal of Organizational Behavior,* March 1996, pp. 191–196.

35. J. S. Becker, "Empirical Validation of Affect, Behavior, and Cognition as Distinct Components of Attitude," *Journal of Personality and Social Psychology,* May 1984, pp. 1191–1205; the components or structure of attitudes is thoroughly discussed by A. P. Brief, *Attitudes in and around Organizations* (Thousand Oaks, CA: Sage, 1998), pp. 49–84.

36. L. Festinger, *A Theory of Cognitive Dissonance* (Stanford, CA: Stanford University Press, 1957).

37. J. Hempel, "Big Blue Brainstorm," *BusinessWeek Online,* July 28, 2006, p. 70.

38. IBM Jam Events page, https://www.collaborationjam.com (accessed May 5, 2008).

39. C. Salter, "Fast 50 2008: IBM," *Fast Company.com,* http://www.fastcompany.com/fast50_08/ibm.html (accessed May 5, 2008).

40. These five job dimensions are developed by researchers at Cornell University as part of the Job Descriptive Index. For a review of the development of the JDI, see P. C. Smith, L. M. Kendall, and C. L. Hulin, *The Measurement of Satisfaction in Work and Retirement* (Skokie, IL: Rand McNally, 1969).

41. See A. J. Kinicki, F. M. McKee-Ryan, C. A. Schriesheim, and K. P. Carson, "Assessing the Construct Validity of the Job

Descriptive Index: A Review and Meta-Analysis," *Journal of Applied Psychology,* February 2002, pp. 14–32.

42. "Middle Managers Unhappy," *HR Magazine,* July 2006, p. 16.

43. The various models are discussed in T. A. Judge, C. J. Thoresen, J. E. Bono, and G. K. Patton, "The Job Satisfaction–Job Performance Relationship: A Qualitative and Quantitative Review," *Psychological Bulletin,* May 2001, pp. 376–407.

44. Ibid. Also see M. Riketta, "The Causal Relation between Job Attitudes and Performance: A Meta-Analysis of Panel Studies," *Journal of Applied Psychology,* March 2008, pp. 472–481.

45. See S. P. Brown, "A Meta-Analysis and Review of Organizational Research on Job Involvement," *Psychological Bulletin,* September 1996, pp. 235–255.

46. This recommendation is supported by K. W. Thomas, *Intrinsic Motivation at Work* (San Francisco: Berrett-Koehler, 2000).

47. Survey of adults conducted for Adecco Staffing North America, reported in K. Gurchiek, "Good News for Moms Reconsidering Work," *HR Magazine,* July 2006, p. 30.

48. See N. Podsakoff, J. A. LePine, and M. A. LePine, "Differential Challenge Stresssor-Hindrance Stressor Relationships with Job Attitudes, Turnover Intentions, Turnover, and Withdrawal Behavior: A Meta-Analysis," *Journal of Applied Psychology,* March 2007, pp. 438–454; M. Riketta, "Attitudinal Organizational Commitment and Job Performance: A Meta-Analysis," *Journal of Organizational Behavior,* March 2002, pp. 257–266.

49. See J. E. Mathieu and D. Zajac, "A Review and Meta-Analysis of the Antecedents, Correlates, and Consequences of Organizational Commitment," *Psychological Bulletin,* September 1990, pp. 171–194; see also M. Riketta, "Attitudinal Organizational Commitment and Job Performance: A Meta-Analysis," *Journal of Organizational Behavior,* March 2002, pp. 257–266.

50. See R. D. Hackett, "Work Attitudes and Employee Absenteeism: A Synthesis of the Literature," *Journal of Occupational Psychology,* 1989, pp. 235–248.

51. Costs of turnover are discussed by R. W. Griffeth and P. W. Hom, *Retaining Valued Employees* (Thousand Oaks, CA: Sage, 2001).

52. M. Littman, "Best Bosses Tell All," *Working Woman,* October 2000, pp. 48–56.

53. 2000 study by Development Dimensions International, Pittsburgh, reported in "Replacing Key People Has Many Hidden Costs," *San Francisco Chronicle,* December 24, 2000, p. J1; reprinted from *Boston Globe.*

54. D. W. Organ, "The Motivational Basis of Organizational Citizenship Behavior," in B. M. Staw and L. L. Cummings, eds., *Research in Organizational Behavior* (Greenwich, CT: JAI Press, 1990), p. 46.

55. See B. J. Hoffman, C. A. Blair, J. P. Meriac, and D. J. Woehr, "Expanding the Criterion Domain? A Quantitative Review of the OCB Literature," *Journal of Applied Psychology,* March 2007, pp. 555–566; and T. D. Allen, "Rewarding Good Citizens: The Relationship between Citizenship Behavior, Gender, and Organizational Rewards," *Journal of Applied Psychology,* January 2006, pp. 120–143.

56. D. S. Ones, "Introduction to the Special Issue on Counterproductive Behaviors at Work," *International Journal of Selection and Assessment* 10, no. 1–2 (2002), pp. 1–4.

57. B. Leonard, "Study: Bully Bosses Prevalent in U.S.," *HR Magazine,* May 2007, pp. 22, 28.

58. See J. Chamberlin, A. Novotney, E. Packard, and M. Price, "Enhancing Worker Well-Being," *Monitor on Psychology,*

May 2008, pp. 26–29; and C.M.S. Mitchell and M. L. Ambrose, "Abusive Supervision and Workplace Deviance and the Moderating Effects of Negative Reciprocity Beliefs," *Journal of Applied Psychology,* July 2007, pp. 1159–1168.

59. "Taking Bullies to the Woodshed," *HR Magazine,* May 2008, p. 12.

60. C. Hymowitz, "Bosses Have to Learn How to Confront Troubled Employees," *The Wall Street Journal,* April 23, 2007, p. B1.

61. J. Janove, "Jerks at Work," *HR Magazine,* May 2007, pp. 111–117.

62. S. Dilchert, D. S. Ones, R. D. Davis, and C. D. Rostow, "Cognitive Ability Predicts Objectively Measured Counterproductive Work Behaviors," *Journal of Applied Psychology,* May 2007, pp. 616–627.

63. J. R. Detert, L. K. Treviño, E. R. Burris, and M. Andiappan, "Managerial Modes of Influence and Counterproductivity in Organizations: A Longitudinal Business-Unit-Level Investigation," *Journal of Applied Psychology,* July 2007, pp. 993–1005.

64. Canadian Cancer Society 2002 study, cited in J. Gillum, "Strong Words, Images Target Smoking," *USA Today,* July 13, 2004, p. 10D.

65. D. Dearborn and H. Simon, "Selection Perception: A Note on the Departmental Identification of Executives," *Sociometry* 21 (1958), pp. 140–144.

66. Definition adapted from C. M. Judd and B. Park, "Definition and Assessment of Accuracy in Social Stereotypes," *Psychological Review,* January 1993, p. 110. See also D. T. Wegener, J. K. Clark, and R. E. Petty, "Not All Stereotyping Is Created Equal: Differential Consequences of Thoughtful Versus Nonthoughtful Stereotyping," *Journal of Personality and Social Psychology,* January 2006, pp. 42–59.

67. I. K. Broverman, S. Raymond Vogel, D. M. Broverman, F. E. Clarkson, and P. S. Rosenkrantz, "Sex-Role Stereotypes: A Current Appraisal," *Journal of Social Issues,* 1972, p. 75.

68. B. P. Allen, "Gender Stereotypes Are Not Accurate: A Replication of Martin (1987) Using Diagnostic vs. Self-Report and Behavioral Criteria," *Sex Roles,* May 1995, pp. 583–600.

69. J. Landau, "The Relationship of Race and Gender to Managers' Ratings of Promotion Potential," *Journal of Organizational Behavior,* July 1995, pp. 391–400.

70. S. R. Rhodes, "Age-Related Differences in Work Attitudes and Behavior: A Review and Conceptual Analysis," *Psychological Bulletin,* March 1983, p. 38.

71. See T.W.H. Ng and D. C. Feldman, "The Relationship of Age to Ten Dimensions of Job Performance," *Journal of Applied Psychology,* March 2008, pp. 392–423; and R. J. Grossman, "Keep Pace with Older Workers," *HR Magazine,* May 2008, pp. 39–46.

72. J. J. Martocchio, "Age-Related Differences in Employee Absenteeism: A Meta-Analysis," *Psychology and Aging,* December 1989, pp. 409–414; and M. C. Healy, M. Lehman, and M. A. McDaniel, "Age and Voluntary Turnover: A Quantitative Review," *Personnel Psychology,* Summer 1995, pp. 335–345.

73. Central Intelligence Agency, *The World Factbook, 2008,* https://www.cia.gov/library/publications/the-world-factbook/geos/us.html (accessed May 5, 2008).

74. See H. Dolezalek, "Boomer Reality," *Training,* May 2007, pp. 16–21.

75. K. Helliker, "The Doctor Is Still In: Secrets of Health from a Famed 96-Year-Old Physician," *The Wall Street Journal,* March 8, 2005, p. D1.

76. Statistics are reported in "Job Types by Race in the U.S.," *MSN Encarta,* http://encarta.msn.com/media_461546975/Job_Type_by_Race_in_the_U._S.html (accessed May 5, 2008).

77. J. C. Brigham, "Limiting Conditions of the 'Physical Attractiveness Stereotype': Attributions about Divorce," *Journal of Research and Personality* 14 (1980), pp. 365–375; H. Hatfield and S. Sprecher, *Mirror, Mirror . . . The Importance of Looks in Everyday Life* (Albany, NY: State University of New York Press, 1986).

78. M. M. Mobius and T. S. Rosenblat, "Why Beauty Matters," *American Economic Review,* March 2006, pp. 222–235.

79. Ibid.

80. M. M. Clifford and E. H. Walster, "The Effect of Physical Attractiveness on Teacher Expectation," *Sociology of Education* 46 (1973), pp. 248–258.

81. T. Cash and L. H. Janda, "The Eye of the Beholder," *Psychology Today,* December 1984, pp. 46–52.

82. H. R. Varian, "Beauty and the Fattened Wallet," *The New York Times,* April 6, 2006, http://www.nytimes.com/2006/04/06/business/06scene.html?ex=1301976000&en=a5f0aa1131668f77&ei=5090&partner=rssuserland&emc=rss (accessed August 26, 2008).

83. S. J. Linton and L. E. Warg, "Attributions (Beliefs) and Job Satisfaction Associated with Back Pain in an Industrial Setting," *Perceptual and Motor Skills,* February 1993, pp. 51–62.

84. W. S. Silver, T. R. Mitchell, and M. E. Gist, "Responses to Successful and Unsuccessful Performance: The Moderating Effect of Self-Efficacy on the Relationship between Performance and Attributions," *Organizational Behavior and Human Decision Processes,* June 1995, pp. 286–299; and D. Dunning, A. Leuenberger, and D. A. Sherman, "A New Look at Motivated Inference: Are Self-Serving Theories of Success a Product of Motivational Forces?" *Journal of Personality and Social Psychology,* July 1995, pp. 58–68.

85. L. Woellert, "The-Reporter-Did-It Defense," *BusinessWeek,* May 8, 2006, p. 34.

86. See D. Eden and Y. Zuk, "Seasickness as a Self-Fulfilling Prophecy: Raising Self-Efficacy to Boost Performance at Sea," *Journal of Applied Psychology,* October 1995, pp. 628–635. For a thorough review of research on the Pygmalion effect, see D. Eden, *Pygmalion in Management: Productivity as a Self-Fulfilling Prophecy* (Lexington, MA: Lexington Books, 1990), ch. 2.

87. D. B. McNatt, "Ancient Pygmalion Joins Contemporary Management: A Meta-Analysis of the Result," *Journal of Applied Psychology,* April 2000, pp. 314–322.

88. See B. Schlender, "How Bill Gates Keeps the Magic Going," *Fortune,* June 18, 1990, pp. 82–89.

89. These recommendations were adapted from J. Keller, "Have Faith—in You," *Selling Power,* June 1996, pp. 84, 86; and R. W. Goddard, "The Pygmalion Effect," *Personnel Journal,* June 1985, p. 10.

90. *The Wirthlin Report,* reported in "Job Stress Can Be Satisfying," *USA Today,* April 19, 1999, p. 1B.

91. Study by The Medstat Group appearing in the *American Journal of Health Promotion,* October 3, 2000, reported in K. Fackelmann, "Stress, Unhealthy Habits Costing USA," *USA Today,* October 3, 2000, p. 5A.

92. American Institute of Stress, cited in J. W. Upson, D. J. Ketchen Jr., and R. D. Ireland, "Managing Employee Stress: A Key to the Effectiveness of Strategic Supply Chain Management," *Organizational Dynamics* 36 (2007), pp. 78–92.

93. Study in *Circulation,* March 1998, reported in "Managers at Risk from Work Stress," *San Jose Mercury News,* April 12, 1998, p. 5E; reprinted from *The New York Times.*

94. See M. A. Cavanaugh, W. R. Boswell, M. V. Roehling, and J. W. Boudreau, "An Empirical Examination of Self-Reported Work Stress among U.S. Managers," *Journal of Applied Psychology,* February 2000, pp. 65–74; A. J. Kinicki, F. M. McKee-Ryan, C. A. Schriesheim, and K. P. Carson, "Assessing the Construct Validity of the Job Descriptive Index: A Review and Meta-Analysis," *Journal of Applied Psychology,* February 2002, pp. 14–32; A. Weintraub, "Inside Drugmakers' War on Fat," *BusinessWeek,,* March 17, 2008, pp. 41–46; and M. R. Frone, "Are Work Stressors Related to Employee Substance Use? The Importance of Temporal Context in Assessments of Alcohol and Illicit Drug Use," *Journal of Applied Psychology,* January 2008, pp. 199–206.

95. R. S. Lazarus, *Psychological Stress and Coping Processes* (New York: McGraw-Hill, 1966); and R. S. Schuler, "Definition and Conceptualization of Stress in Organizations," *Organizational Behavior and Human Performance,* April 1980, p. 1980.

96. H. Selye, *Stress without Distress* (New York: Lippincott, 1974), p. 27.

97. R. S. Lazarus and S. Folkman, "Coping and Adaptation," in W. D. Gentry, ed., *Handbook of Behavioral Medicine* (New York: Guilford, 1982).

98. R. S. Lazarus, "Little Hassles Can Be Hazardous to Health," *Psychology Today,* July 1981, p. 61.

99. Selye, 1974, pp. 28–29.

100. M. Beck, "When Fretting Is in Your DNA: Overcoming the Worry Gene," *The Wall Street Journal,* January 15, 2008, p. D1. See also L. M. Hilt, L. C. Sander, S. Nolen-Hoeksema, and A. A. Simen, "The BDNF Val66Met Polymorphism Predicts Rumination and Depression Differently in Young Adolescent Girls and Their Mothers," *Neuroscience Letters,* December 2007, pp. 12–16.

101. M. Friedman and R. H. Rosenman, *Type A Behavior and Your Heart* (Greenwich, CT: Fawcett Publications, 1974), p. 84.

102. See M. S. Taylor, E. A. Locke, C. Lee, and. M. E. Gist, "Type A Behavior and Faculty Research Productivity: What Are the Mechanisms?" *Organizational Behavior and Human Performance,* December 1984, pp. 402–418; S. D. Bluen, J. Barling, and W. Burns, "Predicting Sales Performance, Job Satisfaction, and Depression by Using the Achievement Strivings and Impatience–Irritability Dimensions of Type A Behavior," *Journal of Applied Psychology,* April 1990, pp. 212–216.

103. S. Booth-Kewley and H. S. Friedman, "Psychological Predictors of Heart Disease: A Quantitative Review," *Psychological Bulletin,* May 1987, pp. 343–362; S. A. Lyness, "Predictors of Differences between Type A and B Individuals in Heart Rate and Blood Pressure Reactivity," *Psychological Bulletin,* September 1993, pp. 266–295; and T. Q. Miller, T. W. Smith, C. W. Turner, M. L. Guijarro, and A. J. Hallet, "A Meta-Analytic Review of Research on Hostility and Physical Health," *Psychological Bulletin,* March 1996, pp. 322–348.

104. J. O'Donnell, "Wanted: Retail Managers," *USA Today,* December 24, 2007, pp. 1B, 3B.

105. M. Richtel, "In Web World of 24/7 Stress, Writers Blog Till They Drop," *The New York Times,* April 6, 2008, new section, pp. 1, 23.

106. T. D. Schellhardt, "Company Memo to Stressed-Out Employees: 'Deal with It,'" *The Wall Street Journal,* October 2, 1996, pp. B1, B4; see also L. A. Wah, "An Executive's No. 1 Fear," *American Management Association International,* January 1998, p. 87.

107. J. A. Davy, A. J. Kinicki, and C. L. Scheck, "A Test of Job Security's Direct and Mediated Effects on Withdrawal Cognitions," *Journal of Organizational Behavior,* July 1, 1997, p. 323.

108. G. Graen, "Role-Making Processes within Complex Organizations," in M. D. Dunnette, ed., *Handbook of Industrial and Organizational Psychology* (Chicago: Rand McNally, 1976), p. 1201.

109. M. Culp, "Coping When Co-Worker Is Under Stress," *The Hartford Courant,* February 25, 2008, courant.com/business/hc-midred0225.artfeb25,0,4210457.story.com (accessed February 25, 2008).

110. T. D. Wall, P. R. Jackson, S. Mullarkey, and S. K. Parker, "The Demands-Control Model of Job Strain: A More Specific Test," *Journal of Occupational and Organizational Psychology,* June 1996, pp. 153–166; and R. C. Barnett and R. T. Brennan, "The Relationship between Job Experiences and Psychological Distress: A Structural Equation Approach," *Journal of Organizational Behavior,* May 1995, pp. 250–276.

111. "Lousiest Bosses," *The Wall Street Journal,* April 4, 1995, p. A1. For more about bad managers, see J. Sandberg, "Had It Up to HERE? Despite Risk, Some Say Quitting Is Way to Go," *The Wall Street Journal,* August 14, 2007, p. B1; G. G. Scott, *A Survival Guide for Working with Bad Bosses: Dealing with Bullies, Idiots, Back-Stabbers, and Other Managers from Hell* (New York: AMACOM, 2005); and A. Dobson, "Working It Out: Fixing a Strained Relationship with Your Boss," *San Francisco Chronicle,* March 2, 2008, p. H1.

112. J. Schaubroeck and D. C. Ganster, "Chronic Demands and Responsivity to Challenge," *Journal of Applied Psychology,* February 1993, pp. 73–85; E. Demerouti, A. B. Bakker, F. Nachreiner, and W. B. Schaufeli, "The Job Demands Resources Model of Burnout," *Journal of Applied Psychology,* June 2001, pp. 499–512.

113. J. M. Plas, *Person-Centered Leadership: An American Approach to Participatory Management* (Thousand Oaks, CA: Sage, 1996).

114. M. Patsalos-Fox, quoted in W. J. Holstein, "Tension Headaches in the Corner Office," *The New York Times,* March 12, 2006, sec. 3, p. 1.

115. N. E. Adler, T. Boyce, M. A. Chesney, S. Cohen, S. Folkman, R. L. Kahn, and S. L. Syme, "Socioeconomic Status and Health: The Challenge of the Gradient," *American Psychologist,* January 1994, pp. 15–24.

116. The link between stress and depression is discussed by P. Freiberg, "Work and Well-Being: Experts Urge Changes in Work, Not the Work," *The APA Monthly,* January 1991, p. 23.

117. M. Staver, quoted in C. H. Deutsch, "Winning the Battle Against Burnout," *The New York Times,* August 27, 2006, sec. 3, p. 5.

118. See C. H. Deutsch, "Winning the Battle Against Burnout," *The New York Times,* August 27, 2006, sec. 3, p. 5.

119. Absenteeism and stress are discussed by S. Shellenbarger, "Work & Family: Was That 24-Hour Flu That Kept You Home Really Just the Blahs?" *The Wall Street Journal,* July 24, 1996, p. B1.

120. S. L. Larson, J. Eyerman, M. S. Foster, and J. C. Gfroerer, *Worker Substance Use and Workplace Policies and Programs* (Rockville, MD: Substance Abuse and Mental Health Service Administration, Department of Health and Human Services, June 2007), http://oas.samhsa.gov/work2k7/toc.cfm#All (accessed May 5, 2008).

121. M. Ferri, L. Amato, and M. Davoli, "Alcoholics Anonymous and Other 12-Step Programmes for Alcohol Dependence (Review)," *Cochrane Database of Scientific Reviews,* 2006, Issue 3. See also report in N. Bakalar, "Review Sees No Advantage in 12-Step Programs," *The New York Times,* July 25, 2006, p. D6.

122. Recommendations for reducing burnout are discussed by M. Wylie, "Preventing Worker Burnout while Supporting the Users," *MacWeek,* October 4, 1993, pp. 12–14; and "How to Avoid Burnout," *Training,* February 1993, pp. 15, 16, 70.

123. These examples and techniques are discussed by L. Landon, "Pump Up Your Employees," *HR Magazine,* May 1990, pp. 34–37; and R. L. Rose, "Time Out: At the Menninger Clinic, Executives Learn More About Themselves—and Why They're So Unhappy," *The Wall Street Journal,* February 26, 1996, p. R5.

124. See R. Kreitner and A. Kinicki, *Organizational Behavior*, 8th ed. (Burr Ridge, IL: McGraw-Hill, 2008); and A. Novotney, "The Happiness Diet," *Monitor on Psychology,* April 2008, pp. 24–25.

125. R. Kreitner, "Personal Wellness: It's Just Good Business," *Business Horizons,* May–June 1982, p. 28.

126. See J. J. Medina, "The Science of Thinking Smarter," *Harvard Business Review,* May 2008, pp. 51–54; R. Riney, "Heal Leadership Disorders," *HR Magazine,* May 2008, pp. 62–66; and M. Fugate, A. J. Kinicki, and G. E. Prussia, "Employee Coping with Organizational Change: An Examination of Alternative Theoretical Perspectives and Models," *Personnel Psychology,* Spring 2008, pp. 1–36.

CHAPTER 12

1. Kleiman, "Work-Life Rewards Grow," *San Francisco Examiner,* January 16, 2000, p. J-2; reprinted from *Chicago Tribune.*

2. M. Buckingham and C. Coffman, *First, Break All the Rules: What the World's Greatest Managers Do Differently* (New York: Simon & Schuster, 1999).

3. Kimberly Scott, project leader for Hewitt Associates, which helps compile the *Fortune* list, reported in D. Murphy, "Can Morale Contribute to Safer Skies?" *San Francisco Examiner,* February 11, 2000, p. J-1.

4. These and other employee perks are described in A. Johnson, "It's True: A Nicer Office Can Boost Morale," *The Arizona Republic,* September 3, 2007, pp. D1, D3; S. Covel, "Telemarketer Bucks High Turnover Trend," *The Wall Street Journal,* November 19, 2007, p. B4; A. Bruzzese, "Family-Friendly Employers," *The Arizona Republic,* November 25, 2007, p. EC1; T. Sharples, "Who's the Boss?" *Time,* January 14, 2008, p. 61; K. Shevory, "The Workplace as Clubhouse," *The New York Times,* February 16, 2008, p. B5; S. Armour, "Day Care's New Frontier: Your Baby at Your Desk," *USA Today,* March 31, 2008, pp. 1A, 2A; S. Roberts "Shifts in Pregnancy and Work," *The New York Times,* February 26, 2008, p. A11; A. Lallande, "Recognize Your Investments," *HR Magazine,* April 2008, pp. 91–94; and M. Meece, "Doing the Unusual to Help Workers Solve Personal Problems," *The New York Times,* April 3, 2008, p. C4.

5. Adapted from definition in T. R. Mitchell, "Motivation: New Directions for Theory, Research, and Practice," *Academy of Management Review,* January 1982, p. 81.

6. See R. M. Ryan and E. L. Deci, "Intrinsic and Extrinsic Motivations: Classic Definitions and New Directions," *Contemporary Educational Psychology,* January 2000, pp. 54–67.

7. S. E. Needleman, "The Latest Office Perk: Getting Paid to Volunteer," *The Wall Street Journal,* April 29, 2008, p. D1.

8. See P. W. Hom, L. Roberson, and A. D. Ellis, "Challenging Conventional Wisdom about Who Quits: Revelations from Corporate America," *Journal of Applied Psychology,* January 2008, pp. 1–34; J. B. Olson-Buchanan and W. R. Boswell, "An Integrative Model of Experiencing and Responding to Mistreatment at Work," *Academy of Management Review,* January 2008, pp. 76–96; and M. Riketta, "The Causal Relation Between Job Attitudes and Performance: A Meta-Analysis of Panel Studies," *Journal of Applied Psychology,* March 2008, pp. 472–481.

9. K. Down and L. Liedtka, "What Corporations Seek in MBA Hires: A Survey," *Selections,* Winter 1994, pp. 34–39; see

also S. Armour, "Companies Get Tough on Absent Employees," *The Arizona Republic,* February 7, 2003, p. A2; reprinted from *USA Today.*

10. T. Van Tassel, "Productivity Dilemmas," *Executive Excellence,* April 1994, pp. 16-17.

11. A. Maslow, "A Theory of Human Motivation," *Psychological Review,* July 1943, pp. 370-396. A more recent expression of Maslow's theory can be found in C. Conley, *Peak: How Great Companies Get Their Mojo from Maslow* (San Francisco: Jossey-Bass, 2007).

12. H. Benson, "In an Era of High Technology, Low Commitment, One Man Says He's Found a Way to Measure Integrity," *San Francisco Chronicle,* June 21, 2006, pp. El, E3.

13. P. H. Ray and S. R. Anderson, *The Cultural Creatives: How 50 Million People Are Changing the World* (New York: Harmony Books, 2000).

14. D. E. Meyerson, *Tempered Radicals: How Everyday Leaders Inspire Change at Work* (Boston: Harvard Business School Press, 2003). For examples of the need for achievement, see M. R. della Cava, "Answering Their Calling," *USA Today,* March 13, 2006, pp. ID, 2D.

15. Conley, 2007.

16. For a complete review of ERG theory, see C. P. Alderfer, *Existence, Relatedness, and Growth: Human Needs in Organizational Settings* (New York: Free Press, 1972).

17. D. C. McClelland, *Human Motivation* (Glenview, IL: Scott, Foresman, 1985).

18. D. McClelland and H. Burnham, "Power Is the Great Motivator," *Harvard Business Review,* March/April 1976, pp. 100-110.

19. S. W. Spreier, M. H. Fontaine, and R. L. Malloy, "Leadership Run Amok," *Harvard Business Review,* June 2006, pp. 72-82.

20. Recent studies of achievement motivation can be found in H. Grant and C. S. Dweck, "A Goal Analysis of Personality and Personality Coherence," in D. Cervone and Y. Shoda, eds., *The Coherence of Personality* (New York: Guilford Press, 1999), pp. 345-371.

21. S. A. Flaum and J. A. Flaum, with M. Flaum, *The 100-Mile Walk: A Father and Son on a Quest to Find the Essence of Leadership* (New York: Amacom, 2006). See also J. C. Mead, "How to Succeed in Business: Walk," *The New York Times,* January 29, 2006, sec. 14LI, p. 6; and S. Berfield, "Walk 100 Miles in My Shoes," *BusinessWeek,* June 26, 2006, pp. 80-81.

22. F. Herzberg, B. Mausner, and B. B. Snyderman, *The Motivation to Work* (New York: Wiley, 1959); and F. Herzberg, "One More Time: How Do You Motivate Employees?" *Harvard Business Review,* January–February 1968, pp. 53-62.

23. J. S. Adams, "Toward an Understanding of Inequity," *Journal of Abnormal and Social Psychology,* November 1963, pp. 422-436; and J. S. Adams, "Injustice in Social Exchange," in L. Berkowitz, ed., *Advances in Experimental Social Psychology,* 2nd ed. (New York: Academic Press, 1965), pp. 267-300.

24. See B. Baird, "Don't Get Mad: Get Even," *The Arizona Republic,* April 20, 2008, pp. DI, D5; C. Hymowitz, "In the Lead: Pay Gap Fuels Worker Woes," *The Wall Street Journal,* April 28, 2008, p. B8; and G. Colvin, "Rewarding Failure," *Fortune,* April 28, 2008, p. 22.

25. U.S. Department of Commerce, cited in A. Salkever, "An Easy Antidote to Employee Theft," *BusinessWeek online,* May 20, 2003, www.businessweek.com/smallbiz/content/may2003/sb20030520_9328_sb018.htm (accessed May 11, 2008). See also J. Greenberg, "Employee Theft as a Reaction to Underpayment Inequity: The Hidden Cost of Pay Cuts," *Journal of Applied Psychology* 75 (1990), pp. 561-568.

26. See J. Choi and C. C. Chen, "The Relationship of Distributive Justice and Compensation System Fairness to Employee Attitudes in International Joint Ventures," *Journal of Organizational Behavior*, August 2007, pp. 687-703; S. W. Whiting, P. M. Podsakoff, and J. R. Pierce, "Effects of Task Performance, Helping, Voice, and Organizational Loyalty on Performance Appraisal Ratings," *Journal of Applied Psychology,* January 2008, pp. 125-139; and S. Tangirala and R. Ramanujam, "Employee Silence on Critical Work Issues: The Cross-Level Effects of Procedural Justice Climate," *Personnel Psychology,* Spring 2008, pp. 37-68.

27. See R. A. Posthuma, C. P. Maertz Jr., and J. B. Dworkin, "Procedural Justice's Relationship with Turnover: Explaining Past Inconsistent Findings," *Journal of Organizational Behavior,* May 2007, pp. 381-398; Y. Cohen-Charash and J. S. Mueller, "Does Perceived Unfairness Exacerbate or Mitigate Interpersonal Counterproductive Work Behaviors Related to Envy?" *Journal of Applied Psychology,* May 2007, pp. 666-680; and H. Moon, D. Kamdar, D. M. Mayer, and R. Takeuchi, "Me or We? The Role of Personality and Justice as Other-Centered Antecedents to Innovative Citizenship Behaviors within Organizations," *Journal of Applied Psychology,* January 2008, pp. 84-94.

28. V. H. Vroom, *Work and Motivation* (New York: Wiley, 1964).

29. C. Wallis, "How to Make Great Teachers," *Time,* February 25, 2008, pp. 28-34; and N. Zuckerbrod, "Tenure, Evaluation Process Get Poor Grades in Teacher Survey," *The Arizona Republic,* May 7, 2008, p. AIO.

30. A Hudson survey of 10,000 employees March 20-26, 2006, found that 48% of managers but only 31% of nonmanagers agreed with the statement "Employees who do a better job get paid more"; 46% of managers but only 29% of nonmanagers agreed with the statement "My last raise was based on performance." Information cited in "Reasons for Raises," *BusinessWeek,* May 29, 2006, p. 11.

31. Research supporting the need to establish a direct relationship between pay and performance can be found in M. L. Williams, M. A. McDaniel, and N. T. Nguyen, "A Meta-Analysis of the Antecedents and Consequences of Pay Level Satisfaction," *Journal of Applied Psychology,* March 2006, pp. 392-413. Also see B. Colvin, "AmEx Gets CEO Pay Right," *Fortune,* January 21, 2008, pp. 22-24; and S. Banjo, "Shared Goals," *The Wall Street Journal,* April 14, 2008, p. R3.

32. Community Training and Assistance Center, *Catalyst for Change: Pay for Performance in Denver—Final Report,* January 2004; http://www.ctacusa.com/denvervol3-front-section.pdf (accessed May 11, 2008). See also Community Training and Assistance Center, "Teacher Pay for Performance: Catalyst for Change," press release, *CTAC News,* February 9, 2004; http://www.ctacusa.com/news3.html (accessed May 11, 2008).

33. M. Philips and P. Tyre, "A Bonus, Sir, with Love," *Newsweek,* September 24, 2007, p. 53.

34. P. Whoriskey, "Fla. to Link Teacher Pay to Students' Test Scores," *Washington Post,* March 22, 2006, p. Al; R. Tomsho, "More Districts Pay Teachers for Performance," *The Wall Street Journal,* March 23, 2006, pp. BI, B5; E. W. Green, "More Apples for the Very Best Teachers," *U.S. News & World Report,* September 18, 2006, p. 40 ; and "States Experiment with Pay for Performance," *Education Week,* January 10, 2008, http://www.edweek.org/login.html?source=http%3A%2F%2Fwww.google.com%2Fsearch%3Fhl%3Den%26q%3Dteacher%2Bpay%2Bfor%2Bperformance%2B2008&destination=http%3A%2F%2Fwww.edweek.org%2Few%2Farticles%2F2008%2F01%2F10%2F18pay_side.h27.html&levelId=1000&baddebt=false (accessed May 9, 2008).

35. G. Toppo, "Kids' Good Grades Pay Off—Literally," *USA Today,* January 28, 2008, p. 3A. See also the National Math and Science Initiative, which runs the seven-state program, http://test.nationalmathandscience.org/component/option,com_frontpage/Itemid,110/ (accessed May 9, 2008).

36. For a thorough discussion of goal-setting theory and application, see E. A. Locke and G. P. Latham, "Building a Practically Useful Theory of Goal Setting and Task Motivation," *American Psychologist,* September 2002, pp. 705–717.

37. See A. L. Kalleberg, "The Mismatched Worker: When People Don't Fit Their Jobs," *Academy of Management Perspectives,* February 2008, pp. 24–40.

38. S. Melamed, I. Ben-Avi, J. Luz, and M. S. Green, "Objective and Subjective Work Monotony: Effects on Job Satisfaction, Psychological Distress, and Absenteeism in Blue-Collar Workers," *Journal of Applied Psychology,* February 1995, pp. 29–42; and B. Melin, U. Lundberg, J. Söderlund, and M. Granqvist, "Psychological and Physiological Stress Reactions of Male and Female Assembly Workers: A Comparison between Two Different Forms of Work Organization," *Journal of Organizational Behavior,* January 1999, pp. 47–61.

39. M. A. Campion and C. L. McClelland, "Follow-Up and Extension of the Interdisciplinary Costs and Benefits of Enlarged Jobs," *Journal of Applied Psychology,* June 1993, pp. 339–351.

40. Herzberg et al., 1959.

41. S. Phillips and A. Dunkin, "King Customer," *BusinessWeek,* March 12, 1990, p. 91.

42. J. R. Hackman and G. R. Oldham, *Work Redesign* (Reading, MA: Addison-Wesley, 1980).

43. See S. E. Humphrey, J. D. Nahrgang, and F. P. Morgeson, "Integrating Motivational, Social, and Contextual Work Design Features: A Meta-Analytic Summary and Theoretical Extension of the Work Design Literature," *Journal of Applied Psychology*, September 2007, pp. 1332–1356. Also see A. M. Grant, "The Significance of Task Significance: Job Performance Effects, Relational Mechanisms, and Boundary Conditions," *Journal of Applied Psychology,* January 2008, pp. 108–124; and F. W. Bond, P. E. Flaxman, and D. Bunce, "The Influence of Psychological Flexibility on Work Redesign: Mediated Moderation of a Work Reorganization Intervention," *Journal of Applied Psychology,* May 2008, pp. 645–654.

44. Dr. Paul H. Grundy, I.B.M.'s director of Health Care Technology and Strategic Initiatives, quoted in M. Freudenheim, "A Model for Health Care That Pays for Quality," *The New York Times,* November 7, 2007, p. C3.

45. See E. L. Thorndike, *Educational Psychology: The Psychology of Learning, Vol. II* (New York: Columbia University Teachers College, 1913); B. F. Skinner, *Walden Two* (New York: Macmillan, 1948); *Science and Human Behavior* (New York: Macmillan, 1953); and *Contingencies of Reinforcement* (New York: Appleton-Century-Crofts, 1969).

46. J. Sandberg, "A Modern Conundrum: When Work's Invisible, So Are Its Satisfactions," *The Wall Street Journal,* February 19, 2008, p. B1.

47. This is a "blended definition" proposed by the Conference Board from many definitions, cited by S. Roesler, "What Does Employee Engagement Really Mean?" *All Things Workplace*, March 12, 2007, http://www.allthingsworkplace .com/2007/03/what_does_emplo.html (accessed May 11, 2008).

48. This figure comes from T. R. Clark, "Engaging the Disengaged," *HR Magazine,* April 2008, pp. 109–112.

49. Statistic from study by Towers Perrin, cited by B. Kiviat, "The Rage to Engage," *Time,* April 28, 2008, p. Global 10. See also *2007 Towers Perrin Global Workforce Study,* October 9, 2007, www.towersperrin.com/tp/getwebcachedoc?webc=HRS/USA/2007/200710/GWS_Fact_Sheet_draft_10_9_07_v5.pdf (accessed May 11, 2008).

50. Taisdeal, quoted in Benson, 2006. For an article about the importance of congeniality, see D. Brady, "Charm Offensive," *BusinessWeek,* June 26, 2006, pp. 76–80.

51. A. Zipkin, "The Wisdom of Thoughtfulness," *The New York Times,* May 31, 2000, pp. C1, C10.

52. Gallup Organization study, reported in Zipkin, 2000. This differs from a survey by the Society for Human Resource Management, *2007 Job Satisfaction Survey Report,* in which employees said the top five "very important" aspects of job satisfaction were compensation, benefits, job security, work/life balance, and communication between employees and senior management. See S. Miller, "HR, Employees Vary on Job Satisfaction," *HR Magazine,* August 2007, pp. 32, 34. The magazine *Workspace* reported that employees said benefits were more important, followed by compensation and then by "growth and earning potential," as reported in P. B. Brown, "Same Office, Different Planets," *The New York Times,* January 26, 2008, p. B5.

53. E. White, "The Best vs. the Rest," *The Wall Street Journal,* January 30, 2006, pp. B1, B3; and J. Pfeffer, "Stopping the Talent Drain," *Business 2.0,* July 2006, p. 80.

54. See, for example, J. Anderson, "Tying One's Pay to Performance: What a Concept," *The New York Times,* July 15, 2005, p. C7; and G. Farrell and B. Hansen, "Stocks May Fall, but Pay Doesn't," *USA Today,* April 10, 2008, pp. 1B, 2B. See also M. J. Canyon, "Executive Compensation and Incentives," *Academy of Management Perspectives,* February 2006, pp. 25–44.

55. P. Hodson, *2008 Proxy Season Foresights #2—Performance Targets Targeted,* February 15, 2008, Corporate Library, http://www.thecorporatelibrary.com/info.php?id=88 (accessed May 9, 2008). This study by Corporate Library, an independent governance research organization for the Securities and Exchange Commission, is reported in E. Simon, "How Execs Get Bonus Not Clear," *San Francisco Chronicle,* February 21, 2008, p. C3.

56. B. E. Graham-Moore and T. L. Ross, *Productivity Gainsharing* (Englewood Cliffs, NJ: Prentice-Hall, 1983).

57. "Take Stock of Stock Options," *Human Resource Executive Magazine,* June 3, 2004, workindex.com; www.workindex.com/editorial/hre/hre0406-03.asp (accessed July 12, 2006).

58. K. Clark, "Too Safe a Bet?" *U.S. News & World Report,* June 19, 2006, pp. 37–38. For more on backdating of stock options, see J. Ledbetter, "Backdating: It Ain't Over," *Fortune,* March 20, 2008, http://dailybriefing.blogs.fortune.cnn .com/2008/03/20/backdating-it-aint-over (accessed May 9, 2008); and H. W. Jenkins Jr., "One Last Backdating Whipping Boy?" *The Wall Street Journal,* April 30, 2008, http:// online.wsj.com/article/SB120951511131354625.html (accessed May 9, 2008).

59. PricewaterhouseCoopers survey, reported in S. Shellenbarger, "What Job Candidates Really Want to Know: Will I Have a Life?" *The Wall Street Journal,* November 17, 1999, p. B1. See also S. F. Premeaux, C. L. Adkins, and K. W. Mossholder, "Balancing Work and Family: A Field Study of Multi-Dimensional, Multi-Role Work-Family Conflict," *Journal of Organizational Behavior,* August 2007, pp. 705–727; S. Cummins, "Life, Liberty, and the Pursuit of Balance," *BusinessWeek,* October 23, 2007, http://www.businessweek. com/managing/content/oct2007/ca20071023_799034 .htm?campaign_id=rss_daily (accessed May 11, 2008); J. Herzlich, "Work/Life Balance Tops List," *The Arizona Republic,* January 6, 2008, p. EC1;

60. K. W. Smola and C. D. Sutton, "Generational Differences: Revisiting Generational Work Values for the New Millennium," *Journal of Organizational Behavior,* June 2002, p. 379.

61. Hira, 2008, p. 42.

62. Walker Information Global Network and Hudson Institute, *2000 Global Employee Relationship Report,* in "Global Workforce Study Highlights Alarming Trends," September 19, 2000, http://www.hudson.org/index.cfm?fuseaction=publication_details&id=697 (accessed May 11, 2008).

63. Spherion and Louis Harris Associates 1999 survey, reported in Zipkin, 2000.

64. See P. Falcone, "Doing More with Less: How to Motivate and Reward Your Overworked Staff During Lean Times," *HR Magazine,* February 2003, pp. 101–103; D. Kehrer, "Here Are Some Keys to Keeping Good Employees," *Reno Gazette-Journal,* March 30, 2004, p. 4D; and J. Noveck, "Do Bosses Need to Be Mean to Get Work Done?" *Nevada Appeal,* July 9, 2006, pp. D1, D2.

65. B. L. Ware, quoted in Zipkin, 2000.

66. K. Lingle, quoted in C. Kleiman, "Work-Life Rewards Grow," *San Francisco Examiner,* January 16, 2000, p. J-2; reprinted from *Chicago Tribune.*

67. S. Shellenberger, "Companies Retool Time-Off Policies to Prevent Burnout, Reward Performance," *The Wall Street Journal,* January 5, 2006, p. D1.

68. See A. Fisher, "The Rebalancing Act," *Fortune,* October 6, 2003, pp. 110–113; D. Cadrain, "Cash vs. Non-cash Rewards," *HR Magazine,* April 2003, pp. 81–87; C. Hymowitz, "While Some Women Choose to Stay Home, Others Gain Flexibility," *The Wall Street Journal,* March 30, 2004, p. B1; J. Shramm, "Fuel Economy," *HR Magazine,* December 2005, p. 120; S. Armour, "Cost-Effective 'Homesourcing' Grows," *USA Today,* March 13, 2006, p. 1B; S. E. Needleman, "Pick Worker Rewards Carefully," *The Wall Street Journal,* March 28, 2006, p. B8; M. P. McQueen, "Employers Expand Elder-Care Benefits," *The Wall Street Journal,* July 27, 2006, pp. D1, D6; A. Pomeroy, "The Future Is Now," *HR Magazine,* September 2007, pp. 46–51; S. Shellenbarger, "Good News for Professionals Who Want to Work at Home," *The Wall Street Journal,* November 15, 2007, p. D1; S. Armour, "As Dads Push for Family Time, Tensions Rise in Workplace," *USA Today,* December 11, 2007, pp. 1A, 2A; K. R. Lewis, "Getting Time Off and Getting Work Done a Balancing Act," *San Francisco Chronicle,* December 16, 2007, p. E6; and D. Hudepohl, "Working from Home: Mapping Out Your First 90 Days," *The Wall Street Journal,* February 19, 2008, p. B8.

69. A. Hedge, quoted in P. Wen, "Drab Cubicles Can Block Workers' Creativity, Productivity," *San Francisco Chronicle,* March 10, 2000, pp. B1, B3; reprinted from *Boston Globe.*

70. See Johnson, 2007, which describes a study by Harvard Medical School psychologist Nancy Etcoff that reinforces the idea that a person's physical environment has a big impact on his or her mood at work. Also see I. DeBare, "Shared Work Spaces a Sign of the Times," *San Francisco Chronicle,* February 19, 2008, pp. A1, A7.

71. J. Sturges, N. Conway, D. Guest, and A. Liefooghe, "Managing the Career Deal: The Psychological Contract as a Framework for Understanding Career Management, Organizational Commitment, and Work Behavior," *Journal of Organizational Behavior,* November 2005, pp. 821–838; and J. Badal, "'Career Path' Programs Help Retain Workers," *The Wall Street Journal,* July 24, 2006, pp. B1, B4.

72. J. P. Smith, "Sabbaticals Pervade Business Sector," *Reno Gazette-Journal,* February 22, 2004, p. H1; M. Arndt, "Nice Work If You Can Get It," *BusinessWeek,* January 9, 2006, pp. 56–57; and L. Chao, "Sabbaticals Can Offer Dividends for Employers," *The Wall Street Journal,* July 17, 2006, p. B5.

CHAPTER 13

1. D. L. Duarte and N. T. Snyder, *Mastering Virtual Teams: Strategies, Tools, and Techniques That Succeed,* 3rd ed. (San Francisco: Jossey-Bass, 2006).

2. C. Sandlund, "Remote Control," *Business Week Frontier,* March 27, 2000, pp. F.14–F.20; A. Salkever, "Home Truths about Meetings," *BusinessWeek,* April 24, 2003, http://www.businessweek.com/smallbiz/content/apr2003/sb20030424_0977_sb010.htm?chan=search (accessed May 12, 2008); B. J. Alge, C. Wiethoff, and H. J. Klein, "When Does the Medium Matter? Knowledge-Building Experiences and Opportunities in Decision-Making Teams," *Organizational Behavior and Human Decision Processes* 91 (2003), pp. 26–37; B. Snyder, "Teams That Span Time Zones Face New Work Rules," *Stanford Business Magazine,* May 2003, http://www.gsb.stanford.edu/news/bmag/sbsm0305/feature_virtual_teams.shtml (accessed May 12, 2008); M. K. Brown, B. Huettner, and C. James-Tanny, *Managing Virtual Teams: Getting the Most from Wikis, Blogs, and Other Collaborative Tools* (Plano, TX: Wordware Publishing, 2007); M. Goldsmith, "Crossing the Cultural Chasm," *BusinessWeek,* May 30, 2007, http://www.businessweek.com/careers/content/may2007/ca20070530_521679.htm?chan=search (accessed May 12, 2008); and L. Noeth, "Supervising a Virtual Team Is Still All about Basics," *Rochester Democrat & Chronicle,* April 27, 2008, http://www.democratandchronicle.com/apps/pbcs.dll/article?AID=/20080427/BUSINESS01/804270332/-1/COLUMNS (accessed May 12, 2008).

3. "Once the Best, U.S. Settles for Bronze," *The New York Times,* September 3, 2006; http://www.nytimes.com/aponline/sports/AP-BKO-Worlds-U.S.html (accessed September 4, 2006). See also G. Colvin, "Why Dream Teams Fail," *Fortune,* June 12, 2006, pp. 87–92.

4. A. Bagnato, "Greek Tragedy: Team USA's Dreams of Gold Gone," *Reno Gazette-Journal,* September 2, 2006, p. 2B.

5. M. Sokolove, "One Team, Indivisible?" *Play* (special edition of *The New York Times Magazine*), September 2006, p. 18.

6. P. F. Drucker, "The Coming of the New Organization," *Harvard Business Review,* January–February 1988, pp. 45–53.

7. "Top 10 Leadership Tips from Jeff Immelt," *Fast Company,* April 2004, p. 96.

8. T. Kelley, quoted in P. Sinton, "Teamwork the Name of the Game for Ideo," *San Francisco Chronicle,* February 23, 2000, pp. D1, D3. Kelley is coauthor, with J. Littman, of *The Art of Innovation: Lessons in Creativity from IDEO, America's Leading Design Firm* (New York: Random House, 2001) and of *The Ten Faces of Innovation: IDEO's Strategies for Defeating the Devil's Advocate and Driving Creativity Throughout Your Organization* (New York: Currency/Doubleday, 2005).

9. This definition is based in part on one found in D. Horton Smith, "A Parsimonious Definition of 'Group': Toward Conceptual Clarity and Scientific Utility," *Sociological Inquiry,* Spring 1967, pp. 141–167.

10. E. H. Schein, *Organizational Psychology,* 3rd ed. (Englewood Cliffs, NJ: Prentice-Hall, 1980), p. 145.

11. J. R. Katzenbach and D. K. Smith, *The Wisdom of Teams: Creating the High-Performance Organization* (Boston: Harvard Business School Press, 1993), p. 45.

12. J. R. Katzenbach and D. K. Smith, "The Discipline of Teams," *Harvard Business Review,* March–April 1995, p. 112.

13. D. Krackhardt and J. R. Hanson, "Informal Networks: The Company Behind the Chart," *Harvard Business Review,* July–August 1993, p. 104.

14. Study by Center for Workforce Development, Newton, MA, reported in M. Jackson, "It's Not Chitchat, It's Training," *San Francisco Chronicle,* January 7, 1998, p. D2.

15. Center for Workforce Development, *The Teaching Firm: Where Productive Work and Learning Converge* (Newton, MA: Education Development Center, 1998). For more on informal learning, see D. W. Livingstone and R. Roth, "Workers' Knowledge: An Untapped Resource in the Labour Movement," paper presented at the International Conference on Union Growth, Toronto, April 30–May 1, 2001, http://www.oise.utoronto.ca/depts/sese/csew/nall/res/31workers.htm (accessed September 4, 2006); V. J. Marsick and K. E. Watkins, "Informal and Incidental Learning," *New Directions for Adult and Continuing Education,* February 26, 2002, pp. 25–34; and M. B. Twidale, "Over the Shoulder Learning: Supporting Brief Informal Learning," *Computer Supported Cooperative Work,* December 2005, pp. 505–547.

16. K. K. Spors, "Getting Workers to Share Their Know-How with Peers," *The Wall Street Journal,* April 3, 2008, p. B6. For more on virtual knowledge sharing, see B. Rosen, S. Furst, and R. Blackburn, "Overcoming Barriers to Knowledge Sharing in Virtual Teams," *Organizational Dynamics* 36 (2007), pp. 259–273.

17. See E. Krell, "HR Challenges in Virtual Worlds," *HR Magazine,* November 2007, pp. 85–88; and R. King, "The (Virtual) Global Office," *BusinessWeek,* May 2, 2008, http://*msnbci .businessweek.com/technology/content/may2008/ tc2008052_842516_page_2.htm* (accessed May 12, 2008).

18. E. Sundstrom, K. P. DeMeuse, and D. Futrell, "Work Teams," *American Psychologist,* February 1990, pp. 120–133.

19. See K. Buch and R. Spangler, "The Effects of Quality Circles on Performance and Promotions," *Human Relations,* June 1990, pp. 573–582; and E. E. Lawler III, "Total Quality Management and Employee Involvement: Are They Compatible?" *Academy of Management Executive,* February 1994, pp. 68–76.

20. G. L. Stewart and M. R. Barrick, "Team Structure and Performance: Assessing the Mediating Role of Intrateam Process and the Moderating Role of Task," *Academy of Management Journal,* April 2000, p. 135. See also S. E. Humphrey, J. R. Hollenbeck, C. J. Meyer, and D. R. Ilgen, "Trait Configurations in Self-Managed Teams: A Conceptual Examination of the Use of Seeding for Maximizing and Minimizing Trait Variance in Teams," *Journal of Applied Psychology,* May 2007, pp. 885–892.

21. Good background discussions can be found in P. S. Goodman, R. Devadas, and T. L. Griffith Hughson, "Groups and Productivity: Analyzing the Effectiveness of Self-Managing Teams," in J. P. Campbell, R. J. Campbell, and Associates, eds., *Productivity in Organizations* (San Francisco: Jossey-Bass, 1988), pp. 295–327; E. G. Rogers, W. Metlay, I. T. Kaplan, and T. Shapiro, "Self-Managing Work Teams: Do They Really Work?" *Human Resource Planning,* no. 2, 1995, pp. 53–57; and R. Rico, M. Sánchez-Manzanares, F. Gil, and C. Gibson, "Team Implicit Coordination Processes: A Team Knowledge-Based Approach," *Academy of Management Review,* January 2008, pp. 163–184.

22. See K. Kraiger, "Perspectives on Training and Development," in W. C. Borman, D. R. Ilgen, and R. J. Klimoski, eds., *Handbook of Psychology,* vol. 12 (New York: John Wiley, 2003), pp. 176–177; and C. Douglas and W. L. Gardner, "Transition to Self-Directed Work Teams: Implications of Transition Time and Self-Monitoring for Managers' Use of Influence Tactics," *Journal of Organizational Behavior* 25 (2004), pp. 47–65.

23. C. Douglas and W. L. Gardner, "Transition to Self-Directed Work Teams: Implications of Transition Time and Self-Monitoring for Managers' Use of Influence Tactics," *Journal of Organizational Behavior* 25 (2004), pp. 47–65.

24. See B. W. Tuckman, "Developmental Sequence in Small Groups," *Psychological Bulletin,* June 1965, pp. 384–399; and B. W. Tuckman and M.A.C. Jensen, "Stages of Small-Group Development Revisited," *Group & Organization Studies,* December 1977, pp. 419–427. An instructive adaptation of the Tuckman model can be found in L. Holpp, "If Empowerment Is So Good, Why Does It Hurt?" *Training,* March 1995, p. 56. See also C. Gersick, "Marking Time: Predictable Transitions in Task Groups," *Academy of Management Journal,* June 1989, pp. 274–309; and S. Wait, "Team Building Is Critical for Successful Growth," *Reno Gazette-Journal,* August 5, 2006, p. 5E.

25. See F. P. Morgeson, M. H. Reider, and M. A. Campion, "Selecting Individuals in Team Settings: The Importance of Social Skills, Personality Characteristics, and Teamwork Knowledge," *Personnel Psychology,* Autumn 2005, pp. 583–611.

26. Practical advice on handling a dominating group member can be found in M. Finley, "Belling the Bully," *HR Magazine,* March 1992, pp. 82–86; see also B. Carey, "Fear in the Workplace: The Bullying Boss," *The New York Times,* June 22, 2004, pp. D1, D6.

27. Techniques for team building are discussed by P. Falcone, "On the Brink of Failure," *HR Magazine,* February 2008, pp. 82–84; and "Sound of Teambuilding," *Training,* February 2008, p. 16.

28. J. Schaubroeck, S.S.K. Lam, and S. E. Cha, "Embracing Transformational Leadership: Team Values and the Impact of Leader Behavior on Team Performance," *Journal of Applied Psychology,* July 2007, pp. 1020–1030.

29. "Is Your Team Too Big? Too Small? What's the Right Number?" *Knowledge@Wharton,* June 14, 2006, Wharton School, University of Pennsylvania, http://knowledge.wharton.upenn.edu/article.cfm?articleid=1501&CFID=1653072&CFTOKEN=14318984 (accessed September 1, 2006).

30. "A Team's-Eye View of Teams," *Training,* November 1995, p. 16.

31. M. E. Shaw, *Group Dynamics,* 3rd ed. (New York: McGraw-Hill, 1981); G. Manners, "Another Look at Group Size, Group Problem-Solving and Member Consensus," *Academy of Management Journal* 18 (1975), pp. 715–724.

32. H.-S. Hwang and J. Guynes, "The Effect of Group Size on Group Performance in Computer-Supported Decision Making," *Information & Management,* April 1994, pp. 189–198.

33. S. J. Karau and K. D. Williams, "Social Loafing: Research Findings, Implications, and Future Directions," *Current Directions in Psychological Science,* October 1995, pp. 134–140; S. J. Zacarro, "Social Loafing: The Role of Task Attractiveness," *Personality and Social Psychology Bulletin* 10 (1984), pp. 99–106; P. W. Mulvey, L. Bowes-Sperry, and H. J. Klein, "The Effects of Perceived Loafing and Defensive Impression Management on Group Effectiveness," *Small Group Research,* June 1998, pp. 394–415; and L. Karakowsky and K. McBey, "Do My Contributions Matter? The Influence of Imputed Expertise on Member Involvement and Self-Evaluations in the Work Group," *Group & Organization Management,* March 2001, pp. 70–92.

34. J. Welch and S. Welch, "When a Star Slacks Off," *BusinessWeek,* March 17, 2008, p. 88.

35. B.-C. Lim and K. J. Klein, "Team Mental Models and Team Performance: A Field Study of the Effects of Team Mental Model Similarity and Accuracy," *Journal of Organizational Behavior,* January 2006, pp. 403–418.

36. J. L. Yang, "The Power of Number 4.6," *Fortune,* June 12, 2006, p. 122.

37. Deutschman, 1994.

38. J. R. Hackman, *Leading Teams: Setting the Stage for Great Performances* (Boston: Harvard Business School Press, 2002).

39. J. R. Hackman and N. J. Vidmar, "Effects of Size and Task Type on Group Performance and Member Reactions," *Sociometry* 33 (1970), pp. 37–54.

40. K. J. Klein, cited in "Is Your Team Too Big? Too Small? What's the Right Number?" June 14, 2006.

41. K. D. Benne and P. Sheats, "Functional Roles of Group Members," *Journal of Social Issues,* Spring 1948, pp. 41–49. See also E. C. Dierdorff and F. P. Morgeson, "Consensus in Work Role Requirements: The Influence of Discrete Occupational Contest on Role Expectations," *Journal of Applied Psychology,* September 2007, pp. 1228–1241; and D. J. McAllister, D. Kamdar, E. W. Morrison, and D. B. Turban, "Disentangling Role Perceptions: How Perceived Role Breadth, Discretion, Instrumentality, and Efficacy Relate to Helping and Taking Charge," *Journal of Applied Psychology,* September 2007, pp.1200–1211.

42. D. C. Feldman, "The Development and Enforcement of Group Norms," *Academy of Management Review,* January 1984, pp. 47–53.

43. D. Kahneman, "Reference Points, Anchors, Norms, and Mixed Feelings," *Organizational Behavior and Human Decision Processes,* March 1992, pp. 296–312.

44. Adapted from N. Byrnes, "The Art of Motivation," *BusinessWeek,* May 1, 2006, pp. 57–62.

45. "Nucor Named Top U.S. Steel Manufacturer," *Charlotte Business Journal,* April 24, 2008, http://www.bizjournals .com/charlotte/stories/2008/04/21/daily34.html?q= Nucor%20Corp. (accessed May 12, 2008).

46. "Nucor Makes BusinessWeek's List of Top Performers," *Charlotte Business Journal,* April 2, 2008, http://www.biz-journals.com/charlotte/stories/2008/03/31/daily37.html (accessed May 12, 2008).

47. Feldman, 1984.

48. A big part of cohesiveness is building trust. See D. De Cremer and T. R. Tyler, "The Effects of Trust in Authority and Procedural Fairness on Cooperation," *Journal of Applied Psychology,* May 2007, pp. 639–649; J. A. Colquitt, B. A. Scott, and J. A. Lepine, "Trust, Trustworthiness, and Trust Propensity: A Meta-Analytic Test of Their Unique Relationships with Risk Taking and Job Performance," *Journal of Applied Psychology,* July 2007, pp. 909–927; and R. Ilies, D. T. Wagner, and F. P. Morgeson, "Explaining Affective Linkages in Teams: Individual Differences in Susceptibility to Contagion and Individualism–Collectivism," *Journal of Applied Psychology,* July 2007, pp. 1140–1148.

49. See, for example, P. Jin, "Work Motivation and Productivity in Voluntarily Formed Work Teams: A Field Study in China," *Organizational Behavior and Human Decision Processes* 54, no. 1 (1993), pp. 133–155.

50. L Janis, *Groupthink,* 2nd ed. (Boston: Houghton Mifflin, 1982), p. 9. See also K. D. Lassila, "A Brief History of Groupthink," *Yale Alumni Magazine,* January–February 2008, pp. 59–61, www.philosophy-religion.org/handouts/pdfs/BRIEF-HISTORY_GROUPTHINK.pdf (accessed May 12, 2008).

51. V. Kemper, "Senate Intelligence Report: Groupthink Viewed as Culprit in Move to War," *Los Angeles Times,* July 10, 2004, p. A.17.

52. J. Surowiecki, quoted in J. Freeman, "Books," *The Christian Science Monitor,* May 25, 2004; www.csmonitor.com/2004/0525/p15s01-bogn.html (accessed July 12, 2004). Also see J. Surowiecki, *The Wisdom of Crowds: Why the Many Are Smarter Than the Few and How Collective Wisdom Shapes Business, Economies, Societies, and Nations* (New York: Doubleday, 2004).

53. V. H. Palmieri, quoted in L. Baum, "The Job Nobody Wants," *BusinessWeek,* September 8, 1986, p. 60.

54. Surowiecki, quoted in Kemper, 2004. See also J. A LePine, "Adaptation of Teams in Response to Unforeseen Change: Effects of Goal Difficulty and Team Composition in Terms of Cognitive Ability and Goal Orientation," *Journal of Applied Psychology* 90 (2005), pp. 1153–1167.

55. M. R. Callway and J. K. Desser, "Groupthink: Effects of Cohesiveness and Problem-Solving Procedures on Group Decision Making," *Social Behavior and Personality,* no. 2, 1984, pp. 157–164.

56. Adapted from N. Byrnes, P. Burrows, and L. Lee, "Dark Days at Dell," *BusinessWeek,* September 4, 2006, pp. 26–29.

57. G. A. Moore, quoted in Byrnes, Burrows, and Lee, 2006, p. 27. Moore is author of *Dealing with Darwin: How Great Companies Innovate at Every Phase of Their Evolution* (New York: Portfolio/Penguin, 2006).

58. K. Chan, "Worst Stock for 2008: Dell," *The Motley Fool,* January 14, 2008, http://www.fool.com/investing/value/2008/01/14/worst-stock-for-2008-dell.aspx (accessed May 12, 2008). See also M. Richtel, "Profit Falls as Dell Tries to Grow and Limit Costs," *The New York Times,* February 29, 2008, http://www.nytimes.com/2008/02/29/technology/29dell.html?_r=1&adxnnl=1&oref=slogin&adxnnlx=1210781074-6yUkhsVaGozRxnSrdRLD4A (accessed May 12, 2008).

59. D. H. Freedman, "Collaboration Is the Hottest Buzzword in Business Today. Too Bad It Doesn't Work," *Inc. Magazine,* September 2006, pp. 61–62.

60. B. Rosner, "How to Avoid Violence from a Fired Worker," *San Francisco Sunday Examiner & Chronicle,* November 15, 1998, p. CL-13.

61. S. A. Hendricks, E. L. Jenkins, and K. R. Anderson, "Trends in Workplace Homicides in the U.S., 1993–2002: A Decade of Decline," *American Journal of Industrial Medicine* 50 (2007), pp. 316–325.

62. J. A. Wall Jr. and R. Robert Callister, "Conflict and Its Management," *Journal of Management,* no. 3 (1995), p. 517.

63. C. Alter, "An Exploratory Study of Conflict and Coordination in Interorganizational Service Delivery Systems," *Academy of Management Journal,* September 1990, pp. 478–502; S. P. Robbins, "'Conflict Management' and 'Conflict Resolution' Are Not Synonymous Terms," *California Management Review,* Winter 1978, p. 70.

64. Cooperative conflict is discussed in D. Tjosvold, *Learning to Manage Conflict: Getting People to Work Together Productively* (New York: Lexington, 1993); and D. Tjosvold and D. W. Johnson, *Productive Conflict Management Perspectives for Organizations* (New York: Irvington, 1983). See also A. C. Amason, K. R. Thompson, W. A. Hochwarter, and A. W. Harrison, "Conflict: An Important Dimension in Successful Management Teams," *Organizational Dynamics,* Autumn 1995, pp. 20–35; and A. C. Amason, "Distinguishing the Effects of Functional and Dysfunctional Conflict on Strategic Decision Making: Resolving a Paradox for Top Management Teams," *Academy of Management Journal,* February 1996, pp. 123–148.

65. L. Lange, quoted in J. Noveck, "Do Bosses Need to Be Mean to Get Work Done?" *Nevada Appeal,* July 9, 2006, pp. D1, D2. See also D. Brady, "Charm Offensive," *BusinessWeek,* June 26, 2006, pp. 76–80; and A. Dobson and R. Berman, "Building a Better Boss," *San Francisco Chronicle,* September 23, 2007, p. H-1.

66. G. Namie, *U.S. Workplace Bullying Survey,* September 2007, conducted by Workplace Bullying Institute and Zogby International, using 7,740 online interviews, for Waitt Institute for Violence Prevention, www.healthyworkplacebill.org/pdf/WBIsurvey2007.pdf (accessed May 12, 2008).

67. K. L. Zellars, B. J. Tepper, and M. K. Duffy, "Abusive Supervision and Subordinates' Organizational Citizenship Behavior," *Journal of Applied Psychology,* December 2002, pp. 1068–1076.

68. B. J. Tepper and E. C. Taylor, "Relationships Among Supervisors' and Subordinates' Procedural Justice Perceptions and Organizational Citizenship Behaviors," *Academy of Management Journal,* February 2003, pp. 97–105; B. J. Tepper, M. K. Duffy, J. Hoobler, and M. D. Ensley, "Moderators of the Relationship between Coworkers' Organizational Citizenship Behavior and Fellow Employees' Attitudes," *Journal of Applied Psychology,* June 2005, pp. 455–465; B. J. Tepper, M. Uhl-Bien, G. F. Kohut, S. G. Rogelberg, D. E. Lockhart, and M. D. Ensley, "Subordinates' Resistance and Managers' Evaluations of Subordinates' Performance," *Journal of Management,* April 1, 2006, pp. 185–209; B. J. Tepper, M. K. Duffy, C. A. Henle, and L. S. Lambert, "Procedural Injustice, Victim Precipitation, and Abusive Supervision," *Personnel Psychology,* March 2006, pp. 101–123; B. J. Tepper, S. E. Moss, D. E. Lockhart, and J. C. Carr, "Abusive Supervision, Upward Maintenance Supervision, and Subordinates' Psychological Distress," *Academy of Management Journal* 50 (2007), pp. 1169–1180; and B. J. Tepper, "Abusive Supervision in Formal Organizations: Review, Synthesis, and Research Agenda," *Journal of Management,* June 1, 2007, pp. 261–289.

69. R. I. Sutton in "Breakthrough Ideas for 2004: The HBR List," *Harvard Business Review,* February 2004, pp. 13–24, 32–37. Sutton's topic was headed "More Trouble Than They Are Worth." His book based on these ideas is *The No Asshole Rule: Building a Civilized Workplace and Surviving One That Isn't* (New York: Warner, 2007).

70. R. I. Sutton, "R. I. Sutton: Nasty People," *CIO Insight,* May 1, 2004, http://www.cioinsight.com/c/a/Past-Opinions/Robert-I-Sutton-Nasty-People (accessed May 12, 2008).

71. A. M. O'Leary-Kelly, R. W. Griffin, and D. J. Glew, "Organization-Motivated Aggression: A Research Framework," *Academy of Management Review,* January 1996, pp. 225–253. See also G. A. Van Kleef and S. Côté, "Expressing Anger in Conflict: When It Helps and When It Hurts," *Journal of Applied Psychology,* November 2007, pp. 1557–1569.

72. L. R. Pondy, "Organizational Conflict: Concepts and Models," *Administrative Science Quarterly* 2 (1967), pp. 296–320.

73. P. Burrows, "Carly's Last Stand?" *BusinessWeek,* December 24, 2001, pp. 63–70. See B. Pimentel, "Heftier HP Is Ready to Forge Ahead," *San Francisco Chronicle,* May 5, 2002, pp. G1, G4.

74. K. W. Thomas, "Conflict and Conflict Management," in *Handbook of Industrial and Organizational Psychology,* M. Dunnette, ed. (Chicago: Rand McNally, 1976), pp. 889–935; K. W. Thomas "Toward Multiple Dimensional Values in Teaching: The Example of Conflict Behaviors," *Academy of Management Review,* July 1977, pp. 484–490; and M. A Rahim, "A Strategy for Managing Conflict in Complex Organizations," *Human Relations,* January 1985, p. 84.

75. Rahim, 1985.

76. R. A. Cosier and C. R. Schwenk, "Agreement and Thinking Alike: Ingredients for Poor Decisions," *Academy of Management Executive,* February 1990, p. 71. Also see J. P. Kotter, "Kill Complacency," *Fortune,* August 5, 1996, pp. 168–170.

77. See "Facilitators as Devil's Advocates," *Training,* September 1993, p. 10; and C. R. Schwenk, "Devil's Advocacy in Managerial Decision Making," *Journal of Management Studies,* April 1984, pp. 153–168.

78. S. G. Katzenstein, "The Debate on Structured Debate: Toward a Unified Theory," *Organizational Behavior and Human Decision Processes,* June 1996, pp. 316–332.

79. W. Kiechel III, "How to Escape the Echo Chamber," *Fortune,* June 18, 1990, p. 130.

CHAPTER 14

1. H. Lancaster, "If Your Career Needs More Attention, Maybe You Should Get an Agent," *The Wall Street Journal,* October 20, 1998, p. B1. See also L. K. Hardie, "Joelle K. Jay: Leadership Coach Inspires Businesspeople to Succeed," *Reno Gazette-Journal,* January 15, 2006, pp. 1E, 13E; R. Berman, "Coached Toward Brighter Management," *San Francisco Chronicle,* March 5, 2006, pp. G1, G6; A. S. Wellner, "Do You Need a Coach?" *Inc. Magazine,* April 2006, pp. 85–93; and N. Brozan, "Top Brokers Hire Coaches to Climb Higher," *The New York Times,* May 7, 2006, sec. 4, p. 9.

2. R. L. Knowdell, "The 10 New Rules for Strategizing Your Career," *The Futurist,* June–July 1998, pp. 19–24.

3. C. A. Schriesheim, J. M. Tolliver, and O. C. Behling, "Leadership Theory: Some Implications for Managers," *MSU Business Topics,* Summer 1978, p. 35. See also G. Yukl, "Managerial Leadership: A Review of Theory and Research," *Journal of Management* 15 (1989), pp. 251–289.

4. T. Peters and N. Austin, *A Passion for Excellence* (New York: Random House, 1985), pp. 5–6; but see also B. Kellerman, "Leadership—Warts and All," *Harvard Business Review,* January 1, 2004, pp. 40–45.

5. B. M. Bass, *Bass & Stogdill's Handbook of Leadership: Theory, Research, and Managerial Applications,* 3rd ed. (New York: Free Press, 1990), p. 383.

6. J. P. Kotter, "What Leaders Really Do," *Harvard Business Review,* December 2001, pp. 85–96; the role of leadership within organizational change is discussed in J. P. Kotter, *Leading Change* (Boston: Harvard Business School Press, 1996).

7. F. Smith, quoted in "All in a Day's Work," *Harvard Business Review,* December 2001, pp. 54–66.

8. L. H. Chusmir, "Personalized versus Socialized Power Needs among Working Women and Men," *Human Relations,* February 1986, p. 149.

9. A. Wong, quoted in "My Journey to the Top," *Newsweek,* October 15, 2007, pp. 49–65.

10. R. M. Kramer, "The Great Intimidators," *Harvard Business Review,* February 2006, pp. 88–96.

11. R. E. Tedlow, "The Education of Andy Grove," *Fortune,* December 12, 2005, pp. 117–138. Tedlow is also the author of *Andy Grove: The Life and Times of an American* (New York: Portfolio, 2006).

12. A. S. Grove, *Only the Paranoid Survive: How to Exploit the Crisis Points That Challenge Every Company and Career* (New York: Random House, 1999). Grove is also the author of *High Output Management* (New York: Vintage, 1995) and of *Swimming Across: A Memoir* (New York: Grand Central Publishing, 2002).

13. "Remaking Intel from Top to Bottom," *BusinessWeek,* January 9, 2006, p. 49.

14. Tedlow, 2005, p. 138.

15. S. Harrison, "Deliberate Acts of Decency," *HR Magazine,* July 2007, pp. 97–99.

16. Based on Table 1 in G. Yukl, C. M. Falbe, and J. Y. Youn, " Patterns of Influence Behavior for Managers," *Group & Organization Management,* March 1993, pp. 5–28.

17. G. Yukl, H. Kim, and C. M. Falbe, "Antecedents of Influence Outcomes," *Journal of Applied Psychology,* June 1996, pp. 309–317.

18. B. Schlender, "A Conversation with the Lords of Wintel," *Fortune,* July 8, 1996, p. 44.

19. R. M. Stogdill, "Personal Factors Associated with Leadership: A Survey of the Literature," *Journal of Psychology* 25 (1948), pp. 35–71; and R. M. Stogdill, *Handbook of Leadership* (New York: Free Press, 1974).

20. B. Bass, *Stogdill's Handbook of Leadership,* rev. ed. (New York: Free Press, 1981).

21. See S. J. Zaccaro, "Trait-Based Perspectives of Leadership," *American Psychologist*, January 2007, pp. 6-16; and R. Sternberg, "A Systems Model of Leadership," *American Psychologist*, January 2007, pp. 34-42. Recent discussions of the trait approach are provided by D. B. Peterson, "High Potential, High Risk," *HR Magazine*, March 2008, pp. 85-88; and "Timeless Leadership: The great Leadership Lessons Don't Change," *Harvard Business Review*, March 2008, pp. 45-49.

22. Executive coaching is discussed by S. Labadessa, "Now Go Out and Lead!" *BusinessWeek*, January 8, 2007, pp. 72-73.

23. Leadership development programs are discussed in G. M. Spreitzer, "Leading to Grow and Growing to Lead: Leadership Development Lessons from Positive Organizational Studies," *Organizational Dynamics*, November 2006, pp. 305-315; and E. White, "Manager Shortage Spurs Small Firms to Grow Their Own," *The Wall Street Journal*, February 15, 2007, pp. B1, B4.

24. J. M. Kouzes and B. Z. Posner, "The Credibility Factor: What Followers Expect from Their Leaders," *Business Credit,* July–August 1990, pp. 24–28; J. M. Kouzes and B. Z. Posner, *Credibility* (San Francisco: Jossey-Bass, 1993); and J. M. Kouzes and B. Z. Posner, *The Leadership Challenge: How to Get Extraordinary Things Done in Organizations* (San Francisco: Jossey-Bass, 1995).

25. Study by Catalyst, New York, reported in J. S. Lublin, "Women Aspire to Be Chief as Much as Men Do," *The Wall Street Journal,* June 28, 2004, p. D2.

26. R. Sharpe, "As Leaders, Women Rule," *BusinessWeek,* November 20, 2000, pp. 75–84.

27. Study by Hagberg Consulting Group, Foster City, California, reported in Sharpe, 2000, p. 75.

28. B. R. Ragins, B. Townsend, and M. Mattis, "Gender Gap in the Executive Suite: CEOs and Female Executives Report on Breaking the Glass Ceiling," *Academy of Management Executive,* February 1, 1998, pp. 28–42.

29. L. Tischler, "Where Are the Women?" *Fast Company,* February 2004, pp. 52-60.

30. P. Sellers, "Power: Do Women Really Want It?" *Fortune,* October 13, 2003, p. 88.

31. See M. Conlin, "Self-Deprecating Women," *BusinessWeek,* June 14, 2004, p. 26. For more on this subject, see also "The 'Masculine' and 'Feminine' Sides of Leadership and Culture: Perception vs. Reality," *Knowledge@Wharton,* http://knowledge.wharton.upenn.edu/index.cfm?fa=printArticle & ID (accessed May 23, 2008); "Guiding Aspiring Female Execs Up the Ladder," *HR Magazine,* January 2006, p. 14; T. G. Habbershon, "It's a Man's World," *BusinessWeek SmallBiz,* Spring 2006, p.16; Q. M. Roberson and C. K. Stevens, "Making Sense of Diversity in the Workplace: Organizational Justice and Language Abstraction in Employees' Accounts of Diversity-Related Incidents," *Journal of Applied Psychology,* March 2006, pp. 379-391; E. Porter, "Women in Workplace—Trend Is Reversing," *San Francisco Chronicle,* March 2, 2006, p. A2, reprinted from *The New York Times*; T. L. O'Brien, "Up the Down Staircase: Why Do So Few Women Reach the Top of Big Law Firms?" *The New York Times,* March 19, 2006, sec. 3, pp. 1, 4; "Breaking into the Boardroom," *The Wall Street Journal,* March 27, 2006, p. B3; E. White, "Why Few Women Run Plants," *The Wall Street Journal,* May 1, 2006, pp. B1, B5; J. Zaslow, "A New Generation Gap: Differences Emerge Among Women in the Workplace," *The Wall Street Journal,* May 4, 2006, p. D1; W. A. Holstein, "Glass Ceiling? Get a Hammer," *The New York Times,* June 18, 2006, sec. 3, p. 12; C. Hymowitz, "Women Swell Ranks as Middle Managers, but Are Scarce at Top," *The Wall Street Journal,* July 24, 2006, p. B1; S. Vedantam, "Glass Ceiling Breaks When Women Are in Charge, Study Says," *San Francisco Chronicle,* August 13, 2006, p. A17, reprinted from *Washington Post.*

32. B. Groysberg, "How Star Women Build Portable Skills," *Harvard Business Review,* February 2008, pp. 74-81. See also R. D. Arvey, Z. Zhang, B. J. Avolio, and R. F. Krueger, "Developmental and Genetic Determinants of Leadership Role Occupancy among Women," *Journal of Applied Psychology,* May 2007, pp. 693-706. Some popular treatments on the subject of woman and leadership are C. V. Flett, *What Men Don't Tell Women about Business: Opening Up the Heavily Guarded Alpha Male Playbook* (New York: Wiley, 2008) and N. DiSesa, *Seducing the Boys Club: Uncensored Tactics from a Woman at the Top* (New York: Ballantine Books, 2008).

33. R. House, M. Javidan, P. Hanges, and P. Dorfman, "Understanding Cultures and Implicit Leadership Theories Across the Globe: An Introduction to Project GLOBE," *Journal of World Business,* Spring 2004, p. 4.

34. R. Likert, *New Patterns of Management* (New York: McGraw-Hill, 1961); and R. Likert, *The Human Organization* (New York: McGraw-Hill, 1967).

35. C. A. Schriesman and B. J. Bird, "Contributions of the Ohio State Studies to the Field of Leadership," *Journal of Management Studies* 5 (1979), pp. 135–145; and C. L. Shartle, "Early Years of the Ohio State University Leadership Studies," *Journal of Management* 5 (1979), pp. 126–134.

36. V. H. Vroom, "Leadership," in M. D. Dunnette, ed., *Handbook of Industrial and Organizational Psychology* (Chicago: Rand McNally, 1976).

37. M. Stettner, *Skills for New Managers* (New York: McGraw-Hill, 2000); J. H. Grossman and J. R. Parkinson, *Becoming a Successful Manager: How to Make a Smooth Transition from Managing Yourself to Managing Others* (New York: McGraw-Hill, 2001); and L. A. Hill, *Becoming a Manager: How New Managers Master the Challenges of Leadership,* 2nd ed. (Boston: Harvard Business School Press, 2003). For more on becoming a leader, also see B. Kellerman, "What Every Leader Needs to Know about Followers," *Harvard Business Review,* December 2007, pp. 84-91; M. Gottfredson, S. Schaubert, and H. Saenz, "The New Leader's Guide to Diagnosing the Business," *Harvard Business Review,* February 2008, pp. 63-73; "Timeless Leadership: A Conversation with David McCullough," *Harvard Business Review,* March 2008, pp. 45-49; S. D. Friedman, "Be a Better Leader, Have a Richer Life," *Harvard Business Review,* April 2008, pp. 112-118; and B. Reeves, T. W. Malone, and T. O'Driscoll, "Leadership's Online Labs," *Harvard Business Review,* May 2008, pp. 58-66.

38. F. E. Fiedler, "Assumed Similarity Measures as Predictors of Team Effectiveness," *Journal of Abnormal and Social Psychology* 49 (1954), pp. 381-388; F. E. Fiedler, *Leader Attitudes and Group Effectiveness* (Urbana, IL: University of Illinois Press, 1958); and F. E. Fiedler, *A Theory of Leadership Effectiveness* (New York: McGraw-Hill, 1967).

39. A review of the contingency theory and suggestions for future theoretical development is provided by R. Ayman, M. M. Chemers, and F. Fiedler, "The Contingency Model of Leadership Effectiveness: Its Levels of Analysis," in F. Dansereau and F. J. Yamminrino, eds., *Leadership: The Multiple-Level Approaches*

(Stamford, CT: JAI Press, 1998), pp. 73–94. Also see M. V. Vugt, R. Hogan, and R. B. Kaiser, "Leadership, Followership, and Evolution," *American Psychologist*, April 2008, pp. 182–196.

40. R. J. House, "A Path-Goal Theory of Leader Effectiveness," *Administrative Science Quarterly*, September 1971, pp. 321–338; and R. J. House and T. R. Mitchell, "Path–Goal Theory of Leadership," *Journal of Contemporary Business*, Autumn 1974, pp. 81–97. The most recent version of the theory is found in R. J. House, "Path-Goal Theory of Leadership: Lessons, Legacy, and a Reformulated Theory," *Leadership Quarterly*, Autumn 1996, pp. 323–352.

41. These studies are summarized in House, 1996.

42. Supportive results can be found in D. Charbonneau, J. Barling, and E. K. Kelloway, "Transformational Leadership and Sports Performance: The Mediating Role of Intrinsic Motivation," *Journal of Applied Social Psychology*, July 2001, pp. 1521–1534.

43. Results can be found in P. M. Podsakoff, S. B. MacKenzie, M. Ahearne, and W. H. Bommer, "Searching for a Needle in a Haystack: Trying to Identify the Illusive Moderators of Leadership Behaviors," *Journal of Management*, 1995, pp. 422–470.

44. A thorough discussion is provided by P. Hersey and K. H. Blanchard, *Management of Organizational Behavior: Utilizing Human Resources*, 5th ed. (Englewood Cliffs, NJ: Prentice-Hall, 1988).

45. Results can be found in J. R. Goodson, G. W. McGee, and J. F. Cashman, "Situational Leadership Theory," *Group & Organization Studies*, December 1989, pp. 446–461.

46. C. Adams, "Leadership Behavior of Chief Nurse Executives," *Nursing Management*, August 1990, pp. 36–39.

47. See D. C. Lueder, "Don't Be Misled by LEAD," *Journal of Applied Behavioral Science*, May 1985, pp. 143–154; and C. L. Graeff, "The Situational Leadership Theory: A Critical View," *Academy of Management Review*, April 1983, pp. 285–291.

48. For a complete description of the full range leadership theory, see B. J. Bass and B. J. Avolio, *Revised Manual for the Multi-Factor Leadership Questionnaire* (Palo Alto, CA: Mindgarden, 1997).

49. A definition and description of transactional leadership is provided by J. Antonakis and R. J. House, "The Full-Range Leadership Theory: The Way Forward," in B. J. Avolio and F. J. Yammarino, eds., *Transformational and Charismatic Leadership: The Road Ahead* (New York: JAI Press, 2002), pp. 3–34.

50. E. MacDonald and C. R. Schoenberger, "The World's Most Powerful Women: The Top 10," *Forbes*, September 17, 2007, pp. 126–127.

51. B. Morris, "What Makes Pepsi Great?" *Fortune*, March 3, 2008, pp. 54–66.

52. U. R. Dundum, K. B. Lowe, and B. J. Avolio, "A Meta-Analysis of Transformational and Transactional Leadership Correlates of Effectiveness and Satisfaction: An Update and Extension," in B. J. Avolio and F. J. Yammarino, eds., *Transformational and Charismatic Leadership: The Road Ahead* (New York: JAI Press, 2002), p. 38.

53. Supportive results can be found in T. A. Judge and J. E. Bono, "Five-Factor Model of Personality and Transformational Leadership," *Journal of Applied Psychology*, October 2000, pp. 751–765.

54. Supportive research is summarized by Antonakis and House, 2002.

55. Morris, 2008.

56. H. Schultz, "Indra Nooyi," *Time*, April 30, 2008, http://www.time.com/time/specials/2007/article/0,28804,1733748_1733758,00.html (accessed May 19, 2008). See also D. Brady, "Keeping Cool in Hot Water," *BusinessWeek*, June 11, 2007, p. 49.

57. These definitions are derived from R. Kark, B. Shamir, and C. Chen, "The Two Faces of Transformational Leadership: Empowerment and Dependency," *Journal of Applied Psychology*, April 2003, pp. 246–255. See also R. T. Keller, "Transformational Leadership, Initiating Structure, and Substitutes for Leadership: A Longitudinal Study of Research and Development Project Team Performance," *Journal of Applied Psychology*, January 2006, pp. 202–210; J. Schaubroeck and S.S.K. Lam, "Embracing Transformational Leadership: Team Values and the Impact of Leader Behavior on Team Performance," *Journal of Applied Psychology*, July 2007, pp. 1020–1030; H. Liao and A. Chuang, "Transforming Service Employees and Climate: A Multilevel, Multisource Examination of Transformational Leadership in Building Long-Term Service Relationships," *Journal of Applied Psychology*, July 2007, pp. 1006–1019; S. J. Shin and J. Zhou, "When Is Educational Specialization Heterogeneity Related to Creativity in Research and Development Teams? Transformational Leadership as a Moderator," *Journal of Applied Psychology*, November 2007, pp. 1709–1721; and A. E. Colbert, A. L. Kristof-Brown, B. H. Bradley, and M. R. Barrick, "CEO Transformational Leadership: The Role of Goal Importance Congruence in Top Management Teams," *Academy of Management Journal*, February 2008, pp. 81–96.

58. B. Nanus, *Visionary Leadership* (San Francisco: Jossey-Bass, 1992), p. 8. See also J. Murphy, "Ghosn Hedges Bets on Emissions," *The Wall Street Journal*, May 15, 2008, p. B2; and D. Enrich, "Citigroup Pandit Faces Test as Pressure on Bank Grows," *The Wall Street Journal*, May 6, 2008, pp. A1, A20.

59. See R. E. Quinn, "Moments of Greatness: Entering the Fundamental State of Leadership," *Harvard Business Review*, July–August 2005, pp. 75–83.

60. Morris, 2008.

61. See H. Lui, and A. Chuang, "Transforming Service Employees and Climate: A Multilevel, Multisource Examination of Transformational Leadership in Building Long-Term Service Relationships," *Journal of Applied Psychology*, July 2007, pp. 1006–1019; and J. Schaubroeck, S.S.K. Lam, and S. E. Cha, "Embracing Transformational Leadership: Team Values and the Impact of Leader Behavior on Team Performance," *Journal of Applied Psychology*, July 2007, pp. 1020–1030.

62. Results can be found in Dundum, Lowe, and Avolio, 2002; and Erez, V. F. Misangyi, D.E. Johnson, M. A. LePine, and K. C. Halverson, "Stirring the Hearts of Followers: Charismatic Leadership as the Transferal of Affect," *Journal of Applied Psychology*, May 2008, pp. 602–615.

63. See Kark, Shamir, and Chen, 2003.

64. Supportive results and can be found in B. M. Bass, B. J. Avolio, D. I. Jung, and Y. Berson, "Predicting Unit Performance by Assessing Transformational and Transactional Leadership," *Journal of Applied Psychology*, April 2003, pp. 207–218; P. Wang, and F. O. Walumbwa, "Family-Friendly Programs, Organizational Commitment, and Work Withdrawal: The Moderating Role of Transformational Leadership," *Personnel Psychology*, Summer 2007, pp. 397–427; and D. M. Herold, D. B. Fedor, S. Caldwell, and Y. Liu, "The Effects of Transformational and Change Leadership on Employees' Commitment to Change: A Multilevel Study," *Journal of Applied Psychology*, March 2008, pp. 346–357.

65. See A. J. Towler, "Effects of Charismatic Influence Training on Attitudes, Behavior, and Performance," *Personnel Psychology*, Summer 2003, pp. 363–381; and B. J. Avolio, R. J. Reichard, S. T. Hannah, F. O Walumbwa, and A. Chan, "A Meta-Analytic Review of Leadership Impact Research: Ex-

perimental and Quasi-Experimental Studies," *Leadership Quarterly,* in press; M. Weinstein, "Leadership Leader," *Training,* February 2008, pp. 41-46.

66. These recommendations were derived from J. M. Howell and B. J. Avolio, "The Ethics of Charismatic Leadership: Submission or Liberation," *The Executive,* May 1992, pp. 43-54.

67. G. Graen and J. F. Cashman, "A Role-Making Model of Leadership in Formal Organizations: A Developmental Approach," in J. G. Hunt and L. L. Larson, eds., *Leadership Frontiers* (Kent, OH: Kent State University Press, 1975), pp. 143-165; F. Dansereau Jr., G. Graen, and W. J. Haga, "A Vertical Dyad Linkage Approach to Leadership Within Formal Organizations: A Longitudinal Investigation of the Role-Making Process," *Organizational Behavior and Human Performance,* February 1975, pp. 46-78; and R. M. Dienesch and R. C. Liden, "Leader-Member Exchange Model of Leadership: A Critique and Further Development," *Academy of Management Review,* July 1986, pp. 618-634.

68. See D. Duchon, S. G. Green, and T. D. Taber, "Vertical Dyad Linkage: A Longitudinal Assessment of Antecedents, Measures, and Consequences," *Journal of Applied Psychology,* February 1986, pp. 56-60.

69. See B. Erdogan, M. I. Kraimer, and R. C. Liden, "Work Value Congruence and Intrinsic Career Success: The Compensatory Roles of Leader-Member Exchange and Perceived Organizational Support," *Personnel Psychology,* Summer 2004, pp. 305-332; and T. N. Bauer, B. Erdogan, R. C. Liden, and S. J. Wayne, "A Longitudinal Study of the Moderating Role of Extraversion: Leader-Member Exchange, Performance, and Turnover During New Executive Development," *Journal of Applied Psychology,* March 2006, pp. 298-310; O. Epitropaki and R. Martin, "From Ideal to Real: A Longitudinal Study of the Role of Implicit Leadership Theories on Leader-Member Exchanges and Employee Outcomes," *Journal of Applied Psychology,* July 2005, pp. 659-676; W. Lam, X. Huang, and E. Snape, "Feedback-Seeking Behavior and Leader-Member Exchange: Do Supervisor-Attributed Motives Matter?" *Academy of Management Journal,* April 2007, pp. 348-363; and S. A. Furst and D. M. Cable, "Employee Resistance to Organizational Change: Managerial Influence Tactics and Leader-Member Exchange," *Journal of Applied Psychology,* March 2008, pp. 453-462.

70. A turnover study was conducted by G. B. Graen, R. C. Liden, and W. Hoel, "Role of Leadership in the Employee Withdrawal Process," *Journal of Applied Psychology,* December 1982, pp. 868-872. The career progress study was conducted by M. Wakabayashi and G. B. Braen, "The Japanese Career Progress Study: A 7-Year Follow-Up," *Journal of Applied Psychology,* November 1984, pp. 603-614.

71. R. J. House and R. N. Aditya, "The Social Scientific Study of Leadership: Quo Vadis?" *Journal of Management* 23 (1997), pp. 409-473.

72. A thorough discussion of shared leadership is provided by C. L. Pearce, "The Future of Leadership: Combining Vertical and Shared Leadership to Transform Knowledge Work." *Academy of Management Executive,* February 2004, pp. 47-57.

73. This research is summarized in B. J. Avolio, J. J. Soskik, D. I. Jung, and Y. Benson, "Leadership Models, Methods, and Applications," in W. C. Borman, D. R. Ilgen, and R. J. Klimoski, eds. *Handbook of Psychology,* vol. 12 (Hoboken, NJ: John Wiley & Sons, 2003) pp. 277-307.

74. L. L. Berry, "The Collaborative Organization: Leadership Lessons from Mayo Clinic," *Organizational Dynamics,* August 2004, pp. 230-231.

75. A. Taylor III, "Bill's Brand-New Ford," *Fortune,* June 28, 2004, p. 74.

76. A. Ignatius, "Meet the Google Guys," *Time,* February 12, 2006, http://www.time.com/time/magazine/article/0,9171,1158956,00.html (accessed May 23, 2008); and Google Corporate Information, "Google Management," http://www.google.com/corporate/execs.html (accessed may 23, 2008).

77. P. Sellers, "MySpace Cowboys," *Fortune,* September 4, 2006, pp. 66-74. See also B. Stelter, "From MySpace to Your Space," *The New York Times,* January 21, 2008, http://www.nytimes.com/2008/01/21/technology/21myspace.html (accessed May 19, 2008).

78. An overall summary of servant leadership is provided by L. C. Spears, *Reflections on Leadership: How Robert K. Greenleaf's Theory of Servant-Leadership Influenced Today's Top Management Thinkers* (New York: Wiley, 1995).

79. D. L. Moore, "Wooden's Wizardry Wears Well," *USA Today,* March 29, 1995, pp. 1C, 2C.

80. B. Saporito, "And the Winner Is Still . . . Wal-Mart," *Fortune,* May 2, 1994, pp. 62-70.

81. M. De Pree, quoted D. Gergen, "Bad News for Bullies," *U.S. News & World Report,* June 19, 2006, p. 54. The quote is from M. De Pree, *Leadership Is an Art* (New York: Dell, 1989).

82. Gergen, 2006.

83. See B. J. Avolio, J. J. Sosik, D. I. Jung, and Yair Berson, 2003, pp. 295-298.

84. D. MacRae, "Six Secrets of Successful E-Leaders," *Business Week online,* September 6, 2001; www.businessweek.com/technology/content/sep2001/tc2001096_619.htm (accessed May 23, 2008).

85. D. Q. Mills, *E-Leadership: Guiding Your Business to Success in the New Economy* (Paramus, NJ: Prentice Hall Press, 2001). See also R. Hargrove, *E-Leader: Reinventing Leadership in a Connected Economy* (Boulder, CO: Perseus Books Group, 2001); T. M. Siebel, *Taking Care of eBusiness: How Today's Market Leaders Are Increasing Revenue, Productivity, and Customer Satisfaction* (New York: Doubleday, 2001); S. Annunzio, *eLeadership: Bold Solutions for the New Economy* (New York: Free Press, 2002); and B. J. Avolio and S. S. Kahai, "Adding the "E" to E-leadership: How It May Impact Your Leadership," *Organizational Dynamics* 31 (2003), pp. 325-338.

86. L. Capotosto, "Millenial Management," *Darwin,* www2.darwinmag.com/connect/books/book.cfm?ID-188 (accessed July 24, 2004).

CHAPTER 15

1. C. Vinzant, "Messing with the Boss' Head," *Fortune,* May 1, 2000, pp. 329-331.

2. M. Price, "Effective Communication Begins with Listening," *Reno Gazette-Journal,* November 27, 2000, p. 1F.

3. D. Stiebel, *When Talking Makes Things Worse! Resolving Problems When Communication Fails* (Dallas, TX: Whitehall & Nolton, 1997). Reported in O. Pollar, "Talk Is Cheap If You Have Big Disagreements," *San Francisco Examiner & Chronicle,* February 21, 1999, p. J-3.

4. Employee, high-tech communications, on "Business Exchange," AllBusiness Web site, http://www.allbusiness.com/management/customer-experience-management/3904798-1.html (accessed May 20, 2008).

5. See K. Gurchiek, "Survey: 'Key Skills Advance HR Career," *HRMagazine,* April 2008, p. 38.

6. September 1998 survey by Office Team, reported in S. Armour, "Failure to Communicate Costly for Companies," *USA Today,* September 30, 1998, p. B1.

7. J. R. Hinrichs, "Communications Activity of Industrial Research Personnel," *Personnel Psychology,* Summer 1964, pp. 193-204.

8. J. Kotter, "Power, Dependence, and Effective Management," *Harvard Business Review* 55 (1977), pp. 125–136.

9. J. Sandberg, "From Crib to Cubicle, a Familiar Voice—Our Own—Reassures," *The Wall Street Journal,* March 25, 2008, p. BI.

10. R. L. Daft, and R. H. Lengel, "Information Richness: A New Approach to Managerial Behavior and Organizational Design," in B. M. Staw and L. L. Cummings, eds., *Research in Organizational Behavior* (Greenwich, CT: JAI Press, 1984), p. 196; and R. H. Lengel and R. L. Daft, "The Selection of Communication Media as an Executive Skill," *Academy of Management Executive,* August 1988, pp. 225–232.

11. E. Goode, "Old as Society, Social Anxiety Is Yielding Its Secrets," *The New York Times,* October 20, 1998, pp. D7, DII.

12. See T. J. Bruce and S. A. Saeed, "Social Anxiety Disorder: A Common, Underrecognized Mental Disorder," *American Family Physician,* November 15, 1999, pp. 2311–2320, 2322; and S. Reinberg, "15 Million Americans Suffer from Social Anxiety Disorder," *BusinessWeek,* April 9, 2008, http://www.businessweek.com/lifestyle/content/healthday/614405.html?chan=top+news_top+news+index_lifestyle (accessed May 20, 2008).

13. S. Merchant, quoted in S. Srivastava, "Why India Worries about Outsourcing," *San Francisco Chronicle,* March 21, 2004, p. E3.

14. The role of jargon in communication is discussed by R. Spragins, "Don't Talk to Me That Way," *Fortune Small Business,* February 2002, p. 26; and C. Hymowitz, "Mind Your Language: To Do Business Today, Consider Delayering," *The Wall Street Journal,* March 27, 2006, p. BI.

15. J. Blais, "Mind Your Manners, Even If You're at Work," *USA Today,* January 17, 2000, p. 5B; M. Brody, "Test Your Etiquette," *Training & Development,* February 2002, pp. 64–66; S. Jayson, "Are Social Norms Steadily Unraveling?" *USA Today,* April 13, 2006, p. 4D; and C. Binkley, "Americans Learn the Global Art of the Cheek Kiss," *The Wall Street Journal,* March 27, 2008, pp. DI, D8.

16. P. Post and P. Post, *Emily Post's The Etiquette Advantage in Business: Personal Skills for Professional Success,* 2nd ed. (New York: HarperCollins, 2005); and A. M. Sabath, *One Minute Manners: Mastering the Unwritten Rules of Business Success* (New York: Broadway Books, 2007). Also see B. Y. Langford, *The Etiquette Edge: The Unspoken Rules for Business Success* (New York: AMACOM, 2005); J. Whitmore, *Business Class: Etiquette Essentials for Success at Work* (New York: St. Martin's Press, 2005); and S. Fox, *Business Etiquette for Dummies*, 2nd ed. (New York: John Wiley & Sons, 2008).

17. Some of these barriers are discussed in J. P. Scully, "People: The Imperfect Communicators," *Quality Progress,* April 1995, pp. 37–39.

18. A. Farnham, "Trust Gap," *Fortune,* December 4, 1989, p. 70.

19. C. R. Rogers and F. J. Roethlisberger, "Barriers and Gateways to Communication," *Harvard Business Review,* July–August 1952, pp. 46–52.

20. Rogers and Roethlisberger, 1952, p. 47.

21. W. D. St. John, "You Are What You Communicate," *Personnel Journal,* October 1985, p. 40.

22. The importance of nonverbal communication is discussed by D. Arthur, "The Importance of Body Language," *HRFocus,* June 1995, pp. 22–23; and N. M. Grant, "The Silent Shroud: Build Bridges, Not Barriers," *HRFocus,* April 1995, p. 16. Problems with interpreting nonverbal communication are discussed by A. Pihulyk, "Communicate with Clarity: The Key to Understanding and Influencing Others," *The Canadian Manager,* Summer 2003, pp. 12–13.

23. This statistic was provided by A. Fisher, "How Can I Survive a Phone Interview?" *Fortune,* April 10, 2004, p. 54.

24. See N. Morgan, "The Kinesthetic Speaker: Putting Action into Words," *Harvard Business Review,* April 2001, pp. 113–120.

25. "How Cultures Collide," *Psychology Today,* July 1976, p. 14.

26. Norms for cross-cultural eye contact are discussed by C. Engholm, *When Business East Meets Business West: The Guide to Practice and Protocol in the Pacific Rim* (New York: John Wiley & Sons, 1991).

27. See J. A. Russell, "Facial Expressions of Emotion: What Lies Beyond Minimal Universality?" *Psychological Bulletin,* November 1995, pp. 379–391.

28. Related research is summarized by J. A. Hall, "Male and Female Nonverbal Behavior," in A. W. Siegman and S. Feldstein, eds., *Multichannel Integrations of Nonverbal Behavior* (Hillsdale, NJ: Lawrence Erlbaum, 1985), pp. 195–226.

29. A thorough discussion of cross-cultural differences is provided by R. E. Axtell, Gestures: The *Do's and Taboos of Body Language Around the world* (New York: John Wiley & Sons, 1998). Problems with body language analysis also are discussed by C. L. Karrass, "Body Language: Beware the Hype," *Traffic Management,* January 1992, p. 27; and M. Everett and B. Wiesendanger, "What Does Body Language Really Say?" *Sales & Marketing Management,* April 1992, p. 40.

30. Results can be found in Hall, 1985.

31. J. N. Cleveland, M. Stockdale, and K. R. Murphy, *Women and Men in Organizations: Sex and Gender Issues at Work* (Mahwah, NJ: Lawrence Erlbaum, 2002), p. 108.

32. P. Leo, "Thorny Etiquette Problem for Men: Hug, Kiss, or Handshake?" *Pittsburgh Post-Gazette,* March 23, 2006, http://www.post-gazette.com/pg/06082/675002-294.stm. See also R. Marin, "Hug-Hug, Kiss-Kiss: It's a Jungle Out There," *The New York Times,* September 19, 1999, http://query.nytimes.com/gst/fullpage.html?res=9906E0D8123CF93AA2575AC0A96F958260 (accessed May 21, 2008); J. W. Lee and L. K. Guerrero, "Types of Touch in Cross-Sex Relationships between Coworkers: Perceptions of Relational and Emotional Messages, Inappropriateness, and Sexual Harassment," *Journal of Applied Communication Research* 29 (2001), pp. 197–220; D. Jones, "Female Bosses Can Touch More Freely," *USA Today,* February 19, 2002, p. 9B; and D. Brown, "Men Are Hugging Men More, but Rules Aren't Always Clearly Defined," *Seattle Post-Intelligencer,* July 11, 2005, http://seattlepi.nwsource.com/lifestyle/231855_guyhugs.html (May 21, 2008).

33. See J. S. Lublin, "Women Fall Behind When They Don't Hone Negotiation Skills," *The Wall Street Journal,* November 4, 2003, p. BI. See also "Do Women Shy Away from Competition, Even When They Can Win?" *Knowledge@Wharton,* November 16, 2005, http://knowledge.whart.upenn.edu/article.cfm?articleid=1308 (accessed May 21, 2008); and J. R. Curhan and A. Pentland, "Thin Slices of Negotiation: Predicting Outcomes from Conversational Dynamics within the First 5 Minutes," *Journal of Applied Psychology,* May 2007, pp. 802–811.

34. J. C. Tingley, *Genderflex: Men & Women Speaking Each Other's Language at Work* (New York: American Management Association, 1994), p. 16.

35. C. Clarke, quoted in A. Pomeroy, "Female Executives May Have a Business Edge," *HR Magazine,* August 2005, p. 16. See also C. Clarke, "A (Necessary) End to Male Dominance," *post-gazette.com,* March 21, 2006, http://www.post-gazette.com/pg/06080/673640-334.stm (accessed September 21, 2006).

36. R. Sharpe, "As Leaders, Women Rule," *BusinessWeek,* November 20, 2000, pp. 75–84.

37. A. Cummings, reported in "The 'Masculine' and 'Feminine' Sides of Leadership and Culture: Perception vs. Reality," *Knowledge@Wharton,* October 5, 2005, knowledge.wharton. upenn.edu/article.cfm?articleide=1287 (accessed May 21, 2008).

38. D. Tannen, "The Power of Talk: Who Gets Heard and Why," in *Negotiation: Readings, Exercises, and Cases,* 3rd ed., R. J. Lewicki and D. M. Saunders eds. (Burr Ridge, IL: Irwin/ McGraw-Hill, 1999), pp. 147–148. Research on gender differences in communication can be found in V. N. Giri and H. O. Sharma, "Brain Wiring and Communication Style," *Psychological Studies* 48 (2003), pp. 59–64; and E. L. MacGeorge, A. R. Graves, B. Feng, S. J. Gillihan, and B. R. Burleson, "The Myth of Gender Cultures: Similarities Outweigh Differences in Men's and Women's Provision of Responses to Supportive Communication," *Sex Roles* 50 (2004), pp. 143–175.

39. D. Jones, "Male Execs Like Female Coaches," *USA Today,* October 24, 2001, p. 3B.

40. G. M. Goldhaber, *Organizational Communication,* 4th ed. (Dubuque, IA: W. C. Brown, 1986).

41. Early research is discussed by K. Davis, "Management Communication and the Grapevine," *Harvard Business Review,* September–October 1953, pp. 43–49; and R. Rowan, "Where Did *That* Rumor Come From?" *Fortune,* August 13, 1979, pp. 130–137. The most recent research is discussed in "Pruning the Company Grapevine," *Supervision,* September 1986, p. 11; and R. Half, "Managing Your Career: 'How Can I Stop the Gossip?'" *Management Accounting,* September 1987, p. 27.

42. T. J. Peters and R. H. Waterman Jr., *In Search of Excellence* (New York: Harper & Row, 1982); and T. Peters and N. Austin, *A Passion for Excellence: The Leadership Difference* (New York: Random House, 1985).

43. C. Gibbons and A. Johnson, "The Tasks at Hand," *Arizona Republic*, September 19, 2007, pp. D1, D2.

44. N. L. Reinsch Jr., J. W. Turner, and C. H. Tinsley, "Multicommunicating: A Practice Whose Time Has Come?" *Academy of Management Review,* April 2008, p. 391.

45. See Reinsch, Turner, and Tinsley, 2008, pp. 391–403, for a complete discussion of multicommunicating.

46. Study by World Economic Forum, reported in R. Kim, "U.S. Info Tech Ratings Improving, Study Says," *San Francisco Chronicle,* April 10, 2008, pp. C1, C2. See also C. Holahan, "The Sad State of U.S. Broadband," *BusinessWeek,* May 22, 2008, http://www.businessweek.com/technology/content/may2008/tc20080522_340989.htm?chan=top+news_top+news+index_news+%2B+analysis (accessed May 22, 2008).

47. D. Kirkpatrick, "Life in a Connected World," *Fortune,* July 10, 2006, pp. 98–100.

48. See J. T. Arnold, "Improving Intranet Usefulness," *HR Magazine,* April 2008, pp. 103–106; and D. M. Owens, "Managing Corporate Politics Online," *HR Magazine,* May 2008, pp. 69–72.

49. J. Scheck and B. White, "'Telepresence' Is Taking Hold," *The Wall Street Journal,* May 6, 2008, http://online.wsj.com/article/SB121003318054369255.html (accessed May 20, 2008).

50. J. S. Lublin, "Some Dos and Don'ts to Help You Hone Video-conference Skills," *The Wall Street Journal,* February 7, 2006, p. B1.

51. Results can be found in S. A. Rains, "Leveling the Organizational Playing Field—Virtually: A Meta-Analysis of Experimental Research Assessing the Impact of Group Support System Use on Member Influence Behaviors," *Communication Research,* April 2005, pp. 193–234.

52. Challenges associated with virtual operations are discussed by S. O'Mahony and S. R. Barley, "Do Digital Telecommunications Affect Work and Organization? The State of Our Knowledge," in R. I. Sutton and B. M. Straw, eds. *Research in Organizational Behavior,* vol. 21, (Stamford, CT: JAI Press, 1999), pp. 125–161.

53. D. E. Baily and N. B. Kurland, "A Review of Telework Research: Findings, New Directions, and Lessons for the Study of Modern Work," *Journal of Organizational Behavior,* June 2002, pp. 383–400.

54. Report by the Reason Foundation, reported in "Will More of Us Be Telecommuting?" *The Week,* January 13, 2006, p. 11.

55. See E. Garone, "How to Make Working at Home Work for You," *The Wall Street Journal,* April 29, 2008, p. D4; and R. S. Gajendran and D. A. Harrison, "The Good, the Bad, and the Unknown about Telecommuting: Meta-Analysis of Psychological Mediators and Individual Consequences," *Journal of Applied Psychology,* November 2007, pp. 1524–1541.

56. See S. Shellenbarger, "Some Companies Rethink the Telecommuting Trend," *The Wall Street Journal,* February 28, 2008, p. D1.

57. K. Maney, "One Fine Day a Cellphone Could Find You a Parking Spot," *USA Today,* May 3, 2006, p. 3B; and J. Markoff and M. Fackler, "With a Cellphone as My Guide," *The New York Times,* June 28, 2006, pp. C1, C7.

58. M. Weinstein, "Mobility Movement," *Training,* September 2007, pp. 14–16.

59. N. Cohen, "Technology Can Be a Blessing for Bored Workers," *The New York Times,* February 18, 2008, p. C3.

60. See M. Gunn, "The Original Executive Blogger," *The Always On Generation,* March 13, 2006, http://www.alwayson-network.com/comments.php?id=13807_0_1_0_C (accessed September 21, 2006). See also R. Buckman, "How Tech Start-Ups Tap Blogs as Cheerleaders," *The Wall Street Journal,* February 9, 2006, p. B6.

61. S. Banjo, "Attention, Bloggers," *The Wall Street Journal,* March 17, 2008, p. R5.

62. J. Fine, "Polluting the Blogosphere," *BusinessWeek,* July 10, 2006, p. 20. See also L. Gomes, "Employee Blogging: What's the Purpose?" *The Wall Street Journal,* March 4, 2008, p. B3.

63. Survey by Salary.com and America Online, reported in S. Toomey, *Suntimes.com,* August 9, 2006; http://www.suntimes.com/output/news/cst-nws-slack09.html (accessed May 22, 2008). See also D. H. Freedman, "Worried That Employees Are Wasting Time on the Web? Here's Why You Shouldn't Crack Down," *Inc. Magazine,* August 2006, pp. 77–78; A. Fox, "Caught in the Web," *HR Magazine,* December 2007, pp. 35–39; and J. McGregor, "A Way to Tell If They're Slaving Away or Surfing," *BusinessWeek,* January 14, 2008, p. 56.

64. B. White, "The New Workplace Rules: No Video-Watching," *The Wall Street Journal,* March 4, 2008, pp. B1, B3.

65. N. H. Nie, A. Simpser, I. Stepanikova, and L. Zheng, *Ten Years After the Birth of the Internet, How Do Americans Use the Internet in Their Daily Lives?* (Stanford, CA: Stanford Institute for Quantitative Study of Society, 2004).

66. J. Tierney, "Why Nobody Likes a Smart Machine," *The New York Times,* December 18, 2007, pp. D1, D4.

67. K. Maney, "No Time Off? It's Tech Giants' Fault," *USA Today,* July 21, 2004, p. 4B.

68. D. Greenfield, quoted in M. Conlin, "Take a Vacation from Your BlackBerry," *BusinessWeek,* December 20, 2004, p. 56.

69. See M. Burley-Allen, "Listen Up," *HR Magazine,* November 2001, pp. 115–120.

70. Online Survey conducted July 2007 by Society for Human Resource Management, reported in Gurchiek, 2008.

71. Burley-Allen, 2001; see also C. G. Pearce, "How Effective Are We as Listeners?" *Training & Development,* April 1993, pp. 79–80; and R. A. Luke Jr., "Improving Your Listening Ability," *Supervisory Management,* June 1992, p. 7.

72. Research by The Discovery Group, reported in "Hey, I'm Talking Here," *Training,* December 2005, p. 9.

73. See the discussion on listening in G. Manning, K. Curtis, and S. McMillen, *Building Community: The Human Side of Work* (Cincinnati, OH: Thomson Executive Press, 1996), pp. 127–154.

74. Derived from J. R. Goldon, *A Diagnostic Approach to Organizational Behavior,* 2nd ed. (Boston: Allyn and Bacon, 1987), p. 230; P. Slizewski, "Tips for Active Listening," *HRFocus,* May 1995, p. 7; G. Manning, K. Curtis, and S. McMillen, *Building the Human Side of Work Community* (Cincinnati, OH: Thomson Executive Press, 1996), pp. 127–154; and J. Sandberg, "What Exactly Was It That the Boss Said? You Can Only Imagine," *The Wall Street Journal,* September 19, 2006, p. B1.

75. M. Just, P. A. Carpenter, and M. Masson, reported in J. Meer, "Reading More, Understanding Less," *Psychology Today,* March 1987, p. 12.

76. K. Alesandrini, *Survive Information Overload* (Homewood, IL: Irwin, 1992), pp. 191–202.

77. Alesandrini, 1992, p. 197.

78. K. Tyler, "Toning Up Communications," *HR Magazine,* March 2003, pp. 87–89.

79. T. Alessandra and P. Hunsaker, *Communicating at Work* (New York: Fireside, 1993), p. 231.

80. Alessandra and Hunsaker, 1993, p. 241.

81. Cited in Alessandra and Hunsaker, 1993, p. 169.

82. G. Lindenfield, "Don't Be Nervous," *Management Today,* June 2003, p. 81.

83. P. Theibert, "Speechwriters of the World, Get Lost!" *The Wall Street Journal,* August 2, 1993, p. A16. This section adapted from C. Wahlstrom and B. Williams, *Learning Success: Being Your Best at College & Life,* 3rd ed. (Belmont, CA: Wadsworth, 2002), pp. 243–245.

84. L. Waters, *Secrets of Successful Speakers: How You Can Motivate, Captivate, and Persuade* (New York: McGraw-Hill, 1993), p. 203.

CHAPTER 16

1. Some new ideas are found in J. Quittner, "How Jeff Bezos Rules the Retail Space," *Fortune,* May 5, 2008, pp. 127–134; A. Taylor III, "Can This Car Save Ford?" *Fortune,* May 5, 2008, pp. 170–178; M. V. Copeland, "Boeing's Big Dream," *Fortune,* May 5, 2008, pp. 180–191; and R. J. Grossman, "Keep Pace with Older Workers," *HR Magazine,* May 2008, pp. 39–46.

2. See, for example, G. Colvin, "Who Wants to Be the Boss?" *Fortune,* February 20, 2006, pp. 76–78.

3. When labor costs rise, productivity slows down, unless other variables are changed. See M. Crutsinger, "Growth of Productivity Slows Down," *San Francisco Chronicle,* August 9, 2006, p. C3.

4. J. Welch, quoted in T. A. Stewart, "U.S. Productivity: First but Fading," *Fortune,* October 1992, p. 54.

5. Office of Macroeconomic Analysis, U.S. Treasury, "Profile of the Economy," March 2008, www.fms.treas.gov/bulletin/b2008-1 poe.doc (accessed May 26, 2008). See also "Productivity Rises More Than Expected," CNN Money.com, May 7, 2008, http://money.cnn.com/2008/05/07/news/economy/productivity_ap.ap (accessed May 26, 2008).

6. L. Uchitelle, "Productivity Finally Shows the Impact of Computers," *The New York Times,* March 12, 2000, sec. 3, p. 4; J. Reingold, M. Stepanek, and D. Brady, "Why the Productivity Revolution Will Spread," *BusinessWeek,* February 14, 2000, p. 112–118; G. S. Becker, "How the Skeptics Missed the Power of Productivity," *BusinessWeek,* January 1, 2004, p. 26; and J. Aversa, "Bernanke Bullish on Productivity Gains," *Business-Week Online,* August 31, 2006, http://www.businessweek.com/ap/financialnews/D8JRJTJOO.htm?chan=search (accessed September 19, 2006).

7. See study by B. P. Bosworth and J. E. Triplett, "Productivity Measurement Issues in Services Industries: 'Baumol's Disease' Has Been Cured," *The Brookings Institution,* September 1, 2003, www.brookings.org/views/articles/bosworth/200309.htm (accessed August 1, 2006). Also see H. R. Varian, "Information Technology May Have Been What Cured Low Service-Sector Productivity," *The New York Times,* February 12, 2004, p. C2.

8. See W. W. Lewis, *The Power of Productivity: Wealth, Poverty, and the Threat to Global Stability* (Chicago: University of Chicago Press, 2004). Also see V. Postrel, "Why Do Certain Countries Prosper? A New Study Looks at Productivity and Comes Up with Some Contrarian Conclusions," *The New York Times,* July 15, 2004, p. C2.

9. W. Taylor, "Control in an Age of Chaos," *Harvard Business Review,* November–December 1994, pp. 64–70.

10. B. Horovitz, "Can Eateries Go Green, Earn Green?" *USA Today,* May 16, 2008, pp. 1B, 2B.

11. V. O'Connell, "Reversing Field, Macy's Goes Local," *The Wall Street Journal,* March 6, 2008, pp. B1, B8.

12. A. P. Sloan Jr., *My Years with General Motors* (New York: Doubleday, 1964).

13. D. Foust, "Big Brown's New Bag," *BusinessWeek,* July 19, 2004, pp. 54–56. See also M. Brewster and F. Dalzell, *Driving Change: The UPS Approach to Business* (New York: Hyperion, 2007).

14. I. G. Seidenberg, quoted in S. E. Ante, "Giving the Boss the Big Picture," *BusinessWeek,* February 13, 2006, pp. 48–51.

15. R. S. Kaplan and D. P. Norton, "The Balanced Scorecard—Measures That Drive Performance," *Harvard Business Review,* January–February 1992, pp. 71–79.

16. Kaplan and Norton, 1992.

17. R. S. Kaplan and D. P. Norton, "Having Trouble with Your Strategy? Then Map It," *Harvard Business Review,* September–October 2000, pp. 167–176. See also R. Kaplan and D. Norton, "Plotting Success with 'Strategy Maps,'" *Optimize,* February 2004, http://www.optimizemag.com/article/show-Article. jhtml?articleId=18200733 (accessed September 18, 2006).

18. R. Quinn, quoted in J. H. Lingle and W. A. Schiemann, "From Balanced Scorecard to Strategic Gauges: Is Measurement Worth It?" *American Management Association,* March 1996, pp. 56–61.

19. Lingle and Schiemann, 1996.

20. See G. L. Neilson, K. L. Martin, and E. Powers, "The Secrets to Successful Strategy Execution," *Harvard Business Review,* June 2008, pp. 61–70.

21. For discussions of how to measure services and intangible assets, see R. S. Kaplan and D. P. Norton, "Measuring the Strategic Readiness of Intangible Assets," *Harvard Business Review,* February 2004, pp. 52–63; K. M. Kroll, "Repurposing Metrics for HR," *HR Magazine,* July 2006, pp. 65–69; and B. Hindo, "Satisfaction Not Guaranteed," *BusinessWeek,* June 19, 2006, pp. 32–36.

22. W. G. Ouchi, "The Transmission of Control Through Organizational Hierarchy," *Academy of Management Journal,* June 1978, pp. 173–192; and R. E. Walton, "From Control to Commitment in the Workplace," *Harvard Business Review,* March–April 1985, pp. 76–84.

23. A description of Genentech's culture is provided by B. Morris, "The Best Place to Work Now," *Fortune,* January 23, 2006, pp. 79–86.

24. J. V. Pearson and R. J. Michael, "Zero-Based Budgeting: A Technique for Planning Organizational Decline," *Long Range Planning,* June 1981, pp. 68–76; P. A. Pyhrr, "Zero-Based Budgeting," *Harvard Business Review,* November–December 1970, pp. 111–118; and "Zero-Based Budgeting," *Small Business Report,* April 1988, pp. 52–57; and L. J. Shinn and M. S. Sturgeon, "Budgeting from Ground Zero," *Association Management,* September 1990, pp. 45–58.

25. For more about Ritz-Carlton, see C. Gallo, "How Ritz-Carlton Maintains Its Mystique," *BusinessWeek,* February 13, 2007, http://www.businessweek.com/smallbiz/content/feb2007/sb20070213_171606.htm?chan=search; and C. Gallo, "Employee Motivation the Ritz-Carlton Way," *BusinessWeek,* February 29, 2008, http://www.businessweek.com/smallbiz/content/feb2008/sb20080229_347490.htm?chan=search (both accessed May 26, 2008).

26. D. Jones, "Baldrige Winners Named," *USA Today,* November 24, 1999, p. 3B. See also D. Jones, "Baldrige Award Honors Record 7 Quality Winners," *USA Today,* November 26, 2003, p. B6; and R. O. Crockett, "Keeping Ritz Carlton at the Top of Its Game," *BusinessWeek Online,* May 29, 2006, http://www.businessweek.com/magazine/content/06_22/b3986130.htm?chan=search(accessed September 20, 2006). For more about the Baldrige awards, go to the Baldrige National Quality Program Web site at http://www.quality.nist.gov.

27. W. E. Deming, *Out of the Crisis* (Cambridge, MA: MIT press, 1986), p. 5.

28. Larry Coburn, quoted in B. Kenney, "Whatever Happened to Quality?" *IndustryWeek,* April 2008, pp. 42–47.

29. R. N. Lussier, *Management: Concepts, Applications, Skill Development* (Cincinnati, OH: South-Western College Publishing, 1997), p. 260.

30. The Japanese have taken efficiency to a high level. See the example of Matsushita Electric Industrial Co., described in K. Hall, "No One Does Lean Like the Japanese," *BusinessWeek,* July 10, 2006, pp. 40–41.

31. O. Port, "The Push for Quality," *BusinessWeek,* June 8, 1987, pp. 130–136.

32. M. Maynard, "Quality Is Major Concern of Toyota's Visiting Chief," *The New York Times,* January 15, 2008, p. C5.

33. See H. Liao and M. Subramony, "Employee Customer Orientation in Manufacturing Organizations: Joint Influences of Customer Proximity and the Senior Leadership Team," *Journal of Applied Psychology,* March 2008, pp. 317–328. Also see P. Hellman, "Rating Your Dentist," *Management Review,* July–August 1998, p. 64.

34. S. Lohr, "Academia Dissects the Service Sector, but Is It a Science?" *The New York Times,* April 18, 2008, http://www.nytimes.com/2006/04/18/business/18services.html (accessed June 6, 2008).

35. F. X. Frei, "The Four Things a Service Business Must Get Right," *Harvard Business Review,* April 2008, pp. 70–80.

36. J. Goldstein, "As Doctors Get a Life, Strains Show," *The Wall Street Journal,* April 29, 2008, pp. A1, A14.

37. H. Rothman, "You Need Not Be Big to Benchmark," *Nation's Business,* December 1992, pp. 64–65.

38. K. Chang, "Enlisting Science's Lessons to Entice More Shoppers to Spend More," *The New York Times,* September 19, 2006, p. D3.

39. J. Pfeffer and R. I. Sutton, *Hard Facts, Dangerous Half Truths & Total Nonsense: Profiting from Evidence-Based Management* (Boston: Harvard Business School Press, 2006).

40. I. Austen, "In a Chevy, Engine from China and Transmission from Japan," *The New York Times,* March 26, 2008, pp. C1, C8.

41. C. L. Mann, "Globalization of I.T. Services and White-Collar Jobs: The Next Wave of Productivity Growth," December 2003, International Economics Policy Briefs, No. PB03-11, www.iie.com/publications/pb/pb03-11.pdf (accessed August 1, 2006). See also V. Postrel, "A Researcher Sees an Upside in the Outsourcing of Programming Jobs," *The New York Times,* January 29, 2004, p. C2.

42. H. Menzies, "Quality Counts When Wooing Overseas Clients," *Fortune,* June 1, 1997, www.fortune.com/fortune/subs/article/0,15114,378797,00.html (accessed August 1, 2006).

43. B. Ekeler, quoted in Menzies, 1997. See also M. V. Uzumeri, "ISO 9000 and Other Metastandards: Principles for Management Practice?" *Academy of Management Executive* 11, no 1. (1997), pp. 21–28; and T. B. Schoenrock, "ISO 9000: 2000 Gives Competitive Edge," *Quality Progress,* May 2002, p. 107.

44. A. Fisher, "Rules for Joining the Cult of Perfectability," *Fortune,* February 7, 2000, p. 206.

45. J. E. Morehouse, quoted in C. H. Deutsch, "Six Sigma Enlightenment," *The New York Times,* December 7, 1998, pp. C1, C7. For more on Six Sigma, see M. S. Sodhi and N. S. Sodhi, "Six Sigma Pricing," *Harvard Business Review,* May 2005, pp. 135–142; and J. Gordon, "Take *That* to the Bank," *Training,* June 2006, p. 41.

46. D. Jones, "Firms Aim for Six Sigma Efficiency," *USA Today,* July 21, 1998, pp. 1B, 2B.

47. See M. Poppendieck, "Why the Lean in Lean Six Sigma?" *The Project Management Best Practices Report,* June 2004, www.poppendieck.com/pdfs/Lean_Six_Sigma.pdf (accessed August 1, 2006).

48. Arner and Aston, 2004; and A. Aston, J. Carey, and O. Kharif, "Online Extra: The New Factory Floor, and Tomorrow's," *BusinessWeek Online,* May 3, 2004; www.businessweek.com/ =@@vr3DfocQkImUSwOA/magazine/content/04_18/b3881601. htm (accessed August 1, 2006).

49. K. Day and J. Howard, "Albertsons Officials to Implement New Efficiency Program," *Reno Gazette-Journal,* February 25, 2004, pp. 1D, 3D.

50. Six Sigma has come under fire for hurting creativity, yet it was adopted as a major initiative by the conglomerate Textron in 2002, and since then the stock has soared. See B. Hindo and B. Grow, "Six Sigma: So Yesterday?" *BusinessWeek,* June 11, 2007, http://www.businessweek.com/magazine/content/07_24/b4038409.htm (accessed May 26, 2008); and D. Jones, "CEO Expects Good Things as Textron Does Six Sigma Right," *USA Today,* January 21, 2008, p. 3B.

51. See R. J. Aldag and T. M. Stearns, Management (Cincinnati, OH: South-Western Publishing, 1987), pp. 653–654; D. Robertson and E. Anderson, "Control System and Task Environment Effects on Ethical Judgment: An Exploratory Study of Industrial Salespeople," *Organizational Science,* November 1993, pp. 617–629.

52. K. A. Merchant, *Control in Business Organizations* (Boston: Pitman, 1985), pp. 10–11; K. M. Bartol and D. C. Martin, *Management,* 3rd ed. (Burr Ridge, IL: Irwin/McGraw-Hill, 1998),

pp. 533–534; and J. R. Schermerhorn Jr., *Management for Productivity,* 3rd ed. (New York: John Wiley & Sons, 1993), p. 592.

53. See D. Rice, "Climate Now Shifting on a Continental Scale," *USA Today,* May 15, 2008, p. 4D; and annual Rechargeable Recycling Corporation green guilt survey, reported in J. Kornblum, "Survey: More Americans Feel Guilty for Not Living Greener," *USA Today,* May 8, 2008, p. 5D.

54. E. Iwata, "Companies Discover Going Green Pays Off," *USA Today,* May 21, 2008, p. 4B. See also M. Weinstein, "It's Not Easy Being Green," *Training,* April 2008, pp. 20–25; M. Lavelle, "Three Ways That Firms Can Save," *U.S. News & World Report,* April 28, 2008, pp. 46–47; C. Laszlo, "Sustainability for Competitive Advantage," *San Francisco Chronicle,* May 14, 2008, p. B9; and I. DeBare, "Firms Honored for Green Ingenuity and Commitment," *San Francisco Chronicle,* May 21, 2008, pp. C1, C4.

55. Bartol and Martin, 1998, pp. 532–533; S. C. Certo, *Modern Management,* 8th ed. (Upper Saddle River, NJ: Prentice Hall, 2000), pp. 435–436; and Griffin, 1997, pp. 384–386.

56. J. P. Kotter, L. A. Schlesinger, and V. Sathe, *Organization: Text, Cases, and Readings on the Management of Organizational Design and Change* (Homewood, IL: Irwin, 1979).

57. K. Merchant, *Control in Business Organizations* (Boston: Pitman, 1985).

EPILOGUE

1. G. Hamel, with B. Breen, *The Future of Management* (Boston: Harvard Business School Press, 2007), p. 6.

2. "The Top Gurus," *The Wall Street Journal,* May 5, 2008, p. B6.

3. G. Hamel, "Break Free!" *Fortune,* September 19, 2007, http://money.cnn.com/magazines/fortune/fortune_archive/2007/10/01/100352608/index.htm (accessed May 26, 2008).

4. Hamel, "Break Free!" 2007.

5. A. R. Rasbury, "New Kid on the Job: How to Get Off to a Good Start," *Black Enterprise,* May 1, 2008, http://www.thefreelibrary.com/New+kid+on+the+job:+how+to+get+off+to+a+good+start.-a0178674810 (accessed May 26, 2008).

6. K. Holland, "For the Chief, a Little Skepticism Can Go a Long Way," *The New York Times,* May 25, 2008, business section, p. 14.

7. B. Taylor, "Why Zappos Pays New Employees to Quit—And You Should Too," *Harvard Business Publishing,* May 19, 2008, http://discussionleader.hbsp.com/taylor/2008/05/wy_zappos_pays_new_employees_t.html (accessed May 26, 2008).

8. E. White, "Art of Persuasion Becomes Key," *The Wall Street Journal,* May 19, 2008, p. B5.

9. See, for instance, Hamel, *The Future of Management,* 2007, pp. 200–204.

glossary

A

absenteeism When an employee doesn't show up for work.

accountability Describes expectation that managers must report and justify work results to the managers above them.

acquired needs theory Theory that states that there are three needs—achievement, affiliation, and power—that are the major motives determining people's behavior in the workplace.

action plan Course of action needed to achieve a stated goal.

adaptive change Reintroduction of a familiar practice, the kind of change that has already been experienced within the same organization.

adaptive perspective Perspective of organizational culture that assumes that the most effective cultures help organizations anticipate and adapt to environmental change.

adhocracy culture Type of organizational culture that has an external focus and values flexibility.

adjourning One of five stages of forming a team; the stage in which members of an organization prepare for disbandment.

administrative management Management concerned with managing the total organization.

affective component of an attitude The feelings or emotions one has about a situation.

affirmative action The focus on achieving equality of opportunity within an organization.

Americans with Disabilities Act Passed by the U.S. in 1992, act that prohibits discrimination against the disabled.

Analyzers Organizations that allow other organizations to take the risks of product development and marketing and then imitate (or perhaps slightly improve on) what seems to work best.

analytics (business analytics) Term used for sophisticated forms of business data analysis, such as portfolio analysis or time-series forecast.

anchoring and adjustment bias The tendency to make decisions based on an initial figure.

Asian-Pacific Economic Cooperation (APEC) Group of 21 Pacific Rim countries whose purpose is to improve economic and political ties.

assessment center Company department where management candidates participate in activities for a few days while being assessed by evaluators.

attitude A learned predisposition toward a given object; a mental position with regard to a fact, state, or person.

audits Formal verifications of an organization's financial and operational systems.

authority The right to perform or command; also, the rights inherent in a managerial position to make decisions, give orders, and utilize resources.

availability bias Tendency of managers to use information readily available from memory to make judgments; they tend to give more weight to recent events.

B

balance sheet A summary of an organization's overall financial worth—assets and liabilities—at a specific point in time.

balanced scorecard Gives top managers a fast but comprehensive view of the organization via four indicators: (1) customer satisfaction, (2) internal processes, (3) the organization's innovation and improvement activities, and (4) financial measures.

base pay Consists of the basic wage or salary paid employees in exchange for doing their jobs.

behavior Actions and judgments.

behavioral component of an attitude Also known as *intentional component,* this refers to how one intends or expects to behave toward a situation.

behavioral leadership approach Attempts to determine the distinctive styles used by effective leaders.

behavioral science Relies on scientific research for developing theories about human behavior that can be used to provide practical tools for managers.

behavioral viewpoint Emphasizes the importance of understanding human behavior and of motivating employees toward achievement.

behavioral-description interview Type of structured interview in which the interviewer explores what applicants have done in the past.

behaviorally anchored rating scale (BARS) Employee gradations in performance rated according to scales of specific behaviors.

benchmarking A process by which a company compares its performance with that of high-performing organizations.

benefits (fringe benefits) Additional nonmonetary forms of compensation.

Big Five personality dimensions They are (1) extroversion, (2) agreeableness, (3) conscientiousness, (4) emotional stability, and (5) openness to experience.

birth stage The nonbureaucratic stage, the stage in which the organization is created.

blended value The idea that all investments are understood to operate simultaneously in both economic and social realms.

blog Online journal in which people write about whatever they want about any topic.

bonuses Cash awards given to employees who achieve specific performance objectives.

boundaryless organization A fluid, highly adaptive organization whose members, linked by information technology, come together to collaborate on common tasks; the collaborators may include competitors, suppliers, and customers.

bounded rationality One type of nonrational decision making; the ability of decision makers to be rational is limited by numerous constraints.

brainstorming Technique used to help groups generate multiple ideas and alternatives for solving problems; individuals in a group meet and review a problem to be solved, then silently generate ideas, which are collected and later analyzed.

break-even analysis A way of identifying how much revenue is needed to cover the total cost of developing and selling a product.

break-even point The amount of sales revenue at which there is no profit but also no loss to your company.

budget A formal financial projection.

buffers Administrative changes that managers can make to reduce the stressors that lead to employee burnout.

bureaucratic control The use of rules, regulations, and formal authority to guide performance.

burnout State of emotional, mental, and even physical exhaustion.

business plan Document that outlines a proposed firm's goals, the strategy for achieving them, and the standards for measuring success.

C

cascading Objectives are structured in a unified hierarchy, becoming more specific at lower levels of the organization.

causal attribution The activity of inferring causes for observed behavior.

Central American Free Trade Agreement (CAFTA) Trade agreement involving the United States and Costa Rica, the Dominican Republic, El Salvador, Guatemala, Honduras, and Nicaragua and which is aimed at reducing tariffs and other barriers to free trade.

centralized authority Organizational structure in which important decisions are made by upper managers—power is concentrated at the top.

change agent A person inside or outside the organization who can be a catalyst in helping deal with old problems in new ways.

charisma Form of personal attraction that inspires acceptance and support.

clan culture Type of organizational culture that has an internal focus and values flexibility rather than stability and control.

classical viewpoint In the historical perspective, the viewpoint that emphasizes finding ways to manage work more efficiently; it has two branches—scientific and administrative.

closed system A system that has little interaction with its environment.

code of ethics A formal, written set of ethical standards that guide an organization's actions.

coercive power One of five sources of a leader's power that results from the authority to punish subordinates.

cognitive component of an attitude The beliefs and knowledge one has about a situation.

cognitive dissonance Term coined by social psychologist Leon Festinger to describe the psychological discomfort a person experiences between what he or she already knows and new information or contradictory behavior, or by inconsistency among a person's beliefs, attitudes, and/or actions.

cohesiveness The tendency of a group or team to stick together.

collaborative computing Using state-of-the-art computer software and hardware to help people work together.

collective bargaining Negotiations between management and employees regarding disputes over compensation, benefits, working conditions, and job security.

common purpose A goal that unifies employees or members and gives everyone an understanding of the organization's reason for being.

communication The transfer of information and understanding from one person to another.

compensation Payment comprising three parts: wages or salaries, incentives, and benefits.

competitive intelligence Gaining information about competitors' activities so that one can anticipate their moves and react appropriately.

competitive advantage The ability of an organization to produce goods or services more effectively than its competitors do, thereby outperforming them.

competitors People or organizations that compete for customers or resources.

computer-assisted instruction (CAI) Training in which computers are used to provide additional help or to reduce instructional time.

conceptual skills Skills that consist of the ability to think analytically, to visualize an organization as a whole and understand how the parts work together.

confirmation bias Biased way of thinking in which people seek information to support their point of view and discount data that does not.

conflict Process in which one party perceives that its interests are being opposed or negatively affected by another party.

conglomerate Type of organization in which a large company does business in different, quite unrelated areas.

consensus General agreement; group solidarity.

constructive conflict Functional conflict that benefits the main purposes of the organization and serves its interest.

contemporary perspective In contrast to the historical perspective, the business approach that includes three viewpoints—systems, contingency, and quality-management.

content perspectives Also known as *need-based perspectives;* theories that emphasize the needs that motivate people.

contingency approach to leadership The belief that the effectiveness of leadership behavior depends on the situation at hand.

contingency design The process of fitting the organization to its environment.

contingency leadership model Fiedler's theory (1951) that leader effectiveness is determined by both the personal characteristics of leaders and by the situations in which leaders find themselves; the leader's style is either task-oriented or relationship-oriented, and it must be determined which style fits the situation at hand.

contingency planning Also known as *scenario planning* and *scenario analysis;* the creation of alternative hypothetical but equally likely future conditions.

contingency viewpoint In opposition to the classical viewpoint; a manager's approach should vary according to—that is, be contingent on—the individual and the environmental situation.

continuous improvement Ongoing, small, incremental improvements in all parts of an organization.

continuous-process technology A highly routinized technology in which machines do all of the work, to produce highly routinized products.

control process The four steps in the process of controlling: (1) establish standards; (2) measure performance; (3) compare performance to standards; and (4) take corrective action, if necessary.

control standard The first step in the control process; the performance standard (or just standard) is the desired performance level for a given goal.

controlling Monitoring performance, comparing goals, and taking corrective action as needed.

coordinated effort The coordination of individual efforts into a group or organization-wide effort.

core principles of TQM In total quality management, (1) everyone involved with the organization should focus on delivering value to customers (people orientation), and (2) everyone should work on continuously improving the work processes (improvement orientation).

corporate social responsibility (CSR) The notion that corporations are expected to go above and beyond following the law and making a profit, to take actions that will benefit the interests of society as well as of the organization.

cost-focus strategy One of Porter's four competitive strategies; to keep the costs, and hence prices, of a product or service below those of competitors and to target a narrow market.

cost-leadership strategy One of Porter's four competitive strategies; keeping the costs, and hence prices, of a product or service below those of competitors and targeting the wider market.

counterproductive work behaviors (CWB) Types of behavior that harm employees and the organization as a whole.

countertrading Bartering goods for goods.

cross-functional team A team that is staffed with specialists pursuing a common objective.

culture A shared set of beliefs, values, knowledge, and patterns of behavior common to a group of people.

culture shock Feelings of discomfort and disorientation associated with being in an unfamiliar culture.

customer division A divisional structure in which activities are grouped around common customers or clients.

customers Those who pay to use an organization's goods or services.

D

database Computerized collection of interrelated files.

decentralized authority Organizational structure in which important decisions are made by middle-level and supervisory-level managers—power is delegated throughout the organization.

decentralized control An approach to organizational control that is characterized by informal and organic structural arrangements, the opposite of bureaucratic control.

deciding to decide A manager agrees that he or she must decide what to do about a problem or opportunity and take effective decision-making steps.

decision A choice made from among available alternatives.

decision making The process of identifying and choosing alternative courses of action.

decision-making style A style that reflects the combination of how an individual perceives and responds to information.

decision tree Graph of decisions and their possible consequences, used to create a plan to reach a goal.

decisional role One of three types of managerial roles: managers use information to make decisions to solve problems or take advantage of opportunities. The four decision-making roles are entrepreneur, disturbance handler, resource allocator, and negotiator.

decline stage The fourth stage in the product life cycle; period in which a product falls out of favor and the organization withdraws from the marketplace.

decoding Interpreting and trying to make sense of a message.

Defenders Experts at producing and selling narrowly defined products or services.

defensive avoidance When a manager cannot find a good solution and follows by (a) procrastinating, (b) passing the buck, or (c) denying the risk of any negative consequences.

defensive strategy Also called *retrenchment strategy;* one of three grand strategies, this strategy involves reduction in the organization's efforts.

delegation The process of assigning managerial authority and responsibility to managers and employees lower in the hierarchy.

Deming management Ideas proposed by W. Edwards Deming for making organizations more responsive, more democratic, and less wasteful.

demographic forces Influences on an organization arising from changes in the characteristics of a population, such as age, gender, ethnic origin, and so on.

development The education of professionals and managers in the skills they will need to do their jobs.

devil's advocacy Taking the side of an unpopular point of view for the sake of argument.

diagnosis Analysis of underlying causes.

dialectic method The process of having two people or groups play opposing roles in a debate in order to better understand a proposal.

differentiation The tendency of the parts of an organization to disperse and fragment.

differentiation strategy One of Porter's four competitive strategies; offer products or services that are of a unique and superior value compared to those of competitors and to target a wide market.

discrimination Prejudicial outlook; when people are hired or promoted—or denied hiring or promotion—for reasons not relevant to the job.

distributor A person or an organization that helps another organization sell its goods and services to customers.

diversification Strategy by which a company operates several businesses in order to spread the risk.

diversity All the ways people are unlike and alike—the differences and similarities in age, gender, race, religion, ethnicity, sexual orientation, capabilities, and socioeconomic background.

division of labor Also known as *work specialization;* arrangement of having discrete parts of a task done by different people. The work is divided into particular tasks assigned to particular workers.

divisional structure The third type of organizational structure, whereby people with diverse occupational specialties are put together in formal groups according to products and/or services, customers and/or clients, or geographic regions.

downward communication Communication that flows from a higher level to a lower level.

dumping A foreign company's practice of exporting products abroad at a price lower than the home-market price, or even below the costs of production, in order to drive down the price of the domestic product.

E

e-business Using the Internet to facilitate every aspect of running a business.

e-commerce Electronic commerce; the buying and selling of goods and services over computer networks.

e-mail Electronic mail; text messages and documents transmitted over a computer network.

e-leadership Leadership that involves one-to-one, one-to-many, and within and between-group and collective interactions via information technology.

economic forces General economic conditions and trends—unemployment, inflation, interest rates, economic growth—that may affect an organization's performance.

effective To achieve results, to make the right decisions, and to successfully carry them out so that they achieve the organization's goals.

efficient Using resources—people, money, raw materials, and the like—wisely and cost-effectively.

electronic brainstorming (brainwriting) Technique in which members of a group come together over a computer network to generate ideas and alternatives.

embargo A complete ban on the import and/or export of certain products.

emotional intelligence The ability to cope, to empathize with others, and to be self-motivated.

employee assistance programs (EAPs) Host of programs aimed at helping employees to cope with stress, burnout, substance abuse, health-related problems, family and marital issues, and any general problems that negatively influence job performance.

employee engagement A heightened emotional connection to an organization that influences an employee to exert greater discretionary effort at work.

employment tests Tests legally considered to consist of any procedure used in the employment selection process.

enacted values Values and norms actually exhibited in the organization.

encoding Translating a message into understandable symbols or language.

entrepreneur Someone who sees a new opportunity for a product or service and launches a business to try to realize it.

entrepreneurship The process of taking risks to try to create a new enterprise.

environmental scanning Careful monitoring of an organization's internal and external environments to detect early signs of opportunities and threats that may influence the firm's plans.

Equal Employment Opportunity (EEO) Commission U.S. panel whose job it is to enforce antidiscrimination and other employment-related laws.

equity theory In the area of employee motivation, the focus on how employees perceive how fairly they think they are being treated compared to others.

ERG theory Theory proposed by Clayton Alderfer that assumes that three basic needs influence behavior—existence, relatedness, and growth—represented by the letters E, R, and G.

escalation of commitment bias When decision makers increase their commitment to a project despite negative information about it.

espoused values Explicitly stated values and norms preferred by an organization.

ethical behavior Behavior accepted as "right" as opposed to "wrong" according to recognized ethical standards.

ethical dilemma A situation in which you have to decide whether to pursue a course of action that may benefit you or your organization but that is unethical or even illegal.

ethics Generally accepted standards of right and wrong that influence behavior; these standards may vary among countries and cultures.

ethics officer A person trained about matters of ethics in the workplace, particularly about resolving ethical dilemmas.

ethnocentric managers Managers who believe that their native country, culture, language, and/or behavior are superior to others.

ethnocentrism The belief that one's native country, culture, language, abilities, and/or behavior are superior to those of another culture.

European Union (EU) Union of 25 trading partners in Europe.

evidence-based management Form of management that believes in translating principles based on best evidence into organizational practice, bringing rationality to the decision-making process.

exchange rate The rate at which one country's currency is exchanged for another country's currency.

execution As proposed by Larry Bossidy and Ram Charan, execution is not simply tactics, it is a central part of any company's strategy; it consists of using questioning, analysis, and follow-through in order to mesh strategy with reality, align people with goals, and achieve results promised.

expatriates People living or working in a foreign country.

expectancy The belief that a particular level of effort will lead to a particular level of performance.

expectancy theory Theory that suggests that people are motivated by two things: (1) how much they want something and (2) how likely they think they are to get it.

expert power One of five sources of a leader's power, resulting from specialized information or expertise.

exporting Producing goods domestically and selling them outside the country.

external audit Formal verification by outside experts of an organization's financial accounts and statements.

external communication Communication between people inside and outside an organization.

external dimensions of diversity Human differences that have an element of choice; they consist of the personal characteristics that people acquire, discard, or modify throughout their lives.

external recruiting Attracting job applicants from outside the organization.

external stakeholders People or groups in the organization's external environment that are affected by it. This environment includes the task environment and the general environment.

extinction The withholding or withdrawal of positive rewards for desirable behavior, so that the behavior is less likely to occur in the future.

extranet An extended intranet that connects internal employees with selected customers, suppliers, and other strategic partners.

extrinsic reward The payoff, such as money, that a person receives from others for performing a particular task.

F

Fair Labor Standards Act Legislation passed in 1938 that established minimum living standards for workers engaged in interstate commerce, including provision of a federal minimum wage.

feedback The receiver's expression of his or her reaction to the sender's message. Also, the information about the reaction of the environment to the outputs that affect the inputs; one of four parts of a system, along with inputs, outputs, and transformational processes.

financial statement Summary of some aspect of an organization's financial status.

first-line managers One of three managerial levels; also called *supervisory managers;* they make the short-term operating decisions, directing the daily tasks of nonmanagerial personnel.

fit perspective Perspective of organizational culture that assumes that an organization's culture must align, or fit, with its business or strategic context.

fixed budget Allocation of resources on the basis of a single estimate of costs.

focused-differentiation strategy One of Porter's four competitive strategies; to offer products or services that are of unique and superior value compared to those of competitors and to target a narrow market.

forced ranking performance review systems Performance review systems whereby all employees within a business unit are ranked against one another, and grades are distributed along some sort of bell curve, like students being graded in a college course.

forecast A projection of the future.

formal appraisals Appraisals conducted at specific times throughout the year and based on performance measures that have been established in advance.

formal communication channels Communications that follow the chain of command and are recognized as official.

formal group A group, headed by a leader, that is established to do something productive for the organization.

forming The first of the five stages of forming a team, in which people get oriented and get acquainted.

four management functions The management process that "gets things done": planning, organizing, leading, and controlling.

franchising A form of licensing in which a company allows a foreign company to pay it a fee and a share of the profit in return for using the first company's brand name and a package of materials and services.

free trade The movement of goods and services among nations without political or economic obstruction.

full-range leadership Approach that suggests that leadership behavior varies along a full range of leadership styles, from take-no-responsibilty (*laissez-faire*) "leadership" at one extreme through transactional leadership, to transformational leadership at the other extreme.

functional managers Managers who are responsible for just one organizational activity.

functional structure The second type of organizational structure, whereby people with similar occupational specialties are put together in formal groups.

fundamental attribution bias Tendency whereby people attribute another person's behavior to his or her personal characteristics rather than to situational factors.

G

gainsharing The distribution of savings or "gains" to groups of employees who reduce costs and increase measurable productivity.

general environment Also called *macroenvironment*; in contrast to the task environment, it includes six forces: economic, technological, sociocultural, demographic, political-legal, and international.

general managers Managers who are responsible for several organizational activities.

geocentric managers Managers who accept that there are differences and similarities between home and foreign personnel and practices and that they should use whatever techniques are most effective.

geographic division A divisional structure in which activities are grouped around defined regional locations.

glass ceiling The metaphor for an invisible barrier preventing women and minorities from being promoted to top executive jobs.

global economy The increasing tendency of the economies of the world to interact with one another as one market instead of as many national markets.

global outsourcing Using suppliers outside the United States to provide labor, goods, and/or services.

global village The "shrinking" of time and space as air travel and electronic media make it easier for the people of the globe to communicate with one another.

globalization The trend of the world economy toward becoming a more interdependent system.

GLOBE project Massive, ongoing cross-cultural investigation of nine cultural dimensions involved in leadership and organizational processes. Started by Robert J. House, GLOBE stands for Global Leadership and Organizational Behavior Effectiveness.

goal Also known as *objective;* a specific commitment to achieve a measurable result within a stated period of time.

goal displacement The primary goal is subsumed to a secondary goal.

goal-setting theory Employee-motivation approach that employees can be motivated by goals that are specific and challenging but achievable.

government regulators Regulatory agencies that establish ground rules under which organizations may operate.

grand strategy Second step of the strategic-management process; it explains how the organization's mission is to be accomplished. Three grand strategies are growth, stability, and defensive.

grapevine The unofficial communication system of the informal organization.

greenfield venture A wholly-owned foreign subsidiary that the owning organization has built from scratch.

group Two or more freely interacting individuals who share collective norms, share collective goals, and have a common identity.

group cohesiveness A "we feeling" that binds group members together.

group support systems (GSSs) Use of state-of-the-art computer software and hardware to help people work better together.

groupthink A cohesive group's blind unwillingness to consider alternatives. This occurs when group members strive for agreement among themselves for the sake of unanimity and avoid accurately assessing the decision situation.

growth stage The second stage of the product life cycle. This, the most profitable stage, is the period in which customer demand increases, the product's sales grow, and (later) competitors may enter the market.

growth strategy One of three grand strategies, this strategy involves expansion—as in sales revenues, market share, number of employees, or number of customers or (for nonprofits) clients served.

H

halo effect An effect in which we form a positive impression of an individual based on a single trait.

hero A person whose accomplishments embody the values of the organization.

heuristics Strategies that simplify the process of making decisions.

hierarchy culture Type of organizational culture that has an internal focus and values stability and control over flexibility.

hierarchy of authority Also known as *chain of command*; a control mechanism for making sure the right people do the right things at the right time.

hierarchy of needs theory Psychological structure proposed by Maslow whereby people are motivated by five levels of needs: (1) physiological, (2) safety, (3) love, (4) esteem, and (5) self-actualization.

high-context culture Culture in which people rely heavily on situational cues for meaning when communicating with others.

historical perspective In contrast to the contemporary perspective, the view of management that includes the classical, behavioral, and quantitative viewpoints.

Hofstede model of four cultural dimensions Model proposed by

Geert Hofstede that identified four dimensions along which national cultures can be placed: individualism/collectivism, power distance, uncertainty avoidance, and masculinity/femininity.

holistic wellness program Program that goes beyond stress reduction by encouraging employees to strive for a harmonious and productive balance of physical, mental, and social well-being brought about by the acceptance of one's personal responsibility for developing and adhering to a health promotion program.

horizontal communication Communication that flows within and between work units; its main purpose is coordination.

human capital Economic or productive potential of employee knowledge, experience, and actions.

human relations movement The movement that proposed that better human relations could increase worker productivity.

human resource inventory A report listing an organization's employees by name, education, training, languages, and other important information.

human resource (HR) management The activities managers perform to plan for, attract, develop, and retain a workforce.

human skills The ability to work well in cooperation with other people in order to get things done.

hygiene factors Factors associated with job dissatisfaction—such as salary, working conditions, interpersonal relationships, and company policy—all of which affect the job context or environment in which people work.

I

import quota A trade barrier in the form of a limit on the numbers of a product that can be imported.

importing Buying goods outside the country and reselling them domestically.

incentives Benefits used to move people to action, such as commissions, bonuses, profit-sharing plans, and stock options.

income statement Summary of an organization's financial results—revenues and expenses—over a specified period of time.

incremental budgeting Allocating increased or decreased funds to a department by using the last budget period as a reference point; only incremental changes in the budget request are reviewed.

incremental innovations The creation of products, services, or technologies that modify existing ones.

incremental model One type of nonrational model of decision making; managers take small, short-term steps to alleviate a problem.

indigenization laws Laws that require that citizens within the host country own a majority of whatever company is operating within that country.

individual approach One of four approaches to solving ethical dilemmas; ethical behavior is guided by what will result in the individual's best long-term interests, which ultimately is in everyone's self-interest.

informal appraisals Appraisals conducted on an unscheduled basis and consisting of less rigorous indications of employee performance than those used in formal appraisals.

informal communication channels Communication that develops outside the formal structure and does not follow the chain of command.

informal group A group formed by people seeking friendship that has no officially appointed leader,

although a leader may emerge from the membership.

information overload An overload that occurs when the amount of information received exceeds a person's ability to handle or process it.

informational role One of three types of managerial roles: managers receive and communicate information with other people inside and outside the organization as monitors, disseminators, and spokespersons.

innovation Introduction of something new or better, as in goods or services.

inputs The people, money, information, equipment, and materials required to produce an organization's goods or services; one of four parts of a system, along with outputs, transformation processes, and feedback.

instrumentality The expectation that successful performance of the task will lead to the outcome desired.

integration The tendency of the parts of an organization to draw together to achieve a common purpose.

interacting group A problem-solving technique in which group members interact and deliberate with one another to reach a consensus.

internal audit A verification of an organization's financial accounts and statements by the organization's own professional staff.

internal dimensions of diversity The human differences that exert a powerful, sustained effect throughout every stage of people's lives (gender, age, ethnicity, race, sexual orientation, physical abilities).

internal locus of control The belief that one controls one's own destiny.

internal recruiting Hiring from the inside, or making people already employed by the organization aware of job openings.

internal stakeholders Employees, owners, and the board of directors, if any.

international forces Changes in the economic, political, legal, and technological global system that may affect an organization.

international management Management that oversees the conduct of operations in or with organizations in foreign countries.

International Monetary Fund (IMF) One of three principal organizations designed to facilitate international trade; its purpose is to assist in smoothing the flow of money between nations.

Internet Global network of independently operating but interconnected computers, linking hundreds of thousands of smaller networks around the world.

interpersonal role One of three types of managerial roles; managers interact with people inside and outside of their work units. The three interpersonal roles include figurehead, leader, and liaison activities.

intervention Interference in an attempt to correct a problem.

intranet An organization's private, internal Internet.

intrapreneur Someone who works inside an existing organization who sees an opportunity for a product or a service and mobilizes the organization's resources to try to realize it.

intrinsic reward The satisfaction, such as a feeling of accomplishment, a person receives from performing a task.

introduction stage The first stage in the product life cycle; a new product is introduced into the marketplace.

intuition Making a choice without the use of conscious thought or logical inference.

intuition model Form of nonrational decision making whereby a manager quickly sizes up a situation and makes a decision based on his or her experience or practice.

ISO 9000 series Set of company quality-control procedures, developed by the International Organization for Standardization in Geneva, Switzerland, that deals with all activities—from purchasing to manufacturing to inventory to shipping—that can be audited by independent quality-control experts, or "registrars."

J

jargon Terminology specific to a particular profession or group.

job analysis The determination of the basic elements of a job.

job characteristics model The job design model that consists of five core job characteristics that affect three critical psychological states of an employee that in turn affect work outcomes—the employee's motivation, performance, and satisfaction.

job description A summary of what the holder of the job does and how and why he or she does it.

job design The division of an organization's work among its employees and the application of motivational theories to jobs to increase satisfaction and performance.

job enlargement Increasing the number of tasks in a job to increase variety and motivation.

job enrichment Building into a job such motivating factors as responsibility, achievement, recognition, stimulating work, and advancement.

job involvement The extent to which one is personally involved with one's job.

job posting Placing information about job vacancies and qualifications on bulletin boards, in newsletters, and on the organization's intranet.

job satisfaction The extent to which one feels positively or negatively about various aspects of one's work.

job simplification The process of reducing the number of tasks a worker performs.

job specification Description of the minimum qualifications a person must have to perform a job successfully.

joint ventures Organizations that join forces to realize strategic advantages that neither could have achieved alone; a U.S. firm may form a joint venture, also known as a *strategic alliance,* with a foreign company to share the risks and rewards of starting a new enterprise together in a foreign country.

justice approach One of four approaches to solving ethical dilemmas; ethical behavior is guided by respect for impartial standards of fairness and equity.

K

knowledge management Implementation of systems and practices to increase the sharing of knowledge and information throughout an organization; also, the development of an organizational structure—and the tools, processes, systems, and structures—that encourages continuous learning and sharing of knowledge and information among employees, for the purpose of making better decisions.

knowledge worker Someone whose occupation is principally concerned with generating or interpreting information, as opposed to manual labor.

L

large-batch technology Routinized products made by highly mechanized organizations; mass-production assembly-line technology.

leader–member exchange (LMX) model of leadership Model proposed by George Graen and Fred Dansereau that emphasizes that leaders have different sorts of relationships with different subordinates.

leadership The ability to influence employees to voluntarily pursue organizational goals.

leading Motivating, directing, and otherwise influencing people to work hard to achieve the organization's goals.

lean Six Sigma Quality-control approach that focuses on problem solving and performance improvement—speed with excellence—of a well-defined project; *see also* Six Sigma.

learned helplessness The debilitating lack of faith in one's ability to control one's environment.

learning organization An organization that actively creates, acquires, and transfers knowledge within itself and is able to modify its behavior to reflect new knowledge.

legitimate power One of five sources of a leader's power that results from formal positions with the organization.

licensing Company X allows a foreign company to pay it a fee to make or distribute X's product or service.

line managers Managers who have the authority to make decisions and usually have people reporting to them.

locus of control Measure of how much people believe they control

their fate through their own efforts.

loss Total costs exceed total sales revenue.

low-context culture Culture in which shared meanings are primarily derived from written and spoken words.

M

macroenvironment Also called *general environment;* includes six forces: economic, technological, sociocultural, demographic, political-legal, and international.

maintenance role Relationship-related role consisting of behavior that fosters constructive relationships among team members.

management The pursuit of organizational goals efficiently and effectively by integrating the work of people through planning, organizing, leading, and controlling the organization's resources.

management by exception Control principle that states that managers should be informed of a situation only if data show a significant deviation from standards.

management by objectives (MBO) Four-step process in which (1) managers and employees jointly set objectives for the employee, (2) managers develop action plans, (3) managers and employees periodically review the employee's performance, and (4) the manager makes a performance appraisal and rewards the employee according to results.

management by wandering around (MBWA) Style of management whereby a manager literally wanders around the organization and talks with people across all lines of authority.

management process Performing the planning, organizing, leading, and controlling necessary to get things done.

management science Sometimes called *operations research;* branch of quantitative management; method of solving management problems by using mathematics to aid in problem solving and decision making.

maquiladoras U.S. manufacturing plants allowed to operate in Mexico with special privileges in return for employing Mexican citizens.

market culture Type of organizational culture that has a strong external focus and values stability and control.

matrix structure Fourth type of organizational structure, which combines functional and divisional chains of command in a grid so that there are two command structures—vertical and horizontal.

maturity stage A stage when the organization becomes very bureaucratic, large, and mechanistic. Also the third stage in the product life cycle; period in which the product starts to fall out of favor, and sales and profits fall off.

means-end chain A hierarchy of goals; in the chain of management (operational, tactical, strategic), the accomplishment of low-level goals are the means leading to the accomplishment of high-level goals or ends.

mechanistic organization Organization in which authority is centralized, tasks and rules are clearly specified, and employees are closely supervised.

media richness Indication of how well a particular medium conveys information and promotes learning.

medium The pathway by which a message travels.

Mercosur The largest trade bloc in Latin America, with four core members: Argentina, Brazil, Paraguay, Uruguay.

message The information to be shared.

meta-analysis Statistical pooling technique that permits behavioral scientists to draw general conclusions about certain variables from many different studies.

middle managers One of three managerial levels; they implement the policies and plans of the top managers above them and supervise and coordinate the activities of the first-line managers below them.

midlife stage A period of growth evolving into stability when the organization becomes bureaucratic.

mission An organization's purpose or reason for being.

mission statement Statement that expresses the purpose of the organization.

modular structure Seventh type of organizational structure, in which a firm assembles product chunks, or modules, provided by outside contractors.

monochronic time The standard kind of time orientation in U.S business; preference for doing one thing at a time.

moral-rights approach One of four approaches to solving ethical dilemmas; ethical behavior is guided by respect for the fundamental rights of human beings.

most favored nation This trading status describes a condition in which a country grants other countries favorable trading treatment such as the reduction of import duties.

motivating factors Factors associated with job satisfaction—such as achievement, recognition, responsibility, and advancement—all of which affect the job content or the rewards of work performance.

motivation Psychological processes that arouse and direct goal-directed behavior.

multicommunicating The use of technology to participate in several interactions at the same time.

multinational corporation Business firm with operations in several countries.

multinational organization Nonprofit organization with operations in several countries.

N

National Labor Relations Board Legislated in 1935, U.S. commission that enforces the procedures whereby employees may vote to have a union and collective bargaining.

need-based perspectives Also known as *content perspectives;* theories that emphasize the needs that motivate people.

needs Physiological or psychological deficiencies that arouse behavior.

negative conflict Conflict that hinders the organization's performance or threatens its interests.

negative reinforcement Removal of unpleasant consequences following a desired behavior.

network structure Sixth type of organizational structure, whereby a central core is linked to outside independent firms by computer connections, which are used to operate as if all were a single organization.

noise Any disturbance that interferes with the transmission of a message.

nonrational model of decision making A model of decision-making style that explains how managers make decisions; they assume that decision making is nearly always uncertain and risky, making it difficult for managers to make optimum decisions.

nonverbal communication Messages in a form other than the written or the spoken word.

norming One of five stages of forming a team; stage three, in which conflicts are resolved, close relationships develop, and unity and harmony emerge.

norms General guidelines or rules of behavior that most group or team members follow.

North American Free Trade Agreement (NAFTA) Formed in 1994, the trading bloc consisting of the United States, Canada, and Mexico.

not bat an eye To not seem to see; to not react.

O

objective See *goal.*

objective appraisal Also called *results appraisal;* form of performance evaluation that is based on facts and that is often numerical.

open system System that continually interacts with its environment.

operating plan Typically designed for a 1-year period, this plan defines how a manager will conduct his or her business based on the action plan; the operating plan identifies clear targets such as revenues, cash flow, and market share.

operational control Monitoring performance to ensure that operational plans—day-to-day goals—are being implemented and taking corrective action as needed.

operational goals Goals that are set by and for first-line managers and are concerned with short-term matters associated with realizing tactical goals.

operational planning Determining how to accomplish specific tasks with available resources within the next 1-week to 1-year period; done by first-line managers.

operations management A branch of quantitative management; effective management of the production and delivery of an organization's products or services.

opportunities Situations that present possibilities for exceeding existing goals.

organic organization Organization in which authority is decentralized, there are fewer rules and procedures, and networks of employees are encouraged to cooperate and respond quickly to unexpected tasks.

organization A group of people who work together to achieve some specific purpose. A system of consciously coordinated activities or forces of two or more people.

organization chart Box-and-lines illustration of the formal relationships of positions of authority and the organization's official positions or work specializations.

organization development (OD) Set of techniques for implementing planned change to make people and organizations more effective.

organizational behavior (OB) Behavior that is dedicated to better understanding and managing people at work.

organizational citizenship behaviors Employee behaviors that are not directly part of employees' job descriptions—that exceed their work-role requirements—such as constructive statements about the department.

organizational commitment Behavior that reflects the extent to which an employee identifies with an organization and is committed to its goals.

organizational culture Sometimes called *corporate culture;* system of shared beliefs and values that develops within an organization and guides the behavior of its members.

organizational life cycle Four-stage cycle with a natural sequence of stages: birth, youth, midlife, and maturity.

organizational opportunities The environmental factors that the organization may exploit for competitive advantage.

organizational size Measurement of a group's size according to the number of full-time employees.

organizational strengths The skills and capabilities that give the organization special competencies and competitive advantages in executing strategies in pursuit of its mission.

organizational threats The environmental factors that hinder an organization's achieving a competitive advantage.

organizational weaknesses The drawbacks that hinder an organization in executing strategies in pursuit of its mission.

organizing Arranging tasks, people, and other resources to accomplish the work.

orientation Process of helping a newcomer fit smoothly into the job and the organization.

outputs The products, services, profits, losses, employee satisfaction or discontent, and the like that are produced by the organization; one of four parts of a system, along with inputs, transformation processes, and feedback.

outsourcing Subcontracting of services and operations to an outside vendor. Using suppliers outside the company to provide goods and services.

owners Those who can claim the organization as their legal property.

P

panic Situation in which a manager reacts frantically to get rid of a problem that he or she cannot deal with realistically.

parochialism Also known as *ethnocentrism;* narrow view in which people see things solely from their own perspective.

participative management (PM) The process of involving employees in (1) setting goals, (2) making decisions, (3) solving problems, and (4) making changes in the organization.

path–goal leadership model Contingency approach that holds that the effective leader makes available to followers desirable rewards in the workplace and increases their motivation by clarifying the paths, or behavior, that will help them achieve those goals and providing them with support.

pay for knowledge Situation in which employees' pay is tied to the number of job-relevant skills they have or academic degrees they earn.

pay for performance Situation in which an employee's pay is based on the results he or she achieves.

PDCA cycle A plan-do-check-act cycle using observed data for continuous improvement of operations.

perception Awareness; interpreting and understanding one's environment.

performance appraisal Assessment of an employee's performance and the provision of feedback.

performance management The continuous cycle of improving job performance through goal setting, feedback and coaching, and rewards and positive reinforcement.

performing The fourth of five stages of forming a team, in which members concentrate on solving problems and completing the assigned task.

personality The stable psychological traits and behavioral attributes that give a person his or her identity.

personalized power Power directed at helping oneself.

philanthropy Act of making charitable donations to benefit humankind.

piece rate Pay based on how much output an employee produces.

planning Setting goals and deciding how to achieve them. Also, coping with uncertainty by formulating future courses of action to achieve specified results.

planning/control cycle A cycle that has two planning steps (1 and 2) and two control steps (3 and 4), as follows: (1) Make the plan. (2) Carry out the plan. (3) Control the direction by comparing results with the plan. (4) Control the direction by taking corrective action in two ways—namely, (a) by correcting deviations in the plan being carried out, or (b) by improving future plans.

policy Standing plan that outlines the general response to a designated problem or situation.

political-legal forces Changes in the way politics shape laws and laws shape the opportunities for and threats to an organization.

polycentric managers Managers who take the view that native managers in foreign offices best understand native personnel and practices, and so the home office should leave them alone.

polychronic time Kind of time orientation common in Mediterranean, Latin American, and Arab cultures; preference for doing more than one thing at a time.

Porter's four competitive strategies (four generic strategies) (1) Cost-leadership, (2) differentiation, (3) cost-focus, (4) focused differentiation. The first two strategies focus on wide markets, the last two on narrow markets.

Porter's model for industry analysis Model proposed by Michael Porter for determining competitiveness within a particular industry; suggests that business-level strategies originate in five primary competitive forces in a firm's environment: (1) threats of new entrants, (2) bargaining power of suppliers, (3) bargaining power of buyers, (4) threats of substitute products or services, and (5) rivalry among competitors.

positive reinforcement The use of positive consequences to encourage desirable behavior.

power The measure of the extent to which a person is able to influence others so that they respond to orders.

predictive modeling Data mining technique used to predict future behavior and anticipate the consequences of change.

proactive change Planned change; making carefully thought-out changes in anticipation of possible or expected problems or opportunities; opposite of *reactive change.*

proactive personality Someone who is apt to take initiative and persevere to influence the environment.

problems Difficulties that inhibit the achievement of goals.

procedure Also known as *standard operating procedure;* a standing plan that outlines the response to particular problems or circumstances.

process innovation A change in the way a product or service is conceived, manufactured, or disseminated.

process perspectives Theories of employee motivation concerned with the thought processes by which people decide how to act: expectancy theory, equity theory, and goal-setting theory.

product division A divisional structure in which activities are grouped around similar products or services.

product innovation A change in the appearance or the performance of a product or a service or the creation of a new one.

product life cycle A model that graphs the four stages of a product or service during the "life" of its marketability: (1) introduction, (2) growth, (3) maturity, and (4) decline.

profit The amount by which total revenue exceeds total costs; a valuable return.

profit sharing The distribution to employees of a percentage of the company's profits.

program A single-use plan encompassing a range of projects or activities.

programmed conflict Conflict designed to elicit different opinions without inciting people's personal feelings.

project A single-use plan of less scope and complexity than a program.

project life cycle Cycle of a project with four stages from start to finish: definition, planning, execution, and closing.

project management Achieving a set of goals by planning, scheduling, and maintaining progress of the activities that constitute a project.

project management software Programs for planning and scheduling the people, costs, and resources to complete a project on time.

project planning Preparation of single-use plans, or projects.

Prospectors Managers who develop new products or services and seek out new markets, rather than waiting for things to happen.

punishment The application of negative consequences to stop or change undesirable behavior.

Q

quality The total ability of a product or service to meet customer needs.

quality assurance A means of ensuring quality that focuses on the performance of workers, urging employees to strive for "zero defects."

quality circles Small groups of volunteer workers and supervisors who meet intermittently to discuss workplace and quality-related problems.

quality control A means of ensuring quality whereby errors are minimized by managing each state of production.

quality-management viewpoint Perspective that focuses on quality control, quality assurance, and total quality management.

quantitative management An evolutionary form of operations research whereby quantitative techniques, such as statistics and computer simulations, are applied to management. Two branches of quantitative management are management science and operations management.

R

radical innovations New products, services, or technologies that replace existing ones.

radically innovative change Change involving a practice that is new to the industry.

RATER scale Scale enabling customers to rate the quality of a service along five dimensions—reliability, assurance, tangibles, empathy, and responsiveness—each on a scale from 1 (for very poor) to 10 (for very good).

ratio analysis The evaluation of financial ratios (the relationship of two or more things); includes liquidity ratios, debt management ratios,

asset management ratios, and return ratios.

rational model of decision making Also called the *classical model;* the style of decision making that explains how managers should make decisions; it assumes that managers will make logical decisions that will be the optimum in furthering the organization's best interests.

reactive change Change made in response to problems or opportunities as they arise. Compare *proactive change.*

Reactors Managers who make adjustments only when finally forced to by environmental pressures.

readiness The extent to which a follower possesses the ability and willingness to complete a task.

realistic job preview A picture of both positive and negative features of the job and organization given to a job candidate before he or she is hired.

receiver The person for whom a message is intended.

recruiting The process of locating and attracting qualified applicants for jobs open in the organization.

reduced cycle time The reduction of steps in the work process.

referent power One of five sources of a leader's power deriving from personal attraction.

reinforcement Anything that causes a given behavior to be repeated or inhibited; the four types are positive, negative, extinction, and punishment.

reinforcement theory The belief that behavior reinforced by positive consequences tends to be repeated, whereas behavior reinforced by negative consequences tends not to be repeated.

related diversification Strategy by which an organization under one

ownership operates separate businesses that are related to one another.

relaxed avoidance The situation in which a manager decides to take no action in the belief that there will be no great negative consequences.

relaxed change The situation in which a manager realizes that complete inaction will have negative consequences but opts for the first available alternative that involves low risk.

reliability Degree to which a test measures the same thing consistently, so that an individual's score remains about the same over time, assuming the characteristics being measured also remain the same.

representativeness bias The tendency to generalize from a small sample or a single event.

responsibility The obligation one has to perform the assigned tasks.

reward power One of five sources of a leader's power that results from the authority to reward subordinates.

risk propensity Willingness to gamble or to undertake risk for the possibility of gaining an increased payoff.

rites and rituals The activities and ceremonies, planned and unplanned, that celebrate important occasions and accomplishments in an organization's life.

role A socially determined expectation of how an individual should behave in a specific position; set of behaviors that people expect of occupants of a position.

rule Standing plan that designates specific required action.

S

sales commissions The percentage of a company's earnings as the result of a salesperson's sales that is paid to that salesperson.

Sarbanes-Oxley Act of 2002 Often shortened to *SarbOx* or *SOX;* act establishing requirements for proper financial record keeping for public companies and penalties for noncompliance.

satisficing model One type of nonrational decision-making model; managers seek alternatives until they find one that is satisfactory, not optimal.

scenario analysis Also known as *scenario planning* and *contingency planning;* the creation of alternative hypothetical but equally likely future conditions.

scientific management Management approach that emphasizes the scientific study of work methods to improve the productivity of individual workers.

selection process The screening of job applicants to hire the best candidate.

selective perception The tendency to filter out information that is discomforting, that seems irrelevant, or that contradicts one's beliefs.

self-efficacy Personal ability to do a task.

self-esteem Self-respect; the extent to which people like or dislike themselves.

self-fulfilling prophecy Also known as the *Pygmalion effect;* the phenomenon in which people's expectations of themselves or others leads them to behave in ways that make those expectations come true.

self-managed teams Groups of workers who are given administrative oversight for their task domains.

self-monitoring Observing one's own behavior and adapting it to external situations.

self-serving bias The attributional tendency to take more personal responsibility for success than for failure.

semantics The study of the meaning of words.

sender The person wanting to share information.

servant leaders Leaders who focus on providing increased service to others—meeting the goals of both followers and the organization—rather than on themselves.

sexual harassment Unwanted sexual attention that creates an adverse work environment.

shared leadership Simultaneous, ongoing, mutual influence process in which people share responsibility for leading.

simple structure The first type of organizational structure, whereby an organization has authority centralized in a single person, as well as a flat hierarchy, few rules, and low work specialization.

single-product strategy Strategy by which a company makes and sells only one product within its market.

single-use plan Plan developed for activities that are not likely to be repeated in the future; such a plan can be either a program or a project.

situational interview A structured interview in which the interviewer focuses on hypothetical situations.

situational leadership theory Leadership model that holds that leaders should adjust their leadership style according to the readiness of the followers.

Six Sigma A rigorous statistical analysis process that reduces defects in manufacturing and service-related industries.

skunkworks A project team whose members are separated from the normal operation of an organization and asked to produce a new, innovative product.

small-batch technology System in which goods are custom-made to customer specifications in small quantities.

SMART goal A goal that is Specific, Measurable, Attainable, Results oriented, and has Target dates.

social capital Economic or productive potential of strong, trusting, and cooperative relationships.

social loafing The tendency of people to exert less effort when working in groups than when working alone.

social responsibility Manager's duty to take action that will benefit society's interests as well as the organization's.

socialized power Power directed at helping others.

sociocultural forces Influences and trends originating in a country, society, or culture; human relationships and values that may affect an organization.

spam Unsolicited e-mail jokes and junk mail.

span of control The number of people reporting directly to a given manager.

special-interest groups Groups whose members try to influence specific issues.

special-purpose team A team that meets to solve a special or one-time problem.

stability strategy One of three grand strategies, this strategy involves little or no significant change.

staff personnel Staff with advisory functions; they provide advice, recommendations, and research to line managers.

stakeholders People whose interests are affected by an organization's activities.

standing plan Plan developed for activities that occur repeatedly over a period of time; such a plan consists of policies, procedures, or rules.

statistical process control A statistical technique that uses periodic random samples from production runs to see if quality is being maintained within a standard range of acceptability.

stereotype A standardized mental picture resulting from oversimplified beliefs about a certain group of people.

stereotyping The tendency to attribute to an individual the characteristics one believes are typical of the group to which that individual belongs.

stock options The right to buy a company's stock at a future date for a discounted price; often a benefit given to key employees.

storming The second of five stages of forming a team in which individual personalities, roles, and conflicts within the group emerge.

story A narrative based on true events, which is repeated—and sometimes embellished upon—to emphasize a particular value.

strategic allies Describes the relationship of two organizations that join forces to achieve advantages that neither can perform as well alone.

strategic control Monitoring performance to ensure that strategic plans are being implemented and taking corrective action as needed.

strategic goals Goals that are set by and for top management and focus on objectives for the organization as a whole.

strategic human resource planning The development of a systematic, comprehensive strategy for (1) understanding current employee needs and (2) predicting future employee needs.

strategic management A five-step process that involves managers from all parts of the organization in the formulation and implementation of strategies and strategic goals: establish the mission and the vision; establish the grand strategy; formulate the strategic plans; carry out the strategic plans; maintain strategic control.

strategic planning Determining what an organization's long-term goals should be for the next 1–10 years with the resources it expects to have available; done by top management.

strategic positioning Strategy that, according to Michael Porter, attempts to achieve sustainable competitive advantage by preserving what is distinctive about a company.

strategy A large-scale action plan that sets the direction for an organization.

strategy formulation The process of choosing among different strategies and altering them to best fit the organization's needs.

strategy implementation The execution of strategic plans.

strategy map A visual representation of the four perspectives of the balanced scorecard that enables managers to communicate their goals so that everyone in the company can understand how their jobs are linked to the overall objectives of the organization.

strength perspective Perspective of organizational culture that assumes that the strength of a corporate culture is related to a firm's long-term financial performance.

stress The tension people feel when they are facing or enduring extraordinary demands, constraints, or opportunities and are uncertain about their ability to handle them effectively.

stressor The source of stress.

structured interview Interview in which the interviewer asks each applicant the same questions and then compares the responses to a standardized set of answers.

subjective appraisal Form of performance evaluation based on a manager's perceptions of an employee's traits or behaviors.

subsystems The collection of parts that make up the whole system.

sunk-cost bias (sunk-cost fallacy) Biased way of thinking in which managers add up all the money already spent on a project and conclude it is too costly to simply abandon it.

supplier A person or organization that provides supplies—raw materials, services, equipment, labor, or energy—to other organizations.

sustainability Economic development that meets the needs of the present without compromising the ability of future generations to meet their own needs.

SWOT analysis The search for the Strengths, Weaknesses, Opportunities, and Threats that affect an organization.

symbol An object, act, quality, or event that conveys meaning to others.

synergy Situation in which the economic value of separate, related businesses under one ownership and management is greater than the businesses are worth separately.

system A set of interrelated parts that operate together to achieve a common purpose.

systems viewpoint Perspective that regards the organization as a system of interrelated parts.

T

360-degree assessment A performance appraisal in which employees are appraised not only by their managerial superiors but also by peers, subordinates, and sometimes clients.

tactical control Monitoring performance to ensure that tactical plans—those at the divisional or departmental level—are being implemented and taking corrective action as needed.

tactical goals Goals that are set by and for middle managers and focus on the actions needed to achieve strategic goals.

tactical planning Determining what contributions departments or similar work units can make with their given resources during the next 6 months to 2 years; done by middle management.

tariff A trade barrier in the form of a customs duty, or tax, levied mainly on imports.

task environment Eleven groups that present you with daily tasks to handle: customers, competitors, suppliers, distributors, strategic allies, employee groups, local communities, financial institutions, government regulators, special-interest groups, and mass media.

task role Behavior that concentrates on getting the team's task done.

team A small group of people with complementary skills who are committed to a common purpose, performance goals, and approach to which they hold themselves mutually accountable.

team-based structure Fifth type of organizational structure, whereby teams or workgroups, either temporary or permanent, are used to improve horizontal relations and solve problems throughout the organization.

technical skills Skills that consist of the job-specific knowledge needed to perform well in a specialized field.

technological forces New developments in methods for transforming resources into goods or services.

technology All the tools and ideas for transforming material, data, or labor (inputs) into goods or services (outputs). It applies not just to computers but any machine or process that enables an organization to gain a competitive advantage in changing materials used to produce a finished product.

telecommute To work from home or remote locations using a variety of information technologies.

telepresence technology High-definition videoconference systems that simulate face-to-face meeting among users.

top managers One of three managerial levels; they make the long-term decisions about the overall direction of the organization and establish the objectives, policies, and strategies for it.

total quality management (TQM) A comprehensive approach—led by top management and supported throughout the organization—dedicated to continuous quality improvement, training, and customer satisfaction. It has four components: (1) Make continuous improvement a priority. (2) Get every employee involved. (3) Listen to and learn from customers and employees. (4) Use accurate standards to identify and eliminate problems.

trade protectionism The use of government regulations to limit the import of goods and services.

trading bloc Also known as an *economic community;* a group of nations within a geographical region that have agreed to remove trade barriers with one another.

training Educating technical and operational employees in how to better do their current jobs.

trait approaches to leadership Attempts to identify distinctive characteristics that account for the effectiveness of leaders.

transactional leader One who focuses on the interpersonal transactions between managers and employees.

transactional leadership Leadership style that focuses on clarifying employees' roles and task requirements and providing rewards and punishments contingent on performance.

transformation processes The organization's capabilities in management and technology that are applied to converting inputs into outputs; one of four parts of a system, along with inputs, outputs, and feedback.

transformational leadership Leadership style that transforms employees to pursue organizational goals over self-interests.

trend analysis A hypothetical extension of a past series of events into the future.

turnover The movement of employees in and out of an organization when they obtain and then leave their jobs.

two core principles of TQM (1) *People orientation*—everyone involved with the organization should focus on delivering value to customers; and (2) *improvement orientation*—everyone should work on continuously improving the work processes.

two-factor theory Herzberg's theory that proposes that work satisfaction and dissatisfaction arise from two different work factors—work satisfaction from so-called motivating factors and work dissatisfaction from so-called hygiene factors.

Type A behavior pattern Behavior describing people involved in a chronic, determined struggle to accomplish more in less time.

U

underemployed Working at a job that requires less education than one has.

unity of command Principle that stresses an employee should report to no more than one manager in order to avoid conflicting priorities and demands.

unrelated diversification Operating several businesses that are not related to one another under one ownership.

unstructured interview Interview in which the interviewer asks probing questions to find out what the applicant is like.

upward communication Communication that flows from lower levels to higher levels.

utilitarian approach One of four approaches to solving ethical dilemmas; ethical behavior is guided by what will result in the greatest good for the greatest number of people.

V

valence The value or the importance a worker assigns to a possible outcome or reward.

validity Extent to which a test measures what it purports to measure and extent to which it is free of bias.

value system The pattern of values within an organization.

values Abstract ideals that guide one's thinking and behavior across all situations; the relatively permanent and deeply held underlying beliefs and attitudes that help determine a person's behavior.

variable budget Allowing the allocation of resources to vary in proportion with various levels of activity.

variable costs Expenses that vary directly depending on the numbers of the product that one produces and sells.

videoconferencing Using video and audio links along with computers to enable people located at different locations to see, hear, and talk with one another.

virtual bank A bank with no building to go to; an Internet bank.

virtual organization Organization whose members are geographically apart, usually working with e-mail, collaborative computing, and other computer connections, while often appearing to customers and others to be a single, unified organization with a real physical location.

vision A long-term goal describing "what" an organization wants to become; it is a clear sense of the future and the actions needed to get there.

vision statement Statement that expresses what the organization should become and where it wants to go strategically.

W

whistleblower An employee who reports organizational misconduct to the public.

wholly-owned subsidiary A foreign subsidiary, or subordinate section of an organization, that is totally owned and controlled by the organization.

work teams Teams that engage in collective work requiring coordinated effort; they are of four types, which may be identified according to their basic purpose: advice teams, production teams, project teams, and action teams.

World Bank One of three principal organizations designed to facilitate international trade; its purpose is to provide low-interest loans to developing nations for improving transportation, education, health, and telecommunications.

World Trade Organization (WTO) One of three principal organizations designed to facilitate international trade; it is designed to monitor and enforce trade agreements.

Y

youth stage The stage in which the organization is in a prebureaucratic phase, one of growth and expansion.

Z

zero-based budgeting (ZBB) Forcing each department to start from zero in projecting its funding needs for the coming budget period.

credits

CHAPTER 1

Photos: Page 4, AP Photo/Joe Cavaretta; 5, © Dynamic Graphics/PictureQuest/DAL; 6, Chip Somodeville/Getty Images; 7, Eric Audras/PhotoAlto/PictureQuest/DAL; 9, Robyn Beck/AFP/Getty Images; 10, © Brian Williams & Stacy Sawyer; 12, AP Photo/Pat Sullivan; 14, AP Photo/Christophe Ena; 16, AP Photo/Mark Lennihan; 17, AP Photo/Ben Margot; 18, © Mark Leet Photography; 19, Eric Audras/PhotoAlto/PictureQuest/DAL; 20, AP Photo/John Todd; 21, AP Photo/Frederick Smith; 23, AP Photo/Mark Sakuma; 25 , © 2008 Morton Buildings, Inc/Courtesy of Woodward Camp. All rights reserved; 26, AP Photo/Manish Swarup; 28, AP Photo/Jeff Christensen.

CHAPTER 2

Photos: Page 43, © Bettmann/CORBIS; 44, © Underwood & Underwood/CORBIS; 45, Sean Gallup/Getty Images; 46, © Bettmann/CORBIS; 47, Courtesy of AT&T Archives and History Center, Warren, NJ; 48, Courtesy of Debra's Natural Gourmet; 50, Justin Sullivan/Getty Images; 54 Top, © Mark Richards/PhotoEdit; 54 Bottom, © Kayte M. Deioma/PhotoEdit; 59, Courtesy of MIT Press.

CHAPTER 3

Photos: Page 72, © Mark Peterson/CORBIS; 74, © The McGraw-Hill Companies, Inc./John Flournoy, photographer/DAL; 75, Tom Boyle/Getty Images; 78 Top, © Andre Jenny/The Image Works; 78 Bottom, © The McGraw-Hill Companies, Inc./John Flournoy, photographer/DAL; 79, © age fotostock/SuperStock; 81, © Comstock Images/PictureQuest/DA; 85, © Reuters/CORBIS; 87, © Mike Segar/CORBIS; 88, © Eric Millette Photography; 93, © Royalty-Free/CORBIS/DAL; 94, AP Photo/Haraz Ghanbari; 95, Scott T. Baxter/Getty Images/DAL; 96, Courtesy of Johnson & Johnson.

CHAPTER 4

Photos: Page 108, Joseph Van Os/Getty Images; 109, AP Photo/Michael Probst; 110, Jacobs Stock Photography/Getty Images/DAL; 112, © Royalty-Free/CORBIS/DAL; 113, Chung Sung-Jun/Getty Images; 117, AP Photo/Steven Senne; 118, John A. Rizzo/Getty Images/DAL; 122, AP Photo/Gerald Herbert; 129, © 2008 Toyota Motor Sales, U.S.A., Inc.

CHAPTER 5

Photos: Page 141, © Corbis/SuperStock/RF; 143, © The McGraw-Hill Companies, Inc./Jill Braaten, photographer/DAL; 152, © David Young-Wolff/PhotoEdit; 158, Image100/PunchStock/DAL.

CHAPTER 6

Photos: Page 168, © Roberts Publishing Services; 170, AP Photo/Ric Francis; 173, AP Photo/Frank Franklin II; 175, © Reuters/CORBIS; 177, © Roberts Publishing Services; 181, © The McGraw-Hill Companies, Inc./Jill Braaten, photographer/DAL; 182, Courtesy of Southwest Airlines; 185, Steve Mason/Getty Images/DAL; 187, © Brian Williams & Stacy Sawyer; 190, AP Photo/Paul Sakuma.

CHAPTER 7

Photos: Page 202, AP Photo/Robert E. Klein; 204, Courtesy of Southwest Airlines; 207, © Royalty-Free/CORBIS/DAL; 209, AP Photo/Boeing; 210, AP Photo/Rene Macura; 213, AP Photo/Yakima Herald-Republic, Kris Holland; 215, © The McGraw-Hill Companies, Inc./John Flournoy, photographer/DAL; 216, AP Photo/Marcus R. Donner; 220, Digital Vision/Getty Images/DAL; 222, Photodisc/PunchStock/DAL; 224, Photodisc/PunchStock/DAL.

CHAPTER 8

Photos: Page 240, Ryan McVay/Getty Images/DAL; 241, Courtesy of HP; 249, Tsuno Yoshkazu/APF/Getty Images; 251, Eric Audras/Paloalto/PictureQuest/DAL; 253, Digital Vision/RF; 255, Skip Nall/Getty Images/DAL; 261, Mike Clark/APF/Getty Images; 263, © Najlah Feanny/CORBIS; 265, John MacDougall/APF/Getty Images.

CHAPTER 9

Photos: Page 278, AP Photo/John Amis; 279, © Chevron Corporation and used with permission; 283, Ablestock/Alamy/RF; 290, Courtesy of Lafayette Instrument Company, Inc.; 291, BananaStock/PictureQuest/DAL; 293, © Digital Vision/Getty Images/DAL; 294, Ryan McVay/Getty Images/DAL; 298, Photodisc/Getty Images/RF; 299, © Royalty-Free/CORBIS/DAL.

CHAPTER 10

Photos: Page 313, © The McGraw-Hill Companies, Inc./John Flournoy, photographer/DAL; 318, Sony Ericsson/Getty Images; 321, © OJO Images/SuperStock/RF; 323, AP Photo/Paul Sakuma; 331, Rick Gershon/Getty Images.

CHAPTER 11

Photos: Page 340, © Royalty-Free/CORBIS/DAL; 347, Courtesy of New School University; 348, © Najlah Feanny/CORBIS; 350, © Ben Van Hook Photography; 355, Stockbyte/PunchStock Images/DAL; 357, © Royalty-Free/CORBIS/DAL; 360, Ryan McVay/Getty Images/DAL.

CHAPTER 12

Photos: Page 372, © Tony Freeman/PhotoEdit; 381, AP Photo/Colin Anderson/Jupiterimages/RF; 383, AP Photo/The Canadian Press, Frank Gunn; 384, Stockbyte Platinum/Getty Images/DAL; 387, © Digital Vision/Getty Images/DAL; 391, Keith Brofsky/Getty Images/DAL; 393, Photo by Howard Sokol/Courtesy of The Boppy Pillow; 397, Photodisc/Getty Images/RF.

CHAPTER 13

Photos: Page 408, Digital Vision/DAL; 410, © Gerhard Joren/ OnAsia Images; 413, © Electronic Arts, Inc.; 417, © Tom Pretty- man/PhotoEdit; 420, © The McGraw-Hill Companies, Inc./John Flournoy, photographer/DAL; 422, AP Photo/Damian Dovarga- nes; 426, © Brand X Pictures/PunchStock/DAL.

CHAPTER 14

Photos: Page 437, Thomas Engstom/Getty Images; 439, Anne Knudsen/Getty Images; 446, John A. Rizzo/Getty Images/RF; 448, Photodisc/Getty Images/DAL; 452, AP Photo/Elaine Thompson; 454, Doug Menuez/Getty Images/RF; 456, AP Photo/Virgin America/Bob Riha, Jr.

CHAPTER 15

Photos: Page 470, Ryan McVay/Getty Images/DAL; 474, Photo- disc/Getty Images/RF; 478, Photodisc/Getty Images/RF; 482, Image Source/Getty Images/RF; 484, © Digital Vision/DAL; 487, Zigy Kaluzny/Getty Images; 490, Photodisc/Getty Images/RF; 491, © Comstock/CORBIS/RF; 493, © moodboard/CORBIS/RF.

CHAPTER 16

Photos: Page 505, © Royalty-Free/CORBIS/DAL; 510, © im- age100/CORBIS; 517, © Royalty-Free/CORBIS/DAL; 518, Oscar Abetta/Getty Images; 521, AP Photo/ Kevork Djansezian; 525, Courtesy of Viking Corporation; 531, Courtesy of Instituto Pro- Natura; 533, Kim Steele/Getty Images/DAL.

name index

Page numbers followed by n indicate material found in notes.

company index

subject index

Constancy of purpose, 59
Constitutional rights, 82
Constructive conflict, **421**, 422–423, 425–427
Consultation, 440, 441
Contemporary perspectives of management, **41**, 52–59
Content perspectives on motivation, **372**–378
Contests, 426
Contingency approaches to leadership, 441, **448**–453
Contingency design, **262**–266
Contingency factors in job characteristics model, 388
Contingency leadership model (Fiedler), **448**–449
Contingency planning, **180**–182
Contingency viewpoint, 52, 56–**57**
Contingency workers, 395
Continuing education, 293, 396; *see also* Learning
Continuous improvement, 59, **525**; *see also* Quality
Continuous-process technology, **265**–266
Control
    defined, **14**, **506**
    effective management, 531–533
    financial, 511–512, 517, 518–521
    levels and areas of, 516–517
    locus of, 26, 342
    as management function, 437
    of meetings, 178
    over factors creating dissonance, 347
    purposes and processes of, 506–510
    span of, 253
    strategic, 177
    stress from lack of, 358
    tools for, 511–515, 518–521, 536–538
Control charts, 530
Control freaks, 375
Control process steps, **508**–510
Control standards, **509**
Controlling, **14**, **506**
Controversial issues, writing about, 492
Conventional morality, 84
Cooperation, 46–47, 49
Cooperative conflict, 421
Coordinated effort, **252**
Coordination, 141–142
Core business, defending, 142
Core competencies, 264
Core job characteristics, 387–388
Core processes, 191–192
Corporate buyers, computer sales to, 155
Corporate culture; *see* Organizational culture
Corporate scandals; *see* Ethics; Executive
    misconduct
Corporate social responsibility, **86**–90
Corrective actions, 154, 177, 510
Cost-benefit analyses, ethics based on, 82
Cost controls, 507
Cost-focus strategy, **185**
Cost-leadership strategy, **184**
Counterproductive work behaviors, **351**
Countertrading, **117**
Coursematch, 23
Cramming, 29
Creativity, 206; *see also* Innovation
Credibility, 227, 477; *see also* Trust
Credit cards, cell phones as, 318
Credit Mobilier scandal, 83
Crises
    as catalyst for strategic management, 173–174
    handling personally, 239
    responses as reflection of culture, 247
    as stressors, 358
Criticism, 297, 420
Cross-cultural communications, 472, 475–476
Cross-functional teams; *see also* Teams
    advantages, 258
    defined, 409, **410**
    in TQM approach, 524, 527
Cruise ships, 185
Cuba, U.S. embargo, 119
Cubicles, 396, 397, 474, 475
Cultural adaptability, 130

Cultural areas of control, 517
Cultural changes, 79–80
Cultural creatives, 374
Cultural differences; *see also* Diversity;
    Organizational culture
    as communication barriers, 475–476
    interpersonal space, 127, 478
    as key management challenge, 10
    major types, 127–128
    models, 123–125
    respecting, 105, 111, 122–123
    within virtual teams, 405
Culture shock, 122–123
Cultures, **122**; *see also* Organizational culture
Current assets, 520
Curse of knowledge, 205, 322
Customer divisions, **256**
Customer experience, 76
Customer service
    Amazon.com emphasis, 76
    competitive importance, 8–9, 513
    cost of problems, 207
    improving at T-Mobile, 400–401
Customer value, 524
Customers
    changing experience for, 171
    compensating for bad experiences, 173–174
    defined, **75**
    employee conflicts with, 402–403
    foreign, 111
    impact of company ethics on, 90
    listening to, 59, 65–66
    loyalty as strength, 181
    performance appraisal by, 295, 296
    responsiveness to, 8, 322, 513
    role in TQM, 522, 524
    strategy role of, 461
Cycle times, 529

D
- -
Dabble time, 541
Dashboards, 511, 536–538
Data analysis, 214–215
Data gathering, 233–234
Data-mining software, 56, 214
Databases, **11**, 278
Deadlines, 153, 159, 423, A3
Debt management ratios, 520
Decentralized authority, **254**, 508
Decentralized control, **517**
Deception on résumés, 286
Deciding to decide, **226**–227
Decision making
    barriers to, 225–229
    bias in, 201, 227–229
    centralized versus decentralized, 254, 508
    defined, **202**
    delays in, 230, 464–465
    employee involvement approaches, 527
    ethical guidelines, 216–218
    evidence-based principles, 212–215
    in groups, 219–224, 419–420, 427, 429
    impact of technology on, 11
    management science approach, 50
    nonrational model, 209–211
    painful, 167
    rational model, 205–209
    reversing big decisions, 229
    types and styles, 202–204
Decision-making styles, **203**
Decision trees, **216**–218
Decisional roles of management, **21**, 22
Decisions, **202**
Decline stage (product life cycle), **186**
Declining careers, 139
Decoding, **471**, 475
Defect reduction, 523–524, 530
Defenders, **142**
Defensive avoidance, **226**
Defensive strategies, **176**

Definition stage (project life cycle), 158
Delays, 177, 230, 464–465
Delegating
    defined, **254**
    guidelines for, 239
    in Hersey-Blanchard theory, 453
    of reading, 491
Deming management, 522–523
Demographic forces, **80**, 93–95, 316
Demonstrators, 78, 120
Demotion, 301
Depression, stress and, 360
Deregulation, 107
Descriptive models of decision making, 208, 209
Design of jobs for motivation, 385–388
Desktop publishing software, 278
Development (employee), **292**, 293
Deviations from standards, 509–510
The Devil Wears Prada, 422
Devil's advocacy, **426**
Diagnosis, **206**, 319–320
Dialectic method, **426**–427
Diamonds in the Data Mine, 214
Differential rate systems, 43
Differentiation of organizations, **264**
Differentiation strategy, **184**–185
Difficulty of goals, 150, 153
Digital document storage, 89
Digital video disks, 187
Dignity of human life, 218
Direction setting, 170, 437
Directive decision-making style, 203
Directive leadership, 450
Directness, 480
Directors as stakeholders, 74
Disabled workers, 95
Discipline, 301
Discontinuous change, 197
Discrimination
    avoiding in promotions, 300
    current trends, 94–95
    defined, **282**
    laws against, 280–282
    reverse, 96
    rise in complaints, 282
Dismissals; *see* Firings
Disneyland, 175
Disobedience, 253
Displaying confidence, 480
Disruptive innovation, 313
Dissatisfaction, 316–317, 377–378
Disseminator role, 21, 22
Distorted perceptions, 352–356
Distractions, 20, 21, 29, 490
Distress, 358
Distributors, **76**
Disturbance handler role, 21, 22
Diversification, opposition to, 162
Diversification strategies, **188**–189
Diversity; *see also* Cultural differences
    barriers to, 95–97
    in cultural behavior, 124–125
    defined, **91**
    dimensions, 91–93
    encouraging, 503
    as key management challenge, 10, 300
    trends, 93–95
Division of labor, **252**, **414**
Divisional structures
    basic types, **256**, 257
    diversification through, 188, 256
    managing size of, 265
DivX disk, 187
DMAIC, 530
DocBase Direct, 529
Doctors
    ethics, 81–82
    evidence-based practice, 39, 62
    gifts from drug salespeople, 336
Doha Round, 119
Downsizing, 301
Downward communication, **483**

Dreamliner aircraft, 208–209, 212
Dress, 105, 287
Dress, culturally sensitive, 105
Dropouts, 95
Drug abuse, stress and, 360–361
Drug-benefit programs, 195–196
Drug sales, 336
Drug testing, 289
Dumping, **119**
DVDs, 187, 324
Dysfunctional conflict, 421
Dyslexia, 20

E

E-business, **11**
E-commerce, **11**, **107**, 183
E-leadership, **460**–461
E-learning, 293
E-mail
    benefits of, 486
    defined, **11**
    effective writing in, 492
    executives' use of, 19
Eagle feathers, 236
Early behaviorism, 46–48
Echo Boomers, 55
Econometrics, 88
Economic communities, 120–121
Economic forces, **79**
Economic performance, cultures promoting, 245–248
Economic value of organizations, 87–88
Economies, national, 107–108
Economies of scale, 264
Edsel mistake, 55
Education, 293, 396; *see also* Learning; Training
Education levels, 95, 116, 286
Effectiveness, **5**, 207, 471
Efficiency
    as classical management goal, 42–45
    in communications, 471
    competitive importance, 10
    defined, **5**
    of group decision making, 220
    impact of company ethics on, 90
Effort-to-performance expectancy, 382
Egos, 477
85-15 rule, 59
Electronic brainstorming, **223**
Embargoes, **119**
Embarrassment, avoiding, 417
Emergencies; *see* Crises
Emotional intelligence, **344**, 365
Emotional stability, 340
Emotional stress, 357, 360
Emotions, influence on decisions, 225
Empathy, 344
Employee assistance programs, **361**
Employee benefits; *see* Fringe benefits
Employee-centered behavior, 446
Employee engagement, **392**
Employee fraud, 90
Employee involvement, 292, 527
Employee replacement, 300–302
Employee Retirement Income Security Act (ERISA), 281
Employee stock ownership plans, 74
Employees; *see also* Human resource management; Performance appraisal
    ability to execute strategy, 191
    collective bargaining with, 280
    as company stakeholders, 72, 74
    conflicts with customers, 402–403
    creation of project teams by, 429
    diversity, 91–97
    excessive control of, 532–533, 539
    fitting jobs to, 385–386
    as human capital, 61, 277, 291
    ill-suited to jobs, 305–306
    impact of company ethics on, 90

involving in decision making, 221, 524, 527, 533, 540–541
involving in quality management, 59, 524, 527, 540–541
listening to, 496–497
monitoring off-hours behavior, 432, 539
needs for change, 317
as partners, 181, 543
performance objectives, 150–152
predicting needs for, 279
promoting loyalty, 71
recruiting among, 284, 285
recruiting by, 285
resistance to change, 327, 328–331, 515
as resources, 276–279
theft by, 379, 533
Theory X and Theory Y views of, 48–49
as whistleblowers, 85, 99–101
Employment; *see* Jobs
Employment histories, lying about, 286
Employment tests, **289**–290
Enacted values, **242**
Encoding, **471**, 475
Encouragers, 416
Energy cycles, 28–29
Energy drinks, 143
Energy levels, 26, 28–29
Energy-saving measures, 89, 532
Energy Star products, 89
Engineering problems, 143
Enlargement of jobs, 385–386
Enrichment of jobs, 386
Entrepreneur role, 21, 22
Entrepreneurial problems, 143
Entrepreneurs, **24**
Entrepreneurship
    common lack of planning, 168
    defined, **24**
    elements of, 23–26
    innovation in, 324
Enumerations, 31
Environmental groups, 120, 531
Environmental protection
    businesses supporting, 88–89, 152, 531–532
    demonstrations supporting, 120
    organizational development for, 320–321
Environmental scanning, **179**
Environments
    in contingency viewpoint, 57, 262–264
    general forces of, 79–80
    impact on communications, 479
    opportunities and threats in, 179–180, 181
    promoting learning in, 62
    responses to uncertainty in, 142–143
    as stressors, 359
    supportive, 361
    sustainability, 88–89
    task environment forces, 75–78
Equal Employment Opportunity (EEO) Commission, **280**–282
Equal Pay Act, 281
Equity sensitivity, 401–402
Equity theory, **379**–381
ERG theory, **374**–375
Errors, controlling for, 51, 507
Escalation of commitment bias, **229**
Espoused values, **242**
Essay test-taking skills, 31–32
Esteem needs, 373
Ethical behavior, **81**
Ethical dilemmas, **81**
Ethics; *see also* Social responsibility
    approaches to, 82–83
    benefits to companies, 90
    as decision-making criterion, 206, 216–218
    defined, **81**
    guiding principles, 101–102
    as key management challenge, 11–12, 81
    promoting, 84–85
    training in, 83–84
    in transformational leadership, 456, 457
Ethics officers, **216**

Ethnic diversity, 10, 94; *see also* Diversity
Ethnic stereotypes, 354
Ethnocentrism, **96**, **112**
Etiquette, 476
European Union, 80, **121**
Euros, 121
Eustress, 358
Evaluation; *see also* Performance appraisal
    of organization development efforts, 320
    in rational decision making model, 206–207, 208
Evidence-based decision making, 212–215
Evidence-based management
    by Andy Grove, **439**
    defined, **40**
    elements of, 39
    growing emphasis on, 62
    tools for, 511
EWorkbench software, 11
Exam taking, 30–32
Exception, management by, 510
Exchange tactics, 440
Execution of strategies, 177, **190**–192
Execution stage (project life cycle), 158
Executive coaches, 481
Executive misconduct, 12, 83–84, 216; *see also* Ethics
Executive summaries, 491
Executives; *see* Chief executive officers; Top managers
Exercise, 360
Existence needs, 375
Expatriate managers, **129**–130
Expectancy theory, **381**–384
Expectations
    conflicting, 359
    influence on behavior, 356
    influence on decisions, 225
    for virtual teams, 405
Expense budgets, 519
Expenses, 520
Experience, openness to, 340
Expert power, **438**
Expertise, 205, 210, 322
Exporting, **116**
External audits, **521**
External communication, **484**
External dimensions of diversity, **93**
External forces of change, 316
External locus of control, 26, 342, 450
External opportunities and threats, 180, 181
External recruiting, **284**–285
External stakeholders, **75**–80
Extinction, **390**
Extinction threats, 82
Extranets, **486**
Extreme-sports retreats, 25
Extrinsic rewards, **371**
Extroversion, 340, 341
Exxon Valdez incident, 78
Eye contact, 478

F

Face-to-face communication, 473
Face-to-face contact jobs, 116
Facemash, 23
Facial expressions, 479
Fact gathering, 230
Fads, 167
Failure
    fear of, 329
    as necessary risk, 325, 326
    personality and, 342
    role in learning, 213–214, 230, 311
Fair Labor Standards Act, **280**
Fair Minimum Wage Act, 281
Fairness
    as common ethical dilemma, 83
    of control systems, 532
    as decision-making principle, 102, 218

Hersey-Blanchard situational leadership theory, 452–453
Herzberg's two-factor theory, 377–378, 385 386
Heuristics, **227**–229
Hierarchies
    communicating through, 482–483
    of needs, 48, 372–374
    of objectives, 152
    in organizational structures, 250, 252
    traditional support and alternatives, 41
Hierarchy cultures, **241**
Hierarchy of authority, **252**
Hierarchy of human needs, 48
High-context cultures, **123**
High-control situations, 449
High-performance cultures, 245–248
High school dropouts, 95
Higher-level needs, 373
Highlighting in written pieces, 493
Hinduism, 129
Hiring
    for commitment, 543
    discrimination prohibited, 280–282
    as management function, 436
    selection process overview, 285–290
Hispanics, 10, 80, 94
Histograms, 530
Historical perspectives of management
    behavioral, 46–49
    classical, 42–45
    defined, **41**
    quantitative, 50–51
Hofstede model, **123**–124
Holistic hunches, 210
Holistic wellness programs, **361**
Hollow organizations, 258–260
Homebuilding firms, 272
Homicides, 421
Homosexual workers, 94–95
Honesty, 218, 443
Hora peruana, 128
Horizontal command structures, 257
Horizontal communication, **483**–484
Horizontal loading, 386
Horizontal specialization, 250
Horse trading, 222
Hospital management, 51
Host countries, 105
Hostile environment harassment, 283
Hotels, 24, 51
Hours of work, 19–20
House's path-goal leadership model, 449–452
HP Way, 242, 246
HR generalists, 307
HRIS professionals, 307
Human capital, **61**, 277, 291
Human hair extensions, 106
Human life, respecting dignity of, 218
Human relations movement, **48**–49
Human resource inventories, **279**
Human resource management; *see also* Employees;
    Performance appraisal; Training
    advancement and discipline issues, 300–302, 305–306
    career paths, 307
    compensation and benefits issues, 298–299
    control tools for, 517
    defined, **276**
    legal issues in, 280–283
    major elements, 276–279
    orientation, training and development, 291–293
    performance appraisal, 294–297
    recruitment and selection, 284–290
Human skills, **27**–28
Humane orientation, 124, 125
Humaneness, 218
Hygiene factors, 377, **378**
Hypocrisy, 347

I

Idea generation; *see also* Innovation
    brainstorming, 223
    groupthink impact on, 419
    in learning organizations, 62
    through strategic planning, 170
Identity, from organizational culture, 244
Ignoring-randomness bias, 201
Illegal immigration, 94
Illiteracy, 95
Illnesses, stress-related, 357; *see also* Health
Illusion of unanimity, 419
The Illusions of Entrepreneurship, 324
Imagery, 29
Immigration Reform & Control Act, 281
Impartial controls, 532
Implementation, 177, 190–192, 207
Import quotas, 114, **119**
Importing, **115**
Improvement objectives, 151
Improvement orientation of TQM, 524, 525
In-group collectivism, 124, 125
In-group exchange, 458
Incentives; *see also* Motivation; Rewards
    aligning with company goals, 299
    defined, 298
    for drug purchases, 336
    for innovation, 326
    need for change, 317
    personality and, 342
    popular approaches, 392–397
    to spur constructive conflict, 426
Income statements, **520**
An Inconvenient Truth, 88
Incremental budgeting, **518**
Incremental innovations, **323**
Incremental model of decision making, **210**
Independent learning opportunities, 339
India
    as export market, 108
    general impact on markets, 313–314
    software services, 111–112, 114
Indirectness, 480
Individual approach to ethics, **82**
Individualism, 123, 124, 125
Indonesian currency crisis, 120
Industrial psychology, 46
Ineffective responses to problems, 225–226
Infection control, 51
Infiltration strategies, 186
Influence, leadership and, 439–441
Informal appraisals, **297**
Informal communication channels, **484**
Informal groups, **408**
Information overload, 473, **489**
Information resource controls, 517
Information sharing, 481
Information technology; *see also* Technology
    historic development, 106–107
    impact on Gen Y, 55
    impact on globalization, 108
    key management challenges of, 10–11, 61
    leadership based on, 460–461
    overview of communication tools, 485–489
    productivity gains from, 505
    teamwork via, 11, 405, 410
    use in recruiting and selection, 285
Informational roles of management, **21**
Ingratiating tactics, 440
Initiating structure, 447
Initiative, 3
Injury lawsuits, 366–367
Innovate system, 323
Innovation; *see also* Change
    ability to manage, 311
    attitudes toward, 348
    defined, **8**
    disruptive, 313
    growing emphasis on, 61
    loss under yes men, 364
    in management processes, 540–542

means of promoting, 322–327, 503, 513
medium-sized firm advantages, 262
organizational cultures promoting, 157, 241, 244, 323, 325 326, 541 542
overcoming resistance to, 328–331
planning for, 161–163
as strategic planning benefit, 170–171
from teams, 414
Innovation Jam, 348
Innovative change, **328**
Innovator's dilemma, 157
The Innovator's Dilemma, 313
Inputs, **53**, 379, 505
Inspections, 529
Inspiration; *see* Motivation
Inspirational appeals, 440, 441
Institutional collectivism, 124, 125
Institutional power, 375
Instrumentality, **382**
Insurance industry, 269–270
Integrated product development, 260
Integration, 47, **264**
Integrity, 341, 456
Intellectual stimulation, 219
Intelligence, emotional, 344, 365
Intelligence tests, 289
Interaction facilitation, 451
Interaction in teams, 414
Internal audits, **521**
Internal dimensions of diversity, **92**
Internal forces of change, 316–317
Internal locus of control, **26**, 342, 450
Internal processes, monitoring, 513
Internal recruiting, **284**, 285
Internal stakeholders, **74**
Internal strengths and weaknesses, 180, 181
International forces in business environment, **80**
International management challenges, 110–112
International Monetary Fund, **120**
International Organization for Standardization, 529
Internet
    background checking on, 287
    broadband services' impact, 227
    car buying via, 183
    competitive intelligence on, 189
    defined, **11**
    forces of change for, 318
    impact on communications, 11, 485–486
    impact on Gen Y, 55
    impact on print media, 314–315
    key management challenges of, 11, 61
    leadership based on, 460–461
    as personal computer sales channel, 76
    popularization of, 107
    use in recruiting and selection, 285
Internet Relay Chat, 260
Internships, 244
Interpersonal roles of management, **20**, 22
Interpersonal skills, 27–28
Interpersonal space, 127, 478
Interruptions, 20
Interventions for organizational problems, **320**
Interviewing, 286–289
Intimidation in groups, 219–220
Intranets, **485**–486
Intrapreneurs, **24**, 25, 326
Intrinsic rewards, **371**
Introduction stage (product life cycle), **186**
Introductions, making, 476
Introductions to verbal messages, 493
Intuition in hiring, 288
Intuition model of decision making, **210**–211
Inventory management controls, 517
Inverted U relationships, 357
Investment, globalization of, 108
Investors, employees as, 369
Involvement with jobs, 350
Invulnerability, sense of, 419
iPhones, 162
iPods, 68, 155, 162, 318

Maturity stage (product life cycle), **186**
MBO technique, 150–152
McClelland's acquired needs theory, 375–376
Means-end chains, **147**
Means versus ends, in control process, 533
Measurability of goals, 152–153
Measurement
     in basic control process, 509, 513–515
     of goals, 152–153
     for improving productivity, 503
     in performance appraisal, 294
     transmitting culture through, 248
Measurement-managed firms, 513–515
Meat industry, 80
Mechanistic organizations, 262–**263**
Media
     in communication process, **471**, 475
     for effective communication, 472–473
     as stakeholders, 78
Media richness, **473**
Medical Expense Manager, 246
Medical imaging, 67–68
Medical model of organization development, 319–320
Medical practice, 39, 62, 81–82
Medium-size companies, 262
Meetings, 178, 405, 487
Megamergers, 109
Memory chips, 439
Memory skills, 29
Mental imagery, 29
Mentoring, 251
Mercosur, **121**
Mergers and acquisitions
     as force for change, 318, 319
     global effects, 108–109
     in health care industry, 195, 196
Messages, **471**, 489
Metro 7 jeans, 55
Mexico, 114, 120
Microbreweries, 170
Microprocessors, 439
Middle managers, **16**–**17**, 146, 147
Midlife stage of organizations, **266**
Millennium Generation, 55, 339
Mindfulness, 57
Mindguards, 419
Mindlessness, 57
Minifirms, 109
Minimum wage, 280, 281
Minnesota Multiphasic Personality Inventory, 366
Minorities, 94, 282; *see also* Discrimination; Diversity
Mintzberg's study, 19–22
Mission
     as constancy of purpose, 59
     defined, **145**
     establishing, 174–176
     importance to motivation, 542
     introducing new employees to, 292
Mission statements
     basic purpose, 144–146, 174–175
     continuing importance, 167
     defined, **145**
     guidelines for creating, 175
Mistake proofing, 51
Mistakes, 51, 507; *see also* Failure
Mistrust, climates of, 329
Misunderstandings, 424
Misuse of technology, 488
Modeling, 215, 418
Moderate-control situations, 449
Modular structures, **261**
Momentum, 170
Moneyball, 214–215
Monitor role, 21, 22
Monochronic time, **127**
Moods, 225
Moral development, 84; *see also* Ethics
Moral principles, 218
Moral-rights approach, **82**, 101–102

Morale, 414, 537; *see also* Attitudes; Motivation
Most favored nation trading status, **121**
Motion studies, 43, 44
Motivating factors, in Herzberg's theory, 377, **378**
Motivating potential score, 388
Motivation; *see also* Incentives; Productivity; Rewards
     to accept change, 330
     compensation for, 383–384, 392–394
     importance to behavioral viewpoint, 46–49
     job design and, 385–388
     as leadership function, 437, 456
     MBO technique, 150–152, 295
     mission-based, 542
     needs-based theories, 372–378, 385–386
     from organizational culture, 243–244
     overview, **370**–371
     process views of, 379–384
     reinforcement perspectives, 389–391
     for team performance, 413
Movements, in communication, 479
Movie rentals, 324
MP3 players, 68
MRI technology, 67–68
Multicommunicating, **485**
Multinational organizations, 109, **110**; *see also* Large firms
Multiplier effect, 5–6
Multitasking, 21, 128, 481
Multivariable testing, 528
Mutual accountability, 413
Mutual-benefit organizations, 18, 249
Mutual funds, 216
Myers-Briggs Type Indicator, 289
Myths, 247

N

Namibia, 117
Narrow markets, 184
Narrow span of control, 253
National cultures, 122; *see also* Cultural differences
National Labor Relations Board, **280**
Native American students, 236
Natural beef, 315
Necessity entrepreneurs, 26
Need for achievement, 26, 376
Needs, role in motivation, 370–371, **372**–378
Needs hierarchy, 48, 372–374
Negative conflict, **421**, 422
Negative reinforcement, **389**–390
Negative stress, 358, 359–360
Negotiations, 479
Negotiator role, 21, 22
Nervousness while speaking, 493
NetSuite software, 537, 538
Network structures, **258**–261
Network television, 9
Networking, 3
Neuromarketing, 68
New competitors, 183
New jobs, 275
News leaks, 155
News media, 314–315
Newspaper advertising effectiveness, 528
Newspaper reading tips, 491
Newton Messagepad, 54
Niche products, 312–313
Nintendo, 55
No-jerk rule, 422
Noise, in communication process, **472**
Nonmonetary budgets, 519
Nonmonetary incentives, 394–397
Nonprofit organizations
     basic attributes, 18, 249
     boards of directors, 74
     economic value of, 87
     general management, 18
Nonrational decision making, **209**–211
Nonverbal communications
     cultural differences, 123

elements of, **478**–479
     manners as, 476
     noise in, 472
Nonwork demands, 359
Norming stage (team), **412**
Norms, **416**–417
North American Free Trade Agreement, **120**
Note taking, 30
Numbered lists, 31

O

Oakland Athletics, 214–215
Obedience, 253
Obesity, 80
Objective appraisals, **294**–295
Objective controls, 532
Objective test-taking skills, 31
Objectives; *see also* Goals
     conflicts over, 424
     defined, **147**
     imprecise, 515
     management by, 150–152, 295
     motivation and, 383, 384
Observable artifacts, 241–242
Observing performance, 509
Occupational Safety and Health Act, 280, 281
Occupational Safety and Health Administration, 85
Off-the-job training, 293
Office politics, 240
Office retail stores, 171
Offshoring, 115–116, 132–134, 313–314; *see also* Outsourcing
Ohio State leadership model, 446–447
On-demand TV technologies, 9
On-the-job training, 293
Onboarding, 291
One-call resolution, 401
100 Best Companies, 276
Online auctions, 109
Online bookstores, 107
Online commerce, 11, 107, 183
Online distribution of personal computers, 76
Online training, 293
Open body positions, 479
Open-book management, 71
Open-source software, 322–323
Open systems, **54**–55
Openness to experience, 340
Operant conditioning, 389
Operating budgets, 519
Operating plans, **147**
Operational control, **516**
Operational goals, **147**, 148
Operational planning, 144, **146**, 147, 192
Operations management, **51**
Operations process, 192
Operations research, 50
Opportunities
     defined, **206**
     organizational, 180, 181
     recognizing, 327, 507
Opportunity entrepreneurs, 26
Optimism, excessive, 213, 419
Options, abandoning, 159
Oral communication skills, 493–494
Oral foods, 315
Oral reports, 509
Organic foods, 315
Organic organizations, **263**, 265, 266
Organization charts, **249**–250
Organization development, **319**–321
Organizational behavior, **345**
Organizational citizenship behaviors, **351**
Organizational commitment, **350**; *see also* Commitment
Organizational culture
     applicants' fit with, 288
     basic types and levels, 241–243
     building execution into, 192
     constructive conflict in, 426

Procrastination, 21, 226, 230
Product development, 161–163
Product divisions, **256**
Product innovation, **323**; *see also* Innovation
Product integration, 9
Product life cycle
    defined, **185**
    as force for global expansion, 113–114
    need for planning in, 142
    strategies in, 185–186
Production teams, 409
Productivity; *see also* Motivation; Quality
    age and, 353
    attitude and, 349–350
    as classical management goal, 42–45
    controlling for, 507
    cooperation and, 49
    growth rates, 79, 505
    Hawthorne effect, 47–48
    human relations and, 48–49
    impact of gains on employment, 115
    measuring, 350
    organizational cultures promoting, 245–248
    overview and importance, 504–505
    technology barriers, 488–489
    tips for improving, 503
Professional associations, 76–77
Profit sharing, **394**
Profitability of projects, A6
Profits, 87, 90, 511–512, A5
Programmed conflict, **426–427**
Programs, **149**
Progress, role of plans in assessing, 141
Project life cycle, **157**–159
Project management, **156**
Project management software, **11**
Project planning, **156**–159, A1–A6
Project teams, 410
Projects defined, **149**
Promotions, 20, 248, 300–301
Prospect theory, 229
Prospectors, **142–143**
Protectionism, **118**–119
Protective tariffs, 118
Protestants, 128
Protestors, 78, 120
Prototypes, treating organizations as, 212–213
Psychological stress, 360
Psychology, 46
Public services, outsourcing, 528
Public speaking skills, 493–494
Puget Sound Chinook, 82
Punishment, **390**, 391, 438
Purpose, 144, 492
Pygmalion effect, 356
Pyramid model of management, 15–17, 41

Q

Quality; *see also* Productivity
    competitive importance, 8–9
    defined, **58**
    management focused on, 52, 58–59
    methods for promoting, 410, 522–530
Quality assurance, 52, **58**
Quality circles, 409, **410**, 527
Quality control, 52, **58**, 507
Quality-management viewpoint, 52, **58**–59
Quantitative viewpoints of management, **50**–51
Questioning, 30, 480, 490
QuickBooks, 246
Quicken, 246
Quid pro quo harassment, 283
Quotas, 114, 119, 282

R

Race discrimination, 282
Racial diversity, 10, 91, 94
Racial stereotypes, 354; *see also* Stereotypes
Radical innovations, **323**, **329**

Radically innovative change, **329**
Random sampling, 529
Range of variation, 509–510
RATER scale, 526
Ratio analysis, **520**
Rational decision making, **205**–209
Rational persuasion, 440, 441
Rationalization, 419
Raw materials, 113
RAZR phone, 260
Reactive change, **314**–315
Reactors, **143**
Readiness of employees, **452**
Reading, 30, 491–492
Ready-mix concrete, 234–235
Real estate sales, 229
Realism, 192
Realistic controls, 532
Realistic job previews, **285**
Receivers, **471**, 475
Reciting, 30
Recognition, 71
Recommendations, checking, 286
Recruiting; *see also* Hiring; Human resource
        management
    basic approaches, 284–285
    for commitment, 543
    costs, 351
    defined, **284**
    discrimination prohibited, 280–282
Recycling, 89
Reduced cycle times, **529**
Reference checks, 286
Referent power, **438**
Refreezing stage (Lewin model), 330
Regents, 74
Regional trade organizations, 120–121
Registars, 529
Regulatory agencies, **77**–78
Rehearsing, 29
Reinforcement, defined, **389**
Reinforcement perspectives on motivation,
        389–391
Reinforcement theory, **389**
Related diversification, **188**–189
Relatedness needs, 375
Relationship behavior, in Hersey-Blanchard theory,
        452
Relationship management, emotional intelligence
        and, 344
Relationship-oriented leadership, 448, 449
Relationships in leader-member exchange model,
        458
Relaxed avoidance, **225**–226
Relaxed change, **226**
Reliability of tests, 290
Religion, 91, 128, 129
Renewable energy, 89
Repetitive jobs, 385
Replacing employees, 300–302
Reports, 509, 533
Repossessed homes, 327
Representation and networking, 451
Representativeness bias, **228**
Reprimands, 391
Research and development, 503
Research papers, 158
Resentment over promotions, 301
Resistance
    to innovation, 327, 328–331, 515
    to strategy implementation, 177
Resource allocator role, 21, 22
Resources
    budgeting, 436, 518–519
    conflicts over, 423
    large team advantages, 414
    people as, 524
    providing for innovation, 325–326
Respect, rituals of, 105
Responsibility, **253**, 386; *see also* Authority; Power
Restaurants, 507
Results appraisals, 294–295

Results-oriented goals, 153
Résumés, screening, 286
Retention, 71, 110, 129–130; *see also* Turnover
Retrenchment strategies, **176**
Return ratios, 520
Revenue tariffs, 118
Revenues, 90, 519, 520, A5
Reverse discrimination, 96
Reversing big decisions, 229
Reviewing for exams, 30–31
Reward power, **438**
Rewards; *see also* Incentives; Motivation
    basic types, 371
    creating dissonance, 347
    in equity theory, 379–380
    in expectancy theory, 383
    failure to support change, 330
    importance to execution, 192
    for innovation, 326, 327
    leadership based on, 454–455
    monetary and nonmonetary types, 392–397
    personality and, 342
    as positive reinforcement, 389, 391
    to spur constructive conflict, 426
    for study, 29
    for teams, 429–430
    transmitting culture through, 248
    for whistleblowers, 85
Rework, avoiding, 525
Richness of media, 473
Rights theory, 101–102
Risk
    denying, 226
    in entrepreneurship, 24–25, 26
    innovation and, 323, 325
Risk propensity, **202**
Risk reduction, 188–189
Risk tolerance, 26, 515
Rites and rituals, 105, **243**
Rivalry among competitors, 184
Role ambiguity, 359
Role conflict, 359
Role modeling, 247
Role overload, 358–359
Role-playing, 426–427
Roles
    norms for, 417
    as stressors, **358**–359
    on teams, 411–412, **415**
Root-cause analysis, 51
Routine decisions, 239
Routines, introducing new employees to, 292
Rubicon Programs, 18
Rules, **149**
Rules of thumb, 227–229
Rumors, 329
Run charts, 530
Russia, 125

S

Sabbaticals, 397
Sabotage, 469, 533
Safety hazards, reporting, 85, 99–101
Safety laws, 280, 281
Safety needs, 373
Salaries, 6, 16, 298; *see also* Compensation
Sales, impact of company ethics on, 90
Sales budgets, 519
Sales commissions, **393**
Sales force peer learning, 408
Sales revenues, A5
Salt River Pima-Maricopa Indian Community, 236
Samples, 201, 529
Sarbanes–Oxley Act, **83**, 281
Satisfaction, 371, 378; *see also* Job satisfaction;
        Motivation
Satisficing, **210**, 220, 226
Scandals; *see* Ethics; Executive misconduct
Scanlon plan, 394
Scatter diagrams, 530